B&T

THE WRITER'S HANDBOOK

The Writer's Handbook

2001 Edition

Edited by

SYLVIA K. BURACK
Editor, The Writer

Publishers   THE WRITER, INC.   Boston

CONTENTS

ACKNOWLEDGMENTS

I am indebted to Elizabeth Preston, Managing Editor of *The Writer,* and to Ann-Margaret Caljouw, its Senior Editor, for their unfailing energy, enthusiasm, and dedication in making this volume a reality.

Sylvia K. Burack, Editor

Background
for Writers

❑ 1

DEALING WITH PRAISE

BY T. ALAN BROUGHTON

RECENTLY ONE OF MY STUDENTS SENT ME THREE TOUGH QUESTIONS. I didn't answer her immediately. I like questions when they show engagement, but the nearly unanswerable ones are best of all because then we get to share our ignorance, and often they help me to form tentative answers.

The student asked: "1) When you write 'good' or 'fine' beside a line or image or sometimes at the end of the poem, does that mean you don't think I should change it, or does it mean just that I'm on the right track? 2) Do those words mean I'm doing 'fine' as a student writer, or have I reached some level beyond the 'good' work you see over the years from students? 3) Why do I sometimes find it even harder when you praise my work than when you find things wrong with it? I don't think I know what to do with something when you like it." I knew she wasn't being angry or ironic. In the conversations we'd had previously, in class or my office, she had always been straightforward, serious (about her work—not humorlessly self-serious), and trusting. She was not accusing me of evasion.

What she wanted to know was, "Where am I standing in the world of poets and poetry? How can I see where I am in this daily fog of my work, my hopes, my dreams, and above all my need to know if all this is really panning out?" I took time answering her because I knew one response immediately, but I did not want to give that too quickly. I wanted to reach it after some discussion because at first it might seem glib or evasive. I could have told her that I'd been writing and publishing for about forty years, but the implications in her questions were ones in my own literary life that I had not found a way to resolve. The difference between her and me was that I no longer expected any definitive answers, although that did not mean I could throttle the questions or the angst they rose out of.

What I do remember is that when one is beginning to write seriously—that is, when one has understood that writing takes each of us to places we could never imagine our minds possessed and that we hope we will never stop going there through whatever words we can find— the problem of knowing whether one really has the talent is matched by the insecurity of not knowing whether one has the persistence. If only committing oneself to an art were as irreversible and inevitable as paying taxes or signing the line on a mortgage agreement! At least from those forty years of writing, I can say that I am far more certain now than when I began that I will be continuing to write until I drop in my tracks. There is some security in that, I suppose. I'm proud to be a lifer. But I also remember my ambitions to be a concert pianist, and although I gave it up after I spent some years at Juilliard and saw the competition and also had a chance to judge the depth of my talent, I still sit down at the piano every day, and some days I feel that twitch of amputated dreams. It would be safer for me to tell her those experiences, I thought, than be more direct and tell her that I've had writing students whose talents were superb but who did not continue to write after their college years. She might think that was a vague adumbration on my part, a quiet hint that I did not think she had that persistence herself.

But I circled back to the question concerning my praise of her work and had to admit that I've not resolved that either in my life as writer: Why is it that when an editor rejects my work and I am at first defensive, then abjectly certain that he or she is right, I am finally able to walk away either by revising the manuscript or looking at it with new eyes and deciding that the person was simply not reading the work correctly? I have learned to incorporate rejection, and now sometimes my initial reaction is even very calm and accepting. If the person is right, I wouldn't want the work published; if wrong, then I'll find a place for it elsewhere, even if that means on the shelf in my closet among other works I like a great deal because they did something special for me—maybe just opening a way to do the next piece that was very much better because of the previous attempt.

But acceptances are another matter, and if accompanied by praise, I find myself enormously pleased but deeply suspicious. I know that I can do some pretty good work, but already, picking up my copy and looking at it carefully after I've reread the acceptance, I can see flaws, see the ways it came out all right, but not at all as well as I had wanted it to. Believe me, I want that praise and acceptance. The act of writing is not complete until the work has passed from the writer to a reader, and only that reading makes it as whole as it needs to be. If the reader likes the experience, the circle can seem quite complete. I don't have the self-assurance, determination, even stubborn despair (to say nothing of the abilities) of an Emily Dickinson to write, bind up my poems, and hope the attic doesn't burn down before someone stumbles across my work. But I've come to mistrust praise—not because of the giver but because of what I can or cannot do with it in my own life. Rejection is a hard wall I do my flip turns against. I push off and get a good start toward reaching the other end of the pool. Praise, I sink through and might never come up again. It feeds my ambition, leads me outward to look for the security that can never really be found there. I've learned never to stop revising a piece just because it has been accepted and published, no matter how good the place is.

Finally, neither rejection nor praise provides the persistence or answers the questions the student was asking. I probably only compounded her insecurities by praising her for asking the questions, at the same time that I tried to give her some of the fumbling answers hinted at in the paragraphs above. Certainly I could tell her that from my many years of teaching she was among the best students. I could also give her every encouragement to continue to write, since I knew she sensed her talent as much as I did. I remember with life-long gratitude a teacher I had when I was seventeen who gave me that much information and helped me cast loose from shore and try myself out on longer voyages. But with the other questions, I could only share my own confusions and let her know that I hoped she might resolve them sooner than I, or at least come up with more articulate answers. I think the best advice, however, was that if she was already finding her way into essential questions, ones that would vex her in varied ways for the rest of her writerly life, then perhaps she really was a writer at heart. I think many artists are people who perceive very early in their lives what the persistent questions of the art are, and they continue because they take joy in finding new answers for them.

I left her with a few sentences from one of the letters written by Rilke to a young poet that I often console myself with when as vexed as she was:

You ask whether your verses are good. You ask me. You have asked others before. You send them to magazines. You compare them with other poems, and you are disturbed when certain editors reject your efforts. Now (since you have allowed me to advise you) I beg you to give up all that. You are looking outward, and that above all you should not do now. Nobody can counsel and help you, nobody. There is only one single way. Go into yourself. Search for the reason that bids you write; find out whether it is spreading out its roots in the deepest places of your heart, acknowledge to yourself whether you would have to die if it were denied you to write. This above all—ask yourself in the stillest hour of your night: *must* I write? Delve into yourself for a deep answer. And if this should be affirmative, if you may meet this earnest question with a strong and simple *"I must,"* then build your life according to this necessity; your life even into its most indifferent and slightest hour must be a sign of this urge and a testimony to it.*

This is demanding advice. But I've never used it quite the way that Rilke might have intended. I don't see this as a one-time search. I think it happens often in the life of a writer. One keeps checking in, year after year, asking the questions, finding the answers in new forms, new wordings—always provisional, but if the answers keep coming up with new ways to say "yes," who knows? It could go on for a whole lifetime.

---

*Rainer Maria Rilke. *Letters to a Young Poet*, trans. Norton, Norton & Co., 1963

□ 2

Wooing the Muse

By Eileen Herbert Jordan

I AM SITTING AT MY DESK GAZING AT A PICTURE ON THE WALL FACING me; let me tell you why. Tucked in the frame of the picture is a headline I clipped from *The New York Times*. ALWAYS ASKING, WHAT IS THIS REALLY ABOUT? I have no idea what this question once meant to an editor—I only know that now it is mine. It is the first thing I see when I start to write and the last when I stop. In between, it is what keeps my eye on the ball. It is my latest gimmick.

Maybe you wonder why I don't simply write a guideline of my own and tack it up. That wouldn't work for me. To be viable it must be something already in print and something that, when I see it, hits me like a ton of bricks. Gimmicks are intensely personal. Writers, of course, are a little crazy: We all know that.

There are some tricks of the trade and writers use them shamelessly. Here are a few I know about—maybe one will work for you.

Silence and sound. Some very smart writers use music as a third dimension in their work, treating it almost like the musical score of motion picture. They spend a good deal of time picking the right selections to accompany their writing—great blues or jazz for a mood piece, an old song for a period story, a torch song for the end of a love affair. If this approach does nothing more than make you sit and moon over Gershwin, it's not for you; otherwise, try it.

My own choice is listening to a classical piece in the background. I can do this without being distracted because I know almost nothing about classical music; a tinny Bach fugue will never bother me. Instead, the air around me fills with silver shavings as I listen, and that's so much lovelier than silence that it makes me want to work.

There are talented writers who cannot finish a line unless they are in a room that is as still as a cell; I wish I could help them. Unfortunately, one of Murphy's laws is that noise will follow you anywhere, so these writers end up moving from pillar to post, always looking for better acoustics. Sometimes a room at your local library is your answer. It's worth investigating. And your permanent gimmick? A pair of very good ear plugs.

What should I wear? I never thought I would write this sentence. I never would have, either, had I not recently heard Sue Grafton on the "Today" show. Grafton (the hugely successful author of the alphabet mysteries (*A Is For Alibi, B Is For* . . . etc.) was wearing what obviously was a designer suit. Her face was a cameo by Lancôme, her hair tousled as only professionals can tousle. Furthermore, she was telling Katie Couric that, when she was working, she dressed and groomed herself this way every day. *Every day.* She considered writing her job, and she prepared for it every morning, just as any working woman would. She could function no other way. It was a whole new idea to me. I pass it along because, when all else fails, looking good may be the thing that gives you back what every writer needs—faith in yourself.

I must confess that, before I could brood very long about my career being killed by my wardrobe, I remembered what another successful writer had said to me when I started freelancing: "Oh, what you have to look forward to. You haven't known bliss until you've gone to work in your nightgown!"
Each meant what she said. Take your pick!

Before you put it on paper, put it on paper. I'm not going into the subject of outlines; I deal in gimmicks. This is one used by a writer I know, to keep her characters in check. Before she starts a piece of fiction, she prepares resumés of everyone she is writing about. They are, in fact, thorough case histories, covering everything from temperament, family background, and medical reports to horoscopes—the latter because she is also an astrologer. She keeps the "case histories" in a file, always at hand. They give a writer a strong sense of security, especially in a long piece when you tend to forget who has blue eyes and who has brown. But they can be dangerous, too. Characters have the habit of taking matters into their own hands—falling in love with the wrong man, running off to Europe, dropping out of college. Unless you keep these things straight, you're going to lose them and probably the story, too. So keep a file if it helps, but have plenty of blank pages for revising as you go along.

Memorabilia. Yankee baseball caps! Lucky shirts! Old dance programs! Silver dollars! Four-leaf clovers! There's a writer for every one of them. I'm only going to discuss two areas that cry *memory*—and might be worth second thoughts.

Scent. A scented candle needs only a match. Today there are so many of them that with a flick of your fingers you can evoke total recall of almost anything, from the gardenia corsage you wore at your senior prom to Mom's apple pie. The seashore in a shell works, too. And, best of all, try a few sprays of a certain after-shave lotion or a special perfume.

Pictures. There are pros and cons about pictures. Some writers see them as graphic reminders of their subject and therefore a big plus. Others say, nonsense! Pictures are not Post-it notes. When you write, you're in a different place. Memory and imagination are all you need. Personally, I'm in the middle. I will have pictures of buildings and landscapes and such nearby, for accuracy. Faces are such a small part of a character that I describe them without looking.

Going on-line. I know someone, successful in her writing, who is steeped in the world of her computer, as skilled in using it as a race car driver competing in the Indy 500. With this ideal combination of man and the machine, could there possibly be need for more help?

"I do 'Let's Pretend,' " she says. "I pretend that I'm writing an e-mail letter. That's the only way I can get started."

I am so excited to hear that "Let's Pretend" has entered the electronic age that I almost forget to tell her it is a wonderful idea—even if you don't have a computer. Writing a letter to someone not only calms you down, but also sharpens the tools of your trade. Call it batting practice, if you will; it works.

Once, in my youth, I worked for a writer on a magazine. Every morning he arrived at the office carrying a large, dog-eared, brown manuscript envelope covered with notes scribbled in pencil. The notes were, in fact, ideas for stories that had come to him in the night. He would empty the envelope and place it on my desk. My job was to take a pair of scissors and cut out each note, as if I were creating a jigsaw puzzle. I would make a pile, then type each note on a separate piece of paper, and present the results to him.

I heard, via the grapevine, that I was secure in my position because I was the only person he had found who could read his handwriting. I didn't feel secure; I felt doomed. Had I mastered *Beowulf* for this? Had I read Emily Dickinson on the subway to end up here? At last one day I got up my courage, picked up the uncut envelope, and walked with it into his office.

"Did you ever think of keeping a notebook on your night table?" I asked. "They have them in the supply room, and I'd be glad to go get you one."

At first, he gave me the look one gives somebody who has come up with a suggestion that is utterly mad. Then, very slowly, his face softened. He was picking up on the fact that I was only a kid and had absolutely no idea of the craziness I was walking into when I started hanging out with writers. It was going to be a long road, and he knew it; I didn't know it then.

"Oh, no," he said at last, but his voice was gentle, "I couldn't do that. That wouldn't work for me . . . oh, no . . . that wouldn't work for me at all."

So the message doesn't change: *Whatever works for you works.* And I was true to my headline: If you find just one thing here that helps on any day you are writing, I'll be delighted.

❑ 3

WRITERS: SEE HOW THEY RUN

BY JOYCE CAROL OATES

RUNNING! IF THERE'S ANY ACTIVITY HAPPIER, MORE EXHILARATING, more nourishing to the imagination, I can't think of what it might be. The mysterious efflorescence of language seems to pulse in the brain, in rhythm with our feet and the swinging of our arms. Ideally, the runner who's a writer is running through the land- and cityscapes of her fiction, like a ghost in a real setting.

The structural problems I set for myself in writing, in a long, snarled, frustrating and sometimes despairing morning of work, for instance, I can usually unsnarl by running in the afternoon.

On days when I can't run, I don't feel "myself"; and whoever the "self" is I feel, I don't like nearly so much as the other. And the writing remains snarled in endless revisions.

Writers and poets are famous for loving to be in motion. The English Romantic poets were clearly inspired by their long walks, in all weather: Wordsworth and Coleridge in the idyllic Lake District, for instance. The New England Transcendentalists, most famously Henry David Thoreau, were ceaseless walkers; Thoreau boasted of having "traveled much in Concord," and in his eloquent essay "Walking" acknowledged that he had to spend more than fours hours out of doors daily, in motion; otherwise he felt "as if I had some sin to be atoned for."

My favorite prose on the subject is Charles Dickens's "Night Walks." Written with his usual brilliance, this haunting essay seems to hint at more than its words reveal. Dickens associates his terrible night restlessness with what he calls "houselessness": under a compulsion to walk and walk and walk in the darkness and pattering rain.

It isn't surprising that Walt Whitman should have tramped impressive distances, for you can feel the pulse beat of the walker in his slightly breathless, incantatory poems. Henry James also loved to walk for miles in London.

I, too, walked (and ran) for miles in London years ago. Much of it in Hyde Park. Regardless of weather. Living for a sabbatical year with my husband, an English professor, in a corner of Mayfair overlooking Speakers' Corner, I was so afflicted with homesickness for America, and for Detroit, I ran compulsively; not as respite for the intensity of writing but as a function of writing.

As I ran, I was running in Detroit, envisioning the city's parks and streets, avenues and expressways, with such eidetic clarity I had only to transcribe them when I returned to our flat, recreating Detroit in my novel *Do With Me What You Will* as faithfully as I'd recreated Detroit in *Them* when I was living there.

What a curious experience! Without the bouts of running, I don't believe I could have written the novel; yet how perverse, one thinks, to be living in one of the world's most beautiful cities, London, and to be dreaming of one of the world's most problematic cities, Detroit. But of course, writers are crazy. Each of us, we like to think, in her own inimitable way.

Both running and writing are highly addictive activities; both are, for me, inextricably bound up with consciousness. I can't recall a time when I wasn't running, and I can't recall a time when I wasn't writing.

(Before I could write what might be called human words in the English language, I eagerly emulated grown-ups' handwriting in pencil scribbles. My first "novels"—which I'm afraid my loving parents still have in a trunk or a drawer—were tablets of inspired scribbles illustrated by line drawings of chickens, horses, and upright cats. For I had not yet mastered the trickier human form, as I was years from mastering human psychology.)

My earliest outdoor memories have to do with the special solitude of running or hiking in our pear and apple orchards, through fields of wind-rustling corn towering over my head. Through childhood I hiked, roamed, tirelessly explored the countryside: neighboring farms, a treasure trove of old barns, abandoned houses and forbidden properties of all kinds, some of them presumably dangerous, like cisterns and wells covered with loose boards.

These activities are intimately bound up with storytelling, for always there's a ghost-self, a "fictitious" self, in such settings. For this reason I believe that any form of art is a species of exploration and transgression. (I never saw a "No Trespassing" sign that wasn't a summons to my rebellious blood. Such signs, dutifully posted on trees and fence railings, might as well cry, "Come Right In!")

To write is to invade another's space, if only to memorialize it. To write is to invite angry censure from those who don't write, or who don't write in quite the way you do, for whom you may seem a threat. Art by its nature is a transgressive act, and artists must accept being punished for it.

If writing involves punishment, at least for some of us, the act of running even in adulthood can evoke painful memories of having been, long ago, as children, chased by tormentors. (Is there any adult who hasn't such memories? Are there any adult women who have not been, in one way or another, sexually molested or threatened?) That adrenaline rush, like an injection to the heart!

I attended a one-room country schoolhouse in which eight very disparate grades were taught by a single overworked woman. The teasing, pummeling, pinching, punching, mauling, kicking, and verbal abuse that surrounded the relative sanctuary of the schoolhouse simply had to be endured, for in those days there were no protective laws against such mistreatment. I don't believe I was singled out, and I came to see years later that such abuse is generic, not personal. It must prevail through the species; it allows us insight into the experiences of others, a sense of what a more enduring panic, entrapment, suffering, and despair must be truly like. Sexual abuse seems to us the most repellent kind of abuse, and it's certainly the abuse that nourishes a palliative amnesia.

Beyond the lines of printed words in my books are settings in which the books were imagined and without which the books could not exist. Sometime in 1985, for instance, running along the Delaware River south of Yardley, Pennsylvania, I glanced up and saw the ruins of a railroad bridge and experienced in a flash such a vivid, visceral memory of crossing a footbridge beside a similar railroad trestle high above the Erie Canal in Lockport, New York, when I was 12 to 14 years old, that I saw the possibility of a novel. This would become *You Must Remember This*, set in a mythical upstate New York city very like the original.

Yet often the reverse occurs: I find myself running in a place so intriguing to me, amid houses, or the backs of houses, so mysterious, I'm fated to write about these sights, to bring them to life (as it's said) in fiction. I'm a writer absolutely mesmerized by places; much of my writing is a way of assuaging homesickness, and the settings my characters inhabit are as crucial to me as the characters themselves. I couldn't write even a very short story without vividly "seeing" what its characters see.

Stories come to us as wraiths requiring precise embodiments. Running seems to allow me, ideally, an expanded consciousness in which I can envision what I'm writing as a film or a dream. I rarely invent at the typewriter but recall what I've experienced. I don't use a word processor but write in longhand, at considerable length.

By the time I come to type out my writing formally, I've envisioned it repeatedly. I've never thought of writing as the mere arrangement of words on the page but as the attempted embodiment of a vision: a complex of emotions, raw experience.

The effort of memorable art is to evoke in the reader or spectator emotions appropriate to that effort. Running is meditation; more practicably it allows me to scroll through, in my mind's eye, the pages I've just written, proofreading for errors and improvements.

My method is one of continuous revision. While writing a long novel, every day I loop back into earlier sections to rewrite, in order to maintain a consistent, fluid voice. When I write the final two or three chapters of a novel, I write them simultaneously with the rewriting of the opening, so that, ideally at least, the novel is like a river uniformly flowing, each passage concurrent with all the others.

My most recent novel is 1,200 finished manuscript pages, which means many more typed-out pages, and how many miles of running, I dare not guess!

The twin activities of running and writing keep the writer reasonably sane and with the hope, however illusory and temporary, of control.

❏ 4

WRITING WITH JOY

BY JANE YOLEN

THERE ARE WRITERS WHO BELIEVE THAT WRITING *IS* AGONY, AND that's the best anyone can say of it. Gene Fowler's famous words are quoted all the time: "Writing is easy: All you do is sit staring at a blank sheet of paper until the drops of blood form on your forehead." Or Red Smith's infamous creed: "There's nothing to writing. All you do is sit down at a typewriter and open a vein."

But that's a messy way of working! And blood is extremely hard to get off of white paper.

Now, I am one of those people who makes a distinction between being a writer and being an author. A writer puts words on a page. An author lives in story. A writer is conversant with the keyboard, the author with character.

Roland Barthes has said: "The author performs a function; the writer an activity." We are talking here about the difference between desire and obsession; between hobby and life. But in either case, I suggest you learn to write not with blood and fear, but with joy.

Why joy?

It's a personal choice.

First of all, I am not a masochist willing to submit myself day after day to something that brings me pain. And I do mean day after day. Like an athlete or a dancer, I am uncomfortable—and even damaged—by a day away from my work.

Second, one need not have an unhappy life to write tragedy. Or conversely, one need not be deliriously happy all the time to write comedy. (In fact, many stand-up comics admit to being miserable much of the time.) Shakespeare was neither a king nor a fool, not a Moor or a Jew. He never saw a real fairy, and he was never asea in a tempest. His life was somewhere between happy and sad, as are most authors' lives. Yet he could write tragedy, comedy, and all between.

Authors are like actors; we get under the skins of our characters, inhabiting their lives for a while. We just don't have to live on and on with them forever. I have written about dragons, mermaids, angels, and kings. Never met any up close. I have even written a murder mystery, but I did not have to murder someone in order to write it. Still—don't mess with me. After doing my research, I *do* know how!

Third, writing for a living is much easier than spending a lot of time in a therapist's chair. Cheaper, too. Authors get to parade their neuroses in public disguised as story. If we are lucky, we get paid for doing it. And we get applause as well. As Kurt Vonnegut said: "Writers get to treat their mental illnesses every day."

Writing fiction—and poetry—is a bit like dreaming. You can find out what is troubling you on a deeper level. That one's writing goes out and touches someone else on that same level—though differently—is one of the pieces of magic that attends to art.

But I speak of *choosing* joy as if it were truly a matter of choice. For some people it is not. For some, agony oils the writing machine.

So—if you find that writing with pain is part of your process, I will not try and talk you out of it. After all, who am I to argue when Susan Sontag proclaims: "You have to sink down to a level of hopelessness and desperation to find the book that you can write." Or when Fran Lebowitz complains: "I just write when fear overtakes me." Or when Georges Simenon confesses: "Writing is not a profession but a vocation of unhappiness."

I may consider them whiners more than writers, but it is simply their way. Just don't ask me to stand by and give them a literary Heimlich maneuver when they get a bit of plot stuck in their throats.

□ 5

Writing Matters

By Julia Alvarez

One of the questions that always comes up during question-and-answer periods is about the writing life. The more sophisticated, practiced questioners usually ask me, "Can you tell us something about your process as a writer?"

In part, this is the curiosity we all have about each other's "processes," to use the terminology of my experienced questioner. We need to tell, and we also want to know (don't we?) the secret heart of each other's life. Perhaps that is why we love good novels and poems—because we can enter, without shame or without encountering defensiveness or embarrassment, the intimate lives of other people.

But the other part of my questioner's curiosity about the writing life has to do with a sense we all have that if we can only get a hold of the secret ingredients of the writing process, we will become better writers. We will have an easier time of it if we only find that magic pencil or know at which hour to start and at which hour to quit and what to sip that might help us come up with the next word in a sentence.

I always tell my questioners the truth: Listen, there are no magic solutions to the hard work of writing. There is no place to put the writing desk that will draw more words out of you. I had a friend who claimed that an east-west alignment was the best one for writing. The writing would then flow and be more in tune with the positive energies. The north-south alignment would cause blocks as well as bad dreams if your bed was also thus aligned.

See, I tell my questioners, isn't this silly?

But even as I say so, I know I am talking out of both sides of my mouth. I admit that after getting my friend's tip, I lined up my writing desk (and my bed) in the east-west configuration. It wasn't that I thought my writing or my dream life would improve, but I am so impressionable that I was afraid that I'd be thinking and worrying about

17

my alignment instead of my line breaks. And such fretting would affect my writing adversely. Even as recently as this very day, I walk into my study first thing in the morning, and I fill up my bowl of clear water and place it on my desk. And though no one told me to do this, I somehow feel this is the right way to start a writing day.

Of course, that fresh bowl of water sits on my desk on good *and* bad writing days. I know these little ceremonies will not change the kind of day before me. My daily writing rituals are small ways in which I contain my dread and affirm my joy and celebrate the mystery and excitement of the calling to be a writer.

I use the word *calling* in the old religious sense: a commitment to a life connected to deeper, more profound forces (or so I hope) than the marketplace, or the academy, or the hectic blur of activity that my daily life is often all about. But precisely because it is a way of life, not just a job, the writing life can be difficult to combine with other lives that require that same kind of passion and commitment—the teaching life, the family life, the parenting life, and so on. And since we writers tend to be intense people, whatever other lives we combine with our writing life, we will want to live them intensely, too. Some of us are better at this kind of juggling than others.

After twenty-five years of clumsy juggling—marriages, friendships, teaching, writing, community work, political work, child caring—I think I've finally figured out what the proper balance is for me. Let me emphasize that this is not a prescription for anyone else. But alas, I'm of the Gerald Ford school of writers who can't chew gum and write iambic pentameter at the same time. I can do two, maybe three intense lives at once: writing and being in a family; writing and teaching and being in a family; writing and teaching and doing political work; but if I try to add a fourth or fifth, I fall apart, that is, the writing stops, which for me is the same thing as saying I fall apart.

But still, I keep juggling, picking up one life and another and another, putting aside the writing from time to time. We have only one life, after all, and we have to live so many lives with it. (Another reason the writing life appeals so much is that you can be, at least on paper, all those selves whose lives you can't possibly live out in the one life you've got.)

Living other lives enriches our writing life. The tension between them can sometimes exhaust us, this is true—but the struggle also makes the hard-won hours at the writing desk all the more precious. And if we are committed to our writing, the way we lead our other lives can make them lives-in-waiting to be writing lives.

For me, the writing life doesn't just happen when I sit at the writing desk. It is a life lived with a centering principle, and mine is this: that I will pay close attention to this world I find myself in. "My heart keeps open house," was the way the poet Theodore Roethke put it in a poem. And rendering in language what one sees through the opened windows and doors of that house is a way of bearing witness to the mystery of what it is to be alive in this world.

This is all very high-minded and inspirational, my questioner puts in, but what about when we are alone at our writing desks, feeling wretchedly anxious, wondering if there is anything in us worth putting down?

Let me take you through the trials and tribulations of a typical writing day. It might help as you also set out onto that blank page, encounter one adventure or mishap after another, and wonder—do other writers go through this?

The answer is probably yes.

Not much has happened at six-twenty or so in the morning when I enter my writing room above the garage. I like it this way. The mind is free of household details, worries, commitments, voices, problems to solve.

My mood entering the room depends on what happened with my writing the day before. If the previous day was a good one, I look forward to the new writing day. If I was stuck or uninspired, I feel apprehensive. In short, I can't agree more with Hemingway's advice that a writer should always end his writing day knowing where he is headed next. It makes it easier to come back to work.

The first thing I do in my study every morning is read poetry (Jane Kenyon, George Herbert, Rita Dove, Robert Frost, Elizabeth Bishop, Rhina Espaillat, Jane Shore, Emily Dickinson . . .). This is the first music I hear, the most essential. Interestingly, I like to follow the reading of poetry with some prose, as if, having been to the heights I need to come back down to earth.

I consider this early-morning reading a combination of pleasure-reading time when I read the works and authors I most love and finger-exercise reading time, when I am tuning my own voice to the music of the English language as played by its best writers. There's an old Yiddish story about a rabbi who walks out in a rich neighborhood and meets a watchman walking up and down. "For whom are you working?" the rabbi asks. The watchman tells him, and then in his turn, he asks the rabbi, "And whom are you working for, rabbi?" The words strike the rabbi like a shaft. "I am not working for anybody just yet," he barely manages to reply. Then he walks up and down beside the man for a long time and finally asks him, "Will you be my servant?" The watchman says, "I should like to, but what would be my duties?"

"To remind me," the rabbi says.

I read my favorite writers to remind me of the quality of writing I am aiming for.

Now, it's time to set out: Pencil poised, I read through the hard copy that I ran off at the end of yesterday's writing day. I used to write everything out by longhand, and when I was reasonably sure I had a final draft, I'd type it up on my old Selectric. But now, I usually write all my prose drafts right out on the computer, though I need to write out my poems in longhand, to make each word by hand.

This is also true of certain passages of prose and certainly true for times when I am stuck in a novel or story. Writing by hand relieves some of the pressure of seeing something tentative flashed before me on the screen with that authority that print gives to writing. "This is just for me," I tell myself, as I scratch out a draft in pencil. Often, these scribblings turn into little bridges, tendrils that take me safely to the other side of silence. When I'm finally on my way, I head back to the computer.

But even my hard copies look as if they've been written by hand. As I revise, I begin to hear the way I want a passage to sound. About the third or fourth draft, if I'm lucky, I start to see the shape of what I am writing, the way an essay will go, a character will react, a poem unfold.

Sometimes if Bill and I go on a long car trip, I'll read him what I am working on. This is a wonderful opportunity to "hear" what I've written. The process of reading my work to someone else does tear apart that beauteous coating of self-love in which my own creation comes enveloped. I start to hear what I've written as it would sound to somebody else.

When I'm done with proofing the hard copy of the story or chapter or poem, I take a little break. This is one of the pleasures of working at home. I can take these refreshing breathers from the intensity of the writing: go iron a shirt or clean out a drawer or wrap up my sister's birthday present.

After my break, I take a deep breath. What I now do is transcribe all my handwritten revisions on to my computer, before I launch out into the empty space of the next section of the story or essay or the chapter in a novel. This is probably the most intense time of the writing day. I am on my way, but I don't know exactly where it is I am going. But that's why I'm writing: to find out.

On the good days, an excitement builds up as I push off into the language, and sentence seems to follow sentence. I catch myself smiling or laughing out loud or sometimes even weeping as I move through a scene or a stanza. Certainly writing seems to integrate parts of me that are usually at odds. As I write, I feel unaccountably whole; I disappear! That is the irony of this self-absorbed profession: The goal finally is to vanish. On bad days, on the other hand, I don't disappear. Instead, I'm stuck with the blank screen before me. I take more and more breaks. I wander out on the deck and look longingly south toward the little spire of the Congregational church and wish another life for myself. Oh, dear, what have I done with my life?

I have chosen it, that's what I've done. So I take several deep breaths and go back upstairs and sit myself down and work over the passage that will not come. As Flannery O'Connor attested: "Every morning between 9 and 12, I go to my room and sit before a piece of paper. Many times, I just sit for three hours with no ideas coming to me. But I know one thing: If an idea does come between 9 and 12, I am there ready for it." The amazing thing for me is that years later, reading the story or novel or poem, I can't tell the passages that were easy to write, the ones that came forth like "greased lightning" from those other passages that made me want to give up writing and take up another life.

On occasion, when all else fails, I take the rest of the day "off." I finish reading the poet or novelist with whom I began the day or I complain to my journal or I look through a picture book of shoes one of my characters might wear. But all the while I am feeling profound self doubt—as if I were one of those cartoon characters who runs off a cliff, and suddenly looks down only to discover, there's no ground beneath her feet!

At the end of the writing day (about two-thirty or three in the afternoon), I leave the room over the garage. I put on my running clothes, and I go for a run. In part, this exercise does make me feel better. But one of the best perks of running has been that it allows me to follow Hemingway's advice. I don't always know where I am headed in my writing at the end of the work day, but after I run, I usually have one or two good ideas. Running helps me work out glitches in my writing and gives me all kinds of unexpected insights. While I run down past the Fields's house, through Tucker Development, down to the route that goes into town, and then back, I've understood what a character is feeling or how I'm going to organize an essay or what I will title my novel. I've also had a zillion conversations with dozens of worrisome people, which is much better than trying to have these conversations with them while I am trying to write. Also, since I am not near a phone, I am not tempted to call them up and actually have it out with them. I've saved a lot of friendships and relationships and spared myself plenty of heartaches this way.

After the run, the rest of the workday is taken up by what I call the writing biz part of being a writer. What this involves, in large part, is responding to the publicity machine that now seems to be a necessary component of being a published writer. Answering mail, returning phone calls, responding to unsolicited manuscripts from strangers or to galleys from editors who would so appreciate my putting in a good word for this young writer or translation or series. Ironically, all this attention can sometimes amount to distraction that keeps me from doing the work that brought these requests to my door in the first place.

I could just ignore these requests. But all along the way, I found helpers who did read my manuscript, did give me a little of their busy day. These are favors I can never pay back, I can only pass on. And so I do try to answer my own mail and read as many galleys by new writers as I possibly can and return phone calls to those who need advice I might be able to give.

When I'm finally finished with my writing biz or I've put it aside in the growing pile for tomorrow, I head to town to run errands or see a friend or attend a talk at the college. As the fields and farms give way to houses and lawns, I feel as if I'm reentering the world. After having been so intensely a part of a fictional world, I love this daily chance to connect with the small town I live in, to find out how everybody else is doing.

How's it going? everyone asks me, as if they really want to know all about my writing day.

At the end of a good reading, the audience lingers. It's late in Salt Lake City or Portland or Iowa City. Outside the bookstore windows, the sky is dark and star-studded. Then, that last hand goes up, and someone in the back row wants to know, "So, does writing really matter?"

This once really happened to me on a book tour. I felt as if I'd just been hit "upside the head," an expression I like so much because it sounds like the blow was so hard, the preposition got jerked around, too. Does writing matter? I sure hope so, I wanted to say. I've published six books. I've spent most of my thinking life, which is now over thirty years, writing. *Does writing really matter?* It was the hardest, and the best, question I've been asked anywhere.

Let's take out the *really*, I said. It makes me nervous. I don't *really* know much of anything, which is why I write, to find things out. Does writing matter?

It matters, of course, it matters. But it matters in such a small, almost invisible way that it doesn't seem very important. In fact, that's why I trust it, the tiny rearrangements and insights in our hearts that art accomplishes. It's how I, anyhow, learned to see with vision and perplexity and honesty and continue to learn to see. How I keep the windows and doors open instead of shutting myself up inside the things I "believe" and have personally experienced. How I move out beyond the safe, small version of my life to live other lives. "Not only to be one self," the poet Robert Desnos wrote about the power of the imagination, "but to become each one."

And this happens not because I'm a writer or, as some questioners put it, "a creative person." I'll bet that even those who aren't writers, those who are concerned with making some sense of this ongoing journey would admit this: that it's by what people have written and continue to write, our stories and creations, that we understand who we are. In a world without any books, we would not be the same kind of critter. "Art is not the world," Muriel Rukeyser reminds us, "but a knowing of the world. It prepares us."

Prepares us for what? I have to admit that I don't really know what it prepares us for. For our work in the world, I suppose. Prepares us to live our lives more intentionally, ethically, richly. A hand shoots up.

"You mean to say that if Hitler had read Tolstoy he would have been a better person?"

Let's say that it would have been worth a try. Let's say that if little Hitler had been caught up in reading Shakespeare or Tolstoy and was moved to the extent that the best books move us, he might not have become who he became. But maybe, Tolstoy or no Tolstoy, Hitler would still have been Hitler. We live, after all, in a flawed world of flawed beings. In fact, some very fine writers who have written some lovely things are not very nice people.

But I still insist that while writing or entering into the writing of another, they were better people. If for no other reason than they were not out there, causing trouble. Writing is a form of vision, and I agree with that proverb that says, "Where there is no vision, the people perish." The artist keeps that vision alive, cleared of the muck and refuse and junk and little dishonesties that always collect and begin to cloud our view of the world around us.

It is the end of the reading. My readers, who for this brief evening have become real people with questions about my writing life, come forward to have their books signed and offer some new insight or ask a further question. That they care matters. That they are living fuller versions of themselves and of each one because they have read books matters. This is why writing matters. It clarifies and intensifies; it reduces our sense of isolation and connects us to each other.

❑ 6

WRITING AND INSPIRATION

BY JAY PARINI

FOR THIRTY YEARS OR SO, I'VE BEEN SITTING DOWN AT MY DESK EVERY morning to write. I stay there, usually for three or four hours, whether or not anything comes. It's much like being a grocer: You have to open the shop and wait for customers; if any come, all is well and good. But even if nobody turns up, the obligation to keep business hours remains.

Despite this discipline, and the consolations of literary shopkeeping, I do—like all writers—fret over inspiration. The eternal question that faces everyone in this profession is where do stories, poems, and novels come from? Then comes the further, more vexing, question: Once you've got the idea for a poem or piece of fiction, how do you actually embody that idea in a fully realized work of art? That is, how do you "give to airy nothings," as Shakespeare wrote in *A Midsummer Night's Dream*, "a local habitation and a name"?

It should be obvious that the chief source of inspiration for any writer is experience. William Faulkner was once asked how much of his fiction came from his personal life, and he responded:

"I can't say. I never counted up. Because 'how much' is not important. A writer needs three things, experience, observation, and imagination, any two of which, at times any one of which, can supply the lack of the others. With me, a story usually begins with a single idea or memory or mental picture. The writing of the story is simply a matter of working up to that moment, to explain why it happened or what it caused to follow. A writer is trying to create believable people in credible moving situations in the most moving way he can. Obviously he must use as one of his tools the environment he knows."*

I write poetry and fiction, with no sense of preferring one to the other. Poetry, at least for me, is a way of paying attention to the daily

---

*Writers at Work: The Paris Review Interviews, ed. Malcolm Cowley. (New York: Viking, 1958), 133

25

fluctuations of experience. It is a seeking after grace. Poetic language is not, like the language of fiction, necessarily a vehicle for communication in the strictest sense. Poetry embodies, and often extends, the experience of the writer. Wallace Stevens once spoke of "The poem of the mind in the act of finding / What will suffice," and I think any poet can understand what he meant by those suggestive lines. In an age of disbelief, when there is so little solace or consolation in the culture at large, poetry is about finding a language adequate to our experience. Poets write to make sense of their own experience, to give it body and shape; ideally, others will read their poems and find them "useful" in some way, but the main use is always for the poets themselves. (Perhaps this explains why so much poetry is obscure?)

Fiction, on the other hand, seems to derive from a very different impulse: the wish to tell a story, to communicate experience within the generic boundaries of narrative. The desire to tell a story is ancient, and most writers do not have to look for ideas so much as wonder how to isolate and contain those springing forth naturally. (Writers block, I submit, is not so much the lack of a story to tell as a lack of confidence to tell it.)

When Robert Penn Warren, the great poet and novelist, was in his early eighties, he told me that he still had five or six novels in his head. They were, he said, "like airplanes circling an airport, waiting for permission to land." I find myself in much the same predicament.

With poems, I have always found that receptivity is everything. You have to be on the lookout for poems; in a way, they are there already, but you can't snag them unless you have your pen in hand, your notebook open. My ritual over many years has been to go to a local diner for breakfast and sit with a notebook open. I wait patiently, sometimes making lists of favorite words, thinking up titles for unwritten poems, or trying out phrases. The poems spring from those phrases, one phrase building upon another.

Thomas Campion (1567–1620) once usefully defined poetry as "a system of linked sounds." I like to build poems on that notion, linking sounds by various means, including the most obvious, such as rhyme (I love slant rhymes best) or alliteration. But there are other ways to link sounds: You might create interlocking metaphors, or—if you have a bent for philology—think of the roots of words, linking them by a principle of association.

Let me give an example of linking from a recent poem of my own, "Rain Before Nightfall."

Late August, and the long soft hills
are wet with light;
a silken dusk, with shifting thunder
in the middle distance. Chills
of fall have not yet quite
brought everything to ruin.

And I stop to look, to listen
under eaves. The yellow rain
slides down the lawn,
it feathers through the pine,
makes lilacs glisten,
all the waxy leaves. The air
is almost fit for drinking,
and my heart is drenched,
my thirst for something
more than I can see
is briefly quenched.

The circumstances under which I wrote this poem come vividly to mind. I was visiting the summer home of Robert Frost, in Ripton, Vermont. It was early evening, and I was alone. A sudden rain had recently swept the fields and forest, and the house was dripping as I sat on the little screened-in porch. As often happens in New England, the weather changed dramatically, and now a bright yellow sun flooded the landscape; I could hardly believe the yellowness of everything, even the grass and trees. I was overcome with a fierce sense of longing and joy, one of those exquisite and painfully mixed emotions that occasionally overwhelm us. My urge to get this experience down on paper was almost uncontainable.

I remember writing "a silken dusk," then waiting for a long time. Then I wrote, "the long soft hills are wet with light." With these phrases in hand, I was able to push forward, adding the "shifting thunder"—a gift from the skies. I kept telling myself to describe whatever was before me, remembering Wallace Stevens' great line: "Description is revelation." More than anything else, I wanted not to lose focus, to keep my eye on the object: the landscape, which through meditation would yield a spiritual essence. I wanted to find what Seamus Heaney has called "the music of what happens."

Soon I began linking the sounds of this poem, letting the l-sounds and s-sounds recur, almost like a pulse. I decided, instinctively, not to follow any rigid rhyme scheme but to rhyme as needed, so in the fourth line "hills" married "Chills." "Light" hitched up with "quite." These were traditional end-rhymes, but I hooked up "thunder," which concludes the third line, with "under," the first word in the eighth line. Internal rhyming is essential, I think, in stitching together poems. One should always think of rhyming as a form of echo, just as rhythm should be considered a pulse, not a metronomic tick-tock. I especially enjoyed rhyming "rain" with "ruin," a slant rhyme.

One hears a lot about the "New Formalism" these days, but there is nothing behind this phrase. Good poets have always used form as needed. Likewise, they have broken forms when the demand, which issues from the internal requirements of the poem, insisted that the form be abandoned. As anyone who has tried writing poetry knows (or ought to), no verse is really free if the poet hopes to construct a memorable poem. Those who choose to write in free verse should be aware that every line has a meter, and that words invariably create a music as their vowels and consonants collide. The poet has to manage these collisions with skill and tact.

Rhythms beget rhythms. In "Rain Before Nightfall," I recall starting with that line of "sprung" blank verse: "Late August, and the long soft hills," then quickly deciding to vary the pace with "are wet with light." As usual with me, I counted the stresses in each line, letting the unstressed syllables fall or gather as they would. This technique has its roots in Anglo-Saxon and Middle English poetry, and it allows for a more natural mesh of speaking voice with rhythmical unit.

The frightening thing about writing is that rules often get you nowhere. Poets and writers of fiction must, finally, achieve that mysterious thing called "a voice" on their own. But how do they do that? In truth, it's hard *not* to do it. All human beings have a distinct and original voice, as unique as their own thumbprints. When you hear someone you know speaking over the phone, even with your hand over the receiver so that the words themselves are indistinct, you can still tell who is talking. People have a particular way of hanging words together, of generating syntax; the rhythms in every speaking voice are almost invariably unique. The point of good writing is to utilize these individual aspects of a writer's voice, and that is where technique comes in. In poetry, it is where the discipline of language enters: knowing how to control the flow, the pulse of the line; keeping the imagery fresh and concrete; following the metaphors as far as they will go, but breaking them off when they have gone too far. Again, there are no rules here: You learn by trial and error. You must write badly at first, then revise, drawing closer and closer to the unique voice that is already latent but somehow obscured.

For writers of fiction, many of the same issues obtain, although the demands of storytelling are different from those of lyric poetry. Faulkner is on the mark when he says a writer must draw on "experience, observation, and imagination." But experience is foremost. The texture of daily life must find its way into all good fiction. Some writers—John Updike is a perfect example—have created a vast shelf of books devoted to this principle. He evokes the world with such astonishing particularity, as when (in a story called "Leaf Season") he describes driving through Vermont in the fall to experience "the leaves, whole valleys and mountains of them—the strident pinks and scarlets of the maples, the clangorous gold of the hickories, the accompanying brasses of birch and beech—on both sides of the road, rise after rise, a heavenly tumult tied to our dull earth only by broad bands of evergreen and outcropping of granite." The translation of experience into language must be, for Updike, almost instinctual by this point in his career.

For most writers—myself included—mere description of the world's glittering surface is not enough. I find myself eager to tell a story, to feel that surge through plot as characters entangle themselves in situations and need rescuing. Like Warren, I usually have five or six novels in my head, and I feel perpetually pressed for time to get them down on paper. This isn't to say there are not many days when, as I suggested earlier, I don't sit in the grocery store without customers. After thirty years, I still find myself puzzled by this thing called "inspiration." Why does the energy flow from unseen, bountiful sources one day, then dry up the next? I doubt that anyone can answer this, but there are ways of dealing with a seeming lack of inspiration.

Let me stay with the grocery store metaphor. The grocer can always do other things when nobody comes into the shop: He can study his accounts or wash the vegetables; he can sweep the floor and check his inventory. I find the parallel duties in writing extremely calming and useful. That is, I like to make lists of future characters or draw diagrams of plots. I can always go back and groom old passages, improving the rhythms of awkward sentences, finding glitches, substituting fresh metaphors and adjectives for clichés, which inevitably occur. If worse comes to worse, I can always read. For inspiration, I turn to Updike, Vidal, Marquez, Borges, Heaney, Frost. I have a private shelf of favorite writers, and I have spent blissful days rereading passages that I have virtually committed to memory. This reading often sparks my own writing.

When I'm working on a novel or story, I like to keep that "slight forward tilt" in the plot that Updike once mentioned. But how to keep the narrative moving, generate narrative momentum, that *sine qua non* without which any work of fiction is dead on the page?

I once spent a year on the Amalfi coast of Italy, and by lucky chance my neighbor was Gore Vidal. We became friends, and I learned a good deal about the writing life from him. One day I was working on a piece of fiction in which two characters were discussing the philosophy of Heidegger. I asked Gore if it were possible for two characters in a novel to discuss Heidegger for about twenty pages without losing the reader's interest. He looked at me with a droll smile and said, "Only if the characters are sitting in a railway car, and the reader knows there is a bomb under their seat."

I often recall that comment. In fact, I make a point to ask myself at regular intervals as I'm working: Is there a bomb under the seat? Without it, I know I may lose the narrative compulsion essential to good fiction.

More so than in poetry, fiction demands a vast commitment to the desk. I don't think it's possible to succeed in writing fiction without a huge capacity to sit in a desk chair and keep your attention focused on the task at hand for long periods. But this is also the reward of the art: that sense of being swept into a wholly separate world that is nevertheless contingent upon the one outside. You come to appreciate the intense pleasure of giving "a local habitation and a name" to vague intimations, those "airy nothings" that accost us daily in the shower, as we fall asleep or stumble awake, as we drive the children to school or sip a mug of coffee in the neighborhood diner.

You also come to realize that inspiration is only the beginning. As Alfred North Whitehead once said, "The art of literature, vocal or written, is to adjust the language so that it embodies what it indicates." That is, the poem or story, the novel or play, must somehow enact what it seeks to evoke. And here, the writer's craft comes into play, a discipline learned by trial and error, reading, writing, and revising, and long empty hours when the clock ticks slowly on the wall, and the cash register seems woefully, terrifyingly empty.

❑ 7

ADVICE FROM *STUART LITTLE*

BY PATRICIA WILES

STUART LITTLE, E. B. WHITE'S STORY ABOUT A MOUSE BORN INTO A human family, has always been one of my favorite books from childhood. I enjoyed the movie version of the book that released last year, but the experience of watching the story on the big screen couldn't equal the fondness I have for the book and the idea it planted in my head so many years ago—that no person is too small to have big adventures! And while growing up, I was fortunate enough to have many adventures, thanks to some wonderful books and the authors who wrote them.

Whether you're a child or an adult, it's easy at times to feel small and overwhelmed by the world. I did then, and still now, admire Stuart Little, who was only two inches tall. As important to his family as any full-sized person, his size was an asset and never considered a disability. He performed vital tasks around the house, like retrieving his mother's wedding ring from the bathtub drain and maneuvering stuck piano keys. By the time he was ready to venture out of his family's New York apartment, he had developed a sensible, not arrogant, self-confidence. While waiting for his first bus ride, Stuart thought, "I'm not tall enough to be noticed, yet I'm tall enough to want to go to Seventy-second Street."

I recently reread *Stuart Little*. This time, reading it as a writer, I admired the crisp prose and the apparent ease with which the story seemed to flow. The commandments set down by E.B. White in the writer's bible, *The Elements of Style*, echoed in the back of my head: "Write with nouns and verbs . . . Do not overwrite. . . . Avoid the use of qualifiers. . . . Do not affect a breezy manner." How could he make this look and sound so easy?

When you're a writer, it's easy at times to feel small and overwhelmed by all the words out there in the world. Compared to the giants, your voice seems only two inches tall. As I studied the illustration on the book's dustjacket, the copy I'd checked out from the library looked just like the one I'd read so many years ago—and it probably was, since it was published in 1973. But I didn't remember the text on the back:

> Mr. White finds writing difficult and bad for one's health, but he keeps at it even so. He would like, more than anything, to be a poet. The poets, he thinks, are the great ones. He began to write *Stuart Little* in the hope of amusing a six-year-old niece of his, but before he finished it she had grown up and was reading Hemingway.

Intrigued, I perused a reference book or two and came across White's explanation of why he wrote *Charlotte's Web*:

> I haven't told why I wrote the book, but I haven't told why I sneeze, either. A book is a sneeze.

For all the negatives stacked up against Stuart, his childhood was positive. He grew up and left home feeling confident in the route he had decided to take. The last lines of the book read: "As he peered ahead into the great land that stretched before him, the way seemed long. But the sky was bright, and he somehow felt he was headed in the right direction." We all want to trust our instincts, follow those inner promptings that tell us to journey into territories uncertain but reassuredly appealing. E. B. White must have felt compelled to write, despite his struggles. I like to think that maybe these last lines from *Stuart Little* expressed his truest feelings about his chosen profession.

E. B. White died in 1985, but his words remain behind to inspire, cheer, entertain, and uplift young and old alike. How glad I am that he, like Stuart, peered into the bright morning sky and followed the writer's path. And as I wait at the stops where a writer must choose to board the bus alone and venture into the unknown territories where words must be tamed and destiny fulfilled, I will remember the thoughts of a gallant mouse and remind myself that although I think that my voice may be too small to be noticed, I am not too small to want to go to Seventy-second Street.

❏ 8

THE JOURNEY INWARD

BY KATHERINE PATERSON

"DO YOU KEEP A JOURNAL?" NO, I ANSWER A BIT RED-FACED, BECAUSE I know that *real* writers keep voluminous journals so fascinating that the world can hardly wait until they die to read the published versions. But it's not quite true. I do make journal-like entries in used schoolgirl spiral notebooks, on odd scraps of paper, in fairly anonymous computer files. These notations are all so embarrassing that I am hoping for at least a week's notice to hunt them down and destroy all the bits and pieces before my demise.

I write these entries, you see, only when I can't write what I want to write. If they were collected and published, the reader could logically conclude that I was not only totally inept as a writer but that I lacked integration of personality at best, and at worst, was dangerously depressed.

If I had kept a proper journal, these neurotic passages would be seen in context, but such is not the case. If my writing is going well, why would I waste time talking about it? I'd be doing it. So if these notes survive me, they will give whatever segment of posterity might happen upon them a very skewed view of my mental state.

The reason I am nattering on about this is that I have come to realize that I am not alone. As soon as my books (after years of struggle) began to be published, I started to get questions from people that I had trouble answering in any helpful way: "Do you use a pen and pad or do you write on a typewriter?" (Nowadays, "computer" is always included in this question, but I'm talking about twenty years ago.)

"Whatever works," I'd say. Which was true. Sometimes I wrote first drafts by hand, sometimes on the typewriter; often I'd switch back and forth in an attempt to keep the flow going. The questioner would thank me politely, but, looking back, I know now that I had failed her.

"Do you have a regular schedule everyday or do you just write when you feel inspired?" the person would ask earnestly. I am ashamed to say, I would often laugh at this. "If I wrote only when I was inspired," I'd say, "I'd write about three days a year. Books don't get written in three days a year."

Occasionally, the question (and now, I know, all these were the same question) would be framed more baldly. "How do you begin?" "Well," I would say, "you sit down in front of the typewriter, roll in a sheet of paper and . . ."

If I ever gave any of you one of those answers, or if any other writer has ever given you similar tripe, I would like to apologize publicly. I was asked, in whatever disguise, a truly important question, and I finessed the answer into a one-liner.

How *do* you begin? It is not an idle or trick question. It is a cry from the heart.

I know. That's what all those aborted journal notes are about. They are the cry when I simply cannot begin. When no inspiration ever comes, when neither pen, nor pencil, nor typewriter, nor state-of-the-art computer can unloose what's raging about inside me.

So what happens? Well, something must. I've begun and ended over and over again through the years. There are several novels out there with my name on the cover. Somehow I figured out how to begin. Once the book is finished, the memory of the effort dims—until you're trying to begin the next one.

Well, I'm there now. I have to begin again. What have I done those other times? How have I gotten from that feeling of stony hopelessness? How do I break through that barrier as hard as sunbaked earth to the springs of creativity?

Sometimes, I know, I have a conversation with myself on paper:

What's the matter?
What do you mean "what's the matter?" You know perfectly well. I want to write, but I can't think of a thing to say.
Not a single thing?
Not a single thing worth saying.
You're scared what you might say won't be up to snuff? Scared people might laugh at you? Scared you might despise yourself?
Well, it is scary. How do I know there's still anything in here?
You don't. You just have to let it flow. If you start judging, you'll cut

off the flow—you've already cut off the flow from all appearances—
before it starts.

Grump.

Ah yes, we never learn, do we? Whatever happened to that wonderful
idea of getting up so early in the morning that the critic in you was still
asleep?

How do I know it will work this time?

You won't know if you don't try. But then, trying is risky, and you
do seem a bit timid to me.

You don't know what it's like pouring out your guts to the world.

I don't?

Well, you don't care as much as I do.

Of course I do. I just happen to know that it is so important to my
psychic health to do this that I'm willing to take the risk. You, my
friend, seem to want all the creative juices inside you to curdle and
poison the whole system.

You're nothing but a two-bit psychologist.

Well, I've been right before.

But how do I begin?

I don't know. Why don't we just get up at five tomorrow, come to
the machine and type like fury for an hour and see what happens? Could
be fun. Critic won't be up, and we won't ever have to show anybody
what we've done.

Now you understand why I have to burn this stuff before I die. My
posthumous reputation as a sane person of more than moderate intelligence hangs in the balance. But living writers, in order to keep writing,
have to forget about posthumous reputations. We have to become, quite
literally, like little children. We have to remember our early griefs and
embarrassments. Talk aloud to ourselves. Make up imaginary companions. We have to play.

Have you ever watched children fooling with play dough or finger-
paint? They mess around to see what will emerge, and they fiddle with
what comes out. Occasionally, you will see a sad child, one that has
decided beforehand what he wants to do. He stamps his foot because
the picture on the page or the green blob on the table falls short of the
vision in his head. But he is, thankfully, a rarity, already too concerned
with adult approval.

The unspoiled child allows herself to be surprised with what comes out of herself. She takes joy in the material, patting it and rolling it and shaping it. She is not too quick to name it. And, unless some grownup interferes, she is not a judge but a lover of whatever comes from her heart through her hands. This child knows that what she has created is marvelous simply because she has made it. No one else could make this wonderful thing because it has come out of her.

What treasures we have inside ourselves—not just joy and delight but also pain and darkness. Only I can share the treasures of the human spirit that are within me. No one else has *these* thoughts, *these* feelings, *these* relationships, *these* experiences, *these* truths.

How do I begin? You could start, as I often do, by talking to yourself. The dialogue may help you understand what is holding you back. Are you afraid that deep down inside you are really shallow? That when you take that dark voyage deep within yourself, you will find there is no treasure to share? Trust me. There is. Don't let your fear stop you. Begin early in the morning before that critical adult within wakes up. Like a child, pour out what is inside you, not listening to anything but the stream of life within you. Read Dorothea Brande's classic *On Becoming a Writer,* in which she suggests that you put off for several days reading what you have written in the wee hours. Then when you do read it you may discern a repeated theme pointing you to what you want to begin writing about.

Begin, Anne Lamott suggests in her wonderful book *Bird by Bird,* in the form of a letter. Tell your child or a trusted friend stories from your past. Exploring childhood is almost always an effective wedge into what's inside you. And didn't you mean to share those stories with your children someday anyhow?

While I was in the midst of revising this article, my husband happened to bring home Julia Cameron's book, *The Artist's Way.* Cameron suggests three pages of longhand every morning as soon as you get up. I decided to give the "morning pages" a try and heartily recommend the practice, though these pages, too, will need to be destroyed before I die.

When I was trying to begin the book which finally became *Flip-Flop Girl* (and you should see the anguished notes along the way!), I just began writing down the name of every child I could remember from the fourth grade at Calvin H. Wiley School. Sometimes I appended a note that explained why that child's name was still in my head. Early-morn-ing exercises explored ways the story might go, and I rejected most of them, but out of those fourth-grade names and painful betrayals a story began to grow. Judging from the notes, it was over a year in developing and many more months in the actual writing. But I did begin, and I did finish. There's a bit of courage for the next journey inward.

Now it's your turn. Bon voyage.

□ 9

TOOLS OF THE WRITER'S TRADE

By Christopher Scanlan

IN SHAKESPEARE'S TIME, ITINERANT ACTORS WHO TOOK THEIR PLAYS from village to town carried bags bulging with the tools of their art—scraps of costume, props, jars of paint. A writer's tools can be every bit as colorful and creative, and they won't take up as much room. Rummage through your memory and imagination to see if you find long-forgotten tools you can dust off.

Here are the tools I found and use: a tightrope, a net, a pair of shoes, a loom, six words, an accelerator pedal, and a time clock.

A tightrope

Take a risk with your writing every day. Submit to the magazine of your dreams. Conceive the next Great American Novel. The risks I've taken as a writer—pitching an ambitious project, calling for an interview with a reputed mobster, sending a short story back out in the mail the day it returned in my self-addressed envelope—have opened new doors and, more important, encouraged me to take other risks. Stretch an imaginary tightrope above your desk and walk across it every day.

A net

The best writers I know cast trawler's nets on stories. And they cast them wide and deep. They'll interview ten people, listening and waiting, to get the one quote that sums up the theme. They'll spend hours trolling for the anecdote that reveals the story. They'll sift through records and reports, looking for the one specific that explains the universal or the detail that captures the person or conveys the setting. I once wrote a story about a family in Utah whose daughter was a suspected victim of serial murderer Ted Bundy. During my visit, I noticed that a light switch next to the front door had a piece of tape over it so no one could turn it off. When I asked about it, the mother said she always left the light on until her daughter came home. The light had been burning for twelve years, a symbol of one family's unending grief.

A pair of shoes

Empathy, an ability to feel what another person feels, may be the writer's most important tool. Empathy is different from sympathy: It's one thing to feel sorry for a rape victim; it's another to imagine and write persuasively to recreate the constant terrors and distrust sown in the victim's mind. To write about a young widow in my story "School Uniform," I had to imagine the problems of a woman coping with her own grief and that of her children:

> After the funeral, Maddy had made sure that each child had something of Jim's. It was torture to handle his things, but she spread them out on their bed one night after the children were asleep and made choices. Anna draped his rosary from the mirror on her makeup table; Martin kept his paper route money secured in his father's silver money clip. Brian filled the brass candy dish that Jim used as an ashtray with his POGS and Sega Genesis cartridges. Daniel kept his baseball cards in Jim's billfold. There were days she wished she could have thrown everything out, and had she been alone, she might have moved away, started somewhere fresh with nothing to remind her of what had been, all she had lost when he died, leaving her at 38 with four children. And on nights like this, when there was trouble with Daniel, again, she wanted to give up.

When you write about a character, try to walk in that person's shoes.

A loom

Writers, like all artists, help society understand the connections that bind us. They identify patterns. Raymond Carver said, "writing is just a process of connections. Things begin to connect. A line here, a word here." Are you weaving connections in your stories? In your reading? In your life? Are you asking yourself what line goes to what line, and what makes a whole? "Only connect!" urged E.M. Forster. Turn your computer into a loom that weaves stories.

Six words

Thinking is the hardest part about writing and the one writers are likeliest to bypass. When I'm writing nonfiction, I try not to start writing until I've answered two questions: "What's the news?" and "What's the story?" Whatever the genre—essay, article or short story—effective writing conveys a single dominant message. To discover that theme or focus, try to sum up your story in six words, a phrase that captures the tension of the story. For a story about a teenage runaway hit by a train and rescued by another teen, my six words are "Lost, Then Found, On the Tracks." Why six words? No reason, except that in discipline, there is freedom.

An accelerator pedal

Free writing is the writer's equivalent of putting the pedal to the metal. I often start writing workshops by asking participants to write about "My Favorite Soup." It loosens the fingers, memory, and imagination. I surprised myself recently by describing post-Thanksgiving turkey soup:

> Most holidays have a "Do Not Resuscitate" sign on them. At the end of Christmas everybody vows that next year will be different, we'll pick names, not buy for everybody. It's too expensive, too time-consuming. But turkey soup puts a holiday on a respirator for a few more days of life, enough time to remember and savor the memories of the family around the table.

Speeding on a highway is a sure-fire route to an accident, but doing it on the page or computer screen creates an opportunity for fortunate accidents—those flashes of unconscious irony or insight that can trigger a story or take you and your readers deeper into one.

A time clock

Writers write. It's that simple—and that hard. If you're not writing regularly and for *at least* 15 minutes before your day job, then you're not a writer. Many times I resist; the writing is terrible, I'm too tired, I have no ideas, and then I remember that words beget other words. I stifle my whining and set to work, just for a little while, I tell myself. Almost always, I discover writing I had never imagined before I began, and those are the times I feel most like a writer. Put an imaginary time clock on your desk, right next to your computer. Punch in.

□ 10

Write from Where It Hurts

By Anne Bernays

THE FIRST TIME I TAUGHT A WRITING CLASS I WAS SCARED STIFF. NOTH-
ing I had done before—editing a magazine, publishing five novels—
prepared me for trying to explain how I'd done it or, more daunting
still, to translate what I worked at every day into curriculum.

I was a cook with nothing to measure with and no recorded recipes.
Whatever I knew about constructing a piece of fiction lay in an unsorted
jumble in what a shrink would call the unconscious but I prefer to think
of as the cellar. This was the place I dipped into optimistically whenever
I needed something.

If I had been asked how you build characterization or indicate motive,
I would have been at a loss. I was like the centipede who, when asked
which foot it moved first, froze. How could I teach others to write?
Well, you can't really teach people how to write, can you? They either
have it or they don't.

The five teenagers I met in a bright and cozy classroom wore expectant faces. What to do? "Write a story," I said, aware of how incredibly
hard it is to write a story, harder than a novel. Every piece must fit
snugly; each word must carry the weight of three or four words spoken
aloud, carelessly.

The students did their homework. They came back with stories about
extraterrestrials or about young people waking up in the morning, walking barefoot across a cold floor while smelling the coffee brewing
below, then into the bathroom to look at themselves in the mirror and
wonder who they were and why they were here. It didn't take long to
realize that they were making the same mistakes over and over again. I
wasn't teaching them anything.

Suppose I asked them all to do the same exercise, like scales for a
singer? So I made up an exercise as arbitrary and demanding as solfège,
gave them a word limit, 600, and sent them off. I thought they would

chafe at being reined in, having their imaginations severely clipped. But they surprised me by asking for another exercise and another. They were like first-graders completing a page in an arithmetic workbook and getting a gold star for it.

Making up these prose drills forced me to start organizing and classifying the elements of fiction that lay in that messy heap. This was salutary for me, and I began to see that about half the student's battle is learning basic skills, while the other half involves tapping into imagination, memory, and a singular view of life and the world, a view no one else shares until you put it into words.

My assignments sounded simple enough, but they were hard to bring off with style and conviction. One was an emotional childhood memory, to be told in the present tense, using the language and perceptions of a child, to be followed the next week by the same memory, this time in the past tense and from the point of view of an adult who, presumably, has learned something in the meantime.

From that time, 1975, I've taught writing at one place or another, always using exercises that focused on isolated elements of the craft, like dialogue, plot, point of view, characterization, revision, language. (The students hated the one in which they were not allowed to use any adjectives or adverbs, but it made them realize how strong verbs and nouns are, especially when they stand alone.)

You can teach almost anyone determined to learn them the basics required to write sentences and paragraphs that say what you want them to say clearly and concisely. It's far more difficult to get people to think like a writer, to give up conventional habits of mind and emotion. You must be able to step inside your character's skin and at the same time to remain outside the dicey circumstances you have maneuvered her into. I can't remember how many times I advised students to stop writing the sunny hours and write from where it hurts: "No one wants to read polite. It puts them to sleep."

The idea that people aren't always what they seem was a startling notion to more beginning students than I like to acknowledge. I thought everyone knew that a person who smiles all the time may very well have a troubled and even murderous heart. This in turn leads to an analysis of what it means to be a) cynical and b) skeptical, and how, if you're going to write fiction it's more productive to be b than a.

If you're going to write fiction that's even vaguely autobiographical—and which of us hasn't?—in trying to decide what to put in and what to leave out, don't consider what your friends, neighbors and especially your immediate family are going to think and/or say, assuming, that is, that they ever read what you write. You don't want to hurt people deliberately; if you've got the proper skills, you can disguise most people so they won't recognize themselves.

There's a sureness to good writing even when what's being written about doesn't make that much sense. It's the sureness of the so-called seat of an accomplished horseback rider or a sailor coming about in a strong wind. The words have both muscle and grace, familiarity and surprise. If forced to choose one writer of the 20th century who has these qualities most abundantly, I would name Vladimir Nabokov, who makes me want to take back everything I said about adjectives, except that each of his is chosen as carefully as an engagement ring: "On her brown shoulder, a raised purple-pink swelling (the work of some gnat) which I eased of its beautiful transparent poison between my long thumbnails and then sucked till I was gorged on her spicy blood."

You can't teach that kind of sureness; it comes only after writing every day, sometimes for years. The stock questions—"How will I know when to stop?" "How much detail is enough?"—can only be answered by "You'll know," trusting that as they acquire skill their mean self-editors are developing real muscle.

You can't teach someone who is tone deaf how to sing. But those people don't turn up for singing lessons. Students learn pretty fast whether or not they can carry a tune. When they can't, they leave the class.

And there's this to teaching: It's a public act. You're on, people listen to you, watch you, endow you with an authority you don't deserve. Most good teachers have a streak of the theatrical, myself not excluded. My mother wanted me to be a musical comedy actress-singer and to this end sent me to a celebrated singing teacher who had trained a good many Broadway and concert hall voices.

I took lessons from this woman until I appeared triumphantly as Papagano in my girls' school production of "The Magic Flute." It was, I confess, a high point in my life, almost as exhilarating as the sale of my first short story.

My most recurrent anxiety dream is not about writing but about getting up onstage and realizing I haven't learned my solo. The writer ultimately took over from the singer, and I'm not at all sorry about that. After 45 or so the singing voice begins to thin and waver. A writer's voice, God willing, is clear and strong until she's carried out feet first.

❑ 11

BUILDING A LASTING WRITERS' GROUP

BY D.M. ROSNER

OFTEN, A WRITER IS HIS OWN WORST CRITIC. AS A MEMBER OF A WRITers' group since its inception in 1989, I've found that participation in a good critique group is not only helpful in keeping my perspective and polishing my work, but is also inspirational during those inevitable dry spells. Experience has also taught me, however, that there are a number of pitfalls any new writers' group should be careful to avoid. If you're thinking about starting a writers' group, here are some ideas that may help.

Forming your group

All you really need to start your writers' group are other writers and a place to meet with them. Here are some ideas:

- If you know any writers, ask them if they would like to form a writers' group. If you don't know any other writers, try visiting a local college campus (evening writing classes draw writers of all ages and abilities). Another good place to meet writers is at writers' conferences, listings of which can be found in most writers' magazines.
- Try to keep the group small. More than five or six members may limit the ability of the group to critique one another's work. (Some groups are much larger; but if you choose to have a larger group, you may need to limit critiques to only a few members' work per meeting.)

Once you've gathered some writers, hold an initial meeting. You'll need to make the following decisions:

- How often to meet; what time; where; and for how long. (For instance, our group meets at 7:00 every other Monday night at members' homes or at coffee bars, for approximately two hours.)

46

- What kind of writing you wish as the focus of your group. (My group, for example, is for fiction writers. Some groups are for poetry only, while others cover a wide range of forms.)
- How much material each author can submit for critique at each meeting. (Ten pages per person per meeting is generally a good place to start.)
- Whether members prefer to read the work to be critiqued at home and bring comments to the meeting, or have authors read their work aloud at the meeting and invite comment. (We bring our work to the meetings and read it aloud—this can be helpful to the authors in catching errors, getting the rhythm of a sentence, or feeling out dialogue.)
- What ground rules to use, including choosing a leader or mediator.
- Whether or not you wish to write bylaws, to establish clearly the group's expectations of new members. These can come in handy as your group grows.
- Whether or not you wish to have each member report in on what he or she has accomplished since the previous meeting, and if so, who will keep a record of this information.

A word about critiques

The purpose of a critique group is to provide honest comments on members' work. Don't forget that many writers—new writers in particular—have fragile egos, but there is such a thing as being too nice. If something about a member's piece isn't working for you, it's important to share that with the writer, in a direct but gentle way.

Here are some things to remember when critiquing:

- Be honest when critiquing one another's work, but be diplomatic in your approach when offering suggestions.
- Give a balanced critique, taking care to point out the parts that work well, as well as those that don't.
- Explain the reasons for your comments or suggestions.
- Don't argue with another member's opinion of your work. If you don't agree with the changes suggested, just don't use them. (If you don't understand why the suggestion was made, you may politely ask the person giving the critique to clarify the comment.)

If your members are new to the art of tactful critiquing, you may want to create a checklist, or guidelines, for critiquing. This could be helpful in reminding members to share positive opinions, point out areas that need work, and provide reasons for each.

Common pitfalls

It's been rare that we've had to ask a member to leave our group, but it has happened. We've learned from our mistakes over the years, and have established bylaws and a screening process for new members, to avoid potential problems. Here are some tips that might help you avoid such problems:

- Be very clear about *exactly* what you expect from your members. Something as simple as expecting them to come to every meeting can cause misunderstanding and resentment.
- Be sure your members all share the same level of dedication. Your group can be serious or informal, but it's best not to try to mix the two.
- Every member should be expected to put an equal level of effort into critiquing one another's work.
- If you have a problem with a member's level of participation in the group (or method of critique, or anything else), the leader or mediator should talk to him or her about it, as diplomatically as possible. This may not always work (and the member may choose to drop out of the group), but sometimes what seems to be a major problem is nothing more than a minor misunderstanding blown out of proportion.

Keeping your group alive

My writers' group has stayed together so long because luckily, our members are serious writers who are dedicated to one another. Sure, we've had some members who have come and gone, but many have left only because they've moved out of state, and we all still keep in touch.

If you want your group to last, it's important to find others who share your level of dedication. Whenever new members join, explain to them how you feel about your group, to avoid potential problems later.

Don't feel that your group has to be limited to its scheduled meetings, either. In addition to regular meetings, our group also holds a variety of special events, such as:

- *Novel's Day*, during which we meet for a full day of work on our own individual projects. Writing in a room full of other working writers is very inspiring. (We hold three or more such days each year.)
- *Annual Halloween party*, for which we write a story to be read at the party (and come dressed as one of our characters).
- *Annual retreat,* held over long a weekend, usually at a bed & breakfast, and which is rather like an extended Novel's Day.

Writer's groups can be helpful, inspiring, and a lot of fun. For more ideas, stop by our website at: http://pages.cthome.net/6ft_ferrets/

❏ 12

AN END TO WRITER'S BLOCK!

BY SANDRA SCOFIELD

I'M IMPATIENT WITH THE VERY IDEA OF WRITER'S BLOCK, BUT IT doesn't mean I don't know it when I see it—or feel it. Panic, lassitude, depression: any or all may be symptoms, but whatever the version, the sure thing is the writing stops and heartache starts. The late poet William Stafford used to say, "Lower your standards, and write." He wasn't one to wait around for the perfect moment. Dig for ore, and maybe you'll find a gem. He wasn't encouraging inferior writing, and neither am I, but he was right in saying that you can't just sit it out. The way to end writer's block is to replace it with habits that keep you confident and productive.

After years of experience and observation, I've identified these factors as primary contributors to writer's block: *(1) Lack of research; (2) Lack of imagination; (3) Lack of focus; (4) Lack of confidence.*

Before I talk about the problems separately, I have to say that they all have a common thread: Too often, the writer starts writing too soon, with unreasonable expectations. I've heard many writers say they just "start writing and see where it goes," and if that works for you, well, you're one of the lucky ones. But many writers—especially beginners—tell me that just jumping in at the start of a particular story (or, heaven help them, a novel) is a sure route to a dead end. I'm all for free writing, *as long as you have no expectations or standards.* There are dozens of books to give you ideas for writing practice, but practice, by definition, isn't the actual game. The harder it is for you to write a "real story," the more you probably need to do the kind of writing that has no pressure, no criteria for success. Find a stimulus, and "warm up" this way, every day if you like. The writer Carol Bly tells her students to write an autobiography, a fine way to write past your hang-ups, to explore the fertile ground of memory, and to put words on a page without the burden of invention. I tell writers to write a "credo," a statement

50

of beliefs: What values mean the most to you? What scares you? What "news" would you like to spread? *What are you trying to figure out about the world?* You'll learn things about yourself, and you'll have concepts to help you evaluate the *content* of your work. I do it once a year; my credo is always evolving.

Research

Writing historical fiction carries the obvious dictum to learn as much as you can about your subject. What you may not realize, however, is that "research" includes all the information and observations that will help you develop characters and structure in any story. When I knew I wanted to set my novel in a Mexican village near an expatriate colony, I read about retirement in Mexico. I talked to several people who had spent time in Chapala, near Guadalajara, and others who knew San Miguel de Allende. Finally, I flew down and spent ten days exploring the region around Lake Chapala. I took the cheap buses; I hired taxi drivers to take me to remote villages. I sat in squares and talked my observations into a microcassette recorder. I took photographs of buildings and panoramas, market stalls, and the like. (I prefer to jot down notes about people unobtrusively.) I tried foods I hadn't eaten before. When I wanted to show my character Mr. Riley growing braver—he's too timid to go to Egypt!—I put him in those buses, and set a plate of tripe in front of him.

Of course, we can't always travel. When I was researching *Plain Seeing*, in order to write the 39 pages that take place in 1942 Hollywood, I read biographies of film stars and looked at books of photographs. I viewed a dozen movies from that period. I didn't know what I was looking for, yet I found it: a movie for my character to act in; the ambiance of a screen test; the details of a starlet's contract. It took a pleasurable month, and at the end, I had the confidence to write the chapter. If you feel "dry," you may just need to feed yourself from the springs of research.

Imagination

You must cultivate an agile mind. Learn that the elements of a story are all malleable. Stretch your creativity. Form a story group, in which writers share oral stories. Use family stories, memories of "embarrassing moments" or "something you lost." Fill in the unknown in a newspaper clipping. Read a published story and have everyone make up a different ending. Many books suggest story starters. Play with them *orally* so that you push yourself to work nimbly without worrying about style. Before I wrote *A Chance to See Egypt*, which I thought of as a kind of folk tale, I participated in a workshop in which we made up our own fairy tales and myths.

Apply these same playful principles to work in progress. When I feel stuck, I get out a big sheet of paper and write my characters' names and everything I know about them. Then I set about changing one feature about each to see what effect it has on their interactions. Try brainstorming questions and answering them in as many ways as you can. The most creative question is *What if . . . ?* Don't get attached to an idea too quickly; the next idea might be better. When something clicks, get right back to writing.

Focus

Here's my prejudice: When I set out, I want to have some idea of where I'm going. I may amend my story ten times over before I've finished it. Tell the story simply, in a few pages, knowing it's only a sketch. Go back to your credo, and ask yourself if you're pursuing something that really matters to you. (A false goal will kill your story.) Try to "see" a strong image in the story, and describe it. Where does it fit? Are you moving *from* it or *toward* it? In *A Chance to See Egypt*, I imagined a young woman in a moving Jeep on a dusty road, her long black hair blowing. That became an important moment of transition in the novel. In *Plain Seeing*, the picture of a young pregnant girl stepping down from a train reverberates throughout the novel, which is about the ways the loss of a parent haunts a child's life ever after.

Confidence

You can see by now that I believe "writing-aerobics" build muscles, i.e., skills; those skills build confidence. Nevertheless, writers are much affected by emotions. Publishing is tough. You've been rejected more times than you can count. You see writers whose work you don't like reaping rewards, or you see so many writers you admire you can't imagine there's any room for you. Your day is crammed, and you aren't giving writing enough time. You don't want to write, and you don't want to quit.

Give yourself a break. Remind yourself of what you have accomplished. Look through your notebooks (you *do* keep a notebook!); you'll be amazed at the ideas you've had. Make a fresh copy of a successful story (or a successful scene), and ask a friend to read it and tell you it's good. That's right; ask for praise. You can look at your weaknesses some other time. Read about the craft. Go to a writers' conference, and hang out with people who love what you love.

Also, kid yourself into offhandedness. I keep index cards by my bed and by the couch, and any time of day or night I jot down ideas. I'm not committed to them, so it's easy, and later, when I have a pile, I transcribe them and see what I've got. I write little playlets of dialogue instead of a scene, so I can hear the characters; of course it's not going into my novel that way, so I don't feel self-conscious. Before I write a scene, I daydream it over and over. I write jacket copy for the book this is going to be someday, even a review or two! Write one line you hope will be said about your work, and tack it above your desk.

Do your drafting on the back of used pages, or on cheap colored paper, so you are fully aware that it doesn't really count; it's just a first try. Team up with a friend and check in every week (every day?) and tell one another one idea you've had. No time? No ideas? Write one sentence. That's right, one sentence. Maybe it'll grow to one paragraph, or you'll discover a fresh idea. Set a timer for ten minutes and get up guiltlessly when it rings. I've written seven novels in ten years, and I've hardly ever worked longer than two hours at a sitting. The thing is, I sit down often!

You're the only one who knows how important writing is to you. You don't have to hurry; you *shouldn't* hurry. Seek the pleasure of discovery, and breathe through the tough times. Writer's block isn't a wall of bricks; it's as ephemeral as dust motes. Walk right through.

❑ 13

TELLING STORIES

BY PATTY DANN

"I STOPPED LYING WHEN I TURNED SEVENTY," CONFIDED ONE OF MY students. For the past ten years, spring, summer, fall and winter, in a bare room at the local YMCA, I have had my socks knocked off by the stories the students write and read aloud. They are all older than I am. The only requirement to get into my class is to be at least fifty years old. My main role is that of a willing ear. The students are butchers and bakers and candlestick makers from Brooklyn and Bialystok; they have survived wars and marriages and the twentieth century. For eight years, as I preached the necessity of writing boldly and honestly about real life, I could write only fiction. Until two years ago, when real life intervened.

In a time of sound-bites and web sites, instant rewind and fast-forward, when people take pictures of their babies being born, and one hour later lie in the recovery room gazing at the photos from the Quik-Pix down the block, the workshops are based on the primitive notion of telling stories around the campfire. This process of writing and then reading aloud has a kind of magical force.

I didn't always confine my classes to the older crowd. One April afternoon, as the students trickled out of the classroom, an older woman, who had not shown me her writing, waited hesitantly at the door.

"Excuse me," she said. "I grew up in Vladivostok, that's Eastern Siberia. I was born the year of the Russian Revolution. One evening my father bumped into Lenin on the street . . ."

The next morning I asked the director if I could limit my workshops to students fifty years and over.

"I don't think you'll get anybody, but give it a try," he said.

There were four students in my first class. I was assigned to a pottery studio with high counters. We all sat hunched on stools over the sinks. "Write about a memory of food. Ten minutes," I said with authority.

After the allotted time, I asked the students to read their work aloud. The stories flowed, from a Chinese woman who as a child ate fried-egg sandwiches with her uncle in the back of a laundromat; an Irish painter with a hearing aid the size of a cigarette pack who nursed six babies; a man who wrote of a parakeet who ate ice cream and spoke French; a woman who hid from the Nazis in a barn for a winter and had only chestnuts to eat . . .

These stories always had some kind of curative effect on me. They filled me with a kind of inner peace, even though the stories had as much heartache as happiness.

I left them again to write about a memory of shoes. As I sat outside the class, I thought of the blue sneakers left in the cubbyhole of my friend, Billy, who fell off a horse and died in the fourth grade. I could not bring myself to write even his name. When I returned to the classroom the students read their stories aloud. I felt as if I were listening to a celestial radio; every time I turned the dial I was enchanted.

"My grandparents were both mute and wore high-button shoes. They invented their own sign language. They came to this country from Poland when they were fifteen and were married for seventy years," read the first woman.

"My father was a carpenter in South Africa. He left raw planks of wood out in the yard to age, and when it rained, the sweet smell of wet cedar and his work boots filled our house," read the second woman.

The poet, Marian Moore, said that a writer has to have "the courage of your peculiarities," and I certainly have enough peculiarities, but they always came out in fiction. I was frightened to try life on the other side.

The classes grew and it seemed essential for everyone to read aloud each time, as if they were bearing witness to their lives, so I began to limit the classes to twelve people.

Once, a student walked out of my class. The assignment I'd given was to write about Roosevelt's death, and miraculously, an argument ensued about Eleanor Roosevelt. There were shouting and clenched fists between two women debating whether Eleanor should have spent more time with her children. At this point the woman who believed Eleanor should have stayed home more bolted out the door, never to be heard from again.

While many people said they'd signed up for the class to write something for their children or grandchildren, halfway through the semester the same questions always arose. "What should I do if my family finds my work? Where can I hide my disks? How can I guarantee that after I die my work will be destroyed?"

The students rarely wrote about their children or even their marriages, but instead about experiences they'd had years ago. Girdles and spats, washboards and propeller planes, the first electric lights on the block . . . the nineteenth century seemed closer than the twenty-first. Over ten years, only four things have been constant in the class:

1. Most of the students are women.

2. Most of them apologize before they read their work aloud for the first time.

3. If I give the assignment of "Religion," they all say they are not religious.

4. If I give the assignment of "Mother," at least one person weeps.

"What about *your* life?" a bold student asked at the start of a class.

"Oh, no," I demurred. "I'm too young."

That was so until my husband and I took a long journey to Vilnius, Lithuania, and I began to keep a journal.

Did my transatlantic voyage, becoming a mother, and having a son whose story has been so different from my own make me write about real life? Possibly. I can't be certain.

When I was a little girl one of my favorite stories was about a girl who desperately wanted to have hair long enough for a pony tail. She cried and cried until miraculously, one day, her hair was long enough. Time had passed. And that is the simple and wise lesson I have learned from my students. Perhaps I started writing about my own life when I finally became a mother, but perhaps it is because I am finally old enough to remember.

❏ 14

GIVING UP YOUR DAY JOB

BY ROBERTA ROESCH

IS THERE A WRITER WITH SOUL SO DEAD WHO NEVER TO HIMSELF—OR herself—has said, "I can't wait to give up my day job"?

From my encounters with writers—in editing, writing, and teaching—I doubt that there are many who don't experience the utopian dream of a full-time free-lance life. But whether you currently free-lance full-time or envision that for the future, the following baker's dozen of ongoing rules and refreshers are the "Go" signs to free-lance success.

Rule 1: Stick to those two **S Words**—SCHEDULE and SELF-STARTER. Admittedly they're overused and sometimes dirty phrases, in many people's minds. But they're *still* the *only* way to get to your day's writing. It doesn't matter whether you begin at 5:00 a.m., 9:00 a.m., or 3:00 in the afternoon. The *essential* is to start and keep going. One of my first interviews as a new writer was with Fannie Hurst, a famous novelist of her time, and I'll always remember her advice: "Give yourself the gun—and begin."

Rule 2: Line up an ongoing bread-and-butter project for a base income, unless you're made of money or have a rich uncle. There's no denying that free-lancing can be a feast or famine affair so, especially in the beginning, it's smart to have one sure thing that will bring in enough money on a regular basis, and won't take too much time.

Rule 3: Keep your place of work *organized.* This big O for organization applies to the space in which you work, your desk and desktop, your files and supplies and equipment you need. You don't have to be neat, but you do have to have hands-on accessibility to what will help you work efficiently. A writer new to free-lancing telephoned me one day to ask *me* to look up a word in *my* dictionary. His excuse? He worked in his basement and his dictionary was on the third floor.

Rule 4: Use technology. Even though there are still some yellow-pad writers—and even though you don't have to be a dyed-in-the-wool techie—you'll usually find that the electronic products and software that are right for you and your work help you accomplish more. Mastering Internet resources and on-line research techniques saves lots of time.

Rule 5: Be firm about interruptions. One writer decided her first task as a new free lancer was to train her family to respect her working hours. She had to lay down the law: She was to be interrupted only in case of an emergency. Then, with tongue in cheek, she defined an emergency as "something involving blood and smoke—and lots of it." Even when you threaten blood and smoke, it's not easy to get people to respect your working time. But set and stick to boundaries. Let your answering machine take all phone calls except top priority ones. See that people know when you're *not* available. Then if you still get interruptions—as you inevitably will—say firmly, "It's not a good time," "I can't do it now," or "It will have to wait."

Rule 6: Get assignments and deadline work to editors and clients on time. Become known for your reliability. To succeed as a free lancer, you usually need several projects and multiple deadlines going simultaneously. This means requesting sufficient time to do each job and, then, adding in a little extra time for good measure. It also means starting projects on time, tracking your progress, and being realistic about how much you can accomplish in each work session.

Rule 7: Remember the two words "Good enough" and forget the idea that you have to work on every piece of writing till it's A+ perfect. Even though it's ideal to give your best to every project, the reality-and-time element is that it's often more important to get B and C jobs done and delivered on time rather than hanging on to them longer than it takes to do a *good* job. Know when A+ is required and when "Good enough" is more productive and appropriate.

Rule 8: Say "No" when you should say "No." Too often your golf buddies think you can drop your writing every time they need an extra player. Or your mother expects you to meet her at the mall because your time is your own. As a "No" reminder, one writer friend has "No" pasted to his phone. My phone reminder that encourages a "No" states, "The business of a writer is to write."

Rule 9: Make your time do double duty by doing two tasks at once. While waiting on the phone, delete files you no longer need from your computer's hard disk, skim "To Read" material, or sort through the mail. While watching TV at night, set yourself up with 100 postpaid envelopes, plus labels or a rubber stamp with your return address. When you need to send out mail during the day, the envelopes will be ready to address and mail.

Rule 10: Perform a postmortem at the end of a writing project. Record what went well and what didn't. Ask yourself what you liked about your work on the project and what you didn't like. If all went well and you were pleased with your working methods, continue doing—and improving on—the procedure that worked. If you didn't like your handling of the project and the end results, revise your plan of action for future projects.

Rule 11: During your writing hours, take breaks to restore your energy. Get a cup of coffee, walk around your workplace, or go outside for a few minutes of fresh air. Sneak in five minutes of daily exercise by stretching or lifting small weights while waiting for manuscripts to be printed.

Rule 12: Stay connected to other people, since full-time free-lancing is an "alone" life. Join professional writers' organizations and interact with their programs and members. Use Internet newsgroups or bulletin boards to stay in touch with peers. Get out of your workplace on a regular basis for meals or contacts with others when you can compare notes with writers who share the free-lance life. Try to arrange your appointments and outside contacts for one trip—instead of running in and out of your workplace for separate appointments all week long.

When someone asks for a meeting on a day when you've decided "No outside trips," just say you're committed; no need for explanations.

Rule 13: Forgive yourself (and the world around you) when, despite your best laid intentions and plans, your free-lance schedule, organization, and time management do not work as you had hoped. Major and minor crises and frustrations throw free-lancing off the track. But since they are bound to happen at times, roll with the punches when they do. When the "Go" sign is green again, get back on track with the rules and refreshers.

Most of all, when you *can* free-lance full-time, *enjoy* your writing and work because, when you give up your day job and become a full-time free lancer, life is about as good as it gets.

❏ 15

ARE YOU READING ENOUGH?

BY MAGGIE MURPHY

WE TAKE IT AS A GIVEN THAT THOSE OF US WHO LONG TO SEE OUR words in print love to read, but are you reading *enough?* We'd be surprised if an art student rarely visited art museums, or a would-be actor repeatedly turned down free theatre tickets. Yet it's a common lament among editors that many aspiring writers desperate to sell their manuscripts have scant acquaintance with the wonderful literary works already in libraries and bookstores.

Reading inspires us, sparks new ideas, and teaches us by example how to write effectively. The best writers I know, published and unpublished, are voracious readers. When you read interviews with accomplished writers, take special note of how frequently they describe themselves as *readers* in love with books.

If you aren't nurturing yourself as a reader, you're short-changing yourself as a writer. Here are ten tips to invigorate your reading program:

1) Read widely

The best literary menu provides plenty of variety. Most writers do have special loves: One of mine is children's literature. Still, you don't want to limit your reading to only your favorite literary field.

Read widely, and you'll discover galaxies of exciting worlds to explore.

In addition, reading plays, poems, fairy tales, and myths is invaluable to writers crafting in quite different fields. As just two examples, take plays and poetry.

Whether you're writing a mystery, a science fiction novella, or the Great American Novel, you can learn a great deal about dynamic writing from reading William Shakespeare's *Macbeth* or any other powerful play. In plays, you'll find excellent examples of dialogue that develops character and speeds the plot along. You'll also get a feel for presenting your story in scenes and, by examining the way a playwright handles entrances and exits, get your characters in and out of those scenes smoothly.

Then there's the oft-neglected world of poetry, a magical realm of vivid imagery and fanciful leaps. Reading poetry, everything from the delicate word-web of a Matsuo Bashō haiku to Samuel Taylor Coleridge's enchanting *Christabel*, will encourage you to weave more artful and inimitable tapestries with your prose.

2) Keep a "books finished" list

I started such a list in college nearly 20 years ago, and it's been a good way to monitor my reading life. If you suddenly stop adding to a "books read" list, you're more likely to head for the library or bookstore instead of letting several bookless weeks slide by.

It's rewarding to see your list grow. Remember that reading is an accomplishment as well as an enjoyable activity. There is no round of applause when you finish the last page of a marathon read like Victor Hugo's *Les Misérables*, but adding it to your "books finished" list is a small way to celebrate your reading success.

3) Always bring a book along

How often have you found yourself in a crowded waiting room wishing you had a book with you?

To make book-carrying more convenient, look for some "light reading" that is literally just that. If the hardback you're reading is too heavy, buy the same book secondhand in paperback, if available, and slip it into your bag. Choose slim books to read on your daily travels, such as Robert Louis Stevenson's classic novella *Dr. Jekyll and Mr. Hyde*.

4) Listen to books on tape

Audio books can transform a boring car trip into a literary adventure. Books on tape are also excellent for people who feel too tired to read in bed at night.

You'll find a tempting selection of audio books available in bookstores and public libraries. You can listen to the poems of Emily Dickinson, or a full-cast performance of Shakespeare's *A Midsummer Night's Dream*.

The sound of a well-trained voice reading to you is entrancing. Just slip in a cassette, and it's like having Scheherazade entertain you. It's especially meaningful to put yourself under the spell of the spoken word. With your own writing, you're striving to create polished work that stands the "read it out loud" test.

5) Read to a friend

Enjoy the experience of reading out loud to a friend, relative, child, or other book lover. This is a rewarding way to share a book.

6) Create your own reading theme

Focus on time travel, sea or ghost stories. Save the theme reading lists you find in magazines, and on library flyers and bookmarks. Read Charlotte Brontë's *Jane Eyre,* and then Jean Rhys's *Wide Sargasso Sea,* a haunting novel with an inventive tie-in to the Brontë classic. Read writers associated with places you're visiting, such as Dickens when you're in London.

One of my reading themes centered on Newbery Medal-winning children's books. Without this self-assignment, I doubt I'd have bought a used copy of Dhan Gopal Mukerji's *Gay-Neck: The Story of a Pigeon,* the Newbery award winner in 1928, now a little-known book, but rich with achingly beautiful descriptions of India.

7) Find book buddies

When a friend recommends a book she's just finished, I try to read it soon after so it will still be fresh in her mind for discussion.

One of my friends and I have had interesting conversations about works as different as Banana Yoshimoto's lyrical novel *Kitchen* and Jon Krakauer's gripping *Into Thin Air: A Personal Account of the Mt. Everest Disaster.*

And there's nothing like visiting with a book friend who shares your literary tastes. My mother is my children's book buddy because she understands that good children's books can be literature. We've talked about children's stories set on islands, brave storybook mice, and the verse of Mother Goose.

8) Join a book group

As a member of a book group, you have the opportunity to share the joy of books with others, while stretching yourself as a reader. Check listings in bookstore, library, and community center newsletters.

9) Go online

The Internet is an amazing resource for bibliophiles. For example, the online bookseller Amazon.com features just about every literary offering you can imagine, including book lists, author interviews, and even free e-mailed book recommendations.

Just one caution here: Exploring the Internet is like flipping through an enchanted magazine that will never have a last page. Don't be lured into doing so much reading *about* reading that you wind up staring at your computer screen for hours instead of opening a good book.

10) When you can't read a lot, at least read a little

People with frantic daily schedules often make little headway reading demanding tomes, become discouraged, and stop reading much at all. If you're facing a particularly hectic time, avoid this trap by reading plays, poems, or the fine short stories in good literary journals or collections. Try reading children's books such as C.S. Lewis's *The Lion, the Witch and the Wardrobe*. This book is packed with adventure and wisdom, yet it is written for shorter attention spans. In just six pages, you've left England and entered the magical land of Narnia.

When I'm very busy, I also like to set out certain books that don't need to be read cover to cover but are ideal for dipping into again and again, titles like *Grimms' Fairy Tales*, Ingri and Edgar Parin d'Aulaire's *Norse Gods and Giants*, and *The Arabian Nights*. (Even Sindbad the sailor's narrative is conveniently broken up into seven voyages.) For writers, such myths and tales are the bedrock of storytelling.

❏ 16

FINDING THE RIGHT CONFERENCE FOR *YOU*

BY DOROTHY WINSLOW WRIGHT

WHAT DO YOU WANT FROM A WRITERS CONFERENCE? POETRY? MAR-keting? Basic writing techniques? Do you want to attend one nearby, perhaps in a downtown hotel, or do you prefer a quieter setting—the pine-scented woods or a beach by a rolling surf? In my twenty-five years as a published writer, I have attended conferences from New England to Hawaii, some lasting only a day, others a week. Some gave me far more than I expected, others left me unsatisfied.

This doesn't mean there was anything wrong with the conferences; they just weren't what I needed at the time. In my early days, I sought the basics: How to prepare a manuscript for submission—margins, format, font. What goes into a query letter? Is an SASE necessary? Now, as a more seasoned writer, I look for conferences slanted toward my particular interests.

Selecting a conference should be done with careful consideration for what will meet your needs:

How much time can you invest? Can you afford the accommodations? What does the conference cover? Who are the speakers? What workshops are offered? What genres are covered? Do you want a no-nonsense, down-to-earth conference in casual surroundings, or one with some amenities? Some conferences take place at posh resorts, where meals and rooms are expensive.

Conferences keep you current about books being published, and you begin to see trends. You learn that publishing a book today is far more costly than it was ten years ago. What impact does this have on a first-time novelist? What are the chances of having your book accepted by an agent or publisher? Is your theme marketable? Is it timely or dated? Have trends changed since you began writing your book? If so, how can you update it? Do you need powerful sex scenes, or is that scaling back? How do spiritual books fit into the market place? What are magazines buying? What is out, and what is in? These are the sorts of things you ferret out at writers' conferences, either in lectures, informal workshops, or discussed over lunch.

At one conference I attended, I found a solution to a problem I hadn't been able to solve: How could I interest an editor in an adult book that opens in the voice of a sixteen-year-old? The two editors who considered it saw it as a young adult novel. It wasn't, but they hadn't read past the first ten pages. At the conference, suggestions came quickly: Add a preface, use the last chapter as the first then flash back, rewrite the beginning with an adult scene. What I will do, I'm not sure, but the conference met my needs.

The very first conference I attended opened doors for me. Madeleine Costigan, who conducted the fiction workshop, read one of my manuscripts and advised me to send it to *Ford Times* Magazine. It was accepted and published the following spring. Until then, I had little knowledge about writing and submission techniques. Many benefits came my way because I attended a conference that treated beginners with such tenderness. I returned for two more years, then decided it was time to branch out and attend a week-long conference.

There, I realized immediately that a large conference lacks intimacy. The workshops were held in a chapel, which doubled as an auditorium. Although there was time for questions at the close of each lecture, there was little interaction with the instructors. It was not the cosseting environment that existed at my first conference, yet it was stimulating in a different way. I still remember author Dennis Hensley, whose high-powered talk convinced me that luck had little to do with getting published—that there was an art to marketing. If your work is good, it will sell. Just keep sending it out. A dozen items circulating at once would bring results. My fingers burned as I wrote down the work habits he deemed essential, habits I still use. I write every day and send out at least two items a week, either new work, a rejected manuscript to a new publisher, or a query letter.

When I moved to Hawaii, I lost my ties with east coast conferences, but found a new one through the Honolulu Branch of the National League of American Pen Women. The one-day conference scheduled eight workshops, two at the same time, some geared to beginners, others toward experienced writers. It concluded with a panel of local editors seeking free-lance material. This informed me of local needs, and a few weeks later my article, "In Search of Olivine," appeared in the travel pages of a Honolulu newspaper.

Because of the informality at a large California writers conference I attended, it was easy to find qualified people willing to help solve problems. This could occur at a beach party, in the dining room, or in workshops, all in more or less informal settings. For memoirs, we sat around a long table in a conference room. There was a relaxed, give-and-take atmosphere as different people presented their work. For fiction, we sat movie-house style in an auditorium, the enthusiasm contagious. The poetry session took place in a beach-front cottage as writers read their poems to the thrum of the surf.

One evening, biographer A. Scott Berg focused on the research that went into his *Lindbergh* book. As I listened, it struck me that research is a long, arduous task, and that well-known authors go through the same struggles beginners do. This applies to comedy writers as well, which became clear as we listened to a humor panel. Although one-liners leapt across the platform, keeping us in stitches, the seriousness of their writing came through. Even established authors spend hours at their keyboards, and continue to have doubts about the success of a work-in-progress.

During the long flight home from California, I realized I had lucked into the conference that was right for me at this stage in my writing. But as I thought about it, I realized it wasn't luck, it was a carefully considered choice. A little research via friends, the Internet or publications such as *The Writer*, will help you zero in on the appropriate conference for you. If you do, you'll have an experience that will brighten and enrich your writing life, an experience that will leave you wanting more.

How To Write—
Techniques

❑ GENERAL FICTION

□ 17

EVERYTHING YOU NEED TO KNOW ABOUT WRITING SUCCESSFULLY— IN TEN MINUTES

BY STEPHEN KING

I. The First Introduction

THAT'S RIGHT. I KNOW IT SOUNDS LIKE AN AD FOR SOME SLEAZY WRITers' school, but I really am going to tell you everything you need to pursue a successful and financially rewarding career writing fiction, and I really am going to do it in ten minutes, which is exactly how long it took me to learn. It will actually take you twenty minutes or so to read this article, however, because I have to tell you a story, and then I have to write a *second* introduction. But these, I argue, should not count in the ten minutes.

II. The Story, or, How Stephen King Learned to Write

When I was a sophomore in high school, I did a sophomoric thing which got me in a pot of fairly hot water, as sophomoric didoes often do. I wrote and published a small satiric newspaper called *The Village Vomit*. In this little paper I lampooned a number of teachers at Lisbon (Maine) High School, where I was under instruction. These were not very gentle lampoons; they ranged from the scatological to the downright cruel.

Eventually, a copy of this paper found its way into the hands of a faculty member, and since I had been unwise enough to put my name on it (a fault, some critics would argue, of which I have still not been entirely cured), I was brought into the office. The sophisticated satirist had by that time reverted to what he really was: a fourteen-year-old kid who was shaking in his boots and wondering if he was going to get a suspension . . . what we called a "three-day vacation" in those dim days of 1964.

I wasn't suspended. I was forced to make a number of apologies— they were warranted, but they tasted like dog-dirt in my mouth—and spent a week in detention hall. And the guidance counselor arranged what he no doubt thought of as a more constructive channel for my talents. This was a job—contingent upon the editor's approval—writing sports for the Lisbon *Enterprise*, a twelve-page weekly of the sort with which any small-town resident will be familiar. This editor was the man who taught me everything I know about writing in ten minutes. His name was John Gould—not the famed New England humorist or the novelist who wrote *The Greenleaf Fires,* but a relative of both, I believe.

He told me he needed a sports writer, and we could "try each other out," if I wanted.

I told him I knew more about advanced algebra than I did sports.

Gould nodded and said, "You'll learn."

I said I would at least try to learn. Gould gave me a huge roll of yellow paper and promised me a wage of 1/2¢ per word. The first two pieces I wrote had to do with a high school basketball game in which a member of my school team broke the Lisbon High scoring record. One of these pieces was a straight piece of reportage. The second was a feature article.

I brought them to Gould the day after the game, so he'd have them for the paper, which came out Fridays. He read the straight piece, made two minor corrections, and spiked it. Then he started in on the feature piece with a large black pen and taught me all I ever needed to know about my craft. I wish I still had the piece—it deserves to be framed, editorial corrections and all—but I can remember pretty well how it went and how it looked when he had finished with it. Here's an example:

Last night, in the ~~well-loved~~ (gymnasium) of Lisbon High

School, partisans and Jay Hills fans alike were stunned by

an athletic performance unequalled in school history: Bob

Ransom, ~~known as "Bullet" Bob for both his size and~~

~~accuracy,~~ scored thirty-seven points. He did it with grace

and speed. . .and he did it with a odd courtesy as well,

committing only two personal fouls in his ~~knight-like~~ quest
                                                vs basketball team
for a record which has eluded Lisbon ~~thinclads~~ since 1953.

When Gould finished marking up my copy in the manner I have indicated above, he looked up and must have seen something on my face. I think he must have thought it was horror, but it was not: It was revelation.

"I only took out the bad parts, you know," he said. "Most of it's pretty good."

"I know," I said, meaning both things; yes, most of it was good, and yes, he had only taken out the bad parts. "I won't do it again."

"If that's true," he said, "you'll never have to work again. You can do *this* for a living."

Then he threw back his head and laughed.

And he was right: I *am* doing this for a living, and as long as I can keep on, I don't expect ever to have to work again.

III. The Second Introduction

All of what follows has been said before. If you are interested enough in writing to be a purchaser of this book, you will have either heard or read all (or almost all) of it before. Thousands of writing courses are taught across the United States each year; seminars are convened; guest lecturers talk, then answer questions, and it all boils down to what follows.

I am going to tell you these things again because often people will only listen—really *listen*—to someone who makes a lot of money doing the thing he's talking about. This is sad but true. And I told you the story above not to make myself sound like a character out of a Horatio Alger novel but to make a point: I saw, I listened, and I *learned*. Until that day in John Gould's little office, I had been writing first drafts of stories that might run 2,500 words. The second drafts were apt to run 3,300 words. Following that day, my 2,500-word first drafts became 2,200-word second drafts. And two years after that, I sold the first one.

So here it is, with all the bark stripped off. It'll take ten minutes to read, and you can apply it right away . . . if you *listen*.

IV. Everything You Need to Know About Writing Successfully

1. Be talented

This, of course, is the killer. What is talent? I can hear someone shouting, and here we are, ready to get into a discussion right up there with "What is the meaning of life?" for weighty pronouncements and total uselessness. For the purposes of the beginning writer, talent may as well be defined as eventual success—publication and money. If you wrote something for which someone sent you a check, if you cashed the check and it didn't bounce, and if you then paid the electric bill with the money, I consider you talented.

Now some of you are really hollering. Some of you are calling me one crass money-fixated creep. Nonsense. Worse than nonsense, off the subject. We're not talking about good or bad here. I'm interested in telling you how to get your stuff published, not in critical judgments of who's good or bad. As a rule, the critical judgments come after the check's been spent, anyway. I have my own opinion, but most times I keep them to myself. People who are published steadily and are paid for what they are writing may be either saints or trollops, but they are clearly reaching a great many someones who want what they have. Ergo, they are communicating. Ergo, they are talented. The biggest part of writing successfully is being talented, and in the context of marketing, the only bad writer is one who doesn't get paid. If you're not talented, you won't succeed. And if you're not succeeding, you should know when to quit.

When is that? I don't know. It's different for each writer. Not after six rejection slips, certainly, nor after sixty. But after six-hundred? Maybe. After six thousand? My friend, after six thousand pinks, it's time you tried painting or computer programming.

Further, almost every aspiring writer knows when he is getting warmer—you start getting little jotted notes on your rejection slips, or personal letters . . . maybe a commiserating phone call. It's lonely out there in the cold, but there *are* encouraging voices . . . unless there is nothing in your words that warrants encouragement. I think you owe it to yourself to skip as much of the self-illusion as possible. If your eyes are open, you'll know which way to go . . . or when to turn back.

2. Be neat

Type. Double-space. Use a nice heavy white paper. If you've marked your manuscript a lot, do another draft.

3. Be self-critical

If you haven't marked up your manuscript a lot, you did a lazy job. Only God gets things right the first time. Don't be a slob.

4. Remove every extraneous word

You want to get up on a soapbox and preach? Fine. Get one, and try your local park. You want to write for money? Get to the point. And if you remove the excess garbage and discover you can't find the point, tear up what you wrote and start all over again . . . or try something new.

5. Never look at a reference book while doing a first draft

You want to write a story? Fine. Put away your dictionary, your encyclopedias, your World Almanac, and your thesaurus. Better yet, throw your thesaurus into the wastebasket. The only things creepier than a thesaurus are those little paperbacks college students too lazy to read the assigned novels buy around exam time. Any word you have to hunt for in a thesaurus is the wrong word. There are no exceptions to this rule. You think you might have misspelled a word? O.K., so here is your choice: Either look it up in the dictionary, thereby making sure you have it right—and breaking your train of thought and the writer's trance in the bargain—or just spell it phonetically and correct it later. Why not? Did you think it was going to go somewhere? And if you need to know the largest city in Brazil and you find you don't have it in your head, why not write in Miami, or Cleveland? You can check it . . . but *later*. When you sit down to write, *write*. Don't do anything else except go to the bathroom, and only do that if it absolutely cannot be put off.

6. Know the markets

Only a dimwit would send a story about giant vampire bats surrounding a high school to *McCall's*. Only a dimwit would send a tender story about a mother and daughter making up their differences on Christmas Eve to *Playboy* . . . but people do it all the time. I'm not exaggerating; I have seen such stories in the slush piles of the actual magazines. If you write a good story, why send it out in an ignorant fashion? Would you send your kid out in a snowstorm dressed in Bermuda shorts and a tank top? If you like science fiction, read science fiction novels and magazines. If you want to write mysteries, read the magazines. And so on. It isn't just a matter of knowing what's right for the present story; you can begin to catch on, after a while, to overall rhythms, editorial likes and dislikes, a magazine's slant. Sometimes your reading can influence the *next* story, and create a sale.

7. Write to entertain

Does this mean you can't write "serious fiction"? It does not. Somewhere along the line pernicious critics have invested the American reading and writing public with the idea that entertaining fiction and serious
ideas do not overlap. This would have surprised Charles Dickens, not
to mention Jane Austen, John Steinbeck, William Faulkner, Bernard
Malamud, and hundreds of others. But your serious ideas must always
serve your story, not the other way around. I repeat: If you want to
preach, get a soapbox.

8. Ask yourself frequently, "Am I having fun?"

The answer needn't always be yes. But if it's always no, it's time for
a new project or a new career.

9. How to evaluate criticism

Show your piece to a number of people—ten, let us say. Listen carefully to what they tell you. Smile and nod a lot. Then review what was
said very carefully. If your critics are all telling you the same thing
about some facet of your story—a plot twist that doesn't work, a character who rings false, stilted narrative, or half a dozen other possibles—
change it. It doesn't matter if you really like that twist or that character;
if a lot of people are telling you something is wrong with your piece, it
is. If seven or eight of them are hitting on that same thing, I'd still
suggest changing it. But if everyone—or even most everyone—is critic-
izing something different, you can safely disregard what all of them
say.

10. Observe all rules for proper submission

Return postage, self-addressed envelope, etc.

11. An agent? Forget it. For now.

Agents get 10% to 15% of monies earned by their clients. 15% of
nothing is nothing. Agents also have to pay the rent. Beginning writers
do not contribute to that or any other necessity of life. Flog your stories
around yourself. If you've done a novel, send around query letters to
publishers, one by one, and follow up with sample chapters and/or the
complete manuscript. And remember Stephen King's First Rule of
Writers and Agents, learned by bitter personal experience: *You don't
need one until you're making enough for someone to steal . . .* and if

you're making that much, you'll be able to take your pick of good agents.

12. If it's bad, kill it

When it comes to people, mercy killing is against the law. When it comes to fiction, it *is* the law.

That's everything you need to know. And if you listened, you can write everything and anything you want. Now I believe I will wish you a pleasant day and sign off.

My ten minutes are up.

❑ 18

WELCOME TO MY STUDY

BY MAEVE BINCHY

AS THEY SAY IN IRELAND, A HUNDRED THOUSAND WELCOMES TO MY study. Or my half of the study. I share a big, bright room with my husband Gordon Snell, a children's writer, and we find that the discipline of working side by side is a great help.

You can't suddenly turn on the radio, file your nails, or get lost in reading someone else's novel if you have announced that you're going to get 1,200 words done today. It's much easier to fool yourself than to find an excuse to fool someone else. And as writers, we all know we are aching for an excuse not to write. So this is why I'm taking time off from my next book to pause and tell you all the things you should be doing. I was a schoolteacher for eight years, and old habits die hard. Once a bossy schoolmarm, always a bossy schoolmarm.

You want to know how to write a novel. All right, sit up and pay attention. Here we go.

Timing

The secret of the Universe is timing, and it's especially true for writing a novel. Before you start you must decide how long you think it's going to take. Make a realistic timetable, and stick to it. My pages are 250 words each and I think I write five pages a day. A book is around 500 pages, so in theory it should take one hundred days to write a book. But we all know that is madness. We don't write every day; in my case I write four days a week. So that's more like 20 pages a week, and to get 500 pages you have to work for 25 weeks. Good, you say; that's not too bad—about six months. But that's madness, too. You have to plan a book first, and to my mind that takes ten weeks. And when it's finished, you have to spend five more weeks tidying it up before you send it off. So—a total of forty weeks. How does that sound?

Planning

I think of some emotion, like friendship, betrayal, eagerness for an education, the class system. Then I sit for days thinking of a story with a beginning, middle, and end to hang it on. This is the hardest bit, but it's easier if you remember you don't *have* to stick to it, it just has to be there, like some kind of scaffolding for putting up a building.

Now make up the main characters—about four or five of them, not a cast of thousands. And when I say make up, *do* make them up: Don't put your friend, your mother-in-law, your colleague into it. Put yourself in, of course; you can't sue yourself. Also, you're familiar with the way you react, so it's dead easy to write yourself into books. I always put idealized versions of myself in, younger, thinner, more beautiful, nicer, more saintly. (Whenever you find a good, warm, kind-hearted teacher in one of my books, that's me!)

Next, get some pastel-colored paper—I choose pale-green—and write down each character's name and birthday, and draw a picture of where they live. I have found this to be hugely helpful. Whenever I mention someone, I just check the green pages to make sure I don't put her in the wrong house or make her five years younger than she should be!

The last thing to do in the planning phase is to take a piece of pale-pink paper and write down the chapter endings—say things like, "By the end of Chapter Three, we must know what she is going to do about this situation, and she has begun to act on it," or "By the end of Chapter Five he must have discovered the missing money and realized that only one person could have taken it." Otherwise, you could have the next four chapters drifting on and on with someone trying to resolve a situation and the whole audience out there fast asleep.

Now, you're ready to begin writing.

Write quickly

You probably don't write any better when you write slowly than when you write quickly, so make it speedy. Don't pause for breath, punctuation, too much analysis. Imagine you can hear the people speaking, and try to get it down as quickly as possible. To get dialogue right, listen to everyone, everywhere—eavesdrop, follow people so you can hear what they are saying. To get a scene right for *Tara Road,* I spent two days watching mothers and teenage daughters buying clothes in a store. Never hang up on a crossed telephone line, watch people in planes and trains, and be vigilant the whole time. When the people in your books speak, try to hear their voices in your head. Don't give them fake Deep South accents, or bad pronunciation, or lisps, but pretend you are listening at the door, and somehow it comes easier. In a conversation between two people, I often put my head on one side when I'm writing what one character is saying, and on the other when the second one is speaking.

Are they real people?

I usually make most of my characters people that I would like to meet and know, but put a fair sprinkling of rotten apples in, as well. Funnily, people always remember the bad guys, the ones who prove "there ain't no good in men," but there must be strong, brave people as well, people who make the right decisions and don't abandon friends or loves or duty.

If you pretend they *are* real people, they will become so. I don't say I wonder what I will make Marilyn do here, as if my character were a puppet. Instead I say, "I wonder what she would do here," as if she had a life of her own. It really does work.

If you give your characters lots of clothes and records and hobbies and pets of their own . . . even though you don't mention all these things, somehow they make characters more believable.

I never let all the good people become sickeningly good; I give them a few slightly irritating habits, as everyone in real life has, and the same goes for the villainous ones. They can't be truly bad; they must have some redeeming features, as even the worst people I ever met seem to have.

Is it any good?

I have no idea whether anything I write will be of the remotest interest to anyone else. Some mornings when I read what I wrote the previous day I think it's fairly entertaining; other times I think it's pure rubbish. The main thing is not to take any notice, not to get elated or upset, just keep going.

If you write what you know about, you will always be on safe ground. I am very edgy and nervous about going into territories I know nothing about. That's why you don't find much high finance, group sex, or yachting parties in my stories.

And I write exactly as I speak; I don't roll each sentence around and examine it carefully before letting it loose! If you speak in your own voice, you can never be accused of being pretentious or showing off; you can just be yourself, and that's a huge advantage in anybody.

And finally . . .

Keep to your forty weeks. And remember that when you have finished, that's only the first draft. If you have no publisher yet, then the horrible bit of being rejected starts. But stick with it; those who quit are just leaving the coast clear for those of us who didn't quit. Remember, the really famous writers who were rejected time after time got up, and dusted themselves off, and started again.

If you *do* have publishers, they will want you to change things here and there. If you trust them, then change what they ask you. My publishers *always* ask me to change things, and say exactly the same two things to me on every single book. Fourteen books, and I can never remember to put in a physical description of anyone, and I have to do it all at the end. Fourteen books, and I always forget that one thing should lead to another, rather than having lots of incidents flying in formation.

But I have remembered some of the other advice: If you're telling a story, get on with it; don't delay too long, rambling down little byways; and you often learn a lot about the main characters from little things that minor characters say about them. I know things in my own heart, for example, there is nobody really ordinary if you know where to look. We are all the heroes and heroines of our own life story. Stand at a railway station, in a shopping mall, in an airport, and watch the faces. Everyone has some kind of a dream, a hope, a plan. Some may have nightmares and regrets, but there isn't one person out there in that crowd who is uninteresting. Believe that, and you will never be without a plot, a character, or indeed, an interesting life.

□ 19

MINING FAMILY GOLD FOR FICTION

BY EILEEN GOUDGE

THERE'S USUALLY ONE IN EVERY BUNCH. I'LL BE GIVING A SPEECH AT some literary event and someone in the audience will raise his or her hand to comment, "You write so well about dysfunctional families!" To which I give my standard reply: "Is there any other kind?" It always gets a laugh—the uneasy laughter of those for whom the joke hits a little too close to home. Tolstoy said it best: "Happy families are all alike; every unhappy family is unhappy in its own way."

Which isn't to say there aren't *some* truly happy families or that there are no good times even in unhappy ones. It's just that my experience has been colored by the unique and not always cozy ties in my family. Usually, it's centered on mother-daughter conflict or sibling rivalry. Broken mother-child bonds as well as feelings of abandonment feature largely in my novels. And let's not forget marital strife.

I never set out to exact revenge through the sharpened point of my pen. It's not about getting the last word in, either (though it has occurred to me, on more than one occasion, that writing is a pretty nifty way to kill two birds with one stone). If I had to liken it to anything, I'd compare the process to a Ouija board. You don't always know who (or what) is controlling the planchette; all you know is that it's somehow giving answers your conscious mind may not be ready, or able, to supply. As my plot thickens, I'm not always prepared for the direction in which it's guided. All I know for certain is that those thorny issues are there, lurking below the surface, waiting to pop up like mischievous imps to wreak havoc with the most carefully crafted outline. And having recently completed my sixth adult novel, I can safely, if somewhat uneasily, say the themes that form a continuum in all my novels have something—if not everything—to do with families.

The point of all this is that there's gold in them thar hills. The old adage, write what you know, is never truer than when family relationships come into play. Everything we know, feel, think, or believe is colored by how we were brought up. Most of our angst centers on unresolved family conflicts. Sibling rivalry that began in early childhood continues undiminished into adulthood. Lost opportunities and unrequited love loom large in the imagination. And somewhere amid this labyrinth of memories, experiences, and conflicts lies the mother lode: the unique blend of fact and fiction, the alchemy, so to speak, that makes a story, your story, come to life.

Attempting to put that story down on paper, however, is a feat as deceptively, and sometimes maddeningly, simple as the principle behind gold mining: Just because it's out there doesn't mean it's easy to get to. And don't forget the ever-hovering specter of familial disapproval, otherwise known as, "What would Uncle Frank think?" To help you get past these roadblocks and reach your goal—a richly emotional story that will engage the reader's interest while tugging on his or her heartstrings—I've outlined a few key steps, starting with some common misconceptions.

- **My life is boring. No one will be interested in what happened to me.** Wrong. Everyone's story is potentially interesting. My husband, a reporter for a radio news station, occasionally lectures on the subject of media training. His favorite example is a segment entitled "Everybody Has a Story." First, a location is chosen by a dart tossed willy-nilly at a map of the United States. When the reporter arrives at his destination, he opens the phone book and plucks a name at random. Then he asks that person to tell his or her story. One week, it was an elderly woman who spoke of the terrible time in her life when her only son left home as a teenager, vowing never to return. She became so depressed, she attempted suicide. Yet today, many years later, that son lives just a mile down the road, and they see each other nearly every day.

The point is that you don't have to be a mountain climber or a lion tamer or even a doctor to tell a fascinating story. Sometimes the most harrowing conflicts arise from extraordinary events in the lives of very ordinary people. The millions of readers who love Stephen King will agree, I think, that it's not the monsters, ghosts, or demons that make his novels so compelling; it's his depiction of small-town life in Maine and the dilemmas that beset his characters—dilemmas readers can identify with.

I recently wrote a short story for an anthology entitled *Fathers and Daughters*, in which I recall the Cold War frenzy surrounding that brief spell in the mid-sixties when everyone with a back yard was putting in a bomb shelter. I had briefly considered using a real-life family as the subject of a somewhat different story—that of the only black family in our cul-de-sac—but in the end discarded the idea. In my ten years on Roan Place, I never once laid eyes on the Greens, though they lived directly across the street. On Halloween, we were told by our parents not to trick-or-treat at their house. My father explained that they were "private" people who didn't wish to be "bothered." The truth had far more to do with bigotry, I'm sure. And, yes, there's a story here—one filled with racial tension and the end of an era. But it's not mine, you see. At heart, it belongs to the Greens.

• **I really wanted to be an astronaut**. Yes, but in reality you're a dentist—or homemaker—or insurance broker. And when you imagine that someone else has had a more exciting life, it's quite often a case of the grass being greener on the other side of the fence. Anyway, who's to say there isn't an angle to your own story that's even more compelling than a trip to the moon? More compelling, in some ways. Which isn't to say you can't sprinkle your tale with elements of wishful thinking, or use a dramatic framework by which your characters are propelled through the story. Only that at the heart of your story there must be real emotions that derive from real-life experiences.

In my first novel, *Garden of Lies*, I wrote about two baby girls switched at birth during a daring rescue from a hospital fire. I never gave up either of my children at birth, but I do know what it's like to be a mother, so I could well imagine the anguish Sylvie would feel at having to make such a choice. I also know what it's like to hunger, as an adult, for something you were deprived of as a child. My parents and I have always had a difficult and often contentious relationship. My mother and I will never see eye to eye on just about any subject. I've made peace with it for the most part, and I try to accept things as they are. But deep down, there's a little part of me that mourns the loss of innocence that comes with recognizing one's parents to be deeply flawed, and weeps for what never was and can never be. And it is that longing with which I imbued Rose Santini, my abandoned baby grown to womanhood.

The parent-child conflict materialized again in my novel, *One Last Dance*. When Lydia Seagrave, on the eve of her fortieth anniversary, fatally shoots her husband (whom everyone, including her three daughters, assumed she was devoted to), it's the proverbial Pandora's box opening to reveal a host of family secrets. Oddly enough, while I was in the midst of writing the book, my father passed away. I'd already completed the first draft, but when I went back over it, a curious thing happened. As I was rewriting the funeral scene, details I hadn't consciously remembered from my dad's funeral came vividly to mind. Emotions to which I'd been numbed at the time gripped me. More than mourning my father's passing, I realized I was grieving for what had been missing in my life. Suddenly, the scene became far more powerful, and I saw a way to make the death of this somewhat remote and not altogether likable character truly tragic.

The death of a loved one can also be the catalyst that brings submerged half-truths and unspoken resentments exploding to the surface. And just as it was for my siblings and me, Daphne and her sisters discover that each has very different and often conflicting memories of her childhood. As they struggle to find the through line amid these disparate views, the experience proves cathartic—and ultimately redeeming.

I used this theme again (or perhaps it used me) in *The Second Silence*. Mary Quinn has done her best to put aside painful memories of her past. But when her grown daughter is caught in a terrible crisis that draws her back to her hometown, Mary has no choice but to confront those unresolved conflicts, most of which center around her mother. How she does it and what comes of it goes very much to the core of my relationship with my own family. It provides not only the hub to which the spokes of my story are affixed, but the momentum that propels it.

Another theme that many of you, I'm sure, can relate to is sibling rivalry. The earliest and best example in literature is Cain and Abel. John Steinbeck used it effectively in *East of Eden*. Shakespeare tapped this rich vein of ore in many of his plays, notably *The Tempest* and *Hamlet*. And what would Louisa May Alcott's *Little Women* have been without the memorable scene in which Amy, in a fit of jealous pique, destroys Jo's manuscript? Siblings have a unique relationship that an only child can't fully comprehend. Part of it is that no one will ever know you as well as the sister who remembers all the intimate details of your childhood.

I come from a big family—five girls and one boy (pity my poor brother!)—so I'm familiar with the turf. I used those emotions in *One Last Dance*. Though Daphne is the sister to whom Kitty feels closest, it also frustrates her that Daphne is so "blind" to the truth: that all wasn't as hunky-dory as she imagined growing up. And their younger sister, Alex, is tormented by the fact that she was their mother's least favorite. Oddly enough, Kitty believes that *she* was the least favorite. A feeling common among siblings, I've found. As the time of their mother's trial approaches, however, the three sisters are drawn together, and by story's end, each arrives at a different sort of truth.

- **How do I know which experiences and emotions to tap?** Think of it more as letting those emotions tap you on the shoulder. Often, I don't know where the emotional core of a scene lies until I start to tell my story. What works best, I've found, is to simply begin putting it down on paper. If you can write it dry-eyed, without so much as a lump in your throat, maybe it's not as powerful as you thought. Sometimes, though, it's just a matter of knowing which point of view to choose.

In the first draft of *One Last Dance*, I'd told a pivotal scene from Kitty's point of view, which I later switched to Daphne's. Why? Because Daphne is the sister with the most invested in what Kitty refers to as the "Myth of the Ideal Childhood." Therefore, when we first visit Lydia behind bars, the scene—as viewed through Daphne's eyes—is more emotionally wrenching. She can hardly believe this is the same mother who baked cookies and tenderly nursed her when she was sick. Thus, it becomes an almost surreal experience—one that ultimately turns out to be just the jump-start she needs, not only to come to Lydia's aid, but to leave her loveless marriage.

A simple test you can apply when in doubt is to ask yourself, "Which of my characters has the most to lose—or gain—from this experience?" The answer is usually apparent right off, but if it doesn't come to you immediately, put it on the back burner to simmer a bit. Eventually, your scene will take its proper course. Because, in the end, the experiences closest to your heart are the ones your muse most often guides you toward.

- **How can I look my parents in the eye after they've read what I've written?** This is the most common fear that plagues even writers who've gotten past the first few roadblocks. An extreme form of self-consciousness sets in when you imagine everyone in your family— gasp!—reading what is so personal to you and perhaps not so flatteringly drawn from real life. While writing, you must be very strict in booting from your mind any fantasies of the horrified reactions of friends and family. In my experience, no one ever recognizes himself in a novel unless the portrait is a good one—then everyone stakes claim to it.

Sometimes, a deeply-felt experience alone is enough to give shape to a character. The villain in *Garden of Lies*, a nasty and self-absorbed doctor named David Sloane, is purely fictional. Yet something like the scene in which he learns Rachel is pregnant actually happened to me. When I told my first husband that I was going to have a baby, he was less than pleased. We were young expatriates living in a foreign country, barely scraping by. I remember feeling terribly crushed, and though he eventually came around (sort of), the initial joy I'd felt was never fully recaptured. When David Sloane insists heartlessly that Rachel have an abortion, she reacts unexpectedly. After much agonizing, she says she'll have one—but only if David performs it. That way, he'll know full well that what they're doing is profound and wrenching. Until I actually wrote that scene, it hadn't occurred to me that that was exactly how I'd felt: I wanted my husband to walk a mile in my moccasins. When those long-buried feelings finally surfaced, it was very cathartic for me, but not in the least slanderous of anyone dead or alive.

At the same time, I would be less than honest to say that what we write doesn't have an effect on those around us. Occasionally, a character or subject can rub someone the wrong way. In my case, it wasn't what I was writing but what I was saying. Shortly after the publication of *Garden of Lies*, I began giving interviews about having been a welfare mom when my son was a baby. For years, I'd felt ashamed of this episode in my past and kept it carefully hidden from those who hadn't known me then. But the more I spoke out about it, the better I felt. My story also proved inspiring to other women who were struggling financially. I received letters from many who thanked me for giving them hope.

The trouble arose when my parents complained that these interviews were "making them look bad." I never blamed my predicament on them, either in thought or word, but in retrospect I can see that perhaps they felt guilty for not doing more to help. At any rate, they gave me an ultimatum: If I didn't stop doing those interviews, I would be disowned. It was a tough choice, but in the end I knew I'd be giving up too much of my hard-won self-respect if I were to cave in. As a result of my decision, it was five years before I had any contact with either of my parents.

Did I grieve? More than anyone can know. Do I regret either my choice—or writing the novel that led me to it? Not for an instant. Because I believe that, above all else, one must never flinch from looking reality in the eye, however painful.

I believe the same about writing: To thine own pen be true. In order to create memorable stories and characters you must be willing to travel deep into the mineshaft of your own memories. You must endow your characters with the best of what you yourself hope for—and the worst of what you fear. In the end, you will be rewarded by the knowledge that redemption, in fiction as in life, is almost always possible and the human spirit indeed indomitable.

❏ 20

HOW TO WRITE A NOVEL:
QUESTIONS AND ANSWERS

BY SIDNEY SHELDON

Q. *What is the hardest part of a novel for you to write?*
A. The hardest part of a book is the beginning. When I begin a book, I have no plot in mind, only a character. I start dictating to my assistant, and as I talk, the character comes to life and gets involved with the other characters. I have no idea where the story is going to lead me.

I want to emphasize that I do not recommend this way of working for any but the most experienced writers, since writing without an outline can lead to a lot of blind alleys. For a beginning writer, I think an outline is very important. Novels should have a beginning, a middle, and an end, and it is a good idea to have a road map to tell you where you are going. Without an outline, it's very easy to wander all over the place. At best, you can get lost; at worst, you can go over a cliff and find out you do not have a novel.

Q. *How do you get readers emotionally involved in your characters, or make them share the characters' emotions and reactions?*
A. You get your readers emotionally involved in your characters by being emotionally involved yourself. Your characters must come alive for you. When you are writing about them, you have to feel all the emotions they are going through—hunger, pain, joy, despair. If you suffer along with them and care what happens to them, so will the reader.

Q. *What roles can minor characters play in a novel, and how are they best used to highlight the actions and goals of the main characters?*
A: Someone once said that in movies there are no small parts—only small actors. In a sense, there are no minor characters in novels, meaning that every character should be as distinctive and colorful as possible.

91

Make that character physically unusual, or give him an exotic background or philosophy. The reader should remember the minor characters as well as the protagonists.

Q. *Creating and releasing tension seem to be important aspects of your novels. You often seem to let your readers relax, but not too much; when this happens, you pull them back with sometimes unrelieved tension. Are there specific ways of doing this?*

A. I love writing cliff-hangers, and yes, there are certain techniques that can be used. The most important thing is to create characters in whom readers are interested. Because if they are not interested in your characters, they will be indifferent to whatever dangers those characters might be subjected to. If you are writing a suspense novel, a good trick is to create a dangerous situation for your characters and end the chapter on that note. Start your next chapter with another group of characters, if possible. But do not immediately get your protagonist out of trouble. Build the suspense, and keep building it.

Q. *Much has been said about writing about what you know, from your own experience. Some novelists, however, feel that this is too limiting and constricting, and that the good novelist uses his or her imagination and inventiveness and turns parts of what he knows into the story for his characters to act out. How do you feel about this?*

A. It is an axiom that writers should write only out of their own experience. Whether you do or not depends on how much you believe in axioms. By all means write about what you know. Use your experiences. However, very few writers experience murder, rape, or suicide, and few of us have traveled to Tibet or Fiji, or have pillaged ancient villages or taken over conglomerates. All of us, however, can experience these things in our imaginations, for that is the world where writers live. There are certain cautions that must be taken. If you are going to write about ancient Cathay, research it. In the libraries of the world and on the internet are the answers to any possible questions you might have. If you want a locale or an event to be real to the reader, it must first be real to you. You must be able to see it, touch it, smell it, before you can expect the reader to believe in it. When that happens, it will have beocme an actual experience for you.

Q. *Does it help writers as they develop to read their work aloud to others?*

A. I know writers who like to read aloud their works in progress, and the reactions from their audience are helpful to them. Many writing workshops use this technique where the listeners critique the work of the authors. Personally, I would find this approach very disconcerting. I prefer to work in private. Once my publishers have approved an idea for a novel of mine, they don't see a word until about two and a half years later, when I have completed and polished the book.

Q. *Is there any special checklist that you use to determine that your manuscript is right, satisfies you, and is ready to send off to the publisher?*

A: Every artist has to have his own sense of when his work is ready. My own personal checklist is rewriting. I rewrite my manuscripts up to a dozen times, and I will spend from a year to a year and a half rewriting. The manuscript is not sent to the publisher until I am satisfied that it is as good as I know how to make it.

Q. *How can a writer best develop the skill for self-criticism?*

A: There are two phases to writing a novel: the creative phase and the editorial phase. I feel that it is very important for them not to occur simultaneously. When you are putting words on paper, don't be a critic, because that is inhibiting. When you have finished the novel, then you must be ruthlessly critical of what you have done. That first wonderful flush of creativity is over, and you are faced with the reality of what is on paper. I think the best way to become self-critical is to read major writers and try to measure up to their standards.

Q. *Should fiction ever teach a lesson, preach, or be didactic in any way, even indirectly trying to convey a message?*

A. I think it is dangerous to write a novel that is purely propaganda. On the other hand, I think that every writer has the right, if not the obligation, to put forth his or her views. I happen to believe that we treat our elderly shabbily by shutting them away in institutions of one kind or another when they are no longer able to be useful members of society. In *A Stranger in the Mirror,* I wrote a scene in which my protagonist goes to visit his father, who is in such a place. I was able to convey my feelings to the reader, but it was all part of the novel, not a detour for preaching. I am appalled by the way our court system works, and in *Rage of Angels* I tried to convey some of my feelings. I think it is very healthy for characters to express your point of view, but your message will be much stronger if you do it entertainingly.

It comes back to that old question of reality: If your characters are real, then everything they do and say will feel and sound right to the reader. If unsuitable points of view are superimposed on your characters, then you have created a false note that the reader most certainly will be aware of.

Q. *Most successful writers have experienced failure early on, and intermittently throughout their careers. Do you see early failures or successes as somehow detrimental to beginning writers? Is there any way to use these extremes to the writer's advantage?*

A. The effect of early failure or success depends on the person to whom it happens. Failure spurs some people on and discourages others. I think the saddest thing is when a writer has an enormous early success and is never able to achieve it again. I firmly believe that if a person has talent in any field, and perseveres, nothing can stop that person from succeeding.

□ 21

THE CRUCIAL FIRST PAGE

BY ANN HOOD

HERE IS MY PREMISE: YOUR FIRST PAGE IS YOUR MOST IMPORTANT PAGE. Whether you are writing a ten-page short story or a four-hundred-page novel, your biggest task is getting the first page perfect. Consider for a moment all of the firsts in your life: your first day of school; your first best friend; the day you first learned to read; your first love; your first kiss; your first broken heart; the first person you loved who died; your first baby; your first apartment; your first car; the first time you saw Paris or New York City, the Taj Mahal or the Grand Canyon. Each of these firsts paved the way for all of the seconds and thirds and thousandths that followed. Each of these firsts changed you in some way. Every "first" sets the tone, the pace, the mood, the voice, the place, the stakes in life and in writing. Contemplating getting your first page exactly right is enough to bring on permanent writer's block.

But let me give you the good news: Your first first page, the one you wrote yesterday when you got a great idea for a new story, or the one you wrote last year when you began the novel that is almost finished, does not need to be perfect. In fact, it shouldn't be. It is almost impossible to write the right first page until you are finished with all the other pages, even if you have a solid outline or a crystal-clear vision of what you want to do.

Here's why. A first page must do all of the following things, only some of which writers know when they begin:

• It must establish point of view. Who is telling this story? A first-person narrator? If so, is it that narrator's story? Or is the narrator an observer, like Nick Carroway in F. Scott Fitzgerald's *The Great Gatsby*? Will you tell the story in the third person? A limited third-person or omniscient? Or maybe your story is to be told by multiple characters, and you will shift points of view among two or three or

95

many. Then you have to decide which of these characters will begin the novel and why. After all, if you use more than one point of view, why does the one on the first page have to come first?

• A first page must also establish setting. In a novel it is possible to move through time and place; it's even possible to cover many settings in a short story. But there is a reason for stories to begin where and when they do, and it's important to have the setting clear. Margaret Atwood described a first page as a train: You don't get on unless you know where you're going. Imagine reading a novel and discovering on page 20 or page 220 that it's taking place on Mars sometime in the future. Perhaps that discovery tells you that you're on a journey you do not want to take, and that you will get off that train as quickly as possible.

• Every story dictates how specific its setting must be. In Barbara Kingsolver's novel, *The Poisonwood Bible*, the setting needs specificity. It isn't just somewhere in Africa; it's the Congo at a particular time. Imagine if Margaret Mitchell neglected to reveal her setting for *Gone With the Wind*. What setting do you need for your story? And how can you inform the reader what the setting is on the first page?

• The first page should establish the tone for the rest of the novel. Read the first page of *A Catcher in the Rye*, and you know what the tone—sassy, cynical, opinionated—of the entire novel will be. If Holden Caulfield became sweet and innocent in Chapter Two, the reader would know that the writer had not paid attention to what was required on his first page.

• The first page must also show readers the conflict, so they will know what's at stake for the protagonist. Sometimes the conflict is told in plain language, as in Raymond Carver's short story, "Cathedral": "This blind man, an old friend of my wife's, he was on his way to spend the night." It's clear that the blind man's visit is going to cause conflict in the narrator. And often it's not just on the first page; it's in the first line. Think of the first line of Tolstoy's *Anna Karenina*: "Happy families are all alike; every unhappy family is unhappy in its own way." Think of Dickens, the first line of *A Tale of Two Cities*, "It was the best of times, it was the worst of times." In his novel, *The Prince of Tides*, Pat Conroy shows the conflicts that stem from being a southern male: "My wound is geography."

Before you turn to page two, you as the writer must know the most basic things about your protagonist. Is the main character a man or a woman? What's her age? Name? Maybe even her race, her socio-economic status, and where she lives. The author certainly has to know why she's your protagonist. Sometimes readers are given clues to all the facts, and it is up to them to put these facts together.

Suppose you haven't settled on a name for the protagonist. You can't decide between Debra and Claire. Use both. Or use neither. A character's name often evolves as you write and discover more about your character. At some point the right name will come to you. Also, you aren't sure what kind of work Debra/Claire does. In fact, you don't know much about her at all. What you have that makes you want to write this story is a vague idea that excites you, and a really good first line, perhaps an image that haunts you, an image of a lonely woman in a city.

That's enough to get you started. Write that great first line. Describe that image. And you are on your way. Your writing will be a process of discovery, and you will write your way into your story. If you do know a lot about your protagonist, or have a long detailed outline, or a great first line, good! Begin writing and see how and where the story deviates from that original idea and that strong outline. In both cases, your first page will fall short of what a first page must ultimately accomplish for the story to be successful. What's important about the *first* first page is that it got you writing.

When you have finished your entire first draft, you will write your true first page. By then you will realize that your protagonist is neither Debra nor Claire, but Linda, and you will understand enough about her and about your story to enable you to reveal everything a good first page must. Or you will have learned that your strong outline fell apart at some point, and you need a completely different first page. In fact, your novel may really take hold somewhere around page 120. In most cases, it will be clear that you need a new beginning, and you will embrace that task because you are so excited about what you've written, that you've finished this draft.

The thing you will fight to keep no matter what is that great first line. You will believe that in a million drafts this is the most perfect first line, not just for this book, but the best first line ever written. And you will hold on to it much longer than you should.

Maybe your instinct is right. But ask yourself if, after you've rewritten the rest of the page, the first line still fits at all. Now that you know the ending of the novel, should this first line really open it? Does it actually encapsulate the entire book's meaning the way Tolstoy and Dickens and countless others have managed to do? If you can honestly say it does, then leave it in—but not because you are attached to it, or because it is so clever or beautiful or snappy that no reader could resist it. All of those are reasons that it *isn't* working, rather than that it is.

Let me share with you the history of the first pages of one of my own novels to demonstrate how the perfect first page is born. My first novel, *Somewhere Off the Coast of Maine*, began as series of interconnected short stories. The first one became the first and last chapter of the novel after months of sitting with all the stories spread before me and shuffling and reshuffling them. It took me close to a year to discover that the beginning of that one story was also the beginning of the novel.

Waiting to Vanish, my second novel, began with an image I had of a young woman driving up to a house in winter and staring at it with great sadness. Whose house was it? And why did it evoke such powerful memories? I discovered the answers to those questions only as I wrote. Eventually, that opening scene, which had so intrigued me, ended up as part of a flashback in Chapter Two.

When I wrote a novel with multiple points of view, the protagonist's point of view was given only through her letters to the family she had deserted. One of those letters opened the novel, and I wrote and rewrote that letter dozens of times. When a copy editor at my publisher's read *Places to Stay the Night*, she wrote a note saying, "I love this novel. It has wonderful characters and great emotional depth, and that is why I am asking you to please get rid of the letters. They are too glib, and they undermine all of the really good writing here. They also obscure the main character's personality. I know that you can bring Libby to life, because everyone else here is so alive." After I got angry and cried a lot—after all, the letters were the skeleton from which the rest of the novel grew—I discarded all of those letters and rewrote them as full-blown chapters, including the first chapter, which I wrote last.

Always willing to repeat mistakes, I discarded over 200 pages of my next novel, *The Properties of Water*, rewrote them, and decided that rather than a coming-of-age novel, it was the story of adult sisters. I rewrote it again, and then realized that my true first page was really the first page of Chapter Two; I discarded Chapter One altogether.

This brings me to my latest novel, *Ruby*, which began with a sentence, not just any sentence, but the most beautiful, sad, and evocative sentence I'd ever written. "Olivia kept her husband's voice in her jewelry box, beside the pearl ring her grandmother had given her, two expired passports, a key to her apartment in Manhattan." Any reader, I thought, would want to read on. The story was about Olivia, a 37-year-old woman whose husband was struck by a car driven by a college student. One day Olivia comes home and finds a pregnant teenager in her kitchen.

In the opening chapter, the reader learned that Olivia was a painter of carousel ponies, that she and her husband had been married for ten years, that her best friend was a zany editor for a women's magazine who was having an affair with a married man. Olivia had not worked or done much of anything for about six months. When my agent read the manuscript, she told me that Olivia's job was dumb, her friend was obnoxious, and nobody could sit in a house for six months, no matter how depressed she was.

Several months and many revisions later, Olivia had become a milliner, her friend was less kooky, and Olivia and her husband were newlyweds when he was killed. I had taken care of many of the first chapter's problems and still managed to keep my beautiful first line. But, despite the changes, the first chapter remained sluggish and dull; the novel sold, no doubt, on the strength of the following nine chapters, and my editor told me how much she loved the book—except for the first chapter. I wrote and rewrote it, always certain that with such a great first line the chapter would ultimately soar. But it was not until I had so rewritten the first chapter that the first line no longer made sense that I was literally forced to write a new first line—"Olivia had so many things to tell the girl that killed her husband that she didn't know where to begin." Then I was able to get that first chapter absolutely right. The first first line is not even in the book.

All of the things that must be accomplished on a first page really have to be accomplished on every page in a story. You must always tweak the protagonist, reminding the reader of who she is and what she wants. You must keep the tone consistent, the setting alive, the conflict accelerating, the writing honest. In a way, every page is the first page. It's just that the real first page must hold all of the promise and expectation for what's to come.

❑ 22

VISIONS AND REALITIES

BY THOMAS FLEMING

HALF AWAKE IN THE DAWN, I KNEW I WAS IN A BEDROOM IN BERLIN. In the bed an attractive young German woman was having a bad dream. She tossed and turned and uttered anguished cries. Suddenly, I was in the dream. A U-boat with a knight's head on the conning tower was cruising through the Atlantic's gray depths. Around it exploded a half dozen *wabos*—depth charges. The boat tilted on its side and began to sink.

Now I—and the woman—were inside the U-boat, watching the drowning men gasp for a last breath as the water rose around them. We swam through the chaos until we reached the control room, where the captain, the woman's husband, awaited death with stoic defiance.

Then we were outside the U-boat again. Out of the depths swam a gigantic angel, as large as the boat, with huge staring eyes and a fixed hieratic smile. This incredible creature embraced the dying boat in its immense arms. Back in the Berlin bedroom, the woman awoke and thought: *The Path. The angel is part of the Path.*

I awoke in my New York City bedroom and raced to my computer. In an hour, I had written the first chapter of my 1994 novel, *Loyalties.* In succeeding years, I've puzzled more than once about where this vision came from. It utterly defies rational analysis. I was not thinking about writing a novel about the German Resistance to Hitler—which is what the book became. I had only the dimmest knowledge about those tragic patriots, gleaned from reading Anthony Cave Brown's *Bodyguard of Lies*, two or three years earlier. Why did that image (which was not in the Brown book) erupt in my imagination?

I had a similar experience with my 1992 novel, *Over There.* This was a book I had planned to write for years. It was going to be about my father, who had been promoted from sergeant to lieutenant during the battle of Argonne. "Teddy Fleming as the Immortal Sergeant" was the way I summed it up.

100

Instead, one morning I awoke with a vision of a drunken colonel driving a car down a highway outside San Antonio, Texas, at suicidal speed. Beside him sat a frowning black sergeant. The colonel had a name: Malvern Hill Bliss. He was the son of a Maryland Confederate who had lost a leg in the Civil War battle of the same name. He was a Catholic, whose wife and son had recently been killed by a Moro guerrilla in the Philippines. He was driving to a brothel where (I knew) General John J. Pershing would interrupt his drunken amours to tell him President Wilson had made Pershing head of the AEF, and he was taking Bliss to Europe with him to command a division.

In this whirling kaleidoscope, Teddy Fleming as the immortal sergeant virtually vanished. In the final version of the novel, he had little more than a walk-on part. This outburst of imagination was almost as mysterious as the birth of *Loyalties*. But I could at least glimpse what my imagination was telling me. In most histories and novels, World War I seemed to be the triumph of death over life. My imagination was urging me to write a different book. Pershing was taking Bliss to Europe with him because he too had been wounded by death—the soldier's enemy. He had lost his wife and three children 15 months before, in a fire in their San Francisco quarters. He was summoning Bliss, the one man who understood what he felt, to help him confront death's terrific challenge—as well as the awesome task of rescuing the French and British from the brink of collapse and defeat. In a landscape of death, *Over There* became a life-affirming book.

Such experiences have convinced me that Cushing Strout, the Cornell critic, knows whereof he speaks in his brilliant book, *The Veracious Imagination*. Strout argues that the imagination is not simply a mental device that "makes things up." On the contrary, it is an intellectual tool, closely wedded to the writer's intelligence. What it imagines for a novel is integrally connected to the essence of what the writer, consciously or unconsciously, wants to say about the subject.

Important as the vision may be, there is also the reality of writing the whole novel. That is where craft comes into the picture. The vision has to be nurtured by a lot of hard work. A first chapter may leap from a writer's fingers onto the computer screen, as if by magic. Maybe even a second chapter (which was the case in my writing *Loyalties*). Thereafter, the writer has to start thinking more as an artist and less as a mystic.

The vision may require a great deal of research to sustain it. In the case of *Loyalties*, I spent endless hours reading about World War II Berlin, Madrid, and Washington, DC, where much of action takes place. I also acquired a veritable library on the German Resistance to Hitler. For *Over There*, I went to France and drove and hiked along much of the 1918 western front—and read widely about the relatively unknown role of women in that much misunderstood war. In the course of finishing both these books, I built up enough notes and Xeroxes to fill an entire filing cabinet.

At least as important was keeping a journal of the novel as it evolved. I used to do this in notebooks; now I do it on the computer. The vision that compels you to write the book may be followed by many more glimpses of what is going to happen, far ahead of where you are in writing the story. I call these glimpses "flash-aheads" and note them down, no matter what hour of the day or night they occur.

I keep a tape recorder beside my bed and dictate these ideas if they appear in the midnight hours or at dawn. Not all these flashes turn out to be germane to the story, but a surprising number can or will play a vital role in supplying you with turning points or even the ending toward which you are groping.

A TV script writer once told me that writing a novel seemed to him like getting in a small boat and rowing out to sea hoping eventually you'll hit land. In many ways, a novel is a voyage into the unknown. But a good sailor/writer can deal with the anxiety if he keeps track in his journal where he is going and where he has been.

As the novel grows, another vital component comes into play: the lineup. I create a summary of each chapter, which enables me to go back and quickly recall what has happened to a certain character or how a theme was introduced for the first time. It's not only a way of avoiding repetition. The lineup gives you a sense of control over this torrent of words spilling onto the screen. I found a lineup useful back in my typewriter days. With a computer, which makes previous chapters less accessible, a lineup is essential.

The computer poses another problem that even the most visionary novelist has to keep in mind. Writing and rewriting on a computer are so easy, you can develop a sense of complacency about what you are producing. Especially when you can print it out on clean pages, in neat lines, with none of the smudges and underlining and clips and paste-ups that the typewritten manuscript inevitably acquired. I call this prob-

lem "The tyranny of the written." It looks so good, you may start thinking it is as good as it looks.

Stay tough-minded about your work-in-progress. Writing is still nine-
tenths or at least seven-tenths rewriting. I find it useful to put the manuscript away for several days after I've printed it out so I come back to it
in a less mesmerized state of mind. I also value the opinion of my agent,
my editor, and perhaps a reliable friend, who can see it without the
glow of my original vision, which may still be burning in my eyes but
has not quite gotten to the page.

Several of the devices can also be very useful in bringing a novel to
life when it tiptoes into your imagination, without any initial fireworks.
Sometimes a novel emerges simply as a voice, saying something that
sounds almost silly at first. In the late Sixties, I spent four years writing
a history of the U.S. Military Academy at West Point. I met many officers' wives and found them fascinating. They saw the Army experience
in ways dramatically different from their husbands' perceptions. For the
next few years, I heard a voice whispering:

> *The officers' wives*
> *The officers' wives*
> *That's what we'll be*
> *For the rest of our lives.*

It didn't make much sense, but I put it in my notebook every time it
appeared. In 1979, my agent and I sat down to discuss my next book.
Suddenly I said: "I've got an idea for a novel called *The Officers'
Wives*."

"Great title," my agent said. "Go for it."

When I started writing, the three very different women who were
main characters, their husbands, their children, emerged with amazing
ease. The song was sung at a party in the first chapter. It didn't play
that much of a role in the overall book. But if I hadn't put it in my
notebook, I might well have forgotten it—and I wouldn't have written
a novel that sold two million copies.

Liberty Tavern, my 1975 novel set in Revolutionary New Jersey, had
an even stranger genesis. I saw a man making a toast: "Here's to all
those that we love. Here's to all them that love us."

A crowded room responds: "Here's to all them that love those that love them. Love those that love them that love us!"

These words turned out to be the last lines of the novel. They were the key to the main character, Jonathan Gifford, the ex-British officer who dominates the book. To get to the ending, I had to do a lot of research on the American Revolution in New Jersey. But I always knew I was heading toward that moment when Gifford would raise his glass and peace would descend on an independent America.

My latest novel, *Hours of Gladness*, first emerged from a single word: *Mick*. Then it became *Mick O'Day*. The name kept pushing against my consciousness. Slowly, the character appeared—an Irish-American spiritually wounded by Vietnam, living with his fellow Irish-Americans in a New Jersey shore town, with the Vietnamese woman he loved now a refugee living nearby, untouchable, alienated forever.

I filled pages of my journal about Mick. I found out what Marines went through in Vietnam, living in the villages with the Vietnamese people, fighting the Viet Cong night after night. I went down to the Jersey shore and talked to people about the way the slime from Atlantic City's gambling casinos oozed into their daily lives. By the time I started telling Mick's story, I felt like a member of his family.

The name of the game is turning the vision into the reality called a novel. To do it, you have to be realistic about working at it day by day, using down-to-earth common sense tools as well as that wonderful creature called the veracious imagination.

□ 23

ADULT AND YOUNG READERS: WHAT DO THEY HAVE IN COMMON?

BY JOAN AIKEN

PEOPLE WHO KNOW THAT I WRITE BOOKS FOR BOTH ADULTS AND CHILdren sometimes ask me: What is the difference between those kinds of writing? Do you have a different attitude toward what you write? Is the vocabulary different? What about the plots? The characters? Why do you *want* to write for both sets of readers?

As I grow older, I find these questions harder to answer, perhaps because the gap between the two sets of readers grows narrower—either in reality or in my mind. Looking about at other writers who also produce books read by both sets of readers—Russell Hoban, Peter Dickinson, Nina Bawden, Judy Blume—I suspect that the same thing is happening to them: They are beginning to write for a non-age reader who falls somewhere between the two groups—or, and this is just as likely, the readers themselves are changing. (For instance, there is now a vast readership who grew up forty years ago on the works of C.S. Lewis and Tolkien, and now have that built-in addiction.) Younger readers are turning to older books, and older readers go back to the pleasures found in fantasy and adventure stories.

It is like Kipling's wonderful change-over in *The Story of the Armadillos:*

> Can't curl but can swim
> Slow-Solid, that's him
> Curls up but can't swim
> Stickly-prickly, that's him

Perhaps I have it the wrong way 'round, but it doesn't matter, that is really the point of the story. It is no use learning a formula to help you with your work because, inevitably if you do so, a whole set of circumstances will change and the formula will fail you.

One thing we can be sure of: Older readers grow lazier, while younger readers are more adventurous and prepared to work harder. My grandchildren tackle books that I would not have the stamina to attempt, but our tastes still overlap. When they visit me, I read them my favorite passages from classic fiction—the shipwreck from Masefield's marvelous *Bird of Dawning*, or the gripping episode in Hugo's *Les Misérables* when Jean Valjean rescues poor little Cosette from the rapacious Thénardier family—and we have that unmatchable feeling of silent rapport when everybody's imagination is equally engaged.

But, although the area of common enjoyment is, I think, growing larger, there are still no-go areas on both sides. Few adults, for instance, would read Louisa Alcott these days; she is too sanctimonious, too quick to point a moral, though her plots and characters are still full of life, and young readers, girls especially, are still held by them. Few readers under twenty undertake Marcel Proust or Henry James with much enjoyment, because the action is too slow, the emphasis lies in character analysis.

There is one rule that still holds firm: In a story for young readers, the action *must* be swift, continuous, and immediately gripping. I was proud to find myself recently included in the new *Oxford Dictionary of Quotations* for my remark that Sir Walter Scott's leisurely opening of *Ivanhoe* ("In that pleasant district of merry England . . . etc.") would, these days, be accompanied by the sound of books slapping shut all over the library.*

And there are plenty of universal themes that still and always will engage the emotions and sympathies of both young and adult readers.

Injustice, for example. Injustice is the unbearable pain throughout the story that made *Jane Eyre* an instant bestseller and has kept it in print from 1847 to 1999. Why should poor little Jane, who has done nothing wrong, be treated so harshly by the odious Reed family? Once the reader's sympathies are engaged on Jane's behalf, the trick is done, there is no chance of closing the book until her wrongs have been righted. Arthur Ransome is an English writer whose children's adventure stories have somewhat gone out of fashion now, perhaps because several of them are written to formula. The children set themselves, or are set, a project, to make a map of the locality, or whatever, and by hard work,

---

The Way to Write for Children, St. Martin's Press

it is just completed as the story ends. But one, *The Big Six*, is very different from the others because in it the group of children who are the main characters are unjustly accused of theft and vandalism and the whole neighborhood turns against them. They become pariahs and have to clear themselves and nail their accusers by a series of heroic efforts. The fact that there are actual villains to contend with, instead of just the forces of nature, makes this book outstanding among the others.

Shakespeare has an elegant and skillful touch in mingling an injustice theme with a comedy motif, as in *The Merchant of Venice*, where the very grim Shylock-Antonio legal case focused on the horrifying pound-of-flesh penalty is contrasted with the light-hearted nonsense over rings and caskets. The injustice is done, first to Antonio, then to Shylock, giving a deeper resonance to the whole. Similarly in *Much Ado About Nothing*, the absurd Beatrice-Benedick story would hardly hold water on its own, if it were not counterpointed by Claudio's totally unjust accusations against poor Hero and the (highly improbable) unmasking of his scheme by Dogberry & Co. (It really takes Shakespeare to get away with this plot.)

Injustice is of course the theme of many classic folktales, starting from Cinderella. My favorite is a Croation story, "Stribor's Forest," in which a poor old mother is abominably treated by her daughter-in-law, who is really a snake turned into a girl, and has a snake's nature. She sets her mother-in-law impossible tasks, such as going to the forest for strawberries on a snowy winter's day. The good old mother is helped with her tasks by a tribe of benevolent forest elves, who finally offer to rescue her from her plight by restoring her to her girlhood in a magically created village in the enchanted forest. But realizing that, if this happens, her son would no longer exist, she chooses to go back to her life of hardship. This unprecedented choice undoes all the magic, and the son's wife becomes a snake again. This story, as well as having the classic folktale ingredients, is genuinely touching. Injustice has also formed the basis of many thriller and mystery stories, and can make the difference between a flat whodunit and an engrossing page-turner. Dorothy Sayers's *Strong Poison*, for instance, has terrific tension because Harriet Vane, the central character, is standing trial for her lover's murder. The jury can't agree, and there is only one month before the retrial in which to find proof that Harriet didn't commit the murder. The time element, and the fact that the reader is sure from the start that

Harriet is innocent, make this one of Sayers's best. Dick Francis, in his thriller *Enquiry*, uses a similar situation: His hero/narrator and the trainer he works for are barred from racing after being falsely accused of cheating in a race; owners are taking their horses away from the trainer (time element again), so there is only a limited period in which to prove that the accusation is false. Having the narrator as hero is an advantage here because he is able to tell the reader from the start that the charge is an unjust one.

I used the injustice theme myself in my Felix Brooke trilogy. Crossed wires seem to happen more in historical fiction than in contemporary work; perhaps because it is so much easier now to pick up the telephone and sort matters out. (As Stephen Leacock said, if only, when Othello had demanded, "Where is that handkerchief?," Desdemona had the presence of mind to answer, "I sent it to the laundry, darling," much trouble would have been saved.)

In my Felix Brooke stories I have the goodhearted but wild and impetuous hero run away from his uptight, strait-laced Spanish family because they are harsh with him, believing him to be illegitimate. When that situation is straightened out, he goes off to rescue the children of a man who is accused of being mad, and a traitor to his country. Felix very soon begins to realize that these are false accusations being circulated by the man's malevolent wife. In fact, the situation is the exact reverse of what he has been told, but by the time Felix is aware of this, he is on top of a cliff in the Pyrenees with three children, one seriously ill and one killed by poison.

Reconciliation is another universal theme that operates equally well in juvenile and adult fiction—the slow (or it may be sudden) coming together of two characters who have been opposed, if not actual enemies, throughout the story.

Dumas uses it in *The Three Musketeers*. All through the story, a character called Rochefort has been opposing and hindering D'Artagnan at every turn. They are mostly prevented by circumstances from actually fighting; but on the very last page, the epilogue, when all has been tidied up and a great many people have died, Dumas nonchalantly mentions to the reader: "D'Artagnan fought three duels with Rochefort and wounded him three times." D'Artagnan tells Rochefort, "If we have another fight, I shall probably kill you." Rochefort replies, "In that case it would be better for us both to forgive and forget . . . upon which they shook hands, this time in friendship."

In *Our Mutual Friend*, Dickens has a terrific cat-and-dog relationship between one of the heroines, spoiled little Bella Wilfer, and the hero, Rokesmith, whose real name is Harmon. He has been left a fortune on condition that he marry Bella, at that time unkown to him. Objecting to this arbitrary arrangement, Harmon contrives the pretense that he has been drowned, and presents himself to Bella merely as her family's lodger, somebody's unimportant secretary. Dickens has a lot of fun over this situation, as Bella first slights, teases, and spurns the humble Rokesmith, and then can't help falling in love with him (as he has with her already) and finally agrees to marry him, still without knowing that he is the real heir. The final revelation is enough to make the modern reader squirm with embarrassment, but Victorian readers lapped it up.

Georgette Heyer used the theme in half a dozen of her novels: A hates B adapts well to a Regency setting. And so did Jane Austen in *Pride & Prejudice*. Of course the fact that the antipathy is based on sexual attraction pushes the story up toward the adult market. Similarly, in E.M. Forster's *A Room with a View*, until the last chapter Lucy thinks she can't stand George; and the very same situation turns up in *Anne of Green Gables*, with Anne detesting the uppish, teasing Gilbert Blythe who puts her down at school. Hostilities crackle on briskly throughout the plot until Gilbert self-sacrificingly gives up a job so that Anne can have it, and the scene is set for romance to spring up between them.

It is much more entertaining for the writer—and the reader—to set the two main characters at loggerheads so they can display all their worst characteristics. In my school library, we used to have a wonderful weepie, *The Flight of the Heron* by D.K. Broster, about the Scottish clans rising against the English. The Scots hero mistakenly thinks that his English counterpart has betrayed him, and the misunderstanding is cleared up only at the very end when the dying Englishman, before he breathes his last, has just enough time to gasp out, "I always liked you!"

Must adult and juvenile characters differ? Obviously, characters in adult fiction can be more complex, can be depicted at greater depth and length, while young readers want to get on with the plot; they are not in the market for deep motivation and analysis, but the *type* of character may be basically the same for both age groups. King Arthur and Sir

Gawaine and Robin Hood, after all, began as heroes of adult fiction before they were adopted into the juvenile library. And an untidy, impatient problem-solver such as Sara Paretsky's V.I. Warshawski is equally welcome in both.

Reviewing the theme of overlap from children's to adult novels and vice versa, it struck me that I have a character who seems to have established himself with a foot in both camps. He is a somewhat inept, but intelligent and well-meaning British peer of the realm who wandered out of my last Jane Austen sequel, *The Youngest Miss Ward*, where, as Lord Camber, he goes off to found a Utopian community on the banks of the Susquehanna river. In *Dangerous Games*, my latest Dido Twite novel, as Lord Herondale, he is on a Pacific island searching for games to amuse the ailing King James III; and now he has turned up as the brother of Lady Catherine de Bourgh in yet another Austen spin-off. Vague, chatty, floundering, his heart in the right place and liable to cause his friends untold trouble, he is a kind of Sorceror's Apprentice. I have no idea where he came from, he is like no one I know, but I think it highly probable that he will turn up again, no doubt where least expected, whether in a juvenile or an adult story, who can say? Writing is like that. It continually takes the writer by surprise.

❑ 24

You Can Do It All with Dialogue

By Barnaby Conrad

Charles Dickens once said that writers must be actors—they must act out their stories. And nowhere in the writing of fiction is acting more of a prerequisite than in the creating of effective dialogue.

Plausibility is high on the list of requirements for good dialogue; the reader must come away with the impression that he is eavesdropping, and not that he is being manipulated as to plot and character (which he most surely is). Dialogue is certainly one of the easiest, quickest, and most indelible ways to etch a character into a reader's mind; sometimes a character will say something so revealing that no subsequent statements or acts will redeem him or her. For example, if a veterinarian said to his nurse: "There are pain killers and sedatives in this drawer, but I never use them, because animals have no souls and can't feel pain like humans," would you take your pet to him? Just as when Hannibal Lecter tells Clarice Starling in *The Silence of the Lambs* that he ate a man's liver with a little chianti and some fava beans, readers won't think he's a swell fellow even if he should later on become the head monk in the Monastery of Our Lady of the Unusual.

Dialogue can do so much! As Elmore Leonard has said, "All the information you need can be given in dialogue."

How right he is! Look at some of the functions one can accomplish when characters talk:

1. *Weather and setting*
"Damn, but it's cold in this damn city! As Mark Twain said, 'the coldest winter I ever spent was one summer in Frisco.' "

2. *Back story and character delineation*
In *The Postman Always Rings Twice*, by James M. Cain, a master of tough dialogue, Frank Chambers is a twenty-four-year-old drifter who

lands a job at a "roadside sandwich joint, like a million others in California," run by Nick Papadakis and his hormonal young wife, Cora.

Within two short chapters Frank and Cora are lovers. In Chapter Three we learn something of Cora's character, background, and the fact that she is up to no good (in fact, they soon will kill her husband):

> "Look out, Frank. You'll break a spring leaf."
> "To hell with the spring leaf."
> We were crashing into a little eucalyptus grove beside the road. The Greek had sent us down to the market to take back some T-bone steaks he said were lousy, and on the way back it had got dark. I slammed the car in there, and it bucked and bounced, but when I was in among the trees I stopped. Her arms were around me before I even cut the lights. We did plenty. After a while we just sat there. "I can't go on like this, Frank."
> "Me neither."
> "And I hate that Greek."
> "Why did you marry him? You never did tell me that."
> "I haven't told you anything."
> "We haven't wasted any time on talk."
> "I was working in a hash house. You spend two years in a Los Angeles hash house and you'll take the first guy that's got a gold watch."

A lesser writer might have devoted a gratuitous and a more-than-we-need-to-know chapter to what Cain does in the line: "We did plenty."

Did you notice that in this excerpt there are no "he saids" or "she saids"? They are not necessary; the reader always knows who is talking.

And certainly there is no "he retorted" or "she sneered" or "she whispered" or "she chortled." If one character in a kitchen says to another, "You ain't no Julia Child," there is no need to add "he said sarcastically." One of the few times when *how* someone says something is valid is when a character speaks, as they say in the theater, "against the line" (viz: "I love you," he said savagely.).

Elmore Leonard says, "These days about the only adverbs I use with dialogue are 'loudly' or 'softly'."

3. *Burgeoning romance*

In F. Scott Fitzgerald's novel, *Tender is the Night*, Dick Diver, a married doctor, becomes involved with Rosemary Hoyt, a *very* young actress.

> Her room in the hotel was diagonally across from theirs and nearer the elevator. When they reached the door she said suddenly:

"I know you don't love me—I don't expect it. But you said I should have told you about my birthday. Well, I did, and now for my birthday present I want you to come into my room a minute while I tell you something. Just one minute."

They went in and he closed the door, and Rosemary stood close to him, not touching him. The night had drawn the color from her face—she was pale as pale now, she was a white carnation left after a dance.

"When you smile—" He had recovered his paternal attitude, perhaps because of Nicole's silent proximity, "I always think I'll see a gap where you've lost some baby teeth."

But he was too late—she came close up against him with a forlorn whisper.

"Take me."

"Take you where?"

Astonishment froze him rigid.

"Go on," she whispered. "Oh, please go on, whatever they do. I don't care if I don't like it—I never expected to—I've always hated to think about it but now I don't. I want you to."

This is the beginning of a revealing scene and is worth your looking it up and reading it in its entirety. How much the author accomplishes here! By eavesdropping on their conversation, we learn so much about Rosemary's and Dick's characters.

And we even get a little laugh:

> "Take me."
> "Take you where?"

Which leads us to,

4. Poignant humor

Noel Coward's name is synonymous with witty dialogue, yet he rarely sacrifices the thrust of conflict or character development simply to make a bon mot or a quick quip. His 1930 play *Private Lives* is called a comedy, but there are many poignant love scenes. Amanda and Elyot, a divorced couple, are on their honeymoons on the Riviera with their new spouses. Not only are they staying at the same hotel, coincidentally, but they have adjoining suites.

(Remember that while it is unwise to *end* a story with a coincidence, one may *start* one with a coincidental happening. "Don't look now, darling, but I think that man you sent to prison is on the very same plane with us!)

This is the dialogue that ensues when Noel Coward's protagonists find themselves very nervous and awkwardly alone for a few minutes on the moonlit porch:

> AMANDA (*Not looking at him*): What have you been doing lately? During these last years?
> ELYOT *(Not looking at her)*: Travelling about. I went round the world you know after—
> AMANDA (*Hurriedly*): Yes, yes, I know. How was it?
> ELYOT: The world?
> AMANDA: Yes.
> ELYOT: Oh, highly enjoyable.
> AMANDA: China must be very interesting.
> ELYOT: Very big, China.
> AMANDA: And Japan—
> ELYOT: Very small.
> AMANDA: Did you eat sharks' fins, and take your shoes off, and use chopsticks and everything?
> ELYOT: Practically everything. (*He turns to her.*)
> AMANDA: And India, the burning Ghars, or Ghats, or whatever they are, and the Taj Mahal. How was the Taj Mahal?
> ELYOT (*Looking at her*): Unbelievable, a sort of dream.
> AMANDA (*Facing him*): That was the moonlight I expect, you must have seen it in the moonlight.
> ELYOT (*Never taking his eyes off her face*): Yes, moonlight is cruelly deceptive.
> AMANDA: And it didn't look like a biscuit box, did it? I've always felt that it might.
> ELYOT (*Quietly*): Darling, darling, I love you so.

5. Creating tension and warning of impending actions

The following is from Dashiell Hammett's 1929 novel *The Maltese Falcon.*

> "Another thing," Spade repeated, glaring at the boy: "Keep that gunsel away from me while you're making up your mind. I'll kill him. I don't like him. He makes me nervous. I'll kill him the first time he gets in my way. I won't give him an even break. I won't give him a chance. I'll kill him."
> The boy's lips twitched in a shadowy smile. He neither raised his eyes nor spoke.
> The fat man said tolerantly: "Well, sir, I must say you have a most violent temper."

When John Huston made his film of that novel he took the dialogue virtually intact from the book.

A frequently asked question is, "How much dialogue should there be?"

One could answer glibly "half and half," but in truth there is no formula for the ratio of the spoken word to exposition either in novels or short stories. Entire stories have been written in dialogue, and others have been written without a word of dialogue. (I know of no *novels* that have gone to either extreme, but they may exist.)

Notice the balance of dialogue to exposition in the following tense excerpt from Elmore Leonard's novel *Stick* (and no one is better than he at imbuing dialogue with tension). Cecil, the fired chauffeur, has come drunkenly to make trouble for Barry, the employer, who is having a garden party. Stick, the low-keyed protagonist, has been hired to replace Cecil as chauffeur and gofer; he appears on the scene carrying a can of gasoline:

> Stick placed the can on the ground. He picked up the glass, filled to the brim, turned carefully and came over to Cecil with it. Cecil stared at him, weaving a little, pressing back against the cart as Stick raised the glass.
>
> "You doing? I don't drink gasoline, for Christ sake. Is it reg'ler or ethyl?"
>
> Stick paused, almost smiled. Then emptied the glass with an up-and-down toss of his hand, wetting down the front of Cecil's shirt and the fly of his trousers.
>
> There was a sound from the guests, an intake of breath, but no one moved. They stared in silence. They watched Cecil push against the bar, his elbow sweeping off bottles, watched him raise the fifth of Jack Daniel's over his head, the sour mash flooding down his arm, over the front of his shirt already soaked. He seemed about to club down with the bottle . . .
>
> Stick raised his left hand, flicked on a lighter and held it inches from Cecil's chest.
>
> "Your bag's packed," Stick said, looking at him over the flame. "You want to leave or you want to argue?"

Notice how Leonard leaves out words—"You doing?"—the way people do in real life.

Some stories call for a great deal of dialogue; a John Updike cocktail party would indicate a lot of talk, while in a Robinson Crusoe-type story one would expect less.

6. *To begin*

An effective way to begin a story or a novel is with someone speaking. Larry McMurtry likes to begin *in medias res*, as in this opening of his 1989 novel *Some Can Whistle*, about a writer's long-lost daughter suddenly entering his life:

> "Mister Deck, are you my stinkin' Daddy?" a youthful, female's furious voice said into the phone.
> I could not have been more startled if I had looked up into the blue Texas sky and seen a nuclear bomb on its way down.

Catherine Ryan Hyde, author of the novel *Pay It Forward*, says: "Whether beginning or ending with dialogue, my biggest challenge is to get out of its way." Remember the scene in *The Wizard of Oz* when Toto pulls back the curtain to reveal the harmless old man? ("I'm not a bad man, my dear—just a bad wizard.") One glimpse behind the curtain, and the illusion is ruined. To me, a mistake in dialogue is anything that reminds the reader that a bad wizard is at work behind the scenes.

7. *Using summary dialogue*

That is where the author *describes* the dialogue rather than recording it word by word, sentence by sentence. Summary dialogue can be very useful at times, especially when the actual dialogue would be tedious to the reader because *he already knows the information.*

> "Tom! Oh, Tom!" She came into his arms sobbing, her clothes torn and singed from the fire. And little by little the story came out in choking words, about how the fire started, how she'd found Jed, the itinerant they'd taken in and been kind to, standing there laughing with the can of gasoline in his hand.
> "You poor baby," Tom murmured, holding her close.

Presumably, in this version, the reader has already "seen" the described action and doesn't need to hear it twice in detail. But if this were all new to the reader, as well as to Tom, we would want to hear the actual words for ourselves, like this:

> "Darling! Your clothes—what happened?"
> "Awful!" she managed to gasp. "Jed—it was Jed—I couldn't believe it— our house, our beloved house . . . Hold me, hold me."
> "Jed? What'd that bastard do?"
> "After all we've done for him! I found him standing there—just standing there with a can of gasoline—"
> "I'll kill him—"

"And Tom, he was laughing! Yes, laughing as our house burned to the ground!"

"You poor baby," he said, holding her close, and already choosing the weapon with which to kill Jed.

8. To indicate background or regional origins

For regional dialogue or dialect, Annie Proulx is difficult to top. You'll find useful examples on almost any page of her collection of stories about the West, *Open Range*:

> "Oh, lord," said Bliss, finishing with the mare." I'm done here. I'll warsh that stuff off a your rig."
> As he straightened up Jaxon tossed him the sack of tobacco. "There you go, brother boy. And I find the good shears I'll cut your lousy hair. Then I got a go."

A little dialect can do wonders for a character ("Are you wantin' real buttah or just I Can't Believe?").

But one must be careful about overdoing dialect. In *How to Talk Pure Ozark*, Dale Freeman goes into the spelling and pronunciation of certain words that would be irritating in a serious manuscript:

> *Bag* is used as in "He bagged her to marry up with him"; *dork*, what it gets when the sun goes down; *flar*, a rose is about the prettiest flar there is; *hern*, it ain't hern, it's his'n; *oral*, your car needs two quarts of oral; *rah cheer*, he was born rah cheer; *retch*, as in "If I'd knowed it was you, I'd have retch out and wove."

9. To end

Ending a story or novel with dialogue is a tried-and-true practice. Here is Hemingway's bittersweet end to his novel *The Sun Also Rises*. The impotent Jake and the sex-driven English girl know their affair can go nowhere. They are in a taxi in Madrid:

> Brett moved close to me. We sat close against each other. I put my arm around her and she rested against me comfortably. It was very hot and bright, and the houses looked sharply white. We turned out onto the Gran Via.
> "Oh, Jake," Brett said, "we could have had such a damned good time together."
> Ahead was a mounted policeman in khaki directing traffic. He raised his baton. The car slowed suddenly, pressing Brett against me.
> "Yes." I said. "Isn't it pretty to think so?"

10. *Humor and comic relief*

Of course, dialogue has always been a staple of humor throughout literature even in dramatic scenes. In his bestseller, *Havana Bay*, Martin Cruz Smith sends his Russian detective, Arkady Renko, to Cuba on a missing-persons matter:

> In one case he advises a Cuban woman not to try to cut her own throat because it so rarely works. "Interesting," she replies. "A Cuban man would have said, 'Oh, but it's such a pretty throat.' Everything with them leads to sex, even suicide. That's why I like Russians, because with them suicide is suicide." "Our talent," replies Arkady.

SOME DIALOGUE TIPS

• After writing down the essential dialogue for the information that must be conveyed to the reader, try reading it aloud, to another person.

• Does it sound stilted or does it seem natural? Remember, most of us tend to talk in short choppy sentences—we repeat words, we leave out words, rarely in perfect sentences with nouns and verbs and adjectives in proper order.

• Are the words consistent with the character who speaks it? John Steinbeck's Lenny in *Of Mice and Men* doesn't talk like Henry Higgins in *Pygmalion*. Scarlett O'Hara doesn't sound like Liza Doolittle.

• Does the dialogue advance the plot?

• Does it characterize the speaker or another character?

• Does it help us *see* what is going on?

• Can some of the less important talk be put into "summary dialogue" so as not to tax the reader's attention unduly with mundane trivia? ("After asking pleasantly for some minutes about Bill's family and his job, Clara said quietly: 'Why *did* you kill him, Bill?' ")

• Jot down overheard snatches of conversation in a restaurant, theater, or bus. ("Syndrome? I say, is that"—wheezy laugh—"a brothel near the airport?")

• Copy choice selections of dialogue from favorite books, plays, and films and put them in your notebook. (Fred Astaire grumbling to Judy Garland: "Why didn't you *tell* me I was in love with you?")

• Above all: Train yourself to listen for the unexpected, the poignant, and the insightful.

❑ 25

QUESTIONS OF CHARACTER

BY DENNIS LEHANE

IN HER BOOK ON WRITING, *MYSTERY AND MANNERS*, FLANNERY O'Connor relates an oft-quoted anecdote about writing the story "Good Country People," in which a Bible salesman steals the wooden leg of a lonely, unattractive woman. O'Connor stated that she herself didn't know her character was going to commit the theft until ten or twelve lines before he actually did it, at which point she realized it had been "inevitable" all along. Studying her craft, applying and reapplying its principles, working not only to convey a vision of the world, but to develop one in the first place—all those things and more, O'Connor stressed, went into the "accident," so that it wasn't accidental at all.

Often one reads advice about how to structure a plot, or create scenes with oomph, or craft dialogue that singes the ear, and all of this is relevant, yet it's useless if you don't know how to build character. As Aristotle wrote two centuries ago, "Character is action." In other words, character is plot; character is dialogue; character is scene. You must have one before you can have the other, and character is the only element intrinsic to the equation. It is the sole building block; everything else rises from it.

Character, then, is your foundation. All other components—dialogue, your facility with language, an original storyline—are merely floors. And while a solid foundation doesn't make a building (and thus, plenty of stories with strong central characters can still fail because the rest of the structure leaks), no building can survive without one. Yet, countless buildings can and do survive without an eighth or ninth floor. That is to say, a story with a few strong characters can occasionally survive a weak plot, but a story with a strong plot cannot—ever—survive weak characters. Because if you don't care about Who the What is happening to, then you won't care about the What in the first place.

This is not to contend that all characters must be "likable." They

119

don't, not even main characters. They just have to be real, vivid, multi-dimensional, recognizable as members of the human race, so that their actions, no matter how potentially bizarre—stealing a woman's wooden leg, for example—are ultimately understandable and seemingly inevitable. When someone speaks of an unsuccessful book or movie or play and says, "It didn't make sense," often what he or she means is, "The characters' actions didn't make sense," and the reason the actions (read: plot) didn't make sense is because the characters themselves weren't fully drawn.

Plot, you see, is nothing but the acting out of the main character's internal struggle. All drama, eventually, is about explicating one or more characters' souls. That's it. *The Silence of the Lambs concerns* a serial killer and the race to catch him before he kills again, but it is *about* Clarice Starling's coming to terms with who she is in relation to both her past (the lambs) and her present (their eventual silence at the book's end). *The Great Gatsby concerns* a guy named Gatsby who chases a lost love and ultimately loses everything because of it, but it is *about* the effect of Gatsby's fall on the evolution and self-awareness of Nick Carroway and Nick's realization that the "foul dust that preyed on Gatsby" is a dust he himself is a part of, if not by action then at least by birthright. Without Clarice Starling's evolution, *Silence* is just another serial killer book; without Carroway's evolution, *Gatsby* is just a perverse Horatio Alger story with a depressing coda. The plots of the books are not what set them apart; the character is.

When I wrote my first novel, *A Drink Before the War,* I started with a character. That's all I had. And the character in my head was not Patrick Kenzie, the protagonist of the novel; it was his deceased father, Edgar, AKA "The Hero," a man who was, in Irish-American vernacular, a "street angel/house devil." I created a man who was a hero fireman and, later in life, a beloved city councilor, cherished by all except his family whom he abused and tortured and generally treated in a very, very bad manner. Yet, as I wrote about him, I found myself slipping into the first-person point of view, which told me the character I was really writing about was his son. And so, in the best biblical sense, Patrick was begot by Edgar.

So, now I had this guy, a private investigator whose father was evil, yet loved by the general public. What kind of man would the son be?

He'd hate hypocrisy, for one. He'd have a mistrust of politicians. He'd have a keen sense of injustice and an identification with those who are abused—by families, by government, by society in general. He would also, logic told me, have his father's temper. And maybe, I told myself, he'd be a bit self-righteous; he'd have a lot of anger, and anger often turns into self-righteousness. O.K. I had my character. What kind of case would explicate him?

He gets hired by politicians to find a black cleaning woman who, it turns out, is being sought for far different reasons than the ones Patrick was given. When she dies, he realizes he's been used not only to find her but also to lead her to the spot of her assassination. He also discovers she has an abused son, who's grown into a feared gang leader locked in a death struggle with his father, who's in bed with the politicians. And because Patrick is white and caught in the middle of a black-on-black gang war, he also has to (involuntarily) confront his own racism. And the result isn't one he'd have necessarily hoped for.

The process of defining my main character ultimately led me into the core of what my novel was about: race warfare as class warfare; violence as a multi-generational disease; white-collor crime as a far more insidious transgression than blue-collar crime; child abuse as a hamster wheel from which no one—victim or victimizer—can vacate once they've stepped on and started pedaling. And all of this—along with some hopefully whizz-bang shoot-outs, car chases, betrayals and un-maskings—stemmed from one character. Who begot another. Who begot another.

So, character is the foundation, yes. But how do we build a solid character?

A former professor of mine, the novelist John Dufresne, expressed one theory I've always liked a lot. Mr. Dufresne used to teach that one way to successfully envision a character is to imagine her in a room of her home and then make a list of the items you see there. It seems implausibly simple, but that's the beauty of it. Are her clothes on the floor or neatly hung, and what kind of clothes are they? What's in her CD rack? What magazines fan out across her coffee table? What titles line her bookcase, or does she have a bookcase?

Once you've answered some of these questions, you haven't created a character yet, but you have found a way in to her psyche. You've laid brick #1 of the foundation.

For more bricks, go back to Aristotle. If character is action, have your character in this room you've designed, do something. Have her cook or answer the phone or go out, or whatever you choose, but have her *act* and act as soon as possible. A telltale sign of student fiction tends to be pages and pages of character description—what the character looks like, what's in her room, what she ate for breakfast—without any action. Frankly, that's boring, and worse, it shows lack of confidence: It shows the writer trying to figure out the character on the page, as opposed to knowing the character *before* the first page is written and then gradually defining her for the reader. All of those details—looks, room, eating habits, etc.—can come out through action. A character can see her reflection in the window of her car as she's walking toward it. And you can then describe what she looks like with the narrative already in motion. (Where is she going? Why? And how come she's driving so fast?)

This isn't to say that you, the writer, have to know the character inside and out before you write about her. Half the fun of writing comes in the discovery process. Usually, you write your way into a character. Now, if this seems to contradict what I mentioned above—that the writer should know the character before the first page is written—let me explain that when I refer to that first page, I'm referring to the first page you'd actually allow someone to read, the first fit-to-be-published page, which is usually about the twentieth page you write. Which is one way of saying, that if you don't rewrite, you don't write. You type.

The core to building character is rewriting. *You* need to know everything that's in your character's apartment, so write it down. You need to know who her first boyfriend was, what her first car smelled like, the name of her childhood pet, if she got along with her parents, why she doesn't like mustard. And you learn all those things by writing them down. And then when you know them—when you, in fact, know your character—you cut most of that stuff out or shape it into moments of action, thereby creating plot. Hemingway called it the tip-of-the-iceberg theory: What shows up in fiction in regard to character is the very tip of an iceberg peeking up above the waterline. But there's a whole lot of iceberg below the waterline that the audience never sees—and that is what *you* know about your character. And as Hemingway put it, if there isn't more iceberg beneath the surface, the audience might not be able to see it, but they can sense it, and they will put your book or story aside. But if you do know your character the audience will sense that, too, feel it in the confidence of your prose and the certainty of your narrative arc, and your readers will then follow wherever you lead.

Less ultimately equals more. The more you know about your character, the less you have to show. I know what my main protagonist, Patrick Kenzie, looks like, but it's only recently that fans have begun noticing that they don't. Because he's a first-person narrator, I would find it odd if he described himself, so the only physical descriptions the reader gets of him come from other characters, and those descriptions are few and far between. I know who his childhood sweetheart was, which sports he played badly as a child, what's in his kitchen cupboard, who his favorite high school teachers were, and what his college GPA was, but none of that, thus far, has been germane to the plots of the five novels in which he's appeared, and so, it stays in my head, not on the page.

When you tell a story, think of it as if you're doing it live, sitting around the proverbial campfire. You're trying to keep people entertained, and if you don't, they'll nod off, or wander back into their tents, or go find someone else to entertain them. So, in order to hold them at your side, hanging on your words, you have to make those words count. You have to make them vivid and enticing and brief. You have to get to the heart of all your narrative elements—character, plot, dialogue—concisely.

If you learn how to do that, through the creation of fully fleshed-out characters and stringent, merciless rewriting, then your "happy accidents" will occur. And by the time you're really good at what you do, they won't seem all that accidental.

□ 26

MAKING CONNECTIONS

BY HAL BLYTHE AND CHARLIE SWEET

LAST SUMMER AS INSTRUCTORS AT A CREATIVE-WRITING CONFERENCE, we had an experience that made us better writers. While critiquing a promising piece of fiction, we became frustrated because we couldn't put our finger on why the story didn't quite work. The tale, which centered around a young soldier's baptismal firefight in Vietnam, at first seemed solid. The main character was believable, the setting was described in gritty realism, and the plot had a beginning, middle, and end.

But although the story was technically correct, it didn't really capture our interest. We found we couldn't get involved with the writer's grunt in Southeast Asia. Finally, the problem hit us: *The story lacked emotional impact.*

As we helped the writer revise his story, we came to look on the fiction-writing process from a new perspective. And that led us to adopt a different approach—*an approach you can use to insure you engage readers more deeply in your fiction.*

A good model for this approach is Walt Whitman's "A Noiseless Patient Spider." The arachnid, which the poet compares to the human soul perched on an isolated promontory, launches filament, filament out of itself, "seeking spheres to connect them." How true! Don't we, solitary beings all, spend a great deal of time trying to be part of the world around us? Don't we all seek emotional rapport with our family, our friends, and our co-workers?

Similarly, effective fiction most often centers on characters trying to make connections, seeking to build emotional bridges, whether to people, causes, objects, or nature. Conflict occurs when these bridges are broken or never quite span to the other side.

The story we critiqued lacked these connections. The young infantryman didn't even try to connect to a single "sphere—a cause (war), his fellow soldiers, people back home, people in country, or to his own goals. In fact, his character existed in an emotional vacuum because the writer was not aware of his protagonist's inner life.

Consider how this "connections" approach relates to readers. How can an audience identify with a character so lacking in basic human skills, and not even be aware of them? Simply put, *no emotion for the character, no emotion for the reader.*

Effective writers have always used this connections model in order to create powerful, emotional fiction. Even Oedipus tries to connect with his beloved Thebes, his family, and the will of the gods. His tragedy occurs because he severs all three connections through his act of patricide, and at the end he is led away from the city he loves into exile, the final bond broken. Classic nineteenth-century heroines, such as Hedda Gabler and Emma Bovary, are dissociated from their society and the men who care for them. They try to belong by adopting such conventional means as marriage, but are thwarted. Their filaments never truly attach.

A popular twentieth-century story that also deals with the subject and can also be understood in terms of connections is Hemingway's "Big Two-Hearted River." In fact, Hemingway has omitted any specific reference to the story's emotional core, Nick Adams's negative experience on World War I battlefields. As a result, on the surface the story seems to be simply the account of a fishing trip.

Actually, however, it is about Nick's trying to make connections. Shell-shocked and isolated by his wartime experiences, Nick tries to establish a relationship with the real world. To accomplish this, he returns to a familiar haunt of his youth. At first, his attempt to connect fails, for the familiar town of Seney has burned to the ground. Gradually, as Nick treks into the country, sets up camp, and fishes, he reconnects with his past. Going through the minute ritual of campcraft puts him in touch with the person he was before the war, and his wounds start to heal. Ultimately, as readers experience these details, they begin to connect with Nick. Successfully depicted emotion, even at Hemingway's subdued level, engenders emotion in the readers.

Can making these connections approach help explain some contemporary stories that affect us deeply? A widely praised but often misunderstood story is Bobbie Ann Mason's well-known short story "Shiloh." Her depiction of the strained marriage of Norma Jean and

Leroy Moffitt begins in a small, rented house in Western Kentucky and concludes with the husband watching his wife stand on a bluff overlooking the Shiloh battlefield. In between, nothing seems to happen: Leroy merely dreams of building a cabin, while Norma Jean lifts weights and takes courses at the community college. Yet this story haunts us—why? What holds its apparent lack of action together?

The author bases her story on two spiders trying to connect. Now back home and disabled, Leroy wants to relate more closely to his wife ("There is a connection between him and Norma Jean.") by developing his feminine side (he even tries needlepoint). Norma Jean, on the other hand, is trying to connect to her masculine side (she is a bodybuilder). Ultimately, the two spouses end up disconnecting. While Leroy has come home to roost, Norma Jean is ready to fly.

The story's emotional impact derives from the two characters struggling in opposite directions. As they connect to other sides of their being, they sever the tenuous filament of their marriage.

By the end of the conference, our student's revision focused on an 18-year-old, introspective rookie who feels extremely cut off from his home, his family, friends, and a special girl. These *frayed connections* become more poignant each time he pulls out his wallet to show pictures of his brother, his farmhouse, his car, and Sheila. Obviously he's using these photographs to hold on to old connections as well as *to make* new connections with the men in his rifle squad.

Unfortunately, he finds the only way he can truly belong with his comrades is to do what soldiers do well—kill. But shooting the enemy goes against *another connection*—the moral code with which he was reared. In the writer's climax, his protagonist overrides his scruples, and, going against orders to maintain silence, he shoots an enemy soldier. In the aftermath, he searches the dead man's body only to discover a wallet containing pictures of a smiling baby and a pregnant woman. The final scene depicts the young man in a profound despair, for now ironically, he is *totally disconnected* from his family, his basic values, his rifle squad, and even from humanity.

The next time you begin to write a piece of fiction, start by focusing on your protagonist and try to figure out with what connection he or she would most like to make. Is it something personal, part of business, or an object?

Now try to discover why your protagonist wants to make the connection in the first place. What fuels the engine? Suppose, for instance, your female lead wants to connect to a male through marriage. Why? Does she want children? Does she really want to prove to her parents that she can do what they couldn't and stay married? Does she only want to be like her friends, who are all married? Maybe, you decide, she romantically believes that some day she will meet her prince.

The next step is to depict the female protagonist actively trying to make her connection. Does she pick a co-worker, an old boyfriend, or the first man who smiles at her? Be certain that the prospective bonds are emotional: She must have a sense of her feelings being affected. Place obstacles in her way, especially those that heighten the emotional intensity of her quest. Does the male she chooses not like her? Does she suddenly realize that her quest has been flawed from the start because it's not real?

Move on. Do some of these filaments connect? Is she frustrated? Does she understand why she wants to connect? If thwarted, does she give up or try again? Keep raising the emotional stakes.

Making—and unmaking connections in writing a story has one major advantage: *It forces you to add an emotional dimension to your fiction.* In addition, using this technique can . . .

• Keep you from being mechanical (always a well-defined beginning-middle-ending)
 • Create a variety of new conflicts (you explore nuance)
 • Force you to focus on developing character (internally and in terms of relationships)
 • Prevent you from relying too much on a staple of popular fiction—purely surface external conflict.

Ultimately, this technique will help your readers connect with your story.

❏ 27

TURNING HISTORY INTO FICTION

BY CARYL RIVERS

CREATING A FICTIONAL JOHN FITZGERALD KENNEDY FOR MY NOVEL *Camelot* was a daunting challenge, because some see him as the gallant young champion of civil rights, while others see the reckless womanizer and cynical politician who appears in *The Dark Side of Camelot*.

My book is set in 1963, as the civil rights movement is moving to a climax. I had to get inside the mind of Kennedy, who is only one of the characters. The others are a 25-year-old woman journalist trying to make it in a man's world, a young black civil rights worker torn between his career as a writer and his devotion to the movement, and a photojournalist wrestling with his own demons about committing to anything other than his Nikon.

When using a historical character, you have to decide whether to be faithful to history or to attempt a fanciful or satiric approach. I chose a realistic, flesh-and-blood Kennedy, as true to the historical record as possible. To do that, I drew on my own experiences, and on extensive research.

I was lucky because as a very young journalist, I had actually covered JFK. The first time I interviewed him, I was in college, and he was in the Senate, and I got all dressed up and tried to be a real reporter. He was very kind, and told me he had wanted to be a journalist, too. We rode together in the Senate subway from his office building to the floor, and one of my clip earrings fell off and rolled out of sight under the seat. (I learned a valuable lesson—never wear anything that can fall off when you are doing an interview.) He started grubbing for it under the seat, and I was mortified. He found it and gave it back, with a grin. Later, when he was killed on that terrible day in Dallas, all I could think of was being able to go back in time to the subway car, so I could say, "Please, please don't go to Dallas in 1963."

When I joined a Washington bureau, I got to spend time around the

White House, seeing JFK in action, meeting Martin Luther King, the astronauts, and a fabulous cast of characters. For aspiring writers, journalism is a very good trade to take up, because it gives you a ticket of admission to so many disparate worlds. Writers broaden their repertoire by getting to places where things are happening. Taking creative writing courses is fine, but don't forget to live, so you'll have something to write about. Also, as a reporter, you have to listen hard to people to recreate the rhythms of their speech, which makes it easy to create dialogue for fictional characters.

The structure of *Camelot* is complex. For Mary Springer and Jay Broderick, the journalist and photographer in my novel, the reader has to see them doing things, especially at a civil rights march that turns violent. The third-person, omniscient narrator device is very good when you want to see people acting, and to present that action from different points of view. Don, the black activist, presented a different challenge. I wanted readers to experience his growing up in a very segregated Washington and living through events in the civil rights movement before the time the novel actually begins. I finally chose a diary format, which allowed me to go to the past without confusing flashbacks.

For JFK, I chose first-person interior monologue, in italics, because I wanted to set him apart as a special character. I wanted to explore his ruminations on the crises he was facing as President, his problematic relationships with his father and his older brother Joe, and his close relationship with his sister, Kathleen, who was killed in a plane crash. Italics are a good way to let the reader know right away that a portion of your narrative is set aside from the rest, but the sections can't be too long; italics are hard to read after a while.

I pored through all the major histories and biographies of the JFK era, and I also visited the Kennedy library. For any writer wanting to plunge into a historical period, presidential libraries are great sources, because they house diaries, interviews, videotapes and artifacts of the era. Good research gives you the confidence that you are creating a valid character. I decided to present Kennedy as a man conflicted by the two sides of his nature: His wish to be a bold, idealistic hero warred with his instinctive caution. Kennedy grew up as a sickly child often alone with his books, reading about the knights of the round table performing heroic deeds. Like Teddy Roosevelt, another sickly boy who willed himself to become the Rough Rider, Kennedy projected an image of youthful vitality, often while in great pain. Through much of his life he struggled to move out of the giant shadow of his father, and the ambassador's conservative politics. When push came to shove, he usually did the decent thing . . . especially where basic fairness was concerned.

Since JFK could—and often did—swear like the sailor he was, I allowed his thoughts to be sometimes profane. "That damned preacher is going to fuck me out of a second term," he says to himself about Martin Luther King. Kennedy was both awed by King's courage and irritated by his persistence. Kennedy knew that he risked losing his whole civil rights package if he alienated the Southerners who ran the Senate. But of course, it was the constant pressure that forced the country to move forward.

My JFK, a history buff, is acutely aware that both he and King would be forever linked. He walks to the window of the oval office, thinking about the shades of all the great men who had been in that office.

> It was dusk, his favorite time, and the ghosts were beginning to stir. He had the strange sensation that he and the preacher would be a part of those stirrings one day, that the two of them were locked together in some strange dance that would probably last as long as they lived. Where it would lead, he had no idea. He only knew the music would not stop.

At first, I decided not to put JFK's assassination in the book, but then I realized that the dramatic structure really called for it. And I knew that many readers would not be familiar with the terrible drama that played out that day. I chose William Manchester's *The Death of a President* as my guide to November 22, 1963, because it is an exhaustive chronicle of the events of that day. I read the Manchester account, and then put it away, recreating the facts in my own language. Although I gave Manchester ample credit in the introductory notes, I didn't want my novel to be seen as using his cadence, his words, his rhythms. My editor found one place where I used the same phrase Manchester did in his book to describe the gunman, and I changed it.

One eerie coincidence surprised me. I created a fictional "shadow" that Kennedy could see in his peripheral vision—death, with which he had become well acquainted through family tragedies and war. I was startled, as the book was about to come out, when Kennedy's secretary, Evelyn Lincoln, died, and in her effects was a note showing that JFK had a premonition of his own death before he went to Dallas.

That shadow, it seems, was more than fiction.

❏ 28

PACING YOUR NOVEL

BY MARGARET CHITTENDEN

WHEN I BEGIN TO PLOT A NOVEL, I TEND TO THINK OF MY BRAIN AS A stockpot: I just throw ideas into it and let them simmer. It's no coincidence that one of my favorite quotes from the I Ching is, "Before the beginning of great brilliance, there must be chaos."

At first, I don't believe in being too organized. Eventually however, I get ready to write my synopsis—my plan—my plot, try to combine all the elements and make order out of the chaos.

The writer of popular fiction usually sets up a situation that creates suspense and anticipation, then shows what the fallout from that is, using cause and effect: If this happens, what would be the result, and what would that cause to happen, and what would be the consequence, until the situation is resolved and the loose ends are tied up. That's a very basic outline for a novel, but it gets the plot off to a good start.

One of the flaws I've seen most often when reading other writers' manuscripts is a beginning that's too slow. I don't think your characters have to show up on page one in the middle of a gunfight, but there should be a sense that something is happening or is about to happen. No reader is going to read patiently on while waiting for the suspense to begin.

Here are a few things to look at that have to do with pacing; I'll leave it up to you to decide if you should consider them before plotting, before writing, during writing, after you have finished the first draft . . . never. No one who writes for a living has gone up a mountain and been given a set of stone tablets with the rules of writing etched into them. If anything I suggest doesn't work for you, discard it and work it out your own way.

Try to have an opening that will engage your reader's attention right away. It is often the first page that sells a book to an editor or to a reader. It has to be interesting. What works best for me is to have more than one person on the scene and people *doing* things, rather than sitting around talking or thinking. Don't have anyone musing in a bathtub. Flying around waiting to land in an airplane is another dangerous situation—dangerous for boredom, that is.

People often talk about starting with a narrative hook, which is O.K. if it works. Unfortunately, some writers interpret that to mean starting with an enormously dramatic action scene, whether it belongs in the story or not. I'm happy if a book starts with something intriguing.

Earl Emerson, author of the Thomas Black mystery series and the Mac Fontana mystery series, always comes up with intriguing beginnings. For example:

> On Saturday, some ghoul murdered my dog. It surprises you when they do something like that. I expect to be flattened by snarling eighteen wheelers on the freeway. I expect to be lunged at by booze hounds with broken beer bottles in taverns. I expect to be slapped by loose women who aren't quite as loose as I thought. But it surprises you when some spook caves in your dog's skull on a rainy Saturday evening. (*The Rainy City*, Avon Books)

> It was raining when they rolled me out of the big Lincoln and into the ditch. (*Yellow Dog Party*, Ballantine Books)

I always check my first sentences to make sure they will generate questions in the reader's mind. This sets my plot in motion, because I have to answer those questions.

If your pace seems too slow at any point in the book, think action. Your characters don't have to be battling savage hordes—unless that's an integral part of the story—but it helps if they are doing *something*. This doesn't necessarily have to be vital for the story. Sometimes you need a scene in which two people are simply swapping information, or getting to know each other, or perhaps having an argument. And it doesn't have to be while they are eating lunch. Most books have too many meals in them. (Mine do. I have to cut out several meals when I'm revising.) The reader will understand that your characters eat. You can even say, "They ate dinner, then. . . ."

Your story also gets much more interesting and thus speeds up the pace if you put your characters in a variety of scenes. The first time I remember noticing this was in Sue Grafton's novel, *A is for Alibi*, in which the main character, Kinsey Millhone, has lunch with one person, then goes to visit the office of another. My interest really perked up when Kinsey goes to question a dog groomer. The constant references to what the woman is doing and what the dogs are doing brought this scene alive, and taught me about the importance of using a variety of settings. In my mystery, *Dead Beat and Deadly* (Kensington), there are a couple of meals, but there's also an interview with a former homeless person after he's found a place to stay—and the "furniture" is a little unusual. There's a scene at a hair stylist's salon; one at a veterinarian's clinic; one in a women's rest room; one in an alley; and then, because my series is set in a country-western tavern, there are scenes on the dance floor and at the bar.

In *Dying to Sing* (Kensington), I had my sleuth, Charlie Plato, and her sidekick Zack Hunter hike over the Golden Gate Bridge with a doctor from whom they're trying to get some information about the murder victim. The Golden Gate Bridge had nothing to do with the story, nor did the freighter that passed under the bridge, or the waves people were riding below them, but those activities added interest to what might otherwise have been a rather dry question-and-answer scene, thus increasing the pace of the story.

Pacing does not always mean going fast; sometimes it's actually necessary to slow it down. Check your story (preferably after you have written it) to see if the pace of each section seems right. If the scene is an important one with all kinds of ramifications, you might want to slow the pace a bit. If the scene follows one of lickety-split action, you might want to slow that down, too, to give the reader a bit of a rest. Non-stop action can get just as boring as no action at all.

I discussed the subject of pacing with Dale Furutani, author of the Samurai Trilogy and the Ken Tanaka Mystery Series, and he wrote, "I think the biggest mistake writers make is in thinking they have to move at a frenetic pace throughout a book. In classical music, there are beautiful, quiet interludes to set a level from which the more vigorous passages can ascend. Without setting this base, you just have forty minutes of loud noise. In writing, we talk about the tricks to increase pace (shorter sentences, ever ascending action, more action verbs, shorter chapters, etc.), but we don't usually talk about the techniques to create the interludes (poetic language, appeal to emotions like solitude and love, interesting diversions from the main plotline, etc.)."

I agree with this, though I'd add a caveat. You shouldn't play too much beautiful music without having something going on. One place you must think about timing is at the end of your story. It must not be too abrupt, or the reader might not believe it could happen that way. It must not drag on too long, either. You have to study the pacing of your endings carefully to make sure they will satisfy the reader.

If, however, people have been sitting around talking for a while, you'll want to speed things up. And if you have an action scene, you don't want to insert extraneous details that will slow it down. Or make it unbelievable.

Every once in a while I'll read a book in which the action is hot and heavy, with the villain breathing down the hero and heroine's neck—this is no time for the hero to notice what beautiful eyes the heroine has. Or for the heroine to wonder how old the hero is and if he's married. Nor is it the time to describe the snow melting off the pine branches.

If you want to create atmosphere and stretch out suspense by having the heroine hide behind a tree in the forest while the villain creeps slowly toward her, then by all means have the snow melting off the pines. It's a question of balancing the atmosphere with the action.

You'll slow down a story if you stop the action to show what a character looks like. However, if you want to show the person in a way that brings him or her to life, don't give a complete description all at once, but rather note the things you would note when you first meet someone—height, approximate age, general physique, coloring. You may notice the color of the eyes the next time you meet, along with a mouth set in a grim expression, a weak chin, or hairstyle.

The way a person dresses tells a lot about him or her, so take the time to describe the clothing. In *Dead Beat and Deadly*, here is how I presented Zack Hunter, who stars in a weekly TV series. We're in Charlie Plato's viewpoint:

> He looked great. He always does. Unfortunately. His long legs and lean hips were packed into his jeans just right. As Sheriff Lazarro, Zack had dressed in all black clothing—jeans, cowboy hat, Western shirt, Tony Lama Boots. This outfit had worked as well for Lazarro as it had for Johnny Cash, and it proved so successful in snaring the ladies that Zack had made it his signature suit, as much a part of him as his green eyes and wry smile and the straight black eyebrows that slanted whimsically upward above his nose.

Now, that's quite a lot of words, but I think you get a lot of information about Zack and a little about Charlie, too, and it's not necessary for me to talk much about Zack's appearance after that. If I have him put on or take off his cowboy hat, or raise those slanted eyebrows, you'll see him the way I want you to see him. So I'm really saving words in the long run.

Although I've noted that pacing also refers to slowing the story down from time to time, the flaw in many stories is that they move with the pace of a snail; most need speeding up. When I've finished a book, I go over each scene and ask myself, "What is happening?" And if nothing is, I look carefully to see if action is necessary.

Using transitions is the best way to pick up the pace. Transitions get you from place to place or person to person without your having to give all the details. "Later," "The following day," "Meanwhile back at the ranch." Quite often there is no need to tell how the character or characters got from here to there; you can just start another chapter or scene without worrying about what happened in between. You can even hop over a whole week, if the adjoining scenes lend themselves to that.

But here again, there will be times when you should make a slower transition. In some cases, there has to be a complete change of mood, and you have to prepare the reader for it. Or in a particular case, you might not want to hop over several days with a single word. You just have to examine the scene before and the scene after, listening to the internal rhythm of each, and then decide how long the transition should be. Think of a transition as the stepping stone that gets you from one place or one time period to another.

I began by talking about the sort of primordial soup I start with when I'm plotting a novel. Getting out of that soup is sometimes a problem, but if you keep the setup, anticipation, action, and resolution in mind, you'll bring order out of the chaos, and pick up—or slow down—your pace as necessary.

❏ 29

Capture the Reader's Imagination

By Karin McQuillan

Reading is a collaboration between the imagination of the writer and the imagination of the reader. It is the writer's challenge to enable readers to create in their own minds the characters and the events the author has imagined. Given the necessary cues, the reader will be transported to an imaginary world, moved to tears or laughter, and be caught up in the story till the last word. If the author breaks the illusion by faulty writing, the reader will lose conviction.

The common advice "show, don't tell" is the key to success, but it can take years for beginning writers to work out what this actually means. The urge to explain instead of to fictionalize is natural, because it is the way we communicate in conversation. When we tell people about our experiences, they are learning it secondhand: We tell what happened; we don't recreate it in words. We add our thoughts, our analysis, describe our reaction.

The fictional illusion

In fiction, the writer's task is to create the illusion of a firsthand experience. This is the rendering of a scene that unfolds before readers' eyes as if they were there. It is a bit of magic, a tour de force that transforms black marks on a page into vivid settings, peopled by living characters caught up in a web of relationships and action. In fiction, "getting the idea across" is the enemy of that experiential illusion. Readers don't want an abstract idea; they want reality. That is the writer's challenge.

Writers often report that they watch the scene taking place in their mind's eye like a movie, and write it down. If only this were so! All too often, by the time this "movie" gets on the page, it is visually static; having scene after scene with characters talking about something exciting that happened offstage, or interminable close-ups of the main character's face with a voice-over narrating her thoughts about the off-stage event, would never hold an audience's attention.

The challenge is to write as if you're watching a movie unfold before you, *with the sound turned off.* Write as if you cannot use exposition or interior monologue; these have their place, but your writing will be stronger if you do not rely on them to create the story. Explanations cannot create the living dream that will capture your reader's imagination. From the action, setting, and body language, the reader should be able to grasp what's happening and feel the emotional impact of the scene. If you can't "turn the sound off" in your fictional narrative and have the visualized elements carry the scene, then those elements are not strong enough.

Readers want to be there

A key rule for writing a successful novel flows immediately from this discipline. You have to show events happening in front of the reader. This means putting the major scenes, the exciting scenes, the revealing scenes, the love scenes, the violent scenes—the difficult-to-write scenes—in your novel. To enlist the reader's imagination, you must have the courage to imagine scenes far outside your own experience. That is the challenge and reward of being a fiction writer.

I have read many unpublished manuscripts of murder mysteries by beginning writers in which the discovery of the body occurs offstage, the arrival of the police occurs offstage, the quarrels between characters take place offstage. The detective is kept busy hearing about all this in snappy dialogue from colorful characters. But it isn't enough. Readers want to hear, see, smell, taste and touch it themselves. They want to see more than just people talking, no matter how witty or belligerent they are.

Dramatize your ideas

The writer must show the reader many things, some concrete, some conceptual. Use your imagination to dramatize the concepts, giving them outward form in behavior, gesture, and setting so that the character's inner feelings can be rendered as graphically as the shape of his nose. Not only do you show where the characters are, and how they look, but you show who they are, what they are feeling, how they relate to other people, using all the tools available: setting, dialogue, viewpoint, voice, stage action, plot, sentence structure, and even word choice.

"Show, don't tell" means that you never put your ideas about the character on the page; those belong in your note file. You put down exactly the right information to give your readers the experience, so they come to the idea themselves. For example, you don't write, "She was a beautiful woman." That is an idea. It could apply to a million women, all different. The reader doesn't know what to imagine.

You don't write, "She was a tall, gorgeous blond." That is a generic description, lacking the uniqueness of life. Clichés are by definition ideas worn thin from overuse, a shorthand that replaces imagination. No matter how vivid a cliché may seem, it will not evoke anything fresh or personal in the readers' mind.

Show your blond with spare, powerful details of action, setting, and body language. If your details are well chosen, the reader will fill in the entire picture and visualize her as a specific, living woman, and see her beauty and feel its impact.

Here is the readers' first look at the model, Candy Svenson, in my African mystery, *Deadly Safari*:

> The staff were craning their necks to peer past the dining tent. I turned to see what they were staring at.
> Candy Svenson emerged from her afternoon nap. She stood framed by the tent awning. A mane of tawny hair stood out wildly from her head. A yellow robe with enormous padded shoulders and bird tracks all over it hung open and revealed a skintight green satin nightgown underneath. She stepped forward and stretched languorously.

There are only two sentences actually describing Candy's mane of hair and tight satin nightgown. The rest shows her in action, and the effect she has on the male staff, thus creating a strong impression in the reader's mind of a striking, unrestrained, sensual woman who likes to attract attention.

Notice I left almost everything to the reader's own imagination: the shape of Candy's features, the color of her eyes, the shape of her figure, whether voluptuous or willowy. Is her skin soft and yielding, or smooth and muscular? I don't say, but my reader knows. The reader will fill in all those details with her own imagination's lexicon of a sexy, beautiful woman, more vivid and convincing than any tracing of Candy's nose and breasts and skin that I could do. Each reader will have created her own Candy, but they will all have the essential elements necessary for the story.

The five rules of effective rendering

How do you know what details to select? Here are five basic rules: *Do not describe the obvious*; *visualize the scene through your viewpoint character*; *choose details that are unique in time and place*; *appeal to the five senses*; and *select details that evoke emotion*.

Extended description calls attention to the writing, thus blurring the reader's illusion of simply being there. Control the urge to write long blocks of description. Readers may enjoy that in Jane Austen, but they will skip over such paragraphs in a contemporary book. The solution: Work description into sentences involving stage action, plot or characterization. Make every word work triple time.

Effective details don't state the obvious. You can't create the illusion of a specific beach, or the feeling of being at the beach, by saying the sky was blue with puffy white clouds, and there were seagulls. When you don't demand anything of your own imagination, you won't enlist the reader's capacity for fantasy, either. Such a commonplace description doesn't set off personal associations or sense impressions to give life to this particular imaginary beach. It is an abstraction of a beach, in no place and no time, and it will never seem real.

The second rule is to see the scene through your narrator's eyes and attitude. Not all summer days are alike, and they are not the same to all people, or even to the same person at different moments. What would your point of view character notice, given his or her personality and what is happening in the story? The actual words you choose will have to be in your character's voice, that is, using the vocabulary, sentence structure, and pacing that suit your character's identity. What your character will notice on a particular sunny day will depend on her frame of mind, and will communicate her feelings to the reader. It must be congruent with both plot and character.

Here is my heroine Jazz as she radios in the discovery of the murdered body of her friend. I don't say Jazz is terribly upset. I describe sunlight and two birds. Those concrete details enable the reader to visualize Jazz as a physical being at a particular time and place, feeling a burden of pain and horror:

> I called in and gave detailed instructions on how to find Emmet's camp. The sun came in through the open roof hatch and fell in a burning patch on my back. I could feel sweat trickling between my shoulder blades. . . . A shadow passed over me, then another, bird-swift. Two vultures fell from the sky. They tipped their wings from side to side to hasten their descent, greedy to share in the possible spoils.

Notice I did not explain that a Land Rover has a roof hatch. Respect readers' ability to construct the image of something they are familiar with, like car sun roofs. I focus on the sense impression of the sun burning her back and sweat trickling down her skin. This is not a friendly, happy sun, because Jazz is feeling the oppression and hostility of the world at that moment. Appealing to the five senses makes the idea of a hot African sun take on an oppressive physical reality.

I don't state the idea that vultures began to gather. I help the reader see them from Jazz's perspective, and with her careful observation of animals: She feels the shadow, sees how vultures tip their wings to fall to earth as quickly as possible, because as a safari guide, she is a person who notices such things. Readers visualize and recoil from the greedy vultures, and I leave the rest to their imagination.

Anytime you anchor your reader in a unique moment in time, you are recreating the experience of real life. Here's a sunny morning later in the book, when Jazz is in a very different mood. I don't need to mention the sun for the reader to imagine it and feel in a sunny frame of mind. The sun is indicated by the detail of the golden grass, anchored in the specificity of Kenya's dry season. Again, there is a bird, not generic, but a particular one, standing too close to the road:

> Once I set off, my spirits rose. I love driving by myself. We were nearing the end of the dry season, and the grass was sere, straw white and pale gold. A yellow-billed stork stood stiff and unmoving inches from the car as I whisked by. His gaudy yellow bill was topped with a band of bright red across his face, and I couldn't help but smile at such a cheerful sight.

Through describing Jazz driving past grass and a bird, I have given the reader a setting so vivid they feel the wind of the car, feel the vastness of Africa, feel themselves smile inwardly. I have also shown the reader Jazz's mood, her intimate observation of wildlife and the seasons, a sense of her natural vitality and her independence. Concepts (It was a sunny day. Jazz cheered up because she likes to drive. The grass was yellow. She saw a stork.) tend to be unidimensional, while living details mimic the rich, multi-layered experience of reality.

The importance of accuracy

Accuracy is absolutely essential for illusion. You probably have never found a corpse, but if you describe the discovery of a murder victim with the authority of accurate sights, sounds, smells, and plausible behavior, the reader will readily follow along. If you count on your readers not knowing anything relevant to a crime scene themselves and make it all up, you will lose readers who *do* know something about the topic—doctors, lawyers, cops. Multiply this effect through all the scenes in your book, all the areas of in-depth knowledge you touch on, and that "accuracy doesn't matter" will lose you a lot of readers.

For example, like millions of other Americans, I am an avid gardener. If your hero is walking up the steps to his beloved's house in Boston, humming a tune and stopping to sniff April's roses, I will not be smelling roses with him. Nor will I be enjoying his romantic mood, as I was a moment before. That "April's rose" has popped me right out of the story. Instead of being caught up in the fictional illusion, I am aware of the ignorant author, who doesn't know that April in Boston gives us daffodils, or maybe a doorstep container of pansies. I know that roses don't arrive till June, and are the promise of summer, not heralds of spring. In other words, a single word of careless, inaccurate writing has broken the illusion for countless readers.

Do I have to do research on every single statement? the beginner wails. Obviously that's both impractical and death to the imagination. What is called for is respecting what you know and what you don't. If you don't know about the progression of bloom through the seasons, then don't use flowers to convey the ardor of spring.

It is better to choose a detail you personally know: It will not only be accurate, it will have the lifelike quality of uniqueness and specificity. Perhaps the roses you're thinking of actually are a sign of spring, in the person of a flower vendor who appears in April at the top of the subway stairs: Put the vendor in the book, and it will come to life, instead of the phony garden roses that killed the scene.

If you need to be specific about something outside your experience—as in the make of a gun at the scene of the crime—then some research is called for. Looking up guns in a book will do, but if you make the effort to go to a shop and handle actual handguns, or even better, go to a range and do some shooting, your imaginary gun will become far more convincing. You will not only learn the proper make, size, and so on, you will have the heft of it in your hand, the smell in your nostrils, your inner sensations of holding or shooting a gun.

In some mystery novels, the kind of gun used is not terribly important, and you can get away with vagueness, respecting the cardinal rule of not stating anything that's actually false. But if you're writing a tough private eye tale in which your main character would know and care about firearms, then you must educate yourself so you can ground your fantasies in reality.

Fiction allows us to transcend our lonely individuality and glimpse the world through another's eyes. The author gives the gift of an imagined world. Readers can receive the gift only if they join in with their imagination to realize that world. The tools of this magic are prosaic elements of the writing craft: point of view, dialogue, action, description, well-written prose, research. Readers want to discover your imagined world. Do your job, and they will do the rest.

□ 30

MATTERS OF FACT:
FICTION WRITERS AS RESEARCHERS

BY SHARON OARD WARNER

A FEW INTERESTING FACTS ON HONEY BEES:

1. Worker bees irritate the queen to prepare her to fly. She has to lose a little weight before she can take to the air.
2. The queen flies only once, going a distance of seven or eight miles so as not to mate with her brothers.
3. Mating occurs in the air, and after the act is completed, the drone dies and falls to the ground. (I could make all sorts of wise cracks here, but I'll refrain.)

This is the first use I've had for a whole legal pad full of notes I took in a beekeeping class a few summers ago. I registered for the class because I intended to write about a beekeeper, and to that end, I took faithful notes. More than two years have passed, and my beekeeper has yet to show himself. I do have firm possession of a radiologist who reads tarot cards, and I'm hoping to give her the beekeeper for a husband. As of this morning, she has yet to embrace him, but I'm optimistic about working it out. I intend to use some of this material on bees, but it's obvious that I'm not going to do all of it justice. If you need a stray bee fact or two, you're welcome to the above. Interesting though these facts are, I doubt that I'll find a place for them.

A few additional facts:

1. Bees don't like carbon dioxide, so when you work with them, be sure to breathe out the side of your mouth. (Try doing that, just to see how it feels.)
2. When a bee stings, she will die, but in the process she'll leave a "mad bee" smell on your skin, a smell that makes other bees want to sting you as well.
3. The mad bee smell is easy to identify: It smells for all the world like bananas with a little solvent mixed in.

143

Keep your hands off these facts. I can almost guarantee I'll use them sooner or later, and probably sooner. These are the kinds of facts that authenticate character and offer opportunities to advance a plot. They're active facts that carry a sensory charge. Let me show you what I mean: Once the radiologist acquiesces and agrees to be married to the bee-keeper, one of the first things he'll do is lumber out to the hives and check on his bees. Maybe he has someone else with him, his daughter Sophie say, and he'll tell her a little about how to handle the combs. Already, I can predict that Sophie will insist on getting stung. She's that sort of girl. And there we have it: the "mad bee" smell all over Sophie, enticing the other bees to sink their stingers into the soft skin of her upper arm and to swarm menacingly about her face. "Get away, Sophie!" her father will yell, wresting the comb from her hands. But Sophie will refuse because she's sixteen and more hormones than good sense.

This one little scene requires more facts than might be readily appar-ent. The three I've listed will launch the scene, but they won't complete it. Almost immediately, others will be necessary. Without them, the scene will lose steam, and the plot will stall. As it turns out, fiction and fictional characters take their vitality from facts, from real-life detail, which means that writers of fiction are in the business of research. We're fact hoarders—accumulating, sorting, and storing details that give our stories life.

Some of the fact-finding is rather mundane, but research need not be dull. The beekeeping class and my trip to the beekeeper's house to "handle" the bees were recent highlights. (No, I did not get stung while I held the combs, nor did I wear gloves or a veil. Are you impressed? Well, you shouldn't be. These were gentle bees.) I think of this early research as a sort of "grounding" because I use these facts to situate my main characters in their milieu. Where do these people I'm writing about live? In which city, on what street, in this house or that? What do they do for a living? What are their hobbies, besides beekeeping, of course? Their fears? Their joys? To answer these questions, it's neces-sary to leave the computer and enter the world.

Sometimes, these forays take me only as far as the local library or bookstore. Books, newspapers, and magazines often provide sufficient information. For instance, I recently bought a book called *Beekeeping*, which advertises itself as a "Complete Owner's Manual," all you need to be a beekeeper or to create one. Like everything else, it's not what it claims to be, but it will answer some of my questions. What sort of questions? Well, here's one: To write the scene where stubborn Sophie invites a bee sting, I need to know the season, and the decision can't be arbitrary. From my bee class, I learned that bees winter, a state akin to hibernation, and that wintering lasts longer in certain areas of the country than in others. The farther north you live, the trickier this wintering process can be, but I digress.

And digress again: It's important to know facts, yes, but it's just as important to recognize when enough is enough. Lengthy and in-depth research carries its own liabilities. Think about it. Having spent time, energy and *el dinero* on acquiring precious facts, how likely are you to squander them? Not bloody likely. Which leads perfectly good writers to stuff their narratives with tangential information, just to justify that expensive tome on medieval bedroom practices or the weekend trip to Amarillo for local color. Don't overdo it; that's my advice. I almost quit reading that wonderful novel *Snow Falling on Cedars* for exactly this reason. There's only so much I want to know about fishing boats, and David Guterson tested my patience more than once. (I realize he won the PEN Faulkner and all, but no one is perfect.)

But don't let's go to Puget Sound, beautiful though it is. Let's stay in arid Albuquerque with the beekeeper. He lives right in town with me, in the North Valley, on the other side of the Rio Grande. So we've established place. What about the season? Checking my handy-dandy beekeeping book, I note that by mid-April the hive will be quite active. The desert is blooming, and nectar is plentiful. (Before I write this scene, I'll need to know exactly which plants bloom in April in Albuquerque, because the beekeeper is not only concerned with his insects; he's also concerned with their food sources. Lumbering out to check the hive, he'll be thinking about goldenrod, prickly pear, and Palmer lupine.) By April, the old bees that wintered over are dying off, and the young bees are taking their place. The brood nest will have swelled to six to eight combs, providing the beekeeper with something to check. And I'm guessing that the young bees are more likely to sting. I'll have to check to make sure, but if they're anything like teenage Sophie, they're hotheaded and impulsive.

To tell the truth, Sophie is the real subject of my book, and I'll let you in on a secret not even her parents know. Sophie's pregnant. Now

I've been pregnant, twice actually, so I don't need to research the various stages of pregnancy. I remember them all too well. But I've never been pregnant as a teenager, and certainly not as a teenager in 1998, and this does require some investigation. Before I began to work on this project—so far, I've written two short stories on these characters, and the stories themselves are a kind of research, a way of developing characters and familiarizing myself with the material—I read *Reviving Ophelia: Saving the Selves of Adolescent Girls*. The author, Mary Pipher, is a clinical psychologist in private practice in Lincoln, Nebraska. I also went to a reading and talk Ms. Pipher gave at a local bookstore, which proved helpful in a larger sense. It provided context and some sense of urgency. Ms. Pipher is very concerned about plight of teenage girls in the 1990s.

> Girls know they are losing themselves. One girl said, "Everything good in me died in junior high." Wholeness is shattered by the chaos of adolescence. Girls become fragments, their selves split into mysterious contradictions. They are sensitive and tenderhearted, mean and competitive, superficial and idealistic. They are confident in the morning, and overwhelmed with anxiety by nightfall. They rush through their days with wild energy and then collapse into lethargy. They try on new roles every week—this week the good student, next week the delinquent, and the next, the artist. . . . Much of their behavior is unreadable. Their problems are complicated and metaphorical—eating disorders, school phobias, and self-inflicted injuries. I need to ask again and again in a dozen different ways, "What are you trying to tell me?"

This is precisely the question I'm asking of Sophie, again and again, and the answers she provides will do much to shape the material for the novel. Thus, *Reviving Ophelia* provides me with a necessary cultural perspective, one I will certainly find useful, but this "grounding" I'm talking about is something more elemental. It's a matter of territory, of the actual earth on which a character walks.

So where does Sophie walk? Well, she walks around high school for one thing. Sophie goes to Valley High School in Albuquerque, which is, not so coincidentally, where my son goes to school as well. My son Corey is a sophomore, and Sophie is a senior, so it's not likely they'll run into one another, which is just as well because Sophie is not, as mothers say, a "good influence." She's got troubles, that girl. Still, my son's attendance at Valley is as useful to me as Ms. Pipher's book. Maybe more useful. I go to the high school frequently, and whenever I do, I take note of the place itself and of the kids who spend their days there.

Valley is one of the oldest high schools in Albuquerque. From all appearances, the main buildings date from the fifties. The campus has been maintained over the years, but in piecemeal fashion: In "senior circle," new picnic tables hunker up to crumbling cement benches. The library is now labeled the Media Center, but it houses a modest collection of moldy-looking books, not a computer in plain sight. The carpet in the Media Center is a horrible shade of puke green, and appears to have been laid down in the late sixties or early seventies when all the adults went temporarily color blind. I was around then, but still coming of age, and so I don't have to take responsibility for that carpet. At the last meeting of the Parent's Advisory Council—yes, I'm a member— the principal, a gracious and energetic man named Toby Herrera, voiced his hope that the carpet would soon be replaced. We all nodded vigorously and tried not to look down.

At an earlier meeting this year, Mr. Herrera happened to mention that Albuquerque has a high school specifically designed for pregnant teens. (Is this a step forward or backward? I can't decide.) The school is called New Futures, and the facility includes counseling for new and expectant mothers as well as on-site day care. When Mr. Herrera mentioned this school, I thought of Sophie, for whom New Futures will be an option, and I also thought of my own high-school career, when the girls who got pregnant had no options whatsoever. By and large, they did not have abortions, unless they crossed the border into Mexico—we're talking pre-Roe vs. Wade here—and they did not stay in school. What they did do, I suppose, was to get married, if the boy in question had the presence of mind or the generosity to propose, or else they slipped away to a home for unwed mothers in Fort Worth. I used to hear girls whisper about that place. It might have been, might still be, a humane and cheerful alternative to living at home or jumping off a cliff; I don't know. But at the time, it seemed a sort of prison where everything was stripped away, first your identity, your family and your friends, and finally, your baby, as well.

But Sophie lives in a different world, and it's one I need to know about. As Mr. Herrera was quick to point out, pregnant girls can choose to go to school at New Futures or they can stay at their home school. In other words, Sophie can continue to attend Valley, and knowing Sophie,

I imagine that's what she'll do. Of course, that decision will simplify my research tasks a bit because it means I won't have to scout out New Futures. One of the most important aspects of this "grounding" is to gain a firm sense of place, and here we're talking about everything from the time period to the city to the weather.

Naturally, Sophie blames her several bee stings on Daddy, then runs sobbing into the house. Ahh, yes, the house. What color is the back door Sophie slams behind her? And is her room at the front of the house or the back? For me, identifying home is one of the most important early research tasks. Before I can accomplish much in the way of characterization and plot, I must know where my characters live, and by this, I mean a particular house with particular windows that look out on particular plants and alleys and streets. Imagining the house does not work for me. It's too ephemeral—made-up people in a made-up house. The walls begin to waver and shift before my eyes, the kitchen to slide from one end of the house to the other, the garage to attach then unattach. Just where did I put that third bedroom, I wonder, and what was on the walls? Sooner or later, the occupants feel a tremor beneath their feet; they're threatened with imaginary collapse. Everything has its limits, you see, my imagination included.

So where to find a real house? My own doesn't work. I live there, my husband and children live there. We don't have room for a fictional family, and besides, they're bound to have entirely different tastes from mine. They're better housekeepers; they find time to dust thoroughly and not just swipe at the surfaces of things. Or maybe they're worse: Maybe pet hair gathers in the corners of the rooms, and dirty plates and coffee cups collect beside the bed and on top of the toilet tank. What I need, you see, is somebody else's home, full of furniture and magazines and knick knacks, but without occupants. A ready-made set.

For my first novel, I had a piece of luck. My family was in Austin, Texas, for the holidays, which is where the novel takes place, and my husband and I spent New Year's Eve with a friend who just happened to be house-sitting for an entire year. So there we were, drinking a little wine and listening to The Gypsy Kings, my husband and his friend Mark discussing, yawn, the University of Texas basketball team. An hour passed, and they moved on to the Dallas Cowboys. To keep from nodding off, I got up and had a look around. I took note of the flamingoes in the study, a whole motley crew of flamingoes—plastic ones, metal ones, and a wooden flamingo that swung from the ceiling. I puzzled over a small black and white TV on the counter in the bathroom, and the red tile floor in the kitchen. I peered out the bedroom windows and weighed myself on the scales. Nosy, you say. Yes, you're absolutely right, but I didn't open the medicine chest or any of the drawers. I didn't try on clothes, like the main character in Raymond Carver's story, "Neighbors." I just made a leisurely stroll around the premises. Later, when the characters in my first novel took up residence in this house, I had only to turn on The Gypsy Kings to bring it all back. Perfect.

For the second novel, I had to take action. No gift houses this time around. So I "feigned" and pretended to be a potential home buyer. Dragging my husband along to make it look good, I scouted several houses. I had ideas about where the beekeeper and his family would live. For one thing, I wanted them to reside in the North Valley, because I like it there, and because Sophie is already enrolled at Valley High School. She has friends there. We wouldn't want to move her at this late date. And the beekeeper requires land with flowering plants around his house, as well as a nearby water source. Bees have to drink.

Beforehand, I studied newspaper ads, choosing houses for description, location, price, and size. All these houses were occupied and previously owned. In each case, a real estate person was hosting an open house, so no one would be inconvenienced. The first houses we saw were all wrong. In a strange turn of events, we happened to go to a house which was the scene of a terrible murder, a story that had been on the news and in the papers for weeks, a death befitting a Dostoevsky novel. I won't go into details, as they will plunge you into despair. The real estate agent, who was clearly ill at ease, referred to the crime obliquely, mentioning it to us in order to be "up front." He'd been ordered by the court to sell the house, he said. What could he do? Indeed, I thought. His situation deserved its own novel. Before, the house had seemed dreary, broken up in odd ways, old and neglected. But afterwards, it seemed more than gloomy; it seemed downright haunted. Naturally, my husband and I hightailed it out of there, retreating to the car where we sat in shock for a few minutes before pulling slowly away, leaving the real estate agent to pace back and forth in the family room, an honest man who would surely be trapped in this tragic house for countless Sundays to come.

Quite naturally, we were tempted to abandon house hunting, for that day anyway, but we decided to forge on, and now I'm glad we did. The third house was perfect, or close to perfect, more expensive than the house I imagined for Sophie and her parents, but otherwise ideal. I took away a real estate brochure that I covered with notes. Here's the real-tor's description: "This wonderful custom adobe home offers a quiet private retreat with views, Northern New Mexico decor, and room for horses." Or bees, lots of bees. The house is situated on 1.3 acres. It's a territorial style home with a pitched metal roof, a long front porch, brick floors and window ledges, vigas, latillas, and tile accents. (Live in Albuquerque for a few years, and you'll be able to sling these terms, too.) The house is shaped in an L; one wing is eighteen years old, the other only seven, but it was constructed to look old. The upstairs win-dows offer a view of the bosque, which is Spanish for woods. Whenever you see the bosque, you know the river is close by. Beyond the bosque, two inactive volcanoes rise like the humps of a camel's back. You want to move there, right? So did I, but I didn't have an extra $332,500. Yep, that was the asking price.

Though I can't have the house in reality, I've taken possession of it in my imagination. Sophie and her parents live there, and in order to give the family the financial wherewithal to afford this little hacienda in the midst of the city, I gave the mother, Peggy, a career that would bring in the big bucks, or at least the medium-sized bucks. Hence, her job as a radiologist. Actually, my reasons for making her a radiologist are a bit more complicated. I imagine Peggy to be a woman of extraor-dinary insight, someone who can see into people, very nearly a psychic.

Not surprisingly, Peggy's profession and her interest in tarot cards were suggested to me by some of the paraphernalia I noted in the house. The back upstairs bedroom was occupied by a young woman named Zoe (test papers in evidence), whose interests in Buddhism and acu-puncture were also on display. An altar stood at one end of the room, and among the books on Zoe's desk was *The Book of Shiatsu* as well as a plastic body model for both the meridianal and extraordinary points. I made notes quickly because my husband insisted we not linger. He had compunctions about my nosiness, but I maintain that I did no one any harm, and again, I only looked at the things that were out in the open. Already, I've altered the particulars. Peggy is not a Buddhist, nor does she do acupuncture. But she does concern herself with what can't be seen on the surface, and it was Zoe's room that put this idea in my head. Thank you, Zoe.

But nothing comes free. I know about tarot cards because I took a class when I was seventeen and intent on the future. I still have the cards and the books. But here's a piece of research I have yet to do. I have to learn about the daily life of a radiologist: hours, tasks, and so forth. Having been to one fairly recently, I have a general sense of what radiologists do, but I need to know a great deal more. Already, I've lined up a lunch date with an acquaintance who used to work for a group of radiologists. And I have library sources. That won't be enough, of course, but it will get me started. The task is to find out how radiologists *think,* how they integrate their work in their day to day lives. Because radiologists aren't just radiologists at work. Like the rest of us, they carry their work away with them, and use it to understand the world.

The same is true for writers, of course, and for visual artists, photographers, assistant principals, day care workers, police officers, and doctors. A few years back, I asked my gynecologist so many questions about abortion that he quipped I could write off the visit as research, which, not so coincidentally, is exactly what it was.

Fiction writers are researchers. We can't help it. It's part and parcel of who we are. In restaurants, we crane our heads to listen to conversations taking place around us; we note accents and idiosyncratic speech patterns. At the mall, we stare at the strangers milling about, all of them people with homes to go to, children to care for, lives to lead. They have secrets these strangers, and we imagine what they are. It turns out that research isn't a distinct process, something with a beginning and end. It's ongoing, part and parcel of our lives. It is, in some sense, *our* secret.

One more interesting bee fact:

> When working with bees, wear white or light-colored clothing. Bees are attracted to red and black.

They're bees, you see. They can't help it.

❏ 31

THE POWER OF DIALOGUE

BY SOL STEIN

DIALOGUE IS A LANGUAGE THAT IS FOREIGN TO MOST WRITERS OF NON-fiction and to many newcomers to fiction writing. It is also a triumphant language. It can make people unknown to the author cry, laugh, and believe lies in seconds. It is succinct, but can carry a great weight of meaning. In a theater, dialogue can draw thunderous applause from people who have paid heavily for the privilege of listening to it. At its best, as in Shakespeare's best, dialogue provides us with memorable—and beautiful—guides to understanding human behavior. Fortunately, the techniques of dialogue can be learned by writers eager to please their readers.

I'm lucky in having started out as a playwright, where the only words the audience hears are dialogue. It had better be good. When I write novels, I am tempted to use dialogue often. The minute characters talk, the reader sees them. And we know readers prefer to see what's happening, rather than to hear about it through narration. Not to be lightly dismissed are those white spaces on the page created by exchanges of dialogue. They make the reader feel the story is moving fast.

Dialogue is meant to be *experienced* by the reader, not *studied*. Halting over a line of dialogue can interrupt the reader's experience. It is important to understand that the reader perceives thoughts serially, one at a time, which is why dialogue that builds is so effective when characters fling sentences one after another, each adding to the force of the whole. Dialogue that is short, snappy, and punchy engages other characters as well as the reader.

Life is full of routine exchanges. "How are you?" "I am fine." "How's the family?" All those usual greetings are boring as dialogue, which thrives on surprise and indirection. For example:

She: Hello there! How are you?
He: On my way to jail.

152

She: Good God, what are you planning to do?
He: It's done.

This exchange raises more questions than it answers, and that is good. The main purpose of dialogue is to reveal character and to move a story along. The example obviously gets a story going.

Let's look at a simple example of dialogue that reveals character:

She: I see you're feeling better.
He: Since when can you see what I feel?
She: I thought this was going to be a peaceful discussion.
He: That was yesterday.

With only two lines for each character, it is safe to say that the woman is temperate and wants a harmonious relationship. The man is intemperate, difficult, and quick to anger.

Dialogue is at its best when it is confrontational and adversarial—either or both. Talk is an action. And when talk is tough and combative, it can be much more exciting than physical action. In that excitement, the writer is likely to make a mistake. He will take sides with one of the characters.

Does the writer take sides?

Indeed he does; he takes *both sides* and gives each its due. And here's a hint: If in a verbal duel you find yourself wedded to the beliefs of one of the characters, try your damnedest to make the other character win the argument. You won't succeed, but you should try to conceal your prejudices. It will make your exchanges far more interesting.

Character most reveals itself in dialogue under stress. Stressed characters will blurt things out that they never meant to say. They can also be defensive, as in the following example:

I am not nervous, I just can't stand being called for jury duty. I walk into the courthouse, I think I'm the one that's on trial. For what? I've never even gone through a yellow light.

Characters also reveal themselves when they are angry. Example:

My missus and me been in this jammed waiting room for two solid hours. Not one person has been ushered in. What's the doctor doing? How many patients does a doctor need in his waiting room to satisfy his ego? Our kid, he was supposed to be picked up fifteen minutes ago. I can't phone the sidewalk outside the school, I've got to get out of here and leave the missus to hear the bad news of her tests all alone. Jesus, why can't these stethoscope generals keep appointments like other people?

The aim of dialogue is to create an emotional effect in the reader, and one of the things a writer has to learn is that dialogue may sound artificial when it is coherent and logical. You want thoughts that are loose, words that tumble out.

In life, we try to avoid shouting because it shows that we are out of control. And we don't like it when other people shout at us. Someone else's anger makes us uncomfortable. Readers love shouting if the tone is carried by the words rather than by the author telling the reader that a character is shouting.

Shouting can be dramatic if anger is responded to by anger, but perhaps even more dramatic if the anger is met with an attempt to pacify or to resolve, especially if the anger continues. Listen to the supervisor in the following exchange:

> "Don't you knock before you come in?"
> "I'm sorry, I—"
> "Can it. I've heard all the excuses, you blew your
> last chance, that's it."
> "It wasn't my fault. Judy can tell you—"
> "I don't want you involving Judy, George, Carey, anybody; it was you who didn't . . . look, I've had enough! Just pack, get your things, and get out of here."

Without the context, readers don't know who did what, but they get a sense of the supervisor's anger, not only from what he says, but also from the looseness of his disjointed comments. What comes across is the strength of his emotion, and to the extent that what he says seems unfair to the other person, the emotion transfers to the reader.

What can you say about the student below?

> Teacher: Tell me about yourself.
> Student: I'm just a boy.
> Teacher: All the boys here are boys. What's different about you?
> Student: Nothing, I have a mother and a sister and I do my homework every day.
> Teacher: You left out your father.
> Student: It's not my fault. He left himself out.

Teacher: Did you forget to mention him?
Student: He took off. He doesn't even phone.
Teacher: Do you know where he is? Can you get in touch?
Student: He isn't anywhere. He could be dead and I wouldn't know!

The boy is trying not to reveal to his teacher or classmates the secret thing that makes him different. When the boy is eventually forced to reveal it, the reader is immediately sympathetic toward him. A character who reveals *not enough* reveals much.

To sum up, a character reveals himself most readily when under stress, blurting things out, saying things in anger that are normally suppressed, saying not enough, saying too much.

Before you begin writing any new dialogue, know the purpose of the exchange. How will you orchestrate it to make it adversarial? If a conflict between the characters speaking already exists, does the exchange exacerbate that conflict or at least increase the tension between the characters? After completing an exchange, or when revising a scene, check to see if the lines spoken by each character are consistent with that character's background. Weed out any unnecessary words. Loosen stiff sentences. Substitute colloquial expressions for formal ones. And perhaps most important, check to see what's going on between the lines.

Three underused techniques for making dialogue interesting are as follows: showing impatience, conveying a misunderstanding between characters, and differing underlying attitudes that rise to the surface.

As a refresher, let's review some basic guidelines for dialogue:

1. What counts in dialogue is not what is said but what is meant.

2. Whenever possible, dialogue should be adversarial. Think of dialogue as confrontations or interrogations. Remember, combat can be subtle.

3. The best dialogue contains responses that are indirect, oblique.

4. Dialogue is illogical. Non sequiturs are fine. So are incomplete sentences, and occasional faulty grammar suited to the character.

5. Dialogue, compared to actual speech, is terse. If a speech runs over three sentences, you may be speechifying. In accusatory confrontations, however, longer speeches can increase tension if the accusations build.

6. The use of misunderstandings and impatience in your characters' dialogue will help increase tension.

7. Characters reveal themselves best in dialogue when they lose their cool and blurt things out.

8. In life, adversarial or heated exchanges tend to be repetitive; in dialogue, such exchanges build. In life, adversarial exchanges vent the speakers' emotions; in dialogue, such exchanges are designed to move a story forward.

9. Avoid dialect. It makes readers see words on the page and interrupts their feeling them.

10. In dialogue every word counts. Be ruthless in eliminating excess verbiage. All talk is first draft. Dialogue is not talk.

❏ 32

WRITERS AND THEIR READERS

BY NORMA FOX MAZER

A NOVEL I WROTE OVER A NUMBER OF YEARS, *WHEN SHE WAS GOOD*, is the story of Em Thurkill and her struggle to live with and then come out from under the shadow of her abusive older sister, Pamela. Since the novel was published (fall, 1997) to the kind of reviews writers dream about, a shadow seems to have fallen over Em's story, one characterized mainly by the word "bleak." Questions were raised: Why do writers write these bleak books? Do young readers want to read bleak books? Or will they be repelled by them?

I don't choose to write bleak books. Writing a novel is, for me, like a kind of marriage that I enter in a somewhat dazed state of love, believing that this will be (at last!) a perfect union, blessed by all—relatives and readers. This is the honeymoon phase.

Then reality intervenes: I got married to this idea; now I have to live with it. Frustration enters the relationship. I dream of divorce, but being of a faithful nature, I stick with what I've chosen. And often, I'm rewarded: I find myself back once more in a state of bliss: ideas come; language, images.

But long before all this, there's something else: I'll call it the courtship. How we got to know each other. How I decided to take to this idea, to stay true to it. My courtship with *When She Was Good* had its first stirrings years ago. We had four kids and a two-family house shared with my parents, in the old working-class section of Syracuse, with its crowded, flat-roofed houses, churches on every corner, and tiny brilliant gardens.

After 10 years in the apartment below my parents, we were itchy from being constantly under the parental eye. No one said any of this in so many words. We were an almost Puritanically restrained and inhibited bunch. We all adored books and from grandparents to youngest child read voraciously. But when it came to feelings, too often we went mute or glowered at each other.

157

My husband and I realized we had to break free. Driven by equal amounts of guilt, love, and irritation, we found them a good apartment in a good building in a pleasant neighborhood.

My mother had a gift for friendship, and quite soon made friends in the new building. One of these was a woman who lived with her sister. The sister did some kind of knitting—dolls, perhaps. Once, I met the friend, a tall, gawky woman who seemed younger than her years, and a little frightened beneath her sudden, on-and-off smile.

Sometime later, my mother showed me a note the woman had written her. Something about this note, its tone of clenched intensity, made me think that she was in love with my mother. I didn't say this. My mother would have been shocked and embarrassed.

A few years later, I read an article on loneliness in America. The evidence pointed to the existence of two single older women for every single older man. A sad picture for women, if they believed happiness lay in pairing up. But why did people always have to be in pairs? I began to plan a novel about three older people who would fall in love with each other in various combinations. Like the statistics, two women, one man. Each one alone, each lonely. There was overweight Warren, a shoe salesman, who'd grown up in the shadow of his two older brothers. And Louise, feisty and energetic, with two disappointed and disappointing daughters. And Em, who lived with her domineering older sister, who busily knit doll-like figures.

For years I worked on this novel whenever I could. As time went on, I stayed with it even in the most extreme moments of despair at how long I'd been dallying and getting nowhere, or at least not where I wanted to go—which was to The End. As happens, over a long period of intimacy with anyone, I came to know my characters well. I knew, for instance, Em's childhood in detail.

I introduced my three characters to each other. They had a dinner party. They went to the beach. They took a trip. One of them had a heart attack. Things happened, which is good. Things must happen in a novel. But I could never get to the end of their story. Every time I approached it, a leaden feeling overtook me. It wasn't a structural problem, but more that something was emotionally lacking. I wasn't convinced.

I wrote other books. I wrote articles and short stories. But this story and those three people were always with me. At any moment, walking home from a movie, driving to the dentist, standing in line in the supermarket, I would be mentally writing and revising. This went on for years. I became disgusted. Why couldn't I finish this story? I wanted to hate it. I did hate it. I announced to my husband that I was through with it. It was unwritable. I was going to delete it from my computer. Kill it. No mercy. Dead.

"Don't do that," he said. "There's too much good stuff there." He was telling me to get back in the harness. I bared my teeth and made sulking, resentful noises, but back I went, writing and rewriting, inventing new scenes, finding out more things about my character. But, really, what else did I have to know? I was already better acquainted with these people than with any of my friends. I could write a book about each one of them, I said. But stubbornly, I kept trying to cram them all into the same story.

Then I went to a Christmas party in New York City. A few hundred literary types were jammed into a small space, everyone shouting to be heard over the din, everyone smiling and waving—exactly the kind of scene that makes me want to creep into a corner. Someone I knew stopped me. "It's barbaric, isn't it?" I shouted.

"What?" he shouted back. "A barbershop? I've been looking for a good one."

"Bar-bar-ic!" I mouthed.

"Barbara? I haven't seen her. She looks great, though."

"I thought so, too," I said.

He looked pleased that I agreed with him. At that moment, I would have agreed with anything. Because, behind me, I had just heard—or thought I heard—someone say "real tough young adult stuff." Maybe I heard the words "real tough." Maybe I didn't. Maybe I just needed to hear those words. Whatever. In that instant, I knew that I should write the novel around Em alone. And I felt—absurdly, and wrongly, but thrillingly—that her story had sprung full blown into my mind.

I went to work the next morning around 3:30. It was impossible for me to sleep. From the pages I'd written over the years, I pulled every scene and incident in which Em figured. A lot of pages. In these pages were Em's childhood, her life with her sister, scenes alone, scenes with her and Louise, with her and Warren, with the three of them together. I had more than I needed and much less than I needed. I had written in third person, but now I wanted a closer, more intimate voice. Months later, I heard or found the line, "I never thought Pamela would die," and from that moment the form my book would take—which was not a straightforward linear narrative—became entirely clear to me.

As I wrote on, I worried. I worried about getting the book published. Everyone—whoever Everyone is—was saying no one wanted young adult books anymore. What was wanted were stories for younger kids, scary stories, funny stories, lighthearted stories. What I was writing might be scary, but not goosebump-scary, and it sure wasn't cute or adorable or lovable. It was a domestic story, like almost everything I've written, but more intense, starker, honed down to the bone.

Is this the definition of bleak? And if so, who did I think the audience was? I envisioned older readers, both adults and those people caught between *what is, what was, and what will be*—in other words, teens. No longer children, not yet adults, bright, imaginative, bewildered, and buffeted by emotions, hormones, adults, and everyone else's ideas—by everything, in fact, which we, as adults, presumably have put in place, dealt with, and understand.

Being a writer for this audience means entering a teenage mind, maybe the mind I once had, and yet never leaving the one I have now. While I write, I'm adult, teenager, and writer, and a struggle goes on among these selves.

As a teenager, my view is restricted. As a writer, I can hope for my characters, but promise nothing. While I know that the world is not as grim as it sometimes looks, at times it is even grimmer. I can't get in there and prop up my character. I have to stay with her, with who *she* is and what *she* perceives. I have to follow the scent, keep my nose to the trail, even if it begins in sorrow and fear and ends without much hope; even if it's bleak, because bleak is part of the world, too. The real world.

As things turned out, I didn't have a hard time finding a publisher. One editor told me he cried when he read the manuscript. Although another editor was interested, the first won my heart with his tears. He was a careful, and I might even say, loving editor for my book. I was so lucky. I lived with Em for a long time, and I was happy to let her go into the world.

My analogy of novel writing to marriage is faulty. Marriages often end with sadness—the death of the marriage or the death of a partner. But writing a book and finding a publisher brings about the opposite—a kind of birth. No, wrong again. Newborns are not pitched into the world and bid goodbye, Godspeed, and good luck. But that's more or less the way it goes with books. It's no longer up to the writer, but to the readers to embrace our books, to nourish them, to keep them alive. Though I love readers—how could I exist without them?—rather than my going where they are, I want them to come along with me.

Writing and publishing books that have been labeled "bleak" implies our faith in our readers, faith that they are hungry for and ready for more than a TV gloss on life. And a belief that it's important to give it to them. Faith, too, that they are ready to see a larger world or a different world, maybe not an ideal world, but a world that I believe is true and real.

□ 33

WRITING ABOUT YOUR
OWN BACKYARD

BY SHELBY HEARON

WE'RE TOLD TO WRITE ABOUT WHAT WE KNOW. BUT OFTEN IT IS DIFFI-
cult to write about a place you know too well, a place that was home to
you. I lived in this house, we say, on this street, and my parents were,
well, my parents. My conclusion, after a recent trip back to Austin,
Texas, attempting to write about a house and town I lived in for so
many years, is that we have to distinguish what we know from what our
characters know.

For example, suppose you go back to the hillside where you used to
sit with your high scool love (long since gone), and you find it now the
site of one of a cluster of overpriced, oversized homes with a view. In
this case, you don't want to write about How Things Have Changed or
Aren't Developers Awful.

You want your early memory to be *something your character doesn't
know and learns about.* Say she's living in that fine home, trying to
adjust to being on the rich side of town looking down on where she
used to live, and she finds out that years ago someone in the story used
to sit on that very slope in her garden, when there wasn't a home in
sight, and dream about the future. Who was the dreamer? Her mother?
The girl in high school who took her beau? Her husband, with someone
that he can't forget? In any case, you are letting your character learn
something you already know. You are sharing with the reader the freshness of her discovery, her glimpse at the hope, the scent in the air, the
longing, that you once experienced. So, *even though you know it already, your character doesn't.*

Here's a real example from my past, which I used in my novel *Ella
in Bloom.* Years ago, after a divorce, I rented an apartment in Austin
that backed onto a springed stream called Barton Creek. Right outside
the sliding glass doors of my otherwise ordinary, tiny efficiency, was a

162

deck high in the treetops, with the sound of the rushing stream down below. I loved the place, and it was there I experienced the joy of living alone for the first time in my life. So, in the book, my narrator does not know there are apartments now built on what was once just a grassy bluff. She ends up there quite by accident; she learns about the place I knew so well.

Conversely, the other way you can bring to life a place almost too familiar to begin to write about, is by discovering *something you don't know but your character does*. Because she has to know everything about this topic/activity/locale, and you don't know anything, you have to research it in order to give your character authentic details and feelings concerning it.

The Austin I lived in and reared my children in was a country-music-loving community centered around the University of Texas and the state Capitol. Now, however, Austin is primarily a high-tech city, a silicon valley. There are nine hundred computer companies in the city and abutting townships. All this part of the larger Austin area is unknown to me, and, therefore, has to be a part of the lives of some of my characters; and as they live and work in that part of the county, the reader (and I!) learn about it, too.

I'll give an example. Poring over the newest *Texas Almanac* (a most marvelous fact-filled source), I noticed that Pflugerville, which I recall as a tiny German wide-spot-in-the-road with a good bakery and about 150 people, had become a town of 15,000, many of whom worked for Dell. Since this looked like a good, concrete, manageable place to start learning (you can't start with something large and vague like "the computer industry"), I subscribed to the local newspaper—who could resist receiving the weekly *Pflugerville Pflag?*—to learn about the news and schools and real estate in the language of the people who lived there. I also hung around a realty office, ate a few wonderful plates of barbeque, took a roll of film, and, finally, placed my narrator's boyfriend *in a neighborhood new to me, but not to him*.

Sometimes what helps you bring a familiar place to life is finding out what new things people do to make a living; changes in economics are as much a part of conveying a sense of place as changes in population or rainfall. Again, perusing the *Texas Almanac*—in this case to refresh my memory about the towns and waterways and precipitation levels of some of the counties where my people's people were from—I happened upon an item under agribusiness: raises *ratites*. A word I'd never even heard before. The term refers to birds that can't fly (resist that metaphor!), in other words, ostriches and emus. Emus! A new world.

I called the Texas Fish, Game and Wildlife Commission and found out that emus were considered livestock, not game. When I called the Extension Division of Texas A & M, they referred me to a branch office in Ector County (home of the University of Texas, Permian Basin). But it wasn't the reams of material that these agreeable people sent that went into the story, but their language, their responses. I found there was a "Save the Emus" group that considered emus an endangered species; that the people who raised them for food thought them "nothing but overgrown chickens"; that the ranchers who bred them to tan for leather raged with frustration because they needed the tanned leather to make the chaps and gauntlets to protect them against the emus' slashing claws. As is usually the case with "place setting" details, not a lot of this information got into the text, but, then, when the inevitable Texas drought hit, the effect of the baking dry skies was made more concrete, more specific. The emus all had to be slaughtered along with the cattle.

There is a third case you should consider in writing about your own backyard: When you know the place and people and your character needs to know also, you make this distinction: *You knew them as they were; your character knows them as they might have been.* My parents' home, once mine, sprawling, in disrepair—with its secret stairway from the attic, its oversized closets that let you slip into other rooms from the back, its sixty-foot-long screened porch and squirrels in the crawlspace—now has new owners. It has a new address, fronting on a side street, a new glassed-in porch, a smart structural face-lift, upscale interiors. I wanted to use that house in my novel, to fix it on the page much as you might fix a photo in an album, a bee in amber. But I did not put the remembered house or my real remembered parents in the story, rather, I put the couple they might have been, the home they might have furnished. The old father, an historian, always at his desk writing his own past, is not my daddy, a geologist with a non-human view of time; the mother, always in her garden watching her winged and four-legged visitors, living only in the present, is not my mama, whose mind was focused on her and the world's troubled past.

Sometimes you write about your own home place to recover it, sometimes to redress it, sometimes merely to recall it. But in any case, such a remembrance of things past is a dialogue between you and your story-teller. Either you introduce her to your homesickness for that hillside where you used to sit with your love under the stars, or she takes you to a country café, where, over a plate of green-mesquite smoked ribs, she tells you what's new in your own backyard.

□ 34

PUTTING EMOTION INTO
YOUR FICTION

BY BHARTI KIRCHNER

LAUGH, SCREAM AND WEEP BEFORE YOUR KEYBOARD; MAKE YOUR reader feel. I kept this in mind when I started writing my first novel, *Shiva Dancing*. In developing characters, plot, and setting, I looked for every opportunity to make an emotional impact on the reader. Often, as I composed a sentence or paragraph, I felt the emotion myself.

Why are emotions important? Because they're more compelling than ideas, facts, and reasoning, which are the stuff of nonfiction. In fiction, the character must act from emotion, rather than from reason. And emotional truth is the reward readers hope to get from a novel. They will not turn to the next chapter or even the next page unless the material engages their emotions.

What emotions? Love and hate, joy and despair, fear and hope. Those are the significant ones to develop over a novel or chapter. But there are others—pride, timidity, shame, and humiliation—that move people and characters minute to minute, word to word.

Whether simple and understated or complex and dramatic, emotions need to be conveyed in a story, first by developing sympathetic characters. The more readers identify or sympathize with your protagonist, the more they'll feel her emotions and be curious enough to turn the page.

In the first chapter of *Shiva Dancing,* for example, seven-year-old Meena is kidnapped by bandits from her village in Rajasthan on the night of her wedding. The girl cries as she's snatched away from her mother's loving embrace by two big men on camels. Her old grandfather, who shuffled after them, looks on helplessly. This incident is meant to draw an emotional response from the reader. At the end of the chapter Meena's found by an American couple in a train far away from her village. They're about to take her to their home in New Delhi, where they're temporarily posted, when the chapter ends. The reader is likely to ask at this point: What's going to happen to Meena? Will she ever find her village? Where will she end up?

Turn to the next chapter.

If emotion is important, the question is: How do you, the writer, actually depict it on paper? And how does the reader know what that emotion is? The cardinal rule is: *Show, don't tell.* In other words, stating a mental condition directly may not convince the reader. For example:

> She was anxious.

In real life, you observe someone's behavior and draw appropriate conclusions. The example below from *The Power of the Sword* by Wilbur Smith *shows* that the character is agitated:

> Centaine was too keyed up to sit down. She stood in the center of the floor and looked at the pictures on the fireplace wall without actually seeing them.

You can also *show* an emotion through a character's thought. This is often effective, since a person may not reveal his true feeling in his speech. Use a simile, as Alice Hoffman does in *Second Nature:*

> He just couldn't shake the feeling of dread; he was like an old woman, waiting for disaster to strike.

Notice how much more effective the above is than saying:

> He was afraid.

Use physical symptoms. Readers are convinced of an emotion only when they recognize a physical reaction similar to one they've experienced themselves: a racing heart, stiff legs, or cold palms. Here's one of Meena's reactions in *Shiva Dancing,* but first a bit about the story and the scene where she finds herself.

Meena is adopted by the American couple, who raise her in San Francisco. When we meet her again, she's 35, a software techie, working for a Bay Area company. In one scene, Meena goes to a bookstore to attend a reading by Antoine Peterson, a celebrity novelist she has met briefly on one previous occasion. After the reading, he invites her for tea. Just when the chai is tasting "creamy smooth," and the tabla music has reached a crescendo, Antoine mentions his upcoming marriage to Liv and their honeymoon. Meena's reaction?

> Her tea tasted cold and weak. She set her cup down, trying to keep her hand steady.

An emotion, however, is not an end in itself. Describing it in a vacuum is never enough. You have to combine facts and action with emotion to create an illusion of reality. Here's an example from *The Rest of Life* by Mary Gordon.

> She gets into the train, one of the first to board. [action and fact] Everything is still and quiet. [fact] Then the train starts up with an insulting lurch. [emotion]

Though I try to bring out a character's feelings even during the first draft, I find I never catch them one hundred per cent. Revision is the perfect time to check for the following: What are the various emotional situations in which the protagonist has found herself? How does she react to the stimulus? Look for a sentence, some piece of dialogue, or a flashback where emotions can be injected. Nostalgia, a milestone in life, a return to some place previously visited, are potential sources.

In *Shiva Dancing,* Meena returns to her village after an absence of three decades. As she arrives with her driver, she notices that the thatched-roof houses have been replaced by newer buildings. She can't recognize any of the sights. She's eager to find her mother. The reader knows—but Meena doesn't—that her mother is long dead. Meena meets a schoolboy on the street and asks, in one poignant moment, about her mother:

> "My mother made clothes for the kids. She embroidered their names on their baby sari. Everyone in the village came to her."
> The shocking reply that comes to Meena through her driver is:
> His mother buys ready-made clothes for him.

Use sizzle in your dialogue: Inane comments, yes-and-no answers might do in real life, but speech in fiction must have the effect of potential shockers. In *Shiva Dancing,* Antoine returns from a book tour and immediately goes to visit Meena at her apartment. There, he finds Carlos, a close friend of Meena's, who tells him Meena has left for India.

Antoine doesn't like Carlos in the first place, and now he has the task of finding out where she is actually staying. Carlos, protective of Meena, has been unwilling up to this point to share any information about her. Finally, the outwardly polite Carlos explodes:

> "She had strong feelings for you. I've never seen Meena get so excited about a man. And what do you do? You build up her hopes, then dump her the day Liv comes back. Pardon me if I'm getting a little emotional. Meena's my friend. It hurts me to see her cut up like that."
> "I didn't mean to hurt her," Antoine said. "My situation is different now."
> "It better be."

The words used in a dialogue can be simple, but just repeating a phrase can intensify the emotion. Here's Alice Hoffman in *Second Nature:*

> "Help me up," Richard Aaron shouted over the sound of the hooves hitting against the earth. "Just help me up."

A person's words may be a smoke screen, but her voice, facial expression, and gestures can be a dead giveaway. Notice how Gail Godwin does this in *The Finishing School:*

> Her chin shot up so fast that it set in motion the crest of her feathery haircut. "Where did you hear about them?"

Another place where an emotional quality can be imparted is in the setting. *Create an atmosphere:* A dark house on a stormy night has a sinister connotation, whereas a sunny day on a beach is quite the opposite. You can make effective use of the environment to set a mood. This is equivalent to using background music in a movie to highlight the action on the screen. In this example from *Shiva Dancing,* Meena is about to attend a staff meeting at Software International Company. There's tension among her coworkers. The scene opens with a short description of the conference room:

> Sunlight streamed in through the room's only window, casting shadows of the saucerlike leaves of the potted plants on the wall *without warming the room.*

The italics is mine. When selecting from a number of details in a surrounding, pick only those elements relevant for the character, those that bring an emotional surge. Here's novelist Antoine in *Shiva Dancing* arriving in Calcutta in pursuit of Meena. He feels lonely and uncertain. Everything he sees through his taxi window on the way to the hotel is colored by his present mental condition:

> Antoine's eyes watered as acrid charcoal smoke from a clay oven on the sidewalk drifted in through the open car window. Along with the smoke came the smell of freshly baked flat bread. A young woman in a yellow-orange sari browned the puffy *roti* rounds over the fire. Her deep eyes and rhythmic gestures reminded him of Meena. He yearned for fresh bread made just for him.

Use symbolism. A symbol is a habit, an object, an event, almost anything charged with a hidden meaning that stems from association. In *Shiva Dancing,* a symbol used for Meena is her thirst, which, in effect, is her longing for her desert homeland. In her San Francisco office, she always keeps a glass of water on her desk and sips from it often. The true meaning of this ritualistic habit is revealed to her only after she finally returns to her village.

> "Tubewell," the boy said, pointing. He rushed to it and levered the handle until water gushed out. Meena made a cup of her hands, drank deeply and splashed the remainder on her face. As she did so, she went back in time when she was tiny. Mataji would hold a glass of well water to her mouth. This clear earth water tasted the same. She had missed it. Without knowing it, she had been thirsty all these years.

Collect "feeling" words: Avoid overusing common words, such as "loving," "calm," or "blissful." Consider cataloguing your own feelings in a notebook and using them for your characters. Here are some examples:

Animated	Exasperated
Diffident	Sated
Bubbly	Petrified
Refreshed	Crushed

Regardless of what techniques are used, ultimately it's the writer's own emotions that set the tone of a scene or piece of fiction. As a preparation for writing, it might be necessary for you to revisit an incident in the past and try to identify and relive an emotion. Or, like an actor, you might assume a new role and experience a new set of emotions. The choice of words, the length of a sentence, the pacing of paragraphs all broadcast to readers how they should feel. In general, short sentences and paragraphs heighten the drama, whereas longer, more leisurely writing gives the reader more breathing space.

Avoid sentimentality. As important as emotions are, don't overemphasize powerful ones such as loss and grief. Readers feel manipulated when presented with one misery after another. You may summarize such happenings or provide relief by using humor and insight. In general, the stronger the emotion, the more you need to restrain your passion in describing it.

To sum up, don't be afraid to transfer one or more emotional experiences of laughter, pain, or agony to your readers. They may curse you because they burned the rice, dropped their aerobics routine, and were late for work, but they won't put your book down.

❑ 35

POINT OF VIEW

BY ROBIN WHITE

IN FICTION, THE HIDDEN PERSUADER BEHIND ANY STORY IS A POINT OF view that focuses your narrative, involves your reader, and temporarily suspends all other realities, save the one on the page. Your prose may be artful, and your story clever, but if your point of view is ineffective, the work can seem like so many rows of flat black letters on a dull white page. On the other hand, there may be nothing special about your prose or story, but if your point of view is arresting, your words will spring to life.

Since point of view is so important, how do we go about choosing the right one—apart from just stumbling upon it? First, you must recognize that for any given story there are many different points of view, not merely the shift from third person to first, first to omniscient. And it can be creatively stimulating to try different ones until you find the one that will not let you (or your reader) go. Because every individual is unique, no two people ever see things in quite the same way, and shifting the viewpoint from one to another can enhance how readers see what writers want them to see.

For example, let's take the story of "Little Red Riding Hood." As the story goes, a little girl named after her riding cape sets out one day to take a basket of treats to her grandmother, who lives alone in a gloomy forest patroled by an English-speaking wolf. We don't know why Grandma doesn't stay with Riding Hood's parents (one of whom has to be her child); and we have no idea why our young heroine has been sent off by herself through wild-animal territory. We are told only that she is confronted by the wolf, who stupidly fails to eat her at once and instead sneaks around to Grandma's house, strips and devours the old lady, dons her clothes, gets into her bed, and soon manages to snack on the grandchild. Then a huntsman comes to the rescue, kills the wolf, and saves Grandma and Red Riding Hood, removing them alive, we're told, from the wolf's belly.

So, how do you handle this story? One way is to see things from the little girl's point of view: Her father is a deadbeat, her mother is having an affair, and Grandma is desperately in need of food and company. So off goes Little Red on a good will mission and discovers that the world away from home can be hazardous. This point of view rests on the premise that smart girls who venture into wolf territory need to befriend the local huntsman.

But how do things look from the wolf's point of view? There is Mrs. Wolf—yes, *Mrs.*—just trying to get food for her cubs, maybe change the way people tend to look on all wolves as male, when along comes a chance to engage in intergenerational dialogue, persuade young and old to save the forest, and be kind to wild animals. Unfortunately, before the dialogue can begin, Huntsman knocks on the door, hoping to sell Grandma some venison. Mrs. Wolf runs for her life, and Riding Hood makes the news by telling everyone that she and Grandma had been eaten alive. This point of view might advance the argument that everyone's little darling was nothing but a liar, responsible for starting a lot of bad PR for timber wolves, who are really shy creatures who avoid people.

Events can also be seen from Grandma's point of view, the huntsman's, the parents', the neighbor's, even a wolf cub's, as well as that of a psychologist, social worker, reporter, and so on. To turn things around—not assume that life has only one reality—is the surest way to discover your internal reality and create an illusion of reality that will grip the reader.

In addition to inspiring new insights, the effort to explore various points of view can also help you avoid offending someone unintentionally. For example, if you have seen things from the huntsman's point of view, you may be less likely to tackle the side issues of animal rights and the NRA, infuriating the proponents and opponents of both. Or if you have seen things from Grandma's point of view, you won't tend to say something that annoys the AARP. But an even more important reason to explore differing viewpoints is that writing itself is an act of faith—faith in the unseen, faith that an evolving truth does exist, and that fragmented sensory evidence is the external symptom of it. We seek the truth, believe in the truth as if it were singular, yet is there ever a whole, single, unchanging truth?

When giving testimony in a court of law, for instance, those who testify are asked to swear to tell "the truth, the whole truth, and nothing but the truth," and everyone usually so swears. But whose truth? What makes the difference between individual truths? What might be true for one, might not be true for another? Two people can witness the same event and give conflicting accounts of it. Even family members can experience something together and later on disagree about what happened.

The more writers grapple with viewpoint, the better they understand that what they see is conditioned by what they believe. Personal beliefs in turn are conditioned by time and by group beliefs. The truth thus tends to be encompassed rather than known, and a writer's ability to encompass it is a process that involves point of view.

One ironclad rule about point of view states that in a short story the writer should never switch from first- to third-person, or vice versa. J. D. Salinger is the only writer I know of who broke this rule, and did so successfully in his famous short story, "For Esmé—with Love and Squalor," when he changed his first-person narrator into a third-person protagonist. He did this by disarming the reader with humor: "I'm still around, but from here on in, for reasons I'm not at liberty to disclose, I've disguised myself so cunningly that even the cleverest reader will fail to recognize me." Thereafter, Staff Sergeant X takes over, and readers are moved, not put off. But what would happen if Salinger had chosen to see things not from the viewpoint of an adult male but through the eyes of Esmé, or her little brother, or perhaps a relative or close friend? Could the shift from first- to third-person have worked? And how would the impact have changed if the story had been told entirely in first person or entirely in third person?

Another interesting choice of viewpoint is Hemingway's, in "The Short Happy Life of Francis Macomber." The story opens: "It was now lunch time and they were all sitting under the double green fly of the dining tent pretending that nothing had happened." "They" includes Macomber, his wife, and Wilson the safari leader. The action could be viewed through the eyes of any one of them, or of one of the servants. Instead, Hemingway elects the omniscient point of view, which allows him to shift from one person to another, for the most part favoring Wilson, and thus avoiding literary disaster when Mrs. Macomber sleeps with him and later on "accidentally" shoots her husband. This detached, often dry way of seeing things is what conveys a profound sense of irony.

Now let's consider Fitzgerald's curious use of third-person adult male to tell a clearly autobiographical story, "Babylon Revisited," in which Charlie, a recovering alcoholic, fails to regain custody of his daughter, Honoria, from the Peters, relatives with whom the child is living. Some writers might be tempted to tell the story from Honoria's point of view to show how it feels to live with relatives who blame your father for your mother's death. Others might choose Mrs. Peters' point of view to dramatize her seething rage against Charlie. And I would have chosen Charlie's point of view in first- instead of third-person to help him vent his grief: wife dead, only child in her sister's custody. But Fitzgerald chose third person in order to convey a sense of total sadness—glitter gone, old friendships fled—making it one of his most memorable short stories.

I can also cite one of my own stories, "First Voice," as an example, because it involved a struggle with point of view. The story was about what happens when Aaron, the eldest son of American missionaries in South India, decides to become a sannyasi, or Hindu holyman (tantamount to what might happen if the first son of a prominent American surgeon decided to become a witch doctor). While the story eventually aroused the interest of American youth in Hindu culture, I had to shift point of view until I found the one that came alive for me. Since I am the eldest son of American missionaries, the logical viewpoint might have been Aaron's, in first- or third-person.

That did not work; it left me feeling uninvolved. So did the viewpoints of Aaron's parents, his sister, and one of his Indian friends. Then I created Samuel, a younger brother close enough to be a caring go-between, who looked at things from his point of view, so the story took off, in first person. Although the events narrated never occurred, readers continue to think that I must have gone through some revolutionary experiences in India. I did, but trying to become a Hindu holyman was not one of them.

When your point of view is working, it will draw into its vortex a host of sensory details—the evidence of touch, smell, taste, sight, and sound—that will breathe life into your words and validate what you are trying to say. And once this happens, your characters—not you—take charge, controlling the story. That is a great moment, well worth working for.

❑ SPECIALIZED FICTION

□ 36

WRITING THE HISTORICAL MYSTERY

BY ANNE PERRY

ATTENDING WRITERS' CONFERENCES IS ALMOST ALWAYS ENJOYABLE, and at the best of them one may learn a great deal. For me, most of it has come from two sources: One is listening to others, sometimes writers, sometimes editors or agents. The other is in being asked questions, and having to think of the answers. Other people have a great gift for putting their finger on the hole in your argument, or the gap in your self-knowledge. It obliges you to think, and the courtesy that people will listen obliges you to be as honest as you can.

As a writer of historical mysteries, I am most often asked this question:

"Where do you do your research?"—to which the answer is mostly in books. Looking at clothes, places, artifacts can be helpful, but they are only the dressing, the props, for a scene. You need to know about people more than things. By all means have the feel, the smell, and the sounds correct. Never use even the most trivial inventions before their time. Note especially those that we take for granted: fabrics, pens and paper, postal systems, forms of heating, transport, spectacles, etc. Medicine is a great key to a period; so is food. It is remarkable how choice and taste have widened with refrigeration and flight, not to mention education and immigration.

But far more than material things, I think one should research beliefs, values, and attitudes of mind. A present-day mind in a period costume is not a historical story. Ask yourself a few questions about the period you are working in. For example, what were political expectations? Had anybody even imagined "one man vote," let alone women's rights? Few people are outraged by lack of what they have not ever imagined having. We take one step of progress at a time. No 1990s consciences in 1890—or 1790!

What did people, particularly women, hope from marriage? And what

179

did they reasonably expect? Again, not 1990s: equality, freedom, or constant romance. But perhaps greater loyalty, to be protected (or suffocated) from certain unpleasant realities.

What medicines were available? But more important, what diseases were endemic, what were the usual sanitary conditions? What knowledge or ignorance was there about infection, childbirth, contraception, even anatomy and physiology?

What were people afraid of? What did they hope for, dream of? What embarrassed them or made them laugh?

Many of the facts you find will be the same as today, which is how you make the readers identify with your characters. Other facts are different—which is where your exploration begins.

How much of your research do you include, and how do you know what to leave out? I think one of my greatest mistakes (which I have now recognized, and, I hope, addressed) was somehow to weave in everything that interested me, and that was far too much.

Anyone who wishes to read a social history will buy one. What a novelist is aiming for is a *drama* about people who happen to have lived in another time, and possibly another place.

The single most important thing I know about plot, again discovered through constructive criticism from others, is that *all* characters must have a reason for everything they do (and "because the author needs them to" is not a reason). The questions to ask yourself are—"would you do that if you were in their place?" and "why?"

Every scene must have a purpose. "It was a great event in history—I would love to have been there" is *not* a purpose. It was one of the most consistent mistakes I made. I hope I have learned not to repeat it, but I am still tempted! I can feel myself slither toward the precipice. How can you resist a royal execution, a great betrayal, the meeting of two figures who will become lovers, or enemies who destroy a nation? You had better resist it, if they have nothing to do with your story!

The lesson I learned from someone else and from which I benefit most is to remember yourself as a reader, as well as a writer. What do you enjoy reading? Why? What sort of plots do you like? What sort of characters? What makes you laugh, cry? Why do you have to turn the page? What gives you greatest satisfaction or excitement?

What do you skip over? What irritates you? What makes you feel loved, or cheated, or disappointed?

Think of your favorite books, and why you like them. Is it a compulsive plot that makes sense, complex characters with passion, humor, vulnerability, the power to love, a setting that is used but not obtrusive?

That is what I like, too.

Perhaps that is what we should try to write.

❏ 37

WRITING THE MODERN WESTERN

BY PETER BRANDVOLD

THE GRAND OLD MAN OF HARD-BOILED FICTION, JAMES M. CAIN, ONCE told an aspiring writer that if his writing wasn't keeping him up nights, it probably wouldn't keep others up nights, either. Meaning, of course, that one should write first for oneself. An audience would follow naturally.

You wouldn't think that so simple a recipe would be so hard to follow. But what do we aspiring writers do? We go to college and get a bunch of highfalutin ideas. We read writers like James Joyce and Henry James and Bobbie Ann Mason, and we learn that the only way to write a novel is by detailing the droll lives of the people across the street or exploring our middle-class angst. We frown and nod and sigh, lick our pencils, and flip to the next page of Raymond Carver for inspiration. And what comes out of our typewriters and computers are dry-as-dust imitations of "Araby," "Shilo," and "What We Talk About When We Talk About Love."

Don't get me wrong. Those are fine stories by fine writers, but they're not the kind of stories most of us saw ourselves writing when we were twelve years old and eating up Edgar Rice Burroughs, Max Brand, and Robert Louis Stevenson as fast as we could.

When writers go to college and are introduced to elitist views about what is literature and what is not literature, what is acceptable and not acceptable, we get stymied and confused. Such a great distance yawns between what initially made us want to write and what is acceptable to write that we can't write anything at all.

I know. It happened to me.

After earning a B.A. in English and an MFA in creative writing from a prestigious writing program, I promptly got blocked. Ten years later, three books published, three more about to be, and with a contract for two more, I'm over it.

And you know how I did it? I went back to what made me want to be a writer in the first place. I went back to the dreamy summer I was twelve years old and was reading as though my life depended on it, harassing the local librarians with pleas for more sea stories and frontier stories. I went back to genre fiction, the forbidden entertainment I read only when my literary friends weren't looking.

Because I always loved the myth of the Old West, and had read nearly every novel and story Louis L'Amour and Luke Short ever wrote, I decided to try a Western. O.K., I had a genre. Now, needing to know what was happening in the genre of late, I checked out an armful of paperbacks from the local library.

What I learned from that reading spree was that the Western genre needed one hell of a shot in the arm. I couldn't find any compelling heroes I hadn't met when I was twelve. I found few new twists on the old plots and nary a heroine lovely enough and real enough to make my heart hurt.

No, aside from Larry McMurtry and too few others, the new Western writers couldn't create the dream. The genre needed a writer writing to entertain himself to attract readers who would sit up into the wee hours of the morning, being entertained.

I eventually figured out that what I needed was an unexpected hero. No clichés. I didn't want John Wayne or Matt Dillon or any of the Cartwrights. They've been done. My guy had to be larger-than-life, but at the same time he had to be *different*.

After much deliberating I finally decided to make my hero an ex-Marshal—a drunken ex-Marshal who gambles. Why ex-Marshal? Because he got shot. By whom? A whore. Yes! And not just any whore—a drunken whore who wasn't even aiming at him. A drunken whore who shot my hero by mistake. No Matt Dillon, this guy. I was entertaining myself by coming up with new twists to old characters, working against the clichés.

The heroine of a genre novel also needs to be entertaining. What's more entertaining than a beautiful woman? Answer: a beautiful woman who isn't merely beautiful but who lives and breathes and acts and reacts the way a real woman would, and who isn't just there to give the hero something to fight for. You don't find many of those in today's—or even yesterday's—Westerns, which is one reason the genre has fallen on hard times.

In my third book, *Dakota Kill*, I wanted to make Jacy Kincaid more than just a pretty face. She's lovely, to be sure, but she doesn't just stand around wringing her hands while the men ride off to fight the evil cattle baron trying to kill off the smaller ranchers on the Canaan Bench. She rides off *with* them, toting a well-oiled Henry rifle in her saddle sheath and a Remington revolver on her hip. After all, she lives here too, and feels the need to protect her ranch just as strongly as the men feel the need to protect theirs.

Jacy's tough enough to stand up to any man in spurs—or longjohns.

In one scene, she and my hero, Mark Talbot, are drinking whiskey in her cabin, getting drunk as they reminisce about the old days, when they were both kids growing up on the Bench. She gets a little tipsy, and Talbot helps her to bed. She invites him to stay, and pats the bed beside her. Now I've set up what could be a predictable bedroom scene. Yawn. Instead, I decided to have fun with it:

> "Come on—I don't bite," she said. He crawled under the covers and snuggled up to her.
> "It's been a long time since I've had a man to keep me warm," she said drowsily, getting comfortable against him.
> He kissed her ear, ran his hand down her thigh.
> She looked up suddenly. "What's that?"
> "Sorry . . . I, uh . . . seem—"
> "I'm not a loose woman, Mr. Talbot," she said haughtily. "Here, I'll take care of it."
> She thrust her hand through the front opening in his longjohns, grabbed his member, and squeezed, slowly pressing it down.
> "There—how's that?" she asked.
> He gave his head a quick shake and smiled against the pain. "Yeah . . . yeah . . . that should . . . do it," he said with a sigh.
> "Good."
> Then she wedged her head against his chest and went to sleep.

Another thing I try to do to keep myself and readers entertained is create fresh villains. To be entertaining, they have to be foul. I mean, they really have to make you clench your jaws whenever they swagger into a scene. They can't just kick cats and shoot dogs or boast facial scars. That's been done. They have to be over-the-top different, bizarre, creepy—without being goofy. They have to be the kind of people you have nightmares about waking up and finding them in your house.

In my first Western, *Once a Marshal*, I struggled with this problem of creating an expected yet unexpected Western villain. I knew he had to be a gunfighter. Nothing nastier than a gunfighter. In keeping with tradition, I gave him the name Weed Cole and made him as fast on the draw as Doc Holliday, but I also made him funny and unpredictable. He relentlessly pursues his boss's wife, our lovely heroine Fay Beaumont. With as much charm as a tobacco plug, he stalks her like a lusty tomcat, and really gives her the creeps:

> Dipping her pen, Fay heard a man's muffled, singsong voice outside. She placed the pen in the ink jar, stood, and parted the curtains. A man in a Stetson hat and duster sat in the tree swing below, swinging with the casual industry of a boy playing hooky from school.
>
> He pulled back on the ropes and swung forward, boots straight out in front of him, duster blowing out behind. He lifted his head, revealing the dark, bristled cheeks, scarred nose, and lewd leer of Weed Cole.
>
> "I . . . gotta . . . seeecret. . . . I . . . gotta seeecret . . ."

How many gunfighters have you seen in tree swings? I had fun writing that scene, more fun than I would have had if I'd settled for something easy. I stayed up late writing it, and I'm confident a few readers have stayed up late reading it. Isn't that what it's all about?

So forget everything you learned in school. I hereby grant you permission to write about another time and place, to create larger-than-life heroes, tough, beautiful heroines, and villains villainous enough to keep you glancing over your shoulder as you write.

Just use your imagination.

And remember, if your writing isn't keeping *you* up nights, it's not going to keep anyone else up, either.

38

WRITING FICTION ON TWO LEVELS

BY KATHERINE HALL PAGE

WHEN TRUMAN CAPOTE'S *IN COLD BLOOD* WAS PUBLISHED IN 1965, an immediate debate ensued. Was it fact or fiction? Inevitably, the word "faction" entered the list of literary genres. Capote took the information he'd gathered from extensive research on the case and presented it from his own very particular, non-objective point of view. In so doing, he added a new dimension to "Write about what you know." The end result wasn't a true crime book. It wasn't a mystery. It was faction.

The challenge for me as a mystery writer has always been to write about what I *don't* know—to write purely from my imagination, asking innumerable "What ifs?" along the way as part of the process. When I write a mystery, I'm writing on two levels. I'm describing a fictional occurrence, a murder, as if it really happened. There's a logical sequence of events and it all has to make sense. I can't produce the evil twin from Australia in the last chapter. What does have to happen in the last chapter is for the reader to say to himself or herself, "I should have guessed that."

At the same time that I'm telling the story, I'm writing on another level, doing everything I can to keep the reader both engrossed and totally in the dark. It's here that the tendency to run amok can affect even the best mystery writers—too many suspects, overly complicated plot twists, in short, an overflowing creel of red herrings.

In writing *The Body in the Bookcase*, I completely departed from the way I'd always written and produced a piece of faction. The whole process took place in my mind, but this time the voices and large portions of the plot were not the products of pure imagination, but reality recalled.

Our home was burglarized in January 1995. We lost every piece of jewelry, silver, and similar valuables we'd owned. The sense of loss and violation was second only to the grief we'd felt at times of a death.

Mourning gave way to rage and this in turn to action. Suddenly the "What if?" was real life. Once again, I was imagining scenes, but this time instead of putting them down on paper, we went out and lived them. After a string of coincidences, we began turning up our items in large antique markets and fairs. All the booths belonged to the same dealer. We'd gotten some of our own back, although it represented only a tiny fraction of what was taken. What I'd also been given, I soon realized, was a ready-made plot.

One of the best pieces of advice I've ever received about writing was from a journalist friend. "Remember," she said, "all is fodder." In fiction, the "fodder" is processed—often beyond recognition. Something that may have happened to us or someone we know is filtered through the writer's imagination until the experience becomes unique. Joyce Maynard wrote directly about her affair with J.D. Salinger. Reading that account, a writer of fiction begins to spin it into something quite different, yet the same. The older author might become a musician; the young woman a promising student glimpsed at a recital. The fan letter from him to her might remain pivotal, as well as the unraveling of the relationship. The plot is there, the fodder—the raw material. The difficulty lies in creating something new, something that is not so derivative that the reader remarks at page two, "Oh, this is just a rehash of the Salinger-Maynard story," and shuts the book.

The Body in the Bookcase was an enormously satisfying book for me to write—and not simply because I could punish the wicked, unlike what occurred in real life. Taking the events and adding whatever my imagination conjured up was like focusing the lenses of a pair of binoculars to suit one's own specific vision.

What I took away from the experience was a renewed appreciation for the role of fact in fiction and the notion that an entire plot could evolve from a single reported or observed event. Of course, there's nothing new in this advice. Writers have long scanned the headlines for inspiration, for what's hot. Judith Rossner's 1975 novel, *Looking For Mr. Goodbar,* hit the bookstores as young singles—and their parents—were waking up to the realization that courtship rituals were not what they had been. What writers starting out may not fully realize, however, is what *they* may be bringing to the headlines. Anyone can take the facts and write an account of what happened, embellishing here and there, but only a few can give voice to the characters and create a mirror image of truth that seems more believable than the original truth itself.

Fortunately, we do not have to experience everything we write about. Far less painful is keeping a file of newspaper clippings. Mine is filled with all sorts of items—things that strike me as funny, tragic, odd, frightening. It's bulging, and some of the items are many years old. A random sampling reveals the following, any one of which could be expanded into a full-length story:

• A bigamist who changed the locks on his two houses, so they'd be the same and he'd have only one key on his ring. Also, identical wardrobes at each, so he'd never face the question, "Honey, where did you get that tie?"

• A court ruling against a would-be buyer who'd signed a purchase agreement for a Victorian house in New York State. The buyer claimed that the seller had failed to disclose the existence of three ghosts in residence.

• The disappearance of a 69-year-old suburban Boston woman vacationing in Maine reported by her husband, the last to see her, after he stopped at a variety store so she could use the bathroom. Provocative detail—back home, the daughter noticed that the groceries were not put away where her mother normally stored items.

• Headline: "Golfers Play Past Corpse"

• An actor, Brandon Lee, killed on the set by a prop gun filled with .44 caliber bullets instead of blanks.

The seemingly small detail of the groceries put away out of their normal places in the story of the woman who disappeared offers an example of the way a fact can be expanded into a full-blown fiction. I'd have the daughter voice her suspicions to my sleuth and soon be on the trail of the person most likely to have access to the house—the husband. He'd use the vacation as a cover, having really killed his wife in the kitchen during an argument—before she put the groceries away. He couldn't simply leave them out. She wouldn't have gone away with ice cream melting on the counter. He couldn't throw them away. She might have run into a friend at the market, or the check-out person in the small town might recall the purchases. Soon, I'd be back to my original mode—writing on two levels, chronicling a believable sequence of events and at the same time, creating smoke screens for the reader.

A writer need look no further than today's paper to start a clipping file. A front-page headline reads, "Phantom Insurance Empire Was Built on Trail of Aliases." Martin R. Frankel may well have pulled off one of the largest insurance frauds in history when he duped not only a string of savvy executives and backers, but also the Roman Catholic Church. Frankel had apparently used the St. Francis of Assisi Foundation, a philanthropy he'd founded with the church's wholehearted approval, as a front for taking control of a network of insurance companies. Means, motive, opportunity? There's more. Firefighters responding to an alarm at his Greenwich, Connecticut, mansion found the charred remains of documents and evidence that Frankel had researched showing which foreign countries do not have extradition treaties with the United States. Frankel, of course, was not home. Now add the body of a young woman, a supposed suicide, found at Frankel's home in 1997, and you won't have to look any further for a plot.

❏ 39

FIRST-PERSON NARRATORS IN HISTORICAL FICTION

BY WILLIAM MARTIN

REACH INTO YOUR WALLET. TAKE OUT A DOLLAR BILL. LOOK AT THE face:

George Washington, just as you've always known him: a distant old man with gray hair, ill-fitting dentures, and the hard, humorless eyes of the schoolmaster who's just caught you making spitballs at the back of the classroom.

Now look more closely, remembering the words of Gilbert Stuart, who painted the portrait that the government engravers borrowed. Stuart said Washington's features were "indicative of the strongest and most ungovernable passions. Had he been born in the forests, he would have been the fiercest of all the savages."

So . . . maybe the expression on Washington's face is less an outward sign of inner calm than a cold plaster mask concealing hot fires beneath.

Read a little bit about him. You'll learn that he had a volcanic temper and struggled all his life to keep it in check. He had an almost foolhardy sense of courage on the battlefield, driven by the belief that providence, or fate, would work its will no matter what. For all the adulation he enjoyed, he had a skin so thin that even as president, he considered any kind of criticism a personal affront. This first American commander-in-chief aspired, in his youth, to be a British officer. This paragon of honesty could shade the truth whenever he had to. In his youth, he loved another man's wife, but his own marriage lasted forty years. In the first half of his life, he focused his energies on acquisition of land, of slaves, of the material wealth that would bring him respect, but his legacy was secured by all that he gave up—an army at the end of the Revolution, political power at the end of a presidency, and a population of slaves in his last will and testament.

The truth is that no one, not even George Washington, goes from youth to old age without changing or growing, oblivious to the working of time and experience, never deviating from the course. The man behind the dollar-bill face was filled with what the writing teachers call "consistent inconsistencies," those logical contradictions of personality that we should always try to look for to make a character more interesting, more dramatic, and more human.

But how to convey that humanity, those "consistent inconsistencies," when the frozen face seems always before us, when the marble man dominates on pedestals and in display cases from the Boston Public Garden to California's Huntington Museum?

I first asked the question back in 1991, when I wrote a documentary about Washington for PBS. I asked it again when I decided that the Washington I'd met on PBS would make a wonderful subject for a novel. That was when people started asking me why I would write a novel instead of a straight biography.

Well, there are plenty of Washington biographies already. Not so many novels. And I'm a novelist. I wasn't put on earth to live by the hard code of the footnote. I prefer the seductive mistress of story. The historian serves the truth of his subject. The novelist serves the truth of his tale. And as a novelist, I have tools no historian should touch: I can manipulate time and space, extrapolate from the written record to invent dialogue and incident, create fictional characters to bring you close to the historical figures, and fall back on my imagination when the research runs out.

I've always said that a historical novel should never let the facts get in the way of a good story, but the best historical novels respect the spirit of the times if not the letter. And the facts of Washington's life are better than anything you could make up: the modest beginnings, the possessive mother, the adventures in the French and Indian War, the years as a social-climbing Virginia planter, the Revolution, the presidency, the denouement on the Potomac.

Washington left thousands of pages behind, in the form of letters, diaries, documents, reports. Scholars have been sifting them for two hundred years, looking for keys to his personality and an explanation for his greatness. Finding answers has not been easy. I once asked a famous Washington scholar what forces of character came together to make Washington so reliable, so prudent, so trustworthy with the future of America. She thought for a moment and said, "No one really knows." I think that Washington wanted it that way. Remember, that face on the dollar bill gives up very little in the way of emotion or psychological insight.

So, back to the central queston. How to get at him in fiction?

The process of starting a novel is seldom linear—one idea leading to another with a kind of cold geometric logic. I find it all to be more circular. Ideas about plot, character, and technique spiral about as if dropped into a funnel inside your head, while you lean over the keyboard, waiting.

With *Citizen Washington*, a little nugget of research dropped out of the funnel first: After Washington died, Martha burned all of their letters. What, I wondered, might the letters have contained? What insights into the evolution of Washington's character? What perceptions about his life? And why did Martha burn them?

As I answered those questions, the funnel deposited a plot on my desk: An anti-Washington newspaper editor named Hesperus Draper learns of the burned letters. He decides that Martha must have been hiding a scandal. He sends a young writer out to interview people who knew Washington, in the hopes of uncovering it. If he does, he'll use it against Washington's Federalist political descendants in the next election.

A young man seeks to solve a mystery; an old man waits for the solution. Out of plot had spun fictional characters who would be changed by their brush with history, the kind of characters who give historical fiction its dramatic heart, serving as foils for the historical figures and surrogates for the modern reader. But if they're our surrogates, what do they see for us, and how do they see it? Out of character spins point of view.

Every time we sit down to write, we must decide on an angle from which to tell the story. Will we use our own reliable authorial voice and move freely through the minds of all our characters? Or will we tell the tale from the first-person, through the eyes of a main character who may or may not be reliable, whose impressions will be colored by his personality, background, education, and experience?

I have usually used a technique I learned from reading the master of the Revolutionary War saga, Kenneth Roberts. In books like *Arundel* or *Oliver Wiswell*, he allowed his narrator to explore the thoughts, emotions, and internal desires of his primary fictional characters, but he kept a respectful distance from historical characters like Benedict Arnold or Benjamin Franklin, developing them only through word, gesture, and action.

I had always found this approach the safest course with people who once were alive in the real world and not just in the pages of my fiction. I had never gone into the minds of historical figures. I had put words in their mouths, yes, but I had always tried to extrapolate from something they had thought or written, or something that had been written by eyewitnesses to their lives.

I could not imagine writing, "Washington thought it was cold, colder than a well-digger's ass. He sat in the boat, wiggled his toes to keep them from turning into pieces of lead, and hoped desperately that this crazy plan to cross the Delaware would work."

There's an intimacy about such a passage that's fine for a fictional character (if you dump the adverbs and the clichéd metaphor), but it seems a little too personal for my relationship with a historical figure, especially one like Washington, who seldom invited intimacy of any kind.

Nevertheless, my young narrator, no matter how fictional, could not explore Washington's life if he spoke only to other fictional characters. And as *Citizen Washington* took shape, I began to see it as a tapestry of intertwined stories told by the people around Washington, colorful threads that would weave a picture of Washington without ever going into his mind. Our narrator would have to meet people like John Adams, Thomas Jefferson, Washington's close friend Dr. James Craik, and Martha herself, and I would have to write from their points of view, whether I wanted to or not.

But part of being a good writer is to be a good reader. So I reread Michael Shaara's *The Killer Angels*, in which he brings the Battle of Gettysburg to life from the fictional but carefully researched points of view of historical figures like Robert E. Lee and Joshua Lawrence Chamberlain. I made him my inspiration.

Like all disciplines, the first-person point of view brings constraints that, paradoxically, can be liberating. Because we can describe only what one person saw and felt, we are freed from worrying about any other set of opinions or emotions. Find the right level of diction for your narrator, decide how honest he's going to be about himself and the people around him, and start writing.

In *Citizen Washington*, I found it easy to drop into the voices of my twelve narrators, eight historical and four fictional. The historical figures had left written records that gave me their tones of voice, their personal concerns, and their observations of Washington. So Thomas Jefferson would speak somewhat more circumspectly than the blunt-as-a-hammer John Adams. And Martha Washington, indifferently educated as most eighteenth-century women were, would tell her tale with less refinement than the well-read Abigail Adams.

Martha's surviving letters capture her as she once described herself—"homey, happy, cheerful as a cricket, and busy as a bee." Her writing is dotted with grammatical errors, yet it is full of homespun wisdom and an optimism derived from a faith so powerful in "the Divine Being" that it enabled her to survive the death of both her children and never falter in her devotion to her husband.

Consider this scene with Martha: It is March, 1776. Washington is depressed that he could not bring about a decisive battle in Boston, and he fears what lies ahead. His dialogue is taken from one of his letters, but in my version, Martha elicits it from him:

> Even news that American mothers were naming their newborn sons George, in honor of the successful siege of Boston, did not amuse my husband. He told me, "We could have ended the war right here . . ."
> We were alone in the room where we had spent so much of our private time during the siege. The British had sailed off . . . and my husband was convinced that when they appeared again, 'twould be in New York.
> He looked out the window at a line of troops beginning the long walk south. "Howe will be reinforced. More regulars. Mercenaries. . . ."
> I told him he would succeed again, as he had in Boston.
> He smiled. "We beat them in a most shameful manner, didn't we."
> "Yes.
> "Beat them out of a place that might be the strongest to defend on the whole continent."
> "Yes."
> "Fortified in the best manner, at enormous expense."
> I said yes again, emphatically. When a man's spirit falters, 'tis the role of a good wife to restore him. "So go to New York. I shall follow . . ."

The scene is simple and simply written, befitting my characterization of its narrator. Washington could be a man of gloomy apprehensions, but he always overcame them to do his job. This scene shows the apprehensions and lets Martha's optimism break them down. Without going into his head, Martha brings you closer to her husband, and in the process, she unconsciously characterizes herself as one of those wellsprings of Washington's almost supernatural endurance.

But what of my fictional characters? After Gilbert Stuart, the most famous image of George Washington may be the painting by Emmanuel Leutze, "Washington Crossing the Delaware." I looked at that painting hundreds of times before I noticed that the oarsman in front of Washington is black. History is full of anonymous oarsmen who help advance the great plot and are then forgotten. In *Citizen Washington*, I resolved to remember a few of them.

I also believe the old saying that if you want to know the master, see him through the eyes of a servant. So I created Jacob, a fictional Mount Vernon slave, as a narrator. And his son, who runs away in search of his freedom, ends up as that oarsman, face-to-face with Washington on the most famous Christmas night in American history.

But how would Jacob sound? I wanted the reader to be able to identify every narrator by voice alone. That's why Martha speaks simply and makes regular references to her faith; why John Adams is sharp and opinionated; why Hesperus Draper begins sentences without subjects and fills his talk with scatalogical metaphors. For Jacob, I worked on a dialect that would approximate though not mimic the speech of an eighteenth-century slave. My job was not to create perfect history or perfect dialect, remember, but to approximate the experience, so the modern reader can approach and slip easily into the world the characters inhabit.

I read some *Huck Finn*, though I had no intention of going so far over the top (for a twentieth-century reader) as Twain had with Jim. I studied remembrances of Mount Vernon slaves set down by white writers. And I asked this: Why do some African Americans, even today, speak in the present tense? Is it simply the result of poor education? Or is it a linguistic tradition passed down from certain African languages? Or does it reflect a slave culture in which there was no future and the past was too painful to contemplate?

I decided I would not rely on misspellings to give Jacob's voice, but on syntax and tense. He would speak only in the present. His son, however, who runs off and fights for freedom, would speak a better brand of English, containing both past and future tenses. Their language would evolve as their hopes rose, but their observations would always be sharp.

In this scene from Washington's youth, he has just been told by his mother that he can't go off and join the British navy. He's furious. Jacob, who is Washington's age, narrates, and I play with the legend about Washington throwing things across rivers:

> George go down the hill, down the path through the trees, down to the river-bank. And all the way, he's kickin' at stones and whisperin' to hisself 'bout how he damns that farm and damns his mother and damns hisself for not runnin' away.
>
> He's fifteen, don't forget, and they's no better age for feelin' sorry for yourself, even if you got nothin' to feel sorry 'bout.
>
> He pick up a stone and he fling it out at the river. Now, the Rappahannock be slow, and not near so pretty as the P'tomac, nor near so wide. But wide enough, 'bout seventy yards or so. And that stone jess drop and splash. Then he pick up another one and fling it harder, and I swear it split the diff'rence 'tween the first splash and the far bank. Then he try agin, and he git even closer.
>
> I watch from behind a tree and he jess put all his mad into throwin' them stones, till finely I swear he throw a apple-sized stone all the way 'crost that damn river. All the way. And I thinks, damn but he's strong.

Strong indeed. And strong-tempered. And determined, at the end of that scene, to move out of his mother's control. He tells Jacob to fetch the surveying tools, and he moves on to the next phase of his life.

So, in two short scenes, given life by first-person narrators, we have met an apprehensive man cheered by his wife before facing an insurmountable task and a boy who seethes at the whole oppressive adult world that keeps him from fulfilling his ambition. First-person narrators have brought us close to the character and illuminated him as best they could, but they have not entered his mind, respecting instead the essential mystery at the core of every human being.

Now take out that dollar bill again. Take another look. I think the face is starting to move. Next thing you know, he'll be talking to you.

❏ 40

TIME TRAVEL AND FANTASY

BY CHRISTINA HAMLETT

TIME. WHO AMONG US HASN'T LONGED FOR THE ABILITY TO SPEED UP the clock, turn it back, or make it stand still? Even the concept of a "virtual vacation" holds wide appeal—the chance to view ancient or future realms through contemporary eyes. Until technology makes such options available, of course, we have the power of the pen and the availability of three distinctly different genres—romance, fantasy, and science fiction—to make time travel an enjoyable escape.

Some common themes

Timeless love: Hero or heroine meets soulmate in another century and must deal with the dilemma of whose era is better.

Saving the planet: Protagonist needs to prevent global destruction, recover a magical object from pesky trolls, or thwart an arch-villain-scientist-power-mogul.

Accidental segue: The lead character didn't intend to go anywhere that day, but it's always fortuitous that he/she did.

Crime-busters: Any premise that involves going back in time to resolve a past wrongdoing, or jumping forward to pursue an enterprising antagonist.

Leaps of faith

Foreshadowing is a critical component in any time-travel story, regardless of which genre you select. It not only provides the protagonist with valuable clues (lightning strikes the old clock tower at a specific hour) or imbues readers with dread (pennies left in pockets can cause major time-suck). It's also important that whatever conditions are present to jump-start the journey need to be replicated in order to make the return trip.

Even though you're writing in a surrealistic vein, certain elements of your plot need to be grounded in logic or at least have a plausible explanation. For instance, how did your characters get there (wherever "there" is)? Can they get back on their own, or do they need outside help (witchcraft, electrical storms, plutonium, etc.)? Does time, as they know it, stand still in the present, or does it progress at the same pace, thus necessitating an excuse for them to be gone three years without paying the rent?

Included below are some examples of particularly bad time-travel writing:

• A heroine who discovers a shrinking "time-hole" in the countryside and conveniently steps back and forth whenever she needs to get lip gloss or clean lingerie from her apartment. (Do not succumb to the contrivance of letting your characters "visit"; plant them somewhere and make them cope accordingly.)

• A romance in which Lancelot and Mordred are transported to the 1990's. Lancelot starts to age and grow weak; Mordred does not. (Whatever parameters you set for your characters need to be consistent.)

• A despondent futuristic cop goes back ten years, prevents the death of his pregnant wife, and returns "home" to find his wife and ten-year-old son cheerfully asking how his day at work went. (Shouldn't his memory banks have adjusted upon reentry?)

• A Scottish laird quickly sheds 700 years of brutish demeanor and his brogue and appears in turtlenecks and tight jeans, carries a Walkman, and uses cool phrases like, "How should I know? I'm not a scientist," and "I'll have another latté." (How does this stuff get published?)

Yesterday v. tomorrow

Regardless of direction or destination, time travel presents a trio of challenges to the writer:

    1) Knowledge of history
    2) Social consciousness
    3) Empathy

Unless your story takes place in a totally fabricated realm, you'll need to bone up on the dates, places, and events that shape your plot.

While it may appear that writing about the past is easier than speculating about the future, remember that much of the history we've learned was interpreted by subsequent generations who put their own spin on its significance and value.

At the opposite end of the spectrum is science fiction that paints an idyllic or dark view of our destiny. In spite of this, however, the core conflict necessary for reader identification still must hinge on social concerns that have plagued mankind for thousands of years: hunger, freedom, crime, and prejudice. Even in fantasy novels, there exists a defined pecking order of power and limitations on individual liberty.

Finally, there is the writer's own sympathy with the time traveler's plight. Traveling backward would be akin to having a city dweller forced to go wilderness camping; the awareness of what she was missing in terms of civilized amenities like blow-dryers and voice mail would either force her to learn to live without them or to invent workable substitutes. Traveling forward might be likened to being plopped into a strange place where everyone around her speaks a foreign language but seems to be functioning just fine. How-oh-how can she find the library or order a piece of toast?

Dr. Livingston, I presume

Time travel provides an intriguing site in which your novel's fictional characters can interact with real people and/or their fictional ancestors. Such scenarios, however, are replete with complications—for example, the film *Back to the Future*, in which young Marty McFly unintentionally becomes a rival with his nerdy father, thus threatening to blot out his own existence. Entanglements also ensue with a protagonist's specialized knowledge—and the accompanying frustration—regarding events to come. Although the historical facts themselves can't be altered, you can have fun hinting that your characters had input into to the development; i.e., "I know you've got your heart set on the next battle in Parma, Ohio, sir, but have you considered Gettysburg as a possibility?"

One-way or round-trip?

While science fiction, fantasy, and time-travel all pose the question of whether your characters will return to their own time, fantasy and science fiction are more likely to address time-travel as "just part of the job." The quest completed or humanity saved, they amble back to whatever they were doing at the start. In romantic time-travels, however, the journey is invariably precipitated by loneliness, betrayal, or boredom. If the character thought they had problems before, what do they do when the age difference between them and their lovers spans eons? And how do they decide where to spend Thanksgiving?

In books and film, the resolution of such long-distance passion has been handled in a variety of ways. In H.G. Wells's *Time After Time*, the main character decides her lover's century could use a little enlightenment about women's lib and she hops in the time machine to go back with him. In *Knight in Shining Armor*, Jude Devereaux used the device of a look-alike descendant to reunite the heroine with the man of her dreams. Diana Gabaldon's imaginative *Outlander* series has the heroine travel to the past, return to the present, then orchestrate a second journey to save her beloved Jamie's life and tell him about the daughter she had conceived in Trip #1.

Whatever route you choose, the resolution must be emotionally satisfying in terms of sacrifice, compromise, and whether it's credible that a warrior whose only talent is skull-bashing could be happy with a nice desk job in Manhattan.

❏ 41

SECRETS OF
ROMANTIC CONFLICT

BY VANESSA GRANT

ROMANCE IS A MASSIVE MARKET, WITH THOUSANDS OF DEVELOPING writers struggling to crack it. Those who succeed know how to create and resolve romantic conflict to sustain suspense.

Romance literature tells us that love is the most powerful force in our lives. A story that does not convey this message is not a romance, although it may contain a romantic subplot.

Even romances that end unhappily, like *Casablanca* and *Bridges of Madison County,* show readers how love can help one achieve personal growth. In the best romances, this powerful love-message is inseparable from story conflict and suspense.

What is romantic conflict?

In a romance, falling in love creates problems for both hero and heroine, but ultimately love's power provides the solution. During their romantic journey, characters must experience both internal and external conflict as they struggle to achieve their goals.

Internal conflict is the result of a character's wanting two incompatible things. A hero wants love, yet fears being vulnerable. A heroine must keep a secret, although her moral code demands honesty.

In my novel, *Hidden Memories,* my heroine Abby has a secret. Her daughter Trish was conceived with Ryan, a stranger she met when she was in shock after her husband's death. Abby knows she should be honest about her daughter's real father, but fears the consequences of telling the truth. She wants to be an honest person, but she wants to hide the truth. Because she can't have both, she struggles inwardly.

If your characters don't experience internal conflict, you're telling the reader that the issues in this story aren't important enough to worry

201

about. Internal conflict is essential, but external conflict generates excitement. If your hero and heroine don't experience *external* threats to their goals, they'll spend the book agonizing about the internal struggle and your reader will become impatient. External conflict occurs when characters struggle with each other over opposing goals. When characters with opposing goals have transactions with each other, conflict moves out in the open, becoming visible to readers and other characters.

Whenever a character experiencing internal conflict acts in response to that struggle, it becomes externalized and may create conflict with other characters. Abby's internal conflict, when she acts on it, has the potential to affect Ryan, her daughter, her daughter's grandfather, and her parents.

In Chapter One, Abby tries to hide when she recognizes Ryan across a crowded room. He could expose her secret and throw her life into turmoil. Even before Abby makes the first move in her struggle with this hero, she's fighting with her conscience, Ryan's right to know his child, and her desire to avoid exposure. When Ryan recognizes Abby, his attempt to learn all he can about her threatens to expose her secret even more. She fears he'll learn she has a daughter and realize he's the father. Abby's frightened response to the external conflict generates intensifying internal conflict.

In your novel, external conflict should always intensify the internal conflict.

Ryan wants to know why Abby disappeared after their brief affair. Once he learns she's had his child, he wants to form a strong relationship with his daughter. Because Abby wants to maintain the fiction that Trish is her dead husband's daughter, she can't let him have what he wants. Their opposing goals create both internal and external conflict.

Every step in the external struggle between Ryan and Abby makes Abby's internal conflict worse. Because of her internal conflict, when the external conflict begins, her reactions are instinctive, not logical. Characters experiencing heightened internal conflict often behave irrationally.

Abby is under stress, attacked from outside by Ryan, from inside by her own conscience. She tries to hide, to pretend, to evade. Ryan becomes suspicious. Abby's mother, who likes Ryan, makes things worse when she tries some matchmaking. As Abby and Ryan fall in love, both internal and external conflict skyrocket.

With strong internal conflict and strong interlinking external conflict, the stakes rise. The reader fears it won't work out for these characters. Will Abby drive Ryan away with her inability to live openly with the truth? Will Ryan become angry and leave? The more uncertainty readers feel over the outcome, the more satisfied they will be when hero and heroine come together in the end.

As your story progresses, the conflict must change and develop. Your hero and heroine must have trouble getting what they want, they must worry about it, doubting whether their relationship can work. For good reasons, they must offend one another. We all commit offenses against people we love because we're tired, worried, or afraid we're not loved as much as we love. Those are valid emotional reasons arising from our internal conflicts. They generate transactions that are part of external conflict.

In a love story, the conflict eventually develops to make the reader ask: "Do hero and heroine care enough about each other to make the necessary compromises? Can they trust each other enough to reveal their inner selves and commit to a believable, lasting relationship?

How to create conflict

Conflict is created when goals meet obstacles. To create conflict, first give your character an important goal, then have someone oppose that goal.

Every strong desire has its corresponding fear. If you combine your character's goal to a fear, you'll achieve a high level of internal conflict when things begin to go wrong. Abby's goal of keeping her secret is attached to her fear of what will happen if the truth becomes known. Her late husband was a famous artist, and although he destroyed Abby's sense of self, the world believed their marriage was idyllic. Now, however, if the truth is exposed, both Abby and her daughter will suffer.

Strong goals conceal strong fears.

By the time Ryan discovers Abby's lie, they are struggling with their own new relationship. The external conflict issues have grown. They are in conflict over Ryan's desire to be acknowledged as Trish's father, Abby's fear of committing to another disastrous relationship, and his insistence that they marry and become a family.

To create conflict in your story, give your character a goal, then ask yourself what fear hides behind that goal. The more powerful the fear, the higher the level of conflict. If your hero's goal is financial power, why is money so important to him? What does he fear? Did he live in severe poverty as a child? Perhaps he vowed never to be poor again. If he fears poverty, intensify the fear by making it personal. Perhaps his baby brother had a disease requiring expensive medical care. The hero worked a paper route, mowed lawns, and dug ditches for extra money, but it wasn't enough. The brother died.

This hero has a deep emotional fear that someone he loves will suffer again, and he won't be able to provide enough. With this fear behind his drive to achieve wealth, any threat to his financial security will create strong internal conflict. If this hero must choose between money and the woman he loves, all his fears about poverty will be aroused, and he'll be thrown into severe conflict. If he chooses money, he'll lose his love and the joy in life. If he chooses love, he'll lose the money and may be unable to keep his love safe. Unless your story is a tragedy, the hero will have to win the battle against his demons and choose love. His struggle will involve pain, suffering, and sacrifice.

From conflict to resolution

A good story begins by putting forth a *story question* in the reader's mind. In a romance novel, the story question is usually, "Will heroine and hero overcome the obstacles to love—*their conflict issues*—and find happiness?"

In *Hidden Memories,* Abby's opening conflict arises from her internal struggle between honesty and fear. As the story progresses, the conflict changes and develops. When Ryan discovers Trish is his daughter, he wants Abby to marry him so that they can be a family, but she believes their marriage would be a disaster. Abby and Ryan still struggle over their daughter's identity, but a new element has been added: Abby's fear of the pain she risks if she surrenders to her growing love for Ryan and agrees to marry him.

As your story progresses, new problems should continue to emerge as the romantic conflict moves through several stages: beginning, middle, black moment, and ending. Ideally, the beginning of your story will create suspense and curiosity in your reader by showing or hinting at internal or external conflict. If you didn't put conflict in the first page of your manuscript, try beginning the story at a different point.

Here are a few examples from the opening paragraphs of my own stories:

It couldn't be him!
Abby had dreamed him in nightmares, dreams suppressed and almost forgotten. A man's head and shoulders glimpsed across a room . . .

from *Hidden Memories*

Eight hours was too long. She should have walked right up to Connar and faced him this morning at the exhibition. "Let's talk," she should have said.

from *Yesterday's Vows*

"We may have to turn back!" the pilot shouted over the engine noise.
"Can't you give it a try?" Sarah squinted to see through the windscreen and wished herself back in her Vancouver office.

from *Nothing Less Than Love*

If you begin your story by tossing your characters into strong conflict—with themselves, each other, or circumstances—you'll be off to a good start. As your story progresses, your characters should face a series of problems that create increasing conflict, thus forcing them to wrestle with the real issue. A satisfying novel pits characters against overwhelming odds, then leaves them to struggle through disaster after disaster until victory is won.

Heroine and hero may have a wonderful time on a date. They may laugh, make love, even get married, but despite their ultimate victories, the problems keep coming until happiness seems impossible. The harder you make life for your characters, the better your readers will like the book. Until you reach the final scene, every transaction must present new problems, or new developments to old problems. Forget everything you ever learned about being nice to people. To be a good storyteller, you must treat your characters terribly, throwing their worst fears in their faces

In a satisfying romance, the suspense between hero and heroine culminates in a black moment when all seems lost. To be powerful, the black moment must emerge from the personality and fears of your characters, and it must be deeply related to the conflict issue. The more powerful your moment, the more satisfying the resolution.

It is only after the black moment, when hero and heroine realize that they've lost each other, that they can experience the full strength of their love. In the aftermath of the black moment, hero and heroine each realize that their relationship matters more than the convictions they held so rigidly. After this realization, they are willing to make the necessary sacrifice to achieve their happy ending.

Panicked by Ryan's demands for marriage and her own fears, Abby finally succeeds in driving Ryan away, only to realize how bleak life will be without the man she loves. If the conflict is based on your characters' fears and personal history, the sacrifice must be related. The hero who fears poverty must sacrifice the illusion that money can prevent personal loss. Abby, who fears exposure, must embrace truth and risk herself.

To achieve a happy ending, lovers must always sacrifice their need to protect themselves against abandonment. They must allow themselves to become vulnerable, to risk broken hearts and grief, before they can win the prize of true intimacy.

It is only at the end of the romance novel, when hero and heroine make their sacrifices and emerge victorious over the conflicts that threaten their future, that the reader's suspense is ended with the satisfying answer to the story question.

Can this couple overcome the obstacles to love and find a happy ending?

Yes, they can, but it isn't easy.

❏ 42

WRITING MYSTERY NOVELS: SOME MODEST HINTS AND WARNINGS

BY GWENDOLINE BUTLER

THE MYSTERY NOVEL, MUCH MORE THAN THE MAINSTREAM NOVEL, must appear spontaneous, but it cannot be so. No one was better at this than its begetter, Wilkie Collins, Agatha Christie in her prime, and my favorite writer, Elizabeth Daly. At the moment I would award the palm to the English writer Reginald Hill, and I wish Raymond Chandler was not dead, but Ross Macdonald took his place marvelously (in a slightly different mystery style), and so did his wife Margaret Millar. Her books read as if they were just happening to someone she knew.

Contrivance is necessary, because the mystery novel must contain a puzzle, a problem to be solved. A question must be raised for the reader to brood over, and then it must be resolved, logically, so the reader believes. There is an unspoken contract with the readers that they will be treated fairly by the author and given an honest answer somewhere in the book. There is trust between the writer and the reader: You do not cheat. At the same time, you cannot be totally straightforward. After all, this is a mystery novel, so you have to sustain reader interest. I've found that it is often wise to make several mysteries hang upon one big one, say, a death in unusual circumstances. Or you know there is a body, but it has completely disappeared. How? Why? Or a body may be found, hidden in another grave. Either a modern one or a stone age tumulus that is being excavated. Again, how and why? Perhaps the body has red socks on—and nothing else.

All these "clues" help because as one after another of the minor puzzles is solved, they are steps to the main solution. No fudging is allowed; there must be a good, practical reason for the killer to dispose of the body in this way. Not just a mad murderer with a taste for a stone age burial mound and red socks!

You can see from all this that the mystery cannot just resolve itself;

it must have a solver or a detective, a person who is believable and who uses techniques that are real. You cannot pretend or invent techniques, especially as readers grow ever more sophisticated. What sort of a detective? Well, the days of amateur detectives, like Lord Peter Wimsey, are over—much enjoyed but finished—so as the writer, you have a choice: You can keep the action brisk and compressed so that your non-professional detective can clear up everything before the police get there, or you can have a pro, either a policeman or scientist of some sort, or a lawyer. If you have a police officer, it is advisable to read up on police procedure or get to know a police detective, because readers today are very knowledgeable. I like to have a police officer, myself, but if you do so, you must remember to make your detective story entertaining as well as accurate. The mystery novel is very elastic: It is not just a puzzle; it should also reflect society, its manners, and its problems. The spy story or the thriller can, to a certain extent, be a fairy story; the crime story never can.

The detective stories of the 30's and 40's tended to be puzzles, such as those solved by the New York detective Inspector Queen and his son Ellery. The Queen novels posed a problem and then demanded the reader solve it. To a certain extent, this was even the case with Hercule Poirot, as depicted by Agatha Christie, but she had an engaging way of winding the reader into her stories. To my mind, the modern detective story reads better if the plot does not depend on a cunning alibi.

All the same, it is still a puzzle story with which you want to tantalize readers before letting them see the truth. It's good if they can gradually work the problem out, bit by bit; but technically, I think it is much better, more satisfying, if readers come up with the answers by degrees, rather than in one great denouement—although a final thunderbolt, if you can manage it, is splendid.

Because a mystery story raises questions, you have to be careful of your technique. To my mind it is vital to know the end before you write the beginning, although within that framework, I like the plot to grow toward its ending. I would feel it dishonest to begin with one murderer in mind, but then to change it halfway through; that would mean that any killer would do, provided there was a surprise. Not everyone would agree with me there. Some writers might consider this too strict a rule.

In my crime novels, the detective is the questioner, so I give him (or her) the focus, and tell the story mainly through his or her eyes. You may prefer to have the narrator an innocent before whose eyes the story unfolds, but make sure that such a story is told in the first person. There are drawbacks here: Since the narrator cannot be everywhere, he or she will have to rely on reported evidence. The first-person narrator has been suspect ever since Agatha Christie, in *The Murder of Roger Ackroyd*, used the device in a devastating way. No writer has dared to do it quite like that again.

It is probably wiser to avoid too crowded a Dickensian scene, but you do need some interesting secondary characters among whom to hide the victim and the killer. A surprise victim is always a welcome touch, so the reader can say: "I didn't expect *that* one to get killed!" But secondary and minor characters have other uses besides providing handy victims. They can help explain plot points and push the action forward. And I feel that they must have real reason for being a part of the plot, indeed for being in the novel at all. I even like a walk-on character to have a real reason for being in the story. You can't always do this, of course, and part of being a writer is inventing a likable, amusing character, so don't deny yourself this pleasure. I have to admit that I have several times invented a cat or a dog as a character for my amusement. Of course, I try to give them some plot point: They can find a body or bite the killer. Others could do that, of course, but the animals are my present to myself.

Minor characters can present a problem: You as the writer can get too interested in them and upset the balance of the plot. Take, for example, this imaginary plot: A woman newspaper editor is stabbed in her office. The murderer is, in fact, her estranged husband, but the false clues suggest it is a political killing, since she is famous for her right-wing views and has quarreled with an MP with whom she has had an affair. He is suspect number one. But the dead woman's daughter is a fashion editor for another paper and might interest the writer who enjoys using models, photographers, and eccentric couturiers as characters. Great fun, but they are not the main plot. You may be tempted to develop this aspect of the plot, but you should control it. Though it may be amusing, plotwise it is a dead end. Go back to the mainstream—the daughter and her relationship with her father and mother. It is a family murder, not a political one.

Very important, too, is the setting of the crime. Make it as real as possible and know your way around it. There was a period when maps were popular, and they do make the scene concrete, but the mystery novel has widened its territory and no longer is confined to, say, a country house or a college. Even the books about the Oxford colleges where Inspector Morse works do not provide a map, as did the Oxford book introducing Inspector Appleby of long ago. Today the emphasis is more psychological and scientific, rather than on alibis and maps.

Finally, there are a few very practical points that you should remember as you write your mystery:

If you find it hard to remember names, you should write them down as soon as you have the characters on the scene; keep a handwritten list at your elbow. Also, be sure to avoid names that are too much alike or begin with the same letter.

If you have a character who is part of a series—for example, the detective with his or her friends, secretaries, and assistants—it is wise to keep a list with a short biography for each one!

All this is a gospel of perfection, but I must confess that I have just written the first chapter of a novel in which a character meant to be secondary has walked onto the page with such energy that I know he means to stay there.

❏ 43

You Don't Need a History Degree to Write Historical Fiction

By Cynthia Bass

READERS WHO LOVE HISTORICAL NOVELS DEMAND MORE FROM THEIR fiction than good stories with compelling characters. They hope to relive the past. They expect accuracy; they value atmosphere; they search for interesting bits of information. They want to look up from a book and say, "I didn't know they had pretzels during the Civil War!"

For writers of historical fiction, this means that we need to know some real history. But even if your primary memory of high school history is a lot of naps, don't panic! It isn't necessary to know everything. There are several easy ways to get all the information you need to help you write a detailed, informative, high-quality historical novel— without a history degree. Here's how you do it:

Master the basic facts

The first (and most difficult) step is to learn the major facts about your time period. For this you need some trustworthy *secondary sources.*

A "secondary source" is a history or biography written by an expert in the field. *Battle Cry of Freedom*, by James MacPherson, and *A Distant Mirror*, by Barbara Tuchman, are examples of excellent secondary sources. Libraries and bookstores are full of choices for every conceivable time and place.

A good secondary source uses information that is cited, either in footnotes or annotations in the back of the book. There also should be a bibliography, with references to other sources. Footnotes and a bibliography are of crucial importance: They show that the author is not just presenting a partisan viewpoint without any serious research. Also, they're useful in helping you locate further research materials.

I use three simple tests to judge the "trustworthiness" of a secondary source. First, is it cited by *other* secondary sources? This practice is known as cross-citing. If a book is not cross-cited, it's unlikely that its interpretation can be used with confidence.

My second test for trustworthiness is the publisher. Reputable publishers may seem to publish a lot of bad fiction, but they don't, as a rule, bring out bad history.

Example: Recently, when researching my new novel about German physicists and the atomic bomb, I found a book at my library that argued that England, not Nazi Germany, started World War II. In view of the fact that WW II began when the Nazis invaded Poland, this assertion sounded suspicious. So I checked the publisher and found no listing for them. Later, I found out they're known for publishing pro-Nazi books—definitely the kind of sources to avoid.

My third test is the writing. Trustworthy secondary sources are seldom exciting, and they're often even a little boring, because what's important to the writers is the information, not the style.

How do you tell when you've read enough secondary sources? When you feel that you know what happened during the time period you've chosen. This may take one book or a dozen, but the day will come that your period holds no more surprises. Now for the fun: the details.

Making the jump from overview to close-up

A historical novel is successful if it makes you feel you're living in the period. As a writer, you can achieve that success by using *primary sources*. A "primary source" is a source created in the past for the use of the people living at that time. Primary sources have the immediacy and freshness of something intended for daily consumption, and using them extensively gives your novel the specificity of real life. Three primary sources are invaluable for historical novelists:

1. *Newspapers and magazines*

Newspapers and magazines tell a lot about a society. Don't read *only* the news, though; read advertisements, letters to the editor, "human interest" stories and help-wanted ads. You're not so much seeking information as immersion. You want to know what everyday life was like.

Consider advertisements. When researching my second novel,

Maiden Voyage, which took place on the *Titanic*, I checked out a copy of *Collier's*—a once-popular, now defunct magazine—in which I saw an ad for catsup. This ad opened up my main character's world for me. It showed me that 1912 was an era of mass production and that people splurged on non-essential items. On the label I saw a "pure food" stamp and a "wholesomeness rating." This meant people were worried about food purity and contamination of manufactured goods. Then I read the copy. Catsup is being touted as "good for the female figure—high in nutrients, promotes slimness." Oh, my—they were already pushing weight loss. All this from one ad!

Besides regular advertisements, check the help-wanted ads, to learn not only what jobs were available and how much they paid, but as a microcosm of a society. For example, in 1912, help-wanted ads in Boston routinely excluded Irish applicants; in New York, Italians; in Seattle, Chinese. They also describe 60-hour work weeks, mandatory church attendance, and minimum height and weight requirements (these positions often required some heavy lifting). References to any of this will do wonders for the authenticity of your fiction.

Letters to the editor and special-interest articles are also gold mines. They tell you what people of the time thought important. For example, most letters to the editor in Great Britain on the eve of the First World War concern Ireland, not Germany, while in France, special-interest articles all center on a murder trial. Only in Germany and Austria do the letters and articles mention a possible war.

2. Fiction

Reading fiction published in your time period will help you discover how people of the time spoke. One of the worst mood-breakers in fiction is the anachronism. It's also one of the most obvious; even the most non-historically-minded reader will catch these goofs (the word "goof," by the way, is from World War I; don't have a lady-in-waiting for Catherine the Great say it!).

Another benefit of reading fiction of your time period is that you sometimes discover expressions you think of as "modern" have been around for a long time. I never realized that use of the verb "make" to mean "seduce" was a time-honored practice till I saw it in Balzac's *Cousin Bette*.

Read both "good" and "popular" fiction from the period—good because it shows standards of the day, popular because it shows how people actually spoke in everyday life.

3. *Letters and diaries*

Letters and diaries are incredibly rich sources for the details of daily existence—food, fashion, health, family, love. Because letters and diaries were written for private consumption, they often brought up topics not seen as fit to print. Thus, they can provide you with an intimate knowledge of your period never found in the more self-conscious primary sources mentioned above.

Example: One of the narrators of my first novel, *Sherman's March*, is General Sherman ("War is hell") himself. At the outset, I knew quite a bit about his Civil War exploits: the burning of Atlanta, the March to the Sea. What I didn't know (and never would have dreamed) is how many female "acquaintances" he had in the South. I learned about these women from his letters, and I used the information to write a chapter in which he meets an old lover.

How far back should you go?

Your research should go further back than the main time period of your novel, because characters often remember events from their pasts, and you need to know what those memories are. For a main character, I would go back to when he or she is approximately three years old. For instance, all the action in *Sherman's March* takes place during the three weeks of Sherman's March to the Sea (1864); still, I had to go back to 1823 (when Sherman was three years old) to know what sort of memories he had, so that his reveries would sound like those of a real person.

And don't think you can avoid this research by creating only young characters! If *any* character is older, you need insight into his memories, too. One of the most boring clichés in fiction is the generic geezer, spouting off about the good old days, without giving a concrete example of those good old days, because the author stopped her research too soon. If a character reminisces about her teen-age years during the Great Depression, don't have her remember a romantic dance with a long-lost beau; have her remember dancing to "Tangerine."

When can you stop the research and start writing?

This one's easy. You stop when the period you've been researching feels real to you. And as soon as you reach this point, make sure you *do* stop: Don't use endless research as an excuse not to write your novel. Find some reliable secondary material and a variety of primary sources; learn what you can; gain confidence; and then start writing.

One final word about research: Research can make history come alive, but it can't by itself do the same for your characters. That's because the essence of character isn't the facts of the past but your characters' passions as they respond to that past. So make sure to fill your head with facts before you start, but make doubly sure that your heart goes into your fiction.

❏ 44

SELLING SPECULATIVE FICTION

BY LESLIE WHAT

THE GENRE KNOWN AS SCIENCE FICTION AND FANTASY IS MUCH MORE than rocket ships, dystopias, and elves. This might explain why some critics and writers prefer to call it "the literature of the fantastic" or "speculative fiction"—SF for short. SF magazines and anthologies publish a mix of unclassifiable fiction, magical realism, urban fantasy, alternative history, high fantasy, and hard science fiction. No matter what you call it, speculative fiction is a great field for the new writer.

Editors actively seek out talent: They attend conventions; make virtual appearances on-line; teach at workshops or conferences; and read unsolicited submissions from unknowns—unceremoniously known as "slush." Leading SF magazines publish only ten to twelve of every thousand manuscripts submitted; fortunately for new writers, every editor is a reader hoping to find precious words in that mountain of paper. And there are ways to make your work stand out, at least long enough for the editor to notice your name.

My first professionally published story, "King for a Day" (*Asimov's Science Fiction*), postulated that there were so many Elvis impersonators in Hell, the *real* Elvis had a hard time finding work. In my satiric vision of the afterlife, John Lennon waited in line to see himself. The acceptance was a bit of a surprise, because I hadn't been sure if "King for a Day" was *really* science fiction. But I was sure about the important things: The story was fast-paced, original, and lively; the manuscript proofread to the best of my ability. The rest was up to the editor.

Though the creative side may be in the writing, selling fiction is business, and in business, deals can be broken by a clumsy introduction. Take time to come up with a title that creates interest and excitement in the story. A knockout line from the text might do, or a portion of a quote that has always intrigued you. Titles can mirror the concept of the story. "Designated Hater" (*Magazine of Fantasy and Science Fic-*

216

tion) took its cue from the American League, but twisted the rules for the sake of the plot. "The Goddess is Alive, and Well, Living in New York City" (*Asimov's Science Fiction*) reworked a bumper sticker I saw on pre-1980 VW vans. Titles work best when they reflect both the tone and language of the story. "A Dark Fire, Burning from Within" (*Realms of Fantasy*) tells the reader not to expect one of my lighthearted pieces, while "How to Feed Your Inner Troll" (*Asimov's Science Fiction*) suggests not only an encounter with a magical being, but a satire of pop psychology.

Think of the opening paragraphs of your story as an introduction to a prospective employer. Picture yourself standing face to face with the employer while you mumble on for pages before getting down to what you both mean and want to say. Not the most effective use of time. Rambling openings can keep an editor from reading to the end and giving your work the attention it deserves.

Analyze your beginning carefully. It should:

1) Evoke a sense of time and place. A reader expects a story to take place in the here and now, unless you say otherwise. If your story is set in the Italy of 2507, mention this at the start, or offer enough clues to prevent the revelation from coming as a surprise on page six. Clues can take the form of metaphor, dialogue, or straight narrative description.

2) Establish tone and authority through voice, word choice, theme, imagery, and detail. Prove that you are in control of your story by a correct use of grammar and a healthy respect for the conventions of language.

3) Introduce major character(s), hint at ages, gender, socioeconomic background. This can be the barest introduction, to be elaborated upon throughout the story.

4) Foreshadow major story problems and introduce minor ones.

A beginning that accomplishes as much of the above as possible will increase its chances for publication. Here's an example from "Smelling of Earth, Dreaming of Sky" (*Asimov's Science Fiction*):

Sunday at church:
In his sermon, the minister preaches that the first man was made from earth.

"Adamah," he begins, "common clay begat Adam, common man." Adam of
earth, who thought he knew better than God and was forced to leave Paradise.
    "We all—every one of us—came from that very clay," says the minister.
"With this humble beginning, the Bible teaches that not one of us is better
than the rest."
    I groan, disagreeing. The minister must be referring to the commoners.

This opening makes clear who the story is about, and also hints at
possible conflicts. Each new piece of information builds on what has
previously been established. The next few paragraphs reveal that the
narrator is an angel, sent back to perform one good deed. The somber
tone of the writing, the deliberate use of present tense to magnify the
feelings of a character who is trapped, the angry voice coupled with the
spare choice of details, suggest that she will be unlikely to fulfill her
mission. (Note: The title came from an earlier work that another editor
had rejected with a note, "Title great, story stinks." The truth hurt, but
he was right. I kept the title, tossed the story, then wrote a better one in
its place.)

Selling wonders

Gardner Dozois, the editor of *Asimov's Science Fiction,* compares
himself to P. T. Barnum, who sold wonders and marvels for money. "If
there's no wonder or marvel in the content of your story," says Dozois,
"then it's going to be a hard sell."
    Editors want stories that are interesting and entertaining, unique, and
logically consistent in their own way. Read what is being published
now for clues of where to send your work. Magazines like *Analog* and
Science Fiction Age are unlikely to publish a "Gnomes on Vacation"
story, while *Realms of Fantasy* might not be the first place to send a
story featuring "Physicists Who Save Themselves Before the Sun Goes
Nova." Of course, there are always exceptions.
    Instead of trying to clone what you read, view ideas through a prism
to see them in a different light. For "Mothers' Day," (*Realms of Fantasy*), I took the legend of the Pied Piper one step further. What would
it *really* be like, I wondered, for a man stuck inside a cave with all those
children? The resulting story was a sympathetic yet satiric look at a
man living with what he *never* bargained for.
    It's fine to reuse a premise if you do something different. You must
take the premise where no writer has gone before. A story cannot have

time travel or virtual reality as the only focus; it must use the idea as background setting, what editor Dozois calls "The furniture of plot." In "Compatibility Clause" (*Fantasy and Science Fiction*), I borrowed heavily from William Gibson, my experiences and observations at video arcades, and themes of married life. The story is about a wife (Mrs. Claus on the night before Christmas), desperate to communicate with her husband, a busy man with an addictive personality. I combined real-life tensions with a fantasy world and a science fiction gimmick to create a story.

Hard sells

You might have trouble selling what is known as a *Translation Story:* the Western set on Alpha IV, with blasters instead of shotguns, and spaceships instead of horses. As a general rule, the fantastic or scientific idea must be an integral part of the story and not put there just to set up your theme or add interest to the plot.

Other hard sells include the surprise ending: the *deus ex machina*, where the resolution occurs as if by the hand of God; the story set in virtual reality (unbeknownst to the characters, who are revealed as imaginary only at story's end); stories that take place in dreams; Adam and Eve at the end of the world; stories with joke endings. If you've written one of the above, send it out anyway, but if you get back form letter rejections, you might try changing tactics. You will not be able to sell stories based on Star Trek or any licensed characters, or stories that are spin-offs from trademarked games.

Stories about ghosts are said to be a hard sell, though I've sold several. The key to selling a ghost story might be figuring out what the ghost represents on a symbolic level, as well as knowing why the ghost is needed in the story. Little-known legends reinterpreted through your unique vision can be a source of ideas for new and inventive ghost stories. "Beside the Well" (*Bending the Landscape: Fantasy,* White Wolf Publishing 1997) was based on a Korean folk tale, but with a few unexpected twists that fit the theme of the anthology. "Clinging to a Thread" (*Fantasy and Science Fiction*) presented ghosts through their physical connection to the objects they once touched. Vampires have been done to death (sorry), but an inventive writer might come up with a way to make them fresh.

Your story must be about the day, the person, and the event—not just any day or any person who happens to be trapped in some fascinating scenario. If another person could just as easily replace the central character, if the angel is merely symbolic and could be replaced by a Western Union man, if the effect of time travel is the same as if your character just got out of jail, you'd better rethink what you've written.

Why this person? Why today? Why is THIS fantastic element necessary? In general, these questions must be answered for the story to sell. Otherwise, let yourself go wild. In the field of speculative fiction, stories are limited only by imagination.

DEFINITIONS

Cyberpunk: Combines street-smart punks with the hi-tech world of computers and neural networks.

Hard Science Fiction: SF where the scientific idea is central to the plot, conflict, and resolution in the story.

Urban Fantasy/Contemporary Fantasy: Magic in modern-day settings, also called "North American magical realism."

High Fantasy: Often set in feudal or medieval societies where magical beings reside.

Alternative History: Looking at how an alternative past would change the present.

WEB SITES OF INTEREST

1) <http://critique.org/users/critters> On-line workshop, support, critiques, advice.

2) <http://www.sff.net> Author newsgroups, marketing information, and a private on-line critique group.

3) <http://www.speculations.com> News of open anthologies, magazine guidelines.

❏ 45

How To Generate
Suspense in Fiction

By John Lutz

Suspense in fiction has been defined as the reader wondering what happens next. But for the writer, it has to be something much more than that, something better understood, and something the writer knows how to generate.

One way to help understand suspense is to realize that it is not simply curiosity. Curiosity keeps the readers turning pages by holding out the promise that they will eventually get answers to questions. In a classic puzzle mystery novel, this might happen in the last chapter, where the detective gathers all the characters in the drawing room and explains how the victim was found shot to death in his locked study without a gun being present and with no sound being heard, and who the murderer is and why. All loose ends will be tightly knotted, and the reader will be satisfied. But a good mystery, like any good novel or short story, requires something more—suspense.

Suspense is emotional. It is the reader experiencing vicariously what the story's main character is experiencing. Of course, this requires the reader to identify with the character. When the character feels emotional tumult, so on a certain level will the reader, and when the character suffers physical pain, maybe mild, sympathetic, and unconscious pain will cause the reader's grip to tighten on the book cover.

The first challenge for the suspense writer is to get the reader to identify with your character. You do this by giving the reader more than merely a description of the character and his surroundings. You want the reader—as soon as possible—to think, *Yes, I understand, I've been there, I know exactly how that feels.* The writer has to find common denominators in order to engage reader emotion.

Here's an example from my short story "High Stakes" (originally published in *The Saint Mystery Magazine*):

221

Ernie followed the bellhop into the crummy room at the Hayes Hotel, was shown the decrepit bathroom with its cracked porcelain, the black-and-white TV with its rolling picture. The bellhop, who was a teenager with a pimply complexion, smiled and waited. Ernie tipped him a dollar, which, considering that Ernie had no luggage other than the overnight bag he carried himself, seemed adequate. The bellhop sneered at him and left.

While all of us haven't checked into that kind of a hotel under those circumstances, most of us have traveled less than first-class and encountered a disdainful bellhop. The important points here are that the reader learns something about Ernie and his situation, and on a certain level, identifies with him and is beginning to feel what Ernie feels.

A story that relies mainly on clues and curiosity sends a different sort of initial signal to the reader. Compare the above with the opening paragraph of my puzzle mystery "Shock," that portends curiosity rather than suspense (from the 1996 anthology *Unusual Suspects*):

It was odd the way people in shock had a protective, calming armor against emotion, almost like a powerful deadening drug. And this was a shocking scene. Every lamp in the beach cottage blazed, illuminating detail and making it all the more vivid, the deeper to be etched into memory.

No emotion here—not even the introduction of the main character— but mostly an objective observation leading to the second paragraph in which the details referred to above are described for the reader to ponder. Curiosity, not suspense, which will come later. In this story, the reader primarily wants to learn more facts and what they mean; in "High Stakes," the reader mainly wants to learn more about Ernie and his predicament. The writer, of course, knows what the reader doesn't, and decides how the reader should feel about Ernie. In "Shock," I wanted the reader to feel sympathy for Ernie, to see him as one of life's underdogs:

He had spent most of his forty years in the starkly poor neighborhood of his birth; and if he wasn't the smartest guy around, he did possess a kind of gritty cunning that had enabled him to make his own erratic way in the world. And he had instinct, hunches, that led to backing the right horse sometimes, or playing the right card sometimes. Sometimes. He got by, anyway. Getting by was Ernie's game, and he just about broke even. He was not so much a winner as a survivor. There were people who resented even that.

No suspense here yet, but the groundwork is being laid. I wanted the reader's sympathy for Ernie because he's going to be forced out onto a high ledge by thugs, the window closed and locked behind him, his way to the left and right blocked, his only available direction down, and Ernie without wings. If the reader already feels sorry for Ernie, the reader is out on that ledge with him, vicariously feeling his terror. Paragraphs of detailed description aren't the slightest substitute for that kind of empathy:

> Vertigo hit him with hammer force. Twelve stories seemed like twelve miles. He could see the tops of foreshortened street lights, a few toylike cars turning at the intersection. His mind whirled, his head swam with terror. The ledge he was on seemed only a few inches wide and was barely visible, almost behind him, from his precarious point of view. His legs quivered weakly; his boots seemed to become detached from them, seemed to be stiff, awkward creatures with their own will that might betray him and send him plunging to his death. He could see so far—as if he were flying. Ernie clenched his eyes shut. He didn't let himself imagine what happened to flesh and bone when it met the pavement after a twelve-story drop.

Of course curiosity plays a role in this. Readers wonder how Ernie's going to get out of his predicament. But that isn't the primary hook here. Readers want Ernie to get safely off that ledge because they felt sorry for him even before he found himself in danger—and that's what places readers on the ledge, trembling in Ernie's boots.

Once you've established the essential character-reader identification, there are several techniques for generating and heightening suspense. One of them is the ticking clock: Your character has a time limit and must accomplish something difficult and dangerous, maybe something that means life or death, and time is fast ticking away. That's the situation in my *Alfred Hitchcock's Mystery Magazine* story, "Dead Man," when the main character realizes that the heavy door of an airtight vault has just swung shut behind him, sealing him inside with little hope of rescue:

> Masters had never in his life panicked, but never in his life had he had a harder time fighting panic than now. No one was due in the house until tomorrow morning, when Margaret would arrive to prepare breakfast, and the vault was completely airtight and escape-proof. Add to that the fact that someone had obviously set out to imprison him in the vault until he suffocated, and his chances of breathing fresh air again were negligible. Always one to face things squarely and calculate instantly, accurately, and realistically where he stood, Masters arrived at the conclusion that he was a dead man.

The goal here is to put the reader in the vault with Masters while time and oxygen dwindle. Here suspense must transcend mere curiosity. *How* Masters escapes shouldn't be more important to the reader than *if* he will somehow find a way to defy time and the odds against him.

Another way to create suspense is to let the reader know something your character doesn't suspect. Perhaps a time bomb can be ticking away in a minivan full of children, while the car-pooling mother drives, happy and unaware, toward a school. In this situation, we've combined the character's unawareness of impending danger along with the (this time literally) ticking clock. At this point, the reader should already care about your character and in addition will be concerned for the lives of the children and be drawn deeper into the story. Somewhere in the back of the reader's mind should be silent screaming: *Stop the van! Take the children and run!* In the best of circumstances for the writer, that's what comes of letting the reader know more than your character.

In my short story "Hector Gomez Provides," published in *Mike Shayne's Mystery Magazine*, a poor man, who earns his money diving from a high cliff into a tiny, rocky cove for the amusement of rich tourists, has been drugged but doesn't know it (though the reader does). His survival depends on his precise timing of an oncoming wave so the water in the cove is momentarily deep enough for him to knife into it safely and not be bashed to death on the rocks:

> At last, Hector saw an oncoming swell that would provide enough water when it entered the cove. He watched it approach, a rolling, glittering vast hill of water, shot with sunlight as if it contained thousands of diamonds.
> It seemed to take forever to reach the point Hector had chosen, where he knew it would begin to curl into a green, sloping wall for its assault on the cove. The point from where it would enter the cove only a moment before the plummeting Hector sliced into its cool depths.

The reader should of course be standing on the high, rocky ledge with Hector, not lounging safely below as a spectator.

And the reader must dive along with Hector:

> Hector didn't want to dive . . . But his right arm was already raised, signaling the turistas, all watching through admiring, apprehensive eyes. Many were peering through camera lenses, hastily setting F-stops and shutter speeds, not admitting to the secret desire to record on film a brave man's death. It was too late for Hector to turn away with self respect.
> As soon as he launched himself into the air . . .

If the writer's done a good job, maybe the reader will unconsciously catch his or her breath here.

Now let's combine the ticking clock with another way of creating suspense—atmosphere.

In this instance the reader knows that a killer lurks in the apartment of an unsuspecting woman arriving home. This isn't just any woman; the reader has gotten to know and like her. And it isn't just any apartment building, but an ornate, converted 19th-century bordello where long ago a grisly murder occurred and a similar murder might be committed tonight. Its floors and doors creak, and its walls are in need of paint and marked with ominous graffiti. The reader wants to know, needs to know, whether the woman will enter her apartment and be killed. Her key is already in her hand.

Then she's stopped in the dim hall by a neighbor who has a crush on her and wants her to go back outside with him and walk around the corner for a cup of coffee. The woman has always been a little leery of this guy and is undecided. We know he's nothing more than a love-struck, amiable pest, but she doesn't know that. Will she go back outside with the neighbor instead of inside to her apartment and almost certain death? Everything rides on what is to her a trivial decision. And if the reader cares enough about the woman to be standing in her shoes, we have suspense, generated not only by atmosphere, but by the fact that we're aware of something terrible and momentous that she doesn't suspect.

There are plenty of variations and combinations of these techniques used to create suspense in mystery stories, from Poe's "Pit and the Pendulum," in which with each repetitive swing a blade drops closer to a bound man's exposed throat, to a single woman living an outwardly normal life day after day with a new roommate she doesn't suspect (but the reader knows) is a psychotic killer.

The secret is to reach beyond curiosity and engage the reader's emotions. That's not always an easy thing for a writer to do, but armed with some easily obtained knowledge, it's certainly possible. The question everyone serious about writing good fiction has to ask him or herself is whether the effect is worth the effort.

There should be no suspense involved in waiting for the answer.

❏ 46

THE SUPPORTING CAST
IN YOUR NOVEL

BY BARBARA DELINSKY

WHEN I BEGAN FICTION WRITING, I DIDN'T HAVE TO THINK ABOUT minor characters and their role in a novel. In those days, I wrote 200-page novellas that were too short to allow for minor characters. That changed with my shift into full-length fiction. Suddenly my books were twice as long and twice as deep. They definitely called for a cast of characters that went beyond two or three stars.

So I began adding secondary characters. I had no formal training in creative writing, but common sense told me that the purpose of a supporting cast was to flesh out my hero and heroine by giving them lives independent of one another. To that end, I created parents who had raised those main characters, and siblings with whom they had grown up and competed. I created friends who shaped their early adulthood and former spouses who left them burned. I created children who affected not only their present, but their future.

In doing this, I instinctively applied the same rule that trial-and-error had taught me about fiction writing in general: Just as every scene has to have a purpose, so every character, no matter how minor, has to have a purpose. Tossing in a character solely for the sake of making a book longer is pure filler and unacceptable. Readers see through this ploy in no time flat—and feel cheated.

Looking back, now that I have over sixty full-length books to my credit, I can see method to my madness in creating a supporting cast. Minor characters add richness to a novel, no doubt about that, but there are dozens of ways in which they do so. For simplification's sake, I offer three general categories that describe what the supporting cast contributes: depth, breadth, and movement.

Let's start with movement, since it is the most obvious of the three. Minor characters are often introduced to propel a plot forward, and in

226

this role, they serve a specific purpose: to provide information or create a complication; as a sounding board, to help a major character work through an emotional dilemma; as an all-out villain whose evil deeds must be answered.

Plots in which minor characters have a role are most often action-driven. Mysteries fall into this category, as do legal thrillers, westerns, science fiction. Of my own recent books, *A Woman's Place* does so, too.

In this first-person novel, the main character, Claire Rafael, is a successful businesswoman whose husband, Dennis, sues her for divorce, demanding sole custody of the children, possession of their house, and huge alimony. Much of the story centers on Claire's fight to regain custody of the children.

Most of the minor characters in *A Woman's Place* are tools for moving the plot forward. Carmen Niko, Claire's lawyer, sets the legal wheels in motion. Judge E. Warren Selwey hears the case and makes decisions that have a direct impact on the plot. Dean Jenovitz is the psychologist whose role it is to interview Claire and Dennis, gain insight into them, and make a custody recommendation to the court. Phoebe Lowe, as Dennis's lawyer and potential significant other, is responsible for many of Dennis's actions, to which Claire must then respond.

A Woman's Place is more action-driven than some of my other novels. In *Three Wishes*, which I wrote immediately after it, minor characters serve a very different purpose: They bring breadth to the novel.

By breadth, I mean color—color, atmosphere, backdrop. *Three Wishes* is set in a small town in northern Vermont that itself is a vital part of the story. How to bring out the flavor of this oh-so-crucial-to-the-plot small town? Minor characters. They create the environment in which the major characters operate. Flash O'Neill, who owns the diner where the heroine works, adds the twist of modern chic that sets the tone of the town. Various regulars at the diner describe the businesses that keep the town solvent. Emma McGreevy, Eliot Bonner, and Earl Yarum represent the traditional, old-time triumvirate of power. Dotty Hale is the obligatory gossip; Julia Dean is the newcomer who illustrates the town's capacity for warmth; Verity Greene is the bohemian who pushes the town's limits of trust.

These minor characters add breadth to *Three Wishes* in the form of a physical environment, but minor characters can also add emotional breadth. This often takes the form of a sub-plot or two that echo—and hence reinforce—the major theme of the book.

My novel *Coast Road* is the best example I can give of the emotional element. It is the story of Rachel and Jack, artist and architect respectively, who have been divorced for six years, after ten years of marriage. When Rachel is in a near fatal accident, Jack receives a middle-of-the-night call that brings him to her bedside and puts him in charge of their two teenage daughters. During sixteen days of trying to coax Rachel out of her coma, he becomes immersed in an in-depth analysis of not only of his marriage, but of parenthood.

Loyalty—as in fighting for what matters most—emerges as a major theme in this examination. Loyalty is also the theme of several subplots driven by the supporting characters. Just as Jack comes to realize that he wasn't there emotionally for his wife during the later years of their marriage, he finds himself talking about loyalty with his fifteen-year-old daughter as she straddles a social crossroad; with his thirteen-year-old daughter, as she cares for her sick cat; and with his ex-wife's best friend as she tries to explain the deepest meaning of friendship. This echoing of the theme among the supporting cast helps Jack understand and resolve his own larger issue of loyalty.

Coast Road is also a good example of the third type of contribution minor characters can make—depth. Depth is crucial to novels like this that are heavily emotional and largely character-driven. The starring players in such novels must be three-dimensional. The supporting cast is instrumental in making them so.

Each supporting cast member is chosen to illuminate some aspect of the life or personality of a major character. In the case of family members, the illumination has to do with the passage of time. Family members share a history with the major character. Their thoughts and personalities help explain the "why" of the main character's behavior. They offer glimpses of the main character in childhood, adolescence, adulthood, and serve as a mechanism that allows the writer to reach into the past or imagine the future.

But depth has another dimension as well. Here, minor characters help round out a picture of the major characters in the present tense. These would be friends, neighbors, colleagues—all of whom, through words, action, or mere presence, say something about who and what the main character is as the story unfolds.

Again, *Coast Road* is an apt illustration. The female lead lies comatose for nine-tenths of the book. How, then, is her voice heard? This was the challenge I set for myself in writing the book. The answer? Through the supporting cast. Rachel may lie in a coma, but she remains the main character through a depth offered by her daughters, her best friend, her book group, her mother, and, yes, the husband she divorced six years before.

One of the questions I'm most frequently asked is whether I create the plot before the characters, or vice versa. A natural follow-up to that question is whether star players are created before the supporting cast. My answer to both questions is the same: It depends on the novel. The general assumption would be that major characters are created first, and minor characters are added as needed, rather like salt and pepper, for flavor; yes, this is what happens most often. But there are exceptions. I recently finished writing a book with another small-town setting, and I actually had half a dozen members of the supporting cast already chosen, while I was still grappling with the major theme of the book and, hence, the identity of the stars.

Neither way is right or wrong. What *is* wrong is if a writer gets so hung up on which should come first that he or she is stalled and can't write at all!

A note here on point of view. Some very successful writers brain-hop, relating the innermost thoughts of even the most peripheral minor character. I am uncomfortable doing that. For one thing, I like to write an entire scene from one point of view, that of the character with the most at stake emotionally. For another, I think that introducing so many diverse—and often irrelevant—elements dilutes the effectiveness of the emotions. Since my novels have become known for their emotional impact, this method is working for me. The bottom line is that you must think about what the strength of your book will be, and make point-of-view decisions accordingly.

Making the wrong point-of-view decision is but one of several dangers I would caution you against, where the supporting cast is concerned.

Another is introducing the supporting cast at the outset of the book, before you introduce a main character or two. Readers can be like ducklings. They will imprint on the first character they meet. If that character is a peripheral one, there will be confusion and a delay in their relating to the main character. Too long a delay, and the reader becomes detached emotionally, closes the book, and is lost.

Similarly, if the supporting cast is so much more likable than the leading players that readers don't care about the leading players, they won't read on, you've lost them. If part of your plot makes the good guys look bad for a while, that's fine, but keep in mind that you walk a tightrope. The reader has to care what happens. If your supporting cast can make the reader care enough to keep reading until the major characters pick up the ball, your problem is solved.

Conversely, a minor character who is overly loud, bad, quirky or glaring may divert the reader's attention from the flow of the plot. I call this the "cauliflower breast" issue, named after a love scene I once read, a beautifully lyrical piece in which the author suddenly likened the heroine's breast to cauliflower. That stopped me short, ice water on any passion I might have imagined. Jarring minor characters can have the same effect. Keep in mind that every minor character must have a role in supporting the major characters. If the jarring has a definite purpose, it may work. If, however, you have simply created a wonderfully weird minor player on the spur of the moment, think twice about it. Such a player may drag the reader too far afield, and might best be saved for its own starring role.

Those caveats aside, I can't stress strongly enough the positive role that the supporting cast can play. Alone, a major character is like the right hand picking out single notes on a piano. The notes may have rhythm and a tune; in the hands of a maestro, they may even have feeling and heart. But the tune remains largely one-dimensional until a second player, the left hand, joins in. When that left hand picks out single notes of a complementary theme, you have a pleasant duet. Add chords by either or both hands, and you have a full-bodied song. The supporting cast in a novel supply the notes in those chords. They shouldn't overpower, jar, or bore. Used to their fullest, they turn a song into a song that is beautiful, meaningful, and memorable.

❏ 47

Writing the Supernatural Novel

By Elizabeth Hand

I'VE ALWAYS THOUGHT THAT THE OLDEST PROFESSION WAS THAT OF storyteller—in particular, the teller of supernatural tales. A look at the cave paintings in France or Spain will show you how far back our hunger for the fantastic goes: men with the heads of beasts, figures crouching in the darkness, skulls and shadows and unblinking eyes. Take a glance at the current bestseller list, and you'll see that we haven't moved that far in the last twenty thousand years. Books by Anne Rice, Stephen King, Joyce Carol Oates, and Clive Barker, among many others, continue to feed our taste for dark wine and the perils of walking after midnight. But how to join the ranks of those whose novels explore the sinister side of town?

First, let me distinguish between supernatural fiction and its tough (and very successful) younger cousin, the horror novel. Horror novels depend heavily upon the mechanics of plot, less-than-subtle characterizations, and shock value—what Stephen King calls "going for the gross-out." In spirit and execution, they aren't that different from the "penny dreadfuls" of a century ago, crude but effective entertainments that tend to have a short shelf life. Unlike more stylized works such as *Dracula, The Turn of the Screw* or *The Shining,* most horror novels lose their ability to chill the second time around—they just don't stand up to rereading. As Edmund Wilson put it, "The only horror in these fictions is the horror of bad taste and bad art."

In the wake of Stephen King's success, the 1980's was a boom decade for horror fiction. But the market was flooded with so many books—and so many second-rate Stephen King imitators—that publishers and readers alike grew wary. With the dwindling reading public, it's far more difficult today to get a supernatural novel into print.

But the readers *are* there. And they're quite a sophisticated audience, which makes it both more challenging, and more fun, to write the sort

231

of novel that will appeal to someone who prefers *The Vampire Lestat* to the *The Creeping Bore*.

More than other genres, supernatural fiction is defined by *atmosphere* and *characterization*. By atmosphere, I mean the author's ability to evoke a mood or place viscerally by the use of original and elegant, almost *seductive* language. Science fiction and fantasy also rely heavily upon unusual settings and wordplay, often against a backdrop of other, imagined, worlds. But the most successful supernatural novels are set in *our* world. Their narrative tension, their very ability to frighten and transport us, derives from a conflict between the macabre and the mundane, between everyday reality and the threatening *other*—whether revenant, werewolf, or demonic godling—that seeks to destroy it.

The roots of supernatural fiction lie in the gothic romances of the eighteenth and nineteenth centuries with their gloomy settings, imperiled narrators and ghostly visitations. Even today these remain potent elements. Witness Anne Rice's vampire Lestat during a perambulation about prerevolutionary Paris:

> The cold seemed worse in Paris. It wasn't as clean as it had been in the mountains. The poor hovered in doorways, shivering and hungry, the crooked unpaved streets were thick with filthy slush. I saw barefoot children suffering before my very eyes, and more neglected corpses lying about than ever before. I was never so glad of the fur-lined cape as I was then. . . .

Much of the pleasure in Rice's work comes from her detailed evocations of real, yet highly romanticized, places: New Orleans, Paris, San Francisco. It pays to have firsthand knowledge of some desirable piece of occult real estate: Readers love the thrill of an offbeat setting, but they also like recognizing familiar landmarks. So, Stephen King has staked out rural Maine as his fictional backyard. The incomparable Shirley Jackson (whose classic "The Lottery" has chilled generations of readers) also turns to New England for the horrific doings in *The Haunting of Hill House*, *The Bird's Nest* and *We Have Always Lived in the Castle*. Daphne du Maurier's novella "Don't Look Now" gives us a tourist couple lost amidst the winding alleys of Venice, a notion creepy enough to have inspired Ian McEwan's nightmarish *The Comfort of Strangers*. Just about any setting will do, if you can imbue it with an aura of beauty and menace. My neo-gothic novel *Waking the Moon* takes place in that most pedestrian and bureaucratic of cities, Washington, D.C. But by counterpointing the city's workaday drabness with exotic descriptions of its lesser-known corners, I was able to suggest that an ancient evil might lurk near Capitol Hill:

> From the Shrine's bell tower came the first deep tones of the carillon calling the hour. I turned, and saw in the distance the domes and columns of the Capitol glimmering in the twilight, bone-colored, ghostly; and behind it still more ghostly buildings, their columned porticoes and marble arches all seeming to melt into the haze of green and violet darkness that descended upon them like sleep.

Style, of course, is a matter of taste and technique, and as with all writing, your most important tools should be a good thesaurus and dictionary. (Good taste in reading helps, but is probably not necessary.) A thesaurus can transform even the oldest and most unpalatable of chestnuts. "It was a dark and stormy night" becomes "Somber and tenebrous, the vespertine hour approached."

The danger, of course, is that such elevated diction easily falls into self-parody. But when well-done, it can quickly seduce the reader into believing in—well, in any number of marvelous things:

> Last night I dreamt that I woke to hear some strange, barely audible sound from downstairs—a kind of thin tintinnabulation, like those coloured-glass bird scarers which in my childhood were still sold for hanging up to glitter and tinkle in the garden breeze. I thought I went downstairs to the drawing room. The doors of the china cabinets were standing open, but all the figures were in their places—the Bow Liberty and Matrimony, the Four Seasons of Neale earthenware, the Reinecke girl on her cow; yes, and she herself—the Girl in a Swing. It was from these that the sound came, for they were weeping.

This is from Richard Adams's superb *The Girl in a Swing,* to my mind the best supernatural novel I've ever read. One of the problems in writing supernatural fiction stems from the fact that "ghost stories" are nearly always better when they are really *stories,* rather than full-length novels. Indeed, many of the classic works of dark fantasy—*The Turn of the Screw,* Charlotte Gilman's "The Yellow Wallpaper," Oliver Onions's "The Beckoning Fair One"—are novellas, a form that particularly suits the supernatural, but which is a hard sell: too short for publishers looking for meaty bestsellers, too long for a magazine market that thrives on the 5,000- to 7,000-word story. It is very difficult to sustain a high level of suspense for several hundred pages. Chapter after chapter of awful doings too often just become awful, with the "cliff-hanger" effect ultimately boring the reader.

Characterization is one way of avoiding this pitfall. If your central characters are intriguing, you don't need a constant stream of ghoulish doings to hold a reader's attention. Think of Anne Rice's Lestat, whose melancholy persona has seen him through several sequels. Or the callow student narrator of Donna Tartt's *The Secret History,* a novel which has only a hint of the supernatural about it, but which is more terrifying than any number of haunted houses:

> Does such a thing as "the fatal flaw," that showy dark crack running down the middle of a life, exist outside literature? I used to think it didn't. Now I think it does. And I think that mine is this: a morbid longing for the picturesque at all costs.

The Secret History is told in the first person, as are *The Girl in a Swing,* Rice's *Vampire Chronicles,* and *Waking the Moon.* In supernatural fiction, it is not enough that the protagonist compel our interest. Readers must also be able to truly *identify* with him, to experience his growing sense of unease as his familiar world gradually crumbles in the face of some dark intruder, be it spirit or succubus. That is why the first-person narrator is so prevalent in supernatural tales. It is also why most uncanny novels feature individuals whose very *normalcy* is what sets them apart from others. Like us, they do not believe in ghosts, which makes it all the worse when a ghost actually does appear.

But "normal" does not necessarily mean "dull." Richard Papen, the narrator of *The Secret History,* is drawn into a murderous conspiracy when his college friends seek to evoke Dionysos one drunken winter night. In *The Girl in a Swing,* Alan Desland is a middle-aged bachelor whose most distinguishing characteristic is his extraordinary *niceness*—until he becomes obsessed with the beautiful Kathe, who may be the incarnation of a goddess—or of a woman who murdered her own children. And in C. S. Lewis's classic *That Hideous Strength,* an entire peaceful English village is besieged by the forces of darkness.

As with all good fiction, it is important that the central characters are *changed* by their experiences, whether for good or ill. Lazy writers often use mere physical transformations to effect this change: The heroine becomes a vampire. Or the heroine is prevented from becoming a vampire. Or the heroine is killed. Far more eerie is the plight of the eponymous hero of Peter Ackroyd's terrifying *Hawksmoor,* a police detective who finds himself drawn into a series of cult murders that took place in London churches two hundred years before:

> Hawksmoor looked for relief from the darkness of wood, stone and metal but he could find none; and the silence of the church had once again descended as he sat down upon a small chair and covered his face. And he allowed it to grow dark.

While he is very much a twentieth-century man, Nicholas Hawksmoor's unwanted clairvoyance gives him a glimpse of horrors he is unable to forget, and forever alters his perception of the power of good and evil in the world and in his work.

In many ways, the intricacies of *plot* are less central to supernatural fiction than is *pacing* (another reason why short stories usually work better than novels). A careful balance must be achieved between scenes of the ordinary and the otherworldly. Usually, a writer alternates the two, with the balance gradually tipping in favor of the unreal: Think of Dracula moving from Transylvania to London, and bringing with him a miasma of palpable evil that slowly infects all around him. In *Waking the Moon,* my heroine's involvement with the supernatural parallels her love affair in the real world. However you choose to do it, don't let the magical elements overwhelm your story completely.

Especially, don't let the Big Supernatural Payoff come too *soon.* (The only thing worse that killing off all your werewolves fifty pages before the end is penning these dreadful words: IT WAS ALL A DREAM.) Think of your novel in musical terms: You wouldn't really want to listen to one Wagnerian aria after another, would you? Well, neither would you want to read page after page of mysterious knockings, stakes through the heart, and screams at midnight.

Finally, dare to be different. Does the world really need another vampire novel? How about a lamia instead? Or an evil tree? As always, it's a good idea to be well-read in your chosen genre, so that you don't waste time and ink reinventing Frankenstein's monster. In addition to the works mentioned above, there is a wealth of terrific short supernatural fiction that can teach as well as chill you. *Great Tales of Terror and the Supernatural* (edited by Herbert A. Wise and Phyllis Fraser) is perhaps the indispensable anthology. There are also collections by great writers such as Poe, Robert Aickman, John Collier, Edith Wharton, Isak Dinesen, Sheridan Le Fanu, M. R. James, and many, many others. Jack Sullivan has written two books that I refer to constantly: *Elegant Nightmares* and *Lost Souls,* classic studies of English ghost stories that can serve as a crash course on how to write elegant horror. These, along with Stephen King's nonfiction *Danse Macabre,* should put you well on your way to creating your own eldritch novel. Happy haunting!

❑ 48

STRESS-FREE TURKEYS
AND MURDER

BY ANNE GEORGE

A COUPLE OF THANKSGIVINGS AGO, WHEN I TOOK MY TURKEY FROM the freezer, I discovered a card attached to the yellow plastic netting. It proclaimed that this was a "stress-free turkey raised in the shade of pecan trees." Since I was about to do all sorts of terrible things to this bird, including stuffing and eating it, the fact that it had had a happy youth was hardly comforting. The card, instead of assuring me that the meat would be tender, turned the frozen lump in my kitchen sink into a turkey with a past.

I'm not crazy. I stuffed it, cooked it until the thermometer popped out, and served it on the turkey platter I bring out twice a year. We all enjoyed it.

But, oh, the power of words. As soon as I read the card, I rushed for my notebook and copied it down. And the "stress-free turkey" shows up several times in my novel *Murder Gets a Life*. It even gave me the name of one of the families, Turkett.

In the notebook I keep in my purse at all times, I jot down things that strike me as funny or unusual. Recently, three men, two from Bangladesh and one from Cincinnati, were trapped in the elevator in the huge iron statue of Vulcan that overlooks Birmingham, Alabama. I used the incident in my last book, but I put Mary Alice Tate Sullivan Nachman Crane, one of the sisters in my Southern Sisters Mystery series, in with them. Mary Alice is six feet tall, admits to weighing two hundred fifty pounds and, as her brother-in-law says, has the nerve of a bad tooth. She has also been widowed by three wealthy men, all of whom were twenty-eight years older than she. The other sister, Patricia Anne Tate Hollowell, is a retired school teacher, petite, long-married to a husband she adores. They live in Birmingham, are in their sixties, and keep stumbling over bodies.

237

I know these women. I know their families, their friends, the communities in which they live. I know what they order at Morrison's Cafeteria. I wouldn't dare write about them otherwise. This is the old "write what you know about" advice. Well, it's true. I received a letter from a woman in Arizona telling me that you couldn't drive down Lakeshore from a shopping center and turn left into Samford University. You can. They've built a new shopping center since the lady left Birmingham. But it reminded me of how important it is not to be careless when you're writing about a specific location.

I began writing humorous mystery novels after twenty years of writing serious poetry. From that background, I learned the importance of each word; that concrete words are the foundation of all good writing, and that a sense of place is a necessity. Poems, short stories, novels—all must be grounded in a place.

From my poetry background, I also picked up what I consider the necessary habit of reading aloud what I've written. When you're reading a poem aloud and you stumble, you know the rhythm isn't right. Now I do the same thing with my novels. Each day when I sit down to write, I read aloud what I wrote the day before. If I stumble badly over the dialogue or some part of a paragraph, I usually find that it's too wordy. Rhythm is an essential element of writing not emphasized enough. Not that you want to be sing-songy. Not at all. But smooth. Then a sharp, deliberate change in rhythm can be used to signify something important to your reader. Reading aloud is especially important for dialogue. We don't talk the way we write. We talk in half-sentences, with exclamations and contractions.

My characters talk with southern accents. They say, "I'm fixing to go to the store," or "Do you reckon he's coming?" My copy editor appreciates the colloquialisms and has stopped me only a few times, once for "He stuck his head in the door" (she added "way"), and "Let's pick up the house" (changed to "straighten"). My dialogue has been described as being right on the money. Do they think I could do a British accent? I'll stick to what I know. Believe me, it's safer. And I'll keep reading it out loud.

Each of the two sisters in this mystery series has her own way of speaking. I'm working on my seventh novel in the series now, and I know them so well, that it's no problem. Mary Alice, the older, larger, bossier sister tends to make pronouncements. Patricia Anne, who has been known to correct her sister's grammar, is slightly more hesitant. She'll say, "I think." Mary Alice just says, "It is." In *Murder on a Bad Hair Day*, Patricia Anne and Mary Alice are in a barbecue restaurant and Patricia Anne is worried about the dirty windows. Mary Alice announces it's not dirt, it's just grease, and eats happily.

On the other hand, when faced with a real emergency, it's Patricia Anne who is the stronger one. Mary Alice tends to fall apart. Sometimes, though, she surprises me, which is the joy of writing a series. There is room for the characters to grow, for their families to change, for me to get to know them better.

My novels are character driven. I know that if you can get the murder on the first page, it's great. P.D. James can do this; I can't get a body in until the third or fourth chapter. First I have to introduce the sisters, let my readers get to know them as I do. I usually keep them as the only two characters in the first chapter. I don't want to confuse the reader by throwing too many people in too soon. I do try to establish the basis of the story early on, and I usually do this by having the sisters talk about it. In *Murder on a Girls' Night Out*, the first in the series, Mary Alice announces that she has bought a country-western bar. This is what sets everything in motion. In the book I am working on now, their cousin Pukey Lukey, so called because of his childhood carsickness, shows up with the news that his wife of forty years has run off with another man. It will take them several chapters to find a body. If you can go the P.D. James route, though, get that body in there quickly.

In writing, we don't have the luxury of using body language to help us communicate. But we do have simple words, which are the paint with which we create our word pictures. Years ago, I had a great teacher who made me cut every word of four or more syllables, and every three-syllable word (ing's and ed's weren't counted).

"Now," he said, "what's left is the gold. Use it."

It's a lesson I've never forgotten. What I had to work with were words of Anglo-Saxon derivation. Of course we can't limit ourselves to nothing but these words, but I still think of them as the "gold," especially the strong verbs, the most important words in every sentence. The men and women in my novels walk at the edge of a cliff. They don't perambulate beside the precipice.

People often ask me how I came to write mysteries. Actually, the sisters made their first appearance in a short story entitled "Where Have

You Gone, Shirley Temple," based on a true incident. They were in an antique mall looking for a Shirley Temple doll to replace the one Mary Alice swore Patricia Anne had lost over fifty years before. A tornado hit (Patricia Anne hadn't been watching the Weather Channel; it was all her fault), and they ended up under a drop-leaf Duncan Phyfe table, fussing. The sisters were so well received, and I was so fond of them, that I knew I wanted to do more with them. I'm not good at plotting, so I challenged myself to see if I could write a mystery. And I did. I actually fit all of the pieces together and sold it.

"It was the voice," my editor said. "And I laughed at the sisters by page two."

Voice. Your voice. The distinctive quality that announces, "Hey, it's ME writing this. This is what I believe. This is what I am." You owe it to your readers to show them who you are. And that takes courage. It takes baring a little of your soul.

In *Murder Makes Waves*, the sisters witness a turtle laying her eggs. This is the way Patricia Anne describes it:

> On the horizon, lightning streaked across a cloud, and moments later we heard distant, muffled thunder. I looked at the dark water of the Gulf, at the turtle laying her eggs, at my daughter, her face filled with awe as she knelt in the sand, at all of us caught in a small pool of light on this beach on this primal night. It was something I'll always remember.

This is my voice. I hope my readers recognize it as true.

But when you're writing a murder mystery, even a cozy, you've got to kill somebody off. And what did I, the real-life Patricia Anne, know about that? I knew I'd better not try to have someone killed with a gun. I'd make a fool of myself. My husband has an old B.B. gun, the only weapon in our house. So I realized that the people in my novels would have to die some other way.

My veterinarian came through for the second book in the series. I took my cat in for her shots and asked him how I could kill a woman with hair products. He knew exactly how and was delighted to tell me.

The Okaloosa County Sheriff's department kept me from making a bad mistake in *Murder Makes Waves*. The sisters find a body on the beach, and I assumed the county sheriff would investigate, but something told me I'd better check it out. I got my chance at a mall in Fort Walton Beach, Florida, where I happened to notice that there was a sheriff's substation. I asked the employees there who would investigate a body on the beach.

"Is it wet?" they wanted to know.

I said yes, it was on the beach.

"The Florida Marine Patrol investigates the wet ones."

They seemed so disappointed, I put two bodies in that book; one was snug and dry in a condo so the Okaloosa County sheriff could be involved, too.

Big lesson learned. I now call about anything that's questionable. My local fire department helped me with an arson question. I'm on a first-name basis with my neighborhood policemen, who are an invaluable resource. Fortunately my daughter is a lawyer, so I get a lot of answers from her about criminal procedures.

I don't outline. I know I should, and I recommend it. But when I do, the person who is the designated murderer invariably gets killed about halfway through the book. So around chapter thirteen, I begin to get panicky. I have to decide who did it. I have several good friends who have been kind enough to read what I've written and say who they think did it. Though they usually choose different people, it's still helpful to get their comments. If there is a writing group available close to you, join it. It doesn't have to be a mystery writing group. We all need support and advice. For instance, my group advised me while I was writing the third book that I should let the sisters find the body, that their different reactions would tell so much about their characters. They were absolutely right, and I've done that in every book since.

I wish I could say I write every day, but I don't. That doesn't mean I'm not working. A lot of a writer's work is done while she's cooking supper or exercising. Plots must be thought out, characters developed. But get to the notebook or the computer as soon as you can to put those thoughts down.

One final piece of advice that seems so simple: Send your work to publishers. Don't be hesitant. But know your market. A friend and I owned Druid Press for ten years, and for listings in the literary market directories, we were very specific about what we published: We wanted short fiction and unrhymed poems under forty lines in length. Period. We received nonfiction manuscripts, epic novels, autobiographies. Sometimes the postage on these tomes ran three or four dollars. A total waste. We also received many query letters with no SASE included, and we simply couldn't afford to respond. We sold the company seven years ago, and we're still getting manuscripts. Don't waste your money and time. Make sure your mystery goes to a publisher who publishes mysteries. And if that manuscript is returned, send it out again. A clean copy. When I was in publishing, I actually received manuscripts with other editors' comments on them. Be professional. Follow the rules.

And keep that notebook handy. The world is full of stress-free turkeys waiting for you to write about. Just do it!

❏ 49

THE PLOT THICKENS

BY BARBARA SHAPIRO

SOME WRITERS CAN SIT DOWN AND BEGIN A NOVEL WITHOUT KNOWING where it will end, trusting in the process to bring their story to a successful conclusion. I'm not that trusting. And I'm not that brave. I don't have the guts to begin a book until I know there *is* an end—and a middle, too. I need to have a rough outline that allows me to believe my idea might someday be transformed into a successful novel. Some writers need a working title; I need a working plot.

A substantial segment of the writing community turns its collective nose up at the mere mention of the word "plot"—particularly if that plot is devised before writing has begun. "Plot is not what novels are about," they claim. "Novels are about feelings and characters and ideas. Plot is for TV movies." Novels *are* about feelings and characters and ideas, but novels are, above all else, stories, and it is through the story that the characters' feelings and the author's ideas are revealed. A handy equation is: Story equals plot equals novel. But what exactly *is* a story?

A story is a tale with a beginning, a middle, and an end. It's a quest. Your protagonist goes after something she wants very badly— something she gets, or doesn't get, by the end. Whether it's returning to Kansas (Dorothy in *The Wizard of Oz*) or killing the witch ("Hansel and Gretel"), this journey is the story, the plot, the means by which your characters' strengths and weaknesses are unveiled, his or her lessons learned. It is the trip you and your protagonist and your reader all make together.

All human beings have the same features, yet the magic of the human race is that we all look different. The same holds true for plot. While the specifics of your plot are unique, there is an underlying structure that it shares with other stories—and it is this structure that you can use to develop your working plot.

243

Human beings have been telling stories and listening to stories as long as there have been human beings, and there is a structure to these stories. Tell the story without the right structure and risk losing your listeners. Find this structure, and your job as a novelist will be easier; you will understand your readers' expectations and be able to meet them. Follow this plot structure and add your own voice, your own words, your own creativity, and you will have a unique novel that works.

Discovering and understanding the underlying structure of the novel will help you develop your working plot even before you begin writing. It will get you moving by assuring you that you are on the right path. In my career, I have used this concept to come up with a number of tricks to help me discover where my novel is going—and to get myself going. These tricks can be translated into four exercises: (1) classical structure; (2) plot statement; (3) the disturbance; and (4) the crisis.

Step 1: Classical structure

There is a long-running argument among writers as to exactly how many different stories there are. Some say there are an infinite number, some say there are 47 or 36 or 103, and others say there is only one. I am a member of the "only one story" school. I believe this one story is the skeleton upon which almost all successful novels are hung—this story *is* the underlying structure. If I can figure out how *my* story hangs on this skeleton, I can begin to move forward. This is how the story goes:

> There once was a woman who had a terrible problem enter her life (*the disturbance*). She decided that she was going to solve/get rid of her problem so she devised a plan (*goal*). But whenever she put this plan into action, everything around her worked against her (*conflicts*) until the problem had grown even worse and she seemed even further then ever from reaching her goal. At this darkest moment (*crisis*), the woman made a decision based on who she was and what she had learned in the story. Through this decision and the resulting action (*climax*), her problem was resolved (*resolution*) in either a positive (*happy ending*) or negative way (*unhappy ending*).

The first step to understanding and using story structure is to break the classic story into its component parts. The key elements are: the disturbance; the goal; the conflicts; the crisis; the climax—the sacrifice and the unconscious need filled from the backstory; and the resolution. Once this is clear to you, then you can transpose these components into your particular story. To accomplish this, ask yourself the following five questions:

What is the disturbance? Some terrible or wonderful or serendipitous event that comes into your protagonist's life, upsets her equilibrium and causes her to develop a goal that propels her through your story. A tornado, for instance.

What is the protagonist's goal? To get out of Oz and return to Kansas.

What are some of the conflicts that stand in her way? The key to creating a successful story is putting obstacles in your protagonist's path—external, internal, and interpersonal. Create opposition and frustration to force her to fall back on who she is, and what she knows, to overcome the hurdles you have created. No hurdles, no conflict, no story. Conflict is what moves your story forward and what develops your protagonist's character.

What specific crisis will she face in the end?
How will she resolve this crisis?

Once you have answered these questions, you will have the skeletal outline for a story that is the basis for almost every successful novel written, and you may find you are ready to begin. If this is the case, dive right in. Unfortunately, for me, this is not enough. I need to do a bit more.

Step 2: Plot statement

A plot statement is a one-sentence, high-concept summary of the set-up of your story. It is what you might pitch to a producer to whom you were trying to sell a movie—or to an agent to whom you are trying to sell a book. To write this statement all you need to know is your protagonist, the disturbance, his goal, and what is at stake.

"Dorothy Gale (protagonist) must find her way home (goal/stakes) after a tornado blows her into the strange land (disturbance) full of evil witches and magical wizards," is the plot statement for Frank Baum's *The Wizard of Oz*.

"Jay Gatsby (protagonist) must win back the love of Daisy Buchanan (goal) to give meaning to his meaningless life (stakes) after he buys a mansion across the water from the one in which Daisy lives (disturbance)," is the plot statement for F. Scott Fitzgerald's *The Great Gatsby*.

"Delia Grinstead (protagonist) must create a new life for herself (goal/stakes) after she impulsively walks away from her three children and long-term marriage," is the plot statement for Anne Tyler's *Ladder of Years*.

"Suki Jacobs (protagonist) must discover what really happened on the night Jonah Ward was killed (goal) before her teenage daughter is arrested for a murder she didn't commit (stakes), but that she did predict (disturbance)," is the plot statement for my latest book, *Blind Spot*.

What's the plot statement for yours?

Step 3: The disturbance

Although you already have a rough idea of what the disturbance of your story is, it is useful to make it more specific. This isn't just any disturbance: It is a particular event that begins the action of your particular story, throws your protagonist into turmoil, and forces her to devise a specific goal that will place her on the path that will lead her to *her* crisis. It is the "particular" aspect of these events that makes your story unique. To discover your disturbance—and, in many ways, your character—ask yourself the following question: "What is the worst thing that can happen to my protagonist, but will ultimately be the best thing that could happen to her?"

What does your protagonist need to learn? Her lesson is your readers' lesson: It is the theme of your book. What life lesson do you want to teach? Once you have answered these questions, you will be able to develop a character whose story resonates to your theme—a character whose backstory reflects what she needs to learn and whose journey within your story teaches it to her.

The disturbance in my second book, *Blameless*, occurs when Dr. Diana Marcus' patient, James Hutchins, commits suicide. It is the worst thing for Diana because it tears her life apart:

She begins to question herself as a psychologist.
A wrongful death and malpractice suit is filed by the Hutchins family, jeopardizing Diana's teaching position and practice as a psychologist.

She is publicly humiliated when the media disclose her unprofessional behavior.

Her husband Craig becomes suspicious, and their marriage is jeopardized.

Diana's inability to save James mirrors her childhood tragedy when she was unable to save her younger sister, and taps into all of her deepest insecurities.

This all sounds pretty terrible, but, like life, it's not all bad. James' death is also a good thing for Diana, because it forces her to face her tragic flaws and try to correct them:

She acknowledges her professional mistakes, making her a better therapist.

She and her husband rediscover their relationship.

She learns that she cannot cure everyone.

She forgives herself for her sister's death.

In order to come up with this disturbance, I had to delve deeply into Diana's present life and develop a past for her that would create a character who needed to learn this lesson. This process deepened both Diana and my plot.

How is your disturbance the best and worst thing that could happen to your protagonist?

Step 4: The crisis

The crisis of your novel is the major decision point for your protagonist. It reveals who she really is and what the experience has taught her. Its seeds are in the disturbance, and all the conflicts lead inexorably to this specific crisis, this specific decision and its specific resolution. But the decision can't be a simple one. If the choice is too easy, your reader will be unsatisfied. Therefore, you must create a decision that has both good and bad consequences, that has both gains and sacrifices, so that your reader will not know which choice your protagonist will make. To determine the crisis in your story, ask yourself the following questions:

What is the event that precipitates the crisis?
What is the decision the protagonist must make?

What does she learn in the decision-making process?
How does the decision reveal who she is (the backstory)?
How does her decision reflect on what happened to her in this story?
What does she lose in the decision (the sacrifice)?
What does she gain from her decision?
How is the decision turned into action?
How does the decision resolve the plot?

When I was developing the plot for *Blameless,* I asked myself the above questions and came up with these answers:

James shows up at Diana's apartment and holds a gun to his head; he tells her that if she tells him not to shoot himself, he won't.

Diana must decide whether to stop James from killing himself.

Diana learns that everyone cannot be saved, that she cannot save everyone, and she is not responsible for James.

Diana overcomes her belief that it is her mission to save everyone, realizes that she is not responsible for her sister's death, and ultimately forgives herself for it.

Diana struggles with her need to control her career, her marriage, her patients, and herself.

James will be dead, and she will be responsible for not stopping him.

A dangerous murderer will be dead, and Diana will remove the threat to herself and her unborn baby.

Diana doesn't say anything, and James blows his brains out.

James really is dead, and Diana is cleared of his murder.

So if you aren't as brave a writer as you'd like to be—or if that mythical muse just won't appear—try these four exercises. You just might discover that you aren't that cowardly after all. And that novel might just get finished.

❏ NONFICTION: ARTICLES AND BOOKS

☐ 50

IMAGINED LIVES

BY LINDA SIMON

AS A WRITING PROJECT, BIOGRAPHY SEEMS SIMPLE: AFTER ALL, THERE is a built-in plot, a ready-made cast of characters, and, if we choose our subjects with care, a significant story to tell. Anyone who made a discovery (think Pasteur), enacted some daring feat (Lindbergh, Earhart), was much in the public eye (any of the Kennedys), or contributed to culture (writers, artists, dancers, musicians, actors) seems a foolproof choice for any biographer. Such subjects may—or may not—be foolproof for you.

A sense of connection

No matter how famous or acclaimed a potential subject may be, a biographer needs to feel a sense of connection and understanding. It's not enough to admire a subject; a biographer needs to believe that he or she can truly understand that individual's experiences, motivations, needs, and problems. In any historical writing, of which biography is part, evidence becomes colored, shaped, and interpreted through the particular lenses that the biographer brings. Those lenses may be honed by personal experiences and cultural context; the biographer becomes increasingly aware of the power of those lenses as research and writing progress. As Mark Schorer, biographer of Sinclair Lewis, once remarked, "biography itself has two subjects, and two subjects only—the figure whose life is being recreated, of course, and the mind that is recreating it . . . ." It's important, then, to feel some sympathy or empathy for your subject before you begin to write.

For some biographers, that feeling of empathy becomes so intense that they feel "possessed" by their subject. When Stephen B. Oates wrote about Abraham Lincoln, he admitted that he "identified powerfully" with his subject and felt that he had penetrated behind the myths and public images of Lincoln to find the essence of a complex, troubled,

251

brilliant man. "I became so involved in his life that I got depressed when he did; I hurt when he hurt. When I left my study after a day's writing in his world, with brass bands playing Civil War music in my head, I was stunned to find myself in the twentieth century." Sometimes such immersion is helpful, when it allows a biographer to develop a sense of intuition about the person's feelings and motivations, but sometimes such identification prevents a biographer from making judgments; the biographer feels like a conduit for the subject's telling of his or her own autobiography. I think that all biographers struggle both to immerse themselves in another life and to keep themselves from the perils of overly identifying with their subject.

Research and discovery

When choosing a subject, it's important to know that you'll have ample evidence to document and analyze the life. Everyone leaves a paper trail: Think about the documents you've accumulated—birth and marriage certificates, medical records, tax records, canceled checks, school transcripts, not to mention letters. If you keep a diary or journal, so much the better for your biographer. For some subjects, documents can be found in the collections of major university libraries. For literary figures, the Houghton Library at Harvard University, the Beinecke Library at Yale, the Harry Ransom Humanities Research Center at the University of Texas at Austin, the Huntington Library in California, and the Barrett Library of the University of Virginia are just a few libraries with significant literary collections. If you know that your subject is represented in these collections, you may write to the library and request a catalogue; there is usually a nominal charge for such material.

If your subject already has been written about, the first step to finding material is examining the bibliography and acknowledgments of that book, dissertation, or article. Without that kind of background source, you may need to do some detective work by writing to or visiting local historical societies or collections, by tracing your subject in various reference sources (such as *The National Union Catalog of Manuscript Collections* or the *Directory of Archives and Manuscript Repositories in the United States*), or, if your subject is contemporary, by placing a notice in *The New York Times Book Review* or *The New York Review of Books*.

Once you locate sources, however, don't think that you will ever know everything about your subject. Even if you are writing about a former President, with access to a presidential library, you will find gaps, especially relating to childhood and adolescent experiences. Usually, when you read a biography, you'll notice that the subject seems to spring to life as an adult very quickly. Some biographers fill in childhood gaps by creating a textured portrait of the place in which the subject grew up, or giving historical background. Sometimes, that kind of material can be interesting, but only if it is relevant to understanding the subject. "It is gaps," wrote Paul Murray Kendall, biographer of Richard III, "that tempt the fledgling biographer to speculate, the 'artistic' biographer to invent, the scholarly biographer to give a lecture on history." Recognizing gaps should not dissuade you from choosing a particular subject, but you need to be honest with your reader about what you do not know. "To fill gaps by wondering aloud, lying, padding—or simply to leave them for the reader to tumble into," adds Kendall, "is not to fill the shoes of a true biographer."

Gaps may occur even if you are faced with mountains of material. Henry James and William James, for example, left thousands of letters, but they or their heirs burned thousands more. The story we tell about them, then, reflects what they felt safe to leave us. We will never know what went up in flames, nor how that material might substantially change the story we take to be "truth."

If gaps are one biographical obstacle, witnesses to a life may prove another. When I researched the life of Alice B. Toklas, for example, I found that many of her friends had written memoirs in which she and her companion Gertrude Stein were featured among the cast of characters. These memoirs were useful in helping me recreate events in the two women's lives, but I was careful to test one version against another in attempting to verify the "truth" of what occurred. I place "truth" in quotation marks, because, as any historian knows, the truth, at any time, is simply what can be substantiated. How your subject felt, what he or she thought, usually cannot be known. What you *believe* your subject felt or thought comes by developing a sense of biographical intuition.

Witnesses may or may not be reliable, may or may not have their own reasons for presenting a version of events. Biographers need to be skeptical about testimony, whether they find it in published works, in unpublished archival documents (letters, diaries), or by interviewing people who knew your subject. When I wrote a biography of Thornton Wilder, some people who knew him agreed to talk with me. I was grateful, of course, for their time and interest in my work, but often I found that they knew the "public" versions of Wilder's experiences, which they had read or heard from Wilder himself, and offered little information that was more intimate or personal.

When a subject is someone still living, readers will expect that a biographer will interview people involved in the person's life. But these interviewees may or may not be available. If your subject has decided not to cooperate with your biographical project, he or she may instruct friends, colleagues, relatives, and other associates to refuse to speak with you. Even if your subject encourages your project, not all of those friends, colleagues, and others may feel comfortable about speaking with you, knowing that their words and views will be recorded. You may have to be diplomatic and persuasive to enlist their cooperation. Writing about a living person is in some ways more difficult and challenging than writing about a historical figure. But in any research, you will accumulate information, test one version of "truth" against another, and develop your own intuition about the reality of your subject's life.

Beginning biographers, faced with gaps or unreliable witnesses, may worry that they cannot find enough material to write a life story. More experienced biographers know that there is never enough; research is never complete. But at some point, the biographer believes that a coherent, interesting, compelling story can emerge from the files and notes that he or she has collected. Biographers have different ways of transforming research into a manuscript: Some complete all research before beginning to write; others write and do research at the same time. I do most of my research before I begin the first chapter, but usually supplement that research as I write. A chapter that may be five pages long with information I collected at one point will grow to twenty-five pages with information I find later. It's helpful to envision the manuscript as a growing body of work rather than as a linear production that you *must* write from beginning to end.

Organizing your material

Writers need to be disciplined, and part of that discipline applies to files and notes. Devise whatever system makes sense for you: Some writers use computer files, some use handwritten index cards stored in a wooden box; some writers scan all written material into their computer, others use file folders stuffed with photocopied material. Don't feel that you must keep up with the latest technology; you should instead match your system of organization to your system of research and the way you process what you find. The latest computer software won't help you if you haven't found a way to read the material you've uncovered, record whatever information is relevant to your work, and have easy access to that information when you need it.

Just as there is no single formula for organizing your notes, there's no formula for organizing a biography. Most writers begin at the beginning and end with the subject's death. But you may decide to open your story with a scene from mid-life that captures the essence of your subject's personality. When I wrote a biography of William James, I began the book with an anecdote about James's speech at a Memorial Day service in 1897, when James was fifty-five years old. James was very nervous about the speech, and he did not yet realize just how famous he really was. I chose to start with this story because it revealed a vulnerability and fear that dogged James throughout his life; because he emerged triumphant; and because it allowed me to introduce the 19th-century culture in which he lived. After presenting this anecdote, I returned to a chronology that began with his grandfather (most biographies provide some genealogical background) and ended just after his death. The opening scene served to set the stage for the drama of his life.

However you decide to organize your biography, aim to write it as well as you can. Most biographers learn their craft from novelists: Word choice, metaphor and imagery, sentence rhythm all contribute to style and can make a difference between an exciting, compelling tale and a dull, perfunctory rendering of a life. The biographer, said Paul Mariani, whose subjects include poet William Carlos Williams, "is as much the inventor, the maker, as the poet or the novelist when it comes to creating a life out of *prima materia* we call words . . . ." As researcher and writer, Mariani tells us, the biographer sifts through "words, words transcribed, written, uttered, words, words, and more words, which the biographer must shape and select and reorder, until a figure begins again to live in our imagination." This shaping, selecting, and reordering of words is the biographer's ultimate imaginative task in order to give, as Mariani puts it, "the *illusion* of a life"—which is as near as we can come to the reality.

□ 51

WRITE BY REWRITING

BY TOM JENKINS

UNLIKE SOME FORMS OF FICTION, THE WELL-WRITTEN ARTICLE IS OR-derly. It is built according to an organized pattern of sentences and paragraphs. To achieve this order, you must keep in mind that writing is a process with integral and sequential links: thinking, organizing, writing, and rewriting. It is rewriting that ties it all together.

Before you start to write, you plan your article, its amorphous information taking shape in your mind as you collect it. Information and insights are incubated as you begin to organize your ideas. When speaking, you can get away with crashing clichés and disorganized digressions, but when you write articles, you must be clear and logical. You can achieve this with a brief or skeletal outline of your ideas, to show the relationship of the parts to the whole as you write.

As you proceed with your writing, daily drafts reveal false starts and changes, a mess to anyone else's eyes or brain. But your thoughts are being transmuted into the visual form that will eventually become your finished article. The substance is there. After you complete that first version, you should step back from your early drafts for at least a short time before you begin the curative treatment of *rewriting.*

Then the rearrangement and removal of sentences and paragraphs can begin. In some instances, you are rewording the early mistakes in sentences written quickly to "get them down." In other cases, you are making up for inadequate organizing. But rewriting is more deep-seated than sentence refinement. You are realigning the flow of your ideas to maintain your original focus and to provide the right sequence of illuminating details.

No amount of planning can totally eliminate the need for rewriting. The reason is simple. Writing an orderly article is a visual process that takes place, ultimately, on the page (or the terminal). You don't write it in your head (as we are sometimes prone to think), but on the page. It needs planning for its birth but rewriting for its life.

To convey the orderliness you want, you must see the whole (however flawed at that point) before you can alter its parts. You must see the total composition before you know what elements are missing, what paragraphs need strengthening, and what sentences need removing. By reviewing and changing, and then more reviewing and simplifying, you reach toward perfection, at least in terms of what you want in your article. Rewriting is, by definition, repeat writing.

Here's an example of this process. An article I wrote for *Westways* illustrates the value of rewriting both by its initial failure and its final success. In writing about the historic (and first) photograph ever made of the now famous Mount of the Holy Cross (in Colorado) in 1873 by William H. Jackson, I made a brief outline, including an introduction, Jackson's background, the search for the legendary mountain, the final photo, and a conclusion. It seemed complete to me.

I opened with the following two paragraphs.

> A man was born in Keeseville, New York, in 1843 who changed legend into fact and mystery into reality with his precocious field photograhy. William Henry Jackson photographed remote areas of the West, bringing to the world for the first time spectacular visual representations of some of America's natural miracles.
>
> During his lifetime, Jackson took more than 100,000 photographs. But perhaps his most notable achievement was his photograph of the 14,000-foot Mount of the Holy Cross in the Sawatch Range of north central Colorado. How Jackson obtained that now-famous picture has itself become a legend.

This opening—the first item in my outline—gives an introductory overview, a promise of the details to come. But I failed to develop the second section, which was only a token of what was needed. Upon completion of the article, I reviewed it and saw its inadequacy: In my desire to grab the readers' attention with Jackson's tough wilderness trek to find the mountain whose existence no one had to date verified (my third section), I rushed through the second, omitting important details. I had left out the background that the reader needed to understand Jackson's nature and his compulsion to reach his goal.

So I rewrote the earlier section, giving additional specifics, and sent the manuscript to the publisher. It was returned. Fortunately, the senior editor was patient enough to ask for more details. "Though the story of Jackson's photographing the Mount of the Holy Cross is interesting," she wrote, "I would suggest emphasizing the man rather than the mountain. This will require more historical data about Jackson."

Again, I rewrote the article, giving details about Jackson's childhood and a romantic relationship that revealed much more about the man. Two paragraphs ran as follows:

> They soon became engaged, but a lover's quarrel took place. "She had spirit, I was bull-headed, and the quarrel grew," Jackson later related. On the front porch, she spoke an icy, "Good night, Mr. Jackson," to which he replied, "Good night, Miss Eastman," bowing from the hip. After a week of misery, he attempted a reconciliation, but without success. Thus he prepared to go West.
>
> But he never forgot Caddie Eastman. He carried a small daguerreotype of her throughout his expeditions in the West. None of his family knew of its existence until it was discovered among his private papers after his death.

In the earlier draft, I had failed to give enough supporting details. Later, I did the opposite by writing too much, allowing my own experience of having climbed up the vertical portion of the "cross" to affect—unwisely—my account of Jackson's discovery. It was wordy, as follows:

> Suddenly before them, bright and clear, was the awesome cross of snow in the face of the 14,000-foot mountain across from them. They disbelieved their eyes, for its magnitude and beauty were unlike anything they had ever seen. The legend was not a legend: Both the mountain and the cross were real. The upright couloir of the cross stretched approximately 1,500 feet, a formidable challenge to mountain climbers who attack it before dawn with ropes, ice axes, and crampons. The crossarm is about 500 below the summit, extending 750 feet on both sides. Its size added to its impact upon the men. They were struck by its magnificence.

Review of the "completed" manuscript once again led me to more rewriting. The paragraph was wordy, so I revised it in the following way:

> Suddenly before them, bright and clear, was the awesome cross of snow in the face of the 14,000-foot mountain across from them. The legend was not a legend: Both the mountain and the cross were real. The upright couloir of the cross stretched approximately 1,500 feet. About 500 feet below its top, the arms intersected, each slightly lifted and extending almost 750 feet on both sides. It was magnificent.

Although rewriting is not easy, we should welcome the chance to refine our work. It's our job. Why should an editor have to do it? Some editors, justifiably, won't. Actually, we improve our own writing by doing the rewriting ourselves. As it has been often and wisely said, good rewriting demands a kind of unhurried tinkering with words. Each unsuccessful try eliminates another wrong solution and leads you to the right one. Writing leads to rewriting, which is rethinking and restructuring, bringing you closer to the orderliness you want

In rewriting, be hard on yourself. Be an editor for a while and cut out everything that does not add directly to the reader's understanding. Someone has said that words are like inflated money; the more you use, the less each one is worth. Just committing words to paper or electronic storage does not make them sacred and immutable. They must be measured and fitted to the idea you have in mind. Sometimes, using a quote in place of your own words can sum up what you want to say. Near the end of my Jackson article, I added a quote of *his* response on first seeing the snowy cross, inserting two sentences that were not in my first draft:

> When I first saw the cross, time seemed to stand still; only a gentle breeze murmured in the solitude of this incomparable place. It was a long time before we came back to our earthly thoughts and packed our things for the descent. (His party was on the summit of a mountain two miles across a canyon; it was from this spot he first saw and photographed the Mount of the Holy Cross.)

I attempted the "ideal minimum expression" in closing my Jackson article with a two-sentence paragraph from which no words could be removed without losing what I considered to be relevant facts:

> Jackson was drawn to the mountain, climbing up to photograph it again in 1880 and 1893, and with his son, Clarence, in 1897 and 1905. But subsequent photos never surpassed his first photograph in 1873, one of the most celebrated mountain photos ever made.

Even if you never attain perfection, rewriting indicates your attempt to achieve it. It also indicates your concern for your reader. In writing magazine articles, you are not writing for yourself but for your anticipated readers. No technical skill or love of language can make up for the need to "see" your message through the readers' eyes. They don't want to work their way through a pile of words; they want only accurate and simple words so they can understand your message. That requires cutting all that are not necessary. It requires editing. In a word, re-writing.

You can be your own final reader. *Scribendo disces scribere*: By writing, one learns to write. Also, by rewriting, one learns to write better.

❏ 52

THE ISSUE OF ISSUES

BY RUTH SELIGMAN

SHOULD THE TOWN COUNCIL REVISE THE ZONING RESTRICTIONS IN certain neighborhoods? Should the city impose a curfew for teenagers on weekend nights? Should the state abolish the death penalty? How much information regarding their condition should doctors give their patients? Should recycling facilities be mandated for every community?

What do all these questions have in common? They can serve as the focus for issue-oriented articles, those that examine matters of public concern and do so from as many different angles as possible. The market for these articles is very broad: It ranges from consumer publications targeted to specific audiences to trade, business, and professional journals, and includes the weekend magazines of both local and national newspapers, as well as the daily pages of those papers.

If, however, you are new to the writing game, your best bet may be your local newspaper. True, they don't pay as much as established magazines, but the experience you will gain from writing for this market can be invaluable. You will acquire a great number of skills, from learning how to develop such an article to discovering where and how to look for material and statistical data to strengthening the "pros" and "cons" of your argument.

There are other advantages to concentrating first on your local scene:

1) As a member of your community, you generally know the concerns of your fellow citizens.

2) Access to primary source material, such as the people who can give you informal opinions, is relatively easy. You may actually know people personally or have contacts who do and can ease your entry to them.

3) Your audience will be receptive to this type of material for, as a rule, most people are more interested in what is happening in their own community than in what is going on in the next state or even in the next town.

4) Finally, a good issue-oriented article in a local newspaper may be picked up by a regional publication or even a national one. Thus, your initial piece can serve as an entry or calling-card for a broader market. At the least, it can be used as a sample when submitting a query to these markets.

In looking for topical subjects, many frequently surface just before a municipal election, when the electorate will vote on certain proposals. For example, they may be asked to vote on whether the safety regulations in the public schools are adequate or should be updated. This gives you a chance to research the existing regulations to determine whether or not new ones are needed.

Often, a brief item in your local newspaper, perhaps one stating that a local hospital is cutting back on staff, can be developed into an in-depth piece, leading you to explore the adequacy or inadequacy of health-care facilities in your community. As a starting-point for this particular article, you might interview a veteran nurse on the staff or a family who now has to travel quite far for medical treatment. Anecdotal material for an opening gambit enables readers to relate easily and instantly to the situation. It makes for a livelier opening than merely stating the issue, either in question or declarative form.

No matter what their personal feelings are, writers should strive to present a balanced piece. An issue-oriented article is not an op-ed piece in which only one opinion is presented. It is mandatory to present as many different angles as possible. There are always two sides—and sometimes more—to every story. For example, counterbalance the remarks of a nurse opposing staff cutbacks with an interview with the head of the hospital, who may explain why the action that was taken will not affect the quality of health-care provided by the hospital.

In many ways, issue pieces are akin to investigative reporting. In both fields, writers must be scrupulously careful to see that their facts are correct, to check and double-check. They should be wary of using secondary sources. A news report that four nurses have been dismissed must not be taken at is face value. A visit to the hospital may reveal the exact number and show that two of the nurses have merely been transferred to another facility. This fact was either ignored and overlooked in the initial news story or, perhaps, just not known.

As in investigative reporting, issue-oriented writing entails leg work

THE ISSUE OF ISSUES

and "digging." This "digging" makes for a richer, more comprehensive, and meaningful article. Frequently, one contact leads to another. The mayor may refer you to the Chief of Police, or the company's Chief Financial Officer may send you to the head of the Human Resources Department.

You may build your article around any issue—social, political, economic, medical, or psychological. Articles in which the issue is both timely and controversial and of valid concern to the audiences for whom it is intended have the best chance of attracting the attention of an editor. A magazine for teenagers will not be in the market for a piece on subsidizing daycare facilities for working mothers, but a publication that is geared to these young mothers will.

Issue pieces differ from straight news reportage, which traditionally works according to a pyramid format, with the first paragraph giving the conventional "who, what, where, why, and when" information, with each successive paragraph merely expanding on the points made in the first paragraph. The result: In a news story each paragraph becomes successively less important, enabling editors who need to cut the story to chop off as many of the latter paragraphs as space limitations require.

In any feature, and especially in an issue-oriented one, the first paragraph should just set the scene, whetting the reader's appetite for more. The body of these articles is usually based on personal interviews with people concerned about the issue, and especially with those actively pushing or opposing it. In choosing whom to interview, go, if possible, to the top—to the chief executive officer of a company, the director if it is a nonprofit organization, or if it is a political question, to the mayor or head of the town council. If these people are impossible to reach, it is OK to settle for a lower-level one, such as a department head. Generally, however, it is unwise to depend on a clerk or a secretary or even the official spokesperson, since the information he or she gives may be less reliable.

Although some writers find that they can interview via telephone, face-to-face contact is infinitely better. Use the telephone only when a certain fact has to be checked or you need to ask one or two simple questions.

An excellent source for material are professors and instructors at local colleges. Many may actually be engaged in serious research on the topic you are investigating and are often more than willing to share some of their findings with you. If they are not working on your topic, they often know of other professionals who are.

When seeking information, be very careful to avoid giving the impression that you are planning to do a "hatchet job." Assure your contacts that you are looking at both sides of the issue.

Quoted material may be supplemented by statistical data, including comparative information. If, for example, you are discussing an issue of specific concern to your town, it is often a good idea to find out how other communities have dealt with a similar problem.

For background material, don't forget your local libraries and their back copies of newspapers. Become friendly with the local librarian, who can help you find information, since they are familiar with reference books and related periodicals.

Today, an increasing number of writers are discovering the value of the Internet. If you aren't connected to the Internet, find someone who is. Since I don't have access to it, I use the help of a fellow journalist who is willing to look up information for me. In return, I edit his material.

In summary, here's my recipe for issue-oriented pieces:

1) Use a catchy opening, often a human interest anecdote.

2) Give a balanced presentation that shows both sides of the issue.

3) Write a conclusion that briefly summarizes the main points covered in your article.

Ideally, the article should end giving the readers sufficient material and information with which to make up their own minds.

□ 53

CREATING A MEMOIR

BY NATALIE ROTHSTEIN

"WHERE DO I COME FROM, GRAMMA?," MEGAN ASKED. MY ANSWER was *An American Family*, a three-generation family history incorporating the Jewish immigrant experience. I wrote it so that she would know about her background, about some long-ago people who were, unmistakably, irrevocably connected to her. Surely there was a story to tell, but if the devil is in the details, then I was about to have a devilish time of it.

What manner of book was this to be? The shores of bookland were littered with memoirs and self-serving confessions, many in the guise of "setting the record straight." A recent *New Yorker* cartoon has Isabella saying to Columbus, "Just tell me about the new continent. I don't give a damn what you've discovered about yourself."

A personal story is different, of course. There is supposed to be an element of discovery about it. That's why people read memoirs. And, I believe, it is why people write them: to find meaning in a life of one's own.

"I matter; I was here," is every writer's cry for immortality. We want to leave a record, but what sort of a record is the question. In this tabloid-era society, down-and-dirty accounts are what, all too often, pass as legitimate stories. Sensationalism has co-opted the market, and we have become too much like the starlet who wants publicity at any price. "I don't care what they say about me; just be sure they spell my name right." Well, I knew I did care what was said about me.

So there were choices to be made. Would I make the right choices? What to put in; what to leave out? Was this to be a very personal book, one exclusively for my family, or would it be of interest to a wider reading-audience? Would *anyone* want to read it?

In writing this book, I wanted to be able to tell the simple truth. And yet I knew that the truth was never simple. Remember the folk tale concerning the blind men and the elephant? In that account, each person, by feeling the giant pachyderm, discovered only a part of the whole: a tail, a trunk, a floppy ear. And based solely on their piecemeal discoveries, each person made a different assumption about the true nature of the beast. And each and every one of them was wrong. I viewed this yarn as a cautionary tale. In other words: Don't make assumptions based on a portion of the whole.

Having decided that I wanted to get as close to the whole truth as possible, I realized that I had a very large problem. Gathering family data was, at this point, a paper chase. My mother and her nine siblings were all gone. My father and his generation—also gone. There was no one left to talk to; there were no oral histories to take. I have no siblings, but I could—and did—call or write my cousins who are scattered all over the country, asking for photos, anecdotes, records, anything that would shed more light on our shared history.

What if the details were meager? In certain instances, they were. To date, I have never been able to uncover the name of the ship my grandfather sailed on when, in 1892, he left his wife and three small children in the little Russian village of Korzangorodok to make a new start in America. I hope that, with continued research, I may one day find the name of that ship. But what is forever lost is the knowledge of what life was like for my grandparents during the five years that they were separated by an ocean.

But I could imagine. I imagined Grandpa toiling to earn enough money to bring his family over from the Old Country to the New World. And I wondered: Did he find work right away? Where and with whom? How lonely was he?

Pondering these questions, I knew that I had found something of an answer, if not to the past, at least to my current problems. What, I had wondered, if I wrote the book as fiction, imagining conversations and situations for my characters? A fill-in-the-blanks kind of story with me filling in the blanks.

Certainly there was ample precedent. Fictive portrayals of historical characters were done all the time. Think of the historical novels of Gore Vidal's *Burr* or E.L. Doctorow's *Ragtime*. I did. I thought of them. And I knew I couldn't do it.

It wasn't just the fear of flying—the worry of *could* I do it; it was the concern about *should* I do it. And the answer for me was "no." The book was not going to be a novel; Grandma and Grandpa were not to be messed with. I was going to have to tell their story straight.

"Where did I come from, then? Ah, where indeed?/This is a riddle monstrous hard to read . . ." wrote Samuel John Stone [1839–1900] in a piece called "Soliloquy of a Rationalistic Chicken," an ironic little verse I happened upon. I was dealing with the same question, but the answers I sought to write must be of a less whimsical nature.

The book started to develop as a hybrid: part history, part biography, part memoir. What informs a memoir are impressions of a life. Through what one hopes is an artful rendition, a portrait emerges. In a memoir, it is as if you came upon the proverbial shoebox full of family photos, and you decided to arrange them so that they would tell a story. Some snapshots are duplicates; some are not clear; some are overexposed, and some you omit. So you must make choices and decide which ones best illuminate and illustrate your story.

I thought of some of my favorite memoirs. Lillian Hellman's *An Unfinished Woman*. [Even if Mary McCarthy did once famously remark that every word Hellman wrote was a lie, including "and, if, or but."] Willie Morris's *New York Days,* Philip Roth's *Patrimony*, Russell Baker's *Growing Up*. And, yes, Mary McCarthy's own book, *Memories of a Catholic Girlhood*. These narratives offer not just mere recitations of dates and events, but rather, in the words of Denise Levertov, "testimonies of lived life." The best of the genre, these memoirs are compelling, vivid, and bravely unsentimental.

I do not put myself in the same category with these luminaries. Anyway, I had enough problems of my own to figure out because, "mere" or not, I knew I was going to need some of that "recitation of events and dates" to tell my story. Part memoir, part history, I would write of my family's lives by relating the story of their world and by recounting some of the events taking place in the larger world, events that influenced their lives.

It is always fascinating to contemplate our choices. We hope we are being thoughtful in weighing our options, but instincts and desires are also a part of the equation. Sometimes you just have to trust the visceral as well as the cerebral reactions. And so while the book evolved in its hybrid form, I thought of that development as a reasonable plan, while acknowledging that it was also something of an accident. A happy one, I hoped.

One of the reasons we write is to find out what we're really thinking. It is an attempt to see things whole. When you set yourself the task of looking back at the roads taken—and those not taken—then a certain picture emerges.

"What's it all about, Alfie?" Surely, a question for the ages. It's why we write; it's why we read. So that we can try to figure it out. In my case, it took a while.

It took over a year of reading and research before I ever began the writing. I had five bulging folders of resource material including letters, a family tree, and documents such as birth certificates, death certificates, and my grandfather's Change of Name document from Boston City Hall. Somewhere in there was the making of a book.

I read other memoirs even though I was nervous about whether I was being inspired by other writers or, heaven forbid, overwhelmed by them. Great writing is stimulating, but it is a gold standard that can be hard for us mortals to reach. I was reminded of a remark that Dorothy Parker made when she was once compared to Edna St. Vincent Millay. "I may be following in her footsteps," Parker said, "but unfortunately, in my own ugly sneakers." I know what she meant.

However, I figured that if I laced up my own ugly sneakers every day, I had a good chance of getting where I wanted to go. Talent will take you only so far; perseverance can propel you to your goal. Once, in talking to a classroom of fifth graders about the writing life, when they asked about how you could possibly manage to write a book—I mean, you could dream about it, but how could you actually do it?—I told them that if you just wrote a page a day, at the end of the year you would have a 365-page book. Why, you could even take some time off for weekends and still have a sizeable manuscript! The kids were wreathed in smiles as they realized that a dream was like a sailboat: It required some work and skill but if you make the effort, your dream might take you to faraway places.

Some of the issues in dealing with the book were practical; some were not. For instance, what to call it? During most of the process I referred to it as *The Book.* But then, inspiration hit at four o'clock one morning, waking me up. I would call it *An American Family,* since it was the story of how an immigrant family evolved into an American family.

I worried about certain chapters, about some of the transitions. I wrote and rewrote and rewrote. Meeting with my once-a-month writers group, I bounced ideas off of them, asking and receiving guidance.

As I began writing, I experienced a combination of exhilaration and nervousness. Excited to be starting but anxious, nevertheless. I felt something like those fifth graders who did not know how it was possible to sail a dream into port. I believed then—and even more so now—that you have to arm yourself with the practical knowledge of your trade and beyond that, you have to dare. I thought about a movie actor trying out for a part in a western. "OK, you've got the role," says the director, "and, by the way, you do ride a horse, don't you?" Well, like that apocryphal actor, I didn't know how to ride a horse either. But, I was going to. Or put another way, Nike was right. "Just do it."

So I mounted that horse every morning and went to work. And I realized that I was happy, happy to be writing the story, to see the pages mounting up. It was slow, very slow; I am not a speed runner but rather a marathoner. I knew it would be a long haul and it was. Five years.

I wondered if I would know when I would be ready to write *The End*. I did.

I did three rewrites and thought that, finally, I was finished. I wasn't.

Putting aside the writer's hat and donning that of the editor, I asked if the questions I started out with had been answered. Who were these people? What had their lives been like? What was the meaning of it all? I found myself listening to the voices of the past and hoped I was properly tuned in.

In writing the book, I had tried to tell my own story as part of a continuum, as just one of the parts in a three-generation family history. And I tried to be authentic without being exploitive. You have to examine what is important to you in this kind of personal history. I felt that it was appropriate to omit the very personal if it were to cause pain or if it seemed to me self-indulgent.

There is always a dichotomy between honesty and discretion. Too much of one, and the other suffers.

An old adage admonishes that to die without leaving a record is to die without an inheritance. The people I come from have always abided by that dictum. Each spring, at Passover, throughout the generations, we are instructed to tell our children the story of the Exodus. As writers, we too tell stories about where we came from and how we got here. Wherever that "here" may be.

❏ 54

THE MAKER'S EYE

BY DONALD M. MURRAY

WHEN BEGINNING WRITERS COMPLETE THEIR FIRST DRAFT, THEY USUally read it through to correct typographical errors and consider the job of writing done. When professional writers complete their first draft, they usually feel they are at the start of the writing process. Now that they have a draft, they can begin writing.

That difference in attitude is the difference between amateur and professional, inexperience and experience, journeyman and craftsman. Most productive writers share the feeling that the first draft (and most of those that follow) is an opportunity to discover what they have to say and how they can best say it.

To produce a progression of drafts, each of which says more and says it better, writers have to develop a special reading skill. In school we are taught to read what is on the page. We try to comprehend what authors have said, what they meant, and what are the implications of their words.

The writers of such drafts must be their own best enemy. They must accept the criticism of others and be suspicious of it; they must accept the praise of others and be even more suspicious of it. They cannot depend on others. They must detach themselves from their own page so they can apply both their caring and their craft to their own work.

Detachment is not easy. It takes ego to write. I need to say, "I am here. Listen. I have something important to say." Then, after our egos have produced a draft, we must read when our judgment may be at its worst, when we are close to the euphoric moment of creation. Writers must learn to protect themselves from their own egos.

Just as dangerous as protective writers are despairing ones, those who think everything they do is terrible, dreadful, awful. If they are to publish, they must save what is effective on the page while cutting away what doesn't work. Writers must hear and respect their own voice.

Remember how each craftsperson you have seen—the carpenter eyeing the level of a shelf, the mechanic listening to the motor—takes the instinctive step back. This is what writers have to do when they read their own work.

It is far easier for most beginning writers to understand the need for rereading and rewriting than it is to understand how to go about it. Published writers don't necessarily break down the various stages of rewriting and editing, they just go ahead and do it.

There is nothing virtuous in the rewriting process. It is simply an essential condition of life for most writers. There are writers who do very little rewriting, mostly because they have the capacity and experience to create and review a large number of invisible drafts in their minds before they get to the page. And many writers perform all of the tasks of revision simultaneously, page by page, rather than draft by draft. But it is still possible to break down the process of rereading one's own work into the sequence most published writers follow and which beginning writers should follow as they study their own pages.

Seven elements

Many writers just scan their manuscript at first, reading as quickly as possible for problems of subject and form. They stand back from the more technical details of language so they can spot any weaknesses in content or in organization. Each writer works in an individual way, but I know from my studies of the writing process that most writers read their manuscripts as I do, paying close attention to seven key elements of effective writing.

The first is *subject*. Do I have anything to say? If I am lucky, I will find that I do have something to say, often more than I expected. If the subject is not clear, or if it is not yet limited or defined enough for me to proceed, I step back and try to catch the focus of what I *may* say in a line that may become a title or the first sentence of the piece. If not, I write my way toward meaning with discovery drafts that usually make the subject come clear.

The next point I check is *audience*. Like most writers, I write first for myself, to explore and then share my world. But the aim of writing is communication, not just self-expression. I ask myself if there is an audience for what I am writing, if anyone will need or enjoy what I have to say.

Form is usually considered after audience. Form, or genre, is the vehicle that will carry what I have to say to my readers, and it should grow out of my subject. If I have a character, my subject may grow into a short story, a magazine profile, a novel, a biography, or a play. It depends on what I have to say and to whom I wish to say it. When I reread my manuscript, I ask if the form is suitable, if it works, if it will carry my meaning to my reader.

Once I have the appropriate form, I survey the *structure*, the order of what I have to say. Every good piece of writing is built on a solid framework of logic or argument or narrative or motivation; it is a line that runs through the entire piece of writing and holds it together. If I read my manuscript and cannot spot this essential thread, I stop writing until I find something to weave my writing together.

The manuscript that has order must also have *development*. Each part of it must be built in a way that will prepare the reader for the next part. Description, documentation, action, dialogue, metaphor—these and many other devices flesh out the skeleton so that the reader will be able to understand what is written. How much development? That's like asking how much garlic. It depends on the cook, the casserole, and to whom it is going to be served. This is the question that the writer will be answering as he reads his piece of writing through from beginning to end, and answering it will lead him to the sixth element.

The writer must be sure of his *dimensions*. This means that there should be something more than structure and development, that there should be a pleasing proportion among all of the parts. I cannot decide on a dimension without seeing all of the parts of writing together. I examine each section of the writing in its relationship to all of the other sections.

Finally, I listen for *tone*. Any piece of writing is held together by that invisible force, the writer's voice. Tone is my style, tone is all that is on the page and off the page, tone is grace, wit, anger—the spirit that drives a piece of writing forward.

Potentialities and alternatives

When I have a draft that has subject, audience, form, structure, development, dimension, and tone, then I am ready to begin the careful process of line-by-line editing. Each line, each word has to be right.

Now I read my copy with infinite care. I often read aloud, calling on my ear's experience with language. Does this sound right—or this? I read and listen and revise, back and forth from eye to page to ear to page. I find I must do this careful editing at short runs, fifteen or twenty minutes, or I become too kind to myself.

Slowly, I move from word to word, looking through the word to see the subject. Good writing is, in a sense, invisible. It should enable the reader to see the subject, not the writer. Every word should be true— true to what the writer has to say. And each word must be precise in its relation to the words that have gone before and the words that will follow.

This sounds tedious, but it isn't. Making something right is immensely satisfying, and the writer who once was lost in a swamp of potentialities now has the chance to work with the most technical skills of language. And even in the process of the most careful editing, there is the joy of language. Words have double meanings, even triple and quadruple meanings. Each word has its own tone, its opportunity for connotation and denotation and nuance. And when I connect words, there is always the chance of the sudden insight, the unexpected clarification.

The maker's eye moves back and forth from word to phrase to sentence to paragraph to sentence to phrase to word. I look at my sentences for variety and balance in form and structure, and at the interior of the paragraph for coherence, unity and emphasis. I play with figurative language, decide to repeat or not, to create a parallelism for emphasis. I work over my copy until I achieve a manuscript that appears effortless to the reader.

I learned something about this process when I first wore bifocals. I thought that when I was editing I was working line by line. But I discovered that I had to order special editing glasses, even though the bottom section of my bifocals have a greater expanse of glass than ordinary glasses. While I am editing, my eyes are unconsciously flicking back and forth across the whole page, or back to another page, or forward to another page. The limited bifocal view through the lower half of my glasses is not enough. Each line must be seen in its relationship to every other line.

When does this process end? The maker's eye is never satisfied, for he knows that each word in his copy is tentative. Writing, to the writer, is alive, something that is full of potential and alternative, something that can grow beyond its own dream. The writer reads to discover what he has said—and then to say it better.

A piece of writing is never finished. It is delivered to a deadline, torn out of the typewriter on demand, sent off with a sense of frustration and incompleteness. Just as writers know they must stop avoiding writing and write, they also know they must send their copy off to be published, although it is not quite right yet—if only they had another couple of days, just another run at it, perhaps. . . .

❑ 55

Writing "Double-Life" Articles

By John Lenger

Don Quixote, Dr. Strangelove, Underdog, and Darth Vader. *The Scarlet Pimpernel* and Hester Prynne of *The Scarlet Letter*. Wonder Woman and Superman. Dr. Jekyll and Mr. Hyde, Rosalind of *As You Like It*, Walter Mitty, the Count of Monte Cristo and Jean Valjean of *Les Misérables*.

Fiction is full of characters who hide their pasts, assume secret identities, lead double lives, or otherwise are not quite who readers think they are. And so is nonfiction. Publications as different as *The Wall Street Journal*, *Boston Magazine*, *The New Republic*, and *Sky & Telescope* are publishing articles that make readers do double-takes.

From Boston's Billy Cohn, pioneer heart surgeon by day and hard-rocking bass guitar player by night, to Canada's Grey Owl, once the most famous Native American in the world (though he was really an Englishman named Archie Belaney), people with dual identities fascinate readers—and provide rich material for nonfiction writers.

Once you start looking, you'll find double-life stories everywhere: among co-workers, friends, and people with whom you do business. These stories tend to be the best type of article for beginners to write, as my journalism students at the Harvard University Extension School have demonstrated time and time again. For instance, when one of my students discovered that her hair stylist was also a trained jazz vocalist, she sold an article about the stylist/singer to a local newspaper. The newspaper received such a positive response to the piece that it hired the writer as a columnist. Another student, a university program administrator/free-lance writer, has sold articles to a number of university publications about her colleagues' dual identities as researchers and artists. Yet another student had his first free-lance piece, about a police photographer who is also a Harvard night school student, published in the Boston Police Patrolmen's Association newspaper.

275

Once you identify a likely candidate for a double-life story, writing and marketing the article you write will be easy if you follow these five steps:

1) Understand why readers are fascinated by double lives. Readers wonder if the people around them are *really* who we think they are. *The Wall Street Journal* features a double-life article in almost every issue, from the tale of the politically left-leaning professor who now employs servants, to the article about the high-flying entrepreneur whose secret past as a drug smuggler finally caught up to him.

Readers of your local newspaper or regional magazine will also be excited to discover that the kindly old gentleman working at the hardware store was a World War II hero, and are reassured to find out that the neighbor's big secret is that he does woodworking as a hobby, and that noise coming from his garage is quite innocent.

As much as we speculate about others, we also wonder about ourselves. Like Walter Mitty in the classic James Thurber story, we imagine stepping outside our everyday lives and pursuing adventures. Reading about other people's escapades allows us to live vicariously, and sometimes gives us courage to try new identities for ourselves.

2) Search out people who have particularly interesting dual identities. A person may be a mother, a wife, a daughter, an accountant, a supervisor, an athlete, a volunteer, and so on. The key is to identify two facets that seem to contrast strongly with each other. The greater the contrast, the better the article.

The Boston Globe once ran an article about a high-powered leader in Washington who became the top official at Harvard University's Kennedy School of Government. At his job, the official interacted with the world's most powerful political leaders; in his spare time, he raised chickens. Another time, *The Boston Globe* ran a front-page story about a documentary filmmaker's controversial project to prove African ancestry for Britain's Queen Elizabeth. "This upsets the whole paradigm of the social ladder where black is at the very bottom and royal houses at the very top," said the filmmaker.

Yet another *Boston Globe* story profiled a Hasidic grand rabbi who had been a business magnate before assuming his religious duties. As the *Globe* reporter wrote about the grand rabbi's transformation, "The man whom old acquaintances recall as a clean-shaven, jet-setting, competitive international businessman and lawyer now looks like an Old World mystic who probably never laid eyes on a laptop."

It's also possible to turn the formula upside down and write about people who would be expected to have very interesting lives, but don't. *The Wall Street Journal* profiled a man whose business is transporting exotic dancers to and from the clubs where they work. The driver confided this private fact to a reporter. His love life suffers because of his job. He won't date strippers because doing so in the past hurt his business, and most other women won't date him when they find out what he does for a living.

3) Don't turn a cliché into an article. All grade school teachers have hearts of gold and all part-time performers are waiting for their big break. And sure, you could write that someone who once worked as a translator in military intelligence was "a spy like James Bond," but at best it's a tired cliché; at worst it's a misrepresentation. Instead of relying on clichés, you should instead describe what your subject did in that other fascinating life. The people you interview, your editors, and most of your readers will appreciate your article more if it's not laced with trite stereotypes.

4) Deal with ego problems that arise, or head them off if possible. Identity is a sensitive matter, and even if your story is written with great sympathy and understanding, the subject or someone close to the subject may have a disappointing reaction to it. For example, there was an article about a high school honor student who, apart from her normal teen-age life, was a musical prodigy. The prodigy's mother complained because the article did not list *all* her daughter's honors. It's sometimes difficult to write about co-workers because they may have unrealistic expectations—but you still have to see them every day.

It's advisable to explain the process of writing an article before the interview, telling the subject that it's the writer's responsibility to write for *readers* rather than for the person being profiled. In all cases, the writer must make clear that he will determine what information is used. Most people will cooperate with such a directive; those who don't are probably more trouble than their stories are worth.

5) Identify the right market for your article. This is particularly important when writing double-life stories. The main question is "What audience will care about this person's dual identity?" Although the revelation that famed 19th-century writer and medical professor Oliver Wendell Holmes was fascinated by astronomy and wrote many poems celebrating the sky might not appeal to some editors, *Sky & Telescope* magazine published a free-lance article about the topic.

If your profile subject—in at least one of her lives—is a doctor, lawyer, teacher, parent, tennis player, etc., you should investigate topic-specific magazines for that aspect of the subject's personality. One writer targeted running magazines and parenting magazines for an article about mothers who run marathons.

Smaller magazines and newspapers dedicated to local coverage are always in the market for double-life stories about people who live in their areas. What reader wouldn't be fascinated to know that the person seen regularly in the grocery store just published her second novel?

And it is possible to have your double-life story appear in a national publication. During his first week as a freshman at Harvard, a student answered a knock on his dorm room door from a fellow student who said that a bunch of athletes were reading poetry to counteract their "dumb jock" image. He went to the poetry reading—and wrote articles about it for *The New York Times* and *Sports Illustrated*.

The more you look around you, the more people you will discover who are living double lives. Whom do you know at work or in your community who is living a double life?

Recognize those people, write about them, and you'll more than double your chances of getting published—and in the process, you'll have twice as much fun.

❑ 56

WRITING PERSONAL EXPERIENCE ARTICLES

BY DEBORAH NEWTON

AFTER NORA EPHRON EXPERIENCED A PAINFUL INCIDENT IN HER youth, her mother told her to buck up, because "everything that happens to you is copy." Copy. Isaac Bashevis Singer once said, "If you write about the things and the people you know best, you discover your roots." And Ben Franklin's autobiography contains these words: "The next thing most like living one's life over again seems to be a recollection of that life, and to make that recollection as durable as possible by putting it down in writing."

Sift through all those suggestions and what advice do you get? You should write about what you know. What you've experienced. And what better form to write about your life's happenings than in a personal experience article.

You've experienced things that can interest others. We all have. These experiences don't have to be world-shattering, just incidents that readers can relate to, and find meaningful. As long as you learned something from the experience—even something as small as seeing the experience in a new light—readers will be able to relate to it. If the incident changed your life in a profound way, all the better. If you give it the right spin and structure, you can turn your personal experience into a salable article.

Women's magazines such as *Redbook* and *Ladies' Home Journal*, and religious magazines such as *Guideposts* and *The Lutheran*, use true personal experience pieces. Confession magazines such as *Black Secrets* and *True Love* are always on the lookout for fictionalized versions of personal experiences, though this market is somewhat limited.

Here's how you go about it:

A tight structure is imperative for the personal experience article. Your focus must be strong. The first step is to decide on the point or theme you want to emphasize with your piece, and everything in your article must build to prove this point. *Crime doesn't pay*, for example, is too broad a theme for a personal experience piece, but narrow that focus to, *My ex-husband kidnapped our young daughter, and my faith in the justice system was strengthened because he was sent to jail when he was caught*, and you've got the makings for an excellent personal experience article.

So, is there a formula for writing one of these pieces? The following structure works well for a wide variety of personal experience articles:

Always start your piece on the day that something different happens to you (the "I" character of your story if you're writing in the first person, or the viewpoint character if you are describing someone else's experience). This incident becomes the "hook" on which you capture the reader's interest. Try to make the hook provocative so the reader wants to know what will happen to the viewpoint character. A shocking statement works well as a personal experience hook ("I didn't think it would feel so good to pull the trigger and watch my target lurch and fall to the ground."), or an anecdote that leaves a question in the reader's mind ("When I was ten and snooping through my mother's dresser drawer, I found out that she wasn't a woman at all!"). Because of this incident or situation, you or your focus character has to react and decide how to handle the problem. Often, the decision your character makes will be wrong and will cause him or her stress and suffering. But he made that choice for a reason that seemed right to him at the time. The viewpoint character continues on the course charted by this decision until something happens to change his attitude. A dark moment or turning point forces him to make a sacrifice or a choice that teaches him a lesson. The article can then continue to a satisfactory conclusion, resolving the original problem. As long as your viewpoint character learns something about himself or changes in some way, your article has done its job.

Confused? Don't be. Let's take this one step at a time with an example from an article published in *Ladies' Home Journal*.

• *The problem or original conflict (your hook).* Your story or article always opens with an occurrence that forces your main character to make a decision. She's sailing along in life and suddenly, the problem pops up. This is the starting point for your piece (and not a moment sooner). For example, in Andrea Warren's "Can This Marriage Be Saved?" column in *Ladies' Home Journal*, the focus character, Rita, has remarried Ken after her first husband, the father of her two young children, was killed in an accident. Her problem is that she can't forget her first husband. The hook is a direct quote that makes the reader want to keep reading to find out how she solves her problem. ("Ken doesn't know this, but lately I've been visiting the cemetery where Charlie is buried.")

• *The reaction or bad decision.* Your focus character reacts to the problem in a way that moves the story along and continues the tension. She makes a bad choice of action. Rita's wrong decision is overindulging her children, and when Ken tries to discipline them, she takes their side against their stepfather. (This renders him lower in the new family's hierarchy than he should be.) Readers may at first see the folly of Rita's ways and wonder why she has reacted this way, but they will understand why she does it once they learn what has motivated her to do it.

• *Motivation.* This is the reason your character made that bad choice. Rita's motivation, told in a flashback, is the story of how Charlie was killed. Because of the grief she still suffers over Charlie's death, she has become a pushover with her kids and spoils them. She still sees her first marriage and family as the main relationship in her life, and her second husband as just that—secondary.

Motivation is often slipped into the personal experience piece by way of a flashback, as in our example, but it may also be woven in by means of introspection—the character's inner thoughts—as long as this doesn't break up the flow of the narrative.

• *The body of the story.* Build your article with events that have been put into motion by your main character's original choice, including what has direct bearing on your article. Don't bog the piece down with incidentals such as what the focus character had for breakfast last Tuesday, unless that menu in some way contributes to the outcome of the piece. The body of Rita's story describes the bitter arguments that take place over the discipline of the children when Ken arrives on the scene.

• *The dark moment or crisis.* Your focus character can't go on living with this choice he's made, because if he does, there's no story, and he or she can't learn or change from his original (wrong) decision. So, a crisis occurs. Rita's crisis occurs when Ken begins to withdraw from the family unit and Rita fears she may lose him.

• *Sacrifice or decision.* Your focus character must make some sort of sacrifice or decision in order to learn her lesson and change. Rita does so when she goes to a marriage counselor, and follows his advice of putting her new husband above her children in the family dynamic.

• *Satisfactory ending.* Note, I didn't say *happy ending* because the conclusion of your personal experience piece doesn't necessarily have to be *happy*. It needs only be the *right* ending for the particular situation. If you or your viewpoint character's bad decision was something horrible like injuring another person, you don't deserve to live happily ever after. Your ending must show that while you have suffered and learned this lesson, that may not keep you from suffering further consequences in your life. The satisfactory ending in the *Ladies' Home Journal* example shows Rita's and Ken's attempts at making time for each other and building strength as a couple. The second part of the story is told from Ken's point of view, showing his problem, reaction, motivation, and decision.

• *Theme.* After you've drafted your personal experience piece, go back over it to see if you've developed the theme you set out to tackle. If you've gone off on a tangent, rework the piece to eliminate any digressions. For a tight personal experience piece, only one theme should dominate.

"A writer wastes nothing," F. Scott Fitzgerald said. Don't waste your personal experiences. Look into your own life or the life of someone close to you for personal experiences—and write about them. There's a good market for these articles.

□ 57

WRITING A SALABLE OP-ED PIECE

BY JAMES H. PENCE

WE ALL HAVE OPINIONS, AND MOST OF US LIKE TO EXPRESS THEM. IF you don't believe that, just flip through your local newspaper's *Letters to the Editor* section. On any given day you will find a variety of people—not usually writers—expressing all sorts of opinions on every issue from national politics to local leash laws. Whether or not we have acted on it, we have all felt the desire to fire off a letter to the local paper when something in the news touched us. But if you're a writer, and all you do is send a letter to the editor, you're missing a great opportunity. Next time an issue comes along that you absolutely *must* comment on, write an op-ed piece. But before you do, make sure you understand what makes an op-ed article salable.

Choice of topics

Essential in the process of crafting a salable opinion piece is the ability to choose topics well. Column space in a newspaper is at a premium. If the editors aren't convinced of the relevance of your topic to their readers, it doesn't matter how well you write it, it will be rejected. So, you must give careful attention to your subject matter.

Be relevant

The key to relevance in op-ed pieces is choosing a topic that touches on a larger issue. For example, if you are responding to a local library's decision to filter its Internet service to prevent children from accessing pornographic sites, don't merely offer an opinion on the propriety of the decision. That's the stuff of a letter to the editor. Instead, address the larger issue, in this case personal freedom versus a desire to protect our children. As you learn to address the issues behind the news, you will increase your chances of selling your piece.

Be unique and timely

As important as relevance is, it is often not sufficient to make your column salable. You must address the events of the world around you through your unique perspective. Let your background, your interests, your personal areas of expertise color your piece. Address your topic as only you can. Are you an attorney? Give an attorney's perspective. Are you a parent? Look at issues through a parent's eyes. It is your distinctive viewpoint that makes your piece stand out, and increases its salability.

In writing op-eds, you need to write your piece quickly for two reasons. If you wait too long, the editor may not consider the matter newsworthy. Also, if you don't write your piece quickly enough, someone else may write one on your subject first.

A while back, I delayed writing a commentary on Dr. Jack Kevorkian's appearance on *60 Minutes* in which he euthanized a man before a national audience. A week later, when I was just about ready to begin working on the piece, I opened the *Dallas Morning News* "Viewpoints" section to discover the very article I was planning to write!

Try to have your finished article ready within forty-eight hours of the time you write your rough draft. Also, check with your local newspaper on submissions. Many papers now allow fax and even e-mail submissions for op-ed pieces. If you can save the time that mailing your piece would have taken, you increase your chances of being at the front of the line on a particular issue.

Once you've decided to write op-ed pieces, develop the habit of watching the news for items suitable for your unique commentary. With the easy access to on-line newspapers and magazines through the Internet, you can keep abreast of local, national, and worldwide events. And remember to choose your topics carefully, filtering them through your own personality and background. You won't be qualified to write on every issue, but find those you are qualified to comment on, and start writing.

I stumbled into op-ed writing in the middle of President Clinton's much-publicized problems with Monica Lewinsky. One of the main topics of discussion was whether or not the people of the United States should forgive him. Some people compared the President to the biblical

King David. Since David had committed adultery and had been forgiven and restored, they argued, we should likewise forgive Clinton for his indiscretions.

I had no problems with forgiving the President, but from my perspective as a minister, I felt that flawed reasoning led people to identify President Clinton with King David. So, I decided to write my first op-ed piece, comparing the president to a different biblical king, Saul. I penned some eloquent barbs and angry responses to what I thought was a gross misapplication of the biblical story.

A few hours later, I read my first draft—and threw it away.

In the process of writing that piece, I learned *three* important characteristics of good op-ed writing. A salable op-ed piece must have the proper tone. Tone reflects your *attitude* toward your topic and your readers, and if it is abusive or antagonistic, it's unlikely to be published.

Letter or op-ed?

One characteristic that distinguishes a letter to the editor from an op-ed piece is that while a letter can be filled with angry rhetoric and even name-calling, an op-ed piece must present a reasoned argument. There is no place in op-ed writing for irrationality or ad hominem argument (although syndicated columnists often get away with it). If you want your piece to be considered, you must learn to filter out emotion without losing passion. The best way to accomplish this is to get your anger out on the first draft. Let your emotions flow. Express your anger, your outrage, your frustration. Set it aside for a few hours, then, when you've cooled down, edit mercilessly. Remove the anger and the irrationality, but leave in the passion for your subject that caused you to write the piece in the first place.

Be constructive

As you write the piece, and especially as you rewrite it, make sure you are not merely being critical. It's easy to focus on problems and, while it's not always possible to offer a solution, a good opinion piece will at least challenge readers to find one. If you just want to criticize, write a letter to the editor. If you write an op-ed piece, be constructive.

Try to avoid writing in the first-person singular. There is no quicker way to doom your piece than to fill it with phrases like, "I think," "in my opinion," or even just the pronoun "I." There's a strange irony here. On the one hand, an op-ed piece offers your opinion, but if it's written in the first person, it stands a good chance of being rejected. In fact, the guidelines that editors issue for op-ed pieces will often specify "no first-person" pieces, because overuse of the first person tends to give the piece a "know it all" tone. Stick to writing in the third person or the first-person plural. Editors want *opinion*, not opinionated pieces.

Style

Newspapers have certain requirements of the material they publish. One of the toughest constraints the op-ed writer must deal with is that of word count. Usually, the acceptable range is between 500 and 800 words. That means that you don't have unlimited space to make your point. It can be a daunting task to address an issue about which volumes could be written, and to accomplish it in roughly 700 words. The trick is in learning to focus.

When you write an op-ed piece, you don't have the luxury of using a scattershot approach. Nor do you have the space to touch on every aspect of your topic. Often it's hard even to hit the highlights. Instead, you must address your issue with laser precision by focusing on the central issue or "kernel" of your opinion, or you can choose a peripheral issue to be your subject.

For example, had you wished to respond to Dr. Kevorkian's televised assisted suicide on *60 Minutes*, you might have raised the question of journalistic impropriety or the implications of Dr. Kevorkian's act. In a single op-ed piece you could not convey both points effectively. The narrower your focus, the better.

As you write your piece, don't forget to document thoroughly any references or quotations you make. You don't need to submit the documentation with the piece, but you must be able to back up any statements you attribute to others. Newspapers hold their writers to high standards where their sources are concerned. Although you are not *reporting* news, you must still hold yourself to similar standards when you use reference material.

Writing op-ed pieces is a wonderful way for a writer to express an opinion in a powerful forum. Perhaps syndication might even be in your future—all because you decided to express your opinion.

□ 58

THE BUSINESS OF CRAFT WRITING

BY KATHLEEN PEELEN KREBS

IN THE PAST THREE DECADES, THE HANDCRAFT MOVEMENT HAS SPAWNED an interest in and appreciation of fine crafts for the consumer, and big business for the artist. The proliferation of art and craft fairs in almost every town, city, state, and province across the United States and Canada is a testament to the ever-growing demand for original, handmade merchandise. The publishing world is racing to keep pace with this market, and a wide variety of books, magazines, and periodicals carry articles pertaining to craft.

As a fiber artist and basket maker for over ten years, I have contributed numerous "how-to" articles on various aspects of my craft: from locating, gathering, and preparing natural materials to step-by-step instructions in basketry techniques, such as coiling, twining, and weaving. And selling my art through museum stores, art galleries, and fine craft fairs has inspired me to write articles on the business of craft.

Based on my experience as an artist and writer, I offer the following seven steps for entering the craft writing market:

1) *Write what you know.*

If you have ever turned a bowl, knit a sweater, crafted a candle, woven a basket, built a birdhouse, or braided a rug, you may have the how-to basics of writing about your craft. The market for craft how-to's is broad. A multitude of specialized craft publications offer techniques on quilting, knitting, woodworking and carving, embroidery, metal-smithing, ceramics, and weaving. A number of general craft magazines feature instructions on how to make anything from stained-glass lampshades to mosaic flowerpots. Home and garden magazines offer well-written articles on subjects ranging from herbal wreaths from your backyard, to building your own bent-willow garden furniture.

I have written instructions for making hats from lily leaves and mats

287

from scented herbs. My article on drying pine needles to coil a natural green basket was featured as a cover story for a national craft magazine, and brought me $300.

2) Tap the children's market.

Do you remember those beanbag squares, potato prints, and paper-bag masks you made in second grade? Most children's magazines have a "crafts corner" and welcome new ideas (or variations upon old ones). This is an easy way for crafting amateurs to enter the craft writing market. If you have ever helped a child make a tissue-paper kite, a newspaper mâché animal, an egg-carton caterpillar, or a felt finger puppet, you can write an article with an original twist on your project. An article I wrote on Southwest-style, woven newspaper baskets earned me $250 from a national family craft magazine.

3) Record your research.

You have spent hours in art museums admiring antique Chinese porcelain or seventeenth-century Japanese kimonos. You seek out contemporary expressions in wood in countless art galleries. Many fine art and craft publications accept well-researched articles on a particular area of interest. *Fiberarts Magazine* published an article on the sari collection of one of the last Ottoman princesses, as well as a feature on collecting early "aloha shirts" from Hawaii. For an article on Huichol Indian bead and yarn art published as a colorful cover story for *Bead & Button Magazine*, I earned $375.

Read extensively in your field of interest and focus your article for a particular publication. You may wish to call experts or collectors in the field to add details and depth.

4) Profile an artist.

You are captivated by the one-of-a-kind brass door-knockers of a local metalsmith and linger longingly over the tilework of a well-known ceramist. Call or write the artist to request an interview, and then query one of the art and craft publications that frequently feature artist profiles. Ask about photo requirements.

5) Review a crafts show.

If you are well-informed about a particular area of craft, reviewing an art gallery or museum show that exhibits work in your field may prove profitable. (Shows and openings are often listed in local newspapers.) Target your market. Several craft and art publications, as well as newspapers, accept free-lance reviews. Well-crafted impressions backed by knowledge are always acceptable.

6) *Evaluate a craft fair.*

Craft is big business, and the major venues for a majority of craft artists are the juried craft shows held throughout the U.S. and Canada. Professional artists and all of those concerned with the business of craft, as well as consumers of handcrafts, welcome articles evaluating and appraising these shows. There is an ever-increasing free-lance market for such evaluations in craft publications.

Visit your favorite show, noting attendance, quality of the artists' work, the originality and appeal of booth display. Jot down a few questions to ask artists or request a card and an O.K. to contact the artists after the show. Always ask permission to use an artist's name, and offer to send a copy of the article, if published. Ask how long the artist has exhibited at the show; try to find out if the show was profitable; did the artist have better wholesale or retail sales; what were the show's costs vs. profits, etc. You might also interview customers, as well as show staff and promoters.

7) *Offer craft business advice.*

Whether you sell your craft in galleries, gift shops, at professional craft shows, or through your local church or school bazaar, you know something about the business of craft. Tips on pricing, booth set-up, photography for jurying, advertising, bookkeeping for tax purposes, and travel expenses are well-received by the craft trade magazines.

I sold my article, "Beneficial Booth Behaviors," to *The Crafts Report* for $200, and I'm currently writing articles on craft booth design and counter-productive sales attitudes for another publication.

Writing for the crafts market is an enjoyable way to share your professional know-how, your part-time hobby, or your special field of interest with others. The demand for well-written, informed articles has never been higher.

❑ 59

WRITING ABOUT PETS

BY ROBERTA SANDLER

IF YOU LIVE WITH A PET, OR IF YOU LIKE ANIMALS, WRITING ABOUT them may be the *purrrfect* venue for you. According to Barry Sinrod, author of *Do You Do It When Your Pet's In The Room?*, pet-lovers kiss, cook for, give gifts to, and unashamedly slobber over their pets just as surely as pets slobber over their human companions. There are about 92 million pets in American households, creating a large readership for pet articles, both in print and electronic markets. Pet-lovers like articles that explain how to keep their animals healthy, happy, and well-trained. They like humorous or poignant first- and third-person articles about the special bond between people and pets, and also the relationship between celebrities and their pets. What tugs at readers' heartstrings? Articles about dogs who become lost or abandoned far from home and somehow find their way back home; articles about sick or injured animals who recover; articles about pets who save the lives of their human companions. Readers are inspired by articles about animal activists and about people who do something to encourage appreciation of pets.

The markets for pet articles

Pet publications attract people who share their lives with a domesticated animal. These publications vary from breed-specific, such as *The Retriever Journal* and *The Gaited Horse*, to the more generic *Pet Life, Pets, Part of the Family, Dog Fancy, I Love Cats, AKC Gazette, The Chronicle Of The Horse, Doggone, Good Dog*, and *Reptile and Amphibian Hobbyist*. But you needn't limit yourself to writing only for pet magazines; consumer, lifestyle, and health publications use pet articles, as well. Here are examples:

• Jeanne Strack serves as a foster mom to abandoned puppies. As head of P.U.P.S. (Puppies Under Protection), she nurtures them until

290

they're old enough to be turned over to the local animal shelter to be put up for adoption. I contacted Jeanne after I saw her newspaper ad requesting donations of blankets and other items for P.U.P.S., and the resulting article was published in *Dog Fancy*. I revised it, added more anecdotes and quotes, and sold the article to my daily newspaper.

• My veterinarian told me about Jordie, a Lhasa apso whose heart condition was corrected by a pacemaker. My filler about Jordie appeared in *Palm Beach Life* magazine.

• The Epilepsy Foundation searches for dogs with a special ability to predict when a person is about to have a seizure. Through the Foundation, I contacted a young woman named Victoria, who had suffered from daily multiple seizures since being injured in a car accident, and who was "reborn," thanks to a golden retriever who was trained as a seizure-alert dog. I interviewed Victoria by phone (we lived on opposite ends of the country). My goal was to show readers the dependency and loyalty between human beings and animals. My article appeared in *Woman's World*.

• Ten-year-old Buddy could have died from the bite of a poisonous rattlesnake in his back yard. Instead, his Rottweiler, Apache, jumped between the snake and Buddy, and took the bite. For three days, it was unclear whether Apache would live. My article about this dog who was willing to die to save his human friend also appeared in *Woman's World*.

• In Brevard County, Florida, the ASPCA has a Meals On Wheels program for pets who live with older people. I wrote about the program for *Successful Retirement* magazine.

My life with my beautiful golden retriever, Thumper, became a humorous, first-person piece published in a Canadian regional magazine, *Okanagan Life*, and later appeared in *Good Housekeeping*.

• A stray dog who lived in Juneau, Alaska, in the 1930s, was adopted by the entire city. Although deaf, she could somehow "hear" when a ship was approaching the harbor. The statue of Patsy Ann that sits facing the harbor motivated me to write about this inspiring little dog, and my articles about her were published in *Hearing Health*, and in two travel magazines for cruise lines, *Crown & Anchor* and *Destinations*.

• In Riverfront Park in Daytona Beach, Florida, there is a solitary gravestone on which these words are engraved: "Brownie, the town dog. 1940–1955. A good dog." Brownie was a stray dog who wandered into Daytona Beach in 1940, remained, and was loved by everyone. My article about Brownie appeared in *50 Plus Lifestyles.*

Do you see how many markets there are for articles about pets?

Topics that amuse and help

Articles about pet antics will always sell. *Good Dog* published my humorous essay about my West Highland terrier, Friday, who tries to climb inside the TV when she sees animals on the screen. "Dog Day Afternoons," about my Cairn terrier, Bambi, appeared in *American Kennel Gazette,* and *Family Circle* ran my essay, "Purrfect Pet Project," about how my daughter came home with a stray kitten—an orphan we couldn't refuse. I've lived with many pets through the years and have written about them all. Some pet behavior is universal, and people who live with a large dog like mine will laughingly identify with his behavior. Here's how I humorously described my chagrin over my golden retriever Thumper's insistence that she sleep with me:

> When I awakened in the morning, the first thing that assaulted my vision was a big, fat, hairy red derrière. I groaned and buried my head under my pillow. Thumper, believing she'd stumbled onto a game, shoved her snout under the pillow and exhaled me out of bed.

Another type of pet article that sells well is the "how to." For example, the *Sun Sentinel* published my article about how to cope with the loss of a pet. I've written articles for *50 Plus Lifestyles* about pet care and how to travel with a pet. *The* (Bergen) *Record* and the (Fort Myers) *News Press* travel sections published my article about on-site pet kennels at Florida's theme parks, and I've submitted a short article about hotels that cater to pet guests ("Southern Hospitality Goes to the Dogs") to a pet publication and a lifestyle publication.

Service articles

Service articles include straightforward advice from pet experts, but can be livened with anecdotes. In a piece on coping with the loss of a pet, I showed how a woman handled the grieving process by keeping a journal in which she wrote poems to her deceased pet.

Serious articles about people and pets and the wonderful relationship betweeen them should elicit an emotional response from readers. Poignancy and drama are two key elements that draw readers into the story. In my article, "Here Come the Pet Therapists" (*CATS* Magazine), I used this illustration:

> Hobie likes to work with babies. He is Briana's 4-year-old longhaired, silver classic tabby. Briana was holding him one morning at the center (a pediatric residence for children with severe medical disabilities) when he showed interest in 9-week-old baby Andrew, who was born with multiple birth defects.
> Andrew was resting in his young mother's arms. Briana brought Hobie closer to the infant, who had never reacted to any stimuli. Andrew suddenly reached out to knead Hobie's fur. Stunned, his mother burst into tears. "I can't believe it," she sobbed. "I didn't think he was capable of responding to anything. It's like a miracle."

In my article, "She's Got 8 Lives Left," which appeared in *Woman's World*, Bonnie Kinley's son Scott notices that their kitten, Bootsie, has suddenly stopped breathing. Bonnie resorts to CPR, a situation reflecting drama and urgency.

> Bonnie inserted a finger into Bootsie's mouth. Nothing was blocking the kitten's breathing passage. Then, she covered Bootsie's mouth and nose with her own mouth, and blew two tiny puffs of air into the cat's lungs. Nothing happened. Desperately, Bonnie repeated the procedure. "C'mon, Bootsie," she whispered. Her cheeks were wet with tears as she continued to breathe air into Bootsie. Bonnie saw Bootsie's chest rise faintly. "Bootsie's back! You did it, Mom," Scott shouted.

Do your own pets or relatives' and friends' pets do stupid pet tricks or have a funny habit? Is there a neighborhood bakery, park, or camp that caters to pets? Can a local veterinarian tell you about a pet who beat the medical odds, or about a citizen involved in a pet program such as Paws To Help? These are good article subjects.

Need ideas? Search your local newspaper for articles about animals, interview the people cited there, and write your own articles. This is how I learned of the K-9 police dog who had hip replacement surgery paid for by residents who rallied to his aid (my article about this appeared in *Arthritis Today*) and the hearing-impaired woman whose "hearing" (service) dog was rejected by residents of the woman's condo (*50 Plus Lifestyles* bought my piece on this).

Articles about pets can pay as little as $35 and more than $1,000, depending on the length and the publication. If you are a true pet lover, you'll find, to your delight, that when you emBARK on an article about pets, pursuing this subject can be the cat's meow.

❑ 60

THE $$$ AND SENSE OF TRAVEL WRITING

BY JANE EDWARDS

PEOPLE OFTEN JUMP TO THE CONCLUSION THAT TRAVEL WRITERS ARE constantly being showered with free trips and deluxe accommodations in return for a few kind words in print!

Nothing could be further from the truth. While staff writers at the top glossies undoubtedly have their travel expenses underwritten by the magazine, the vast majority of travel writers are free lancers who must finance their own research trips. Even featured columnists for major newspapers pay their own way.

Hilda Anderson, a past president of the Society of American Travel Writers, has been writing her acclaimed "Short Trips" column for the *Seattle Post-Intelligencer* every week for almost two decades. Recently, she assured me that wherever she travels in search of material to write about, she foots the bill. "Newspapers," she said emphatically, "do not pay the expenses of travel writers, or even travel columnists."

Furthermore, most reputable publications have stringent rules prohibiting writers from accepting "perks"—complimentary transportation, lodging, etc.—in conjunction with any article they publish. Designed as a safeguard for readers, the ban guarantees that items about cruises, hotels, restaurants and other tourist attractions are the authors' honest opinions, unbiased by their expectation of future favors.

To put it bluntly, there's no free ride for travel writers!

However, if you're not daunted by these bald facts but still have a passion for geography and a yen to write about faraway places with strange-sounding names, then travel writing is for you. Whether your métier is fiction or nonfiction, the themes and techniques of travel writing can add panache to your work, a "little something extra" editors and readers will find hard to resist.

Fair warning: At least in the beginning, travel writing can seem more like an expensive hobby than a remunerative career. Consider those first months or years spent learning your craft as higher education, as if you were working your way through college. Keep your day job; earning a regular salary lets you focus on improving your craft as a writer rather than worrying about ways to keep the roof over your head. During this apprenticeship period it's important to seize every opportunity for publication that comes your way. Markets accessible to newcomers are often low paying. Don't let this deter you. Few experiences in life are as rewarding as seeing your byline in print. Equally important, your first-published efforts provide "clips," eventual springboards to higher-paying markets.

Yes, I can hear you saying, but with an attitude like that, how can I afford a top-of-the-line computer? I'll tell you a secret: *You don't really need one*! This statement might be considered downright blasphemous by proponents of the Information Age, but in truth, high tech has very little to do with writing success. I know many, many wannabe writers who are convinced that as soon as they acquire the world's most sophisticated new keyboard and all the software ever invented to go with it, they will automatically become best-selling authors.

They're only kidding themselves. Writing success comes from practice and perseverance. From trial and error. From sending out your work, having it come back with a rejection slip, then rewriting it over and over, better each time, and sending it out again. It doesn't matter if your first drafts are scrawled in pencil on the back of junk mail. As long as they're neatly typed, editors don't really care if the manuscripts you submit were done on the portable Underwood your Grandma used in college.

Content is what counts. Words. Each of them the best it can possibly be.

My first five published novels and at least a dozen early short stories were typed on a manual Royal typewriter. For the next 15 books and much more short fiction, I used an IBM Selectric II (still one of my prized possessions). Not until 1995, when I began writing nonfiction for a newspaper editor who expected articles to be turned in on disk, did I add a word processor to my equipment. The Canon StarWriter 400 cost $$$, compared to the $$$$$ needed to purchase a "name" brand computer plus modem and all the other accessories. This article is being written on that machine, which still functions perfectly.

Research trips don't have to cost a fortune, either. When I began writing and selling fiction in my twenties, I created fictional backgrounds based on interesting nearby settings. Then as now, travel for me was both passion and goal. Whenever the family finances would allow a trip, we went. So, inevitably, did my heroes and heroines. First to the Monterey Peninsula, two hours down the road. In time, to Hawaii, the San Juan Islands, Florida, Ireland, Venice, Mykonos, Bora-Bora.

It makes sense even for experienced travel writers to target the less expensive, close-to-home locales for most of their articles. The majority of newspaper travel articles are tailored to fit the lifestyles of average readers: time-starved, budget-conscious readers who pick up the Sunday paper hoping to find descriptions of short, affordable getaways they and their families can enjoy.

While these locations are generally within a few hours' drive, the cost of your research and photographs for a mini-holiday destination piece will still usually exceed the "stringer" fee the newspaper pays for your piece. Therefore, as a free lancer hoping to make travel writing pay its way (and yours, too), you need to make sure each trip does the work of three or four more.

One way to get started is to find enough interesting features about a place you intend to visit *anyway* to warrant turning your trip into a travel article. An early article I wrote about Seaside, Oregon, came about because my husband and I participated in a holiday arts and crafts show there. The many attractions of this delightful beach town made it a natural for a "come and bring the family" story.

After completing research for the piece, it occurred to me that the popular annual event might also interest the readers of *Oregon Coast*. Yes, said the editor when I queried; write it up for the following November. Next, learning that new baby seals were due to be born at Seaside's aquarium at about the same time that this attraction celebrated its 60th anniversary, I sent another proposal to the same magazine. The result was a second "go-ahead-on-spec."

Particularly when they aren't well acquainted with a writer's work, editors will often cautiously agree to take a look at an article on speculation. Never let the lack of a guarantee keep you from doing a thorough job of research and submitting your very best work. Turn in a piece the editor loves, and your next query may result in a contract up front. Similarly, don't be put off by the fact that an otherwise ideal market pays "on publication," rather than "on acceptance." Anticipating a check due months after you've done the work gives you something solid to look forward to. Earmark it for a special journey!

That trip to Seaside resulted in three published articles, one for the newspaper and two others in a good regional magazine. These days, I don't wait until I arrive at a destination to start my research. Instead, I contact the Chamber of Commerce as far ahead as possible and ask them to send me all the promotional material on the region. Then I start counting the "plusses."

What kind of plusses? Travel plus all the different categories included in *The Writer's* market listings. Let me give you a few examples that have worked for me.

Travel + art = an article on how Western murals turned a dying town into one of the state's top tourist attractions. Travel + animals = a piece on sending our kitties to camp (a.k.a. The Sandbox Ranch) while we went on vacation. Travel + ethnic minorities = a story about how the Yakama Indians of central Washington changed the spelling of their name in a bid for tribal identity. Travel + gardening = a round-up linking a bonsai garden in Canton, China, with several similar attractions near Puget Sound. Travel + history = the tale of the U.S. Army's Bicycle Infantry stationed at Fort Missoula, Montana, in 1897. Travel + religion = a funny vignette about water from the Sea of Galilee. Travel + sports = a profile of a female senior citizen who launched the first woman's kayaking club in America.

Each of those plusses along with many others resulted in articles with my byline. Once I started looking at every destination as if it were a rich gold mine, full of nuggets, I turned them into tales of interest to editors and readers. You can tap into that gold mine, too. When you decide to visit a spot, research it thoroughly in advance. Before leaving home, query publications whose interests match a particular facet of that destination—their own special "travel-plus."

Don't wait until you return from a trip to record your expenses. Keep track of mileage, and carry along a notebook to record every travel expenditure. Keep receipts in a zippered envelope; you'll need them to fill out your 1040 form. It's a "$$$ and Sense" approach to accounting. That's just one more "plus" of being a travel writer.

❏ 61

TRICKS OF THE TRADE (JOURNALS)

BY FRASER SHERMAN

PERHAPS YOU'VE HEARD THAT TRADE JOURNALS—MAGAZINES GEARED to specific industries—are good markets to write for, but when you flip open the market listings you're baffled. How could you ever come to know enough to write for magazines such as *Journal of Emergency Medical Services*, *Journal of Court Reporting*, or *Construction Marketing Today*?

I had that feeling a decade ago, when I first looked at the trade journal market, but having sold articles to many trade magazines, I've found it possible to write about keeping roads free of weeds and grass (*Transportation Builder*), fraud in workers' compensation insurance (*Foundations*), and the use of computerized maps in law enforcement (*Law Enforcement Technology*). And while trade magazines don't bring the high profile or pay rate of an article in *Esquire*, they have helped me accumulate a solid collection of clips.

Where to get ideas for trade journal articles

If your profession has its own trade magazine, you shouldn't have too much trouble getting ideas. Is there an industry-wide problem your company is trying to solve? A new technology that doubles your productivity? A new regulation you think is hare-brained? Do you have a strong opinion on a current hot-button issue? It's never essential to write only what you know, but it can make the work easier.

Of course, drawing on your profession will give you material for only two or three magazines. What about magazines for the fields in which you have no experience?

Check the newspaper

Newspapers routinely report how problems or developments in a particular industry affect the public; give that information a spin, and you may have a trade article. After my local newspaper described the problems caused when pet-owners abandoned animals during hurricanes—or refused to evacuate without them—I queried *Emergency* on the subject from the emergency-management standpoint: How can overextended emergency officials deal with dozens of strays after a catastrophe? If owners evacuate, where can they take their pets? *Emergency* not only bought the piece, they featured it on their cover.

The world around you

Contact some of the local public relations people; learn about the seminars offered at the next convention in town; talk to a local business owner. You may find information that can be turned into an article. My first sale to *Emergency* came when I covered a presentation at a local hospital's seminar on emergency medicine.

Study the market

Once you know what you want to write about, consult the market listings at the back of this *Handbook* (or the trade journal market list in the February issue of *The Writer*), and list every trade magazine that might be interested in your piece. For instance, an article on problems with 911 systems might sell to magazines for firefighters, for police, and for EMTs.

Then order at least one sample copy or more of the magazines you want to query and ask for their writers' guidelines. Trade journals are far more likely to offer free sample copies than consumer publications.

Read the guidelines, then study the magazine itself. Is it a regional or national magazine? Do the editors use profiles of industry leaders? How-to articles? Do they cover new regulations and controversial issues? Do they expect authors to have hands-on experience in the profession?

Refine the idea

Let's say you've been fascinated by a local mall's approach to deterring shoplifters. Before you send off any queries, call the mall manager and ask for some background. Is this approach unique, or standard operating procedure around the country? Did their shoplifting problem result from some universal problems other malls had to solve, or was it unique to the local situation? You don't want to propose an idea everyone in the industry has already heard about—or one that nobody else in the industry can use.

Even if you get a go-ahead, your idea may still need some refining. My original query to *Law Enforcement Technology* was based on how local police used computer-generated maps to make up for the lack of detailed, up-to-date commercial area maps. After talking to the software supplier, I learned about other police departments using the maps in other ways; that made for a much more informative article than I'd originally conceived.

Finding information

Once you get a go-ahead from the magazine, you'll need to get in-depth information for your article. If you're not in the field professionally, where do you do your research?

a) *Local professionals.* Even if they don't know anything about your particular topic, they can steer you toward people who might.

b) *Trade associations.* In my work for *Foundations*, I request a lot of information from the public relations office of the National Association of Home Builders, which has explained the impact of new environmental regulations, the industry position on construction-related legislation, insurance problems for builders, and other useful topics.

c) *Bureaucrats.* Contrary to popular myth, I've found many people in state and local governments who are well-informed and helpful, willing to translate arcane regulations into everyday speech, or give me the rationale for new government policies. It can take several phone calls to find the right person in the right department, but it's worth it.

d) *Researchers.* If your initial research turns up the name of a researcher (pollster, scientist, statistician) with an interest in your particular topic, by all means call him or her and if possible, arrange for an interview.

When holding interviews, keep two things in mind. First, bias: I've never met a builder who didn't think new regulations on the industry were unfair and irrational, and I've never met a bureaucrat who didn't think the new rules were fair and viable. When interviewees make statements about "fairness," ask for details—what exactly makes the rule fair (or unfair)?

Second, keep in mind that many of your interviewees won't be PR professionals or politicians, and won't be used to talking with the press. Don't be confrontational; be patient if the interviewee is nervous; and make your questions as specific as possible: "What effect will cheap, quick-drying concrete have on the homebuilding industry?" will net more information than "What's new in concrete houses?"

More study

After you've gathered enough information to start drafting the article, take another look at the magazine. Do articles open with a concrete example, a broad overview, a quote? Do they favor a dry, scholarly style with minimal quotes, or a more sprightly, light tone? What technical details can you assume your readers know, and what do you have to explain? If you can shape your style until it's close to the magazine's, your chance of a sale will increase.

Multiple submissions

Many topics and issues are relevant to various trade journals: For example, the basic principles of preventing employee theft or keeping the IRS happy may be the same for different businesses. Nonetheless, your piece should be written specifically for the magazine to which you are submitting. If you have written an article on 911 systems for *Emergency*, you may consider refocusing the article, and making the requisite changes in tone and format, to fit the style of *Chief of Police*. If you're willing to make the changes, multiple submissions can pay off.

Follow the rules

All the rules of manuscript and query format, on treating editors with respect, about doing only your best work and being willing to rewrite—they're as true for *Masonry* as they are for *Law Enforcement Technology*. Don't kid yourself that trade magazines are a substandard genre that will take substandard work; treat them with respect and professionalism, and you may find plenty of opportunities to practice your own trade—writing—for pay.

□ 62

Military Money: Cashing In On Old War Stories

By Lance Q. Zedric

IF YOU'VE ALWAYS WANTED TO WRITE FOR MILITARY MAGAZINES, BUT never considered yourself an expert, relax—you don't have to be an expert or even a veteran to break into this well-paying free-lance market. It's easier than you think, and often the best material can be found in an old history book or even right next door.

There are plenty of topics bivouacked out there. All you have to do is ask. Everyone knows a family member, friend or neighbor who served in the military. And they all have an old war story to tell. The kind old man next door might have been a celebrated war hero or a Medal of Honor winner! Your grandfather, father, aunt or uncle might have served aboard a ship with Admiral Nimitz, eaten Christmas dinner with General Patton, or participated in a historic event. Millions of stories are waiting to be told.

After you've blown the dust off *U.S. History 101,* turn to the sections on World War I, World War II, Korea, the Vietnam War, and even the more recent military ventures, and you will find accounts of important battles, commanders, or military events that, with a little research and a fresh angle, will provide ideal material for an interesting article.

Recon the market. Research military publications, and become familiar with their readership. A sound battle plan will prevent having your article become a rejection slip casualty.

The military market ranges from general to specific. For example, *VFW Magazine* (Veterans of Foreign Wars) and *American Legion Magazine* have readerships of more than two million veterans from every branch of the military. They publish various articles on training, weaponry, tactics, veterans legislation, active and former units, military personalities and nostalgia. Publications with such large readerships prefer articles that appeal to as many of their readers as possible. They focus on events involving large military units, such as Army and Marine divisions, Navy fleets, and Air Force Squadrons. Smaller publications, on the other hand, cater to more defined audiences. *Behind The Lines: The Journal of U.S. Special Operations,* specializes in articles on elite U.S. units, such as the Green Berets and Navy SEALs; others focus on respective branches of the military. *Army Magazine* appeals to Army veterans; *All Hands* and *Navy Times* to the Navy; and *Air Force Times* to the Air Force. Magazines like *Civil War Illustrated, World War II* and *Vietnam,* among others, appeal to enthusiasts of a particular war.

Editors are always on the lookout for articles offering new insights on prominent military leaders and for anniversary articles commemorating notable battles and events. But most publications prefer articles on major anniversaries, such as the fifth, tenth, twenty-fifth, fiftieth, and one-hundredth.

But military publications aren't limited to anniversary themes. Anything to do with the home front is also desirable. Whether it's an article on industrial war production, sending care packages to a family member overseas, or collecting "sweetheart pins," the possibilities are endless. Read past issues and look for a theme.

It will save time and effort to consult a calendar. Since most magazines require at least four months' lead time, allow ample time to query, research, and write an article. If you're writing a 50th-anniversary article on the armistice during the Korean War, which occurred in June 1953, send your query or article to the editor by February 2003.

But be careful. War recollections can be a professional minefield. Here are a couple of tips to remember when interviewing a war veteran for an article:

Never write a military article based solely on a personal recollection. As years pass, war stories tend to be exaggerated and important details omitted. Whether intentional or not, veterans often "embellish" their experiences and recollections. What might have been a five-minute skirmish with a squad of enemy troops armed with pistols in 1944, may, more than fifty years later, become a bloody, year-long siege against two divisions of crack troops armed with automatic rifles! So, beware. Ask the veteran you're interviewing for specific times, dates, locations, books, articles, documents, and for the name of anyone who could "help verify" the account.

Use tact when interviewing a veteran. War is often the most traumatic event in a person's life, and it can be an ongoing source of great pain. Don't begin an interview with "how many people did you kill?" or "tell me what it's like to kill somebody." Insensitivity will guarantee failure. Ease into the interview, and allow the person time to relax and learn more about you. For example, ask an open question, such as "tell me what you were doing before you left for military service." As your subjects relax, ask specific questions. But steer clear of potentially sensitive questions until a solid rapport is established. Always put the veteran's feelings first.

If you want to research a specific military unit, but can't find anyone who served in it, don't give up. Most units have a veterans' association and are listed with the Office of the Chief of Military History in Washington, D.C. Another approach is to consult reunion announcements listed in military magazines; these usually provide a phone number to call for information. Explain that you are researching an article on their unit, and chances are a membership roster will be in the mail.

When you need detailed accounts of a particular unit, government institutions are the best source. The National Archives at Suitland, Maryland, contains enough information for the most ambitious military article. The United States Military History Institute at Carlisle Barracks, Pennsylvania, is an outstanding repository for unit histories and contains the personal papers of some of the country's most outstanding military figures. Service academy libraries at West Point, Annapolis, and Colorado Springs, along with military post libraries across the nation, also have extensive unit histories and rare documents. But call first and obtain clearance. Admittance is not guaranteed.

Good photographs can sell an article. In many cases, military photographs are easy to obtain. Most veterans have a few snapshots and will eagerly show them or lend them to you to be copied. With luck, a rare one-of-a-kind photo might turn a reluctant would-be editor into an eager, all-too-happy-to-write-you-a-check editor!

Photographs can also be purchased from several government sources. The Still Photo Branch of the National Archives in College Park, Maryland, is one. It will research its photo files and provide a partial listing on three topics. You then select a commercial contractor from a list to produce the photographs.

Other government sources in the Washington, D.C., area maintain extensive photo files and offer similar services. The Department of Defense Still Media Records Center provides Army, Navy, Air Force, and Marine Corps photographs from 1954 to the present. The Smithsonian's National Air and Space Museum has Air Force photographs prior to 1954. Coast Guard photographs are available through the Commandant at Coast Guard Headquarters.

If time is short, consult the ad sections of military magazines. Military photo catalogues are available from a number of private suppliers. The photos might cost more, but they will arrive much faster than if they were ordered from Uncle Sam. And an 8 x 10 B&W photo may sell a $500 article.

After concluding your research and obtaining photographs, it's time to write. Here are a few more helpful tips:

1. Write tight and factually. The military audience is knowledgeable and will not be won over with flowery prose or fluffy writing. They appreciate facts and hate filler. Most readers are veterans and know how to cut through fat to get to the point.

2. Use quotes from participants when possible. Put the reader in a muddy foxhole alongside a bedraggled infantryman. Put him or her in the cockpit of a bullet-ridden F-14 screaming toward a Soviet MIG at mach 1 with guns blazing! Let the reader take part in the action.

3. Extol duty, honor and country. Patriotism sells, especially with readers of military magazines. Don't be afraid to wave the flag responsibly.

Whether you write about an elite unit fighting its way out from behind enemy lines against insurmountable odds, recount the monumental invasion of Normandy, or retell the sad story of a soldier's loneliness far from home, if you do your homework and follow a few simple rules, you should be well on your way to breaking into this lucrative market. Salute!

❏ 63

CREATIVE NONFICTION WRITING

BY RITA BERMAN

WHAT IS CREATIVE NONFICTION? IS IT A NEW GENRE OF WRITING? AN oxymoron? Fictionalized facts? While it sounds like a contradiction in terms, creative nonfiction is a new description for an old skill: that of writing well-crafted salable articles. For today's market, however, nonfiction writers are allowed, even encouraged, to incorporate certain fiction techniques and to use the first-person "I."

Formerly, the formal style, using a neutral voice, is now recognized as distancing the writer from the reader, whereas writing from the first-person viewpoint can help with reader identification that is further magnified if the writer's experiences or comments resonate or connect with the reader's life. That is why seemingly ordinary concerns of everyday life, such as health, diet, sex, money, and travel can provide good potential topics for creative nonfiction. The range of creative nonfiction includes feature articles, memoirs, essays, personality profiles, travel pieces, how-to's and even contemporary, political, or other social issues pieces.

Because editors have switched from asking "just give me the facts," to "tell me a story," *how* you tell the story is where creative nonfiction comes in. In other words, the article remains nonfiction because the content is based on fact and is not created or made up, but you have more freedom in the actual writing of it. That calls for embellishing and enhancing, narrating instead of reporting, dressing up the bare facts by using fiction techniques such as setting of mood, providing description of place, expressing emotion, and often incorporating dialogue or flashbacks.

Before describing some of the fiction elements you could use, it might be helpful to review the basic structure of an article. You must catch the reader's interest in the introduction; in the next section identify your topic; in the body of the piece present your material; and close by drawing a conclusion or repeating a key point.

Your task is to write your article like a storyteller, not as a gatherer of facts. Take those facts and filter them through your eyes. Provide details so that you add to, but don't change the information you have gathered. And as you write, keep your potential readers in mind, so that you angle the story to their needs.

My article on graphology, "Unlocking Secrets in Handwriting Can Help Hiring" (*Triangle Business*), began with an opening quote from my source, Mary Gallagher, a handwriting expert:

> "Looking at how applicants cross their t's or dot their i's is one way to decide whether to hire an individual." So said Mary Gallagher, a certified graphoanalyst. More than 5,000 companies use handwriting analysis as a hiring aid. . . . Employers need the edge to know not only what the applicant projects but also what he or she is capable of doing.

Having aroused the readers' interest, a brief summary about the history of graphology came next, and then I continued with examples of what handwriting might reveal. Quotes from other people who had used Gallagher's services, including a manager who had ignored her findings, gave balance to the piece.

Framing the story

For this particular piece, I used the technique of framing the story to make a satisfactory ending: I circled around to the beginning by referring to the opening paragraph. For creative nonfiction, this is an excellent way of tying the article together, satisfying the curiosity you have aroused and leaving the reader with a resonant image of all that has gone before. You might draw a conclusion, make an evaluation, or point out a question that still needs an answer.

In this instance I ended by informing readers of how companies obtain a sample of handwriting from applicants in order to study it; they have prospective employees state in their own handwriting why they believe they are qualified for the job.

Atmosphere and mood

Specific details are highly significant in nonfiction to help the reader visualize the place or the event you are describing. They add interest and color and convey atmosphere and mood to the setting, locale, time of year, and even the weather in your article. General statements, such as, "We went to a museum, which we found interesting," fall flat without supporting detail. Use fiction techniques to describe what you saw in the museum.

Make note of your impressions and reactions as you conduct your research. Whether you are taking a tour, arriving at a new destination, or interviewing someone for a personal profile, these impressions and observations may turn out to be the lead or heart of your piece when you come to write it.

Example: In a piece about redevelopment and housing in Jamaica for *Town and Country Planning Journal,* I opened with a description of what I had seen in the drive from the airport:

> The coast road from the airport is a narrow lane overlooked by small and large estates. Plantations, old great houses, and tiny country towns dot the hillside. Snaking by resort hotels and sugar-cane fields, some of which are now being developed into housing estates, the life of the country appeared before us as we turned each bend on the main north-coast road.

Writing in first person

Your nonfiction pieces will come alive creatively when you incorporate your personal observations. Use all of your senses. Tell your readers what you tasted, saw, touched, heard. . . . By personalizing the piece, it becomes your own. No other article will have that voice—your voice.

Instead of saying that there were vendors at the site and leaving it at that, I described my encounter with them in "Spain, New and Old Faces," published in *Leader Magazine:*

> . . . As we stepped down from the bus, we were accosted by a group of women darting in front of us, each waving a lace tablecloth. Having caught our attention, they shouted prices at us in Spanish, jabbing their fingers in the air to indicate how many thousands of pesetas they wanted.
>
> To indicate that I wanted a smaller cloth, and round, I made a circle with my hands. They understood. An older woman held up a tablecloth while a young girl held up five fingers, 50,000 pesetas. I countered with two fingers. She shook her head and held up four fingers. I then showed cash—25,000 pesetas (approximately $25). She took two bills, but wanted "another finger," total of $30. No deal. I pointed to an embroidered rectangular cloth and the finger shaking started all over again. . . . I got both tablecloths for $53.

By revealing the interaction that took place, I enhanced the story and by adding color and humor, made the piece more interesting than if I had baldly stated that I spoke no Spanish, but we came to a deal.

Reveal your characters

Creative nonfiction is frequently about people. We're all curious about how other people live, what they do, and how they think. For personality profiles, draw on the external cues that you observed while doing the interview. Describe the subject's quirks, mannerisms, or appearance, what he wore, how he moved his body as he spoke. Movement can reveal and imply at the same time. "Shifting in his chair" conveys an image quite different from "settling in his chair."

Dialogue

The fiction writer makes up dialogue, but in creative nonfiction you take the dialogue from your interview notes or tapes, using direct quotes from your sources, instead of paraphrasing. This adds verbal color to your piece and encourages your readers to draw their own conclusions—an excellent way to present a controversial topic or viewpoint.

I used provocative statements about women and their reactions to conflict as my lead for a piece for *Women Executive's Bulletin:*

> Most women fear conflict—perhaps more than men fear it. . . . Many women give contradictory signals. For example, when they are under stress and trying to communicate, they often smile, unconsciously suggesting to the other person that this isn't such a serious situation, according to Dr. Ruth D. Anderson, Associate Professor of Speech Communication.

Next, I offered some significant details on how we learn to communicate:

> The communication skills we learn early in life are those that we use when we reach managerial and executive positions: to accept conflict as a normal, everyday occurrence, then to understand how to handle conflict. Think back to how your mother, or any other female authority figure in the household you grew up in, dealt with conflict. If she screamed, do you scream?

Here's another "tell me more" quote that I used for a general-interest article on buying or selling a house, a concern of many Americans:

"The consumer has the right to bargain," said Andrew M. Barr, a real estate broker. "It isn't a rigid situation. Some houses are easier to sell than others. Why charge 6% when you can do it for 3% and sell it in a week? That's fair to the consumer and fair to us."

Published in the *Virginia Cardinal,* my article explored the sensitive topic of brokers' commission and informed the reader about available alternatives in the Washington D.C. area, the flexible fee system, or using a consumer-oriented advisory service.

Flashbacks

Flashbacks are another fiction device you might consider using to provide a change of pace. By means of the flashback you can expand your story and take the reader in a direction different from where you began. Example: "As the train drew into the station, I remembered the last time I visited London. . . ." Or, "As he spoke of his father I was remembering our first meeting, more than 20 years ago. . . ."

With this technique, you can introduce something significant from the past that has bearing on the present. To help the reader make the transition back to the present, insert a transitional phrase or word, such as "now" or "today," and continue with the present-day account.

Writing about my own experience as a temporary worker some years ago, I used a flashback to go back to when the Kelly Girl organization began in 1946, transitioning to a change of name of Kelly Temporary Services in the 1980's, then continued with more of my work experiences and ended with a forecast about the future direction of temporary work.

Know your readership

As you write, keep in mind the readers you want to reach; you need to know for whom you are writing. This calls for studying your possible markets before you commence writing, research that will be helpful when you shape the story. For example, some magazines publish only descriptive essays, while others prefer nuts-and-bolts information. After you have studied the market listings as well as writers' guidelines and read several issues of the magazine, you will know what the readers like and how to aim your articles to their preferred style.

Knowing my readership helped me slant my piece, "Pick up on the

Shell Game," for *The Army, Navy, Air Force Times Magazine*. I opened with:

> When Navy man Jim Wadsworth was stationed in New Guinea 30 years ago, he stooped over and picked up a shell on the beach. By that simple act, he found himself hooked on a hobby—shell collecting.
> Shelling has given many military families special pleasures. Any number can play; there are no sex or age barriers. You don't have to be an expert or spend a cent, unless you want to become a professional shell collector. Shells can be traded with other collectors or bought like stamps from a dealer.

That paragraph linked the hobby of shell collecting to military families, who were the readers of this particular magazine. By focusing the angle of the story to those readers, I achieved publication.

Creative nonfiction is not a new genre, but a new description for articles based on fact but written in fictional form. Creative nonfiction uses mood, setting, descriptions of place, action, people, senses, thoughts, and feelings. It may use dialogue and flashbacks. The first-person viewpoint adds to reader identification, catches their attention. Your personal impressions and comments can help make your nonfiction unique.

□ 64

THE KEY TO INTERVIEWING SUCCESS

BY JOY PARISE

IF YOU WANT TO ADVANCE IN YOUR ARTICLE WRITING, INCORPORATE the opinions of outside professionals to enliven and enrich your work. If done properly, a good interview provides not only plenty of material that will add depth to an article, but also valuable ideas and sources for future projects.

The actual interview is no place for on-site training. Much of the success of an interview will depend on your behind-the-scenes preparation to make sure that your subject is enough at ease to talk freely and openly to you. With experience, you'll learn techniques that work best for you. The following are some methods that can help you on your way to interviewing success.

1. If at all possible, arrange for a face-to-face interview. While a telephone call can give you the information you need, an in-person interview will more than pay off. Eye contact with your subject will help relax him or her, and being able to describe his or her gestures, appearance, and surroundings can make your writing come alive.

Once you have phoned and arranged the interview, follow up with a note thanking the person and confirming the time and place, and enclose a simple business card, if you have one. If you'll need any specific information, photos, statistics, or phone numbers, alert your subject in your note so that he or she can have them handy. Don't send specific questions that you'll be asking. Nothing is worse than sitting down in front of the subject who reads stilted and scripted answers to you.

2. Make the most of your interviewing time, and give your subject the maximum amount of time to talk. Prepare your questions in advance so that you don't flounder. To create an atmosphere of easy conversation, don't keep the list of questions in front of you. Tuck them inside the cover of your notepad or place them discreetly to the side to peek at now and then. Be familiar enough with your questions in advance to be flexible if new material from your subject's comments and responses pops up, if your interview takes an interesting new slant, or if your prepared order doesn't work. Although your prepared questions will help keep you on course, don't be close-minded. Keep alert. You may find a whole line of discussion to pursue spontaneously.

3. Structure your questions around a preliminary outline. Try to keep the outline of your article in your mind before you go into the interview so that you ask your questions in sequence. This will make it easier later to work from your notes rather than facing a hodgepodge of information you have to organize.

When I interview someone for a feature, I structure my articles in a specific way. Drawing a picture in words of the gestures, appearance, or surroundings tells why this person is interesting enough to be written about. That's how I try to capture the readers' attention so that they will become interested enough to want to know more about this person—and keep reading.

I then go into the subject's area of expertise and give enough objective and colorful information so that readers say, "I didn't know that." (Editors often tell me that they found my articles very informative; they learned a lot.) Then I swing back to the person I'm interviewing and ask about his or her goals for the future.

Whatever your style, make a plan in advance so that you have a good idea where you want to steer your interview.

4. Dress for success. Making a good appearance begins with being on time. If you're interviewing someone important enough to be interviewed, then his or her time is important, too. Respect it.

Dress in a way to put your subject at ease. Don't underestimate this step. If you're going to a corporation, wear a suit. If you're going to a small business, try a sports jacket. If you're going to a cowboy barn, try jeans. For a sports club, neat slacks. The idea is to make your subject comfortable enough to relate to you and want to help you write a good article.

5. Let your instincts take over. If for some reason you're having a really hard time with the interview, let your subject know it. Some years ago, I was sent to cover a riding clinic at an out-of-state stable. The owner was very rude and cold. After trying to get quotes from him—to make him look good—and getting nowhere, I looked at him and lightly said, "Come on, give me a break. Help me out here." Since he knew he was being obnoxious (but was probably never called on it), he immediately tuned in and started talking.

Another time, I was asked to do an article on a whole family. The editor had tried to write a piece about them but had found them almost impossible to interview. Though they were willing to sit down with me, they found it hard to make anything other than the "name, rank, and serial number" types of comments.

When I walked into their house, to my horror I found the whole family sitting around the table. Self-conscious in front of each other, no one spoke. From the corner of the table, one person would meekly add a bit of information. I went home and waited for a few days, then phoned that person. I told him that he sounded as if he had so much background to tell me about (which he did), and I asked if I could meet with him alone so that I could write a "good" article. We met again at his house, sat under a lovely tree, and talked for an hour about the family history and their achievements in the horse world. The tree became the central symbol for the stability of the family, and the article turned out much better than I'd ever imagined it would.

Don't be afraid to ask for more if you are not getting what you need, but do so tactfully and honestly.

6. Bring a tape recorder. Be prepared to take notes to back up what's on the tape. The recorder is good for capturing the exact ways that people speak, as well as names and figures and other information that takes too much time to write. This is important in drawing a picture of your subject. Furthermore, the flow of your subject's speech as opposed to yours in your writing will help keep the rhythm of your article interesting.

A third and more subtle use of the tape recorder comes in when it is shut off. I've gotten some of my best quotes when the interview appears to be formally over and the people you're interviewing tend to relax and open up.

Once, when I was interviewing a successful professional horseman, he walked me to the door of his stable, and looking out over his forty-acre farm, he waved his arm and said, "I'm so lucky. I'm so lucky. I'm forty years old and doing what I love!"

I began the article with that gesture and those words. Since the article showed that he had attained what he had through hard work and dedication, not luck, his humility endeared him to the readers. In fact, he said he never got so much positive feedback from any other article written about him. The fact was that he was a nice guy, and it showed—particularly when the interview was "officially" over.

7. Let your subject really talk. Ask your subject what he or she thinks is important, and what he or she would like you to write. You'll be amazed!

Once when I was interviewing a man who had won at a horse show, I asked him what he would like me to say. He talked about his stable's successful breeding program—something few people knew about, although it was highly successful.

Not only did it add more information to the article, but it provided me with material for a second article on that stable—an eight-page piece I wrote the next year for a national magazine.

8. Show your appreciation. Get to your interview on time, leave on time, and be polite. Remember, you're not the important person here; the person you're interviewing is. Send a copy of your published article with a thank-you note.

9. Look inside yourself. If you're not getting a successful interview after careful preparation, then look inside. Were you sincerely interested in the person you interviewed? Dogs, horses, and kids know when someone dislikes them, but they warm up with people they know they can trust. People being interviewed do, too. Put your best foot forward, and you can't fail.

□ 65

HOW TO WRITE AND SELL HUMOROUS GREETING CARDS

BY DONNA GEPHART

WRITING GREETING CARDS FOLLOWS THE FOUR SIMPLE BASICS OF OTHER types of writing:

1. Read published greeting cards.
2. Write intensely and creatively.
3. Edit mercilessly.
4. Submit professionally.

First things first

Read greeting cards. Before I sit to write a batch of greeting cards, I'll spend an hour and a half in a card shop or any other store that sells greeting cards reading every funny card I can find. After all, if you write romances, you read romances. If you write horror, you read horror.

Also, read anything that might give you an idea for a card; copy on a cereal box, ads, slogans, billboards, or poems might inspire a card idea.

You should also send for submission guidelines. Simply send a self-addressed, stamped envelope to the editorial department of a greeting card company with a note saying, "Please send guidelines." You can obtain addresses from various sources. Look on the back of the cards on the racks. Consult market lists of greeting card companies. Visit the web site of the National Greeting Card Association which offers its members an online list of companies at http://www.greetingcard.org.

Before putting pen to paper, keep a few things in mind:

- Though women purchase between 80–90% of all greeting cards, many men are successful in the field because they are able to think like women.
- When writing, keep a real person in mind, whether it's a best

316

friend, sister, ex-boyfriend, etc., and write as though you're going to give the card to this person. It's a sure-fire trick to guarantee your card is salable.

- Finally, write what editors need. Birthday is the most popular occasion.

Editors are starving for fresh, innovative ways to wish someone a happy birthday. Christmas and Valentine's Day are the most popular seasonal occasions. (Remember, though, that even smaller companies buy seasonal ideas up to a year ahead of time.)

I usually write surrounded by things to inspire me. If I'm writing birthday cards, I browse lists I've created that have to do with birthdays, for instance, one which details the physical aspects of aging: false teeth, age spots, the need to wear glasses, etc. I'll pair items on the list and try to find connections or think of multiple meanings for an item. For example, glasses can mean reading glasses or drinking glasses. That thought inspired this card. (O = outside or front of card; I = inside of card.)

O: Here' s a birthday present you can really sink your teeth into . . .
I: (Drinking glass containing false teeth)
(Kalan, Inc.)

Besides the lists I've created about particular topics, I love to read through humorous quotations. Clichés can always be twisted into a new way to say something. A rhyming dictionary and thesaurus should be close at hand. And I collect fascinating facts. Did you know a cat has thirty-two muscles in each ear? And a goldfish has a memory span of three seconds? I even knew a writer who kept old love letters and various kinds of cologne in her desk to inspire her when she wrote cards for Valentine's Day.

It's all in the format

As you read greeting cards, you'll notice that certain formats or setups are used again and again. There are several formats into which you can try to fit your ideas with examples from cards I've published. Use these as a guide, but don't let them restrict your creativity.

1. *Lists.* "Top ten" lists were quite popular for awhile and some still are, such as the Top Ten Reasons to be Glad You're Having Another Birthday or Top Ten Reasons I Love You. Shorter lists also work well. Example:

> O: You' re 21—an adult now. It' s time to make some very serious decisions about your future . . .
> I: bottles or cans
> domestic or imported
> by itself or with a shot
> top shelf or the cheap stuff
> shaken or stirred
> dry or on the rocks
> with a twist or without
> straight or with a mixer (Gibson Greetings)

2. *A pun or play on words.*

> O: Congratulations on your pregnancy.
> I: You deserve a standing ovulation. (InnoVisions)

3. *Using the physical properties of the card itself, such as color, weight, measurements, etc.*

> O: (Hunk photo) Your Christmas present is exactly seven inches long . . .
> I: by five inches wide. And when you're done staring at it, you can put it back in the envelope. (Gibson Greetings)

4. *Riddles with a personal twist. A question ending with an unexpected answer.*

> O: Valentine's Day Riddle: What would it mean if you were hot, sweaty and panting heavily?
> I: It would mean the batteries in the remote control died and you had to get up and change the channel yourself. (Gibson Greetings)

5. *Statement of "fact" that can begin with "Did you know . . ." or "Statistics prove . . ."*

> O: Hey Bachelorette! Studies prove there are many devices to increase a man's sexual desire. Leave it to you to find one that reduces it.
> I: A wedding ring. Congratulations! (Smart Alex)

6. *Short poem, often with a twist ending.*

O: Happy birthday to you.
You live in the zoo.
You look like a monkey.
I: But you're really my sister. (Gibson Greetings)

7. *Exaggeration*

O: Is it possible for you to read this birthday card without wearing glasses?
I: Sure, if you can stretch your arm to Cleveland. Happy Birthday. (Oatmeal Studios)

8. *Comparison. Finding the similarities or dissimilarities between two separate items.*

O: What's the difference between men and birthdays?
I: We can live without men. (Gibson Greetings)

9. *Parody a well-known document or expression.*
The following is a parody of the Miranda Rights that an officer must read to a person being arrested:

O: HALT! Valentine's Day Police. Your complete cooperation will be appreciated.
I: You will be confined overnight in the bedroom. A thorough strip search and frisking will be provided. You have the right to remain naked. Anything I have can and will be held against you. Any questions? (Gibson Greetings)

Editing

After you've written your hot new greeting cards, let them cool completely. Take the dog for a walk. Throw in a load of laundry. Discover the joys of in-line skating. Go on a cruise. Just get away from your ideas. Far away. Pull them out again after several days or even weeks. Now edit your card as you would any other type of writing. Eliminate words that don't work. If your punch line seems flat, stretch to find something more original or cut it. Make sure the card is one you would send to someone or would enjoy receiving. Do you think you heard this joke somewhere before? If so, strike it. On the other hand, if your card idea still makes you laugh out loud after time away from it, you've got a winner, and you're ready to organize your ideas into a professional presentation.

Submitting like a pro

Editors at greeting card companies are swamped with misspelled submissions, flat ideas and poor grammar. These are returned immediately. On the other hand, every editor has several writers with whom she works closely and often; writers who submit original ideas, presented professionally. They are your competition. Here's how to compete:

After editing your card ideas, type each one on a 3″ x 5″ index card. On the top corner of each index card, put a code number. For example, a simple one like B-37 would be the 37th Birthday card I've written. Or V-98 is the 98th Valentine's Day card. An editor will refer to your ideas using these code numbers.

Type two identical index cards for each idea. One card stays in your files. (On the back of the one you keep, list the companies to whom you send it.) The other index card goes to the greeting card company. (On the back of this one, type your name, address and phone number so the editor can contact you when she wants to buy your card.)

Gather a batch of card ideas, and put them in an envelope along with a SASE. For your records, keep a copy of every card you're sending out with a cover sheet listing date, name of company, and which ideas you sent.

The waiting period

Having spent nearly seven years as the editor at a greeting card company, I can tell you what happens to your submission after it reaches an editor's desk.

First, your envelope is dropped into a drawer with dozens of other envelopes.

Second, after your friendly editor is back from attending meetings, analyzing sales data, working on the latest new product line, and proofreading finished cards, she'll pull out the envelopes from her drawer, and read the contents of each one.

You can expect one of three responses:

1) A form rejection letter. Editors can't accept all the good cards they receive because of space and budget constraints, so if your ideas are returned to you, make a note of it on your records and get them out to another company . . . the same day.

2) A hold letter. An editor may hold one or two ideas from your batch and return the rest. It will take several weeks to make the rounds at meetings to seek approval to purchase them. Not all "holds" are purchased, but your odds are often very good.

Make a note of the holds on your records, and send the others to the next company on your list.

3) A contract will be sent to you for one or more of your card ideas. Sign it. Wait a couple of weeks for the check. (You can expect to earn anywhere from fifty to a hundred and fifty dollars for each one accepted, depending on the rates of a particular company. No royalties are paid, and the company buys all rights.) Be happy! You're a published greeting card writer. In several months, you may receive samples of the card(s) you sold.

General do's and don'ts

1. Don't submit artwork. If an illustration is integral to understanding the joke, describe it briefly.

2. Do wait six to eight weeks before mailing a polite reminder note. And another four to six weeks to withdraw your ideas if you haven't heard a word.

3. Don't submit simultaneously to several companies. You're in a bad position if two editors want the same idea.

4. Do remove a card idea from circulation once it's sold. Remember: The greeting card company buys all rights.

5. Don't call, question or harangue an editor about her decision.

6. Do have as much fun writing and submitting greeting cards as thousands of people will have reading and sending your published cards.

7. Don't give up after a few rejections. Even top-selling greeting card writers get rejections. Keep reading, writing, revising, and submitting.

Finally, if you enjoy writing greeting card copy, you might also enjoy creating novelty products—key rings, T-shirts, etc. Although the markets for these products have shrunk over the past few years, there are still a few companies seeking Post-It notepads and novelty buttons (witty one-liners).

Writing greeting cards is a profitable field, highly receptive to innovative, professional writing, even if you've never sold a greeting card before.

❏ 66

How to Break Into Newspaper Writing

By Lisa Coffey

HAVE YOU EVER READ A NEWSPAPER ARTICLE, OPINION PIECE, OR FEATURE story and said to yourself, "I could write something like that, only about 100 times better"? If so, you've clearly got the confidence; now save the hyperbole for the supermarket tabloids and let's get started.

The first step is to study the newspaper for which you wish to write. Note content, flavor, style, and approximate word count for different types of pieces. Ask yourself: Would my article/column fit well in this newspaper? Because of ad layouts and page designs, editors must adhere to certain word count constraints. So, if opinion columns on the editorial page generally run 750 words, don't submit something twice that length.

No writing method is set in stone, but one sound approach is to tackle a topic in stages. Follow the 4 R's: *Reflection, Reporting, Reconstruction*, and *Revision*.

Reflection involves pondering an issue and determining whether there is in fact a conflict or problem requiring focus, investigation, and resolution. For example, a former Section 8 (housing program designed to create affordable housing) program manager phoned our newspaper about a disturbing trend he had seen: Tenants who trashed their rental units were rightly evicted, only to be recertified to obtain housing at other Section 8 units. Was that a problem? Yes. Landlords, unable to recoup damages from impoverished tenants, were pulling out of the Section 8 program. Fewer landlords meant a growing shortage of such housing for those who truly needed it. Further, destructive tenants were never punished for their behavior—no penalty, no deterrent. This is where you define the issue, establishing the premise of your piece. Now you're ready for your next step.

Reporting involves getting the who, what, when, where, why, and how of the story, in addition to establishing for readers why they should care. For the Section 8 editorial series, I contacted numerous Section 8 landlords, tenants, the Indiana Department of Human Services, and the Legal Services Organization, and I acquired photos and a wealth of other information from the former program manager who initially called the newspaper. I also enumerated solutions—one of which was adopted by the then Housing and Urban Development Secretary Jack Kemp after he read the series—and the ramifications to U.S. taxpayers if they didn't demand accountability from the government's entitlement program administrators. Sources of information for your article or column are available from experts and laymen on both sides of an issue, from your local library, on-line databases such as NEXIS and Data Times (often available through your local library), and public records (with most documents available through the federal Freedom of Information Act and state companion "sunshine" laws). Try to get as much information as possible during your reflection stage. You probably won't use everything, but the more you gather and review, the more likely you are to write a balanced, well-rounded story.

Reconstruction involves arranging your material into a logical, coherent, and attention-grabbing form readers can understand. Break down the reconstruction phase into four S's: the Stopper, the Synopsis, the Supporting Material, and the Summary.

• *The Stopper* is that eye-catching lead, the opening statement or paragraph that makes the reader want to read more. For my Section 8 series, I began with a quote from a Section 8 landlord: "It's like a swarm of locusts going through an area. . . . There are places here in the city where Section 8 tenants have literally destroyed the community." It was an ugly comment, but it was the heart of the series' raison d'être: to tell an ugly story and to try to do something about it. Or how about this lead to a story about the U.S. Department of Agriculture sending subsidies to deceased farmers: "The dead don't tell tales; they're too busy collecting USDA benefits." Sometimes light humor may be appropriate to draw attention to a serious story. Make the lead the most arresting part—not necessarily the meat, but the attention-grabber that will make readers want to continue.

• *The Synopsis* is a focus statement, a clarification of the issue at hand. "Legal Services Organization's summer victory, which prevents termination of destructive tenants from the Section 8 housing program, could turn into a winter defeat for the very group whom Legal Services and the courts sought to protect—low-income tenants." It is from the synopsis—the statement of the problem or conflict, the issue you wish to address in your writing—that the rest of your article will flow. The synopsis isn't meant to be exciting or cute: It explains, defines, and steers your readers toward what is to come.

• *Supporting material* is just that—the quotes, statistics, hard facts, examples and other documentation that build your piece and help the reader form a truly informed opinion on the issues under discussion. Don't forget to cite all sources and always get permission before quoting someone directly.

• *The Summary* is a simple restatement of the issues, with proposed action.

Revision involves eliminating the extraneous or repetitious material, checking your facts, and double-checking your sources. This is where you may discover that you should shift your story in a totally new direction. Don't be afraid to do that. Be flexible. Let what will help readers the most be your guide.

What to write

Write a news feature or column describing a personal event that gave you new insight or a greater degree of compassion for others. Write a travel piece about an unusual place you or your family recently visited. Do a local celebrity profile from an unusual angle—the state legislator whose toughest "race" was against cancer. Offer to cover school board meetings or other news in your neighborhood; most newspapers have sections featuring "zoned" news from specific parts of town or a region and often are in the market for "correspondents" from those areas. Write a how-to column on a topic the paper doesn't regularly feature: tax strategies, dog grooming, housecleaning tips, ethnic cooking, summer/winter automotive maintenance, gardening, child-rearing, single parenthood. If your article is good, you may be asked to write a column on the subject on a regular basis. But be sure to do your homework.

When to write it

If the President just signed a welfare bill, and you've been following the welfare debate in Congress and can offer cogent analysis of the pros and cons of the legislation that now is law, opinion editors want to hear from you—right away. Speed is of essence. Many issues will be around for a long time—crime, education, the national debt, foreign policy—but when a news event occurs, the media must respond and do so quickly, explaining, analyzing, predicting, and offering articles that tie into the event. Fresh voices are often welcome, especially if a national event can be reported from a local angle.

Where to submit

Call a newspaper in which you'd like to see your work published. Have a finished piece or well-defined proposal ready. Ask to speak to the city, state, sports, fashion or opinion page (op-ed) editor, depending on whether your submission is city news, state news, sports news, etc. The editor may ask you to send your material by e-mail, regular mail or fax; conversely, they may not be interested. You'll never know until you try. In fact, that's how I—with no journalism credentials—ended up working at *The Indianapolis News*; I made a cold call to the editor, proposing a weekly column idea. He liked it, I started writing it, and several months later, when a position opened up on the paper's editorial staff, he offered it to me, and I've been working there for almost ten years. Take a chance; the worst thing that can happen is for an editor to say no.

In what format to submit

Help the editor! For many newspapers, the faster you can get your story or column in, and the sooner it can be put into their typesetting/pagination system, the more inclined the editor will be to buy it. Some publications, however, may not use the Internet for copy transmission; be sure to ask. Also, submit your material in the format (single-spaced vs. double-spaced, etc.) requested by the newspaper, which will have its own preferences.

Some words to the wise

* Write the way you talk. Be concise and precise. Don't try to impress with big words and long sentences. Communicate clearly and authoritatively.

* Bone up on grammar, spelling, and punctuation. Get a copy of *The Elements of Style* by Strunk and White and *The Associated Press' Stylebook*, which nearly all newspapers follow. Some writers with the most to say have the least chance of saying it in print because their grammar, spelling and punctuation are so poor that an editor is turned off immediately.

* Get a good thesaurus or book of synonyms. You'll learn about precise writing as you study synonyms and their subtle semantic differences. Your ability to convey various shades of meaning through your words is akin to an artist's ability to create meaning through his or her brush strokes, shading techniques, and color palette. Write what you want to convey, nothing more, nothing less.

* Do not depend on your spellchecker! It cannot differentiate words that are correctly spelled but have completely different meanings.

The key

Newspapers strive for truth, fairness and accuracy, not only because libel laws demand it, but because the philosophical and constitutional justification for a free press crumbles without it. Always remember, "If in doubt, cut it out," until you can verify the information.

* If you were a mother, would you want to read that your son, in custody, but not yet convicted, is: 1) a "murderer"; or 2) an "alleged murderer"? Neither one, but if you had a choice, you'd probably prefer the latter. Watch your wording, not just to avoid libel, but to be sure it's true and accurate.

* If a reporter quoted you in the newspaper, how would you feel if your words were twisted, even if unintentionally? Do the best, most accurate job you can, but also know that mistakes may be made— printed corrections and a personal apology are the proper responses in those cases. Newspapers, especially dailies, have a great impact on the community; their circulation alone gives them the power to create consensus on the issues of the day. They can uncover truth or fuel gossip; they capture the spirit of the age, and they also help shape it. It should be every newspaper journalist's solemn goal to disseminate truth in a way that elevates, not degrades, that spirit.

❏ 67

SNOOPING IN THE PAST: WRITING HISTORICAL BIOGRAPHIES

BY LAURIE WINN CARLSON

THE PAST FEW YEARS HAVE SEEN BIOGRAPHIES OF PEOPLE FROM THE past propelled onto bestseller lists across the country: *Undaunted Courage,* Stephen Ambrose's biography of Meriwether Lewis; *Unredeemed Captive,* by John Demos, the story of Eunice Williams and the French and Indian War; *No Ordinary Time,* the story of Franklin and Eleanor Roosevelt by Doris Kearns Goodwin, and several biographies of Jane Austen, to name only a few.

The spectacular sales of historical biographies prove that the public wants stories about heroes and heroines, whether their lives involved statesmanship, exploration, or writing literature. People read biographies for many of the same reasons they read novels: to be entertained, to be informed, to be comforted or inspired, to identify with successful people, to live somebody else's life for a while. There's every reason to write historical biographies if you like historical research, enjoy learning about people, and can master the elements of good storytelling.

How does a writer go about retelling the life of a historical person in a way that grabs first an editor, then the reader? Even the most intriguing person's life can be incredibly boring unless presented with creativity and skill. Writing historical biographies requires a combination of techniques from nonfiction and fiction writing, and like the novelist, the first decision the biographer makes is, "Whose story can I tell?" Just like creating a main character in a novel, choosing the subjects for biographies is all-important. Who they are, the times they lived in, and the choices they made are what keeps the narrative going.

The main character

The person you choose to write about must be someone with whom readers will want to identify. That doesn't mean they have to be saints—

readers like to read about "bad guys," too, and biographies of history's villains can make compelling reading. Just be careful to select someone whose life and character pique your interest. I decided to write about women missionaries in the West because they were different from our commonly held perceptions—they were feminists rather than conventional nineteenth-century wives and mothers—and that makes their story intriguing and interesting to today's readers.

Avoid stereotypes: They are too boring. Challenge your preconceptions, search for people who tried to break the mold society had created for them, who strived to do something different and worthwhile, even if they made poor decisions or met with failure. Similar to a protagonist in a novel, good biographies follow the "hero's journey." Writers need to examine a person's life, the hurdles and obstructions he or she met, and how that person overcame them. If he or she failed miserably, perhaps that failure can be understood better or differently from today's perspective.

Like the novelist, as a biographer you want to reveal a person's character bit by bit, showing rather than telling. Using the subject's own writings (diaries, letters) as well as what others wrote or said about the person can be very revealing, but, of course, other people's opinions can be biased, based on personal resentments or jealousies. How you interpret the facts determines whether or not your biography will have true depth and dimension. You'll want to reveal details about your subject's life throughout your book, looking for ways to stir readers' emotions by creating drama and tension, even some suspense, to propel them forward.

Setting

For historical biographies, time and place are extremely important to the picture of the subject's life. What best-selling biographies have in common is that they examine lives of people who lived in periods of turmoil and action, and are carefully researched and scrupulously accurate. In addition, they are written in a lively narrative style that engages and holds readers' interest.

As you choose the person to write about, look at the geographic setting and the time period and social class in which they lived. Time and place achieve a symbolic importance in a biography, as they do in a novel. In biographies, the setting is another character of sorts; it provides hurdles the protagonist must overcome. An impoverished childhood, geographic isolation, ramifications of social class—these all become part of the setting in a biography. When writing about a woman of the early nineteenth century, it makes a great deal of difference whether she lived in a settled New England village or on the Ohio frontier. Where and when she lived is part of her life's story.

When you're casting about for a particular subject for your biography, look for people who lived in exciting times. That will make the entire story much more interesting and provide conflicts outside the person's inner character.

Other characters

Biographies, like novels, have antagonists or villains. Your subject may be young, idealistic, duty-bound; the "bad guys" can be treacherous weather, distance, rugged terrain, armed and dangerous dissidents, time running out, lack of funds, or simply the dark side of human nature. You will also need to identify and include people who helped the protagonist: lovers, mentors, siblings, rescuers, friends, or confidants. Adding these elements will enrich the biography—you will not simply be retelling chronological events in a dead person's life—and will eventually give the biography a sort of climactic resolution.

When you choose a suitable subject to write about, be careful not to choose someone you're in love with—and be sure not to fall in love with the subject as you write. Be alert for evidence of character failings in even the most righteous subject's life: Those natural flaws, mistakes, and weaknesses make the character more well-rounded and real.

Theme

Once you've selected the subject for your biography, ask yourself: Why do I want to write about this person? It's an important question because it gives you the theme for the book. What topics, besides the facts of the person's life, will you include? What broader issues will you address as you tell about this particular person and the times he or she lived in? The theme is really the story you are telling, whether it's about an ordinary person trying to save the farm, a business, society, or whether the theme is one of family devotion, escape from intolerable conditions, or how to overcome adversity and become a leader. These are the overall themes you should really be exploring when you write a person's life from the past.

Study psychological motivation, and place the person's life within the times in which he or she lived. Don't judge his or her efforts (or lack of them) by today's social standards, but determine the expectations of the period in which your subject lived and how he or she did or did not live up to them.

Structure

Most biographies are pretty much chronological, because that's how lives are lived. But you can jump around or diverge somewhat to keep the narrative dramatic as well as realistic. What you're trying to do is to write in scenes, like a playwright. Plan your story around the incidents or events with the most dramatic potential. Select scenes that are visual, full of conflict, danger, failure, suffering, turning points, beginnings, discoveries, and successes. You can't recount all the events in the person's life, but only the most important, dramatic ones; perhaps limit the scope of the book to a span of only a few years or a decade, rather than an entire lifetime. Omit details of childhood, education, old age, or other times when your subject's life held little conflict or excitement. Focus your narrative on the times and events that shaped the subject's life.

Research

Research strongly affects your selection of a subject. You certainly can't select someone about whom there's practically nothing known, because then you have to invent the facts, in which case you should switch from writing a biography to writing a historical novel.

If you want to write about someone with an extensive written record—diaries, court records, letters, and military records—you'll have no problem with research. If, however, you choose a female subject who wasn't famous enough to have left behind lots of written records (and most women in history would fall into this category), you'll need to search harder for information, and can perhaps write a group biography, as I did. This will enable you to use what several women wrote about each other, and by comparing and contrasting their lives, you'll be able to produce a strong narrative.

Researching the biography is all-important in giving your writing authenticity; the use of specialized jargon of the day, and specific details gleaned from your research will help make your book credible. The foods people ate, the fabric used in the clothing they wore, the specific illnesses and medicines they were subject to—these all help the reader become more involved in the story you are telling and make your words ring true. This research takes time, but these tiny details makes the subject's life become more real to you, too. The words I found in missionary hymns of the 1830s made me see how women connected becoming a missionary with going to far-off lands for adventure. I would have never discovered that fact if I'd simply accepted that they sang "generic" church hymns. The exact words in the hymns provided a rich resource for understanding the people who sang them. As you do your research, you should at times be surprised, or else you simply aren't digging enough.

A last question to ask as you set about writing a biography: Why would anyone else want to read about this person? Your answer will help you identify your theme and focus, and maintain the energy and effort it takes to complete a project as time-consuming and difficult as writing a historical biography. A satisfying mix of personality, historical setting, and human nature, moving along a chronological continuum, gives you (and your readers) a story to enjoy and remember.

If there's one other thing a historical biographer needs, it's a passion for digging into the lives of people, finding out all you can about them and the times in which they lived—along with the drive to tell others about it. An unquenchable desire for gossip (backed up by research, mind you) goes a long way, too!

❑ 68

THE HOW-TOS OF
HOW-TOS

BY LINDA SLATER

I HAVE BEEN WRITING AND SELLING HOW-TO ARTICLES FOR ABOUT twenty years. Most editors are willing to consider a well-crafted article that helps other people learn how to do something well. I have sold many articles and have not been immune to rejection either, so I feel I have been through the School of Hard Knocks several times! Here are my best tips for selling that how-to article:

1. **Never give up.** If an article is rejected by *Mother Earth News,* try *Back Home* or *Countryside*. I once sent an article to eight different magazines before it sold. Your article won't be published gathering dust on the shelf.

2. **Revise.** If an article is rejected, reread it and see what might make it sparkle. Does it need better, more detailed photographs? Do you need a few more quotes from other, more varied experts? Is the article dated?

3. **Read at least ten issues** of the magazine you are aiming to sell to. What style do they favor? Are the articles formal or informal and conversational? Carefully study the photographs. Are the articles fifty percent text and fifty percent photos? Does humor fit this magazine's style? Now you know how to slant your article.

4. **Try new markets** that had been unknown to you. I once sent a garden article to a small magazine I found in my doctor's office. I am now the garden editor of that magazine! Risk-taking is healthy for all writers. You might be surprised where you might sell your article on flyfishing for women. I took a risk once and sent an article on self-esteem to a magazine for large women, *Big Beautiful Woman,* and sold it. Spend ten minutes every day studying market lists on books on writing at your library or at home. You may be amazed at which magazine or newspaper will buy your how-to article.

5. **Keep an "idea file"** for those days when inspiration won't come. Several kinds of articles from various publications get me going. For example, I keep a garden idea file, a self-help idea file, and a general human-interest idea file. If I read about a local artist or unusual character, I cut out the article so that I'll remember to try an article similar to that or in more depth about that subject. A news story about a flood or fire might turn into a human-interest piece or an article on flood or fire insurance, with examples of people who have lost everything because they weren't insured.

6. **Ask for feedback.** Ask friends or family to read your article and give you good or bad feedback. Is the piece clear and easy to read? Do the photographs help tell the reader how to do something? You will learn from each feedback you receive. Take a deep breath and try it.

7. **Stay in touch with local events.** Keep a calendar of local and state fairs, festivals, competitions, and events. Visit some of these events and see whom you can meet and talk to. Take photos of local artists, musicians, crafts-people, and writers. Could you turn any of these interviews into a how-to piece on drawing or painting? Sewing or fishing? Quilting or boating? One woman in my area compiled and self-published a booklet on "How to Compete in Art Fairs and Festivals and Sell Your Work," and sold several thousand copies at art fairs and through the mail. I once took photos of four weavers at a show and sold an article about them to a regional publication, and another time, I did a profile of a woman who paints on gourds and sells them for hundreds of dollars.

8. **Write about your passionate interests.** I am wild about gardening, so I love interviewing area gardeners, talking to people who run nurseries, and telling others how to garden. I make my own herbal teas, so I sent an article on this topic to *Mother Earth News*. They bought it, used it in the magazine, then paid me again when they reprinted it in an anthology. I sold an article to an environmental magazine on gardening with my children, and one on how to quit smoking to a health food publication. If you love angels or miracles, you have the germ of an article idea. (Hint: Anything with the word "soul" in it seems to sell these days!)

9. **Solve a problem.** This type of article tells readers how to overcome a problem or solve a dilemma in their everyday lives. It could be about how to take out coffee stains or cleaning the house with non-

toxic chemicals, how to catch bass or grow spinach. This kind of article may require some research or interviews with local or national experts. I find that if I have at least five quotes in an article from experts who live all over the country, it has more credibility. I check the library for names of experts in the field and write or call them. Once Joyce Brothers called me back while I was baking cookies and surprised me with her promptness. For ideas, ask your friends or relatives what kinds of problems they are trying to solve. (Hint: Many of my friends are struggling with how to communicate with their teenager and how to pay for their children's college education. Remember, there are 40 million baby boomers now thinking about these problems.)

10. **Tailor your article to a specific market.** Check and recheck your article for spelling, grammar, and punctuation. Ask people to proof it, read it, give you feedback. Enclose an SASE, and send your article out! If it is rejected, revise and send it out the next day to another market. Your article will not sell sitting on your desk or waiting for you to make it perfect.

❏ POETRY

❑ 69

Four Tricks of the Poet's Trade

By David Kirby

You've probably spent some time wool-gathering and thinking about the future—specifically, your future as a poet. And no doubt you've asked yourself some version of the question, "What do editors really want?"

To answer that question, let's begin by considering what it's like to be an editor right now. Editing a poetry magazine these days is like turning on a fire hydrant. Only it's poems that gush out, not water: Even the littlest magazine receives a half-dozen manuscripts every day, and the big ones like *Poetry* attract tens of thousands of submissions over the course of a year.

The way I see it, the flood of poetry into editorial offices is only going to get stronger. More people are going to school and learning to write well. Too, the economy's booming, and that's going to leave more time for artistic pursuits. Finally, the appearance of new markets every day is going to encourage new talent: Every year there are more listings in *The Directory of Poetry Publishers* (Dustbooks); a recent edition lists 2,336 poetry publishers. And electronic publication is just starting to take off; as more on-line journals appear, and more people acquire Internet service, it won't be long before poetry web pages are as inundated with submissions as the traditional poetry magazines are.

My guess is that, as far as market changes go, the big trend in poetry over the next few years is going to involve not variety but quantity. The development of any significant new type of poetry seems unlikely, because there is already so much variety among the dominant types— free verse, formal poetry, prose poetry, Language poetry, performance poetry—and also still much work to be done in these areas. So I'm predicting that the tendency will be not toward some new variety of poem, but toward more of the same—much more.

Where does this leave poets who want to share their work with others but are aware that the competition is ferocious? Let's begin by remind-

339

ing ourselves that the editors of the world are not our enemies: They love poetry passionately or they wouldn't be the underpaid, overworked people they usually are. And the editors I know are pretty open-minded; they don't care what kind of poetry you write, as long as you write it well. They're simply looking for the best work out there. In fact, they demand it.

But they're overwhelmed. Let's imagine an editor is sitting in his office and looking at a stack of, say, 20 submissions from twenty poets, and it's not even lunchtime yet. Let's also say there are three or four poems in each submission, and that among these 60–80 poems are several of yours. How are you going to make your poems stand out? How are you going to get that editor to put the other poems aside and give your work a good, close read?

As a poet, teacher, contest judge, and, mainly, a fan of poetry, I read dozens of poems every week, hundreds every month, and thousands every year, and I can tell you this: A poem either engages my interest immediately or it doesn't. Too, a poem also either sustains that interest or it fails to.

How? There are actually four very simple tricks of the trade that every poet should know and that any poet can use to write the type of poem that he or she wants to. So let me tell you what they are, and then I have a couple of surprises for you.

I think I can best illustrate my points if we first take a look at a poem of mine that was published in the magazine *Amelia* and later appeared in my book *Saving the Young Men of Vienna*, which won the Brittingham Prize in Poetry:

Fallen Bodies

The night of the Franklinton game
the bus breaks down, the seniors cry
because they will never play football again,
and we all go home with our parents and girlfriends.
Billy Berry lies in the back of my father's Buick,
covered with bruises, unable to lift his right arm,
and tells stories he swears are true:

that apple seeds cure cancer,
that a giant dove hovered over the van
the night his church group
came back from Mexico,

that Hitler left Germany by submarine
after the war and established a haven
in Queen Maud Land, near the South Pole.

The air comes in through windows
that won't quite close
as we drive up the dark highway to Baton Rouge,
through towns where tired old men
sell peaches on the corners of used car lots
or doze in diners that sag by the roadside,
spacecraft cooling in the Louisiana night.

Using "Fallen Bodies" as our text, let's look at the four tricks of the trade that will make your poem stand out from all the others:

(1) **The Hook.** What catches the reader's attention and makes this poem different from all others? The answer is something concrete and slightly mysterious; in this instance, it's a broken-down bus and a bunch of unhappy high-school football players. Immediately you get a mental picture, and then you ask, "What next?"

(2) **The Voice.** What vocabulary (formal or streetwise), sentence length (long, short, mixed), tonal qualities (wistfulness, confidence, horror, humor) do you want to use to get the effect you desire? In "Fallen Bodies," the voice is world-weary; look at all those negative words and phrases, like "breaks down," "cry," "never," "bruises," "unable," "cancer," "won't quite," "dark," "tired old," "used," and "sag," not to mention the word "night," which occurs in the first and last lines of the poem and one other time as well. Yet this voice is also thoughtful: There are only three sentences in the poem, and each is packed with ideas and images, as though the speaker has composed his thoughts very carefully. So the overall effect is of a world-weary yet philosophical observer.

(3) **Saturation.** The first draft of a poem is usually a skinny draft. Fatten it with details: The ones in this poem speak for themselves, from the capsule picture of the defeated team to the outlandish story of Hitler's submarine voyage to the portraits of the old men in the car lots and diners.

(4) **The Big Theme.** Whenever I use that phrase, I always capitalize the first letters of the words to remind myself that The Theme must

always be Big. A pretty poem can still be a trivial poem, so make sure your poem deals with something of consequence. That doesn't mean you should be obvious about it; you'll always want to present your argument by means of images rather than editorial statements. In the case of "Fallen Bodies," I wanted to say that, even in defeat, one can still see that the world is filled with strange wonders, and this realization can be consoling. Hence my final image: not chrome-and-glass diners per se, but spacecraft that seem to come from another dimension, as if by magic.

And that's it. Once you know what you want to say, you figure out the best way to start, you decide what voice you want to use, you saturate your writing with plenty of details, and you arrange everything so your Big Theme will emerge. You can test this scheme on other poems, your own or someone else's; my guess is that your favorites will all have the four elements I've outlined above and the ones that don't work quite as well will be lacking in one or more areas.

And now for the surprises. The first you've probably guessed already, which is that my four tricks of the trade, which are intended to help you write the poetry of the future, are also characteristic of the great poetry of the past. Take Dante's *Inferno*. It begins with a man getting lost in the woods at night: What a hook! Then there's the poet's voice, which ranges from comic to angry to pitying to devout but is, for the most part, simply awestruck at all the bizarre figures in the underworld. As for detail, if giants and harpies and dragons aren't enough, not to mention some of the greatest celebrity sinners of all time, there's Satan himself, frozen in the ice of Hell's basement. And while there's more than one Big Theme (after all, it's a Big Poem), certainly the immortality of true love is the greatest of these.

The second surprise is that the four tricks of the trade essential to any good poem are also indispensable to any piece of good writing. For example, a good novel has a good hook. (What would *Moby Dick* be without "Call me Ishmael"?) Each hit song has an unmistakable voice; you could play "Somewhere Over the Rainbow" loud and fast, but the version most people remember is the wistful one that Judy Garland sang. Every good play is saturated with details: If *Macbeth* didn't have all those witches and sword fights, it would just be a dull treatise on Scottish politics. And each of these has its own Big Theme: pride, nostalgia, ambition.

The fact that these four tricks have characterized every good piece of writing, regardless of its genre or the period in which it was written, is especially good news, since it means that, if you use them in your own writing, you will, in effect, "market-proof" your work against any changes in editorial taste that may occur.

Say I'm wrong in my earlier predictions and editors begin to demand some new kind of poetry that we can't even conceive of at the moment. It won't matter, because you'll be writing work that uses four elements that have always worked.

❏ 70

POETIC LEAPS AND MOVEMENTS

BY JAMES PLATH AND ZARINA MULLAN PLATH

FOR A POEM TO "BEGIN IN DELIGHT AND END IN WISDOM," AS ROBERT Frost suggested, the poem must have some movement, so that it can draw life and vitality from the poetic "leaps" it includes—leaps that can impart the same variety, connection, and complication as the movements in a symphony.

For example, a poet wanders into a public library and sees an arrangement of sea shells, coconut berries, and a handful of sand scattered on a reading table, obviously arranged. There are a number of ways for the poet to respond initially, and to "shift gears" throughout the poem he or she may write about this scene. The types of movements below are suggested not as a prescribed formula or sequence, but as *possibilities*—just as a painter has a palette of colors to choose from. A combination of these movements can quickly transform a prosaic description into something deeper and more richly textured—in short, something more *poetic*.

• **Straight (sensory) description:** One of the most common starting points is to describe, using sensory detail. What does the scene look like, as a whole, and in its individual parts—size, shape, color, sight, smell, sound, texture, taste? It could be argued that the image, and not the word, is the basic unit of poetic language, for so much is dependent upon this level of description. In "The Walk" (from *Leaving Yuba City*), for example, Chitra Banerjee Divakaruni quickly establishes a scene through her memory of the details of her girlhood landscape: "We climbed carefully / in our patent-leather shoes up hillsides looped / with trails the color of earthworms. Below, / the school fell away, the sad green roofs / of the dormitories, the angled classrooms." But straight description is observation, and that in itself may not lead a poet to insights without his or her first making a leap in another direction or two.

344

- **Contextual description:** How does an object look in relation to other things in the room, or outside the room? Many of the things we describe change in value or appearance when they are examined in the context of other objects. A six-footer may seem tall in a high school classroom, but on the NBA hardcourts? A poet might first describe the "seashore" arrangement, then pull back the camera to describe a wider view, with people walking past, noses pressed into books, everyone apparently unaware or unconcerned. Consider Sharon Olds's poem, "The One Girl at the Boys' Party" (from *The Dead and the Living*). The situation is ripe for contrasts and contextualization, which Olds uses to full effect: "I set her down among the boys. They tower and / bristle, she stands there smooth and sleek, / her math scores unfolding in the air around her."

- **Metaphoric description:** A figurative language leap. To what can the object/scene be compared, either the whole or the parts? Does it resemble a museum diorama or a tiny oasis? Is one clam shell shaped like an oriental fan? Metaphoric description—including simile, metaphor, symbol, allusion—is another layer of poetry that the poet might, in a sentence or two, explore, e.g., the coconut berries on the table might look like cherry pits. In another poem by Sharon Olds, "Armor" (*The Dead and the Living*), a young boy's fascination with medieval weaponry in a museum serves as a metaphor for his mother's fear of losing him—both literally, as in war, and figuratively, as a small child becomes a man.

- **Associative description:** What does the object or action remind you of? Something you've read? Someone you know? Something a friend or family member has? Another place or object? If the berries remind the poet of cherry pits, he or she might deliberately strive to recall poetically events from childhood involving cherry pits, and shift to a stanza that might begin, "When I was young, we used to spit cherry pits, our fingers pulp-red, at cardboard targets, at each other." The introduction of this element compels or challenges the poet to draw a connection between the initial object or scene and the comparisons. In Jorie Graham's "Salmon" (from her collection *Erosion*), she begins with one memory of watching a nature show about salmon swimming upstream, then meditates on the fish's "helplessness" in the face of its desire, before finally moving to an associated childhood memory of witnessing a sexual act. The childhood memory, when recalled in light of the salmon, takes on more resonance than if it alone formed the central image of the poem.

• **Literary description:** A poet could easily use words or phrases that refer to Oliver Wendell Holmes' famous poem about the nautilus seashell to add another layer of meaning and complexity to a poem about this little library diorama. A literary—or for that matter, any cultural—allusion can serve as a new "lens" through which the reader can view the scene. Richard Jackson's "Homeric" is set in the decidedly ordinary landscape of a fast food restaurant in Chattanooga, Tennessee, yet in this environment the speaker recalls the year he "discovered Homer's / rosey fingered dawn, as preached by Sister Michael, / was really the bloody one Hector, Ajax and the others / made for themselves" (in *New American Poets of the '90s*). Here, allusions to *The Odyssey* and its ancient battles serve as a bridge between the action taking place in the restaurant, where a small fight breaks out, and the speaker's own recollection of defending himself against boyhood bullies.

• **Lyric and meditative description:** Consider the quality of sand or shell, or sandness/shellness, or celebrate the objects with emotional appreciation or euphoria. What's the poet's reaction to the object or action? What *is* sand, or a shell? More important, what's the *tone*, or how does the poet feel about the object? Elizabeth Bishop's "The Fish" (*The Complete Poems: 1927–1979*) is a long, lush, lyrical tribute to a "tremendous fish" hooked half out of the water. The speaker takes in every nuance of the fish's body, from the brown skin "hung in strips / like ancient wallpaper" through the "frightening gills / fresh and crisp with blood" into the "coarse white flesh / packed in like feathers." The fish is not merely scrutinized, but glorified and admired as well—so much so that the speaker, humbled, feels compelled to release it back into the water.

• **Speculative description:** This type of description is usually causal, temporal, or spatial. What can the object or person become? Where is it going, or where has it been? In the case of the sand, berry and shell arrangement, who might have put it there? For what purpose? Who left it? Why won't library staff, patrons, or janitors remove it?

What might that suggest about the atmosphere, climate, human nature? What will happen if it is left? Or removed? A common technique is to fast-forward into the future to describe the same scene speculatively, or to go in reverse to describe the past of an object or scene. For example, consider Galway Kinnell's "The Milk Bottle" (from his *Selected Poems*), in which the speaker imagines he "can actually remember one certain / quart of milk which has just finished clinking / against three of its brethren / in the milkman's great hand."

• **Negation:** Describe or consider what the object(s) is *not*, or what it will not be used for, will never do or become. For example, this sand will never find its way back to the sea, spilled from a river onto a delta of silt and crushed rock. Or it may not be scraped into a plastic bag and added to a sandbox where toddlers doze imaginary subdivisions or their older siblings pretend to lie on exotic beaches, awaiting rescue. Rita Dove uses negation in "Great Uncle Beefheart" (*Selected Poems*) to underscore the subject's eroding health and dignity as he ages. She writes, "It was not as if he didn't try / to tell us: first he claimed / the velvet armchair, then the sun / on the carpet before it."

• **Concrete/specific/narrow to abstract/general/broad description** (and vice versa): After describing the objects or action on a literal level, move to the world of ideas or "types." If you described the library diorama metaphorically, as an oasis, perhaps move to rumination on what an oasis *is* or isn't. It's a refuge, but in miniature does it act as a refuge for students? Not literally, for it's too small. But what about mentally? Does it send them places? Does sand by itself have no mystical power, but the suggestion of shells and sand have an associative power of place? You may then wish to meditate on what makes a refuge. In "The Cleaving" (*The City in Which I Love You*), Li-Young Lee begins with the concrete and deceptively ordinary description of a Chinese butcher at work, "his shining face grinning / up at ducks dangling single file." But the sight of the butcher carving duck meat sends the speaker on a lyrical and philosophical mind-journey, moving from contemplation of his own judgment day, to the noise a body makes when it meets the soul "over the soul's ocean and penumbra," and even a fantasy of eating Emerson, "his transparent soul, his / soporific transcendence." In the end, the speaker realizes that the soul "is cleaved so that the soul might be restored"—quite a leap from the rough butcher shop imagery which opens the poem.

- **Inside/internal to outside/external description** (and vice versa): Given an opening description of the sand arrangement, the next stanza or movement might begin, "Outside, students lie under the lazy umbrella of maple branches" and then shift to that exterior subject, then perhaps back again to the original internal/inside meditation or consideration, or another aspect of it. It sets up a contrast, a juxtaposition, that again forces the reader to consider how the situations and descriptions relate to one another: ironically similar, opposite, etc. Galway Kinnell uses this device in section two of "Under the Maud Moon" (*Selected Poems*). The solitary speaker first is shown sitting by a fire in the rain, remembering songs he once sang for his small daughter, then turning his thoughts outward into the possibilities of the darkness: "Somewhere out ahead of me / a black bear sits alone."

- **Parallel description:** Juan Gris had a technique in which he used "echoes" of objects—smaller, unrelated items that were shaped or colored to "echo," parallel, or remind the viewer of the initial object. Applied to poetry, such echoes prompt readers to recall the original image and draw comparisons. Given the library "seashore" diorama, a poet might describe children huddled in a corner in such a way as to remind us that their arrangement is similar to the diorama on the table. Consider Ron Wallace's poem "Oranges" (in *Plums, Stones, Kisses & Hooks*). The speaker begins by recalling the tang of his breakfast orange and its lingering concrete images. But, the orange imagery is later scent on his hands as he leaves the house—strictly echoed throughout the poem far more metaphorically: "The sun ripens in the sky. / The wind turns thin and citrus." Fishermen pursue perch "quick / and bright as orange slices," and when the speaker arrives at his lover's house, they "peel off" their clothes, and "slice through / that wordy rind."

Some of the most successful poets are jugglers. If a poem seems to say little or go nowhere, it may be that there are not enough balls in the air to make the poem interesting. Bringing in another element or two forces the writer to consider the emerging poem in a different light, which, in turn, urges the reader to make those connections as well, to see the subject/object in a new way. And that, after all, is what poetry is all about.

❑ 71

DISCOVERING THE POWER OF METAPHOR

BY JOYCE PESEROFF

GOOD POETRY REQUIRES POWERFUL LANGUAGE. DRAFTING A POEM, WE want our verbs to be energetic; our adjectives need to surprise as well as describe. A brilliant constellation of images, such as the ones readers find in any number of Shakespeare's sonnets, allows a poem to develop its own imaginative landscape. And figures of speech allow the poet who creates them to extend this landscape further.

Commonly used figures of speech include simile, metaphor, metonymy, synecdoche, and personification. Metonymy substitutes the name of one thing for another closely associated with it, often replacing an abstraction with a concrete noun, as when "birth to death" becomes "cradle to grave." Synecdoche uses the part to stand for the whole: "Lend me your ears," Shakespeare writes, when Antony wants the crowd's complete attention. Personification can give a human face to the world, as when Jane Kenyon praises the "cheerful worm in the cheerful ground." Simile and metaphor are both figures of comparison. "Shall I compare thee to a summer's day?" Shakespeare asks in his sonnet. His similes make comparisons by using the terms "like" or "as"; metaphors dispense with these words altogether.

It seems to me that the act of comparison is both preverbal and basic to human development. I watch a very young infant in her crib, gazing at the fists she brings close to her face, looking from one to the other. The hands are similar but not quite identical. When babies learn to talk, every animal is, at first, a "doggy" (or "kitty," or "buh-ie"). Older babies learn to discriminate between doggy and kitty, horsie and moo-cow, elaborating distinctions that become more and more sophisticated. Like/unlike is built into the brain, and language that makes connections along these paths strikes deep into human experience.

Of the two figures of speech offering comparison, metaphor provokes more complex and various associations in the reader's mind. Similes

349

often associate themselves with one or two individual features. "Cheeks like roses" have petals but no thorns, and in the phrase, "small as the ear of a mouse," no aspect of mousiness—color, scent, or the sound of one skittering across your kitchen counter—matters other than size. Or take the statement, "She's like a sunset." The reader may associate sunsets primarily with natural beauty, with pink and golden hues, or with a certain flamboyance. Compare this to the sentence, "She is sunset." Added to the associations mentioned before, and deepening them, is the prospect of the day's decline. Beauty and the end of beauty cohabit in metaphor.

Shakespeare's sonnet "That Time of Year" is an example of comparison without the use of "like" or "as":

That Time of Year

That time of year thou mayst in me behold
When yellow leaves, or none, or few, do hang
Upon those boughs which shake against the cold,
Bare ruined choirs where late the sweet birds sang.
In me thou see'st the twilight of such day
As after sunset fadeth in the west,
Which by-and-by black night doth take away,
Death's second self that seals up all in rest.
In me thou see'st the glowing of such fire
That on the ashes of his youth doth lie,
As the deathbed whereon it must expire,
Consumed by that which it was nourished by.
    This thou perceiv'st, which makes thy love more strong,
    To love that well which thou must leave ere long.

Each of the sonnet's three quatrains uses a single metaphor. In the first four lines, the poem's speaker compares himself to a time of year-early winter. In lines 5—8, the speaker compares himself to a time of day-twilight, after sunset, night coming on fast. In the last quatrain, the speaker is a dying fire on a bed of ash.

Imagine that Shakespeare had made a list of questions concerning his speaker and his predicament. His list might have begun like this:

If I were a time of year, which season would I be?
If I were a time of day, what hour would I be?
If I were a form of fire, what kind of fire would I be?

You can create such a list when you are contemplating a situation or an individual you want to write about. Consider these questions:

If this subject were a form of water, what form would it be? Would it be a peaceful lake or spring freshet? Ocean or trout stream? Tap water or well water, waterfall, puddle?

If this subject were an animal, what animal would it be? A tiger or hare? A rooster or a jackass?

If this subject were a flower, would it be joe-pye-weed or rose? Burgundy lily or snapdragon?

If this subject were a form of shelter, would it be a tent, a mansion, cabin in the woods, penthouse suite, mobile home, or studio apartment?

Continue by responding, as quickly as possible and in the same manner, to the rest of this list:

> Tree or fruit?
> Form of transportation?
> Kind of weather or climate?
> Article of clothing?
> Color of the rainbow?
> Historical period?
> Food or drink?
> Musical instrument?
> Art or sport?
> Geographical feature?
> Astronomical feature?
> Room in the house?
> Age?
> Kind of work?

Depending upon the person or situation in your poem, you can vary this list to include books and movies, popular songs, kitchen appliances, comic book superheroes, vegetables, board games, cities. Be careful to avoid familiar or overused phrases like "raging river" or "torrential rain"; don't let your words congeal into dead metaphors. It's important to finish with a list of at least twenty answers to your group of questions.

Your responses—all of them concrete, specific nouns and adjectives—will provide the metaphors for you to work with. The longer your list, the more aspects of the subject your poem will reveal. The question, "What kind of animal would this subject be?" might suggest a physical resemblance: "John is a Florida panther." Your answer to, "What form of water would this subject be?" might describe emotional depth with, "John is a still pond." If your flower is a snapdragon, read-ers will be affected by the sound of the word as well as by its visual image.

Although this method might seem best for a poem with an individual as its subject, John Davidson's ballad, "Thirty Bob a Week," uses a series of metaphors to describe a situation—the plight of the underpaid British workingman:

> It's a naked child against a hungry wolf;
> It's playing bowls upon a splitting wreck;
> It's walking on a string across a gulf
> With millstones fore-and-aft about your neck.

Davidson and Shakespeare suggest two ways of structuring a collec-tion of metaphors into a poem. Davidson uses a simple list, rapidly making three metaphors in four lines. Shakespeare extends his into a fourteen-line sonnet by answering each question in gorgeous detail. Creating a narrative from your cache of words is a third strategy. I wouldn't worry about how the narrative evolves—your Florida panther might yodel while rafting across a still pond—but it is important, in the first draft, to include every answer to the questions on your list. It's fine if some of these look paradoxical: Can that same John be a large wildcat and a placid lake? Perhaps, through these figures, you've discovered something about your subject you didn't know before.

In subsequent revisions, you can decide which—and how many—metaphors to include. Whatever strategy you choose, you have discov-ered a technique to draw the power of metaphor into the language of your poems.

❏ 72

REVISING POETRY

BY PEGGY MILLER

REVISION HAS AN UNDESERVED REPUTATION OF DRUDGERY AND DIFFI-
culty. Every time you put a pen to paper, you are already revising—not
just the visible revisions of crossing out and arrows and writing along
the margins of a first draft. Each time you choose a word, you are
choosing not to use another, or many others.

Writers engage in a constant process of mental revision, a sort of
rehearsal process that may extend well beyond the writing itself. All
day you might be trying out lines, or having titles or first lines or ideas
for poems occur to you. So it's a very good idea to keep a pen and
notebook handy. Ideas that occur when you are away from your desk
are so easily forgotten and lost forever. It may be that even in our sleep
we go on writing. Sometimes I go to bed stymied for how to end a
poem I am working on, or with some line of a poem still grinding
around in my mind, only to wake in the morning with a really exciting
solution.

Thinking and dreaming up poems becomes more and more frequent
when you write regularly. Few people actually write every day, but
when they write often enough, they fall into the habit of keeping an eye
open for ideas. It is as if the subconscious knows that it will be called
on soon again for some writing ideas, so it stays limber and ready. Thus
the prospect of revising a poem should not distress you. It is more of
the same mysterious creative process. And, it is often only in the revising that the finest poems emerge.

Revising and recycling

Beyond grammatical and spelling corrections, workshop suggestions
often deal with what you can omit. Tightening the poem is usually a
good idea. Take out all unnecessary words and phrases. If you are un-
sure, read the poem without the phrase and see if it still expresses your

intent. Use adjectives and adverbs sparingly, since they may diminish the directness of nouns and water down the poem's impact. Try to use strong verbs; especially avoiding *to be* and *to have*. Always strive for fresh language.

There are limitless ways to say what you mean. Find the most creative and original words to express an idea or build an image: This is what poetry is. Keep a good dictionary and thesaurus handy and use them. (The computer dictionaries are extremely limited.) Most of all, take yourself seriously. A poem is worth a lot of work.

But play with your writing, too. Experiment for the most effective line breaks. Sometimes rearranging is helpful. Often a first stanza can be deleted, because it represents your first thoughts, before you knew where the poem was going. Or a first stanza can be moved to last so that the poem ends on its strongest point, with the idea that inspired the poem.

Always read your poem aloud to yourself. There is a different part of your mind that hears and can help you recognize places where the words aren't right yet. Say the words aloud when you first write a poem and at every step of your revision. A great deal of smoothing and revision can take place immediately after you write the first draft.

Sometimes, before you can revise a poem you need to put it in a dark closet for six months until the details of the poem have faded from memory. Then the mistakes you made, the inconsistencies, the places that definitely need to be fixed become more evident to you. Even the best parts of the poem—the images and magical language—might become clearer to you after a good rest in the closet. Knowing what works in the poem is as important as knowing what doesn't.

Poems that just don't make it can also benefit from six months in a closet. *Never* throw away "failed" poems! They didn't fail; maybe it just wasn't their time yet. Recycle your unrealized fragments of writing: Take two poems that don't seem to be working and interweave their lines, alternating between poems. Read the new construction. Sculpt it until you make it work. It is possible that you will find amazing expressions of poetry that you would not have otherwise thought to place next to each other.

Another way to use that unfinished material you have written is to look closely at each of your unfinished poems. Within them you may find three-line or five-line poems already complete in themselves. They might have been your favorite lines in a poem that just didn't jell. Look for the fine little poem in your original rough draft.

There are ways to help you look at your poems in a different light. For example, you might rearrange your poem so that each line has the same number of words. Then vary the number of syllables and accents from line to line while adhering to the same word count. Or try arranging your poem with the same number of syllables in each line, or putting the whole poem into three- or four-line stanzas. Try putting your draft into a poetic form such as a sonnet or a limerick, or in rhymed couplets. See how it sounds rewritten into iambic meter. Conversely, if your poem was written in such a form to begin with, try changing it to free verse. You may be able to see the words differently and find ways to say it better. Then you can revert to the original form, or keep the new form.

These are not the only approaches to revision. Sometimes your poem needs more material, or new material to replace sections. This is always the more difficult kind of revision. Write notes about what you need to do: "Describe back yard near the tamarack" or "Add a section about the ballet lesson" or "Ending?" Then try to go back into the mood or place you were in when you first wrote the poem, and begin again. Think about it all day long, while you do the dishes, and even just before you go to sleep. (Keep a pad or a small recorder by the bed and record your mental composing so you don't forget! This is a risky time to think about writing because you might fall asleep and lose your ideas, but the pre-sleep state is also very often the most productive.)

Coming up with new material for a poem is not something that you can do as rapidly as revisions in the workshop. Use everything you know. Be patient. This phase of revision may take a lot longer than writing the original draft. You need to look at the present version of the poem with a careful and discerning eye. What did you intend to say? Did you actually say it, or did you go in a different direction altogether, and never get back to the first impulse?

How do you know when your poem is finished? A "finished" poem should be greater than the sum of its words; it should express itself in a magical, individual way. It should, at the same time, speak clearly to the reader. All aspects of the finished poem should be intentional. The language should be elegant or efficient or potent—a little tighter than prose. If the language is diffuse, its lightness should accomplish part of what the poem communicates. The poem should say something you know, something that is important to you. It should be pleasing to you both in what it accomplishes, and how it does so. *Revision* is so important. It is what separates the good poem from the fine poem. It can be tremendously rewarding as you see your writing gain power and depth.

What if you can't think of anything to write?

One of the most famous poets to advise "free" or "undirected" writing was William Stafford, who said, simply record your thoughts. Exercise that part of your mind that is involved with forming ideas and putting them into words and onto paper. Many successful writers believe that the activity of writing is a process of discovery. Your mind is never devoid of ideas.

Sometimes the inspiration for a poem is already there and you urgently want to express it, but that does not happen frequently. You must practice your craft, get into the habit of writing. It is wise to develop a routine of writing for its own sake, and not to expect that each time you write something profound will result.

Write with no particular direction in mind. Put down whatever occurs to you. It keeps the connection from mind to pen to page well-oiled. Do this as often as you can, as many days in a row as your life permits. The objective here is not to write a poem, but to record whatever is streaming through your mind at the moment. If it turns out to be important or crucial or poetic, fine, but it does not have to be. Consider this writing habit an exploration of your thinking. You may be surprised by what you find. And if such undirected writing does not have a poem as its immediate aim, almost any idea or image, because it is the product of the complex human mind, can be the seed for a poem. Write with confidence. Write from the heart. Enjoy your writing. Poetry is the fertile ground of thought. Don't let any rules or suggestions inhibit the intentions of your poem, your creative vision.

Starting over

The process of writing is complex. Every word you put on paper is a decision among the uncountable things you could have said, and among the uncountable ways you could have said it. You never really know which path you will take when you begin to write a poem, and if you are like me, you wonder about those roads not taken; you'll worry if there might have been a wisp of a thought that would have made it a better poem. One way to recapture those "wisps" you may have missed is simply to "start over." Write a poem until you reach its end. Put the page aside and begin the poem again, immediately. The ideas and words you wrote and those you decided against will be fresh in your mind. The little things that surfaced briefly and didn't make it to the page are still there. In the second writing, remember those lost pieces, and this time, write them down, though they may not have seemed useful when you first thought of them.

When you get to the end, put the page aside and begin the poem yet again. Immediately. Work for the same goal. Pick up the ideas that were still lost from the first writing but didn't make the second one because they didn't fit logically or they seemed to stray from the subject. And in this third version you can also pick up the wisps that fluttered by while you wrote the second version.

When you finish the third version of the poem, begin again. Continue to start fresh versions until you absolutely cannot think of anything else that you didn't use. This includes seemingly unrelated ideas. Six versions is a good number, but maybe two will be all you can manage until you get into the habit. You should write all of the versions in a single sitting, one after another.

This process can be more powerful than the common habit of writing a first draft and revising it until you are satisfied. Those little details that you miss disappear rapidly, and you can begin to think that the way you wrote the poem is the only possible one. If you have written a smashingly fine poem, then it's no problem. This process won't work in all cases; it seems to work best with the complicated poem. The starting-over process can provide abundant material for you.

This manner of writing recognizes the complexity and elusiveness of the creative process. You will have allowed your mind to wander into other subjects and to try other approaches and use other words. And when you take all of your versions in hand, you are ready to write the poem. You may even have material for another.

❏ *73*

The Instant of Knowing

By Josephine Jacobsen

I AM NEITHER SO IMPERTINENT NOR SO NAÏVE AS TO WORK TOWARD A definition of poetry, but I want to tell a story, a true story that implies as much of a definition as I have come by.

The center of everything is the poem. Nothing is important in comparison to that. Anything that in some valid way is not directly connected with that current of energy which is the poem is dispensable.

The naming of things, which is the poet's function, is not, like a science, progressive. It is circular, and each passage of the circle is unique.

Often the poet brings back very little from the instant of knowing. Sometimes—rarely—he brings back something that combines two worlds: something germane to what Yeats called "the artifice of eternity"—the made and the eternal. Such poetry may wear any mode: the august, the raucous, the witty, the tragic. Nothing could matter less. Poetry is energy, and it is poetic energy that is the source of that instant of knowing that the poet tries to name. The test for the true poetic energy is, it seems to me, the only universal test that can be applied to poetry.

In the process of naming things, the poet is caught at once in the problem of naming his own time, the problem of what was called "relevancy" until that word's exhaustion gave everyone empathetic fatigue. In naming his own time, the poet may be one of those rare writers who reach community in a working solitude, though seldom in a personal one. Ionesco writes: "For solitude is not *separation* but *meditation*, and we know that social groups . . . are most often a collection of solitary human beings. . . ."

For solitary writers, the group experience in the pursuit of their own work is a negative experience. They work alone; the poem's inception and execution is as secret as a film's development in a darkroom. They learn, ravenously, from their fellows, their betters, the great dead, their own guts; from talk, from print, by osmosis; but they are not, and can never be, group members. Most poets, on the other hand, as John Ciardi pointed out, have at some phase of their working life as poets been part of a group, and these have the stimulation and reinforcement that fly like sparks from the contact with congenial minds with the same general approach, objectives, and dislikes. But groups can also generate group-think—that curious amalgam that bounces back and forth, carrying always some measure of other-directed debris.

The brief story I want to tell is completely concerned with that energy and how it travels and the mysterious fact that certain words, in a certain arrangement, and with a certain cadence, start up a chain reaction explained by nothing in the words themselves or in their content.

Once, after a speech I gave, a hot controversy arose as to what degree of analysis of a poem is possible without destroying the life of the poem. A number of teachers in the audience felt that poems could be, and were, dismembered to the point of death. Others held out, very stoutly indeed, for the belief that the more you studied the poem, the more it meant to you. I understand very well the first point of view, having some years ago had a class for teachers of poetry who had been so disheartened by the poetry analysis to which they themselves as students had been subjected, that they cordially disliked poetry and were now trying to learn to reapproach it. On the other hand, it is impossible to denigrate the joy and comprehension that come from a close textual reading. It seems to me that the solution of the basic problem—as Robert Frost has pointed out—lies in acknowledging as the most important element that point of mystery which is the core of the poem, that untranslatable quasar that can never fully be put into the prose of exposition. Certain words, in a certain cadence.

"Ah sunflower! weary of time, who countest the steps of the Sun." It would be impossible to find simpler or more daily words. Or, "I have been one acquainted with the night." It is something that is not music and is not talk and is both; but what it does, every single time, is touch the nerve that knows. It is, literally, an instant of knowing—of something simultaneously strange and familiar; something already known but now discovered.

More than fifty years ago, on a cold autumn afternoon, my husband and I were exploring some of the small side roads in the northern mountains of New Hampshire. One such road went over the crest of a hill and past a small and thoroughly overgrown cemetery, which obviously hadn't been used in the past decade. We stopped the car, and got out, and started wandering around in the tall grass, reading some of the tombstones. Some of them were tilted at angles, and some had lost letters to the weather. They said all the usual things—"Beloved wife of . . . " "He giveth his beloved rest . . . " A few said "Infant Son" or "Infant Daughter," and there were quite a lot of children. It was cold in the wind, and we started back to our car. Just before we got to the gate, which was rusted and rather lopsided, I saw a carving of a pair of clasped hands, on a leaning stone, and stooped down to look at the inscription. There was a woman's name but no relationship, and under the name and the date were carved two lines of poetry. They said:

> It is a fearful thing to love
> What Death can touch.

Eleven words, ten of them monosyllables. Immediately I thought, I know those lines; but I didn't, in the sense of placing them, and neither did my husband, though he had had exactly the same sense of recognition. They hung in my mind as though every hour they were going to place themselves. I quoted them a few times to people I thought might recognize them; always there was the same reaction: "Yes, I know that . . ." But no one did.

A few months later, I wrote a longish and unsatisfactory poem about a wartime cemetery, and in it, I quoted the epitaph from the tombstone. Later, I forgot about the poem, but I didn't forget the two lines I did not write; they were there.

About four or five years later, after an illness, I came home from the hospital and found some piled-up issues of *Commonweal*. Leafing through them, I noticed a review of a play that had just opened in New York, by a poet whose work had interested me when I saw his Pulitzer Prize-winning play, *Hogan's Goat*. The poet was William Alfred and the verse-play under review was his *Agamemnon*. The review, a very favorable one, after praising the poetry and the stature of the play, went on to say that the play reached its climax in Cassandra's cry, "It is a fearful thing to love what death can touch."

I don't think I have ever had such an eerie sensation. I kept reading the words over, waiting for them to change in some particular. Then I sat down, in a sort of superstitious panic, and wrote a letter to William Alfred, and asked him where he had gotten those two lines, as I had a special reason for wanting to know. He wrote back at once to say that evidently the copy of the published play, which he had sent me, hadn't arrived. It came in the next day, and there was a note in the front which said that Cassandra's cry, "It is a fearful thing to love what death can touch," was from a poem by Josephine Jacobsen and had been quoted to him by C. Page Smith, the historian.

When I was preparing this piece, I did what I had waited many years to do—I wrote to William Alfred and asked him what, exactly, he remembered. This is what he wrote me, as new to me then as it is to you now:

It was Columbus Day, 1950. C. Page Smith had arranged a trip under the aegis of Samuel Eliot Morison, to Plymouth, to look at where the Mayflower had first landed. Professor Morison had recently lost his wife. Part of the tour, on that gray cold day, was the graveyard . . . of the pilgrims, on a small hill above the harbor. As we looked out over the sea from the rise, Page told Professor Morison of that poem of yours and of the New Hampshire tombstone . . . it haunted me as it haunts me still.

Those eleven words, put together by an unknown human being, carved by someone's hand on a grassed-over tombstone, in a deserted New Hampshire graveyard, had struck—in a chain of energy, unbelievable but natural—into my mind, then into my poem; had extricated themselves from that inferior substance, and struck through the mind of another writer so forcefully that he had been compelled to speak them to a poet-dramatist, who put them at the core of the poem that was his play; and the reviewer found them rising from that play to arrest him and put them, as the play's climax, onto the page of a magazine, later held by the person who had received their impact from the stone in the grass in the graveyard.

I think that the whole meaning of the instant of knowing lies in that circuit. A knowledge of what we already knew becomes for an instant so devastatingly fresh that it could be contained no more than a flash of lightning. The arrangement of the oldest human fact into certain special sounds, in a certain sequence. It is the thing that cannot be argued with. And I have always felt almost superstitious about the story, because it is such a complete one; it is, to me, of the essence of poetry. Whenever I hear someone trying to define poetry or hear myself working toward a definition, I think of that carved stone sending out its terrible energy to that nerve of knowledge in the hearer, the reader, which transmits it.

This is the live energy that keeps the mass from corruption: the venal poet who writes, the editor who publishes, the critic who analyzes, the reader who reads. What that energy speaks to is our knowledge, but a dormant, denied-by-habit knowledge that is kindled to response in the rare instant.

That energy is the common quality that brings poets together.

❏ 74

THE SHOCK OF GOOD POETRY

BY JANE HIRSHFIELD

WHAT IS THE MEANING OF A "LITTLE" MAGAZINE IN THE LIFE OF poetry in American culture today? Is it a forum for the inquisitive reader to see what is being written, what kinds of thoughts and forms of thought are occupying the minds and hearts of writers both established and unknown? Is it a place for those writers to put their work forward first to the doorkeeping editors, then to readers—a kind of gladiatorial testing ground, perhaps? Is it, as the deconstructionists might pro-pose, a locus for the prevailing cultural tendencies of mind and style to im-pose themselves further, or, as the experimentalist avant-garde might propose, a place where the marginal can find a small space in which to be heard, to wedge a clearing amid established patterns of speech and of being?

These are real questions, even interesting ones, but they are also tired ones. I will confess that when opening the envelopes of poems sent on to me by the unfailingly gracious staff of *Ploughshares*, I did not con-sider my activity as guest editor a chance to impose or explore any theory of art and culture. I did not consider the role of the words I read in regard to the culture at large. I did not consider the role of "poetry," or whether or not it "matters." I did not consider—though I did no-tice—the way certain themes and types of poems recurred from submis-sion to submission. What I considered was the poems: the words on the page, and the effect they had on my heart and mind and body as I let them enter my being. And what I hoped for, each time I turned to a fresh page, was nothing less than to find myself moved and transformed.

Make no mistake: I consider such a moment of transformation a radi-cal event. Radical in both senses of the word—an extraordinary poem requires of its reader a fundamental revolution in being, and also returns the reader to some deep root of being which has been present in us from the start. It may be that both senses are necessary for our survival: We live so much of the time in a state of estrangement from ourselves. Estranged from the possibility of a real knowledge of our own experience, estranged from our own hearts, we wander the hours and years in a kind of day-blindness, lost in the alleyways of an expected life. It is easier, certainly, to navigate a life we believe is predictable, is knowable, is known. And the costs? Bearable—until some event forces us to realize it has all been a dream, a falseness, and we must recover the ability to see not what we wish to see, but what is: a wholly surprising world.

A good poem offers always some entrance into and reminder of the fact that genuine experience is unexpected. A good poem shocks us awake, one way or another—through its beauty, its insight, its music, it shakes or seduces the reader out of the common gaze and into a genuine looking. It breaks the sleepwalking habit in our eyes, in our ears, in our mouths, and sets us adrift in a small raft under a vast night-sky of stars. We feel ourselves moving, too, above a vast, cold-streaming current carrying inner-lit sea creatures, tangles of kelp strands, fishes. Thus we learn the deep clefts of the mid-ocean land-rifts; thus the wave-blanketed mountains rise up before us as islands, a new habitation for heart and mind.

We depart the known ease in order to arrive somewhere other than where we were. We travel by poem, as by any other means, in order to see for ourselves more than was seen.

The record of those travels matters—one person's word-wakened knowledge becomes another's. We seed poems into magazines, into books, onto the Internet, over the radio, whether to be met by two million people or two hundred, because we are beings who learn from one another how to become our full selves. The pages of *Ploughshares*, filled year by year with new poems and new stories chosen by new selectors, matter to me immensely because on any of them I may meet the few words that will suddenly cast me into a widened humanness, a widened knowledge and range of being.

This encounter of words and reader occurs in privacy, in silence; if any of these pages becomes such a moment of liberation for any of its readers, it is unlikely that I or the words' author will ever hear of it. Yet I have utter confidence that the sum of such moments is one of the essential ways that both individuals and cultures move forward—into awakening; into first the recognition of and then responsibility for our kinship with others; into agreement that this life in all its harshness and beauty is one we want not merely to get through blindly, but make our own. And so we say of a good poem, of a good story, "powerful."

Recently, Czeslaw Milosz mentioned to me his theory that Walt Whitman was responsible for the First World War. "You see," he said, "by the end of the nineteenth century, Whitman began to be widely translated, and all the young revolutionaries of Europe read eagerly and took to heart this new cry for democratic being . . ." Then there is the letter I once received from a woman who had read *The Ink Dark Moon*:* "I heard in those ancient poems what was missing from my life, and ended my marriage." I remember, too, my own return from a period of prolonged depression, a dark hibernation of being; after months of not reading anything, I found one voice I could tolerate—Rilke's. Slowly, surely, his intimate, inward murmuring guided me back to the terrifying shoals of aliveness.

I offer this powerful and dangerous thing into your hands, a "little" magazine. It has been a pleasure to be part of its coming into existence.

---

* *The Ink Dark Moon* is a collection of translations by Jane Hirshfield of two women poets of the 9th- and 10th-century Japanese Court, who were among the creators of the Japanese lyric.

❏ 75

STARTING A POEM

BY PETER MEINKE

MOST BEGINNING POETS DON'T HAVE TROUBLE STARTING A POEM; YOU probably have started hundreds. It's *finishing* a poem that's difficult, and more challenging. But sometimes everyone gets stuck: the dread writer's block.

I no longer worry about this, knowing from experience that a little fallow time is sometimes needed, to let the soil rejuvenate. The Romantic poets had a favorite metaphor for creativity, the Aeolian harp—a harp with stretched strings often placed in windows so that when the wind blew, it would make music. Many of these poets looked upon themselves as writers who waited passively for inspiration to blow through them:

> And what if all of animated nature
> Be but organic Harps diversely framed,
> That tremble into thought, as o'er them sweeps
> Plastic and vast, one intellectual breeze,
> At once the Soul of each, and God of all?
>
> (from "The Eolian Harp," by Samuel Taylor Coleridge)

Well, we *are* harps, and inspiration is real, but we can fan the breeze a little ourselves. The first way is to relax and be patient. Something will come, the breeze will pick up again. To help this along, however, it's good to have a regular time and place for writing poems. Just as you can train yourself to remember dreams, you can train yourself to be receptive to the poetic ideas circulating around and inside you.

A notebook can be a great help; just pick a phrase out of it, transfer it to your computer, or typewriter, or legal pad, and see what comes. The simple act of carrying a notebook around and writing in it can make you a more observant person, and more likely to write poetry.

Poets are natural spies and eavesdroppers; they should be seers (*see-ers*), as well.

Figure out whether silence or music sparks your creative energy. I need silence before I can concentrate, but many writers prefer working while listening to music, usually classical. Hart Crane was famous for writing his poems to the strains of Ravel's "Bolero"; Frank O'Hara turned on Rachmaninoff concertos. I've known several city poets who couldn't write in the country: too quiet, or the birds and crickets bothered them.

Poetry can and does get written anywhere, and under any conditions. Some poets write standing up, some write in bed, many have written in prison, but it makes sense to help your writing along however you can. If you have a place where you regularly go to write—spending hours and hours in a room of your own—you should make it comfortable: a good chair at the right height to avoid back problems or carpal tunnel syndrome; a desk with enough room to spread out; a good light; a window (unless you're like Marcel Proust and prefer a cork-lined room); the usual supplies: pencils, pens, paper, envelopes, stapler, Scotch tape, scissors, calendar.

I have a file cabinet, which every poet needs after writing for several years: drafts, letters from editors, letters from writers, correspondence, articles to save, deadlines. The business of poetry churns out a lot of paperwork!

You may like some pictures or photos on your desk and walls. On my wall there's a blown-up photograph my wife took of Yeats's tombstone in Drumcliff churchyard: "Cast a cold eye / On life, on death. / Horseman, pass by!" Also on my wall is a James Thurber sketch of himself and a poster/photograph of my favorite artist, Camille Pissarro. A couple of beer coasters from Neuchâtel protect the much-scarred desk from new coffee stains. It's far from plush, but it's comfortable; it's the place I go to write.

The need, as always, is to be able to clear your mind and concentrate, and try to sink deep within yourself to find the poem, which can appear from anywhere. Robert Frost said, "A poem begins as a lump in the throat, a sense of wrong, a homesickness, a lovesickness. . . . It finds the thought and the thought finds the word." Sometimes you can't control your surroundings, and you just have to give writing your best shot, from wherever you are.

Recipe

Let's say you want to write a poem
yes?
a good poem maybe not The Second Coming but
your hair is getting thin already and
where's your Dover Beach?

Everything seems somehow out of reach
no?
all of a sudden everyone's walking faster than you and
you catch yourself sometimes staring not at girls

You live in at least two worlds
yes?
one fuzzy one where you always push
the doors that say pull and
one clear cold one where you live alone

This is the one where your poem is
yes?
no
It's in the other one
tear your anthologies into small pieces
use them as mulch for your begonias and
begin with your hands

(first published in Poetry)

    This poem speaks for itself, but I can perhaps get it to talk faster by saying a little about it. The image of the poet isolated in his or her own world is pervasive in our society: the "clear cold one where you live alone." And it's true that for the most part, you're alone when writing. But Yeats was right when he wrote, in "The Circus Animals' Desertion," "I must lie down where all the ladders start, / In the foul rag-and-bone shop of the heart." That is to say, poems should come from the crowded real world, not the rarefied romantic one. And although you should read as much as you can of the great poets who have gone before you, if you hope to write poetry over any length of time, you must also grow *out* of the anthologies and find your own voice. Your poems must emerge from your own experience, even—or perhaps particularly—from your most painful experience. So "begin with your hands" means you should 1) sit down and begin to write, and 2) dig into the roots of your own life (the anthologies will make excellent mulch).

"Recipe" also has a subliminal message: *Poetry is that special language with which much care is taken.* Although the lines may seem to be written in light chatty free verse, closer inspection will show it's not all that "free." Rhymes or near-rhymes link the stanzas (beach/reach, girls/worlds, alone/poem). The next-to-last line of each stanza ends with the conjunction "and." A five-line structure is repeated up to the last stanza when the two-line reversal ("no/It's in the other one") extends that stanza to seven. Also notice the alliteration (cold/clear, begonias/begin), the odd hyphenation (walk-/ing), the disjointed sentence structure ("staring not at girls").

All of these details represent decisions I had to make, ideas I had, effects—successful or not—that I was consciously striving for while writing "Recipe." The reader shouldn't even be aware of them, at least not at first. But they're important. They make the poem a poem.

Your story is interesting to you because of what happened. What will make your story interesting to others is the way you tell it. What you should always be looking for when starting a poem is finding and using fresh language. In "Recipe," the perky "yes/no" structure with its reversal was enough to get me going. Almost all poets have their "Writing a Poem" poem—there must be thousands of them!—so why add another? My job as a writer was to make it verbally lively, funny, sad, helpful—*worth reading.* Some poems aren't worth reading, just as, in a sense, some people aren't worth meeting, although these judgments and reactions vary widely with the individual. To make your poem readable, attack it, as you begin, with the same physical intensity and pleasure that a child uses working with Play-Doh, or building blocks, putting it together a handful at a time. The energy that goes into writing your poem will be the energy that shines out of it.

Many writers, finding themselves stuck, are able to get going again by concentrating on some ordinary object around them. I might look out my window and describe the live oak there. Two kinds of Spanish moss, hanging and balled, cling to it. A limb looks dead. A bald patch is spreading on the main trunk. One limb is much longer than the others, reaching toward the sun; a bluejay on it is eyeing a mockingbird with suspicion. I can say so much about this tree! You can do the same with a waste basket or a bottle of Liquid Paper or the wires leading to your electric outlets. Poems begin with close observation, so the act of describing something within view is a good exercise, and with luck and care, you can find yourself writing a real poem.

One other suggestion I should add about starting. Write as fast as you can think and feel, uncritically, for as long as you can. Just let it all flow out. See where the poem's going, and try to get there. Afterwards, you can take all the time you want to rewrite.

I mentioned before that I often write past the point that I need to; when I reread what I've written, I see I've repeated myself, or spelled out the obvious. Usually in rewriting, my poems shrink. Of course, many poets don't work that way. Apparently Dylan Thomas would labor all morning on a single line, perfect it, and then head to the pub. The next day, another line, and so on until a poem was done. But most poets do it the other way around: Write the first draft fast, then spend however much time it takes on making a poem out of it.

Beginning a poem may be like diving into a strange lake. You can look all you want, you can prepare all morning, you can study the water, you can stick your toe in, but sooner or later you have to jump. This takes courage, as does any important act that has no guarantee of a successful conclusion. Still, when you hit that water and look around, there's nothing else quite so exciting.

□ 76

THE POET AS HYBRID MEMOIRIST

BY MOLLY PEACOCK

FOR SOME PEOPLE KEEPING THEIR GIRLHOOD PROMISES MAKES A DEFINI-
tion of hell on earth, but abiding by my promises became a definition
of heaven. By the age of eight I had already decided: a) not to have
children, b) to marry Humankind's Best Friend (I had my eye on the
collie down the street), c) to become a painter with an easel and a real
beret, and d) to use at least gigantic, at best colossal words. Now it is a
deep pleasure to glance up at my husband (whom I can easily call my
best friend), then look across the desk to see the four books of poetry
I've written, and know that I've become a word-painter—sans easel and
beret. But when I wrote my fifth book, a memoir called *Paradise, Piece
by Piece* all about the choices I've made in my life, I had to learn a new
skill—writing prose. Like a painter attempting to make a sculpture, I
didn't know at first how to construct a prose book.

Should I, like a sociologist, conduct interviews about how *other* people made crucial choices? Or, like a journalist, make a cultural essay?
Or was I really on a poet's search, a quest for understanding? I quickly
realized that I couldn't do interviews and cull statistics. I would have to
use a poet's skills.

One way poets understand what they discover is by tenderly examining that discovery with words. This examination must have the lightest
touch—the poet as physician, with deft hands. The process of describing, even though it is exterior, draws on the deeply unconscious interior
of the describer. My challenge was to examine aspects of my life un-
mentioned and buried; I would have to feel my way toward them, relying on my senses and intuitions to provide language for my
descriptions. So much in the culture would have you fight or ignore
your own instincts that it is a relief and an adventure to have only them
to trust.

Even though I was planning to write about how I came to construct my life as an adult, I knew I had to go to the place where the senses are sharpest: childhood. When I entered scenes of my growing up in working-class Buffalo in the 1950s and in rural upstate New York, my senses rang with truths, and I began hearing again what I had forgotten for decades, the voices of my family imprinted from long ago. I was their duckling.

As soon as I made myself small, crouched under the kitchen table on the green linoleum floor where I often played with my coloring books and crayons, I could picture the feet on the floor, taste the wax of the crayon I wasn't supposed to put in my mouth, and most importantly, hear their voices. Critics have wondered how people can put dialogue in their memoirs—surely they don't remember the actual words and their sequence. But as a poet learns to listen to deeply internal rhythms, I listened to the deeply internalized voices of my family. I could "hear" them speak. I could mimic them the way only a child mimics a parent or a teacher, with—as any teacher knows—appalling accuracy. Thus, as I remembered each situation and reinserted myself into it, remaking myself small, reattuning myself to the feelings of being in that place and at that time, I reheard their voices, now coming out of my own heart, that is, my own mouth. (Sometimes my heart *was* in my mouth as I felt my way into my past.) I discovered that what I heard was crucial to the assembling of the reasons for my most unusual choice to be childfree—especially when I remembered the voices of the grownups as they reiterated, "Don't ever have children, Molly," and all the contradictory feelings I felt when that statement was repeated.

Thus, the dialogue I made up for the memoir isn't "invented" like the dialogue of a novel; it is reconjured from an attunement with the past. I do know the difference, because later on in the writing of my book, I created characters and did indeed invent dialogue. I found myself writing a hybrid memoir, one that incorporated fictional characters. I wanted to be careful of other people's privacy, even though, as a poet who has used my life freely in my work, I understood I would be interrupting my own.

But how would my apprehensions become a book? Would the discoveries be discrete and individual, like poems? Surely not, I worried, afraid of putting a big, huge prose book together. Surely so, another voice inside me said, why not use the same principle? So I did what anyone does to get a big job done: made the book step by step. I would go to a place and time in my life and just start writing; because I'd picked a certain moment, the writing had a natural border. Then, like beads, I began stringing the sections together. Of course, I made many of these "necklaces" over time. After all, the book took me six years to write—just about as long as a book of my poems takes. But each time I reassembled the pieces of the book, I was reacknowledging, and coming first to understand, and then to love, all the people and circumstances of my life, even the really terrible ones.

As a matter of fact, it was the terrible times I started off with. The first scene I wrote was where my Dad, in a rage, tears off the legs of the maple kitchen table after throwing a hot pan of corn at the wall, just missing my head. These times were dark beads, blue-black like lapis lazuli. I did not have the gold beads, the humor, the love and friendship, the art that I also joyfully experienced and embodied. The early "necklaces" had grouped all the things that prevented me from developing normally in a relentless line before me. Seeing them made me understand a crucial aspect of my choice not to have children: I had not made only a reactive, negative decision; this was the dark side of a galaxy that was also lit by positive choices, ambitions, and desires.

When I began to supply the light to the book, I wrote about the funny, happy, spiritual, and sloppily artistic side of my personality and my life. Suddenly I was laughing out loud. This humor swathed cold situations with the love that became apparent to me only after I realized how only partially true the coldness was.

And there had been aspects of my life that were obscure to me because I had a full palette. All the pieces were coming into place, especially that essential aspect of being that my first tries had ignored: spirituality. Now religion, with all my goofy interpretations, and art, the activity that had saved my life by enabling me to focus, were vitally present as choices toward a healthy whole. I was getting a complete picture—and I had really become a complete woman: a poet, a wife, a friend, a daughter, a sister, a teacher, a public person with opinions and goals she understood with zest and without apology.

As my roles became clear to me, so did aspects of certain characters. And this is where the novelistic side to this nonfiction book comes in. My goal of concentrating on the many facets of a single issue made me up the level of craft from beading to the techniques of the jeweler. Not only did I have to give emeralds their complex faces, I had to provide settings for them. Because my parents and sister were dead, I felt I could set them in a context that would tell the truth because I was free to explore the ambiguities of love and hatred that made our family what it was. My husband Mike, a literature professor, understood very well what my work was all about, and he both trusted and permitted me to say anything I wanted about him. My cousin, likewise, trusted me to represent him as he was. My friends also trusted me, but who was I to tell their stories baldly and from the outside? Now the book was becoming more of an artful enterprise, full of themes, motifs, and balancing. I have many and varied friends. Could they all be given appropriate character portraits and numbers of pages? Could I remain loyal and also air their stories? In response, I melded composites of all my dearest friends into two characters, Maggie and Lily. Opposing them is another fictional character, the novelist Mariah Moore. She is a product of all the negative voices that were inside me, the noisy jury of criticism in my head. My poet's training in narrowing, and structuring, was at work, creating a hybrid memoir that took the excitement of scenes from my life and set them against the decisions—sometimes wacky, sometimes wise—that resulted.

Yet I hated the idea of precious "poetic" prose. I wanted to write straight to the heart of an ordinary reader, because I myself am an ordinary human who found herself under extraordinary pressure. This demanded metaphor.

Single metaphors, infrequently placed so that they pop up in the landscape like errant flowers, let each character bloom. When my sister—in an antique beaded flapper dress and bare dirty feet—accosts me in an Upper East Side supermarket, she winks one conspiratorial eye, "just like a macaw." With that comparison, she becomes the complex person she was: bred in a kind of jungle, but willing, within her own wildness, to become a tame pet. Very often in poetry, when an animal is evoked, the "natural" self of the speaker is about to appear.

I had to turn the light of metaphor on myself, too. Food and sex, the signs of life, flourish everywhere in *Paradise, Piece by Piece*. Was I conscious of these metaphors? Oh, yes—and no. Once I found myself using them, I tried to continue. Our intuition operates in spite of us, but when we become aware of it, and let it guide us through the rest of our conscious life—our freedom shapes our destiny.

The rhythm of language is part of the *hap* of the book. ("Hap" is the

Old English root of "happen" and "happiness" and means "fate" or "fortune.") I began *Paradise, Piece by Piece* just after I reunited with my lost lover from high school, the man who, a year later, would become my husband. To rest in the grasp of a love that went its own secret way through a wilderness of years and suddenly revealed itself, gave intimate meaning to my experience of fate and hap. And so I was able to write through the panoply of feelings in all the stages of my life so far—smelling, touching, and tasting them.

❏ 77

A SERIOUS LOOK AT LIGHT VERSE

BY ROSEMARIE WILLIAMSON

I HAVE BEEN WRITING AND SELLING LIGHT VERSE FOR NEARLY THIRTY years. As an art school graduate (who had always enjoyed humorous writing), I had been undecided about my career choice until I enrolled in a creative writing course at a then-nearby New Jersey university. When my professor, who was both knowledgeable and enthusiastic, happened to spot a few of my verses lying around on the table beside my assignment pad, she got very excited. "These are great," she said. "Send them out—flood the market!"

I will never forget her words. I did indeed send my light verse out, to two of the markets she had suggested. To my utter amazement, within a week I received an acceptance from both *Good Housekeeping* magazine and *The Saturday Evening Post*. Hallelujah—I was hooked!

An early acceptance by *The Saturday Evening Post* was "Cost Plus":

> She sells
> Sea shells
> By the sea shore.
> Sam sells
> Clam shells
> For a bit more.

A sale to *Good Housekeeping* from the same period was "Mob Psychology":

> You join the bargain-hunting group,
> Grabbing and unfolding—
> Then find the only thing you want
> Is what some stranger's holding.

This is all well and good, you may be thinking, but how does the verse itself come about? Surely it doesn't evolve full-blown? Not at all. There are a few simple rules to remember, and within these confines, your creativity can run wild. First, you must have a funny idea. (If you find something amusing, chances are others will, too.) Everyday events provide one of the richest sources for humor; the office, supermarket, church, sporting events, shopping mall—all can produce laughable situations.

Possibly the easiest and most common poetic form for humor is the four-line verse, called the quatrain. The quatrain is a neat little package whose length makes it ideal for use as a magazine filler, or for other spots where space is limited. Its brevity is particularly suited to telling a "joke in rhyme," which essentially defines light verse. Making each word count, the first three lines build up to the fourth line, the all-important punch line.

Second in importance is the title, which can serve one or more functions. Titles can provide background material, act as lead-ins, or simply be relevant wordplay. Remember that a clever title is your first chance to catch an editor's eye.

Following are two favorite titles of mine—which may have been instrumental in selling the verses:

Of All the Gauls!

Caesar's legions, so we're told,
Were famous for their marches.
Which may account for Rome today
Being full of fallen arches.

(*The Wall Street Journal*)

Handwriting on the Cave

A caveman's life was fraught with fear,
His world was full of predators,
And it's much the same for modern man,
Except we call them creditors.

(*The American Legion Magazine*)

A word about meter

In a humorous poem the meter (or rhythm or beat) should be regular and simple, to make sure that readers' (or listeners') attention will focus on the words and not be distracted by unexpected changes in rhythm.

Otherwise, double entendres and other forms of wordplay could easily be missed. Irregular and even innovative meter certainly has a place in the poetic scheme of things. Long, rambling epics, elegiac stanzas, and free verse are all perfectly acceptable forms, but they're *not* light verse—whose format is quite different.

Two examples of uncomplicated metric lines come to mind. Familiar to most of us, the first line is from a nursery rhyme, and the second from a Christmas carol:

MAry, MAry, QUITE conTRAry

and its inverse

it CAME upON a MIDnight CLEAR

You will notice that I have capitalized the accented or "stressed" syllables; the unaccented or "unstressed" syllables are in lower case. The first line starts with a stressed syllable, the second with an unstressed one. Either would be a splendid vehicle for light verse. (No need, here, to go into the intricacies of "iambic tetrameter," etc. Life is complicated enough! I just remembered that years ago I wrote a short verse called "They Trod on My Trochee"—which remains unsold!)

So far we have a boffo title and a knee-slapping punch line, but what about the other lines? Not to mention the rhyme scheme—what is appropriate for light verse? The first three lines of a humorous quatrain should provide fodder for the grand finale in the fourth line. If the last line concerns a dog, the build-up lines could be full of canine humor— "Dry Bones," old sayings, puppy puns, etc. When my children were growing up, we had a family dog. Kids-plus-dog inspired the following poem, which ran in *The Saturday Evening Post*:

Dog Days

School is out, the weather's nippy—
They forecast snow; the kids yell "Yippee!"
And greet the flakes with eager glance,
But Fido views the scene askance—
"Although for kids it has its assets,
It's enough to BURY us poor bassets!"

I had more to say about the subject than usual, so I extended it into a set of three couplets.

The most common rhyme scheme for a quatrain is to have the second and fourth lines rhyme. Frequently, the first and third lines also rhyme (but with a different end-rhyme sound from lines #2 and #4). The following verse (which I sold to *The Wall Street Journal*) demonstrates the most common rhyme scheme:

Gag Rule

While dental work for some is painful,
And frequently induces squawking,
My complaint is somewhat different—
It means I have to give up talking!

While you'll be aware of the second/fourth line rhyme in this poem (a copy of which hangs in my dentist's office!), there are other things going on as well. You'll note the dentist-related wordplay of the title. The word "squawking" is funny-sounding—even more so when associated with supposedly mature adults. The last line, however, is the real clincher, with its surprise ending.

Endowed with a good sense of humor, you're already halfway there, and the rest of the trip is fun.

Markets

An investment that's sure to pay long-term dividends is the purchase of a few books: an introduction to poetry that explains basic terms and concepts, as well as that perennial poet's pal, a rhyming dictionary. Public libraries are virtual wellsprings of information about and examples of light verse by well-known humor writers—from the amiable Robert Benchley to the tart-tongued Dorothy Parker.

Several of the so-called slick magazines are good markets for light verse. This can be an off again-on again situation, however, so it's best to check recent issues to determine their current editorial policy.

Literary and college magazines can be good markets for beginning as well as established verse writers. *Cimarron Review,* a publication of Oklahoma State University, bought two of my verses, one of which follows:

From "A" to Zebra

Our kids described their zoo trip to us,
Excitedly, at home that night:
"We saw most animals in color—
But the striped one was in black and white."

A real plus in writing light verse is the fact that the entire process can be just plain FUN! Not many professions can offer such an enticing "perk." With practice, you can learn to view life's little annoyances as raw material for humor—it becomes positively addictive. After writing—and selling—light verse for nearly thirty years, I find the challenge just as exciting today as when I started out, and that's saying quite a bit.

□ 78

WRITING A POEM: TECHNIQUE AND INTUITION

BY GREG GLAZNER

ANY SUCCESSFUL WRITER NEEDS, AMONG OTHER THINGS, TWO RADICALLY different abilities: technique and intuition. Technique is learned consciously; it gives us the ability to make conscious decisions about craft and criticism. Intuition must be enhanced unconsciously; it makes use of our attitudes, chance happenings that nevertheless "work" in a poem, and that baffling experience no one understands and which we sometimes call "inspiration."

The following exercises focus on technique, but they also encourage intuitive writing. Exercises are one way of making it possible for poems to happen *through* us, of getting us in condition for those unpredictable times when intuition pushes us toward lines we didn't think we were capable of.

One exercise that helps writers incorporate surprise and spontaneity in their work was developed by my co-editor at *Countermeasures* magazine, Jon Davis. I sometimes use it in my classes, but it works just as well for the solitary writer as it does for a group of students.

First, write twenty or so unrelated words and phrases on individual slips of paper—"In Her Room," "Jungle Plants," and "Cable Television," for example—again, phrases that seem completely unrelated. Select several phrases at random. Now, incorporate the random phrases in successive lines of a poem. The object is to make the unrelated phrases relate somehow—through image, tone, style, narrative, or some combination of these. The exercise often produces lines that are surprising and intuitive, yet oddly coherent as well. These qualities give power to Jon Davis's own poetry. In this section of his "The Ochre World," I've italicized connecting words and associations in lines that seem, at first glance, to leap from one unconnected image to the next: "The *star*-nosed mole popped out of the earth like a *log*, flopped on its belly. / Its

381

progress across the hardpan was like the progress of a *canoe* paddled by children. / In Vermont, in summer, my brother and I commandeered our host's *canoe* and paddled into the *starry* night. / If meaning is a stew, these nouns, these verbs, this handful of adjectives must *float* in a broth before they can be digested. / Were we, that night, the *lake's* intelligence?" (This last line is, as well, an allusion to a famous passage in Wordsworth's *Prelude* in which he "borrows" a canoe.)

While this exercise encourages the poet to incorporate unpredictable connections in a poem, I sometimes use a quite different one that sharpens the writer's ear for rhythms. In a class in graduate school that focused on Walt Whitman and Philip Levine, our professor, poet Patricia Goedicke, asked us to take a famous short poem as a model and mimic in a poem of our own every aspect of its rhythms—using the model's syllable count, its placement of accented and unaccented syllables, and the pauses indicated by commas and periods.

The most common difficulty with this exercise is trying to *hear* the play of stressed and unstressed syllables in a poem. If this is the case for you, take this first step: Mark the accented and unaccented syllables of multi-syllabic *words*—not of entire poems. Then check yourself against the dictionary's markings. When you can mark single words successfully, you'll have much less trouble marking lines of poetry. Hearing stressed syllables in a poem is exactly like hearing them in individual words.

I chose section 9 of Whitman's "Song of Myself" as a model because I'd been feeling imprisoned by iambs (˘ ´) and wanted to explore freer rhythmic possibilities. Whitman's last two lines seemed, in particular, both free in their rhythms and extremely well-written. How so? Listen to the play of iambs (˘ ´) and anapests (˘ ˘ ´). "Ĭ júmp frŏm thĕ cróssbeăms ănd seíze thĕ clŏveř ănd tímŏthў , / Ănd řoll heád ovĕř heéls ănd tánglĕ mў háir fŭll ŏf wísps." The last two lines of my imitation (opposite in tone, but almost identical in rhythm) went "Ĭ walk tŏ thĕ creékbĕd ănd tośs iň grável ănd wórrў thiňgs, / Ănd tĕll nó oňe bŭt crows ănd grackles hŏw dárklў ĭt góes." Not "finished lines" by a longshot, but the feel of that exercise must have resurfaced to help me later, when I wrote, in iambs, the opening lines of "The Metaphysician's Weekend"—"Tŏ soóthe mўsélf, I've steṕped oŭtside, / bŭt évĕn heře, it's chemĭstrў: /" and then immediately broke that rhythm with something quite different: "boóze ĭn thĕ blóodstřeam, thĕ blínd lawn / rísiňg undĕrnéath me ăs the stréetlight / ĭs dĕlivéred dośnwărd." Look at all those anapests playing off of the line's other rhythms. The exercise had compelled me to take Whitman's rhythms into my head and send them back out, later, in my poem.

I don't want to overstate the case. Writing several drafts of original poems (I wrote more than fifty drafts of the first section of "The Metaphysician's Weekend") is probably the most important way, overall, to learn to write poetry. But exercises *are* an efficient means for addressing specific aspects of poetry.

One I've invented may help you get past the hurdle that almost all beginning poets struggle with: writing in a stiff, stilted voice.

To begin with, make a tape recording of yourself telling some sort of colorful anecdote. Now play it back and take note of the kinds of words, rhythms, and phrases you used most naturally. That is, take note of the kind of *voice* you've used. For example, you may have used a chummy voice full of farfetched comparisons: "You couldn't have beat sense into his head any more than you could have beat rocket science into a pit bull." You may have leaned on trendy phrases: "He was a totally rad head-banging type of guy with black tattoos and rings hanging out of him everywhere." Maybe you spoke in an earnest voice using emphatic repetitions: "I couldn't say that to her, not with so many people watching us. I just couldn't. There was no way to say anything about it until the next day." (This stage of analysis is even more enjoyable if you can find a writing partner. In this case, you'll analyze each other's voice.) Once you've arrived at a preliminary understanding of the kind of voice you chose naturally, try writing a poem making use of it.

Clearly, the oral voice is not any sort of end-all. Many other kinds of voice might serve you as well. And no one would claim an exercise as an accomplished work of poetry. But I'd count "a rad head-banging type of guy with black tattoos and rings hanging out of him" as a dramatic improvement over "His dark rage, despair, and empty longing were more infinite than the eternal black sky"—the sort of lines beginning writers often come up with before working through the exercise.

Sometimes writers are encouraged to think of technical exercises as a way to generate finished pieces and to publish them or read them in public, if possible. I'd like to suggest a different approach. So much of the focus in the poetry world these days is on quick self-gratification. When you pour your energy into writing a merely competent poem, one that is more or less "publishable" or one that seems to express how you were feeling at a given moment, or a poem flashy enough to conjure up applause at an open mike or a poetry slam—then an atmosphere alien to real poetry takes hold. Narrow self-interest starts to choke everything else out.

But if the growing interest in poetry were to move somehow in a different direction, toward, say, the love of all accomplished writing—no matter who writes it—then the development of technique and intuition through exercises would become steps on a long, rich journey one never completes. If by some extremely unlikely combination of will and inspiration and talent and good luck, you write a poem brilliant enough to last, then obviously, the devotion has been worth the effort. Less obviously, however, even if one's own work falls short, the effort has still been worthwhile. There's still that irreplaceable, strenuous pleasure, that rare kind of understanding we encounter when we take art seriously.

What's wrong with this as a kind of incantation for poets of all stripes?: *We paid attention in great detail to the work we loved, through close reading and sometimes, through imitations. We knew the marvelous singing qualities of our language intimately, knew them in our minds and in our hands. We understood the best poetry to be such a fine thing that poets—beginning poets working on technical exercises, mid-career poets working on a third or fourth book, even great poets like Walt Whitman—had, at their best, worked not primarily for short-lived attention, but to serve a vibrant, powerful art.*

With some attention to a broader purpose, writing exercises are far from being a quick fix. They become part of a slow, deepening intensification of experience that's only possible through language.

❑ 79

What Makes a Good Poetry Workshop?

By Elizabeth Biller Chapman and Eve Sutton

It is early evening on a quiet street in a California suburb. If you were standing outside the front door of one home, you'd hear a mixture of voices from the living room—giddy, firm, accusing, tender—punctuated by silence, and laughter raucous as a freshman dorm.

Peering through the front window, you'd see a cozy circle of couches and chairs, a small table of refreshments, stacks of paper, and ten or twelve adults who banter with the easy familiarity of old friends. Welcome to the Thursday Night Poets.

Much has been written about the vicious world of workshops, wolf packs that leave their victim's entrails on the floor. At the other extreme are gatherings so "supportive" that one's ego is coddled at the expense of one's writing.

We are fortunate to belong to a group that is both gentle and constructive. Here are our hints for starting a critique group, and for making it successful.

When and where

Choose a consistent time, day, and location: We meet on Thursday evenings, September to June, a holdover from the years when most of us were enrolled in a poetry class offered by a local community college.

What's available: reference books, especially dictionaries; assorted poetry—Shakespeare, Norton anthologies, lots of contemporary writers; food and drink.

Who's in, and why

Size: The group should be large enough for productive discussion, small enough so it doesn't feel impersonal or overwhelming. Not everyone can attend every week. We've found that if our group includes

385

12–15 people, we're likely to have a good number—eight or more—at each meeting.

Level: We've made a decision not to include poets who were still learning the elementary skills of the craft, because we wished to work at a more advanced level. However, we do have some members who started writing poetry just a few years ago, along with some who have decades of experience.

Diversity: Our group includes both genders, and a range of ages, backgrounds, occupations, income levels, and living situations. When a poem makes a reference to a particular place, religion, or experience, it's likely that at least one member of the group will recognize it from an insider's perspective, and at least one member will not. We can discuss how to present that reference in a way that is clear, but not condescending.

Guidelines

This is our customary format—it is not unique. As members arrive, they place their poems, enough copies to go around, face down on the table. This is the Stack, which is passed around 15 minutes after the official Start Time—not as simple as it sounds, since people want to stop and read the poems!

The poet reads his or her poem aloud. A silence follows. If they wish, members write comments on their copies to hand back to to the poet later. Then we discuss, beginning with a "holistic" comment on the overall poem or effect, positive attributes, what works well. Other comments, suggestions, changes. A basic axiom: Every criticism implies its opposite.

Workshop atmosphere: energy

The most important thing: generosity of tone and spirit. This is not the same as sappy: "You're a nice person, and this is a nice poem." It means everyone must be willing to make an effort to find something positive to say about each poem. It is more important than laser-like wit or "being right."

Examples

1. A helpful suggestion for change, from "Shedding a Layer" by S. Gaines:

> Torn from an old magazine
> this richly colored advertisement:
> "The Timelessness of Diamonds."

Comment: It would be stronger without the second line (which "tells" more than it "shows").
Revised version:

> Torn from an old magazine
> "The Timelessness of Diamonds."

2. A revision, based on a workshop comment, from "Parting" by E. B. Chapman, written for a mentor, about to move away:

> Last night I heard an owl, clearly, five hoots.
> Difficult thatched bird, was that you?
> announcing your departure all along the creekbed . . .

Comment: The second adjective modifying "bird" was originally "wise"; triter and more "mental" than the other imagery.

3. A poem we all agreed on: It works as is; leave it alone:

Saving Time
by E. Sutton

> I hoard each fragment
> against winter dark: gilt-edged
> notch of mountain at dawn, glint
> of blue-lake afternoon, evening's book
> for dessert outdoors. I'll never return
> the daylight I've saved.

In conclusion

We'd like to end with some advice from our former poetry teacher, who, though comfortably retired, still follows our progress. Here, then, are two of Richard Maxwell's Maxims:

1. Dive in; if you pussyfoot around, testing the water, you'll never get wet.
2. Remember, you don't have to be doing this, but you really like to.

P. S. Have fun!

❑ 80

The Poet's Choice: Lyric or Narrative

By Gregory Orr

Poets are haunted by the dream of perfection in a way that writers in no other literary art form are. And unity is one of those mysterious elements interwoven with poetry's fatal dream of its own perfection.

Unity is something almost all poets and those writing about poetry have insisted upon as an essential element. But things become complicated when we decide to define unity, because there are many definitions leading to many different kinds of poems.

Suppose we begin with two kinds of poems and the distinct kind of unity each might aspire to: *lyric poems* and *narrative poems*. They aren't different kinds of poems; they actually exist on a spectrum with (pure) lyric on one end and (pure) narrative on the other. I've put the adjective "pure" in parentheses because there is no such beast; every lyric has some element of narrative in it, even if it is only an implied dramatic context for its words. Similarly, every narrative has some lyric element, if only a metaphor placed at a crucial point or the heightening of its rhythmic texture, as it approaches its narrative climax. Lyric and narrative are part of a continuum, and it is extremely interesting to take a number of your poems and try to locate them along this spectrum. Ask yourself: Is this sonnet more lyric than narrative? And how does it compare with any of my other poems in terms of lyric and narrative elements? Which is dominant?

Lyrics and narratives are the products of different sensibilities or of the same sensibility operating in two distinct ways. These differences can be understood by comparing them with the making of a sculpture. There are two basic ways of making a piece of sculpture: carving and modeling.

The carving method involves taking a piece of stone or wood and cutting away toward some desired or intuited shape *within* the original block. The finished piece emerges as the extra material is stripped away.

The modeling method requires the sculptor to construct a skeletal structure out of wood or metal that essentially defines the shape of the piece, much as our skeleton defines the shape of our bodies. This structure is called an armature. Once the armature is constructed, the sculptor proceeds by slapping lumps of clay or plaster on it to flesh out the shape. This modeling technique is one of accretion: The sculptor has added material to make his piece, and the finished piece is larger than what he or she began with. Also, the carving technique results in a piece that is smaller than the original stone the sculptor began with.

What do these two techniques have to do with poetry? They correspond to the lyric and narrative modes. The lyric poem is created like the carved sculpture—the poet intuits a hidden, compelling shape within the language of the first draft. The secret is to carve away, to eliminate the excess as you work your way toward the lyric's secret center. The motto of the lyric is somewhat mystical: "Less is more."

The author of narrative, on the other hand, has a different purpose: If the lyric poet seeks a hidden center, then the narrative poet wants to tell a story—this happened, and then that happened. He or she wants to add material, to keep moving, to find out what is over the next hill. The narrative poem is a kind of journey, and it needs to add action to action, event to event, line to line. Narrative poems get longer as they are rewritten, because the narrative poet discovers his or her meanings by asking, "What next?" and pushing a poem's protagonist further by adding one line to the next. One of the cleverest definitions of narrative thinking comes from contemporary poet Frank O'Hara, who spoke of his work as his "I-did-this-and-then-I-did-that" poems. O'Hara's remark sounds almost glib, but he's articulating the secret of how a narrative gets made. The narrative poet's motto is the sensible: "More is more."

The narrative poem wanders across a landscape, propelled by verbs and unified by the need to have a beginning, middle, and end that relate to each other. The narrative poem is searching for something and won't be happy (complete, unified) until it has found it. The lyric poem has a different shape—it *constellates* around a single center, usually an emotional center: a dominant feeling. If the shape of a narrative is a line meandering down the page, then the shape of a lyric is that of a snowflake or crystal. The lyric is not searching, because it already knows what it knows, what it feels. Browning caught this already-knowing when he said "the lyric poet digs where he stands." The lyric poet digs into his or her emotion, a single, centered thing.

Needless to say, neither the narrative nor the lyric is "right"; each can be merely a direction a poet might take a poem. But they also reflect inclinations a poet has, and as such, they can be more deeply rooted in the dominant psychology of a poet.

Robert Frost is a prime modern example of a narrative temperament—not that his poems contain no lyric moments, but that the lyric was seldom his aim, and lyric unity was not what he usually sought. William Carlos Williams would be my candidate for a poet whose primary temperament is lyric.

What do I mean by lyric and narrative unity? Aristotle, who in the fifth century B.C. became the first poet-friendly critic with his *Poetics,* knew that unity was essential to the dramatic effectiveness of poetry. His idea of poetry was essentially narrative, and he proposed that what could unify narrative poetry was this: that it describe a single action. He further insisted that there had to be a beginning, a middle, and an end to this action, and that these three parts should be in a harmonious relationship.

When Robert Frost writes his poem "Directive," he is giving us a quintessential narrative poem, which will take the form of a journey, the poet-speaker offering himself to us as a guide. We travel over a landscape toward the ruins of a vanished village (we are also, in a sense, traveling backward in time). It is the narrative as journey, the narrative as a series of actions where *verbs,* those action words, move us forward from one sentence to the next. How will Frost's "Directive" achieve narrative unity? By arriving at a significant location (the village, the spring behind the deserted house) and making a significant discovery (the cup hidden in the hollow tree). We have journeyed a long way, we have journeyed from being "lost" and disoriented to being "found" and located.

Here is Edmund Waller's 17th-century lyric "On a Girdle." The girdle he celebrates is an embroidered sash or belt women then wore around their waists, not the "foundation garment" in modern use:

On a Girdle

That which her slender waist confined
Shall now my joyful temples bind;
No monarch but would give his crown
His arms might do what this had done.

It was my heaven's extremest sphere,
The pale which held that lovely deer;
My joy, my grief, my hope, my love
Did all within this circle move.

A narrow compass! and yet there
Dwelt all that's good, and all that's fair.
Give me but what this ribband bound,
Take all the rest the sun goes round.

(1664)

Waller's poem achieves lyric unity through two methods. One is through the single emotion that motivates and animates the poem: praise of the beloved. The poet is at pains to tell us how enraptured he is at the thought of his beloved: He'd rather have her in his arms than the whole world in his possession. Notice that Waller sticks with the single emotion and takes it all the way through the poem. Lyrics tend to do that—locate their single, central emotion and take it to the limit.

The second unifying element in Waller's poem is "technical," i.e., the recurring use of circle images and metaphors. Almost everything is a circle starting (and ending) with the sash that encircles his beloved's waist. He puts the sash around his head, and that reminds him of the circle of a king's crown and arms around a woman's waist. In stanza two he thinks of heavenly spheres and the circle of fence (pale) that might confine a deer; in stanza three, he thinks of her waist again, and (the final line) the giant orbit of the sun around the earth (here he's using the old earth-centered cosmic scheme).

The reason I chose Waller's poem rather than, say, a William Carlos William lyric is this: The very technique that unifies Waller's lyric—a series of metaphors—would work *against* narrative unity.

Why? How? Simply this: Metaphors slow a poem down. The more metaphors, the slower the going. The reader has to stop and think about (and savor) the comparisons. But narrative poems thrive on momentum; they need to keep moving. A good narrative poet knows to beware of metaphors and use them sparingly. Metaphors are a lyric poet's friend, but they can disrupt narrative unity, which is based on unfolding action.

A lyric poem can go wrong in many ways: Most commonly, the first draft has not sufficiently surrounded its emotional or imagistic character. (In this situation, when the sculptor revises by carving the block of wood, he ends up with no more than a toothpick, or even less.)

Similarly, when a narrative poem goes wrong, it can get completely lost and wander aimlessly. Remember that in Frost's poem, the speaker/poet/guide knows exactly where his poem is taking readers, even if they don't.

If a poem you're working on is giving you trouble, try to locate it on the spectrum that goes from lyric to narrative. If your poem aspires to narrative, then keep it moving with verbs and action, and ask yourself where this story best begins, how it develops, how it is resolved. If your poem aspires to lyric, ask where its emotional or imagistic center is, and see if you can strengthen it by stripping away extra material.

❑ 81

POETS SPEAK IN MANY VOICES

BY GEORGE KEITHLEY

WRITERS OF THE PERSONA POEM—A DRAMATIC MONOLOGUE SPOKEN IN the voice of a character created by its author—often find it one of the most rewarding of poetic forms. And often for the same reasons that delight readers: At its best, the poem may be surprising, insightful, and dramatic, all at the same time.

While *persona* may refer to the speaker of any poem, the term *persona poem,* in current usage, refers to a poem spoken by a central character other than the author. Immediately you see one of its attractions: It invites us to enter the consciousness of a creature other than oneself. Who hasn't, at some time, wondered what it would be like to be someone else? Or tried to understand how the world might look when viewed from a perspective other than our own? Well, for the duration of each persona poem, the poet thinks and feels and speaks as someone else; perhaps a person of a different sex, age, nationality, or culture.

Because of this different perspective, in which the poet assumes the role of someone else, the persona poem differs essentially from a lyric poem (in which the speaker is the author) or a narrative poem (written in the third person about other people and their experiences).

Among the best-known examples of the persona poem are some of the most admired poems in the English language: Robert Browning's "My Last Duchess," T.S. Eliot's "Journey of the Magi," W.B. Yeats's "Crazy Jane Talks with the Bishop," and Hart Crane's "Repose of Rivers" (a monologue in the mind of the Mississippi River).

As that last example suggests, the *persona,* or speaking-consciousness of the poem, needn't be a person. Poems in this form have also been written from the imagined intelligence of rain, snow, fog, fire, sheep, frogs, bears, horses, whales, characters from fairy tales, and the constellations in the night sky.

Whether they are historical figures or fictional ones, human or nonhuman, the speakers of these poems bring to both the poet and the reader many voices that might otherwise have remained silent, not only in the world around us, but also within ourselves.

A few of the many successful persona poems written by modern poets are Linda Pastan's "Old Woman," Galway Kinnell's "The Bear," Louise Bogan's "Cassandra," James Wright's "Saint Judas," and Gwendolyn Brooks's "We Real Cool" and "Big Bessie Throws her Son into the Street." The telling nature of these titles is no accident. The reader of a persona poem should learn from the title or the first lines of the poem exactly who is speaking, and perhaps—something of the situation that has moved the speaker to address us.

Keep the identity of the speaker clear and direct. Since you're asking the reader to embark on a journey into the consciousness of another being, often one in inner turmoil, let the identity of that figure be clear from the start. The poem's essential mystery lies in what the speaker reveals to readers, and in the language in which the revelation is expressed. In one of the most famous persona poems, Browning offers the title "My Last Duchess," and the speaker, the Duke, begins:

> That's my last Duchess painted on the wall,
> Looking as if she were alive. I call
> That piece a wonder now . . .

Immediately the reader knows that the Duchess has died, and her widowed husband cares more about her portrait than he cared for her.

In my book, *Earth's Eye,* I included a poem, "Waiting for Winter," which begins:

> I think of my name, Julia Grahm,
> and hold my hands so in a circle,
> making my mind obey my mind.

In the first line the speaker gives readers her name and invites them to see that introspection and self-restraint are her significant features. (She'll go on to reveal that, in her forties, living alone, she's keenly attuned to the promptings of her body and soul.)

Similarly, in the same book, my poem, "In Early Spring," begins with a young woman saying:

In early spring I felt the weight
of his legs
upon my own. I undid my dress,
we watched the wind row
across the water . . .

At this point, I hope the poem has established the voice of its central character and has suggested her situation.

About the speaker's situation—remember that the persona poem is a *dramatic* monologue. Ask yourself: What is it about this situation that causes my character to experience an intensity of insight and emotion? What is the urgency that compels this person to speak? What makes us eager to reveal ourselves to others? When you can answer these questions, you're ready to write the poem and hope to see it published.

Once the nature of your central character is apparent to you, and the figure has begun to reveal itself, you then have the speaking-consciousness that is vital to the persona poem, and you're ready to move on, within the life of that character. I often visit a diner where a waitress, as she places food before her customers, smiles, and says: "There you go!" As if she's recognizing our hunger, our anticipation, and our readiness to begin. That feeling of release, of freedom to explore, is typical of the poet and the reader, meeting each other in the persona poem. For the poem offers a wide range of physical and psychological experience not often accessible to us. Writing it, or reading it, we inhabit another life—or perhaps a part of our own consciousness of which we're usually unaware.

I tend to write the persona poem for two different purposes. One is to allow myself to enter a state of feeling, a state of being, and to speak from within that context, which previously had been unknown to me. It might mean empathizing with a character of a far different nature, but by assuming the thoughts and feelings of that speaker, to the extent that I give voice to them, I might come to a better understanding of the "character" of that figure. On the other hand, the persona might be very compatible, but I find it difficult to write about myself in the first person, so the dramatic figure, the persona, is a mask that allows me to speak, free of an otherwise stifling inhibition.

A word of caution. Much has been said about the ethics of appropriating someone else's culture or history: a poet pretending to be someone he or she is not, in order to capitalize on a history of suffering that the writer hasn't endured. The rule is simple: Don't do it. You write with your head and your heart. Your conscience will tell you if your empathy is authentic. Or not. A virtue of the persona poem is that it affords both poet and reader an opportunity for understanding and compassion.

A second reason for writing the persona poem is that often the central figure is involved in a dramatic situation or story. Taking on the character of the figure is a way of entering the story. The speaking figure is itself our invitation to enter the poem.

So the persona poem will be most compelling if the main figure, the speaking-consciousness, is at the center of a dramatic situation, for the moral and psychological pressures of a conflict will bring thought and feeling into focus. Why is that persona compelling to us? Why at this particular moment? If the poem's central character, its speaking voice, is encountered at a moment of dramatic tension, or moral consequence, or significant insight, the answer will be evident to the poet and the reader alike.

The drama that compels our interest may or may not be apparent from the character's actions. What's vitally important is the poet's understanding of the character's inner nature at the moment when it's revealed to the reader. In "The Pleading Child," another poem in *Earth's Eye,* I tried to evoke the troubled joy a young boy experiences one winter night with his parents and his sister, in what might otherwise seem a very peaceful environment:

> After Christmas Mass the strains
> of carols call us to the flesh
> and blood figures in the stable crèche:
> "Joy to the world! the Savior reigns . . ."
>
> Joseph, Mary, and the Child in white.
> Kneeling, the Kings set down their pomp
> and gifts. We troop into the night—
> Moon, lift up your little lamp.
>
> The stone bridge straddles the stiff creek.
> Skate blades slung back, two sharp boys slip
> off the ice. Beyond the bridge we grip
> each other's hands to climb the bleak
> hill. My sister whispers, "Look!"
> Fresh tracks pock the snow, dogs romp
> down the road in a ragged pack—
> Moon, lift up your little lamp.
>
> Something more than the snow or chill

makes my mother stop and weep.
Something her heart had hidden deep
within the winter pulses still:
Silent in the sparkling dark,
lovers bundle past the pump
house and pause. Only their eyes speak—
Moon, lift up your little lamp.

Father shoulders Julia over
a steep drift. Why do I cry?
Mother's singing, ". . . the sounding joy,
Repeat the sounding joy." I shiver
in my short coat and she stoops to fold
her arms around me. Gladly we tramp
home across the glittering cold—
Moon, hold up your happy lamp!

Whether the resulting persona poem is a character study or the evolving of a story, there is, at the heart of the poem, a figure who compels our attention. The writer's interest in this figure might be an impulse toward compassion, or humor, or the desire to come to understand different aspects of human nature or the natural world. Or it might be a desire to explore the drama of the character's situation.

Each of these is a fundamental motive for writing, and the persona poem results from the combination of introspection, examination, and drama. It is a dramatic form, and a poetic medium, but it is also, and essentially, a poem. So it must live and prosper according to those qualities of language, rhythm, tension, and imagery that we give it.

The possibilities for subjects in the persona poem are limited only by our imagination and our willingness to take risks—which is another way of saying that it's time to get to work. Now, for however long it takes to write the poem, you find yourself becoming (and giving voice to):

- A teacher facing her third-grade class on the first morning of the school year.
- A man watching a baseball game with his father who is recovering from a stroke.
- The almost silent snowfall that settles upon a pine forest.
- A parent attending the military funeral of an only son, killed in combat.
- A woman riding the subway home to her apartment while she con-

siders a recent marriage proposal that she's not quite willing to accept. Or reject.

- A river flowing swiftly under a fine spring rain.
- A child walking thoughtfully through the dappled shade of a fruit orchard on a summer morning.
- A man who stands in a public parking lot looking at his red pickup truck, while two police officers pull his arms behind his back and handcuff his wrists.
- An owl gliding over a frozen field at twilight.
- A stand-up comic waiting to go on stage in a small theater.
- An elderly woman picking her way through a city park, a bag of groceries in her arms, while her granddaughter skips ahead of her into the deepening dusk.
- A colt running through a field of grass glossy with sunlight.

"There you go!"

❏ Playwriting

❏ 82

TRANSFORMING STORY INTO PLOT

BY DAVID COPELIN

WHAT *IS* A PLOT, ANYWAY? WHAT'S THE DIFFERENCE BETWEEN A PLOT and a story? And how do you create one from another?

Here's a classic distinction: "The queen died, and then the king died" is a story. "The queen died, and then the king died *of grief*" is a plot. *Story*, then, is the events of a play, in whatever order you choose to tell them. *Plot* concerns the relationship among these events and the characters who enact them.

We can infer that our king and queen had more than a political marriage, that their public relationship contained (and probably concealed) a powerful emotional bond. In such a case, our hypothetical king's death may be explained to his subjects as an emotional response to the loss of his queen. How sad! How moving! But what if, behind the scenes, a darker political struggle is taking place? What if the king's death means the end of one dynasty and the establishment of another, with a civil war to decide which dynasty will rule? Yes, the king's grief was deep, but did it *really* cause his death? Or was it a convenient coincidence? As Shakespeare put it (cynically): "Men have died from time to time, and worms have eaten them; but not for love." Then how *did* the king die? For that matter, how did the *queen* die? What if . . . ? Or could the king's grief and a political struggle be *simultaneous truths?* Of course they could.

As you see, the dramatic possibilities inherent in this situation are limitless.

In such a case, plot and character influence each other in many ways, and as the playwright, you determine which influences are most important.

As a practical matter, the story of your play is likely to develop well before its plot does, because all the linkages among events and characters—both obvious and subtle—that make up an effective plot are usu-

401

ally a result of several drafts. Getting the story elements right, and presenting them in the most effective order, is hard enough; but making a plot out of the story, a plot in which every moment gives just enough information and no more, in which the play's forward movement is both unmistakable and compelling, is even harder.

Fortunately, the complicated and lengthy process of creating a play from an idea, or an image, or a character, or whatever you start from, is ultimately more fascinating than frustrating. Don't worry if your plot isn't completely clear to you at the outset. Don't worry if you don't know all there is to know about each character before you start writing your script. Some playwrights create random lists of character traits, then sculpt each list into a person. Try this, and see if it works for you. Or you may be more comfortable imagining a character as a whole, and discovering additional traits as they reveal themselves in the course of your writing the play.

Alternatively, you may start with an event, then say, "What kind of character would most likely be involved in such an event?" Or (and better) "What kind of character would be highly *un*likely to be involved in such an event, and what would happen if he or she *were* so involved?"

In your first draft, feel free to begin with bits and pieces of your story. Don't worry, at this point, about unity, coherence, or emphasis. Step by step, make each event or transaction into a scene; each scene into a series of scenes that fit together according to your dramatic vision; each series of scenes into an act; each act into a play. Take your time, building the overall structure out of smaller units. You need not write the play in chronological order. In later drafts, you can cut, add, rearrange, expand, contract—do whatever is necessary to make those bits and pieces fit together seamlessly.

Traditionally, a play is supposed to have a beginning, a middle, and an end; plays that do so are highly satisfying to most audiences. But you can make an arbitrary choice of where in a story to start and where to end. Those choices will define the middle. Remember, you can always use a *flashback* or *flash-forward,* as the structure of your play may require.

One common test for the effectiveness of a play is whether or not it has *forward motion*, but while *most* plays need to move forward through time with some urgency, there are some really great plays that do not.

Their motion is circular or spiral, their force centripetal. Their action meanders, and their characters seem stuck in time and place.

Consider Anton Chekhov's plays, in which the leisure of the landed Russian gentry conceals a dim, anguished perception that nothing they do will keep their world from coming to an end. A lot happens in Chekhov, but it tends to happen *offstage*. Chekhov dramatizes a world that seems to have no drama, except for the occasional intense moment; deftly, he turns the typical plot-rich 19th-century play into examinations of character so subtle, yet so powerful, that generations of actors have found exploring roles in his plays to be indispensable for their training. Chekhov's plays don't have much forward motion in the traditional sense, because they reveal a world that is autumnal, burnt out, yet they manage to proceed to their dramatically logical end with seemingly effortless grace.

Nevertheless, many dramatic authors today, and many audiences, expect a play to move forward clearly and quickly, partly because they have been conditioned by thousands of hours of film and television to mistake *action* for *drama*. In our daily lives, we learn to experience time primarily as linear. In our dreams, however, we experience time in many other ways, so plays with dream-like, imaginative structures tend to be less linear than plays that attempt to replicate the recognizable external world. Hamlet says that the purpose of theatre is "to hold, as 'twere, the mirror up to nature." You, the playwright, get to decide what sort of mirror, and what aspect of nature. For example, Harold Pinter's play *Betrayal* begins after its events have taken place, and tells its story backwards. The audience experiences how memory revises our lives, and how actions that destroy human relationships may begin in a chance word here, a careless gesture there. In a different mode, Tennessee Williams created *The Glass Menagerie* consciously as a dream-play. Time swirls, history repeats itself, "real" objects become symbols, and so on. On stage, private dreams may become public magic.

Most playwrights follow a "forward motion" model, in which story elements are kept or discarded to the degree that they move the plot toward its climax and conclusion. Forward motion gathers momentum, so that a play seems to move faster and faster as it nears its most revealing moment. This is the technique Sophocles used in as early a play as *Oedipus Rex*: He created the sensation of increasing speed by making each successive scene shorter (and therefore more intense) than the preceding one, until the play's ultimate, inexorable revelation.

Sophocles' invention is thoroughly adaptable to our time. *Glengarry Glen Ross,* David Mamet's feisty, funny play about sleazy Chicago real-estate salesmen, is an excellent contemporary example of the Sophoclean model of forward motion—and yet Sophocles is probably the last influence you'll think of if you read or see Mamet's play. *Glengarry's* combination of verbal jazz, lean structure, and ruthless analysis of petty capitalism seems utterly American and up-to-date.

This is an important reason for you to acquaint yourself with as many plays as possible. Imagine using a 2,500-year-old technique for thoroughly modern purposes! There's no need to reinvent the wheel, but rediscovering what makes it turn can be very helpful to any playwright.

Sometimes a plot is described in terms of "rising action," "climax," and "falling action," generally to show how dramatic stories move from A to B to C. Plays structured this way often have impressive power and clarity, but not all viable dramatic paths are linear. These days, more and more dramatic material that is fragmented, or repetitive in subtle ways, or is simply a series of blackout sketches, finds its way to successful performance. Nevertheless, because "forward motion" has such power over us, many playwrights' work is criticized for what it *doesn't do* rather than appreciated for what it *does*—especially if the play's motion is seemingly static. Any play, no matter how much it seems to hold an objective mirror up to everyday reality, is in fact an imaginative creation in which the playwright has the option of reaffirming the commonly accepted rules of time, space, and behavior, or inventing new ones. Whatever the playwright's choice, the more consistently and tellingly these rules are applied, the more persuasive the play will be.

Plays that appear to be about the world we all share are easier to appreciate than plays about worlds that exist only in the writer's mind, but of course this depends on the writer. August Strindberg worked quite effectively in both modes. *The Father* is ruthlessly objective, while *The Ghost Sonata* is much more obviously a dream play. The same dark comic sensibility informs both dramas, but in the first, forward motion is relentless. In the second, motion comes in many diverse forms. If you compare these texts to Canadian playwright George F. Walker's *Suburban Motel* cycle, you'll see how forward motion and circular repetition can be combined. I wouldn't have thought of mixing together the sensibilities of Sam Shepard and the Marx Brothers, but Walker did, and the result is wacky, preposterous theatre with a great core of human truth.

If your talent is for writing non-linear and/or non-realistic plays, it's up to you to provide alternate sources of dramatic energy. Here are a few such sources: progressive revelation of character (e.g., Emily Mann's *Still Life*), increasing emotional intensity (e.g., Sam Shepard's *Buried Child*), more powerful imagery of states of inertia (e.g. Samuel Beckett's *Happy Days*), vivid theatrical poetry (e.g. Federico Garcia-Lorca's *Blood Wedding*). *Something* has to take the place of forward motion, or your play will be wan and tepid.

You can, of course, combine linear and non-linear elements in your play, or realistic scenes and non-realistic scenes. This sort of dramatic counterpoint has exciting theatrical possibilities.

There are many techniques that will help you turn your story into a plot:

1. *Follow your instincts about which elements of your story deserve the most stage time.*

2. *As you draft and redraft, you will notice patterns emerging in your story. Make linkages among these patterns through the repetition and development of language, symbols, and sounds, as appropriate to the characters and situation—so that you are working on verbal, visual, and aural dimensions of your play simultaneously.* How does Shakespeare use the witches in *Macbeth* to create atmosphere, provide information, and dramatize the interplay between the ordinary and the occult? How does David Mamet's *American Buffalo* make verbal repetition and the focus on small rituals coexist in a wholly appropriate and resonant context? Read Mamet's description of the play's setting, and notice how the setting and the dialogue complement each other.

3. *If your plot is starting to feel too convoluted, try "storyboarding" it.* Borrow a technique from film writing: Put units of action on index cards, then put each index card on your wall. Does the first way you arranged each card make sense to you? Do you need all the cards? Are there gaps in the pattern? If so, do you need to fill these gaps? How can you rearrange the cards so that a different, perhaps more provocative, pattern begins to emerge? Follow that trail!

4. *As the playwright, only you know which events in the early part*

of a play will in retrospect be seen as significant. Theatre people refer to such an event as a *setup.* To complete the structural (and emotional) circle, a setup must be followed, usually at some distance, by a *payoff.* This is usually some sort of surprise, some event or revelation that in retrospect is inevitable, without having been predictable in advance. Oscar Wilde's preposterous coincidences, late in *The Importance of Being Earnest,* are wonderful examples of payoffs, absurd and delightful at the same time.

Make sure, therefore, that your setups stay concealed, but don't forget that there must be a payoff—unless you choose, for some good reason, *not* to pay off a setup, to leave the structural-emotional circle unclosed. To look at it from another angle: In writing a payoff, make sure that you go back and locate the setup. If there isn't one, invent one. Then hide it.

Hidden setups that are paid off openly and tellingly occur in Edward Albee's *Who's Afraid of Virginia Woolf?,* when the offstage child is revealed as a fantasy with the emotional impact of reality; in Shakespeare's *Macbeth,* when Birnam Wood *does* come to Dunsinane, though not in the form we expect; and in Bertolt Brecht's *Mother Courage,* when the significance of Swiss Cheese's nickname becomes chillingly clear.

5. *What can you cut without weakening your play's structure?* If your first answer is "Nothing!"—look again.

6. *Be careful about #5.* August Wilson's plays, such as *Fences, The Piano Lesson,* and *Seven Guitars,* are characterized by a loose, open architecture and a lot of rambling discourse that can seem repetitive and verbose. But since Wilson is dramatizing a culture with a complicated attitude about time and how best to pass it, it makes some sense for his plays to unfold slowly, with a lot of fits and starts and blind alleys. The rough edges of Wilson's writing, the meandering and curlicues, become attributes of an identifiable individual *style* of playwriting. This style may not be suitable for every playwright, but it is an artistic choice.

In other words, don't be too quick to homogenize your work. You have a right to your idiosyncrasies; in the end, they may be more valuable than you expected.

7. *There is a certain satisfaction to tying up all the loose ends of a play neatly, as in the much-abused, little-appreciated "well-made" play; but this sort of tightly contrived and controlled playwriting has*

few advocates today. It survives most obviously in TV sitcoms and movies. A looser structure seems to suit many contemporary playwrights. There may be a greater satisfaction in leaving some elements unresolved, so that the audience is left wanting to know what happens to the characters even after the play is over. This is more like life itself, in which few questions are answered totally and unambiguously.

For example, in Arthur Miller's *Death of a Salesman*, the author focuses most of our attention on Willy Loman, his (anti)hero. But this major focus is buttressed by a strong secondary focus on Willy's family. What happens to Linda, Biff, and Happy after Willy's suicide? We never really learn, so part of the significance of Willy's choice is lost to us. But, you can't write about everything at once. Choosing *which* elements to leave unresolved is the mark of a master, and this mastery is the result of practice.

After reading *Death of a Salesman*, read Donald Margulies' *The Loman Family Picnic*. There's a lesson here about the constructive use of an older play to inspire a new one, and the illumination of the older play by the newer one. Tom Stoppard's plays *Rosencrantz and Guildenstern are Dead, The Real Inspector Hound*, and *Travesties* are both tributes to and parodies of, respectively, Shakespeare's *Hamlet*, any Agatha Christie murder mystery, and Oscar Wilde's *The Importance of Being Earnest*. The most significant fact to keep in mind, though, is that each of Stoppard's plays stands perfectly well on its own. You don't need to have read or seen the plays that inspired them, but if you have, you get an extra measure of enjoyment from the echoes, and can learn from the ways this approach has been used.

8. *Make your exposition serve multiple purposes. Exposition* is information about characters and events from the past or present that an audience needs to know to appreciate onstage action fully.

Although audiences *want* to know what's going on at every moment, they don't *need* to know. Suspense is an important attribute in a play, because it reinforces an audience's curiosity and helps provide some of the forward motion. So when should you provide vital information? For many purposes, at the latest possible moment. This does *not* mean that you save all crucial information until the play's last five minutes, then tell the audience everything you've withheld; but make sure you've explored indirect ways of giving information before you do so directly.

One of the most effective ways to do this is to have your characters discuss what actions they are *going to* take, rather than what they have done in the past. You'll find that any necessary background or character information will emerge organically, so that you don't have to slow your play down by giving the audience chunks of the past.

In contemporary plays, exposition is almost never *just* exposition; it often contains action as well as other kinds of information. Emily Mann's *Execution of Justice* dramatizes the famous and controversial murder trial of Dan White, the San Francisco politician who shot Mayor George Moscone and gay activist Harvey Milk in 1975. The play's strategy is to give us a kaleidoscopic view of the community in which it takes place. The profusion and sprawl of actual events, the candid reminiscences of people involved in the trial, and volumes of court testimony are all challenges to the playwright's need for dramatic economy. They were also her raw material.

Given this complexity, every moment in *Execution of Justice* had to serve several purposes simultaneously. The drama opens with two characters speaking. They are both onstage, close to each other, yet they seldom acknowledge each other's presence. They represent two opposing factions in the community and in the play. One of the characters is an unnamed San Francisco policeman who wears a "Free Dan White" T-shirt under his uniform; the other is Sister Boom-Boom, a gay transvestite in a nun's habit. From the first moment of the play, we are confronted with a kind of civic schizophrenia. The scene sets the tone for the play, and introduces us to its larger subject: the conflict of different value systems within the same community. It is exposition disguised as action.

You may never confront the challenge of effective exposition to such a degree in your own work, but *Execution of Justice* is a good example of how to rise to such a challenge.

9. *"Show, don't tell" means don't say directly in words what you can convey indirectly through behavior, and never, ever sermonize.* This is generally gospel for contemporary playwrights. But, as Sportin' Life says of that *other* gospel, "It ain't necessarily so." There are exceptions. Look at Tony Kushner's play *Slavs! (Thinking About the Problems of Virtue and Happiness)* for a recent example of "breaking the rules" and getting away with it. This play begins with a character reading to the audience out of a book! There are few clearer ways of saying outright, "Let's save time. This is what you need to know." I admire the

playwright's nerve, his willingness to do whatever he felt the situation required, and "show, don't tell" be damned. You may never start a play with a lecture, and I hope that doing so never becomes fashionable; but it *is* part of the available stock of playwriting strategies.

There are many ways of turning a story—whether totally fictional or taken from headlines like *Execution of Justice*—into a plot, then into a play. Whether character, structure, theatricality, or mood predominates depends very much on choices you make and the sort of effect you are trying to achieve: Even the most rigid dramatic structure is really quite malleable.

Consider, for example, what Ibsen did with the "well-made" play of his time, and what Shakespeare did with the Elizabethan dramatic forms he inherited. Look at the idiosyncratic contemporary comedies of the late Charles Ludlam, plays such as *Camille (A Tearjerker), Der Ring Gott Farblonjet, The Bourgeois Avant-Garde, The Mystery of Irma Vep*—unique, yet clearly inspired by such older dramatic forms as Restoration comedy and Victorian melodrama. Bertolt Brecht was famous for updating older dramatic structures into contemporary forms. His *Mother Courage* and *The Caucasian Chalk Circle,* for example, revised an open, Shakespearean, "epic" way of writing plays. Don't be afraid to mine the past for intriguing ways to turn your stories into play plots. Don't be afraid to invent new ways to do so, either.

□ 83

THE DEVIL'S IN THE REWRITE

BY JULIE JENSEN

REWRITING IS LIKE MILK OR EXERCISE—EITHER YOU LIKE IT OR YOU don't. Also like milk and exercise, it's necessary. So it's best if we all learn to like it. Better yet, if we all learn to love it.

Because theater is a collaborative art form, writing for the stage is full of rewriting: Directors, actors, designers all play a part. They all have opinions, and they all affect the play, either overtly or covertly. Some of them will actually tell you how to rewrite; others will just make choices that make the text changes necessary.

It's wise to be open-minded about rewrites. The best playwrights listen, cull the suggestions, and make the changes they find genuinely helpful. Unwise playwrights take all suggestions and try to incorporate them. Foolish playwrights listen to no one and make no changes at all.

Here are a few suggestions, things to keep in mind during the rewriting process.

The first concerns **plot**. Ask yourself this question: What's the difference between the character at the beginning of the play and at the end? In other words, did something happen? Think back on your favorite plays. Compare the leading character at the beginning with the one at the end. Look at Romeo and Juliet when we first meet them. By the end, of course, they are dead. But they have done more than just die. They've been through a lot. And that's good. One sign of a good plot.

The second test concerns **structure**. Are the events in an arc? Arc implies an arch. But arc is also more elastic than that. Arc is a bubble in the wind, stretching. It's a good shape for a play.

Next, make sure you've written **beats**. Beats are the small units of a play. Beats in a play correspond to paragraphs in prose. They should have beginnings, middles, and ends. It's easiest to define a beat as the time between a character's starting to pursue a goal and the point at which he achieves it, changes it, or stops. That section or segment is a beat.

Can a beat be short? Of course. Sometimes a piece of stage business is a whole beat. The character reads the note, thinks a second, wads it up, and tosses it into the fire. That's a beat. A beat might also be a page or two long. A woman wants her husband to wrap a present for their child. Her pursuit of that goal is a beat. Her reasons compose the element of the beat. She's running late, she's got to change her clothes, and the child will be home at any moment. When she grabs the box, tosses it on the couch, and decides to wrap it herself, that's the end of the beat.

The reason you write in beats is simple: You want your play to be made up of sections rather than isolated lines. It's also easy for actors to play beats. They understand them instinctively and will endeavor to supply them if you don't. The structure of the action is also easier to apprehend if it's divided into beats. Could you have a good piece of prose in which there were no paragraphs? Well, perhaps, but I doubt it. We think in sections. We feel in sections. Sections help us divide up an experience.

Now then, a radical suggestion: Don't think about *expanding* your play. Think about *cutting* it. If expansion is really a goal, think about adding events, not expanding dialogue. In general, playwrights worry entirely too much about their work being too short. Most people in the audience worry about a play being too long. Try packing a lot of events into a small section of time rather than scattering a few events over a long period of time.

Recently, I was standing in a theater lobby, waiting to see a new play. Someone came out with news that the play was only 95 minutes long, with one intermission. We were buoyant. And yet, I'll bet anything that the playwright had tormented herself about whether the play was long enough.

I had a similar experience at the opening of a college production of a musical. "It's three hours and twenty minutes long," someone said. We were all disappointed. I myself was inconsolable. One couple frowned and left.

Theater experiences need to be intense and, in general, shorter than they were in the past. Audiences just won't put up with a lot of talk. They certainly can't put up with the boredom. And overlong plays threaten both.

My best advice is to rewrite the play to please the audience and yourself. Examine your own responses to experiences in the theater. Then go ahead and be ruthless. Cut any scene not necessary to the story, even if it contains some of your favorite bits, lines, or ideas. *Especially* if it contains your favorite bits, lines, or ideas, cut it. If it doesn't further the story, it sticks out as "writerly," calls attention to itself, to the writing. And that is a no-no, the writer equivalent to a show-off child. Embarrassing rather than impressive.

Cut also any repeated beats. That means any beats in which the character repeats the same tactics in pursuit of a goal. Say, for example, that a character wants his sister to leave the room. His first tactic is to lure her out, his second is to threaten her, his third is to insult her. If he threatens her twice, it is less effective than if he threatens her only once.

Now we are at the micro-editing stage. Pare down the individual lines. Make sure they're economical. What if a character says something like, "Oh, hell, Bill, how many times do I have to tell you? You just don't understand anything." All right. But check to see if the line would be better if it read, "Hell, Bill, you just don't understand anything." Then take a look at that version. Maybe it would be better yet if it read, "You understand nothing." Make sure you've tested every line every possible way. Almost always, the most economical version is the best.

A writer with a particularly good ear will often imitate speech, and that can be wonderful. But it can also lead to extra beats in a line, especially at the beginning. For example, a character will say something like, "Well, yes, I know, but I also like horses." Far better if the character says, "I also like horses." It's cleaner, sharper, in some way more surprising. But most of all, it moves the scene along. It steps forward rather than marching in place, and then stepping forward.

You can also sharpen the individual lines by letting a character go on the offensive. What if the line reads, "I don't know. I don't think you understand." We know already that the lead-in sentence is unnecessary. But the second sentence is inert. What if, instead, it reads, "You. What do you understand?" You've said the same thing, you've shortened the speech, and you've also issued a challenge. The line is sharper, cleaner, better. And probably the scene is, too.

On the other hand, the character might surprise you, and say, "It smells like Campbell's Vegetable Soup in here." Good for him. Surprises are wonderful. Most plays have too few of them.

That leads me to another suggestion. Note the images you're using. (Images are figures of speech that appeal to one of the five senses.) Quite consciously, make sure that your images are interesting, subtle, fun. And while you're at it, check to see if they appeal to at least four of the five senses. Of the senses—sight, touch, smell, taste, and hearing—we tend to overdo images of sight and neglect all the others.

This next suggestion is quite radical: If you're having trouble with a section you've rewritten several times, try using iambics (a two-syllable foot, the first unaccented, the second accented). They are very easy rhythm structures, quite natural to English. They make the language rock, give it a sense of momentum. (By the way, you need not worry about the pentameter part or any other number of feet to the line. The important thing is the iambic.)

Practice some lines. Don't worry about meaning. Pay attention only to the rhythm: Ta-DUM, ta-DUM, ta-DUM. Here's an example: "In fact, the words are in my mind. But God himself could hardly give them voice." Good old iambic. Write more lines, just for practice. "You can't believe I'm dead tonight. I've gone and said too much." Language is pure sound and rhythm. Just practice the rocking motion.

Now take a look at some of your awkward lines. See if letting them rock back and forth will help you move the scene along.

One final suggestion (I like to apply this one after I've been playing with the details, the mechanics, because it is a marked contrast): Test your play for truth. Is what you're saying true? Is what this character says and does true? You can learn to finesse anything, but make sure you don't lose your soul in the process. All the technical expertise in the world can't compensate for a play that lies.

❏ 84

WHEN THE WELL RUNS DRY

BY KENT R. BROWN

YOU'VE FINISHED THAT SCATHING DIATRIBE AGAINST SOMETHING OR other, and that hysterical comedy about the time you and three longtime women friends from Cape May, New Jersey, were stranded in a country 'n western bar in Amarillo, Texas. Now what? Your audience is hungry for something new, original, daring, funny but not silly, silly but not stupid, serious but not a complete downer, and your blank computer screen is daring you to knock its socks off. And nothing's coming. You've run dry!

It's a fact. As storytellers, you sometimes get stuck, run out of steam. Or perhaps you find yourself writing the same play over and over again, using similar themes, situations, and characters. You need to expand your skills by varying your plots and characterizations. Where then do you go for artistic stimulation? The answer? Everywhere. History, myth, biographies, diaries, letters, newspapers, obituaries, and the yellow pages—all are possible sources of inspiration.

Reading history, whether ancient or current, places us at the center of the social, political, scientific, and military revolutions that left their mark on human development. We can explore the public and private lives of Jefferson, Lincoln, Madame Curie, or Louis XIV. We can research the Ming Dynasty, Alexander's conquest of the western world, the Great Depression, the role of women in science or the influence of immigration on the social fabric of America. The possibilities are endless. We can continue our fascination with whatever our favorite themes might be, but we must draw our characters, accurately or with artistic embellishments, from the fabric of history.

History is full of fascinating people, but perhaps you don't have the time or, truthfully, the interest to wade through scholarly analyses. You're willing to be enriched and all that, but you really want to write the five- to six-character play with no more than one or two settings. If

414

so, start reading the newspaper. You do read the newspaper, you say, but nothing leaps out at you. Why would it? *You* have to improvise, speculate.

Over several mornings, with *The New York Times* and two local newspapers before me, I decided to see what plots and characters might be hiding within the articles I read. I tried to keep an eye out for conflict, that situation in which two energies go up against one another. Without conflict, without making choices, there is little drama. Here goes.

• **Article:** The opening of a new art gallery. The drama: A photographer/artist who "sees" life as a set of flat planes and surfaces has difficulty communicating his/her own heart. Maybe a parent is dying and the artist tries to convey emotion through drawings or photographs. But the parent is blind. The play takes place in the gallery, perhaps, or in the summer cottage where the artist, estranged over the years, has come to say goodbye. What might happen? The possibilities are endless.

• **Article:** A biographer has elected to focus on embarrassing/sexual behavior engaged in by the subject of the biography. The drama: The biographer is approached by the subject's last surviving family member and is asked to expunge this unflattering period/episode/event in the subject's background. But the biographer needs the publication to break into an august circle of celebrity biographers. The issues are fascinating. Does any singular action actually reflect the essence of an individual? Are reputations built upon truths or fiction? Is honesty really the best policy?

• **Article:** The need to establish an investment strategy at an early age to insure that a child's college tuition will be fully funded. The drama: A single father/mother, having made disastrous financial decisions, resolves to take money from a teen-age child's education fund to cover loans or bad debts. Where is the play set? In the living room, fine, but how about a playground? On a teeter-totter? It might be dynamic to see an adult and fully-grown child coming to terms with the parent's flaws, surrounded by toys of symbolic innocence and hope. Maybe this is really a play for young people focusing on two children who set out to help their father/mother who is ill at home and has lost his/her job. How might they help out? What difficulties might they encounter?

- **Article:** Legal vs. emotional claim to items in an estate. The drama: A niece or long-distant relative appears after a funeral claiming title to an object that has been willed to her sister with whom she has had a stormy relationship. What rights do the sisters really have? What evidence will they each produce? What do they know about the family, the deceased, each other? What are the *real* stakes here?

- **Article:** A longtime social club has been meeting in an old house that is up for sale. The members face displacement. The drama: One of the club members is the buyer but does not want the others to continue meeting there. Why? I don't know yet, but if I started to explore the energy inherent in the situation, something would emerge.

- **Article:** A mother and two sick children are stranded by the side of the road in bad weather. The drama: A grown daughter, her ailing mother, and her two teen-age children are stranded at a roadside picnic rest stop. Two men approach and offer their assistance, which requires one of the stranded family members to go with one of the men while the second man stays with the family. I'm intrigued.

- **Article:** A retrospective piece looking at the Mars Rover and efforts of the engineers and scientists. The drama: What must it be like to devote one's life effort to a machine? Is it to benefit the human race, or is it motivated by a desire for celebrity? What about the scientists' families and the time the scientists spent away from loved ones? Perhaps a scientist tries to excite his children to share his enthusiasm for the work, but the children rebel because of his absence. Maybe this play is set in the backyard in a tent or a lean-to the father helped build. And the children refuse to come inside the house.

For a little comedy, try the absurd:

- **Article:** Older children in greater numbers seek money and financial assistance from their parents. The comedy: A scruffy, slightly degenerate father seeks financial aid from his grown child. But the grown child is such a poor manager of money that the father moves in with him or her and tries to manage not only the child's financial life but the child's love life as well.

• **Article:** A feature on an unfamous writer of famous jingles. The comedy: A quiet, unassuming writer of greeting cards and jingles is approached by a mobster/unsavory character to write a tribute for the mob/gang's boss on the eve of . . . something or other. I haven't figured it out quite yet, but maybe the writer falls in love with the gangster's daughter or wife or mistress!

At the core of these speculations must always be the search for an energy opposite to that generated by the protagonist. And don't require all the questions you may have about the material to be fully known before you begin to write. Many writers launch into their work letting the impulse and energy guide their inquiry. Often, too, the ending is not what they originally thought it was going to be. That's not necessarily bad. The exploration most likely will unearth future plot or character possibilities.

I used several issues of USA Today in writing my play, *The Phoenix Dimension*. The inciting event was actually supplied by a friend who answered his phone one morning and heard a woman's voice plead, "Help me." My friend didn't recognize the voice, thought it was a prank, and hung up. But he couldn't get back to sleep. What if the plea was genuine, what if he had stayed on the phone longer? Concurrently, I had become increasingly fed up with America's obsession with violence. Indulgent and confessional talk shows, depressing nightly news, and hundreds of articles about how we damage ourselves in so many ways in this country—all this had been fueling my frustration. *The Phoenix Dimension* fused together these two separate but thematically related states.

A ringing telephone is heard in the dark. A man in his 50s answers it. A woman's voice is heard. He hangs up. She calls back. He is hooked. She has a seductive voice and seems to know a great deal about his life, even warning him that his job is in jeopardy. A man of simple means, his full identity has been invested in his work. He becomes wary. She calls him at his office, but he never gave out his work number. His world begins to come apart. Younger employees want his job, and the boss seems eager to see the man leave the company. By the end of the play, and without ever having met her directly, the woman has persuaded him to kill his boss, who happens to be the woman's husband.

To create the impression of being off-center and no longer in control of a stable environment, I wrote a series of sound bites influenced by jingles, discount and grocery store announcements, radio and television talk shows, and predominantly, from those thumbnail news items *USA Today* lists under the heading of each state. These were interspersed throughout the play, between scenes, as my central character dressed, went to work, stared out the window, sat in a bar, and so on. Also, I never allowed him to leave the stage, thus intensifying his sense of being assaulted by the frantic and often absurd dimensions of life. For several months, I read these news snippets to learn about murders, bizarre marital difficulties, gang killings, killer bee attacks, and a host of other actual events. Each was tailored to underscore specific moments in the play, or to serve as ironic counterpoints to the action. I don't believe I could have made up all the items I used. In this instance, truth was stranger than fiction but served my fictional needs perfectly.

Besides history, biography, personal observations, and journalism, what's left? Obituaries. Here's what you'll find:

• A rural farmer who fought in W.W. II, fathered seven children, lost his farm in a major Midwest flood, played Santa Claus at annual Rotary Christmas festivities, sang with a barbershop quartet, survived three wives, and lived to be ninety-seven years of age. And that's just what was printed in the obituary! What influence might his W.W. II experiences have had on his attitude toward life? What made him want to play Santa Claus?

• A single mother in the south, with three adopted children of mixed heritage, who earned her living as a professional mourner, a tutor in Italian, a nurse, and a choir singer who often sang at ten church services per week. She served on the state's Welfare Commission and generated funding initiatives for the Special Olympics. What conflicts did she have with her children, her employers? How did she spend whatever quiet time came her way, or was she driven to prove something to herself or to someone else?

• A Ph.D. university scholar of hard sciences who was a sports photographer and National Science Foundation Fellowship recipient, a Formula 1 race car driver, and loved ballet and classical music. Was this a man who valued control and precision but enjoyed dealing with risky variables as he raced around the track?

Finally, if you are really pressed for time, and are fed up with the alcoholic fathers, insensitive psychiatrists, and arrogant teachers that always seem to turn up in your cast lists, try this: Open a telephone book and turn to the yellow pages. You'll be amazed at the countless occupations, associations, and businesses that keep this country moving but seldom walk the stage: air conditioning contractors, termite controllers, animal welfare directors, antique dealers, architects, auto supply owners/workers/secretaries, bank examiners, birth center directors, private bodyguards, billiard parlor owners, bookbinders, burial vault salespersons, caterers, chiropractors, ministers, crane operators, kitchen designers, elevator inspectors—I'll stop here.

Imagine the options! You can mix and match your characters as you do your wardrobe. How about a crane operator father who is an opera buff? Why not? Or a chiropractor who studied film in college and knows the dialogue to all the films by John Ford and plays out a different scene each time he's working on a client. Or maybe there's a play about a burial vault salesperson who meets an antique dealer/mortician/ bookbinder who wants to be buried in a specially designed vault that plays Dixie whenever the doors are opened. Well, this last idea may or may not fly, but give it a try. The point here is that what we do and how we elect to spend our time and our energy tells volumes about our values—and our characters' values, as well.

To develop a rich appreciation for how fascinating people's lives can be, read the oral histories compiled by Studs Terkel: *The Good War, Hard Times, Working,* and *American Dreams.* The personal tales of fear, joy, aspiration, and regret are riveting, superior tributes to human tenacity. Also, for a personal perspective on history, take a look at *Eyewitness to History,* edited by John Carey, for examples of life as it was lived from the siege of Jerusalem in 70 A.D. to the fall of Ferdinand Marcos in 1986.

To see how history and nonfiction can inform the theatrical imagination, take a good look at Robert Bolt's *A Man for All Seasons;* Robert Schenkkan's *The Kentucky Cycle;* James Goldman's *The Lion in Winter; Clarence Darrow,* by David Rintels; *Becket,* by Jean Anouilh; the musical *Quilters,* by Molly Newman (book) and Barbara Damashek (book, music and lyrics); and *Across the Plains,* by Sandra Fenichel Asher.

Root your work in reality, but remember, fact alone is not drama. You have to push it, shape it, tease it into a dramatic work that can be more truthful to the spirit of human condition than the facts that created it.

❑ 85

FINDING A THEME
FOR YOUR PLAY

BY PETER SAGAL

USUALLY WHEN PEOPLE ASK ME WHAT MY PLAYS ARE ABOUT, I HEM
and haw and squint off into the sky and then come up with something
like, "Well, there's this guy, and he has this dog. . . . and then this army
invades. . . . well, it's really kind of a love story, in the end." I feel
silly, and my questioner hasn't learned anything, which may be right,
because if he wants to know what the play is about, he should see
the thing. I mean, we write immortal works of dramatic literature, not
slogans.

But I recently wrote a play that could be summarized in a single
sentence.* This was a first for me, and because of this, and because the
sentence in question invoked some political and moral questions, I became instantly known as a Dramatist of Serious Theme. This makes me
bristle, because like every other normal writer, I resent any praise that
is not universal. What are my comedies, chopped liver?

Nonetheless, I'm now known as a guy with something to say, and
I've been asked here to give some tips on how to say it, that is, how to
approach the problem of Theme in playwriting. (That raises the ancil-
lary question of how you write a play when you have *nothing* to say,
which is a problem I face daily.) Somebody—I think it was Woody
Allen quoting Samuel Goldwyn—said that people go to the theater for
entertainment; if you want to send a message, call Western Union. But
the theater has changed a lot and seems to be surviving only because of
its toehold in Meaning; i.e., movies and TV may give you cleavage and
explosions, etc., but if you want to learn something, come to the theater.
Somebody else said—and this time I know, it was the actor Simon

---

*"A Jewish lawyer defends the First Amendment rights of a man who says the Holo-
caust did not happen." (*Denial*, Long Wharf Theater, Dec. 1995)

Callow—that in this day and age, going to the theater for "entertainment" is like going to a restaurant for indigestion.

So how to approach the theme play, the political or "problem" play? First of all, it seems to me that the playwright should always begin not from a statement, but a question. It is boring to be told an opinion, but it is interesting to be asked for your own. Thus, a writer who sets off to tell us, "Racism is bad!," for example, will probably ultimately irritate the audience, because they know that racism is bad and they're sorry, but frankly they don't feel that they had to pay $20 or whatever to be told again. But a writer who asks the audience, "Why is racism bad?" or even "Is racism ever justified?" will hold the playgoers' attention, because they may never have thought about it before, and their answers may surprise or please or horrify the playwright.

Once you have framed your question in an interesting and provocative way, how do you dramatize it? Here we fall into the great Unknown, because the answer depends on your particular vision of drama and the theater, and my answer may not suit you and your purposes. For example, if you're Brecht, you'll pose your question by writing it on a banner and hanging it upstage center. What I do is try to make the Thematic Problem into a personal one.

Sometimes it's obvious how to do this, sometimes it's not. If you're writing about True Love, then clearly your play will need some lovers. If it's about racism, then a racist or two will be in order. More complicated questions require more complicated solutions, but part of your job as a dramatist (some would say your *whole* job) is to find that telling situation, that moment of crisis and decision plucked from the entire span of an infinite number of imaginary lifetimes, that perfectly distills the essence of the question you're addressing. For example, let's say you want to write about the tension between duty to self and duty to country. You want to write about a solider. But which solider, in which war? An Englishman fighting in World War I? A Jew fighting in World War II? An Asian American fighting in Vietnam? Any situation will give different emphases to different sides of your question. How do you choose?

In considering this choice, remember that the worst sin the dramatist can commit is to lie to an audience. In this context, it means putting a question out there and then making the answer easy or simple when it's not. There's a great temptation when asking an important question—

"Will True Love Always Triumph?"—to go immediately for the best and most comforting answer—"Yes!"—and ignore all the evidence to the contrary that's in the world, in your heart, in your own play. Consider *King Lear.* Its answer to that particular question would be a resounding *No,* so during the 17th century, the play was rewritten by Nahum Tate to answer *Yes:* Cordelia, quite alive at the end, united with Edmund and her loving father. That rewritten version was rejected by history for, among other things, being a lie.

So if you are going to ask a tough question, and you should, you must be merciless in your search for the answer. Let the situation of the play be rife with ambiguity and doubt. Let your characters be contradictory, holding both bad and good within them. Let the most horrible opinions be held by the most pleasant and attractive people. Let good people do terrible things to one another; let them react to kindness with anger and to attacks with fear. Because that's what happens in the real world, and if by chance you do want to say, ultimately, something good—that Love will triumph, that freedom is precious and worth fighting for—it won't help your case to set your play in a fantasy world where these things come easier than they actually are.

What I've often done is to take a character I admire and like, and then either put that character in a very difficult position, or cause him or her to do something rather unpleasant and then have to deal with the results. In my play *Denial* I took a character who was very confident in her support of free speech and confronted her with another character— very charming, by the way—who made her want to scream and strike out every time he opened his mouth. In *Angels in America,* by Tony Kushner, a lead character, who is charming and sympathetic and funny, abandons his lover in time of crisis, so we are left to ask ourselves—we, who think of ourselves as charming and sympathetic and funny—if when the time came, we might do the same thing.

The second worst sin in the theater, after lying, is to be boring. In fact, it's often in the pursuit of not being boring that we end up telling our worst lies. There's a strong temptation—driven by the market and our own inclination to be cheerful—to preach to the choir. The theater of today desperately wants to say something Useful and Good about the world; it wants to condemn what needs condemning and praise what needs praising, according to the mores of the day. But the problem is that unless you do that from a deeply informed, dramatically charged, almost universally comprehending place, you're going to bore the heck out of your audience.

How do you achieve that kind of aesthetic Buddha-nature, where you comprehend everything, where all forces balance, where the true strengths and faultlines of the universe reveal themselves?

Work hard, write every day, and tell the truth. It may not work, but nothing else will.

❏ Juvenile and Young Adult

❏ 86

Writing Children's Books for Today's Readers

By James Cross Giblin

Many writers for children have been upset by the changes that have occurred in book publishing in recent years. Long-established imprints like Macmillan, Scribners, Lodestar, and Bradbury have vanished from the scene. A number of publishers have stopped reading unsolicited manuscripts—those that do not come from literary agents. And publishers are less patient with slower-selling titles; if a book doesn't take off strongly, chances are it will be declared out-of-print after a year or so.

Then there's the Internet. Already it has had a tremendous impact on the way people, young and old, acquire the information they want and need. It's also changed the way many people buy books. Some go so far as to predict that the Internet, and related technologies such as the electronic book, will eventually render the conventional book obsolete.

Will that happen? No one can say with any certainty, although I personally doubt it. In the meantime, I'm happy to report on some positive developments in the children's book field that help not only to counterbalance the negatives, but also expand the opportunities for writers.

One development is the launching of new publishing programs. Front Street Books has joined forces with *Cricket Magazine* to publish a new line of fiction for the 8–12 age group. North-South Books of Switzerland has enlarged its American operations and started a new imprint, David Reuther Books, headed by the former editor-in-chief of William Morrow.

Children's publishing is also becoming more decentralized, with houses like Chronicle Books in San Francisco, Carolrhoda Books in Minneapolis, and Peachtree Publishers in Atlanta, proving that a publisher doesn't have to be located in the Northeast to be a success.

But even with these increased publishing opportunities, many beginning writers have a hard time finding homes for their first books, and many experienced writers who have lost their editors and publishers through acquisitions or mergers have an equally hard time finding replacements. Here are a few observations on the current publishing scene that I hope will be helpful to both groups of writers.

Picture Books

Publishing houses still open to unsolicited submissions receive more picture book manuscripts than any other kind. Of the 5,000 or so submissions that we screened each year at Clarion when I was editor-in-chief, at least 4,000 were picture books. And we were then publishing no more than twelve picture books a year. So, the competition in the picture book field is extremely fierce.

Several types of picture book stories are in demand, however. These include:

- Stories with an "edge," like Jon Sczieska's skillful parodies of the classic nursery tales, William Steig's playful *Pete's a Pizza*, and Jack Gantos's stories about that naughty feline, Rotten Ralph. The hope is that such tales will be popular with both children and with the adults who have to read them aloud over and over again.
- Stories that lend themselves to bold illustration in oversize formats that will catch the eye of adult book buyers in bookstores. Examples are two stories by Margie Palatini, *Piggie Pie* and *Zak's Lunch*.
- Brief, simple stories that can be turned into board books directed toward the youngest listeners and viewers.
- Stories that can be illustrated with warm, cuddly pictures that will appeal to grandmothers and great aunts. Examples include books like Marion Dane Bauer's *If You Were Born a Kitten*, Lindsey Tate's *Teatime with Emma Buttersnap*, and Bijou Le Tord's *God's Little Seeds: A Book of Parables*.

Sometimes it may seem that where picture books are concerned, children are the last concern of marketers. That's because it's adults, not small children, who select and buy the vast majority of picture books.

However, it's the books that young children take to their hearts that enjoy the longest lives on publishers' backlists. Other picture books, with larger formats and flashier illustrations, may make a stronger initial impact in bookstores. But their sales often fall off sharply after the first selling season.

Meanwhile, it's the steady reorders from school and public libraries that keep most picture books alive. And what generates those reorders? Usually it's reader demand, based on the qualities children have always loved in picture books—appealing characters, fast-paced action, and generous doses of humor. So the trick for the picture book writer today is to come up with a story that lends itself to showy illustration, but also has the qualities that will enable it to endure. That's no easy challenge.

Fiction

The situation in hardcover fiction publishing is quite different from the one prevailing in picture books. For one thing, most hardcover novels are still sold in the so-called institutional market of public and school libraries. That explains why the Newbery Medal, awarded annually by the children's section of the American Library Association, remains the single most effective promotional instrument in generating hardcover fiction sales.

Paperback fiction is another matter. Young readers, not adult librarians, purchase the bulk of paperback fiction titles either through book clubs like Scholastic's or in bookstores. Librarians may decry series like the "Goosebumps" and "Fear Street," but young readers make them into bestsellers. Fortunately, many readers are open to individual titles, too—especially those written by authors they know and like, such as Lois Lowry, Gary Paulsen, Katherine Paterson, and so on.

What sorts of novels are editors looking for today? It may be easier to say what they're *not* looking for:

(a) Routine family and school stories with nothing fresh or striking in terms of characterization or plot.

(b) Mild mysteries in which there's little of importance at stake.

(c) Stories told in the first person in a casual, slangy style. Such stories may possess a certain immediacy, but too many have a flat, dull tone, lacking in flavor and vivid description.

(d) Lightweight teen romances that seem to be taking place in the 1950s, although they are usually set in the present.

(e) Stories that are too determined to teach a moral lesson, whether it be about drugs, or drinking, or teenage sex. These topics are all deserving of treatment in novels for young people, but they have to emerge from fully grounded characters in convincing and realistic situations. Young readers quickly dismiss stories that seem to be written from the outside, in the hectoring tone of a critical adult.

Editors *are* looking for stories for all age groups that have something new to say, and that are written in a distinctive voice. "Voice" is a quality that's hard to define, but for me, it is often linked with a feeling of authenticity. For example, you can tell immediately from the choice of details whether a writer knows the setting he's writing about. Details of clothing and gesture, along with the rhythm and choice of words in the dialogue, also tell you whether the writer knows his characters.

A distinctive voice is an essential element in all types of fiction, from a gritty realistic story set in the inner city to a historical novel about a boy or girl living in Renaissance Italy. It's also what makes a story for any age group stand out, from the ten-page manuscript for an easy reader to a 200-page novel for young adults.

Speaking of young adult fiction, it may be about to experience a resurgence. After years in which many commentators said the genre was all but dead, the American Library Association recently established a new award, on a par with the Newbery, that will be presented each year to the book an ALA committee finds to be the best in the YA category.

This comes at a time when many people aren't sure exactly where the young adult field begins and ends. Twenty years ago, there was common agreement that young adults were teens of fourteen and up, and Judy Blume was regarded as the quintessential young adult novelist. Today Judy Blume is read by nine- and ten-year-olds, and many think the young adult category starts at age eleven or twelve.

I find it helpful to think of young adult books as books directed toward young people who are going through the painful transition from childhood to adulthood. This period starts earlier for some, later for others. Consequently, I believe everyone concerned with books for young adults—and that includes parents, teachers, librarians, reviewers, and editors as well as writers—should be flexible when it comes to deciding whether a story idea or published book is suitable for a young adult audience. Young adult books that may be too harsh for one youngster to absorb may be just what another person of the same age wants and needs.

Nonfiction

Children's nonfiction offers some of the most promising opportunities for writers. For one thing, there's less competition in it. Most publishers receive relatively few nonfiction submissions. This is probably because many writers think nonfiction isn't as much fun to do as a picture book story or a novel.

They forget that some of the best picture books are nonfiction. For example, *Snowflake Bentley*, which won the coveted Caldecott Medal for illustration in 1999, is a picture book about the scientist who discovered that no two snowflakes are alike. Written by Jacqueline Briggs Martin and illustrated with woodcuts by Mary Azarian, *Snowflake Bentley* exemplifies a new trend in both picture books and nonfiction. It works equally well with younger and older children, as do a growing number of nonfiction picture books. These books range from biographies to science books to studies of animal life such as Laurence Pringle's prize-winning book about the Monarch butterfly.

I've had some happy experiences myself with nonfiction picture books. When I wrote the picture book biographies of George Washington and Thomas Jefferson, my editor at Scholastic and I thought the chief audience for them would be second- and third-graders. We were pleasantly surprised to discover that young people of eleven, twelve, and even thirteen were enjoying the books, too.

Obviously, the long-held truism that older children consider picture books babyish is no longer accurate. I imagine this is because youngsters today are used to getting so much of their information visually from television and the Internet.

The nonfiction books that I've discussed so far were all published as individual titles. But there's another segment of nonfiction publishing that is more receptive to writers, especially beginners. This is the segment that issues nonfiction books in series.

A number of publishers specialize in nonfiction series. Among the best known are Lerner Publications, Children's Press, Franklin Watts, and Enslow Publishers. Among them, they offer books for a wide range of readers from preschool to young adult. Most of their books are aimed at the school and library market; some are not even available in bookstores. Teachers use series nonfiction books to supplement textbooks, and librarians recommend them to children who have to write book reports for a science or social studies class.

Almost every conceivable topic is explored in one or more of the series. Some deal with the different states, some cover foreign countries and cultures. Others are made up entirely of biographies, and there are also series devoted exclusively to scientific subjects, as well as such social problems as bigotry and sexual harassment. Responding to their primary market in schools, series nonfiction books relate closely to the curriculum.

Editors of series nonfiction are always on the lookout for new writers who can do solid research and present their findings in a clear, lively way that communicates to a young audience. Generally, the editors want to see queries and writing samples rather than complete manuscripts, since most series books are written on assignment. If the editors like your writing style, they may ask you to do an outline and sample chapter for a future title in one of their series. And you can take it from there.

The Future of Children's Books

Recently I read a news feature in *The New York Times* on the state of children's book publishing that offered some solid reasons to be hopeful about the future of the field.

The article explored a publishing phenomenon—the fantastic popularity of the Harry Potter novels, written by a hitherto unknown British author, J.K. Rowling. The hardcover edition of the first title in the series, *Harry Potter and the Sorcerer's Stone*, published in the United States by Scholastic, has been a *New York Times* bestseller for nearly two years (and a paperback bestseller for a year); it has been joined by *Harry Potter and the Chamber of Secrets* and *Harry Potter and the Prisoner of Azkaban*, racking up sales in the millions.

What accounts for the amazing success of these books about the adventures of an orphan boy, Harry Potter, who attends an unusual boarding school, the Hogwarts School for Witchcraft and Wizardry? Was it the enthusiasm of the book's editor? Or was it the marketing campaign devised by Scholastic?

While helpful in launching the "Harry" books, something besides marketing was responsible for lofting them into the outer reaches of publishing success. That something was word of mouth. What first made children, and then adults, want to spread the word about "Harry"?

The answer to that question should give us all hope, for it was nothing more nor less than the books themselves. Not a movie tie-in, not a Harry doll or sweatshirt or wizard's wand—at least not yet. No, it was just a compelling story, published in the format of a plain, old-fashioned book.

Most of us will never come close to writing anything as popular as these books. But their triumph can serve as an inspiration to us. For it says that in an age when technology is king and the future of publishing often seems uncertain, words printed on pages bound together with glue and thread still have the power to thrill and delight readers.

❑ 87

Is It Good Enough for Children?

By Madeleine L'Engle

SEVERAL YEARS AGO, WHEN I WAS TEACHING A COURSE ON TECH-niques of fiction, a young woman came up to me and said, "I do hope you're going to teach us something about writing for children, because that's why I'm taking this course."

"What have I been teaching you?" I asked her.

"Well—writing."

"Don't you write when you write for children?"

"Yes, but—isn't it different?"

No, I assured her, it isn't different. The techniques of fiction are the techniques of fiction, and they hold as true for Beatrix Potter as they do for Dostoevsky.

But the idea that writing for children isn't the same as writing for adults is prevalent indeed, and usually goes along with the conviction that it isn't quite as good. If you're a good enough writer for adults, the implication is, of course, you don't write for children. You write for children only when you can't make it in the real world, because writing for children is easier.

Wrong, wrong, wrong!

I had written several regular trade novels before a publisher asked me to write about Swiss boarding school experiences. Nobody had told me that you write differently when you write for children, so I didn't. I just wrote the best book I possibly could; it was called *And Both Were Young*. After that, I wrote *Camilla*, which was reissued as a Young Adult novel, and then *Meet the Austins*. It's hard today for me to understand that this simple little book had a very hard time finding a publisher, because it's about a death, and how an ordinary family reacts to that death. Death at that time was taboo. Children weren't supposed to know about it. I had a couple of offers of publication if I'd take the death out. But the reaction of the family—children as well as the parents—to the death was the core of the book.

Nowadays what we offer children makes *Meet the Austins* seem pale, and on the whole, I think that's just as well, because children know a lot more than most grown-ups give them credit for. *Meet the Austins* came out of my own family's experience with several deaths. To have tried to hide those deaths from our children would have been blind stupidity. All hiding does is to confuse children and add to their fears. It is not subject matter that should be taboo, but the way it is handled.

A number of years ago—the first year I was actually making reasonable money from my writing—my sister-in-law was visiting us, and when my husband told her how much I had earned that year, she was impressed and commented, "And to think most people would have had to work so hard for that!"

Well, it is work, it's most certainly work; wonderful work, but work. Revision, revision, revision. Long hours spent not only in the actual writing, but in research. I think the best thing I learned in college was how to do research, so that I could go right on studying after I graduated.

Of course, it is not *only* work; it is work that makes the incomprehensible comprehensible. Leonard Bernstein said that for him music was cosmos in chaos. That is true for writing a story, too. Aristotle wrote that what is plausible and impossible is better than what is possible and implausible.

That means that story must be true, not necessarily *factual*, but true. This is not easy for a lot of people to understand. When I was a child, one of my teachers accused me of telling a story. She was not complimenting me on my fertile imagination; she was accusing me of telling a lie.

Facts are fine; we need facts. But story takes us to a world that is beyond facts, out on the other side of facts. And there is considerable fear of this world.

The writer Keith Miller told me of a young woman who was determined that her three preschool children were going to grow up in the real world. She was not, she vowed, going to sully their minds with myth, fantasy, fairy tales. They were going to know the truth—and for truth, read fact—and the truth would make them free.

One Saturday, after a week of rain and sniffles, the sun came out, so she piled the children into her little red VW bug and took them to the Animal Farm. The parking lot was crowded, but a VW bug is small, and she managed to find a place for it. She and the children had a wonderful day, petting the animals, going on rides, enjoying the sunshine. Suddenly, she looked at her watch and found it was far later than she realized. She and the children ran to where the VW bug was parked, and to their horror, found the whole front end was bashed in.

Outraged, she took herself off to the ranger's office. As he saw her approach, he laughed and said, "I'll bet you're the lady with the red VW bug."

"It isn't funny," she snapped.

"Now, calm down, lady, and let me tell you what happened. You know the elephant your children had such fun riding? She's a circus-trained elephant, and she was trained to sit on a red bucket. When she saw your car, she just did what she was trained to do and sat on it. Your engine's in the back, so you can drive it home without any trouble. And don't worry. Our insurance will take care of it. Just go on home, and we'll get back to you on Monday."

Slightly mollified, she and the kids got into the car and took off. But she was later than ever, so when she saw what looked like a very minor accident on the road, she didn't stop, but drove on.

Shortly, the flashing light and the siren came along, and she was pulled over. "Lady, don't you know that in this state it's a crime to leave the scene of an accident?" the trooper asked.

"But I wasn't in an accident," she protested.

"I suppose your car came that way," the trooper said, pointing to the bashed-in front.

"No. An elephant sat on it."

"Lady, would you mind blowing into this little balloon?"

That taught her that facts alone are not enough; that facts, indeed, do not make up the whole truth. After that she read fairy tales to her children and encouraged them in their games of Make Believe and Let's Pretend.

I learned very early that if I wanted to find out the truth, to find out why people did terrible things to each other, or sometimes wonderful things—why there was a war, why children are abused—I was more likely to find the truth in story than in the encyclopedia. Again and again I read *Emily of the New Moon*, by Lucy Maud Montgomery, because Emily's father was dying of diseased lungs, and so was mine.

Emily wanted to be a writer, and so did I. Emily knew that there was more to the world than provable fact, and so did I. I read fairy tales, the myths of all nations, science fiction, the fantasies and family stories of E. Nesbitt. I read Jules Verne and H.G. Wells. And I read my parents' books, particularly those with lots of conversation in them. What was not in my frame of reference went right over my head.

We tend to find what we look for. If we look for dirt, we'll find dirt, whether it's there or not. A very nice letter I received from a reader said that she found *A Ring of Endless Light* very helpful to her in coming to terms with the death of a friend, but that another friend had asked her how it was that I used dirty words. I wrote back saying that I was not going to reread my book looking for dirty words, but that as far as I could remember, the only word in the book that could possibly be construed as dirty was *zuggy*, which I'd made up to avoid using dirty words. And wasn't looking for dirty words an ugly way to read a book?

One of my favorite books is Frances Hodgson Burnett's *The Secret Garden*. I read it one rainy weekend to a group of little girls, and a generation later to my granddaughters up in an old brass bed in the attic. Mary Lennox is a self-centered, spoiled-rotten little heroine, and I think we all recognize at least a little of ourselves in her. The secret garden is as much the garden of Mary's heart as it is the physical walled garden. By the end of the book, warmth and love and concern for others have come to Mary's heart, when Colin, the sick boy, is able to walk and run again. And Dickon, the gardener's boy, looks at the beauty of the restored garden and says, "It's magic!" But "magic" is one of the key words that has become taboo to today's self-appointed censors, so, with complete disregard of content, they would add *The Secret Garden* to the pyre. I shudder. This attitude is extreme. It is also dangerous.

It comes down to the old question of separate standards, separate for adults and children. The only standard to be used in judging a children's book is: *Is it a good book?* Is it good enough for me? Because if a children's book is not good enough for all of us, it is not good enough for children.

❏ 88

THE OUCH FACTOR

BY SID FLEISCHMAN

WHEN I FIRST BEGAN TO WRITE FICTION, I MADE EVERY MISTAKE known to the world of moveable type. I even pioneered mistakes as yet undiscovered. In my haste to keep a story moving, I was apt to leap from action to action, unwilling to pause for reactions. If one of my characters hit his thumb with a hammer, I didn't give him time to say ouch.

I hadn't a clue to the story muscle that reactions provide. They are, of course, dramatic punctuation, focusing and intensifying passing moments. But they may be more. Somewhere along the way, I discovered the power of reaction to reveal character, to jump start a dying scene—and even, as I will explain, to give an unexpected direction to a story-in-progress. I regard reaction as one of a writer's loyal company of friends.

Take this situation: A nine-year-old boy is sent to a foreign city, to be met at the airport by a grumpy uncle. When Uncle Grump fails to turn up, the boy hops a bus and walks in on the relative. Grump dismisses the matter with not even an apology. All this dramatic fodder is told, not shown, at the speed of light in a couple of narrative paragraphs.

What's wrong here? The "ouches" are missing. Discovering no one there to meet him at the airport—a strong dramatic situation—the abandoned boy *must* react. Is he scared? Does he wonder if his uncle is sick? Dead? Didn't the old man receive the letter to say he would be arriving? Maybe Uncle Grump really doesn't want him to visit. What should he do? Reaction would jump start the scene.

And how about that cardboard uncle? The way he responds will peg his character. *Arrogant*: "You're a day early, boy!" *Addled*: "Dear me, dear me, who'd you say you were?" *Guilt-stricken*: "You poor lad, you must be starved! Mollie, set a plate for the boy and bring a dunce cap for me."

I'm not certain what wised me up to the full range and impact of reaction. My education may have started with the famous World War II news picture of the Frenchman on a Paris boulevard trying to hold back his tears as he watches the invading Germans come goose-stepping by.

That face, caught in a moment of profound tragedy, was a reaction shot. One could read a life story into it.

Reaction! How had I managed to treat it so cavalierly?

Motion pictures have been described as the art of *action and reaction.* There is even the well-defined "reaction shot." The next time you watch a movie on TV, turn off the sound and watch the reaction shots flicker by like exclamation points. To punch up the moment, savvy comedians invented a trunkload of reactions: "takes," "double takes," mouth-spraying "spit takes." Who could forget Edgar Kennedy's slow burn?

And then I saw an amazing newspaper item (one that seems to recur about every twenty years) about a convict, about to be let out of prison, *who doesn't want to leave.* There blossomed in my head that marvel of them all—what I have come to call the "contrary reaction."

When a character's response is contrary to the normal and the expected, but somehow made logical—that's pure story oxygen.

Isn't that what makes O. Henry's story, "The Ransom of Red Chief," such a charmer and so memorable? An insufferable nine-year-old kid, you'll recall, is kidnapped and forced to hide out in a cave—to his utter delight! There he plays Indian chief. Finally:

"Red Chief," says I to the kid, "would you like to go home?"

"Aw, what for?" says he. "I don't have any fun at home. I hate to go to school. I like to camp out. You won't take me back home again, Snake-eye, will you?"

In due time, the family demands a "ransom" from the kidnappers to take the tyke *back.* How's that for contrary reaction?

I use these reversals whenever I see a good opportunity. In my Gold Rush novel, *Bandit's Moon* (Greenwillow Books), my eleven-year-old heroine, Annyrose, should flee for her life at the sight of the notoriously bloodthirsty bandit, Joaquín Murieta and his gang. She does the reverse. Standing her ground, she pleads, "Sir . . . take me with you!"

Naturally, I had to set up a situation and a rationale so that the reader would not regard the girl as certifiable. That was easy. I made Joaquín her immediate opportunity to escape from a greater villain, that horror in petticoats, O.O. Mary. At the same time the reverse "take" enabled me to establish Annyrose's feisty, unflappable and resourceful character. It all worked beautifully, and the novel was designated a Notable Book by the American Library Association.

In an earlier novel, *By the Great Horn Spoon!* (Little, Brown), I opened the story with two stowaways, Jack and the family butler, Praiseworthy, on a ship bound for California. They rise from two potato barrels where they have been hiding. Watch the reverse reaction:

> "I suggest that we see what can be done about improving our accommodations," said Praiseworthy, tapping his bowler hat firmly in place. "Shall we go?"
> "Go?" Jack replied. "Go where?" He fully expected to pass the voyage below decks with the cargo. He had read dire accounts of the treatment handed out to stowaways on ships of the sea.
> "Why, to pay our respects to the captain," said Praiseworthy.
> "*The captain!*" The words very nearly caught in his throat. "But he'll put us in chains—*or worse!*"
> "Leave that to me," said Praiseworthy, with an airy lift of the eyebrow. "Come along. . . ."

The direction of another one of my novels was profoundly changed when I tried out a bit of contrary reaction in a boy and dog story, *Jim Ugly* (Greenwillow Books). Here I was dealing with the reaction of a one-man dog, Jim Ugly, to the death of his master. The dog, half wolf, might normally mourn the death at the nearby gravesite. Then I wondered how it would play if I reversed the reaction, with the dog showing no interest in the spot. Here it reaches a climax:

> I hauled up on the rope and pointed to the burying ground. "This way, Jim Ugly. Dad's in there."
> Jim Ugly gave me a twitchy look, as if to say I didn't have enough brains to know my way outdoors without printed instructions. . . .
> My eyes tightened on the tombstones leaning up against the sunset. I knew for a sudden fact what Jim Ugly had known all along. My dad wasn't buried there. His scent wasn't on that rough, hammered-together coffin. The hair on my neck shot up.

If the boy's father wasn't in the pine box, where was he? That became the novel, thanks to Jim Ugly's contrary reaction.

And you'll remember what happened to the fellow who bit into a savory French pastry. The remembered taste of that *petite madeleine* in childhood, as Proust described his reaction, set the narrator off on a six-volume memory trip.

Shake hands with the ouch factor. It's an author's friend.

❑ 89

SAILING THE CRAFT OF
CHILDREN'S POETRY

BY J. PATRICK LEWIS

NOT LONG AGO, A YOUNG WOMAN WHO WANTED DESPERATELY TO write children's poetry asked me for some advice. "Which poets do you enjoy reading?" I asked her encouragingly. "Good heavens," she said, "I never *read* poetry. After all, I wouldn't want to be affected by what others have written."

That little encounter brought to mind my own benighted, late-in-life experience when I first discovered "Lady Poetry." I was just on the sunlight side of forty, laboring in other fields (professing Economics!) for most of my adult life. Don't ask what or who turned my head. I honestly don't remember, though to that source or gentle soul I now extend a swashbuckling bow.

Enthusiasm and commitment, hard work and long hours at the writer's trade I offered in spades, as the making of poems, especially children's verse, took hold of me—obsessively. My first efforts so startled me with their brilliance that I couldn't wait to show the world what I had wrought: "Going down and down/For the good turf. Digging," as Seamus Heaney memorably put it. Needless to add, it wasn't long before I escaped that rarefied air and realized that what I'd penned was abominable doggerel. Forgive the redundancy, but I am at pains to emphasize the true awfulness of my mid-life "juvenilia," now, mercifully, mulch in a landfill.

What was absent was a sense of craft, because I had read almost no poetry. I didn't know that poems are, as Mary Oliver says, "fires for the cold, ropes let down to the lost, something as necessary as bread in the pockets of the hungry." What to do? What I did was to stop writing. For three years. I immersed myself in the bone and the marrow of poetry—adult's and children's, classics and new—before I dared to take up a pen again.

I'm not sure if any of that experience justifies pontificating on "what children's poets should do." So these few tips I offer humbly to those who would plow these fields:

Never fear failure, that cold, hardhearted friend, but friend nonetheless. The novelist Allan Gurganus has said, in another context, that, "In America, the true 'F-word' is Failure." When I make school visits I emphasize how important it is to fail—regularly. What comes easy is cheesy. Schools should award prizes to kids who say, "Hey, I failed three times today—and that was before lunch!" A lesson for grown-up poets, too. Every writer's toolkit should come with a regulation, extra-large wastebasket.

Learn the rules of prosody—metrics, verse forms, rhythm, rhyme. Most people learn to play the guitar by first understanding chords. Or they become plumbers by learning the trade's techniques. Poets are no exception.

Once you know the rules, go ahead and break them. Especially for children who are cutting their teeth on language, sound is vital to sense *and* nonsense. Most of my children's verses do indeed rhyme. But I encourage teachers to *dis*courage the very young from rhyming. As T. S. Eliot says of the naming of cats, rhyming "is not one of your holiday games." It takes time and skill, two essentials that children have precious little of. They invariably opt for the cheap nonsense neologism that they mistakenly believe to be poetry. If, as an adult cobbler of children's verse, you choose to write in rhyme, beware: The bar of excellence rises a notch or two because contrived rhymes are so easy to write—yet painful to read.

Let me elaborate. A well-intentioned children's magazine once gave a different word—one word each—to three other children's poets and me. Our charge was to rhyme that word four times in a quatrain within one minute over the telephone! "We will then publish the results," the editor said, "as a challenge and an inspiration to our young readers." Foolishly, all four of us rose to the bait, and all four "poems" appeared in the next issue of the magazine. I don't know if there were any subsequent howls to the editor, but there should have been. Each poem was, how should I say this? Horrid. And a poor lesson for aspiring poets. Writing poetry is not a race against time. It is composition, not competition. Like painting, poetry requires a slow hand.

Keep children's poems fairly short. For better or (in my opinion) worse, the increasing speed of the world no longer provides shelter or comfort to epics, ballads, long narrative poems. Publishers find little to like about them. And after a trying day at home or office, parents are unlikely to relish a bedtime reading of, say, even the masterful eighteen (*18!*) stanzas of Lewis Carroll's "The Walrus and the Carpenter."

When I am asked where ideas come from, I state the obvious: everywhere. Generally, the sources are three: reading; observing; and remembering your own childhood or experiences with your children. Look for inspiration around the corner, in a food court, at a soccer game, in the grocery line, at the aquarium. Muses hang out everywhere, but most notably in the pages of books. What I told the young lady I mentioned at the outset is that, quite apart from the sheer thrill of reading, another poet's words or lines might be the catalyst for her own magnum opus.

To increase your chances of publication, look to themes that have general appeal: holidays; seasons; birthdays; food; colors; sports. There are far too few poems on math and science. If you can write a love poem that isn't "sincere," more power to you. An anthologist recently asked me for a poem about school. Does this qualify?

> Knives can harm you, heaven forbid!
> Axes may disarm you, kid.
> Guillotines are harmful, but . . .
> There's nothing like a paper cut.

Apparently not. The poem didn't make it into the school anthology, but, happily, it found worthy homes elsewhere.

This little ditty of mine appeared in the Food Section of several regional newspapers:

> God made the rooster,
> God made the hen,
> But Ma made the chicken
> Pot pie! Amen.

Even the sky—and pie—is not the limit. Unanchor your imagination. No subject is out of bounds for poetry.

Or choose a theme of your own. Last year, thumbing through *The Guinness Book of World Records*, I was inspired to write a collection of "extreme poems." *A Toast of Mosts & A Feast of Leasts* (Harcourt/ Creative) should appear in time for Y2K.

Write a bookmark poem (long and skinny), a dream poem, or an acrostic poem:

Libraries
Are
Necessary
Gardens,
Unsurpassed
At
Growing
Excitement.

Write a list poem by starting with a color:

Violet is . . .

my cat's tongue
lavender out on a holiday
blush pears
bruised peaches
pain gone away
Earth from six miles high
the color of dreams after midnight
the afternoon glancing off a grackle's back
the flower that bears her name

To write for children, be the child that still lives in you. How often do children find themselves talking to someone or something that can't talk back? An uncooperative soccer ball, spilled orange juice, a cozy doll? If you write a poem in a voice that addresses the voiceless, this is an apostrophe poem. Left alone, children often speak in an apostrophe voice, addressing the moon, a mouse, a blade of grass, even an absent person. For instance:

Sea, Who Are You?

A quilt of blue on blue?
An ocean in disguise?
An endless mirror to
The self-important skies?
The city of the strange?

The country of the deep?
The wind's first practice range?
The secrets seagulls keep?
The home to buried hills . . .
Oh what's a mystery for?
The empire that builds
Gold borders on a shore.

Don't be afraid to imitate! Pianists learn by practicing other people's works; so can poets. You may discover that what you have written is actually better than the original, or a scintillating parody of it, duly acknowledged, of course.

Do you like riddles? I can tell you from my school visit experiences, riddles are a natural vein to mine. Kids love them, perhaps because they are tickled to be an interactive part of guessing the answer:

To folks in Maine,
They're red and round,
And you can find 'em
Underground.
In Idaho,
They're brown and big.
They still grow under-
Ground. You dig?

Immediately obvious to you, but not necessarily to second-graders. Like all forms of poetry, riddle poems are more difficult to write than they seem.

Children are extremely visual, which is why concrete poetry is another exciting avenue for them—and for you—to explore. It's impossible to make great claims for shape poems, apart from their cleverness on the page. But again, it's the aspect of the word play that students find, well, playful, and that sets them to thinking.

Haiku, cinquains, limericks, double dactyls—try them all on for size. And don't forget the first rule you learned, probably at a much younger age than I did: Find your own voice. Better yet, find your own voices.

The great Dr. Seuss certainly had a distinctive, recognizable style. You always know a Seuss poem when you meet one. But he was a most notable and very successful exception, which is why, I suppose, too many people writing for children try in vain to substitute his voice for their own. It has always seemed to me more virtuous, or more fun at least, to write in so many styles that no single poem can be traced back to you. There is a challenge so daunting that you are bound to fail over and over again.

And that's the best part. Nothing succeeds like failure.

❑ 90

How to Research and Write Nonfiction for Children

By Susan Goldman Rubin

During the past few years I've discovered the excitement and satisfaction of researching and writing nonfiction for children—and getting it published. Many editors are looking for lively, nonfiction manuscripts ranging in areas from biographies to art, science, nature, history and social issues. They want books for the youngest children as well as for middle-grade readers and young adults. The field is wide open. Yet many aspiring writers and experienced pros stick to fiction.

According to Steve Mooser, President of the Society of Children's Book Writers and Illustrators (SCBWI), the ratio of all children's books published is about 60% fiction to 40% nonfiction. So why not give nonfiction a try as a way of breaking in or as a new challenge?

Start by finding a subject that interests you. Perhaps it's a biography of an unsung hero or heroine. Or a historical incident that will be celebrated in the next two or three years. (Remember that it takes at least a year to produce a children's book from the time the contract is signed, and it may take another year to do the research and writing.) Maybe you have an idea for a book that could fit into an existing series. This happened to me when I proposed my first nonfiction manuscript, a biography of architect Frank Lloyd Wright. I thought it belonged in a young adult series called First Impressions published by Harry N. Abrams; the editor agreed.

For me, finding the subject is a snap. I love art and feel passionate about sharing my enthusiasm with children, but you don't necessarily have to know everything about the subject you choose. In fact, part of the pleasure of writing nonfiction is in learning more about something or someone that you're greatly interested in. When I began researching my Frank Lloyd Wright biography, I wasn't even sure whether he had been born in the United States or Europe! But when our family set out for a repeat visit to Wright's Hollyhock House in Barnsdall Art Park, Los Angeles, I knew then that I wanted to do a book about him.

The next stop was the library to see what had been published and when. *The Subject Guide to Children's Books in Print* (now on the Internet) provides a list of titles and dates of publication. Perhaps a book on your topic came out many years ago and is now outdated. Maybe books on your subject were for an older age group but had never been done as a picture book for young readers. See what's out there and come up with a fresh angle.

"Get the hook and you've got the book," said my editor at Holiday House when I told her I wanted to write more about architecture for middle-grade readers. I dimly remembered hearing in an interior design class that the Eiffel Tower had stirred up controversy when it was first built. Parisians had actually protested! Maybe there were more stories like that. So I came up with the idea for *There Goes the Neighborhood! Ten Buildings People Loved to Hate.* (A catchy title helps, too.) The trick was to find nine other stories like the one about the Eiffel Tower, and to feature different kinds of buildings throughout the world.

It is possible to sell a nonfiction book without having completed it. What you have to do is write the proposal, and sometimes an outline and sample chapters. Caroline Arnold, author of more than 100 nonfiction books for children, calls this stage becoming a "temporary expert."

Include a partial bibliography of the materials you've consulted so far. If you're planning a book illustrated with vintage photographs, or reproductions of art, find out what the pictures may cost. Make some calls and state sample prices in your proposal to reassure your intended publisher that permissions for illustrations will be affordable. Some houses do their own photo research, but I prefer doing it myself.

Unless you already have a publisher who has expressed interest in your project, it's acceptable to send out multiple queries or proposals. Consult the list of book publishers in the July issue of *The Writer* Magazine. See who's looking for nonfiction for the age group you're targeting, and send your proposal to more than one house.

If and when an editor shows serious interest, you have to buckle down and start researching in earnest before even writing your first draft. Read everything you can find about your subject—books, magazine articles, newspaper clippings—whether written for adults or children. The bibliographies of other authors' books often contain good leads for further reading. Look at videos. Listen to CDs. Immerse yourself! Keep a big box for the project and toss in anything you come across that may be useful. It's amazing how newspapers seem to print stories with just the information you need when you're doing a book. And who knows? You may come up with an idea for your next book. Be alert to other possibilities.

Make a list of your sources. Note the libraries from which you borrowed materials so that you can find them again. If you come across quotations that you may want to use, jot down the names of the publications and page numbers. Some authors keep this information on index cards. Others use their computers. I confess to being less well-organized and have suffered for it when frantically searching through my scribbled notes to find sources of quotes.

All of this research is called "secondary." But *primary* research means visiting a site, conducting interviews, and reading letters and diaries.

When I started work on a biography of photographer Margaret Bourke-White, I went to the University of Syracuse to examine their archives. There were more than one hundred boxes of prints, writings, correspondence, notes, personal documents, and memorabilia such as cameras, lenses and scrapbooks! Where to begin?

Fortunately, I had received a description from the Syracuse archivist of Bourke-White's papers so I had a chance to browse through and make some preliminary choices.

Next I made many phone calls and talked to people who had known Bourke-White: her nephews, who manage her estate; her sister-in-law, who took care of her during the last months of her life; and numerous photographers, reporters, editors and assistants who worked with her at *Life* magazine. Although most of these interviews amounted to only a few lines of text, they gave me fresh insights into facets of Bourke-White's personality. I even consulted with a professional photographer who set up an old fashioned 8″ × 10″ view camera like the one Bourke-White used so that I could better understand the technical problems she faced when taking pictures.

The research can become absorbing and costly, so it's important to know when to stop researching and start writing. After all, you want to honor the deadline set in your contract and turn in your manuscript on time.

In nonfiction as well as in fiction, the principles of good writing apply: clarity, simplicity, liveliness. Trust your own voice. Write your manuscript as if you're talking directly to the readers. Organize the material into a sequence that makes sense. Follow your outline. If it's a biography, a chronological order works best.

Most nonfiction writers try to use storytelling techniques—that is, they present their information with a beginning, middle, and end. Anecdotes and scenes dramatize events and grab the readers' interest. Quotations help bring characters and situations to life. In writing about architect Philip Johnson's Glass House in New Canaan, Connecticut, for *There Goes the Neighborhood!* I quoted from an interview with him. When I asked Mr. Johnson how he felt when his neighbors criticized his design, he chuckled and said, "I rejoice in rejection."

When you've completed your manuscript, go over it and see if it flows smoothly. Read it from start to finish. Is it too long? Does it need cutting? Have you repeated certain words, phrases or stylistic devices (such as parentheses) too often? If you're using quotations, have you copied them accurately? Are events presented in correct chronological order?

Your bibliography may include a list of video cassettes, sound recordings and Web sites, as well as the dates of those expensive phone interviews. Place an asterisk next to works suitable for children. Finally, write the introduction. One of my editors says that the best time to do this is *after* the whole book is done. Only then do you have a clear sense of what you wanted to say and what the book is about. Perhaps it needs a personal note to explain why you decided to write it in the first place.

Now your manuscript is ready to send off. This doesn't mean it's finished. Your editor will be going over it, flagging pages and asking questions that will send you scurrying back to the library, and studying your original notes in order to come up with the answers. You may disagree with some of the editor's suggestions. It's your book, and you have the right to keep what you feel belongs and omit what you think doesn't fit. But everyone wants the best book possible. As one copyeditor told me after I had to wade through hundreds of her notes and Post-It flags without fainting, "We only want to make *you* look good."

At last the manuscript goes back to the publisher and gets set into type. Meanwhile, you clear your desk, pay your overdue library fines, and start researching your next nonfiction book for children.

❑ 91

WRITING AN EARLY CHAPTER BOOK

BY COLBY RODOWSKY

AS WITH SO MANY OTHER THINGS IN MY LIFE, I LEARNED TO WRITE AN early chapter book by doing it. I had already had seventeen novels for children and young adults published and was, in a mild sort of way, casting about for something else to try.

"Write an early chapter book," an editor suggested.

"What exactly is an early chapter book?" I asked.

She then went on to explain that it was a book a child would read after the I-Can-Read books and before the heftier middle-grade novels. That it would have everything a novel for older readers would have—plot, action, characterization—only on a smaller scale, and, most important, it would have chapters, something of tremendous importance to young readers.

My first stop was my local children's bookstore, where I looked over the display of chapter books and questioned the owner, hearing, once again, about plot and characters and action. I read the collection of books my editor sent me, trying to dissect them but, more often than not, getting caught up in the story. I called a writer friend and told her what I was about to try and she said, "Write about a dog. Everybody likes dogs."

A dog? Long after we hung up I turned the idea over in my mind. I had already written one dog book for middle-grade readers, and certainly didn't want to duplicate that book. A dog, a dog, I thought. What to do with a dog? At the time, one of my granddaughters was begging for a puppy, but so far her parents had resisted, and I toyed with that idea. But nearly all children want puppies, and many parents resist. No plot there.

Still, it seemed to be a logical starting point. A girl desperately and single-mindedly wanted a puppy. But suddenly, as is the way with writing fiction, she was no longer just "a girl" but was now eight-year-old

Ellie Martin. Just as suddenly, Ellie had a mother and a father and an older sister named Karen (who was sometimes a pain). Mr. and Mrs. Martin had promised Ellie that when she was nine she could have a puppy. All well and good, but obviously still no plot there—unless . . .

Then all my writer what-ifs took over. Because our own children are grown, and our house is too big, my husband and I occasionally talk about moving to a smaller place, maybe an apartment. The conversation always ends when one of us says, "But of course we can't move; the dog needs the house and the yard."

What if the Martin family had an elderly relative (one Ellie didn't even know) who really did have to move to an apartment where no pets were allowed—and she had a dog? And what if Great-aunt Margaret (because by now she was clearly Great-aunt Margaret who lived in Hagerstown, Maryland) asked Ellie's parents to take her dog? And what if they said yes, and then told Ellie that she could indeed now have a dog, Great-aunt Margaret's dog Preston, who would (fairly or unfairly) take the place of the puppy she had hoped for, because her parents were firmly convinced that they were a one-pet-at-a-time family?

As these bits and pieces came together I knew, without hesitation, that Ellie would think that any dog named Preston was sure to be "a sort of square, boring brown dog with sticking-up ears and a skinny tail." When she saw him for the first time her fears were confirmed: Preston was indeed square, and boring, and brown; and he did have sticking-up ears and a skinny tail.

Here was a plot.

Leaping ahead to the ending, I knew that, despite Ellie's protestations about Preston not being her dog, she and Preston would bond. I also knew that none of this could or would happen overnight. I, as the writer, and children, as readers, would have to deal and empathize with Ellie's disappointment, her consternation, her angst. Her eventual appreciation of Preston would have to grow by baby rather than giant steps. (All in a book that was to run only about thirty-some manuscript pages.)

I started to write, and the story went—as all my writing projects go—smoothly a small fraction of the time and not so smoothly (almost limpingly) the rest of the time. Some days (rarely) I seemed to skim along, plucking out of the air words that were just waiting there for me. Other times I agonized, staring at the computer screen, writing hesitantly, and often clicking on the delete key, much the way I do when I'm writing for older readers.

Aspects of the story unfolded as I went along. Ellie's acceptance of Preston was gradual: She reluctantly threw a ball to him and he brought it back; he kept her company during a scary TV movie she couldn't bear to turn off; he came to her aid when she got lost taking the long way home from her friend Amy's house.

When the book was finished I sent it to my editor, who liked it and agreed to publish it, adding, almost as an afterthought, that there was a problem with the ending, and the resolution seemed abrupt. Then, in subsequent letters, she talked about fleshing out the characters and went on to say that though it was "a sweet, well-written story . . . it could be even better," and "that chapter ten should really be chapter eleven, which means that ten still needs to be written."

It was then I realized that if my book had been a picture, the people in it would have been stick figures, and that the phrase "bare-boned" had no place in a description of an early chapter book. I went back to work, digging deeper, learning more about my characters and how they interacted with one another. I discovered that Mr. and Mrs. Martin weren't merely Ellie's parents, but that he was a lawyer who also played the bagpipes while she was a quilt maker. I learned that Great-aunt Margaret loved Preston too much just to hand him over to Ellie and forget about him; the old woman and the child would now be irrevocably involved in each other's lives. I wrote the elusive chapter ten, then rearranged all the chapters into seven.

While over the course of several chapters Ellie and Preston inched closer together, both my editor and I found that somehow that wasn't enough. There had to be more. Maybe Ellie would have to almost lose Preston to find out how much she cared about him. This led me to write a new scene in which Ellie overhears her parents discussing the fact that though they had been sure Ellie would come to love Preston, it didn't seem to be happening, and perhaps it was now time to find a new home for the dog. "When Ellie heard that, she felt as if she had a big empty hole right in the middle of her stomach."

The next day in school, Ellie and her classmates are asked to write compositions about "Someone Important in My Life," and on hearing Ellie read hers aloud, her teacher asks, "But you forgot to tell us who Preston is."

It is then that Ellie Martin proudly proclaims, "Preston? . . . Preston is my dog."

Writers often wonder about the vocabulary in early chapter books . . . do you have to use special words? I found in writing *Not My Dog* that I almost instinctively chose language that was appropriate to the story I was telling. It wasn't long after this that the characters took over, dictating (as characters often do) the tone of the book. All the revisions notwithstanding, at no time during this process was it ever suggested that I change any particular word for a simpler one, though occasionally overly long sentences were broken into two.

I did have to bear in mind that no matter how involved or engaging I thought my story was, I had to keep it to an unintimidating length, and I had to remember those all-important chapters for the just-reading-on-their-own set. Much about writing has to be learned by *doing*. Doing it one way, and if that doesn't work going back and trying something else. Again, and then again.

Writing an early chapter book takes as much care and love and attention and plain hard work as writing any other novel for young readers. And don't forget those well-rounded characters, dialogue that's as real as if spoken by the kid next door, and, of course, a plot.

❏ 92

WRITING SHORT STORIES FOR TEENS

BY DONALD R. GALLO

KNOWING THAT MANY TEENAGERS HAVE SHORT ATTENTION SPANS, you've decided to write short stories aimed at teens rather than attempting a novel. Short stories seem easier because you have to write only a few pages, perhaps 3,000 to 5,000 words, compared with two hundred or more pages for a novel. If the writing goes well, you could complete a story in a week, maybe less, instead of the months, or even years, you might spend constructing a novel. On the other hand, a novel gives you space in which to create characters, build tension, resolve conflicts, while in a short story, all that has to be done in just a few pages. As a result, short stories are both easier and harder to write than novels.

As with writing novels, there is, of course, no formula for writing good short stories, though there are qualities you can aim for. The following advice does not come as a result of my being a successful or prize-winning writer of short stories. I have never written a publishable short story, though I have edited and published the short stories of many of the top writers in the field, so I can tell you what makes their stories good. In addition, what authors and editors might say about their work is not as important as what readers say about the stories they read: We can think a story we've written is great, but if our intended readers don't think so, what have we accomplished? Thus, much of the advice I will provide here is based on what teenage readers say they look for in stories and novels.

Teenagers—especially so-called reluctant readers—react to many of the same qualities I react to when I open a large manila envelope submitted by a writer, and I read for the first time a never-before-published short story for a new collection I've planned.

Catchy title

The title usually isn't the first thing you write when you're starting a new story; for some writers, in fact, it's the last thing they struggle with. Nevertheless, it is the first thing readers see. If a reader is leafing through a collection of stories, one title is going to catch that reader's attention more than the others. You want that title to be yours. (When the novel *Snow Falling on Cedars,* by David Guterson, was first published, I knew I wanted to read it. I had no idea what it was about. I didn't care. The title fascinated me.)

Which story in each of the following pairs of titles would you read first?

"The Child" or "The Boy with Yellow Eyes"?

"Shotgun Cheatham's Last Night Above Ground" or "Dancer"?

"The All-American Slurp" or "Dawn"?

"Hamish Mactavish Is Eating a Bus" or "The Wedding Cake in the Middle of the Road"?

Except in the last case, where both sound weirdly interesting, the decision is easy. This is not to suggest that the stories with less interesting titles are not good stories. These are all real titles of stories published in well-reviewed collections. But at this point, we are just interested in getting the attention of the reader.

Attention-getting opening

Whether your title is or is not enticing, your opening lines must grab readers by the sleeve and lead them into your story. If you are writing a novel, you can take your time getting into it—though if you are writing for teenagers, I don't recommend you dally too long. With a short story, you don't have time to be leisurely. You have to hook your readers with those opening lines and keep them reading. Notice how the opening lines of the following stories grab your attention immediately and make you want to read on. (Incidentally, all of the passages I quote are from books I have edited, all published in hardcover by Delacorte Press and in paperback by Dell.)

> Dad came down with the flu that week, so I had to go down to the subway and feed the unicorns.
> (from "Midnight Snack," by Diane Duane in *Sixteen*)

> From the very beginning, I knew the place was haunted. I wasn't frightened. Far from it. Ghosts were the company I came to count on.
> (from "Shadows," by Richard Peck in *Visions*)

> Ms. Morgan was a witch. At any rate she certainly looked like a witch. She wore baggy dresses and had stringy black hair and a pinched face, and

if you could have stood to look into her beady eyes long enough, you would have seen that they were violet. With a little putty on her nose, she would have been a shoo-in for the Margaret Hamilton role in a revival of *The Wizard of Oz*.
(from "Ethan Unbound," by Gary L. Blackwood in *Short Circuits*)

Interesting characters

It's probably a toss-up whether the characters or the conflicts are more important in good stories. When you are thinking about what to write, you can begin to formulate your story either by creating an interesting character or a thought-provoking conflict. But a good story needs both.

Richard Peck created two memorable characters in his now famous "Priscilla and the Wimps" (in *Sixteen*): the bully Monk Klutter, leader of a gang called Klutter's Cobras, who terrorize classmates and shake down fellow students for their lunch money, and his nemesis, Priscilla Roseberry. Peck's narrator describes Priscilla this way: "Priscilla was, hands down, the largest student in our particular institution of learning. I'm not talking fat. I'm talking big. Even beautiful, in a bionic way."

Priscilla is surely not someone easy to forget. Even more interesting from a writing perspective, though, is that in Peck's story, both Monk Klutter and Priscilla Roseberry are more memorable than the narrator. That's not usually the case in fiction for teenagers. More typically, the narrator is the main character, as is the case in the following excerpt from Chris Crutcher's "Superboy" (in *Ultimate Sports*):

> Pa Kent says I ain't probly gonna ever win no prizes for smarts, but I ain't been in no contests. Long as I'm not in one, I could probly tell everone I coulda got maybe a Third or so, and who'd know?

That's Clark, whom everyone views as a dummy. So he lashes out at other kids who make fun of him, until ironman contestant Bo Brewster (Crutcher's main character in his novel *Ironman*) helps Clark learn to channel his anger through athletic competition.

Just a side note here—though an important one: In all of the short story collections for teenagers I have edited, with very few exceptions, teenagers are the main characters; the narrators, also, are almost always teenagers. This is not the case in many other short story collections aimed at teenagers. In some of those stories, young children or adults are the main characters, and other stories are told from an adult perspective looking back. There's nothing wrong with any of those approaches, if the resulting story is good. But most teenagers want to read about characters who are like themselves or even a bit older, so the main focus of your stories ought to be teenagers and their problems. But the choice is yours: You have to balance what you want to say with whom you expect to read it.

Characters who are unusual, like Clark and Monk and Priscilla, are likely to be memorable. But readers also like characters with whom they can identify, who are in situations almost every teenager is likely to face. One such character is Seth in Todd Strasser's very popular story "On the Bridge" (in *Visions*). Seth is an ordinary, pretty good kid who admires Adam, the tough guy in his school. But emulating Adam leads Seth into trouble that he didn't expect—perfect for middle school kids, especially boys who want to act macho but follow a leader who deserves no respect.

Even though your main character is someone out of the ordinary, like Saeng, a Laotian refugee, in "The Winter Hibiscus," by Minfong Ho (in *Join In*), it is helpful if that character has something in common with ordinary teenage readers. Saeng is about to take the test for her driver's license, something almost every American teenager does, and she's so worried about failing that she does just that. Easy for 16-year-olds to identify with.

A thought-provoking conflict

Your story should have some conflict, and if that conflict or the main issue in your story makes readers think, so much the better. In Ron Koertge's "Duet" (in *No Easy Answers*), the conflict between two dating high school students is evident from the story's first line: "Betsy, you've got to sleep with me. I'm going crazy." He's ready for sex, and she isn't. How will they deal with the sexual tension? (She suggests he have sex with her promiscuous girl friend.)

Will Weaver's "The Photograph" (in *No Easy Answers*) begins this way:

> "Naked?"
> "Yes."
> "Ms. Jenson? Our beloved phys ed teacher and girls' track coach?"
> "Skinny-dipping. Absolutely. She was in the lake totally naked."

Three guys check out this irresistible situation and find it's true. The teacher does skinny-dip, and one guy gets photographs of her . . . and a lot more. What they do with those photographs makes the story even more interesting. *No* male in high school will be able to resist that!

The conflicts in both stories aren't just entertaining; they also provide readers with the opportunity to think about making sensible choices and being responsible for the consequences of their actions.

Lively dialogue, preferably with humor

You can tell your story in a variety of ways, but remember that kids hate lengthy descriptions and love lively dialogue. Here's a little more of the beginning of Ron Koertge's "Duet":

> "Betsy, you've got to sleep with me. I'm going crazy."
> There was this long silence at the other end of the line. Then she said, "Okay."
> I couldn't believe my ears. "You mean it?"
> "Right now. This instant. Drop everything and get over here."
> I looked out my bedroom door, as if I could see down the hall, down the stairs to the dining room.
> "But Mom's got dinner on the table."
> "Well, then I guess you've missed your chance, haven't you?"
> "Can't you wait until tonight?"
> "And play second fiddle to a pork chop? No way."

There's no way I can teach you to write such clever dialogue, but that's the kind of example you have to aim to emulate.

All of the above

The very best stories—of course—have all these characteristics:

- a catchy title
- an attention-getting opening
- interesting characters
- a thought-provoking conflict
- lively dialogue, preferably with a good amount of humor

If it all comes together, then you might be lucky and create a story like Chris Crutcher's now famous "A Brief Moment in the Life of Angus Bethune" (in *Connections*), which later became a movie.

May you all be fortunate enough to find an Angus character in your imagination, with a thought-provoking conflict to challenge him and entertain readers for years to come.

❏ 93

CREATING BELIEVABLE
TEEN-AGE SLEUTHS

BY JOAN LOWERY NIXON

IN THE ADULT MYSTERY NOVEL PROTAGONISTS COME IN MANY VARIE-
ties: the law enforcement professional, attorney, or private investigator—all of whom have the training and resources to conduct believable
investigations—and the amateur detectives, who may not have a badge
or license but who do have backgrounds of skills and life experiences
that give them the necessary authority to solve crimes.

In the young adult mystery, however, the situation is entirely different. For young readers (usually from fifth grade through high school) to
relate totally to the main character, that main character must be a teenager, too. This means that the protagonist, who is too young to have
mastered professional skills, is limited solely to the role of amateur
detective.

To be believable, stories for young adults must mirror reality as much
as possible. Suspension of disbelief can go only so far. In the real world,
we read about young people as victims of crimes or perpetrators of
crimes, but it's rare to read of a teenager actually solving a crime. So
how do we, as writers, make young readers believe that an inexperienced kid their own age with problems very much like their own—
someone who procrastinates, who has trouble passing geometry, who
has just broken up with a boyfriend, or who can't get along with her
parents—can actually best law enforcement professionals at their own
work? How can we make the fictional actions of our teen-age sleuths
ring true?

The first step is to develop the main character's personal problem.
Let readers get to know her well. Her flaws are every bit as important
as her good points, because they make her more "human" and easy to
like. You want readers to cheer on your main character, to want her to
solve her personal problem.

462

My novel *Who Are You?* opens with Kristi Evans having an argument with her parents. The dialogue will be familiar to teenagers who have heard and said the same things in disagreements with their own parents:

> The doorbell rings, but Mom, Dad, and I just stare at each other. We've been building walls of angry words, slathering them over with shouts of "That's a completely unreasonable request!" and "You don't even try to understand!" and "Use your brain, Kristi! Do you think we're made of money?" and "You don't know anything about me. You don't care!"
>
> The loud chime of the doorbell intrudes and suddenly we're silent. The noise is a shock, like being caught naked in the shower room after gym class. Dad clears his throat, turns, and walks to open the door.

Two homicide detectives have come to question Kristi's family. A wealthy River Oaks resident named Douglas Merson has been seriously wounded in what seems to have been an attempted robbery at his home. The Evanses are puzzled by the detectives' insistence that they must have some connection with Merson, or at the very least, be acquainted with him, because none of them knows who the man is. Their confusion turns to complete astonishment when Sergeant Balker tells them that on Douglas Merson's coffee table they found a file with a birth announcement, notations about a school play, awards in art shows in middle school and high school and current photographs. "The clippings all have to do with your daughter," Sergeant Balker tells the Evanses. "The file is labeled 'Kristin Anne Evans.' "

We're now into the mystery element of the novel, but as the chapter develops, the reason for the family argument develops, too. Holly's disagreement with her parents isn't just a side issue: It plays a strong part in the solution of the mystery itself.

I also opened my novel *Spirit Seeker* with the main character's personal problem:

> Saturday. 2:00 a.m. Through the silence of the house came the creaking of the front door, the thud of dead bolts slapping into place, and the padding of muffled footsteps toward the kitchen. I had been lying in bed, waiting for him. With only a cold hollow where my stomach ought to be, I slid out of bed, threw a robe over my T-shirt, and ran barefoot down the stairs to confront my father.
>
> Even though I was furious, I was frightened, too. Don't get me wrong. I wasn't afraid of my father. I was scared of what he was doing to Mom . . . and to me.

Holly Campbell begins to berate her homicide detective father for once again hurting her mother—this time by forgetting to come home for their anniversary celebration—but she soon discovers that the case that had demanded her father's undivided attention was the double murder of the parents of one of Holly's close friends, Cody Garnett.

Holly is torn. As the story progresses she begins to waver in her firm conviction that her father's preoccupation with his job is destroying her parents' marriage. When she becomes involved in saving her friend from arrest, she realizes how demanding the solution of a murder can be.

Some young adult mystery novels are written with a light touch, with humor used throughout the story to break the tension of suspense, as in the opening of *Murdered, My Sweet*:

> It's not easy being related to a woman who's famous for murdering people.
> Don't get me wrong. Mom's not a real murderer. She's Madeline Jakes, the most famous mystery writer in the United States—maybe the world. She's a good writer, too. I've never met anyone who could read one of Mom's novels late at night and not have to sleep with the bathroom light on.
> So many people have seen Mom's picture on the back of her book jackets and watched her being interviewed on TV that they recognize her in public places. "There's Madeline Jakes!" some whisper. Some point. Maybe because they've been watching too much television, I notice some glance around to see if Mom's with the police, helping to solve a murder at that very moment.
> Solve a murder? Mom? It's actually funny. My mom is a woman who half the time can't even figure out where she put her car keys or placed her glasses. . . . Mom has never solved a murder in her life, except for the murders in her books. Because she makes those up, she knows from the very beginning "whodunnit." I don't count them.
> Try telling that to Mom. She's actually started to believe what she reads about herself.

Jenny Jakes and her mystery writing mother are suddenly plunged into a situation in which a group of relatives count on the famous Madeline to solve a murder that has taken place. It's all very public—front-page news—so Madeline Jakes's reputation is at stake.

Motive—a strong motive for investigating a crime—is not only necessary for each young main character; along with believability of character, it's one of the two most important elements of the young adult mystery novel.

Kids are smart and savvy. While the very young can easily accept detectives who are cats, dogs, or kindergarteners who look for footprints with magnifying glasses, teenagers are more demanding. They won't tolerate a main character who heedlessly goes into a dark tunnel to search for clues. They want to identify with someone like themselves—someone who gets scared, who recognizes a dangerous situation when he sees it and takes precautions, who thinks the situation through logically, and who knows how to call for help when he has to.

In *Who Are You?* Kristi has a compulsion to know who the man is who has kept a secret file about her. Without her knowledge, he has even taken photographs of her. Angry at this invasion of her privacy, she needs to find out what *he* looks like. Is it possible she might recognize him? And, even more important to her, *why* has he kept this file with information about her? What was his reason for doing so?

Kids would understand Kristi's motivation. They'd probably feel exactly the same way and take similar action.

In *Spirit Seeker,* Holly is upset when her father says he suspects Cody of the crime because in most family murders it's the surviving member who is guilty, and Cody's alibi is weak.

Holly is horrified. She is sure that her friend couldn't have committed murder. With everyone against Cody, including the police, he doesn't seem to have a chance, so Holly is determined to do what she can to prove that Cody is innocent.

Readers identify with Holly. They feel as outraged as she does and would take the same actions, if it were up to them.

Jenny Jakes, too, has a strong motive for solving the crime. She loves her mother, and she doesn't want to see her fail in a very public, embarrassing way. Relying on knowledge she's picked up from her Uncle Bill, a homicide detective, Jenny does her best to make her mother's investigation look good.

Haven't most teenagers, at one time or another, been embarrassed by something their parents have done or said? Here's Jenny's mother—who thinks she's a sleuth and isn't—ready to embarrass Jenny and herself big-time. Young readers can definitely relate to Jenny's need to help her mother out of this tough situation.

Kids like to know that one of their own is clever enough to pick up on a clue that police have missed. In *Nobody's There*, Edna Merkel, an elderly woman who lives alone, is attacked. Police search her house, calling in Abbie Thompson, a teenager who's been assigned to assist elderly people through a teen support group. While the police have ignored a lone coffee cup on the kitchen counter, assuming it had been used by Edna, it's Abbie who snaps to the fact that it couldn't be Edna's. Edna had mentioned once that she didn't like coffee. She drank only tea.

"The coffee cup in the kitchen," Abbie said. "It wasn't hers. Someone else drank half that cup of coffee. You need to take it in for fingerprints."

The police listen and take action. Wow! An adult in authority actually pays attention to what a teenager has to say. Kids feel good about that.

It's also Abbie who uses the same kind of logical, deductive reasoning any teenager might use to discover not only the identity of the unusual weapon used in the attack, but also to determine where the weapon is hidden, and why it hasn't been simply tossed in the Gulf where it couldn't be found. Does this make sense to young readers? Completely. Given the chance, they could do it, too.

Teen-age main characters don't always try to go it alone. They confide in their best friends, they bounce ideas off them, and in some sticky situations, they even take along these friends for support. Wouldn't anybody?

In *The Haunting*, Lia's best friend Jolie is terrified that something terrible will happen when Lia and her parents set foot inside an inherited plantation house that's known to be haunted. Jolie takes Lia to a voodoo shop in New Orleans, where the proprietor sells Lia a small bag of gris-gris to wear around her neck—gris-gris that is supposed to protect Lia from whatever evil spirits might be in that plantation.

As the girls leave the shop, Lia says,

"It looks weird. It even smells a little funny. What if it's got dead stuff in it or ground-up bones?"

Jolie stopped and faced me. "Don't back off now, Lia," she said. "Promise me that you'll wear it. Promise, or I won't be able to sleep or eat or do anything except worry until you come home. Promise!"

"All right," I said reluctantly. "I promise."

Teen-age sleuths can't drop everything else in their lives in order to try to solve a crime. There are exams, homework, curfews, babysitting, soccer practice, and ballet lessons. And sometimes there are difficult adults who get in the way. But these handicaps can actually be a help to writers in that they make the fictional lives of teen-age protagonists even more recognizable and acceptable to young readers.

If you give your main characters familiar personal problems and strong motivation for entering the world of detection, you will have created believable teen-age sleuths.

❑ 94

What I Learned By Writing My First Children's Book

By Nancy McArthur

When I began my first children's book, all I had was a funny title for a middle-grade novel, *The Plant That Ate Dirty Socks*, and a general idea of what it would be about. I plunged in, determined to figure it all out. What I learned in the process was a priceless education in the realities of writing a publishable book for children.

You have to work within the requirements for the type of children's book you want to write. You can write anything you want, of course, but if you hope to get published, don't do a fifty-page manuscript for a short chapter book that requires no more than 30 manuscript pages. It's amazing how many aspiring writers don't check out the basic requirements and formats for the different categories of children's books. Reading James Cross Giblin's *Writing Books for Young People* (Kalmbach Publishing Co.) helped get me on track. I also learned techniques by analyzing the work of excellent authors. (See page 472.)

You don't have to wait for inspiration. If you do, you might wait a long time—or forever. Sometimes an idea comes to you out of the blue. Make the most of that when it happens, but it seldom happens often enough to make a whole book. If you make an effort to get ideas, they will come when you need them. If you are serious about writing books, you need to acquire the habit of getting, saving, and developing ideas.

Write down and save anything interesting that occurs to you, regardless of whether it is useful for your current project. You never know what will come in handy. Some of the items I've saved or jotted down in my idea files that provided jumping-off points for my imagination include a robot dinosaur exhibit; an article about a shuttle astronaut's teleconference from space with students at his old elementary school; a woman wearing musical Christmas socks; and a college student of mine who came to class on Halloween in a rubber gorilla head.

Other reliable ways to develop ideas are free-writing, making lists, doing research for facts and authentic detail, and brainstorming (a.k.a. "mapping" or "webbing").

Writing a rough draft is a process of discovery. First, sort through the chaos of your idea notes and make an informal list of what you want to include. As you write, you'll keep adding to and rearranging the list. Many more ideas and connections between them will emerge—things that never would have occurred to you otherwise. The old adage that one thing leads to another really proves true in the writing process. My motto for doing a rough draft is: "Try anything. You can always change it."

You don't have to begin at the beginning. Start by drafting any scenes you have a clear picture of in your mind, even small fragments, regardless of where in the book they may ultimately fit in. This approach prevents procrastination or fear of finishing.

Setting practical goals prevents inaction. Choose the number of pages you feel you could comfortably finish in a single writing session. At first I inadvertently set too high a goal. By the fourth day, I was six pages behind. Then I realized that even one hour or page per session will eventually add up to a completed manuscript. I spurred myself on by keeping a progress chart on graph paper, marking the number of pages to be done for each successive draft. Filling in a square for each page completed gave me a sense of accomplishment.

Participating in a writers' group can provide a regular deadline, because you are expected to bring something you have written to each meeting. The objective feedback on manuscripts is very helpful. Or you can attend a writers' conference where manuscripts can be evaluated, and use that as your deadline.

Revise, revise, revise. Published books give no clue to the process the authors went through. No one could guess that the many drafts of *The Plant That Ate Dirty Socks* made a stack nine inches high and weighed eight pounds, quite a contrast to the three-eighths-of-an-inch-thick paperback book that it produced. Whenever I read about major revisions by an author whose work I admire, it is a comfort, an encouragement, and a confirmation of what experience has taught me: Revising is a powerful and effective technique, truly one of the secrets of good writing. The *Charlotte's Web* that we read was E. B. White's eighth draft!

For me, a complete rewrite (not just tinkering) for the second draft helped immensely to firm up the story. Some parts didn't need changing, but many did. Some scenes clearly fit into the whole, revealing where transitions were called for. New scenes were obviously needed; others that meandered or led nowhere had to be cut.

At this point, I was looking at structure, asking myself such questions as, Does everything make sense? Does every part of the story have a reason for being there? Does every scene serve some purpose—move the story forward or establish or develop character or situation? Do any parts need more information or more detail so readers can picture what I'm writing about? How have I introduced and portrayed each main character? Are their motivations believable? Does my beginning engage the reader right away? Are chapter lengths within the average number of pages for books of this type?

The third draft was more of a polishing process. Now I was really hunting for cross-outs and every superfluous word. Next, I read the whole manuscript aloud. Many things not obvious in silent reading popped out—more unnecessary words and phrases, even whole paragraphs, word repetitions, dialogue that wandered or didn't sound lifelike, and sentences difficult to read aloud. Some authors read their manuscripts into a tape recorder and use the playback to accomplish this phase.

For the final, acid test, I read my book to a small group of children the ages of my intended audience. (Since the reading was going to take a little over two hours, we took a halftime pizza break.) I asked them to stop me at any word or part they didn't understand. Sitting opposite them so I could keep looking up from my pages and watch their faces, I could see, sentence by sentence, when they were engrossed in the story and when their interest flagged, even for a moment.

If they started looking around the room, I was losing them. I jotted check marks at the parts that held them or made them laugh, x's at the spots that needed deleting, and question marks at places that needed clarification. This reading showed me things that needed fixing that I couldn't find any other way.

If the manuscript needs major work, you can revise and test again with a new batch of children. In the best-case scenario, when you find that your story went over well with your test audience, you polish the small things you discovered in the read-aloud, and then send your book to an editor (or in the case of my first book, to one editor after another until one accepted it).

Just when you think you're finished, ha! Finally, my dream started to come true. An editor responded, "We love this book, and we want to buy it," and added, "We'd like you to make some revisions." When the letter arrived with detailed suggestions, my euphoria was swept away by a feeling of %$#*?! (as old comics characters used to say in stressful moments). More revising? Oh, no! Oh, yes. This is a normal part of the professional relationship between editor and author. Regard this as help, not hindrance, whether the editor wants you to change a few words or perform a massive renovation. My editor gave me valid advice on how to make my book better. We discussed the suggestions, most of which I agreed with.

Writing my first book took four years, off and on (mostly *off*), and eight or nine drafts. Now my books take about four months and about four drafts, because I write steadily instead of in fits and starts. I learned that I had to be my own cheerleader to keep going, and that patience and persistence in revising are essential. And although publishing decisions are made by adults, trying out my manuscripts on children has taught me volumes on how to connect with my intended audience.

During those four years, when I went into libraries and bookstores, I would look at the intermediate fiction and fantasize, "When my book is published, it will go right there among the other authors whose names start with M." Then, at last, when *The Plant That Ate Dirty Socks* was really there, it was a dream that I had made come true.

How to analyze published books

The so-called secrets of good writing are available right under our noses—in good books. Ask your children's librarian to recommend books of the type you aspire to write, and study them.

To analyze picture books, which look deceptively simple, make a list of what happens on each page so you can see how the book is structured across the two-page spreads. Note what the illustrations show in addition to what the words tell. Count the number of sentences or words in several picture books to get a realistic estimate for manuscript length.

For books for beginning readers, note the very simple sentences (no clauses). For chapter books for second- and third-grade level, note that sentences are predominantly simple, with some complex ones blended in. To analyze short chapter books and middle-grade books, write a chapter-by-chapter summary. This will reveal the structure and pacing of the plot. Note the average chapter lengths and how chapters usually end with something that makes the reader want to read on.

To learn how to write great beginnings, read the first pages of a dozen or more good books. Notice how the readers' interest is engaged right away. What has the writer established about the characters and situation by the end of the first page?

Buy paperback copies of the some of the best examples and mark them up with colored pens or pencils to track various techniques the authors used. For example, to learn about characterization, follow each character with one color through all the aspects of the book that portray that character—appearance, actions, reactions, his own words or thoughts, how other characters regard him, and if and how he changes or grows. (For a masterful example of characterization techniques, examine in this way Wilbur in *Charlotte's Web*.)

To learn descriptive techniques, underline the details that draw pictures with sensory words so readers can see, hear, feel, touch, smell or even taste. Mark comparisons, another effective description method. Observe how much or how little description the author used. Sometimes only a few details are needed to be vivid.

Read dialogue aloud. How has the author made it sound lifelike? Do different characters have individual speech patterns? Check the variety of attribution verbs (said, warned, whined, shouted, murmured, complained, etc.), and note how each suits exactly what is being said. "Said" is such a neutral word that you can use it often without being monotonous; but judicious use of appropriate synonyms greatly enhances dialogue.

□ 95

GET YOUR READER INVOLVED

BY ANNE WARREN SMITH

CERTAIN STORIES INVITE READERS IN AND HOLD THEM TIGHT; THEY feel magnetized or glued, unable to put the book down. They connive to outwit the villains, guffaw at the protagonist's antics, and long after they've finished reading, they catch themselves still living in that other world, still caring for the characters. If you can write that kind of book for young adults, your story will win out over all the other enticements today's young adults face.

The best writing for young adults is interactive; it forges a partnership with the reader. How do writers achieve this? The answer lies in the language—specifically in the nouns and verbs and sensory details they use. Small stuff, you may think, but I'm talking here about *final* revisions. Once you are satisfied that your characters and plot are as good as you can make them, take time to look at individual words. Every word has the power to magnetize.

Make your nouns specific

At first, you're lazy and may write, "Eat all your vegetables," or "Don't tease that dog." How much more effective if you say, "Eat all your beet greens," or "Don't tease that pit bull." Name every vegetable and dog—every generic noun—in your prose. In his award-winning book, *Blue Skin of the Sea,* although Graham Salisbury speaks of "rubble" as his characters enter a disaster area, he gets specific right away:

> The rubble crammed up into the back end of the river was incredible— splintered buildings, boulders, cars, bent and twisted steel beams, dead fish, telephone poles, and cane trash. And a sampan as long as Dad's, red hull to the sky. . . . Steel parking meters were bent flat to the sidewalks. Where buildings had once been, there were only vacant cement pads. The houses, shops, and boats lay farther back, in shattered heaps, with men digging through them. Fish trapped in puddled gutters flopped hopelessly in brown, foot-deep ponds.

Another kind of specificity—proper nouns—will also engage your young adult readers. Here are the enticing first lines of Salisbury's novel:

> A noon-high Hawaiian sun poured over the jungled flanks of the Big Island, spreading down into the village of Kailua-Kona and the blistering metal bed of Uncle Harley's fish truck. Keo and I sat across from each other on the black rubber inner tubes that Uncle Harley, Keo's father, had gotten for us at the Chevron Station in Holualoa.

Actual places that exist on a map and an uncle with a real name lend verisimilitude and flavor to the story. And a Chevron station isn't just a generic gas station; the name instantly evokes a red and white picture in the minds of most readers.

Choose strong verbs

In my own early drafts, I use the first verb that occurs to me. For example, I may have written that Tom, my young adult hero, *walked* through the forest. I need then to consider whether he *staggered, marched, moseyed, crept, sauntered,* or *strode* through the forest. Or did he *skip, trudge, amble,* or *tiptoe?* Each of these verbs evokes a different picture of what Tom was really doing and, most important, how he felt about it. This is where the writer turns the reader into a partner. If I choose *amble,* my reader thinks, "Tom's relaxed, not a bit worried." Furthermore, the reader is more apt to *believe* Tom is relaxed than if I had simply told him so.

In a second reading of my story, I find I've written that Tom's friend Linda ate a hamburger, but it's more likely that, depending on her frame of mind (and the condition of her braces), she *munched, gummed, pigged out, picked at, wolfed, gulped, chomped,* or *chewed.* Choose any one of these verbs and you can *see* her. Paul Zindel's creepy fantasy, *Doom Stone,* teems with evocative verbs. Notice how *sprang, shrieked, fled,* and *burst* work for him:

> Like a tick on a burning match cover, the monster sprang whole from the cage, landing against the far wall. It shrieked, its flesh on fire as it fled for the cellar door. With a single motion it burst the doors from their hinges.

Reading Salisbury's *Blue Skin of the Sea* again, you see how he uses powerful verbs to show his character's fear of deep water and at the same time his fascination with it:

The mask pushed in on my face and small streams of water dripped in at my temples. The ocean filled my ears and pressed in painfully. We floated in an air of watery space with a crackling, snapping, buzzing sound all around us. A small puddle began to gather in the mask, below my nose, nearly panicking me.

But for a moment I looked beyond the puddle, amazed at the islands of coral that broke the sandy ocean floor. Silent fish circled and hung in small schools far beneath my feet, their backs dark and bullet shaped. A huge parrot fish nibbled at the edge of a mass of coral, then suddenly darted away and sailed to a stop farther out.

As if the verbs *pushed, filled, pressed, floated, circled, hung, nibbled, darted,* and *sailed* aren't enough, Salisbury adds *crackling, snapping, buzzing, and panicking.*

Add power with sensory details

Never underestimate the power of sensory details. I always need to add and refine the sensory details in my own final drafts, and the work is well worth the effort. Sensory details are the warhorses that crank up tension, create mood and atmosphere, and breathe life into our characters.Here are some examples:

In my hypothetical story, Tom's younger brother Jerry, normally a happy-go-lucky kid, is walking down a dark alley. I already know enough to use *creeping* instead of *walking* since I want the reader to know that Jerry's afraid. Now, suppose I increase Jerry's (and therefore the reader's) fear by adding carefully selected sensory details: I choose the smell of urine, the rasp of a garbage can on the pavement, the flash of a cat's eyes from the top of the fence, and the prickly chill of bricks against Jerry's back as he presses against the wall. Smells, sounds, sights, textures. Did I forget taste? Here is a possible one: "He tasted sour apple fear—acid, rancid—worse than anything he'd ever tasted before." As you incorporate more sensory details into a scene you are writing, watch the tension thermometer rise.

Sensory details also increase tension by forcing your narrative into slow motion, like nightmares in which you can barely move your leaden feet to avoid being run over by the speeding locomotive. In *Probably Nick Swansen,* Virginia Euwer Wolff stops time by heightening background sounds that otherwise might not be noticed:

There was a fierce quiet in the living room. You could hear the lawn sprinkler ticking and a fly angry on the windowsill looking for a way out. Nick looked at his mother and dad. If he got killed, they wouldn't have any children left at all.

In *Alias,* by M.E. Ryan, the protagonist knows he's not supposed to look in a box that belongs to his mother. Here's how his sense of hearing is heightened:

> The box was old and worn from years of travel. The stars and crescents were faded, the cardboard lid frayed at the edges.
> My hands were shaking so badly, I almost dropped it.
> I paused a moment and listened. Was something ticking inside the box?
> Nope—just the alarm clock in the corner. I swallowed a few times, took a deep breath, and opened the box.

In *The True Confessions of Charlotte Doyle,* the author, Avi, could have told the reader that Charlotte, the fourteen-year-old protagonist, was excited. Instead he lets the reader participate. Notice the details:

> Everywhere I looked great canvas sails of gray, from mainsail to main royal, from flying jib to trysail, were bellied out. Beyond the sails stretched the sky itself, as blue as a baby's bluest eyes, while the greenish sea, crowned with lacy caps of foaming white rushed by with unrelenting speed. The *Seahawk* had gone to sea.

Readers share Charlotte's excitement as her adventure begins. A few pages later, however, Avi describes the same scene, this time, with details and verbs that foretell disaster:

> Though the *Seahawk* heaved and rolled, creaked and groaned, her sails hung limply. The sky was different too; low, with a heavy dampness that instantly wet my face, though I felt nothing so distinct as rain. As for the sea, it was almost the same color as the sky, a menacing claylike gray. And yet, it was in constant motion, its surface heaving rhythmically like the chest of some vast, discomforted sleeper.

Gary Paulsen in *Sisters/Hermanas* uses sensory details to characterize fourteen-year-old Rosa, an illegal immigrant who is a prostitute on the streets of Houston. He doesn't tell his readers that Rosa is a sympathetic character; they *know* she is when they read the following:

> In the middle [of her room] was a bed made of wood with burned edges and covered with burned brands that she sometimes ran her fingers over in the late mornings when she awakened. . . . The bed was a kind of nest for

her. Sometimes when she was hurt, when the men hurt her, she would come back to the room and curl into the center of the bed with the blanket that had the soft, silky edge wrapped around her and take comfort there, rubbing the silk between her fingers until she slept.

Be selective with your details. Discard those that readers will automatically understand. In *Probably Nick Swansen*, Virginia Euwer Wolff carefully chooses the sensory details that are most likely to take us into the mind of a young man who is learning disabled. Here's her very successful first paragraph:

Room 19 was dressed up. It crackled with sounds, and party smells came from everywhere. Green streamers hung from the ceiling, two tables were covered with junk food, and more things were arriving every time you turned around—hot dogs, homemade brownies, three kinds of potato chips. A giant homemade poster was trying to come unhinged from its masking tape over the blackboard, and it said in huge red letters, "Yay, Shana."

Consider the details Wolff does *not* put in. Any teenager can fill in the ordinary blanks of chalk dust or desktop graffiti. Wolff uses the space to introduce a character in whose mind a room might be "dressed up," or where a poster might seem to be alive—in short, the kind of person many teenage readers might avoid in real life.

Practice

Beyond being aware of the amazing power of specific nouns and verbs and sensory details when writing for young adults, here are some ideas that may help you improve your young adult stories:

- Read the prize-winning books I've quoted here and ask your librarian about other outstanding books for young adult readers. Read them once for enjoyment and then again, paying particular attention to nouns, verbs, and sensory details.
- Write pairs of sentences using weak verbs and strong verbs.
- Write a paragraph that uses general nouns, then rewrite it using specific ones.
- Write a scene in which you incorporate every one of the five senses. Write it over and over using different sensory details each time to evoke a different emotion: joy, sadness, fear, or horror.
- Scrutinize your current writing. Evaluate each noun and verb. See

what sensory details you can add. Remember that just any verb or any detail won't do. Use artistic judgment to select ones that increase tension, evoke pictures, conjure atmosphere, and give characters their identity and sympathetic qualities.

Think of the young adult reader as your partner. Give your readers the best raw material, and they will leap into your story and stay with you to The End.

❑ 96

TEN TIPS ON WRITING PICTURE BOOKS

BY DIANE MAYR

AS A CHILDREN'S LIBRARIAN, I DO STORY HOURS FOR PRESCHOOLERS ages 3 to 5. Children this age have developed language skills, but aren't yet able to read on their own. After more than 1,500 story hours, I know what these children like. By sharing this knowledge I hope to improve the chances of my wowing young patrons with some great picture book—yours.

Tip #1: READ. When wannabe writers tell me they have written a book for children, I ask them to compare their book to something already in print. I'm usually met with a blank stare, or "I haven't read many children's books." If you haven't read what's out there, how do you know if your book is better than—or as good as—the rest? How do you know your version of "The Three Little Pigs" is different enough from the traditional one to attract a child's (or publisher's) attention? [Suggestions of titles to "study" will be shown in brackets.]

Tip #2: BE BRIEF. Good books for preschoolers run 800 words or less—sometimes considerably less. Look at the word counts of some of the "classics": *The Very Hungry Caterpillar* (Eric Carle)—225; *If You Give A Mouse A Cookie* (Laura Joffe Numeroff)—291; *The Snowy Day* (Ezra Jack Keats)—319; and *Corduroy* (Don Freeman)—708.
Don't use a lot of description, the illustrator will fill in the details. (You may, though, wish to provide notes, separate from the text, about illustrative elements crucial to your story.) A balance of dialogue and narration works best.

Tip #3: TELL A GOOD STORY. If your forte is "mood" pieces, then you're not aiming for the preschool audience. For them, something has to happen, and the story must have a beginning, a middle, and an end. The ending must not be ambiguous; predictability is expected.

Have you heard of the "rule of three"? The main character must complete three tasks, or face three foes, before winning the day. The rule has worked for generations of talespinners; try letting your heroine face the monster under the bed three times before she develops the courage to banish it. [Read: *The Wolf's Chicken Stew*, by Keiko Kasza]

Tip #4: KNOW THE PRESCHOOL PSYCHE. Preschoolers are strongly tied to their homes and family. They enjoy hearing about situations they're familiar with such as the arrival of a new baby. It's your task to develop a twist on a familiar theme, but make the twist believable. [Read: *Julius, The Baby Of The World*, by Kevin Henkes]

As adults, we have a tendency to dismiss a preschooler's fears and "problems" as inconsequential, but they're very real. They need to be addressed and dealt with reassuringly. [Read: *Rosie's Baby Tooth*, by Maryann Macdonald]

The problems adults see as significant—death, divorce, abuse, etc.— are topics for bibliotherapy; such books have a place, but are not for the general audience. Nor are 3-to 5-year-olds the audience for a picture book that tries to explain the Holocaust. Childhood is short but critical in the development of character. Preschoolers deserve to feel secure.

Animals often appear as the characters in picture books, but don't allow the talking animals in your stories to do things a child wouldn't do. For example, don't have Baby Monkey cross a busy street by herself. If you do, preschoolers will invariably ask, "Where's the Mommy?" If Baby Monkey needs to cross the street without Mom in order to advance your plot, leave it in, but don't arbitrarily dismiss a young monkey's (child's) need to depend on responsible adults. [Read: *Baby Duck And the Bad Eyeglasses*, by Amy Hest]

Tip #5: SUREFIRE PLEASERS. Preschoolers love humor! But, they're not looking for subtlety. Think pratfalls without pain. Sophisticated punning is out, but nonsense words draw a laugh. [Read: *Froggie Gets Dressed*, by Jonathan London; *Contrary Mary*, by Anita Jeram; *Tacky The Penguin*, by Helen Lester; *Mother Makes A Mistake*, by Ann Dorer]

Noises are always a hit. Preschoolers will "moo" and "quack" along with the reader—and love doing it! [Read: *Is This A House For Hermit*

Crab?, by Amy McDonald; *Peace At Last,* by Jill Murphy; *Small Green Snake,* by Libba Moore Gray]

Allow the audience to discover a "secret" before the main character does. Little kids, so frequently put down by older siblings, more advanced peers, and even by adults, appreciate the opportunity to feel "smarter" than someone else. This device is often used by puppeteers who have the audience see the villain before the lead puppet does. If you've ever heard the gleeful screams, "Look behind you! He's behind you!", then you know how successful this can be with preschoolers. [Read: any of Frank Asch's books about Bear. Two good examples: *Mooncake* and *Bread And Honey*]

Questions scattered throughout the story—for example, "Should he look under the bed?"—allow interaction between the child and the story. Kids love to interact! [Read: *The Noisy Book,* by Margaret Wise Brown]

Tip #6: PICTURES ARE ESSENTIAL. If your story makes sense without visual clues, then it is not a picture book. Text and pictures must contribute equally to telling the story. (One note of caution: Unless you are an accomplished artist/illustrator, do not attempt to illustrate your own work if you plan to submit it to a trade publisher. You need not seek out an illustrator, the illustrator will be selected by your publisher.) [Read: *King Bidgood's In The Bathtub,* by Audrey Wood, illustrated by Don Wood]

Tip #7: WATCH YOUR LANGUAGE! Preschoolers tend to take what you say literally. If I read aloud—" 'Look, it's snowing!' he cried."—without a doubt, a child will interrupt me to ask, "Why is he crying?" Use "he said" or "he shouted."

Nothing destroys the flow of a story like having to stop to explain an unfamiliar term. Use language with which today's children are comfortable. Don't use "frock" for dress or "dungarees" for jeans.

Tip #8: LEARN THE 3 "R's." Repetition, rhythm, and rhyme work well with the younger set. Traditional folktales like "The Little Red Hen" still appeal to them because of the repetition. Rhyme, unfortunately, can kill a story if it's not done well. Rather than write a story entirely in rhyme, try a few repetitive rhyming sentences. [Read: *Millions Of Cats,* by Wanda Gag; *A Cake For Barney,* by Joyce Dunbar]

Tip #9: READ ALOUD. Read your story out loud and listen. If you stumble, nine times out of ten, there's something wrong with the writing. When it finally sounds right to you, try reading it to someone else for continuity and clarity.

Tip #10: MAKE A DUMMY. Fold eight pieces of paper in half and staple at the fold. You now have a 32-page dummy. Cut and paste your words onto the pages, leaving the first three pages blank for front matter. You'll need to make decisions on length. Is the story too short? Too long? Does it flow smoothly? You may want to make notes about the pictures you envision for each page or spread. The suspense in a story could be jeopardized by raising a problem in the text on a left-hand page and having a picture on the right-hand page provide the solution. Remember, preschoolers are "reading" the illustrations as you're reading the words. It's preferable to have a page turn before providing resolutions or answers.

Bonus Tip: Make Friends with Your Children's Librarian. She can introduce you to the classic picture books, as well as to the best of what's currently being published. She'll have review journals and publishers' catalogues for you to look at, and she can double as a critical reader.

I've been waiting more than ten years for the perfect picture book to share with my story hour kids; I can wait a little longer for you to write it!

❑ 97

BRINGING HISTORY TO LIFE FOR CHILDREN

BY DEBORAH M. PRUM

DID YOU KNOW PETER THE GREAT PRACTICED DENTISTRY ON HIS SUBjects? That Botticelli means "little barrel"? Or that Ivan III's new wife was so heavy, she broke her bed the first night she stayed at the Czar's palace?

With marvelous facts like these at our disposal, there is no excuse for subjecting children to boringly written history. Of course, the primary purpose of writing history for kids is to instruct, not to entertain. However, once you lose a child's interest, you risk losing your audience. A good writer achieves a balance, presenting facts and concepts in a way that will entice a young reader to read on cheerfully and willingly.

Keep them awake with verbs

Nothing puts someone to sleep faster than the use of boring verbs. Granted, when you are writing about past events, you naturally tend to use verbs like "was, were, had been," but entangling your prose in passive constructions will slow down forward movement in your piece.

Whenever you can, use active image verbs. Consider these two sentences:

By the mid-sixteenth century, the unhappy serfs were hungry and became violent.
Starving serfs stormed the palace, destroying furnishings and attacking the royal guards.

Make them laugh

Use humor liberally in your writing. Catchy subtitles help, especially when you have to discuss subjects that ordinarily may not appeal to children. The subtitle "The Burning of the Papal Bull—*Not* a Barbecue!" will attract more interest than "Martin Luther Rebels."

When appropriate, include a cartoon. A cartoon will draw a child's eyes to a page. You can use a cartoon to poke fun with your material (i.e. a picture of Botticelli dressed in a barrel, apropos of his nickname). Or, you can use a cartoon to make a point. A cartoon depicting the disputing political parties prior to the Civil War may serve to inform your reader as effectively as a paragraph on the subject.

Highlighting an amusing fact makes children more likely to plow through less interesting information. For example, in a discussion of the Gutenberg press, you can start by mentioning that Johann Gutenberg started out life as "John Gooseflesh" (Gensfleisch). Once you have grabbed their attention, then you can go on to talk about the somewhat drier details of your topic.

Be careful when using humor. Avoid the temptation to distort fact in order to be funny.

Using sidebars

Not all factual information or lists may fit smoothly into your text, and may slow the pacing of your piece. For material that is tangential to your primary point, sidebars are a useful way to handle these problems.

A sidebar enables you to include greater detail on a topic without disrupting your narrative flow. Sidebars can give your reader an in-depth view of the period you are discussing. For a piece on the Civil War, you might include a few recipes of the dishes popular at the time. Or, if you are discussing Leonardo Da Vinci, you might include a list of all his inventions. Every once in a while, it doesn't hurt to include a nonsensical sidebar, like this one:

Places Marco Polo did *not* explore:
1. Lizard Lick, North Carolina
2. Walla Walla, Washington
3. Newark, New Jersey

When writing about history for children, you can easily get bogged down in confusing details. Good organization of your material is essential. A young child reading about the first few centuries of Russian history will be tempted to think that every last Russian of importance was named Ivan or Fedor. Of course, that's not true. But, you have to provide a way to sort through potentially confusing material. There are several ways to help your readers:

One is to show a detailed family tree at the beginning of your chapter, including dates, actions for which the person is famous, and nicknames (i.e. Ivan the Great, Ivan the Terrible, Fedor the Feebleminded).

If you must discuss many events occurring over several years, consider using a time line to show the "who, what, and when" of any era in a clear and simple way.

Another way to help a child understand some of the forces contributing to an event is to tell a story. How did a lightning storm change Martin Luther's life? Talk about the time Borgia betrayed the Duke of Urbino: Borgia borrowed, then used the Duke's own weapons to attack his city. Mention that Peter III played with lead soldiers and dolls, and ultimately lost the Russian Empire to his wife, Catherine the Great. By telling these stories, you will make your material far more interesting and you will give children a better sense of history.

Controversy

Don't shy away from controversy. Make it your ally. Use the tension controversial issues create to add excitement to your text. When possible, tell both sides of the story. Readers know that historians disagree. Help your readers form their own opinions by including direct quotes from the controversial figures, quotes of correspondence, or transcripts of debates. Give the children a chance to hear both sides and an opportunity to develop their critical thinking skills.

Not all historians agree, but you can make controversy work for you. That statement will not come as a shock to most adults, yet it does pose a problem for writers. Which side of the story do you present to young readers? Maybe the "facts" are clear (although, not always), but one historian may slant a discussion in a completely different way from another.

For example, what about Machiavelli? Was he an ogre, an opportunist with dangerous political ideas? Was he a practical political scientist who merely described reality? Does the answer lie somewhere in between? Those are good questions, debated by one and all. How should you present the topic to children?

Fascinating beginnings

You must capture your young reader's attention at the beginning of a chapter and end it in a way that will make that child want to go on to the next chapter.

Begin with an interesting fact or a question: "What does the word 'Medici' mean to you? 1) an interesting pasta dish, 2) a new foreign convertible, 3) a deadly tropical disease, or 4) none of the above."

Capture your reader's attention by opening a chapter with a scene from everyday life at the time your book takes place. (Make it clear that this event "might" have happened but don't veer from accepted fact.) For example, you could start a chapter on Thomas Jefferson by describing him playing his violin for some guests in his drawing room at Monticello.

Ending your chapter well is just as important as beginning well. You want your reader to finish your book. Make a statement that will pique the child's curiosity.

Insofar as possible, make your book a visual pleasure. If you are writing about Ben Franklin, see if you can find museum photographs of his pot-bellied stove. Look for pictures of Catherine the Great's crown or Galileo's telescope. If you are discussing a war or an explorer, include colorful maps.

When writing history for children, be certain that you know your audience. Spend some time around the age group for whom you are writing. Listen to the words they use. Pay attention to how they form their sentences. Figure out what they think is funny. Then, in your own writing, use syntax slightly more complex than what they used. Include a few unfamiliar terms, but be certain to highlight and define any new word. When you are presenting a concept that is foreign to your readers, compare it with one they already understand.

Once your material is written, test it on a child you know. Find a curmudgeonly person who is a reluctant reader. You will be sure to get some valuable comments. A grumpy child will provide a good first test for your material. Then, if you have the opportunity, read your manuscript in front of a classroom of kids. Are your words greeted with excitement and interest, or just yawns and glassy-eyed stares? If you see tired looks and drooping eyelids, enliven your prose accordingly. However, if the children want to know more, you've got a winner.

❏ 98

WHEN YOU WRITE HUMOR
FOR CHILDREN

BY JULIE ANNE PETERS

CHILDREN ARE BORN TO LAUGH. IN FACT, HUMOR IS THOUGHT TO BE the first expressive form of communication. Good writers understand the value of humor when they write for children. Not only does humor entertain and amuse them, but it lures the most reluctant reader.

When my first book, *The Stinky Sneakers Contest,* was selected by third-grade children in Greater Kansas City as their favorite book of 1995, I was delighted—and shocked. Humorous books rarely win awards. In the kingdom of exalted literature, humor is relegated to serfdom. But the award confirmed my belief that even though funny books infrequently win prestigious literary prizes, they do become children's favorites.

Writers often tell me, "I'm not a funny person. I can't write humor." Piffle! Betsy Byars, grandmistress of humorous children's books, reveals the secret. "The funniest word in the vocabulary of a second grader," she says, "is 'underwear.' " Use it liberally. "Poo poo" works for preschoolers. Or you can rise above so-called potty humor and choose one of the standard humor devices that follow.

Surprise

Writers and illustrators of picture books are guaranteed laughter or smiles by springing the unexpected on their young readers. Books are the perfect vehicle for creating humor through surprise. James Stevenson demonstrates this very effectively in his book, *Quick! Turn the Page.*

To bring about surprise, take an expected event or consequence and create the unexpected. A boy bounces a ball. He expects it to go up and come down. Page one: Ball goes up. Page two: A wild monkey in a banyan tree snatches the ball and steals off to . . . ? Next page. Surprise can delight page after page, intermittently, or just once, with a surprise ending. Read Judith Viorst's poem, "Mother Doesn't Want a Dog," for a classic example of a surprise ending.

Exaggeration

The earliest American humor used exaggeration in its purest form: larger-than-life heroes performing superhuman feats. Remember Pecos Bill, Paul Bunyan, and John Henry? The American tall tale is still a favored form of humor for children. Anne Isaac's *Swamp Angel* moves this classic genre into the 1990s with her female superheroine. Not only does Swamp Angel fend off Thundering Tarnation, the marauding bear, she has to prove herself to taunting backwoodsmen who'd have her stay at home, quilting.

Transcendental toasters, madcap Martians, and articulate animals are all examples of truth stretching. My favorite mouthy mammal is the mutt, Martha, in Susan Meddaugh's *Martha Speaks*. After Martha dog eats a bowl of alphabet soup, she becomes quite the loquacious pooch. "You people are so bossy. COME! SIT! STAY! You never say please."

Journey beyond the bounds of possibility to create exaggerated humor. How about a plucky petunia? A daring doormat? Even preschool children can differentiate between the real and unreal as they gleefully embrace the fun in make-believe.

Word and language play

With wordplay, language is key to the rhythm, sound, and rhyme that carries your story forward. Readers become reciters. Jack Prelutsky, Shel Silverstein, and Joyce Armor are wizards of wordplay in their witty poetry. Nancy Shaw's "Sheep" books are shear joy (yes, pun intended).

If you're not a poet and you know it, try your hand at literal translation. *Amelia Bedelia* books by Peggy Parish teach you how. Amelia Bedelia, the indomitable maid, takes every order, every conversation, every suggestion literally, and sets herself up for catastrophe. Children love trying to predict the consequences of Amelia's misunderstandings.

Role reversal

Eugene Trivizas chose role reversal to retell a classic fairy tale in his *The Three Little Wolves and the Big Bad Pig*. To make the most effective use of role reversal, choose familiar characters acting out of character. Turn everyday events topsy-turvy. Harry Allard uses children's perceptions about substitute teachers (whether true or not) when he changes meek, mild Miss Nelson into bleak, vile Viola Swamp. You may choose to switch family members, as Mary Rodgers did with her mother/daughter exchange in *Freaky Friday,* or people and their pets, aliens with automobiles, princes and paupers. Stay away from twins, though. It's been done and done and done.

Nonsense

Nonsense includes incongruity and absurdity, ridiculous premises, and illogical series of events. What makes a nonsense book funny is its weirdness. *Imogene's Antlers,* by David Small, is the story of a young girl who wakes up one day to find she's grown antlers. This is a problem. Imogene has trouble getting dressed; she can't fit through narrow doorways; her antlers get caught in the chandelier. Even worse, her mother keeps fainting at the sight of her. Though children recognize the absurdity of Imogene's situation, they also see how well she copes with her sudden disability. This book speaks to children's physical differences, which is a fundamental value of humor.

Literary humor helps children grow. It offers distancing from pain, from change and insecurity, from cruelty, disaster and loss. Children are not always sophisticated or mature enough emotionally to laugh at themselves. Humorous books with subtle serious themes offer children ways to deal positively with life's inequities. They offer a magic mirror, through which children's problems—and their solutions—can be reflected back.

Slapstick

Farce and horseplay have been part of the American humor scene since vaudeville—maybe before. Who knows what Neanderthals did for fun? Physical humor appeals to the child in all of us. Hectic, frenetic chases and bumbling, stumbling characters cause chaos in the pages of children's books. Your plot will immediately pick up pace if you include a frantic fiasco or two. Check out Betsy Byars' *Golly Sisters.* May-May and Rose's calamitous capers are rip-roaring fun. Avi used slapstick masterfully in his book *Romeo and Juliet Together (And Alive)*

At Last! His high schoolers' rendition of Shakespeare's masterpiece would make The Bard weep (with tears of laughter).

Satire

You can achieve humor by poking fun at human vices, human foibles or the general social order, which rarely makes sense to children, so they love to see it pulverized on paper. My favorite satirical series is "The Stupids," by Harry Allard. I swear these people lived next door to me when I was growing up. James Marshall's illustrations add hilarity to the humor.

To write effective satire for children, you must recognize the ridiculous in youngsters' lives. Make fun of uppity people's pretensions, lampoon restrictions, and spoof the silly societal mores children are expected to embrace. Create characters who teeter on the edge, who challenge the status quo—and thrive. Read Sid Fleischman's *The Whipping Boy* for a lesson in writing satire.

Adolescent angst

Family and school stories, growing up and coming-of-age novels make up the bulk of children's humorous fiction. Adolescence just seems to lend itself to humor. Laughter helps older children deal with life's larger dilemmas: death, divorce, disability, senility, loss, and unwelcome change. Reading about characters who successfully and humorously overcome obstacles provides children with painless lessons on how to handle their own problems.

For my book *B.J.'s Billion-Dollar Bet,* I started with a troublesome topic—betting. Frequently, I overhear conversations between kids who are placing bets: "Oh, sure. I bet you," or "Wanna bet? Come on, let's bet on it." And they bet away valuable items—clothing, sports card collections, lunch money. To show the consequences of betting, I created B.J. Byner, a compulsive gambler who bets and loses all of his possessions, then begins to bet away his family's belongings. When B.J. loses his mother's lottery ticket in a wager, then finds out the ticket is a fifty-million-dollar winner, he has to get that ticket back!

I hope young readers will see that the risks of gambling are considerable; the losses more than they may be willing or able to pay. Betting can result in loss of friendship, family conflict, and, as with any addiction, loss of control and self-respect. If I hadn't chosen a humorous premise for this book, it would have been too preachy.

Middle-grade and young adult novels include more urbane, cerebral humor. These young people are developing their own individual views of the world, and social relationships take on a major role.

For my middle-grade novel, *How Do You Spell Geek?*, I began with a funny, offbeat character, Lurlene Brueggemeyer, the geek, and built the story around her. The issues are serious ones—judging people by their appearance, shifting alliances between friends, peer pressure, and self-examination, but I gave my main character, Ann, a sarcastic sense of humor and a wry way of watching her world get weird, which seems to lighten the load.

Read the masters of middle-grade humor: Ellen Conford, Barbara Park, Beverly Cleary, Betsy Byars, Daniel Pinkwater, and Jerry Spinelli, among many, many others.

There are humor writers who defy classification; they relate to their audiences through rebellion, radicalism, and general outrageousness. Three young adult authors who fall into this special category are M.E. Kerr, Richard Peck, and Paul Zindel. Their books validate an emerging adult's individuality, passion, and self-expression.

If you plan to try your hand at humor, steer clear of targeting a specific age group. I've received letters from eight-year-olds who are reading my junior high novel, *Risky Friends*. And I'm sure you know high schoolers who still get a hoot out of Dr. Seuss. Even though sense of humor evolves as we grow older, we never lose appreciation for the books that made us laugh when we were younger.

Humor writing is a spontaneous act. It comes from deep within, from your own wacky way of looking at the world. One word of caution: Humor has power. What we laugh at, we make light of. What we laugh at, we legitimize and condone. Cruelty is never funny. Violence isn't funny. Torture, torment, neglect, war, hatred, and preying on others' misfortunes are not subjects for children's humor. There's a fine line between sarcasm and cynicism; between light-spirited and mean-spirited. So be aware. If you do write humor for children, observe the limits.

There's more than one way to connect with children through humor (beyond using "underwear"). In fact, with all the techniques available, and given the fact that children laugh easily, your chances of eliciting gleeful responses are excellent.

❑ EDITING, MARKETING,
AND AGENTS

❏ 99

The Author/Editor Connection

By Eve Bunting

At a writers' conference once, I heard an author state: "Make no mistake. The writer and the editor are enemies. He's always on the side of the publisher and not on yours." I was astonished and appalled. This has never been my experience. Never.

As a children's book writer who "publishes around," I have several editors, male and female, young and older. Since I don't work through an agent, my contacts are directly author to editor. I have always been treated fairly and have always had the assurance that we are a team, striving for the best possible book.

This is not to say there have not been disagreements. Of course there have. But with compromise on both sides we have always been able to work a problem out.

To establish and keep a good relationship, there are some things the author should bear in mind.

1) Be prepared to listen when your editor suggests changes. Yes, the book is yours. Yes, every word is as perfect as you have been able to make it. But the editor has had a lot of experience, knows what works and what doesn't, and is as anxious as you are for a quality book. **But**, be prepared to take a stand if you feel you are right. Present your case. Be factual. Be reasonable. Chances are she (I'm using the generic "she" because I have more female editors than male) will come around to your thinking. Be gracious if you are proven wrong. The best editors during discussion will be careful to ask: "Do you agree?" and will often say: "Of course, you have the last word." That may not be exactly true, but it leaves room for further discussion.

2) Try to realize that your editor is a person who works hard. Do not burden her with unnecessary questions and complaints. Yes, you want to know how your book is coming along. It's O.K. to ask. But not every

495

week. When it's finally published, you want to know how it is selling. Call the royalty department. Yes, you are upset that you can't find a copy in your local bookstore. Call the sales department and ask if they know why.

You don't think your work has been promoted with enough enthusiasm? (A lot of us feel that way. I was going to say *most* of us, but perhaps many authors are totally satisfied. I don't know any of them!) Talk to the Promotions Department to suggest what they might do, as well as what you are willing to do: bookstore signings, school visits, visits to your local library. Perhaps it can be a joint project between you and the publisher.

3) If you submit a new manuscript to your editor, try not to be irate if she doesn't get back to you right away. Understand that she has a workload that allows only a small percentage of her time to be spent reading manuscripts—even yours. She has meetings coming out of her ears!

4) If your editor tells you that your book will not be published this year, and possibly not until the following fall, or the spring after that, bite the bullet. Publishers' lists fill up, and you have to realize that you are going to have your book scheduled where (a), there is a slot for it, or (b), where the publisher feels it will sell best. There's no point in ranting and raving in your very understandable impatience. Your editor will bless you for not being difficult.

5) When you are asked to make corrections on a manuscript or galleys, do them promptly. The editor is making deadlines herself. Being on time can determine whether or not your book makes that list where it's slotted. If your manuscript is not ready, another book may replace yours.

6) Be absolutely certain of your facts. An error in a nonfiction book is unforgivable, and it is equally unforgivable in fiction. A reader or reviewer is going to pick up on it. Children's books are particularly open to scrutiny. The embarrassment of an error falls on the editor and copy editor, but yours is the primary accountability. A mistake will not endear you to anyone. In my very first middle-grade novel, I made an

incredible blunder: I put the Statue of Liberty in New York Harbor a year before it was actually there! Horrors! No one caught it, except an astute librarian who challenged me on it while I stood at a podium, talking about the book. Double horrors! I will never forget that moment nor the lesson I learned. Since I was a fairly recent immigrant from Ireland, I managed to exclaim, "Oh! Forgive me! I thought that wonderful statue was always there, welcoming the tired and the poor as she welcomed me." That got applause instead of boos! It was corrected in the next printing.

7) For picture book writers who are not fortunate enough to be able to illustrate their books, the key words are "be reasonable." Of course, we want the very best artists in the country—in the world—to illustrate our books. Surely, this is not too much to ask! You pine for Trina Schart Hyman. You know she'd do an exquisite job. You lust after Barbara Cooney. Her style would be just perfect for your book. And how about Chris Van Allsburg? But if you are reasonable, you will know that every picture book author wants those illustrators and others equally wonderful, equally famous. The reality is that we are probably not going to get any one of them. It is all right to ask, but don't be aggrieved or petulant if it doesn't happen. Usually the artist is chosen by the editor in consultation with the art department and after much perusal of sample art and already published picture books. They are usually very good at choosing just the right artist. Perhaps they come up with a "first time" artist, and your first reaction is likely to be, "Oh, no! Not for *my* book!" But all wonderful illustrators start somewhere. I personally have discovered the thrill of having newish, relatively unknown artists turn out to be smash hits and lift my books beyond the ordinary to the extraordinary. I thank them. And I thank my editors. They know I trust them.

8) Try to accept the fact that you are not your editor's only author. She is juggling four, six, eight other writers and illustrators, too. She can't give you her undivided attention. You may think another author is getting more than her fair share of attention. That may be true. But that author may have paid her dues in many years of good books. One of her books may have made a million dollars for the company. It may have earned a lot of money and prestige-making awards. It's been said that 20% of a publisher's list supports the other 80%. Another author's

book and the attention it gets may be making it possible for your book to get published.

9) If, by unfortunate chance, your editor has to turn down your next manuscript, take a deep breath and swallow your disappointment. When she says she's sorry, she probably is. An editor does not easily reject a book, especially if she has worked with the author before. It is easier to be the bearer of pleasant news. Your editor may have fought for your book with a publishing committee and lost. Say, "I'm sorry, too. Can you give me any idea why you decided against it?" Listen to what she says. You may want to make changes before you submit it elsewhere. And remember, you may want to try her with another manuscript in the future, so keep that relationship cordial.

10) Remember that your editor is human. Show appreciation for her efforts in making your book the thing of beauty that it is. Flowers, candy, or other gifts are unnecessary. A simple thank-you note is sufficient.

Ten points about how to keep that author/editor relationship warm and cordial. A word or two about the editor/author relationship. What should an author expect to get from her editor?

- As quick a reading of a new manuscript as possible.
- As quick a response as possible.
- Enthusiasm.
- Open-mindedness.
- Support of the book with the sales and publicity departments.
- Attentiveness to your misgivings, if any.
- A commitment to keep in touch. Not to hear what is happening to your book is horrible, and since you would be out of line to bug her, she should be courteous and keep you informed.
- Praise. Insecure as we are, we need a certain amount of TLC.
- The assurance that author and editor are in this together. It's *your* book.
- To be a person of her word. If she says she'll call, write, see you, then you have the right to assume she is dependable, as you are.

So . . . we have a good author/editor relationship, and a good book. Working together, with consideration for one another, we've done it!

❏ 100

QUERY LETTERS THAT WORK

BY HOWARD SCOTT

HAVE YOU EVER WONDERED WHY YOUR QUERIES AREN'T HITTING? ARE rejection letters piling up? Does it seem that breaking into a new publication is an impossible dream? Do you suspect that certain editors spot your name on the envelope and slip a rejection notice in your SASE without even reading the proposal? If so, read on.

The biggest problem with queries is that they do not have an arresting slant. A slant isn't the subject; it's the author's particular take on the subject, the central thread that ties the story together. The trick is to come up with a slant that presents the subject in a fresh light and hooks the reader into finishing the whole article.

For example, the subject of quilt-making has no intrinsic allure or excitement unless you come up with a slant and make sure the slant connects to the readers. A query on how the computer has aided quilt makers would be an appropriate slant for a computer magazine. Why quilt-making is a good hobby for senior citizens would be an appropriate slant for a seniors magazine. How new dyes have changed quilt-making design would work for an arts/hobby periodical. Each of these proposed slants has an inherent story, and suggests that an answer or solution exists. Moreover, each slant narrows the subject to suggest a particular audience.

I recently wrote an article for *Nation's Business* on raising prices. My query letter did not read, "Are you interested in seeing an article about raising prices?" Instead, I wrote: "I will focus on how to incur minimum customer resistance to raising prices." Do you see the difference between the two approaches? The first proposal is a subject query. The second proposal is a slant in which I set up an investigatory path, which sets up an expectation, namely, how to achieve minimal customer dissatisfaction, and therefore lose the fewest number of customers to competition.

499

Consider the harried editor for a moment. He or she receives dozens of proposals every day/week/month. She chooses those few proposals that excite her. It's not a science, and very often, her choice depends on something that stops her. Yes, experience and clips count, but if you excite the editor with a "wow, I never thought of that!" slant, your chances are good for a go-ahead on spec.

To create a strong slant, ask yourself these six questions and answer them affirmatively before you write the query:

1. Does my slant presuppose a question? In the quilting examples, the editor is left with a question. Why is quilt-making a good hobby for senior citizens? How do computers change quilt-making? How do dyes affect quilt patterns? The question makes the editor curious enough to assign the article.

I queried the editor of *The Rotarian* about house-swapping (vacationing by exchanging houses, cars, and information), promising that I would provide a formula to determine who is best suited to house-swapping and who should never consider the idea. The editor was intrigued with the formula aspect and asked me to spell that part out. If I had just suggested a story about house-swapping, a *subject* query, she might not have given me the go-ahead. My query made her wonder just what type of person swaps homes. The piece was accepted for publication.

2. Does my slant hint at a useful answer? This is a close cousin to the first question, but there is an important distinction. The good slant asks a question that can be answered. *The Rotarian* editor above felt that the question would deliver a prescriptive answer, which readers could put to immediate use. So make sure that your question has an answer that will be useful to the reader.

My query to *Family Life* proposing an article on why ferrets are better pets than rabbits, guinea pigs, mice, or gerbils told the editor that she could expect some factual reasoning on the preferable pet, and that the reader would be able to make an informed decision based on my answers. This was so much better than a query on ferrets as pets, which, in the mind of the editor, wouldn't supply answers.

3. Does the slant sufficiently narrow the topic? You don't want to cover too broad a topic. The reader doesn't learn much, nor is the writer challenged to get down to the essence of the subject. In a more narrowly conceived focus, you must dig beneath the surface for underlying reasons, for explanations, and for the story behind the story.

4. Does the slant offer an unusual perspective? This is a hard one, because you probably haven't read the last several years' issues of that magazine, which would tell you if the approach is unique. The subject matter doesn't have to be unique, but the particular slant should not have been used before. If you have not come across your particular focus in any publication, if you think it's an interesting approach to the subject, if the slant interests you, then the idea is probably a fresh one.

I decided to write an article for *Sky Magazine*, the Delta Airlines in-flight publication, about the Massachusetts Institute of Technology (MIT) Enterprise Forum. The Forum is a monthly get-together of venture capitalists, consultants, and other interested parties that analyze a company, often with the intention of funding the firm. I knew a query on the Enterprise Forum as a profile would not work because *Sky's* articles focus on trends. So I came up with the slant of unusual ways to raise money, calling it "adventure capital." I used the MIT Enterprise Forum as one method; for other examples I found a playwright who raised money by hosting a pre-performance party; and a small business that borrowed equipment from its suppliers to start up. I wove all three examples into the article, drawing from my slant to title the piece "Adventure Capital."

5. Can you state the slant in a single sentence? This exercise shows that you have a bona fide concept. If you can't do so, it means that you don't really have an idea, or that it's too broad in scope, or it is not well-formulated. If you have to explain your slant in long-winded prose, you probably can't communicate it clearly to the reader.

In the proposal for my article "How to Get Kids Interested in Bees," which appeared in *Bee Culture,* my slant was that kids are naturally interested in insects, thus their curiosity would be piqued by a discussion of the hard science part—bee colonization, bee leadership, flower pollination, etc. My query stated, "Since children are natural insect fans, it's easy to imagine them getting excited about bees," and I proposed to offer several bridge-creating strategies. "How to Get Kids Interested in Bees" appeared in *Bee Culture*'s June, 1999 issue.

6. Can you restate the slant into a catchy article title? This exercise tests whether your idea is as concise and as interesting as you think. By creating a catchy title, you can see how your idea stands up, compared to the other articles in the table of contents. Remember, some readers scan the contents page first to see if they want to read an article, and

dismiss those that don't interest them. Finally, a working title, or handle, helps the editor keep the piece in his mind.

I always thought one reason the *Providence Journal Sunday Magazine* editor gave me a spec go-ahead on an article about being a life-drawing model was my proposed title, "The Naked Truth." In fact, when he published the piece, he didn't change my title, which is rare; I imagine that when he received my query, he was captivated by the double entendre aspect of the title.

One final note: No matter how good your queries are, don't expect a 100% response. Last fall, I sent out 46 queries to 46 trade magazines. The queries were about the tax changes in 1999, so all the magazines could use this information. With each query, I included a previously published tax clip and SASE. Eighteen publications, or 39%, responded. Five, or 11%, gave me an assignment. Those five assignments led to five published pieces. The moral is—writing is still a numbers game.

□ 101

WHAT DO AGENTS WANT?

BY NANCY LOVE

AGENTS SAY THEY WANT NEW WRITERS, BUT WHEN YOU SEND A QUERY or a proposal, they fire back, "No thanks!" What are you to make of this mixed message? Aside from those agents who really do not welcome new clients, the rest of us need a continuous supply of fresh offerings to submit to publishers, but since we are in the publishing business to sell books, we are constantly trying to select those we think publishers want. The question we ask is: *What do publishers want?*

Death by mid-list

The conventional wisdom these days is, *Publishers do not want mid-list books.* The term "mid-list" refers to the place a book has in a publishing house catalogue. It is a book that is not "front-list" (books listed in the first few pages of the catalogue and declared thereby best-seller material), and it is not "back-list" (perennials listed in the back of the catalogue and kept in print season after season). Translation: Only best sellers need apply. That leaves high and dry the nice, little literary or commercial novel with no break-out potential. And what about first novels?

The reality is, mid-list and first novels *do* get published, often by smaller publishing houses, many of which have fine reputations for discriminating taste, and then the authors are poached by the mainstream houses that didn't have the guts to take a chance themselves. Or they are championed by stubborn editors at the larger houses who want to nurture a talented writer or who have enough clout to bulldoze through the disapproval of sales and marketing departments.

Another reality is that it is often easier to get a first novel accepted than a second if the first one bombed. Enter the Dread Sales Record. Once you have a sales history documented in bookstore computers everywhere, it will follow you around for the rest of your publishing

503

life, and can be amended only by subsequent successes that balance out the failures, or by changing your name.

One of the dirty little secrets of agentry is that many agents will avoid novels with either of the above potential problems (i.e., a mid-list book or a second book that follows a wipe-out first book), but might be less than candid about sharing these reasons for rejection.

Appetite for nonfiction

Sure, publishers want front-list nonfiction titles, too, but are more welcoming to a mid-list book that has a potential of being back-listed. Most fiction is here today, gone tomorrow, but a nonfiction title that yields even modest, but steady, revenue may be kept around for a number of years. Many publishers will take on a "small" book they believe will not only earn out, but will generate income in the long run.

But before you rejoice prematurely, remember that today publishers have an insatiable appetite for credentials attached to nonfiction books. Backing by an authority or institution is important, and for some books, essential. A health book needs a genuine medical (doctor, hospital, or health organization) imprimatur, foreword, or co-authorship. A cookbook needs a food establishment tie-in (restaurateur, chef, or TV or print food personality. For large publishers, credentials are a must for an offer of even a minimal advance on a nonfiction book. To really hit pay dirt, you might need more than credentials; it will also help if you have a "platform"—a following or a guaranteed promise of advance sales. In this scenario, the author is not just a gardening authority, but she can also attach the name of the Garden Clubs of America to her book and a promise that the organization will offer it as a premium to their members.

The agent connection: Do you even want one?

If you write short fiction or articles, academic or textbooks, or poetry, you don't need or want an agent. Often, writers of literary fiction also do better on their own when approaching smaller publishers or college presses that agents may not deal with because of slow response time and low or non-existent advances.

I know writers of both fiction and nonfiction who—initially, anyhow—like to represent themselves and do well at it. But be prepared to spend a lot of downtime with the nitty-gritty of that process. You might also come out ahead if you have connections and are more comfortable being in control.

Getting in the agent's door

What makes the difference?

Agents often specialize. First, research your target. Find out if you are in the right place before you waste your stamp and everyone's time. Use listings in authors' source books. Scan books that are similar to yours for an acknowledgment of an agent. Use the name of the workshop leader or fellow writer who referred you. Go to writers' conferences where you might meet appropriate agents. Collect their cards and use the connection when you are querying.

Winning queries and proposals

There are whole books devoted to this subject, so I will stress just a few points:

- Queries need to be positive, succinct, yet contain the facts about who you are and what the book is about. A query is like a short story in which every word has to count. A novel can ramble a bit, but short stories and queries don't have that luxury.
- There is no excuse for bad spelling or grammar. If you and your computer can't be counted on to proofread, ask a friend to read your work.
- Proposals and summaries of novels can be more expansive, but they also should be professionally crafted. Your writing ability and skills are being judged in everything you submit.
- There is nothing in a nonfiction proposal more important than a marketing plan. Make suggestions for how the publisher can promote the book, and even more essential, tell the publisher how you can help. Do you have media contacts? Are you an experienced speaker? Do you have lists of newsletters in your field that might review or write about the book? Do you lecture at meetings where the book can be sold or flyers can be distributed? Do you have a web site or belong to an organization that does and will promote your book? You get the idea.

Authors frequently respond to a request for this information by saying, "I write the book. That's my job. Selling the book is the job of the publisher." Unfortunately, while that might have been true at one time, it is no longer. Even when large advances are involved, I have discovered that publishers need and expect input from authors, and their cooperation and willingness to pitch in with ideas and commitment.

As an agent, I have to be sensitive to that point of view, so I find myself making decisions on whether or not to take on an author based not only on what she has to say and how well she says it, but on her credentials, her visibility, and on her ability to promote and become involved in publicity. Also, if you are able to put aside some of your advance to pay for publicity and perhaps a publicist, be sure to let the agent know this.

A marketing plan is not usually expected from a novelist, but it is a pleasant and welcome surprise if one is forthcoming. Fiction is promoted, too, by in-store placement, author appearances, book jacket blurbs. Sales of mysteries are helped by authors who are active in such organizations as the Mystery Writers of America (regional branches), Sisters in Crime, and other mystery writer organzations that support their members and boost their visibility. All novelists can start a minor groundswell by making themselves known at local bookstores, by placing items in neighborhood newspapers, and by using other local media. Some writers have reached out to store buyers with mailings of postcards, bookmarks or reading copies. Signal your readiness to participate, and make known what contacts you have, when you are approaching an agent.

Start out by writing the big, the bold, the grabber novel every agent is going to want. This works only if an author feels that option is viable. I strongly believe a writer has to have a passion for the book she is writing, whether it is fiction or nonfiction, or it probably isn't going to work.

Till death do us part

You've succeeded in attracting an agent; now what? I would advise waiting until an agent indicates an interest before plunging in with such nuts-and-bolts questions as, What is your commission? Which other writers do you represent? Do you use a contract?

I'm in favor of author-agent contracts, because they spell out the understanding and obligations of the two parties, not the least of which is how either one can end the relationship. Basically, unless an agent commits a serious breach, she is on the contract with the publisher for the life of the contract. There should be, however, an agreed-upon procedure for dissolving the author-agent contract.

After all, the author-agent relationship is the business equivalent of a marriage. Attracting the partner is just the beginning.

❑ 102

GETTING A SCREENPLAY AGENT

BY BONNIE SANDERS AND ALAN A. ROSS

LAWYER JOKES RANK NUMBER ONE. GAGS ABOUT AGENTS RUN A CLOSE second. The saying goes that the amount of sincerity in Hollywood could fit into a flea's navel, with enough room left over for an agent's heart.

Although literary agents are not all heartless, here are six reasons they don't want your script.

(1) Most literary agents are closed agencies

This means unsolicited manuscripts are not accepted. Many new writers, unaware of this, spend time and money to mail their scripts off to agents only to be disappointed when those scripts are either returned unopened or never returned at all. And don't expect agents to return phone calls regarding your material.

There are several reasons most agencies are closed. For one, they already have a cadre of writers under contract, and selling their material and procuring writing spots and projects for them is a full-time job. It is easy to understand why they prefer to concentrate on writers they know rather than writers they don't.

And who can blame them? Sadly, many new writers don't write up to basic industry standards. The wail heard from agents time and again is how can "writers" expect to sell their scripts if they haven't even learned the correct screenplay format, or at the very least, taken the time to check the spelling? Quite frankly, they just aren't willing to let their paid readers take the time to cull the good from the bad.

Despite the fact that these agents just might miss out on the next hit movie, they prefer to play it safe. In Hollywood you are only as good as "what you did last." Established agents are not willing to risk their reputations with studios by pitching stories from unknowns.

These closed agencies also pay their readers a fee of at least $50

508

dollars per script to provide "coverage," consisting of a brief description of the story, a checklist on character development, plot, style, and dialogue, and a grid that rates the entire piece from poor to excellent. Each script receives either a pass (in this business the same as fail) or a "consider" or "recommend." Scripts good enough to warrant one of the latter two evaluations are afforded the very rare O.K. to be "kicked upstairs," because the first reader thinks the script is worthy of a second read.

(2) Most "open" agents who do accept unsolicited material require a one-page query

Writing a good query letter is an art unto itself. Some of you may have already learned that writing short is more difficult than writing long, yet that is what agents want. To prove this point, here is just a smattering of what agents said when queried by *The Hollywood Scriptwriter*, a long-running periodical for writers:

CHARLOTTE GUSAY LITERARY AGENCY states, "One-page query letter/synopsis is best."

EARTH TRACKS ARTISTS AGENCY is open to new writers, but will not accept, read, or return unsolicited scripts. Instead, a query letter with **short** synopsis is required.

HOHMAN/MAYBANK/LIEB AGENCY says, "This group is not currently considering unsolicited material. However, if you can write a brief, effective query letter about your feature-length script, it will be read."

B. R. FLEURY AGENCY requires a query letter prior to submitting a complete script (upon request). "We have strict guidelines, and writers may ask for them. Work will not be read if guidelines are ignored."

SANDRA WATT & ASSOCIATES say, "Send a query letter and synopsis, but keep your synopsis to **under** half a page."

LYNN PLESHETTE AGENCY is interested only in features or TV movies. A query letter is the best way to start, and SASE must accompany it or there will be no chance of response.

So, the message from these agents, and many others not included here is clear. Query letter! Query letter! Query letter!

It is a tough assignment to introduce yourself in a query, and to impart in one page the synopsis, the essence of your characters, and the heart of your story. Agents want to be enticed, especially since they receive as many as fifteen of these letters a day, and they just don't have the time to read them all.

But, let us assume your query does get read, does entice, and your one-pager brings a positive reply: The agent asks to see the entire script. Having broken through the first hurdle, it is with barely confinable excitement that you mail off your manuscript, only to be thwarted by the next barrier: getting your script read by someone who really knows how to read scripts.

Because many of these open agencies are just starting out—which is of course the reason they will accept unsolicited material in the first place—they can't afford to employ readers at $50 dollars plus per script. Consequently they often use temps or secretaries, some of whom know very little about screenwriting.

(3) Open agents not requiring queries get deluged

Imagine a small agency that wants to encourage unknown writers and deems itself as open. It isn't reaching too much to picture a mail carrier making multiple trips into the office to deliver half a ton of manuscripts. Do the math. The average 120-page script weighs almost one and a half pounds. Multiply that by 500, and that half-ton isn't much of an exaggeration. One agent we know tried being a totally open agency and he received at least 500 scripts every month. Visualize the space that much material takes up. Right now, in our office, we are staring at eighty-six scripts that fill two shelves 40″ x 12″.

Many of these less established agents have offices that could be described as glorified closets stuffed with an avalanche of scripts. And who will read this mound of material? Unpaid readers. In this business *you get what you pay for*. In most instances unpaid readers do not have the necessary sense of obligation to the job. What job? They squeeze script reading into their spare time.

Are these readers qualified?

Sometimes yes. Sometimes no.

Why do they do it? Most of them are writers, and they read to learn. This is an important, smart, and valid thing to do. There is always something valuable to be gained from reading scripts, both good and bad;

perhaps an exciting style, a new way with words, or how not to write a script. An agent's biggest carrot is that if an unpaid reader finds that next blockbuster, he or she will be entitled to a small percentage of the sale. But, as good as this is, unpaid workers just cannot always find the time to give it their all.

Other unpaid readers for open agencies are interns who hope to get jobs as paid readers or story editors one day. Most are young and have never taken a course in screenwriting, or have never written a script. And unless they have taken a course on how to do coverage, they really can't do an adequate job of giving a script this type of evaluation.

The result of too many manuscripts and too few qualified readers means that your chances of hearing anything about your script soon (if at all) is remote. It is sad but true; with scripts being scattered about to various readers, it isn't uncommon for some of them to get lost along the way.

(4) The legal issue

Accepting unsolicited screenplays from unknown writers is a risky proposition for agents. In fact, even accepting unsolicited treatments is chancy, because we live in an increasingly litigious society. Plagiarism lawsuits are becoming more and more common, and fear of being sued abounds in the industry.

Because many scripts have similar themes, it is more than possible for a movie to get made with a plot almost identical to that of another script still making the rounds. If that floating script had made its way to some of the same production houses as the other, it is easy to see how the number-two writer could feel his or her idea had been stolen. *Voilà*, lawsuit.

Whether coincidental or nefarious, lawsuits are expensive and time-consuming to defend. It is much easier to refuse to read unrepresented material. That is why you must register your screenplay either with the U.S. Copyright Office or with the Writers Guild of America (addresses on next page), and why agents and production houses demand that un-agented writers sign release forms protecting both agents and writers.

U.S. Copyright Office
Library of Congress
101 Independence Ave. S.E.
Washington, DC 20559
(202) 707-3000
Web site: www.loc.gov/copyright/

Writers Guild of America, West, Inc.
7000 West Third St.
Los Angeles, CA 90048
(323) 782-4500
Web site: www.wga.org

(5) Writers Guild signatory agents may not charge reading fees

All of the agents we have discussed so far are Writers Guild signatory agents, meaning that they may not charge reading fees. In actuality it might make more sense and probably work out better for fledgling screenwriters if agents were allowed to charge a reading fee. That way, most new screenwriters would at least get the opportunity to be read by an agent or by one of his or her paid readers. As it is, agents don't want to lay out money for uncertain sources of revenue.

It is the stance of the Writers Guild that the 10% commission agents receive for each sale as well as that same percentage made on their clients' residuals is adequate. The Guild publishes a list of agents who have signed a contract that categorically states they will not charge a reading fee or refer writers to evaluators who do, either. The fear is that unscrupulous people may set up shop as screen doctors and screenplay evaluators. Often unqualified, these supposed experts are unable to offer real help to novice screenwriters, but they are more than able to take their money.

(6) Many agents are specialists

What this means is that an already very narrow field becomes even narrower. *The Hollywood Scriptwriter* did a survey on what kinds of screenplays agents were looking for. Here are a few partial responses:

BERG AGENCY is interested in children's programming as well as dramas and comedies.

STEWART TALENT MANAGEMENT: "Comedy features are the only projects of interest here."

THE KAPLAN-STAHLER AGENCY: "We represent only writers of half-hour and hour television series. No features. No TV movies. No pilots by uncredited writers."

LEGACIES: "Query on feature-length or TV movies, dramas only."

There you have it—the facts; the odds you are bucking. There are more than 500 Writers Guild of America agencies, over 180 in California alone. Fewer than 10 percent will accept unsolicited screenplays, and most require a query letter first.

Whether it is a query letter or a script you manage to send to one of these rare "open agencies," the turnaround you can expect is typically three to six months. Of course, there are exceptions. A single quarter in a slot machine has been known to yield a small fortune, and on rare occasions unknown writers do get agents, but the odds against that are high.

It isn't that agents, as in the joke, "lack sincerity." It is just that they are in business and need to do what is most cost effective.

And getting exceptional screenplays into the hands of producers is not difficult. The keyword is exceptional.

❑ 103

Killing Off Characters . . . and Other Editorial Whims

By Louise Munro Foley

EDITORIAL COMMENTS ARE SELDOM GREETED WITH ENTHUSIASM BY writers, but most writers drag themselves—however ungraciously—back to the keyboard to make the changes requested by the editors. Over the years I have often gnashed my teeth as I capitulated to editors' suggestions, but found that in most cases the points they made were valid. Furthermore, the editors' advice aided me on future books as well, helping me to identify recurring pitfalls of my own making—sort of a signal to keep me from repeating errors over and over again.

Did I learn from my mistakes? Yes, indeed.

My first mistake was selling the first book I ever wrote. After dropping over half a dozen transoms and being promptly being shipped back to me, it finally sold to Random House. That was the good news. The bad news was my attitude. This is a snap, right? Knock out a book, persevere in sending it out, and you'll eventually get a check in the mail. Not quite. My next three book manuscripts and their numerous form rejection slips still reside in my filing cabinet, silent reminders against getting too cocky.

Lesson 1: Respect the craft and the competition.

I learned something else from that first book: The letter I received from Random House expressing their interest led off with a mysterious line. "Several of us have enjoyed reading this chapter. When may we see the rest of the book?"

Well! Obviously there was a difference of opinion here about what age group I was writing for. I was thinking in terms of a picture book, but the vocabulary I had used prompted the editor to see it as a book for older readers. I did what any anxious writer would do: Using the same characters, I sat down and wrote more "books" (to me), "chapters" (to them), and sent them off.

Lesson 2: Know the age level you're writing for.

O.K. I was learning to follow the rules, and one piece of advice we've all heard repeatedly is *write what you know.* I could do that. With two sports-playing sons, I set out to cash in on those hot-dusty—cold-rainy (take your seasonal pick) hours I had spent on bleachers in local parks. I wrote a picture book about baseball. This time, I had the language level right, but the opening was all wrong. Delacorte expressed an interest. An editor called me, saying, "Your story starts out on page eleven." The first ten pages were cut before *Somebody Stole Second* was published, with my page eleven as page one.

I still tend to go through a narrative "warming-up" process when I start a new book, but a sign on my office wall—"Your story starts on page 11"—reminds me to do some heavy editing before sending out a manuscript.

Lesson 3: Introduce the protagonist and the problem quickly.

If you think that losing ten pages is bad, listen up. Figuring that I was on a sports roll, I turned my attention to football. (*Tackle 22*, Delacorte) This time the editor didn't stop at cutting pages. "You don't need this many kids," he groused. "Young readers will get confused." He killed off characters. Three of them. And had the survivors deliver the dialogue of my three excised players. In retrospect, I felt he was right.

Lesson 4: Don't overpopulate your book.

My next editorial lesson came when an editor I had previously worked with invited me to write a story about sibling rivalry. Would I give it a try? Would I?! Piece of cake! As the middle daughter in a family of three girls, I knew everything there was to know about sibling rivalry.

I wrote the book. Five-year-old Sammy finds restrictions are imposed on his lifestyle after the arrival of his baby sister: He doesn't go to the park as often; he has to curtail noisy activities during her naps; he gets less attention from neighbors and family.

But even with a relatively satisfying ending—after he came to grips with the changes—the book was a hard sell. Although the idea had been suggested by the editor, the folks at Western Publishing sensed there was something wrong with my manuscript. Several editors had a go at it, and the rewrites were drudgery. Finally, the correct diagnosis was made: The problem was with the flashbacks. In making comparisons, Sammy would think back to what it was like before baby sister's arrival. And picture-book kids don't handle flashbacks very well.

I solved the problem by introducing Grandma and a friend who could talk (in the present) with Sammy, about how it used to be, thus eliminating the flashbacks.

Lesson 5: Avoid flashbacks in books for readers eight years old or younger.

Then there was was my "now you see it, now you don't" picture book—the vanishing act of my repertoire. By the time the editor got through writing her "suggestions," my locale was changed from rural to suburban; neighbors became family friends; a brother was now a neighbor; and a number of plot elements were dumped and replaced. The editor's letter ran over half as long as the book; I shelved my manuscript and wrote *her* book.

A cop-out? No, for this compelling reason. The editor had a slot in a series for the book she outlined, and I wanted to make the sale.

She hadn't asked me to write something to which I was philosophically or ethically opposed; "her" book wasn't better or worse than mine, it was just different.

Lesson 6: If you get an assignment, write it to spec.

Should we, as writers, always be compliant? Should we just roll over and play dead when editorial fingers snap? No, of course not. But be aware that putting up a fight doesn't always assure a win. Here's my horror story.

After teaching a class for six years on "Writing and Selling Non-Sexist Books for Children" at the university and community college level, I considered that I knew the language and nuances of sexism that creep into books for kids, sending subtle but lasting skewed messages. And I conscientiously kept them out of my work . . . unless I deliberately wanted them there for a good reason.

Such was the case with *Ghost Train* (Bantam), in which one of my male characters uttered a sentence that upset the editor (the third one to work on the book, thanks to the transient nature of publishing people).

The storyline goes like this: In a desperate attempt to salvage some of the peach crop when a trucker's strike halts shipping in the Okanagan Valley, my character suggests they have a Peach Festival to lure tourists.

Harry, the orchard owner, excited about the idea, says: "I'll get some of my lady friends to bake pies. . . ."

"No," says the editor. "Delete 'lady.' It's sexist."

"Wait a minute," I argued. "Harry's fifty years old. A bachelor. A farmer. He doesn't know any *men* who bake pies. It's perfectly logical for him to say 'lady friends.' This is the way he would normally talk. It has to do with the integrity of his character."

I lost. In the published book, the editor has Harry saying that his housekeeper can get some of her friends together to bake pies . . . a statement that has its own sexist connotation.

Lesson 7: Fight to keep your character's dialogue in sync with his or her personality, and don't willingly sacrifice a persona in order to suit the editor.

The most puzzling piece of advice I've ever had from an editor came when I was working on book four in *The Vampire Cat Series* (TOR) for middle-aged readers.

In my outline, I had the villainous vampire come down with chicken pox, transmitted by the little brother of the girl protagonist.

"I don't think so," said the editor.

"Why not?" I asked.

"It's not realistic," she replied.

"Oh. Realistic," I repeated.

I hung up the phone, promising to give it some thought.

In a series that featured a talking cat, a host of vampires, and a feline underground spy network, her response called for some intense deliberation on my part. I'm still working on it.

Lesson 8: Don't ever lose your sense of humor.

❏ 104

CONFESSIONS OF A CONTEST JUDGE

BY BEVERLY LAUDERDALE

AS A WRITER PRIVILEGED TO ACT AS A CONTEST JUDGE (MOST RE-cently in a national first-chapter-of-a-novel category), I find my "almost" stack is always high. Many submissions in that pile will switch to the "keep" pile when their authors do some of the following:

Begin with the right character

If a single narrator tells the story—and in most contest entries that's the case—then the central character must appear early so readers know for whom to cheer (or occasionally hiss).

Entry 1: Taxi driver Ben dominates pages one to ten and immediately charms me. I worry about his financial concerns, share his eagerness to get home to his family, appreciate quips exchanged with his last fare. However, when Ben drops this customer at a cruise ship, Ben vanishes.

His sole purpose has been to drive the main character to the destination point for her adventure. I feel cheated and sorry because Ben will have to be omitted if the writer wishes to sell the story.

Entry 2: A driver and his wife disagree for five pages until Driver, enraged by the escalating argument, runs off the road into a river. Only then does the writer reveal that their child Mark is in the back seat. He swims to safety and, as the synopsis attached to the entry explains, grows to troubled adulthood.

Since this is Mark's story, he should be on stage first. Have him listen to his parents, and react before, during, and after impact. Because this is a crucial scene, the basis for everything that occurs in Mark's life, he must be immediately involved.

Entry 3: Jacob paces his apartment. Because of the skillful writing, I see and smell Jacob's fear, as I gradually learn that he and his girlfriend Lisa have stumbled upon secret papers. Lisa phones and whispers that someone is after her. Gunshots are heard, and suddenly Lisa stops talking, but since she's played a small part I'm not so shaken at her death as convinced of Jacob's peril. "Run, Jacob," I silently urge. As he hurries out the door, an assailant blasts him with a shotgun.

While some may believe that the death of a likable character will make readers more desperately desire the murderer's capture, there are more honest ways to engage readers. Furthermore, in the first few chapters of the book, readers expect to identify with the character in whom they'll invest their emotions. It's the writer's job to create a protagonist who leaves an impression—who when not in the forefront, still remains on readers' minds.

Weeks later, I still feel disappointed and tricked with Jacob's death. I'd falsely assumed that this was Jacob's story. An old but valid question to ask is, "Whose story is this, and who's the most effective person to tell it?"

Maintain a single viewpoint

A single viewpoint allows readers to identify with the character; to experience what she does. Alas, that's also a pitfall, for readers, too, wear the character's blinders. We accept that the author's in control and knows more than we do, but the writer should never directly show that he can't extend the character's field of vision.

Entry 1: "I" (nameless in the chapter's opening) is at the beach. "I" smiles at a woman mistaken for Denise. "She thinks I'm insulting her and yells at me," the next sentence states. Hold it. "I" can't know what strange woman thinks because "I" am not privy to her thoughts. "I" can say, "Apparently, she thinks I've insulted her." Small matter? Perhaps, but anything that weakens this fictive setting, weakens the entire piece.

Entry 2: Samantha climbs a staircase accompanied by her mother-in-law. Samantha glances at the older woman. "But she guesses her son stands waiting for us," reads this sentence, "and she means to give the appearance that she and I are friends." How can Samantha be certain of mother-in-law's intentions? Truer to say, "I feel that she guesses . . ." or "I sense that . . ." or "Intuitively, I know . . ."

Entry 3: "Samuel studies his scarred back." Unless he has a mirror, that's just not possible.

Do reread a draft of your manuscript with one purpose: to spot anything, even minor, that lies beyond a character's boundaries.

Avoid blocks of explanation

A delightful part of reading first chapters was the discovery that action or intriguing situations launched every one. Obviously, these writers have mastered the dynamic hook. The difficulty arose when the writer faced the task of filling in what happened before that moment. Time after time, he stopped the narrative's momentum with a barrage of exposition.

Entry 1: "Ann sat stoically quiet all the way from Pennsylvania to California." Shortly after this initial sentence, the writer—compelled to provide motivation for Ann's silence—supplies a seven-page summation. In May Ann's husband receives news of a West Coast transfer; he's thrilled, because that's his home. Ann, on the other hand, spends a painful summer alternately loving and hating her spouse as she tells family and her Pennsylvania friends goodbye. Then the narrative resumes with the couple's arrival in San Francisco.

Why not lead off with husband's announcement? Let chapter one unfold showing Ann's conflicts. Involve readers. End with her shutting the car door as they leave Pennsylvania.

Entry 2: Mr. Rodriguez, new boss, summons J.J., a long-time employee, into a book-lined office. In harsh dialogue that contrasts effectively with the sophisticated atmosphere, Rodriguez fires J.J., who suddenly embarks on a long, introspective reminiscence in which he reviews years with the company. Clunk.

Entry 3: Cynthia steps into a restaurant and chooses a table beside a cowboy, Randy. Their character-revealing conversation sparkles until the writer outlines how and why Cynthia arrived at this café. The sketch, just twenty lines long, freezes the action and breaks the mood. When Randy's joke reestablishes the *now*, as a reader, I'm aware that I'm an outsider, holding sheets of paper.

Some remedies? Select an exciting, but less dramatic beginning. With less to explain, there's more opportunity to build suspense. Or, weave in essential background facts, and thus avoid shattering an evolving spell. Always consider: What is the minimum the reader must know at this moment?

Often, details can suggest a background that makes exposition unnecessary. For instance, if a dog flinches when the owner raises a hand, that reaction intimates the dog/master relationship.

Use all five senses

Most contest entries contained graphic images, but many failed to make use of sounds, tastes, textures, and smells. The world in which we, and our characters, live is a composite of senses. Therefore, when writers avoid sensory impressions or concentrate exclusively on sight, the world is incomplete. Some places beg for more than visual description. For example, doesn't a bakery demand aromas?

Entry 1: Father Ryan walks slowly toward the altar. He surveys the church, notes flickering candles, light softened by stained glass, elderly worshippers randomly seated in oak pews.

Fine, but he never notices the scent of candle wax, the rustle of his cassock, the texture of the stone floor beneath his shoes.

Entry 2: Janie, a young girl in 1887, enters a general store. She comments on its darkness, its uneven floor, on "stuff stacked all round the sides," on men who whittle, chew, and spit by the fireplace. As she steps forward does the floor protest? The fire snap? Do the men need a bath? When they spit does their spittle hiss upon striking the hearth?

Entry 3: After work each evening, Tim stops at his neighborhood bar to shoot pool and drink beer. What odors pervade this room? How does the bar stool feel as he sinks down on it? How does the pool cue feel as he slides his hand along the shaft?

Naturally, writers must employ senses judiciously. They should examine each scene to make sure at least one other sense besides sight could add to its effect.

While focusing on these four areas won't guarantee winning a contest (or selling that novel), such attention will ensure a more finely-crafted work.

❑ INTERVIEWS

❏ 105

A Conversation with Maeve Binchy

By Lewis Burke Frumkes

Lewis Burke Frumkes: Maeve Binchy is the author of *Light a Penny Candle, Evening Class, The Glass Lake, The Copper Beech, The Lilac Bus, Circle of Friends, Silver Wedding, Firefly Summer, Echoes,* three volumes of short stories, two plays, and a teleplay, which won three awards at the Prague Film Festival. Her latest book, *Tara Road* (Delacorte Press), is an Oprah Book Club selection. Maeve, tell us a bit about *Tara Road.*

Maeve Binchy: It is the story of two women—one Irish and one American—and the problems they face in one particular year of their lives. The Irish woman is Ria Lynch. She's married to a drop-dead handsome man named Danny, a real estate agent. They have two children and live on Tara Road, a street on which the houses are becoming worth more every week in the newly affluent Ireland. Ria is perfectly happy, and thinks it's time to have another baby, that's the only thing she'd like. When she starts to tell her husband about this, she gets the most terrible shock in the world: He tells her that *he* is having a child with another woman and he's about to leave her. So that's the first big bang on the solar plexus. I tried to imagine what I would do if such an awful thing happened to me. I think I'd probably want to get away from the pity and the sympathy of everybody in familiar surroundings. So I decided that Ria would swap houses with an American woman named Marilyn who has a totally different problem: She is bereaved, can't get over it, needs some space, and decides to leave America.

LBF: It's a wonderful premise, and the book is a very good read. Now, I want to talk a little about you, Maeve. Your books have sold more copies than those of James Joyce, Samuel Beckett, Brendan Behan or William Butler Yeats. That's an incredible statistic. Did you have a breakout book, or did you sell well right from the beginning?

MB: I started with two books of short stories. Though people seemed to like them, they weren't very successful; apparently people don't like short stories unless they are by very well-known writers. I find that odd because I buy short stories by people who are not well-known, thinking that if I don't like the first story, I might like the second one. But this is not the way it happened. When my first novel was published in 1982–83, things suddenly became very different. It was translated into twenty languages. It wasn't what I expected. I take all this publicity about "more than James Joyce" and "more than Yeats" very lightly in the sense that it is true, of course, it is true in terms of sales. I mean, they were not writing for airports. The thing is, if you were going on a journey and you were thinking, I must read something on the plane, and if you had read any of my books before you would think, well, she tells a good story. It's very unlikely that you would take *Finnegans Wake* to get you across the Atlantic. Therefore, these books are read by an entirely different clientele. So it really isn't comparing like with like. It's a function of today's kind of marketing of books.

LBF: People everywhere love your books.

MB: For some reason I have hit upon a form of story telling that appeals to people in different languages. But I always say to myself, why would these people really be interested in the stories I tell? But then having asked myself the question, I answer it by saying that I suppose they have also felt love and hope and pain, and they have had dreams and had the delight of close families and the more irritating aspects of close families. They have, perhaps, also loved people who haven't loved them in return and also might have wanted to go up to the bright lights of a big city—it might be Tokyo or Seoul or Athens or Dublin—but the principle is the same. You have people who are young and enthusiastic and want to try to achieve their dream, and I think that is why people everywhere like them.

LBF: Ireland has a great literary history. The Irish have always been able to tell a good tale, but Americans are becoming more and more aware of good Irish writing.

MB: There is indeed a resurgence in Irish writers. When I was a young woman going into bookshops in Ireland there were only two Irish woman writers—Mary Lavin and Kate O'Brien. In the sixties, Edna

O'Brien came and that meant three. Now, when you go into an Irish bookshop the walls are full of them.

LBF: Do you think some of this had to do with the fact that recently there have been a number of Irish Booker Prize winners?

MB: I think it has a lot to do with the Irish having become a lot more confident in themselves. We don't apologize for being Irish. We don't have to write about deprivation and loss anymore. Ireland is a country that has come out into the sunshine. I never feel that the past is always looking over my shoulder because I think that everybody is writing differently. New people are writing, young people are writing. They've found a voice for themselves; their own voice.

LBF: How did you get into writing?

MB: By accident, as an awful lot of people do. My accident was ludicrous. When I was young I was going to be a saint. There was going to be a Saint Maeve's day, like Saint Patrick's Day, and people were going to walk in a procession after a statue of me tottering along through the streets. Then I wanted to be a judge because my father was a lawyer and we always knew that the judges were the most important people. And then I became a teacher, and I was very happy. I loved teaching.

LBF: What did you teach?

MB: I taught History and Latin in a girls' Catholic school. And I taught French in a Jewish school in Dublin.

LBF: An interesting mix.

MB: A great mix. The Jewish parents were so pleased with me and the way I taught their children—for instance, I taught them little songs that had to do with Israel for Chanukah—that they gave me a ticket to go to Israel. I wrote my parents all about the lovely time I was having: I told them about how the communal farms in Israel worked and how the children didn't sleep with their parents and they had to learn how to be grown-up and independent from their parents. I remember talking about the extraordinary dining. I was in the desert and it was near the time of the war, so there were air raids and I wrote all about it. My father in particular was so impressed by my letters, he had them typed up and sent them to the newspaper, and they were impressed as well, and published them. I didn't think I was writing for anybody except my parents. So when I came home my work was there in print, and it was then I realized I was a writer. What I discovered in writing those letters was that if you write as you speak and you write what you know about in your own voice rather than trying to imitate anybody else, then you're much more authentic and people are going to like it.

❏ 106

A Conversation with
James Patterson

By Lewis Burke Frumkes

Lewis Burke Frumkes: After much success with his past thrillers *Along Came a Spider, Kiss the Girls, Jack & Jill,* and *When the Wind Blows,* James Patterson has published *Pop Goes the Weasel,* another in the series featuring detective Alex Cross. Jim, tell us how you stumbled across Alex Cross, and how did that evolve?

JP: When I set up the series, I wanted to write books that people couldn't put down, because I didn't find enough of them myself. Second, I was interested in creating a larger-than-life black hero. I just didn't think there were many of those; they tended not to show up in the movies. If you think about Cross, he's an anti-stereotype, he's raising two kids by himself, he has a great relationship with his grandmother. He is a trained psychologist who's also a detective, fearless, a little too obsessive about his work; he's got his downsides, but he's bigger than life. The other part, which I didn't figure out until later, has to do with the whole Cross family, including Alex.

When I was a kid I grew up in upstate New York, and my grandparents had a small restaurant. The cook was a black woman. At one point, when I was about two or three, she was having trouble with her husband, and my parents and grandparents said, "Move in with us." She moved into our house, and she lived with us for about four years. She didn't have any duties in the house, she just worked in the restaurant, but she and I became unbelievably close. I spent incredible amounts of time with her and her family, her aunts and uncles, nephews and nieces, that whole thing. She was like a mother to me. She eventually went back to Detroit, where she was from originally, and that was the closest I had felt to there being a death in the family, we had been so close. But that's where my notion of the Cross family comes from. It comes from her family. I don't believe that I could write convincingly

529

about what goes on on street corners on 110th Street right now. I mean, I can write in a superficial way about it, but I can write about that family. I know that family.

There are two things readers always say about the Alex Cross books. One is that they are hard to put down—you know, I like to try to keep readers on the edge of their seats for the whole six or seven hours they spend with the book—and the second is they like the Cross family. I am constantly being warned that nothing bad must ever happen to anybody in the family, including the cat Rosie. So, I'm very careful with them.

LBF: *Pop Goes the Weasel, When the Wind Blows, Jack & Jill*— these titles come from children's nursery rhymes. How do you select them?

JP: Well, having a young child helps! We have a big book of nursery rhymes at home. Originally *Along Came a Spider* was called *Remember Maggie Rose*, but my editor didn't think that was a great title. *Along Came a Spider* was the title of one of the sections in the book. Once we went with that, we realized it was a lot easier. It would be easier for people to remember James Patterson, the one who wrote all those books with the nursery-rhyme titles. It also seems to counterpoint nicely against the books, which can be pretty scary.

LBF: Absolutely. Jim, you've already said you love page turners, and you write that way; there is nobody that does that better. When you are not writing, whom do you read, and whom did you read who might have influenced you?

JP: That question comes up when I am touring, and initially I didn't have an answer because I couldn't think of who had influenced me as a writer. It wasn't mystery writers; I didn't really read mysteries. But when I first started getting involved in literature, the writers who really opened up my world and said to me, people are different, it's not like the way you grew up in the Hudson Valley, were Jean Genet, John Rechy, Beckett. They got me excited about writing, excited about ideas, and probably helped me open my head up so I could create these crazy bad guys. I didn't read a lot of commercial fiction either growing up or in college, but there were two page turners I read—*Day of the Jackal* and *The Exorcist*—that gave me this notion that you can write a book that people can't wait to get back to.

LBF: Most people may not be aware of the fact that you have been very successful in the advertising business. I wonder if you could just briefly talk about that, how you got into advertising, and whether the lessons you used in that field in any way have an impact on how you write.

JP: I wanted to write novels, but I thought it was presumptuous to think that I could write them and get them published, so I thought I'd better get a job. I had a friend who had a friend in advertising. I went and talked to her. She was running around her office in a T-shirt, she was funny, she was making a lot of money, and she said, this is easy. So I said, OK, I can do that while I'm trying to write novels. And I got into it, and I found it very nice and eventually as I moved up the ladder I hired only one kind of person, talented and nice to be around. So it was really kind of like a liberal arts environment. Eventually I was chairman of J. Walter Thompson, then I said, Enough! Let's do something else!

LBF: And you've just hit it big with these books. Did it surprise you with the first one, how fast it caught on?

JP: Yes, it did. I thought we had a good shot because the publisher for *Along Came a Spider* went out and did what they had to do: They had enough books out there—people didn't have to go hunting around in the bookstores and find it on the back shelves; they promoted it very nicely. We were fortunate that people picked it up, and then that they liked the books a lot. I mean, you can sell them one time, but if they don't like the books, that's the end of it.

LBF: Jim, do you have favorite words that you either return to more often than other words or that appeal to you more than other words?

JP: I haven't thought about it, but probably. In the beginning, I really worried a lot about the sentences in my books. But at some point—and I think it's one of the reasons that I sell a lot of books—I stopped writing sentences and started writing stories. And that's the advice I give to new writers. Sentences are really hard to write. Stories flow. If you've got an idea, the story will flow. Once you have the story down if you want to go back and polish it for the next ten years, you can do that. But don't start with the sentences, you'll just drive yourself crazy. You also will put a lot of sentences down that you ought to take out but you can't because you say, Oh, I love that paragraph! Oh, I love that page! Oh, I love that chapter! But it's not really part of the story and it shouldn't be in there. Write the story.

LBF: Along with this wonderful advice, tell us about your habits. Do you write at night, during the day? Do you work on a computer?

JP: The main discipline I have is that I write every day. I try to write in the morning because it was my habit when I was in the advertising business. Now I have a lot more time to think about the books, and also if I happen to have some free time, dead time, I just go and write. I do use an outline; outlines are great. If you want to write a novel where plot is important you must outline it first, or you will waste an incredible amount of time and energy. I deviate from the outline; I always change the endings. I never know until I've written the whole thing. To me it's a lot like editing film, which I used to do a lot of in advertising, where I put all the pieces down and say, well let's look at it. It's not a movie, yet it needs something. Fortunately I can go out and reshoot, so to speak, write another chapter without getting the actors back.

LBF: Because you are having such an enormous success with the Alex Cross books, there must be terrific pressure on you to turn out similar books. Have you ever entertained the idea of doing what you did with *Miracle on the 17th Green*, of doing something different?

JP: I'm involved with a lot of things right now. I'm writing a love story that I am very excited about, it's a really good story. I just couldn't resist it. I'm creating a new series that takes place in San Francisco. It features four women who get involved in solving murders.

LBF: That sounds fabulous. It's amazing how you can keep all of it straight. James Patterson's new book, *Pop Goes the Weasel*, is the perfect novel if you want to stay up all night because it's incredible, and you can't put it down.

❏ 107

A CONVERSATION WITH
MELINDA HAYNES

BY LEWIS BURKE FRUMKES

Lewis Burke Frumkes: Melinda Haynes has written a very special book, beautifully written, called *Mother of Pearl*. It's an Oprah Book Club selection and it's four hundred and fifty pages of literary talent. Anyway, Melinda, it's an interesting story and I'd like you to introduce *Mother of Pearl* for us.

Melinda Haynes: It's set in 1956 in Petal, Mississippi, a real town. My first memories are of Petal. My father was a pastor there, and I felt that it was really important to go back, and let that be the place for my book to begin. It is about a black man, Even Grade, who was abandoned at birth on the steps of a Lutheran orphanage in Memphis. All he has from his mother is a note she pinned to him. He decides to head south to try to find her, but really to try to find family. He ends up working for Hercules Powder. His nearest neighbor is Canaan Mosely, and a deep friendship develops there. Canaan is self-taught. His formal education ended in the eighth grade. But he works as a janitor for the library. He is working on his thesis; it's his life work, which he calls *The Reality of the Negro*. It's a stack that is about five inches tall, and it keeps changing, the reality keeps changing so it's marked through in red. Canaan is really the opposite of Even. Even is quiet and contemplative, a poet at heart. But Canaan is very vocal, very skeptical. Even Grade is in love with a seer, who lives down by the creek. It's a risky love; he's never loved anyone before. He is reaching out to her and they are drawn closer. Instead of finding his mother he is finding a true family. On that side of the story are these individuals.

LBF: I love the names.

MH: The names were really given to me, I felt. I decided on the name Valuable Korner for one of my characters while I was headed to

533

Bellingrath Gardens. We came to an intersection and headed south and there was the nastiest corner you had ever seen in your life. It was very trashy. And someone had put a sign in the center that said "Valuable Corner, Property for Sale," and they had planted roses underneath. The name just hit me. The force for me, in writing the book, is that I really believe that in each of us there is the ability for kindness, and the ability to do the right thing. This is just a story that I developed. I didn't have an outline; I didn't really know where I was going. Originally, it was just a gift for my husband for Christmas.

LBF: What a gift!

MH: Yes. Ray believed in me. He bundled up the first one hundred and sixteen pages, had me write a cover letter, and I was in a panic! He told me to just write it, and I said, "Ray, I really don't want you to send this off! This is for you." He said, "Don't worry about it then. We'll wait till it's finished." So I finished it, and he dated it. Then Ray sent it to the agent Wendy Weil without my knowledge.

LBF: How did he know Wendy?

MH: Well, I subscribe to the magazine, *Poets and Writers*, and in it was a feature on her, so he sent it to her. She called and said, "Hi, this is Wendy Weil in New York." It was just incredible. She said, "I have your manuscript here. I would love to represent you; this is marvelous." I wrote it and they received it that Saturday and it was sold to Hyperion. I believe it probably ran the risk of being too clichéd if the storyline had been handled any differently. But it really is how the black and white community in low Mississippi come together and form a union that is better than blood.

LBF: Well, it is marvelous. And the writing is wonderful, which makes me want to ask, what kind of training did you have, Melinda? This is the first novel that you wrote. Where did you get this writing talent?

MH: I don't know. I painted for years. I was a commissioned portrait artist. I gave it up because I had a breakdown and ended up in the hospital. I was supporting the family at that time. I have three daughters, my husband was not working, my former husband. For a variety of reasons, we had to file for bankruptcy. But I am so thankful for that. It really drew the line on that part of my life. It was the creative energy that I had but it had died a long time ago because I was doing it for someone else. When I stumbled into writing, it was like being trapped inside a song. And I was there, and for the first time I could verbalize that internal world. I spent a lot of time there, because of panic disorder. When you have that, you are locked, your room and your ceiling in your life get smaller and smaller, and you spend a lot of time in imagination.

LBF: You obviously don't have panic disorder anymore. You are traveling around very comfortably.

MH: I love writing. I love this new person named Melinda Haynes; I never met her before. I learned to forgive myself. I felt like I failed for a long time because my painting could not do it for my family. But I thank God for it now because it just opened up a completely new avenue for me.

LBF: Good for you. It is one thing to escape, but to write a blockbuster book and exhibit your talent around the world and be acclaimed for it! And deservedly so. Now, tell us a little about Oprah. She is really good at this, selecting excellent books.

MH: Yes. The day she called, I was working. It was 5:30 and the phone rang and this woman with this low voice said, "I just read your book, *Mother of Pearl*, and I loved it. How did you do it?" And I just rattled on! Seven minutes later I looked down at my watch and I said, "I'm sorry, I forgot to ask your name," and she said, "This is Oprah Winfrey."

LBF: Wow! What a surprise!

MH: I said, "No, it's not!" And then I thought well, how nice, she called to tell me she liked my book. It still didn't register. A few minutes later she said, "Not only do I love it but it's going to be our summer selection." I was pretty coherent up until that point. Then, I couldn't say anything! It is a challenge to read this book, I realize that, but so many more people have met Even Grade, Canaan Mosely, Valuable Korner and Grace Johnson, thanks to Oprah.

LBF: You deserve all the fame and attention you are getting. I'm sure your agent and readers are clamoring for you to do another novel after the success of *Mother of Pearl*. But after hearing your story, I would think a memoir would be special.

MH: Someone mentioned that. The strange thing is that when I was in the final third of *Mother of Pearl*, it was such a life force for me that I thought, what if this doesn't happen again? So I started the second novel, *Chalktown*.

LBF: *Chalktown*?

MH: Yes, it is a street in George County, Mississippi, where no one talks. They sling insults and recipes on chalkboards set up outside their houses. Hyperion purchased it. I'm on the second draft now. Someone did mention a memoir. When I was young, everyone thought I should keep a journal. But it's so hard for me to write about myself. It's easier to transfer all these things I feel into some other character.

LBF: Obviously, from the rich language that you use it is clear that you love words. Do you have any favorites, words that you use more than others perhaps or appeal to you more often?

MH: Words saved my life. Reading really made a difference. There are sentences that I can hold onto when things really get tough. One of my favorite sentences is, "Memory believes before knowing remembers." I used that in the quote at the beginning of my novel. It really speaks to me about what we know that is instinctive. That certainness. I'm sure it means certain things to certain people. I believe that the last three pages of Faulkner's *The Mansion* are the most beautiful words ever. I think one of my favorite lines in my book is when Even has had his friendship with Canaan a little bit fractured. He wakes up and is sad, and he is thinking, "I am man born of woman, but I carry no proof with me." The melancholy there touches me and tells a lot about his nature.

LBF: Melinda, who might have inspired you? Who besides Faulkner did you read that you admired a great deal?

MH: I read James Joyce at an early age. Because of the panic disorder I was internal, and books became my life line. I also read Flannery O'Connor. My favorite short story is "The Turkey." Annie Proulx. Toni Morrison. Mary Hood, she wrote *Familiar Heat*. There are a lot of them.

LBF: How do you work when you are writing a book? Do you use a word processor, and do you work during the night or day?

MH: While I was working at the *Catholic Week*, Ray took over everything. I would come home and start writing at 7:30 and work until 2:30 in the morning. But now that I am not working there, the day begins around 9:30. I make myself available for writing, I sit there. It doesn't always come. A lot of reading is involved. Then I take a break for lunch and do some work during the afternoon. Then I spend a lot of time on the tractor. The tractor is a big deal in my life.

LBF: A real tractor?

MH: Yes, a real tractor. A bush hop. We live out in the woods and we have to keep the field grass down, because of the rats. It takes about two hours, and during that time I can think things through a little more clearly. That is pretty much how things work on a normal schedule. This is not normal, the touring. This is a first. I look forward again to those quiet times.

LBF: What advice would you give to young writers starting out?

MH: To read. Read everything. When you come across that sentence that seems to really connect, read it over and over again and find out why. The second piece of advice is to forget about the rules. Don't worry about them. There is an honesty that exists inside the characters in such a way that you have to be honest to what the characters want to do. In one situation part of me wanted one of the characters to react a different way, but I couldn't allow them to do it. You have to be honest to what the story is saying.

❏ 108

AN INTERVIEW WITH BRIAN JACQUES

BY STEPHANIE LOER

Stephanie Loer: What inspired the "Redwall" series?

Brian Jacques: I wrote the first "Redwall" book for the children in The School for the Blind in Liverpool. I wanted the story to be a fast-paced, exciting adventure, where the heroes pull themselves up by the bootstraps and have hair-breadth escapes. I was on my way to read it to the children, when I met a former schoolmaster, who asked to read it first. He read it, but instead of returning it, he took it to a London publisher, who took the book on the spot. And so began my own adventure. I still read many of my stories to the kids at The School for the Blind; they can take credit for launching me into the world of children's books.

SL: Why are your characters animals, and why do mice play a particularly significant role in your stories?

BJ: Children identify with animals. They can recognize human nature and good and evil more easily in animals, because virtues and vices can be more simply shown. Mice are my heroes because, like children, mice are little and have to learn to be courageous and use their wits.

SL: Why do you think your books are so popular?

BJ: I think that kids who read my books want to be in the world of "once upon a time, long, long ago, and far away." I want my stories to transport children away from the angst of the modern world and I think the tales I concoct do that.

SL: When you have an idea, what drives and develops the storyline—the characters or the plot?

BJ: Usually the characters come first. Some enter my mind as good guys, others as bad guys; still others start as the nasties and end up as the goodies. Then I look for central themes, such as the value of friendship, honesty, courage, or as in my new book *Marlfox*, gaining self-respect. Although the settings are similar, the plots, themes, action, and the characters must work together to create a totally new tale. Each story must be strong and hold together by itself. And the book must give kids a rousing, good adventure—or they will shut the cover and never read it.

SL: How are you able to pack so many details into the writing and still keep the story exciting?

BJ: Think of an artist. An artist uses brushes, pens, and colors to make exciting pictures. Because I'm a writer, I paint with words and these "word pictures" must be interesting. The words I use in the details and descriptions are my brushes, pens, and colors. Words are what I use to make my verbal pictures exciting.

SL: Do you plan to continue the series?

BJ: I have just finished the next book, *The Legend of Luke*. As I tell the children I meet in school, if you keep reading the "Redwall" books, I'll keep writing them. Because there is no place I'd rather be than within that world I've been lucky enough to create.

❑ 109

A CONVERSATION WITH ETHAN CANIN

BY LEWIS BURKE FRUMKES

Lewis Burke Frumkes: Ethan Canin, whose most recent novel, *For Kings and Planets,* is published by Random House, is widely regarded as one of our finest writers. *For Kings and Planets* is an extraordinary coming-of-age story. I want to begin by asking where the title comes from.

Ethan Canin: One of the characters in the novel, Orno Tarcher, is a Midwesterner living in New York. He's a rather serious, hardworking, intelligent man seeking contentment in his life. He finds himself in the company of a wild, energetic, creative, artistic New Yorker named Marshall Emerson. That's sort of what the book is about—contentment versus ambition.

Orno ends up becoming a dentist. Marshall asks him if he's learned the names of teeth yet and Orno responds, "Yes, I have, and I think it will be a disappointment for you. They are *not* named for kings and planets."

LBF: Are Marshall and Orno based on people you have known?

EC: No. Like any character a fiction writer has created, they are parts of me drawn out and enlarged. But I don't think I *consciously* write about anybody I know.

LBF: You are a physician, but not practicing right now. How much do you incorporate your medical knowledge into your literary work?

EC: I try not to use the medical knowledge, because to me that would be a failure of imagination. I don't want to write a book about medicine . . . maybe thirty years from now I'll write one. Because to invent anything at all, you have to invent everything. The world you actually know, the world of memory and present relationships, is so much more powerful than the world of imagination, that you will just naturally gravitate toward what you know.

LBF: Did you know anyone like Marshall Emerson? I know you said he's part of you, enlarged and exaggerated. Exactly how much of you is in him?

EC: Marshall has an eidetic memory; I have a really good memory, but not an eidetic memory. I did know a guy in medical school who was sort of square, very rigid, literal, and I was surprised to find out that as an undergraduate at Harvard, he had won the Shakespeare award, and it didn't really mesh with the literal intelligence I saw in him. It turns out that he had memorized all of Shakespeare's plays! But, I don't think that he could really have invented anything.

LBF: Of the two major characters in this novel—Orno and Marshall—is one more appealing to you than the other?

EC: Actually, I've got to choose both. Orno values kindness and diligence. Marshall values invention and nonconformity.

LBF: At the very end of the book, somebody is crying. Is that symbolic of anything special or some view of you?

EC: Someone *is* crying at the very end of the book. A child is crying, and that child has the seed in him of other characters in the book. In the next book, I want to write about how, as a parent looking at that child, you see your friend, who was a dangerous and alluring friend; and you see your wife, who is both good and tainted by the same friendship.

LBF: Do not let me put words in your mouth with this next one, but are you thinking of a trilogy?

EC: Yes. You are not putting words in my mouth. That's exactly what I was thinking of. I want to wait ten years and write this book about when these people are parents, and then ten more years, and write about them again.

LBF: You first came onto the literary scene with *Emperor of the Air.* Tell us a little about how that came about. You were obviously studying medicine and writing at the same time.

EC: I actually started out in college as an engineering major. I wandered into an English class one day simply because it was listed on the next page in the course catalogue after engineering. I was looking for another class and ended up taking a creative writing course.

LBF: Where was that?

EC: Stanford. I began reading the stories of John Cheever, and that changed my life. Suddenly I just wanted to be a writer. I would read those stories and I would type them out just to imagine I had written them, just to *feel* what it was like. The language is beautiful and he makes art out of the rhythm of the words.

LBF: What an unusual thing to do, to have done it as an exercise. I have never heard of anyone doing that before. That's wonderful.

EC: It's interesting because you learn things. Something simple about Cheever is that his paragraphs are longer than yours would have been. His sentences are longer. He pushes everything farther than I would have pushed them. He also has a shape to his paragraphs. It's always the same: It's small when it opens, then it gets large, then it's small. So, you learn things. Anyway, how did I get from there to writing? I actually decided I would become a writer late in college. So I went to the University of Iowa as a graduate student, to try to write, was immediately humiliated, and didn't write a word for two years.

LBF: Humiliated how?

EC: John Irving came to give a class. He read one of my stories and didn't like it at all. So I took biology classes instead at the University of Iowa and fulfilled my pre-med requirements.

LBF: Is John Irving responsible for your becoming a doctor?

EC: He is. I wondered, "What have I done here?" I had a scientific background. I liked people, basically. And in a colossal failure of imagination, I went to medical school, and my first year I wrote a book because I wasn't supposed to be doing it. I think I was rebelling against that kind of minute learning, where your mind has to memorize, memorize, memorize. As a result, I had a really inventive period.

LBF: You were never tempted to use that knowledge to write a medical thriller?

EC: Yes, I was tempted. I mean, you can make a ton of money doing that. But I make enough money now to live on my writing and I don't want to change that. I would like to write literary novels; what moves me are literary novels.

LBF: The human condition, relationships, characters?

EC: Yes. Characters. That's what I want to write and right now I am fortunate enough to be able to pay the rent doing that. Ten years from now I might write a thriller.

LBF: It must have been difficult to turn away from medicine.

EC: It was very difficult. I had given years of my life, a dozen years of my life, all my time, a hundred thousand dollars, just to walk away from it. I wake up every morning as a writer and I don't know whether today's the last day I will write. Very difficult for me. Very insecure.

LBF: Is writing a struggle for you?

EC: It is very difficult for me to start writing, but once I start I don't even pause. And I write for about half an hour a day.

LBF: You write for only half an hour a day?

EC: Yes. It's almost non-stop. I sit down, write about five hundred words, and then stop. It takes about half an hour.

LBF: On a word processor?

EC: Yes.

LBF: Morning or night?

EC: Morning; I don't want it to hang over me.

LBF: That's funny, because I do the same thing. I'm working on a memoir. I've got about two hundred pages. I do about five hundred words, about half an hour every morning before I go to work.

EC: Everyone is always surprised at only half an hour a day. But if you do that every day, it's just a book a year, really.

LBF: You are quite right. I hear some writers say, "Well, I start working about eight in the morning and at four in the afternoon I put my manuscript away." I don't know how they do that.

EC: Most writers do that. I do *not* know how they do it. I mean, for me the moment of invention is sort of a single burst. To write eight hours a day is a different kind of writing—choosing words, taking one out, putting one back in. But to me writing is a stream.

LBF: You are considered one of our very best writers. Is your head inflated at all?

EC: No praise has ever changed anyone's self perception. I think it gives you enough to keep an even keel. It's still very, very hard for me. I'm plagued by doubt all the time. I can't imagine ever getting so much praise that it would make writing easy for me. Writing is exceptionally difficult for me. It is so much more difficult than medicine!

LBF: What are you reading these days?

EC: All kinds of writers. I'm reading a Barry Unsworth novel right now—*Sacred Hunger*. I've been reading Alice Munro, who is an exquisite writer; so is Barry Unsworth, for that matter.

LBF: What advice would you give to new writers starting out?

EC: I would give this advice to new writers: Read books that you love. Learn to nurture your imagination. Learn what nurtures your imagination because the physical world of television, of people you know, of what the next guy is saying on the bus, is so much more powerful than your imagination that you need to find out early what nurtures your imagination. I spent years figuring that out. I tried to travel; I tried spending time in the jungle; I tried building houses, and I discovered that, at least for me, that doesn't work. The only thing that nurtures imagination is reading, and reading good books. When I say good books I mean books that speak to you. That is invaluable. That will provide you with the right inspiration.

❑ 110

A CONVERSATION WITH DORIS LESSING

BY LEWIS BURKE FRUMKES

Lewis Burke Frumkes: Doris Lessing, one of the most distinguished writers living today, has published over 30 books, probably the most well-known of them *The Golden Notebook*. Her newest books are *Mara and Dan: An Adventure,* and *Walking in the Shade, 1949–1962,* the second volume of her astonishing autobiography, both published by HarperCollins. Doris, you once submitted a book to your publisher under a pseudonym, Jane Somers. What prompted you to do that little prank?

Doris Lessing: One reason is that writers often feel they're stereotyped and have a set of images stuck to them that they can't get out from under. I thought it might be quite amusing to challenge that a bit.

Two main publishers turned the book down. I know that neither of them read it, and I saw the readers' reports, which were extremely patronizing, and it made me remember how patronized young writers often are. Then a very bright young woman at my very first British publisher, Michael Joseph, took it, not knowing it was mine. She said it reminded her of a young Doris Lessing, and my agent said, "Please, just keep quiet!" Now, what impressed me about that was, two big publishing houses, one in England and one in the United States, could keep the secret, absolutely, whereas I'd only mentioned this in confidence to just one person in the literary world.

LBF: It really shook up the publishing world.

DL: I think they were quite cross with me. It was hilarious. I got the kind of reviews that promising young writers get: "We must keep an eye on this young writer."

LBF: Tell us about yourself, Doris. You had a very unusual childhood.

545

DL: I was born in Persia in a town that was destroyed in the Iran-Iraq war. My father was working for the Imperial Bank of Persia. Then, being a romantic, wanting to be free, he became a farmer in southern Rhodesia. He found himself with a wife, two small children, and a governess, in the middle of unstumped bush in a district that was just being opened up. So I was brought up in the bush, which was the luckiest thing that ever happened to me. I went to a Roman Catholic convent, where I was always ill, and I was a dropout.

LBF: What drew you to language and letters?

DL: The bookcases on the farm were full of the best and greatest literature—all the English classics, all the great children's writers from England and America, which my mother ordered, and then I started ordering books on my own. I read all the great Russians and Proust, of course.

LBF: When did you try your own hand at writing?

DL: I wrote a book in southern Rhodesia when I was 24 or 25.

LBF: And you've been writing ever since with increasing success. Is it fun or is it annoying to hear from readers, "Oh I love you," or, "You're not like what I expected." Is it tiresome after a while or do you enjoy it?

DL: I really don't think it's got much to do with me. It's not what I'm about. What I'm about is writing my books when I'm alone in my room and getting on with it.

LBF: Do you write on a computer, longhand, on a typewriter?

DL: Longhand, no. I still use an old-fashioned typewriter. I can't bring myself to upset my brain by writing on a word processor, but I have to because there are no typists left anymore. What I used to do is hand over a scrappy old manuscript to a typist, but now no one can type, and they can't be bothered to look to see how many mistakes they've made. So I have to learn to use a word processor.

LBF: Do you write at night, or during the day, or once in a while, or all the time?

DL: Ideally, I like to write from 8:00 in the morning to noon or one o'clock. That's my best time. But the trouble is, there's a plumber and a roofer, and a washing machine, so it's very hard to get a straight run.

LBF: If you could have written a book—other than one of your own—that you would have been very proud to have written, what book would it be?

DL: Leaving aside *War and Peace* and all of Dostoevsky, how about Gogol's *The Overcoat*, which is probably the most perfect little book ever written? Have you read it?

LBF: I haven't.

DL: It's the saddest, most beautiful little book.

LBF: I will read it. Doris, what advice would you give to writers starting out?

DL: I always give the same advice, and it's very boring, which is that they have to work hard. There's a great temptation because it's so easy to word-process or whatever to think that they just have to do it and then there it is and it's fine. But in actual fact, you learn to write by writing, and tearing it up, and tearing it up, and doing it again, and by reading a lot of good books. You learn to acquire a style of your own and a sense of discrimination because you've read the best. But a lot of the young writers can't be bothered to do that.

LBF: Do you socialize with other writers?

DL: I don't go in for the literary life. I have good friends, like Margaret Drabble, but I don't go to literary parties very much. I don't have time, you know. I'm an obsessive writer. When one book is finished, the wolf is slapping at my heels.

LBF: Is it more fun for you to do fiction than nonfiction?

DL: Though I have sweated blood over accuracy for my autobiography, I already know it's got three mistakes, and I had a researcher! If you write fiction, it doesn't matter.

Where to Sell

Where to Sell

All information in these lists concerning the needs and requirements of magazines, book publishing companies, and theaters comes directly from the editors, publishers, and directors, but personnel and addresses change, as do requirements. No published listing can give as clear a picture of editorial needs and tastes as a careful study of several issues of a magazine or a book catalogue, and writers should never submit material without first thoroughly researching the prospective market. If a magazine is not available in the local library or on the newsstand, write directly to the editor for the price of a sample copy; contact the publicity department of a book publisher for an up-to-date catalogue, or a theater for a current schedule. Many companies also offer a formal set of writers guidelines, available for an SASE (self-addressed, stamped envelope) upon request.

While some of the more established markets may seem difficult to break into, especially for the beginner, there are thousands of lesser-known publications where editors will consider submissions from first-time free lancers.

All manuscripts must be typed double-space and submitted with self-addressed envelopes bearing postage sufficient for the return of the material. If a manuscript need not be returned, note this with the submission, and enclose an SASE or a self-addressed, stamped postcard for editorial reply. Use good white paper; onion skin and erasable bond are not acceptable. *Always* keep a copy of the manuscript, since occasionally material is lost in the mail. Magazines may take several weeks, or longer, to read and report on submissions. If an editor has not reported on a manuscript after a reasonable length of time, write a brief, courteous letter of inquiry.

Some publishers will accept, and may in fact prefer, work submitted on computer disk, usually noting the procedure and type of disk in their writers guidelines.

ARTICLE MARKETS

The magazines in the following list are in the market for free-lance articles in many categories. Unless listings state otherwise, a writer should submit a query first, including a brief description of the proposed article and any relevant qualifications or credits. A few editors want to see samples of published work, if available.

Submit photos or slides *only* if the editor has specifically requested them. A self-addressed envelope with postage sufficient to cover the return of the manuscript or the answer to a query should accompany all submissions.

GENERAL-INTEREST PUBLICATIONS

AIR & SPACE/SMITHSONIAN—901 D St. S.W., 10th Fl., Washington, DC 20024-2518. George Larson, Ed. General-interest articles, 1,000 to 3,500 words, on aerospace experience, past, present, and future. Pays varying rates, on acceptance. Query. Guidelines at e-mail: editors@airspacemag.com or web site: www.airspacemag.com.

AMERICAN JOURNALISM REVIEW—1117 Journalism Bldg., University of Maryland, College Park, MD 20742-7111. Rem Rieder, Ed. Articles, 500 to 5,000 words, on print, broadcast, and electronic journalism. Query.

THE AMERICAN LEGION—P.O. Box 1055, Indianapolis, IN 46206. John B. Raughter, Ed. Articles, 750 to 2,000 words, on current world affairs, public policy, and subjects of contemporary interest. Payment is negotiable, on acceptance. Query.

AMERICAS—OAS, 19th and Constitution Ave. N.W., Washington, DC 20006. James Patrick Kiernan, Dir. & Ed. Rebecca Read Medrano, Man. Ed. Features, 2,500 to 4,000 words, on Latin America and the Caribbean. Wide focus: anthropology, the arts, travel, science, and development. "We prefer stories that can be well-illustrated." No political material. Pays from $400, on publication. Query. E-mail: americas@oas.org.

ASIAN PAGES—P.O. Box 11932, St. Paul, MN 55111-0932. Cheryl Weiberg, Ed.-in-Chief. Biweekly newspaper tabloid. Profiles and news events, 500 words; short stories, 500 to 750 words; poetry, 100 words; and Asian-related fillers. "All material must have a strong, non-offensive Asian slant." SASE required for response. Pays $40 for articles, $25 for photos/cartoons, on publication. E-mail: asianpages@att.net. Web site: www.asianpages.com.

BET WEEKEND—One BET Plaza, 1900 W. Place N.E., Washington D.C., 20018-1211. Articles, 200 to 500 words, on the lifestyle, arts, education, and entertainment of the African-American community. Do not send complete manuscript; query with SASE. Payment is 50¢ to $1 per word, on publication. Web site: www.msbet.com.

BLACK BOOK—116 Prince St., 2nd Fl., New York, NY 10012-3178. Kevin Bisch, Ed. Quarterly. Entertainment magazine that covers trends, beauty and fashion, news, and cutting-edge journalism. Also, some fiction. Query. Payment varies.

BON APPETIT—6300 Wilshire Blvd., Los Angeles, CA 90048. Barbara Fairchild, Exec. Ed. Articles on fine cooking (sophisticated but approachable; menu format or single focus), entertaining at home, kitchen design, new tableware, food-focused humor, personal essays, cooking classes, and gastronomically focused travel. Pays varying rates, on acceptance; buys all rights. Query with samples of published work. Web site: www.epicurious.com.

BRAZZIL—P.O. Box 50536, Los Angeles, CA 90050-0536. Rodney Mello, Ed. Monthly. Articles, written in English, 800 to 5,000 words, on Brazil and its culture. Features include politics, economy, ecology, tourism, literature, and the arts. Some short stories in Portuguese. Pays $20 to $50 and copies, on publication. Web site: www.brazzil.com. E-mail: brazzil@brazzil.com.

BRILL'S CONTENT—521 Fifth Ave., 11th Fl., New York, NY 10175-1100. Michael Kramer, Ed. Monthly. "The survival guide to the information age." Articles and features on media and information technology from the perspective of the consumer. Pays good rates. Query.

CAPPER'S—1503 S.W. 42nd St., Topeka, KS 66609-1265. Ann Crahan, Ed. Articles, 500 to 700 words: human-interest, personal experience for family section, historical. Payment varies, on publication.

CHANGE: THE MAGAZINE OF HIGHER LEARNING—1319 18th St. N.W., Washington, DC 20036. Attn: Ed. Dept. Well-researched features, 2,500 to 3,500 words, on programs, people, and institutions of higher education; and columns, 700 to 2,000 words. "We can't usually pay for unsolicited articles." E-mail: ch@heldref.org. Web site: www.heldref.org.

THE CHRISTIAN SCIENCE MONITOR—One Norway St., Boston, MA 02115. Articles, 800 words, for "Arts and Leisure," Gregory Lamb, Ed.; "Learning," Amelia Newcomb, Ed.; "Ideas," Jim Bencivengia, Ed.; "Home and Family," April Austin, Ed. Essays and poetry on the "Home Forum Page"; guest columns for "Opinion Page." Pay varies, on acceptance. Original material only, exclusive rights for 90 days. E-mail: oped@csps.com. Web site: www. csmonitor.com.

CHRONICLES—The Rockford Institute, 928 N. Main St., Rockford, IL 61103. Scott P. Richert, Exec. Ed. "A Magazine of American Culture." Articles and poetry that display craftsmanship and a sense of form. "Read the magazine first to get a feel for what we do." No fiction, fillers or jokes. Payment varies.

CIVILIZATION—Library of Congress, 575 Lexington Ave., 33rd Fl., New York, NY 10022. Regan Solmo, Man. Ed. Thought-provoking nonfiction articles and essays; some book reviews and puzzles. "Writers should read the magazine to get a sense of our editorial needs." Guidelines are available. Query. Payment varies.

COLUMBIA—1 Columbus Plaza, New Haven, CT 06507-3326. Tim S. Hickey, Ed. Journal of the Knights of Columbus. Articles, 500 to 1,200 words, on a wide variety of topics of interest to K. of C. members, their families, and the Catholic layman: current events, religion, education, art, etc. Pays $250 to $600, on acceptance. E-mail: info@kofc.org. Web site: www.kofc.org.

THE COMPASS—365 Washington Ave., Brooklyn, NY 11238. J.A. Randall, Ed. True stories, to 1,500 words, on the sea and sea trades. Pays $1,000, on acceptance. Query with SASE. E-mail: randallja@aol.com.

CONSUMERS DIGEST—8001 N. Lincoln Ave., 6th Fl., Skokie, IL 60077. John Manos, Ed. Articles, 500 to 3,000 words, on subjects of interest to consumers: products and services, automobiles, health, fitness, consumer legal affairs, and personal money management. Photos. Pays from 35¢ to 50¢ a word, extra for photos, on publication. Buys all rights. Query with resumé and published clips.

COSMOPOLITAN—224 W. 57th St., New York, NY 10019. Kate White, Ed. Steve Perrine, Exec. Ed. Articles, to 3,000 words, and features, 500 to 2,000 words, on issues affecting young career women, with emphasis on relationships, jobs and personal life. "We only print fiction that is excerpted from a novel being published." Query with SASE. Payment varies.

CULTUREFRONT—150 Broadway, Suite 1700, New York, NY 10038. Attn: Ed. "A Magazine of the Humanities." Nonfiction and occasional fiction articles, to 2,500 words, related to theme. "News and a variety of views on the production, interpretation, and politics of culture." No payment. Query for current themes. Web site: www.culturefront.org.

DIVERSION MAGAZINE—1790 Broadway, New York, NY 10019. Tom Passavant, Ed.-in-Chief. Articles, 600 to 2,000 words, on travel, sports, hobbies, entertainment, food, etc., of interest to physicians at leisure. Photos. Pays from $500, 12 weeks after submission of manuscript. Query. E-mail: tpassavant@hearst.com. Web site: www.diversionmag.com.

EBONY—820 S. Michigan, Chicago, IL 60605. Lerone Bennett, Jr., Exec. Ed. "We do not solicit free-lance material."

THE ELKS MAGAZINE—425 W. Diversey Parkway, Chicago, IL 60614. Anna L. Idol, Man. Ed. Articles, 1,500 to 2,500 words, on technology, business, sports, and topics of current interest, for non-urban audience with above-average income. Pays 20¢ a word, on acceptance. Send manuscript with SASE; no queries please. E-mail: elksmag@elks.org. Web site: www.elks.org/elksmag/.

EMERGE—BET Plaza, 1900 W. Place N.E., Washington, DC 20018. Florestine Purnell, Man. Ed. "Black America's Newsmagazine." Articles, 1,200 to 2,000 words, on current issues, ideas, or news personalities of interest to successful, well-informed African-Americans. Department pieces, 650 to 700 words, on a number of subjects. Pays 50¢ a word, on publication. Query.

ESQUIRE—250 W. 55th St., New York, NY 10019. David Granger, Ed.-in-Chief. Helene F. Rubinstein, Ed. Dir. Peter Griffin, Deputy Ed. Articles, 2,500 to 6,500 words, for intelligent adult audience. Pay varies, on acceptance. Query with published clips; complete manuscripts from unpublished writers. SASE required. Web site: www.esquiremag.com.

ESSENCE—1500 Broadway, New York, NY 10036. Susan L. Taylor, Ed.-in-Chief. Monique Greenwood, Exec. Ed. Provocative articles, 800 to 2,500 words, about black women in America today: self-help, how-to pieces, business and finance, work, parenting, health, celebrity profiles, and political issues. Pays varying rates, on acceptance. Query required.

FAMILY CIRCLE—375 Lexington Ave., New York, NY 10017. Nancy Clark, Deputy Ed. Articles, to 2,000 words, on "women who make a difference," "profiles in courage/love" (dramatic narratives), opinion pieces on topics of general interest, humor essays. Pays top rates, on acceptance. Query required.

FRIENDLY EXCHANGE—P.O. Box 2120, Warren, MI 48090-2120. Dan Grantham, Ed. Articles, 700 to 1,500 words, offering readers "news you can use," on lifestyle issues, such as home, health, personal finance, and travel. Photos. Pays $400 to $1,000, extra for photos. Query required. Guidelines.

THE FUTURIST—World Future Society, 7910 Woodmont Ave., Suite 450, Bethesda, MD 20814. Cynthia Wagner, Man. Ed. Features, 1,000 to 5,000 words, on subjects pertaining to the future: environment, education, business, science, technology, etc. Submit complete manuscript with brief bio and SASE. Pays in copies.

GEIST—1014 Homer St., #103, Vancouver, BC, Canada V6B 2W9. Attn: Editorial Board. Quarterly. "The Canadian Magazine of Ideas and Culture." Creative nonfiction, 200 to 1,000 words; excerpts, 300 to 1,500 words, from works in progress; long essays and short stories, 2,000 to 5,000 words. Payment varies, on publication. Query for longer pieces. E-mail: geist@geist. com. Web site: www.geist.com.

GENERATION—203 N. Wabash, #1618, Chicago, IL 60601. Allen Rafalson, Man. Ed. Bimonthly. Articles that cover topics of interest to both men and women "of the current generation." Insightful first-person opinion pieces. Payment varies. Query.

GLAMOUR—4 Times Sq., New York, NY 10036. Bonnie Fuller, Ed.-in-Chief. Editorial approach is "how-to" for women, 18 to 35. Articles on careers, health, psychology, politics, interpersonal relationships, etc. Fashion, health, and beauty material staff-written. Pay varies per word, on acceptance. E-mail: letters@glamour.com. Web site: www.glamour.com.

GOOD HOUSEKEEPING—959 Eighth Ave., New York, NY 10019. Nancy Bilyean, Articles Ed. Articles, 2,500 words, on a unique or trend-setting event; family relationships; personal medical pieces dealing with an unusual illness, treatment, and results. Pays first-time writers $500 to $750 for short, essay-type articles; $1,500 to $2,000 for full-length articles, on acceptance. "Payment scale rises for writers with whom we work frequently." Queries preferred. Guidelines.

GRIT—Ogden Publications 1503 S.W. 42nd St., Topeka, KS 66609. Donna Doyle, Ed.-in-Chief. Articles, 1,200 to 1,500 words, on people, home and garden, lifestyles, friends and family, reminiscences, grandparenting, Americana. Send complete manuscript with photos (submissions with photos are reviewed and considered first). SASE required; guidelines available. Pays 15¢ to 22¢ a word for features, flat rate for departments, extra for photos, on publication. Allow at least six months for review. Submissions will not be acknowledged, nor will status updates be given. E-mail: grit@cjnetworks.com. Web site: www.grit.com.

HARPER'S BAZAAR—1700 Broadway, 37th Fl., New York, NY 10019. Katherine Betts, Ed.-in-Chief. Articles for sophisticated women on current issues, books, art, film, travel, fashion and beauty. Send queries with one- to three-paragraph proposal; include clips and SASE. Rarely accepts fiction. Payment varies.

HOUSE BEAUTIFUL—1700 Broadway, New York, NY 10019. Elaine Greene, Features Ed. One personal memoir of 3,000 words each month, "Thoughts of Home," with high literary standards. Pays $1 per word, on acceptance. Query with detailed outline and SASE. Guidelines.

IDEALS—P.O. Box 305300, Nashville, TN 37230. Lisa Ragan, Ed. Articles, 800 to 1,000 words; poetry, 12 to 50 lines. Light, nostalgic pieces. Payment varies. SASE for guidelines.

ITALIAN AMERICA—219 E St. N.E., Washington, DC 20002-4922. Brenda K. Dalessandro, Ed. "The Official Publication of the Order Sons of Italy in America." Quarterly. Articles, 1,000 to 2,500 words, and fillers, 500 to 750 words, on people, institutions, and events of interest to the Italian-American community. Also book reviews. Payment varies, on publication. Queries preferred. Web site: www.osia.org.

JOURNAL AMERICA—P.O. Box 459, Hewitt, NJ 07421-0459. Glen Malmgren, Ed. Monthly. Articles on a wide variety of subjects of interest to the American family. Of special interest, articles that deal with all aspects of today's demanding lifestyle, with a touch of humor. Query. Payment varies.

KIWANIS—3636 Woodview Trace, Indianapolis, IN 46268. Chuck Jonak, Man. Ed. Articles, 1,200 to 2,500 words, on home; family; international issues; the social, health, and emotional needs of youth (especially under age 6); career and community concerns of business and professional people. No travel pieces, interviews, profiles. Pays $400 to $1,000, on acceptance. Query. Send SASE for guidelines. E-mail: magazine@kiwanis.org. Web site: www.kiwanis.org/magazine.

LADIES' HOME JOURNAL—125 Park Ave., New York, NY 10017. Pam O'Brien, Articles. Ed. Articles on contemporary subjects of interest to women. "See masthead for specific-topic editors and address appropriate editor." Query with SASE required. Web site: www.lhj.com.

LISTEN MAGAZINE—55 W. Oak Ridge Dr., Hagerstown, MD 21740. Larry Becker, Ed. Articles, 1,000 to 1,200 words, on problems of alcohol and drug abuse, for teenagers; personality profiles; self-improvement articles, and drug-free activities. Photos. Pays 6¢ to 10¢ a word, extra for photos, on acceptance. Guidelines. Sample issues available for $1 and 9x12 envelope. Query.

MCCALL'S—375 Lexington Ave., New York, NY 10017. Attn: Articles Ed. Articles, 1,000 to 1,800 words, on current issues, human interest, family relationships. Payment varies, on acceptance. SASE.

MADEMOISELLE—4 Times Square, 17th Fl., New York, NY 10036. Faye Haun, Man. Ed. Articles, 750 to 2,500 words, on subjects of interest to single, working women in their twenties. Reporting pieces, essays, first-person accounts, and humor; how-tos on personal relationships, work, and fitness. No fiction. Pays excellent rates, on acceptance. SASE required. Query with clips. Web site: www.mademoiselle.com.

METROPOLITAN HOME—1633 Broadway, New York, NY 10019. Attn: Michael Lassell, Articles Dept. Service and informational articles for residents of houses, co-ops, lofts, and condominiums, on real estate, equity, wine and spirits, collecting, etc. Interior design and home furnishing articles with emphasis on lifestyle. Pay varies. Query with clips.

MOTHER EARTH NEWS—49 E. 21st St., 11th Fl., New York, NY 10010. Matthew Scanlon, Ed. Articles for rural and urban readers: home improvements, how-tos, indoor and outdoor gardening, health, food, ecology, energy, and consumerism. Pays varying rates, on acceptance.E-mail: letters@ motherearthnews.com. Web site: www.motherearthnews.com.

MOTHER JONES—731 Market St., Suite 600, San Francisco, CA 94103. Roger Cohn, Ed. Investigative articles, political essays, cultural analyses, multicultural issues. "OutFront" pieces, 250 to 500 words. Query with SASE. Web site: www.motherjones.com.

MS.—20 Exchange Pl., 22nd Fl., New York, NY 10005. Attn: Manuscript Ed. Articles relating to feminism, women's roles, and social change; reporting, essays, theory, and analysis. No poetry or fiction. Pays market rates. Query with resumé, clips, and SASE. E-mail: info@msmagazine.com. Web site: www.msmagazine.com.

NATIONAL ENQUIRER—600 East Coast Ave., Lantana, FL 33464-0002. Attn: C. Montgomery. Mass audience: topical news, celebrities, how-to, scientific discoveries, human drama, adventure, medical news, personalities. Photos. Query (2 to 3 sentences, with source) with SASE.

NAVIGATOR—Pace Communications, 1301 Carolina St., Greensboro, NC 27401. Susanna Rodell, Ed. Bimonthly general interest magazine distributed at Holiday Inn Express Hotels. Aricles on sports, entertainment, and food. Photo essays, news on traveling trends, gear, and information. SASE for guidelines.

THE NEW YORK TIMES MAGAZINE—229 W. 43rd St., New York, NY 10036. Attn: Articles Ed. Timely articles, approximately 3,000 words, on news items, forthcoming events, trends, culture, entertainment, etc. Pays to $2,500 for major articles, on acceptance. Query with clips.

THE NEW YORKER—4 Times Square, New York, NY 10036. Send submissions to appropriate Editor (Fact, Fiction, or Poetry). Factual and biographical articles for "Profiles," "Reporter at Large," etc. Pays good rates, on acceptance. Query.

NEWSWEEK—251 W. 57th St., New York, NY 10019-1894. Attn: My Turn. Original personal (first person) opinion essays, 850 to 900 words, for "My Turn" column; must contain verifiable facts. Submit manuscript with SASE. Pays $1,000, on publication.

PARADE—711 Third Ave., New York, NY 10017. Articles Ed. National Sunday newspaper magazine. Factual and authoritative articles, 1,200 to 1,500 words, on subjects of national interest: social issues, common health concerns, sports, community problem-solving, and extraordinary achievements of ordinary people. "We seek unique angles on all topics." No fiction, poetry, cartoons, games, nostalgia, quotes, or puzzles. Pays from $1,000. Query with two writing samples and SASE.

PENTHOUSE—277 Park Ave., 4th Fl., New York, NY 10172-0003. Peter Bloch, Ed. Lavada B. Nahon, Sr. Ed. General-interest or controversial articles, to 5,000 words. Pays to $1 a word, on acceptance.

PEOPLE WEEKLY—Time-Life Bldg., Rockefeller Ctr., New York, NY 10020. John Saar, Asst. Man. Ed. "Vast majority of material is staff-written." Will consider article proposals, 3 to 4 paragraphs, on timely, entertaining, and topical personalities. Pays good rates, on acceptance.

PLAYBOY—680 North Shore Dr., Chicago, IL 60611. Stephen Randall, Exec. Ed. Sophisticated articles, 4,000 to 6,000 words, of interest to urban men. Humor, satire. Pays on acceptance. Query. E-mail: stephenr@playboy.com.

PLAYGIRL—801 Second Ave., 9th Fl., New York, NY 10017. Daryna McKeand, Man. Ed. Articles, 750 to 3,000 words, on sexuality, relationships, and celebrities for women ages 18 and up. Erotic fantasies, 1,300 to 2,000 words. Query with clips. Pays negotiable rates, after acceptance.

PRESERVATION—1785 Massachusetts Ave. N.W., Washington, DC 20036. Robert Wilson, Ed. Feature articles from published writers, 1,500 to 4,000 words, on the built environment, place, preservation issues, and people involved in preserving America's heritage. Mostly free-lance. Query. E-mail: preservation@nthp.org. Web site: nationaltrust.org.

PRIORITIES—2200 W. Parkway Blvd., Salt Lake City, UT 84119-2099. Mark Cook, Ed. Bimonthly. Profiles of successful individuals and their achievements as well as regular columns covering time management, career development, leadership, communications, personal finance, relationships and family, fitness and health, new product and book reviews. Query. Payment varies.

QUEEN'S QUARTERLY—Queens Univ., Kingston, Ont., Canada K7L 3N6. Boris Castel, Ed. Articles, to 5,000 words, on a wide range of topics, and fiction, to 5,000 words. Poetry; send no more than 6 poems. B&W art. Pays to $400, on publication. E-mail: qquarter@post.queensu.ca. Web site: http:// info.queensu.ca/quarterly.

READER'S DIGEST—Readers Digest Road, Pleasantville, NY 10570-7000. Kenneth Tomlinson, Ed.-in-Chief. Unsolicited manuscripts will not be read or returned. General-interest articles already in print and well-developed story proposals will be considered. Send reprint or query to any editor on the masthead.

REAL PEOPLE—450 7th Ave., Suite 1701, New York, NY 10123-0073. Alex Polner, Ed. True stories, to 500 words, on interesting people, strange occupations and hobbies, eye opening stories about people, places and odd happenings. Pays $25 to $50, on publication; send submissions to "Real Shorts," Brad Hamilton, Ed. Query for interviews, 1,000 to 1,800 words, with movie or TV actors, musicians, and other entertainment celebrities. Pays $150 to $350, on publication. SASE.

REDBOOK—224 W. 57th St., New York, NY 10019. Andrea Bauman, Ed. Articles, 1,000 to 2,500 words, on subjects related to relationships, marriage, sex, current social issues, crime, human interest, health, psychology, and parenting. Payment varies, on acceptance. Query with clips.

ROLLING STONE—1290 Ave. of the Americas, 2nd Fl., New York, NY 10104. Attn: Ed. Magazine of American music, culture, and politics. No fiction. "We rarely accept free-lance material." Query.

THE ROTARIAN—1560 Sherman Ave., Evanston, IL 60201-3698. Charles W. Pratt, Ed. Cary Silver, Managing Ed. Articles, 1,200 to 2,000 words, on international social and economic issues, business and management, human relationships, travel, sports, environment, science and technology; humor. Pays good rates, on acceptance. Query. E-mail: prattc@rotaryintl.org. Web site: www.rotary.org.

RUSSIAN LIFE—89 Main St., #2, Montpelier, VT 05602-2948. Mikhail Ivanov, Ed. Articles, 1,000 to 3,000 words, on Russian culture, travel, history, politics, art, business and society. "We do not want stories about personal trips to Russia, editorials on developments in Russia, or articles that promote the services of a specific company, organization, or government agency." Query. Pays 7¢ to 10¢ a word; $20 to $30 per photo, on publication.

THE SATURDAY EVENING POST—1100 Waterway Blvd., Indianapolis, IN 46202. Ted Kreiter, Exec. Ed. Family-oriented articles, 1,500 to 3,000 words: humor, preventive medicine, health and fitness, destination-oriented travel pieces (not personal experience), celebrity profiles, the arts, and sciences. Pays varying rates, on publication. Queries preferred.

SMITHSONIAN MAGAZINE—900 Jefferson Dr., Washington, DC 20560. Marlane A. Liddell, Articles Ed. Articles on history, art, natural history, physical science, profiles, etc. Query with clips. E-mail: siarticles@aol.com. Web site: www.smithsonianmag.si.edu.

SPORTS ILLUSTRATED—135 W. 50th St., New York, NY 10020. Chris Hunt, Articles Ed. Query. Rarely uses free-lance material. Web site: www.cnnsi.com.

STAR—5401 NW Broken Sound Blvd., Boca Raton, FL 33487. Attn: Ed. Dept. Topical articles, 50 to 800 words, on show business and celebrities, health, fitness, parenting, and diet and food. Pays varying rates.

THE WORLD & I—3600 New York Ave., NE, Washington DC, 20002-1947. Scholarly monthly. Articles, 2,500 words, on current issues, arts, natural science, life, and culture. Submit manuscript on 3.5" disk; via e-mail: input@worldandimag.com; or regular mail, typed and double-spaced. Payment varies according to article, and is made on publication. Send SASE for guidelines. E-mail: editor@worldandimag.com.

THE TOASTMASTER—P.O. Box 9052, Mission Viejo, CA 92690. Suzanne Frey, Ed. Articles, 1,500 to 2,500 words, on decision making, leadership, language, interpersonal and professional communication, humor, logical thinking, rhetorical devices, public speaking in general, profiles of great orators, speaking techniques, etc. Pays $100 to $250, on acceptance.

TOWN & COUNTRY—1700 Broadway, New York, NY 10019. Pamela Fiori, Ed.-in-Chief. Considers one-page proposals for articles. Include clips and resumé. Rarely buys unsolicited manuscripts.

TRAVEL & LEISURE—1120 Ave. of the Americas, New York, NY 10036. Nancy Novogrod, Ed.-in-Chief. Articles, 800 to 3,000 words, on destinations and travel-related activities. Regional pieces for regional editions. Pays varying rates, on acceptance. Query. E-mail: tlquery@amexpub.com. Web site: www.travelandleisure.com.

TV GUIDE—Radnor, PA 19088. Barry Golson, Exec. Ed. Short, light, brightly written pieces about humorous or offbeat angles of television and industry trends. (Majority of personality pieces are staff-written.) Pays on acceptance. Query.

VANITY FAIR—350 Madison Ave., New York, NY 10017. Attn: Submissions (Specify News, Arts, or Culture). Pays on acceptance. Query.

VILLAGE VOICE—36 Cooper Sq., New York, NY 10003. Doug Simmons, Man. Ed. Articles, 500 to 2,000 words, on current or controversial topics. Pays $100 to $1,500, on acceptance. Query or send manuscript with SASE.

WASHINGTON POST MAGAZINE—*The Washington Post,* 1150 15th

St. N.W., Washington, DC 20071. John Cotter, Sr. Ed. Essays, profiles, and Washington-oriented general-interest pieces, to 5,000 words, on business, arts and culture, politics, science, sports, education, children, relationships, behavior, etc. Pays from $1,000, after acceptance.

WOMAN'S DAY—1633 Broadway, New York, NY 10019. Stephanie Abarbanel, Sr. Articles Ed. Articles, 500 to 1,800 words, on subjects of interest to women: marriage, family health, money management, interpersonal relationships, changing lifestyles, etc. Dramatic first-person narratives about women who have experienced medical miracles or other triumphs, or have overcome common problems, such as being overweight. SASE required. Pays top rates, on acceptance. Query; unsolicited manuscripts not accepted.

WOMAN'S WORLD—270 Sylvan Ave., Englewood Cliffs, NJ 07632. Attn: Ed. Articles, 600 to 1,800 words, of interest to middle-income women between the ages of 18 and 60, on love, romance, careers, medicine, health, psychology, family life, travel; dramatic stories of adventure or crisis, investigative reports. Send SASE for guidelines. Pays $300 to $900, on acceptance. Query. E-mail: dearww@aol.com.

YANKEE—Yankee Publishing Inc., P.O. Box 520, Dublin, NH 03444. Jim Collins, Ed. Articles, to 2,500 words, with New England angle. Photos. Pays $150 to $2,000 (average $800), on acceptance. Query required. E-mail: queries@yankeepub.com. Web site: www.newengland.com.

CURRENT EVENTS, POLITICS

AMERICAN CITY & COUNTY—6151 Powers Ferry Rd. N.W., Atlanta, GA 30339-2959. Janet Ward, Ed. Articles, 600 to 2,500 words, on local government issues (wastewater, water, solid waste, financial management, information technology, etc.). "Our readers are elected and appointed local government leaders." Guidelines. E-mail: janet@intertec.com. Web site: www.americancityandcounty.com.

THE AMERICAN LEGION—P.O. Box 1055, Indianapolis, IN 46206. John B. Raughter, Ed. Articles, 750 to 2,000 words, on current world affairs, public policy, and subjects of contemporary interest. Pays $500 to $3,000, on acceptance. Query.

THE AMERICAN SCHOLAR—1811 Q St. N.W., Washington, DC 20009-9974. Anne Fadiman, Ed. Non-technical articles and essays, 3,500 to 4,000 words, on current affairs, the American cultural scene, politics, arts, religion, and science. Pays to $500, on acceptance. No electronic submissions. E-mail: scholar@pbk.org. Web site: www.pbk.org.

THE AMICUS JOURNAL—Natural Resources Defense Council, 40 W. 20th St., New York, NY 10011. Kathrin Day Lassila, Ed. Investigative articles, profiles, book reviews, and essays, related to the environment, especially national and international environmental policy. Also poetry "rooted in nature." Pays varying rates, on publication. Queries with clips required. E-mail: amicus@nrdc.org. Web site: www.nrdc.org.

THE ATLANTIC MONTHLY—77 N. Washington St., Boston, MA 02114. William Whitworth, Ed. Not currently accepting material. Web site: www.theatlantic.com.

BRIARPATCH—2138 McIntyre St., Regina, Saskatchewan, Canada S4P

2R7. George Manz, Man. Ed. "A progressive Canadian newsmagazine." Left-wing articles, 600 to 1,200 words, on politics, women's issues, environment, labor, international affairs for Canadian activists involved in social change issues. Pays in copies. Queries preferred. E-mail: briarpatch@mag@sk. sympatico.ca. Web site: www.briarpatchmagazine.com

CALIFORNIA JOURNAL—2101 K St., Sacramento, CA 95816. Cynthia H. Craft, Ed. "Independent analysis of politics and government." Balanced articles, 1,500 words, related to California government and politics. Advocacy pieces, 800 words. Pays up to $1000 for articles, on publication. (No payment for advocacy pieces.) Query.

CAMPAIGNS & ELECTIONS—1414 22nd St., Washington, DC 20037. Ron Faucheux, Ed. Feature articles, 700 to 4,000 words, related to the strategies, techniques, trends, and personalities of political campaigning. Campaign case studies, 1,500 to 3,000 words; how-to articles, 700 to 2,000 words, on specific aspects of campaigning; items, 100 to 800 words, for "Inside Politics"; and in-depth studies, 700 to 3,000 words, of public opinion, election results, and political trends that help form campaign strategy. Pays in subscriptions and free admission to certain public seminars.

CHURCH & STATE—1816 Jefferson Pl. N.W., Washington, DC 20036. Joseph L. Conn, Ed. Articles, 600 to 2,600 words, on issues of religious liberty and church-state relations, promoting the concept of church-state separation. Pays varying rates, on acceptance. Query.

COMMENTARY—165 E. 56th St., New York, NY 10022. Neal Kozodoy, Ed. Articles, 5,000 to 7,000 words, on contemporary issues, Jewish affairs, social sciences, religious thought, culture. Serious fiction; book reviews. Pays on publication.

COMMONWEAL—475 Riverside Dr., New York, NY 10115. Margaret O'Brien Steinfels, Ed. Catholic. Articles, to 3,000 words, on political, social, religious, and literary subjects. Pays 3¢ a word, on acceptance.

CULTUREFRONT—150 Broadway, Suite 1700, New York, NY 10038. Attn: Ed. "A Magazine of the Humanities." Nonfiction and occasional fiction articles, 2,500 words, related to theme. "News and a variety of views on the production, interpretation, and politics of culture." No payment. Query for current themes. Web site: www.culturefront.org.

EMERGE—BET Plaza, 1900 W. Place N.E., Washington, DC 20018. Florestine Purnell, Man. Ed. "Black America's Newsmagazine." Articles, 1,200 to 2,000 words, on current issues, ideas, or news personalities of interest to successful, well-informed African-Americans. Department pieces, 650 to 700 words, on a number of subjects. Pays 50¢ a word, on publication. Query. E-mail: emerge@bet.net. Web site: www.emerge.com.

FIRST THINGS—156 Fifth Ave., #400, New York, NY 10010-7002. James Nuechterlein, Ed. Published 10 times a year. Essays and general social commentary, 1,500 words or 4,000 to 6,000 words, for academics, clergy, and general educated readership, on the role of religion in public life. Also, poetry, 4 to 40 lines. Pays $300 to $800, on publication.

FOREIGN SERVICE JOURNAL—2101 E. St. N.W., Washington, DC 20037. Articles on foreign policy and international issues of interest to the Foreign Service and the US diplomatic community. Also accepts 600 to 800 word sketches of foreign scenes and incidents for our "Postcard from Abroad"

department. Pays to 35¢ a word, on publication. Query. E-mail: journal@
afsa.org. Web site: www.afsa.org/fsj/index.html

THE FREEMAN—Foundation for Economic Education, 30 S. Broadway, Irvington-on-Hudson, NY 10533. Sheldon Richman, Ed., Beth Hoffman, Man. Ed. Articles, to 3,500 words, on economic, political, and moral implications of private property, voluntary exchange, and individual choice. Pays 10¢ a word, on publication.

IN THESE TIMES—2040 N. Milwaukee Ave., Chicago, IL 60647. Joel Bleifuss, Ed. Biweekly. Articles, 1,500 to 2,500 words, on politics, the environment, labor, women's issues, etc. "A magazine with a progressive political perspective. Please read before querying us." Payment varies, on publication. Query. E-mail: itt@inthesetimes.com. Web site: www.inthesetimes.com.

IRISH AMERICA—432 Park Ave. S., Suite 1503, New York, NY 10016. Patricia Harty, Ed. Articles, 1,500 to 2,000 words, of interest to Irish-American audience; preferred topics include history, sports, the arts, and politics. Pays 10¢ a word, after publication. Query.

MIDSTREAM—633 Third Ave., 21st Fl., New York, NY 10017. Joel Carmichael, Ed. Articles of international and Jewish/Zionist concern. Pays 5¢ a word, after publication. Allow 3 months for response.

MOMENT MAGAZINE—4710 41st St. N.W., Washington, DC 20016. Hershel Shanks, Ed. Sophisticated articles, 2,500 to 5,000 words, on Jewish culture, politics, religion, and personalities. Columns, to 1,500 words, with uncommon perspectives on contemporary issues, humor, strong anecdotes. Book reviews, 400 words. Pays $40 to $600. Web site: www.momentmag.com.

MOTHER JONES—731 Market St., Suite 600, San Francisco, CA 94103. Roger Cohn, Ed. Investigative articles and political essays. Pays $1,000 to $3,000 for feature articles, after acceptance. Query with clips and SASE.

THE NATION—33 Irving Place, 8th Fl., New York, NY 10003. Katrina vanden Heuvel, Ed. Articles, 1,500 to 2,500 words, on politics and culture from a liberal/left perspective. Editorials, 750 to 1,000 words. Pays $75 per published page, to $300, on publication. Query. E-mail: info@thenation.com. Web site: www.thenation.com.

THE NEW YORK TIMES MAGAZINE—229 W. 43rd St., New York, NY 10036. Attn: Articles Ed. Timely articles, approximately 4,000 words, on news items, trends, culture, etc. Pays $1,000 for short pieces, from $2,500 for major articles, on acceptance. Query with clips.

THE NEW YORKER—4 Times Square, New York, NY 10036. Attn: Ed., "Comment." Political/social essays, 1,000 words. Pays on acceptance. Query.

THE PROGRESSIVE—409 E. Main St., Madison, WI 53703. Matthew Rothschild, Ed. Articles, 500 to 4,000 words, on political, social and economic problems. Pays $100 to $500, on publication. E-mail: editorial@progressive.org. Web site: www.progressive.org.

PUBLIC CITIZEN MAGAZINE—1600 20th St. N.W., Washington, DC 20009. Bob Mentzinger, Ed. Investigative reports and articles of timely political interest, for members of Public Citizen: consumer rights, health and safety, environmental protection, safe energy, tax reform, international trade, and government and corporate accountability. Photos, illustrations. Honorarium. E-mail: pcmail@citizen.org. Web site: www.citizen.org.

TIKKUN—2107 Van Ness, Ste. 302, San Francisco, CA 94109. Michael Lerner, Ed. "A Bimonthly Jewish Critique of Politics, Culture & Society." Articles, 2,400 words. "Read a copy to get a sense of what we publish. We are always interested in work pertaining to contemporary culture." Pays in copies. E-mail: magazine@tikkun.org.

VFW MAGAZINE—406 W. 34th St., Kansas City, MO 64111. Richard K. Kolb, Ed. Articles, 1,000 words, related to current foreign policy and defense, American armed forces abroad, and international events affecting U.S. national security. Also, up-to-date articles on veteran concerns and issues affecting veterans. Pays to $500, on acceptance. Query. Guidelines. E-mail: patbrown@vfw.org. Web site: www.vfw.org.

REGIONAL AND CITY PUBLICATIONS

ADIRONDACK LIFE—P.O. Box 410, Jay, NY 12941. Elizabeth Folwell, Ed. Features, to 5,000 words, on outdoor and environmental activities and issues, arts, wilderness, wildlife, profiles, history, and fiction; focus is entirely on the Adirondack Park region of New York State. Pays to 25¢ a word, 30 days after acceptance. Query.

ALABAMA HERITAGE—The Univ. of Alabama, Box 870342, Tuscaloosa, AL 35487-0342. Suzanne Wolfe, Ed. Quarterly. Articles, to 5,000 words, on local, state, and regional history: art, literature, language, archaeology, music, religion, architecture, and natural history. Query, mentioning availability of photos and illustrations. Pays an honorarium, on publication, plus 10 copies. Guidelines.

ALASKA—4220 B St., Suite 210, Anchorage, AK 99503. Bruce Woods, Ed. Articles, 1,500 words, on life in Alaska. Pays varying rates, on publication. Guidelines.

ALBEMARLE—1224 W. Main St., #220, Charlottesville, VA 22903-2858. Hilary Swinson, Ed. Bimonthly lifestyle magazine highlighting the news and events of Virginia. Topics include health and medicine, the arts, home architecture, interior design, and gardening. Write for complete guidelines. Payment varies.

ARIZONA TRENDS OF THE SOUTHWEST—P.O. Box 8508, Scottsdale, AZ 85252-8508. Penny Johnson, Ed. Published ten times per year. Features on fashion, health and beauty, special events, dining, the performing arts, and book reviews. Query for complete guidelines.

ASPEN MAGAZINE—720 E. Durant Ave., #E-8, Aspen, CO 81611-2071. Janet O'Grady, Ed. Bimonthly lifestyle magazine that covers the Aspen and Snowmass area. Outdoor sports, the arts, profiles, the environment, and news and photo essays. Send for guidelines. Pay varies.

ATLANTA —1330 W. Peachtree St., Suite 450, Atlanta, GA 30309-3214. Lee Walburn, Ed.-in-Chief. Articles, 1,500 to 5,000 words, on Atlanta subjects or personalities. Pays $300 to $2,000, on publication. Query.

ATLANTA HOMES AND LIFESTYLES—1100 Johnson Ferry Rd., #595, Atlanta, GA 30342-1746. Attn: Eds. Articles with a local angle. Department pieces for "Around Atlanta," "Short Takes," "House Hunting, "Quick

Fix," and "Cheap Chic." Pays $50 to $300 for departments; $300 to $500 for features, on acceptance.

BACK HOME IN KENTUCKY—P.O. Box 681629, Franklin, TN 37068-1629. Nanci P. Gregg, Man. Ed. Articles on Kentucky history, travel, craftsmen and artisans, Kentucky cooks, and "colorful" characters; limited personal nostalgia specifically related to Kentucky. Pays $25 to $100 for articles with B&W or color photos. Queries preferred.

BALTIMORE MAGAZINE—1000 Lancaster St., Suite 400, Baltimore, MD 21202. Margaret Guroff, Man. Ed. Articles, 500 to 3,000 words, on people, places, and things in the Baltimore metropolitan area. Consumer advice, investigative pieces, profiles, humor, and personal experience pieces. Payment varies, on publication. Query required.

BIG APPLE PARENT—(formerly *The Big Apple Parents' Paper*) 9 E. 38th St., New York, NY 10016. Helen Rosengren Freedman, Man. Ed. Articles, 500 to 750 words, for New York City parents. Pays $35 to $50, on publication. Buys first New York City rights. E-mail: parentspaper@mindspring.com. Web site: www.parentsknow.com.

BIG SKY JOURNAL—P.O. Box 1069, Bozeman, MT 59771. Michelle A. Orton, Man. Ed. Published 5 times a year. Articles, to 2,500 words, and fiction to 4,000 words, on Montana art and architecture, hunting and fishing, ranching and recreation. Payment varies, on publication. Query.

BIRMINGHAM—P.O. Box 10127, Birmingham, AL 35202-0127. Joe O'Donnell, Ed. Monthly publication spotlighting events, people, and activities in and around Birmingham. Also, business features, dining, fashion, and related general interest pieces. Write for complete guidelines. SASE.

BLUE RIDGE COUNTRY—P.O. Box 21535, Roanoke, VA 24018. Kurt Rheinheimer, Ed. Bimonthly. Regional articles, 1,200 to 2,000 words, that "explore and extol the beauty, history, and travel opportunities in the mountain regions of VA, NC, WV, TN, KY, MD, SC, and GA." Color slides or B&W prints considered. Pays $200 for photo-features, on publication. Queries preferred.

BOCA RATON—6413 Congress Ave., #100, Boca Raton, FL 33487. Marie Speed, Ed. Bimonthly that focuses on southern Florida. Fashion, cuisine, travel, finance, health, and profiles of local residents and celebrities. Query. SASE for guidelines.

BOISE MAGAZINE—P.O. Box 1457, Boise, ID 83701-1457. Alan Minskoff, Ed. Quarterly. Lifestyle magazine for the residents and visitors of the Boise area. Dining, cooking, decorating ideas, interviews with local personalities, sports, and fashion. Write for complete guidelines. Payment varies.

THE BOSTON GLOBE MAGAZINE—*The Boston Globe,* P.O. Box 2378, Boston, MA 02107-2378. Nick King, Ed. General-interest articles on regional topics and profiles, 2,500 to 5,000 words. Query and SASE required.

BOSTON MAGAZINE—300 Massachusetts Ave., Boston, MA 02115. Lisa Gerson, Ed. Asst. Informative, entertaining features, 1,000 to 3,000 words, on Boston-area personalities, institutions, and phenomena. Query. Pays to $2,000, on publication.

BROOKLYN BRIDGE—388 Atlantic Ave., Brooklyn, NY 11217-1703. Joe Fodor, Ed. Monthly. Articles on a variety of topics of regional and national interest, including arts and cultural activities, investigative reports, and the "politics" of Brooklyn. Write for guidelines.

BUFFALO SPREE MAGAZINE—5678 Main St., Williamsville, NY 14221. Larry Levite and David McDuff, Pubs. Articles of local interest, to 1,800 words, for readers in the western New York region. Fiction, to 2,000 words; poetry. Pays $125 to $200, $25 for poetry, on publication.

BUSINESS IN BROWARD—P.O. Box 460669, Ft. Lauderdale, FL 33346-0669. Sherry Friedlander, Ed. Published 8 times a year. Articles, 1,000 words, on small business in eastern Florida county. Pay varies, on acceptance.

CANADIAN GEOGRAPHIC—39 McArthur Ave., Ottawa, Ont., Canada K1L 8L7. Rick Boychuk, Ed. "Making Canada Better Known to Canadians and to the World." Articles on interesting places, nature and wildlife in Canada. Payment varies, on acceptance. Query.

CAPE COD LIFE—P.O. Box 1385, Pocasset, MA 02559-1385. Greg O'Brien, Ed. Articles, to 2,000 words, on current events, business, art, history, gardening, and nautical lifestyle on Cape Cod, Martha's Vineyard, and Nantucket. Pays 15¢ a word, 30 days after publication. Query.

CARIBBEAN TRAVEL AND LIFE—330 W. Canton Ave., Winter Park, FL 32789. Bob Friel, Exec. Ed. Articles, 500 to 3,000 words, on all aspects of travel, recreation, leisure, and culture in the Caribbean, the Bahamas, and Bermuda. Pays $75 to $750, on publication. Query with published clips.

CENTRAL PENNSYLVANIA LIFE—P.O. Box 6, Camp Hill, PA 17011-4200. Eric Lund, Ed. Quarterly. Magazine for the Susquehanna Valley's Central Pennsylvania region. Features on the area as well as the following departments: home design, gardening, travel, gourmet food, antiques, the arts, and area events. Write for complete guidelines.

CHARLESTON MAGAZINE—P.O. Box 1794, Mt. Pleasant, SC 29465. Ed. Quarterly. Seeks nonfiction pertaining to Charleston, South Carolina. Past features have discussed topics such as secret winter getaways, holiday gift ideas, and local homeless shelters. Departments include "In Good Taste," "Top of the Shelf," "Midday Recipes," and "Cityscape." Payment varies, on publication. Query for guidelines.

CHARLOTTE—127 W. Worthington Ave., #208, Charlotte, NC 28203-4474. Richard Thurmond, Man. Ed. Monthly magazine that covers the social, economic, and cultural life of the residents of Charlotte and surrounding areas. Includes politics, business, art and entertainment, education, sports, travel, and society. Write for complete guidelines. Payment varies.

CHESAPEAKE BAY MAGAZINE—1819 Bay Ridge Ave., Annapolis, MD 21403. Tim Sayles, Ed. Articles, to 3,000 words, on boating and fishing on Chesapeake Bay. No fiction or poetry. Photos. Pays $100 to $500, on acceptance. Query. E-mail queries and submissions are welcome at cbmediator@aol.com.!

CHICAGO—500 N. Dearborn, Suite 1200, Chicago, IL 60610. Shane Tritsch, Man. Ed. Articles, 1,000 to 5,000 words, related to Chicago. Pays varying rates, on acceptance. Query.

CHICAGO HISTORY—Clark St. at North Ave., Chicago, IL 60614. Rosemary Adams, Ed. Articles, to 4,500 words, on Chicago's urban, political, social, and cultural history. Pays to $250, on publication. Query.

CINCINNATI MAGAZINE—One Centennial Plaza, 705 Central Ave.,

Suite 370, Cincinnati, OH 45202. Kitty Morgan, Ed. Articles, 500 to 3,500 words, on Cincinnati people and issues. Pays $50 to $500. Query with writing sample.

CITY AZ MAGAZINE—2525 E. Camelback Rd., #120, Phoenix, AZ 85016-4223. Vivi Stenberg, Man. Ed. Quarterly aimed at Phoenix area professionals. Covers fashion, beauty, and fitness; local and national profiles; as well as architecture and design. Query. Send for complete guidelines. Payment varies.

COLORADO HOMES AND LIFESTYLES—7009 S. Potomac St., Englewood, CO 80112. Evalyn K. McGraw, Ed. Bimonthly. Articles, 1,300 to 1,500 words, with a focus on Colorado homes and interiors. Features cover upscale homes and unusual lifestyles. Department pieces, 1,100 to 1,300 words, cover architecture, artists, food and wine, design trends, profiles, gardening, and travel. Pays $150 to $300, on acceptance. Guidelines. Query. E-mail: emcgraw@coloradohomesmag.com. Web site: www.coloradohomesmag.com.

COMMON GROUND MAGAZINE—P.O. Box 99, McVeytown, PA 17051-0099. Ruth Dunmire, Pam Brumbaugh, Eds. Quarterly. General-interest articles, 500 to 5,000 words, related to central Pennsylvania's Juniata River Valley and its rural lifestyle. Related fiction, 1,000 to 2,000 words. Poetry, to 12 lines. Fillers, photos, and cartoons. Pays $25 to $200 for articles, $5 to $15 for fillers, and $5 to $25 for photos, on publication. Guidelines.

COMMONWEALTH—177 Tremont St., 5th Fl., Boston, MA 02111. Robert Keough, Ed. Articles, 2,000 to 4,500 words, on politics, government, and public policy issues affecting Massachusetts citizens. Payment varies, on acceptance. Query.

CONNECTICUT—35 Nutmeg Dr., Trumbull, CT 06611. Charles Monagan, Ed. Articles, 1,500 to 3,500 words, on Connecticut topics, issues, people, and lifestyles. Pays $500 to $1,200, within 30 days of acceptance.

CRAIN'S DETROIT BUSINESS—1400 Woodbridge Ave., Detroit, MI 48207. James Melton, Asst. Man. Ed. Business articles, 500 to 1,000 words, about Detroit, for Detroit business readers. Pays $10 per inch, on publication. Query required.

DELAWARE TODAY—P.O. Box 2800, Wilmington, DE 19805. Marsha Mah, Ed. Service articles, profiles, news, etc., on topics of local interest. Pays $150 for department pieces, $200 to $500 for features, on publication. Queries with clips required.

DOWN EAST—Camden, ME 04843. Attn: Manuscript Ed. Articles, 1,500 to 2,500 words, on all aspects of life in Maine. Photos. Pays on acceptance. Query.

EASTSIDE PARENT—Northwest Parent Publishing, 1530 Westlake Ave. N., Suite 600, Seattle, WA 98109. Virginia Smyth, Ed. Articles, 300 to 2,500 words, for parents of children ages 14 and under. Pays $50 to $500, on publication. Queries preferred. Also publishes *Portland Parent, Seattle's Child,* and *Puget Sound Parent.*

FAMILY TIMES—P.O. Box 932, Eau Claire, WI 54702. Nancy Walter, Ed. Articles, from 800 words, for parents in the Chippewa Valley, WI. Pays $35 to $50, on publication. Queries preferred. Guidelines.

FLORIDA WILDLIFE—620 S. Meridian St., Tallahassee, FL 32399-

1600. Attn: Ed. Bimonthly of the Florida Fish and Wildlife Conservation Commission. Articles, 800 to 1,500 words, that promote native flora and fauna, hunting, fishing in Florida's waters, outdoor ethics, and conservation of Florida's natural resources. Pays $55 per published page. SASE for guidelines and how-to-submit memo.

FREDERICK—6 East St., #301, Frederick, MD 21701-5680. Dan Patrell, Man. Ed. Monthly that covers the Mid-Maryland area with emphasis on Frederick County. Local history, business, art, culture, and local personalities. Send for guidelines. Payment varies.

GARDEN SHOWCASE—P.O. Box 23669, Portland, OR 97281-3669. Lynn Lustberg, Ed. Monthly. Articles, to 1,000 words, on gardening. Features cover a wide range of gardening ideas, but all must have a connection to the Pacific Northwest. Also accepts slides or transparencies of trees, shrubs, perennials, and gardens in that area. Payment is $200, on publication. Query. E-mail: editor@gardenshowcase.com. Web site: www.gardenshowcase.com.

GO MAGAZINE—6600 AAA Dr., Charlotte, NC 28212-8250. Tom Crosby, Ed. Focuses on travel and auto safety in North and South Carolina, as well as their neighboring states. Pays 15¢ a published word, on publication.

GOLDENSEAL—The Cultural Ctr., 1900 Kanawha Blvd. E., Charleston, WV 25305-0300. John Lilly, Ed. Quarterly. Articles, 1,000 and 3,000 words, on West Virginia history, folklife, folk art and crafts, and music of a traditional nature. Pays 10¢ a word, on publication. Guidelines.

GRAND RAPIDS—549 Ottawa N.W., Grand Rapids, MI 49503. Carole R. Valade, Ed. Service articles (dining guide, travel, personal finance, humor) and issue-oriented pieces related to Grand Rapids, Michigan. Pays $35 to $200, on publication. Query.

GULF COAST GOLFER—See *North Texas Golfer.*

HIGH COUNTRY NEWS—Box 1090, Paonia, CO 81428. Betsy Marston, Ed. Biweekly. Articles, 2,000 words, and roundups, 750 words, on western environmental issues, public lands management, rural community, and natural resource issues; profiles of western innovators; pieces on western politics. "Writers must take regional approach." B&W photos. Pays 25¢ a word, on publication. Query with clips.

HISPANIC MONTHLY—3006 Garrow St., Houston, TX 77003-2326. Miguel Barrientos, Ed. Monthly that provides news on state and national issues of interest to Hispanics living in Texas. Article topics include business, the community, education, the law, politics, as well as lighter topics such as fashion, entertainment, and health and fitness. Query for complete guidelines. Payment varies.

ILLINOIS ENTERTAINER—124 W. Polk, Suite 103, Chicago, IL 60605. Michael C. Harris, Ed. Articles, 500 to 1,500 words, on local and national entertainment (emphasis on alternative music) in the greater Chicago area. Personality profiles, interviews, reviews. Photos. Pays varying rates, on publication. Query preferred.

THE IOWAN MAGAZINE—504 E. Locust, Des Moines, IA 50309. Jay P. Wagner, Ed. Articles, 1,000 to 3,000 words, on business, arts, people, and history of Iowa. Essays and poetry on life in Iowa. Photos a plus. Payment varies, on acceptance. Query required.

ISLAND LIFE—P.O. Box 929, Sanibel Island, FL 33957. Joan Hooper, Ed. Articles, 500 to 1,200 words, with photos, on wildlife, flora and fauna, design and decor, the arts, shelling, local sports, historical sites, etc., directly related to the islands of Sanibel, Captiva, Marco, Estero, or Gasparilla. No first-person articles. Pays on publication.

JACKSONVILLE—White Publishing Co., 1032 Hendricks Ave., Jacksonville, FL 32207. Ed. Service pieces and articles, 1,500 to 2,500 words, on issues and personalities of interest to readers in the greater Jacksonville area. Department pieces, 1,200 to 1,500 words, on business, health, travel, personal finance, real estate, arts and entertainment, sports, dining out, food. Home and garden articles on local homeowners, interior designers, remodelers, gardeners, craftsmen, etc., 1,000 to 2,000 words. Pays $200 to $500, on publication. Query required. Guidelines.

JOURNAL OF THE WEST—1531 Yuma, Box 1009, Manhattan, KS 66505-1009. Robin Higham, Ed. Articles, to 20 pages, on the history and culture of the West, then and now. Pays in copies.

KANSAS!—Kansas Dept. of Commerce, 700 S.W. Harrison, Suite 1300, Topeka, KS 66603-3957. Andrea Glenn, Ed. Quarterly. Articles, 1,000 to 1,250 words, on attractions and events of Kansas. Color slides. Pays to $350, on acceptance. Query.

KANSAS CITY MAGAZINE—118 Southwest Blvd., Kansas City, MO 64108. Zim Loy, Ed. Articles, 250 to 3,500 words, of interest to readers in Kansas City. Pays to 30¢ a word, on acceptance. Query.

LAKE SUPERIOR MAGAZINE—P.O. Box 16417, Duluth, MN 55816-0417. Paul Hayden, Ed. Articles with emphasis on Lake Superior regional subjects: historical and topical pieces that highlight the people, places, and events that affect the Lake Superior region. Pictorial essays; humor and occasional fiction. Quality photos enhance submissions. "Writers must have a thorough knowledge of the subject and how it relates to our region." Pays to $600, extra for photos, on publication. Query with SASE.

THE LOOK—P.O. Box 272, Cranford, NJ 07016-0272. John R. Hawks, Pub. Articles, 1,500 to 3,000 words, on fashion, student life, employment, relationships, and profiles of interest to local (NJ) readers ages 16 to 26. Also, beach stories and articles about the New Jersey shore. Pays $30 to $200, on publication. E-mail: jrhawks@thelookmag.com. Web site: www.thelookmag.com.

LOS ANGELES MAGAZINE—11100 Santa Monica Blvd., 7th Fl., Los Angeles, CA 90025. Spencer Beck, Ed. Articles, to 3,000 words, of interest to sophisticated, affluent southern Californians, preferably with local focus on a lifestyle topic. Payment varies. Query.

LOUISVILLE—137 W. Muhammad Ali Blvd., Suite 101, Louisville, KY 40202. Dan Crutcher, Ed. Articles, 1,000 to 2,000 words, on community issues, personalities, and entertainment in the Louisville area. Photos. Pays from $50, on acceptance. Query; articles on assignment only. Limited market.

MEMPHIS—Contemporary Media, Box 1738, Memphis, TN 38101. Richard Banks, Ed. Articles, 1,500 to 4,000 words, on a wide variety of topics related to Memphis and the Mid-South region: politics, education, sports, business, history, etc. Profiles; investigative pieces. Pays $50 to $500, on publication. Query. SASE for guidelines. E-mail address: memmag@mem.net.

METROKIDS—1080 N. Delaware Ave., Suite 702, Philadelphia, PA

19125. Nancy Lisagor, Ed. Tabloid. Features and department pieces, 500 to 1,000 words, on regional family entertainment and children's issues in the Philadelphia metropolitan region. Pays $25 to $75, on publication. Web site: www. metrokids.com. E-mail: editor@metrokids.com.

MICHIGAN LIVING—Auto Club of Michigan, 1 Auto Club Dr., Dearborn, MI 48126-9982. Ron Garbinski, Ed. Informative travel articles, 300 to 1,500 words, on U.S. and Canadian tourist attractions and recreational opportunities; special interest in Michigan. Pays $55 to $500 (rates vary for photos), on publication. Send queries only.

MID-WEST OUTDOORS—111 Shore Dr., Hinsdale, IL 60521-5885. Gene Laulunen, Ed. Articles, to 1,500 words, with photos, on where, when, and how to fish and hunt, within 600 miles of Chicago. Pays $30, on publication.

MILWAUKEE MAGAZINE—417 E. Chicago, Milwaukee, WI 53202. John Fennell, Ed. Profiles, investigative articles, and service pieces, 2,000 to 4,000 words; local tie-in a must. No fiction. Pays $400 to $1,000, on publication. Query preferred.

MINNESOTA MONTHLY—Lumber Exchange Bldg., 10 S. Fifth St., Suite 1000, Minneapolis, MN 55402. Pamela Hill Nettleton, Ed. Articles, to 2,000 words, on people, places, events, and issues in or about Minnesota. Pays $150 to $2,000, on acceptance. Query.

MONTANA MAGAZINE—P.O. Box 5630, Helena, MT 59604. Beverly R. Magley, Ed. Recreation, travel, general interest, regional profiles, photoessays. Montana-oriented only. B&W prints, color slides. Pays 15¢ a word, on publication.

MPLS. ST. PAUL—220 S. 6th St., Suite 500, Minneapolis, MN 55402-4507. Brian E. Anderson, Ed. In-depth articles, features, profiles, and service pieces about the Minneapolis-St. Paul area, 300 to 4,000 words. Pays to $2,500.

NEBRASKA HISTORY—P.O. Box 82554, Lincoln, NE 68501. James E. Potter, Ed. Articles, 3,000 to 7,000 words, on the history of Nebraska and the Great Plains. B&W line drawings. Pays in copies. Cash prize awarded to one article each year.

NEVADA MAGAZINE—401 N. Carson St., Carson City, NV 89701. David Moore, Ed. Carolyn Graham, Assoc. Ed. Articles, 500 to 700 or 1,500 to 1,800 words, on topics related to Nevada: travel, history, recreation, profiles, humor, and attractions. Special section on Nevada events and shows. Photos. Pay varies, on publication.

NEW JERSEY REPORTER—The Ctr. for Analysis of Public Issues, 164 Nassau St., Princeton, NJ 08542. Mark Magyar, Ed. In-depth articles, 1,000 to 4,000 words, on New Jersey politics and public affairs. Pays $175 to $800, on publication. Query required.

NEW MEXICO JOURNEY—3333 Fairview Rd., A-327, Costa Mesa, CA 92626. Bimonthly. Travel magazine for AAA New Mexico members. Departments include: "WeekEnder," "DayTripping," "Roads2Roam," "AutoNews" and "TravelNews." Send for guidelines.

NEW MEXICO MAGAZINE—Lew Wallace Bldg., 495 Old Santa Fe Trail, Santa Fe, NM 87501. Attn: Ed. Articles, 250 to 2,000 words, on New Mexico subjects. No poetry or fiction. Pays about 30¢ a word, on acceptance. Query.

NEWPORT LIFE—55 Memorial Blvd., Newport, RI 02840. Lynne Tungett, Publisher. John Pantalone, Ed. Bimonthly. Annual City Guide. Articles, 500 to 2,500 words, on people, places, attractions of Newport County: general-interest, historical, profiles, international celebrities, and social and political issues. Departments, 200 to 750 words: sailing, dining, food and wine, home and garden, and the arts in Newport County. Photos must be available for all articles. Query. SASE.

NORTH DAKOTA HORIZONS—P.O. Box 2639, Bismarck, ND 58502. Lyle Halvorson, Ed. Quarterly. Articles, about 2,500 words, on people, places, and events in North Dakota. Photos. Pays $75 to $300, on publication. E-mail: ndq@sage.und.nodak.edu.

NORTH GEORGIA JOURNAL—P.O. Box 127, Roswell, GA 30077. Olin Jackson, Pub./Ed. History, travel, and lifestyle features, 2,000 to 3,000 words, on north Georgia; need human-interest approach and must be written in first person. Include interviews. Photos a plus. Pays 8¢ to 15¢ per word, on acceptance. Query.

NORTH TEXAS GOLFER—10301 Northwest Freeway, Suite 418, Houston, TX 77092. David Widener, Man. Ed. Articles, 800 to 1,500 words, involving local golfers or related directly to north Texas. Pays from $50 to $350, on publication. Query. Same requirements for *Gulf Coast Golfer* (related to south Texas).

NORTHEAST MAGAZINE—*The Hartford Courant,* 285 Broad St., Hartford, CT 06115. Jane Bronfman, Ed. Asst. Articles spun off the news and compelling personal stories, 750 to 3,000 words, that reflect the concerns of Connecticut residents. Pays $250 to $1,000, on acceptance. Send appropriate SASE. Responds in 2 to 3 months.

NORTHERN LIGHTS—Box 8084, Missoula, MT 59807-8084. Attn: Deborah Clow. Essays, 500 to 2,000 words, about the contemporary West. "We look for finely crafted personal essays that illuminate what it means to live in the American West. We're looking to bust the New York and Hollywood stereotypes." Pays 10¢ a word, on publication.

NORTHWEST REGIONAL MAGAZINES—P.O. Box 18000, 4969 Hwy. 101 N., Florence, OR 97439-0130. Attn: Jim Forst or Judy Fleagle. All submissions considered for use in *Oregon Coast, Oregon Outside* and *Northwest Travel.* Articles, 800 to 2,000 words, pertaining to travel, history, town/city profiles, events, outside activities, and nature. News releases, 200 to 500 words. Articles with photos (slides) preferred. Pays $50 to $300, after publication. Guidelines with SASE.

NORTHWEST TRAVEL—See *Northwest Regional Magazines.*

NOW & THEN—CASS/ETSU, P.O. Box 70556, Johnson City, TN 37614-0556. Jane Harris Woodside, Ed. Fiction and nonfiction, 1,500 to 3,000 words: short stories, articles, interviews, essays, memoirs, book reviews. Pieces must be related to theme of issue and have some connection to the Appalachian region. Also photos and drawings. SASE for guidelines and current themes. Pays $15 to $75, on publication.

OHIO MAGAZINE—62 E. Broad St., Columbus, OH 43215. Alyson Borgerding, Man. Ed. Focuses on travel around the state, with profiles of people, cities, and towns of Ohio; pieces on historic sites, tourist attractions, little-known spots. Lengths and payment vary. Query with clips.

OKLAHOMA TODAY—15 N. Robinson, Suite 100, Oklahoma City, OK 73102. Louisa McCune, Ed. Articles, 250 to 4,000 words: travel; profiles; history; nature and outdoor recreation; and arts. All material must have regional tie-in. Pays $25 to $1,000, on publication. Queries preferred. Guidelines available with SASE. Website: www.oklahomatoday.com

ORANGE COAST—3701 Birch St., Suite 100, Newport Beach, CA 92660. Patrick Mott, Ed. Articles, 2,000 to 3,000 words, of interest to educated Orange County residents. "Escape" (weekend travel) and "Close-Up" (personality profile), approx. 650 words, and 200-word pieces for "Short Cuts" (local phenomena). Query with clips. Pays $400 to $800 for features; $100 to $200 for departments; $50 for "Short Cuts," after acceptance. Guidelines.

ORANGE COUNTY WOMAN—3701 Birch St., #100, Newport Beach, CA 92660-2618. Carroll Lachnit, Ed. Articles, 500 to 1,500 words, for and about women living in Orange County, CA. "Our readers are highly educated, upscale women who are looking for information that will make their busy lives more efficient and gratifying. We cover everything from family issues to health and beauty." Must have strong local angle. No fiction. SASE for guidelines. Pays $50 to $300, on acceptance. E-mail: ocmag@aol.com.

OREGON COAST—See *Northwest Regional Magazines.*

OREGON OUTSIDE—Northwest Regional Magazines, Box 18000, 4969 Hwy 101 N, Suite 2, Florence, OR 97439-0130. Judy Fleagle, Co-Ed. Quarterly. Articles, 1,000 to 1,500 words, on Oregon and the outdoors, "all kinds of adventure, from walks for families to extreme skiing." Prefers to receive manuscript/photo packages. Photos means slide format for color and prints for black and white. Pays $100 to $350, on publication. Query.

ORLANDO MAGAZINE—260 Maitland Ave., Suite 2000, Altamonte Springs, FL 32701. Brooke Lange, Ed. Locally based articles and department pieces, lengths vary, for residents of Central Florida. Query with clips.

OUR STATE: DOWN HOME IN NORTH CAROLINA—P.O. Box 4552, Greensboro, NC 27404. Mary Ellis, Ed. Articles, 1,200 to 1,500 words, on people, history, and travel in North Carolina. Photos. Pays on publication.

PALM SPRINGS LIFE—Desert Publications, 303 N. Indian Canyon Dr., Palm Springs, CA 92262. Stewart Weiner, Ed. Articles, 1,000 to 3,000 words, of interest to "wealthy, upscale people who live and/or play in the desert." Pays $150 to $500 for features, $25 to $75 for short profiles, on publication. Query required. E-mail: stewart@corp.desert-resorts.com. Web sites: www.palmspringslife.com or www.desert-resorts.com.

PENNSYLVANIA MAGAZINE—Box 576, Camp Hill, PA 17001-0576. Matthew K. Holliday, Ed. General-interest features with a Pennsylvania focus. All articles must be accompanied by photocopies of possible illustrations. Query. Guidelines. E-mail: pamag@aol.com.

PERSIMMON HILL—1700 N.E. 63rd St., Oklahoma City, OK 73111. M.J. Van Deventer, Ed. Published by the National Cowboy Hall of Fame. Articles, 1,500 to 2,000 words, on Western history and art, cowboys, ranching, rodeo, and nature. Top-quality illustrations a must. Pays from $100 to $250, on publication. Query by mail only.

PHOENIX MAGAZINE—4041 N. Central Ave., Suite 530, Phoenix, AZ 85012. Kathy Khoury, Man. Ed. Articles, 250 to1,500 words, about people, places, and issues in and around Phoenix. All stories must have strong local connection. No fiction or personal essays. Pays $50 to $750, on publication. Query. E-mail: phxmag@aol.com.

PITTSBURGH—4802 Fifth Ave., Pittsburgh, PA 15213. Attn: Man. Ed. Profiles, from 300 to 3,000 words, feature stories and service pieces, from 1,200 to 3,000 words, and in-depth news features, to 5,000 words, geared primarily to metro Pittsburgh; western Pennsylvania, eastern Ohio, northern West Virginia, and western Maryland. Pays from $300 up, on publication. Query with outline. Brief, timely pieces, to 200 words, pays $50 to $150. Must query first. Web site: www.pittsburghmag.com

PITTSBURGH MAGAZINE—4802 Fifth Ave., Pittsburgh, PA 15213-2957. Ed. Monthly. For residents of western Pennsylvania, eastern Ohio, northern West Virginia, and western Maryland. Covers this region's lifestyle, including entertainment, arts and local events, and recent trends, fashion, and local personalities. Pay varies. Write for guidelines. Query.

PLUS MAGAZINE—(formerly *Senior Magazine*) 3565 S. Higuera St., San Luis Obispo, CA 93401. Attn: Ed. Articles, 600 to 900 words: personality profiles, travel pieces, articles about new things, places, business, sports, movies, television, and health; book reviews (of new or outstanding older books) of interest to seniors. Pays $1.50 per inch; $10 to $25 for B&W photos, on publication.

PORTLAND MAGAZINE—578 Congress St., Portland, ME 04101. Colin Sargent, Ed. "Maine's City Magazine." Articles on local people, legends, culture, and trends. Fiction, to 750 words. Pays on publication. Query preferred.

PORTLAND PARENT—See *Eastside Parent.*

PROVINCETOWN ARTS—650 Commercial St., Provincetown, MA 02657. Christopher Busa, Ed. Annual. Interviews, profiles, essays, 1,500 to 4,000 words. Mainstream fiction and novel excerpts, 500 to 5,000 words. Poems, submit up to 3 at a time. "We have a broad focus on the artists and writers who inhabit or visit Cape Cod." Pays from $125 for articles; $75 to $300 for fiction; $25 to $150 for poems, on publication.

PUGET SOUND PARENT—See *Eastside Parent.*

RANCH & COVE—P.O. Box 676130, Rancho Santa Fe, CA 92121-2766. William Abrams, Ed. Monthly. Local lifestyle publication for residents of the San Diego area. Articles on community leaders, charity fundraisers, and personalities, as well as fashion, art and antiques, and sports. Also includes local music and theatre events. Write for complete guidelines. Query. Payment varies.

RANGE MAGAZINE—106 E. Adams, Suite 201, Carson City, NV 89706. C.J. Hadley, Ed. Quarterly. "The Cowboy Spirit of America's Outback." Articles, 500 to 2,000 words, on issues that threaten the West, its people, lifestyles, lands, and wildlife. "Our main purpose is to present public awareness of the positive presence of ranching operations on America's rangelands." Payment varies, on publication. Query preferred. Web site: www.rangemagazine.com.

RECREATION NEWS—P.O. Box 32335, Washington, DC 20007-0635. Henry T. Dunbar, Ed. Articles, 900 to 2,200 words, on recreation and travel around the mid-Atlantic region for government and private sector workers in the Washington, DC area. "Articles should have a conversational tone that's lean and brisk." Pays $50 for reprints, to $300 for cover articles, on publication.

Queries preferred. Guidelines. E-mail: editor@recreationnews.com. Web site: www.recreationnews.com.

RHODE ISLAND MONTHLY—280 Kinsley Ave., Providence, RI 02903. Sarah Francis, Man. Ed. Features, 1,000 to 4,000 words, ranging from investigative reporting and in-depth profiles to service pieces and visual stories, on Rhode Island and southeastern Massachusetts. Seasonal material, 1,000 to 2,000 words. Fillers, 150 to 500 words, on Rhode Island places, customs, people, events, products and services, restaurants and food. Pays $250 to $1,000 for features; $25 to $50 for shorts, on acceptance. Query in writing.

RURAL LIVING—4201 Dominion Blvd., Suite 101, Glen Allen, VA 23060. Richard G. Johnstone, Jr., Ed. Features, 1,000 to 1,500 words, on people, places, historic sites in Virginia. Queries required. Pays $150 to $200 for articles, on publication.

RURALITE—P.O. Box 558, Forest Grove, OR 97116. Attn: Ed. or Feature Ed. Articles, 800 to 2,000 words, of interest to a primarily rural and small-town audience in OR, WA, ID, WY, NV, northern CA, and AK. "Think pieces" affecting rural/urban interests, regional history and celebrations, self-help, profiles, etc. No fiction or poetry. Pays $30 to $400, on acceptance. Queries required. Guidelines.

SAN DIEGO READER—P.O. Box 85803, San Diego, CA 92186. Jim Holman, Ed. Literate articles, 2,500 to 10,000 words, on the San Diego region. Pays $500 to $2,000, on publication.

SAN FRANCISCO—243 Vallejo, San Francisco, CA 94111. Dale Eastman, Ed. Service features, profiles of local newsmakers, and investigative pieces of local issues, 2,500 to 3,000 words. News items, 250 to 800 words, on subjects ranging from business to arts to politics. Payment varies, on acceptance. Query required.

SAN FRANCISCO BUSINESS TIMES—275 Battery St., Suite 940, San Francisco, CA 94111. Steve Symanovich, Ed. Bay area business-oriented articles, about 20 column inches. Limited free-lance market. Pays $250 to $350, on publication. Query.

SAN FRANCISCO EXAMINER MAGAZINE—*San Francisco Examiner*, 110 Fifth St., San Francisco, CA 94103. Attn: Ed. Articles, 1,200 to 3,000 words, on lifestyles, issues, business, history, events, and people in northern California. Query. Pays varying rates. Web site: www.examiner.com.

SAVANNAH MAGAZINE—P.O. Box 1088, Savannah, GA 31402. Linda Wittish, Ed. Articles, 2,500 to 3,500 words, on people and events in and around Savannah and the region. Historical articles, 1,500 to 2,500 words, of local interest. Reviews, 500 to 750 words, of Savannah-based books and authors. Short pieces, 500 to 750 words, on weekend getaways near Savannah. Pays $75 to $350, after acceptance. Submit complete manuscript. E-mail: lindaw@savannahnow.com. Web site: www.savannahnow.com/savannahmagazine.

SEATTLE MAGAZINE—423 Third Ave. West, Seattle, WA 98119. Rachel Hart, Ed. City, local issues, home, and lifestyle articles, 500 to 2,000 words, relating directly to the greater Seattle area. Personality profiles. Pays $100 to $700, 30 days after publication. Guidelines. E-mail: editor@seattlemag.com. Web sites: www.seattlemag.com, or www.seattlebridemag.com.

SEATTLE'S CHILD—Northwest Parent Publishing, 1530 Westlake Ave. N, Suite 600, Seattle, WA 98109. Ann Bergman, Ed. Articles, 400 to 2,500 words, of interest to parents, educators, and childcare providers of children 14 and under, and investigative reports and consumer tips on issues affecting families in the Puget Sound region. Pays $75 to $500, on publication. Query required.

SENIOR MAGAZINE—See *Plus Magazine.*

SILENT SPORTS—717 10th St., P.O. Box 152, Waupaca, WI 54981. Attn: Ed. Articles, 1,000 to 2,000 words, on canoeing, bicycling, cross-country skiing, running, hiking, backpacking, snowshoeing, inline skating, and other "silent" sports, in the upper Midwest region. "Articles must focus on the upper Midwest. No articles about places, people, or events outside the region." Pays $40 to $100 for features; $20 to $50 for fillers, on publication. Query. E-mail: info@silentsports.net. Web site: www.silentsports.net.

SOUTH CAROLINA HISTORICAL MAGAZINE—South Carolina Historical Society, 100 Meeting St., Charleston, SC 29401-2299. W. Eric Emerson, Ed. Scholarly articles, to 25 pages with footnotes, on all areas of South Carolina history. Pays in copies.

SOUTH CAROLINA WILDLIFE—P.O. Box 167, Columbia, SC 29202-0167. Attn: Man. Ed. Articles, 1,000 to 2,000 words, with regional outdoors focus: conservation, natural history and wildlife, recreation. Profiles. Pays from 15¢ a word. Query. Web site: scwildlife.com.

SOUTHWEST ART—5444 Westheimer, Suite 1440, Houston, TX 77056. Margaret L. Brown, Ed.-in-Chief. Articles, 1,200 to 1,800 words, on the artists, art collectors, museum exhibitions, gallery events and dealers, art history, and art trends west of the Mississippi River. Particularly interested in representational or figurative arts. Pays from $500, on acceptance. Query with at least 20 slides of artwork.

SUNSET MAGAZINE—80 Willow Rd., Menlo Park, CA 94025. Rosalie Muller Wright, Ed. Western regional. Limited free-lance market, but some need for western travel. Query; include clips. Web site: www.sunset.com.

SUNSHINE: THE SUNDAY MAGAZINE OF THE SUN-SENTINAL—*The Sun-Sentinel,* 200 E. Las Olas Blvd., Ft. Lauderdale, FL 33301-2293. Mark Gauert, Ed. Articles, 1,000 to 3,000 words, on topics of interest to south Floridians. Pays $300 to $1,200, on acceptance. Query. Guidelines.

SWEAT—736 E. Loyola Dr., Tempe, AZ 85282. Joan Westlake, Ed. "South West Exercise And Training." Articles, 500 to 1,200 words, on sports, wellness, and fitness with an Arizona angle. "No personal columns or tales. We want journalism. Articles must relate specifically to Arizona or Arizonans." Pays $25 to $60 for articles; $15 to $70 for photos, on publication. Queries required; no unsolicited manuscripts. E-mail preferred: westwoman@aol.com. Web site: www.sweatmagazine.com.

TALLAHASSEE MAGAZINE—P.O. Box 1837, Tallahassee, FL 32302-1837. Kathy Grobe, Man. Ed. Articles, 800 to 1,500 words, on the life, people, and history of the north Florida-south Georgia area. Pays on acceptance. Query.

TEXAS HIGHWAYS MAGAZINE—P.O. Box 141009, Austin, TX 78714-1009. Jack Lowry, Ed. Texas travel, history, and scenic features, 200 to 1,800 words. Pays about 40¢ to 50¢ a word, $80 to $550 per photo. Query. Guidelines. Web site: www.texashighways.com. E-mail: editors@texashighways.com.

TEXAS MONTHLY—P.O. Box 1569, Austin, TX 78767-1569. Gregory Curtis, Ed. Features, 2,500 to 5,000 words, and departments, to 2,500 words, on art, architecture, food, education, business, politics, etc. "We like solidly researched pieces that uncover issues of public concern, reveal offbeat and previously unreported topics, or use a novel approach to familiar topics." Pays varying rates, on acceptance. Queries required. Web site: www.texas monthly.com.

TEXAS PARKS & WILDLIFE—3000 S. Interstate Hwy. 35, Suite 120, Austin, TX 78704. Articles, 400 to 1,500 words, promoting the conservation and enjoyment of Texas wildlife, parks, waters, and all outdoors. Features on hunting, fishing, birding, camping, and the environment. Photos a plus. Pays 30¢ to 50¢ per word, on acceptance; extra for photos. E-mail: magazine@tpwd. state.tx.us. Web site: www.tpwd.state.tx.us.

TIMELINE—1982 Velma Ave., Columbus, OH 43211-2497. Christopher S. Duckworth, Ed. Articles, 1,000 to 6,000 words, on history of Ohio (politics, economics, social, and natural history) for lay readers in the Midwest. Pays $100 to $900, on acceptance. Queries preferred. SASE for guidelines.

TORONTO LIFE—59 Front St. E., Toronto, Ont., Canada M5E 1B3. John Macfarlane, Ed. Articles, 1,500 to 4,500 words, on Toronto. Pays $1,500 to $3,500, on acceptance. Query.

TUCSON LIFESTYLE—Old Pueblo Press, 7000 E. Tanque Verde, Tucson, AZ 85715. Sue Giles, Ed.-in-Chief. Local slant to all articles on businesses, lifestyles, the arts, homes, fashion, and travel in the Southwest. Payment varies, on acceptance. Query preferred. E-mail: tucsonlife@aol.com.

VERMONT LIFE—6 Baldwin St., Montpelier, VT 05602. Tom Slayton, Ed.-in-Chief. Articles, 500 to 3,000 words, on Vermont subjects only. Pays 25¢ a word, extra for photos. Query preferred. E-mail: vtlife@life.state.vt.us. Web site: www.vtlife.com.

VIRGINIA BUSINESS—411 E. Franklin St., Suite 105, Richmond, VA 23219. James Bacon, Pub. Articles, 1,000 to 2,500 words, related to the business scene in Virginia. Pays varying rates, on acceptance. Query required. E-mail: pgaluszka@va-business.com. Web site: www.virginiabusiness.com.

VIRGINIA WILDLIFE—P.O. Box 11104, Richmond, VA 23230-1104. Attn: Ed. Articles, 800 to 1,200 words, with Virginia tie-in, on fishing, hunting, wildlife management, outdoor safety and ethics, etc. Articles may be accompanied by color photos. Pays from 18¢ a word, extra for photos, on publication. Query. E-mail: lwalker@dgif.state.va.us. Web site: www.dgif.state.va.us.

WASHINGTON FLYER—Suite 700, 1707 L St., NW, Washington, DC 20036. Stefanie Berry, Sr. Ed. Bimonthly. Local and travel publication for up-scale Washingtonians and visitors. Nonfiction briefs and features, from 350 to 1,500 words. Color photographs. Pays $150 to $800, on publication. Query. Rarely uses freelance material. Send SASE for guidelines. E-mail: stefanie@ themagazinegroup.com. Web site: www.washingtonflyermag.com.

WASHINGTON POST MAGAZINE—*The Washington Post*, 1150 15th St. N.W., Washington, DC 20071. T. A. Frail, Man. Ed. Personal-experience essays, profiles, and general-interest pieces, to 6,000 words, on business, arts and culture, politics, science, sports, education, children, relationships, behavior, etc. Articles should be of interest to people living in Washington, DC, area. Pays from $750, on acceptance. Limited market.

THE WASHINGTONIAN—1828 L St. N.W., Suite 200, Washington, DC 20036. John Limpert, Ed. Helpful, informative articles, 1,000 to 4,000 words, on DC-related topics. Pays 50¢ a word, on publication. E-mail: editorial@washingtonian.com. Web site: www.washingtonian.com.

WINDSPEAKER—Aboriginal Multi-Media Society of Alberta, 15001 112th Ave., Edmonton, Alberta, Canada T5M 2V6. Debora Lockyer, Ed. Tabloid. Features, news items, sports, op-ed pieces, columns, etc., 200 to 1,000 words, concerning Canada's Aboriginal peoples. Pays from $3 per published inch, after publication. Query. Guidelines.

WINDY CITY SPORTS—1450 W. Randolph, Chicago, IL 60607. Jeff Banowetz, Ed. Articles, to 1,000 words, on amateur sports in the Chicago area. Queries required. Pays $200, on publication.

WISCONSIN TRAILS—P.O. Box 5650, Madison, WI 53705. Scott Klug, Ed./Pub., Kate Bast, Ed. Articles, 1,500 to 2,000 words, on regional topics: outdoors, lifestyle, events, nature, the environment, history, arts, adventure, travel; profiles of artists, craftspeople, and regional personalities, works with previously published writers. Pays 25¢ per word, on publication. Query in writing. Web site: wistrails.com. E-mail: editor@wistrails.com.

THE WREN MAGAZINE—(formerly *Wyoming Rural Electric News*) 340 W. B St., Suite 101, Casper, WY 82601. Kris Wendtland, Ed. Articles, 500 to 900 words, on issues relevant to rural Wyoming. Wyoming writers given preference. Pays to $140, on publication. E-mail: wren@coffey.com.

YANKEE—Yankee Publishing Co., P.O. Box 520, Dublin, NH 03444. Jim Collins, Ed. Articles and fiction, 500 to 2,500 words, on New England and New England people. Pays $500 to $2,500 for features, on acceptance. Query required. E-mail: queries@yankeepub.com. Web site: www.newengland.com.

TRAVEL ARTICLES

AAA GOING PLACES/AAA TODAY—1515 N. Westshore Blvd., Tampa, FL 33607. Sandy Klim, Ed. Bimonthly. Articles, 1,000 to 1,200 words, on travel in Pennsylvania, West Virginia, New York, Massachusetts, and Ohio. International destinations as well. Color photos. Pays $300 to $400, on publication. E-mail: editorial@aaagoingplaces.com.

AIR FAIR: THE MAGAZINE FOR AIRLINE EMPLOYEES—See *Interline Adventures: The Magazine for Airline Employees.*

AIR FORCE TIMES—See *Times News Service.*

ARIZONA HIGHWAYS—2039 W. Lewis Ave., Phoenix, AZ 85009. Rebecca Mong, Sr. Ed. Informal, well-researched travel-experience articles exploring specific areas and aspects of Arizona, including well-known and remote destinations, history, nature, the environment, flora and fauna, anthropology, archaeology, hiking, and recreation. Topics should appeal to families and armchair travelers as well as experienced outdoor recreationists. Third-person preferred. Departments include "Focus on Nature," "Along the Way" (essay-like with a point of view), "Back Road Adventures," "Hike of the Month," and "Great Weekends," which unlike the rest of the magazine encompass guidebook-type service information. Arizona based fiction is occasionally used. Pays 35¢ to 55¢ a word, on acceptance. Written queries. Guidelines at www.arizonahighways.com.

ARMY TIMES—See *Times News Service.*

BIG WORLD—P.O. Box 8743-A, Lancaster, PA 17604. Jim Fortney, Ed. Quarterly. Articles, 500 to 4,000 words, that offer advice on working and studying abroad, humorous anecdotes, first-person experiences, or other "down-to-earth" travel information. "For people who prefer to spend their traveling time responsibly discovering, exploring, and learning, in touch with locals and their traditions, and in harmony with their environment." Pays $10 to $20 for articles, $5 to $20 for photos, on publication. Web page: www.bigworld.com

BLUE RIDGE COUNTRY—P.O. Box 21535, Roanoke, VA 24018. Kurt Rheinheimer, Ed. Bimonthly. Regional travel articles, 750 to 1,200 words, on destinations and backroad drives in the mountain regions of VA, NC, WV, TN, KY, MD, SC, and GA. Color slides and B&W prints considered. Pays to $200 for photo-features, on publication. Queries preferred. Web site: www.blueridgecountry.com. E-mail: info@leisurepublishing.com.

CANADIAN DIVER & WATERSPORT—See *Diver Magazine.*

CARIBBEAN TRAVEL AND LIFE—330 W. Canton Ave., Winter Park, FL 32789-3150. Steve Blount, Ed. Articles, varying lengths, for the upscale traveler. Topics include shopping, dining, arts and entertainment, and sightseeing suggestions. "You need to understand the editorial concept of the magazine; send for writer's guidelines."

COAST TO COAST—2575 Vista del Mar Dr., Ventura, CA 93001. Valerie Law, Ed. Membership publication for Coast to Coast Resorts, private camping and resort clubs across North America. Focuses on "travel, recreation, and good times." Destination features focus on a North American city or region, going beyond typical tourist stops to interview locals. Activity or recreation features introduce readers to a sport, hobby, or other diversion. Also features on RV lifestyle. Send queries or manuscripts. Payment is $350 to $600, on acceptance, for 1,500- to 2,500-word articles. Web site: www.rv.net.

CONDE NAST TRAVELER—360 Madison Ave., New York, NY 10017. Alison Humes, Features Ed. Uses very little free-lance material.

COUNTRY INNS BED & BREAKFAST—P.O. Box 182, S. Orange, NJ 07079-0182. Gail Rudder Kent, Ed.-in-Chief. Bimonthly. Articles, varying lengths, on country inns and bed & breakfast establishments throughout the U.S. Also includes features on antiques, gourmet cuisine, books, art, and regional attractions. Query. Payment varies.

CRUISE TRAVEL—990 Grove St., Evanston, IL 60201. Robert Meyers, Ed. Charles Doherty, Man. Ed. Ship-, port-, and cruise-of-the-month features, 800 to 2,000 words; cruise guides; cruise roundups; cruise company profiles; travel suggestions for one-day port stops. "Photo-features strongly recommended." Payment varies, on acceptance. Query (by mail only) with sample color photos.

DIVER MAGAZINE—P.O. Box 1312, Delta, B.C., Canada V4M 3Y8. Stephanie Bold, Ed. Illustrated articles, 500 to 1,000 words, on dive destinations. Shorter pieces are also welcome. "Travel features should be brief and accompanied by excellent slides and/or prints and a map. Unsolicited articles will be reviewed only from August to October. Guidelines. Limited market. E-mail address: divermag@axion.net. Web site: www.divermag.com.

ENDLESS VACATION—Box 80260, Indianapolis, IN 46280. Laurie D. Borman, Ed. Travel features, to 1,500 words; primarily on North American destinations, some international destinations. Pays on acceptance. Query preferred. Send SASE for guidelines. Limited market.

FRANCE MAGAZINE—4101 Reservoir Rd. N.W., Washington, DC 20007-2186. Karen Taylor, Ed. Quarterly. Articles, varying lengths, on business, culture, and society, for well-educated Francophiles throughout the U.S. Also, sightseeing information and tips on good restaurants and accomodations. Write for complete guidelines. Query.

GO MAGAZINE—6600 AAA Dr., Charlotte, NC 28212-8250. Tom Crosby, Ed. Focuses on travel and auto safety in North and South Carolina, as well as their neighboring states. Pays 15¢ per word, on publication. E-mail: trcrosby@aaaqa.com. Web site: www.aaacarolinas.com.

HAWAII—1210 Auahi St., Suite 231, Honolulu, HI 96814. John Hollon, Ed. Bimonthly. Articles, 1,000 to 2,500 words, related to Hawaii. Pays 10¢ and up a word, on publication. Query.

INDIA CURRENTS—P.O. Box 21285, San Jose, CA 95151. Vandana Kumar, Submissions Ed. First-person accounts, up to 3,000 words, of trips to India or the subcontinent. Helpful tips for first-time travelers. Prefer descriptions of people-to-people interactions. Pays $50 per 1,000 words.

INTERLINE ADVENTURES: THE MAGAZINE FOR AIRLINE EMPLOYEES—(formerly *Air Fair: The Magazine for Airline Employees*) 211 E. 7th St., #1100, Austin, TX 78701. Christina Kosta, Sr. Ed. Travel articles, 800 to 2,500 words, with photos, on shopping, sightseeing, dining, and nightlife for airline employees. Pays $250 to $800, upon publication.

ISLANDS—P.O. Box 4728, Santa Barbara, CA 93140-4728. Joan Tapper, Ed.-in-Chief. Destination features, 2,500 to 4,000 words, on islands around the world as well as department pieces and front-of-the-book items on island-related topics. Pays from 50¢ a word, on acceptance. Query with clips required. Guidelines. E-mail: editorial@islands.com. Web site: www.islands.com.

THE MIDWEST MOTORIST—See *The Midwest Traveler.*

THE MIDWEST TRAVELER—(formerly *The Midwest Motorist*) 12901 N. Forty Dr., St. Louis, MO 63141. Michael Right, Ed. Articles, 1,000 to 1,500 words, with color slides, on domestic and foreign travel. Pays from $150 to $300, on acceptance. E-mail: aaapub@ibm.net. Web site: www.aaa.missouri.com.

MOUNTAIN LIVING MAGAZINE—7009 S. Potomac, Englewood, CO 80112. Attn: Ed. Travel articles, 800 to 1,500 words, on cities, regions, establishments in the mountainous regions of the world. Pays $200 to $300, on acceptance.

NATIONAL GEOGRAPHIC—1145 17th St. N.W., Washington, DC 20036. William Allen, Ed. First-person articles on geography, exploration, natural history, archaeology, and science: 40% staff-written; 60% written by published authors. Does not consider unsolicited manuscripts.

NATIONAL GEOGRAPHIC ADVENTURE—104 W. 40th St., 17th Fl., New York, NY 10018. Features, 4,000 to 8,000 words, on well-known adventures, expeditions, and scientific exploration, and unknown historical tales; department pieces, 2,000 to 3,000 words, including profiles, opinions, or commentaries; and "Compass" pieces, 500 to 2,000 words, about how readers can bring adventure into their own lives. Query with three published clips; send for guidelines. Payment varies. E-mail: adventure@ngs.org. Web site: www.national geographic.com/adventure.

NATIONAL MOTORIST—National Automobile Club, 1151 E. Hillsdale Blvd., Foster City, CA 94404. Jane Offers, Ed. Quarterly. Illustrated articles, 500 to 1,100 words, for California motorists, on motoring in the West, domestic and international travel, car care, roads, news, transportation, personalities, places, etc. Color slides. Pays from 20¢ a word, on acceptance. Pays for photos on publication. SASE required. Query regular mail. Web site: www. nationalautoclub.com.

NAVY TIMES—See *Times News Service.*

NEW MEXICO JOURNEY—3333 Fairview Rd., A-327, Costa Mesa, CA 92626. Bimonthly. Magazine for AAA members in New Mexico. Query for guidelines.

NEW YORK DAILY NEWS—450 W. 33rd St., New York, NY 10001. Linda Perney, Travel Ed. Articles, 700 to 900 words, on all manner of travel. Price information must be included. B&W or color photos or slides. Pays $100 to $200 (extra for photos), on publication.

THE NEW YORK TIMES—229 W. 43rd St., New York, NY 10036. Nancy Newhouse, Travel Ed. Query with SASE required; include writer's background, description of proposed article. Pays on acceptance. E-mail: travel@ nytimes.com.

NORTHWEST REGIONAL MAGAZINES—P.O. Box 18000, 4969 Highway 101, #2, Florence, OR 97439. Attn: Judy Fleagle or Jim Forst. All submissions considered for use in *Oregon Coast* and *Northwest Travel.* Articles, 800 to 2,000 words, on travel, history, town/city profiles, outdoor activities, events, and nature. News releases, 200 to 500 words. Articles with slides preferred. Pays $50 to $300, after publication. Guidelines with SASE. E-mail: judy@ohwy.com or jm@ohwy.com.

NORTHWEST TRAVEL—See *Northwest Regional Magazines.*

OREGON COAST—See *Northwest Regional Magazines.*

OREGON OUTSIDE—Northwest Regional Magazines, Box 18000, 4969 Highway 101, #2, Florence, OR 97439-0130. Judy Fleagle, Jim Forst, Eds. Quarterly. Articles, 1,000 to 1,500 words, on Oregon and the outdoors, "all kinds of adventure, from walks for families to extreme skiing." Prefers to receive manuscript/photo packages. Pays $100 to $350, on publication. Query.

ROUTE 66 MAGAZINE—326 W. Route 66, Williams, AZ 86046-2427. Paul Taylor, Pub. Articles, 1,500 to 2,000 words, on travel and life along Route 66 between Chicago and Los Angeles. Also, fillers, jokes, and puzzles, for the Children's Page. B&W and color photographs. Pays $20 per column, 45 days after publication. Query. E-mail: info@route66magazine.com. Web site: www. route66magazine.com.

SACRAMENTO MAGAZINE—4471 D St., Sacramento, CA 95819. Krista Hendricks Minard, Ed. Articles, 1,000 to 1,500 words, on destinations within a 6-hour drive of Sacramento. Pay varies, on publication. Query.

SPECIALTY TRAVEL INDEX—305 San Anselmo Ave., #313, San Anselmo, CA 94960. C. Steen Hansen, Co-Pub./Ed. Semiannual directory of adventure vacation tour companies, destinations, and vacation packages. Articles, 1,250 words, with special-interest, adventure type travel accounts and information. Pays 20¢ per word, on receipt of complete materials. Slides and photos considered. Queries preferred.

TEXAS HIGHWAYS MAGAZINE—P.O. Box 141009, Austin, TX 78714-1009. Jack Lowry, Ed. Travel, historical, cultural, scenic features on Texas, 200 to 1,800 words. Pays about 40¢ to 50¢ a word; photos $80 to $400. Guidelines. Web site: www.texashighways.com. E-mail: editors@texashighways.com.

TIMES NEWS SERVICE—Army Times Publishing Co., Springfield, VA 22159. Features Ed. Occasional travel articles, 500 to 1,000 words, on mainstream destinations tailored to military people's interests and demographics (not features on military attractions). Query required; send for guidelines. Pays $200 to $350, on acceptance.

TRANSITIONS ABROAD—18 Hulst Rd., Box 1300, Amherst, MA 01004-1300. Nicole Rosenleaf Ritter, Man. Ed. Articles for overseas travelers of all ages who seek an enriching, in-depth experience of the culture: work, study, travel, budget tips. Include practical, first-hand information. Emphasis on travel for personal enrichment. "Eager to work with inexperienced writers who want to share information not usually found in guidebooks. High percentage of material is from free lancers. Also seeking articles from writers with special expertise on cultural travel opportunities for specific types of travelers: seniors, students, families, etc." B&W photos a plus. Pays $2 per column inch, after publication. SASE required for guidelines and editorial calendar. E-mail: editor@transitionsabroad.com. Web site: www.transitionsabroad.com.

TRAVEL AMERICA—World Publishing Co., 990 Grove St., Evanston, IL 60201-4370. Randy Mink, Man. Ed. Robert Meyers, Ed. Features, 800 to 1,200 words, on U.S. vacation destinations. Pays up to $300, on acceptance. Top-quality color slides a must. Query by regular mail.

TRAVEL & LEISURE—1120 Ave. of the Americas, New York, NY 10036. Nancy Novogrod, Ed.-in-Chief. Articles, 800 to 3,000 words, on destinations and travel-related activities. Short pieces for "Smart Going" and "T&L Reports." Pays on acceptance: $3,000 to $5,000 for features; $1,000 to $2,000 for departments; $100 to $500 for short pieces. Query; articles on assignment.

TRAVEL SMART—40 Beechdale Rd., Dobbs Ferry, NY 10522-3098. Attn: Ed. Short pieces, 250 to 1,000 words, about interesting, unusual and/or economical places. Give specific details on hotels, restaurants, transportation, and costs. Pays on publication. "Send manila envelope with 2 first-class stamps for copy and guidelines." Query on longer pieces.

TRAVELERS' TALES, INC.—330 Townsend St., #208, San Francisco, CA 94107. Lisa Bach, Man. Ed. Travel books that inspire, educate, and better prepare travelers with tips and wisdom; original essays collected from prolific writers such as Barbara Kingsolver, Jan Morris, and Jon Krakauer. Accepts unsolicited manuscripts and queries. Payment is on a royalty or flat fee basis. E-mail: submit@travelerstales.com. Web site: www.travelerstales.com.

TRIPS: A TRAVEL JOURNAL—Suite 245, 155 Filbert St., Oakland, CA 94607. Tony Stucker, Ed.-in-Chief. For the active, adventurous traveler. Seeks irreverent articles about unique, interesting travel destinations. Nonfiction, from 500 to 5,000 words; and fillers, from 150 to 500 words. Also accepts photographs and slides. Payment is 20¢ to 25¢ per word, on publication. Query. E-mail: office@tripsmag.com. Web site: www.tripsmag.com.

WASHINGTON FLYER—Suite 700, 1707 L. St. NW, Washington, DC 20036. Stefanie Berry, Sr. Ed. Bimonthly. Travel and local publication for the upscale Washington residents and visitors. Most of the magazine focuses on dining, entertainment, events in the D.C. area. Nonfiction briefs and features, from 350 to 1,500 words. Color photographs. Pays $150 to $800, on publication. Query. Check the web site at: www.washingtonflyermag.com for sample articles. E-mail: stefanie@themagazinegroup.com.

INFLIGHT MAGAZINES

ABOARD—100 Almeria Ave., Suite 220, Coral Gables, FL 33134. Attn: Ed. Dept. Inflight magazine of 7 Latin American international airlines in Chile, Ecuador, Venezuela, Costa Rica, Guatemala, El Salvador, Bolivia, Nicaragua, Honduras, and Uruguay. Articles, 750 words, with photos, on these countries and on science, sports, technology, adventure, wildlife, fashion, business, ecology, and gastronomy. No political stories. Pays 20¢ per word; pay for photos varies, on acceptance and on publication. Query. E-mail: aboard@worldnet.att. net. Web site: www.aboardmagazines.com.

AIRTRAN ARRIVALS—2870 Peachtree Rd. N.E., #161, Atlanta, GA 30305-2918. M.R. Kerley, Ed. Bimonthly. Articles, varying lengths, on dining, hotels, entertainment, lifestyle, and general interest; also, some profiles. Query. Payment varies.

ALASKA AIRLINES MAGAZINE—2701 First Ave., Suite 250, Seattle, WA 98121. Paul Frichtl, Ed. Articles, 250 to 2,500 words, on business, travel, and profiles of regional personalities for West Coast business travelers. Payment varies, on publication. Query.

AMERICA WEST AIRLINES MAGAZINE—Skyword Marketing Inc., 4636 E. Elwood St., Suite 5, Phoenix, AZ 85040-1963. Michael Derr, Ed. Business trends, first-person profiles, destination pieces, fiction, arts and culture, 500 to 2,000 words; thoughtful essays. Pays from $250, on publication. Clips and SASE required. Guidelines. Very limited market.

AMERICAN WAY—P.O. Box 619640, DFW Airport, Fort Worth, TX 75261-9640. Tiffany Franke, Assoc. Ed. Travel, business, food and wine, health, and technology. Departments, 400 to 1,000 words. Sojourns travel stories to 200 words. Features, 1,500 to 2,000 words. Query with SASE. Web site: www.aa.com/away/. E-mail: tiffanyfranke@amercorp.com.

HEMISPHERES—1301 Carolina St., Greensboro, NC 27401. Randy Johnson, Ed. United Airlines inflight magazine. Articles, 1,200 to 1,500 words, on business, investing, travel, sports, family, food and wine, etc., that inform and entertain sophisticated, well-traveled readers. "The magazine strives for a unique global perspective presented in a fresh, strong, and artful graphic environment." Pays good rates, on acceptance. Query by regular mail, no e-mail. Guidelines with SASE. Web site: www.hemispheresmagazine.com.

HORIZON AIR MAGAZINE—2701 First Ave., #250, Seattle, WA 98121-1123. Michele Andrus Dill, Ed. Business and travel articles on the companies, people, issues, and trends that define the Northwest. News items, 200 to 500 words, and profiles for "The Region" section. Other department pieces,

1,800 words, cover corporate and industry profiles, regional issue analysis, travel, and community profiles; main features, 2,500 words. Pays $100 to $600, on publication. Web site: www.horizonair.com.

MERIDIAN—P.O. Box 3344, Palm Beach, FL 33480-1544. Steven Biller, Ed. Monthly. Articles, varying lengths, on such topics as technology, health, adventure, finance, entertainment, and profiles of local celebrities. Editorial features cover a different region in each issue. Query. Guidelines. Payment varies.

US AIRWAYS ATTACHÉ—1301 Carolina St., Greensboro, NC 27401. Jay Heinrichs, Ed. Articles, 400 to 2,500 words, on "the finer things in life." Paragons department offers short pieces touting the best of the best; Informed Sources department contains experts' opinions and knowledge on a variety of topics. No politics or Hollywood issues. Pays $1 a word, on acceptance.

WOMEN'S PUBLICATIONS

BBW: BIG BEAUTIFUL WOMAN—P.O. Box 1297, Elk Grove, CA 95759. Sally E. Smith, Ed.-in-Chief Articles, 800 to 3000 words, of interest to women ages 25 to 45, especially plus-size women, including interviews with successful plus-size women. Payment varies, on publication. Query. E-mail: sesmith@bbwmagazine.com. Web site: www.bbwmagazine.com.

BRAIN, CHILD—P.O. Box 1161, Harrisonburg, VA 22801-1161. Jennifer Niesslein, Stephanie Wilkinson, Eds. *The Magazine for Thinking Mothers.* Quarterly. Fiction and nonfiction, that "focuses on the experience of motherhood. We look for smart, down-to-earth work that's sometimes funny, sometimes poignant. Personal essays, 1,000 to 5,000 words; features, about 3,000 words; fiction, 1,500 to 5,000 words; news items, 200 to 800 words; debates, 700 words; book reviews, 200 words for mini-reviews, 800 to 1,200 for longer ones; and parodies, 800 words. For features, news items, and debates, query. For everything else, send complete manuscript with cover letter. Pays modest rates, on publication.

BRIDAL GUIDE—Globe Communications Corp., 3 E. 54th St., New York, NY 10022. Diane Forden, Ed.-in-Chief. Denise Schipani, Exec. Ed. Laurie Bain Wilson, Travel Ed. Bimonthly. Articles, 1,500 to 3,000 words, on wedding planning, relationships, sexuality, health and nutrition, psychology, travel, and finance. No beauty, fashion articles; no fiction, essays, poetry. Pays on acceptance. Query with SASE.

BRIDE'S—140 E. 45th St., New York, NY 10017. Sally Kilbridge, Man. Ed. Articles, 800 to 3,000 words, for engaged couples or newlyweds, on wedding planning, relationships, communication, sex, decorating, finances, careers, remarriage, health, birth control, religion, in-laws. Major editorial subjects: home, wedding, and honeymoon (send honeymoon queries to Travel Dept.). No fiction or poetry. Pays from 50¢ a word, on acceptance.

COMPLETE WOMAN—875 N. Michigan Ave., Suite 3434, Chicago, IL 60611. Bonnie L. Krueger, Ed. Lora Wintz, Exec. Ed. Articles, 1,000 to 2,000 words, with how-to sidebars, giving practical advice to women on love, sex, careers, health, personal relationships, etc. Also interested in reprints. Pays varying rates, on publication. Please no unsolicited material.

COSMOPOLITAN—224 W. 57th St., New York, NY 10018. Kate

White, Ed. John Searles, Fiction and Books Ed. Articles, to 3,000 words, and features, 500 to 2,000 words, on issues affecting young career women, with emphasis on relationships, jobs and personal life. Fiction on male-female relationships. "We only print fiction that is excerpted from a novel being published." SASE required. Payment varies.

COUNTRY WOMAN—P.O. Box 989, Greendale, WI 53129. Kathy Pohl, Exec. Ed. Profiles of country women (photo-feature packages), inspirational, reflective pieces. Personal-experience, nostalgia, humor, service-oriented articles, original crafts, and how-to features, to 1,000 words, of interest to country women. Pays $25 to $75 for crafts, humor, nostalgia; pays $150 for photo-features, on acceptance.

ELLE—1633 Broadway, New York, NY 10019. Amy Gross, Ed. Dir. Articles, varying lengths, for fashion-conscious women, ages 20 to 50. Subjects include beauty, health, fitness, travel, entertainment, and lifestyles. Pays top rates, on publication. Query required.

ESSENCE—1500 Broadway, New York, NY 10036. Susan L. Taylor, Ed.-in-Chief. Monique Greenwood, Exec. Ed. Provocative articles, 800 to 2,500 words, about black women in America today: self-help, how-to pieces, business and finance, work, parenting, health, celebrity profiles, art, travel, and political issues. Fiction, 800 to 2,500 words. Pays varying rates, on acceptance. Query for articles.

EXECUTIVE FEMALE—135 W. 50th St., New York, NY 10020. Kim Calero, Pres. Articles, 350 to 1,200 words, on managing people, time, money, companies, and careers for women in business. Pays varying rates, on acceptance. Query.

FAMILY CIRCLE—375 Lexington Ave., New York, NY 10017. Nancy Clark, Deputy Ed. Articles, to 2,000 words, on "women who have made a difference," marriage, family, and child-care and elder-care issues; consumer affairs, psychology, and humor. Pays top rates, on acceptance. Query required.

FIT PREGNANCY—21100 Erwin St., Woodland Hills, CA 91367-3712. Peg Moline, Ed. Articles, 500 to 2,000 words, on pregnant women's and postpartum health, nutrition, and physical fitness. No fiction or poetry. Payment varies, on publication. Query. Web site: www.fitpregnancy.com.

GLAMOUR—4 Times Sq., New York, NY 10036. Bonnie Fuller, Ed.-in-Chief. Laurie Sprague, Man. Ed. Articles, from 1,000 words, on careers, health, psychology, politics, current events, interpersonal relationships, etc., for women ages 18 to 35. Fashion, entertainment, travel, food, and beauty pieces staff-written. Pays from $500, on acceptance. Query Articles Ed.

GOLF DIGEST WOMAN—1120 Avenue of the Americas, New York, NY 10018. Rona Cherry, Ed. Interested in previously published authors (in national magazines) who have in-depth knowledge of golf and golf-related subjects. Web site: www.golfdigest.com. Query. Payment varies.

GOOD HOUSEKEEPING—959 Eighth Ave., New York, NY 10019. Articles Ed. No unsolicited material. Best places to break in: "Better Way" (short, advice-driven takes on health, money, safety, and consumer issues) and profiles (short takes on interesting or heroic women or families). No submissions on food, beauty, needlework, or crafts. Short stories, 2,000 to 5,000 words, with strong identification for women. Unsolicited fiction not returned.

HARPER'S BAZAAR—1700 Broadway, 37th Fl., New York, NY 10019.

Katherine Betts, Ed.-in-Chief. Articles, 1,500 to 2,500 words, for active, sophisticated women: the arts, world affairs, travel, families, education, careers, health, and sexuality. Payment varies, on acceptance. No unsolicited manuscripts; query with SASE.

THE JOYFUL WOMAN—P.O. Box 90028, Chattanooga, TN 37412. Joy Rice Martin, Ed. Joanna Rice, Ed. Asst. Fiction, 500 to 1,000 words, for women with a "Christian commitment." Also first-person inspirational true stories, profiles of Christian women, practical and Bible-oriented how-to articles. Pays 3¢ to 4¢ a word, on publication. Queries required.

LADIES' HOME JOURNAL—125 Park Ave., New York, NY 10017. Myrna Blyth, Pub. Dir./Ed.-in-Chief. Articles of interest to women. Send queries to: Deborah Pike, Sr. Ed. (relationships/sex and psychology); Wendy Naugle, Ed. (health/medical); Melina Gerosa, Sr. Ed. (celebrity/entertainment); Pamela Guthrie O'Brien, Articles Ed. (news/general interest); Shana Aborn, Features Ed. (personal experience). Fiction accepted through literary agents only. Guidelines.

MCCALL'S—375 Lexington Ave., New York, NY 10017. Attn: Articles Ed. Human-interest, self-help, social issues, and popular psychology articles, 1,200 to 2,000 words. Also publishes "Couples," first person essays, 1,400 words; "Families," how-to articles, 1,400 words; "Health Sense," short, newsy items; and "Medical Report," health-related items, 1,200 words. Query with SASE. Payment varies, on acceptance.

MADEMOISELLE—4 Times Square, 17th Fl., New York, NY 10036. Faye Haun, Man. Ed. Articles, 1,000 to 3,000 words, on work, relationships, health, and trends of interest to single, working women in their early to midtwenties. Reporting pieces, essays, first-person accounts, and humor. No fiction. Submit query with clips and SASE. Pays excellent rates, on acceptance.

MAMM—Mamm, 349 W. 12th St., New York, NY 10014. Women's monthly focusing on cancer prevention, treatment, and survival. Articles on conventional and alternative treatment and medical news; survivor profiles; investigative features; and essays. Queries are preferred. Writer's guidelines available. Payment varies, and is made within 45 days of acceptance. E-mail address: elsieh@mamm.com.

MIRABELLA—1633 Broadway, New York, NY 10019. Roberta Myers, Ed. Articles, varying lengths, for fashion-conscious women, ages 20 to 50. Subjects include beauty, health, fitness, travel, entertainment, and lifestyles. Pays top rates, on publication. Querywith clips.

MODERN BRIDE—249 W. 17th St., New York, NY 10011. Mary Ann Cavlin, Exec. Ed. Articles, 1,500 to 2,000 words, for bride and groom, on wedding planning, financial planning, juggling career and home, etc. Pays $600 to $1,200, on acceptance.

MS.—20 Exchange Pl., 22nd Fl., New York, NY 10005. Attn: Manuscript Ed. Articles relating to feminism, women's roles, and social change; national and international news reporting, profiles, essays, theory, and analysis. No fiction or poetry accepted, acknowledged, or returned. Query with resume and published clips. E-mail: info@msmagazine.com. Web site: www.msmagazine.com.

NA'AMAT WOMAN—350 Fifth Ave, Suite 4700, New York, NY 10118. Judith A. Sokoloff, Ed. Articles on Jewish culture, women's issues, social and political topics, and Israel, 1,500 to 3,000 words. Short stories with a Jewish theme. Pays 10¢ a word, on publication.

NATIONAL BUSINESS WOMAN—2012 Massachusetts Ave. N.W., Washington, DC 20036-1012. Ed. Quarterly. Articles, varying lengths, of concern to working women. Areas of interest: economic equity and security, business practices and management, political activity, and women in the workplace. Query.

NEW WOMAN—733 3rd Ave., 12th Fl., New York, NY 10017. Attn: Manuscripts and Proposals. Articles for women ages 25 to 49, on self-discovery, self-development, and self-esteem. Features: relationships, careers, health and fitness, money, fashion, beauty, food and nutrition, travel features with self-growth angle, and essays by and about women pacesetters. Pays about $1 a word, on acceptance. Query with SASE.

ORANGE COUNTY WOMAN—3701 Birch St., #100, Newport Beach, CA 92660-2618. Carroll Lachnit, Ed. Articles, 500 to 1,500 words, for women living in Orange County, CA. "Our readers are highly educated, upscale women who are looking for information that will make their lives more efficient and gratifying. We cover everything from workplace and family issues to health and beauty." SASE for guidelines. Payment is $50 to $250, on acceptance. E-mail: ocmag@aol.com.

PLAYGIRL—801 Second Ave., New York, NY 10017. Tascha Church, Ed.-in-Chief. Send queries to: Daryna McKeand, Man. Ed. Erotic entertainment for women. Insightful articles on sexuality and romance; sizzling fiction, humor, and in-depth celebrity interviews of interest to contemporary women. Pays varying rates, after acceptance. Query with clips. Guidelines.

QUE LINDA MAGAZINE—13428 Maxella Ave., #296, Marina del Rey, CA 90292-5620. Marguerita Baca, Ed.-in-Chief. Bimonthly that addresses the needs of today's Latin female. Includes interviews and articles on health, fashion, and romance, and issues of interest to the Latino community. Pay varies. Query.

REAL WOMAN—2423 Camino del Rio South, #111, San Diego, CA 92108-3702. Lisa Williams, Ed.-in-Chief. Bimonthly aimed at women 35 years and older. Includes practical information about diet, health and fitness, relationships, financial matters, and the workplace. "Designed to give readers insight into how other women cope with real issues." Query with SASE. Payment varies.

REDBOOK—224 W. 57th St., New York, NY 10019. Christina Boyle, Sr. Ed. Stephanie Young, Sr. Ed., Health. Dawn Raffel, Fiction Ed. Andrea Bauman, Articles Ed. For mothers, ages 25 to 45. Short stories, 10 to 15 typed pages; dramatic inspirational narratives, 1,000 to 2,000 words. SASE required. Pays on acceptance. Query with writing samples for articles. Guidelines.

SAGEWOMAN—P.O. Box 641, Point Arena, CA 95468-0641. Anne Newkirk Niven, Ed. Quarterly. Articles, 200 to 5,000 words, on issues of concern to pagan and spiritually minded women. Material which expresses an earth-centered spirituality: personal experience, Goddess lore, ritual material, interviews, humor, and reviews. Accepts material by women only. Pays 2¢ a word, from $10, on publication. E-mail: info@sagewoman.com. Web site: www.sagewoman.com.

SELF—4 Times Square, 5th Fl., New York, NY 10036. Attn: Ed. "We no longer accept unsolicited manuscripts or queries." Web sites: www.self.com (marketing) and www.phys.com (editorial).

SPORTS ILLUSTRATED FOR WOMEN—1271 Avenue of the Americas, New York, NY 10020. Bimonthly for women interested and/or participating in sports. The articles, 300 to 1,000 words, are either service items, short profiles, product reviews, or a Question and Answer series. For service pieces send queries to: LizO'Brien@simail.com. For articles, send queries to: Sandy Bailey@simail.com. Pays $1.25 a word, varies per assignment; made on publication. Web site: www.cnnsi.com.

TODAY'S CHRISTIAN WOMAN—465 Gundersen Dr., Carol Stream, IL 60188. Jane Johnson Struck, Man. Ed. Articles, 1,500 to 1,800 words, that are "warm and personal in tone, full of real-life anecdotes that deal with marriage, parenting, friendship, spiritual life, single life, health, work, and self." Humorous anecdotes, 150 words, that have a Christian slant. Payment varies, on acceptance. Queries required. Guidelines. E-mail: tcwedit@aol.com. Web site: www.todayschristianwoman.net.

WOMAN'S DAY—1633 Broadway, New York, NY 10019. Stephanie Abarbanel, Sr. Articles Ed. Human-interest or service-oriented articles, 750 to 1,200 words, on marriage, child-rearing, health, careers, relationships, money management. Dramatic first-person narratives of medical miracles, rescues, women's experiences, etc. "We respond to queries promptly; unsolicited manuscripts are returned unread." SASE. Pays standard rates, on acceptance.

WOMAN'S TOUCH—1445 Boonville Ave., Springfield, MO 65802-1894. Lillian Sparks, Ed. Darla Knoth, Man. Ed. Inspirational articles, 500 to 1,500 words, for Christian women. Pays on publication. Allow 3 months for response. Submit complete manuscript with SASE. Guidelines and editorial calendar. E-mail: womanstouch@ag.org. Web site: www.womanstouch.org.

WOMAN'S WORLD—270 Sylvan Ave., Englewood Cliffs, NJ 07632. Kathy Fitzpatrick, Man. Ed. Articles, 600 to 1,800 words, of interest to middle-income women between the ages of 18 and 60, on love, romance, careers, medicine, health, psychology, family life, travel; dramatic stories of adventure or crisis, investigative reports. Fast-moving short stories, about 1,900 words, with light romantic theme. (Specify "short story" on outside of envelope.) Mini-mysteries, 1,200 words, with "whodunit" or "howdunit" theme. No science fiction, fantasy, horror, ghost stories, or gratuitous violence. Pays $300 to $900 for articles; $1,000 for short stories; $500 for mini-mysteries, on acceptance. Query for articles. Guidelines. E-mail: dearww@aol.com.

WOMEN'S SPORTS & FITNESS—342 Madison Ave., New York, NY 10017. Lucy S. Danziger, Ed.-in-Chief. Articles on fitness, nutrition, outdoor sports; how-tos; profiles; adventure travel pieces; and controversial issues or reported stories in women's sports, 500 to 2,000 words. Pays on acceptance.

WORKING MOTHER—MacDonald Communications, 135 W. 50th St., 16th Fl., New York, NY 10020. Attn: Ed. Dept. Articles, to 2,000 words, that help women in their task of juggling job, home, and family. "We like pieces that solve or illuminate a problem unique to our readers." Payment varies, on acceptance.

WORKING WOMAN—135 W. 50th St., 16th Fl., New York, NY 10020-1201. Articles, 200 to 1,500 words, on business and finance. "Our readers are high level executives and entrepreneurs who are looking for newsworthy information about the changing marketplace and its effects on their businesses and careers." Query. Pays from $250, on acceptance. E-mail: editors@workingwoman.com. Web site: www.workingwoman.com.

MEN'S PUBLICATIONS

ESQUIRE—250 W. 55th St., New York, NY 10019. David Granger, Ed.-in-Chief. Peter Griffin, Deputy Ed. Articles, 2,500 to 4,000 words, for intelligent audience. Pays varying rates, on acceptance. Query with clips and SASE. Web site: www.esquiremag.com.

GALLERY—401 Park Ave. S., New York, NY 10016-8802. C.S. O'Brien, Ed. Dir. Articles, investigative pieces, interviews, profiles, fiction, to 5,000 words, for men. Photos. Query. Guidelines.

GENRE—7080 Hollywood Blvd., Suite 1104, Hollywood, CA 90028. Bryan Buss, Man. Ed. Fiction, 3,000 to 5,000 words, and articles, 750 to 3,000 words, of interest to gay men. "Feature articles should be national in scope and somehow related to the gay male experience." Pays $100 to $400 an article, on publication. Web site: www.genremagazine.com. E-mail: bbuss@genre.com.

GQ—4 Times Square, New York, NY 10036. No free-lance queries or manuscripts.

MEN'S HEALTH—Rodale Press, 33 E. Minor St., Emmaus, PA 18098. Tom McGrath, Dep. Ed. Articles, 1,000 to 2,500 words, on fitness, diet, health, relationships, and careers for men ages 25 to 55. Pays from $1 a word, on acceptance. Query.

MEN'S JOURNAL—1290 Ave. of the Americas, New York, NY 10104-0298. Attn: Editorial. Articles and profiles, 2,000 to 7,000 words, of interest to active men age 25 to 49. Travel, fitness, health, adventure, participatory sports. Service articles for equipment and fitness sections, 400 to 1,800 words. Pays "good rates," on acceptance. Query. Web site: www.mensjournal.com.

NEW MAN—600 Rinehart Rd., Lake Mary, FL 32746. Rob Andresick, Ed. No longer accepting unsolicited manuscripts. Send query letters with an SASE.

PLAYBOY—680 North Shore Dr., Chicago, IL 60611. Stephen Randall, Exec. Ed. Articles, 3,500 to 6,000 words, and sophisticated fiction, 1,000 to 10,000 words (5,000 preferred), for urban men. (Address fiction to Attn: Fiction Ed.) Humor; satire. Science fiction. Pays to $5,000 for articles and fiction, $2,000 for short-shorts, on acceptance. SASE required. E-mail: stephenr@playboy.com.

PLAYERS—8060 Melrose Ave., Los Angeles, CA 90046. David Jamison, Ed. Articles, 2,500 to 3,500 words, for black men: politics, economics, travel, fashion, grooming, entertainment, sports, interviews, fiction, humor, satire, health, and sex. Photos a plus. Pays on publication. E-mail: psi@loop.com.

SENIORS MAGAZINES

AARP BULLETIN—601 E St. N.W., Washington, DC 20049. Elliot Carlson, Ed. Publication of the American Association of Retired Persons. Payment varies, on acceptance. Query required.

ANSWERS: THE MAGAZINE FOR ADULT CHILDREN OF AGING PARENTS—75 Seabreeze Dr., Richmond, CA 94804-7411. Susan R. Keller, Ed. Bimonthly. Articles written for adults caring for their aging parents. Subjects of interest include health, nutrition, finances, housing, and general caregiving advice. Query. Payment varies.

GOOD TIMES—Senior Publications, Inc., 5148 Saint-Laurent Blvd., Montreal, Quebec, Canada H2T 1R8. Denise B. Crawford, Ed.-in-Chief. "The Canadian Magazine for Successful Retirement." Celebrity profiles as well as practical articles on health, beauty, cuisine, hobbies, fashion, leisure activities, travel, taxes, legal rights, consumer protection, etc. Canadian content only. Payment varies. Query.

GOOD TIMES—Robert Morris Bldg., 100 N. 17th St., 9th Fl., Philadelphia, PA 19103. Karen Detwiler, Ed.-in-Chief. Mature lifestyle magazine for readers 50 years and older in Pennsylvania. Articles, to 1,500 words, on medical issues, health, travel, finance, fashion, gardening, fitness, legal issues, celebrities, lifestyles, and relationships. Payment varies, on publication. Query with samples and resume.

HEALTH & MONEY—450 7th Ave., #1701, New York, NY 10123-1799. Marcia McCluer, Ed. Bimonthly. Articles aimed at readers 50 and older who want to remain active during their retirement years. General interest pieces and advice on health, personal finance, and family relationships. Payment varies. Query.

LIFE LINES MAGAZINE—129 N. 10th St., Rm. 408, Lincoln, NE 68508-3627. Dena Rust Zimmer, Ed. Short stories, "Sports and Hobbies," "Remember When . . .," "Travels With . . .," and "Perspectives on Aging," to 450 words. Poetry, to 50 lines. Fillers and short humor, "the shorter the better." No payment.

MATURE LIFESTYLES—4575 Via Royale, #213, Ft. Myers, FL 33919. Kathy J. Beck, Publisher Articles, 500 to 700 words, for readers over 50 in Florida. No fiction or poetry. Florida angle a must. Pays $50, on publication.

MATURE LIFESTYLES—P.O. Box 44327, Madison, WI 53744. Anita J. Martin, Ed. "South Central Wisconsin's Newspaper for the Active 50-Plus Population." Syndicated national coverage and local free lance. E-mail: anitaj@execpc.com.

MATURE LIVING—127 Ninth Ave. N., Nashville, TN 37234-0140. Al Shackleford, Ed. Fiction and human-interest articles, to 1,200 words, for senior adults. Must be consistent with Christian principles. Payment varies, on acceptance.

MATURE OUTLOOK—Meredith Corp., 1716 Locust St., Des Moines, IA 50309. Peggy Person, Ed. Bimonthly. Upbeat, contemporary articles, 75 to 2,000 words, for readers 50 and older. Regular topics include health, money, food, travel, leisure, and stories of real people. Pays $50 to $1,500, on acceptance. Query required. Guidelines. E-mail: outlook@mdp.com.

MATURE YEARS—201 Eighth Ave. S., P.O. Box 801, Nashville, TN 37202. Marvin W. Cropsey, Ed. Articles of interest to older adults: health and fitness, personal finance, hobbies and inspiration. Anecdotes, to 300 words, poems, cartoons, jokes, and puzzles for older adults. "A Christian magazine that seeks to build faith. We always show older adults in a favorable light." Include name, address, and social security number with all submissions. Allow 2 months for response. E-mail: matureyears@umpublishing.org.

MILESTONES—246 S. 22nd St., Philadelphia, PA 19103. Robert Epp, Dir. Cathy Green, Ed. Tabloid published 10 times a year. News articles and features, 750 to 1,000 words, on humor, personalities, political issues, etc., for readers 50 and older. Articles are written by staff and local writers only.

MODERN MATURITY—601 E. St. N.W., Washington, DC 20049. Hugh Delehanty, Ed. Articles, 400 to 2,000 words, on careers, workplace, human interest, living, finance, relationships, and consumerism for readers over 50. Query. Pays $500 to $2,500, on acceptance.

NEW CHOICES: LIVING EVEN BETTER AFTER 50—Reader's Digest Publications, Reader's Digest Rd., Pleasantville, NY 10570. Greg Daugherty, Ed.-in-Chief. Service magazine for people ages 50 and older. Articles on health, personal finance, and travel. Payment varies, on acceptance. Query. E-mail: newchoices@readersdigest.com. web site: www.newchoices.com.

NEW JERSEY 50 + PLUS—See *Spirit +*.

PLUS MAGAZINE—(formerly *Senior Magazine*) 3565 S. Higuera St., San Luis Obispo, CA 93401. Attn: Ed. Articles, 900 to 1,200 words, of interest to men and women 40 +; personality profiles, travel pieces, articles about new things, places, business, sports, movies, television, and health. Reviews of new or outstanding older books. Pays $1.50 per inch; $10 to $25 for B&W or color photos, on publication.

THE RETIRED OFFICER MAGAZINE—201 N. Washington St., Alexandria, VA 22314. Attn: Manuscripts Ed. Articles, 800 to 2,000 words, of interest to military members and their families. Current military/political affairs, recent military history, military family lifestyles, health, money, second careers. Photos a plus. Pays to $1,700, on acceptance. Queries required. Send for guidelines. E-mail: editor@troa.org. Web: www.troa.org/serv/pubs/mag/guidelines.asp.

SECURE RETIREMENT—National Committee to Preserve Social Security and Medicare, 10 G. St., NE, Suite 600, Washington DC, 20002-4215. Denise Fremeau, Ed. Articles, 1,000 to 5,000 words, on age-related and retirement issues. Pay varies, made on acceptance. Query. Web site: www.ncpssm.org.

SENIOR MAGAZINE—See *Plus Magazine*.

THE SENIOR TIMES—The Senior Times Publishing Company, 435 King St., Littleton, MA 01460. Theresa Murphy, Ed. Monthly magazine for seniors with distribution in the greater Boston area emphasizing travel, entertainment, health, finance, senior advocacy issues, opinion, and advice columns, features, and local interviews. No payment.

SPIRIT + —(formerly *New Jersey 50 + Plus*) 1830 US Rt. 9, Toms River, NJ 08755-1210. Pat Jasin, Ed. Articles on finance, travel, and the Internet for people over 45. Pays in copies. Slides and color pictures are accepted. E-mail: spirit50@aol.com.

HOME & GARDEN/FOOD & WINE

AFRICAN VIOLET MAGAZINE—2375 North St., Beaumont, TX 77702. Ruth Rumsey, Ed. Articles, 700 to 1,400 words, on growing methods for African violets; history and personal experience with African violets. Violet-related poetry. No payment.

THE AMERICAN GARDENER—7931 E. Boulevard Dr., Alexandria, VA 22308-1300. David J. Ellis, Ed. Bimonthly. Articles, to 2,500 words, for American ornamental gardeners: profiles of prominent horticulturists, plant research and plant hunting, events and personalities in horticultural history, and plant lore and literature, etc. Shorter, humorous pieces for "Offshoots." "We run very few how-to articles." Pays $100 to $500, on publication. Query with SASE preferred. E-mail: editor@aha.org. Web site: www.ahs.org.

AMERICAN ROSE—P.O. Box 30000, Shreveport, LA 71130-0030. Ed. Articles on home rose gardens: varieties, products, helpful advice, rose care, etc.

ATLANTA HOMES AND LIFESTYLES—1100 Johnson Ferry Rd., #595, Atlanta, GA 30342-1746. Attn: Eds. Articles with a local angle. Department pieces for "Around Atlanta," "Short Takes," "House Hunting," "Cheap Chic," and "Quick Fix." Pays $50 to $300 for departments; $300 to $500 for features, on acceptance.

BETTER HOMES AND GARDENS—1716 Locust St., Des Moines, IA 50309-3023. Jean LemMon, Ed. Articles, to 2,000 words, on health, travel, parenting, and education. Pays top rates, on acceptance. Query.

BIRDS & BLOOMS—5400 S. 60th St., Greendale, WI 53129. Jeff Nowak, Ed. Bimonthly. Articles, 700 to 1,000 words, on personal backyard experiences with wild birds, flowers, gardening, landscaping, etc. ("No bird rescue stories, please!") Shorter pieces for "Backyard Banter." Pays $50 to $400, on publication.

BON APPETIT—6300 Wilshire Blvd., Los Angeles, CA 90048. Barbara Fairchild, Exec. Ed. Articles on fine cooking (menu format or single focus), cooking classes, and gastronomically focused travel. Query with clips. Pays varying rates, on acceptance.

BRIDE'S—140 E. 45th St., New York, NY 10017. Sally Kilbridge, Man. Ed. Articles, 800 to 2,000 words, for engaged couples or newlyweds on wedding planning, home and decorating, and honeymoon. No fiction or poetry. Send travel queries to Travel Dept. Pay starts at 50¢ per word, on acceptance.

CANADIAN GARDENING—340 Ferrier St., Suite 210, Markham, Ont., Canada L3R 2Z5. Rebecca Hanes-Fox, Ed. Features, 1,200 to 2,500 words, that help avid home gardeners in Canada solve problems or inspire them with garden ideas; Canadian angle imperative. How-to pieces, to 1,000 words, on garden projects; include introduction and step-by-step instructions. Profiles of gardens, to 2,000 words. Department pieces, 200 to 400 words. Pays $75 to $700, on acceptance. Queries preferred. E-mail: beckiefox@canadiangardening.com. Web site: www.canadiangardening.com.

CANADIAN SELECT HOMES MAGAZINE—See *Style At Home Magazine.*

CAROLINA GARDENER—P.O. Box 4504, Greensboro, NC 27404. L.A. Jackson, Ed. Bimonthly. Articles, 750 to 1,000 words, specific to southeast gardening: profiles of gardens in the southeast and of new cultivars or "good ol' southern heirlooms." Slides and illustrations should be available to accompany articles. Pays $175, on publication. Query required.

CHEF—Talcott Communications Corp., 20 N. Wacker Dr., Suite 1865, Chicago, IL 60606. Brent T. Frei, Ed.-in-Chief. "The Food Magazine for Professionals." Articles, 800 to 1,200 words, that offer professionals in the foodservice business ideas for food marketing, preparation, and presentation. Pays $300, on acceptance.

COLORADO HOMES AND LIFESTYLES—7009 S. Potomac St., Englewood, CO 80112. Evalyn K. McGraw, Ed. Bimonthly. Articles, 1,300 to 1,500 words, with a focus on primarily upscale Colorado homes and interiors. Department pieces, 1,100 to 1,300 words, cover architecture, artists, design trends, profiles, gardening, food and wine, and travel. Pays $150 to $300, on acceptance. Guidelines. Written query. E-mail: emcgraw@coloradohomesmag. com. Web site: www.coloradohomesmag.com.

CONTEMPORARY STONE & TILE DESIGN—299 Market St., 3rd Fl., Saddle Brook, NJ 07663-5312. Michael Reis, Ed. Quarterly. Articles, 1,500 words, on using stone in architecture and interior design. Photographs and drawings. Payment is $6 per column inch, on publication.

COOKING LIGHT—P.O. Box 1748, Birmingham, AL 35201. Doug Crichton, V.P. and Ed. Articles on fitness, exercise, health and healthful cooking, nutrition, and healthful recipes. Query with clips and SASE.

COOK'S ILLUSTRATED—17 Station St., Brookline, MA 02445. Barbara Bourassa, Man. Ed. Bimonthly. Articles that emphasize techniques of home cooking with master recipes, careful testing, trial and error. Payment varies, within 60 days of acceptance. Query. Guidelines.

COUNTRY GARDENS—1716 Locust St., Des Moines, IA 50309-3023. LuAnn Brandsen, Ed. Bimonthly. Garden-related how-tos and profiles of gardeners, 750 to 1,500 words. Department pieces, 500 to 700 words, on garden-related travel, food, projects, decorating, entertaining. "The gardens we feature are informal, lush, and old-fashioned. Stories emphasize both inspiration and information." Pays $450 to $1,500 for columns; $350 to $800 for features, on acceptance. Query required.

COUNTRY LIVING—224 W. 57th St., New York, NY 10019. Marjorie E. Gage, Sr. Ed. Articles, 800 to 1,200 words, on decorating, antiques, cooking, travel, home building, crafts, and gardens. "Most material is written in-house; limited free-lance needs." Payment varies, on acceptance. Query preferred. E-mail: mgage@hearst.com. Web site: www.countryliving.com.

DESIGN CONCEPTS—See *Your Home.*

FANCY FOOD—Talcott Communications Corp., 20 N. Wacker Dr., Suite 1865, Chicago, IL 60606. Paddy Buratto, Ed. Dir. "The Business Magazine for Specialty Foods, Coffee and Tea, Natural Foods, Confections, and Upscale Housewares." Articles, 2,000 words, related to gourmet food. Pays $250 to $500, on publication.

FINE GARDENING—The Taunton Press, P.O. Box 5506, Newtown, CT 06470-5506. LeeAnne White, Ed. Bimonthly. Articles, 800 to 2,000 words, for readers with a serious interest in gardening: how-tos, garden design, as well as pieces on specific plants or garden tools. "Our primary focus is on ornamental gardening and landscaping." Picture possibilities are very important. Pays $300 to $1,200 per story story on a project basis, part on acceptance, part on completed galley. Photos, $75 to $500. Query. Guidelines.

FLOWER & GARDEN MAGAZINE—4645 Belleview, Kansas City, MO 64112. Attn: Ed. Practical how-to articles, 500 to 1,000 words, on home gardening and landscaping. Photos a plus. Pays varying rates, on acceptance (on publication for photos). Query. E-mail: kcpublishing@earthlink.net. Web site: www.flowerandgardenmag.com.

FOOD & WINE—1120 Ave. of the Americas, New York, NY 10036. Dana Cowin, Ed.-in-Chief. Mary Ellen Ward, Man. Ed. No unsolicited material.

GARDEN GATE—2200 Grand Ave., Des Moines, IA 50312-5306. Steven Nordmeyer, Ed. Bimonthly. Articles on planting, nurturing and harvesting, designs for beautiful landscaping and garden designs, and practical how-to's for growing plants and flowers. Also, information on perennials, annuals, vegetables, shrubs, trees, and indoor plants. Query. Payment varies.

GARDEN SHOWCASE—P.O. Box 23669, Portland, OR 97281-3669. Lynn Lustberg, Ed. Monthly. Articles, to 1,000 words, on gardening. Features cover a wide range of gardening ideas, but all must have a connection to the Pacific Northwest. Also accepts slides or transparencies of trees, shrubs, perennials, and gardens in that area. Payment is $200, on publication. Query. E-mail: editor@gardenshowcase.com. Web site: www.gardenshowcase.com.

GOURMET: THE MAGAZINE OF GOOD LIVING—Conde Nast, 4 Times Square, New York, NY 10036. Attn: Ed. No unsolicited manuscripts; query.

GROWERTALKS—P.O. Box 9, 335 N. River St., Batavia, IL 60510-0009. Chris Beytes, Ed. Articles, 800 to 2,600 words, that help commercial greenhouse growers (not florist/retailers or home gardeners) do their jobs better: trends, successes in new types of production, marketing, business management, new crops, and issues facing the industry. Payment varies, on publication. Queries preferred. E-mail: beytes@growertalks.com. Web site: www.ballpublishing.com.

THE HERB COMPANION—Herb Companion Press, 201 E. Fourth St., Loveland, CO 80537. Robyn Griggs Lawrence, Ed. Bimonthly. Articles, 1,500 to 3,000 words; fillers, 75 to 150 words. Practical horticultural information, original recipes illustrating the use of herbs, thoroughly researched historical insights, step-by-step instructions for herbal craft projects, book reviews. Pays 33¢ per word, on publication.

THE HERB QUARTERLY—P. O. Box 689, San Anselmo, CA 94960. Jennifer Barrett, Ed. Articles, 2,000 to 4,000 words, on herbs: practical uses, cultivation, gourmet cooking, landscaping, herb tradition, medicinal herbs, crafts ideas, unique garden designs, profiles of herb garden experts, and practical how-tos for the herb businessperson. Include garden design when possible. Pays on publication. Guidelines; send SASE.

HOME MAGAZINE—1633 Broadway, 41st Fl., New York, NY 10019. Gale Steves, Ed.-in-Chief. Linda Lentz, Articles Ed. Articles of interest to homeowners: architecture, remodeling, decorating, products, project ideas, landscaping and gardening, financial aspects of home ownership, home offices, home-related environmental and ecological topics. Pays varying rates, on acceptance. Query, with summary of 50 to 200 words.

HORTICULTURE—98 N. Washington St., Boston, MA 02114. Thomas C. Cooper, Ed. Published 10 times a year. Authoritative, well-written articles, 500 to 2,500 words, on all aspects of gardening. Pays competitive rates, on publication. Query.

HOUSE BEAUTIFUL—1700 Broadway, New York, NY 10019. Jane Margoues, Features Ed. & Travel Ed. Service articles related to the home. Pieces on design, travel, and gardening. Query with detailed outline and photos if relevant. Guidelines.

KITCHEN GARDEN—P.O. Box 5506, Newtown, CT 06470-5506. Editorial. Bimonthly. Articles, varying lengths, for home gardeners who "love to grow their own vegetables, fruits, and herbs and use them in cooking." Features include "Plant Profiles," Garden Profiles," Techniques," "Design," "Projects," and "Cooking." Pays $150 per page, half on acceptance, half on publication. Query.

LOG HOME LIVING—P.O. Box 220039, Chantilly, VA 20153. Janice Brewster, Exec. Ed. Articles, 1,000 to 1,500 words, on modern manufactured and handcrafted kit log homes: homeowner profiles, design and decor features. Pays $350 to $550, on acceptance. Web site: www.loghomeliving.com.

THE MAINE ORGANIC FARMER & GARDENER—RR 2, Box 594, Lincolnville, ME 04849. Jean English, Ed. Quarterly. How-to articles and profiles, 100 to 2,500 words, for organic farmers and gardeners, consumers who care about healthful foods, and activists. Tips, 100 to 250 words. "Our readers want good solid information about farming and gardening, nothing soft." Pays about 8¢ a word, on publication. Queries preferred. E-mail: jenglish@midcoast. com. Web site: www.mofga.org.

METROPOLITAN HOME—1633 Broadway, New York, NY 10019. Michael Lassell, Articles Dir. Service and informational articles for residents of houses, co-ops, lofts, and condominiums, on real estate, equity, wine and spirits, collecting, trends, etc. Interior design and home furnishing articles with emphasis on lifestyle. Payment varies. Query.

MOTHER EARTH NEWS—Sussex Publishers, 49 E. 21st St., 11th Fl., New York, NY 10010. Ed. Bimonthly featuring articles on organic gardening, building projects, herbal or home remedies, alternative energy projects, wild foods, and environment and conservation. "We are dedicated to helping our readers become more self-sufficient, financially independent, and environmentally aware." Photos and diagrams a plus. No fiction. Payment varies, on publication. E-mail: letters@motherearthnews.com. Web site: www.mother earthnews.com.

NATIONAL GARDENING MAGAZINE—180 Flynn Ave., Burlington, VT 05401. Michael MacCaskey, Ed.-in-Chief. News, department, and feature articles, 300 to 2,000 words. The magazine of the National Gardening Association, the largest association of home gardeners in the U.S. Published for all home gardeners, beginning or advanced. Informative, how-to articles on all aspects of home gardening. Most articles are assigned.

OLD HOUSE INTERIORS—2 Main St., Gloucester, MA 01930. Regina Cole, Sr. Ed. Articles, 300 to 1,500 words, on architecture, decorative arts, and history. The single most important thing for writers to know is that the magazine is art-driven. When proposing an article, know how it should be illustrated. Professional photos not necessary. Query, with writing clips. Payment is $1 a word, or $200 page minimum, on acceptance.

OVER THE HEDGE—10757 Queensland St., Los Angeles, CA 90034-3412. Siri Kay Jostad, Ed. Bimonthly. Articles, published for all gardening enthusiasts in the state of California. Features include advice from national garden authorities and readers as well. New plant introductions, plant and insect profiles, and a monthly gardening checklist. Query with SASE. Payment varies.

ROCKY MOUNTAIN GARDENER—P.O. Box 18537, Boulder, CO 80308. Susan Martineau, Pub./Ed.-in-Chief. Quarterly. How-to articles, 500 to 1,000 words, on regional techniques and varieties; profiles of regional gardeners and gardens, 500 to 1,000 words; book reviews and production reviews, 300 to

500 words; regional columns (esp. from Utah, Wyoming, and Montana), 200 to 300 words. "Articles must be focused on Rocky Mountain area from New Mexico to Montana. We prefer new, novel, or specific information, not just general gardening topics." Pays 10¢ a word, on publication.

STYLE AT HOME MAGAZINE—(formerly *Canadian Select Homes Magazine*) 25 Sheppard Ave. W., Suite 100, Toronto, Ont., Canada M2N 6S7. Gail Johnston Habs, Ed. How-to articles, profiles of Canadian homes, renovation, decor, and gardening features, 800 to 1,500 words. Canadian content and locations only. Pays from $400 to $900 (Canadian), on acceptance. Query with international reply coupons. Send SASE with international reply coupons for guidelines. E-mail: letters@styleathome.com (for general interest); plore@styleathome.com (guidelines.)

VEGGIE LIFE—1041 Shary Cir., Concord, CA 94518. Deerra Shehabi, Ed. Quarterly. Features, 1,500 to 2,000 words, for "people interested in lowfat, meatless cuisine, natural health, nutrition, and herbal healing." Food features (include 8 to 10 recipes); department pieces, 1,000 to 1,500 words. Payment varies, on acceptance or publication. Queries preferred.

VICTORIAN HOMES—265 S. Anita Dr., Suite 120, Orange, CA 92868-3310. Erika Kotite, Ed. Feature articles, 1,200 to 2,000 words, on decoration, architecture of 19th- and early 20th-century homes that are restored, decorated, and lived in by real people, as well as period museum houses. Other articles explore kitchen and bathroom makeovers with a Victorian flair; paint coverings, gardens, and wall coverings. Query with SASE. Send outline, angle of the piece, and any photos. Allow four to six weeks for a response. Payment varies from $400 to $600, depending on length and complexity, and is made on acceptance. E-mail: ekotite@pacbell.net. Web site: www.victorianhomes mag.com.

WINE SPECTATOR—387 Park Ave. S., New York, NY 10016. Thomas Matthews, Exec. Ed. Features, 600 to 2,000 words, preferably with photos, on news and people in the wine world, travel, food, and other lifestyle topics. Pays from $400, extra for photos, on publication. Query required.

WINES & VINES—1800 Lincoln Ave., San Rafael, CA 94901. Philip E. Hiaring, Ed. Articles, 2,000 words, on grape and wine industry, emphasizing marketing, management, and production. Pays 15¢ a word, on acceptance. E-mail: geninto@winesandvines.com. Web site: www.winesandvines.com.

YOUR HOME—(formerly *Design Concepts*) 820 W. Jackson Blvd., #450, Chicago, IL 60607-3026. Melissa Baker, Ed. Biannual. "A Magazine for Pier 1 Imports' Best Customers." Features: interviews with professional interior designers, 800 to 1,200 words. Pays about 50¢ a word, on publication. Query.

FAMILY & PARENTING MAGAZINES

ADOPTIVE FAMILIES MAGAZINE—255 W. 90th St., Suite 116, New York, NY 10024. Linda Lynch, Ed. Bimonthly. Articles, 1,000 to 1,500 words, on parenting adoptive children and other adoption issues. Payment is negotiable. Query. Web site: www.adoptivefam.org. E-mail: publisher@adoptivefam.com.

AMERICAN BABY—Primedia Consumer Magazines, 249 W. 17th St.,

New York, NY 10011. Judith Nolte, Ed. Articles, 1,000 to 2,000 words, for new or expectant parents on prenatal and infant care. Personal experience, 900 to 1,200 words, (do not submit in diary format). Department pieces, 50 to 350 words, for "Crib Notes" (news and feature topics). No fiction, fantasy pieces, dreamy musings, or poetry. Pays $800 to $2,000 for articles, $500 for departments, on acceptance. Guidelines.

ARIZONA PARENTING—P.O. Box 63922, Scottsdale, AZ 85082-3922. Greg Stiles, Ed. Monthly. Articles covering such topics as pediatric helathcare, regional activities, sports, and education, all aimed at Arizona parents with children between one and 12 years old. Query. Payment varies.

AT-HOME MOTHER—406 E. Buchanan Ave., Fairfield, IA 52556-3810. Jeanette Lisefski, Ed. Quarterly. Articles aimed at women who raise active families, run a home business, manage a household budget, etc.. Articles should be helpful, educational, and supportive. Query. Payment varies.

ATLANTA PARENT—2346 Perimeter Park Dr., Ste. 101, Atlanta, GA 30341. Peggy Middendorf, Ed. Articles, 800 to 2,000 words, on parenting and baby topics. Related humor, 800 to 1,500 words. Photos of parents and/or children. Pays $15 to $30 an article; $15 for photos, on publication.

BABY MAGAZINE—124 E. 40th St., Suite 1101, New York, NY 10016. Jeanne Muchnick, Ed. Bimonthly. Parenting articles, 750 to 1,500 words, geared toward women in the last trimester of pregnancy and the first year of baby's life. "We want how-to and personal articles designed to smooth the transitions from pregnancy to parenthood." Payment varies, on acceptance. Query.

BABY TALK—1325 Avenue of the Americas, New York, NY 10019. Susan Kane, Ed. Articles, 1,000 to 3,000 words, by professionals, on pregnancy, babies, baby care, women's health, child development, work and family, etc. No poetry. Query by mail. Pays varying rates, on acceptance. SASE required.

BAY AREA BABY—See *Bay Area Parent.*

BAY AREA PARENT—401 Alberto Way, Suite A, Los Gatos, CA 95032-5404. Mary Brence Martin, Ed. Articles, 1,200 to 1,400 words, on local parenting issues for readers in California's Santa Clara County and the South Bay area. Query. Mention availability of B&W photos. Pays 6¢ a word, $10 to $15 for photos, on publication. Also publishes *Valley Parent* for central Contra Costa County and the tri-valley area of Alameda County, *Parenting Bay Area Teens, Bay Area Baby, Preschool & Childcare Finder,* and *Education and Enrichment Guide.*

BIG APPLE PARENT—9 E. 38th St., New York, NY 10016. Helen Rosengren Freedman, Man. Ed. Articles, 500 to 750 words, for NYC parents. Pays $35 to $50, the end of the month following publication. Buys first NYC rights. E-mail: parentspaper@mindspring.com. Web site: www.parentsknow.com.

BRAIN, CHILD—P.O. Box 1161, Harrisonburg, VA 22801-1161. Jennifer Niesslein, Stephanie Wilkinson, Eds. *The Magazine for Thinking Mothers.* Quarterly. Fiction and nonfiction "that focuses on the experience of motherhood. We look for smart, down-to-earth work that's sometimes funny, sometimes poignant." Accepts personal essays, 1,000 to 5,000 words; features, 3,000 words; news items, 200 to 800 words; debates, 700 words; fiction, 1,500 to 5,000 words; book reviews, 200 words for mini-reviews, 800 to 1,200 words for longer ones; and parodies, 800 words. For features, news items, and debates, query; for everything else, send complete manuscript with cover letter. Payment is modest, made on publication.

CATHOLIC PARENT—Our Sunday Visitor, Inc., 200 Noll Plaza, Huntington, IN 46750. Woodeene Koenig-Bricker, Ed. Features, how-tos, and general-interest articles, 800 to 1,000 words, dealing with the issues of raising children "with solid values in today's changing world. Keep it anecdotal and practical with an emphasis on values and family life." Payment varies, on acceptance. Guidelines.

CHILDREN MAGAZINE—P.O. Box 251859, Los Angeles, CA 90025-9009. Rachel Lincoln, Ed. Monthly. Articles written for families living is Los Angeles county and surrounding communities. Feature topics include good parenting, child development and safety, entertainment, travel, financial planning, and home improvement. Query. Pay varies.

CHILDSPLAY—See *Today's Family: The Parenting Magazine of Western Massachusetts.*

CHRISTIAN HOME & SCHOOL—3350 E. Paris Ave. S.E., Grand Rapids, MI 49512. Gordon L. Bordewyk, Ed. Articles for parents in Canada and the U.S. who send their children to Christian schools and are concerned about the challenges facing Christian families today. Pays $125 to $200, on publication. Send SASE for guidelines or 9"x12" SASE with 4 first-class stamps for guidelines and sample issue.

CHRISTIAN PARENTING TODAY—4050 Lee Vance View, Colorado Springs, CO 80918. Erin Healy, Ed. Articles, 900 to 2,000 words, dealing with raising children with Christian principles. Departments: "Parent Exchange," 25 to 100 words, on problem-solving ideas that have worked for parents; "Life in our House," insightful anecdotes, 25 to 100 words, about humorous things said at home. Queries preferred for articles. Pays 15¢ to 25¢ a word, on publication. Pays $40 for "Parent Exchange," $25 for "Life in our House." Guidelines.

CONNECTICUT FAMILY—See *New York Family.*

EASTSIDE PARENT—Northwest Parent Publishing, 1530 Westlake Ave. N., Suite 600, Seattle, WA 98109. Virginia Smyth, Ed. Articles, 300 to 2,500 words, for parents of children under 14. Readers tend to be professional, two-career families. Queries preferred. Pays $50 to $600, on publication. Also publishes *Pierce Country Parent, Portland Parent,* and *Puget Sound Parent.*

EDUCATION AND ENRICHMENT GUIDE—See *Bay Area Parent.*

EXCEPTIONAL PARENT—555 Kinderkamack Rd., Oradell, NJ 07649-1517. Maxwell J. Schleifer, Ed.-in-Chief. Articles, to 1,500 words, for parents and professionals caring for children and young adults with disabilities. Practical ideas and techniques on parenting, technology, research, legislation, and rehabilitation. Query. Pays $50, 60 days after publication.

EXPECTING—See *Parents Expecting.*

FAMILY—51 Atlantic Ave., Floral Park, NY 11001. Don Hirst, Ed. Monthly publication for military families including articles on parenting, travel, food, and other issues affecting military families. Query.

FAMILYFUN—Walt Disney Publishing Group, 244 Main St., Northampton, MA 01060. Send queries on articles, to 1,500 words, on family activities to Activities Ed. Payment varies, on acceptance.

FAMILY LIFE—1271 Avenue of the Americas, 41st Fl., New York, NY 10020. Peter Herbst, Ed.-in-Chief. Published 10 times a year. Articles for parents of children ages 5 to 12. Payment varies (generally $1 a word), on acceptance. Limited market. Query required. E-mail: familylife@timeinc.com. Web site: www.parenttime.com.

FAMILY TIMES—P.O. Box 932, Eau Claire, WI 54702. Nancy Walter, Ed. Articles, from 800 words, on children and parenting issues: health, education, raising children, how-tos, new studies and programs for educating parents. Pays $35 to $50, on publication. Query preferred. Guidelines.

GROWING CHILD/GROWING PARENT—22 N. Second St., P.O. Box 620, Lafayette, IN 47902-0620. Nancy Kleckner, Ed. Articles, to 1,500 words, on subjects of interest to parents of children under 6. No personal experience pieces or poetry. Guidelines. E-mail: dnkdunn@aol.com. Web site: www. growingchild.com.

HOME LIFE—127 Ninth Ave. N., Nashville, TN 37234-0140. Jon Walker, Ed.-in-Chief. Monthly. Interviews, how-tos, and features on marriage, family, and parenting, all from a Christian perspective. Payment varies. Query.

INTERRACE—Heritage Publishing Group, P.O. Box 17479, Beverly Hills, CA 90209. Ed. Quarterly. Articles on interracial/intercultural marriage and dating, transracial adoption, multiracial families, and raising multiracial children. Accepts fillers, 100 to 700 words, and features, 700 words or more. Pays $20 plus one-year subscription for features only. Query or send complete manuscript.

JOYFUL TIMES—P.O. Box 20997, Sedona, AZ 86341. Peggy Jenkins, Ed. Bimonthly internet publication "dedicated to activating and nurturing our inner joy, the energy of love." Articles, 500 to 800 words, that "explore how society can more effectively nurture both children and adults to express their fullest potential, thus releasing their inner joy." Pieces should be uplifting and inspirational, exemplifying that joy is attained on the inside. E-mail: joyful@ sedona.net. Web site: www.JOY4U.org.

METROKIDS—1080 N. Delaware Ave., Suite 702, Philadelphia, PA 19125. Amanda Hathaway, Exec. Ed. Tabloid for Delaware Valley families. Features and department pieces, 500 to 1,000 words, on parenting, regional travel, local kids' programs, nutrition, and product reviews. Pays $25 to $50, on publication. E-mail: editor@metrokids.com. Web site: www.metrokids.com.

MOTHERING—P.O. Box 1690, Santa Fe, NM 87504. Ashisha, Sr. Ed. Bimonthly. Articles, to 2,000 words, on natural family living, covering topics such as pregnancy, birthing, parenting, etc. "We're looking for articles that have a strong point of view and come from the heart." Also poetry, 3 to 20 lines. Pays $200 to $500 and higher, on publication. Query. E-mail: ashisha@ mothering.com. Web site: www.mothering.com.

NEW YORK FAMILY—141 Halstead Ave., Suite 3D, Mamaroneck, NY 10543. David Parker, Pub. Betsy F. Woolf, Ed. Articles related to family life in New York City and general parenting topics. Pays $50 to $200. Same requirements for *Westchester Family* and *Connecticut Family.*

PARENTGUIDE NEWS—419 Park Ave. S., 13th Fl., New York, NY 10016. Jenine M. DeLuca, Ed.-in-Chief. Articles, 1,000 to 1,500 words, related to families and parenting issues: trends, profiles, health, education, travel, fashion, calendar of events, seasonal topics, reader's opinions, special programs, products, etc. Humor and women's section.

PARENTING—1325 Avenue of the Americas, New York, NY 10019. Attn: Articles Ed. Articles, 500 to 3,000 words, on education, health, fitness, nutrition, child development, psychology, and social issues for parents of young children. Query.

PARENTING BAY AREA TEENS—See *Bay Area Parent*.

PARENTS EXPECTING—(formerly *Expecting*) 375 Lexington Ave., New York, NY 10017. Elana Lore, Dep. Ed. Not buying any new material in the foreseeable future.

PARENTS EXPRESS—290 Commerce Dr., Fort Washington, PA 19034. Laura Winchester, Ed. and Lynnette Shelley, Assoc. Ed. Articles on children and family topics for parents living in southeastern Pennsylvania and southern New Jersey. Pays $35 to $150 for articles, upon publication.

PIERCE COUNTY PARENT—See *Eastside Parent*.

PORTLAND PARENT—See *Eastside Parent*.

PRESCHOOL & CHILDCARE FINDER—See *Bay Area Parent*.

PUGET SOUND PARENT—See *Eastside Parent*.

RAISING BLACK AND BIRACIAL CHILDREN—Heritage Publishing Group, P.O. Box 17479, Beverly Hills, CA 90209. Ed. Quarterly. Fillers, about 100 words, and articles, about 700 words, related to parenting, caring for, and educating black or biracial children. Transracial adoption stories are also welcome. Query or send complete manuscript; include SASE. Pays $10 for fillers; $20 to $40 for features.

REUNIONS MAGAZINE—P.O. Box 11727, Milwaukee, WI 53211-0727. Edith Wagner, Ed. Positive and instructive articles related to reunions (family, class, military reunions, searching, and some genealogy). Pays honoraria and copies. Web site: www.reunionsmag.com. E-mail: reunions@execpc.com.

SCHOLASTIC PARENT & CHILD—555 Broadway, New York, NY 10012-3919. Susan Schneider, Ed. Bimonthly. Articles, 600 to 900 words, on childhood education and development. "We are the learning link between home and school." Payment varies, on acceptance. Query; no unsolicited manuscripts. SASE.

SEATTLE'S CHILD—Northwest Parent Publishing, 1530 Westlake Ave. N., Suite 600, Seattle, WA 98109. Ann Bergman, Ed. Articles, 400 to 2,500 words, of interest to parents, educators, and childcare providers of children under 12, plus investigative reports and consumer tips on issues affecting families in the Puget Sound region. Pays $75 to $600, on publication. Query.

SESAME STREET PARENTS—One Lincoln Plaza, New York, NY 10023. Susan Lapinski, Ed. Articles, 800 to 2,500 words. Articles on health to Sandra Lee, Sr. Ed.; articles on family finance to Arleen Love, Assoc. Ed.; articles on education, computer material to Karin DeStefano, Lifestyle Ed. Personal essays and other articles of interest to any editor. "Covers parenting issues for families with young children (to 8 years old)." Pays $1 per word, up to 6 weeks after acceptance. SASE for guidelines.

SNOHOMISH COUNTY PARENT—See *Eastside Parent*.

TODAY'S FAMILY: THE PARENTING MAGAZINE OF WESTERN MASSACHUSETTS—(formerly *Childsplay*) 280 N. Main St., E. Longmeadow, MA 01028. Editor. Articles, 300 to 700 words, that address family issues, offers advice and new recipes and daytrip suggestions from readers. E-mail: news@thereminder.com. Prefers writers based in western Massachusetts.

TOLEDO AREA PARENT NEWS—1120 Adams St., Toledo, OH 43624. Erin Kramer, Ed. Articles on parenting, child and family health, and other family topics, 750 to 1,200 words. Writers must be from Northwest Ohio and Southern Michigan. Pays $75 to $100 per article, on acceptance. Query required. E-mail: erin@toledocitypaper.com. Web site: www.toledoparent@family.com.

TWINS—The Magazine for Parent of Multiples, 5350 S. Roslyn St., Suite 400, Englewood, CO 80111. Susan J. Alt, Ed.-in-Chief. Send submissions to Sharon Withers, Man. Ed. Features, 1,100 to 1,300 words, third person. Departments, 750 words, first person. "Articles must be multiples specific and focus on every day issues parents of twins, triplets, and more face. Features should have 2 to 3 professional and/or parental experience sources. Payment is $75 to $250, on publication. Query or send complete manuscript. E-mail: twins.editor@businessword.com. Web site: www.twinsmagazine.com.

VALLEY PARENT—See *Bay Area Parent*.

WESTCHESTER FAMILY—See *New York Family*.

LIFESTYLE MAGAZINES

ABLE—P.O. Box 395, Old Bethpage, NY 11804-0395. Angela Miele Melledy, Ed. Monthly. "Positively for, by, and about the disabled." Nonfiction to 500 words. Pays $25 on publication. Color and B&W photos.

ACCENT ON LIVING—P.O. Box 700, Bloomington, IL 61702-0700. Betty Garee, Ed. Quarterly. Articles, 800 to 1,000 words, for physically disabled consumers, mostly mobility impaired. Topics include travel, problem solving, and accessibility. "We like articles on devices or how-to information that make tasks easier." Pays 10¢ a word, on publication. Query. E-mail: acntlvng@aol.com. Web site: www.accentonliving.com.

AMERICAN HEALTH—Reader's Digest Road, Pleasantville, NY 10570. Attn: Ed. Dept. Lively, authoritative articles, 1,000 to 2,000 words, on women's health, nutrition, mental health, fitness, and a healthy lifestyle. Payment varies, but is made on acceptance. Query with clips.

AQUARIUS: A SIGN OF THE TIMES—1035 Green St., Roswell, GA 30075. Kathryn Sargent, Ed. Articles, 850 words (or 800 words with photos or illustrations), on New Age lifestyles and positive thought, holistic health, metaphysics, spirituality, environment. No payment. E-mail: aquarius-editor@mindspring.com.

AVATAR JOURNAL—237 N. Westmonte Dr., Altamonte Springs, FL 32714. Miken Chappell, Ed. Bimonthly. Articles, 500 words, on self-development, awakening consciousness, and spiritual enlightenment. "Spiritual in nature. Pieces that teach a lesson, paradigm shifts, epiphany experiences, anecdotes with theme of obtaining enlightenment, healing, inspiration, metaphysics." Pays $100 for articles; $50 for poems, on publication. E-mail: avatar@avatarhq.com. Web site: www.starsedge.com.

BACKHOME—P.O. Box 70, Hendersonville, NC 28793. Lorna K. Loveless, Ed. Articles, 800 to 2,500 words, on alternative building methods, renewable energy, organic gardening, livestock, home schooling, home business, healthful cooking. "We hope to provide readers with ways to gain more control over their lives by becoming more self-sufficient: raising their own food, making their own repairs, using alternative energy, etc. We do not promote 'dropping out' of society, but ways to become better citizens and caretakers of the planet." Pays $35 per page; from $20 for photos, on publication. Queries preferred. E-mail: backhome@ioa.com. Web site: www.backhomemagazine.com.

BET WEEKEND—One BET Plaza, 1900 W. Place N.E., Washington D.C., 20018-1211. Articles, 200 to 500 words, on the lifestyle, arts, education, and entertainment of the African-American community. Do not send complete manuscript; query with SASE. Payment is 50¢ to $1 per word, on publication. Web site:www.msbet.com.

CAPPER'S—Editorial Dept., 1503 S.W. 42nd St., Topeka, KS 66609-1265. Ann Crahan, Ed. Human-interest, personal-experience, historical articles, 300 to 700 words. Poetry, to 16 lines, on nature, home, family. Novel-length fiction for serialization. Reader letters on topical subjects, recipes, and hints for "Heart of the Home." Jokes. Children's writing and art section. Pays for poetry, on acceptance; manuscripts, on publication.

THE CHRISTIAN SCIENCE MONITOR—One Norway St., Boston, MA 02115. April Austin, Homefront Ed. Newspaper. Articles on lifestyle trends, women's rights, family, parenting, community, and how-to. Pays varying rates, on acceptance. Web site: www.csmonitor.com.

CONSCIOUS CHOICE—920 N. Franklin, Suite 202, Chicago, IL 60610. Sheri Reda, Ed. Monthly. Articles, 1,500 to 2,200 words, "that encourage people to take personal responsibility for their health, attitudes, growth, and contribution to community life." Subjects include health, science, spirituality, politics, nutrition, and the environment. Pays $75 to $150, on publication. Query.

COUNTRY—5400 S. 60th St., Greendale, WI 53129. Jerry Wiebel, Ed. Pieces, 500 to 1,500 words, on interesting rural and country people who have unusual hobbies; liberal use of direct quotes. Good candid, color photos required. Pays on publication. E-mail: editors@country-magazine.com.

DIALOGUE: A WORLD OF IDEAS FOR VISUALLY IMPAIRED PEOPLE OF ALL AGES—P.O. Box 5181, Salem, OR 97304-0181. Carol McCarl, Ed. Quarterly. Articles, 800 to 1,200 words, and poetry, to 20 lines, for visually impaired youth and adults. Career opportunities, educational skills, and recreational activities. "We want to give readers an opportunity to learn about interesting and successful people who are visually impaired." Payment varies, on publication. Queries preferred. SASE. Web site: www.blindskills.com. E-mail: blindskl@teleport.com.

ENTERTAINMENTEEN—470 Park Ave. South, New York, NY 10016. Hedy End, Ed. Lifestyle monthly for 14- to17-year-old girls. Articles include interviews and profiles of popular teen celebrities: actors, actresses, singers, and musicians. Fillers, humor, and jokes are also welcome. Payment varies and is made on publication.

FATE—P.O. Box 64383, St. Paul, MN 55164-0383. Attn: Ed. Factual fillers; journalistic reports on ghosts, UFOs, psychic phenomena, other paranormal topics, to 3,000 words; personal mystical experiences to 500 words. Pays 10¢ a word. E-mail: fate@llewellyn.com. Web site: www.fatemag.com.

FELLOWSHIP—Box 271, Nyack, NY 10960-0271. Richard Deats, Ed. Bimonthly. Published by the Fellowship of Reconciliation, an interfaith, pacifist organization. Features, 1,500 to 2,000 words, and articles, 750 words, "dealing with nonviolence, opposition to war, and a just and peaceful world community." Photo-essays (B&W photos, include caption information). SASE required. Pays in copies and subscription. Queries preferred. E-mail: fellowship@forusa.org. Web site: www.forusa.org.

FILIPINAS MAGAZINE—363 El Camino Real, Suite 100, S. San Francisco, CA 94080. Mona Lisa Yuchengco, Pub. Monthly. "Aims to provide Filipino-Americans with a sense of identity, community, and pride." Cover stories, 1,500 to 2,000 words; profiles, 900 to 2,000 words; reviews and other features, 600 to 1,200 words. Photos welcome. Query with resumé and three writing samples. Pays $50 to $100, on publication. E-mail: m.yuchengco@filipinas mag.com. Web site: www.filipinasmag.com.

FRIENDLY EXCHANGE—P.O. Box 2120, Warren, MI 48090-2120. Dan Grantham, Ed. Articles, 700 to 1,500 words, offering readers "news you can use," on lifestyle issues such as home, health, personal finance, and travel. Pays $400 to $1,000. Query required. Guidelines.

GENRE—7080 Hollywood Blvd., Suite 818, Hollywood, CA 90028. Bryan Buss, Man. Ed. Fiction, 3,000 to 5,000 words, and articles, 750 to 3,000 words, of interest to gay men. "Feature articles should be national in scope and somehow related to the gay male experience." Pays $100 to $400, on publication. Web site: www.genremagazine.com. E-mail: bbuss@genre.com.

GERMAN LIFE—Zeitgeist Publishing, 1068 National Hwy., La Vale, MD 21502. Carolyn Cook, Ed. Bimonthly. Articles, 500 to 2,500 words, on German culture, its past and present, and how America has been influenced by its German immigrants: history, travel, people, the arts, and social and political issues. Fillers, 50 to 200 words. Pays $300 to $500 for full-length articles, to $80 for short pieces and fillers, on publication. Queries preferred. E-mail: ccook@germanlife.com. Web site: www.germanlife.com.

GOOD TIMES—Robert Morris Bldg., 100 N. 17th St., 9th Fl., Philadelphia, PA 19103. Karen Detwiler, Ed.-in-Chief. Mature lifestyle magazine for people 50 years and older. Articles, 1,200 to 1,500 words, on medical issues, health, travel, finance, gardening, fitness, legal issues, celebrities, lifestyles, and relationships. Guidelines. Payment varies, on publication. Query.

THE GREEN MAN—See *Pan Gaia.*

HEALTH QUEST: TOTAL WELLNESS FOR BODY, MIND & SPIRIT—200 Highpoint Dr., Suite 215, Chalfont, PA 18914. Hilary Beard, Man. Ed. Articles, 500 to 1,500 words, on health issues of interest to African-American men and women. "We focus on total health, so articles cover mind, body, spirit, and cultural wellness." Payment varies, on publication. Query preferred.

HEART & SOUL—BET Publications, One BET Plaza, 1900 W. Place N.E., Washington, DC 20018. Yanick Rice Lamb, Ed. Dir. Articles, 800 to 1,500 words, on health, beauty, fitness, nutrition, and relationships for African-American women. "We aim to be the African-American woman's ultimate guide to total well-being, including body, mind, and spirit." Payment varies, on acceptance. Queries preferred.

HOPE MAGAZINE—Box 160, Brooklin, ME 04616. Kimberly Ridley, Ed. Quarterly. Articles, 150 to 5,000 words, about people making a difference. No nostalgia, sentimental, political, opinion, or religious pieces. Pays 30¢ a word, on publication. Query with clips.

INSIDE MAGAZINE—226 S. 16th St., Philadelphia, PA 19102-3392. Jane Biberman, Ed. Jewish lifestyle magazine. Articles, 1,500 to 3,000 words, on Jewish issues, health, finance, and the arts. Pays $75 to $600 for departments; $600 to $1,200 for features, after publication. Queries required; send clips if available.

INSIDER MAGAZINE—4124 W. Oakton, Skokie, IL 60076. Rita Cook, Ed. Dir. Articles, 750 to 1,500 words, on issues, career, politics, sports, and entertainment. "We are mainly a college publication, but to appeal to college readers you must write above them." Pays 1¢ to 5¢ a word, on publication. Queries preferred. Western Office: 11168 Acama St., #3, N. Hollywood, CA 91602-3039. E-mail: insideread@aol.com. Web site: www.incard.com.

INTERRACE—P.O. Box 17479, Beverly Hills, CA 90209. Candy Mills, Ed. Articles, 800 to 2,500 words, with an interracial, intercultural, or interethnic theme: news, commentary, personal accounts, exposés, historical, interviews, transracial adoption, biracial/multiracial topics, etc. No fiction. "Not limited to black/white issues. Interaction between blacks, whites, Asians, Latinos, Native Americans, etc., is also desired." Pays for features only, all published writers receive up to 5 copies and a one year subscription. E-mail: intrace@aol.com. Web site: www.members.aol.com/intrace.

INTUITION—P.O. Box 460773, San Francisco, CA 94146. Colleen Mauro, Ed. Bimonthy. Articles, 750 to 6,000 words, on intuition, creativity, and spiritual development. Departments, 750 to 2,000 words, include profiles; "Frontier Science," breakthroughs pertaining to parapsychology, creativity, etc.; "Intuitive Tools," history and application of a traditional approach to accessing information. Pays $25 for book reviews to $1,200 for cover articles.

JEWISH CURRENTS—22 E. 17th St., #601, New York, NY 10003. Morris U. Schappes, Ed. Articles and book reviews, 2,400 to 3,000 words, on progressive Jewish culture or history: Holocaust resistance commemoration, Black-Jewish relations, Yiddish literature and culture, Jewish labor struggles. "We are a secular Jewish magazine." No fiction. No payment.

THE JEWISH HOMEMAKER—391 Troy Ave., Brooklyn, NY 11213. Avi Goldstein, Ed. Published 4 times a year. Articles, 1,200 to 2,000 words, for a traditional/Orthodox Jewish audience. Parenting, marriage, humor. Payment varies, on publication. No reprints. Query.

JOURNAL AMERICA—P.O. Box 459, Hewitt, NJ 07421. Glen Malmgren, Ed. Tabloid. Fiction and nonfiction, 200 to 1,000 words, on science and nature or "true but strange stories." Pays in subscription. E-mail: journal@warick.net. Web site: www.ajournal.com.

LINK MAGAZINE: WHERE COLLEGE STUDENTS GET IT—(formerly *Link: The College Magazine*) 32 E. 57th St., 12th Fl., New York, NY 10022. Torey Marcus, Ed.-in-Chief. News, lifestyle, and issues for college students. Short features, 300 to 500 words, on college culture. Well-researched, insightful, authoritative articles, 2,000 to 3,000 words, on academics, education news, breaking stories, lifestyle, and trends; also how-to and informational pieces. Pays $100 to $1,500, on publication. Query. Guidelines. E-mail: editor @linkmag.com. Web site: www.linkmag.com.

LIVING ABOARD—P.O. Box 91299, Austin, TX 78709-1299. Linda Ridihalgh, Ed. Lifestyle magazine for those who live or dream of living on their boats. Articles, 1,000 to 2,000 on personal experience or practical information about living aboard. Photos welcome. Send complete manuscript with bio and credits; e-mail or disk submissions preferred. SASE for guidelines. Pays 5¢ per word, on publication. E-mail: editor@livingaboard.com. Web site: www. livingaboard.com.

MEN'S JOURNAL—1290 Ave. of the Americas, New York, NY 10104-0298. Attn: Editorial. Lifestyle magazine for active men ages 25 to 49. Articles and profiles, 2,000 to 7,000 words, on travel, fitness, health, adventure, and participatory sports. Service articles, 400 to 800 words, for equipment and fitness sections. Pays good rates, on acceptance. Query. Web site: www.mens journal.com.

MOMENT MAGAZINE—4710 41st St. N.W., Washington, DC 20016. Attn: Ed. Dept. A conversation on Jewish culture, politics, and religion. "Notes and News/5760": sharp, surprising 250-word pieces on Jewish events, people, and living. "Olam/The Jewish World": well-written, colorful 800 to 1,500 word first-person "letters from" and sophisticated reporting. Book reviews, to 400 words. Query for 1,500 to 3,500 word features. Pays $50 to $1,000. E-mail: editor@momentmag.com. Web site: www.momentmag.com.

MOUNTAIN LIVING MAGAZINE—7009 S. Potomac, Englewood, CO 80112. Irene Rawlings, Ed. Articles, 800 to 1,500 words, on topics related to mountains: travel, home design, architecture, gardening, art, cuisine, sports, and people. Pays $50 to $400, on acceptance. E-mail: rawlings@winc.usa.com.

NATIVE PEOPLES MAGAZINE—The Arts and Lifeways, 5333 N. 7th St., Suite C-224, Phoenix, AZ 85014-2804. Gary Avey, Publisher/Ed. Bimonthly, full-color on Native Americans. Articles, 1,800 to 2,800 words. Authentic and positive portrayals of traditional and contemporary cultural practices. Pays 25¢ and up a word, on publication. Query, include availability of photos. Guidelines and sample copy. SASE.

NEW AGE, THE JOURNAL FOR HOLISTIC LIVING—42 Pleasant St., Watertown, MA 02472. Jenny Cook, Ed. Articles for readers who take an active interest in social change, personal growth, health, and contemporary issues. Features, 2,000 to 4,000 words; columns, 750 to 1,500 words; short news items, 150 words; and first-person narratives, 750 to 1,500 words. Pays varying rates, after acceptance.

NEW CHOICES: LIVING EVEN BETTER AFTER 50—Reader's Digest Publications, Reader's Digest Road, Pleasantville, NY 10570. Greg Daugherty, Ed.-in-Chief. Service magazine for people ages 50 to 65. Articles on health, personal finance, travel, etc. Payment varies, on acceptance. E-mail: newchoices@readersdigest.com. Web site: www.newchoices.com.

THE NEW YORK TIMES MAGAZINE—229 W. 43rd St., New York, NY 10036. Topical, personal pieces, 900 words, for "Lives." Pays $1,000, on acceptance.

NEWPORT LIFE—55 Memorial Blvd., Newport, RI 02840. Lynne Tungett, Publisher. John Pantalone, Ed. Bimonthly. Annual City Guide. Articles, 500 to 2,500 words, on people, places, attractions of Newport County: general-interest, historical, profiles, international celebrities, and social and political issues. Departments, 200 to 750 words: sailing, dining, food and wine, home and garden, and the arts in Newport County. Photos must be available for all articles. Query. SASE. Web site: www.newportlifemagazine.com.

PALM SPRINGS LIFE—Desert Publications, 303 N. Indian Canyon Dr., Palm Springs, CA 92262. Stewart Weiner, Ed. Articles, 1,000 to 3,000 words, of interest to "wealthy, upscale people who live and/or play in the desert." Pays $150 to $500 for features, $25 to $75 for short profiles, on publication. Query required. E-mail: stewart@corp.desert-resorts.com. Web sites: www.palmspringslife.com or www.desert-resorts.com.

PAN GAIA—(formerly *The Green Man*) P.O. Box 641, Point Arena, CA 95468-0641. Diane Conn Darling, Ed. "Exploring the Pagan World." Articles, 1,500 to 3,000 words. Pays 1¢ per word. Query for guidelines. E-mail: editor@pangaia.com. Web site: www.pangaia.com.

THE PHOENIX—7152 Unity Ave. N., Brooklyn Ctr., MN 55429. Pat Samples, Ed. Tabloid. Articles, 800 to 1,500 words, on recovery, renewal, and growth. Department pieces for "Bodywise," "Family Skills," or "Personal Story." "Our readers are committed to physical, emotional, mental, and spiritual health and well-being. Read a sample copy to see what we publish." Pays 3¢ to 5¢ a word, on publication. Guidelines and calendar. SASE. E-mail: psamples@pioneerplanet.inf.net. Web site: www.gartland.com/phoenix.

PRESENCESENSE—P.O. Box 547, Rancocas, NJ 08073. Attn: Ed. Quarterly. Articles of varying lengths, on social customs, etiquette, and lifestyle. Past issues have included articles on manners, humor, recipes, little known facts, choosing a cigar, wedding planning and life's pleasures & mysteries. Currently seeking material from free-lance writers, artists, and photographers. SASE for guidelines or web site: www.PresenceSense.com.

ROBB REPORT—1 Acton Pl., Acton, MA 01720. Steven Castle, Ed. Consumer magazine for the high-end/luxury market. Features on lifestyles, home interiors, boats, travel, investment opportunities, exotic automobiles, business, technology, etc. Payment varies, on publication. Query with SASE and published clips. Web site: www.robbreport.com.

SAGEWOMAN—P.O. Box 641, Point Arena, CA 95468-0641. Anne Newkirk Niven, Ed. Quarterly. Articles, 200 to 5,000 words, on issues of concern to pagan and spiritually minded women. Material that expresses an earth-centered spirituality: personal experience, Goddess lore, ritual material, interviews, humor, and reviews. Accepts material by women only. Pays 1¢ a word, from $10, on publication. E-mail: editor@sagewoman.com. Web site: www.sagewoman.com.

SAVEUR—100 Ave. of the Americas, 7th Fl., New York, NY 10013. Colman Andrews, Ed. Rarely assigns restaurant-based pieces, and sections such as "Classic" and "Source" are almost always staff-written. Queries should be detailed and specific, and personal ties to the subject mattter are important. Articles, to 2, 000 words. Pays on acceptance.

SCIENCE OF MIND—P.O. Box 75127, Los Angeles, CA 90075. Kenneth Lind, Sylvia Delgado, Assoc. Eds. Articles, 1,500 to 2,000 words, that offer a thoughtful perspective on how to experience greater self-acceptance, empowerment, and a meaningful life. "Achieving wholeness through applying spiritual principles is the primary focus." Inspiring first-person pieces, 1,000 to 2,000 words. Interviews with notable spiritual leaders, 3,500 words. Poetry, to 28 lines. Pays $25 per page. Poetry is seldom printed. E-mail preferred, only accepts will be notified. E-mail: sdelgado@scienceofmind.com.

T'AI CHI—P.O. Box 26156, Los Angeles, CA 90026. Marvin Smalheiser, Ed. Articles, 1,200 to 4,000 words, on T'ai Chi Ch'uan, other internal martial arts and related topics such as qigong, Chinese medicine and healing practices, Chinese philosophy and culture, health, meditation, fitness, and self-improvement. Pays $75 to $500, on publication. Query required. Guidelines. SASE. E-mail: taichi@tai-chi.com. Web site: www.tai-chi.com.

TROIKA—P.O. Box 1006, Weston, CT 06883. Celia Meadow, Ed. Quarterly. Articles, 2,000 to 2,500 words, and columns, 750 to 1,400 words, for arts, health, science, human interest, international interests, business, leisure, ethics, and pro bono. "For educated, affluent baby-boomers, who are seeking to balance their personal achievements, family commitments, and community involvement." Pays $250 to $1,000, on publication. Query or finished manuscript. E-mail: etroika@aol.com. Web site: www.troikamagazine.com.

US AIRWAYS ATTACHÉ—1301 Carolina St., Greensboro, NC 27401. Articles, 400 to 2,500 words, on the finer things in life. "Paragons" department offers short pieces touting the best of the best; "Informed Sources" department contains experts' opinions and knowledge on a variety of topics. No politics or Hollywood issues. Pays $1 a word, on acceptance.

VEGETARIAN VOICE—P.O. Box 72, Dolgeville, NY 13329. Maribeth Abrams-McHenry, Man. Ed. Quarterly. Informative, well-researched and/or inspiring articles, 600 to 1,800 words, on lifestyles and consumer concerns, health, nutrition, animal rights, the environment, world hunger, etc. "Our underlying philosophy is total vegetarian; all our recipes are vegan and we do not support the use of leather, wool, silk, etc." Guidelines. Pays in copies. E-mail: navs@telenet.net. Web site: www.navs-online.org.

VENTURE INWARD—215 67th Ave., Virginia Beach, VA 23451. A. Robert Smith, Ed. Articles, to 4,000 words, on metaphysical and spiritual development subjects. Prefer personal experience. Opinion pieces, to 800 words, for "Guest Column." "Turning Point," to 800 words, on an inspiring personal turning point experience. "The Mystical Way," to 1,500 words, on a personal paranormal experience. "Holistic Health," brief accounts of success using Edgar Cayce remedies. Book reviews, to 500 words. Pays $50 to $400, on publication. Query. E-mail: are@edgarcayce.org. Web site: www.edgarcayce.org.

WEIGHT WATCHERS MAGAZINE—2100 Lakeshore Dr., Birmingham, AL 35209. Exec. Ed. Articles on fashion, beauty, food, health, nutrition, fitness, and weight-loss motivation and success. Pays on acceptance. Query with clips required. Guidelines.

WHOLE LIFE TIMES—21225 Pacific Coast Hwy., Suite B, P.O. Box 1187, Malibu, CA 90265. Kerri Hikida, Assoc. Ed. Tabloid. Feature articles, 2,000 words, with a holistic perspective. Departments and columns, 800 words. Well-researched articles on the environment, current political issues, women's issues, and new developments in health, as well as how-to, humor, new product information, personal growth, and interviews. Pays 5¢ to 10¢ a word for features only, 30 days after publication.

WIRED—520 Third St., San Francisco, CA 94107-1427. Christina

Gangei, Ed. Asst. Lifestyle magazine for the "digital generation." Articles, essays, profiles, fiction, and other material that discusses the "meaning and context" of digital technology in today's world. Guidelines. Payment varies, on acceptance.

YES! A JOURNAL OF POSITIVE FUTURES—Box 10818, Bainbridge Island, WA 98110. Carol Estes, Assoc. Ed. Quarterly. Articles, 1,500 to 2,500 words; poetry, 200 words; photos and drawings. Focus is on "ways people are working to create a more just, sustainable, and compassionate world." Don't simply expose problems; highlight a practical solution. Query. Pays $20 to $50, on publication.

YOGA JOURNAL—2054 University Ave., Berkeley, CA 94704. Kathryn Arnold, Ed. Articles, 1,200 to 4,000 words, on holistic health, spirituality, and yoga. Pays $100 to $3,000, on acceptance. E-mail: karnold@yogajournal. com. Web site: www.yogajournal.com.

SPORTS & RECREATION

ADVENTURE JOURNAL—650 S. Orcas St., Suite 103, Seattle, WA 98108. Kristina Schreck, Man. Ed. Bimonthly. Recreational travel articles, 2,500 to 3,500 words, on risky wild adventures; 700 to 1,200 words, on shorter trips that offer a high degree of excitement; and service pieces, 700 to 1,200 words, on short excursions. Profiles and essays also used. Pays 15¢ a word, on publication. Include clips.

AKC GAZETTE—51 Madison Ave., New York, NY 10010. Mark Roland, Features Ed. "The official journal for the sport of purebred dogs." Articles, 1,000 to 2,500 words, relating to purebred dogs, for serious fanciers. Pays $200 to $450, on acceptance. Queries preferred.

THE AMERICAN FIELD—542 S. Dearborn, Chicago, IL 60605. B.J. Matthys, Man. Ed. Yarns about hunting trips, bird-shooting; articles to 1,500 words, on dogs and field trials, emphasizing conservation of game resources. Pays varying rates, on acceptance.

AMERICAN HUNTER—NRA Publications, 11250 Waples Mill Rd., Fairfax, VA 22030. John Zent, Ed. Articles, 1,400 to 2,000 words, on hunting. Photos. Pays on acceptance. Guidelines.

AMERICAN MOTORCYCLIST—American Motorcyclist Assn., 13515 Yarmouth Drive, Pickerington, OH 43147. Greg Harrison, Ed. Articles and fiction, to 3,000 words, on motorcycling: news coverage, personalities, tours. Photos. Pays varying rates, on publication. Query with SASE. Web site: www.ama-cycle.org.

THE AMERICAN RIFLEMAN—11250 Waples Mill Rd., Fairfax, VA 22030. Mark Keefe, Man. Ed. Factual articles on use and enjoyment of sporting firearms. Pays on acceptance.

AMERICAN SQUAREDANCE MAGAZINE—P.O. Box 777, North Scituate, RI 02857. Ed & Pat Juaire, Eds. Articles and fiction, 1,000 to 1,500 words, related to square dancing. Poetry. Fillers, to 100 words. Pays $1.50 per column inch.

AMY LOVE'S REAL SPORTS—P.O. Box 8204, San Jose, CA 95155-

8204. Jill McManus, Ed. Bimonthly. Articles, on girls' and women's sports with a focus on team sports, and emphasizing the drama of competition. Queries preferred. Pay varies, on publication. Web site: www.real-sports.com. E-mail: jill@real-sports.com.

ATLANTIC SALMON JOURNAL—P.O. Box 5200, St. Andrews, N.B., Canada E5B 3S8. Jim Gourlay, Ed. Articles, 1,500 to 3,000 words, related to Atlantic salmon: fishing, conservation, ecology, travel, politics, biology, how-tos, anecdotes. Pays $100 to $400, on publication. E-mail: asfads@nbnet.nb.ca. Web site: www.asf.ca.

BACKPACKER MAGAZINE—Rodale Press, 33 E. Minor St., Emmaus, PA 18098. Thom Hogan, Exec. Ed. Articles, 250 to 3,000 words, on self-propelled backcountry travel: backpacking, kayaking/canoeing, mountaineering; technique, nordic skiing, health, natural science. Photos. Pays varying rates. E-mail: editor@backpacker.com. Query editor Tom Shealey. Web site: www. backpacker.com. Guidelines on web site.

THE BACKSTRETCH—P.O. Box 7065, Louisville, KY 40257-0065. Sam Ramer, Man. United Thoroughbred Trainers of America. Feature articles, with photos, on subjects related to thoroughbred horse racing. Pays after publication. Sample issue and guidelines on request.

BACKWOODSMAN—P.O. Box 627, Westcliffe, CO 81252. Charlie Richie, Ed. Articles for the twentieth-century frontiersman: muzzleloading, primitive weapons, black powder cartridge guns, woodslore, survival, homesteading, trapping, etc. Historical and how-to articles. No payment. Pays in subscription.

BASEBALL FORECAST, BASEBALL ILLUSTRATED—See *Hockey Illustrated.*

BASKETBALL FORECAST—See *Hockey Illustrated.*

BASSIN'—2448 E. 81st St., Tulsa, OK 74137-4207. Mark Chesnut, Exec. Ed. Articles, 1,200 to 1,400 words, on how and where to bass fish, for the amateur fisherman. Pays $350 to $500, on acceptance. Query.

BASSMASTER MAGAZINE—B.A.S.S. Publications, P.O. Box 17900, Montgomery, AL 36141. Dave Precht, Ed. Articles, 1,500 to 2,000 words, with photos, on freshwater black bass and striped bass. "Short Casts" pieces, 400 to 800 words, on news, views, and items of interest. Pays $200 to $500, on acceptance. Query.

BAY & DELTA YACHTSMAN—4090 S. McCarran, Suite E, Reno, NV 89502. Don Abbott, Pub. Cruising stories and features, how-tos. Must have northern California tie-in. Photos and illustrations. Pays varying rates.

BIKE RACING NATION—See *USA Cycling Magazine.*

BIRD WATCHER'S DIGEST—P.O. Box 110, Marietta, OH 45750. William H. Thompson, III, Ed. Articles, 600 to 2,500 words, for bird watchers: first-person accounts; how-tos; pieces on backyard-related topics; profiles of bird species. Pays from $100, on publication. Submit complete manuscript. SASE for guidelines. E-mail: bwd@birdwatchersdigest.com. Web site: www. birdwatchersdigest.com.

BLACK BELT—P.O. Box 918, Santa Clarita, CA 91380-9018. Attn: Ed. Articles related to self-defense: how-tos on fitness and technique; historical, travel, philosophical subjects. Pays $100 to $300, on publication. Guidelines.

BOW & ARROW HUNTING—265 S. Anita, Suite 120, Orange, CA 92868. Bob Torres, Ed. Articles, 1,200 to 2,500 words, with color slides, B&W or color photos, on bowhunting; profiles and technical pieces, primarily on deer hunting. Pays $250 to $500, on acceptance. Same address and mechanical requirements for *Gun World.*

BOWHUNTER MAGAZINE—6405 Flank Dr., Harrisburg, PA 17112. M.R. James, Ed.-in-Chief. Dwight Schuh, Ed. Informative, entertaining features, 500 to 2,000 words, on bow-and-arrow hunting. Fillers. Photos. "Study magazine first." Pays $100 to $400, on acceptance. E-mail: bowhunter@cowless.com. Web site: www.bowhunter.com.

BOWLERS JOURNAL INTERNATIONAL—122 S. Michigan Ave., #1506, Chicago, IL 60603-6107. Jim Dressel, Ed. Trade and consumer articles, 1,200 to 2,200 words, with photos, on bowling. Pays $75 to $200, on acceptance.

BOWLING—5301 S. 76th St., Greendale, WI 53129. Bill Vint, Ed. Articles, to 1,500 words, on all aspects of bowling, especially human interest angle. Profiles. "We're looking for unique, unusual stories about bowling people and places, and occasionally publish business articles." Pays varying rates, on publication. Query required.

BUCKMASTERS WHITETAIL MAGAZINE—P.O. Box 244022, Montgomery, AL 36124-4022. Russell Thornberry, Exec. Ed. Articles and fiction, 2,500 words, for serious sportsmen. "Big Buck Adventures" articles capture the details and the adventure of the hunt of a newly discovered trophy. Fresh, new whitetail hunting how-tos; new biological information about whitetail deer that might help hunters; entertaining deer stories; and other department pieces. Photos a plus. Pays $250 to $400 for articles. Guidelines.

BUGLE—Rocky Mountain Elk Foundation, P.O. Box 8249, Missoula, MT 59807-8249. Lee Cromrich, Ed. Asst. Bimonthly. Fiction and nonfiction, 1,500 to 4,000 words, on elk and elk hunting. Department pieces, 1,000 to 3,000 words, for: "Thoughts and Theories"; "Situation Ethics"; and "Women in the Outdoors." Pays 20¢ a word, on acceptance. E-mail: bugle@rmef.org. Web site: www.elkfoundation.org.

CANOE AND KAYAK MAGAZINE—P.O. Box 3146, Kirkland, WA 98083. Jan Nesset, Ed.-in-Chief. Features, 1,600 to 2,500 words; department pieces, 500 to 1,000 words. Topics include canoeing or kayaking adventures, destinations, boat and equipment reviews, techniques and how-tos, short essays, camping, environment, safety, humor, health, history, etc. Pays 13¢ a word, on publication. Query preferred. Guidelines. E-mail: editor@canoekayak.com. Web site: www.canoekayak.com.

CAR AND DRIVER—2002 Hogback Rd., Ann Arbor, MI 48105. Csaba Csere, Ed.-in-Chief. Articles, to 2,500 words, for enthusiasts, on new cars, classic cars, industry topics. "Ninety percent staff-written. Query with clips. No unsolicited manuscripts." Pays to $2,500, on acceptance. E-mail: editors@caranddriver.com. Web site: www.caranddriver.com.

CASCADES EAST—716 N.E. Fourth St., P.O. Box 5784, Bend, OR 97708. Geoff Hill, Ed./Pub. Articles, 1,000 to 2,000 words, on outdoor activities (fishing, hunting, golfing, backpacking, rafting, skiing, snowmobiling, etc.), history, special events, and scenic tours in central Oregon Cascades. Photos.

Pays 5¢ to 15¢ a word, extra for photos, on publication. E-mail: sunpub@ sun-pub.com. Web site: www.sun-pub.com.

CHESAPEAKE BAY MAGAZINE—1819 Bay Ridge Ave., Annapolis, MD 21403. Tim Sayles, Ed. Articles, to 2,500 words, on boating, fishing, destinations, people, history, and traditions of the Chesapeake Bay. Photos. Pays $100 to $700, on acceptance. Query at: cbmediator@aol.com. E-mail queries and submissions are welcome. E-mail: cbmeditor@cbmmag.net.

COAST TO COAST—2575 Vista del Mar Dr., Ventura, CA 93001. Valerie Law, Ed. Membership publication for Coast to Coast Resorts, private camping and resort clubs across North America. Focuses on "travel, recreation, and good times." Destination features focus on a North American city or region, going beyond typical tourist stops to interview locals. Activity or recreation features introduce readers to a sport, hobby, or other diversion. Also features on RV lifestyle. Send queries or manuscripts. Pays $350 to $600, on acceptance, for 1,500- to 2,500-word pieces. Web site: www.rv.net.

CROSS COUNTRY SKIER—MD 60 1107 Hazelfine, Chaska, MN 55318. Aaron Kellogg, Ed. Published October through February. Articles, to 2,000 words, on all aspects of cross-country skiing. Departments, 1,000 to 1,500 words, on ski maintenance, skiing techniques, health and fitness. Pays $300 to $700 for features, $100 to $350 for departments, on publication. Query.

CYCLE WORLD—1499 Monrovia Ave., Newport Beach, CA 92663. David Edwards, Ed.-in-Chief. Technical and feature articles, 1,500 to 2,500 words, for motorcycle enthusiasts. Photos. Pays on publication. Query. E-mail: cw1edwards@aol.com.

DANCE SPIRIT—250 W. 57th St., Ste. 420, New York, NY 10107. Sheila Noone, Ed. Monthly. Articles on training, instruction and technique, choreography, dance styles, and profiles of dancers, geared toward dancers of all disciplines. Photos accepted. Payment varies, on publication. E-mail: editor-@lifestyleventures.com. Web site: www.dancespirit.com.

THE DIVER—P.O. Box 28, St. Petersburg, FL 33731-0028. Bob Taylor, Ed. Articles on divers, coaches, officials, springboard and platform techniques, training tips, etc. Pays $15 to $50, $5 to $10 for cartoons, extra for photos, on publication.

DIVER MAGAZINE—P.O. Box 1312, Delta, B.C., Canada V4M 3Y8. Stephanie Bold, Ed. Illustrated articles, 500 to 1,000 words, on dive destinations. Shorter pieces are also welcome. "Travel features should be brief and accompanied by excellent slides and/or prints and a map. Unsolicited articles will be reviewed only from August to October. Pays $2.50 per column inch, on publication. Guidelines. Limited market. E-mail address: divermag@axion.net. Web site: www.divermag.com.

ELYSIAN FIELDS QUARTERLY—P.O. Box 14385, St. Paul, MN 55114-0385. Tom Goldstein, Pub. Articles, to 4,000 words, and poetry, fiction, essays, interviews, humor, and opinion pieces, all related to baseball. Pays in copies. SASE for guidelines. E-mail: info@efqreview.com. Web site: www. efqreview.com.

EQUUS—Fleet Street Corp., 656 Quince Orchard Rd., Gaithersburg, MD 20878. Laurie Prinz, Ed. Articles, 1,000 to 3,000 words, on all breeds of horses, covering their health, care, the latest advances in equine medicine and research.

"Attempt to speak as one horseperson to another." Pays $100 to $400, on publication.

FAMILY MOTOR COACHING—8291 Clough Pike, Cincinnati, OH 45244-2796. Robbin Gould, Ed. Articles, 1,500 to 2,000 words, on technical topics and travel routes and destinations accessible by motorhome. Payment varies, on acceptance. Query preferred.

FIELD & STREAM—2 Park Ave., New York, NY 10016. Duncan Barnes, Ed. Articles, 1,000 to 2,000 words, on hunting, fishing. Short articles, to 1,000 words. Fillers, 75 to 500 words. Cartoons. Pays from $800 for feature articles with photos, $75 to $500 for fillers, $100 for cartoons, on acceptance. Query for articles. E-mail: fsinfo@aol.com. Web site: www.fieldandstream. com.

THE FLORIDA HORSE—P.O. Box 2106, Ocala, FL 34478. Dan Mearns, Ed. Articles, 1,500 words, on Florida thoroughbred breeding and racing. Also veterinary articles, financial articles, and articles of general interest to horse owners and breeders. Pays $200 to $300, on publication. Query.

FLY ROD & REEL—P.O. Box 370, Camden, ME 04843. James E. Butler, Ed. Fly-fishing pieces, 2,000 to 2,500 words, and occasional fiction; articles on the culture and history of the areas being fished. Pays on acceptance. Query.

FOOTBALL DIGEST—Century Publishing Co., 990 Grove St., Evanston, IL 60201. Jim O'Connor, Ed.-in-Chief. William Wagner, Senior Assoc. Ed. Nonfiction articles, 1,500 to 2,500 words, for the hard-core football fan: profiles of pro and college stars, nostalgia, trends in the sport. Pays on publication. Query.

FOOTBALL FORECAST—See *Hockey Illustrated.*

FUR-FISH-GAME—2878 E. Main St., Columbus, OH 43209. Mitch Cox, Ed. Illustrated articles, 800 to 2,500 words, preferably with how-to angle, on hunting, fishing, trapping, dogs, camping, or other outdoor topics. Some humorous or where-to articles. Pays to $150, on acceptance.

GAME AND FISH PUBLICATIONS—P.O. Box 741, Marietta, GA 30061. Attn: Ed. Dept. Publishes 30 monthly outdoor magazines for 48 states. Articles, 1,500 to 2,500 words, on hunting and fishing. How-tos, where-tos, and adventure pieces. Profiles of successful hunters and fishermen. No hiking, canoeing, camping, or backpacking pieces. Pays $125 to $175 for state-specific articles, $200 to $250 for multi-state articles, before publication. Pays $25 to $75 for interior photos. $250 for covers.

GOLF DIGEST—5520 Park Ave., Trumbull, CT 06611. Jerry Tarde, Ed. Currently not accepting material. Web site: www.golfdigest.com.

GOLF DIGEST WOMAN—1120 Avenue of the Americas, New York, NY 10018. Rona Cherry, Ed. Interested in previously published authors (in national magazines) who have in-depth knowledge of golf and golf-related subjects. Pays varying rates, on publication. Web site: www.golfdigest.com.

GOLF FOR WOMEN—125 Park Ave., 15th Fl., New York, NY 10017. Leslie Day Craige, Ed.-in-Chief. Golf lifestyle magazine for avid women golfers. Includes travel, instruction, fashion, equipment, news. Query with clips. E-mail: gfwmag@mdp.com.

GOLF JOURNAL—Golf House, P.O. Box 708, Far Hills, NJ 07931-0708. Brett Avery, Ed. Official publication of the United States Golf Associa- .

tion. Stories and articles relating to golf including its history, lore, rules, equipment, and general information. The focus is on amateur golf. No golf jokes, instruction or travel pieces. Accepts poignant and humorous stories and essays. Pays varying rates, on publication. Send complete manuscript with SASE. Reports in 2 months. E-mail: golfjournal@usga.org. Web site: www.golfjournal.org.

GOLF MAGAZINE—2 Park Ave., New York, NY 10016. Jim Frank, Ed. Articles, 1,000 words with photos, on golf history and travel (places to play around the world); profiles of professional tour players. Shorts, to 500 words. Pays 75¢ a word, on acceptance. Queries preferred.

THE GREYHOUND REVIEW—National Greyhound Assn., Box 543, Abilene, KS 67410. Tim Horan, Man. Ed. Articles, 1,000 to 10,000 words, pertaining to the Greyhound racing industry: how-to, historical nostalgia, interviews. Pays $85 to $150, on publication.

GULF COAST GOLFER—See *North Texas Golfer.*

GUN DIGEST—Krause Publications, Inc., 700 E. State St., Iola, WI 54990. Ken Ramage, Ed. Well-researched articles, to 5,000 words, on guns and shooting, equipment, etc. Photos. Pays from 10¢ a word, on acceptance. Query. E-mail: ramayek@krause.com. Web site: www.krause.com.

GUN DOG—P.O. Box 35098, Des Moines, IA 50315. Rick Van Etten, Ed. Features, 1,000 to 2,500 words, with photos, on bird hunting: how-tos, where-tos, dog training, canine medicine, breeding strategy. Fiction. Humor. Pays $150 to $300 for fillers and short articles, $150 to $450 for features, on acceptance.

GUN WORLD—See *Bow & Arrow Hunting.*

GUNGAMES—Box 516, Moreno Valley, CA 92556. Michael Bane, Ed. Bimonthly. Articles and fiction, 1,200 to 1,500 words, about "the fun side of guns and shooting. No self-defense articles." Related poetry, to 300 words. Pays $150 to $250, on publication.

HANG GLIDING—U.S. Hang Gliding Assn., 31441 Santa Margarita Pkwy., A-256, Rancho Santa Margarita, CA 92688-1836. Gilbert Dodgen, Ed. Articles, 2 to 3 pages, on hang gliding. Pays to $50, on publication. Query.

HOCKEY ILLUSTRATED—Sterling/Macfaden, 233 Park Ave. S., New York, NY 10003. Stephen Ciacciarelli, Ed. Articles, 2,500 words, on hockey players and teams. Pays $125, on publication. Query. Same address and requirements for *Baseball Illustrated, Wrestling World, Pro Basketball Illustrated, Pro Football Illustrated, Baseball Forecast, Pro Football Preview, Football Forecast,* and *Basketball Forecast.*

HORSE & RIDER—1597 Cole Blvd., Suite 350, Golden, CO 80401. Kathy Kadash-Swan, Ed. Articles, 500 to 2,000 words, with photos, on western riding and training, and general horse care geared to the performance horse. Pays varying rates, on acceptance. Buys first N.A. serial rights. Guidelines. Web site: www.horseandrider.com. E-mail hrsenrider@cowles.com.

HOT BOAT—Sport Publications, 8484 Wilshire Blvd., #900, Beverly Hills, CA 90211. Brett Bayne, Ed. Family-oriented articles, 600 to 1,000 words, on motorized water sport events and personalities: general-interest, how-to, and technical features. Pays $85 to $300, on publication. Query.

INSIDE TEXAS RUNNING—9514 Bristlebrook Dr., Houston, TX

77083-6193. Joanne Schmidt, Ed. Articles and fillers on running in Texas. Pays $35 to $100 for articles; $10 for short fillers; $10 to $25 for photos, on acceptance. E-mail: insidetx@aol.com. Web site: www.runningnetwork.com/texas running.

KITPLANES—8745 Aero Dr., Suite 105, San Diego, CA 92123. Dave Martin, Ed. Articles, 1,000 to 4,000 words, on all aspects of design, construction, and performance of aircraft built from kits and plans by home craftsmen. Pays $70 per page, on publication. E-mail: editorial@kitplanes.com. Web site: www.kitplanes.com.

LAKELAND BOATING—500 Davis St., Suite 1000, Evanston, IL 60201-5047. Chad Schlegel, Ed. Articles for powerboat owners on the Great Lakes and other area waterways, on long-distance cruising, short trips, maintenance, equipment, history, regional personalities and events, fishing, and environment. Photos. Pays on publication. Query. Guidelines. E-mail: ibonline@aol.com. Web site: www.lakelandboating.com.

LIVING ABOARD—P.O. Box 91299, Austin , TX 78709-1299. Linda Ridihalgh, Ed. Lifestyle magazine for those who live or dream of living on their boats. Articles, 1,000 to 2,000 on personal experience or practical information about living aboard. Photos welcome. Send complete manuscript with bio and credits; e-mail or disk submissions preferred. SASE for guidelines. Pays 5¢ per word, on publication. E-mail: editor@livingaboard.com. Web site: www. livingaboard.com.

MEN'S HEALTH—Rodale Press, 33 E. Minor St., Emmaus, PA 18098. David Zinczenko, Sr. Ed. Articles, 1,000 to 2,500 words, on sports, fitness, diet, health, nutrition, relationships, and travel, for men ages 25 to 55. Pays from 50¢ a word, on acceptance. Query.

MICHIGAN OUT-OF-DOORS—P.O. Box 30235, Lansing, MI 48909. Dennis Knickerbocker, Ed. Features, 1,000 to 1,500 words, on hunting, fishing, camping, hiking, sailing, wildlife, and conservation in Michigan. Query. Pays $90 to $200, on acceptance. E-mail: mucc@mucc.org. Web site: www. mucc.org.

MID-WEST OUTDOORS—111 Shore Dr., Hinsdale, IL 60521-5885. Gene Laulunen, Ed. Articles, 1,000 to 1,500 words, with photos, on where, when, and how to fish and hunt in the Midwest. No Canadian material. Pays $15 to $35, on publication.

MOTOR TREND—6420 Wilshire Blvd., Los Angeles, CA 90048-5515. C. Van Tune, Ed. Articles, 250 to 2,000 words, on autos, racing, events, histories, and profiles. Color photos. Pay varies, on acceptance. Query.

MOTORHOME MAGAZINE—2575 Vista Del Mar, Ventura, CA 93001. Sherry McBride, Man. Ed. Articles, to 2,000 words, with color slides, on motorhome travel, activities, and how-to pieces. Pays to $600, on acceptance. Web site: www.motorhomemagazine.com.

MUSHING—P.O. Box 149, Ester, AK 99725-0149. Todd Hoener, Ed. Dog-driving how-tos, profiles, and features, 1,500 to 2,000 words; and department pieces, 500 to 1,000 words, for competitive and recreational dogsled drivers, weight pullers, dog packers, and skijorers. International audience. Photos. Pays $20 to $175, on publication. Queries preferred. Guidelines and sample issue on request. Web site: www.mushing.com. E-mail: info@mushing.com.

MUZZLE BLASTS—P.O. Box 67, Friendship, IN 47021-0067. Terri

Trowbridge, Dir. of Pub. Articles, 500 to 1,500 words, on hunting with muzzle-loading rifles, technical aspects of the rifles, historical pieces. Pays $50 to $400, on publication. Send for guidelines. E-mail: mblastdop@seidata.com. Web site: www.nmlra.org.

NATIONAL PARKS MAGAZINE—1776 Massachusetts Ave. N.W., Washington, DC 20036. Linda Rancourt, Ed.-in-Chief. Articles, 1,500 to 2,000 words, on areas in the National Park System, proposed new areas, threats to parks or park wildlife, new trends in park use, legislative issues, and endangered species of plants or animals relevant to national parks. No fiction, poetry, personal narratives, "My trip to . . . ," or straight travel pieces to individual parks. Also, articles, 1,500 words, on "low-impact" travel to national park sites. Pays $400 to $1,000, on acceptance. Query with clips. Guidelines with SASE. E-mail: npmag@npca.org. Web site: www.npca.org.

NORTH TEXAS GOLFER—10301 Northwest Freeway, Suite 418, Houston, TX 77092. Bob Gray, Pub. Articles, 800 to 1,500 words, of interest to golfers in north Texas. Fees and guidelines upon request. Queries required. Same requirements for *Gulf Coast Golfer* (for golfers in south Texas).

OPEN WHEEL—3816 Industry Blvd., Lakeland, FL 33811. Rus S., Ed. Articles, to 6,000 words, on open wheel drivers, races, and vehicles. Photos. Pays to $400 on publication.

OREGON CYCLING—455 W. 1st Ave., Eugene, OR 97401. Jesse Z. Sherman, Ed. Ten times yearly. Informative and entertaining articles related to bicycling and advocacy in the Pacific Northwest. Photos and drawings welcome. No payment for first three articles; pays $20 to $50 for subsequent articles.

OUTDOOR AMERICA—Izaak Walton League, 707 Conservation Ln., Gaithersburg, MD 20878-2983. Ed. Quarterly publication of the Izaak Walton League of America. Articles, 1,500 to 3,000 words on national conservation issues that are top league priorities such as: endangered species, public lands management, and the protection of air quality, water quality and water resources. Other topics include farm-related issues, wildlife and fisheries management controversies of national interest. Pays 30¢ a word. Query with SASE and clips. E-mail: zachh@iwla.org. Web site: www.iwla.org.

OUTDOOR CANADA—340 Ferrier St., Suite 210, Markham, Ont., Canada L3R 2Z5. James Little, Ed. Published 8 times yearly. Articles, 1,500 to 4,000 words, on fishing, hunting, and conservation. Pays $500 and upwards, on acceptance.

OUTDOOR LIFE—2 Park Ave., New York, NY 10016. Todd W. Smith, Ed.-in-Chief. Articles, 1,400 to 1,700 words, and short, instructive items, 900 to 1,100 words, on hunting, fishing, outdoor equipment, and related subjects. Pays $300 to $1500, on acceptance. Query.

OUTSIDE—Outside Plaza, 400 Market St., Santa Fe, NM 87501. No unsolicited material. Web site: www.outsidemag.com.

PADDLER MAGAZINE—P.O. Box 775450, Steamboat Springs, CO 80477. Eugene Buchanan, Ed. Dir. Articles on canoeing, kayaking, rafting, sea kayaking. "Best way to break in is to target a specific department, i.e. 'Hotlines,' 'Paddle People,' etc." Pays 15¢ to 25¢ a word, on publication. Queries preferred. Guidelines. E-mail: editor@aca-paddler.org. Web site: www.paddler magazine.com.

PENNSYLVANIA ANGLER AND BOATER—Pennsylvania Fish and Boat Commission, P.O. Box 67000, Harrisburg, PA 17106-7000. Attn: Art Michaels, Ed. Articles, 500 to 3,000 words, with photos, on freshwater fishing and boating in Pennsylvania. Pays $50 to $300, on acceptance. Must send SASE with all material. Query. Guidelines.

PENNSYLVANIA GAME NEWS—Game Commission, 2001 Elmerton Ave., Harrisburg, PA 17110-9797. Bob Mitchell, Ed. Articles, to 2,500 words, on hunting, wildlife, and other outdoor subjects, except fishing and boating. Photos. Pays from 6¢ a word, extra for photos, on acceptance.

PETERSEN'S BOWHUNTING—6420 Wilshire Blvd., Los Angeles, CA 90048-5515. Jay Michael Strangis, Ed. How-to articles, 2,000 to 2,500 words, on bowhunting. Also pieces on where to bowhunt, unusual techniques and equipment, and profiles of successful bowhunters will also be considered. Photos must accompany all manuscripts. Pays $300 to $400, on acceptance. Query with SASE.

POWER AND MOTORYACHT—260 Madison Ave., 8th Fl., New York, NY 10016. Diane M. Byrne, Exec. Ed. Articles, 1,000 to 2,000 words, for owners of powerboats, 24 feet and larger. Seamanship, ship's systems, maintenance, sportfishing news, travel destinations, profiles of individuals working to improve the marine environment. "For our readers, powerboating is truly a lifestyle, not just a hobby." Pays $500 to $1,000, on acceptance. Query required. No e-mail queries. E-mail: dbyrne@pririediasi.com.

POWERBOAT—1691 Spinnaker Dr., Suite 206, Ventura, CA 93001. Doug Thompson, Ed. Articles, to 2,000 words, with photos, for high performance powerboat owners, on outstanding achievements, water-skiing, competitions; technical articles on hull and engine developments; how-to pieces. Pays $300 to $1,000, on publication. Query and writing samples required. No unsolicited manuscripts. doug@powerboatmag.com

PRACTICAL HORSEMAN—Box 589, Unionville, PA 19375. Mandy Lorraine, Ed. How-to articles conveying leading experts' advice on English riding, training, and horse care. Pays on acceptance. Query with clips. E-mail: prachorse@aol.com.

PRIVATE PILOT MAGAZINE—265 S. Anita Dr., Suite 120, Orange, CA 92868-3310. Bill Fedorko, Ed. Dir. Fly-in destinations, hands-on, how-to, informative articles, 1,500 to 3,000 words, for general aviation pilots, aircraft owners, and aviation enthusiasts. Quality photos. Pays $400 to $700, on publication. Query. Web site: www.privatepilotmag.com.

PRO BASKETBALL ILLUSTRATED—See *Hockey Illustrated.*

PRO FOOTBALL ILLUSTRATED, PRO FOOTBALL PREVIEW— See *Hockey Illustrated.*

RESTORATION—P.O. Box 50046, Dept. TW, Tucson, AZ 85703-1046. W.R. Haessner, Ed. Articles, 1,200 to 1,800 words, on restoration projects in general, as well as restoration of autos, trucks, planes, trains, etc., and related building (bridges and structures). Photos. Pays from $25 per page, on publication. Queries required.

RIDER—2575 Vista Del Mar, Ventura, CA 93001. Mark Tuttle Jr., Ed. Articles, to 2,000 words, with slides, on travel, touring, commuting, and camping motorcyclists. Pays $100 to $750, on publication. Query.

RUNNER'S WORLD—Rodale Press, 33 E. Minor St., Emmaus, PA 18098. Bob Wischnia, Dep. Ed. Articles for "Human Race" (submit to Eileen Shovlin), "Finish Line" (to Beth Eck), and "Health Watch" (to Alisa Bauman) columns. Send feature articles or queries to Bob Wischnia. Payment varies, on acceptance. Query. E-mail: rwedit@rodak.com. Web site: www.runnersworld.com.

RUNNING TIMES—213 Danbury Rd., Wilson, CT 06897-4006. Gordon Bakoulis, Ed.-in-Chief. Articles, 1,500 to 3,500 words, on nutrition, sports medicine, training, and other topics of interest to serious, experienced runners. Payment varies, on publication. E-mail: rtbakoulis@aol.com. Web site: www.runningtimes.com.

SALT WATER SPORTSMAN—263 Summer St., Boston, MA 02210. Barry Gibson, Ed. Articles, 1,200 to 1,500 words, on how anglers can improve their skills, and on new places to fish off the coast of the U.S. and Canada, Central America, the Caribbean, and Bermuda. Photos a plus. Pays $350 to $700, on acceptance. Query. E-mail: editor@saltwatersportsman.com. Web site:www.saltwatersportsman.com.

SEA KAYAKER—P.O. Box 17170, Seattle, WA 98107-0870. Christopher Cunningham, Ed. Articles, 1,500 to 4,000 words, on ocean kayaking. Related fiction. Pays 12¢ a word, on publication. Query with clips and SASE. E-mail: mail@seakayakermag.com. Web site: www.seakayakermag.com.

SILENT SPORTS—717 10th St., P.O. Box 152, Waupaca, WI 54981-9990. Attn: Ed. Articles, 1,000 to 2,000 words, on bicycling, cross country skiing, running, canoeing, hiking, backpacking, and other "silent" sports. Must have regional (upper Midwest) focus. Pays $50 to $100 for features; $20 to $50 for fillers, on publication. Query. E-mail: info@silentsports.net. Web site: www.silentsports.net.

SKI MAGAZINE—929 Pearl St., Suite 200, Boulder, Co 80302. Andy Bigford, Ed. Articles, 1,300 to 2,500 words, for experienced skiers: profiles, and destination articles. Short, 100- to 300-word, news items for "Ski Life" column. Equipment instruction and racing articles are staff-written. Query (with clips) for articles. Pays from $50, on acceptance.

SKI RACING INTERNATIONAL—6971 Main St., Suite No. 1, Waitsfield, VT 05673. Tim Etchells, Ed. Articles by experts on race techniques and conditioning secrets. Coverage of World Cup, pro, collegiate, and junior ski and snowboard competition. Comprehensive results. Photos. Rates vary.

SKIN DIVER MAGAZINE—6420 Wilshire Blvd., Los Angeles, CA 90048-5515. Al Hornsby, Ed. Illustrated articles, 500 to 1,000 words, on scuba diving activities, equipment, and dive sites. Pays $50 per published page, on publication. E-mail: skindiver@petersenpub.com. Web site: www.skin-diver.com.

SKYDIVING MAGAZINE—1725 N. Lexington Ave., DeLand, FL 32724. Sue Clifton, Ed. Timely news articles, 300 to 800 words, relating to sport and military parachuting. Fillers. Photos. Pays $25 to $200, extra for photos, on publication. E-mail: sue@skydivingmagazine.com. Web site: www.skydivingmagazine.com.

SNOWEST—520 Park Ave., Idaho Falls, ID 83402. Lane Lindstrom, Ed. Articles, 1,200 words, on snowmobiling in the western states. Pays to $100, on publication.

SOCCER JR.—27 Unquowa Rd., Fairfield, CT 06430. Joe Provey, Ed. Articles, fiction, and fillers related to soccer for readers in 5th and 6th grade. Pays $450 for features; $250 for department pieces, on acceptance. Query. E-mail: soccerjrol@aol.com. Web site: www.soccerjr.com.

SOUTH CAROLINA WILDLIFE—P. O. Box 167, Columbia, SC 29202-0167. John E. Davis, Ed. Articles, 1,000 to 2,000 words, with state and regional outdoor focus: conservation, natural history, wildlife, and recreation. Profiles, how-tos. Pays on acceptance. Web site: www.scwildlife.com.

SPORTS ILLUSTRATED—135 W. 50th St., New York, NY 10020. Chris Hunt, Articles Ed. Query. Web site: www.cnnsi.com.

SPORTS ILLUSTRATED FOR KIDS—1271 Ave. of the Americas, New York, NY 10020. Steve Malley, Dept. Man. Ed. Articles, 800 words, (submit to Bob Der) and short features, 500 to 600 words, (submit to Erin Egan) for 8- to 13-year-olds. "Most articles are staff-written. Department pieces are the best bet for free lancers." (Read magazine and guidelines to learn about specific departments.) Puzzles and games (submit to Nick Friedman). No fiction or poetry. Pays $500 for departments, $1,000 to $1,250 for articles, on acceptance. Query required.

SPORTS ILLUSTRATED FOR WOMEN—1271 Avenue of the Americas, New York, NY 10020. Bimonthly for active women who are interested and/or participating in sports. The articles, 300 to 1,000 words, are either service items, short profiles, product reviews, or a Question and Answer series. For service pieces send queries to: LizO'Brien@simail.com. For articles, send queries to: SandyBailey@simail.com. Pays $1.25 a word, but varies by assignment; made on publication. Web site: www.cnnsi.com.

STOCK CAR RACING—3816 Industry Blvd., Lakeland, FL 33811. Larry Jewett, Ed. Articles, to 6,000 words, on stock car drivers, races, and vehicles. Photos. Pays to $500, on publication. E-mail: jewettl@emapusa.com. Web site: www.stockcarracing.com.

SURFING—P.O. Box 3010, San Clemente, CA 92674. Jamie Brisick, Exec. Ed. Skip Snead, Ed. Short newsy and humorous articles, 200 to 500 words. No first-person travel articles. "Knowledge of the sport is essential." Pays varying rates, on publication. E-mail: surfing@mcmullenargus.com. Web site: www.surfingthemag.com.

SWEAT—736 E. Loyola Dr., Tempe, AZ 85282. Joan Westlake, Ed. Articles, 500 to 1,200 words, on sports, fitness, or wellness with an Arizona angle. "No personal articles or tales. We want journalism. Articles must relate specifically to Arizona or Arizonans." Pays $25 to $60 for articles; $12 to $70 for photos, on publication. Queries required; no unsolicited manuscripts. E-mail preferred: westwoman@aol.com. Web site: www.sweatmagazine.com.

T'AI CHI—P.O. Box 26156, Los Angeles, CA 90026. Marvin Smalheiser, Ed. Articles, 800 to 4,000 words, on T'ai Chi Ch'uan, other internal martial arts and related topics such as qigong, Chinese medicine and healing practices, Chinese philosophy and culture, health, meditation, fitness, and self-improvement. Pays $75 to $500, on publication. Query required. Guidelines. E-mail: taichi@tai-chi.com. Web site: www.tai-chi.com.

TENNIS—810 Seventh Ave., 4th Fl., New York, NY 10019. Mark Woodruff, Ed. Instructional articles, features, profiles of tennis stars, grassroots articles, humor, 800 to 2,500 words. Photos. Payment varies, on publication. No phone queries

TENNIS WEEK—341 Madison Ave., #600, New York, NY 10017-3705. Eugene L. Scott, Pub. Kim Kodl, Heather Holland, Man. Eds. In-depth, researched articles, from 1,000 words, on current issues and personalities in the game. Pays $300, on publication. E-mail: tennisweek@tennisweek.com. Web site: www.tennisweek.com.

THE REDBONE JOURNAL—P.O. Box 273, Islamorada, FL 33036. Jill Zima, Ed. Quarterly. Fiction, 1,000 to 3,000 words; humorous anecdotes, to 1,000 words; and poetry related to outdoor adventures. Articles and profiles, 1,000 to 3,000 words, on fishing, hunting, travel, the environment, and other outdoor adventures. Slides and photos welcome. Queries with clips or credits and SASE preferred; please indicate availability of artwork. Pays 10¢ per word, on publication. E-mail: redbonejournal@aol.com. Web site: www.the-journal. net.

TRAILER BOATS—20700 Belshaw Ave., Carson, CA 90746-3510. Jim Hendricks, Ed.; Ron Eldridge, Exec. Ed. Lifestyle, technical and how-to articles, 500 to 2,000 words, on boat, trailer, or tow vehicle maintenance and operation; skiing, fishing, and cruising. Fillers, humor. Pays $100 to $700, on acceptance.

TRIATHLETE—2037 San Elijo, Cardiff, CA 92007. Christina Gandolfo, Man. Ed. Published 12 times yearly. Articles, varying lengths, pertaining to the sport of triathlon. No "my first triathlon" stories. Color slides. Pays 20¢ a word, on publication. Query. E-mail: gandolfo@triathletemag.com. Web site: www.triathletemag.com.

USA CYCLING MAGAZINE—(formerly *Bike Racing Nation*) One Olympic Plaza, Colorado Springs, CO 80909. B.J. Hoeptner, Ed. Articles, 500 to 1,000 words, on bicycle racing. Payment depends on nature of article and information included. E-mail: media@usacycling.org. Web site: www.usa cycling.org.

VELONEWS—1830 N. 55th St., Boulder, CO 80301. John Rezell, Ed. Articles, 500 to 1,500 words, on competitive cycling, training, nutrition; profiles, interviews. No how-to or touring articles. "We focus on the elite, competitive asapect of the sport." Pay varies, on publication. E-mail: jrezell@7dogs. com.

THE WALKING MAGAZINE—45 Bromfield St., 8th Fl., Boston, MA 02108. Seth Bauer, Ed. Articles, 1,500 to 2,000 words, on fitness, health, equipment, nutrition, travel, and adventure, famous walkers, and other walking-related topics. Shorter pieces, 500 to 1,500 words, and essays for "Ramblings" page. Photos welcome. Pays $750 to $2,500 for features, $100 to $600 for department pieces, on acceptance. Guidelines.

THE WATER SKIER—799 Overlook Dr., Winter Haven, FL 33884. Scott Atkinson, Ed. Feature articles on water skiing. Pays varying rates, on publication. E-mail: usawsmagazine@usawaterski.org. Web site: www.usawat erski.org.

THE WESTERN HORSEMAN—P.O. Box 7980, Colorado Springs, CO 80933-7980. Pat Close, Ed. Articles, about 1,500 words, with photos, on care and training of horses; farm, ranch, and stable management; health care and veterinary medicine. Pays to $800, on acceptance.

WESTERN OUTDOORS—3197-E Airport Loop, Costa Mesa, CA 92626. Attn: Ed. Timely, factual articles on fishing, 1,200 to 1,500 words, of interest to western sportsmen. Pays $400 to $500, on acceptance. Query. Guidelines. E-mail: woutdoors@aol.com.

WINDY CITY SPORTS—1450 W. Randolph, Chicago, IL 60607. Jeff Banowetz, Ed. Articles, 1,000 words, on amateur sports in Chicago. Pays $200, on publication. Query required.

WOMEN'S SPORTS & FITNESS—342 Madison Ave., New York, NY 10017. Lucy S. Danziger, Ed.-in-Chief. Articles on fitness, nutrition, outdoor sports; how-tos; profiles; adventure travel pieces; and controversial issues in women's sports, 500 to 2,000 words. Pays on publication. E-mail: letters@ cnwsf.com. Web site: www.phys.com.

WRESTLING WORLD—See *Hockey Illustrated*.

YACHTING—20 E. Elm St., Greenwich, CT 06830. Kenny Wooton, Ed. Articles, 1,500 words, on upscale recreational power and sail boating. How-to and personal-experience pieces. Photos. Pays $350 to $1,000, on acceptance. Queries preferred.

AUTOMOTIVE MAGAZINES

AMERICAN MOTORCYCLIST—American Motorcyclist Assn., 13515 Yarmouth Drive, Pickerington, OH 43147. Greg Harrison, Ed. Articles and fiction, to 3,000 words, on motorcycling: news coverage, personalities, tours. Photos. Pays varying rates, on publication. Query with SASE. Web site: www.ama-cycle.org.

CAR AND DRIVER—2002 Hogback Rd., Ann Arbor, MI 48105. Steve Spence, Man. Ed. Articles and profiles, to 2,500 words, on unusual people or manufacturers involved in cars, racing, etc. "Ninety-five percent staff-written. Query with clips. No unsolicited manuscripts." Pays to $2,500, on acceptance. E-mail: editors@caranddriver.com. Web site: www.caranddriver.com.

CAR CRAFT—6420 Wilshire Blvd., Los Angeles, CA 90048. David Freiburger, Ed. Articles and photo-features on high performance street machines, drag cars, racing events; technical pieces; action photos. Pays from $150 per page, on publication.

CYCLE WORLD—1499 Monrovia Ave., Newport Beach, CA 92663. David Edwards, Ed.-in-Chief. Technical and feature articles, 1,500 to 2,500 words, for motorcycle enthusiasts. Photos. Pays $100 to $200 per page, on publication. Query. E-mail: cw1edwards@aol.com.

MOTOR TREND—6420 Wilshire Blvd., Los Angeles, CA 90048-5515. C. Van Tune, Ed. Articles, 250 to 2,000 words, on autos, auto history, racing, events, and profiles. Photos required. Pay varies, on acceptance. Query.

RESTORATION—P.O. Box 50046, Dept. TW, Tucson, AZ 85703-1046. W.R. Haessner, Ed. Articles, 1,200 to 1,800 words, on restoration of autos, trucks, planes, trains, etc., and buildings (bridges, structures, etc.). Photos. Pays from $25 per page, on publication. Queries required.

RIDER—2575 Vista Del Mar Dr., Ventura, CA 93001. Mark Tuttle Jr., Ed. Articles, to 2,000 words, with color slides, on travel, touring, commuting, and camping motorcyclists. Pays $100 to $750, on publication. Query.

ROAD & TRACK—1499 Monrovia Ave., Newport Beach, CA 92663. Ellida Maki, Man. Ed. Short automotive articles, to 450 words, of a "timeless nature" for knowledgeable car enthusiasts. Pays on publication. Query.

FITNESS MAGAZINES

AMERICAN FITNESS—15250 Ventura Blvd., Suite 200, Sherman Oaks, CA 91403. Peg Jordan, R.N., Ed. Articles, 500 to 1,500 words, on exercise, health, research, trends, nutrition, alternative paths, etc. Illustrations, photos.

FIT MAGAZINE—1700 Broadway, New York, NY 10019. Lisa Klugman, Ed. Lively, readable service-oriented articles, 800 to 1,200 words, on exercise, nutrition, lifestyle, and health for women ages 18 to 35. Writers should have some background in or knowledge of sports, fitness, and/or health. Also considers 500-word essays for "Finally Fit" column by readers who have lost weight and kept it off. Pays $300 to $500, on publication. Query.

FITNESS—Gruner & Jahr USA Publishing, 375 Lexington Ave., New York, NY 10017-5514. Sarah Mahoney, Ed.-in-Chief. Articles, 500 to 2,000 words, on health, exercise, sports, nutrition, diet, psychological well-being, alternative therapies, sex, and beauty for readers around 30 years old. Queries required. Pays approximately $1 per word, on acceptance.

IDEA HEALTH & FITNESS SOURCE—6190 Cornerstone Ct. E., Suite 204, San Diego, CA 92121-3773. Ed. Practical articles, 1,000 to 3,000 words, on new exercise programs, business management, nutrition, sports medicine, dance-exercise, and one-to-one training techniques. Articles must be geared toward the group fitness instructor, exercise studio owner or manager, or personal trainer. No consumer or general health articles. Payment is negotiable, on acceptance. Query preferred.

IDEA PERSONAL TRAINER—6190 Cornerstone Ct. E., Suite 204, San Diego, CA 92121-3773. Ed. Association publication for personal fitness trainers. Articles on exercise science; program design; profiles of successful trainers; business, legal, and marketing topics; tips for networking with other trainers and with allied medical professionals; client counseling; and training tips. "What's New" column includes industry news, products, and research. Query. Payment varies, on acceptance. E-mail: member@ideafit.com. Web site: www.ideafit.com.

INSIDE TEXAS RUNNING—9514 Bristlebrook Dr., Houston, TX 77083-6193. Joanne Schmidt, Ed. Articles and fillers on running in Texas. Pays $35 to $100 for articles; $10 to $25 for photos and short fillers, on acceptance. E-mail: insidetx@aol.com. Web site: www.runningnetwork.com/texasrunning.

MEN'S FITNESS—21100 Erwin St., Woodland Hills, CA 91367. Jerry Kindela, Ed.-in-Chief. Features, 1,500 to 1,800 words, and department pieces, 1,200 to 1,500 words, dealing with fitness. Pay varies, 6 weeks after acceptance. Limited market. Web site: www.mensfitness.com.

MEN'S HEALTH—Rodale Press, 33 E. Minor St., Emmaus, PA 18098. Lou Schuler, Fitness Ed. Articles, 1,000 to 2,500 words, on fitness, diet, health, relationships, sports, and travel, for men ages 25 to 55. Pays from 50¢ a word, on acceptance. Query.

THE PHYSICIAN AND SPORTSMEDICINE—4530 W. 77th St.,

Minneapolis, MN 55435. Susan Hawthorne, Exec. Ed. News articles. Sports medicine angle necessary. Pays $300 to $500, on acceptance. Query. Guide lines. E-mail: susanhawthorne@mcgraw-hill.com. Web site: www.phys sportmed.com.

SHAPE—21100 Ewin St., Woodland Hills, CA 91367-3772. Peg Moline, Ed. Dir. Articles, 1,200 to 1,500 words, with new and interesting ideas on the physical and mental side of getting and staying in shape; reports, 300 to 400 words, on journal research. Payment varies, on acceptance. Guidelines. Limited market.

SWEAT—736 E. Loyola Dr., Tempe, AZ 85282. Joan Westlake, Ed. Articles, 500 to 1,200 words, on amateur sports, outdoor activities, wellness, or fitness with an Arizona angle. "No self-indulgent or personal tales. We want investigative pieces. Articles must relate specifically to Arizona or Arizonans." Pays $25 to $60 for articles; $15 to $70 for photos, on publication. Queries required; no unsolicited manuscripts. E-mail: Westwoman@aol.com. Web site: www.sweatmagazine.com.

VEGETARIAN TIMES—4 High Ridge Park, Stamford, CT 06905. Donna Sapolin, Ed. Dir. Articles, 1,200 to 2,500 words, on vegetarian cooking, nutrition, health and fitness, and profiles of prominent vegetarians. "News Items" and "In Print" (book reviews), to 500 words. "Herbalist" pieces, to 1,800 words, on medicinal uses of herbs. Queries required. Pays $75 to $1,000, on acceptance. Guidelines.

VIM & VIGOR—1010 E. Missouri Ave., Phoenix, AZ 85014. Jenn Woolson, Ed. Positive articles, with accurate medical facts, on health and fitness, 1,200 to 2,000 words, by assignment only. Writers may submit qualifications for assignment. Pays $500, on acceptance. Guidelines with SASE.

THE WALKING MAGAZINE—45 Bromfield St., 8th Fl., Boston, MA 02108. Seth Bauer, Ed. Articles, 1,500 to 2,500 words, on fitness, health, equipment, nutrition, travel and adventure, and other walking-related topics. Shorter pieces, 150 to 800 words, and essays for "Ramblings" page. Photos welcome. Pays $750 to $1,800 for features, $100 to $500 for department pieces, within a week of acceptance. Guidelines.

WEIGHT WATCHERS MAGAZINE—2100 Lakeshore Dr., Birmingham, AL 35209. Articles on health, nutrition, fitness, and weight-loss motivation and success. Pays from $1 per word, on acceptance. Query with clips required. Guidelines available.

WOMEN'S SPORTS & FITNESS—342 Madison Ave., New York, NY 10017. Mary Gail Pezzimenti, Man. Ed. Bimonthly. Articles on fitness, nutrition, outdoor sports, and equipment; how-tos; profiles; emerging sports; adventure travel pieces; and controversial issues or reported stories in women's sports, 500 to 2,000 words. Pays on publication. E-mail: letters@cnwsf.com. Web site: www.phys.com.

YOGA JOURNAL—2054 University Ave., Berkeley, CA 94704. Kathryn Arnold, Ed. Articles, 300 to 6,000 words, on holistic health, meditation, conscious living, spirituality, and yoga. Pays $75 to $3,000, on acceptance. E-mail: karnold@yogajournal.com. Web site: www.yogajournal.com.

CONSUMER/PERSONAL FINANCE

CONSUMERS DIGEST—8001 N. Lincoln Ave., 6th Fl., Skokie, IL 60077. John Manos, Ed. Articles, 500 to 3,000 words, on subjects of interest to consumers: products and services, automobiles, travel, health, fitness, consumer legal affairs, and personal money management. Photos. Pays 50¢ a word, extra for photos, on acceptance. Query with resumé and clips.

ESSENCE—1500 Broadway, New York, NY 10036. Susan L. Taylor, Sr. V.P. Monique Greenwood, Ed.-in-Chief. Articles, 800 to 2,500 words, for black women in America today, on business and finance, as well as health, art, travel, politics, and celebrity profiles, self-help pieces, how-tos. Payment varies, on acceptance. Query.

FAMILY CIRCLE—375 Lexington Ave., New York, NY 10017. Ann Matturo, Jennifer Pirtle, Editor-Writers. Enterprising, creative, and practical articles, 1,000 to 1,500 words, on investing, smart ways to save money, and consumer news on smart shopping. Pays $1 a word, on acceptance. Query with clips.

KIPLINGER'S PERSONAL FINANCE MAGAZINE—1729 H St. N.W., Washington, DC 20006. Attn: Ed. Dept. Articles on personal finance (i.e., buying insurance, mutual funds). Pays varying rates, on acceptance. Query required.

KIWANIS—3636 Woodview Trace, Indianapolis, IN 46468. Chuck Jonak, Man. Ed. Articles, 1,200 to 2,500 words, on financial planning for younger families and retirement planning for older people. Pays $400 to $1,000, on acceptance. Query required. E-mail: magazine@kiwanis.org. Web site: www. kiwanis.org/magazine.

THE MONEYPAPER—1010 Mamaroneck Ave., Mamaroneck, NY 10543. Vita Nelson, Ed. Financial news and money-saving ideas; particularly interested in information about companies with dividend reinvestment plans. Brief, well-researched articles on personal finance, money management, saving, earning, investing, taxes, insurance, and related subjects. Pays $75 for articles, on publication. Query with resumé and writing sample.

NEW CHOICES: LIVING EVEN BETTER AFTER 50—Reader's Digest Publications, Reader's Digest Rd., Pleasantville, NY 10570. Greg Daugherty, Ed.-in-Chief. Service magazine for people ages 50 and older. Articles on retirement planning, financial strategies, housing options, as well as health and fitness, travel, leisure pursuits, etc. Payment varies, on acceptance. E-mail: new choices@readersdigest.com. Web site: www.newchoices.com.

OUT—The Soho Bldg., 110 Greene St., Suite 600, New York, NY 10012. Tom Beer, Ed.-in-Chief. Articles, 50 to 8,000 words, on arts, politics, fashion, finance and other subjects for gay and lesbian readers. No fiction or poetry. Guidelines. Query only.

ROBB REPORT—1 Acton Pl., Acton, MA 01720. Steven Castle, Ed. Features on investment opportunities for high-end/luxury market. Lifestyle articles, home interiors, boats, travel, exotic automobiles, business, technology, etc. Payment varies, on publication. Query with SASE and clips. Web site: www.luxurysource.com.

WOMAN'S DAY—1633 Broadway, New York, NY 10019. Stephanie Abarbanel, Sr. Articles Ed. Articles, 750 to 1,500 words, on financial matters of interest to a broad range of women. Pays to $1 per word, on acceptance. Query with SASE. No unsolicited manuscripts.

YOUR MONEY—8001 N. Lincoln Ave., 6th Fl., Skokie, IL 60077. Dennis Fertig, Ed. Informative, jargon-free personal finance articles, to 2,000 words, for the general reader, on investment opportunities and personal finance. Pays 60¢ a word, on acceptance. Query Brooke Hessel, Asst. Ed. with clips for assignment. (Do not send manuscripts on disks.)

BUSINESS & TRADE PUBLICATIONS

ACROSS THE BOARD—845 Third Ave., New York, NY 10022-6679. Kelly Allen, Asst. to the Ed. Articles, 1,000 to 4,000 words, on a variety of topics of interest to business executives; straight business angle not required. Payment varies, on publication. E-mail: Kelly.Allen@conference-board.org. Web site: www.conference-board.org.

ALTERNATIVE ENERGY RETAILER—P.O. Box 2180, Waterbury, CT 06722. Trish Donohue, Ed. Feature articles, 1,000 words, for retailers of hearth products, including appliances that burn wood, coal, pellets, and gas, and hearth accessories and services. Interviews with successful retailers, stressing the how-to. B&W photos. Pays $200, extra for photos, on publication. Query. E-mail: donohue@aer-online.com. Web site: www.aer-online.com.

AMERICAN BANKER—One State Street Plaza, New York, NY 10004. David Longobardi, Ed.-in-Chief. Articles, 1,000 to 3,000 words, on banking and financial services, technology in banking, consumer financial services, investment products. Pays varying rates, on publication. Query preferred.

AMERICAN COIN-OP—500 N. Dearborn St., Chicago, IL 60610-9988. Paul Partika, Ed. Articles, to 2,500 words, with photos, on successful coin-operated laundries: management, promotion, decor, maintenance, etc. Pays from 8¢ a word, $8 per B&W photo, 2 weeks prior to publication. Query. Send SASE for guidelines.

AMERICAN DEMOGRAPHICS—P.O. Box 4949, Stamford, CT 06907. Jill Kirschenbaum, Exec. Ed. Articles, 500 to 2,000 words, on the four key elements of a consumer market (its size, its needs and wants, its ability to pay, and how it can be reached), with specific examples of how companies market to consumers. Readers include marketers, advertisers, and strategic planners. Query.

AMERICAN MEDICAL NEWS—515 N. State St., Chicago, IL 60610. Greg Borzo, Topic Ed. Articles, 900 to 1,500 words, on socioeconomic developments in health care of interest to physicians across the country. Seeks well-researched, innovative pieces about health and science from physician's perspective. Pays $500 to $1,500, on acceptance. Query required. Guidelines.

AMERICAN SCHOOL & UNIVERSITY—P.O. Box 12901, 9800 Metcalf, Overland Park, KS 66212-2216. Joe Agron, Ed. Articles and case studies, 1,200 to 1,500 words, on design, construction, operation, and management of school and university facilities. Queries preferred. Web site: www.asu.com.

ARCHITECTURE—1515 Broadway, New York, NY 10036. Reed Kroloff, Ed. Articles, to 2,000 words, on architecture, building technology, professional practice. Pays 50¢ a word.

AREA DEVELOPMENT MAGAZINE—400 Post Ave., Westbury, NY 11590. Geraldine Gambale, Ed. Articles for top executives of industrial companies on sites and facility planning. Pays 30¢ a word. Query. E-mail: gerri@area-development.com. Web site: www.area-development.com.

AUTOMATED BUILDER—1445 Donlon St., Suite 16, Ventura, CA

93003. Don Carlson, Ed. Articles, 500 to 750 words, on various types of home manufacturers and dealers with slides or color prints. Pays $300, on acceptance, for articles with photos. Query required. E-mail: info@automatedbuilder.com. Web site: www.automatedbuilder.com.

BARRON'S—200 Liberty St., New York, NY 10281. Edwin A. Finn, Jr., Ed./Pres. Investment-interest articles. Query Richard Rescigno, Man. Ed. E-mail: editors@barrons.com. Web site: www.barrons.com.

BARTENDER—P.O. Box 158, Liberty Corner, NJ 07938. Jaclyn W. Foley, Pub./Ed. Quarterly. Articles, 100 to 1,000 words, emphasizing liquor and bartending for bartenders, tavern owners, and owners of restaurants with full-service liquor licenses. Department pieces, 200 to 1,000 words, and related fillers, 25 to 100 words. Pays $50 to $200 for articles, $5 to $25 for fillers, on publication. E-mail: barmag@aol.com. Web site: www.bartender.com.

BICYCLE RETAILER AND INDUSTRY NEWS—502 W. Cordova Rd., Santa Fe, NM 87501. Michael Gamstetter, Ed. Articles, to 1,200 words, on employee management, employment strategies, and general business subjects for bicycle manufacturers, distributors, and retailers. Pays 20¢ a word (higher rates for more complex articles), plus expenses, within 30 days of publication. Query.

BOATING INDUSTRY—National Trade Publications, 13 Century Hill Dr., Latham, NY 12110-2197. John Kettlewell, Sr. Ed. Articles, 1,000 to 2,500 words, on recreational marine products, management, merchandising and selling, for boat dealers and marina owners/operators. Photos. Pays varying rates, on publication. Query. E-mail: jkettlewell@boating-industry.com. Web site: www.boating-industry.com.

BOOKPAGE—ProMotion, Inc., 2143 Belcourt Ave., Nashville, TN 37212. Katherine H. Wyrick, Ed. Book reviews, 500 words, for a consumer-oriented tabloid used by booksellers and libraries to promote new titles and authors. Query with writing samples and areas of interest; Editor will make assignments for reviews. Pays $20 per review. Guidelines.

BUILDER—Hanley-Wood, LLC., One Thomas Cir. N.W., Suite 600, Washington, DC 20005. Boyce Thompson, Ed. Articles, to 1,500 words, on trends and news in home building: design, marketing, new products, etc. Pays negotiable rates, on acceptance. Query.

BUSINESS AND COMMERCIAL AVIATION—4 International Dr., Rye Brook, NY 10573. Attn: Ed. Articles, 2,500 words, with photos, for pilots, on use of private aircraft for business transportation. Pays $100 to $500, on acceptance. Query.

BUSINESS MARKETING—740 N. Rush St., Chicago, IL 60611. Julie Cantwell, Sr. Ed. Articles on marketing, advertising, and promoting products and services to business buyers. Pays competitive rates, on acceptance. Queries required.

BUSINESS START-UPS—2445 McCabe Way, Irvine, CA 92614-6234. Karen E. Spaeder, Man. Ed. Monthly. Articles, 1,200 to 1,500 words, targeted at entrepreneurs ages 23 to 35; focus on starting a new business, motivational ideas, and growth strategies. Pays $400 and up, on acceptance. Guidelines. Query. E-mail: bsumag@entrepreneur.com. Web site: www.bizstartups.com.

BUSINESS TIMES—P.O. Box 580, New Haven, CT 06513. Joel Mac-Claren, Ed. Articles on Connecticut-based businesses and corporations. Query.

CALIFORNIA LAWYER—1145 Market St., 8th Fl., San Francisco, CA 94103. Thomas Brom, Sr. Ed. Articles, 2,500 to 3,000 words, for attorneys in California, on legal subjects (or the legal aspects of a given political or social issue); how-tos on improving legal skills and law office technology. Pays $300 to $2,000, on acceptance. Query.

CHEF—Talcott Communications Corp., 20 N. Wacker Dr., Suite 1865, Chicago, IL 60606. Brent T. Frei, Ed.-in-Chief. "The Food Magazine for Professionals." Articles, 600 to 1,200 words, that offer professionals in the foodservice business ideas for food marketing, preparation, and presentation. Pays $250 to first-time writers, on publication.

CHIEF EXECUTIVE—733 Third Ave., 24th Fl., New York, NY 10017. J.P. Donlon, Ed.-in-Chief. CEO bylines. Articles, 2,000 to 2,500 words, on management, financial, or global business issues of direct concern to CEOs only. Departments, 750 words, on investments, corporate finance, technology/internet, and emerging markets. Pays varying rates, on acceptance. Query required. E-mail: jpdonlan@chiefexecutive.net. Web site: www.chief executive.net.

CLEANING AND MAINTENANCE MANAGEMENT MAGAZINE—13 Century Hill Dr., Latham, NY 12110-2197. Chris Sanford, Man. Ed. Articles, 500 to 1,200 words, on managing efficient cleaning and custodial/maintenance operations; also technical/mechanical how-tos. Photos encouraged. Pays to $300 for commissioned features, on publication. Query. Guidelines.

CLUB MANAGEMENT—107 W. Pacific Ave., St. Louis, MO 63119. Tom Finan, Pub. Teri Finan, Ed. The official magazine of the Club Managers Assn. of America. Features, to 2,000 words, and news items, from 100 words, on management, budget, cuisine, personnel, government regulations, etc., for executives who run private clubs. "Writing should be tight and conversational, with liberal use of quotes." Color photos usually required with manuscript. Query preferred. Guidelines. E-mail: teri@finan.com. Web site: clubmgmt.com.

COLORADO BUSINESS—7009 S. Potomac, Englewood, CO 80112. David Lewis, Ed. Articles, varying lengths, on business, business personalities, and economic trends in Colorado. Preference given to Colorado residents. Pays on acceptance. Query.

COMMERCIAL CARRIER JOURNAL—201 King of Prussia Rd., Radnor, PA 19089. Paul Richards, Exec. Ed. Thoroughly researched articles on private fleets and for-hire trucking operations. Pays from $50, on acceptance. Queries required. E-mail: prichards@cahners.com. Web site: www.ccj magazine.com.

COMPUTER GRAPHICS WORLD—10 Tara Blvd., Suite 500, Nashua, NH 03062-2801. Phil LoPiccolo, Ed. Articles, 1,000 to 3,000 words, on computer graphics technology and its use in science, engineering, architecture, film and broadcast, and interactive entertainment. Computer-generated images. Pays $600 to $1,000 per article, on acceptance. Query.

THE CONSTRUCTION SPECIFIER—Construction Specifications Institute, 99 Canal Center Plaza, Suite 30, Alexandria, VA 22314. Wini Campbell, Ed. Technical articles, 2,000 to 3,000 words, on the "nuts and bolts" of nonresidential construction, for owners/facility managers, architects, engineers, specifiers, contractors, and manufacturers. E-mail: csimail@csinet.org. Web site: www.csinet.org.

CONVERTING MAGAZINE—1350 E. Touhy Ave., P.O. Box 5080, Des Plaines, IL 60017-5080. Mark Spaulding, Ed.-in-Chief. Business articles, 750 to 1,500 words, serving the technical, trends, and productivity information needs of flexible-packaging converting companies, as well as manufacturers of labels, paperboard cartons, and other converted products. Payment varies, on publication. Query required.

COOKING FOR PROFIT—P.O. Box 267, Fond du Lac, WI 54936-0267. Colleen Phalen, Pub./Ed.-in-Chief. Articles, of varying lengths, for foodservice professionals: profiles of successful restaurants, chains, and franchises, schools, hospitals, nursing homes, or other "institutional feeders"; also case studies on successful energy management within the foodservice environment. Business to business articles of interest to foodservice professionals. Payment varies, on publication.

COSTUME! BUSINESS—Festivities Publications, Inc., 815 Haines St., Jacksonville, FL 32206-6025. Sara Summers, Ed. Quarterly. Costume-related articles, 1,200 to 1,500 words, for designers, manufacturers, retailers, and costumers. Queries preferred. Pays 15¢ per word, on publication. Web site: www. festivities-pub.com.

CRAIN'S CHICAGO BUSINESS—740 Rush St., Chicago, IL 60611. David Snyder, Ed. Business articles about the Chicago metropolitan area exclusively.

DAIRY FOODS MAGAZINE—Cahners Publishing Co., 1350 E. Touhy Ave., Des Plaines, IL 60018. Dave Fusaro, Ed. Articles, to 2,500 words, on innovative dairies, dairy processing operations, marketing successes, new products for milk handlers and makers of dairy products. Fillers, 25 to 150 words. Payment varies.

DEALERSCOPE CONSUMER ELECTRONICS MARKETPLACE—North American Publishing Co., 401 N. Broad St., Philadelphia, PA 19108. Janet Pinkerton, Ed. Articles, to 1,000 words, on new consumer electronics, computer and major electronics products, and any associated new technologies coming to retail. Pays varying rates, on publication. Query with clips and resume.

DIVIDENDS—See *Your Business.*

DRAPERIES & WINDOW COVERINGS—666 Dundee Rd., Suite 807, Northbrook, IL 60062-2769. Howard Shingle, Ed. Articles, 1,000 to 2,000 words, for retailers, wholesalers, designers, and manufacturers of draperies and window, wall, and floor coverings. Profiles, with photos, of successful businesses in the industry; management and marketing related articles. Pays $150 to $250, after acceptance. Query. E-mail: info@dwcdesignet.com. Web site: www.dwcdesignet.com.

EMPLOYEE SERVICES MANAGEMENT—ESM Association, 2211 York Rd., Suite 207, Oak Brook, IL 60523. Renee M. Mula, Ed. Articles, 1,200 to 2,500 words, for human resource and employee service professionals on recruitment and retention, becoming an employee of choice, work/life issues, employee services, wellness, management and more. Pays in copies. Web site: www.esmassn.org.

THE ENGRAVERS JOURNAL—26 Summit St., P.O. Box 318, Brighton, MI 48116. Rosemary Farrell, Man. Ed. Articles, of varying lengths, on topics related to the engraving industry or small business. Pays $150 to $300, on acceptance. Query.

ENTREPRENEUR—2392 Morse Ave., Irvine, CA 92614. Rieva Lesonsky, Ed. Dir. Articles for small business owners, on all aspects of running a business. Pay varies, on acceptance. Query required. E-mail: entmag@entrepreneur.com. Web site: www.entrepreneur.com.

EXECUTIVE FEMALE—135 W. 50th St., New York, NY 10020. Kim Calero, President. Articles, 350 to 1,200 words, on managing people, time, money, companies, and careers, for women in business. Pays varying rates, on acceptance. Query.

FANCY FOOD—Talcott Communications Corp., 20 N. Wacker Dr., Suite 1865, Chicago, IL 60606. Carolyn Schwaar, Ed.-in-Chief. "The Business Magazine for Specialty Foods, Confections, and Upscale Housewares." Articles, 2,000 words, related to gourmet food. Pays $250 to $500, on publication.

FARM JOURNAL—1500 Market St., 28th Fl., Philadelphia, PA 19102-2181. Sonja Hillgren, Ed. Practical business articles, 500 to 1,500 words, with photos, on growing crops and raising livestock. Pays 20¢ to 50¢ a word, on acceptance. Query required. Web site: www.farmjournal.com.

FIRE CHIEF—35 E. Wacker Dr., Suite 700, Chicago, IL 60601-2198. Scott Baltic, Ed. Monthly. Articles, 1,000 to 5,000 words and department pieces, 1,000 to 1,800 words, for "Training Perspectives," "EMS Viewpoint," and "Sound Off," for fire officers. SASE or www.firechief.com for guidelines. Pays up to 30¢ per word, on publication. Web site: www.firechief.com.

FITNESS MANAGEMENT—P.O. Box 1198, Solana Beach, CA 92075. Ms. Ronale Tucker, Ed., Edward H. Pitts, Co-Publisher. Authoritative features, 750 to 2,500 words, and news shorts, 100 to 750 words, for owners, managers, and program directors of fitness centers. Content must be in keeping with current medical practice; no fads. Pays 8¢ a word, on publication. Query. E-mail: edit@fitnessmanagement.com. Web site: www.fitnessworld.com.

FLORIST—33031 Schoolcraft Rd., Livonia, MI 48105. Sallyann Moore, Ed. Articles, to 1,500 words, on retail florist shop management.

FLYER—P.O. Box 39099, Lakewood, Wa 98439-0099. Kirk Gormley, Ed. Articles, 500 to 2,500 words, of interest to "general aviation" pilots. Pays to $3 per column inch (approximately 40 words), within a month of publication; $10 for B&W photos; to $50 for color photos. E-mail: kirk.gormly@flyer-online.com. Web site: www.flyer-online.com.

FOOD MANAGEMENT—1100 Superior Ave., Cleveland, OH 44114. John Lawn, Ed. Articles on food service in hospitals, nursing homes, schools, colleges, prisons, businesses, and industrial sites. Trends, legislative issues, how-to pieces with management tie-in, and retail-oriented food service pieces. Query.

FORTUNE SMALL BUSINESS—1271 Ave. of the Americas, Rockefeller Ctr., New York, NY 10020-1393. Hank Gilman, Man. Ed. Articles of interest to small business owners; interviews with CEOs; politics surrounding samll businesses. Query. Payment is on acceptance. E-mail: fsbmail@timeinc.com. Web site: www.fortunesb.com.

GLASS DIGEST—18 E. 41st St., New York, NY 10017-6222. Julian

Phillips, Ed. Articles, 1,200 to 1,500 words, on building projects and glass/metal dealers, distributors, storefront and glazing contractors. Pays varying rates, on publication.

GOLF COURSE NEWS—106 Lafayette St., Yarmouth, ME 04096. Mark Leslie, Ed. Features and news analyses, 500 to 1,000 words, on all aspects of golf course maintenance, design, building, and management. Pays $200, on acceptance. E-mail: mleslie@golfcoursenews.com. Web site: www.golfcourse news.com.

GOVERNMENT EXECUTIVE—1501 M St. N.W., Washington, DC 20005. Timothy Clark, Ed. Articles, 1,500 to 3,000 words, for civilian and military government workers at the management level. E-mail: govexec@govexec.com. Web site: www.govexec.com.

GREENHOUSE MANAGEMENT & PRODUCTION—P.O. Box 1868, Fort Worth, TX 76101-1868. David Kuack, Ed. How-to articles, innovative production and/or marketing techniques, 500 to 1,800 words, accompanied by color slides, of interest to professional greenhouse growers. Pays $50 to $300, on acceptance. Query required.

GROWERTALKS—P.O. Box 9, 335 N. River St., Batavia, IL 60510-0009. Chris Beytes, Ed. Articles, 800 to 2,600 words, that help commercial greenhouse growers (not florist/retailers or home gardeners) do their jobs better: trends, successes in new types of production, marketing, business management, new crops, and issues facing the industry. Payment varies, on publication. Queries preferred. E-mail: beytes@growertalks.com. Web site: www.ballpublish ing.com.

HARDWARE TRADE—10617 France Ave. S., #225, Bloomington, MN 55431. Patt Patterson, Ed. Dir. Articles, 800 to 1,000 words, on unusual hardware and home center stores and promotions in the Northwest and Midwest. Photos. Query. No payment.

HARVARD BUSINESS REVIEW—Harvard Business School Publishing Corp., 60 Harvard Way, Boston, MA 02163. Request a copy of HBR's guidelines for authors, or query editors, in writing, on new ideas about management of interest to senior executives.

HEALTH PRODUCTS BUSINESS—Cygnus Publishing, 445 Broad Hollow Rd., Suite 21, Melville, NY 11747. Judith Desaritz, Ed. Articles, 500 to 1,500 words, on topics related to the health products industry. Photos welcome. Query with SASE preferred. Pays $50 to $200, on publication. E-mail: judith.desaritz@cygnuspub.com.

HEALTH PRODUCTS BUSINESS—445 Broad Hollow Rd., Melville, NY 11747. Judith Desaritz, Ed. Articles that focus on natural/health foods retailers, also interested in information for wholesalers, manufacturers, and others involved in the industry. Includes ideas on sales, marketing, and new trends in the industry.

HEATING/PIPING/AIR CONDITIONING/ENGINEERING—1100 Superior Ave., Cleveland, OH 44114. Michael G. Ivanovich, Ed. Articles, to 3,500 words, on heating, piping, and air conditioning systems and related issues, such as indoor air quality and energy efficiency in industrial plants and large buildings only; engineering information. Pays $70 per printed page, on publication. Query. Web site: www.hpac.com.

HOSPITALS & HEALTH NETWORKS—One N. Franklin St., 29th

Fl., Chicago, IL 60606. Bill Santamour, Man. Ed. Articles, 250 to 1,800 words, for health care executives. Query.

HUMAN RESOURCE EXECUTIVE—LRP Publications Co., 747 Dresher Rd., Horsham, PA 19044-0980. David Shadovitz, Ed. Profiles and case stories, 1,800 to 2,200 words, of interest to people in the human resource profession. Pays varying rates, on acceptance. Queries required. E-mail: dshadovitz@lrp.com. Web site: www.hrexecutive.com.

INDUSTRY WEEK—1100 Superior Ave., Cleveland, OH 44114-2543. John R. Brandt, Ed.-in-Chief. Biweekly. Articles, varying lengths, on business and management. Departments include "Executive Briefing," "Emerging Technologies," "Finance," "Economic Trends," and "Executive Life." Payment varies, on acceptance. Query. Web site: www.industryweek.com

INSTANT & SMALL COMMERCIAL PRINTER—P.O. Box 7280, Libertyville, IL 60048. Anne Marie Mohan, Ed. Articles, 3 to 6 typed pages, for operators and employees of printing businesses specializing in retail printing and/or small commercial printing: case histories, how-tos, technical pieces, small-business management. Pays $150 to $250, extra for photos, on publication. Query.

JEMS, JOURNAL OF EMERGENCY MEDICAL SERVICES—P.O. Box 2789, Carlsbad, CA 92018. A.J. Heightman, Ed.-in-Chief. Articles, 1,500 to 3,000 words, of interest to emergency medical providers (EMTs, paramedics, nurses, and physicians) who work in the EMS industry worldwide. Web site: www.jems.com.

LLAMAS—P.O. Box 250, Jackson, CA 95642. Cheryl Dal Porto, Ed. "The International Camelid Journal," published 5 times yearly. Articles, 300 to 3,000 words, of interest to llama and alpaca owners. Pays $25 to $300, extra for photos, on publication. Query.

MACHINE DESIGN—Penton Publishing Co., 1100 Superior Ave., Cleveland, OH 44114. Ronald Khol, Ed. Articles, to 10 typed pages, on mechanical and electromechanical design topics for engineers. Pays varying rates, on publication. Submit outline or brief description.

MAINTENANCE TECHNOLOGY—1300 S. Grove Ave., Barrington, IL 60010. Robert C. Baldwin, Ed. Technical articles with how-to information on increasing the reliability and maintainability of electrical and mechanical systems and equipment. Readers are managers, supervisors, and engineers in all industries and facilities. Payment varies, on acceptance. Query.

MANAGE—2210 Arbor Blvd., Dayton, OH 45439. Doug Shaw, Ed. Articles, 800 to 1,000 words, on management and supervision for first-line and middle managers. "Please indicate word count on manuscript and enclose SASE." Pays 5¢ a word.

MARKETING NEWS—American Marketing Assn., 311 S. Wacker Dr., Chicago, IL 60606-2266. Lisa M. Keefe, Ed. Biweekly. Articles, 700 to 1,000 words, on every aspect of marketing, including advertising, sales promotion, direct marketing, telecommunications, consumer and business-to-business marketing, and market research. Pays $500 to $1,000, on publication. Query with appropriate clips. E-mail: news@ama.org. Web site: www.ama.org.

MODERN HEALTHCARE—740 N. Rush St., Chicago, IL 60611. Clark Bell, Ed. News weekly covers management, finance, building design and construction, and new technology for hospitals, health maintenance organizations, nursing homes, and other health care institutions. Pays $200 to $400, on publication. Query; very limited free-lance market. E-mail: mhcedit@aol.com. Web site: www.modernhealthcare.com.

MODERN TIRE DEALER—P.O. Box 3599, Akron, OH 44309-3599. Lloyd Stoyer, Ed. Tire retailing and automotive service articles, 1,000 to 1,500 words, with photos, on independent tire dealers and retreaders. Pays $400 to $450, on publication. Query; articles by assignment only.

MUTUAL FUNDS—2200 S.W. 10th St., Deerfield Beach, FL 33442. John J. Curran, Man. Ed. "Writers experienced in covering mutual funds for the print media should send resumé and clips." Pays to $1 a word, on acceptance. E-mail: letters@mfmag.com. Web site: www.mfmag.com.

NATIONAL FISHERMAN—121 Free St., P.O. Box 7438, Portland, ME 04112. Jerry Fraser, Ed. Articles, 200 to 2,000 words, aimed at commercial fishermen and boat builders. Pays $4 to $6 per inch, extra for photos, on publication. Query preferred. Web site: www.nationalfisherman.com.

THE NETWORK JOURNAL—139 Fulton St., Suite 407, New York, NY 10038. Njeru Waithaka, Ed. Monthly newspaper. Articles, 800 to 1,500 words, on small business, personal finance, and career management of interest to African American small business owners and professionals. Profiles of entrepreneurs; how-to pieces; articles on sales and marketing, managing a small business and personal finance. Pays $75 to $150, on acceptance. E-mail: tnj@obe1.com. Web site: www.tnj.com.

NEW CAREER WAYS NEWSLETTER—67 Melrose Ave., Haverhill, MA 01830. William J. Bond, Ed. How-to articles, 1,500 to 2,000 words, on new skills used to move ahead at work in the 21st century and new opportunities for today's home-based businesses. Pays varying rates, on publication. Query with outline and SASE. Same address and requirements for *Workskills Newsletter.*

THE NORTHERN LOGGER AND TIMBER PROCESSOR—Northeastern Logger's Assn., Inc., P.O. Box 69, Old Forge, NY 13420. Eric A. Johnson, Ed. Features, 1,000 to 2,000 words, of interest to the forest product industry. Photos. Pays 15¢ a word, on publication. Query preferred.

NSGA RETAIL FOCUS—National Sporting Goods Assoc., 1699 Wall St., Suite 700, Mt. Prospect, IL 60056. Larry Weindruch, Ed. Members magazine. Articles, 1,000 to 1,500 words, on sporting goods industry news and trends, the latest in new product information, and management and store operations. Payment varies, on publication. Query.

ONCE UPON A TIME—553 Winston Ct., St. Paul, MN 55118. Audrey B. Baird, Ed. "A 32-page support magazine for Children's Writers and Illustrators." Quarterly. Articles, to 800 words: questions, insights, how-to articles, tips and experiences (no fiction) on the writing and illustrating life by published and unpublished writers. Also, short articles, 100 to 400 words. B&W artwork. No payment. E-mail: auderyouat@aol.com. Web site: www.members.aol.com/ouatmag.

OPPORTUNITY MAGAZINE—18 E. 41st St., New York, NY 10017. Ed. How-to articles for people who work at home, small business owners, and people interested in franchising and distributorships. Success stories. Payment varies, on publication. Query.

OPTOMETRIC ECONOMICS—See *Practice Strategies.*

PARTY & PAPER RETAILER—107 Mill Plain Rd., Suite 204, Danbury, CT 06811. Trisha McMahon Drain, Ed. Articles, 1,000 to 1,500 words, that offer employee, management, and retail marketing advice to the party or stationery store owner: display ideas, success stories; advertising, promotion, financial, and legal advice. "Articles grounded in facts and anecdotes are appreciated." Pay varies, on publication. Query with published clips. E-mail: editor@partypaper.com. Web site: www.partypaper.com.

PET BUSINESS—7-L Dundas Cir., Greensboro, NC 27407. Rita Davis, Ed. Brief, documented articles on animals and products found in pet stores; research findings; legislative/regulatory actions; business and marketing tips and trends. Pays 10¢ per word, on publication; pays $20 for photos.

PET PRODUCT NEWS—P.O. Box 6050, Mission Viejo, CA 92690. Mary K. McHale, Ed. Articles, 1,000 to 1,200 words, with photos, on pet shops, and pet and product merchandising. No fiction or news clippings. Pays $150 to $350, extra for photos. Query.

P O B—Business News Publishing Co., 755 W. Big Beaver Rd., Suite 1000, Troy, MI 48084. Jackie Headapohl, Ed. Technical and business articles, 1,000 to 4,000 words, for professionals and technicians in the surveying and mapping fields. Technical tips on field and office procedures and equipment maintenance. Pays $150 to $500, on acceptance.

POOL & SPA NEWS—4160 Wilshire Blvd., Los Angeles, CA 90010. Business and how-to articles for the swimming pool and hot tub construction, retail, and service industries. Pays on publication. Query.

PRACTICE STRATEGIES—(formerly *Optometric Economics*) American Optometric Assn., 243 N. Lindbergh Blvd., St. Louis, MO 63141-7881. Gene Mitchell, Sr. Ed. Articles, 1,000 to 3,000 words, on private practice management for optometrists; direct, conversational style with how-to advice on how optometrists can build, improve, better manage, and enjoy their practices. Short humor and photos. Payment varies, on acceptance. Query. E-mail: rfpicper@theaoa.org. Web site: www.aoanet.org.

PUBLIC RELATIONS QUARTERLY—P.O. Box 311, Rhinebeck, NY 12572. Howard Penn Hudson, Ed. Pub. Articles, 1,500 to 3,500 words, on public relations, public affairs, communications, and writing. No payment. Queries preferred. E-mail: hphudson@aol.com.

PUBLISH—Publish Media, LLC., 462 Boston St., Topsfield, MA 01983. Jennifer Carton, Man. Ed. Features, 1,500 to 2,000 words, and reviews, 400 to 800 words, on all aspects of enterprise communication and publishing technology. Pays according to experience. Payment is 45 days from acceptance.

PUBLISHERS WEEKLY—245 W. 17th St., New York, NY 10011. Daisy Maryles, Exec. Ed. Articles, 900 words, on a current issue or problem facing publishing and bookselling for "My Say" column. Articles for "Booksellers' Forum" may be somewhat longer. Payment varies.

QUICK PRINTING—Cygnus Publishing Inc., 445 Broad Hollow Rd., Melville, NY 11747. Gerald Walsh, Ed. Articles, 1,500 to 2,500 words, of interest to owners and operators of quick print shops, copy shops, and small commercial printers, on how to make their businesses more profitable; include photography/figures. Also, articles on using computers and peripherals in graphic arts applications. Generic business articles will be rejected. Pays from $150, on publication. E-mail: quickptg@aol.com. Web site: www.quick printing.com.

REMODELING—Hanley-Wood, Inc., One Thomas Cir. N.W., Suite 600, Washington, DC 20005. Paul Deffenbaugh, Ed. Articles, 250 to 1,700 words, on remodeling and industry news for residential and light commercial remodelers. Pays on acceptance. Query.

RESTAURANTS USA—1200 17th St. N.W., Washington, DC 20036-3097. Jennifer Batty, Ed. Publication of the National Restaurant Assn. Articles, 1,000 to 2,500 words, on the foodservice and restaurant business. Restaurant experience preferred. Pays $350 to $800, on acceptance. Query. Web site: www.restaurant.org.

THE ROTARIAN—1560 Sherman Ave., Evanston, IL 60201-3698. Willmon L. White, Ed.-in-Chief. Charles W. Pratt, Ed. Cary Silver, Man. Ed. Articles, 1,200 to 2,000 words, on international social and economic issues, business and management, environment, science and technology, sports, and some humor, including cartoons. "No political or religious subjects." Pays good rates, on acceptance. Query. E-mail: prattc@rotaryintl.org. Web site: www.rotary.org.

RV BUSINESS—2575 Vista Del Mar Dr., Ventura, CA 93001. Sherman Goldenberg, Pub. Articles, to 1,500 words, on RV industry news and product-related features. Articles on legislative matters affecting the industry. General business features rarely used. Pays varying rates. E-mail: rub@tl.com. Web site: www.rvbusiness.com.

SAFETY MANAGEMENT—24 Rope Ferry Rd., Waterford, CT 06386. Peter Hawkins, Ed. Interview-based articles, 1,500 words, for safety professionals, on improving workplace safety and health. Pays to 20¢ a word, on acceptance. Query. E-mail: phawkinsp@netscape.net. Web site: www.bbpnews.com.

SMALL PRESS REVIEW—Dustbooks, P.O. Box 100, Paradise, CA 95967. Len Fulton, Ed./Pub. Reviews, 200 words, of small literary books and magazines; tracks the publishing of small publishers and small-circulation magazines. Query. Web site: www.dustbooks.com. E-mail: dustbooks@desi.net.

SOFTWARE MAGAZINE—257 Turnpike Rd., #100, Southboro, MA 01772-1706. Patrick Porter, Ed. Technical features, to 1,800 words, for computer-literate MIS audience, on how various software products are used. Pays about $1,000 to $1,200, on publication. Query required. Calendar of scheduled editorial features available.

SOUTHERN LUMBERMAN—P.O. Box 681629, Franklin, TN 37068-1629. Nanci P. Gregg, Man. Ed. Articles on sawmill operations, interviews with industry leaders, how-to technical pieces with an emphasis on increasing sawmill production and efficiency and new installations. Pays $100 to $250 for articles with B&W photos. Queries preferred. E-mail: ngregg@southern lumberman.com. Web site: www.southernlumberman.com.

SOUVENIRS, GIFTS, AND NOVELTIES MAGAZINE—(formerly *Souvenirs and Novelties*) 7000 Terminal Sq., Suite 210, Upper Darby, PA 19082. Attn: Ed. Articles, 1,500 words, on retailing and merchandising collectible souvenir items for managers at zoos, museums, hotels, airports, and souvenir stores. Pays 12¢ a word, on publication.

STONE WORLD—299 Market St., Suite 320, Saddle Brook, NJ 07663. Michael Reis, Ed. Articles, 750 to 1,500 words, on new trends in installing and designing with stone. For architects, interior designers, design professionals, and stone fabricators and dealers. Pays $6 per column inch, on publication. Query.

SUCCESSFUL FARMING—1716 Locust St., Des Moines, IA 50309-3023. Gene Johnston, Man. Ed. Articles, to 2,000 words, for farming families, on all areas of business farming: money management, marketing, machinery, soils and crops, livestock, and buildings; profiles. Pays from $300, on acceptance. Query required.

TANNING TRENDS—3101 Page Ave., Jackson, MI 49203-2254. Joseph Levy, Ed. Articles on small businesses and skin care for tanning salon owners. Scientific pro-tanning articles and "smart tanning" pieces. Query for profiles. "Our aim is to boost salon owners to the 'next level' of small business ownership. Focus is on business principles with special emphasis on public relations and marketing." Payment varies, on publication. E-mail: joe@smarttan.com. Web site: www.smarttan.com.

TEA & COFFEE TRADE JOURNAL—130 W. 42nd St., Suite 1050, New York, NY 10036. Jane P. McCabe, Ed. Articles, 3 to 5 pages, on trade issues of importance to the tea and coffee industry. Pays 20¢ per word, on publication. Query.

TEXTILE WORLD—6151 Powers Ferry Rd., Atlanta, GA 30339. Mac Isaacs, Ed. Articles, 500 to 2,000 words, with photos, on manufacturing and finishing textiles. Pays varying rates, on acceptance. E-mail: macisaacs@ intertec.com. Web site: www.textileworld.com.

TODAY'S $85,000 FREELANCE WRITER—P.O. Box 543, Oradell, NJ 07649. Brian Konradt, Ed. Bimonthly. Articles, to 1,000 words, on operating a profitable freelance commercial copywriting business and writing for downsized corporations, large and small businesses, ad agencies, and other commercial markets. No fiction. Pays 10¢ a word, on acceptance. Guidelines. SASE.

TODAY'S SURGICAL NURSE—Slack, Inc., 6900 Grove Rd., Thorofare, NJ 08086. Frances R. DeStefano, Man. Ed. Clinical or general articles, from 2,000 words, of direct interest to operating room nurses.

TOURIST ATTRACTIONS AND PARKS—7000 Terminal Sq., Suite 210, Upper Darby, PA 19082. Articles, 1,500 words, on successful management of parks, entertainment centers, zoos, museums, arcades, fairs, arenas, and leisure attractions. Pays 12¢ a word, on publication. Query.

TRAINING MAGAZINE—50 S. Ninth St., Minneapolis, MN 55402. Jack Gordon, Ed. Articles, 1,000 to 2,500 words, for managers of training and development activities in corporations, government, etc. Pays varying rates, on acceptance. Query. E-mail: edit@trainingmag.com. Web site: www.training mag.com.

TREASURY & RISK MANAGEMENT—111 W. 57th St., New York, NY 10019. Anthony Baldo, Ed. Nine issues per year. Articles, 200 to 3,000 words, on treasury management for corporate treasurers, CFOs, and vice presidents of finance. Pays 50¢ to $1 a word, on acceptance. Query. Seeks free lancers.

UNIQUE OPPORTUNITIES—455 S. 4th Ave., #1236, Louisville, KY 40202. Bett Coffman, Assoc. Ed. Articles, 2,000 to 3,000 words, that cover the economic, business, and career-related issues of interest to physicians who are interested in relocating or entering new practices. "Our goal is to educate physicians about how to evaluate career opportunities, negotiate the benefits offered, plan career moves, and provide information on the legal and economic aspects of accepting a position." Pays from 50¢ a word for features, on acceptance. Query. E-mail: tellus@uoworks.com. Web site: www.uoworks.com.

UPSIDE—731 Market St., 2nd Fl., San Francisco, CA 94103. Vince Ryan, Sr. Ed. Business and technology monthly. Short articles about computer and technology businesses and profiles of successful business people. Queries required. Web site: www.upsidetoday.com.

WASTE AGE—(formerly *World Wastes*) 6151 Powers Ferry Rd. N.W., Atlanta, GA 30339. Bill Wolpin, Ed. Dir. Case studies, market analysis, and how-to articles, 1,000 to 2,000 words, with photos of refuse haulers, recyclers, landfill operators, resource recovery operations, and transfer stations, with solutions to problems in the field. Pays from $125 per printed page, on publication. Query preferred.

WINES & VINES—1800 Lincoln Ave., San Rafael, CA 94901. Philip E. Hiaring, Ed. Articles, 2,000 words, on grape and wine industry, emphasizing marketing, management, vinyard techniques, and production. Pays 15¢ a word, on acceptance. E-mail: geninto@winesandvines.com. Web site: www.wines andvines.com.

WOODSHOP NEWS—35 Pratt St., Essex, CT 06426-1185. Thomas Clark, Ed. Features, one to 3 typed pages, for and about people who work with wood: business stories, profiles, news. Pays from $40 to $250 minimum, on publication. Queries preferred. E-mail: woodshopnews@worldnet.att.net. Web site: www.woodshopnews.com.

WORKING WOMAN—135 W. 50th St., 16th Fl.,16th Fl., New York, NY 10020-1201. Articles, 200 to 1,500 words, on business and technology. "We are particularly interested in trend pieces that target a specific industry and demonstrate how it is affected by new technology, business practices, or market situations." No profiles of executives or entrepreneurs. Payment varies, on publication. Query with SASE. E-mail: editors@workingwoman.com. Web site: www.workingwoman.com.

WORLD OIL—Gulf Publishing Co., P.O. Box 2608, Houston, TX 77252-2608. Robert E. Snyder, Ed. Engineering and operations articles, 3,000 to 4,000 words, on petroleum industry exploration, drilling, or production. Photos. Pays from $50 per printed page, on acceptance. Query.

WORKSKILLS NEWSLETTER—See *New Career Ways Newsletter.*

WORLD WASTES—See *Waste Age.*

YOUR BUSINESS—(formerly *Dividends*) Bauer Financial Publishing, 820 W. Jackson, Suite 450, Chicago, IL 60607. Sooji Min, Ed. Features, 1,500 to 1,800 words, of interest to small business owners and executives; departments, 600 to 800 words. Pays 55¢–75¢ a word, on publication. Query. E-mail: baumerfpub@aol.com.

IN-HOUSE/ASSOCIATION MAGAZINES

Publications circulated to company employees (sometimes called house magazines or house organs) and to members of associations and organizations are excellent, well-paying markets for writers at all levels of experience. Large corporations publish these magazines to promote good will, familiarize readers with the company's services and products, and advise them about the issues and events concerning a particular cause or industry.

AARP BULLETIN—601 E St. N.W., Washington, DC 20049. Elliot Carlson, Ed. Publication of the American Assn. of Retired Persons. Payment varies, on acceptance. Query required.

THE AMERICAN GARDENER—7931 E. Boulevard Dr., Alexandria, VA 22308-1300. David J. Ellis, Ed. Bimonthly publication of the American Horticultural Society. Articles, to 2,500 words, for American ornamental gardeners: profiles of prominent horticulturists, plant research and plant hunting, events and personalities in horticulture history, and plant lore and literature, etc. Shorter, humorous pieces for "Offshoots." Pays $100 to $500, on publication. Query preferred. E-mail: editor@ahs.org. Web site: www.ahs.org.

CALIFORNIA HIGHWAY PATROLMAN—2030 V St., Sacramento, CA 95818-1730. Blair Barton, Man. Ed. Articles on the CHP, its personnel, programs, history and mission, or any true-life police-related story that is exciting, action-packed, of great human interest or humorous. Photos a plus. Buys one-time rights; pays 2½¢ a word, $5 for B&W photos, on publication. Guidelines and/or sample copy with 9×12 SASE.

CATHOLIC FORESTER—355 Shuman Blvd., P.O. Box 3012, Naperville, IL 60566-7012. Dorothy Deer, Ed. Official publication of the Catholic Order of Foresters, a fraternal life insurance organization for Catholics. General-interest articles and fiction, 1,000 to 1,200 words, that deal with contemporary issues; no romance moralizing, explicit sex, or violence. Short, inspirational articles, to 500 words. "Need health and wellness, parenting, and financial articles." Pays 20¢ a word, on acceptance. Web site: www.catholicforester.com.

CATHOLIC LIBRARY WORLD—The Catholic Library Assn., 100 North St., Suite 224, Pittsfield, MA 01201-5109. Mary E. Gallagher, SSJ, Ed. Co-Chair. Articles for school librarians, academic librarians, and institutional archivists. No payment. Queries preferred.

COAST TO COAST—2575 Vista del Mar Dr., Ventura, CA 93001. Valerie Law, Ed. Membership publication for Coast to Coast Resorts, private camping and resort clubs across North America. Focus is on "travel, recreation, and good times." Destination features focus on a North American city or region, going beyond typical tourist stops to interview locals. Activity or recreation features introduce readers to a sport, hobby, or other diversion. Also features on RV lifestyle. Send queries or manuscripts. Payment is $350 to $600, on acceptance, for 1,500- to 2,500-word articles. Web site: www.rv.net.

COLUMBIA—1 Columbus Plaza, New Haven, CT 06507-0901. Tim S. Hickey, Ed. Journal of the Knights of Columbus. Articles, 1,200 words, for Catholic families. No fiction. Pays up to $600 for articles, on acceptance. E-mail:info@kofc.org. Web site: www.kofc.org.

THE COMPASS—365 Washington Ave., Brooklyn, NY 11238. J.A. Randall, Ed. True stories (no first-person accounts), to 2,000 words, on the sea, and sea trades. Pays $1,000, on acceptance. Query with SASE. E-mail: randall-ja@aol.com.

THE ELKS MAGAZINE—425 W. Diversey Pkwy., Chicago, IL 60614. Janell Neal, Ed. Asst. Articles, 1,500 to 2,500 words, on technology, sports, history, and topics of current interest; for non-urban audience. Pays 20¢ a word, on acceptance. No queries.

FIREHOUSE—Cygnus Publishing Co., 445 Broad Hollow Rd., Melville, NY 11747. Harvey Eisner, Ed.-in-Chief. Articles, 500 to 2,000 words: on-the-scene accounts of fires, trends in firefighting equipment, controversial fire-service issues, and lifestyles of firefighters. Query. SASE.

THE FURROW—John Deere-North American Agricultural Marketing Center, 11145 Thompson Ave., Lenexa, KS 66219. Karl Kessler, North American Ed. No unsolicited material.

FUTURIFIC INC.—Foundation for Optimism, 305 Madison Ave., #10B, New York, NY 10165. Charlotte Kellar, Ed. Forecasts of what will be. "Only optimistic material will get published. Solutions, not problems. We track all developments giving evidence to our increasing life expectancy, improving international coexistence, the global tendency toward peace, and improving economic trends. We also report on all new developments, economic, political, social, scientific, technical, medical or other that are making life easier, better and more enjoyable for the greatest number of people." Pays in copies. Queries preferred.

HARVARD MAGAZINE—7 Ware St., Cambridge, MA 02138-4037. John Rosenberg, Ed. Articles, 500 to 5,000 words, with a connection to Harvard University. Pays from $100, on publication. Query required. Web site: www.harvard-magazine.com.

IDEA PERSONAL TRAINER—6190 Cornerstone Ct. E., Suite 204, San Diego, CA 92121-3773. Ed. For personal fitness trainers assn. Articles on exercise science; program design; profiles of successful trainers; business, legal, and marketing topics; tips for networking with other trainers and with allied medical professionals; client counseling; and training tips. "What's New" column includes industry news, products, and research. Payment varies, on acceptance. Query. E-mail: member@ideafit.com. web site: www.ideafit.com.

KIWANIS—3636 Woodview Trace, Indianapolis, IN 46268. Chuck Jonak, Man. Ed. Articles, 2,500 words (with 250- to 350-word sidebars), on lifestyle, relationships, world view, children's issues and concerns, education, trends, small business, religion, health, etc. No travel pieces, interviews, profiles. Pays $400 to $1,000, on acceptance. Query. E-mail: magazine@ kiwanis.org. Web site: www.kiwanis.org/magazine.

THE LION—300 22nd St., Oak Brook, IL 60523. Robert Kleinfelder, Sr. Ed. Official publication of Lions Clubs International. Articles, 800 to 2,000 words, and photo-essays, on club activities. Pays from $100 to $700, on acceptance. Query. E-mail: rkleinfe@lionsclubs.org. Web site: www.lionsclubs.org.

NEW HOLLAND NEWS—New Holland, N.A., Inc., P.O. Box 1895, New Holland, PA 17557. Attn: Ed. Articles, to 1,500 words, with strong color photo support, on agriculture and rural living. Pays on acceptance. Query. Web site: www.newholland.com/na.

THE NEW PHYSICIAN—American Medical Student Association, 1902 Association Dr., Reston, VA 20191. Amy Myers-Payne, Ed. Nine issues a year. Articles, 1,200 to 3,500 words, on social, ethical, and political issues for medical students, interns, and residents. Query for departments. Pay is negotiable.

OPTIMIST MAGAZINE—4494 Lindell Blvd., St. Louis, MO 63108. Dena Hull, Man. Ed. Articles, to 1,000 words, on activities of local Optimist

Clubs, and techniques for personal and club success. Pays from $100, on acceptance. Query. E-mail: magazine@optimist.org. web site: www.optimist.org.

RESTAURANTS USA—1200 17th St. N.W., Washington, DC 20036-3097. Jennifer Batty, Ed. Publication of the National Restaurant Assn. Articles, 1,000 to 2,500 words, on the foodservice and restaurant business. Restaurant experience preferred. Pays $350 to $800, on acceptance. No phone queries. Web site: www.restaurant.org.

THE RETIRED OFFICER MAGAZINE—201 N. Washington St., Alexandria, VA 22314. Address the Manuscripts Ed. Articles, 2,000 to 2,500 words, of interest to military retirees and their families. Current military/national affairs, recent military history, health/medicine, and financial topics. No fillers. Photos a plus. Pays to $1,750, on acceptance. Query. Guidelines. E-mail: editor@troa.org. Web site: www.troa.org.

THE ROTARIAN—1560 Sherman Ave., Evanston, IL 60201-3698. Willmon L. White, Ed.-in-Chief. Charles W. Pratt, Ed. Cary Silver, Man. Ed. Publication of Rotary International, world service organization of business and professional men and women. Articles, 1,200 to 2,000 words, on international social and economic issues, business and management, human relationships, travel, sports, environment, science and technology; humor. Pays good rates, on acceptance. Query. E-mail: prattc@rotaryintl.org. Web site: www.rotary.org.

THE SCHOOL ADMINISTRATOR—American Assn. of School Administrators, 1801 N. Moore St., Arlington, VA 22209-1813. Jay P. Goldman, Ed. Articles related to school administration (K through 12). "We seek articles written in a journalistic style about school system practices, policies, and programs that have widespread appeal." Pays in copies. Guidelines available on Web site: www.aasa.org./sa/contents.htm. E-mail address: jgoldman@aasa.org.

VFW MAGAZINE—406 W. 34th St., Kansas City, MO 64111. Richard K. Kolb, Ed. Articles, 1,000 words, related to current foreign policy and defense, American armed forces abroad, and international events affecting U.S. national security. Also, up-to-date articles on veteran concerns and issues affecting veterans. Pays to $500, on acceptance. Query. Guidelines. E-mail: patbrown@vfw.org. Web site: www.vfw.org.

RELIGIOUS MAGAZINES

AMERICA—106 W. 56th St., New York, NY 10019-3893. Thomas J. Reese, S.J., Ed. Articles, 1,000 to 2,500 words, political, social and religious issues. "America, the national Catholic weekly magazine, covers contemporary issues from a religious and ethical perspective." E-mail: articles@america press.org. Web site: www.americapress.org.

AMERICAN BIBLE SOCIETY RECORD—1865 Broadway, New York, NY 10023. David Singer, Man. Ed. Material related to work of American Bible Society: translating, publishing, distributing. All articles staff-written; accepts no free-lance material.

AMERICAN JEWISH HISTORY—American Jewish Historical Society, 2 Thornton Rd., Waltham, MA 02154. Dr. Marc Lee Raphael, Ed. Academic articles, 15 to 30 typed pages, on the settlement, history, and life of Jews in North America. Queries preferred. No payment.

AMIT MAGAZINE—817 Broadway, New York, NY 10003-4761. Rita Schwalb, Ed.; Micheline Ratzersdorfer, Exec. Ed. Patricia Israel, Man. Ed. Articles, 1,000 to 2,000 words, of interest to Jewish women: Middle East, Israel, history, holidays, travel, culture, food.

ANGLICAN JOURNAL—600 Jarvis St., Toronto, Ont., Canada M4Y 2J6. Rev. David Harris, Ed. National newspaper of the Anglican Church of Canada. Articles, to 1,000 words, on news and features of the Anglican Church across the country and around the world, including social and ethical issues and human-interest subjects in a religious context. Pays 23¢ per published word, on publication. Query required.

THE BANNER—2850 Kalamazoo Ave. S.E., Grand Rapids, MI 49560. John D. Suk, Ed. Malcolm McBryde, Assoc. Ed. Fiction, to 2,500 words, non-fiction, to 1,800 words, and poetry, to 50 lines, for members of the Christian Reformed Church in North America. "The magazine's purpose is to inform, challenge, educate, comfort, and inspire members of the church." Also some church-related cartoons. Pays $125 to $200 for articles, $40 for poetry, on acceptance. Query preferred.

BIBLE ADVOCATE—P.O. Box 33677, Denver, CO 80233. Calvin Burrell, Ed. Articles, 1,000 to 1,500 words, and fillers, 100 to 400 words, on Bible passages and Christian living; also teaching articles. Some poetry, 5 to 20 lines, on religious themes. Opinion pieces, to 650 words. "Be familiar with the doctrinal beliefs of the Church of God (Seventh Day). For example, they don't celebrate a traditional Easter or Christmas." Pays $25 to $50 for articles, $20 for poetry, on publication. Send for guidelines and theme list. E-mail: bible advocate@cog7.org. Web site: www.cog7.org/BA.

BREAD FOR GOD'S CHILDREN—P.O. Box 1017, Arcadia, FL 34265-1017. Judith M. Gibbs, Ed. Fiction (to 1,800 words for older children, to 800 words for younger) and articles (to 800 words) that apply the word of God to every situation. "We are an interdenominational teaching magazine for Christian families." Pays $20 for articles; to $50 for fiction, on publication. Guidelines. E-mail: bread@desoto.net.

BRIGADE LEADER—Box 150, Wheaton, IL 60189. Deborah Christensen, Man. Ed. Inspirational articles, 750 words, for Christian men who lead boys in Christian Service Brigade programs. "Most articles are written on assignment by experts; very few free lancers used. Query with clips and we'll contact you if we need you for an assignment. You must understand the Brigade program and be able to address issue Brigade leaders face." Pays $60 to $150.

CATECHIST—330 Progress Rd., Dayton, OH 45449. Patricia Fischer, Ed. Informational and how-to articles, 1,200 to 1,500 words, for Catholic teachers, coordinators, and administrators in religious education programs. Pays $25 to $100, on publication.

CATHOLIC DIGEST—2115 Summit Ave., St. Paul, MN 55105-1081. Attn: Articles Ed. Articles, 1,000 to 3,500 words, on Catholic and general subjects. Fillers, to 300 words, on instances of kindness rewarded; accounts of good deed. Pays from $200 for original articles, $100 for reprints, on acceptance; $4 to $50 for fillers, on publication. Guidelines.

CATHOLIC NEAR EAST MAGAZINE—1011 First Ave., New York, NY 10022-4195. Michael La Civita, Exec. Ed. Bimonthly publication of

CNEWA, a papal agency for humanitarian and pastoral support. Articles, 1,500 to 2,000 words, on people of the Middle East, northeast Africa, India, and eastern Europe: their faith, heritage, culture, and present state of affairs. Special interest in Eastern Christian churches. Color photos for all articles. Pays 20¢ per edited word. Query.

CATHOLIC PARENT—Our Sunday Visitor, Inc., 200 Noll Plaza, Huntington, IN 46750. Woodeene Koenig-Bricker, Ed. Features, how-tos, and general-interest articles, 800 to 1,000 words, for Catholic parents. "Keep it anecdotal and practical with an emphasis on values and family life. Don't preach." Payment varies, on acceptance. E-mail: cparent@osv.com. Web site: www.osv.com.

THE CHRISTIAN CENTURY—407 S. Dearborn St., Chicago, IL 60605. John M. Buchanan, Ed./Pub. Ecumenical. Articles, 1,500 to 3,000 words, with a religious angle, on political and social issues, international affairs, culture, the arts. Poetry, to 20 lines. Photos. Pays about $50 per printed page, extra for photos, on publication. E-mail: main@christiancentury.org. Web site: www.christiancentury.org.

CHRISTIAN EDUCATION COUNSELOR—1445 Boonville Ave., Springfield, MO 65802-1894. Sylvia Lee, Ed. Articles, 600 to 800 words, on teaching and administrating Christian education in the local church, for local Sunday school and Christian school personnel. Pays 5¢ to 10¢ a word, on acceptance.

CHRISTIAN EDUCATION JOURNAL—Trinity Evangelical Divinity School, 2065 Half Day Rd., Deerfield, IL 60015. Dr. Perry G. Downs, Ed. Articles, 10 to 25 typed pages, on Christian education topics.

CHRISTIAN HOME & SCHOOL—3350 E. Paris Ave. S.E., Grand Rapids, MI 49512. Roger Schmurr, Senior Ed. Articles for parents in Canada and the U.S. who send their children to Christian schools and are concerned about the challenges facing Christian families today. Pays $125 to $200, on publication. Send SASE for guidelines. E-mail: rogers@csionline.org. Web site: www.gospelcom. net/csi/chs.

CHRISTIAN PARENTING TODAY—4050 Lee Vance View, Colorado Springs, CO 80918. Erin Healy, Ed. Articles, 900 to 2,000 words, dealing with raising children with Christian principles. Departments: "Train Them Up," 600 to 700 words, on child development (spiritual, moral, character building); "Healthy & Safe," 300- to 400-word how-to pieces on keeping children emotional and physically safe, home and away; "The Lighter Side," humorous essays on family life, 600 to 700 words; "Parent Exchange," 25 to 100 words on problem-solving ideas that have worked for parents; "Life in Our House," insightful anecdotes, 25 to 100 words, about humorous things said at home. (Submissions for "Parent Exchange" and "Life in our House" are not acknowledged or returned.) Pays 15¢ to 25¢ a word, on publication. Pays $25 to $125 for department pieces. Guidelines; send SASE.

CHRISTIAN PUBLICATIONS—Imprint of Horizon Books, 3825 Hartzdale Dr., Camp Hill, PA 17011. George McPeek Adult and young adult nonfiction from 35,000 to 50,000 words, with an evanggelical Christian slant. Queries preferred. Payment is in royalties. Web site: www.cpi-horizon.com.

CHRISTIAN SOCIAL ACTION—100 Maryland Ave. N.E., Washington, DC 20002. Erik Alsgaard, Ed. Articles, 1,500 to 2,000 words, on social justice issues for people of faith. Pays $75 to $125, on publication.

CHRISTIANITY TODAY—465 Gundersen Dr., Carol Stream, IL 60188. Michael G. Maudlin, Man. Ed. Doctrinal social issues and interpretive essays, 1,500 to 3,000 words, from evangelical Protestant perspective. No fiction or poetry. Pays $200 to $500, on acceptance. Query.

CHURCH & STATE—518 C St. N.E., Washington, DC 20002. Joseph L. Conn, Ed. Articles, 600 to 2,600 words, on issues of religious liberty and church-state relations, promoting the concept of church-state separation. Pays varying rates, on acceptance. Query.

CHURCH EDUCATOR—Educational Ministries, Inc., 165 Plaza Dr., Prescott, AZ 86303. Robert G. Davidson, Ed. How-to articles, to 1,750 words, on Christian education: activity projects, crafts, learning centers, games, bulletin boards, etc., for all church school, junior and high school programs, and adult study group ideas. Allow 3 months for response. Pays 3¢ a word, on publication. E-mail: edmin2@aol.com.

CLUBHOUSE JR.—8605 Explorer Dr., Colorado Springs, CO 80920. Jesse Florea, Ed. Articles on Christian values aimed at children ages 4 to 8. Nonfiction, to 500 words, on real people, science, and nature; fiction, from 250 to 1,000 words; Bible stories, 250 to 800 words; rebus stories, to 200 words; poetry, to 250 words; and one-page puzzles. Pays $75 to $200 for all material except poetry, rebus stories, and puzzles. SASE for guidelines.

COLUMBIA—1 Columbus Plaza, New Haven, CT 06510-3326. Tim S. Hickey, Ed. Knights of Columbus. Articles, 1,500 words, for Catholic families. No fiction. Pays up to $600 for articles, on acceptance. E-mail: info@kofc.org. Web site: www.kofc.org.

COMMENTARY—165 E. 56th St., New York, NY 10022. Neal Kozodoy, Ed. Articles, 5,000 to 7,000 words, on contemporary issues, Jewish affairs, social sciences, religious thought, culture. Serious fiction; book reviews. Pays on publication.

COMMONWEAL—475 Riverside Dr., New York, NY 10115. Margaret O'Brien Steinfels, Ed. Catholic. Articles, to 3,000 words, on political, religious, social, and literary subjects. Pays 3¢ a word, on publication.

THE COVENANT COMPANION—5101 N. Francisco Ave., Chicago, IL 60625. Jane K. Swanson-Nystrom, Ed. Articles, 800 to 1,800 words, with Christian implications published for members and attenders of Evangelical Covenant Church "seeking to inform, stimulate thought, and encourage dialogue on issues that impact the church and its members." Pays $35 to $75, on publication. E-mail: companion@covoffice.org.

CRUSADER—P.O. Box 7259, Grand Rapids, MI 49510. G. Richard Broene, Ed. Fiction, 900 to 1,500 words, and articles, 400 to 1,000 words, for boys ages 9 to 14 that show how God is at work in their lives and in the world around them. Also, short fillers. Pays 4¢ to 6¢ a word, on acceptance. Web site: www.gospelcom.net/cadets.

DAILY MEDITATION—Box 2710, San Antonio, TX 78299. Emilia Devno, Ed. Inspirational, self-improvement, nonsectarian religious articles "showing the way to greater spiritual growth," 300 to 1,650 words. Fillers, to 350 words; verse, to 20 lines. Pays 1½¢ to 2¢ a word for prose; 14¢ a line for verse, on acceptance. SASE required.

DECISION—Billy Graham Evangelistic Assn., 1300 Harmon Pl., P.O. Box 779, Minneapolis, MN 55440-0779. Kersten Beckstrom, Ed. Christian testimonies and teaching articles on evangelism and Christian nurturing, 800 to 1,200 words. Vignettes, 400 to 500 words. Pays varying rates, on publication.

DISCIPLESHIP JOURNAL—Box 35004, Colorado Springs, CO 80935. Sue Kline, Ed. Bimonthly. Nonfiction, from 1,500 to 2,500 words. Topics include: teaching on a Scripture passage, teaching on a topic, and how-tos. Focus is on helping believers develop a deeper relationship with Jesus Christ. No book reviews, news articles, or articles about Christian organizations. Send SASE for guidelines. Pays 25¢ a word, on acceptance.

DREAMS & VISIONS—Skysong Press, 35 Peter St. S., Orillia, Ont., Canada L3V 5A8. Steve Stanton, Ed. New frontiers in Christian fiction. Eclectic fiction, 2,000 to 6,000 words, that "has literary value and is unique and relevant to Christian readers today." Pays 1/2¢ per word. E-mail: skysong@bconnex.net. Web site: www.bconnex.net/~skysong.

ENRICHMENT: A JOURNAL FOR PENTECOSTAL MINISTRY— 1445 Boonville Ave., Springfield, MO 65802. Wayde I. Goodall, Ed. Articles, 1,200 to 1,500 words, slanted to ministers, on preaching, doctrine, practice; how-to features. Pays to 10¢ a word, on acceptance.

EVANGEL—Light and Life Communications, Box 535002, Indianapolis, IN 46253-5002. Julie Innes, Ed. Free Methodist. Personal experience articles, 1,000 words; short devotional items, 300 to 500 words; fiction, 1,200 words, showing personal faith in Christ to be instrumental in solving problems. Send #10 SASE for sample copy and guidelines. Pays 4¢ a word for articles, $10 for poetry, on publication.

FAITH TODAY—M.I.P. Box 3745, Markham, Ontario, Canada L3R OY4. Larry Matthews, Man. Ed. Articles, 1,500 words, on current issues and news relating to Evangelical Christians in Canada. Pays negotiable rates (usually 20¢ to 25¢ per word, Canadian), on publication. Queries required. E-mail: ft@efc-canada.com. Web site: www.efc-canada.com/subs.htm.

THE FAMILY DIGEST—P.O. Box 40137, Fort Wayne, IN 46804. Corine B. Erlandson, Ed. Articles, 700 to 1,200 words, on family life, Catholic subjects, seasonal, parish life, prayer, inspiration, how-to, spiritual life, for the Catholic reader. Also publishes short humorous anecdotes drawn from personal experience and gentle light-hearted cartoons. Pays $40 to $60 per article; $25 for personal anecdotes; $40 for cartoons, 4 to 8 weeks after acceptance.

FELLOWSHIP—Box 271, Nyack, NY 10960-0271. Richard Deats, Ed. Bimonthly published by the Fellowship of Reconciliation, an interfaith, pacifist organization, working for peace and justice through non-violence. Articles, 750 and 1,500 to 2,000 words; B&W photo-essays, on active nonviolence, peace and justice, opposition to war. "Articles for a just and peaceful world community." SASE required. Pays in copies and subscription. Queries preferred.

FELLOWSHIP IN PRAYER—See *Sacred Journey: The Journal of Fellowship in Prayer.*

FIRST THINGS—156 Fifth Ave., #400, New York, NY 10010-7002. James Nuechterlein, Ed. Published 10 times a year. Essays and social commentary, 1,500 words or 4,000 to 6,000 words, for academics, clergy, and general educated readership, on the role of religion in public life. Pays $300 to $800, on publication.

FOURSQUARE WORLD ADVANCE—1910 W. Sunset Blvd., Suite 200, P.O. Box 26902, Los Angeles, CA 90026. Ronald D. Williams, Ed. Official publication of the International Church of the Foursquare Gospel. Religious fiction and nonfiction, 1,000 to 1,200 words, and religious poetry. Pays $75, on publication. Guidelines. E-mail: comm@foursquare.org. Web site: www. foursquare.org.

FRIENDS JOURNAL—1216 Arch St., Philadelphia, PA 19107. Susan Corson-Finnerty, Ed. Articles, to 2,500 words, reflecting Quaker life today: commentary on social issues, spiritual reflection, experiential articles, Quaker history, world affairs. Poetry, to 25 lines, and Quaker-related humor and cross-word puzzles also considered. Guidelines.

THE GEM—Box 926, Findlay, OH 45839-0926. Mac Cordell, Ed. Articles, 300 to 1,600 words, and fiction, 1,000 to 1,600 words: true-to-life experiences of God's help, of healed relationships, and of growing maturity in faith. For adolescents through senior citizens. Pays $15 for articles and fiction, $5 to $10 for fillers, after publication.

GOSPEL HERALD—See *The Mennonite.*

GROUP, THE YOUTH MINISTRY MAGAZINE—Box 481, Loveland, CO 80539. Rick Lawrence, Ed. Interdenominational magazine for leaders of junior and senior high school Christian youth groups. Articles, 500 to 1,700 words, about practical youth ministry principles, techniques, or activities. Short how-to pieces, to 300 words. Pays to $200 for articles, $40 for department pieces, on acceptance. Guidelines.

GUIDE—Review and Herald Publishing Assn., 55 W. Oak Ridge Dr., Hagerstown, MD 21740. Tim Lale, Ed. True stories, to 1,200 words, for Christian youth, ages 10 to 14. Pays 10¢ to 12¢ a word, on publication.

GUIDEPOSTS—16 E. 34th St., New York, NY 10016. Catherine Scott, Dept. Ed. True first-person stories, 250 to 1,500 words, stressing how people have used faith to overcome obstacles and live better lives. Anecdotal fillers, to 250 words. Pays $75 to $400 for full-length stories, $25 to $100 for fillers, on acceptance. E-mail: gp4k@guideposts.org. Web site: www.gp4k.com.

INSIDE MAGAZINE—226 S. 16th St., Philadelphia, PA 19102-3392. Jane Biberman, Ed. Jewish lifestyle magazine. Articles, 1,500 to 3,000 words, on Jewish issues, health, finance, and the arts. Paysup to $600 for departments, to $1,200 for features, after publication. Queries required; send clips if available.

JEWISH CURRENTS—22 E. 17th St., #601, New York, NY 10003. Morris U. Schappes, Ed. Articles, 2,400 to 3,000 words, on Jewish history, Jewish secularism, progressivism, labor struggle, Holocaust and Holocaust-resistance, Black-Jewish relations, Israel, Yiddish culture. "We are pro-Israel though non-Zionist and a secular magazine; no religious articles." Overstocked with fiction and poetry. No payment.

THE JEWISH HOMEMAKER—391 Troy Ave., Brooklyn, NY 11213. Abraham M. Goldstein, Ed. Quarterly. Articles, 1,200 to 2,000 words, for a traditional/Orthodox Jewish audience. Payment varies, on publication. Query.

THE JEWISH MONTHLY—B'nai B'rith International, 1640 Rhode Island Ave. N.W., Washington, DC 20036. Eric Rozenman, Exec. Ed. Articles, 500 to 2,500 words, on politics, religion, history, culture, and social issues of Jewish concern with an emphasis on people. Pays $300 to $650 for features, on publication. Query with clips. E-mail: ijm@bnaibrith.org.

THE JEWISH PUBLICATION SOCIETY—1930 Chestnut St., 21st Fl., Philadelphia, PA 19103-4599. Adult nonfiction, juvenile fiction and nonfiction, and young adult fiction and nonfiction on Jewish topics. Query with outline. Payment is in royalties. E-mail address: jewishbooks@aol.com. Web site: www.jewishpub.org.

JOURNAL OF CHRISTIAN NURSING—P.O. Box 1650, Downers Grove, IL 60515-1650. Judy Shelly, Sr. Ed. Articles, 8 to 12 double-spaced pages, that help Christian nurses view nursing practice through the eyes of faith: spiritual care, ethics, values, healing and wholeness, psychology and religion, personal and professional ethics, etc. Priority given to nurse authors, though work by non-nurses will be considered. Pays $25 to $80. Guidelines and editorial calendar. E-mail: jcn@ivpress.com. Web site: www.ncf.jcn.org.

THE JOYFUL WOMAN—P.O. Box 90028, Chattanooga, TN 37412. Joy Rice Martin, Ed. Articles and fiction, 500 to 1,200 words, for Christian women: first-person inspirational true stories, profiles of Christian women, practical and biblically oriented how-to articles. Pays 3¢ to 4¢ a word, on publication. Queries required; no unsolicited manuscripts.

LEADERSHIP—465 Gundersen Dr., Carol Stream, IL 60188. Marshall Shelley, Ed. Articles, 500 to 3,000 words, on administration, finance, and/or programming of interest to ministers and church leaders. Personal stories of crisis in ministry. "We deal mainly with the how-to of running a church. We're not a theological journal but a practical one." Pays $50 to $350, on acceptance. E-mail: ljeditor@leadershipjournal.net. Web site: www.leadershipjournal.net.

LIGHT AND LIFE—P.O. Box 535002, Indianapolis, IN 46253-5002. Doug Newton, Ed. Thoughtful articles about practical Christian living. Social and cultural analysis from an evangelical perspective. Pays 4¢ to 5¢ a word, on publication. E-mail: dougn@fmcna@org.

LIGUORIAN—Liguori, MO 63057-9999. Rev. Allan Weinert, Ed. Catholic. Articles and short stories, 1,500 to 1,700 words, on Christian values in modern life. Pays 10¢ to 12¢ a word, on acceptance. E-mail: aweinert@liguori.org. Web site: www.liguori.org.

THE LIVING LIGHT—U.S. Catholic Conference, Dept. of Education, Caldwell 345, The Catholic Univ. of America, Washington, DC 20064. Theoretical and practical articles, 1,500 to 4,000 words, on religious education, catechesis, and pastoral ministry.

THE LOOKOUT—8121 Hamilton Ave., Cincinnati, OH 45231. David Faust, Ed. Articles, 500 to 1,800 words, on spiritual growth, family issues, applying Christian faith to current issues, and people overcoming problems with Christian principles. Inspirational or humorous shorts, 500 to 800 words. Pays 5¢ to 15¢ a word, on acceptance. E-mail: customerservice@standardpub.com.

THE LUTHERAN—8765 W. Higgins Rd., Chicago, IL 60631. Edgar R. Trexler, Ed. Articles, to 1,200 words, on Christian ideology, personal religious experiences, social and ethical issues, family life, church, and community of Evangelical Lutheran Church in America. Pays $100 to $500, on acceptance. Query required.

MARRIAGE PARTNERSHIP—Christianity Today, Inc., 465 Gundersen Dr., Carol Stream, IL 60188. Ron Lee, Ed. Articles, 500 to 2,000 words, related to marriage, for men and women who wish to fortify their relationship. Humor. Pays $40 to $300, on acceptance. Query required.

MARYKNOLL—Maryknoll, NY 10545. Joseph Veneroso, M. M., Ed. Frank Maurovich, Man. Ed. Magazine of the Catholic Foreign Mission Society of America. Articles, 800 to 1,000 words, and photos relating to missions or missioners overseas. Pays $150, on acceptance. Payment for photos made on publication.

MATURE LIVING—127 Ninth Ave. N., Nashville, TN 37234-0140. Al Shackleford, Ed. Fiction and human-interest articles, to 1,200 words, for senior adults. Must be consistent with Christian principles. Payment varies, on acceptance.

MATURE YEARS—201 Eighth Ave. S., P.O. Box 801, Nashville, TN 37202. Marvin W. Cropsey, Ed. Nondenominational quarterly. Articles, 1,500 to 2,000 words, on retirement or related subjects, inspiration. Humorous and serious fiction, 1,500 to 1,800 words. Travel pieces for seniors or with religious slant. Poetry, to 14 lines. Include social security number with manuscript. Guidelines. E-mail: matureyears@umpublishing.org.

THE MENNONITE—(Merged with *Gospel Herald*) P.O. Box 347, Newton, KS 67114. J. Lorne Peachey, Ed.; Gordon Houser, Assoc. Ed. Articles, 1,200 words, that emphasize Christian themes. Pays 7¢ a word, on publication. Guidelines.

MESSENGER OF THE SACRED HEART—661 Greenwood Ave., Toronto, Ont., Canada M4J 4B3. Articles and short stories, about 1,500 words, for American and Canadian Catholics. Pays from 6¢ a word, on acceptance.

MIDSTREAM—633 Third Ave., 21st Fl., New York, NY 10017. Joel Carmichael, Ed. Jewish/Zionist-interest articles and book reviews. Fiction, to 3,000 words, and poetry. Pays 5¢ a word, after publication. Allow 3 months for response.

MINISTRY & LITURGY—160 E. Virginia St., #290, San Jose, CA 95112. Nick Wagner, Ed. Practical, imaginative how-to help for Roman Catholic liturgy planners. Pays in copies and subscription. Query required.

THE MIRACULOUS MEDAL—475 E. Chelten Ave., Philadelphia, PA 19144-5785. Rev. William J. O'Brien, C.M., Ed. Dir. Catholic. Fiction, to 2,400 words. Religious verse, to 20 lines. Pays from 2¢ a word for fiction, from 50¢ a line for poetry, on acceptance. Web site: www.cmphila.org/camm.

MOMENT MAGAZINE—4710 41st St. N.W., Washington, DC 20016. Hershel Shanks, Ed. Sophisticated articles, 2,500 to 5,000 words, on Jewish culture, politics, religion, and personalities. Columns, to 1,500 words, with uncommon perspectives on contemporary issues, humor, strong anecdotes. Book reviews, 400 words. Pays $40 to $600. Web site: www.momentmag.com.

MOMENTUM—National Catholic Educational Assn., 1077 30th St. N.W., Suite 100, Washington, DC 20007-3852. Margaret Bonilla, Ed. Articles, 500 to 1,500 words, on outstanding programs, issues, and research in education. Book reviews. Pays $25 to $75, on publication. Query.

MOODY MAGAZINE—820 N. La Salle Blvd., Chicago, IL 60610. Andrew Scheer, Man. Ed. Anecdotal articles, 1,200 to 2,000 words, on the evangelical Christian experience in the home, the community, and the workplace. Pays 15¢ to 20¢ a word, on acceptance. Query. No unsolicited manuscripts. E-mail: moodyltrs@moody.edu. Web site: www.moody.edu/moodymag.

NATURE FRIEND—2727 TR 421, Sugarcreek, OH 44681. Marvin Wengerd, Ed. Monthly. Stories, puzzles, activities, experiments about nature for children. Pays 5¢ per word; $15 for fillers and games. Send for guidelines. Sample issues are $5.

NEW ERA—50 E. North Temple, Salt Lake City, UT 84150. Larry A. Hiller, Man. Ed. Articles, 150 to 1,500 words, and fiction, to 2,000 words, for young Mormons. Poetry; photos. Pays 5¢ to 10¢ a word, 25¢ a line for poetry, on acceptance. Query.

OBLATES—9480 N. De Mazenod Dr., Belleville, IL 62223-1160. Mary Mohrman, Manuscripts Ed. Christine Portell, Man. Ed. Articles, 500 to 600 words, that inspire, uplift, and motivate through positive Christian values in everyday life. Inspirational poetry, to 12 lines. Pays $150 for articles, $50 for poems, on acceptance. Send 2 first-class stamps and SASE for guidelines and sample copy. E-mail: cportell@oblatesusa.org. Web site: www.snows.org.

THE OTHER SIDE—300 W. Apsley, Philadelphia, PA 19144. Doug Davidson, Nonfiction Ed. Monica Day, Fiction Ed. Jeanne Minahan, Poetry Ed. Independent, ecumenical, progressive Christian magazine devoted to issues of social justice, Christian spirituality, and the creative arts. Fiction, 500 to 5,000 words, that deepens readers' encounter with the mystery of God and the mystery of ourselves. Nonfiction, 500 to 4,000 words (most under 2,000 words), on contemporary social, political, economic, or racial issues in the U.S. or abroad. Poems, to 50 lines; submit up to 3 poems. Payment is 2 copies, a two-year subscription, plus $20 to $350 for articles; $75 to $250 for fiction; $15 for poems, on acceptance. Guidelines. Web site: www.theotherside.org.

OUR FAMILY—Box 249, Battleford, Sask., Canada S0M 0E0. Marie-Louise Ternier-Gommers, Ed. Articles, 1,000 to 3,000 words, for Catholic families, on modern society, family, marriage, current affairs, and spiritual topics. Humor; verse. Pays 7¢ to 10¢ (Canadian) a word for articles, 75¢ to $1 (Canadian) a line for poetry, on acceptance. SAE with international reply coupons required with all submissions. Guidelines. E-mail: editor@ourfamilymagazine.com. See web site for guidelines and projected themes for 2000: www.ourfamilymagazine.com.

PASTORAL LIFE—Box 595, Canfield, OH 44406-0595. Anthony L. Chenevey, Ed. Articles, 2,000 to 2,500 words, addressing the problems of pastoral ministry. Pays 4¢ a word, on publication. Guidelines.

PENTECOSTAL EVANGEL—1445 Boonville Ave., Springfield, MO 65802. Hal Donaldson, Ed. Assemblies of God. Religious, personal experience, and devotional articles, 400 to 1,000 words. Pays 8¢ to 10¢ a word.

PERSPECTIVE—Pioneer Clubs, P.O. Box 788, Wheaton, IL 60189-0788. Rebecca Powell Parat, Ed. 3 times/year. Articles, 500 to 1,200 words, that provide growth for adult club leaders in leadership and relationship skills and offer encouragement and practical support. Readers are lay leaders of Pioneer Clubs for boys and girls (age 2 to 12th grade). "Most articles written on assignment; writers familiar with Pioneer Clubs who would be interested in working on assignment should contact us." Pays $30 to $120, on acceptance. Guidelines.

PIME WORLD—17330 Quincy St., Detroit, MI 48221. Ed. Articles, 600 to 1,200 words, on Catholic missionary work in South Asia, West Africa, and Latin America. Color photos. No fiction or poetry. Pays 10¢ a word, extra for photos, on publication. Web site: www.pimeusa.org. E-mail: pimeworld@pimeusa.org.

POWER AND LIGHT—6401 The Paseo, Kansas City, MO 64131. Matt Price, Preteen Ed. Fiction and nonfiction, 400 to 800 words, for grades 5 and 6, defining Christian experiences and demonstrating Christian values and beliefs. Pays 5¢ a word for multi-use rights, on publication. E-mail: mprice@nazarene.org.

THE PREACHER'S MAGAZINE—10814 E. Broadway, Spokane, WA 99206. Neil B. Wiseman, Ed. Scholarly and practical articles, 700 to 2,500 words, on areas of interest to Christian ministers: church administration, pastoral care, professional and personal growth, church music, finance, evangelism. Pays 3 1/2¢ a word, on publication. Guidelines.

PRESBYTERIAN RECORD—50 Wynford Dr., Toronto, Ont., Canada M3C 1J7. John Congram, Ed. Fiction and nonfiction, 1,500 words, and poetry, any length. Short items, to 800 words, of a contemporary and often controversial nature for "Vox Populi." The purpose of the magazine is "to provide news, not only from our church but the church-at-large, and to fulfill both a pastoral and prophetic role among our people." Queries preferred. SAE with international reply coupons required. Pays about $50 (Canadian), on publication. Guidelines. E-mail: pcrecord@presbyterian.ca. Web site: www.presbyterian.ca/record.

PRESBYTERIANS TODAY—100 Witherspoon, Louisville, KY 40202-1396. Eva Stimson, Ed. Articles, 1,200 to 1,500 words, of special interest to members of the Presbyterian Church (USA). Pays to $200, before publication. E-mail: today@pcusa.org. Web site: www.pcusa.org/today.

THE PRIEST—200 Noll Plaza, Huntington, IN 46750-4304. Msgr. Owen F. Campion, Ed. Viewpoints, to 1,500 words, and articles, to 5,000 words, on life and ministry of priests, current theological developments, etc., for priests, permanent deacons, and seminarians. Pays $75 to $250, on acceptance. E-mail: tpriest@osv.com. Web site: www.osv.com.

PURPOSE—616 Walnut Ave., Scottdale, PA 15683-1999. James E. Horsch, Ed. Fiction, nonfiction, and fillers, to 750 words, on Christian discipleship and church-year related themes, with good photos; pieces of history, biography, science, hobbies, from a Christian perspective; Christian problem solving. First-person pieces preferred. Poetry, to 12 lines. "Send complete manuscript; no queries." Pays to 5¢ a word, to $2 a line for poetry, on acceptance. E-mail: horsch@mph.org. Web site: www.mph.org.

QUEEN OF ALL HEARTS—26 S. Saxon Ave., Bay Shore, NY 11706-8993. J. Patrick Gaffney, S.M.M., Ed. Publication of Montfort Missionaries. Articles and fiction, 1,000 to 2,000 words, related to the Virgin Mary. Poetry. Pay varies, on acceptance. E-mail: pretre@worldnet.att.net. Web site: www.montfortmissionaries.com.

THE QUIET HOUR—4050 Lee Vance View, Colorado Springs, CO 80919. Gary Wilde, Ed. Short devotionals. Pays $15, on acceptance. By assignment only; query.

RECONSTRUCTIONISM TODAY—30 Old Whitfield Rd., Accord,

NY 12404. Lawrence Bush, Ed. Articles on contemporary Judaism and Jewish culture. No fiction or poetry. Pays in copies and subscription.

REVIEW FOR RELIGIOUS—3601 Lindell Blvd., St. Louis, MO 63108. David L. Fleming, S.J., Ed. Informative, practical, or inspirational articles, 1,500 to 5,000 words, from a Catholic spirituality tradition stemming from charisms of Catholic religious communities. Pays $6 per page, on publication. Guidelines. E-mail: foppema@slu.edu.

SACRED JOURNEY: THE JOURNAL OF FELLOWSHIP IN PRAYER—(formerly *Fellowship in Prayer*) 291 Witherspoon St., Princeton, NJ 08542. Articles, to 1,500 words, relating to prayer, meditation, and the spiritual life as practiced by men and women of all faith traditions. Pays in copies. Guidelines. E-mail: editorial@sacredjourney.org. Web site: www.sacred journey.org.

ST. ANTHONY MESSENGER—1615 Republic St., Cincinnati, OH 45210-1298. Fr. Jack Wintz, O.F.M., Ed. Articles, 2,000 to 2,500 words, on personalities, major movements, education, family, religious and church issues, spiritual life, and social issues. Human-interest pieces. Humor; fiction, 2,000 to 3,000 words. Articles and stories should reflect sound human and religious values, keeping a predominantly Roman Catholic readership in mind. Query for nonfiction. Pays 16¢ a word, on acceptance. E-mail: stanthony@american catholic.org. Web site: www.americancatholic.org.

ST. JOSEPH'S MESSENGER—P.O. Box 288, Jersey City, NJ 07303-0288. Sister Mary Kuiken, Ed. Inspirational articles, 500 to 1,000 words, and fiction, 1,000 to 1,500 words. Verse, 4 to 40 lines. Payment varies, on publication.

SEEK—8121 Hamilton Ave., Cincinnati, OH 45231. Eileen H. Wilmoth, Ed. Articles and fiction, 400 to 1,200 words, on inspirational and controversial topics and timely religious issues. Christian testimonials. Pays 5¢ a word, on acceptance. 6″×9″ SASE for guidelines.

SHARING THE VICTORY—Fellowship of Christian Athletes, 8701 Leeds Rd., Kansas City, MO 64129. David Smale, Man. Ed., Allen Palmieri, Ed. Articles, interviews, and profiles, to 1,500 words, for co-ed Christian athletes and coaches in junior high, high school, college, and pros. Pays from $50, on publication. Query required. E-mail: stv@fca.org. Web site: www.fca.org.

SIGNS OF THE TIMES—P. O. Box 5353, Nampa, ID 83653-5353. Marvin Moore, Ed. Seventh-day Adventists. Articles, 500 to 2,000 words: features on Christians who have performed community services; first-person experiences, to 1,000 words; health, home, marriage, human-interest pieces; inspirational articles. Pays to 20¢ a word, on acceptance. Send 9″×12″ SASE with 3 first-class stamps for sample and guidelines. E-mail: mmoore@pacific press.com.

SOCIAL JUSTICE REVIEW—3835 Westminster Pl., St. Louis, MO 63108-3409. Rev. John H. Miller, C.S.C., Ed. Articles, 2,000 to 3,000 words, on social problems in light of Catholic teaching and current scientific studies. Pays 2¢ a word, on publication.

SPIRITUAL LIFE—2131 Lincoln Rd. N.E., Washington, DC 20002-1199. Edward O'Donnell, O.C.D., Ed. Professional religious journal. Religious essays, 3,000 to 5,000 words, on spirituality in contemporary life. Pays from $50, on acceptance. Guidelines.

STANDARD—6401 The Paseo, Kansas City, MO 64131. Articles and fiction, 300 to 1,200 words; poetry, to 20 lines; fiction with Christian emphasis but not overtly preachy. Pays 3½¢ a word, on acceptance. E-mail: erlead@ nazarene.org or cyourdon@nazarene.org.

TEACHERS INTERACTION—3558 S. Jefferson Ave., St. Louis, MO 63118. Tom Nummela, Ed. Practical, educational, and inspirational articles, 600 to 1,200 words, for Christian teachers and how-to pieces, to 100 words, specifically for volunteer church school teachers. Pays $20 to $100, on publication. Freelance submissions accepted. E-mail: teachersinteraction@cphnet.org.

TEAM NYI MAGAZINE—NYI Ministries, 6401 The Paseo, Kansas City, MO 64131. Editor Quarterly aimed at professional and volunteer Christian youth workers. Lead articles, to 1,500 words; other articles and interviews, to 1,000 words; fillers, to 300 words; all relating to the business of youth ministry. Payment varies. Query via e-mail: TeamNYI@nazarene.org or send query and SASE to above.

THEOLOGY TODAY—Box 29, Princeton, NJ 08542. Patrick D. Miller, Ed. Articles, 1,500 to 3,500 words, on theology, religion, and related social and philosophical issues. Literary criticism. Pays $50 to $200, on publication.

TIKKUN—2107 Van Ness, Ste. 302, San Francisco, CA 94109. Michael Lerner, Ed. "A Bimonthly Jewish Critique of Politics, Culture, and Society." Articles, 2,400 words. "Read a copy to get a sense of what we publish. We are always interested in work pertaining to contemporary culture." Pays in copies. E-mail: magazine@tikkun.org. Web site: www.tikkun.org.

TODAY'S CHRISTIAN WOMAN—465 Gundersen Dr., Carol Stream, IL 60188. Jane Johnson Strud, Man. Ed. Articles, 1,500 to 1,800 words, that are "warm and personal in tone, full of real-life anecdotes" that deal with marriage, parenting, friendship, spiritual life, self, single life, work, and hot issues from an evangelical Christian perspective. Payment varies, on acceptance. Queries required. Guidelines. E-mail: tcwedit@mailcti.com. Web site: www.todays christianwoman.net.

TURNING WHEEL—P.O. Box 4650, Berkeley, CA 94704. Susan Moon, Ed. Quarterly. Articles, poetry, reviews, and artwork. "Magazine is dedicated to Buddhist activism, bringing a Buddhist/spiritual perspective to matters of social and environmental justice." No payment. E-mail: turningwheel@bpf.org. Web site: www.bpf.org.

UNITED SYNAGOGUE REVIEW—155 Fifth Ave., New York, NY 10010. Lois Goldrich, Ed. Articles, 1,000 to 1,200 words, on issues of interest to Conservative Jewish community. Query.

UNITY MAGAZINE—1901 N.W. Blue Pkwy., Unity School of Christianity, Unity Village, MO 64065. Philip White, Ed. Religious and inspirational articles, 1,000 to 1,800 words, on spiritual growth, health and healing, metaphysical, Bible interpretation, and prosperity. Poems. Pays 20¢ a word, on acceptance. E-mail: umag@unityworldhq.org. Web site: www.unityworldhq.org.

VISTA MAGAZINE—6060 Castleway Dr., Indianapolis, IN 46250-0434. Attn: Olivia Seaton, Ed. Articles and adult fiction, on current Christian concerns and issues as well as fundamental issues of holiness and Christian living. Not accepting free lance material at this time.

THE WAR CRY—The Salvation Army, P.O. Box 269, Alexandria, VA 22313. Attn: Man Ed. Inspirational articles, 800 to 1,200 words, addressing modern life and issues. Short fiction, poetry, religious news and trends, Bible study, with emphasis on spiritual discernment and compassionate acts and ministries that correspond to the mission of the Salvation Army. Also short articles on evangelism and devotion, family life, parenting, coping with violence, revival, rehabilitation, and cross-cultural ministries, 350 to 450 words. Color photos. Pays 15¢ to 20¢ a word for articles, $35 to $200 for photos, on acceptance. E-mail: warcry@usa.salvation army.org. Web site: http://publications. salvationarmy.org.

WITH: THE MAGAZINE FOR RADICAL CHRISTIAN YOUTH— 722 Main St., Box 347, Newton, KS 67114. Carol Duerksen, Ed. Fiction, 500 to 2,000 words; nonfiction, 500 to 1,600 words; and poetry, to 50 lines for Christian teenagers. "Wholesome humor always gets a close read." B&W 8x10 photos accepted. Payment is 6¢ a word, on acceptance (4¢ a word for reprints). E-mail: Deliag@gcmc.org.

WOMAN'S TOUCH—1445 Boonville, Springfield, MO 65802-1894. Lillian Sparks, Ed. Darla Knoth, Man. Ed. Articles, 500 to 1,000 words, that provide help and inspiration to Christian women, strengthening family life, and reaching out in witness to others. Submit complete manuscript with SASE. Allow 3 months for response. Payment varies, on publication. Guidelines and editorial calendar. E-mail: womanstouch@ag.org. Web site: www.womans touch.org.

YOUNG SALVATIONIST—The Salvation Army, 615 Slaters Ln., P.O. Box 269, Alexandria, VA 22313. Tim Clark, Man. Ed. Articles, 600 to 1,200 words, that teach the Christian view of everyday living, for teenagers. Short shorts, first-person testimonies, 600 to 800 words. Pays 15¢ a word (10¢ a word for reprints), on acceptance. SASE required. Send 8 1/2 x 11 SASE (3 stamps) for theme list, guidelines, and sample copy. E-mail: ys@usn.salvationarmy.org. Web site: http://publications.salvationarmyusa.org.

YOUR CHURCH—465 Gundersen Dr., Carol Stream, IL 60188. Phyllis Ten Elshof, Ed. Articles, to 1,000 words, about church business administration. Pays about 15¢ a word, on acceptance. Query required. Guidelines. E-mail: yceditor@yourchurch.net. Web site: www.yourchurch.net.

HEALTH

ACCENT ON LIVING—P. O. Box 700, Bloomington, IL 61702. Raymond C. Cheever, Pub. Betty Garee, Ed. Articles, 250 to 800 words, about physically disabled people, including their careers, recreation, sports, self-help devices, and ideas that can make daily routines easier. Good photos a plus. Pays 10¢ a word, on publication. Query. E-mail: acntlvng@aol.com. Web site: www.accentonliving.com.

AMERICAN BABY—Primedia Inc., 249 W. 17th St., New York, NY 10011. Judith Nolte, Ed. Articles, 1,000 to 2,000 words, for new or expectant parents on prenatal and infant care. Personal experience, 900 to 1,200 words (do not submit in diary format). Department pieces, 50 to 350 words, for "Crib Notes" (news and feature topics) and "Medical Update" (health and medicine). No fiction, fantasy pieces, dreamy musings, or poetry. Pays $500 to $1,000 for articles, $100 for departments, on acceptance. Guidelines.

AMERICAN FITNESS—15250 Ventura Blvd., Suite 200, Sherman

Oaks, CA 91403. Peg Jordan, Ed. Articles, 500 to 1,500 words, on exercise, health, trends, research, nutrition, alternative paths, etc. No first person stories. Illustrations, photos.

AMERICAN JOURNAL OF NURSING—345 Hudson St., New York, NY 10014. Santa J. Crisall, Ed. Dir. Articles, 1,500 to 2,000 words, with photos or illustrations, on nursing or disease processes. Query.

AQUARIUS: A SIGN OF THE TIMES—1035 Green St., Roswell, GA 30075. Kathryn Sargent, Ed. Tabloid. Articles, 850 words (or 800 with photo or illustration) on New Age lifestyles and positive thought, holistic health, metaphysics, spirituality, and the environment. No payment. E-mail: aquarius-editor@mindspring.com. Web site: www.aquarius-atlanta.com.

ARTHRITIS TODAY—The Arthritis Foundation, 1330 W. Peachtree St., Atlanta, GA 30309. Cindy McDaniel, Ed. Research, self-help, how-to, general interest, general health, and lifestyle topics, and very few inspirational articles, 750 to 3,000 words, and briefs, 100 to 250 words. "The magazine is written to help people with arthritis live more productive, independent, and pain-free lives." Pays $500 to $2,000 for articles, $75 to $250 for briefs, on acceptance. E-mail: atmail@arthritis.org.

ASTHMA—3 Bridge St., Newton, MA 02158. Rachel Butler, Ed.-in-Chief. Bimonthly. Focus on how to manage asthma. Articles, to 1,200 words, on health and medical news, and human interest stories affecting children, adults, and the elderly. Photographs and drawings are also accepted. Pays on acceptance. Query. E-mail: letters@asthmamagazine.com.

BABY TALK—1325 Ave. of the Americas, New York, NY 10019. Susan Kane, Ed. Articles, 1,000 to 1,500 words, by parents or professionals, on women's health, babies and baby care, etc. No poetry. Pay varies, on acceptance. SASE required.

BETTER HEALTH—1450 Chapel St., New Haven, CT 06511. Cynthia Wolfe Boynton, Pub. Dir. Wellness and prevention magazine published by The Hospital of Saint Raphael in New Haven. Upbeat articles, 2,000 to 2,500 words, that encourage a healthier lifestyle. Articles must contain quotes and narrative from healthcare professionals at Saint Raphael's and other local services. No first-person or personal experience articles. Pays $500, on acceptance. Query with SASE.

CONSCIOUS CHOICE—920 N. Franklin St., Suite 202, Chicago, IL 60610. Sheri Reda, Ed. Monthly. Articles, 1,500 to 2,200 words, "that encourage people to take personal responsibility for their health, attitudes, growth, and contribution to community life." Topics include health, science, business, spirituality, nutrition, and fitness. Pays $75 to $150, on publication.

COPING WITH ALLERGIES & ASTHMA—P.O. Box 682268, Franklin, TN 37068-2268. Attn: Ed. Published six times a year. Provides the "knowledge, hope, and inspiration necessary to help readers learn to live with their conditions in the best ways possible." Seeks original, unsolicited manuscripts and photography. No payment.

COPING WITH CANCER—(formerly *Coping: Living With Cancer.*) P.O. Box 682268, Franklin, TN 37068. Kay Thomas, Ed. Uplifting and practical articles for people living with cancer: medical news, lifestyle issues, and inspiring personal essays. No payment.

CURRENT HEALTH—900 Skokie Blvd., Suite 200, Northbrook, IL

60062-4028. Carole Rubenstein, Ed. Published 8 times a year. Articles, varying lengths, on drug education, nutrition, fitness and exercise, first aid and safety, and environmental awareness. Two editions: *Current Health 1*, for grades 4 to 7, and *Current Health 2*, for grades 7 to 12. Payment varies, on publication. Query with clips and resumé; no unsolicited manuscripts. E-mail: crubenstein @glcomm.com.

DIABETES SELF-MANAGEMENT—150 W. 22nd St., New York, NY 10011. Ingrid Strauch, Managing Ed. Articles, 2,000 to 4,000 words, for people with diabetes who want to know more about controlling and managing it. Up-to-date and authoritative information on nutrition, pharmacology, exercise physiology, technological advances, self-help, and other how-to subjects. "Articles must be useful, instructive, and must have immediate application to the day-to-day life of our readers. We do not publish personal experience, profiles, exposés, or research breakthroughs." Query with one-page rationale, outline, writing samples, and SASE. Pays from $500, on publication. Buys all rights.

FIT PREGNANCY—21100 Erwin St., Woodland Hills, CA 91367-3712. Peg Moline, Ed. Articles, 500 to 2,000 words, on pregnant women's health, sports, and physical fitness. Payment varies, on publication. Query. Web site: www.fitpregnancy.com.

FITNESS—Gruner & Jahr USA Publishing, 375 Lexington Ave., New York, NY 10017. Sarah Mahoney, Ed.-in-Chief. Articles, 500 to 2,000 words, on health, exercise, sports, nutrition, diet, psychological well-being, alternative therapies, and beauty. Average reader is 30 years old. Query required. Pays $1 a word, on acceptance.

FITNESS PLUS—P.O. Box 672111, Bronx, NY 10467. Mathea Levine, Ed. Bimonthly. Articles, 1,000 to 3,000 words, on serious health and fitness training for men. Payment varies, on publication. Queries preferred.

HEALTH PRODUCTS BUSINESS—Cygnus Business Media, Inc., 445 Broad Hollow Rd., Suite 21, Melville, NY 11747. Susan Alberto, Ed. Articles, 900 to 2,700 words, related to the natural health products industry. Photos are welcome. Prefer writers who have credentials in the industry. Please email first. E-mail: susan.alberto@cygnuspub.com.

HERBALGRAM—P.O. Box 144345, Austin, TX 78714-4345. Barbara Johnston, Man. Ed. Quarterly. Articles, 1,500 to 3,000 words, on herb and medicinal plant research, regulatory issues, market conditions, native plant conservation, and other aspects of herbal use. Pays in copies. Query. E-mail: bj@ herbalgram.org.Web site: www.herbalgram.org

HERBS FOR HEALTH—Interweave Press, 201 E. Fourth St., Loveland, Co 80537-5655. Lisa Fleck, Asst. Ed. Bimonthly. Feature articles, 2,000 to 3,000 words; fillers, from 500 to 1,200 words. Publishes helpful, accurate information on the healthful benefits of herbs. Send SASE for guidelines. Pays 33¢ per word, on publication. Web site: www.discoverherbs.com.

IDEA HEALTH & FITNESS SOURCE—6190 Cornerstone Ct. E., Suite 204, San Diego, CA 92121-3773. Ed. Practical articles, 1,000 to 3,000 words, on new exercise programs, business management, nutrition, health, motivation, sports medicine, group-exercise, and one-to-one training techniques. Articles must be geared toward the exercise studio owner or manager, personal trainer, and fitness instruction. No consumer or general health pieces. Payment negotiable, on acceptance. Query preferred. Guidelines.

IDEA PERSONAL TRAINER—6190 Cornerstone Ct. E., Suite 204, San Diego, CA 92121-3773. Michelle Zamora, Asst. Ed. Association publication for personal fitness trainers. Articles on exercise science; program design; profiles of successful trainers; business, legal, and marketing topics; tips for networking with other trainers and with allied medical professionals; client counseling; and training tips. "What's New" column includes industry news, products, and research. Payment varies, on acceptance. Query. E-mail: member@ideafit.com. Web site: www.ideafit.com.

INDEPENDENT LIVING PROVIDER—See *Today's Home Healthcare Provider.*

LET'S LIVE—P.O. Box 74908, Los Angeles, CA 90004. Laura Barnaby, Man. Ed. Articles, 1,500 to 1,800 words, on preventive medicine and nutrition, alternative medicine, diet, vitamins, herbs, exercise. Pays up to $800, depending on length, on publication. Query.

MAMM—Mamm, 349 W. 12th St., New York, NY 10014. Women's monthly focusing on cancer prevention, treatment, and survival. Articles on conventional and alternative treatment and medical news; survivor profiles; investigative features; and essays. Queries preferred. Writer's guidelines available. Payment varies, and is made within 45 days of acceptance. E-mail address: elsieh@mamm.com. Web site: www.mamm.com.

MEDIPHORS—P.O. Box 327, Bloomsburg, PA 17815. Dr. Eugene D. Radice, Ed. "A Literary Journal of the Health Professions." Short stories, essays, and commentary, 4,500 words, related to medicine and health. Poetry, to 30 lines. "We are not a technical journal of science. We do not publish research or review articles, except of a historical nature." Pays in copies. Guidelines. E-mail: mediphors@ptd.net. Web site: www.mediphors.org.

THE NEW PHYSICIAN—American Medical Student Association, 1902 Association Dr., Reston, VA 20191. Rebecca Sernett, Ed. Nine issues a year. Articles, 1,200 to 3,500 words, on social, ethical, and political issues of medical education. Pays $800 to $1,000 per feature-length article.

NUTRITION HEALTH REVIEW—P.O. Box 406, Haverford, PA 19041. Frank Ray Rifkin, Ed. Quarterly tabloid. Articles on medical progress, information relating to nutritional therapy, genetics, psychiatry, behavior therapy, surgery, pharmacology, animal health; vignettes relating to health and nutrition. "Vegetarian-oriented; we do not deal with subjects that favor animal testing, animal foods, cruelty to animals or recipes that contain animal products." Humor, cartoons. Pays on publication. Query.

THE PHOENIX—7152 Unity Ave. N., Brooklyn Ctr., MN 55429. Pat Samples, Ed. Tabloid. Articles, 800 to 1,500 words, on recovery, renewal, and growth. Department pieces for "Bodywise," "Family Skills," or "Personal Story." "Our readers are committed to physical, emotional, mental, and spiritual health and well-being. Read a sample copy to see what we publish." Pays 3¢ to 5¢ a word, on publication. Send SASE for guidelines and calendar.

THE PHYSICIAN AND SPORTSMEDICINE—4530 W. 77th St., Minneapolis, MN 55435. Susan Hawthorne, Exec. Ed. News articles; sports medicine angle necessary. Pays $300 to $500, on acceptance. Query. Guidelines.

PREVENTION—33 E. Minor St., Emmaus, PA 18098. Marty Munson, Man. Ed. Query required. No guidelines available. Limited market.

PSYCHOLOGY TODAY—Sussex Publishing, 49 E. 21st St., 11Fl., New York, NY 10010. Aviva Patz, Exec. Ed. Bimonthly. Articles, 800 to 2,000 words, on timely subjects and news. Pays varying rates, on publication.

RX REMEDY—120 Post Rd. W., Westport, CT 06880. Val Weaver, Ed. Bimonthly. Articles, 600 to 2,500 words, on health and medication issues for readers 50 and over. Regular columns include "The Dispensary" and "The Nutrition Prescription." Query. Pays $1 to $1.25 a word, on acceptance.

TANNING TRENDS—3101 Page Ave., Jackson, MI 49203-2254. Joseph Levy, Ed. Articles on skin care and "smart tanning" for tanning salon owners. "We promote tanning clients responsibly and professionally." Payment varies, on publication. E-mail: joe@smarttan.com. Web site: www.smarttan.com.

TODAY'S HOME HEALTHCARE PROVIDER—(formerly *Independent Living Provider*) 26 Main St., Chatham, NJ 07928-2402. Nancy DelPizzo, Ed. Articles, from 1,200 words, on the home healthcare market. Payment varies, on publication. Send query or resumé.

VEGETARIAN TIMES—4 High Ridge Park, Stamford, CT 06905. Anne Russell, Ed. Dir. Articles, 1,200 to 2,500 words, on vegetarian cooking, nutrition, health and fitness, and profiles of prominent vegetarians. "News Items," to 500 words. "Herbalist" pieces, to 1,800 words, on medicinal uses of herbs. Queries required. Pays $75 to $1,000, on acceptance. Guidelines.

VEGETARIAN VOICE—P.O. Box 72, Dolgeville, NY 13329. Brian Graff, Exec. Ed. Quarterly. Informative, well-researched and/or inspiring articles, 600 to 1,800 words, on health, nutrition, animal rights, the environment, world hunger, etc. Pays in copies. Guidelines. E-mail: navs@telenet.net. Web site: www.navs-online.org.

VIBRANT LIFE—55 W. Oak Ridge Dr., Hagerstown, MD 21740. Attn: Larry Becker, Ed. Features, 600 to 2,000 words, on total health: physical, mental, and spiritual. Upbeat articles on the family and how to live happier and healthier lives, emphasizing practical tips; Christian slant. Pays $80 to $250, on acceptance. E-mail: vibrantlife@rhpa.org. Web site: www.vibrantlife.com.

VIM & VIGOR—1010 E. Missouri Ave., Phoenix, AZ 85014. Sally Clasen, Ed. Positive health and fitness articles, 1,200 to 2,000 words, with accurate medical facts. By assignment only; no queries or unsolicited manuscripts. Writers with feature- or news-writing ability may submit qualifications for assignment. Pays $ .50 per word, on acceptance. Send SASE for guidelines.

THE WALKING MAGAZINE—45 Bromfield St., 8th Fl., Boston, MA 02108. Seth Bauer, Ed. Articles, 1,500 to 2,500 words, on fitness, health, equipment, nutrition, travel and adventure, famous walkers, and other walking-related topics. Shorter pieces, 150 to 800 words, and essays for "Ramblings" page. Color slides welcome. Pays $750 to $1,800 for features, $100 to $500 for department pieces, on acceptance. Guidelines.

YOGA JOURNAL—2054 University Ave., Berkeley, CA 94704. Kathryn Arnold, Ed. Articles, 300 to 6,000 words, on holistic health, meditation, conscious living, spirituality, and yoga. Pays $75 to $3,000, on acceptance. Web site: www.yogajournal.com. E-mail: karnold@yogajournal.com.

YOUR HEALTH—5401 N.W. Broken Sound Blvd., Boca Raton, FL 33487. Susan Gregg, Ed.-in-Chief. Health and medical articles, 1,000 to 2,000 words, for a lay audience. Queries preferred. Pays 20¢ a word, on publication.

EDUCATION

THE ACORN MAGAZINE—8717 Mockingbird Road, Platteville, WI 53818. Attn: Ed. Quarterly. Read by librarians and elementary/preschool teachers. "We're looking for folktales which are interesting. They need dialogue and action. And they have to charm the 4 to 10-year-old child." 200 to 300 words. Payment is two copies of the issue in which you appear.

ACTIVITY RESOURCES—P.O. Box 4875, Hayward, CA 94540. Mary Laycock, Ed. Math educational material only for books geared to mathematics for grades K through 8. Submit complete book manuscript. Royalty. E-mail: info@activityresources.com. Web site: activityresources.com.

AMERICAN SCHOOL & UNIVERSITY—P.O. Box 12901, 9800 Metcalf, Overland Park, KS 66212-2215. Joe Agron, Ed. Articles and case studies, 1,200 to 1,500 words, on design, construction, operation, and management of school and university facilities. Queries preferred. Web site: www.asumag.com.

CABLE IN THE CLASSROOM—214 Lincoln St., #112, Boston, MA 02134. Al Race, Ed. Monthly. Articles, 200 to 1,200 words, for K through 12 teachers and media specialists, on upcoming educational cable television programs and creative ways to use those programs. Pays $100 to $500, on acceptance. Queries required.

CAREERS & THE DISABLED—See *Minority Engineer.*

CHANGE: THE MAGAZINE OF HIGHER LEARNING—1319 18th St. N.W., Washington, DC 20036. Attn: Man. Ed. Columns, 700 to 2,000 words, and in-depth features, 2,500 to 3,500 words, on programs, people, and institutions of higher education. "We can't usually pay for unsolicited articles."

CHRISTIAN EDUCATION JOURNAL—Trinity Evangelical Divinity School, 2065 Half Day Rd., Deerfield, IL 60015. Dr. Perry G. Downs, Ed. Articles, 10 to 25 typed pages, on Christian education topics.

CHRISTIAN EDUCATION LEADERSHIP—P.O. Box 2250, Cleveland, TN 37320-2250. Lance Colkmire, Ed. Quarterly. Articles, 500 to 1,200 words, that "encourage, inform, and inspire those who teach the Bible in the local church." No fiction, poetry, fillers, or artwork. Pays $25 to $55, on acceptance.

THE CLEARING HOUSE—Heldref Publications, 1319 18th St. N.W., Washington, DC 20036. Judy Cusick, Man. Ed. Bimonthly for middle level and high school teachers and administrators. Articles, 2,500 words, related to education: useful teaching practices, research findings, and experiments. Some opinion pieces and satirical articles related to education. Pays in copies.

COMMUNITY COLLEGE WEEK—10520 Warwick Ave., #B-8, Fairfax, VA 27030. Scott Cech, Ed. Biweekly tabloid. Articles, to 1,000 words, related to higher education. Pays 25¢ a word, on publication. Queries preferred. E-mail: scottc@cmabiccw.com. Web site: ccweek.com.

CREATIVE CLASSROOM—149 Fifth Ave., 12th Fl., New York, NY 10010. "Hands-on" magazine for elementary-school teachers. Articles on all curriculum areas, child developmental issues, technology and the Internet in the classroom, professional development, and issues facing elementary teachers. SASE for guidelines and pay rates. E-mail: ccmedit@inch.com. Web site: www.creativeclassroom.com.

EARLY CHILDHOOD NEWS—2 Lower Ragsdale, Suite 125, Monterey, CA 93940. Megan Shaw, Ed. Bimonthly. Fiction, 400 to 600 words; non-fiction, 600 to 2,200 words; and poetry, 400 to 600 words, for child care professionals. "Our purpose is to provide child care professionals with practical information, based upon educational theory, for use inside the classroom." Photographs. Pays $100 to $200, on publication. Query or send complete manuscript.

EQUAL OPPORTUNITY—See *Minority Engineer.*

GIFTED EDUCATION PRESS QUARTERLY—P.O. Box 1586, 10201 Yuma Ct., Manassas, VA 20108. Maurice Fisher, Pub. Articles, to 4,000 words, written by educators, laypersons, and parents of gifted children, on the problems of identifying and teaching gifted children and adolescents. "Interested in incisive analyses of current programs for the gifted and recommendations for improving the education of gifted students. Particularly interested in advocacy for gifted children, biographical sketches of highly gifted individuals, and the problems of teaching humanities, science, ethics, literature, and history to multiple intelligences.. Looking for highly imaginative and knowledgeable writers." Query required. Pays in subscription. Web site: www.giftedpress.com.

THE HISPANIC OUTLOOK IN HIGHER EDUCATION—210 Rt. 4 E., Suite 310, Paramus, NJ 07652. Attn: Man. Ed. Articles, 1,500 to 2,000 words, on the issues, concerns, and potential models for furthering the academic results of Hispanics in higher education. Queries are preferred. Payment varies, on publication. E-mail: sloutlook@aol.com. Web site: www.hispanicoutlook.com.

THE HORN BOOK MAGAZINE—56 Roland St., Suite 200, Boston, MA 02129. Roger Sutton, Ed.-in-Chief. Articles, 600 to 2,800 words, on books for young readers and related subjects for librarians, teachers, parents, etc. Payment varies, on publication. Send complete manuscript. E-mail: info@hbook. com. Web site: www.hbook.com.

INDEPENDENT LIVING PROVIDER—See *Minority Engineer.*

INSTRUCTOR MAGAZINE—Scholastic, Inc., 555 Broadway, New York, NY 10012. Carol Mauro-Noon, Ed. Articles, 300 to 1,500 words, for teachers in grades K through 8. Payment varies, on acceptance.

JOURNAL OF SCHOOL LEADERSHIP—211 Hill Hall, College of Education, Univ. of Missouri-Columbia, Columbia, MO 65211. Dr. Paula M. Short, Ed. Bimonthly. Articulate, accurate, and authoritative articles on educational administration, particularly on translating research and theory into practice. No payment.

LEADERSHIP PUBLISHERS, INC.—P.O. Box 8358, Des Moines, IA 50301-8358. Attn: Dr. Lois F. Roets. Not accepting manuscripts until 2001.

LIBRARY TALK—See *The Book Report.*

MINORITY ENGINEER—1160 E. Jericho Turnpike, Suite 200, Huntington, NY 11743. James Schneider, Ed. Articles, 1,000 to 1,500 words, for college students, on career opportunities; techniques of job hunting, and role-model profiles of professional minority engineers. Interviews. Pays 10¢ a word, on publication. Query. Also publishes: *Equal Opportunity*; *Careers & the Dis-ABLED*, query James Schneider; *Woman Engineer* and *Work Force Diversity*, query Editor Claudia Wheeler. E-mail: info@eop.com. Web site: www.eop.com.

MOMENTUM—National Catholic Educational Assn., 1077 30th St. N.W., Suite 100, Washington, DC 20007-3852. Margaret Bonilla, Ed. Articles,

500 to 1,500 words, on outstanding programs, issues, and research in education. Book reviews. Query or send complete manuscript. No simultaneous submissions. Pays $25 to $75, on publication. E-mail: mbonilla@ncea.org.

PHI DELTA KAPPAN—408 N. Union St., Box 789, Bloomington, IN 47402-0789. Pauline Gough, Ed. Articles, 1,000 to 4,000 words, on educational research, service, and leadership; issues, trends, and policy. Rarely pays for manuscripts. E-mail: kappan@kiva.net. Web site: www.pdkintl.org.

REACHING TODAY'S YOUTH: THE COMMUNITY CIRCLE OF CARING JOURNAL—National Education Service, P.O. Box 8, Bloomington, IN 47402. Alan Blankstein, Sr. Ed. Articles, 1,500 to 2,500 words, that provide an interdisciplinary perspective on positive approaches to reaching and educating youth who are troubled, angry, or disconnected from school, peers, or family. Readers are educators, parents, youth care professionals, residential treatment staff, juvenile justice professionals, police, researchers, youth advocates, child and family psychologists, community members and students. Send SASE for guidelines and current themes.

SCHOLASTIC PARENT & CHILD—555 Broadway, New York, NY 10012-3919. Susan Schneider, Ed. Bimonthly. Articles, 600 to 900 words, on children's education and development. "We are the learning link between home and school." Payment varies, on acceptance. Query; no unsolicited manuscripts. SASE.

THE SCHOOL ADMINISTRATOR—American Assn. of School Administrators, 1801 N. Moore St., Arlington, VA 22209-1813. Jay P. Goldman, Ed. Articles related to school administration (K through 12). "We seek articles written in a journalistic style about school system practices, policies, and programs that have widespread appeal." Pays in copies. Guidelines available on the Web site: www.aasa.org./sa/contents.htm. E-mail address: jgoldman@aasa.org.

SCHOOL ARTS MAGAZINE—50 Portland St., Worcester, MA 01608. Dr. Eldon Katter, Ed. Articles, 800 to 1,000 words, on art education with special application to the classroom: successful and meaningful approaches to teaching art, innovative art projects, uncommon applications of art techniques or equipment, etc. Photos. Pays varying rates, on publication. Guidelines.

SCHOOL SAFETY—National School Safety Ctr., 141 Duesenberg Dr., Suite 11, Westlake Village, CA 91362. Ronald D. Stephens, Exec. Ed. Published 8 times during the school year. Articles, 2,000 to 3,000 words, of use to educators, law enforcers, judges, and legislators on the prevention of drugs, gangs, weapons, bullying, discipline problems, and vandalism; also on-site security and character development as they relate to students and schools. No payment. E-mail: jarnette@nssc1.org. Web site: www.nssc1.org.

TEACHING K-8—40 Richards Ave., Norwalk, CT 06854. Patricia Broderick, Ed. Dir. Articles, 1,000 words on classroom-tested ideas and techniques for teaching students K-8th grade. Pays on publication. No queries.

TEACHING TOLERANCE—The Southern Poverty Law Center, 400 Washington Ave., Montgomery, AL 36104. Jim Carnes, Ed. Semiannual. Articles, teaching ideas, and reviews of other resources available to educators. Payment is $500 to $3,000, on acceptance, for features to 3,000 words; $300 to $800 for essays to 800 words; and $100 to $200, on publication, for "Idea Exchange" articles to 500 words. Query. Web site: www.teachingtolerance.org.

TECH DIRECTIONS—3970 Varsity Drive, Ann Arbor, MI 48108-2223.

Tom Bowden, Man. Ed. Articles, 6 to 10 double-spaced typed pages, for teachers and administrators in industrial, technology, and vocational educational fields, with particular interest in classroom projects, computer uses, and legislative issues. Pays $50 to $150, on publication. Guidelines.

TODAY'S CATHOLIC TEACHER—330 Progress Rd., Dayton, OH 45449. Mary Noschang, Ed. Articles, 600 to 800 words, 1,000 to 1,200 words, and 1,200 to 1,500 words, on education, parent-teacher relationships, innovative teaching, teaching techniques, etc., of use to educators in Catholic schools. Pays $100 to $250, on publication. SASE required. Query. Guidelines. E-mail: mnoschang@peterli.com. Web site: www.catholicteacher.com.

WOMAN ENGINEER—See *Minority Engineer.*

WORK FORCE DIVERSITY—See *Minority Engineer.*

FARMING & AGRICULTURE

AMERICAN BEE JOURNAL—51 N. Second St., Hamilton, IL 62341. Joe M. Graham, Ed. Articles on beekeeping, for professionals. Photos. Pays 75¢ a column inch, extra for photos, on publication.

BEE CULTURE—623 W. Liberty St., Medina, OH 44256. Mr. Kim Flottum, Ed. Basic how-to articles, 500 to 2,000 words, on keeping bees and selling bee products. Slides or B&W prints. Payment varies, on acceptance and on publication. Queries preferred. E-mail address: kim@airoot.com Web site: www.airoot.com/beeculture.

THE BRAHMAN JOURNAL—P.O. Box 220, Eddy, TX 76524-0220. Joe Brockett, Ed. Articles on Brahman cattle only. Photos. Pays $150 to $300, on publication. Queries preferred.

BUCKEYE FARM NEWS—Ohio Farm Bureau Federation, 2 Nationwide Plaza, Box 479, Columbus, OH 43216-0479. Lynn Snyder, Copy Ed. Articles, to 600 words, related to agriculture. Pays on publication. Query. Limited market. E-mail: lnyder@ofbf.org. Web site: www.ofbf.org.

DAIRY GOAT JOURNAL—P.O. Box 10, Lake Mills, WI 53551. Dave Thompson, Ed. Articles, to 1,500 words, on successful dairy goat owners, youths and interesting people associated with dairy goats. "Especially interested in practical husbandry ideas." Photos. Pays $50 to $150, on publication. Query.

FARM AND RANCH LIVING—5400 S. 60th St., Greendale, WI 53129. Nick Pabst, Ed. Articles, 1,000 words, on rural people and situations; nostalgia pieces; profiles of interesting farms and farmers, ranches and ranchers. Pays $10 to $200, on acceptance and on publication. E-mail: editors@farmandranchliving.com. Web site: www.farmandranchliving.com.

FARM INDUSTRY NEWS—7900 International Dr., Minneapolis, MN 55425. Kurt Lawton, Ed. Articles for farmers, on new products, machinery, equipment, chemicals, and seeds. Pays $350 to $500, on acceptance. Query required. Web site: www.homefarm.com.

FARM JOURNAL—1500 Market St., 28th Fl., Philadelphia, PA 19102-2181. Sonja Hillgren, Ed. Articles, 500 to 1,500 words, with photos, on the business of farming. Pays 20¢ to 50¢ a word, on acceptance. Query. Web site: www.farmjournal.com.

FLORIDA GROWER — 1555 Howell Branch Rd., Suite C-204, Winter Park, FL 32789. Michael Allen , Ed. Articles and case histories on Florida citrus and vegetable growers. Pays on publication. Query; buys little free-lance material. E-mail: flgedit@meisternet.com.

THE FURROW—John Deere-North American Agricultural Marketing Center, 11145 Thompson Ave., Lenexa, KS 66219-2302. Karl Kessler, N. American Ed. No unsolicited material.

THE LAND—P.O. Box 3169, Mankato, MN 56002-3169. Kevin Schulz, Ed. Articles on Minnesota agriculture and rural issues. Pays $30 to $60, on acceptance. Query required. E-mail: kschulz@the-land.com. Web site: www.the-land.com.

NATIONAL CATTLEMEN—5420 S. Quebec St., Englewood, CO 80111-1905. Curt Olson, Ed. Articles, 400 to 1,200 words, related to the cattle industry. Payment varies, on publication.

NEW HOLLAND NEWS—New Holland, N.A., Inc., P.O. Box 1895, New Holland, PA 17557-0903. Attn: Ed. Articles, to 1,500 words, with strong color photo support, on agriculture and rural living. Pays on acceptance. Query. Web site: www.newholland.com/na.

OHIO FARMER—117 W. Main St., Lancaster, OH 43130. Tim White, Ed. Technical articles on farming, rural living, etc., in Ohio. Pays $50 per column, on publication.

ONION WORLD—P.O. Box 9036, Yakima, WA 98909-9036. D. Brent Clement, Ed. Production and marketing articles, to 1,500 words (preferred length 1,200 words), for commercial onion growers and shippers. "Research oriented articles are of definite interest. No gardening articles." Pays about $5 per column inch, on publication. Query preferred. E-mail: brent@freshcut.com or brent@onionworld.net. Web site: www.freshcut.com/onion.

PEANUT FARMER—3000 Highwoods Blvd., Suite 300, Raleigh, NC 27604-1029. Mary Evans, Ed. Articles, 500 to 2,000 words, on production and management practices in peanut farming. Pays $100 to $350, on publication. E-mail: mevans@peanutfarmer.com. Web site: www.peanutfarmer.com.

PENNSYLVANIA FARMER—P.O. Box 4475, Gettysburg, PA 17325. John R. Vogel, Ed. Articles on farmers in PA, DE, MD, and WV; timely business-of-farming concepts and successful farm management operations. Short pieces on humorous experiences in farming. Payment varies, on publication.

RURAL HERITAGE—281 Dean Ridge Ln., Gainesboro, TN 38562. Gail Damerow, Ed. How-to and feature articles, 800 to 1,200 words, related to present-day farming and logging with horses, mules, and oxen. Pays 5¢ a word, $10 for photos, on publication. Guidelines. E-mail: editor@ruralheritage.com. Web site: www.ruralheritage.com.

SHEEP! MAGAZINE—P.O. Box 10, Lake Mills, WI 53551. Dave Thompson, Ed. Articles, to 1,500 words, on successful shepherds, woolcrafts, sheep raising, and sheep dogs. "Especially interested in people who raise sheep successfully as a sideline enterprise." Photos. Pays $80 to $150, extra for photos, on publication. Query.

SMALL FARM TODAY—3903 W. Ridge Trail Rd., Clark, MO 65243-9525. Paul Berg, Man. Ed. Agriculture articles, 1,000 to 2,000 words, on preserving and promoting small farming, rural living, and "agripreneurship."

How-to articles on alternative or traditional crops, livestock, and direct marketing. Pays 3 1/2¢ a word, on publication. Query. E-mail: smallfarm@socket.net. Web site: www.smallfarmtoday.com.

SMALL FARMER'S JOURNAL—P.O. Box 1627, Dept. 106, Sisters, OR 97759. Address the Eds. How-tos, humor, practical work horse information, livestock and produce marketing, gardening information, and articles appropriate to the independent family farm. Pays negotiable rates, on publication. Query.

SUCCESSFUL FARMING—1716 Locust St., Des Moines, IA 50309-3023. Gene Johnston, Man. Ed. Articles on farm production, business, and families; also farm personalities, health, leisure, and outdoor topics. Pays varying rates, on acceptance.

THE WESTERN PRODUCER—Box 2500, Saskatoon, Saskatchewan, Canada S7K 2C4. Address News Ed. Articles, to 800 words (prefer under 600 words), on agricultural and rural subjects, preferably with a Canadian slant. Photos. Pays from 23¢ a word; $50 to $100 for color photos, on publication.

THE WREN MAGAZINE—(formerly *Wyoming Rural Electric News*) 340 W. B St., Suite 101, Casper, WY 82601. Kris Wendtland, Ed. Articles, 500 to 900 words, on issues relevant to rural Wyoming. Articles should support personal and economic growth in Wyoming, social development, and education. Wyoming writers given preference. Pays $20 to $140, on publication. E-mail: wren@coffey.com.

WYOMING RURAL ELECTRIC NEWS—See *The Wren Magazine.*

ENVIRONMENT

ALTERNATIVES JOURNAL—Faculty of Environmental Studies, Univ. of Waterloo, Waterloo, Ontario, Canada N2L 3G1. Anicka Quin, Man. Ed. Quarterly. Feature articles, 4,000 words; notes, 200 to 500 words; and reports, 750 to 1,000 words, that focus on Canadian content in areas of environmental thought, policy, and action. No payment. E-mail address: altsed@fes. uwaterloo.ca. Web site: www.fes.uwaterloo.ca/alternatives/

THE AMERICAN FIELD—542 S. Dearborn, Chicago, IL 60605. B.J. Matthys, Man. Ed. Yarns about hunting trips, bird-shooting; articles, to 1,500 words, on dogs and field trials, emphasizing conservation of game resources. Pays varying rates, on acceptance.

AMERICAN FORESTS—910 17th St., Suite 600, Washington, DC 20006. Michelle Robbins, Ed. Looking for skilled science writers for assignments documenting the use, enjoyment, and management of forests. Send clips. E-mail: mrobbins@amfor.org. Web site: www.americanforests.org.

THE AMICUS JOURNAL—Natural Resources Defense Council, 40 W. 20th St., New York, NY 10011. Kathrin Day Lassila, Ed. Quarterly. Articles and book reviews on local, national and international environmental topics. (No fiction, speeches, or product reports accepted.) Pays varying rates, on publication. Query with clips required. E-mail: amicus@nrdc.org. Web site: www. nrdc.org.

ANIMALS—350 S. Huntington Ave., Boston, MA 02130. Paula Abend, Ed. Informative, well-researched articles, to 2,500 words, on animal protection, national and international wildlife, pet care, conservation, and environmental issues that affect animals. No personal accounts or favorite pet stories. Payment is dependent upon amount of research necessary to complete assignment. Payment is made upon acceptance. Query. Web site: www.animalsmagazine.com.

ATLANTIC SALMON JOURNAL—P.O. Box 5200, St. Andrews, N.B., Canada E5B 3S8. Jim Gourlay, Ed. Articles, 1,500 to 3,000 words, related to Atlantic salmon: fishing, conservation, ecology, travel, politics, biology, how-tos, anecdotes. Pays $100 to $400, on publication. E-mail: asfads@nbnet.nb.ca. Web site: www.asf.ca.

AUDUBON—700 Broadway, New York, NY 10003. Lisa Gosselin, Ed. Bimonthly. Articles, 150 to 4,000 words, on conservation and environmental issues, natural history, ecology, and related subjects. Payment varies, on acceptance. Send query with clips and SASE to Ed. Assistant. E-mail: editor@ audubon.org. Web site: www.audubon.org.

THE BEAR DELUXE—P.O. Box 10342., Portland, OR 97296. Tom Webb, Ed. Quarterly. Unique environmental articles, 750 to 3,500 words; essays, 250 to 2,500 words; artist profiles, 750 to 1,500 words; and reviews, 100 to 1,000 words. Fiction, 750 to 4,500 words (2,500 is ideal). Poetry. Pays 5¢ a word, after publication, and subscription. Query for nonfiction. E-mail: bear@ teleport.com. Web site: www.orlo.com.

BIRD WATCHER'S DIGEST—P.O. Box 110, Marietta, OH 45750. William H. Thompson, III, Ed. Articles, 600 to 2,500 words, for bird watchers: first-person accounts; how-tos; pieces on backyard-related topics; profiles of bird species. Pays from $100, on publication. Write for guidelines. Submit complete manuscript with SASE. E-mail: bwd@birdwatchersdigest.com. Web site: www.birdwatchersdigest.com.

BUGLE—Rocky Mountain Elk Foundation, P.O. Box 8249, Missoula, MT 59807-8249. Lee Cromrich, Ed. Asst. Bimonthly. Fiction and nonfiction, 1,500 to 4,000 words, on wildlife conservation, elk ecology and hunting. Department pieces, 1,000 to 3,000 words, for: "Thoughts and Theories"; "Situation Ethics"; and "Women in the Outdoors." Pays 20¢ a word, on acceptance. E-mail: bugle@rmef.org. Web site: www.elkfoundation.org.

CALIFORNIA WILD—(formerly *Pacific Discovery*) California Academy of Sciences, Golden Gate Park, San Francisco, CA 94118-4599. Gordy Slack, Assoc. Ed. Quarterly. Well-researched articles, 1,500 to 3,000 words, on natural history and preservation of the environment. Pays 25¢ a word, on publication. Query. E-mail: calwild@calacademy.org. Web site: www.cal academy.org.

E: THE ENVIRONMENTAL MAGAZINE—Earth Action Network, Inc., P.O. Box 5098, Westport, CT 06881. Jim Motavalli, Ed. Environmental features, 4,000 words, and news for departments: 400 words for "In Brief"; and 1,000 words for "Currents." Pays 20¢ a word, on publication. Query. E-mail: info@emagazine.com. Web site: www.emagazine.com.

FLORIDA WILDLIFE—620 S. Meridian St., Tallahassee, FL 32399-1600. Attn: Ed. Bimonthly of the Florida Fish and Wildlife Conservation Commission. Articles, 800 to 1,200 words, that promote native flora and fauna, hunting, fishing in Florida's waters, outdoor ethics, and conservation of Florida's natural resources. Pays $55 a page, on publication. SASE for "how to submit" memo.

HERBALGRAM—P.O. Box 144345, Austin, TX 78714-4345. Barbara Johnston, Man. Ed. Quarterly. Articles, 1,500 to 3,000 words, on herb and medicinal plant research, regulatory issues, market conditions, native plant conservation, and other aspects of herbal use. Pays in copies. Query. E-mail: bj@herbalgram.org. Web site: www.herbalgram.org.

IN BUSINESS—419 State Ave., Emmaus, PA 18049-3097. Jerome Goldstein, Ed. Bimonthly. Articles, 1,500 words, for environmental entrepreneurs: reports on economically successful businesses that also demonstrate a commitment to the environment, advice on growing a "green" business, family-run businesses, home-based businesses, community ecological development, etc. Pays $100 to $250 for articles; $25 to $75 for department pieces, on publication. Query with clips.

INTERNATIONAL WILDLIFE—National Wildlife Federation, 8925 Leesburg Pike, Vienna, VA 22184. Jonathan Fisher, Ed. Articles, 2,000 words, that make nature, and human use and stewardship of it, understandable and interesting; covers wildlife and related issues outside the U.S. Pays $2,000 for full-length articles, on acceptance. Query with writing samples. SASE for guidelines. E-mail: pubs@nwf.org. web site: www.nwf.com.

MOTHER EARTH NEWS—Sussex Publishers, 49 E. 21st St., 11th Fl., New York, NY 10010. Ed. Bimonthly featuring articles on organic gardening, building projects, herbal or home remedies, alternative energy projects, wild foods, and environment and conservation. "We are dedicated to helping our readers become more self-sufficient, financially independent, and environmentally aware." Photos or diagrams a plus. No fiction. Payment varies, on publication. E-mail: letters@motherearthnews.com. Web site: www.motherearth news.com.

NATIONAL GEOGRAPHIC—1145 17th St. N.W., Washington, DC 20036. William Allen, Ed. First-person, general-interest, heavily illustrated articles on science, natural history, exploration, and geographical regions. Written query required.

NATIONAL PARKS MAGAZINE—1776 Massachusetts Ave. N.W., Washington, DC 20036. Linda Rancourt, Ed.-in-Chief. Articles, 1,500 to 2,000 words, on areas in the National Park System, proposed new areas, threats to parks or park wildlife, new trends in park use, legislative issues, and endangered species of plants or animals relevant to national parks. No fiction, poetry, personal narratives, "My trip to . . . ," or straight travel pieces on individual parks. Articles, 1,500 words, on "low-impact" travel to 4 or 5 national park sites. Pays $400 to $1,000, on acceptance. Query with clips (original slant or news hook is essential to successful query). Guidelines with SASE. E-mail: npmag@ npca.org. Web site: www.npca.org.

NATIONAL WILDLIFE—8925 Leesburg Pike, Vienna, VA 22184. Mark Wexler, Ed. Articles, 1,000 to 2,500 words, on wildlife, conservation, environment; outdoor how-to pieces. Photos. Pays on acceptance. Query. E-mail: pubs@nwf.org. web site: www.nwf.org.

NATURE FRIEND—2727 TR 421, Sugarcreek, OH 44681. Marvin Wengerd, Ed. Monthly. Articles for children that "teach them to be kind to animals, plants, and nature." Also publishes fillers and games. Pays 5¢ per word for nonfiction; $15 for fillers and games. SASE and $4 for guidelines.

NEW HAMPSHIRE WILDLIFE—54 Portsmouth St., Concord, NH

03301. Darrel Covell, Exec. Dir. Bimonthly tabloid. Fiction and nonfiction, 1,700 to 2,000 words. "Dedicated to preserving and protecting hunting, fishing, and trapping and for the conservation of fish and wildlife habitat."

THE NEW YORK STATE CONSERVATIONIST—50 Wolf Rd., Rm. 548, Albany, NY 12233-4502. R.W. Groneman, Ed. "The official magazine of the New York State Department of Environmental Conservation." Bimonthly. Articles, varying lengths, on environmental/conservation programs and policies of New York. Pays $50 to $100 for articles; $15 for photos; and $50 for original artwork, upon publication.

OUTDOOR AMERICA—Izaak Walton League, 707 Conservation Ln., Gaithersburg, MD 20878-2983. Attn: Articles Ed. Quarterly publication of the Izaak Walton League of America. Articles, 1,500 to 3,000 words, on national conservation issues that are of top league priority such as: endangered species, public lands management, and the protection of air and water quality and water resources. Other topics include farm-related issues and wildlife and fisheries management controversies of national interest. Pays 30¢ a word. Query with SASE and clips. E-mail: zachh@iwla.org. Web site: www.iwla.org.

PACIFIC DISCOVERY—See *California Wild.*

SIERRA—85 2nd St., San Francisco, CA 94105. Joan Hamilton, Ed.-in-Chief. Articles, 750 to 2,500 words, on environmental and conservation topics, travel, hiking, backpacking, skiing, rafting, cycling. Photos. Pays from $500 to $4,000, extra for photos, on acceptance. Query with clips. E-mail: sierra.letters @sierraclub.org. Web site: www.sierraclub.org.

SPORTS AFIELD—250 W. 55th St., New York, NY 10019. John Atwood, Ed.-in-Chief. Articles, 500 to 2,000 words, on outdoor sports such as hiking, skiing, kayaking, mountain biking, hunting, fishing, survival, conservation, personal experiences. How-to pieces; humor, fiction. Payment varies, on acceptance.

TEXAS PARKS & WILDLIFE—Fountain Park Plaza, 3000 S. Interstate Hwy. 35, Suite 120, Austin, TX 78704. Susan Ebert, Ed. Articles, 800 to 2,500 words, promoting the conservation and enjoyment of Texas wildlife, parks, waters, and all outdoors. Features on hunting, fishing, birding, camping, and the environment. Photos a plus. Pays to $600, on acceptance; extra for photos. E-mail: magazine@tpwd.state.tx.us. Web site: www.tpwd.state.tx.us.

VIRGINIA WILDLIFE—P.O. Box 11104, Richmond, VA 23230-1104. Attn: Ed. Articles, 500 to 1,200 words, on fishing, hunting, wildlife management, outdoor safety, ethics, etc. All material must have Virginia tie-in and may be accompanied by color photos. Pays from 18¢ a word, extra for photos, on publication. Query. E-mail: lwalker@dgif.state.va.us. Web site: www.dgif. state.va.us.

WHOLE EARTH—1408 Mission Ave., San Rafael, CA 94901. Attn: Ed. Quarterly. Articles and book reviews. "Good article material is often found in passionate personal statements or descriptions of the writer's activities." Pays $40 for reviews; payment varies for articles, on publication.

WILDLIFE CONSERVATION—The Wildlife Conservation Society, Bronx, NY 10460. Nancy Simmons, Sr. Ed. First-person articles, 1,500 to 2,000 words, on "popular" natural history, "based on author's research and experience as opposed to textbook approach." Payment varies, on acceptance. Guidelines. E-mail: nsimmons@wcs.org. Web site: www.wcs.org.

MEDIA & THE ARTS

THE AMERICAN ART JOURNAL—730 Fifth Ave., New York, NY 10019-4105. Jayne A. Kuchna, Ed. Scholarly articles, 2,000 to 10,000 words, on American art of the 17th through the mid-20th centuries. Photos. Pays $200 to $500, on acceptance.

AMERICAN INDIAN ART MAGAZINE—7314 E. Osborn Dr., Scottsdale, AZ 85251. Roanne P. Goldfein, Ed. Detailed articles, 10 to 20 doublespaced pages, on American Indian arts: painting, carving, beadwork, basketry, textiles, ceramics, jewelry, etc. Pays varying rates, on publication. Query.

AMERICAN JOURNALISM REVIEW—1117 Journalism Bldg., University of Maryland, College Park, MD 20742-7111. Rem Rieder, Ed. Articles, 500 to 5,000 words, on print or electronic journalism, ethics, and related issues. Query. Web site: www.ajr.org.

AMERICAN THEATRE—355 Lexington Ave., New York, NY 10017. Jim O'Quinn, Ed. Features, 250 to 2,500 words, on the theater and theaterrelated subjects. Departments include "Profiles," "Books," "Commentary," and "Media". Payment varies, on publication. Query.

AMERICAN VISIONS, THE MAGAZINE OF AFRO-AMERICAN CULTURE—1101 Pennsylvania Ave., NW, Suite 820, Washington, DC 20004. Joanne Harris, Ed. Articles, 1,500 to 2,500 words, and columns, 1,000 words, on African-American culture with a focus on the arts. Pays from $100 to $600, on publication. Query.

ART & ANTIQUES—2100 Powers Ferry Rd., Atlanta, GA 30339. Barbara S. Tapp, Ed. Research pieces, art and antiques in context (interiors), overviews, or personal narratives, 1,500 to 2,000 words, and news items, 250 to 350 words, on art or antiques. Pays 75¢ to $1 a word, on acceptance. Query with resumé and clips.

THE ARTIST'S MAGAZINE—1507 Dana Ave., Cincinnati, OH 45207. Sandra Carpenter, Ed. How-to features, 1,000 to 1,200 words, and department pieces for the working artist. Pays $150 to $350 for articles. Guidelines. Query. E-mail: tamedit@fw.pubs.com. Web site: www.artistsmagazine.com.

BACK STAGE—1515 Broadway, 14th Fl., New York, NY 10036-8901. Sherry Eaker, Ed.-in-Chief. "The Performing Arts Weekly." Service features about learning one's craft, dealing with succeeding in the business; interviews with actors, directors, and playwrights; industry trends. Payment varies, on publication. Queries required; articles on speculation.

BACK STAGE WEST—5055 Wilshire Blvd., 6th Fl., Los Angeles, CA 90036. Robert Kendt, Ed. Weekly. Articles and reviews for actor's trade paper for the West Coast. Query required. Pays 10¢ to 15¢ a word, on publication.

BLUEGRASS UNLIMITED—Box 111, Broad Run, VA 20137-0111. Peter V. Kuykendall, Ed. Articles, to 3,500 words, on bluegrass and traditional country music. Photos. Pays 8¢ to 10¢ a word, extra for photos.

BOMB—594 Broadway, Suite 905, New York, NY 10012. Editor. Quarterly. Articles, varying lengths, on artists, musicians, writers, actors, and directors. Some fiction and poetry. Pays $100, on publication. Send complete manuscript.

CABLE IN THE CLASSROOM—141 Portland St., #8200, Cambridge,

MA 02139-1937. Al Race, Ed. Monthly. Articles, 200 to 1,200 words, for K through 12 teachers and media specialists, on upcoming educational cable television programs and creative ways to use those programs. Pays $100 to $500, on acceptance. Queries required.

THE CHURCH MUSICIAN—See *Church Musician Today.*

CHURCH MUSICIAN TODAY—(formerly *The Church Musician*) 127 Ninth Ave. N., Nashville, TN 37234. Jere V. Adams, Ed. Articles on choral techniques, instrumental groups, worship planning, music administration, directing choirs (all ages), rehearsal planning, music equipment, new technology, drama/pageants and related subjects, hymn studies, book reviews, and music-related fillers. Pays 5½¢ a word for articles on hard copy; 6½¢ per word for articles on diskette, on acceptance.

CINEASTE—200 Park Ave. S., Suite 1601, New York, NY 10003-1503. Attn: Eds. Quarterly. Articles, 2,000 to 3,000 words, on the art and politics of the cinema. "Articles should discuss a film, film genre, a career, a theory, a movement, or related topic, in depth." Interviews with people in filmmaking. Department pieces, 1,000 to 1,500 words. Pays $75 to $100, on publication.

DANCE MAGAZINE—33 W. 60th St., New York, NY 10023. Richard Philp, Ed.-in-Chief. Articles on dancers, companies, history, professional concerns, young dancers, health, and current and upcoming news events. Photos: Query; limited free-lance market.

DANCE TEACHER—(formerly *Dance Teacher Now*) Lifestyle Ventures, 250 W. 57th St., Suite 420, New York, NY 10107. Caitlin Sims, Ed. Articles, 500 to 1,500 words, for professional dance educators, students, and other dance professionals on practical information for the teacher and/or business owner; economic and business issues related to the profession. Profiles of schools, methods, and people who are leaving their mark on dance. Must be thoroughly researched. Photos a plus. Query. Pays $100 to $300. E-mail: csims@lifestyleventures.com. Web site: www.danceteacher.com.

DECORATIVE ARTIST'S WORKBOOK—1507 Dana Ave., Cincinnati, OH 45207. Anne Hevener, Ed. How-to articles, 1,000 to 1,500 words, on decorative painting. "Painting projects only, not crafts." Profiles, 500 words, of up-and-coming painters for "The Artist of the Issue" column. Pays $150 to $300 for features; $100 to $150 for profiles, on acceptance. Query required.

DOUBLETAKE—55 Davis Square, Somerville, MA 02144. Attn: Manuscript Ed. Quarterly. Realistic fiction, narrative poetry, book excerpts, memoirs, essays, and cultural criticism. Color or B&W photo-essays, works in progress, and proposals "in the broadest definition of documentary work. We're looking for new and unexpected insights about the world around us." Payment varies. Guidelines. Query for nonfiction. SASE. Web site: www.doubletakemagazine.org.

DRAMATICS—Educational Theatre Assoc., 2343 Auburn Ave., Cincinnati, OH 45219. Don Corathers, Ed. Articles, interviews, how-tos, 750 to 4,000 words, for high school students of the performing arts with an emphasis on theater practice: acting, directing, playwriting, technical subjects. Prefer articles that "could be used by a better-than-average high school teacher to teach students something about the performing arts." Also publishes plays. Pays $25 to $400 honorarium. Complete manuscripts preferred; graphics and photos accepted. E-mail: dcorathers@etassoc.org.

ELECTRONIC MUSICIAN MAGAZINE—6400 Hollis St., Suite 12,

Emeryville, CA 94608. Patty Hammond, Managing Ed. Monthly. Articles, 1,500 to 3,500 words, on audio recording, live sound engineering, technical applications, and product reviews. Pays $350 to $750, on acceptance. E-mail: emeditorial@intertec.com. Web site: www.emusician.com.

EMMY—5220 Lankershim Blvd., N. Hollywood, CA 91601-2800. Gail Polevoi, Man. Ed. Bimonthly. Articles, 2,000 words, related to the television industry: contemporary issues and trends in broadcast and cable; VIPs, especially those behind the scenes; and new technology. Pays from $900, on publication. "It is easier for newcomers to break in with shorter pieces rather than full-length articles. These items can run 500 to 700 words; pay starts at $250." Query.

THE ENGRAVERS JOURNAL—26 Summit St., P. O. Box 318, Brighton, MI 48116. Rosemary Farrell, Admin. Ed. Articles, varying lengths, on topics related to the engraving industry and small business operations. Pays $75 to $300, on acceptance. Query. E-mail: editor@engraversjournal.com. Web site: www.engraversjournal.com.

ENTERTAINMENT DESIGN—(formerly *Theatrecrafts International*) 32 W. 18th St., New York, NY 10011. Jacqueline Tien, Pub. David Johnson, Ed. Articles, 500 to 2,500 words, on design, technical, and management aspects of theater, opera, dance, television, and film for those in performing arts and the entertainment trade. Pays on acceptance. Query. Web site: www.etecnyc.net.

FILM COMMENT—70 Lincoln Ctr. Plaza, New York, NY 10023-6595. Richard T. Jameson, Ed. Bimonthly. Articles, 1,000 to 5,000 words, on films (new and old, foreign and domestic), as well as performers, writers, cinematographers, studios, national cinemas, genres. Opinion and historical pieces also used. Pays approximately 33¢ a word, on publication.

FILM QUARTERLY—Univ. of California Press Journals, 2120 Berkeley Way, Berkeley, CA 94720. Ann Martin, Ed. Historical, analytical, and critical articles, to 6,000 words; film reviews, book reviews. Guidelines.

GLORY SONGS—127 Ninth Ave. N., Nashville, TN 37234. Jere V. Adams, Ed. For volunteer and part-time music directors and members of church choirs. Very easy music and accompaniments designed specifically for the small church (4 to 6 songs per issue). The Glory Songs kit includes Director's Letter with articles for directors and choir members on leisure reading, music training, worship planning, and choir projects. Pays 5½¢ per word for hard copy; 6½¢ for diskette, on aceptance.

GUITAR PLAYER MAGAZINE—411 Borel Ave., Suite 100, San Mateo, CA 94402. Attn: Lonni Gause, Exec. Ed. Articles, from 200 words, on guitars and related subjects. Pays $100 to $600, on acceptance. Buys all rights.

INDEPENDENT FILM AND VIDEO MONTHLY—304 Hudson St., New York, NY 10013-1015. Patricia Thomson, Ed.-in-Chief. Articles on film, video, and new media. "Technical, practical, legal, and aesthetic coverage of the media arts fields." Pays 10¢ a word, on publication. Query. E-mail: editor@airf.org. Web site: www.airf.org.

INDIA CURRENTS—P.O. Box 21285, San Jose, CA 95151. Vandana Kumar, Managing Ed. Fiction, to 3,000 words, and articles, to 3,000 words, on Indian culture in the United States and Canada. Articles on Indian arts and entertainment. Also music reviews, 800 words; book reviews, 800 words; commentary on national or international events affecting the lives of Indians, 800 words; and travel articles, to 3,000 words. Pays $50 per 1,000 words. E-mail: editor@indiacurrents.com. Web site: www.indiacurrents.com.

INTERNATIONAL MUSICIAN—Paramount Bldg., 1501 Broadway, Suite 600, New York, NY 10036. Attn: Ed. Articles, 1,500 to 2,000 words, for professional musicians. Pays varying rates, on acceptance. Query.

IPI REPORT—132A Neff Annex, School of Journalism, University of Missouri, Columbia, MO 65211. Prof. Stuart Loory, Ed. Quarterly. Short articles on international journalism, press coverage, and free press issues around the world. Queries required. Send SASE for guidelines. (E-mail submissions preferred.) Pay varies, on publication. E-mail: stuartloory@jmail.jour.missouri.edu.

KEYBOARD MAGAZINE—Suite 100, 411 Borel Ave., San Mateo, CA 94402. Marvin Sanders, Ed. Articles, 300 to 5,000 words, on keyboard instruments, MIDI and computer technology, and players. Photos. Pays $200 to $600, on acceptance. Query.

MODERN DRUMMER—12 Old Bridge Rd., Cedar Grove, NJ 07009. Ronald L. Spagnardi, Ed. Articles, 500 to 2,000 words, on drumming: how-tos, interviews. Pays $50 to $500, on publication. E-mail: mdinfo@moderndrummer. com. Web site: www.moderndrummer.com.

NEW ENGLAND ENTERTAINMENT DIGEST—P.O. Box 88, Burlington, MA 01803. Julie Ann Charest, Ed. News and features on the arts and entertainment industry in New England and New York. Pays $15 to $75, on publication, and $5 per print of original photos. E-mail: jacneed@aol.com. Web site: www.jacneed.com.

OPERA NEWS—The Metropolitan Opera Guild, 70 Lincoln Ctr. Plaza, New York, NY 10023-6593. Rudolph S. Ranch, Ed. Articles, 600 to 2,500 words, on all aspects of opera. Payment varies, on publication. Query.

PEI (PHOTO ELECTRONIC IMAGING) MAGAZINE—229 Peachtree St. N.E., Suite 2200, International Tower, Atlanta, GA 30303. Terry Murphy, Exec. Ed. Articles, 1,000 to 3,000 words, on electronic imaging, computer graphics, desktop publishing, pre-press and commercial printing, multimedia, and web design. Material must be directly related to professional imaging trends and techniques. Query required; all articles on assignment only. Payment varies, on publication.

PERFORMANCE—1101 University Dr., Suite 108, Fort Worth, TX 76107. Jane Cohen, Ed.-in-Chief. The leading publication on the touring industry: concert promoters, booking agents, concert venues and clubs, as well as support services, such as lighting, sound, and staging companies.

PETERSEN'S PHOTOGRAPHIC—6420 Wilshire Blvd., Los Angeles, CA 90048-5515. Ron Leach, Ed. Articles and how-to pieces, with photos, on travel, portrait, action, and digital photography, for beginners, advanced amateurs, and professionals. Pays $125 per printed page, on publication.

PLAYBILL—52 Vanderbilt Ave., New York, NY 10017. Judy Samelson, Ed. No unsolicited manuscripts. "Playbill Magazine provides information necessary to the understanding and enjoyment of each Broadway production, certain Lincoln Center and Off-Broadway productions and regional attractions served. In addition to information about the attractions, it features articles by and about theatre personalities, fashion, entertainment, dining, etc." Web site: www.playbill.com.

POPULAR PHOTOGRAPHY—1633 Broadway, New York, NY 10019. Jason Schneider, Ed.-in-Chief. Illustrated how-to articles, 500 to 2,000 words, for serious amateur photographers. Query with outline and photos.

ROLLING STONE—1290 Ave. of the Americas, 2nd Fl., New York, NY 10104. Attn: Ed. Magazine of American music, culture, and politics. No fiction. Query; no unsolicited manuscripts. Rarely accepts free-lance material.

SCULPTURE FORUM—(formerly *Wildlife Art*) P.O. Box 390026, Edina, MN 55439. Robert J. Koenke, Ed. Informative, thought-provoking articles, 500 to 2,500 words, on wildlife and art topics. All media, including wood, bronze, stone, glass, and metal. Many features spotlight individual artists; query with photos or slides of artist's work. Guidelines. Payment varies, on acceptance. Query required. E-mail: publishers@winternet.com. Web site: www.wildlifeartmag.com.

THE SENIOR MUSICIAN—127 Ninth Ave. N., Nashville, TN 37234. Jere V. Adams, Ed. Quarterly music periodical. Easy choir music for senior adult choirs to use in worship, ministry, and recreation. Also includes leisure reading, music training, fellowship suggestions, and choir projects for personal growth. For music directors, pastors, organists, pianists, choir coordinators. Pays 5½¢ a word for hard copy; 6½¢ on diskette, on acceptance.

SOUTHWEST ART—5444 Westheimer, Suite 1440, Houston, TX 77056. Margaret L. Brown, Ed. Articles, 1,200 to 1,800 words, on the artists, art collectors, museum exhibitions, gallery events and dealers, art history, art trends, and Western American art. Particularly interested in representational or figurative arts. Pays from $400, on acceptance. Query with at least 20 slides of artwork.

STAGE DIRECTIONS—SMW Communications, Inc., 250 W. 57th St., Suite 420, New York, NY 10107. Iris Dorbian, Ed. How-to articles, to 2,000 words, on acting, directing, costuming, makeup, lighting, set design and decoration, props, special effects, fundraising, and audience development for readers who are active in all aspects of community, regional, academic, or youth theater. Short pieces, 400 to 500 words, "are a good way to approach us first." Pays 10¢ a word, on publication. Guidelines. E-mail: idorbian@lifestyle ventures.com. Web site: www.stagedirections.com.

STORYTELLING MAGAZINE—116½ W. Main St., Jonesborough, TN 37659. Attn: Eds. Features, 1,000 to 2,500 words, related to the oral tradition. News items, 200 to 400 words, and photos reflecting unusual storytelling events/applications. Query. "Limited free-lance opportunities." Pays in copies. E-mail: nsn@naxs.net. Web site: www.storynet.org.

SURFACE—7 Isadora Duncan Ln., San Francisco, CA 94102. Jeremy Lin, Ed. Dir. Quarterly. Articles, 100 to 3,000 words, including celebrity interviews; reviews of art, music, and fashion. Payment varies, on publication.

TDR (THE DRAMA REVIEW): A JOURNAL OF PERFORMANCE STUDIES—721 Broadway, 6th Fl., New York, NY 10003. Richard Schechner, Ed. Eclectic articles on experimental performance and performance theory; cross-cultural, examining the social, political, historical, and theatrical contexts in which performance happens. Submit query or manuscript with SASE and IBM compatible disk. Pays $100 to $250, on publication.

THEATRECRAFTS INTERNATIONAL—See *Entertainment Design*.

THIRSTY EAR MAGAZINE—P.O. Box 29600, Santa Fe, NM 87592.

Michael Koster, Ed. Bimonthly for music lovers. Short stories, 1,500 to 2,500 words, with music, arts or American culture themes; articles on "non-tuxedo" music; and reviews, 300 to 500 words. Queries are preferred. SASE for writer's guidelines. Submissions to MKoster451@aol.com. E-mail: ThirstyEarMag@yahoo.com.

U.S. ART—220 S. Sixth St., Suite 500, Minneapolis, MN 55402. Sara Gilbert, Ed. Features and artist profiles, 1,200 words, for collectors of limited-edition art prints. Query. Pays $300 to $450, within 30 days of acceptance.

VIDEOMAKER—P.O. Box 4591, Chico, CA 95927. Stephen Muratore, Ed. Authoritative, how-to articles geared to hobbyist and professional video camera/camcorder users: instructionals, editing, desktop video, audio and video production, innovative applications, tools and tips, industry developments, new products, etc. Pays varying rates, on publication. Queries preferred.

WEST ART—P.O. Box 6868, Auburn, CA 95604-6868. Martha Garcia, Ed. Features, 350 to 700 words, on fine arts and crafts. No hobbies. Photos. Pays 50¢ per column inch, on publication. SASE required.

WILDLIFE ART—See *Sculpture Forum.*

HOBBIES, CRAFTS, COLLECTING

ANCESTRY—P.O. Box 990, Orem, UT 84057. Loretto Szucs, Exec. Ed. Jennifer Utley, Managing Ed. Bimonthly for professional family historians and hobbyists who are interested in getting the most out of their research. Articles, 1,500 to 4,000 words, that instruct (how-tos, research techniques, etc.) and inform (new research sources, new collections, etc.). Six hundred word essays (nostalgic, humorous, sentimental) about family history research. No family histories, genealogies, pedigree charts, or queries. Pays $200 to $1,500, on publication. Guidelines.

THE ANTIQUE TRADER PUBLICATIONS—Box 1050, Dubuque, IA 52004. Virginia Hill, Man. Ed. Articles, 1,000 to 2,000 words, on all types of antiques and collectors' items. Photos. Pays from $50 to $250, on publication. Buys perpetual, but non-exclusive rights.

ANTIQUES & AUCTION NEWS—P.O. Box 500, Mount Joy, PA 17552. Denise Sater, Ed. Weekly newspaper. Factual articles, 600 to 1,500 words, on antiques, collectors, collections, and places of historic interest. Photos. Query required. Pays $10 to $35, after publication.

ANTIQUEWEEK—P.O. Box 90, Knightstown, IN 46148. Tom Hoepf, Ed., Central Edition; Connie Swaim, Ed., Eastern Edition. Weekly antique, auction, and collectors' newspaper. Articles, 500 to 2,000 words, on antiques, collectibles, genealogy, auction and antique show reports. Photos. Pays from $40 to $200 for in-depth articles, on publication. Query. Guidelines. E-mail: antiqueweek@aol.com. Web site: www.antiqueweek.com.

AOPA PILOT—421 Aviation Way, Frederick, MD 21701. Thomas B. Haines, Ed. Magazine of the Aircraft Owners and Pilots Assn. Articles, to 2,500 words, with photos, on general aviation for beginning and experienced pilots. Pays to $750. Web site: www.aopa.org.

THE AUCTION EXCHANGE—P.O. Box 57, Plainwell, MI 49080-0057. Attn: Ed. Weekly tabloid. Articles, 500 to 700 words, on auctions, antiques, collectibles, and Michigan history. "We have 10,000 subscribers who collect all sorts of things." Queries preferred. E-mail: auctex@net-link.net.

BECKETT BASEBALL CARD MONTHLY—15850 Dallas Pkwy., Dallas, TX 75248. Mike Payne, Man. Ed. Articles, 500 to 2,000 words, geared to baseball card collecting, with an emphasis on the pleasures of the hobby, but always looking for hardcore market analysis stories. No fiction. Query. Pays $200 to $400, on acceptance. Guidelines.

BECKETT BASKETBALL CARD MONTHLY—15850 Dallas Pkwy., Dallas, TX 75248. Mike McAllister, Man. Ed. Articles, 400 to 1,000 words, on the sports-card hobby, especially basketball card collecting for readers 7 to 70. Query. Pays $100 to $250, on acceptance. Also publishes *Beckett Baseball Card Monthly, Beckett Sports Collectibles & Autographs, Beckett Football Card Monthly, Beckett Hockey Collector,* and *Beckett Racing and Motorsports Monthly.* SASE for guidelines.

BIRD WATCHER'S DIGEST—P.O. Box 110, Marietta, OH 45750. William H. Thompson III, Ed. Articles, 600 to 3,000 words, on bird-watching experiences and expeditions; interesting backyard topics and how-tos. Pays from $50, on publication. Allow 8 weeks for response. E-mail: bwd@birdwatchers digest.com. Web site: www.birdwatchersdigest.com.

BIRDER'S WORLD—P.O. Box 1612, Waukesha, WI 53187-1612. Greg Butcher, Ed. Bimonthly. Articles, 2,200 to 2,400 words, on all aspects of birding, especially on a particular species or the status of an endangered species. Tips on birding, attracting birds, or photographing them. Personal essays, 500 to 1,500 words. Book reviews, to 500 words. Pays $350 to $450 for features, on publication. Query preferred.

BREW YOUR OWN—Battenkill Communications, 5053 Main St., Suite A, Manchester Center, VT 05255. Kathleen James Ring, Ed. Practical how-to articles, 1,000 to 2,500 words, for homebrewers. Pays $50 to $150, on publication. Query. E-mail: byo@byo.com or kath@byo.com. Web site: www. byo.com.

CANADIAN STAMP NEWS—103 Lakeshore Rd., Suite 202, St. Catharines, Ont., Canada L2N 2T6. Virginia St. Denis, Ed. Biweekly. Articles, 1,000 to 2,000 words, on stamp collecting news, rare and unusual stamps, and auction and club reports. Special issues throughout the year; send SASE for guidelines. Photos. Pays from $50 to $85, on publication. E-mail: stamps@trajan.com. Web site: www.trajan.com.

CAR TOY COLLECTIBLES—7950 Deering Ave., Canoga Park, CA 91304-5007. Kevin Boales, Ed. Published 9 times per year. Fun and informative articles on model cars, and automobilia. Focuses on companies and artists that produce cards and accessories. Also, industry news and show/event coverage. Query.

THE CAROUSEL NEWS & TRADER—87 Park Ave. W., Suite 206, Mansfield, OH 44902. Attn: Ed. Features on carousel history and profiles of amusement park operators and carousel carvers of interest to band organ enthusiasts, carousel art collectors, preservationists, amusement park owners, artists, and restorationists. Pays $50 per published page, after publication. Guidelines. E-mail: cnsam@aol.com. Web site: www.carousel.net/trader/.

CHESS LIFE—3054 NYS Rte. 9W, New Windsor, NY 12553-7698. Glenn Petersen, Ed. Articles, 500 to 3,000 words, for members of the U.S.

Chess Federation, on news, profiles, technical aspects of chess. Features on all aspects of chess: history, humor, puzzles, etc. Fiction, 500 to 2,000 words, related to chess. Photos. Pays varying rates, upon publication. Query; limited free-lance market. E-mail: cleditor@uschess.org. Web site: www.uschess.org.

CLASSIC TOY TRAINS—21027 Crossroads Cir., Waukesha, WI 53187. Attn: Ed. Articles, with photos, on toy train layouts and collections. Also toy train manufacturing history and repair/maintenance. Pays $75 per printed page, on acceptance. Query. E-mail: editor@classtrain.com. Web site: www.classtrain.com.

COLLECTOR EDITIONS—170 Fifth Ave., New York, NY 10010. James van Maanen, Ed. Articles, 500 to 1,500 words, on collectibles, mainly contemporary limited-edition figurines, plates, and prints. Pays $150 to $350, within 60 days of acceptance. Query with photos.

COLLECTORS NEWS—P.O. Box 156, Grundy Ctr., IA 50638. Linda Kruger, Ed. Articles, to 1,000 words, on private collections, antiques, and collectibles, especially modern limited-edition collectibles, 20th-century nostalgia, Americana, glass and china, music, furniture, transportation, timepieces, jewelry, farm-related collectibles, and lamps; include quality color or B&W photos. Pays $1.10 per column inch; $25 for front-page color photos, on publication. E-mail: collectors@collectors-news.com. Web site: www.collectors-news.com.

COUNTRY LIVING GARDENER—224 W. 57th St., New York, NY 10019. Lisa W. Quezada, Ed. Bimonthly. Articles on gardens, crafts, decorating ideas, food, entertaining, and travel. Send SASE for guidelines. Payment varies, on publication. E-mail: mgage@hearst.com. Web site: www.countryliving.com.

CRAFTING TRADITIONS—5400 S. 60th St., Greendale, WI 53129. Kathleen Anderson, Ed. All types of craft designs (needlepoint, quilting, woodworking, etc.) with complete instructions and full-size patterns. Pays from $25 to $250, on acceptance, for all rights.

CRAFTS 'N THINGS—2400 Devon, Suite 375, Des Plaines, IL 60018-4618. Nona Piorkowski, Ed. How-to articles on all kinds of crafts projects, with instructions. Send manuscript with instructions and photograph of the finished item. Pays $50 to $250, on acceptance.

CREATIVE QUILTING—450 7th Ave., #1701, New York, NY 10123-1799. Jan Burns, Ed. Bimonthly written for both experienced and novice quilters. Articles should contain detailed instructions and diagrams for making quality quilts. Also, book reviews, articles on quilt exhibitions, and profiles of well-known quilters. Query. Payment varies.

DOLLHOUSE MINIATURES—(formerly *Nutshell News*) 21027 Crossroads Cir., P.O. Box 1612, Waukesha, WI 53187. Kay Melchisedech Olson, Ed. Articles, 1,200 to 1,500 words, for dollhouse-scale miniatures enthusiasts, collectors, craftspeople, and hobbyists. Interested in artisan profiles and how-to projects. "Writers must be knowledgeable about scale miniatures." Color slides or B&W prints required. Payment varies, on acceptance. Query.

DOLLS, THE COLLECTOR'S MAGAZINE—170 Fifth Ave., New York, NY 10010. Nayda Rondon, Ed. Articles, 500 to 1,500 words, for knowledgeable doll collectors; sharply focused with a strong collecting angle, and concrete information (value, identification, restoration, etc.). Include high quality slides or transparencies. Pays $100 to $350, within 30 days of acceptance. Query.

FIBERARTS—50 College St., Asheville, NC 28801. Ann Batchelder, Ed. Published 5 times yearly. Articles, 400 to 2,000 words, on contemporary trends in fiber sculpture, weaving, surface design, quilting, stitchery, papermaking, felting, basketry, and wearable art. Query with photos of subject, outline, and synopsis. Pays varying rates, on publication.

FINE LINES—Box 101447, Pittsburgh, PA 15237. Deborah A. Novak, Ed. Publication of the Historic Needlework Guild. Articles, 500 to 1,500 words, about historic needlework, museums, famous historic needlework, or themes revolving around stitching (samplers, needlework tools, etc.). Pays varying rates, on acceptance. Queries required. E-mail: dnovak3279@aol.com. Web site: www.historicneedlework.com.

FINE WOODWORKING—63 S. Main St., Newtown, CT 06470. Timothy Schreiner, Ed. Bimonthly. Articles on woodworking: basics of tool use, stock preparation and joinery, specialized techniques and finishing, shop-built tools, jigs and fixtures; or any stage of design, construction, finishing and installation of cabinetry and furniture. "We look for high-quality workmanship, thoughtful designs, safe and proper procedures." Departments: "Methods of Work," "Q&A," "Master Class," "Finish Line," "Tools & Materials," and "Notes and Comment." Pays $150 per page, on publication; pays from $10 for short department pieces. Query.

FINESCALE MODELER—P.O. Box 1612, Waukesha, WI 53187. Terry Thompson, Ed. How-to articles for people who make nonoperating scale models of aircraft, automobiles, boats, and figures. Photos and drawings should accompany articles. One-page model-building hints and tips. Pays from $45 per published page, on acceptance. Query preferred.

FRESHWATER AND MARINE AQUARIUM—P.O. Box 487, Sierra Madre, CA 91025. Don Dewey, Ed. "The Magazine Dedicated To The Tropical Fish Enthusiast." How-to articles, varying lengths, on anything related to basic, semi-technical, and technical aspects of freshwater and marine aquariology. Payment is $50 to $350 for features, $50 to $250 for secondary articles, $100 to $200 for columns, and $25 to $75 for fillers. Send for guidelines.

GAMES—P.O. Box 184, Ft. Washington, PA 19034. R. Wayne Schmittberger, Ed.-in-Chief. "The magazine for creative minds at play." Features and short articles on games and playful, offbeat subjects. Visual and verbal puzzles, pop culture quizzes, brainteasers, contests, game reviews. Pays top rates, on publication. Send SASE for guidelines; specify writer's, crosswords, variety puzzles, or brainteasers. E-mail: gamespub@tidalwave.com.

HERITAGE QUEST—A Member of the Sierra Home Family, P.O. Box 329, Bountiful, UT 84011. Leland Meitzler, Ed. Bimonthly. Genealogy how-to articles, 2 to 4 pages; national, international, or regional in scope. Pays $45 to $60 per published page, on publication.

THE HOME SHOP MACHINIST—2779 Aero Park Dr., Box 1810, Traverse City, MI 49685. Joe D. Rice, Ed. How-to articles on precision metalworking and foundry work. Accuracy and attention to detail a must. Pays $40 per published page, extra for photos and illustrations, on publication. Guidelines.

INTERWEAVE KNITS—Interweave Press, 201 E. Fourth St., Loveland,

CO 80537-5655. Melanie Falick, Ed. Quarterly for those who love to knit. "In each issue we present beautifully finished projects accompanied by clear step-by-step instruction." Nonfiction related to knitting; profiles of people who knit. Pays $100 per published page, on publication. Query.

KITPLANES—8745 Aero Dr., Suite 105, San Diego, CA 92123. Dave Martin, Ed. Articles geared to the growing market of aircraft built from kits and plans by home craftsmen, on all aspects of design, construction, and performance, 1,000 to 2,500 words. Pays $70 per page, on publication. E-mail: editorial@kitplanes.com. Web site: www.kitplanes.com.

LEISURE ARTS, THE MAGAZINE—P.O. Box 55595, Little Rock, AR 72215-5595. Anne Van Wagner Childs, Ed. Bimonthly aimed at beginner and expert cross-stitch and knitting enthusiasts. Articles give detailed instructions for projects and designs. Query. Payment varies.

LOST TREASURE—P.O. Box 451589, Grove, OK 74345. Patsy Beyerl, Man. Ed. How-to articles, legends, folklore, and stories of lost treasures. Also publishes *Treasure Cache* (annual): articles on documented treasure caches with sidebar telling how to search for cache highlighted in article. Pays 4¢ a word, $5 for photos, $100 for cover photos. E-mail: managingeditor@lost treasure.com. Web site: www.losttreasure.com.

THE MIDATLANTIC ANTIQUES MAGAZINE—P.O. Box 5040, Monroe, NC 28111. Jennifer Benson, Ed. Articles, 500 to 2,000 words, on antiques, collectibles, and related subjects. "We need show and auction reporters." Queries are preferred. Payment varies, on publication. Please call before writing a story.

MILITARY HISTORY—Primedia History Group, 741 Miller Dr. S.E., Suite D-2, Leesburg, VA 20175. Jon Guttman, Ed. Bimonthly. Features, 4,000 words with 500-word sidebars, on the strategy, tactics, and personalities of military history. Department pieces, 2,000 words, on intrigue, weaponry, and perspectives; book reviews. No fiction. Pays $200 to $400, on publication. Query. SASE for guidelines. E-mail: militaryhistory@thehistorynet.com. Web site: thehistorynet.com.

MINIATURE COLLECTOR—30595 Eight Mile Rd., Livonia, MI 48152-1761. Ruth Keessen, Pub. Articles, 800 to 1,200 words, with photos, on outstanding 1/12-scale (dollhouse) miniatures and the people who make and collect them. Original, illustrated how-to projects for making miniatures. Pays varying rates, within 30 days of acceptance. Query with photos.

MINIATURE QUILTS—See *Traditional Quiltworks.*

MODEL AIRPLANE NEWS—100 E. Ridge Rd., Ridgefield, CT 06877-4623. Larry Marshall, Ed.-in-Chief. Monthly magazine for enthusiasts of radio-controlled model airplanes. Articles include advice from experts in the radio-controlled aviation field, as well as pieces on design and construction of model airplanes, and reviews of new products. Query. Payment varies.

MODEL RAILROADER—21027 Crossroads Cir., P.O. Box 1612, Waukesha, WI 53187. Andy Sperandeo, Ed. Articles on model railroads, with photos of layout and equipment. Pays $90 per printed page, on acceptance. Query. E-mail: mrmag@mrmag.com. Web site: www.modelrailroader.com.

NEW ENGLAND ANTIQUES JOURNAL—4 Church St., Ware, MA 01082. Jamie Mercier, Man. Ed. Well-researched articles, usually by recognized authorities in their field, 2,000 to 5,000 words, on antiques of interest to dealers or collectors; antiques market news, to 500 words; photos required. Pays from $100 to $250, on publication. Query or send manuscript. Reports in 2 to 4 weeks.

NUTSHELL NEWS—See *Dollhouse Miniatures.*

OLD CARS WEEKLY—700 East State St., Iola, WI 54990. Chad Elmore, Ed. Features, to 2,000 words, on the hobby of collectible cars and trucks: restoration, researching, company histories, collector profiles, toys, etc., usually include photos. Pays 3¢ per word and $5 per photo. Query first via regular mail or e-mail: elmorec@krause.com. Web site: www.oldcarsweekly.com.

PETERSEN'S PHOTOGRAPHIC—6420 Wilshire Blvd., Los Angeles, CA 90048. Ron Leach, Ed. How-to articles on all phases of still photography of interest to the amateur and advanced photographer. Pays about $125 per printed page for article accompanied by photos, on publication.

PIECEWORK—Interweave Press, 201 E. 4th St., Loveland, CO 80537. Bimonthly on quilting, knitting, crocheting, embroidery, beadwork, needlepoint, and cross-stitch. Pieces, 1,500 to 2,000 words, on craft history, artist profiles and how-to projects. Photos are welcome. Payment is $100 per printed page, on publication. Send queries or complete manuscripts. Guidelines and theme lists are available on web site: www.interweave.com. E-mail: piecework @interweave.com.

POPULAR MECHANICS—224 W. 57th St., New York, NY 10019. Sarah Deem, Man. Ed. Articles, 300 to 1,500 words, on latest developments in mechanics, industry, science, telecommunications; features on hobbies with a mechanical slant; how-tos on home and shop projects; features on outdoor adventures, boating, and electronics. Photos and sketches a plus. Pays to $1,500; to $500 for short pieces, on acceptance. Buys all rights.

POPULAR WOODWORKING—1507 Dana Ave., Cincinnati, OH 45207. Steve Shanesy, Ed. Project articles, up to 3,000 words; techniques pieces, to 1,500 words, for the "modest production woodworker, small shop owner, wood craftsperson, intermediate hobbyist and woodcarver." Pays $500 to $1,000 for large, complicated projects; $100 to $500 for small projects and other features; pays on acceptance. Query with brief outline and photo of finished project. E-mail: chriss@fwpubs.com. Web site: www.popular woodworking.com.

QUILT MAGAZINE—1115 Broadway, 8th Fl., New York, NY 10010-2803. Jean Eitel, Ed. Quarterly. Traditional quilts, quilting personalities, and various quilting activities. The techniques of articles should appeal to both beginner and expert quilters. Payment varies. Query.

QUILTING TODAY—See *Traditional Quiltworks.*

R/C MODELER MAGAZINE—P.O. Box 487, Sierra Madre, CA 91025. Patricia E. Crews, Ed. "The world's leading publication for the radio control model aircraft enthusiast." How-to articles, varying lengths, on anything related to radio control model aircraft, helicopters, boats, and cars. Payment is $50 to $350 for features; $50 to $250 for secondary articles; and $25 to $75 for fillers. Send for guidelines.

RAILROAD MODEL CRAFTSMAN—P.O. Box 700, Newton, NJ 07860-0700. William C. Schaumburg, Ed. How-to articles on scale model railroading; cars, operation, scenery, etc. Pays on publication. E-mail: bills@ rrmodelcraftsman.com. Web site: www.rrmodelcraftsman.com.

RENAISSANCE MAGAZINE—Phantom Press Publications, 13 Appleton Rd., Nantucket, MA 02554. Kim Guarnaccia, Ed. Feature articles on history, costuming, heraldry, re-enactment, roleplaying, Renaissance faires, interviews, and reviews of medieval and Renaissance books, music, movies, and games. Pays 6¢ a word, on publication.

RESTORATION—P.O. Box 50046, Dept. TW, Tucson, AZ 85703-1046. W.R. Haessner, Ed. Articles, 1,200 to 1,800 words, on restoring and building machines, boats, autos, trucks, planes, trains, buildings, toys, tools, etc. Photos and art required. Pays from $25 per page, on publication. Query.

RUG HOOKING MAGAZINE—Stackpole Magazines, 500 Vaughn St., Harrisburg, PA 17110. Patrice Crowley, Ed. How-to and feature articles on rug hooking for beginners and advanced artists. Payment varies. E-mail: rughook @paonline.com. Web site: www.rughookingonline.com.

SCHOOL MATES—U.S. Chess Federation, 3054 NYS Rt. 9W, New Windsor, NY 12553-7698. Jay Hastings, Publications Dir. Articles and fiction, 250 to 800 words, and short fillers, related to chess for beginning chess players (primarily children, 8 to 15). "Primarily instructive material, but there's room for fun puzzles, cartoons, anecdotes, etc. All chess related. Articles on chess-playing celebrities are always of interest to us." Pays from $20, on publication. Query; limited free-lance market. E-mail: publications@uschess.org. Web site: www.uschess.org.

SEW NEWS—741 Corporate Circle, Suite A, Golden, CO 80401. Linda Turner Griepentrog, Ed. Articles, to 3,000 words, "that teach a specific technique, inspire a reader to try new sewing projects, or inform a reader about an interesting person, company, or project related to sewing, textiles, or fashion." Emphasis is on fashion (not craft) sewing. Pays $25 to $400, on acceptance. Queries required; no unsolicited manuscripts accepted. E-mail: sewnews@sew news.com. Web site: www.sewnews.com.

SPORTS COLLECTORS DIGEST—Krause Publications, 700 E. State St., Iola, WI 54990. Tom Mortenson, Ed. Articles, 750 to 2,000 words, on old baseball card sets and other sports memorabilia and collectibles. Pays $50 to $100, on publication. E-mail: mortensont@krause.com. Web site: www.krause. com/sports.

TEDDY BEAR REVIEW—Collector Communications Corp., 170 Fifth Ave., New York, NY 10010. Eugene Gilligan, Ed. Articles on antique and contemporary teddy bears for makers, collectors, and enthusiasts. Pays $100 to $300, within 30 days of acceptance. Query with photos.

THIRSTY EAR MAGAZINE—P.O. Box 29600, Santa Fe, NM 87592. Michael Koster, Ed. Bimonthly for music lovers. Short stories, 1,500 to 2,500 words, with music, arts or American culture themes; articles on "non-tuxedo" music; and reviews, 300 to 500 words. Queries preferred. SASE for writer's guidelines. Pays $35 for reviews; $75 to $100 for department pieces, 30 days after publication. Submissions to MKoster451@aol.com. E-mail: ThirstyEar Mag@yahoo.com.

THREADS MAGAZINE—Taunton Press, 63 S. Main St., Box 5506, Newtown, CT 06470. Attn: Ed. Bimonthly. Technical pieces on garment construction and embellishment by writers who are expert sewers, quilters, embellishers, and other needle workers. Also covers sewing soft furnishings for home decor. Pays $150 per published page, on publication.

TRADITIONAL QUILTWORKS—Chitra Publications, 2 Public Ave., Montrose, PA 18801. Attn: Ed. Team. Specific, quilt-related how-to articles, 700 to 1,500 words. Patterns, features, and department pieces. Complete manuscripts preferred. Pays $75 per published page, on publication. Also publishes *Quilting Today* and *Miniature Quilts*. E-mail: chitraed@epix.net. Web site: www.quilttownusa.com.

TREASURE CACHE—See *Lost Treasure*.

WEST ART—Box 6868, Auburn, CA 95604-6868. Martha Garcia, Ed. Features, 350 to 700 words, on fine arts and crafts. No hobbies. Photos. Pays 50¢ per column inch, on publication. SASE required.

WESTERN & EASTERN TREASURES—P.O. Box 1598, Mercer Island, WA 98040-1598. Rosemary Anderson, Man. Ed. Illustrated articles, to 1,500 words, on treasure hunting and how-to metal-detecting tips. Pays 2¢ a word, extra for photos, on publication.

WILDFOWL CARVING AND COLLECTING—See *Wildfowl Carving Magazine*.

WILDFOWL CARVING MAGAZINE—(formerly *Wildfowl Carving and Collecting*) Stackpole Magazines, 500 Vaughn St., Harrisburg, PA 17110. Cathy Hart, Ed.-in-Chief. How-to and reference articles, of varying lengths, on bird carving; collecting antique and contemporary carvings. Query. Pays varying rates, on acceptance.

WOODENBOAT MAGAZINE—P.O. Box 78, Brooklin, ME 04616. Matthew Murphy, Ed. How-to and technical articles, 4,000 words, on construction, repair, and maintenance of wooden boats; design, history, and use of wooden boats; and profiles of outstanding wooden boat builders and designers. Pays $200 to $250 per 1,000 words. Query preferred. Web site: www.woodenboat.com.

WOODWORK—42 Digital Dr., Suite 5, Novato, CA 94949. John Lavine, Ed. Bimonthly. Articles for woodworkers on all aspects of woodworking (simple, complex, technical, or aesthetic). Pays $150 to $200 per published page; $35 to $75 for "Techniques," on publication. Queries or outlines (with slides) preferred. E-mail: woodworkmag@aol.com.

YELLOWBACK LIBRARY—P.O. Box 36172, Des Moines, IA 50315. Gil O'Gara, Ed. Articles, 300 to 2,000 words, on boys'/girls' series literature (Hardy Boys, Nancy Drew, Tom Swift, etc.) for collectors, researchers, and dealers. "Especially welcome are interviews with, or articles by, past and present writers of juvenile series fiction." Pays in copies.

YESTERYEAR—P.O. Box 2, Princeton, WI 54968. Michael Jacobi, Ed. Articles on antiques and collectibles for readers in WI, IL, IA, MN, and surrounding states. Photos. Will consider regular columns on collecting or antiques. Pays from $20, on publication. Limited market. E-mail: yesteryear@vbe.com.

ZYMURGY—Box 1679, Boulder, CO 80306-1679. Ray Daniels, Ed. Articles appealing to beer lovers and homebrewers. Pays after publication. Guidelines. Query.

SCIENCE & COMPUTERS

AD ASTRA—National Space Society, 600 Pennsylvania Ave. S.E., #201, Washington, DC 20003-4316. Frank Sietzen, Ed.-in-Chief. Lively, semi-technical features, to 2,000 words, on all aspects of international space exploration. Particularly interested in "Living in Space" articles; commercial space and human space flight technology. Pays $150 to $250, on publication. Query. Guidelines.

AMERICAN HERITAGE OF INVENTION & TECHNOLOGY—60 Fifth Ave., New York, NY 10011. Frederick Allen, Ed. Quarterly. Articles, 2,000 to 5,000 words, on history of technology in America, for the sophisticated general reader. Pays on acceptance. Query. E-mail: it@americanheritage.com. Web site: www.americanheritage.com/i&t.

THE ANNALS OF IMPROBABLE RESEARCH—AIR, P.O. Box 380853, Cambridge, MA 02238. Marc Abrahams, Ed. Science humor, science reports and analysis, one to 4 pages. Brief science-related poetry. B&W photos. "This journal is the place to find the mischievous, funny, iconoclastic side of science." Guidelines. No payment. E-mail: air@improbable.com. Web site: www.improbable.com.

ARCHAEOLOGY—135 William St., New York, NY 10038. Peter A. Young, Ed.-in-Chief. Articles on archaeology by professionals or lay people with a solid knowledge of the field. Pays $500 to $1,000, on acceptance. Query required. E-mail: peter@archaeology.org. Web site: www.archaeology.org.

ASTRONOMY—P.O. Box 1612, Waukesha, WI 53187. Bonnie Gordon, Ed. Dave Eicher, Man. Ed. Articles on astronomy, astrophysics, space programs, recent discoveries. Hobby pieces on equipment and celestial events; short news items. Query with short, detailed article proposal. Pays varying rates, on acceptance.

C/C++ USERS JOURNAL—1601 W. 23rd St., Suite 200, Lawrence, KS 66046-4153. Marc Briand, Editor-in-Chief. Practical, how-to articles, 2,500 words (including up to 250 lines of code) on C/C++ programming. Algorithms, class designs, book reviews, tutorials. No programming "religion." Pay varies, 10¢ to 12¢ a word, on publication. Query. Guidelines.

CLOSING THE GAP—526 Main St., P.O. Box 68, Henderson, MN 56044. Megan Turek, Man. Ed. Bimonthly tabloid. Articles, 700 to 1,500 words, that describe a particular microcomputer product that affects the education, vocation, recreation, mobility, communication, etc., of persons who are handicapped or disabled. Non-product related articles also used. Web site: www.closingthegap.com.

ELECTRONICS NOW—500 Bi-County Blvd., Farmingdale, NY 11735. Carl Laron, Ed. Technical articles, 1,500 to 3,000 words, on all areas related to electronics. Pays $50 to $500 or more, on acceptance.

ENVIRONMENT—1319 18th St. N.W., Washington, DC 20036-1802. Barbara T. Richman, Man. Ed. Analytical articles, 2,500 to 5,000 words, on environmental science and policy issues, especially on a global scale. Detailed queries required. Pays $100 to $300. E-mail: env@heldref.org. Web site: www.heldref.org.

FOCUS—Turnkey Publishing, Inc., P.O. Box 200549, Austin, TX 78720. Geri Farman, Ed. Articles, 700 to 4,000 words, on Data General computers. Photos a plus. Pays to $50, on publication. Query required.

NATURAL HISTORY—American Museum of Natural History, Central Park W. at 79th St., New York, NY 10024. Ellen Goldensohn, Ed.-in-Chief. Informative articles, to 3,000 words, on anthropology and natural sciences.

"Strongly recommend that writers send SASE for guidelines and read our magazine." Pays from $1,000 for features, on acceptance. Query.

NETWORK WORLD—161 Worcester Rd., Framingham, MA 01701-9171. John Gallant, Ed. Articles, to 2,500 words, about applications of communications technology for management level users of data, voice, and video communications systems. Pays varying rates, on acceptance.

POPTRONICS—(formerly *Popular Electronics*) 275-G Marcus Blvd., Hauppauge, NY 11788. Joseph Suda, Man. Ed. Features, 2,000 to 3,500 words, for electronics hobbyists and experimenters. "Our readers are science and electronics oriented, understand computer theory and operation, and like to build electronics projects." Fillers and cartoons. Pays $150 to $500, on acceptance. E-mail: popeditor@gernsback.com. Web site: www.gernsback.com/poptronics.

POPULAR SCIENCE—2 Park Ave., New York, NY 10016. Cecilia Wessner, Ed. Articles, with photos and/or illustrations, on developments in science and technology. Short illustrated articles on new inventions and products; photo-essays, book excerpts. Payment varies, on acceptance.

POPULAR ELECTRONICS—See *Poptronics.*

PUBLISH—Publish Media, LLC., 462 Boston St., Topsfield, Ma 01983. Jennifer Carton, Man. Ed. Features, 1,500 to 2,000 words, and reviews, 400 to 800 words, on all aspects of enterprise communication and publishing technology. Pays according to experience. Payment is 45 days from acceptance.

THE SCIENCES—655 Madison Ave., 16th Fl., New York, NY 10021. Peter G. Brown, Ed. Essays and features, 2,000 to 4,000 words, and book reviews, on all scientific disciplines. Pays honorarium, on publication. Query.

SCIENCEWORLD—Scholastic, Inc., 555 Broadway, New York, NY 10012-3999. Mark Bregman, Ed. Science articles, 750 words, and science news articles, 200 words, on life science, earth science, physical science, environmental science technology, and/or health for readers in grades 7 to 10 (ages 12 to 15). "Articles should include current, exciting science news. Writing should be lively and show an understanding of teens' perspectives and interests." Pays $100 to $125 for news items; $300 to $750 for features. Query with a well-researched proposal, suggested sources, 2 to 3 clips of your work, and SASE (or SASE for guidelines).

SKY & TELESCOPE—Sky Publishing Corp., P.O. Box 9111, Belmont, MA 02178-9111. Bud Sadler, Man. Ed. Articles for amateur and professional astronomers worldwide. Department pieces for "Amateur Astronomers," "Astronomical Computing," "Astro Imaging," "Telescope Plus," "Observer's Log," and "Gallery." Also, 800-word opinion pieces, for "Focal Point." Mention availability of diagrams and other illustrations. Pays 10¢ to 25¢ a word, on publication. Query required.

TECHNOLOGY & LEARNING—Miller Freeman, Inc., 600 Harrison St., San Francisco, CA 94107-1370. Judy Salpeter, Ed. Articles, to 3,000 words, for teachers of grades K through 12, about uses of computers and related technology in the classroom: human-interest and philosophical articles, how-to pieces, software reviews, and hands-on ideas. Payment varies, on acceptance.

TECHNOLOGY REVIEW—MIT, W59–200, Cambridge, MA 02139. John Benditt, Ed. General-interest articles on technology and innovation. Payment varies, on acceptance. Query. E-mail: mitaatr@mit.edu. Web site: www.techreview.com.

YES MAG: CANADA'S SCIENCE MAGAZINE FOR KIDS—4175 Francisco Pl., Victoria, BC, Canada V8N 6H1. Shannon Hunt, Ed. Quarterly. Articles, 250 to 1,200 words, on science and technology topics for children 8 to 14. Topics include do-at-home projects, environmental updates, and profiles on Canadian students or scientists. Query preferred; send for guidelines. Pays 15¢ (Canadian) per word, on publication. E-mail: shannon@yesmag.bc.ca. Web site: www.yesmag.bc.ca.

ANIMALS

ANIMAL PEOPLE—P.O. Box 960, Clinton, WA 98236-0906. Attn: Ed. "News for People Who Care About Animals." Tabloid published 10 times a year. Articles and profiles, "especially of seldom recognized individuals of unique and outstanding positive accomplishment, in any capacity that benefits animals or illustrates the intrinsic value of other species. No atrocity stories, essays on why animals have rights, or material that promotes animal abuse, including hunting, fishing, trapping, and slaughter." No fiction or poetry. Pays honorarium, on acceptance. Query. Web site: www.animalpeoplenews.org. E-mail: anmlpepl@whidbey.com.

ANIMALS—350 S. Huntington Ave., Boston, MA 02130. Paula Abend, Ed. Informative, well-researched articles, to 2,500 words, on animal protection, national and international wildlife, pet care, conservation, and environmental issues that affect animals. No personal accounts or favorite pet stories. Payment is dependent upon amount of research necessary to complete assignment. Payment is made upon acceptance. Query. Web site: www.animalsmagazine.com.

THE ANIMALS' AGENDA—The Animal Rights Network, Inc., P.O. Box 25881, Baltimore, MD 21224. Kristen Rosenberg, Man. Ed. Bimonthly. Features, to 2,500 words; news briefs, to 100 words; true stories, to 400 words; profiles, to 400 words; investigations, to 1,200 words; reviews, to 800 words; and commentaries, to 700 words. No unsolicited manuscripts. Query. E-mail: office@animalsagenda.org. Web site: www.animalsagenda.org.

BIRDS AND BLOOMS—5400 S. 60th St., Greendale, WI 53129. Jeff Nowak, Ed. Articles, 200 to 1,000 words, on backyard experiences, primarily concerning birding or gardening. Preferably written in the first person, conversational style, and short fillers. No rescue or captive bird stories, please. Queries not necessary. Payment varies, on publication. Web site: www.birdsandblooms.com.

CATS—260 Madison Ave., 8th Fl., New York, NY 10016. Jane W. Reilly, Ed. Monthly. Articles, 1,200 to 3,200 words, on the health and welfare of cats. Photos. Pays $50 to $500, on acceptance. Query. E-mail: info@catsmag.com. Web site: www.catsmag.com.

DAIRY GOAT JOURNAL—P.O. Box 10, Lake Mills, WI 53551. Dave Thompson, Ed. Articles, to 1,500 words, on successful dairy goat owners, youths and interesting people associated with dairy goats. "Especially interested in practical husbandry ideas." Photos. Pays $50 to $150, on publication. Query.

DOG FANCY—P.O. Box 6050, Mission Viejo, CA 92690-6050. Steven Biller, Man. Ed. Monthly. Articles, 850 to 1,500 words, on training, health, grooming, behavior, activities, and general pet care for both dog owners and breeders. Pays $200 to $500.

DOG WORLD—Primedia Special Interest Publications, 500 N. Dearborn Ave., Suite 1100, Chicago, IL 60610. Donna Marcel, Ed. Monthly. Articles, 3,000 to 5,000 words, that entertain and educate. Topics include healthcare, training, nutrition, grooming, breeding, and information about shows. Payment varies. Query.

EQUUS—Primedia Inc., 656 Quince Orchard Rd., Suite 600, Gaithersburg, MD 20878. Laurie Prinz, Ed. Articles, 1,000 to 3,000 words, on all breeds of horses, covering their health and care as well as the latest advances in equine medicine and research. "Attempt to speak as one horseperson to another." Pays $100 to $400, on publication.

THE FLORIDA HORSE—P.O. Box 2106, Ocala, FL 34478. Dan Mearns, Ed. Articles, 1,500 words, on Florida thoroughbred breeding and racing. Also veterinary articles, financial articles, and articles of general interest to horse owners and breeders. Pays $200 to $300, on publication.

GOOD DOG!—P.O. Box 10069, Austin, TX 78766-1069. Judi Becker, Ed. Bimonthly. "The Consumer Magazine for Dog Owners." Articles, one to two pages, that are informative and fun to read. No fiction. No material "written" by the dog. Small payment, on publication. E-mail: judi@gooddogmagazine.com. Web site: www.gooddogmagazine.com.

HORSE & RIDER—1597 Cole Blvd., Suite 350, Golden, CO 80401. Kathy Kadash-Swan, Ed. Articles, 500 to 3,000 words, with photos, on western training and general horse care: feeding, health, grooming, etc. Pays varying rates, on acceptance. Guidelines.

HORSE ILLUSTRATED—P.O. Box 6050, Mission Viejo, CA 92690. Moira C. Harris, Ed. Articles, 1,500 to 2,000 words, on all aspects of owning and caring for horses. Photos. Pays $300 to $400, on publication. Query. Web site: www.animalnetwork.com/horses. E-mail: horseillustrated@fancypubs.com.

HORSEMEN'S YANKEE PEDLAR—83 Leicester St., N. Oxford, MA 01537. Kelley R. Small, Pub. News and feature-length articles, about horses and horsemen in the Northeast. Photos. Pays $2 per published inch, on publication. Query. E-mail: info@pedlar.com. Web site: www.pedlar.com.

I LOVE CATS—450 7th Ave., Suite 1701, New York, NY 10123. Lisa Allmendinger, Ed. Fiction, preferably 500 to 700 words, about cats. Articles, to 1,000 words. No poetry, puzzles, or humor. "Read the magazine, then request guidelines with SASE." Pays $40 to $250; $20 to $25 for fillers, on publication. E-mail: yankee@izzy.net. Web site: www.iluvcats.com.

LLAMAS—P.O. Box 250, Jackson, CA 95642. Cheryl Dal Porto, Ed. "The International Camelid Journal," published 5 times yearly. Articles, 300 to 3,000 words, of interest to llama and alpaca owners. Pays $25 to $300, extra for photos, on publication. Query.

MUSHING—P.O. Box 149, Ester, AK 99725-0149. Todd Hoener, Pub. How-tos, innovations, history, profiles, interviews, and features related to sled dogs, 1,200 to 2,000 words, and department pieces, 500 to 1,000 words, for competitive and recreational dog drivers and skijorers. International audience. Photos. Pays $20 to $250, on publication. Send SASE for guidelines. E-mail: editor@mushing.com. Web site: www.mushing.com.

PERFORMANCE HORSE—2895 Chad Dr., Eugene, OR 97408. Cheryl Magoteaux, Ed. Training articles on cutting, reining, and cow horse competition, 1,500 to 2,500 words; profiles, 2,000-word range, that feature a rider, trainer, horse, or event that inspires readers; round-up articles; and interview articles. All articles should include high quality photos. Query with SASE for guidelines. Payment varies from $275 to $550, on publication. E-mail: cherylmagoteaux@performancehorse.com.

PETLIFE MAGAZINE—3451 Boston Ave., Ft. Worth, TX 76102. Allison Fisher, Ed. Bimonthly. How-to pieces and human interest features, 500 to 1,500 words, for pet owners and pet lovers. No first-person pieces. Pays $150 to $300, on acceptance. Web site: www.petlifeweb.com.

PRACTICAL HORSEMAN—Box 589, Unionville, PA 19375. Mandy Lorraine, Ed. How-to articles conveying leading experts' advice on English riding, training, and horse care. Payment varies, on acceptance. Query with clips. E-mail: Prachorse@aol.com.

THE RETRIEVER JOURNAL—Wildwood Press, P.O. Box 968, Traverse City, MI 49685. Steve Smith, Ed. Articles, 1,500 to 2,200 words, on a wide variety of topics of interest to retriever owners and breeders. Pays $250 and up. Query.

SHEEP! MAGAZINE—P.O. Box 10, Lake Mills, WI 53551. Dave Thompson, Ed. Articles, to 1,500 words, on successful shepherds, woolcrafts, sheep raising, and sheep dogs. "Especially interested in people who raise sheep successfully as a sideline enterprise." Photos. Pays $15 to $150, extra for photos, on acceptance. Query.

THE WESTERN HORSEMAN—P.O. Box 7980, Colorado Springs, CO 80933-7980. Pat Close, Ed. Articles, 1,500 to 2,500 words, with photos, on care and training of horses; farm, ranch, and stable management; health care and veterinary medicine. Pays to $800, on acceptance.

WILDLIFE CONSERVATION—The Wildlife Conservation Society, Bronx, NY 10460. Nancy Simmons, Sr. Ed. Articles, 1,500 to 2,000 words, that "probe conservation controversies to search for answers and help save threatened species." Payment varies, on acceptance. Guidelines. E-mail: nsimmons @wcs.org. Web site: www.wcs.org.

YOUNG RIDER—Box 8237, Lexington, KY 40533. Lesley Ward, Ed. Bimonthly. 1,200 word stories about horses and children. No overly sentimental stories, or stories with "goody two-shoes" characters. Photos. Query or send manuscript. Pays $120, on publication. Web site: www.animalnetwork.com.

TRUE CRIME

DETECTIVE CASES—See *Globe Communications Corp.*

DETECTIVE DRAGNET—See *Globe Communications Corp.*

DETECTIVE FILES—See *Globe Communications Corp.*

GLOBE COMMUNICATIONS CORP.—1350 Sherbrooke St. W., Suite 600, Montreal, Quebec, Canada H3G 2T4. Dominick A. Merle, Ed. Factual accounts, 3,500 to 6,000 words, of "sensational crimes, preferably sex crimes, either pre-trial or after conviction." All articles will be considered for *Startling Detective, True Police Cases, Detective Files, Headquarters Detective, Detective Dragnet,* and *Detective Cases.* Query with pertinent information, including dates, site, names, etc. Pays $250 to $350, on acceptance; buys all rights.

HEADQUARTERS DETECTIVE—See *Globe Communications Corp.*

P.I. MAGAZINE: AMERICA'S PRIVATE INVESTIGATION JOUR-NAL—755 Bronx Ave., Toledo, OH 43609. Bob Mackowiak, Ed. Profiles of professional investigators containing true accounts of their most difficult cases. Pays $75 to $100, plus copies, on publication. E-mail: pimag1@aol.com. Web site: www.pimag.com.

STARTLING DETECTIVE—See *Globe Communications Corp.*

TRUE POLICE CASES—See *Globe Communications Corp.*

MILITARY

AIR COMBAT—7950 Deering Ave., Canoga Park, CA 91304-5007. Michael O'Leary, Ed. Bimonthly. Articles on the latest warplanes and the men who fly them, recent air battles, and America's aerial involvement in Vietnam. Send for complete guidelines.

AIR FORCE TIMES—See *Times News Service.*

AMERICA'S CIVIL WAR—Primedia History Group, 741 Miller Dr. S.E., Suite D-2, Leesburg, VA 20175. Roy Morris, Jr., Ed. Articles, 2,000 to 4,000 words, on the strategy, tactics, personalities, arms and equipment of the Civil War. Department pieces, 2,000 words. Query with illustration ideas. Pays from $150 to $300, on publication. Guidelines. SASE.

ARMOR MAGAZINE—4401 Vine Grove Rd., Fort Knox, KY 40121-2103. Terry Blakely, Ed.-in-Chief. Bimonthly that focuses on the research and development aspects of military history and armaments. Covers tactical benefits and strategies, logistics, and related military topics. SASE for guidelines.

ARMY MAGAZINE—Box 1560, Arlington, VA 22210-0860. Mary B. French, Ed.-in-Chief. Features, 1,000 to 1,500 words, on military subjects. Essays, humor, history (especially World War II), news reports, first-person anecdotes. Pays 12¢ to 18¢ a word, $25 to $50 for anecdotes, on publication. Guidelines. E-mail: armymag@ausa.org. Web site: www.ausa.org.

ARMY TIMES—See *Times News Service.*

COAST GUARD—Commandant (G-1PA-1),U.S. Coast Guard, 2100 2nd St. S.W., Washington, DC 20593-0001. Veronica Cady, Ed. Articles on maritime topics, including search and rescue, law enforcement, maritime safety, protection of the marine environment, and related topics. Photos a plus. Pays in copies.

LEATHERNECK—Box 1775, Quantico, VA 22134-0776. William V. H. White, Ed. Articles, to 3,000 words, with photos, on U.S. Marines. Pays $50 per printed page, on acceptance. Query.

MARINE CORPS GAZETTE—Box 1775, Quantico, VA 22134. Col. John E. Greenwood, Ed. Military articles, 500 to 2,000 words; features, 2,500 to 5,000 words; book reviews, 300 to 750 words. "Our magazine serves primarily as a forum for active duty officers to exchange views on professional, Marine Corps-related topics. Opportunity for 'outside' writers is limited." Queries preferred. E-mail: gazette@mca-marines.org. Web site: www.mca-marines.org.

MILITARY—2122 28th St., Sacramento, CA 95818. Lt. Col. Michael Mark, Ed. Articles, 600 to 2,500 words, on firsthand experience in military service: World War II, Korea, Vietnam, and all current services. "Our magazine is about military history by the people who served. They are the best historians." No payment. Accepts articles from subscribers. E-mail: military@ns.net. Web site: milmag.com.

MILITARY HISTORY—Primedia History Group, 741 Miller Dr. S.E., Suite D-2, Leesburg, VA 20175. Jon Guttman, Ed. Bimonthly. Features, 4,000 words with 500-word sidebars, on strategy and tactics of military history. Department pieces, 2,000 words, on intrigue, personality, weaponry, perspectives, and travel. Pays $200 to $400, on publication. Query with illustration ideas. Guidelines. SASE. E-mail: militaryhistory@thehistorynet.com. Web site: www.thehistorynet.com.

NATIONAL GUARD—One Massachusetts Ave. N.W., Washington, DC 20001-1431. John Goheen, Man. Ed. Articles on national defense. Payment varies, on publication.

NAVAL AVIATION NEWS—1231 10th St., S.E., Suite 1000, Washington, DC 20374-5059. Cdr. Jim Carlton, Ed. Bimonthly. Articles on Naval aviation history, technology, and news. No payment. E-mail: nanews@nhc.navy.mil. Web site: www.history.navy.mil.

NAVY TIMES—See *Times News Service.*

OFF DUTY MAGAZINE—3505 Cadillac Ave., Suite 0-105, Costa Mesa, CA 92626. Tom Graves, Man. Ed. Travel articles, 1,800 to 2,000 words, for active-duty military Americans (age 20 to 40) and their families worldwide. Must have wide scope; no out-of-the-way places. Military angle essential. Photos. Pays from 20¢ a word, extra for photos, on acceptance. Query required. Guidelines. Limited market.

THE RETIRED OFFICER MAGAZINE—201 N. Washington St., Alexandria, VA 22314. Attn: Manuscripts Ed. Articles, to 2,000 words, of interest to uniformed services retirees and their families. Current military/political affairs, military history, health, money, military family lifestyles, travel, and general interest. Photos a plus. Pays to $1,350, on acceptance. Queries required; no unsolicited manuscripts. Guidelines available on web site: www.troa.org. E-mail: editor@troa.org.

TIMES NEWS SERVICE—Army Times Publishing Co., Springfield, VA 22159. Features Ed. Articles on food, relationships, parenting, education, retirement, health and fitness, sports, community, personal finance, and personal appearance of interest to military service members and their families for "Lifelines" newspaper section. Also profiles and articles about military life, its problems, and how to handle them. Features, 1,000 words; short features, 500 to 800 words; and shorts to 500 words. Query required; send for guidelines. Pays $200 to $350 for features, on acceptance.

VFW MAGAZINE—406 W. 34th St., Kansas City, MO 64111. Richard K. Kolb, Ed. Articles, 1,000 words, related to current foreign policy and defense, American armed forces abroad, and international events affecting U.S. national security. Also, up-to-date articles on veteran concerns and issues affecting veterans. Pays to $500 on acceptance, unless specially commissioned. Query. Guidelines. E-mail: patbrown@vfw.org. Web site: www.vfw.org.

VIETNAM—Primedia History Group, 741 Miller Dr. S.E., Suite D-2, Leesburg, VA 20175. Col. Harry G. Summers, Jr., Ed. Articles, 2,000 to 4,000 words, on the strategy, tactics, personalities, arms, and equipment of the Vietnam War. Pays from $150 to $300, on publication. Query with illustration ideas. Guidelines. SASE.

WORLD WAR II—Primedia History Group, 741 Miller Dr. S.E., Suite D-2, Leesburg, VA 20175. Michael Haskew, Ed. Articles, 4,000 words, on the strategy, tactics, personalities, arms, and equipment of World War II. Department pieces, 2,000 words. Pays from $100 to $200, on publication. Query with illustration ideas. Guidelines. SASE.

HISTORY

ALABAMA HERITAGE—The Univ. of Alabama, Box 870342, Tuscaloosa, AL 35487-0342. Suzanne Wolfe, Ed. Quarterly. Articles, to 5,000 words, on local, state, and regional history: art, literature, language, archaeology, music, religion, architecture, and natural history. Pays an honorarium, on publication, plus 10 copies. Query, mentioning availability of photos and illustrations. Guidelines.

AMERICAN HERITAGE—60 Fifth Ave., New York, NY 10011. Richard F. Snow, Ed. Articles, 750 to 5,000 words, on U.S. history and background of American life and culture from the beginning to recent times. No fiction. Pays from $300 to $1,500, on acceptance. Query. Web site: www.american heritage.com.

AMERICAN HERITAGE OF INVENTION & TECHNOLOGY—60 Fifth Ave., New York, NY 10011. Frederick Allen, Ed. Quarterly. Articles, 2,000 to 5,000 words, on history of technology in America, for the sophisticated general reader. Query. Pays on acceptance. E-mail: it@americanheritage.com. Web site: www.americanheritage.com/i&t

AMERICAN HISTORY—6405 Flank Dr., Harrisburg, PA 17112. Attn: Tom Huntington. Articles, 3,000 to 5,000 words, soundly researched. Style should be popular, not scholarly, with a good focus and strong anecdotal material. No travelogues, fiction, or puzzles. Pays $300 to $650, on acceptance. Query. No unsolicited manuscripts.

AMERICAN JEWISH HISTORY—American Jewish Historical Society, 2 Thornton Rd., Waltham, MA 02154. Dr. Marc Lee Raphael, Ed. Articles, 25 to 35 typed pages, on American Jewish history. Queries preferred. No payment.

AMERICAN LEGACY—60 Fifth Ave., New York, NY 10011. Audrey Peterson, Ed. Quarterly that celebrates African-American history and culture. Articles, to 3,000 words, on the people and events that have shaped history. Queries preferred; guidelines available. Payment varies, on acceptance. E-mail: amlegacy@americanheritage.com. Web site: www.americanheritage. com/amlegacy.

AMERICA'S CIVIL WAR—Primedia History Group, 741 Miller Dr. S.E., Suite D-2, Leesburg, VA 20175-8920. Roy Morris, Jr., Ed. Articles, 3,500 to 4,000 words, on the strategy, tactics, personalities, arms and equipment of the Civil War. Department pieces, 2,000 words. Query with illustration ideas. SASE for guidelines. Pays from $150 to $300, on publication. Web site: www. thehistorynet.com.

ANCESTRY—P.O. Box 990, Orem, UT 84057. Jennifer Utley, Man. Ed. Bimonthly for professional family historians and hobbyists who are interested in getting the most out of their research. Articles, 1,500 to 3,000 words, that instruct (how-tos, research techniques, etc.) and inform (new research sources, new collections, etc.). Six hundred word essays (nostalgic, humorous, sentimental) about family history research. No family histories, genealogies, pedigree charts, or queries. Pays $200 to $1,500, on publication. Guidelines.

AVIATION HISTORY—Primedia History Group, 741 Miller Dr. S.E., Suite D-2, Leesburg, VA 20175-8920. Arthur Sanfelici, Ed. Bimonthly. Articles, 3,500 to 4,000 words with 500-word sidebars and excellent illustrations, on aeronautical history. Department pieces, 2,000 words. Pays $150 to $300, on publication. Query; SASE for guidelines. Web site: www.thehistorynet.com.

THE BEAVER—167 Lombard Ave., #478, Winnipeg, Manitoba, Canada R3B 0T6. A. Greenberg, Ed. Articles, 500 to 3,000 words, on Canadian history, "written to appeal to general readers." Payment varies, on publication. Queries preferred. Web site: www.historysociety.ca.

CAROLOGUE—South Carolina Historical Society, 100 Meeting St., Charleston, SC 29401-2299. Peter A. Rerig, Ed. General-interest articles, to 10 pages, on South Carolina history. Queries preferred. Pays in copies.

CHICAGO HISTORY—Clark St. at North Ave., Chicago, IL 60614. Rosemary Adams, Ed. Articles, to 4,500 words, on political, social, and cultural history of Chicago. Pays to $250, on publication. Query.

CIVIL WAR TIMES—6405 Flank Dr., Harrisburg, PA 17112. James Kushlan, Ed. Articles, 2,500 to 3,000 words, on the Civil War. "Accurate, annotated stories with strong narrative relying heavily on primary sources and the words of eyewitnesses. We prefer gripping, top-notch accounts of battles in the Eastern Theater of the war, eyewitness accounts (memoirs, diaries, letters), and common soldier photos." SASE for guidelines. Pays $400 to $650 for features, on acceptance.

EARLY AMERICAN HOMES—6405 Flank Dr., Harrisburg, PA 17112. Mimi Handler, Ed. Articles, 1,000 to 3,000 words, on early American life: arts, crafts, furnishings, history, and architecture before 1850. Pays $50 to $500, on acceptance. Query.

EIGHTEENTH-CENTURY STUDIES—Dept. of French and Italian, Kresge Hall 152, Northwestern Univ., Evanston, IL 60208-2204. Bernadette Fort, Ed. Quarterly. Articles, to 7,500 words, on all aspects of the eighteenth century, especially those that are interdisciplinary or that are of general interest to scholars working in other disciplines. Blind submission policy: Submit 2 copies of manuscript; author's name and address should appear only on separate title page. No payment.

GOLDENSEAL—The Cultural Ctr., 1900 Kanawha Blvd. E., Charleston, WV 25305-0300. John Lilly, Ed. Features, 3,000 words, and shorter articles, 1,000 words, on traditional West Virginia culture and history. Oral histories, old and new B&W photos, research articles. Pays 10¢ a word, on publication. Guidelines. Web site: www.wvculture.org/goldenseal.

GOOD OLD DAYS—306 E. Parr Rd., Berne, IN 46711. Ken Tate, Ed. True stories (no fiction), 500 to 1,200 words, that took place between 1900 and 1955. Departments include: "Good Old Days on Wheels," about period autos, planes, trolleys, and other transportation; "Good Old Days in the Kitchen," favorite foods, appliances, recipes; "Home Remedies," hometown doctors, herbs and poultices, harrowing kitchen table operations, etc. Pays $15 to $75, on publication.

THE HIGHLANDER—560 Green Bay Rd., Suite 204, Winnetka, IL 60093. Sharon Kennedy Ray, Ed. Bimonthly. Articles, 1,300 to 2,200 words, related to Scottish history. "We do not use any articles on modern Scotland or current problems in Scotland." Pays $100 to $150, on acceptance. Photos must accompany manuscripts. E-mail: sray5617@aol.com.

JOURNAL OF THE WEST—1531 Yuma, Box 1009, Manhattan, KS 66505-1009. Robin Higham, Ed. Articles, to 15 pages, devoted to the history and the culture of the West, then and now. B&W photos. Pays in copies or subscription. Web site: www.sunflower-univ-press.org.

KENTUCKE: THE MAGAZINE OF BLUEGRASS STATE HERITAGE—P.O. Box 1873, Ashland, KY 41105. William E. Ellis, Ed. Quarterly. Articles, to 2,500 words, on local, regional, and state heritage, including agricultural, architectural, literary, military, natural, pioneer and political history. Pays honorarium plus copies, on publication. Query with clips mentioning availability of photos. E-mail: kentucke@mediaink-ky.com.

LABOR'S HERITAGE—10000 New Hampshire Ave., Silver Spring, MD 20903. Quarterly. Illustrated journal of The George Meany Memorial Archives. Articles, 80 pages, for labor scholars, labor union members, and the general public. Pays in copies.

MILITARY HISTORY—Primedia History Group, 741 Miller Dr. S.E., Suite D-2, Leesburg, VA 20175-8920. Jon Guttman, Ed. Bimonthly. Features, 4,000 words with 500-word sidebars, on the strategy, tactics, and personalities of military history. Department pieces, 2,000 words, on intrigue, weaponry, personalities, and perspectives. Pays $200 to $400, on publication. Query. SASE for guidelines. E-mail: militaryhistory@thehistorynet.com. Web site: www.thehistorynet.com./militaryhistory.

MONTANA, THE MAGAZINE OF WESTERN HISTORY—225 N. Roberts St., Box 201201, Helena, MT 59620-1201. Charles E. Rankin, Ed. Authentic articles, 3,500 to 5,500 words, on the history of the American and Canadian West; new interpretive approaches to major developments in western history. Footnotes or bibliography must accompany article. "Strict historical accuracy is essential." No fiction. Queries preferred. No payment. Web site: www.montanahistoricalsociety.com.

NEBRASKA HISTORY—P.O. Box 82554, Lincoln, NE 68501. James E. Potter, Ed. Articles, 3,000 to 7,000 words, relating to the history of Nebraska and the Great Plains. B&W line drawings. Allow 60 days for response. Pays in copies. Cash prize awarded to one article each year. E-mail: publish@nebraska history.org. Web site: www.nebraskahistory.org.

NOW & THEN—CASS/ETSU, P.O. Box 70556, Johnson City, TN 37614-0556. Jane Harris Woodside, Ed. Fiction and nonfiction, 1,500 to 3,000 words: short stories, articles, interviews, essays, memoirs, book reviews. Pieces must be related to theme of issue and have some connection to the Appalachian region. Also photos and drawings. SASE for guidelines and current themes. Pays $15 to $75, on publication. Web site: http://cass.etsu.edu/n+t/n+t.htm.

OLD WEST—P.O. Box 2107, Stillwater, OK 74076. Marcus Huff, Ed. Does not accept freelance materials.

PENNSYLVANIA HERITAGE—P.O. Box 1026, Harrisburg, PA 17108-1026. Michael J. O'Malley III, Ed. Quarterly of the Pennsylvania Historical and Museum Commission and the Pennsylvania Heritage Society. Articles, 2,500 to 3,500 words, that "introduce readers to the state's rich culture and historic legacy. Seeks unusual and fresh angle to make history come to life, including pictorial or photo essays, interviews, travel/destination pieces." Prefers to see complete manuscript. Pays to $500, up to $100 for photos or drawings, on acceptance.

PERSIMMON HILL—1700 N.E. 63rd St., Oklahoma City, OK 73111. M.J. Van Deventer, Ed. Published by the National Cowboy Hall of Fame. Articles, 1,500 words, on western history and art, cowboys, ranching, and nature. Top-quality illustrations with captions a must. Pays from $150 to $250, on publication.

PROLOGUE—National Archives, NPOL, 8601 Adelphi Rd., College Park, MD 20740-6001. Quarterly. Articles, varying lengths, based on the holdings and programs of the National Archives, its regional archives, and the presidential libraries. Query. Pays in copies.

RENAISSANCE MAGAZINE—Phantom Press Publications, 13 Appleton Rd., Nantucket, MA 02554. Kim Guarnaccia, Ed. Feature articles on Renaissance and Medieval history, reenactments, roleplaying, and Renaissance faires. Interviews, reviews of Medieval and Renaissance books, music, movies, and games. Pays 6¢ a word, on publication. E-mail: renzine@aol.com. Web site: www.renaissancemagazine.com.

RUSSIAN LIFE—89 Main St., #2, Montpelier, VT 05602-2948. Mikhail Ivanov, Ed. Articles, 1,000 to 3,000 words, on Russian culture, travel, history, politics, art, business, and society. "We do not want stories about personal trips to Russia, editorials on developments in Russia, or articles that promote the services of a specific company, organization, or government agency." Pays 7¢ to 10¢ a word; $20 to $30 per photo, on publication. Query.

SOUTH CAROLINA HISTORICAL MAGAZINE—South Carolina Historical Society, 100 Meeting St., Charleston, SC 29401-2299. W. Eric Emerson, Ed. Scholarly articles, to 25 pages including footnotes, on South Carolina history. "Authors are encouraged to look at previous issues to be aware of previous scholarship." Pays in copies.

TRUE WEST—P.O. Box 2107, Stillwater, OK 74076-2107. Marcus Huff, Ed. True stories, 500 to 4,500 words, with photos, about the Old West to 1920. Some contemporary stories with historical slant. Source list required. Pays on acceptance.

VIETNAM—Primedia History Group, 741 Miller Dr. S.E., Suite D-2, Leesburg, VA 20175-8920. Col. Harry G. Summers, Jr., Ed. Articles, 2,000 to 4,000 words, on the strategy, tactics, personalities, arms, and equipment of the Vietnam War. Pays $150 to $300, on publication. Query with illustration ideas. SASE. Web site: www.thehistorynet.com.

THE WESTERN HISTORICAL QUARTERLY—Utah State Univ., Logan, UT 84322-0740. Anne M. Butler, Ed. Original articles about the American West, the Westward movement from the Atlantic to the Pacific, twentieth-century regional studies, Spanish borderlands, Canada, northern Mexico, Alaska, and Hawaii. No payment made.

WILD WEST—Primedia History Group, 741 Miller Dr. S.E., Suite D-2, Leesburg, VA 20175-8920. Gregory Lalire, Ed. Bimonthly. Features, to 3,500 words, with 500-word sidebars, and department pieces, 2,000 words, on Western history from the earliest North American settlements to the end of the 19th century. Pays $150 to $300, on publication. Query with SASE. Web site: www.thehistorynet.com./wildwest.

WORLD WAR II—Primedia History Group, 741 Miller Dr. S.E., Suite D-2, Leesburg, VA 20175-8920. Michael Haskew, Ed. Articles, 3,500 to 4,000 words, on the strategy, tactics, personalities, arms, and equipment of World War II. Pays $100 to $200, on publication. Query with illustration ideas. SASE for editorial guidelines. Web site: www.thehistorynet.com.

COLLEGE, CAREERS

THE BLACK COLLEGIAN—140 Carondelet St., New Orleans, LA 70130. Robert G. Miller, Ed. Articles, to 2,000 words, on entry-level career opportunities, the job search process, how to prepare for entry-level positions, what to expect as an entry-level professional, and culture and experiences of African-American collegians. Audience: African-American juniors and seniors. Pays on publication. Query. E-mail: robert@black-collegiate.com. Web site: www.black-collegian.com.

BYLINE—Box 130596, Edmond, OK 73013. Marcia Preston, Ed.-in-Chief. General fiction, 2,000 to 4,000 words. Nonfiction: 1,500- to 1,800-word features and 300- to 750-word special departments. Poetry, 10 to 30 lines preferred. Nonfiction and poetry must be about writing. Humor, 50 to 600 words, about writing. "We seek practical and motivational material that tells writers how they can succeed, not why they can't. Overdone topics: writers' block, the muse, rejection slips." Pays $10 for poetry; $15 to $35 for departments; $75 for features and $100 for short fiction, on acceptance. Web site: www.byline mag.com. E-mail: bylinemp@flash.net.

CAMPUS CANADA—287 MacPherson Ave., Toronto, Ontario, Canada M4V 1A4. Sarah Moore, Man. Ed. Published four times a year. Articles that inform, entertain, and educate the student community. Payment varies. Query.

CAMPUS LIFE—465 Gundersen Dr., Carol Stream, IL 60188. Chris Lutes, Ed. Articles reflecting Christian values and world view, for high school and college students. Humor, general fiction, and true, first-person experiences. "If we have a choice of fiction, how-to, and a strong first-person story, we'll go with the true story every time." Photo-essays, cartoons. Pays 15¢ to 20¢ a word, on acceptance. Query only. E-mail: cledit@aol.com. Web site: www. campuslife.net.

CAREER DIRECTIONS—21 N. Henry St., Edgerton, WI 53534. Diane Everson, Pres. and Pub. Tabloid. "Current News & Career Opportunities for Students." Career-related articles, 500 to 1,500 words, especially how-to. Pays $50 to $150, on acceptance. Also publishes the newsletter *Career Waves*, for career development professionals.

CAREER WORLD—GLC., 900 Skokie Blvd., Suite 200, Northbrook, IL 60062-4028. Carole Rubenstein, Sr. Ed. Published 7 times a year, September through April/May. Gender-neutral articles about specific occupations and career awareness and development for junior and senior high school audience. Query with clips and resumé. Payment varies, on publication.

CAREERS & COLLEGES—989 Ave. of the Americas, New York, NY 10018. Don Rauf, Ed. Quarterly. Designed to give high school juniors and seniors advice on how to plan their future. Nonfiction, from 800 to 2,500 words. Topics include interesting, new takes on college admission, scholarships, financial aid, work skills, and careers. Payment is $300 to $800 per article, depending on length. Query. E-mail: staff@careersandcolleges.com. Web site: www.careersandcolleges.com.

CAREERS AND THE COLLEGE GRAD—201 Broadway, Cambridge, MA 02139. Kathleen Grimes, Pub. Annual. Career-related articles, 1,500 to 2,000 words, for junior and senior liberal arts students. Career-related fillers, 500 words and line art or color prints. Queries preferred. No payment. Same address and requirements for *Careers and the MBA* (semiannual) for first- and second-year MBA students; *Careers and the Engineer* (semiannual) for junior and senior engineering students; *Careers and the Minority Lawyer* (semiannual) for law school students; *Careers and the International MBA; Careers and the Woman MBA; Careers and the Minority MBA;* and *Careers and the Minority Undergraduate.*

CAREERS & THE DISABLED—See *Minority Engineer.*

CIRCLE K—3636 Woodview Trace, Indianapolis, IN 46268-3196. Shanna Mooney, Exec. Ed. Serious and light articles, 1,500 to 1,700 words, on careers, college issues, trends, leadership development, self-help, community service and involvement. Pays $200 to $400, on acceptance. Queries preferred. E-mail: ckimagazine@kiwanis.org. Web site: www.circlek.org/magazine.

COLLEGE BOUND MAGAZINE—Ramholtz Publishing, Inc., 2071 Clove Rd., Suite 206, Staten Island, NY 10304. Gina LaGuardia, Ed. Six times during the academic year in NY, NJ, and CT; twice each in CA, Chicago, and TX; one national edition. Articles, 200 to 1,000 words, which provide high school students a view of college life. High school and college-related fillers, 50 to 200 words. Send SASE for guidelines. Queries preferred. Pays $20 to $100, 30 days upon publication. E-mail: editorial@collegebound.net. Web site: www.collegebound.net.

DIRECT AIM—3100 Broadway, 660 Pen Tower, Kansas City, MO 64111-2413. Michelle Paige, Ed. Quarterly. Aimed at African American and Hispanic students in colleges, universities, and junior colleges. Topics include career preparation, college profiles, financial aid sources, and interviews with college students across the U.S. Payment varies. Query.

EQUAL OPPORTUNITY—See *Minority Engineer.*

INSIDER MAGAZINE—4124 W. Oakton, Skokie, IL 60201. Rita Cook, Ed. Dir. Articles, 700, 1,500, and 2,100 words, on issues, careers, politics, sports, and entertainment for readers ages 18 to 34. Pays 1¢ to 3¢ a word, on publication. Send SASE for themes. Web site: www.insidermag.com.

LINK MAGAZINE: WHERE COLLEGE STUDENTS GET IT—(formerly *Link: The College Magazine*) 32 E. 57th St., 11th Fl., New York, NY 10022. Torey Marcus, Ed.-in-Chief. News, lifestyle, and entertainment issues for college students. Informational how-to and short features, 300 to 500 words, on education news, finances, academics, employment, lifestyles, trends, entertainment, sports, and culture. Well-researched, insightful, authoritative articles, 2,000 to 3,000 words. Pays 50¢ a word, on publication. Queries preferred. Guidelines. E-mail: editor@linkmag.com. Web site: www.linkmag.com.

MINORITY ENGINEER—1160 E. Jericho Turnpike, Suite 200, Huntington, NY 11743. James Schneider, Ed. Articles, 1,000 to 1,500 words, for college students, on career opportunities; techniques of job hunting; developments in and applications of new technologies. Interviews. Profiles. Pays 10¢ a word, on publication. Query. Same address and requirements for *Woman Engi-*

neer (address Claudia Wheeler), and *Equal Opportunity* and *Careers & the DisABLED* (address James Schneider). E-mail: info@eop.com. Web site: www. eop.com.

SUCCEED—Ramholtz Publishing Inc., 2071 Clove Rd., Suite 206, Staten Island, NY 10304. Gina LaGuardia, Ed.-in-Chief. Quarterly. Feature articles, 1,000 to 1,500 words, on topics of interest to professionals and current students interested in continuing education. Department pieces, 400 to 750 words, on financial advice; career-related profiles; news; book and software reviews; and information on other continuing education-related resources. Query with three writing clips. Guidelines and sample issues available. Pays $50 to $125, 30 days after publication. Responds in 4 to 6 weeks. E-mail: editorial@collegebound.net. Web site: www.collegebound.net.

UCLA MAGAZINE—10920 Wilshire Blvd., Suite 1500, Los Angeles, CA 90024. David Greenwald, Ed. Quarterly. Articles, 2,000 words, must be related to UCLA through research, alumni, students, etc. Pays to $2,000, on acceptance. Queries required.

UNIQUE OPPORTUNITIES—455 S. 4th Ave., #1236, Louisville, KY 40202. Bett Coffman, Assoc. Ed. Articles, 2,000 to 3,000 words, that cover economic, business, and career-related issues of interest to physicians who are looking for their first practice or looking to make a career move. "Our goal is to educate physicians about how to evaluate career opportunities, negotiate the benefits offered, plan career moves, and provide information on the legal and economic aspects of accepting a position." Pays 50¢ a word for features; $200 for profiles, on acceptance. Query. E-mail: tellus@uoworks.com. Web site: www.uoworks.com.

UNIVERCITY MAGAZINE—426 E. 66th St., 2nd Fl., New York, NY 10021-6914. D. Patrick Hadley, Ed. Published ten times a year. Entertainment news, fashion trends, celebrity interviews, music, movie, and book reviews, etc., all aimed at New York City college students. Payment varies. Query.

WOMAN ENGINEER—*Minority Engineer.*

OP-ED MARKETS

THE ATLANTA CONSTITUTION—P.O. Box 4689, Atlanta, GA 30302. Op-Ed Ed. Articles related to the Southeast, Georgia, or the Atlanta metropolitan area, 200 to 600 words, on a variety of topics: law, economics, politics, science, environment, performing and manipulative arts, humor, education; religious and seasonal topics. Pays $75 to $125, on publication. Submit complete manuscript.

THE BALTIMORE SUN—P.O. Box 1377, Baltimore, MD 21278-0001. Marilyn McCraven, Opinion-Commentary Page Ed. Articles, 600 to 1,500 words, on a wide range of topics: politics, education, foreign affairs, lifestyles, etc. Humor. Payment varies, on publication. Exclusive rights: MD and DC.

THE BOSTON GLOBE—P.O. Box 2378, Boston, MA 02107-2378. Marjorie Pritchard, Ed. Articles, to 700 words, on economics, education, environment, foreign affairs, and regional interest. Send complete manuscript. Exclusive rights: New England.

BOSTON HERALD—One Herald Sq., Boston, MA 02106. Attn: Editorial Page Ed. Pieces, 600 to 700 words, on economics, foreign affairs, politics, regional interest, and seasonal topics. Prefer submissions from regional writers. Payment varies, on publication. Exclusive rights: MA, RI, and NH. E-mail: oped@bostonherald.com. Web site: www.bostonherald.com.

THE CHARLOTTE OBSERVER—P.O. Box 30308, Charlotte, NC 28230-0308. Jane Pope, Deputy Ed., Editorial Pages. Well-written, thought-provoking articles, to 700 words. "We are only interested in articles on local (Carolinas) issues or that use local examples to illustrate other issues." Pays $50, on publication. No simultaneous submissions in NC or SC. E-mail: opinion@charlotteobserver.com. Web site: www.charlotte.com.

THE CHRISTIAN SCIENCE MONITOR—One Norway St., Boston, MA 02115. Clara Germani, Opinion Page Ed. Pieces, 400 to 900 words, on domestic and foreign affairs, economics, education, environment, law, media, politics, and cultural commentary. Pays up to $400, on acceptance. Retains all rights for 90 days after publication. For writer's guidelines, call 617-450-2372. E-mail: oped@csps.com Web site: www.csmonitor.com.

THE CLEVELAND PLAIN DEALER—1801 Superior Ave., Cleveland, OH 44114. Gloria Millner, Assoc. Ed. Pieces, 700 to 800 words, on a wide variety of subjects. Pays $75, on publication. E-mail: forum@plaind.com

DENVER POST—P.O. Box 1709, Denver, CO 80201. Bob Ewegen, Ed. Articles, 400 to 700 words, with local or regional angle. No payment for free-lance submissions. Query.

DETROIT FREE PRESS—600 W. Fort St., Detroit, MI 48226. Attn: Op-Ed Ed. Opinion pieces, to 750 words, on domestic and foreign affairs, economics, education, environment, law, politics, and regional interest. Priority given to local writers or topics of local interest. Pays $100, on publication. Exclusive rights: MI and northern OH. E-mail: oped@freepress.com.

THE DETROIT NEWS—615 W. Lafayette Blvd., Detroit, MI 48226. Attn: Richard Burr. Pieces, 500 to 750 words, on a wide variety of subjects. Pays $75, on publication. E-mail: oped@detnews.com. Fax: 313-222-6417.

INDIANAPOLIS STAR—P.O. Box 145, Indianapolis, IN 46206-0145. Andrea Neal, Ed. Articles, 700 to 800 words. Pays $40, on publication. Exclusive rights: IN.

LOS ANGELES TIMES—Times Mirror Sq., Los Angeles, CA 90053. Bob Berger, Op-Ed Ed. Commentary pieces, 650 to 700 words, on many subjects. "Not interested in nostalgia or first-person reaction to faraway events. Pieces must be exclusive." Payment varies, on publication. Limited market. SASE required. E-mail: op-ed@latimes.com.

THE NEW YORK TIMES—229 W. 43rd St., New York, NY 10036. Attn: Op-Ed Ed. Opinion pieces, 650 to 800 words, on any topic, including public policy, science, lifestyles, and ideas, etc. Include your address, daytime phone number, and social security number with submission. "If you haven't heard from us within 2 weeks, you can assume we are not using your piece. Include SASE if you want work returned." Pays on publication. Buys first North American rights.

NEWSDAY—"Viewpoints," 235 Pinelawn Rd., Melville, NY 11747. Noel Rubinton, "Viewpoints" Ed. Pieces, 700 to 800 words, on a variety of topics. Pays $150, on publication. E-mail: oped@newsday.com. Web site: www.newsday.com.

THE REGISTER GUARD—P.O. Box 10188, Eugene, OR 97440. Jackman Wilson, Editorial Page Ed. All subjects; regional angle preferred. Pays $25 to $50, on publication. Very limited use of non-local writers. E-mail: jwilson@guardnet.com

THE SACRAMENTO BEE—P.O. Box 15779, Sacramento, CA 95852-0779. Jewel A. Reilly, Op-Ed Ed. Op-ed pieces, to 750 words; state and regional topics preferred. E-mail: jreilly@sacbee.com. Web site: www.sacbee.com.

ST. LOUIS POST-DISPATCH—900 N. Tucker Blvd., St. Louis, MO 63101. Donna Korando, Commentary Ed. Articles, 700 words, on economics, education, science, politics, foreign and domestic affairs, and the environment. Pays $70, on publication. "Goal is to have at least half of the articles by local writers." E-mail: oped@postnet.com. Web site: www.postnet.com.

ST. PAUL PIONEER PRESS—345 Cedar St., St. Paul, MN 55101. Ronald D. Clark, Ed. Articles, to 750 words, on a variety of topics. Strongly prefer authors or topics with a connection to the area. Pays $75, on publication. E-mail: dtice@pioneerpress.com. Web site: www.pioneerpress.com.

SEATTLE POST-INTELLIGENCER—P.O. Box 1909, Seattle, WA 98111. Sam R. Sperry, Op-ed Page Ed. Articles, 750 to 800 words, on foreign and domestic affairs, environment, education, politics, regional interest, religion, science, and seasonal material. Prefer writers who live in the Pacific Northwest. Pays $75 to $100, on publication. SASE required. Very limited market.

THE WALL STREET JOURNAL—Editorial Page, 200 Liberty St., New York, NY 10281. David B. Brooks, Op-Ed Ed. Articles, to 1,500 words, on politics, economics, law, education, environment, humor (occasionally), and foreign and domestic affairs. Articles must be timely, heavily reported, and of national interest by writers with expertise in their field. Pays $150 to $300, on publication.

WASHINGTON TIMES—3600 New York Ave. N.E., Washington, DC 20002. Frank Perley, Articles and Opinion Page Ed. Articles, 800 to 1,000 words, on a variety of subjects. No pieces written in the first-person. "Syndicated columnists cover the 'big' issues; find an area that is off the beaten path." Pays $150, on publication. Exclusive rights: Washington, DC, and Baltimore area.

ADULT MAGAZINES

CHIC—8484 Wilshire Blvd., Suite 900, Beverly Hills, CA 90211. Scott Schalin, Lisa Jenio, Exec. Eds. Sex-related articles, interviews, erotic fiction, 2,500 words. Query for articles. Pays $150 for brief interviews, $350 for fiction, on acceptance.

GENESIS—210 Route 4 E., Suite 401, Paramus, NJ 07652. Paul Gambino, Ed. Dir. Dan Davis, Man. Ed. Sexually explicit fiction and nonfiction features, 800 to 2,000 words. Celebrity interviews, photo-essays, product and film reviews. Pays on publication. Query with clips.

PENTHOUSE—277 Park Ave., 4th Fl., New York, NY 10172-0003. Peter Bloch, Ed. Lavada B. Nahon, Sr. Ed. Articles, to 5,000 words: general-interest profiles, interviews (with introduction), and investigative pieces. Pays on acceptance.

PLAYBOY—680 North Shore Dr., Chicago, IL 60611. Stephen Randall, Exec. Ed. Articles, 3,500 to 6,000 words, and sophisticated fiction, 1,000 to 10,000 words (5,000 preferred), for urban men. Humor; satire. Science fiction. Pays to $5,000 for articles and fiction, $2,000 for short-shorts, on acceptance. E-mail: articles@playboy.com.

PLAYGIRL—801 Second Ave., New York, NY 10017. Daryna McKeand, Man. Ed. Articles, 750 to 2,000 words, for women 18 and older. Pays varying rates, on acceptance. Web site: www.playgirl.com.

VARIATIONS, FOR LIBERATED LOVERS—11 Penn Plaza, 12th Fl., New York, NY 10001. V. K. McCarty, Ed. Dir./Assoc. Pub. First-person true narrative descriptions of "a couple's enthusiasm, secrets, and exquisitely articulated sex scenes squarely focused within one of the magazine's pleasure categories." Pays $400, on acceptance.

FICTION MARKETS

This list gives the fiction requirements of general- and special-interest magazines, including those that publish detective and mystery, science fiction and fantasy, romance and confession stories. Other good markets for short fiction are the *College, Literary, and Little Magazines* where, though payment is modest (usually in copies only), publication can bring the work of a beginning writer to the attention of editors at the larger magazines. Juvenile fiction markets are listed under *Juvenile, Teenage, and Young Adult Magazines*. Publishers of book-length fiction manuscripts are listed under *Book Publishers*.

GENERAL FICTION

ABORIGINAL SF—P.O. Box 2449, Woburn, MA 01888-0849. Charles C. Ryan, Ed. Stories, 2,500 to 7,500 words, with a unique scientific idea, human or alien character, plot, and theme of lasting value; "must be science fiction; no fantasy, horror, or sword and sorcery." Pays $200. Send SASE for guidelines.

AFRICAN VOICES—270 W. 96th St., New York, NY 10025. Carolyn A. Butts, Exec. Ed., Kim Horne, Fiction Ed., Layding Kaliba, Poetry Ed. Quarterly. Humorous, erotic, and dramatic fiction, 500 to 2,500 words, by ethnic writers. Nonfiction, 500 to 1,500 words: investigative articles, artist profiles, essays, book reviews, and first-person narratives. Poetry, to 50 lines. Include SASE; sample copies available for $5. Pays $25 for fiction, on publication, plus 5 copies of magazine. (Payment varies for nonfiction.) E-mail: africanvoices@ aol.com. Web site: www.africanvoices.com.

AIM MAGAZINE—P.O. Box 1174, Maywood, IL 60153. Myron Apilado, Ed. Short stories, 800 to 3,000 words, geared to proving that people from different backgrounds are more alike than they are different. Story should not moralize. Pays from $15 to $25, on publication. Annual contest. $100 prize.

ALFRED HITCHCOCK MYSTERY MAGAZINE—475 Park Ave. S., New York, NY 10016. Cathleen Jordan, Ed. Well-plotted, plausible mystery, suspense, detection and crime stories, to 14,000 words; "ghost stories, humor, futuristic or atmospheric tales are all possible, as long as they include a crime or the suggestion of one." Pays 8¢ a word, on acceptance. Guidelines with SASE. Web site: www.mysterypages.com.

ANALOG SCIENCE FICTION AND FACT—475 Park Avenue S., New York, NY 10016. Stanley Schmidt, Ed. Science fiction, with strong characters in believable future or alien setting: short stories, 2,000 to 7,500 words; novelettes, 10,000 to 20,000 words; serials, to 70,000 words. Include SASE. Pays 5¢ to 8¢ a word, on acceptance. Query for novels.

ASIMOV'S SCIENCE FICTION MAGAZINE—475 Park Ave. S, 11th Fl., New York, NY 10016. Gardner Dozois, Ed. Short science fiction and fantasies, to 15,000 words. Pays 6¢ to 8¢ a word, on acceptance. Guidelines. E-mail: asimovs@dellmagazines.com. Web site: www.asimovs.com.

THE ATLANTIC MONTHLY—77 N. Washington St., Boston, MA 02114. C. Michael Curtis, Fiction Ed. Web site: www.theatlantic.com.

THE BOSTON GLOBE MAGAZINE—*The Boston Globe,* P.O. Box 2378, Boston, MA 02107-2378. Nick King, Ed. Short stories, to 3,000 words. Include SASE. Pays on publication. Web site: www.boston.com/globe/magazine. No e-mail submissions, please.

BOYS' LIFE—1325 W. Walnut Hill Ln., P.O. Box 152079, Irving, TX 75015-2079. Rich Haddaway, Fiction Ed. Publication of the Boy Scouts of America. Humor, mystery, science fiction, adventure, 1,200 words, for 8- to 18-year-old boys; study back issues. Pays from $750, on acceptance. Send SASE for guidelines. Send complete manuscript; no queries. Web site: www. bsa.scouting.org.

BUFFALO SPREE MAGAZINE—5678 Main St., Williamsville, NY 14221. David McDuff and Laurence Levite, Pubs. Fiction and humor, to 2,000 words, for thoughtful, intelligent readers in the western New York region. Pays $125 to $150, on publication.

BYLINE—Box 130596, Edmond, OK 73013. Marcia Preston, Ed.-in-Chief. Carolyn Wall, Assoc. Fiction Ed. General fiction, 2,000 to 4,000 words. Nonfiction: 1,500- to 1,800-word features and 300- to 750-word special departments. Poetry, 10 to 30 lines preferred. Nonfiction and poetry must be about writing. Humor, 100 to 600 words, about writing. "We seek practical and motivational material that tells writers how they can succeed, not why they can't. Overdone topics: writers' block, the muse, rejection slips." Pays $5 to $10 for poetry; $15 to $35 for departments; $75 for features; and $100 for short fiction, on acceptance. SASE for guidelines or see Web site: www.bylinemag.com. E-mail: bylinemp@aol.com.

CAPPER'S—1503 S.W. 42nd St., Topeka, KS 66609-1265. Ann Crahan, Ed. Fiction, 7,500 to 40,000 words (12,000 to 20,000 words preferred), for serialization. No profanity, violence, or explicit sex. Pays $75 to $300, on publication.

CATHOLIC FORESTER—355 Shuman Blvd., P.O. Box 3012, Naperville, IL 60566-7012. Mary Anne File, Ed. Official publication of the Catholic

Order of Foresters. Humor, light fiction, short inspirational pieces and children's stories, 500 to 1,000 words. No sex, violence, romance, or "preachy" stories; religious angle not required. Pays 20¢ a word, on acceptance. Web site: www.catholicforester.com.

CHESS LIFE—3054 NYS Rte. 9W, New Windsor, NY 12553-7698. Glenn Petersen, Ed. Fiction, 500 to 2,000 words, related to chess for members of the U.S. Chess Federation. Also, articles, 500 to 3,000 words, on chess news, profiles, technical aspects of chess. Pays varying rates, on acceptance. Query; limited market. E-mail: cleditor@uschess.org. Web site: www.uschess.org.

COBBLESTONE: DISCOVER AMERICAN HISTORY—30 Grove St., Suite C, Peterborough, NH 03458-1454. Meg Chorlian, Ed. Historical fiction, 500 to 800 words, for children aged 8 to 14 years; must relate to theme. Pays 20¢ to 25¢ a word, on publication. Send SASE for guidelines. Web site: www.cobblestonepub.com.

COMMENTARY—165 E. 56th St., New York, NY 10022. Neal Kozodoy, Ed. Fiction, of high literary quality, on contemporary social or Jewish issues, from 5,000 to 7,000 words. Pays on publication.

COMMON GROUND MAGAZINE—P.O. Box 99, McVeytown, PA 17051-0099. Ruth Dunmire and Pam Brumbaugh, Eds. Quarterly. Fiction, 1,000 to 2,000 words, related to Central Pennsylvania's Juniata River Valley. Pays $25 to $200, on publication. Guidelines.

COSMOPOLITAN—224 W. 57th St., New York, NY 10019. Alison Broner, Sr. Books Ed. Novel excerpts; submissions must be sent by a publisher or agent. Payment rates are negotiable. SASE.

COUNTRY WOMAN—P.O. Box 989, Greendale, WI 53129. Kathy Pohl, Exec. Ed. Fiction, 750 to 1,000 words, of interest to rural women; protagonist must be a country woman. "Stories should focus on life in the country, its problems and joys, as experienced by country women; must be upbeat and positive." Pays $90 to $125, on acceptance.

CRICKET—P.O. Box 300, Peru, IL 61354-0300. Marianne Carus, Ed.-in-Chief. Fiction, 200 to 2,000 words, for 9- to 14-year-olds. Pays to 25¢ a word, on publication. SASE. Web site: www.cricketmag.com

DISCOVERIES—WordAction Publishing Co., 6401 The Paseo, Kansas City, MO 64131. Attn: Emily Freeburg, Asst. Ed. Weekly take-home paper designed to correlate with Evangelical Sunday school curriculum. Fiction, 500 words, for 8- to 10-year-olds. Stories should feature contemporary, true-to-life characters and should illustrate character building and scriptural application. No poetry. Pays 5¢ a word, on publication. Send SASE for guidelines and theme list. E-mail: vfolsom@nazarene.org (Virgina Folsom, Ed.)

ELLERY QUEEN'S MYSTERY MAGAZINE—475 Park Ave. S., New York, NY 10016. Janet Hutchings, Ed. High-quality detective, crime, and mystery stories, 1,500 to 10,000 words. Also "Minute Mysteries," 250 words, short verses, limericks, and novellas, to 17,000 words. "We like a mix of classic detection and suspenseful crime." "First Stories" by unpublished writers. Pays 3¢ to 8¢ a word, occasionally higher for established authors, on acceptance. Web site: www.mysterypages.com.

ENCOUNTER: MEETING GOD FACE-TO-FACE—(formerly *Straight*) 8121 Hamilton Ave., Cincinnati, OH 45231. Kelly Carr, Ed. Well-constructed fiction, 1,000 to 1,500 words, showing Christian teens using Bible principles in everyday life. Contemporary, realistic teen characters a must. Most interested in school, church, dating, and family life stories. Pays 6¢ to 8¢ a word, on acceptance. Guidelines. No electronic submissions. E-mail: kcarr@standardpub.com. Web site: www.standardpub.com.

ESQUIRE—250 W. 55th St., New York, NY 10019. David Granger, Ed.-in-Chief. Send finished manuscript of short story; submit one at a time. No full-length novels. No pornography, science fiction, poetry, or "true romance" stories. Include SASE. Web site: www.esquiremag.com.

EVANGEL—Light and Life Communications, P.O. Box 535002, Indianapolis, IN 46253-5002. Julie Innes, Ed. Free Methodist. Fiction and nonfiction, to 1,200 words, with personal faith in Christ shown as instrumental in solving problems. Pays 4¢ a word, on publication. Send #10 SASE for sample copy and guidelines.

FICTION INTERNATIONAL—English Dept., San Diego State Univ., San Diego, CA 92182-8140. Harold Jaffe, Ed. Formally innovative and politically committed fiction and theory. Query for themes. Submit between September 1st and December 15th.

FLY ROD & REEL—P.O. Box 370, Camden, ME 04843. James E. Butler, Ed. Occasional fiction, 2,000 to 3,000 words, related to fly fishing. Payment varies, on acceptance. E-mail: jbutler@flyrodreel.com. Web site: www.flyrodreel.com.

GALLERY—401 Park Ave. S., New York, NY 10016-8802. C.S. O'Brien, Ed. Dir. Erotic and general fiction, to 2,500 words, for men's market. "We encourage quality work from unpublished writers." Payment varies, on publication. SASE for guidelines.

GLIMMER TRAIN PRESS—710 S.W. Madison St., #504, Portland, OR 97205. Susan Burmeister-Brown, Ed. Fiction, 1,200 to 7,500 words. "Eight stories in each quarterly magazine." Pays $500, on acceptance. Submit material in January, April, July, and October; allow 3 months for response. "Send SASE for guidelines before submitting." E-mail: info@glimmertrain.com. Web site: www.glimmertrain.com.

GOOD HOUSEKEEPING—959 Eighth Ave., New York, NY 10019. Lee Quarfoot, Literary Ed. Short stories, 2,000 to 5,000 words, with strong identification figures for women, by published writers. Novel condensations or excerpts from about-to-be-published books only. Query; no longer accepts unsolicited manuscripts.

GRIT—Ogden Publications, 1503 S.W. 42nd St., Topeka, KS 66609. Donna Doyle, Ed.-in-Chief. Short stories, 850 to 2,000 words; also historical, mystery, western, adventure, and romance serials (15,000 or less words in 1,000-word installments with cliff-hangers). Articles, 500 to 1,200 words. Serial fiction, 3,500 to 15,000 words. Should be upbeat, inspirational, wholesome and interesting to mature adults. No reference to drinking, smoking, drugs, sex, or violence. Also publishes true-story nostalgia. Pays up to 22¢ a word, on publication. All fiction submissions should be marked "Fiction Dept." Send $4 for sample copy. SASE for guidelines. Submissions will not be acknowledged, nor will status updates be given. E-mail: grit@cjnetworks.com. Web site: www.grit.com.

GUIDEPOSTS FOR KIDS—P.O. Box 638, Chesterton, IN 46304. Mary

Lou Carney, Ed. Value-centered bimonthly for 7- to 12-year-olds. Problem fiction, mysteries, historicals, 1,000 to 1,400 words, with "realistic dialogue and sharp imagery. No preachy stories about Bible-toting children." Pays $300 to $500 for all rights, on acceptance. No reprints. E-mail: gp4k@guideposts.org. Web site: www.gp4k.com.

HARDBOILED—Gryphon Publications, P.O. Box 209, Brooklyn, NY 11228-0209. Gary Lovisi, Ed. Hard, cutting-edge crime fiction, to 3,000 words, "with impact." "It's a good idea to read an issue before submitting a story." Payment varies, on publication. Query for articles, book and film reviews. Web site: www.gyrphonbooks.com.

HARPER'S MAGAZINE—666 Broadway, New York, NY 10012. Attn: Eds. Will consider unsolicited fiction manuscripts. Query for nonfiction (very limited market). No poetry. SASE required.

HIGHLIGHTS FOR CHILDREN—803 Church St., Honesdale, PA 18431-1824. Christine French Clark, Man. Ed. Fiction on sports, humor, adventure, mystery, folktales, etc., 900 words, for 8- to 12-year-olds. Easy rebus form, 100 to 120 words, and easy-to-read stories, to 500 words, for beginning readers. "We are partial to stories in which the protagonist solves a dilemma through his or her own resources." Pays from 14¢ a word, on acceptance. Buys all rights.

THE JOYFUL WOMAN—P.O. Box 90028, Chattanooga, TN 37412. Joy Rice Martin, Ed. First-person inspirational true stories and sketches, 500 to 1,000 words; occasionally uses some fiction. Pays 3¢ to 4¢ a word, on publication.

LADIES' HOME JOURNAL—125 Park Ave., New York, NY 10017. Fiction; only accepted through agents.

THE MAGAZINE OF FANTASY AND SCIENCE FICTION—Box 1806, Madison Sq. Station, New York, NY 10159. Gordon Van Gelder, Ed. Fantasy and science fiction stories, to 25,000 words. Pays 5¢ to 8¢ a word, on acceptance. E-mail: webmaster@fsfmag.com. Web site: www.fsfmag.com.

MATURE LIVING—127 Ninth Ave. N., Nashville, TN 37234. Al Shackleford, Ed. Fiction, 900 to 1,200 words, for senior adults. Must be consistent with Christian principles. Pays $75, on acceptance.

MIDSTREAM—633 Third Ave., 21st Fl., New York, NY 10017. Joel Carmichael, Ed. Fiction with a Jewish/Zionist reference, to 3,000 words. Pays 5¢ a word, after publication. Allow one month for response.

NA'AMAT WOMAN—350 Fifth Ave, Suite 4700, New York, NY 10118. Judith A. Sokoloff, Ed. Short stories, approximately 2,500 words, with Jewish theme. Pays 10¢ a word, on publication.

THE NEW YORKER—4 Times Square, New York, NY 10036. Attn: Fiction Dept. Short stories, humor, and satire. Payment varies, on acceptance.

PLAYBOY—680 North Shore Drive., Chicago, IL 60611. Alice K. Turner, Fiction Ed. Limited market.

PLAYGIRL—801 Second Ave., New York, NY 10017. Daryna McKeand, Man. Ed. Contemporary, erotic fiction, from a female perspective, 3,000 to 4,000 words. "Fantasy Forum," 1,000 to 2,000 words. Pays from $200; $25 to $100 for "Fantasy Forum", after acceptance.

POWER AND LIGHT—6401 The Paseo, Kansas City, MO 64131.

Emily Freeburg, Ed. Asst. Nonfiction, 500 to 800 words, for grades 5 to 6, hot topics and relevant issues. Pays 5¢ a word for multiple-use rights, on publication. E-mail: mprice@nazarene.org.

PURPOSE—616 Walnut Ave., Scottdale, PA 15683-1999. James E. Horsch, Ed. Fiction, up to 750 words, on problem solving from a Christian point of view. Poetry, 3 to 12 lines. Pays to 5¢ a word for fiction; to $2 per line for poetry, on acceptance. E-mail: horsch@mph.org. Web site: www.mph.org.

QUEEN'S QUARTERLY—Queens Univ., Kingston, Ont., Canada K7L 3N6. Attn: Fiction Ed. Fiction, to 5,000 words, in English and French. Pays to $300, on publication. E-mail: qquarter@post.queensu.ca. Web site: http://info.queensu.ca/quarterly.

RANGER RICK—8925 Leesburg Pike, Vienna, VA 22184. Deborah Churchman, Fiction Ed. Photographers and artists wishing to send unsolicited portfolios should first write for photo and art guidelines. No unsolicited article queries or manuscripts. Web site: www.nwf.org/rrick.

ST. ANTHONY MESSENGER—1615 Republic St., Cincinnati, OH 45210-1298. Fr. Jack Wintz, O.F.M., Ed. Barbara Beckwith, Man. Ed. Fiction that makes readers think about issues, lifestyles, and values. Pays 16¢ a word, on acceptance. Queries or manuscripts accepted. E-mail: stanthony@american catholic.org. Web site: www.americancatholic.org.

SEA KAYAKER—P.O. Box 17170, Seattle, WA 98107-0870. Christopher Cunningham, Ed. Short stories exclusively related to ocean kayaking, 1,000 to 3,000 words. Pays on publication. E-mail: mail@seakayakermag.com. Web site: www.seakayakermag.com.

SEVENTEEN—850 Third Ave., New York, NY 10022. Caroline Palmer, Fiction Ed. High-quality, literary short fiction, to 4,000 words. Pays on acceptance. E-mail: carolinepalmer@primediamags.com. Web site: www.seventeen.com.

STEEPLE HILL—300 E. 42nd St., 6th Fl., New York, NY 10017. Romance with an element of faith, 70,000 to 75,000 words, that promote strong family values and high moral standards. Physical interaction should emphasize emotional tenderness rather than sexual desire. Please no sexual intercourse between characters unless they are married. Query with two- to five-page double-spaced synopsis of the story and SASE with sufficient postage. Three "Love Inspired" romances will be published each month. Payment is on a royalty basis.

STRAIGHT—See *Encounter: Meeting God Face-To-Face.*

'TEEN—6420 Wilshire Blvd., Los Angeles, CA 90048-5515. Attn: Fiction Dept. Short stories, 2,500 to 4,000 words: mystery, teen situations, adventure, romance, humor for teens. Pays from $200, on acceptance.

TRUE CONFESSIONS—233 Park Ave. S., New York, NY 10003. Pat Byrdsong, Ed. Timely, emotional, first-person stories, 2,000 to 9,000 words, on romance, family life, and problems of today's young working-class women. Pays 5¢ a word, after publication.

WESTERN PEOPLE—Box 2500, Saskatoon, Sask., Canada S7K 2C4. Attn: Ed. Short stories, 1,200 to 2,500 words, on subjects or themes of interest to rural readers in western Canada. Pays $100 to $200, on acceptance. Enclose international reply coupons and SAE. E-mail: people@producer.com.

WOMAN'S WORLD—270 Sylvan Ave., Englewood Cliffs, NJ 07632. Attn: Fiction Dept. Fast-moving short stories, no more than 1,500 words, with realistic relationship theme. (Specify "romance" on outside of envelope.) Mini-mysteries, to 1,000 words, with "whodunit" or "howdunit" theme. (Specify "mini-mystery" on envelope.) No science fiction, fantasy, or historical romance and no horror, ghost stories, or gratuitous violence. "Dialogue-driven romances help propel the story." Pays $1,000 for romances, $500 for mini-mysteries, on acceptance. SASE for guidelines and manuscript return.

YANKEE—Yankee Publishing Co., P.O. Box 520, Dublin, NH 03444. JIm Collins, Ed. Edie Clark, Fiction Ed. High-quality, literary short fiction, to 3,000 words (shorter preferred), with New England setting; no sap buckets or lobster pot stereotypes. Pays $1,000, on acceptance. E-mail: queries@yankeepub.com. Web site: www.newengland.com.

DETECTIVE & MYSTERY

ALFRED HITCHCOCK'S MYSTERY MAGAZINE—475 Park Avenue S., New York, NY 10016. Cathleen Jordan, Ed. Well-plotted, previously unpublished mystery, detective, suspense, and crime short stories, to 14,000 words. Submissions by new writers strongly encouraged. Pays 8¢ a word, on acceptance. No simultaneous submissions, please. (Submissions sent to *AHMM* are not considered for, or read by, *Ellery Queen's Mystery Magazine,* and vice versa.) Guidelines with SASE. Web site: www.mysterypages.com.

ELLERY QUEEN'S MYSTERY MAGAZINE—475 Park Ave. S., New York, NY 10016. Janet Hutchings, Ed. Detective, crime, and mystery fiction, approximately 1,500 to 10,000 words. Occasionally publishes novelettes, to 20,000 words, by established authors and humorous mystery verse. No sex, sadism, or sensationalism. Particularly interested in new writers and "first stories." Pays 3¢ to 8¢ a word, occasionally higher for established authors, on acceptance. Web site: www.mysterypages.com.

HARDBOILED—Gryphon Publications, P.O. Box 209, Brooklyn, NY 11228-0209. Gary Lovisi, Ed. Hard, cutting-edge crime fiction (suspense, noir, private eye) to 3,000 words. Payment varies, on publication. Query for articles, book and film reviews, and longer fiction. Sample copies $8. Web site: www. gryphonbooks.com.

MURDEROUS INTENT—P.O. Box 5947, Vancouver, WA 98668-5947. Margo Power, Ed./Pub. Quarterly. Mystery and suspense stories and mystery-related articles, 2,000 to 4,000 words; fillers, to 750 words; poems, to 30 lines. "We love humor in mysteries. Surprise us!" Pays $10, on acceptance. No simultaneous submissions. Electronic submissions only. Send query letter with synopsis and length to: madison@teleport.com. Web site: www.murderous intent.com.

MYSTERY TIME—P.O. Box 2907, Decatur, IL 62524. Linda Hutton, Ed. Semiannual. Suspense, 1,500 words, and poems about mysteries, up to 16 lines. "We prefer female protagonists. No gore or violence." Pays $5, on acceptance.

THE STRAND—P.O. Box 1418, Birmingham, MI 48012-1418. A.F. Gulli, Ed. Quarterly. Features, 3,000 to 5,000 words, are modeled after writing styles of Sir Arthur Conan Doyle, Daphne de Maurier, and Robert Louis Stevenson. Send SASE for guidelines. Pays $50 to $150, on publication.

SCIENCE FICTION & FANTASY

ABORIGINAL SF—P.O. Box 2449, Woburn, MA 01888-0849. Charles C. Ryan, Ed. Short stories, 2,500 to 6,500 words, and poetry, one to 2 typed pages, with strong science content, lively, unique characters, and well-designed plots. No sword and sorcery, horror, or fantasy. Pays $200 for fiction, $15 for poetry, $10 for science fiction jokes, and $20 for cartoons, on publication. Web site: www.aboriginalsf.com.

ABSOLUTE MAGNITUDE—P.O. Box 2988, Radford, VA 24143. Warren Lapine, Ed. Quarterly. Character-driven technical science fiction, 1,000 to 25,000 words. No fantasy, horror, satire, or funny science fiction. Pays 1¢ to 5¢ a word, on publication. Guidelines.

ADVENTURES OF SWORD & SORCERY—P.O. Box 807, Xenia, OH 45385. Randy Dannenfelser, Ed. Quarterly. High fantasy and heroic fantasy, 1,000 to 8,000 words. Pays 3¢ to 6¢ a word, on acceptance.

ANALOG SCIENCE FICTION AND FACT—475 Park Ave. S., New York, NY 10016. Stanley Schmidt, Ed. Science fiction with strong characters in believable future or alien setting: short stories, 2,000 to 7,500 words; novelettes, 10,000 to 20,000 words; serials, to 80,000 words. Also uses future-related articles. Pays to 7¢ a word, on acceptance. Query for serials and articles. E-mail: analog@dellmagazines.com. Web site: www.analogsf.com.

ASIMOV'S SCIENCE FICTION MAGAZINE—475 Park Ave. S., 11th Fl., New York, NY 10016. Gardner Dozois, Ed. Short, character-oriented science fiction and fantasy, to 15,000 words. Pays 5¢ to 8¢ a word, on acceptance. Guidelines. E-mail: asimovs@dellmagazines.com. Web site: www. asimovs.com.

FANGORIA—475 Park Ave. S., 8th Fl., New York, NY 10016. Anthony Timpone, Ed. Published 10 times yearly. Movie, TV, and book previews, reviews, and interviews, 1,800 to 2,500 words, in connection with upcoming horror films. "A strong love of the genre and an appreciation and understanding of the magazine are essential." Pays $175 to $250, on publication. No fiction.

FANTASY MACABRE—P.O. Box 20610, Seattle, WA 98102. Jessica Salmonson, Ed. Fiction, to 3,000 words, including translations. "We look for a tale that is strong in atmosphere, with menace that is suggested and threatening rather than the result of dripping blood and gore." Pays 1¢ a word, to $30 per story, on publication. Also publishes *Fantasy & Terror* for poetry-in-prose pieces.

HADROSAUR TALES—Hadrosaur Productions, P.O. Box 8468, Las Cruces, NM 88006. David Summers, Ed. Semiannual. Literary science fiction and fantasy, 1,500 to 6,000 words. Science fiction- or fantasy-based poetry, one to 2 pages. No graphic horror or violence. Pays $6 for fiction; $2 per poem, on acceptance, plus copies. E-mail: info@hadrosaur.com. Web site: www. hadrosaur.com.

THE LEADING EDGE—3163 JKHB, Provo, UT 84602. Douglas Summers Stay, Ed. Semiannual. Science fiction and fantasy, 3,000 to 12,000 words; poetry, to 600 lines; and articles, to 8,000 words, on science, scientific speculation, and literary criticism. No excessive profanity, overt violence, or excessive sexual situations. No simultaneous or electronic submissions. Pays 1¢ a word, on publication. Guidelines available at www.tle.clubs.byu.edu. E-mail: tle@byu.edu.

THE MAGAZINE OF FANTASY AND SCIENCE FICTION—Box 1806, Madison Sq. Station, New York, NY 10159-1806. Gordon Van Gelder, Ed. Fantasy and science fiction stories, to 15,000 words. Pays 5¢ to 7¢ a word, on acceptance. E-mail: webmaster@fsfmag.com. Web site: www.fsfmag.com.

MARION ZIMMER BRADLEY'S FANTASY MAGAZINE—P.O. Box 249, Berkeley, CA 94701. Marion Zimmer Bradley, Ed. Quarterly. Well-plotted stories, 3,500 to 4,000 words. Action and adventure fantasy "with no particular objection to modern settings." Send SASE for guidelines before submitting. Pays 3¢ to 10¢ a word, on acceptance. Web site: www.mzbfm.com.

NIGHT TERRORS—1202 W. Market St., Orrville, OH 44667-1710. Mr. D. E. Davidson, Ed. Stories of psychological horror, the supernatural or occult, from 2,000 to 5,000 words. Pays in copies and by arrangement with professional writers. E-mail: ded3548@aol.com. Web site: www.users.aol.com/ntmagazine/.

OF UNICORNS AND SPACE STATIONS—P.O. Box 200, Bountiful, UT 84011-0200. Gene Davis, Ed. Science fiction and fantasy, to 5,000 words. Poetry related to science fiction, science, or fantasy. "Do not staple or fold long manuscripts." Pays 1¢ per word for fiction; $5 for poems, on publication. Web site: www.genedavis.com/magazine/welcome.jsp.

ON SPEC—P.O. Box 4727, Edmonton, Alberta, Canada T6E 5G6. Jena Snyder, Gen. Ed. Quarterly. Fiction, 1,000 to 6,000 words, and poetry, to 100 lines, including science fiction, fantasy, horror, ghost stories, and magic realism. B&W drawings welcome. SASE for guidelines (IRC outside Canada); one thematic issue per year. Simultaneous submissions accepted, if so marked. Deadlines February 28, May 31, August 31, and November 30. Pays $20 to $180 (Canadian), on acceptance. E-mail: onspec@earthling.net. Web site: www.icomm.ca/onspec/.

OUTER DARKNESS: WHERE NIGHTMARES ROAM UNLEASHED—1312 N. Delaware Pl., Tulsa, OK 74110. Dennis Kirk, Ed. Quarterly. Science fiction and horror, 1,500 to 5,000 words; nonfiction pertaining to legends, myths, folklore, etc., to 1,000 words; poetry, up to two digest-size pages; half-page fillers; and B&W photos and illustrations, to one digest-size page. Query for illustrations only. Pays in copies. No electronic queries. E-mail: outerdarknessmag@hotmail.com.

SCAVENGER'S NEWSLETTER—833 Main, Osage City, KS 66523-1241. Janet Fox, Ed. Flash fiction, 1,500 words, in the genres of science fiction, fantasy, horror, and mystery. Articles, 1,500 words, pertaining to writing and art in those genres. Poems, to 10 lines, and humor, 500 to 700 words, for writers and artists. "Most of the magazine is market information." Pays $4 for fiction, articles, and cover art; $2 for humor, poems, and inside art, on acceptance. E-mail: foxscav1@jc.net. Web site: www.cza.com/scav/index.html.

SCIENCE FICTION CHRONICLE—P.O. Box 022730, Brooklyn, NY 11202-0056. Andrew Porter, Ed. News items, 300 to 800 words, for science fiction and fantasy readers, professionals, and booksellers. Interviews with authors, 3,000 to 5,000 words. No fiction. Pays 3½¢ a word, on publication. Query. Sample issue, $2. E-mail: SFChronicle@Compuserve.com.

THE SFWA BULLETIN—522 Park Ave., Berkeley Heights, NJ 07922. John Betancourt, Ed. Quarterly. Science fiction or fantasy articles to 5,000 words. Pays 8¢ to 10¢ a word, on acceptance. No fiction. E-mail queries preferred: bulletin@sfwa.org.

TALEBONES—Fairwood Press, 5203 Quincy Ave. S.E., Auburn, WA 98092. Patrick and Honna Swenson, Eds. Science fiction and dark fantasy, to 6,000 words. Articles, to 3,000 words, on the state of speculative fiction. Poetry. Cartoons with science fiction or fantasy themes. "We're looking for science fiction and dark fantasy with strong characters and entertaining story lines. Fiction should be more toward the darker side, without being pure horror." Pays 1¢ a word for fiction, 2¢ a word for the lead story, and $7 per poem, on acceptance. Accepts e-mail submissions. E-mail: talebones@nventure.com. Web site: www.fairwoodpress.com.

THE ULTIMATE UNKNOWN—Combs Press, P.O. Box 219, Streamwood, IL 60107-0219. David D. Combs, Ed. Fiction and nonfiction on horror, science fiction, and the future, to 3,000 words. Related poetry, to 20 lines. Payment is one copy. E-mail: ralitsa@sprynet.com.

THE URBANITE: SURREAL & LIVELY & BIZARRE—Box 4737, Davenport, IA 52808. Mark McLaughlin, Ed. Published 3 times a year. Dark fantasy, horror (no gore), surrealism, reviews, and social commentary, to 3,000 words. Free verse poems, to 2 pages. Pays 2¢ to 3¢ a word; $10 for poetry, on acceptance. Query for themes. Web site: www.theurbanite.tripod.com.

WEIRD TALES—DNA Publications, 123 Crooked Ln., King of Prussia, PA 19406-2570. George Scithers and Darrell Schweitzer, Eds. Quarterly. Fantasy and horror (no science fiction), to 8,000 words. Pays about 3¢ to 6¢ per word, on acceptance. Guidelines.

CONFESSION & ROMANCE

BLACK CONFESSIONS—See *Black Romance*.

BLACK ROMANCE—233 Park Ave. S., New York, NY 10003. Marcia Y. Mahan, Ed. Romance fiction, 5,000 to 5,800 words, and relationship articles. Queries preferred. Pays $100 to $125, on publication. Also publishes *Black Secrets*, *Bronze Thrills*, *Black Confessions*, and *Jive*. Guidelines.

BLACK SECRETS—See *Black Romance*.

BRONZE THRILLS—See *Black Romance*.

INTIMACY—233 Park Ave. S., 7th Fl., New York, NY 10003. Marcia Y. Mahan, Ed. Fiction, 5,000 to 5,800 words, for black women ages 18 to 45; must have contemporary plot and contain 2 romantic and intimate love scenes. Pays $100 to $125, on publication. Guidelines.

JIVE—See *Black Romance*.

MODERN ROMANCES—See *True Life Stories*.

ROMANCE AND BEYOND—PMB 9, 3527 Ambassador Caffery Pkwy., Lafayette, LA 70503-5130. Mary Tarver, Ed. Quarterly. Publishes speculative romantic short stories and poetry, combining romance with science fiction, the paranormal, and fantasy. Happy endings only. Articles are 10,000 words. Pays $10 to $15 per story, on acceptance. Send queries. Web site: www. romanceandbeyond.com.

TRUE CONFESSIONS—233 Park Ave. S., New York, NY 10003. Pat Byrdsong, Ed. Timely, emotional, first-person stories, 1,000 to 9,000 words, on romance, family life, and problems of today's young working class women. Very interested in stories highlighting experiences of Asian, African, and Latina Americans. Greatest needs stories, from 5,000 to 8,000 words. Pays 5¢ a word, after publication.

TRUE EXPERIENCE—233 Park Ave. S., New York, NY 10003. Rose Bernstein, Ed. Katherine Edwards, Assoc. Ed. Realistic first-person stories, 1,000 to 12,000 words, on family life, love, romance, overcoming hardships, mysteries. Pays 3¢ a word, after publication.

TRUE LOVE—233 Park Ave. S., New York, NY 10003. Alison Way, Ed. Fresh, young, true-to-life stories, on love and topics of current interest. Must be written in the past tense and first person. Pays 3¢ a word, after publication. Guidelines. In need of stories.

TRUE ROMANCE—233 Park Ave. S., New York, NY 10003. Pat Vitucci, Ed. True or true-to-life, dramatic and/or romantic first-person stories, 5,000 to 10,000 words. All genres: tragedy, mystery, peril, love, family struggles, etc. Topical themes. Love poems. "We enjoy working with new writers." Reports in 3 to 5 months. Pays 3¢ a word, a month after publication.

POETRY MARKETS

As the following list attests, the market for poetry in general magazines is rather limited: There aren't many general-interest magazines that use poetry, and in those that do, the competition to break into print is stiff, since editors use only a limited number of poems in each issue. In addition to the magazines listed here, writers may find their local newspapers receptive to poetry.

While poetry may be scant in general-interest magazines, it is the backbone of a majority of the college, little, and literary magazines (see page 703). Poets will also find a number of competitions offering cash awards for unpublished poems in the *Literary Prize Offers* list.

AMERICA—106 W. 56th St., New York, NY 10019. Paul Mariani, Poetry Ed. Serious poetry in a contemporary prose idiom, free or formal verse, 20 to 35 lines. Submit 2 or 3 poems with SASE. Pays $2 to $3 per line, on publication. Please be advised that we now publish only 10 to 12 high-quality poems a year. Guidelines.

THE AMERICAN SCHOLAR—1785 Massachusetts Ave. NW, 4th Fl., Washington, DC 20036. Anne Fadiman, Ed. Highly original poetry for college-educated, intellectual readers. Pays $50, on acceptance. No electronic submissions. E-mail: scholar@pbk.org. Web site: www.pbk.org.

ASIAN PAGES—P.O. Box 11932, St. Paul, MN 55111-0932. Cheryl Weiberg, Ed.-in-Chief. Poetry, 100 words, with "a strong, non-offensive Asian slant." Pays on publication. E-mail: asianpages@att.net. Web site: www.asian pages.com.

THE ATLANTIC MONTHLY—77 N. Washington St., Boston, MA 02114. Peter Davison, David Barber, Poetry Eds. Previously unpublished poetry of highest quality. Limited market; only 2 to 3 poems an issue. Interested in new poets. Occasionally uses light verse. "No simultaneous, fax, or e-mail submissions; we make prompt decisions." Pays excellent rates, on acceptance. Web site: www.theatlantic.com.

CAPPER'S—1503 S.W. 42nd St., Topeka, KS 66609-1265. Ann Crahan, Ed. Free verse, light verse, traditional, nature, and inspirational poems, 4 to 16 lines, with simple everyday themes. Submit up to 6 poems at a time, with SASE. Pays $10 to $15, on acceptance.

CHILDREN'S PLAYMATE—P.O. Box 567, Indianapolis, IN 46206. Terry Harshman, Ed. Poetry for children, 6 to 8 years old, on good health, nutrition, exercise, safety, seasonal and humorous subjects. Pays from $30, on publication. Buys all rights. Web site: www.childrensplaymatemag.org.

THE CHRISTIAN SCIENCE MONITOR—One Norway St., Boston, MA 02115. Elizabeth Lund, Poetry Ed. Finely crafted poems that explore and celebrate daily life. Seasonal material always needed. No violence or sensuality; no death or disease; no helplessness or hopelessness. Short poems preferred; submit no more than 5 poems at a time. SASE required. Pays varying rates, on publication. Web site: csmonitor.com.

COMMONWEAL—475 Riverside Dr., New York, NY 10115. Rosemary Deen, Poetry Ed. Catholic. Serious, witty poetry. Pays 50¢ a line, on publication. SASE required. No submissions accepted June to September.

COUNTRY WOMAN—P.O. Box 989, Greendale, WI 53129. Kathy Pohl, Exec. Ed. Traditional rural poetry and light verse, 4 to 30 lines, on rural experiences and country living; also seasonal poetry. Poems must rhyme. Pays $10 to $25, on acceptance.

EVANGEL—Light and Life Communications, Box 535002, Indianapolis, IN 46253-5002. Julie Innes, Ed. Free Methodist. Devotional or nature poetry, 8 to 16 lines. Pays $10, on publication. Guidelines available with SASE.

MATURE YEARS—201 Eighth Ave. S., P.O. Box 801, Nashville, TN 37202. Marvin W. Cropsey, Ed. United Methodist. Poetry, to 14 lines, on preretirement, retirement, Christianity, inspiration, seasonal subjects, aging. No "saccharine" poetry. Submit up to 6 poems at a time. Pays 50¢ to $1 per line. E-mail: matureyears@umpublishing.org.

MIDSTREAM—633 Third Ave., 21st Fl., New York, NY 10017. Attn: Poetry Ed. Poetry of Jewish/Zionist interest. "Brevity highly recommended." Pays $25, on publication. Allow 3 months for response.

THE MIRACULOUS MEDAL—475 E. Chelten Ave., Philadelphia, PA 19144-5785. William J. O'Brien, C.M., Ed. Catholic. Religious verse, to 20 lines. Pays 50¢ a line, on acceptance.

THE NATION—33 Irving Place, 8th Fl., New York, NY 10003. Grace Schulman, Poetry Ed. Poetry of high quality. Pays after publication. SASE required. Web site: www.thenation.com.

NATIONAL ENQUIRER—600 East Coast Ave., Lantana, FL 33464-0002. Kathy Martin, Fillers Ed. Short poems, to 8 lines, with traditional rhyming verse, of an amusing, philosophical, or inspirational nature. No experimental poetry. Original epigrams, humorous anecdotes, and "daffynitions." Submit seasonal/holiday material at least 2 months in advance. Pays $25, after publication. Material will not be returned; do not send SASE.

THE NEW REPUBLIC—1220 19th St. N.W., Washington, DC 20036. Attn: Mark Strand, Ed. Pays $100, after publication.

THE NEW YORKER—4 Times Square, New York, NY 10036. Attn: Poetry Ed. First-rate poetry. Pays top rates, on acceptance. Include SASE.

THE PLASTIC TOWER—P.O. Box 702, Bowie, MD 20718. Roger Kyle-Keith Quarterly. Poetry, to 40 lines, in any style. Original and individual subjects preferred. Submit up to 8 poems with SASE. Pays one copy.

PURPOSE—616 Walnut Ave., Scottdale, PA 15683-1999. James E. Horsch, Poetry Ed. Poetry, to 8 lines, with challenging Christian discipleship angle. Pays 85¢ to $2.50 a line, on acceptance. E-mail: horsch@mph.org. Web site: www.mph.org.

ST. JOSEPH'S MESSENGER—P.O. Box 288, Jersey City, NJ 07303-0288. Sister Mary Kuiken, Ed. Light verse and traditional poetry, 4 to 40 lines. Pays $10 to $25, on publication. Very few poems used.

THE SATURDAY EVENING POST—P.O. Box 567, Indianapolis, IN 46206. Steven Pettinga, Post Scripts Ed. Short narratives, jokes, and humorous, clean limericks. No conventional poetry. SASE required. Pays $15, on publication. Writer's guidelines at www.satevepost.org. E-mail address: sateve pst@aol.com.

VERSE—English Dept., Plymouth State College, Plymouth, NH 03264. Brian Henry, Ed. Three times yearly. Poetry (up to 5 poems); and nonfiction, including essays on poetry, interviews with poets, and reviews of poetry. Submit with cover letter and SASE. Pays in copies and subscription. E-mail: verse @versemag.org. Web site: www.versemag.org.

WESTERN PEOPLE—P.O. Box 2500, Saskatoon, Sask., Canada S7K 2C4. Michael Gillgannon, Man. Ed. Weekly circulation, 80,000. Short poetry with Western Canadian themes. Pays on acceptance. Send international reply coupons. E-mail: people@producer.com.

YANKEE—Yankee Publishing Co., P.O. Box 520, Dublin, NH 03444. Jean Burden, Poetry Ed. Serious poetry of high quality, to 30 lines. Pays $50 per poem for first North American Magazine rights, on publication. No e-mail or fax submissions. SASE required. Web site: www.newengland.com.

COLLEGE, LITERARY, & LITTLE MAGAZINES

The thousands of literary journals, little magazines, and college quarterlies published today welcome work from novices and pros alike; editors are always interested in seeing traditional and experimental fiction, poetry, essays, reviews, short articles, criticism, and satire, and as long as the material is well-written, the fact that a writer is a beginner doesn't adversely affect his or her chances for acceptance.

Most of these smaller publications have small budgets and staffs, so they may be slow in their reporting time; several months is not unusual. In addition, they usually pay only in copies of the issue in which published work appears and some (particularly college magazines) do not read manuscripts during the summer.

Publication in the literary journals can, however, lead to recognition by editors of large-circulation magazines, who read the little magazines in their search for new talent. There is also the possibility of having one's work chosen for reprinting in one of the prestigious annual collections of work from the little magazines.

Because the requirements of these journals differ widely, it is always important to study recent issues before submitting work to one of them. Large libraries may carry a variety of journals, or a writer may send a postcard to the editor and ask the price of a sample copy.

For a complete list of literary and college publications and little magazines, writers may consult such reference works as *The International Directory of Little Magazines and Small Presses,* published annually by Dustbooks (P.O. Box 100, Paradise, CA 95967).

ABOUT SUCH THINGS—1701 Delancey St., Philadelphia, PA 19103. Laurel Garver, Man. Ed. Semiannual. Essays and reviews of arts and cultural topics. Free verse poetry. Fiction, to 3,000 words. "We seek contemporary voices that explore how Christian faith affects life in a broken world." Pays in 2 copies. Send SASE for guidelines. Sample $3. E-mail: aboutsuch@home page.com. Web site: www.aboutsuch.homepage.com.

AFRICAN AMERICAN REVIEW—Dept. of English, Indiana State Univ., Terre Haute, IN 47809. Joe Weixlmann, Ed. Essays on African American literature, theater, film, art, and culture; interviews; poems; fiction; and book reviews. Submit up to 6 poems. Pays an honorarium and copies. Query for book review assignments; send 3 copies of all other submissions. Responds in 3 months.

AFRICAN VOICES—270 W. 96th St., New York, NY 10025. Carolyn A. Butts, Exec. Ed. Quarterly. Humorous, erotic, and dramatic fiction, 500 to 2,500 words, by ethnic writers. Nonfiction, 500 to 1,500 words, including investigative articles, artist profiles, essays, and first-person narratives. Pays in copies. SASE. E-mail: annebutts@aol.com. Web site: www.africanvoices.com.

AGNI—Boston Univ., Creative Writing Program, 236 Bay State Rd., Boston, MA 02215. Askold Melnyczuk, Ed. Eric Grunwald, Man. Ed. Short stories, poetry, and reviews. Accepting manuscripts after October 1, 2000.

ALABAMA LITERARY REVIEW—Troy State Univ., 150 Smith Hall, Troy, AL 36082. William E. Hicks, Chief Ed. Annual. Contemporary, literary fiction and nonfiction, 3,500 words; short drama, to 25 pages; and poetry, to 2 pages. Thought-provoking B&W photos. Pays in copies (honorarium when available). Responds within 3 months.

ALASKA QUARTERLY REVIEW—Univ. of Alaska Anchorage, 3211 Providence Dr., Anchorage, AK 99508. Attn: Eds. Short stories, novel excerpts, short plays, and poetry (traditional and unconventional forms). Submit manuscripts between August 15 and May 15. Pays in subscription (and honorarium when funding is available). E-mail: ayaqr@uaa.alaska.edu. Web site: www.uaa.alaska.edu/aqr.

AMELIA—329 E St., Bakersfield, CA 93304. Frederick A. Raborg, Jr., Ed. Poetry, to 100 lines; critical essays, to 2,000 words; reviews, to 500 words; belles lettres, to 1,000 words; fiction, to 4,500 words; fine pen-and-ink sketches; photos. Pays $35 for fiction; $25 for criticism; $10 to $25 for other nonfiction and artwork; $2 to $25 for poetry. Annual contest. E-mail: amelia@lightspeed.net.

THE AMERICAN BOOK REVIEW—Unit for Contemporary Literature, Illinois State Univ., Campus Box 4241, Normal, IL 61790-4241. Rebecca Kaiser, Man. Ed. Literary book reviews, 700 to 1,200 words. Pays $50 or 2-year subscription and copies. Query with clips of published reviews.

AMERICAN LITERARY REVIEW—Univ. of North Texas, English Dept., Denton, TX 76203-1307. Lee Martin, Ed. Short fiction and creative nonfiction, to 30 double-spaced pages, and poetry (submit 3 to 5 poems). Pays in copies. Read: September 1 through May 1. Web site: www.engl.unt.edu/alr.

THE AMERICAN POETRY REVIEW—1721 Walnut St., Philadelphia, PA 19103. Attn: Eds. Highest quality contemporary poetry. Responds in 10 weeks.

AMERICAN QUARTERLY—Dept. of English, Georgetown Univ., Washington, DC 20057. Lucy Maddox, Ed. Scholarly essays, 5,000 to 10,000 words, on any aspect of U.S. culture. Pays in copies.

THE AMERICAN SCHOLAR—1785 Massachusetts Ave. NW, 4th Fl., Washington, DC 20036. Anne Fadiman, Ed. Articles, 3,500 to 4,000 words, on science, politics, literature, the arts, etc. Book reviews. Pays up to $500 for articles, $100 for reviews, on publication. No electronic submissions. E-mail: scholar@pbk.org. Web site: www.pbk.org.

AMERICAN WRITING—4343 Manayunk Ave., Philadelphia, PA 19128. Alexandra Grilikhes, Ed. Semiannual. "We encourage experimentation, new writing that takes risks with form, point of view, and language. We're interested in the voice of the loner, states of being, and initiation. We strongly suggest reading a copy of the magazine before submitting your work." Fiction and nonfiction, to 3,500 words, and poetry. Pays in copies. Sample issue $6, 2 year subscription $10.

ANOTHER CHICAGO MAGAZINE—3709 N. Kenmore, Chicago, IL 60613. Attn: Ed. Semiannual. Fiction, essays on literature, and poetry. "We want writing that's urgent, new, and lives in the world." Pays in copies on acceptance, and small honorarium when possible. Reads February 1 through October 31. Sponsors the Annual Chicago Literary Awards. E-mail: moss67@anotherchicagomag.com. Web site: www.anotherchicagomag.com.

ANTHOLOGY—P.O. Box 4411, Mesa, AZ 85211-4411. Sharon Skinner, Exec. Ed. Bimonthly. Stories, up to 5,000 words, any genre. Poetry, any style, to 100 lines. "We also accept stories based in the fictional city of Haven, where people make their own heroes." Payment is one copy. Send SASE for guidelines. E-mail: info@inkwellpress.com. Web site: www.anthologymagazine.com.

ANTIETAM REVIEW—41 S. Potomac St., Hagerstown, MD 21740.

Ethan Fischer and Susanne Kass, Eds.-in-Chief. Fiction, to 5,000 words. Submissions from natives or residents of MD, PA, WV, VA, DC, DE only. Manuscripts read September through January only. Pays $50 to $100 for fiction, $25 for poems. Literary contest for fiction and poetry. Query for guidelines.

THE ANTIGONISH REVIEW—St. Francis Xavier Univ., P.O. Box 5000, Antigonish, NS, Canada B2G 2W5. George Sanderson, Ed. Poetry; short stories, essays, book reviews, 1,800 to 2,500 words. Pays in copies. E-mail: tar@stfx.ca. Web site: www.antigonish.com/review/.

ANTIOCH REVIEW—P.O. Box 148, Yellow Springs, OH 45387-0148. Robert S. Fogarty, Ed. Timely articles, 2,000 to 8,000 words, on social sciences, literature, and humanities. Quality fiction. Poetry. No inspirational poetry. Pays $10 per printed page, on publication. Poetry considered from September to May; other material considered year-round. Web site: www. antioch.edu/review.

APPALACHIA—5 Joy St., Boston, MA 02108. Parkman Howe, Poetry Ed. Semiannual publication of the Appalachian Mountain Club. Oldest mountaineering journal in the country covers nature, conservation, climbing, hiking, canoeing, and ecology. Poems, to 30 lines. Pays in copies.

ARACHNE—2363 Page Rd., Kennedy, NY 14747-9717. Susan L. Leach, Ed. Semiannual. Fiction, to 1,500 words. Poems (submit up to 7). "We are looking for rural material." Pays in copies. Manuscripts read in January and July.

ARIZONA QUARTERLY—Univ. of Arizona, Main Library B-541, Tucson, AZ 85721. Edgar A. Dryden, Ed. Criticism of American literature and culture from a theoretical perspective. No poetry or fiction. Pays in copies.

ART TIMES—P.O. Box 730, Mt. Marion, NY 12456. Raymond J. Steiner, Ed. Fiction, to 1,500 words, and poetry, to 20 lines, for literate, art conscious readers (generally over 40 years old). Feature essays on the arts are staff-written. Pays $25 for fiction, in copies for poetry, on publication. Responds within six months. E-mail: info@arttimesjournal.com. Web site: www. arttimesjournal.com.

ARTFUL DODGE—College of Wooster, Wooster, OH 44691. Daniel Bourne, Ed. Annual. Fiction, to 20 pages. Literary essays, especially those involving personal narrative, to 15 pages. Poetry, including translations of contemporary poets; submit 3 to 6 poems at a time; long poems encouraged. Pays $5 per page, on publication, plus 2 copies. Manuscripts read year-round.

ASCENT—Dept. of English, Concordia College, 901 8th St. S., Moorhead, MN 56562. W. Scott Olsen, Ed. Three times yearly. Fiction, nonfiction, and poetry. No reviews or editorial articles. Submit complete manuscripts with SASE. Pays in copies. E-mail ascent@cord.edu. Web site: www.cord.edu/dept/english/ascent.

THE ASIAN PACIFIC AMERICAN JOURNAL—The Asian American Writers' Workshop, 37 St. Marks Pl., New York, NY 10003-7801. Hanya Yanagihara, Ed. Short stories, excerpts from longer fiction works by emerging or established Asian American writers. Four copies of each submission in all genres required. Poetry (submit up to 10 poems). Pays in copies. Query required for reviews and interviews; queries preferred for other articles. E-mail: desk@aaww.org. Web site: www.aaww.org.

AURA LITERARY/ARTS REVIEW—P.O. Box 76, Univ. Center, UAB,

Birmingham, AL 35294. Natalie Ann Adams, Ed.-in-Chief. Fiction and essays on literature, to 5,000 words; poetry; artwork in slide or print form. Pays in copies. Guidelines.

BAMBOO RIDGE: JOURNAL OF HAWAII LITERATURE AND ARTS—Bamboo Ridge Press, P.O. Box 61781, Honolulu, HI 96839-1781. Chock and Lum, Eds. Poetry, to 10 pages, and short stories, 25 pages, by writers in U.S. and abroad. Submit with SASE. Reports in 6 to 12 months. Pays 2 copies. Manuscripts read year-round.

BEACON STREET REVIEW—WLP Div., Emerson College, 100 Beacon St., Boston, MA 02116. Attn: Ed. Semiannual. Fiction, poetry, memoir, essays, to 20 pages. "Produced and edited by graduate students. We publish primarily writing by students in MFA programs." Send 3 copies of submission, short bio, and SASE. No payment.

THE BEAR DELUXE— P.O. Box 10342, Portland, OR 97296. Tom Webb, Ed. Quarterly. Unique environmental articles, 750 to 3,500 words; essays, 250 to 2,500 words; artist profiles, 750 to 1,500 words; and reviews, 100 to 1,000 words. Fiction, 750 to 4,500 words (2,500 is ideal). Poetry. Pays 5¢ a word, after publication, and subscription. Query for nonfiction. E-mail: bear@ teleport.com. Web site: www.orlo.com.

THE BELLINGHAM REVIEW—The Signpost Press, MS 9053, Western Washington Univ., Bellingham, WA 98225. Robin Hemley, Ed. Semiannual. Fiction and nonfiction, to 10,000 words, and poetry, any length. Pays in copies and subscription. Manuscripts read October to April. Three annual contests, $1,000 prize for first place. Send SASE for guidelines.

BELLOWING ARK—P.O. Box 55564, Shoreline, WA 98155. Robert R. Ward, Ed. Bimonthly. Short fiction that portrays life as a positive, meaningful process. Pays in copies. Manuscripts read year-round. Please no simultaneous submissions.

THE BELOIT FICTION JOURNAL—Box 11, Beloit College, Beloit, WI 53511. Clint McCown, Ed.; Tenaya Darlington, Man. Ed. Short fiction, one to 35 pages, of all themes (no pornography, political propaganda, religious dogma). Manuscripts read August 1 to December. Pays in copies.

BELOIT POETRY JOURNAL—24 Berry Cove Rd, Lamoine, ME 04605. Strong contemporary poetry, of any length or in any mode. Pays in copies. Guidelines. No simultaneous submissions. Web site: www.bpj.org.

BIBLIOPHILOS—Bibliophile Publishing, 200 Security Bldg., Fairmont, WV 26554. Dr. Gerald J. Bobango, Ed. Quarterly. Fiction and nonfiction, 1,500 to 3,000 words; poetry, to five printed pages (in batches of five). Reviews of history, literature, and literary criticism especially needed. Query. Pays $5 to $25 plus complimentary issue, on publication. Web site: www.personal. umich.edu/~lgmeindl/biblio/bibliophilos.html.

THE BITTER OLEANDER—4983 Tall Oaks Dr., Fayetteville, NY 13066-9776. Paul B. Roth, Ed./Pub. Short stories,1,500 to 2,000 words. Poems, one to 100 lines. "Only highly imaginative poems and stories will suffice." Pays in copies. SASE. E-mail: bones44@ix.netcom.com. Web site: www.bitter oleander.com.

BLACK BEAR REVIEW—Black Bear Publications, 1916 Lincoln St., Croydon, PA 19021-8026. Ave Jeanne, Ed. Semiannual. Contemporary poetry and art work. "We publish poems with social awareness, originality, and strength." Pays in one copy. Web site address: www.home.earthlink.net/~bb review. Submissions with name and address to e-mail address: bbreview@ earthlink.net. No attachments please.

BLACK MOON: POETRY OF IMAGINATION—233 Northway Rd., Reistertown, MD 21136. Alan Britt, Ed. Imaginative poetry, long or short. Payment is one copy. Query. Guidelines.

THE BLACK WARRIOR REVIEW—The Univ. of Alabama, P.O. Box 862936, Tuscaloosa, AL 35486-0027. Laura Didyk, Ed. Fiction; poetry; translations; reviews and essays. Pays about $100 for fiction; about $40 per poem, on publication. Annual awards. Manuscripts read year-round.

THE BLOOMSBURY REVIEW—P.O. Box 8928, Denver, CO 80201. Tom Auer, Ed. Marilyn Auer, Assoc. Ed. Book reviews, publishing features, interviews, essays, poetry. Pays $5 to $25, on publication.

BLUE UNICORN—22 Avon Rd., Kensington, CA 94707. Attn: Ed. Published in October, February, and June. "We are looking for originality of image, thought, and music; we rarely use poems over a page long." Submit up to 5 poems. Artwork used occasionally. Pays in one copy. Guidelines. Contest. SASE.

BLUELINE—English Dept., SUNY, Potsdam, NY 13676. Rick Henry, Ed. Essays and fiction, to 3,500 words, on Adirondack region or similar areas. Poems, to 75 lines; submit up to 5. Pays in copies. Manuscripts read September through November. E-mail: blueline@potsdam.edu. Web site: www.pots dam.edu/engl/blueline.

BORDERLANDS: TEXAS POETRY REVIEW—P.O. Box 33096, Austin, TX 78764. Attn: Eds. Biannual. Outwardly directed poetry that exhibits social, political, spiritual, geographical, or historical awareness coupled with intelligence, creativity, and artistry. Bilingual poems and poems in two languages are acceptable when the poet has written both versions. Submit up to 5 poems with SASE. Also publishes interviews, essays (no more than 3,000 words), and reviews on contemporary poets and poets from the Southwest. Query for guidelines and contests. Pays one copy. Web site: www.border lands.org.

BOSTON REVIEW—E53–407, MIT, Cambridge, MA 02139. Jefferson Decker, Man. Ed. Politics, literature, art, music, film, photography. Original fiction, to 5,000 words. Poetry. Pays $40 to $100. Manuscripts read year-round. E-mail: review@mit.edu. Website: www.bostonreview.mit.edu.

BOTTOMFISH—De Anza College, 21250 Stevens Creek Blvd., Cupertino, CA 95014. Randolph Splitter, Ed. Annual. Short stories, short-shorts, poetry, creative nonfiction, interviews with writers and artists, photography, drawings, comics, and other visual art forms. Pays in copies. Submission period September to December only. Magazine published in April. Web site: www. deanza.fhda.edu/bottomfish.

BOULEVARD—4579 Laclede Ave., #332, St. Louis, MO 63108-2103. Richard Burgin, Ed. Published 3 times a year. High quality fiction, to 30 pages. Pays to $300, on publication. Pieces often reprinted in books and anthologies. No submissions read from April 1 through October 1.

BRIAR CLIFF REVIEW—Briar Cliff College, 3303 Rebecca St., Sioux City, IA 51104. Tricia Currans-Sheehan, Man. Ed. Jeanne Emmons, Poetry Ed. Phil Hey, Fiction Ed. Prose, to 5,000 words: fiction, humor/satire, Siouxland history, thoughtful nonfiction. Also poetry, book reviews, and art. "We're an eclectic literary and cultural magazine focusing on, but not limited to, Siouxland writers and subjects." Pays in copies. Manuscripts read August through October. E-mail: currans@briar-cliff.edu. Web site: www.briar-cliff.edu/bcreview.

THE BRIDGE—14050 Vernon St., Oak Park, MI 48237. Jack Zucker, Ed. Helen Zucker, Fiction Ed. Mitzi Alvin, Poetry Ed. Semiannual. Fiction, to 20 pages, and poetry to 200 lines. "Serious, realistic work with style." Pays in 2 copies.

BUCKNELL REVIEW—Bucknell Univ., Lewisburg, PA 17837. Attn: Ed. Interdisciplinary journal in book form. Scholarly articles on arts, science, and letters. Pays in copies.

CALLALOO—Univ. of Virginia, Dept. of English, 322 Bryan Hall, P.O. Box 400121, Charlottesville, VA 22904-4121. Charles H. Rowell, Ed. Fiction, poetry, drama, and essays by, and critical studies and bibliographies on African-American, Caribbean, and African Diaspora artists and writers. Submit in triplicate: one copy with all contact information and two blind copies. Payment varies, on publication. E-mail: callaloo@virginia.edu. Web site: www.muse.jhu.edu/journals/callaloo.

CALYX, A JOURNAL OF ART & LITERATURE BY WOMEN—P.O. Box B, Corvallis, OR 97339. M. Reaman, Man. Ed. Fiction, 5,000 words; book reviews, 1,000 words (please query about reviews); poetry, to 6 poems. Include short bio. Pays in copies and subscription. Guidelines. SASE. Submissions accepted October 1 to December 15.

THE CAPE ROCK—Dept. of English, Southeast Missouri State Univ., Cape Girardeau, MO 63701. Harvey E. Hecht, Ed. Semiannual. Poetry, to 70 lines, and B&W photography. (One photographer per issue; pays $100.) Pays in copies and $200 for best poem in each issue. Manuscripts read August to April. E-mail: hhecht@sermovn.semo.edu.

THE CAPILANO REVIEW— 2055 Purcell Way, N. Vancouver, B.C., Canada V7J 3H5. Ryan Knighton, Ed. Experimental and literary fiction, 4,000 words; drama; poetry; photos and drawings. Pays $50 to $200, on publication. No electronic submissions. E-mail: tcr@capcollege.bc.ca. Web site: www.cap college.bc.ca/dept/tcr.

THE CARIBBEAN WRITER—Univ. of the Virgin Islands, RR 02, Box 10,000, Kingshill, St. Croix, USVI 00850. Erika J. Waters, Ed. Annual. Fiction, to 15 pages, poems, personal essays, and one-act plays; the Caribbean should be central to the work. Blind submissions policy: place title only on manuscript; name, address, and title on separate sheet. Pays in copies. Annual deadline is September 30. E-mail submissions acceptable: qmars@uvi.edu. Web site: www.uvi.edu/caribbeanwriter/.

THE CAROLINA QUARTERLY—Greenlaw Hall CB#3520, Univ. of North Carolina, Chapel Hill, NC 27599-3520. Brian Carpenter, Ed. Articles, to 5,000 words, by new or established writers. Poetry, to 300 lines; some nonfiction, artwork. Manuscripts read year-round.

THE CENTENNIAL REVIEW—312 Linton Hall, Michigan State Univ., East Lansing, MI 48824-1044. R.K. Meiners, Ed. Articles, 3,000 to 5,000 words, on sciences, humanities, and interdisciplinary topics. Pays in copies.

THE CHARITON REVIEW—Truman State Univ., Kirksville, MO 63501. Jim Barnes, Ed. Highest quality fiction, to 6,000 words. No "relatives" stories, essays, or poems. (Accepts 8 to 12 manuscripts each year.) Pays $5 per printed page.

CHATTAHOOCHEE REVIEW—Georgia Perimeter College, 2101 Womack Rd., Dunwoody, GA 30338-4497. Lawrence Hetrick, Ed. Quarterly. Fiction, essays, interviews, art, book reviews, and poetry. Pays on publication. Send SASE for guidelines and pay schedule. Web site: www.gpc.peachnet.edu/twadley/cr/index.htm.

CHELSEA—Box 773, Cooper Sta., New York, NY 10276. Richard Foerster, Ed. Alfredo de Palchi, Sr. Assoc. Ed. Andrea Lockett, Assoc. Ed. Fresh, original fiction and nonfiction, to 25 manuscript pages. Poems (submit 4 to 6). Translations welcome. "We are an eclectic literary magazine serving a sophisticated international audience. No racist, sexist, pornographic, or romance material." Query for book reviews. Pays $20 per page, on publication. Annual poetry and fiction contests ($1,000 plus publication); send SASE for guidelines for the annual Chelsea Award competitions.

CHICAGO REVIEW—5801 S. Kenwood Ave., Chicago, IL 60637. Eirik Steinhoff, Ed. William Martin, Fiction Ed. Fiction. Pays in copies plus one year subscription. Manuscripts read October through May; replies in 4 to 5 months. E-mail: chicago-review@uchicago.edu. Web site: www.humanities.uchicago.edu/review.

CHIRON REVIEW—702 No. Prairie, St. John, KS 67576-1516. Michael Hathaway, Ed. Contemporary fiction, to 4,000 words; articles, 500 to 1,000 words; and poetry, to 30 lines. Photos. Pays in copies. Poetry and chapbook contests. Web site: www.geocities.com/soho/nook/1748/.

CICADA—329 E St., Bakersfield, CA 93304. Frederick A. Raborg, Jr., Ed. Quarterly. Single haiku, sequences, or garlands; essays about the forms; haibun, tanka, renga, and fiction (one story per issue) related to haiku or Japan. Pays $10 plus one copy for fiction; $10 for "best of issue" poetry. E-mail: amelia@lightspeed.net. Web site: www.cricketmag.com.

CIMARRON REVIEW—205 Morrill Hall, Oklahoma State Univ., Stillwater, OK 74078-0135. Fiction, Nonfiction, or Poetry Editor Fiction. Seeks an individual style that focuses on contemporary themes. Pays $50 for stories and essays; $15 for poems. Manuscripts read year-round. Replies in three months. No simultaneous submissions. E-mail: oklahomafist@hotmail.com. Web site: http://cimarronreview.okstate.edu.

CITY PRIMEVAL—P.O. Box 30064, Seattle, WA 98103. Elizabeth Siddal, Assoc. Ed. Quarterly. Fiction, to 15,000 words, and poetry, to 150 lines, that deals with men and women contending with the evolving urban environment. B&W drawings and photos welcome. Send for guidelines. No simultaneous submissions. Pays one copy.

THE CLAREMONT REVIEW—4980 Wesley Rd., Victoria, BC, Canada V84 1Y9. Eds. Biannual. Fiction with a strong voice, 500 to 3,000 words, and poetry that stirs the heart by young adults 13 to 19. Photos welcome. Submit complete manuscript with SASE (IRC if outside Canada); guidelines available. Pays copy. E-mail: aurora@home.com. Web site: www.members.home.net/review.

THE COA—The Citizens of America, 30 Ford St., Glen Cove, NY

11542. John J. Maddox, Ed. Published 9 times a year. Fiction and nonfiction, 250 to 2,000 words; poetry, to 100 words; fillers. Photos published with article if preferred; drawings also accepted. Pays $40 to $100 using a payment plan. Query for guidelines. E-mail: coamagmc98@webtv.net.

COLLAGES & BRICOLAGES—P.O. Box 360, Shippenville, PA 16254. Marie-José Fortis, Ed. Annual. Fiction and nonfiction, plays, interviews, book reviews, and poetry. Surrealistic, feminist, and expressionistic drawings in ink. "We seek innovation and honesty. The magazine often focuses on one subject; query for themes." B&W photos; photo-collages. Pays in copies. Manuscripts read August through November. E-mail: cb@penn.com. Web site: www. angelrive.com/on2/collagesbricolages.

COLORADO REVIEW—English Dept., Colorado State Univ., Fort Collins, CO 80523. David Milofsky, Ed. Short fiction and poetry on contemporary themes. Pays $5 per printed page for fiction and poetry. Manuscripts read September 1 to April 30. Send SASE for guidelines. Sample issue $10. E-mail: creview@vines.colostate.edu. Web site: www.colostate.edu/depts/english/english-ns4.html.

COLUMBIA: A JOURNAL OF LITERATURE & ART—415 Dodge, Columbia Univ., New York, NY 10027. Attn: Ed. Biannual. Fiction and nonfiction; poetry; essays; interviews; visual art. Pays in copies. SASE for guidelines and contest rules. Manuscripts read September to May.

THE COMICS JOURNAL—Fantagraphics, Inc., 7563 Lake City Way, Seattle, WA 98115. Attn: Man. Ed. "Looking for freelancers with working knowledge of the diversity and history of the comics medium." Reviews, 2,500 to 5,000 words; domestic and international news, 500 to 7,000 words; commentaries, 500 to 1,500 words; interviews; and features, 2,500 to 5,000 words. Query for news and interviews. Pays 3¢ a word, on publication. Guidelines.

CONCHO RIVER REVIEW—Angelo State Univ., English Dept., San Angelo, TX 76909. James A. Moore, Ed. Semiannual. Fiction, essays, and book reviews, 1,500 to 5,000 words. Poetry, 500 to 1,500 words. "We tend to publish traditional stories with a strong sense of conflict, finely drawn characters, and crisp dialogue. Critical papers, articles, and personal essays with a Texas or Southwestern literary slant preferred. Query for book reviews." Payment is one copy. E-mail: james.moore@angelo.edu. Web site: www.angelo.edu/dept/eng.

CONFLUENCE—P.O. Box 336, Belpre, OH 45714-0336. David B. Prather, Poetry Ed. Daniel Born, Fiction Ed. Published annually by Marietta College and the Ohio Valley Literary Group. Poetry and short fiction. Pays in copies. Manuscripts read September through March.

CONFRONTATION—Dept. of English, C.W. Post of L.I.U., Brookville, NY 11548. Martin Tucker, Ed. Serious fiction, 750 to 6,000 words. Pays $15 to $200, on publication. E-mail: mtucker@liu.edu.

THE CONNECTICUT POETRY REVIEW—P.O. Box 818, Stonington, CT 06378. J. Claire White and Harley More, Eds. Poetry, 5 to 20 lines, and reviews, 700 words. Pays $5 per poem, $10 per review, on acceptance. Manuscripts read September to January and April to June.

CONNECTICUT RIVER REVIEW—P.O. Box 4053, Waterbury, CT 06704-0053. Kevin Carey, Ed. Semiannual. Poetry. Submit up to 3 poems. Pays in one copy. Guidelines.

THE CREAM CITY REVIEW—Univ. of Wisconsin-Milwaukee, English Dept., P.O. Box 413, Milwaukee, WI 53201. Peter Whalen, Kyoko Yos-hida, co-eds. Semiannual. Fiction, poetry, essays, reviews, interviews. "We publish work by established and emerging writers. We strive to produce a journal that is engaging, diverse, and of lasting quality." Pays in copies. Reads September 1 through April 30. Send SASE for annual contest guidelines. Web site: www.csd.uwm.edu/dept/english/ccr/index2.html.

CREATIVE NONFICTION—5501 Walnut, Suite 202, Pittsburgh, PA 15232. Lee Gutkind, Ed. "No length requirements; seeking well-written nonfiction prose, attentive to language, rich with detail and distinctive voice on any subject, especially seeking essays that include an informational element using research." Pays from $10 per published page. Send SASE for upcoming themes. E-mail: crn2@pitt.edu. Web site: www.creativenonfiction.org.

CRITICAL INQUIRY—Univ. of Chicago Press, 202 Wieboldt Hall, 1050 E. 59th St., Chicago, IL 60637. W. J. T. Mitchell, Ed. Critical essays that offer a theoretical perspective on literature, music, visual arts, and popular culture. No fiction, poetry, or autobiography. Pays in copies. Manuscripts read year-round.

CUMBERLAND POETRY REVIEW—P.O. Box 120128, Acklen Sta., Nashville, TN 37212. Attn: Eds. High-quality poetry and criticism; translations. Send up to 6 poems with brief bio. No restrictions on form, style, or subject matter. Pays in copies.

CUTBANK—English Dept., Univ. of Montana, Missoula, MT 59812. Attn: Eds. Semiannual. Fiction, to 40 pages (submit one story at a time), and poems (submit up to 5 poems). All manuscripts are considered for the Richard Hugo Memorial Poetry Award and the A.B. Guthrie, Jr. Short Fiction Award. Pays in copies. Guidelines. Manuscripts read August 15 to March 15. E-mail: cutbank@selway.umt.edu.

DENVER QUARTERLY—Univ. of Denver, Denver, CO 80208. Bin Ramke, Ed. Literary, cultural essays and articles; poetry; book reviews; fiction. Pays $5 per printed page, after publication. Manuscripts read September 15 to May 15.

DESCANT—T.C.U. Box 297270, Fort Worth, TX 76129. Dave Kuhne, Ed. Fiction, to 6,000 words. Poetry, to 60 lines. No restriction on form or subject. Pays in copies. Frank O'Connor Award ($500) is given each year for best short story published in the volume. Betsy Colquitt Award ($500) is given each year for best poetry published in the volume. Submit material September through May only. E-mail: descant.tcu.edu.

THE DEVIL'S MILLHOPPER—The Devil's Millhopper Press, USC/Aiken, 471 University Pkwy., Aiken, SC 29801-6309. Stephen Gardner, Ed. Poetry. Send SASE for guidelines and contest information. Pays in copies. E-mail: steveg@aiken.sc.edu.

THE DISTILLERY—Motlow State Community College, P.O. Box 8500, Lynchburg, TN 37352. Niles Reddick, Ed. Semiannual. Fiction, 3,000 words; poetry, submit 4 to 6 poems; essays; photos and art. Responds in 2 to 3 months. Pays in copies. Web site: www.mscc.cc.tn.us/wmw/distillery.

DOUBLE DEALER REDUX—624 Pirate's Alley, New Orleans, LA 70116. Rosemary James, Ed. Quarterly. Fiction, essays, and poetry. "We showcase the work of promising writers." No payment. Query. Contest.

DREAMS & VISIONS—Skysong Press, 35 Peter St. S., Orillia, Ontario,

Canada L3V 5A8. Steve Stanton, Ed. Eclectic fiction, 2,000 to 6,000 words, that is "in some way unique and relevant to Christian readers today." Pays 1/2 ¢ per word. E-mail: skysong@bconnex.net. Web site: www.bconnex.net/~skysong.

EARTH'S DAUGHTERS—P.O. Box 41, Central Park Sta., Buffalo, NY 14215. Attn: Ed. Published 3 times a year. Fiction, to 1,000 words, poetry, to 40 lines, and B&W photos or drawings. "Finely crafted work with a feminist theme." Pays in copies. SASE for guidelines and themes. Reader's fee $5, free submissions for subscribers.

EDGE CITY REVIEW—10912 Harpers Sq. Ct., Reston, VA 20191. T.L. Ponick, Ed. Literary fiction, to 3,500 words; essays, to 2,500 words; formal, metrical poetry. Reviews of small press books. "Prefer metrical poetry to free verse and coherent short fiction to self-consciously styled work. Political slant is conservative." Pays in copies.

EIGHTEENTH-CENTURY STUDIES—Dept. of French and Italian, Kresge Hall 152, Northwestern Univ., Evanston, IL 60208-2204. Bernadette Fort, Ed. Quarterly. Articles, to 7,500 words. Blind submission policy: Submit 2 copies of manuscript; author's name and address should appear only on separate title page. No payment.

EPOCH—251 Goldwin Smith Hall, Cornell Univ., Ithaca, NY 14853-3201. Michael Koch, Ed. Serious fiction and poetry. Pays $5 to $10 a page for fiction and poetry. No submissions between April 15 and September 21. Guidelines.

EUREKA LITERARY MAGAZINE—Eureka College, 300 E. College Avenue, Eureka, IL 61530. Loren Logsdon, Ed. Nancy Perkins, Fiction Ed. Semiannual. Fiction, 15 to 25 pages, and poetry, submit up to 4 poems at a time. "We promote no specific political agenda or literary theory." Pays in copies. E-mail: llogsdon@eureka.edu.

EVENT—Douglas College, Box 2503, New Westminster, BC, Canada V3L 5B2. Calvin Wharton, Ed. Short fiction, poetry, and creative non-fiction. Pays minimum $22 per printed page, on publication. E-mail: event@douglas. bc.ca.

FICTION—c/o English Dept., City College of New York, Convent Ave. at 138th St., New York, NY 10031. Mark Jay Mirsky, Ed. Semiannual. Short stories and novel excerpts, to 5,000 words. "Read the magazine before submitting." Payment varies, on acceptance. Manuscripts not read in the summer. Web site: www.ccny.cuny.edu/fiction/fiction.htm.

FICTION INTERNATIONAL—English Dept., San Diego State Univ., San Diego, CA 92182-8140. Harold Jaffe, Ed. Innovative and politically committed fiction and theory. Query for annual themes. Pays in copies. Manuscripts read from September 1 to December 15.

THE FIDDLEHEAD—Campus House, Univ. of New Brunswick, Fredericton, NB, Canada E3B 5A3. Attn: Ed. Serious fiction, 3,500 words. Pays about $20 per printed page, on publication. Submissions without SASE (IRC, cash, or Canadian stamps only) will not be accepted or returned. E-mail: fid@ nbnet.nb.ca.

FIELD—10 N. Professor St., Oberlin College, Oberlin, OH 44074-1095. Pamela Alexander, Martha Collins, Alberta Turner, David Walker, David Young, Eds. Serious poetry, any length, by established and unknown poets.

Translations by qualified translators. Payment varies, on publication. Manuscripts read year-round. E-mail: oc.press@oberlin.edu. Web site: www.ober lin.edu/~ocpress.

FINE MADNESS—P.O. Box 31138, Seattle, WA 98103-1138. Attn: Ed. Poetry, to 10 pages. Fiction by invitation only. Pays in copies. No simultaneous submissions. Guidelines. Queries to e-mail: beastly@oz.net. Web site: www. scn.org/arts/finemadness.

FIRST INTENSITY: A MAGAZINE OF NEW WRITING—P.O. Box 665, Lawrence, KS 66044. Lee Chapman Biannual. Fiction, to 10 pages, with an "intellectual bite and edgy experimental flavor." No unsolicited poetry. Send complete manuscript with SASE. Pays one copy.

THE FIRST LINE—K Street Ink, P.O. Box 0382, Plano, TX 75025-0382. David LaBounty, Co-Ed. Bimonthly. Fiction based on first line provided (check web site), 300 to 600 words; nonfiction, 300 to 600 words, on favorite first lines. Send complete manuscript. Pays in copies. E-mail: info@thefirst line.com. Web site: www.thefirstline.com.

FIVE POINTS—Georgia State University, University Plaza, Atlanta, GA 30303-3083. Ed. Three times yearly. Fiction, to 7,500 words. No simultaneous submissions. Pays $15 to $50 per printed page and copies, on publication. E-mail: msexton@gsu.edu. Web site: http://webdelsol.com/fivepoints.

THE FLORIDA REVIEW—English Dept., Univ. of Central Florida, Orlando, FL 32816. Russell Kesler, Ed. Semiannual. Mainstream and experimental fiction and nonfiction, to 7,500 words. Poetry, any style. Pays in copies. Web site: www.pegasus.cc.ucf.edu/~english/floridareview/home.htm.

FLYWAY LITERARY REVIEW—(formerly *Flyway*) 206 Ross Hall, Iowa State Univ., Ames, IA 50011. Stephen Pett, Ed. Poetry, fiction, creative nonfiction, and reviews. Pays in copies. Manuscripts read September through May. E-mail: flyway@iastate.edu. Web site: www.engl.iastate.edu/main/ resources/flyway/flyway.html.

THE FORMALIST—320 Hunter Dr., Evansville, IN 47711. William Baer, Ed. Metrical poetry. "Well-crafted poetry in a contemporary idiom which uses meter and the full range of traditional poetic conventions in vigorous and interesting ways. Especially interested in sonnets, couplets, tercets, ballads, the French forms, etc." SASE for writers' guidelines. Sample issue, $6.50. Howard Nemerov Sonnet Award ($1,000); SASE for details.

FOURTEEN HILLS: THE SFSU REVIEW—Creative Writing Dept., San Francisco State Univ., 1600 Holloway Ave., San Francisco, CA 94132-1722. Biannual. Innovative fiction, creative nonfiction, poetry, and drama. Submissions read August through February only. Send complete manuscript and SASE; no simultaneous or e-mail submissions. No payment. Web site: http:// mercury.sfsu.edu/~hill/14hills.html.

FROGPOND—P.O. Box 2461, Winchester, VA 22604-1661. Jim Kacian, Ed. Published 3 times a year plus yearly supplement. Haiku and related writing, plus articles on haiku. Query for articles. E-mail: redmoon@shentel.net. Web site: www.octet.com/~hsa/.

FUGUE—Univ. of Idaho, English Dept., Brink Hall, Room 200, Moscow, ID 83844-1102. Address Exec. Ed. Fiction and nonfiction to 6,000 words. Poetry, any style, 100 lines. Open to new writers. Include SASE. Pays in copies and small honorarium. E-mail: ronmcf@uidaho.edu. Web site: www. uidaho.edu/ls/eng/fugue.

GEORGETOWN REVIEW—P.O. Box 6309 SS, Hattiesburg, MS 39406. Steve Conti, Ed. Semiannual. Fiction and poetry; new exciting voices. Guidelines. Contest.

THE GEORGIA REVIEW—Univ. of Georgia, Athens, GA 30602-9009. Stephen Corey, Acting Ed. Self-contained short fiction. No novel excerpts. Subject matter, style, and length are unrestricted. "All manuscripts receive serious consideration." Pays $40 per printed page, plus one-year subscription. No simultaneous or electronic submissions. Manuscripts accepted September through May. E-mail: bkeen@arches.uga.edu. Web site: www. uga.edu/garev.

THE GETTYSBURG REVIEW—Gettysburg College, Gettysburg, PA 17325. Peter Stitt, Ed. Quarterly. Poetry, fiction, essays, and essay reviews, 1,000 to 20,000 words. Pays $2 a line for poetry; $25 per printed page for prose. Allow 6 months for response. No simultaneous submissions. Web site: www.gettysburgreview.com.

GLIMMER TRAIN PRESS—710 S.W. Madison St., #504, Portland, OR 97205. Susan Burmeister-Brown, Ed. Quarterly. Fiction, 1,200 to 7,500 words. Eight stories in each issue. Pays $500, on acceptance. Submit material in January, April, July, and October. Allow 3 months for response. Short story award for new writers; SASE for details. E-mail: info@glimmertrain.com. Web site: www.glimmertrain.com.

GLOBAL CITY REVIEW—Simon H. Rifkind Ctr. for the Humanties, City College of NY, 138th St. & Convenient Ave., New York, NY 10031. Linsey Abrams, Ed. Biannual. Intellectual and literary forum for women, lesbian and gay, and other culturally diverse writers; writers of color, international writers, activist writers. Thematic issues. Send complete manuscripts. Pays in copies. E-mail: globalcityreview@aol.com.

GRAIN MAGAZINE—Box 1154, Regina, Saskatchewan, Canada S4P 3B4. Elizabeth Philips, Ed. Quarterly. Fresh, startling, and imaginative short stories (or up to 30 pages from a novel-in-progress), creative nonfiction, and poetry. No previously published work accepted. Pays $30 to $100, on publication. Send SASE for guidelines. Web site: www.skwriter.com. E-mail address: grain.mag@sk.sympatico.ca.

GRASSLANDS REVIEW—P.O. Box 626, Berea, OH 44017. Laura Kennelly, Ed. Semiannual. Short stories, 1,000 to 3,500 words. Poetry, any length. "We seek imagination without sloppiness, ideas without lectures, and delight in language. Our purpose is to encourage new writers." Pays in copies. Accepts manuscripts postmarked March or October only. Send SASE for annual contest guidelines. E-mail: glreview@aol.com. Web site: www.hometown.aol.com/g/review/prof/index.htm.

GREEN MOUNTAINS REVIEW—Johnson State College, Johnson, VT 05656. Neil Shepard, Poetry Ed. Tony Whedon, Fiction Ed. Fiction and creative nonfiction, including literary essays, book reviews, and interviews, to 25 pages. Poetry. Manuscripts read September through April. Payment varies (depending on funding), on publication.

GREEN'S MAGAZINE—P.O. Box 3236, Regina, Sask., Canada S4P 3H1. David Green, Ed. Fiction for family reading, 1,500 to 4,000 words. Poetry, to 40 lines. No simultaneous submissions. Pays in copies. International reply coupons must accompany U.S. manuscripts. Manuscripts read year-round.

THE GREENSBORO REVIEW—English Dept., 134 McIver Bldg., UNCG, P.O. Box 26170, Greensboro, NC 27402-6170. Jim Clark, Ed. Semiannual. Poetry and fiction. Submission deadlines: September 15 and February 15. Pays in copies. Guidelines. E-mail: jlclark@uncg.edu. Web site: www. uncg.edu/eng/mfa.

GULF COAST—English Dept., Univ. of Houston, Houston, TX 77204. Attn: Ed. Biannual, Fall and Spring. Fiction (no genre fiction), nonfiction, poetry (submit up to 5), and translations. Payment: $15 poem, $30 essay, short story. Does not read May 15 through August 15.

HALF TONES TO JUBILEE—Pensacola Junior College, English Dept., 1000 College Blvd., Pensacola, FL 32504. Walter F. Spara, Ed. Fiction, to 1,500 words, and poetry, to 60 lines. Pays in copies. Manuscripts read August 15 to May 15. Contest. E-mail: mwernicke@pjc.cc.fl.us.

HAPPY—240 E. 35th St., Suite 11A, New York, NY 10016. Bayard, Ed. Quarterly. Fiction, to 6,000 words. "No previously published work. No pornography. No racist/sexist pandering. No bourgeois boredom." Pays ¢1 per word, on publication, plus one copy.

HAWAII REVIEW—Dept. of English, Univ. of Hawaii, 1733 Donaggho Rd., Honolulu, HI 96822. Attn: Ed. Quality fiction, poetry, interviews, and essays. Manuscripts read year-round. E-mail: hi-review@hawaii.edu. Web site: wwwhawaii.edu/bop/hr.html.

HAYDEN'S FERRY REVIEW—Box 871502, Arizona State Univ., Tempe, AZ 85287-1502. Attn: Ed. Semiannual. Fiction, essays, and poetry (submit up to 6 poems). Include brief bio and SASE. Deadline for Spring/Summer issue is September 30; Fall/Winter issue, February 28. Pays $25 per page, maximum $100. E-mail: hfr@asu.edu. Web site: www.statepress.com/hfr.

THE HEARTLANDS TODAY—Firelands Writing Ctr. of Firelands College, Huron, OH 44839. Larry Smith and Nancy Dunham, Eds. Fiction, 1,000 to 4,500 words, and nonfiction, 1,000 to 3,000 words, about the contemporary Midwest. Poetry (submit 3 to 5 poems). "Writing must be set in the Midwest, but can include a variety of themes." B&W photos. Pays $10 to $20 honorarium, plus copies. Query for current themes. Contest. Manuscripts read January 1 to June 5.

HEAVEN BONE—P.O. Box 486, Chester, NY 10918. Steve Hirsch, Ed. Annual. "The Bridge Between Muse & Mind." Fiction, to 5,000 words. Magazine and book reviews, 250 to 2,500 words. Poetry (submit no more than 10 pages at a time). "Alternative-cultural, post-beat, surrealist, and yogic/anti-paranoiac." Allow 6 months for response. Pays in copies. E-mail: heaven bone@aol.com.

HEROES FROM HACKLAND—1225 Evans, Arkadelphia, AR 71923. Mike Grogan, Ed. Quarterly. Nostalgic articles, 750 to 1,500 words, on B-movies (especially westerns and serials), comic books, grade school readers, juvenile series books, cartoons, vintage autos, country music and pop music before 1956, and vintage radio and television. "We believe in heroes, especially those popular culture icons that serious critics label 'ephemera.'" Pays in copies.

HIGH PLAINS LITERARY REVIEW—180 Adams St., Suite 250,

Denver, CO 80206. Robert O. Greer, Ed. Fiction, 3,000 to 6,500 words, as well as poetry, essays, reviews, interviews. "Designed to bridge the gap between the academic quarterlies and commercial reviews." Pays $10 a page for poetry; $5 a page for fiction, on publication.

THE HIGHLANDER—560 Green Bay Rd., Suite 204, Winnetka, IL 60093. Sharon Kennedy Ray, Man. Ed. Bimonthly. Articles, 1,300 to 1,900 words, related to Scottish history. "We do not want articles on modern Scotland." Pays $100 to $150, on acceptance. E-mail: sray5617@aol.com.

THE HOLLINS CRITIC—P.O. Box 9538, Hollins University, Roanoke, VA 24020. R.H.W. Dillard, Ed. Published 5 times a year. Features an essay on a contemporary fiction writer, poet or dramatist, cover sketch, brief biography, and book list. Also, book reviews and poetry. Pays $25 for poetry, on publication. E-mail: acockrell@hollins.edu. Web site: www.hollins.edu.

HOME PLANET NEWS—P.O. Box 415, Stuyvesant Sta., New York, NY 10009. Enid Dame and Donald Lev, Eds. Quarterly art tabloid. Fiction, to 8 typed pages; reviews, 3 to 5 pages; and poetry, any length. Query for nonfiction. Pays in copies and subscription. Manuscripts read February through May.

THE HUDSON REVIEW—684 Park Ave., New York, NY 10021. Paula Deitz, Ed. Quarterly. Fiction, to 10,000 words. Essays, to 8,000 words. Poetry, submit up to 10. Payment varies, on publication. Guidelines. Reading periods: Nonfiction read January through April. Poetry read April through July. Fiction read June through November. Web site: www.litline.org.

HURRICANE ALICE: A FEMINIST QUARTERLY—Dept. of English, Rhode Island College, Providence, RI 02908. Maureen Reddy, Ed. Articles, fiction, essays, interviews, and reviews, 500 to 3,000 words, with feminist perspective. Emphasis on own-fictional critiques of culture. Pays in copies. E-mail: mreddy@ric.edu.

ILLYA'S HONEY—c/o The Dallas Poets Community, P.O. Box 225435, Dallas, TX 75222-5435. Quarterly. Short fiction, any subject, any style, to 1,000 words; poetry, to 60 lines. "No forced rhyme or overly religious verse." Manuscripts read year-round. E-mail: dpcmail@dallaspoets.org. Web site: www.dallaspoets.org.

INDIANA REVIEW—Ballantine 465, Indiana Univ., 1020 E. Kirkwood Ave., Bloomington, IN 47405-7103. We look for daring stories, poetry, and nonfiction that integrate theme, language, character, and form. We like polished writing, humor, and fiction which has consequence beyond the world of its narrator. Please read the magazine before submitting. Pays $5 per page. Web site: www.indiana.edu/~inreview/ir.html,inreview@indiana.edu.

INDIGENOUS FICTION—P.O. Box 2078, Redmond, WA 98073-2078. Sherry Decker, Ed. Triannual, Feb. June Oct. nontraditional mainstream, fantasy, science fiction, occult, mysteries; 1,000 to 8,000 words (2,000 to 4,500 preferred); poetry (up to 5) to 30 lines. Pays $5 or choice of contributor copy for pieces under 1,000 words; $10 to $20 plus contributor copy for work over 1,000 words; pays on publication. Guidelines for SASE. Sample $6.

INTERIM—Dept. of English, Univ. of Nevada, Las Vegas, NV 89154-5034. Claudia Keelan, Ed. Annual. Poetry, any form or length; fiction, to 7,500 words (uses up to 2 stories per issue), essays, and book reviews. Pays in copies and 2-year subscription. Responds in 3 weeks.

INTERNATIONAL POETRY REVIEW—Dept. of Romance Languages, Univ. of North Carolina, P.O. Box 26170, Greensboro, NC 27402-6170. Attn: Ed. Semiannual. Book reviews, interviews, and short essays, to 1,500 words. Original English poems and contemporary translations of poems. "We prefer material with cross-cultural or international dimension." Pays in copies. E-mail: kmather@uncq.edu. Web site: www.uncq.edu/rom/ipr.htm.

INTERNATIONAL QUARTERLY—P.O. Box 10521, Tallahassee, FL 32302. Van K. Brock, Ed. Fiction and nonfiction, to 5,000 words; poetry. Pays in copies and subscription.

THE IOWA REVIEW—EPB 308, Univ. of Iowa, Iowa City, IA 52242. David Hamilton, Ed. Essays, poems, stories, reviews. Pays $10 a page for prose; $1 a line for poetry, on publication. Manuscripts read September until set for a full year ahead, usually March or April. Web site: www.uiowa.edu/~iareview/.

IRIS: A JOURNAL ABOUT WOMEN—The Women's Ctr., Box 800588, Univ. of Virginia, Charlottesville, VA 22908. Eileen Boris, Ed. Semiannual. Fiction, 2,500 to 7,000 words; personal essays, to 2,500 words; poetry. "Our readers are women; diverse in age and interests." Pays in subscription.

JAPANOPHILE—P.O. Box 7977, Ann Arbor, MI 48107. Susan Aitken, Ed. Fiction, to 4,000 words, with a Japanese setting and at least one Japanese and at least one non-Japanese character. Articles, 2,000 words, that celebrate Japanese culture: "We seek to promote American understanding of Japan and Japanese culture found worldwide. We are not about Japan-bashing or fatuous praise." Also seeks short stories, personal essays, humor, and photos that explore the images, people or experience of Japan, in addition to poetry that utilizes Japanese form, such as haiku. Pays to $25, on publication. Annual short story contest; deadline December 31. Web site: www.japanophile.com for guidelines.

THE JOURNAL OF AFRICAN TRAVEL-WRITING—P.O. Box 346, Chapel Hill, NC 27514. Amber Vogel, Ed. Biannual. Fiction, nonfiction, and poetry on past and contemporary travel in Africa. B&W drawings welcome. Send complete manuscript with SASE. Pays in copies.

JOURNAL OF NEW JERSEY POETS—County College of Morris, 214 Center Grove Rd., Randolph, NJ 07869-2086. Sander Zulauf, Ed. Semiannual. Serious contemporary poetry by current and former New Jersey residents. "Although our emphasis is on poets associated with New Jersey, we seek work that is universal in scope." Pays in copies and a one year subscription. E-mail: szulauf@ccm.edu. Web site: www.ccm.edu/humanities/humanities/journal/html.

KALEIDOSCOPE: INTERNATIONAL MAGAZINE OF LITERATURE, FINE ARTS, AND DISABILITY—United Disability Services, 701 S. Main St., Akron, OH 44311-1019. Darshan Perusek, Ph.D., Ed.-in-Chief. Semiannual. Fiction, essays, interviews, articles, and poetry relating to disability and the arts, to 5,000 words. Photos a plus. "We present balanced, realistic images of people with disabilities and publish pieces that challenge stereotypes." Submissions accepted from writers with or without disabilities. Pays $10 to $125. Guidelines recommended. Manuscripts read year-round; response may take up to 6 months. E-mail: mshiplett@udsakron.org.

KALLIOPE: A JOURNAL OF WOMEN'S LITERATURE & ART—Florida Community College at Jacksonville, 3939 Roosevelt Blvd., Jacksonville, FL 32205. Attn: Ed. Fiction, to 2,500 words; poetry; interviews of women writers, to 2,000 words; and B&W photos of fine art. Query for interviews only. Pays $10 or in copies. Web site: www.fccj.org/kalliope.

KARAMU—Dept. of English, Eastern Illinois Univ., Charleston, IL 61920. Olga Abella, Lauren Smith, Eds. Annual. Contemporary or experimental fiction. Creative nonfiction prose, personal essays, and memoir pieces. Poetry. Pays in copies. Manuscripts read from September 1 to April 1.

KELSEY REVIEW—Mercer County Community College, P.O. Box B, Trenton, NJ 08690. Robin Schore, Ed. Fiction and nonfiction, to 2,000 words, and poetry by writers living or working in Mercer County, NJ. Pays in copies. E-mail: kelsey.review@mccc.edu. Web site: www.mccc.edu.

THE KENYON REVIEW—Kenyon College, Gambier, OH 43022. David H. Lynn, Ed. Published 3 times a year. Fiction, poetry, essays, literary criticism, and reviews. Pays $10 a printed page for prose, $15 a printed page for poetry, on publication. Manuscripts read September through March; however, because of a lengthy backlog of accepted manuscripts, KR will not be accepting unsolicited submissions until September 2000.

KIOSK—c/o English Dept., 306 Clemens Hall, SUNY Buffalo, Buffalo, NY 14260. Kevin Grauke (Fiction), Nathan Goldberg (Poetry), Eds. Fiction, to 20 pages, with a "strong sense of voice, narrative direction, and craftsmanship." Poetry "that explores boundaries, including the formally experimental." Address appropriate editor. Pays in copies. Manuscripts read September 1 to March 1. E-mail: eng-kiosk@acsu.buffalo.edu. Web site: www.wings.buffalo.edu/kiosk.

THE KIT-CAT REVIEW—244 Halstead Ave., Harrison, NY 10528. Claudia Fletcher, Ed. Quarterly. Short fiction, essays, and poetry. Submit complete manuscript with bio and SASE. Pays to $100 for poetry and to $100 for short stories, on acceptance.

THE LARCOM REVIEW—P.O. Box 161, Prides Crossing, MA 01965. Susan Oleksiw, Ed. Biannual of the arts and literature of New England. Short fiction and nonfiction, to 3,000 words; poetry, any length; essays; articles; memoirs; interviews; and the occasional book review. B&W photos of New England are welcome. Query first with SASE. Guidelines. Pays $25, on publication.

LATINO STUFF REVIEW—See *LSR.*

THE LAUREL REVIEW—Northwest Missouri State Univ., Dept. of English, Maryville, MO 64468. William Trowbridge, David Slater, Beth Richards, Catie Rosemurgy, Eds. Semiannual. Fiction, nonfiction, and poetry. Pays in copies and subscription.

THE LEADING EDGE—3163 JKHB, Provo, UT 84602. Doug Summers Stay, Ed. Semiannual. Science fiction and fantasy, to 12,000 words; poetry, to 600 lines; and articles, to 8,000 words, on science, scientific speculation, and literary criticism. No excessive profanity, overt violence, or excessive sexual situations. No simultaneous submissions. Pays 1¢ per word, on publication. Guidelines. Sample copy $4.50. Web site: www.tle.clubs.byu.edu.

THE LEDGE—78–44 80th St., Glendale, NY 11385. Timothy Monaghan, Ed. Poetry; submit 3 to 5 poems at a time. "We publish provocative, well-crafted poems by well-known and lesser-known poets. Excellence is our main criterion." Pays in copies. Sample copy $6. Sponsor of an annual poetry awards competition and an annual poetry chapbook contest. Send SASE for details.

LIGHT—Box 7500, Chicago, IL 60680. John Mella, Ed. Quarterly. Light verse. Also fiction, reviews, and essays, to 2,000 words. Fillers, humor, jokes, quips. "If it has wit, point, edge, or barb, it will find a home here." Cartoons and line drawings. Pays in copies. Query for nonfiction. Web site: www.litline.org/html/lightquarterly.html.

LILITH, THE INDEPENDENT JEWISH WOMEN'S MAGAZINE—250 W. 57th St., New York, NY 10107. Susan Weidman Schneider, Ed. Fiction, 1,500 to 2,000 words, on issues of interest to Jewish women. E-mail: lilithmag@aol.com. Web site: www.lilithmag.com.

LITERAL LATTE—61 E. 8th St., Suite 240, New York, NY 10003. Jenine Gordon Bockman, Ed./Pub. Bimonthly distributed to cafés and bookstores. Fiction and personal essays, to 6,000 words; poetry, to 2,000 words; art. Pays in subscription, honorarium, and copies. Contests and awards. E-mail: litlatte@aol.com. Website: www.literal-latte.com.

LITERARY MAGAZINE REVIEW—Dept. of English Language and Lit., Univ. of Northern Iowa, 117 Baker Hall, Cedar Falls, IA 50614-0502. Grant Tracey, Ed. Reviews and articles concerning literary magazines, 1,000 to 1,500 words, for writers and readers of contemporary literature. Pays in copies. Query. E-mail: grant.tracey@uni.edu.

THE LITERARY REVIEW—Fairleigh Dickinson Univ., 285 Madison Ave., Madison, NJ 07940. Walter Cummins, Ed.-in-Chief. Martin Green, Harry Keyishian, William Zander, Eds. Serious fiction. Open to a variety of imaginative approaches, including translations. Pays in copies. E-mail: tlr@fdu.edu. Web site: www.webdelsol.com/tlr/.

LOLLIPOP—P.O. Box 441493, Boston, MA 02144. Scott Hefflon, Ed. Quarterly. Fiction, essays, and "edgy" commentary on music and youth culture, to 2,000 words; reviews and interviews related to underground culture; fillers; photos and drawings. Queries preferred. Pays $25 (for anything over 1,000 words), and $25 per illustration.

LONG SHOT—P.O. Box 6238, Hoboken, NJ 07030. Dan Shot, Nancy Mercado, Lynne Breitfeller, Andy Clausen, Eds. Fiction, poetry, and nonfiction, to 10 pages. B&W photos and drawings. Pays in copies. Web site: www.longshot.org.

THE LONG STORY—18 Eaton St., Lawrence, MA 01843. Attn: Ed. Stories, 8,000 to 20,000 words; prefer stories about common folks and a thematic focus. Pays in copies. E-mail: rpbtls@aol.com. Web site: www.litline.org/ls/longstory.html.

LONZIE'S FRIED CHICKEN LITERARY MAGAZINE—P.O. Box 189, Lynn, NC 28750. E.H. Goree, Ed. Biannual. Accessible fiction and poetry with a feel for the South. Send only your best work. Up to 5 poems, as many as 15 pages of fiction. Send SASE for return or reply. Pays in copies. Web site: www.lonziesfriedchicken.com.

LSR—(formerly *Latino Stuff Review*) P.O. Box 440195, Miami, FL 33144. Nilda Cepero-Llevada, Ed./Pub. Bilingual publication, English and Spanish, focusing on Latino topics. Poetry, to four poems, 5 to 15 lines each, prefer contemporary with meaning and message. No surrealism, no porn or religious poetry; book reviews to 750 words; interviews to 750 words; line artwork open, up to 5 illustrations, 6x6 for cover or 8x10 for full page inside. Reprints accepted. Do not query. Editor does not comment on submissions. SASE required. Art submissions must be in 3.5″ disk. Pays in copies. No submissions in November, December or January.

LYNX EYE—c/o Scribblefest Literary Group, 1880 Hill Dr., Los Angeles, CA 90041. Pam McCully, Kathryn Morrison, Eds. Quarterly. Short stories, vignettes, novel excerpts, one-act plays, essays, belle lettres, satires, 500 to 5,000 words; poetry, to 30 lines. Pays $10, on acceptance.

THE MACGUFFIN—Schoolcraft College, Dept. of English, 18600 Haggerty Rd., Livonia, MI 48152. Arthur J. Lindenberg, Ed. General, mainstream, and experimental fiction and nonfiction, 400 to 5,000 words. Poetry. "No religious, inspirational, confessional, romance, horror, or pornography." Pays in copies.

THE MALAHAT REVIEW—Univ. of Victoria, P.O. Box 1700 STN CSC, Victoria, BC, Canada V8W 2Y2. Marlene Cookshaw, Ed. Fiction and poetry, including translations. Pays from $30 per page, on acceptance. E-mail: malahat@uvic.ca/malahat. Web site: web.uvic.ca/malahat.

MANOA—English Dept., Univ. of Hawaii, Honolulu, HI 96822. Frank Stewart, Ed. Ian MacMillan, Fiction Ed. Lisa Ottiger, Book Reviews Ed. Fiction, to 30 pages; essays, to 25 pages; book reviews, 4 to 5 pages; and poetry (submit 4 to 6 poems). "Writers are encouraged to read the journal carefully before submitting." Pays $50 for poetry and book reviews; $20 to $25 per page for fiction, on publication.

MANY MOUNTAINS MOVING—420 22nd St., Boulder, CO 80302. Naomi Horii, Ed. Semiannual. Fiction, nonfiction, and poetry by writers of all cultures. Pays in copies. E-mail: mmm@mmminc.org.

MASSACHUSETTS REVIEW—South College, Univ. of Massachusetts, Amherst, MA 01003. Attn: Ed. Short fiction, 15 to 25 pages. Pays $50, on publication. SASE required. Manuscripts read October through May. E-mail: mssrev@external.umass.edu. Web site: www.-unix.oit.umass.edu/~massrev/.

THE MAVERICK PRESS—Rt. 2, Box 4915, Eagle Pass, TX 78852-9605. Carol Cullar, Ed. Short stories, to 1,500 words, and unrhymed poetry. Pays in copies. Query with SASE for themes. Website: www.hilconet.com/~mavpress.

MEDIPHORS—P.O. Box 327, Bloomsburg, PA 17815. Eugene D. Radice, MD, Ed. "A literary journal of the health professions." Short stories, essays, and commentary, 4,500 words. "Topics should have some relation to medicine and health, but may be quite broad." Poems, to 30 lines. Humor. Pays in copies. Guidelines. Web site: www.mediphors.org.

MICHIGAN HISTORICAL REVIEW—Clarke Historical Library, Central Michigan Univ., Mt. Pleasant, MI 48859. Attn: Ed. Semiannual. Scholarly articles related to Michigan's political, social, economic, and cultural history; articles on American, Canadian, and Midwestern history that directly or indirectly explore themes related to Michigan's past. Manuscripts read year-round. E-mail: mihisrev@cmuvm.csv.cmich.edu.

MID-AMERICAN REVIEW—Dept. of English, Bowling Green State Univ., Bowling Green, OH 43403. Wendell Mayo, Ed. High-quality fiction, poetry, articles, translations, and reviews of contemporary writing. Fiction, to 5,000 words, (query for longer work). Reviews, articles, 500 to 2,500 words.

Pays two issues. Manuscripts read September through May. E-mail: wmayo@
bgnet.bgsu.edu. Web site: www.bgsu.edu/midamericanreview.

MIDWEST QUARTERLY—Pittsburg State Univ., Pittsburg, KS 66762.
James B. M. Schick, Ed. Scholarly articles, 2,500 to 5,000 words, on contemporary academic and public issues; poetry. Pays in copies. Manuscripts read year-
round. E-mail: jschick@pittstate.edu. Web site: www.pittstate.edu/engl/mid
west.html.

THE MINNESOTA REVIEW—Dept. of English, Univ. of Missouri,
107 Tate Hall, Columbia, MO 65211. Attn: Eds. Fiction, 1,000 to 6,000 words,
with implicit or explicit political significance. Pays in copies. E-mail: williams
jeff@missouri.edu.

MISSISSIPPI MUD—7119 Santa Fe Ave., Dallas, TX 75223. Joel
Weinstein, Ed. Short stories, to 50 pages, and novel excerpts, 50 to 100 pages;
poetry, any length. Pays $25 for poems; $50 to $100 for fiction, on publication.

MISSISSIPPI REVIEW—Ctr. for Writers, Univ. of Southern Mississippi, Box 5144, Hattiesburg, MS 39406-5144. Frederick Barthelme, Ed. Serious fiction. Pays in copies. E-mail: rief@netdoor.com. Web site: http://
sushi.st.usm.edu/mrw.

THE MISSOURI REVIEW—1507 Hillcrest Hall, Univ. of Missouri-
Columbia, Columbia, MO 65211. Hoa Ngo, Man. Ed. Speer Morgan, Ed. Evelyn Somers, Nonfiction Ed. Fiction. Also poetry, essays, interviews, and book
reviews. Pays $20 per printed page, on contract. Manuscripts read year-round.
E-mail: mr@missourireview.org. Web site: www.missourireview.org.

MODERN HAIKU—P.O. Box 1752, Madison, WI 53701-1752. Robert
Spiess, Ed. Haiku and articles about haiku. Pays $1 per haiku, $200 in awards
each issue, and $5 a page for articles. Manuscripts read year-round. Web site:
www.q-com.com/users/brooksbooks/modernhaiku.html/.

MONTHLY REVIEW—122 W. 27th St., New York, NY 10001. Paul M.
Sweezy, Harry Magdoff, Ellen Meiksins Wood, Eds. Analytical articles, to
5,000 words, on politics and economics, from independent socialist viewpoint.
Pays $25 for reviews, $50 for articles, on publication. Submissions to Vicki
Larson, Asst. Ed.

MYSTERY TIME—P.O. Box 2907, Decatur, IL 62524. Linda Hutton,
Ed. Semiannual. Suspense, 1,500 words, and poems about mysteries, up to 16
lines. "We prefer female protagonists. No gore or violence." Pays $5, on accep-
tance.

NATURAL BRIDGE—Dept. of English, University of Missouri-St.
Louis, 8001 Natural Bridge Rd., St. Louis, MO 63121-4499. Steven Schreiner,
Ed. Biannual. Short fiction, essays, and poetry. Submission periods are July
1 through August 31 and November 1 through December 31. Simultaneous
submissions are accepted. Pays in copies. E-mail: natural@jinx.umsl.edu. Web
site: www.umsl.edu/~natural/index.htm.

NEBO: A LITERARY JOURNAL—Dept. of English, Arkansas Tech.
Univ., Russellville, AR 72801-2222. Attn: Ed. Poems (submit up to 5); mainstream fiction, to 3,000 words; critical essays, to 10 pages. Pays in one copy.
Guidelines. Offices closed May through August. "Best time to submit is September through February."

NEBRASKA REVIEW—Writer's Workshop, FAB 212, Univ. of Nebraska at Omaha, Omaha, NE 68182-0324. James Reed, Ed. Susan Aizenberg, Poetry Ed. Short stories and personal essays, to 7,500 words. Poetry. Pays in copies and subscription. E-mail: jreed@unomaha.edu.

NEW DELTA REVIEW—c/o Dept. of English, Louisiana State Univ., Baton Rouge, LA 70803-5001. Attn: Eds. Semiannual. Fiction and nonfiction, to 5,000 words. Submit up to 4 poems, any length. Also essays, interviews, and reviews. "We want to see your best work." Pays in copies. Also awards prize for best poem and short story for each issue. Manuscripts read September through May.

NEW ENGLAND REVIEW—Middlebury College, Middlebury, VT 05753. Stephen Donadio, Ed. Jodee Stanley Rubins, Man. Ed. Fiction, nonfiction, and poetry of varying lengths. Also, speculative and interpretive essays, critical reassessments, statements by artists working in various media, interviews, testimonials, letters from abroad. "We are committed to exploration of all forms of contemporary cultural expresssion." Pays $10 per page ($20 minimum), on publication. Manuscripts read September through May. E-mail: nereview@middlebury.edu. Web site: www.middlebury.edu/~nereview.

NEW ENGLAND WRITERS' NETWORK—P.O. Box 483, Hudson, MA 01749-0483. Glenda Baker, Ed.-in-Chief. Short stories and novel excerpts, to 2,000 words. All genres except pornography and excessive violence. Personal and humorous essays, to 1,000 words. Upbeat, positive poetry, to 32 lines. Pays $10 for stories; $5 for essays; $3 for poems, plus one copy. Guidelines. Submit fiction, poetry, and essays June 1 to August 31 only. SASE for annual contest details. No electronic submissions. E-mail: newnmag@aol.com. Web site: www.newmag.net.

NEW LAUREL REVIEW—828 Lesseps St., New Orleans, LA 70117. Lee Meitzen Grue, Ed. Annual. Fiction, 10 to 20 pages; nonfiction, to 10 pages; poetry, any length; translation. Library market. No inspirational verse. International readership. Read journal before submitting. Pays in one copy.$10 Individual. $12 Libraries.

NEW LETTERS—Univ. House, Univ. of Missouri-Kansas City, 5101 Rockhill Rd., Kansas City, MO 64110-2499. James McKinley, Ed.-in-Chief. Fiction, 3,500 to 5,000 words. Poetry, submit 3 to 6 poems at a time. SASE for literary awards guidelines. Manuscripts read October 15 to May 15. E-mail: newletters@umkc.edu. Web site: www.umkc.edu/newletters.

NEW ORLEANS REVIEW—Box 195, Loyola Univ., New Orleans, LA 70118. Christopher Chambers, Ed. Serious short fiction; poetry and essays. Experimental work welcome.

NEW TEXAS—University of Mary Hardin-Baylor Box 8008, Beltin, TX 76513. Donna Walker-Nixon, Ed. Short stories under 5,000 words and poetry. Send complete manuscript and disk. Pays in copies. E-mail: dwnixon@umhb.edu.

THE NEW YORK QUARTERLY—P.O. Box 693, Old Chelsea Station, New York, NY 10113. William Packard, Ed. Published 3 times a year. Poems of any style and persuasion, well-written and well-intentioned. Pays in copies. Manuscripts read year-round.

NEXUS—Wright State Univ., W016A Student Union, Dayton, OH 45435. Andre Hoilette, Thomas Poole, Eds. Poetry, short, sudden, or flash fiction, essays, interviews, photography, and art. Specializes in works that highlight the human experience. Pays in 2 copies.

NIGHTSUN—School of Arts & Humanities, Frostburg State Univ., 101 Braddock Rd., Frostburg, MD 21532-1099. Brad Barkley, Barbara Hurd, Karen Zealand, Eds. Annual. Short stories, about 12 pages, and poems, to 40 lines. Payment is 2 copies. Manuscripts read September through April.

NIMROD INTERNATIONAL JOURNAL—Univ. of Tulsa, 600 S. College Ave., Tulsa, OK 74104-3189. Dr. Francine Ringold, Ed.-in-Chief. Quality fiction, experimental and traditional. Also poetry. Publishes 2 issues annually, one awards, one thematic. Pays $6,000 in awards annually. Send SASE for contest (or general) guidelines. E-mail: nimrod@utulsa.edu. Web site: www.utulsa.edu/nimrod.

96 INC.—P.O. Box 15559, Boston, MA 02215. Attn: Ed. Annual. Fiction, 1,000 to 5,000 words; interviews; and poetry of varying length. Pays in subscription, 4 copies, and modest payment, if funding is available.

NO EXPERIENCE REQUIRED—P.O. Box 131032, The Woodlands, TX 77393-1032. Ed. Quarterly. Fiction, to 1,200 words; poetry, to 30 lines. New writers especially welcome. No porn, racist, or sexist material. SASE; sample issues $4.25. Pays 2 copies. Web site: www.members.tripod.com/~jcpiz/index.html.

THE NORTH AMERICAN REVIEW—Univ. of Northern Iowa, Cedar Falls, IA 50614-0516. Peter Cooley, Poetry Ed. Poetry of high quality. Pays from $20 per poem, on publication. Manuscripts read year-round. Manuscripts only returned with an SASE. Reply in 1 to 2 months.

NORTH ATLANTIC REVIEW—15 Arbutus Ln., Stony Brook, NY 11790-1408. John Gill, Ed. Annual. Fiction and nonfiction, to 5,000 words; fillers, humor, photographs and illustrations. A special section on social or literary issues is a part of each issue. No poetry. Pays in copies. Responds in 6 months. E-mail: 75467.1112@computave.com. Web site: www.sunysuffolk.edu/~gillj/.

THE NORTH DAKOTA QUARTERLY—Univ. of North Dakota, Grand Forks, ND 58202-7209. Attn: Ed. Fiction, limited market. Pays in copies. E-mail: ndg@sage.und.nodak.edu.

NORTHEASTARTS—P.O. Box 4363, Portland, ME 04101. Mr. Leigh Donaldson, Ed. Fiction and nonfiction, to 750 words; poetry, to 30 lines; and short essays and reviews. "Both published and new writers are considered. No obscene or offensive material." Payment is 2 copies.

NORTHEAST CORRIDOR—Beaver College, 450 S. Easton Rd., Glenside, PA 19038. Susan Balée, Ed. Semiannual. Literary fiction, personal essays, and interviews, 10 to 20 pages. Poetry, to 40 lines (submit 3 to 5). "We seek the work of writers and artists living in or writing about the Northeast Corridor of America." Pays $25 for stories or essays, $10 for poems, on publication.

NORTHWEST REVIEW—369 PLC, Univ. of Oregon, Eugene, OR 97403. John Witte, Ed. Janice MacRae, Fiction Ed. Published 3 times a year. Serious, original, and vital fiction. "We are very proud of our reputation as a forum for the most talented upcoming young writers." Pays in copies. Send SASE for guidelines. Web site: www.darkwing.uoregon.edu/~engl/deptinfo/nwr.html.

NORTHWOODS JOURNAL: A MAGAZINE FOR WRITERS—P.O. Box 298, Thomaston, ME 04861. Robert W. Olmsted, Ed. Articles of interest to writers; fiction, 2,500 words. Poetry, any length. "Read guidelines first." Pays $4 per page, on acceptance. E-mail: cal@americanletters.org. Web site: www.americanletters.org.

NOTRE DAME REVIEW—Creative Writing Program, English Dept., Univ. of Notre Dame, Notre Dame, IN 46556. Attn: Man. Ed. Semiannual. Fiction, 50 to 60 pages. Essays, reviews, and poetry, 70 to 80 pages. Manuscripts read September through April. Payment varies, on publication.

OASIS—P.O. Box 626, Largo, FL 33779-0626. Neal Storrs, Ed. Fiction and essays, poetry, and translations from any language. "Style is paramount." Pays $15 to $25 for prose, $5 per poem, on publication. Guidelines. Responds same day.

OF UNICORNS AND SPACE STATIONS—P.O. Box 200, Bountiful, UT 84011-0200. Gene Davis, Ed. Science fiction and fantasy, to 5,000 words. Poetry related to science fiction, science, or fantasy. "Do not staple or fold long manuscripts." Pays 1¢ per word for fiction; $5 for poems, on publication. Web site: www.genedavis.com/magazine/welcome.jsp.

OFFERINGS—P.O. Box 1667, Lebanon, MO 65536. Velvet Fackeldey, Ed. Quarterly. Poetry, to 30 lines, traditional and free verse. Students and unpublished writers encouraged. No payment.

THE OHIO REVIEW—344 Scott Quad., Ohio Univ., Athens, OH 45701-2979. Wayne Dodd, Ed. Short stories. Pays a minimum of $5 per page, plus copies, on publication. Manuscripts read September 15th through May 30th. Web site: www.ohiou.edu/theohioreview.

OLD CROW—FKB Press, P.O. Box 403, Easthampton, MA 01027. John Gibney, Pub. Tawnya Kelley Tiskus, Ed.-in-Chief. Semiannual. Fiction and nonfiction, 200 to 6,000 words. Poetry, to 500 lines. "International readership. Our purpose is to publish new and established writers who have something true to say which might horripilate our readers." Pays in copies. Rotating reading period.

OSIRIS—Box 297, Deerfield, MA 01342. Andrea Moorhead, Ed. Multilingual poetry journal founded in 1972, publishing poetry in English, French, German, with other languages in a bilingual format. Translators must have letter of permission from the poet or publisher. Pays in copies. E-mail: moorhead@k12s.phast.umass.edu.

OTHER VOICES—Univ. of Illinois at Chicago, Dept. of English (M/C 162), 601 S. Morgan St., Chicago, IL 60607-7120. Lois Hauselman, Ed. Fresh, accessible short stories and novel excerpts, to 5,000 words. Pays in copies and/or modest honorarium. Manuscripts read October to April. E-mail: othervoices@listserv.uic.edu. Web site: www.othervoicesmagazine.org.

OUTERBRIDGE—College of Staten Island, English Dept. 2S-218, 2800 Victory Blvd., Staten Island, NY 10314. Charlotte Alexander, Ed. Biannual. Well-crafted stories, about 20 pages, and poetry, to 4 pages, "directed to a wide audience of literate adult readers." Pays in 2 copies. Manuscripts read September to June.

PAINTBRUSH: A JOURNAL OF POETRY AND TRANSLATION—Language & Literature Div., Truman State Univ., Kirksville, MO 63501. Ben Bennani, Ed. Annual. Poetry, translations, interviews, and book reviews. Periodically publishes special monograph issues highlighting the work of individual writers. Official sponsor of the $2,000 Ezra Pound Poetry Award. Query. E-mail: pbrush@paintbrush.org. Web site: www.paintbrush.org.

PALO ALTO REVIEW—Palo Alto College, 1400 W. Villaret, San Antonio, TX 78224-2499. Ellen Shull, Ed. Semiannual. Fiction and articles, 5,000 words. "We look for wide-ranging investigations of historical, geographical, scientific, mathematical, artistic, political, and social topics, anything that has to do with living and learning." Interviews; 200-word think pieces for "Food for Thought"; poetry, to 50 lines (send 3 to 5 poems at a time); reviews, to 500 words, of books, films, videos, or software. "Fiction shouldn't be too experimental or excessively avant-garde." Pays in copies. Send SASE for themes and guidelines. E-mail: emshull@aol.com.

PANGOLIN PAPERS—P.O. Box 241, Nordland, WA 98358. Pat Britt, Ed. Literary fiction, 100 to 7,000 words. No poetry or genre fiction. No electronic submissions. Pays in copies. No electronic submissions. E-mail: trtl bluf@olympus.net.

PANHANDLER—English Dept., Univ. of W. Florida, Pensacola, FL 32514-5751. Laurie O'Brien, Ed. Semiannual. Fiction, 1,500 to 3,000 words; poetry, any length. Pays in copies. Responds within 6 months.

PARABOLA: THE MAGAZINE OF MYTH AND TRADITION— 656 Broadway, New York, NY 10012. Attn: Eds. Quarterly. Articles, to 4,000 words, and fiction, 500 words, retelling traditional stories, folk and fairy tales. No poetry. "All submissions must relate to an upcoming theme. We are looking for a balance between scholarly and accessible writing devoted to the ideas of myth and tradition." Send SASE for guidelines and themes. Payment varies, on publication. E-mail: editors@parabola.org. Web site: www.parabola.org.

THE PARIS REVIEW—541 E. 72nd St., New York, NY 10021. Attn: Fiction and Poetry Eds. Fiction and poetry of high literary quality. Pays on publication.

PARNASSUS—205 W. 89th St., Apt. 8F, New York, NY 10024-1835. Herbert Leibowitz, Ed. Critical essays and reviews on contemporary poetry. International in scope. Pays in cash and copies. Manuscripts read year-round.

PARTING GIFTS—3413 Wilshire, Greensboro, NC 27408. Robert Bixby, Ed. Fiction, to 1,000 words, and poetry, to 100 lines. Pays in copies. Manuscripts read January to June. Website: http://users.aol.com/marchst.

PARTISAN REVIEW—Boston Univ., 236 Bay State Rd., Boston, MA 02215. William Phillips, Ed.-in-Chief. Serious fiction. Payment varies. No simultaneous submissions. E-mail: partisan@bu.edu. Web site: partisan review.com

PASSAGER: A JOURNAL OF REMEMBRANCE AND DISCOVERY—c/o Univ. of Baltimore, 1420 N. Charles St., Baltimore, MD 21201-5779. Mary Azrael, Kendra Kopelke, Eds. Fiction and essays, 4,000 words, of "remembrance and discovery." Poetry, to 40 lines. "We publish writers of all ages, but with an emphasis on new older writers." Pays in copies. E-mail: kakopelke@ubmail.ubalt.edu.

PASSAGES NORTH—Northern Michigan Univ., Dept. of English, 1401 Presque Isle Ave., Marquette, MI 49855. Kate Myers Hanson, Ed. Semiannual. Poetry, fiction, interviews, and literary nonfiction. Pays in copies. Manuscripts read September to May.

THE PATERSON LITERARY REVIEW—Passaic County Comm. College, College Blvd., Paterson, NJ 07505-1179. Maria Mazziotti Gillan, Ed. High-quality fiction and poetry, to 10 pages. Pays in copies. Manuscripts read January through May.

PEARL—3030 E. Second St., Long Beach, CA 90803. Marilyn Johnson, Ed. Fiction, 500 to 1,200 words, and poetry, to 40 lines. "We are interested in accessible, humanistic poetry and fiction that communicates and is related to real life. Along with the ironic, serious, and intense, humor and wit are welcome." Pays in copies. Web site: www.pearlmag.com.

PEQUOD—New York Univ., English Dept., 19 University Pl., 2nd Fl., New York, NY 10003. Mark Rudman, Ed. Semiannual. Short stories, essays, and literary criticism, to 10 pages; poetry and translations, to 3 pages. Pays honorarium, on publication.

PEREGRINE: THE JOURNAL OF AMHERST WRITERS AND ARTISTS PRESS—P.O. Box 1076, Amherst, MA 01004. Nancy Rose, Man. Ed. Annual. Fiction and poetry. "We seek unpretentious and memorable writing by new as well as established authors. We welcome work reflecting diversity of voice." Guidelines available with #10 SASE. E-mail: awapress@javanet.com. Website: www.javanet.com/~awapress. Contest.

PIG IRON PRESS—P.O. Box 237, Youngstown, OH 44501-0237. Jim Villani, Ed. Fiction, articles, and living history, to 8,000 words. Poetry, to 100 lines. Thematic anthologies; current theme: The 20th Century. Deadline: September 30, 2000. Pays $5 per page or poem, on publication. Manuscripts read year-round. Responds in 6 months. E-mail: pigironpress@yahoo.com.

THE PIKEVILLE REVIEW—Humanities Div., Pikeville College, 214 Sycamore St., Pikeville, KY 41501. Elgin M. Ward, Ed. Annual. Contemporary fiction, poetry, creative essays, and book reviews. Payment varies on publication. E-mail: eward@pc.edu. Web site: www.pc.edu.

THE PLASTIC TOWER—Box 702, Bowie, MD 20718. Roger Kyle-Keith Quarterly. Poetry, to 40 lines, in any style. Original and individual subjects preferred. Submit up to 8 poems with SASE. Pays one copy.

PLEIADES—Dept. of English and Phil., Central Missouri State Univ., Warrensburg, MO 64093. R. M. Kinder, Kevin Prufer, Eds. Traditional and experimental poetry, fiction, criticism, translations, and reviews. Cross-genre especially welcome. Pays $10 for prose; $3 or contributors copies for poetry, on publication. E-mail: kdp8106@cmsu2.cmsu.edu. Web site: www.cmsu.edu/englphil/pleiades.html.

PLOUGHSHARES—Emerson College, 100 Beacon St., Boston, MA 02116-1596. Attn: Ed. Serious fiction, to 6,000 words, and poetry (submit up to 3 poems at a time). Pays $25 per page ($50 to $250), on publication. Guidelines available with SASE. Manuscripts read August 1st through March 31st. Web site: www.emerson.edu/ploughshares.

POEM—c/o English Dept., U.A.H., Huntsville, AL 35899. Nancy Frey Dillard, Ed. Serious lyric poetry. Pays in copies. Manuscripts read year-round; best to submit December to March or June to September.

POETRY MAGAZINE—60 W. Walton St., Chicago, IL 60610. Joseph Parisi, Ed. Poetry of highest quality. Submit 3 to 4 poems. Allow 10 to 12 weeks for response. Pays $2 a line, on publication. E-mail: poetry@poetrymagazine.org. Web site: www.poetrymagazine.org.

POETS' PAPER—Anderie Poetry Press, P.O. Box 85, Easton, PA 18044-0085. Carole J. Heffley, Ed. Semiannual. "Contemporary poetry that conveys an immediate, clear sense of recognition and thought." Rhymed metered verse as well as free verse. Submit up to 3 poems, any length. $500 annual prize in poetry. Responds in 4 to 6 weeks. SASE. Presently not accepting submissions.

POTOMAC REVIEW—P.O. Box 354, Port Tobacco, MD 20677. Eli Flam, Ed. Regionally rooted quarterly with a conscience and a lurking sense of humor: to inform, challenge, and direct in fresh ways, with ethical depth. Fiction and wide-ranging essays; occasional pieces, to 3,000 words. Poetry, submit 3 poems (to 5 pages total). Pays in copies or modest stipend for assigned nonfiction stories. Fifth annual poetry/fiction writing contest opens January to March 2000; send SASE. E-mail: eliliu@juno.com. Web site: www.meral.com/potomac.

POTPOURRI—P.O. Box 8278, Prairie Village, KS 66208. Polly W. Swafford, Ed. Quarterly. Short stories, to 3,500 words. Literary essays, travel pieces, and humor, to 2,500 words. Poetry and haiku, to 75 lines. "We like clever themes that avoid reminiscence, depressing plots, and violence." Original B&W illustrations. Pays in one copy. Extra copies available at professional discount. E-mail: editor@potpourri.org. Web site: www.potpourri.org.

PRAIRIE SCHOONER—201 Andrews Hall, Univ. of Nebraska, Lincoln, NE 68588-0334. Hilda Raz, Ed. Short stories. Pays in copies and prizes. Manuscripts read September through May. Annual contests. SASE required. E-mail: eflanaga@unlnotes.unl.edu. Web site: www.unl.edu/schooner/psmain.htm.

PRIMAVERA—Box 37–7547, Chicago, IL 60637. Attn: Ed. Board. Annual. Fiction that focuses on the experiences of women; "author need not be female." No simultaneous submissions. SASE required. Pays in 2 copies.

PRISM INTERNATIONAL—E462-1866 Main Mall, Creative Writing Program, Univ. of British Columbia, Vancouver, B.C., Canada V6T 1Z1. Attn: Ed. High-quality fiction, poetry, drama, creative nonfiction, and literature in translation, varying lengths. Include international reply coupons. Pays $20 per published page of prose, $40 per published page of poetry. Annual short fiction contest with $3,000 in prizes. Annual poetry prize of $500. E-mail: prism@interchange.nbc.ca/prism. Web site: www.arts.nbc.ca/prism.

THE PROSE POEM—English Dept., Providence College, Providence, RI 02198. Peter Johnson, Ed. Prose poems. Pays in copies. Manuscripts read after December of 2001. Web site: www.webdelsol.com/tpp.

PUCKERBRUSH REVIEW—76 Main St., Orono, ME 04473-1430. Constance Hunting, Ed. Semiannual. Literary fiction, criticism, and poetry of various lengths. Literary news from Maine, England, France, Italy, etc. Pays in 2 copies. Manuscripts read year-round.

PUDDING MAGAZINE: THE INTERNATIONAL JOURNAL OF APPLIED POETRY—c/o Pudding House Writers Resource Ctr., Bed & Breakfast for Writers, 60 N. Main St., Johnstown, OH 43031. Jennifer Bosveld, Ed. Poems on popular culture, social concerns, personal struggle; articles/essays on poetry in the schools and in human services. Manuscripts read year-round; responds promptly. Check Web site for additional projects: www.puddinghouse.com. E-mail: pudding@johnstown.net.

PUERTO DEL SOL—New Mexico State Univ., Dept. of English, MSC

3E, P.O. Box 30001, Las Cruces, NM 88003-8001. Kevin McIlvoy, Antonya Nelson, Eds. Short stories, to 30 pages; novel excerpts, to 65 pages. Pays in copies. Manuscripts read September 1 to March 1. Web site: www.nmsu.edu/~english/puerto/puerto.html.

QUARTER AFTER EIGHT—Ellis Hall, Ohio Univ., Athens, OH 45701. Attn: Eds. Annual. Short fiction, novel excerpts, essays, criticism, investigations, and interviews, to 10,000 words. Submit no more than 2 pieces. Prose poetry (submit up to 5 poems); no traditional poetry. Pays in copies. Manuscripts read September through March. Guidelines. Annual prose contest. E-mail address: quarteraftereight@excite.com.

QUARTERLY WEST—200 S. Central Campus Dr., Rm. 317, Univ. of UT, Salt Lake City, UT 84112. Margot Schilpp, Ed. Fiction, short-shorts, poetry, essays, translations, and reviews. Pays $25 to $100 for stories, $25 to $50 for poems. Manuscripts read year-round. Biennial novella competition in even-numbered years. E-mail: margot.schilpp@m.cc.utah.edu. Web site: www.chronicle.utah.edu/qw.

RAG MAG—P.O. Box 12, Goodhue, MN 55027-0012. Beverly Voldseth, Ed. Semiannual. Eclectic fiction and nonfiction, art, photos. Poetry, any length. No religious writing. Pays in copies. SASE for guidelines and themes. Not accepting submissions until LATE 2000.

RAIN CROW—Rain Crow Publishing, 2127 W. Pierce Ave., Apt. 2B, Chicago, IL 60622-1824. Michael S. Manley, Pub. Triannual. Short fiction and creative nonfiction, to 8,000 words. Pays $5 per published page, on publication. Guidelines. E-mail: submissions@rain-crow.com. Web site: www.rain crow.com.

RAMBUNCTIOUS REVIEW—1221 W. Pratt Blvd., Chicago, IL 60626. Richard Goldman, Nancy Lennon, Beth Hausler, Eds. Fiction, to 12 pages; poems, submit up to 5 at a time. Pays in copies. Manuscripts read September through May. Contests. Guidelines.

RE:AL, THE JOURNAL OF LIBERAL ARTS—Stephen F. Austin State Univ., P.O. Box 13007, SFA Sta., Nacogdoches, TX 75962. Attn: Eds. Experimental, genre, and historical fiction; reviews and scholarly nonfiction, 250 to 5,000 words. Poetry, to 10 pages. Pays in copies. E-mail: real@titan. sfasu.edu. Web site: www.libweb.sfasu.edu/real/default.html.

RED CEDAR REVIEW—Dept. of English, 17-C Morrill Hall, Michigan State Univ., E. Lansing, MI 48824. Douglas Dowland, Gen. Ed. James Oliver, Fiction Ed. Meg McClure. Poetry Ed. Fiction, to 5,000 words, creative nonfiction, to 5,000 words, and poetry (submit up to 5 poems, no specified length). Pays in copies. Manuscripts read year-round. Web site: www.msu.edu/~rcreview.

RED ROCK REVIEW—Dept. of English, Community College of Southern Nevada, 3200 E. Cheyenne Ave., N. Las Vegas, NV 89030. Dr. Richard Logsdon, Ed. Semiannual. Short fiction, to 5,000 words; book reviews, to 1,000 words; poetry, to 2 pages. "We're geared toward publishing the work of already established writers. No taboos." Payment varies, on acceptance. E-mail: richlogsdon@ccsn.nevada.edu. Web site: www.cccsn.nevada.edu/academics/departments/english/redrockreview/.

RESPONSE: A CONTEMPORARY JEWISH REVIEW—Columbia University Post Office, P.O. Box 250892, New York, NY 10025. Chanita Baumhaft, Ed. Independent journal of Jewish studies, culture, and literature. Publishes articles, essays, and fiction to 3500 words; poetry; book reviews; art; illustrated stories/comics. For nonfiction, query with one to two line abstract/proposal only. Pays in copies. E-mail: Response@Panix.com. Web site: www. responseweb.org.

REVIEW: LATIN AMERICAN LITERATURE AND ARTS—Americas Society, 680 Park Ave., New York, NY 10021. Alfred J. MacAdam, Ed. Semiannual. Work in English translation, 1,000 to 1,500 words, by and about young and established Latin American writers; essays and book reviews. Payment varies, on acceptance. Query. E-mail: dshapico@as-coa.org. Web site: www.americans-society.org.

RIVER CITY—Dept. of English, Univ. of Memphis, Memphis, TN 38152. Thomas Russell, Ed. Poems, short stories, essays, and interviews. No novel excerpts. Pay varies according to grants. Manuscripts read September through April. Guidelines. Contests. E-mail: rivercity@memphis.edu. Web site: www.people.memphis.edu/~rivercity.

RIVER OAK REVIEW—P.O. Box 3127, Oak Park, IL 60303. Semiannual. Address Fiction, Poetry, or Nonfiction Ed. No criticism, reviews, or translations. Limit prose to 20 pages; poetry to batches of no more than 4. Pays in copies, and small honorarium, as funding permits. Web site: www.riveroak arts.org.

RIVER STYX—634 N. Grand Blvd., 12th Fl., St. Louis, MO 63103. Attn: Fiction Ed. Published 3 times a year. Literary fiction. Manuscripts read May through November; reports in 3 to 5 months. Payment is 2 copies, plus one year subscription; $8 per page if possible. Web site: www.riverstyx.org.

ROANOKE REVIEW—Roanoke College, Salem, VA 24153. Robert R. Walter, Ed. Fiction, to 5,000 words, and poetry, to 100 lines. Pays in copies. Allow 10 to 12 weeks for decision. E-mail: walter@roanoke.cdu.

ROCKFORD REVIEW—P.O. Box 858, Rockford, IL 61105. David Ross, Ed.-in-Chief. Published 3 times a year. Fiction, essays, and satire, 250 to 1,300 words. Experimental and traditional poetry, to 50 lines (shorter works preferred). One-act plays and other dramatic forms, to 10 pages. "We prefer genuine or satirical human dilemmas with coping or non-coping outcomes that ring the reader's bell." Submit up to 3 works at a time. Pays in copies; two $25 Editor's Choice Prizes awarded each issue. E-mail: dragonldy@prodigy.net. Web site: www.welcome.to/rwg.

ROSEBUD—P.O. Box 459, Cambridge, WI 53523. Rod Clark, Ed. Quarterly. Fiction, articles, profiles, 1,200 to 1,800 words, and poems; love, alienation, travel, humor, nostalgia, and unexpected revelation. Pays $45 plus copies, on publication. Guidelines. Web site: rsbd.net.

ROSWELL LITERARY REVIEW—JoPop Publications, P.O. Box 8118, Roswell, NM 88202-8118. S. Joan Popek, Ed. Quarterly. Fiction, to 5,000 words, any genre, and poetry. No prose poetry. Pays from $5 to $15 for fiction, $1 to $10 for flash fiction. Poetry earns free copy. All payments made on acceptance. No submissions until mid to late 2000.

SANSKRIT LITERARY-ARTS MAGAZINE—Cone University Ctr., Univ. of North Carolina/Charlotte, Charlotte, NC 28223. Attn: Ed. Annual. Short fiction and poetry. Pays one copy. Manuscripts read in fall only; deadline first Friday in November. E-mail: sanskrit@email.uncc.edu. Web site: www. uncc.edu/life/sanskrit.

SCANDINAVIAN REVIEW—15 E. 65th St., New York, NY 10021-6501. Attn: Ed. Published 3 times a year. Poetry or prose translated from Nordic languages for a lay audience with interest in Nordic countries for annual translation prize competition; write for submission rules. Feature articles on culture, politics, and lifestyle of Scandinavia. Pays from $100+, on publication. Web site: www.amscan.org.

SCRIVENER—McGill Univ.,Arts Bldg., Office 305, 853 Sherbrooke St. W., Montreal, Quebec, Canada H3A 2T6. Attn: Eds. Poems, submit 5 to 10; prose, to 15 pages; reviews, to 5 pages. B&W photography and drawing printed on quality coated paper. E-mail address: scrivener@post.com.

THE SEATTLE REVIEW—Padelford Hall, Box 354330, Univ. of Washington, Seattle, WA 98195-4330. Attn: Fiction Ed. Short stories to 20 pages. Payment varies, usually two contributor's copies. Manuscripts read October 1 through May 31.

SENECA REVIEW—Hobart & William Smith Colleges, Geneva, NY 14456. Deborah Tall, Ed. Poetry, translations, and lyric essays. Pays in copies and 2-year subscription. Manuscripts read September through April. E-mail: senecareview@hws.edu. Web site: www.hws.edu/senecareview/.

SHENANDOAH—Washington and Lee Univ., Troubadour Theatre, 2nd Fl., Lexington, VA 24450-0303. R.T. Smith, Ed. Quarterly. Highest quality fiction, poetry, criticism, essays and interviews. "Read the magazine before submitting." Pays $25 per page for prose; $2.50 per line for poetry, on publication. Web site: www.wlu.edu/~shenandoah.

SKYLARK—2200 169th St., Hammond, IN 46323-2094. Pamela Hunter, Ed. "The Fine Arts Annual of Purdue Calumet." Fiction and articles, to 4,000 words. Poetry, to 21 lines. B&W prints and drawings. Pays in one copy. Manuscripts read November through April for fall publication. E-mail: poet pam49@yahoo.com.

SLIPSTREAM—Box 2071, Niagara Falls, NY 14301. Attn: Ed. Fiction, 2 to 15 pages. Contemporary urban themes encouraged; send SASE for complete guidelines. E-mail: editors@slipstreampress.org. Web site: www.slip streampress.org.

THE SMALL POND MAGAZINE—P.O. Box 664, Stratford, CT 06615. Napoleon St. Cyr, Ed. Published 3 times a year. Fiction, to 2,500 words; poetry, to 100 lines. Pays in copies. Query for nonfiction. Include short bio. Manuscripts read year-round. SASE required.

SMALL PRESS REVIEW—Box 100, Paradise, CA 95967. Len Fulton, Ed. Reviews, 200 words, of small literary books and magazines; tracks the publishing of small publishers and small-circulation magazines. Query. Web site: www.dustbooks.com. E-mail: dustbooks@desi.net.

SNOWY EGRET—P.O. Box 9, Bowling Green, IN 47833. Philip Repp, Ed. Poetry, fiction, and nonfiction, to 10,000 words. Natural history from artistic, literary, philosophical, psychological, and historical perspectives. Pays $2 per page for prose; $2 to $4 for poetry, on publication. Manuscripts read year-round.

SO TO SPEAK: A FEMINIST JOURNAL OF LANGUAGE AND ART—George Mason University, 4400 University Dr., MS2D6, Fairfax, VA 22030-4444. Semiannual. Poetry; plays; fiction entries to 5,000 words; interviews, essays, and reviews to 4,000 words. B&W art, color cover art welcome. Send manuscript with cover letter and SASE or request guidelines. Pays in copies. E-mail: sts@gmu.edu. Web site: www.gmu.edu/org/sts.

SONORA REVIEW—Dept. of English, Univ. of Arizona, Tucson, AZ 85721. Attn: Fiction, Poetry, or Nonfiction Ed. (Address appropriate genre editor.) Annual contests; send for guidelines. Simultaneous submissions accepted (except for contest entries). Manuscripts read year-round.

THE SOUTH CAROLINA REVIEW—Dept. of English, Clemson Univ., Clemson, SC 29634-1503. Wayne Chapman, Ed. Semiannual. Fiction, to 4,000 words. Send complete manuscript (plus diskette on acceptance). Send SASE or E-mail address for guidelines. Pays in copies. Response time is 2 to 3 months. Manuscripts read September through May (but not in December). E-mail: cwayne@clemson.edu. Web site: www.hubcap.clemson.edu/aah/engl/screview.htm.

SOUTH DAKOTA REVIEW—Box 111, Univ. Exchange, Vermillion, SD 57069-2390. Brian Bedard, Ed. Exceptional fiction, 3,000 to 5,000 words; favors work with focus on American West. Pays in copies and one-year subscription. Manuscripts read year-round; slower response time in the summer. Web site: www.usd.edu/engl/sdr. E-mail: bbedard@usd.edu.

THE SOUTHERN CALIFORNIA ANTHOLOGY—c/o Master of Professional Writing Program, WPH 404, Univ. of Southern California, Los Angeles, CA 90089-4034. James Ragan, Ed.-in-Chief. Fiction, to 20 pages, and poetry, to 5 pages. Pays in copies. Manuscripts read September to January.

SOUTHERN EXPOSURE—P.O. Box 531, Durham, NC 27702. Chris Kromm, Ed. Quarterly forum on "Southern politics and culture." Short stories, to 3,600 words, essays, investigative journalism, and oral histories, 500 to 3,600 words. Pays $25 to $250, on publication. Query.

SOUTHERN HUMANITIES REVIEW—9088 Haley Ctr., Auburn Univ., AL 36849. Dan R. Latimer, Virginia M. Kouidis, Eds. Short stories, 3,500 to 15,000 words. SASE required. Submit one story at a time. No simultaneous or e-mail submissions. E-mail: shrengl@auburn.edu. Web site: www.auburn.edu/english/shr/home.htm.

SOUTHERN POETRY REVIEW—Advancement Studies, Central Piedmont Community College, Charlotte, NC 28235. Ken McLaurin, Ed. Poems. No restrictions on style, length, or content. Manuscripts read September through May. E-mail: kenmclaurin@cpcc.cc.nc.us.

THE SOUTHERN REVIEW—43 Allen Hall, Louisiana State Univ., Baton Rouge, LA 70803-5005. James Olney, Dave Smith Eds. Emphasis on highest quality contemporary literature in United States and abroad and with special interest in southern culture and history. Fiction, 4,000 to 8,000 words. Pays $12 a page for fiction, $20 a page for poetry, on publication. No manuscripts read in the summer. E-mail: bmacon@lsu.edu. Web site: www.lsu.edu/guests/wwwtsm.

SOUTHWEST REVIEW—307 Fondren Library W., Box 750374, Southern Methodist Univ., Dallas, TX 75275-0374. Elizabeth Mills, Sr. Fiction Ed. "A quarterly that serves the interests of the region but is not bound by them." Fiction, essays, poetry, and interviews with well-known writers, 3,000 to 7,500 words. Pays varying rates. Manuscripts read September 1 through May 31. E-mail: swr@mail.smu.edu.

SOU'WESTER—Southern Illinois Univ. at Edwardsville, Edwardsville, IL 62026-1438. Fred W. Robbins, Ed. Nancy Avdoian, Assoc. Ed.; Susan Garrison, Fiction Ed.,Scott Heather, Poetry Ed., Allison Funk, Consulting Ed. Fiction, to 8,000 words. Poetry, any length. Pays in copies. Manuscripts not read in August.

THE SOW'S EAR POETRY REVIEW—19535 Pleasant View Dr., Abingdon, VA 24211-6827. Attn: Ed. Quarterly. Eclectic poetry and art. Submit one to 5 poems, any length, plus a brief biographical note. Interviews, essays, and articles, any length, about poets and poetry are also considered. B&W photos and drawings. Payment is two copies. Poetry and chapbook contests. Send SASE for guidelines.

SPARROW: THE YEARBOOK OF THE SONNET—Sparrow Press, 103 Waldron St., W. Lafayette, IN 47906. Felix and Selma Stefanile, Eds./Pubs. Contemporary (14-line) sonnets, and occasionally formal poems in other structures. Submit up to 5 poems. Pays $3 per poem, on publication. A $25 sonnet prize is awarded to a contributor in each issue.

SPECTACLE—Pachanga Press, PMB 155, 101 Middlesex Turnpike, Suite 6, , Burlington, MA 01803-4914. Richard Aguilar, Ed. Semiannual journal of essays, articles, interviews, reportage, cultural criticism, and fiction addressing a broad spectrum of lively and unconventional themes. Send SASE for guidelines. Pays $30 and copies upon publication. E-mail: spectacle journal@hotmail.com.

SPECTRUM—Univ. of California/ Santa Barbara, Box 14800, Santa Barbara, CA 93107. Attn: Ed. Annual. Novel excerpts, short stories, various narrative, poetry, nonfiction essays, slides of art. Annual deadline is February 10.

SPOON RIVER POETRY REVIEW—Dept. of English, Stevenson Hall, Illinois State Univ., Normal, IL 61790-4240. Lucia Cordell Getsi, Ed. Poetry, any length. Pays in copies.

SPSM&H—329 E St., Bakersfield, CA 93304. Frederick A. Raborg, Jr., Ed. Single sonnets, sequences, essays about the sonnet form, short fiction in which the sonnet plays a part, books, and anthologies. Pays $10, plus copies, for fiction and essays; "best of issue" sonnets, $14. E-mail: amelia@lightspeed.net.

STAND MAGAZINE—Dept. of English, Box 2005, VCU,, Richmond, VA 23284-2005. David Latané, U.S. Ed. School of English, Univ. of Leeds, Leeds, LS2 9JT, UK. John Kinsella and Michael Hulse, Eds. British quarterly. Fiction, 2,000 to 5,000 words; also poetry. Web site: www.saturn.vcu.edu/~dla tane/stand.html. E-mail: dlatane@vcu.edu.

STORY QUARTERLY—P.O. Box 1416, Northbrook, IL 60065. Anne Brashler, Marie Hayes, Eds. Short stories. Pays in copies. Sample copy $6. E-mail: theloon@ameritech.net.

THE SUN—The Sun Publishing Co., 107 N. Roberson St., Chapel Hill, NC 27516. Sy Safransky, Ed. Essays, interviews, and fiction, to 7,000 words; poetry; photos. "We're interested in all writing that makes sense and enriches our common space." Pays $300 to $500 for fiction; $300 to $1,000 for nonfiction; $50 to $200 for poetry, on publication.

SYCAMORE REVIEW—Purdue Univ., Dept. of English, West Lafayette, IN 47907. Numsiri Kunakemakorn, Ed.-in-Chief. Semiannual. Poetry, short fiction (no genre fiction), personal essays, drama, and translations. Pays in copies. Manuscripts read September to April. E-mail: sycamore@expert. cc.purdue.edu. Web site: www.sla.purdue.edu/academic/engl/sycamore.

TALKING RIVER REVIEW—Lewis-Clark State College, 500 8th Ave., Lewiston, ID 83501. Attn: Eds. Semiannual. Short stories, novel excerpts, and essays, to 7,500 words. Poetry, any length or style; submit up to 5 poems. "We publish emerging writing alongside established writers." Pays in copies and subscription. Manuscripts read September through February. Send poetry and prose under separate cover.

TAR RIVER POETRY—Dept. of English, East Carolina Univ., Greenville, NC 27858-4353. Peter Makuck, Ed. Poetry and reviews. "We prefer poems with strong imagery and figurative language. No trite, worn-out phrases, vague abstractions, or cliché situations." Pays in copies. Submit September through April.

THE TEXAS REVIEW—P.O. Box 2146, English Dept., Sam Houston State Univ., Huntsville, TX 77341. Paul Ruffin, Ed. Fiction, poetry, articles, to 20 typed pages. Reviews. Pays in copies and subscription. Annual book competitions in fiction and poetry. Write for guidelines. E-mail: engpdr@ shsu.edu. Web site: www.shsu.edu/~engwww/trp.html.

THEMA—Box 8747, Metairie, LA 70011-8747. Virginia Howard, Ed. Theme-related fiction, to 20 pages, and poetry, to 2 pages. Pays $25 per story; $10 per short-short; $10 per poem; $10 for B&W art/photo, on acceptance. Send SASE for themes and guidelines. E-mail: thema@home.com. Web site: www.litline.org/html/thema.html.

THIRD COAST—Dept. of English, Western Michigan University, Kalamazoo, MI 49008-5092. Fiction (Creative Nonfiction) or Poetry Ed. Fiction, creative nonfiction, and poetry (up to 5 poems). SASE; guidelines available. No electronic submissions. Allow 4 months for reply. Pays in copies and subscription. Web site: www.wmich.edu/thirdcoast.

360 DEGREES: ART & LITERARY REVIEW—517 N. Graham St. 3F, Charlotte, NC 28202. Karen Kinnison, Ed. Biannual art and literary review, featuring fiction and poetry (any length), and artwork. Send photocopies and photographs only. Payment is one copy.

THE THREEPENNY REVIEW—P.O. Box 9131, Berkeley, CA 94709. Wendy Lesser, Ed. Fiction, to 5,000 words. Pays to $200, on acceptance. Limited market. Send SASE for guidelines. Manuscripts read September through May. Web site: www.threepenny.com.

TIGHTROPE—Swamp Press, 15 Warwick Ave., Northfield, MA 01360. Ed Rayher, Ed. Limited-edition, letterpress semiannual. Poetry, any length. Pays in copies. Manuscripts read year-round.

TIMBER CREEK REVIEW—3283 UNCG Station, Greensboro, NC 27413. J. M. Freiermuth, Ed. Quarterly. Fiction, 3,000 to 5,000 words; creative nonfiction, 2,000 to 4,000 words; and poetry, to 30 lines. "Not for children, or those easily offended." Pays $5 to $35 plus subscription for prose, author's copy for poetry, on publication. E-mail: timbercreekreview@hoopsmail.com.

TRIQUARTERLY—Northwestern Univ., 2020 Ridge Ave., Evanston, IL 60208-4302. Susan Hahn, Ed. Serious, aesthetically informed and inventive poetry and prose, for an international and literate audience. Payment varies. Manuscripts read October through March. Allow 10 to 12 weeks for reply.

TWO RIVERS REVIEW—215 McCartney St., Easton, PA 18042. Philip Memmer, Ed. Semiannual. Excellent contemporary poetry, any style, from both established poets and astonishing newcomers. Submit 2 to 4 poems, with SASE. Responds in six weeks. E-mail: tworiversreview@juno.com. Web site: http://pages.prodigy.net/memmer/trr.html.

THE URBANITE: SURREAL & LIVELY & BIZARRE—Box 4737, Davenport, IA 52808. Mark McLaughlin, Ed. Published 3 times a year. Dark fantasy, horror (no gore), surrealism, reviews, and social commentary, to 3,000 words. Free verse poems, to 2 pages. Pays 2¢ to 3¢ a word; $10 for poetry, on acceptance. Query for themes. Web site: www.theurbanite.tripod.com.

VERMONT INK—P.O. Box 3297, Burlington, VT 05401-3297. Donna Leach, Ed. Quarterly. Short stories, 2,000 to 3,000 words, that are well-written, entertaining, and "basically G-rated": adventure, historical, humor, mainstream, mystery and suspense, regional interest, romance, science fiction, and westerns. Poetry, to 25 lines, should be upbeat or humorous. Pays to $25 for stories; to $10 for poetry, on acceptance. Send complete manuscript with short bio and SASE. E-mail: vermontink@aol.com. Web site: www.vermontink.com.

VERSE—English Dept., Plymouth State College, Plymouth, NH 03264. Brian Henry, Ed. Three times yearly. Poetry (up to 5 poems); and nonfiction, including essays on poetry, interviews with poets, and reviews of poetry. Submit with cover letter and SASE. Pays in copies and subscription. E-mail: verse@versemag.org. Web site: www.versemag.org.

THE VILLAGER—135 Midland Ave., Bronxville, NY 10708. Lorraine Lange, Ed. Mary Hazzah, Fiction Ed., Jean Buhrig, Articles Ed., Edith Mahoney, Poetry Ed. Fiction, 900 to 1,500 words: mystery, adventure, humor, romance. Pays in copies.

THE VINCENT BROTHERS REVIEW—4566 Northern Cir., Riverside, OH 45424-5733. Kimberly Willardson, Ed. Published 3 times a year. Fiction, nonfiction, poetry, fillers, and B&W art. "Read sample copies/back issues before submitting." Pays from $15 for fiction and nonfiction; $5 for poems; $10 for poetry used in "Page Left" feature. Guidelines. Annual poetry and fiction contests.

VIRGINIA QUARTERLY REVIEW—One W. Range, Charlottesville, VA 22903. Attn: Ed. Quality fiction. Pays $10 per page, on publication. Web site: www.virginia.edu/vqr.

VISIONS INTERNATIONAL—Black Buzzard Press, 1007 Ficklen Rd., Fredericksburg, VA 22405. Bradley R. Strahan, Ed. Published 3 times a year. Poetry, to 50 lines, and B&W drawings. (Query for art.) Read magazine before submitting. Pays in copies (or honorarium when funds available). Manuscripts read year-round.

WASCANA REVIEW OF CONTEMPORARY AND SHORT FICTION—c/o Dept. of English, Univ. of Regina, Regina, Sask., Canada S4S 0A2. Kathleen Wall, Ed. Short stories, 2,000 to 6,000 words; critical articles on short fiction and poetry; poetry. Pays $3 per page for prose, $10 for poetry, after publication. Web address: www.uregina.ca/English/wrhome.htm.

WASHINGTON REVIEW—P.O. Box 50132, Washington, DC 20091-

0132. Clarissa Wittenberg, Ed. Fiction, 2,000 to 2,500 words. Area writers preferred. Pays in copies. Web site: www.washingtonreview.com.

WEST BRANCH—Bucknell Hall, Bucknell Univ., Lewisburg, PA 17837. Auctin Crotola, Man. Ed. Poetry, fiction, nonfiction reviews. Pays in copies and subscriptions, with prize for best of genre. E-mail: ciotola@bucknell.edu.

WESTERN HUMANITIES REVIEW—Univ. of Utah, Salt Lake City, UT 84112. Jenny Mueller, Man. Ed. Semi-annual. Fiction and essays, to 30 pages, and poetry. Pays $5 per page on publication, plus contributor's copies. Manuscripts read October through May; responds in 2 to 4 months. No electronic submissions. E-mail: whr@lists.utah.edu.

WHETSTONE—P.O. Box 1266, Barrington, IL 60011. Attn: Eds. Fiction, poetry, and creative nonfiction, to 20 pages. Poems, submit up to 7. Payment varies, on publication.

WHISKEY ISLAND—Dept. of English, Cleveland State Univ., Cleveland, OH 44115. Attn: Ed. Fiction and nonfiction, under 5,000 words; Poetry up to 10 single-sided pages. We want a well-rounded magazine. Abstract and experimental works welcomed, social and ecological topics as well. Pays in copies. E-mail: whiskeyisland@csuohio.edu. Web site: www.csuohio.edu/whiskeyisland.

THE WILLIAM AND MARY REVIEW—P.O. Box 8795, College of William and Mary, Williamsburg, VA 23187-8795. Brian Hatleberg, Ed. Annual. Fiction, 2,500 to 7,500 words; poetry, all genres (submit 4 to 6 poems); and art, all media. Pays in copies. Manuscripts read September through March. Responds in 3 months.

WIND MAGAZINE—P.O. Box 24548, Lexington, KY 40524. Charlie Hughes and Leatha Kendrick, Eds. Semiannual. Short stories, poems, and essays. Reviews of books from small presses and news of interest to the literary community. Pays in copies. Contests. Manuscripts read year-round. Web site: http://www.wind.wind.org.

WINDSOR REVIEW—Dept. of English, Univ. of Windsor, Windsor, Ont., Canada N9B 3P4. Attn: Ed. Short stories, poetry, and original art. Pays $15 for poetry; $50 for fiction, on publication. Responds in one to 3 months. E-ma il: uwrevv@uwindsor.ca. Web site: www.webnotes1.uwindsor.ca:8888/units/english/English.nsf.

WITNESS—Oakland Community College, 27055 Orchard Lake Rd., Farmington Hills, MI 48334. Peter Stine, Ed. Thematic journal. Fiction and essays, 5 to 20 pages, and poems (submit up to 3). Pays $6 per page for prose, $10 per page for poetry, on publication. E-mail: stinepj@umich.edu.

THE WORCESTER REVIEW—6 Chatham St., Worcester, MA 01609. Rodger Martin, Ed. Poetry (submit up to 5 poems at a time), fiction, and critical articles about poetry with a New England connection. Pays in copies. Responds within 9 months. Web site: www.geocites.com/Paris/LeftBank/6433/.

WRITERS' FORUM—Univ. of Colorado, P.O. Box 7150, Colorado Springs, CO 80933-7150. C. Kenneth Pellow, Ed. Annual. Mainstream and experimental fiction, 1,000 to 8,000 words. Poetry (one to 5 poems per submission). Emphasis on western themes and writers. Pays in copies. Manuscripts read year-round.

WRITERS ON THE RIVER—P.O. Box 40828, Memphis, TN 38174-0828. Mick Denington, Ed. Russell H. Strauss, Prose Ed.; Florence Bruce, Asst. Ed.; Wanda A. Rider, Poetry Ed. Family oriented. Publishes poetry, one page; fiction and nonfiction: adventure, fantasy, historical and regional, mainstream, humor, mystery/suspense, to 2,500 words. Accepts submissions only from states bordering the Mississippi River. Pays in copies. E-mail: tterry@worldnet .att.net or mrdcolonel@aol.com.

YALE REVIEW—Yale Univ., P.O. Box 208243, New Haven, CT 06520-8243. J.D. McClatchy, Ed. Susan Bianconi, Man. Ed. Serious poetry, to 200 lines, and fiction, 3,000 to 5,000 words. Pays average of $400.

YARROW—English Dept., Lytle Hall, Kutztown State Univ., Kutztown, PA 19530. Harry Humes, Ed. Semiannual. Poetry. "Just good, solid, clear writing. We don't have room for long poems." Pays in copies. Manuscripts read year-round.

ZOETROPE: ALL STORY—1350 Avenue of the Americas, 24th Fl., New York, NY 10019. Adrienne Brodeur, Ed.-in-Chief. Stories and one-act plays under 7,000 words. Pays good rates, on acceptance. No submissions from June 1 through August 31. Please include SASE and allow four months for a response. E-mail: info@all-story.com. Web site: www.zoetrope-stories.com.

ZYZZYVA—P.O. Box 590069, San Francisco, CA 94159-0069. Howard Junker, Ed. Publishes work of West Coast writers only: fiction, essays, and poetry. Pays $50, on acceptance. Manuscripts read year-round. E-mail: editor @zyzzyva.org. Web site: www.zyzzyva.org.

GREETING CARDS & NOVELTY ITEMS

Companies selling greeting cards and novelty items (T-shirts, coffee mugs, buttons, etc.) often have their own specific requirements for the submission of ideas, verse, and artwork. In general, however, each verse or message should be typed double-space on a 3×5 or 4×6 card. Use only one side of the card, and be sure to put your name and address in the upper left-hand corner. Keep a copy of every verse or idea you send. (It's also advisable to keep a record of what you've submitted to each publisher.) Always enclose an SASE, and do not send out more than ten verses or ideas in a group to any one publisher. Never send original artwork unless a publisher indicates a definite interest in using your work.

AMBERLEY GREETING CARD COMPANY—11510 Goldcoast Dr., Cincinnati, OH 45249-1695. Dan Cronstein, Ed. Humorous ideas for cards: birthday, illness, friendship, anniversary, congratulations, "miss you," etc. No poems. Send SASE for market letter before submitting ideas. Pays $150. Buys all rights.

AMERICAN GREETINGS—One American Rd., Cleveland, OH 44144.

Kathleen McKay, Ed. Recruitment. Send #10 SASE to receive Humorous Writing guidelines. Current need is for humor only.

BLUE MOUNTAIN ARTS, INC.—See *SPS Studios, Inc.*

BRILLIANT ENTERPRISES—117 W. Valerio St., Santa Barbara, CA 93101-2927. Ashleigh Brilliant, Ed. Illustrated epigrams. Send SASE and $2 for a catalogue and samples. Pays $50, on acceptance. Web site: www.ashleigh brilliant.com.

COMSTOCK CARDS—600 S. Rock, Suite 15, Reno, NV 89502-4115. David Delacroix, Ed. Adult humor, outrageous or sexual, for greeting cards, invitations, and notepads. SASE for guidelines. Payment varies, on publication. Guidelines on web site: www.comstockcards.com.

DAYSPRING GREETING CARDS—P.O. Box 1010, Siloam Springs, AR 72761. Attn: Freelance Ed. Inspirational material for everyday occasions and most holidays. Currently only accepting free-lance copy submissions from published greeting card authors. Qualified writers should send samples of their published greeting cards (no more than 5 cards or copies). Also, the words "Previously Published" must be written on the lower left corner of the mailing envelopes containing copy submissions. Payment is $50 on acceptance. Send SASE for guidelines, or email to: info@dayspring.com, and type in the word "write" for guidelines.

DESIGN DESIGN, INC.—P.O. Box 2266, Grand Rapids, MI 49501-2266. Tom Vituj, Creative Dir. Short verses for both humorous and sentimental concepts for greeting cards. Everyday (birthday, get well, just for fun, etc.) and seasonal (Christmas, Valentine's Day, Easter, Mother's Day, Father's Day, Graduation, Halloween, Thanksgiving) material. Flat fee payment on publication. Please include SASE for return.

DUCK & COVER—P.O. Box 21640, Oakland, CA 94620. Jim Buser, Ed. Outrageous, off the wall, original one-liners for buttons and magnets, no greeting cards. SASE for guidelines. Pays $35, on publication.

EPHEMERA, INC.—P.O. Box 490, Phoenix, OR 97535. Attn: Ed. Provocative, irreverent, and outrageously funny slogans for novelty buttons, magnets, and stickers. Submit typed list of slogans with SASE. Pays $40 per slogan, on acceptance. SASE for guidelines; also available from web site: www.ephemera-inc.com. E-mail: ephemera@mind.net.

FREEDOM GREETING CARDS—75 West St., Walpole, MA 02081. Jay Levitt, Ed. Dept. Traditional and humorous verse and love messages. Inspirational poetry for all occasions. Pays negotiable rates, on acceptance. Query with SASE. Web site: www.freedomgreetings.com.

HALLMARK CARDS, INC.—Box 419580, Mail Drop 288, Kansas City, MO 64141. No unsolicited submissions.

KATE HARPER DESIGNS—P.O. Box 2112, Berkeley, CA 94702. Hand-assembled "quotation" cards. Submit original quotes on index card, one quote per card. No drawings, artwork, or visuals. SASE for guidelines before submitting. Payment varies, on acceptance. Also accepting submissions from children. For guidelines: kateharp@aol.com. Web site: www.hometown.aol.com/kateharp/myhomepage/index.html.

LAFFS BY MARCEL—See *Marcel Shurman Company.*

MARCEL SHURMAN COMPANY—(formerly *Laffs by Marcel*) 101

New Montgomery, 6th Fl., San Francisco, CA 94105. Attn: Deanne Quinones. Sophisticated, humorous birthday, everyday, and seasonal ideas.

OATMEAL STUDIOS—Box 138 TW, Rochester, VT 05767. Attn: Ed. Humorous, clever, and new ideas needed for all occasions. Send legal-size SASE for guidelines.

PANDA INK—P.O. Box 5129, West Hills, CA 91308-5129. Ruth Ann Epstein, Ed. Judaica, metaphysical, cute, whimsical, or beautiful sentiment for greeting cards, bookmarks, clocks, and pins. Currently overstocked; accepting no submissions. Payment varies, on acceptance.

PARAMOUNT CARDS—P.O. Box 6546, Providence, RI 02940-6546. Attn: Editorial Freelance. Humorous, traditional, and inspirational card ideas for birthday, relative's birthday, friendship, romance, get well, Christmas, Valentine's Day, Easter, Mother's Day, Father's Day, and Graduation. Submit each idea (5 to 10 per submission) on 3×5 card with name and address on each, along with SASE. Payment varies, on acceptance.

PLUM GRAPHICS—P.O. Box 136, Prince Station, New York, NY 10012. Yvette Cohen, Ed. Editorial needs change frequently; write for guidelines (new guidelines 3 times per year). Queries required. Pays $40 per card, on publication.

ROCKSHOTS, INC.—632 Broadway, New York, NY 10012. Bob Vesce, Ed. Adult, provocative, humorous gag lines for greeting cards. Submit on 4x5 cards with SASE. Pays $50 per line, on acceptance. SASE for guidelines.

SPS STUDIOS, INC., PUBLISHERS OF BLUE MOUNTAIN ARTS PRODUCTS—(formerly *Blue Mountain Arts, Inc.*) P.O. Box 1007, Boulder, CO 80306. Attn: Ed. Dept. TW. Poetry and prose about love, friendship, family, philosophies, etc. Also material for special occasions and holidays: birthdays, get well, Christmas, Valentine's Day, Easter, etc. Submit seasonal material 5 months in advance of holiday. No artwork. Include SASE. Pays $200 per poem.

VAGABOND CREATIONS, INC.—2560 Lance Dr., Dayton, OH 45409. George F. Stanley, Jr., Ed. Greeting cards with graphics only on cover (no copy) and short punch line inside: birthday, everyday, Valentine's Day, Christmas, and graduation. Mildly risqué humor with double entendre acceptable. Ideas for illustrated theme stationery. Pays $15, on acceptance. E-mail: vagabond@siscom.net. Web site: www.vagabondcreations.com.

WEST GRAPHICS PUBLISHING—1117 California Dr., Burlingame, CA 94010. Attn: Production Dept. Outrageous humor concepts, all occasions (especially birthday) and holidays, for illustrated card lines. Submit on 3x5 cards: concept on one side; name, address, and phone number on other. Pays $60 to $100, 30 days after publication.

HUMOR, FILLERS, & SHORT ITEMS

Magazines noted for their filler departments, plus a cross-section of publications using humor, short items, jokes, quizzes, and cartoons, follow.

However, almost all magazines use some type of filler material from time to time, and writers can find dozens of markets by studying copies of magazines at a library or newsstand.

THE AMERICAN FIELD—542 S. Dearborn, Chicago, IL 60605. B.J. Matthys, Man. Ed. Short fact items and anecdotes on hunting dogs and field trials for bird dogs. Pays varying rates, on acceptance.

AMERICAN SPEAKER—Attn: Current Comedy, 1101 30th St. N.W., Washington, DC 20007. Aram Bakshian, Ed.-in-Chief. Original, funny, performable jokes on news, fads, topical subjects, business, etc., for "Current Comedy" section of *American Speaker* Magazine. Jokes for roasts, retirement dinners, and for speaking engagements. Humorous material specifically geared for public speaking situations such as microphone feedback, introductions, long events, etc. Also interested in longer original jokes and anecdotes that can be used by public speakers. No poems, puns, ethnic jokes, or sexist material. Pays $12, on publication. Guidelines.

THE ANNALS OF IMPROBABLE RESEARCH—AIR, P.O. Box 380853, Cambridge, MA 02238. Marc Abrahams, Ed. Science humor, science reports and analysis, one to 4 pages. B&W photos. "This journal is the place to find the mischievous, funny, iconoclastic side of science. An insider's journal that lets anyone sneak into the company of wonderfully mad scientists." Guidelines. No payment. E-mail: marca@improbable.com. Web site: www. improbable.com.

ARMY MAGAZINE—2425 Wilson Blvd., Arlington, VA 22201-3385. Mary B. French, Ed.-in-Chief. True anecdotes on military subjects. Pays $25 to $50, on publication. Web site: www.ausa.org.

ASIAN PAGES—P.O. Box 11932, St. Paul, MN 55111-0932. Cheryl Weiberg, Ed.-in-Chief. Profiles and news events, 500 words; short stories, 500 to 750 words; poetry, 100 words; and Asian-related fillers, 50 words. "All material must have a strong, non-offensive Asian slant." Pays $40 for articles, $25 for photos/cartoons, on publication. E-mail: asianpages@att.net. Web site: www.asianpages.com.

THE ATLANTIC MONTHLY—77 N. Washington St., Boston, MA 02114. Attn: Ed. Sophisticated humorous or satirical pieces, 1,000 to 3,000 words. Some light poetry. No unsolicited material. Pays from $500 for prose, on acceptance. Web site: www.theatlantic.com.

ATLANTIC SALMON JOURNAL—P.O. Box 5200, St. Andrews, N.B., Canada E5B 3S8. Jim Gourlay, Ed. Fillers, 50 to 100 words, on salmon politics, conservation, and nature. Pays $25 for fillers, on publication. E-mail: asfads. nbnet.nb.ca. Web site: www.asf.ca.

BICYCLING—135 N. 6th St., Emmaus, PA 18098. Attn: Eds. Anecdotes, helpful cycling tips, and other items for "Bike Shorts" section, 150 to 250 words. Pays $25 to $50, on acceptance.

BYLINE—Box 130596, Edmond, OK 73013. Marcia Preston, Ed.-in-Chief. Humor, 50 to 400 words, about writing. Pays $15 to $25 for humor, on acceptance. Web site: www.bylinemag.com. E-mail: bylinemp@aol.com.

CAPPER'S—1503 S.W. 42nd St., Topeka, KS 66609-1265. Ann Crahan, Ed. Letters, to 300 words, sharing heartwarming experiences, nostalgic accounts, household hints, poems, and recipes, for "Heart of the Home." Poetry to 16 lines. Pays on acceptance. Freelance articles on historical, informational, unusual items to 700 words. Pays on publication. Query only for serial fiction. Jokes, submit up to 6 at a time. Pays varying rates (and in gift certificates), on publication.

CATHOLIC DIGEST—2115 Summit Ave., St. Paul, MN 55105-1081. Attn: Filler Ed. Articles, 200 to 500 words, on instances of kindness, for "Hearts Are Trumps." Stories about conversions, for "Open Door." Accounts of good deeds, for "People Are Like That." Humorous pieces, 50 to 300 words, on parish life, for "In Our Parish." Amusing signs, for "Signs of the Times." Jokes; fillers. No fiction. Pays $2 per line, on publication. E-mail: cdigest@ stthomas.edu. Web site: www.catholicdigest.org.

CHICKADEE—179 John St., Suite 500, Toronto, Ont., Canada M5T 3G5. Hilary Bain, Ed. Juvenile poetry, 10 to 15 lines. Fiction, 800 words. Pays on acceptance. Enclose $2.00 money order and IRC for reply. E-mail: jennifer @owl.on.ca. Web site: www.owlkids.com.

CHILDREN'S PLAYMATE—1100 Waterway Blvd., P.O. Box 567, Indianapolis, IN 46206. Terry Harshman, Ed. Articles and fiction, puzzles, games, mazes, poetry, crafts, and recipes for 6- to 8-year-olds, emphasizing health, fitness, sports, safety, and nutrition. Pays to 17¢ a word (varies for puzzles and poems), on publication. Web site: www.childrensplaymatemag.org.

THE CHURCH MUSICIAN—127 Ninth Ave. N., Nashville, TN 37234-0160. Jere V. Adams, Ed. Humorous fillers with a music slant for church music leaders, pastors, organists, pianists, and members of the music council or other planning groups. (No clippings.) Pays $5^{1}/_{2}$¢ a word, on publication. E-mail: churchmusician@lifeway.com.

COLUMBIA JOURNALISM REVIEW—Columbia Univ., 700 Journalism Bldg., New York, NY 10027. Gloria Cooper, Man. Ed. Amusing mistakes in news stories, headlines, photos, etc. (original clippings required), for "Lower Case." Pays $25, on publication.

COUNTRY WOMAN—P. O. Box 989, Greendale, WI 53129. Kathy Pohl, Exec. Ed. Short rhymed verse, 4 to 20 lines, seasonal and country-related. All material must be positive and upbeat. Pays $10 to $15, on acceptance.

CRACKED—Globe Communications, Inc., 3 E. 54th St., 15th Fl., New York, NY 10022-3108. Lou Silverstone, Andy Simmons, Eds. Cartoon humor, one to 5 pages, for 10- to 15-year-old readers. No text pieces accepted. "Queries are not necessary, but read the magazine before submitting material!" Pays from $100 per page, on acceptance. E-mail: dkulpa@globefl.com. web site: www.cracked.com.

CYCLE WORLD—1499 Monrovia Ave., Newport Beach, CA 92663. David Edwards, Ed.-in-Chief. News items on motorcycle industry, legislation, trends. Pays on publication. E-mail: cw1edwards@aol.com.

ELYSIAN FIELDS QUARTERLY—P.O. Box 14385, St. Paul, MN 55114-0385. Tom Goldstein, Pub. Essays, interviews, humor and opinion pieces, varying lengths, all related to baseball. Payment is in copies. SASE for guidelines. E-mail: info@efqreview.com. Web site: www.efqreview.com.

FACES—Cobblestone Publishing, 30 Grove St., Suite C, Peterborough, NH 03458-1454. Elizabeth Crooker Carpentiere, Ed. Puzzles, mazes, crosswords, and picture puzzles for children. Send SASE for list of monthly themes before submitting. E-mail: faces@cobblestonepub.com. Web site: www. cobblestonepub.com.

FAMILY CIRCLE—375 Lexington Ave., New York, NY 10017. Uses some short humor, 750 words. No fiction. Payment varies, on acceptance.

FAMILY DIGEST, THE—P.O. Box 40137, Fort Wayne, IN 46804. Corine B. Erlandson, Ed. Family- or Catholic parish-oriented anecdotes, 10 to 125 words, of funny or unusual real-life parish and family experiences. Pays $25, 4 to 8 weeks after acceptance.

FARM AND RANCH LIVING—5400 S. 60th St., Greendale, WI 53129. Nick Pabst, Ed. Fillers on rural people and living, including farming-related jokes, 200 words. Pays from $25, on acceptance and publication. E-mail: editors@farmandranchliving.com. Web site: www.farmandranchliving. com.

FATE—P.O. Box 64383, St. Paul, MN 55164-0383. Attn: Ed. Factual fillers, to 300 words, on strange, psychic, or paranormal happenings. True stories, to 500 words, on personal mystic experiences. Pays 10¢ a word for fillers (minimum $10), $25 for personal accounts. SASE for guidelines. E-mail: fate@ llewellyn.com. Web site: www.fatemag.com.

FIELD & STREAM—2 Park Ave., New York, NY 10016. Slaton White, Ed. Fillers on hunting, fishing, camping, etc., to 500 words. Cartoons. Pays $75 to $250, sometimes more, for fillers; $100 for cartoons, on acceptance. E-mail: fsinfo@aol.com. Web site: www.fieldandstream.com.

FINESCALE MODELER—P.O. Box 1612, Waukesha, WI 53187. Terry Thompson, Ed. One-page hints and tips on building nonoperating, scale models. Payment varies, on acceptance. E-mail: editor@finescale.com. Web site: www.finescale.com.

GAMES—P.O. Box 184, Ft. Washington, PA 19034. R. Wayne Schmittberger, Ed.-in-Chief. Pencil puzzles, visual brainteasers, and pop culture tests. Humor and playfulness a plus; quality a must. Pays top rates, on publication. E-mail: gamespub@tidalwave.com.

GLAMOUR—4 Times Square, New York, NY 10036. Attn: Viewpoint Ed. Articles, 1,000 words, for "Hear Me Out" the opinion page. Pays $500, on acceptance. Web site: www.glamour.com.

GUIDEPOSTS FOR KIDS—1050 Broadway, Suite 6, Chesterton, IN 46304. Rosanne Tolin, Ed. Inspirational anecdotes, to 250 words. Pays $10 to $75, on acceptance. E-mail: gp4k@guideposts.org. Web site: www.gp4k.com.

MAD MAGAZINE—1700 Broadway, 5th Fl., New York, NY 10019. Attn: Eds. Humorous pieces on a wide variety of topics. Two- to 8-panel cartoons (not necessary to include sketches with submission). Pays top rates, on acceptance. Guidelines strongly recommended; must include SASE for response. Web site: www.madmag.com.

MATURE LIVING—127 Ninth Ave. N., MSN 140, Nashville, TN 37234-0140. Attn: Ed. Brief, humorous, original items. "Grandparents Brag Board" items; Christian inspirational pieces for senior adults, 125 words. Pays $15 to $25.

MATURE YEARS—201 Eighth Ave. S., P.O. Box 801, Nashville, TN 37202. Marvin W. Cropsey, Ed. Poems, cartoons, puzzles, jokes, anecdotes, to 300 words, for older adults. Allow 2 months for manuscript evaluation. "A Christian magazine that seeks to build faith. We always show older adults in a favorable light." Include name, address, social security number with all submissions. E-mail: matureyears@umpublishing.org.

MID-WEST OUTDOORS—111 Shore Dr., Hinsdale, IL 60521-5885. Gene Laulunen, Man. Ed. Where to and how to fish and hunt in the Midwest, 700 to 1,500 words, with 2 photos. Pays $15 to $30, on publication.

NATIONAL ENQUIRER—600 East Coast Ave., Lantana, FL 33464-0002. Kathy Martin, Fillers Ed. Short, humorous or philosophical fillers, witticisms, anecdotes, jokes, tart comments. Original items only. Short poetry, 8 lines or less, with traditional rhyming verse, amusing, philosophical, or inspirational in nature. No obscure or artsy poetry. Submit seasonal/holiday material at least 3 months in advance. Pays $25, after publication.

THE NEW YORKER—4 Times Square, New York, NY 10036. Attn: Newsbreaks Dept. Amusing mistakes in newspapers, books, magazines, etc. Pays $10, on acceptance.

OUTDOOR LIFE—2 Park Ave., New York, NY 10016. Todd W. Smith, Ed. Short instructive items, 900 to 1,100 words, on hunting, fishing, boating, and outdoor equipment; regional pieces on lakes, rivers, specific geographic areas of special interest to hunters and fishermen. Not soliciting materials at present. Web site: www.outdoorlife.com.

PLAYBOY—680 North Shore Dr., Chicago, IL 60611. Attn: Party Jokes Ed. or After Hours Ed. Jokes; short original material on new trends, lifestyles, personalities; humorous news items. Pays $100 for jokes; $50 to $350 for "After Hours" items, on publication.

READER'S DIGEST—Readers Digest Road, Pleasantville, NY 10570-7000. Excerpts Dept. Consult "Wanted: Your Laugh Lines" page for guidelines or go to www.readersdigest.com. Submissions cannot be acknowledged or returned.

REAL PEOPLE—450 7th Ave., Suite 1701, New York, NY 10123-0073. Brad Hamilton, Ed. True stories, to 500 words, about interesting people for "Real Shorts" section: strange occurrences, everyday weirdness, occupations, etc.; may be funny, sad, or hair-raising. Also humorous items, to 75 words, taken from small-circulation newspapers, etc. Pays $25 to $50, on publication.

RHODE ISLAND MONTHLY—280 Kinsley Ave., Providence, RI 02903. Paula M. Bodah, Ed. Short pieces, to 500 words, on Rhode Island and southeastern Massachusetts: places, customs, people and events. Pays $50 to $150. Query.

ROAD KING—Hammock Publishing, 3322 W. End Ave., Suite 700, Nashville, TN 37203. Attn: Fillers Ed. Trucking-related cartoons and fillers. $50, on acceptance. E-mail: roadking@hammock.com. Web site: www.road king.com.

THE ROTARIAN—1560 Sherman Ave., Evanston, IL 60201-3698. Charles W. Pratt, Ed. Occasional humor articles. Payment varies, on acceptance. No payment for fillers, anecdotes, or jokes. E-mail: prattc@rotaryintl.org. Web site: www.rotary.org.

SACRAMENTO MAGAZINE—4471 D St., Sacramento, CA 95819. Krista Minard, Ed. "City Lights," interesting and unusual people, places, and behind-the-scenes news items, to 400 words. All material must have Sacramento tie-in. Payment varies, on publication.

THE SATURDAY EVENING POST—P.O. Box 567, Indianapolis, IN 46206. Steven Pettinga, Post Scripts Ed. Humor and satire, to 100 words, that is upbeat and postive. No lurid references. Light verse, cartoons, jokes, for verse and short narratives. Original material only. SASE required. Pays $15 for verse; $125 for cartoons, on publication.

SKI MAGAZINE—929 Pearl St., Suite 200, Boulder, CO 80302. Andrew Bigford, Ed.-in-Chief. Short, 100- to 300-word items on news, events, and people in skiing for "Ski Life" department. Pays on acceptance.

SPORTS AFIELD—250 W. 55th St., New York, NY 10019. Attn: Almanac Ed. Unusual, useful tips and information, 100 to 300 words, for "Almanac" section: on kayaking, hiking, skiing, mountain biking, rock climbing, fishing, and natural history. Pays on publication.

STAR—660 White Plains Rd., Tarrytown, NY 10591. Attn: Ed. Topical articles, 50 to 800 words, on show business and celebrities, health, fitness, parenting, and diet and food. Pays varying rates.

TECH DIRECTIONS—3970 Varsity Dr., Box 8623, Ann Arbor, MI 48107-8623. Tom Bowden, Man. Ed. Cartoons, puzzles, brainteasers, and humorous anecdotes of interest to technology and industrial education teachers and administrators. Pays $20 for cartoons; $25 for puzzles, brainteasers, and other short classroom activities; $5 for humorous anecdotes, on publication.

THOUGHTS FOR ALL SEASONS: THE MAGAZINE OF EPI-GRAMS—478 N.E. 56th St., Miami, FL 33137. Michel P. Richard, Ed. Epigrams and puns, one to 4 lines, and poetry, to one page. "Writers are advised not to submit material until they have examined a copy of the magazine." Guidelines are free, with SASE. Payment is one copy.

TOUCH—Box 7259, Grand Rapids, MI 49510. Sarah Lynn Hilton, Man. Ed. Puzzles based on the NIV Bible, for Christian girls ages 8 to 14. Pays $10 to $15 per puzzle, on publication. Send SASE for theme update. E-mail: carol@gemsgc.org. Web site: www.gospelcom.net/gems.

TRAVEL SMART—40 Beechdale Rd., Dobbs Ferry, NY 10522-3098. Attn: Ed. Interesting and useful travel-related tips. Practical, specific, information for vacation or business travel. Fresh, original material. Pays $5 to $150. Query for over 250 words.

TRUE CONFESSIONS—233 Park Ave. S., New York, NY 10003. Pat Byrdsong, Ed. Warm, inspirational first-person fillers, to 300 words, about love, marriage, family life, prayer for "Woman to Woman," "My Moment with God," "My Man," and "Incredible But True." Also, short stories, 1,000 to 2,000 words. Pays after publication. Buys all rights.

WISCONSIN TRAILS—P.O. Box 5650, Madison, WI 53705. Attn: Ed. Short articles/fillers, 300 to 800 words, about Wisconsin: places to go, things to do, nature, experiences, etc. Query. No clippings or phone calls. E-mail: editor@wistrails.com. Web site: www.wistrails.com.

JUVENILE & YOUNG ADULT MAGAZINES

JUVENILE MAGAZINES

AMERICAN GIRL—8400 Fairway Pl., P.O. Box 998, Middleton, WI 53562-0998. Kristi Thom, Ed. Barbara Stretchberry, Man. Ed. Bimonthly. Articles, to 800 words, and contemporary or historical fiction, to 3,000 words, for girls ages 8 to 12. "We do not want 'teenage' material, i.e. articles on romance, make-up, dating, etc." Payment varies, on acceptance. Query for articles; include photo leads with historical queries. Web site: www.americangirl.com.

APPLESEEDS—Cobblestone Publishing Co., 99 Perkins Point Rd., Newcastle, ME 04553. Barbara Burt, Co-Ed. Nine times yearly. Multidisciplinary social studies magazine for children 7 to 10. Feature articles, 400 to 600 words; fillers, including short fiction, profiles, and activities, to 300 words. All material must be theme-related. Queries required; send SASE for guidelines and theme list. Pays $50 per page. Web site: www.cobblestonepub.com. E-mail: barbaraburt@post.harvard.edu.

ARCHAEOLOGY'S DIG—135 William St., New York, NY 10038. Stephen Hanks, Ed. Bimonthly for children. Interesting, unusual, informative articles, from 300 to 1,000 words, about archaeology. Queries required. Pays 50¢ a word, on publication. Send SASE for guidelines. E-mail: editor@dig. archaeology.org. Web site: www.dig.archaeology.org.

BABYBUG—Carus Publishing Co., P.O. Box 300, Peru, IL 61354. Marianne Carus, Ed.-in-Chief. Paula Morrow, Ed. Stories, to 4 sentences; poems, and action rhymes, to 8 lines, for infants and toddlers, 6 months to 2 years. Pays from $25, on publication. Guidelines. Web site: www.cricketmag.com.

BOYS' QUEST—P.O. Box 227, Bluffton, OH 45817-4610. Attn: Ed. Bimonthly. Fiction and nonfiction, 500 words, for boys ages 6 to 12. "We are looking for articles, stories, and poetry that deal with timeless topics such as pets, nature, hobbies, science, games, sports, careers, simple cooking, etc." B&W photos a plus. Pays 5¢ a word, on publication. Send SASE for guidelines.

CALLIOPE: WORLD HISTORY FOR YOUNG PEOPLE—Cobblestone Publishing, Inc., 30 Grove St., Peterborough, NH 03458. Rosalie Baker and Charles Baker, Eds. Theme-based magazine, published 9 times yearly. Articles, 750 to 1,000 words, with lively, original approach to world history (East/West) through the Renaissance. Shorts, 200 to 750 words, on little-known information related to issue's theme. Fiction, to 1,200 words: historical, biographical, adventure, or retold legends. Activities for children, to 800 words. Puzzles and games. Pays 20¢ to 25¢ a word, on publication. Guidelines and themes. E-mail: custsvc@cobblestone.mv.com. Web site: www.cobble stonepub.com.

CHICKADEE MAGAZINE—179 John St., Suite 500, Toronto, Ont., Canada M5T 3G5. Ed. Adventure, folktale, and humorous stories and poems for 6- to 9-year-olds. Also puzzles, activities, and observation games. No religious material. Pays varying rates, on acceptance. Submit complete manuscript with $2.00 check or money order for return postage. Send $4.28 (Canadian dollars) for guidelines.

CHILD LIFE—P.O. Box 567, Indianapolis, IN 46206. Lise Hoffman, Ed. Nostalgia and some health-related material, the latter generated in-house or assigned, for 9- to 11-year-olds. Currently not accepting manuscripts for publication. Web site: www.childlifemag.org.

CHILDREN'S DIGEST—1100 Waterway Blvd., P.O. Box 567, Indianapolis, IN 46206. Ed. Published 8 times a year. General interest articles and features for young readers. Of special interest are health, fitness, and nutrition. Query. Payment varies.

CHILDREN'S PLAYMATE—1100 Waterway Blvd., P.O. Box 567, Indianapolis, IN 46206. Terry Harshman, Ed. General-interest and health-related short stories (health, fitness, nutrition, safety, and exercise), 500 to 600 words, for 6- to 8-year-olds. Easy recipes and how-to crafts pieces with simple instructions. Poems, puzzles, dot-to-dots, mazes, hidden pictures. Pays to 17¢ a word, from $30 for poetry, on publication. Buys all rights. Web site: www.childrens playmatemag.org.

CLICK—332 S. Michigan Ave., Suite 1100, Chicago, IL 60604. Attn: Ed. Published ten times a year. Articles, to 850 words for readers 3 to 7, about natural, physical, or social sciences, the arts, technology, math, and history. Fiction that addresses a question about the world. Pays 25¢ a word, on publication. E-mail: click@caruspub.com. Web site: www.clickmag.com.

CLUBHOUSE—Box 15, Berrien Springs, MI 49103. Elaine Trumbo, Ed. Currently overstocked; not considering new material at this time. Action-oriented Christian stories, 800 to 1,200 words. Children in stories should be wise, brave, funny, kind, etc. Pays $25 to $35 for stories. Web site: www.clubhouse magazine.org.

CLUBHOUSE JR.—8605 Explorer Dr., Colorado Springs, CO 80920. Jesse Florea, Ed. Articles on Christian values aimed at children ages 4 to 8. Nonfiction, to 500 words, on real people, science, and nature; fiction, from 250 to 1,000 words; Bible stories, 250 to 800 words; rebus stories, to 200 words; poetry, to 250 words; and one-page puzzles. Pays $75 to $250 for all material except poetry, rebus stories, and puzzles. SASE for guidelines.

COBBLESTONE: DISCOVER AMERICAN HISTORY—30 Grove St., Suite C, Peterborough, NH 03458-1454. Meg Chorlian, Ed. Theme-related articles, biographies, plays, and short accounts of historical events, 700 to 800 words, for 8- to 15-year-olds; also supplemental nonfiction, 300 to 600 words. Fiction, 700 to 800 words. Activities (crafts, recipes, etc.) that can be done either by children alone or with adult supervision. Poetry, to 100 lines. Crossword and other word puzzles using the vocabulary of the issue's theme. Pays 20¢ to 25¢ a word, on publication. (Payment varies for activities and poetry.) Send SASE for guidelines and themes.

CRICKET—P.O. Box 300, Peru, IL 61354-0300. Marianne Carus, Ed.-in-Chief. Articles and fiction, 200 to 2,000 words, for 9- to 14-year-olds. (Include bibliography with nonfiction.) Poetry, to 30 lines. Pays 25¢ a word, to $3 a line for poetry, on publication. Guidelines.

DISCOVERY TRAILS—(formerly *Junior Trails*) 1445 Boonville Ave., Springfield, MO 65802-1894. Sinda Zinn, Ed. Fiction, 800 to 1,000 words, with a Christian focus, believable characters, and moral emphasis. Articles, 200 to 400 words, on science, nature, biography. Pays 7¢ to 10¢ a word, on acceptance. E-mail: discoverytrails@gph.org. Web site: www.radiantlife.org.

DRAGONFLY—1840 Wilson Blvd., Arlington, VA 22201-3000. Christopher Myers, Ed. Bimonthly. Science articles for children in grades 3 to 6. Payment varies. Query.

FACES—Cobblestone Publishing, 30 Grove St., Suite C, Peterborough, NH 03458-1454. Elizabeth Crooker Carpentiere, Ed. In-depth feature articles, 800 words, with an anthropology theme. Shorts, 300 to 600 words, related to themes. Fiction, to 800 words, on legends, folktales, stories from around the world, etc., related to theme. Activities, to 700 words, including recipes, crafts, games, etc., for children. Published monthly, September through May. Pays 20¢

to 25¢ a word. Write for guidelines and themes. E-mail: faces@cobblestone pub.com. Web site: www.cobblestone.pub.com.

FOOTSTEPS—150 Page St., New Bedford, MA 02740. Charles Baker III, Ed. Fiction and nonfiction on African American history and culture, for children 8 to 14. Features, 600 to 750 words; fiction, to 700 words; articles, activities, and fillers, to 600 words. Cultural sensitivity and historical accuracy a must. Query; send SASE for guidelines and theme lists. Pays 20¢ to 25¢ per word, on publication. E-mail: custsvc@cobblestone.mv.com. Web site: www. cobblestonepub.com.

THE FRIEND—50 E. North Temple, Salt Lake City, UT 84150-3226. Vivian Paulsen, Man. Ed. Stories and articles, 1,000 to 1,200 words. Stories, to 250 words, for younger readers and preschool children. Pays from 10¢ a word, from $25 per poem, on acceptance. Prefers completed manuscripts. Guidelines available with SASE.

GIRLS' LIFE—Monarch Avalon, Inc., 4517 Harford Rd., Baltimore, MD 21214. Kelly White, Sr. Ed. Features of various lengths and one-page departments that entertain and educate girls ages 9 to 15. Payment varies, on publication. Query with resumé, clips, and SASE. Send SASE for guidelines. Web site: www.girlslife.com.

THE GOLDFINCH—State Historical Society of Iowa, 402 Iowa Ave., Iowa City, IA 52240-1806. Quarterly. Articles, 200 to 800 words, and short fiction on Iowa history for young people. "All articles must correspond to an upcoming theme." Pays $25 per article, on acceptance. Query for themes.

GUIDEPOSTS FOR KIDS—P.O. Box 638, Chesterton, IN 46304. Mary Lou Carney, Ed. Issue-oriented, thought-provoking articles, 1,000 to 1,500 words. Secondary features: playful and entertaining nonfiction, to 700 words. Fiction: mysteries, contemporary, and holiday stories, 700 to 1,300 words. Not preachy. Child protagonist. Dialogue-filled and value-driven. Pays competitive rates, on acceptance. Query for articles. E-mail: gp4k@guideposts.org. Web site: www.gp4k.com.

HIGHLIGHTS FOR CHILDREN—803 Church St., Honesdale, PA 18431-1895. Beth Troop, Manuscript Coord. Easy-to-read stories, to 600 words for 6- to 8-year-olds; and fiction, to 800 words, for 8-year-olds and up. Humor, adventure, mysteries, sports, history, patriotic tales, first-person accounts, back-to-school issues, biographies, black history, world history and cultures. "We'd also like to see stories that don't fit in any of those categories, but are good, meaningful stories for children." Pays from 14¢ a word, on acceptance. SASE for guidelines.

HOPSCOTCH, THE MAGAZINE FOR GIRLS—P.O. Box 164, Bluffton, OH 45817-0164. Marilyn Edwards, Ed. Bimonthly. Articles and fiction, 600 to 1,000 words, and short poetry for girls ages 6 to 12. Special interest in articles, with photos, about girls involved in worthwhile activities. "We believe young girls deserve the right to enjoy a season of childhood before they become young adults; we are not interested in such topics as sex, romance, cosmetics, hairstyles, etc." Pays 5¢ a word, on publication. Send SASE for guidelines.

HUMPTY DUMPTY'S MAGAZINE—1100 Waterway Blvd., P.O. Box 567, Indianapolis, IN 46206. Nancy Axelrad, Ed. General-interest publication with an emphasis on health and fitness for 4- to 6-year-olds. Easy-to-read fiction, to 300 words, with health and nutrition, safety, exercise, or hygiene as theme; humor and light approach preferred. Creative pencil activities. No-cook recipes using healthful ingredients. Short verse, narrative poems. Pays to 22¢ a word, from $25 for poems, on publication. Buys all rights. Web site: www. humptydumptymag.org.

JACK AND JILL—1100 Waterway Blvd., P.O. Box 567, Indianapolis, IN 46206. Daniel Lee, Ed. Articles, 500 to 800 words, for 7- to 10-year-olds, on sports, fitness, health, nutrition, safety, exercise. Features, 500 to 700 words, on history, biography, life in other countries, etc. Fiction, to 700 words. Short poems, games, puzzles, projects, recipes. Photos. Pays 10¢ to 20¢ a word, extra for photos, on publication.

JUNIOR SCHOLASTIC—Scholastic, Inc., 555 Broadway, New York, NY 10012. Lee Baier, Ed. On-the-spot reports from countries in the news. Payment varies, on acceptance. Query. E-mail: junior@scholastic.com. Web site: www.juniorscholastic.com.

JUNIOR TRAILS—See *Discovery Trails.*

KIDS TRIBUTE—71 Barber Greene Rd., Don Mills, Ont., Canada M3C 2A2. Doug Wallace, Ed. Quarterly. Movie- or entertainment-related articles, 350 words, for 8- to 13-year-olds. Pays $150 to $200 (Canadian), on acceptance. Query required.

KIDS' WALL STREET NEWS: THE NEWS AND FINANCIAL PUB-LICATION FOR THE YOUTH OF OUR WORLD—P.O. Box 1207, Rancho Santa Fe, CA 92067. Ed. Bimonthly. Departments include "Adventure, Sports Arena," "Think about This," "Money & Banking," among others. Articles to 500 words. Submit material on a Mac format disk, with hard copy. Photos, graphs, and artwork. Payment is made on publication. E-mail: email kwsn@aol.com. Web site: www.kidsallstreetnews.com.

KIDZ CHAT—(formerly *R-A-D-A-R*) Standard Publishing, 8121 Hamilton Ave., Cincinnati, OH 45231. Gary Thacker, Ed. Weekly Sunday school take-home paper. Articles, 225 words, on animals and the environment. Fiction, 475 words, dealing with Sunday school lesson themes with 8- to 10-year-old as main character. Pays 5¢ to 7¢ a word, on acceptance. SASE for sample copy, guidelines, and themes.

LADYBUG—P.O. Box 300, Peru, IL 61354-0300. Marianne Carus, Ed.-in-Chief. Paula Morrow, Ed. Picture stories and read-aloud stories, 300 to 750 words, for 2- to 6-year-olds; poetry, to 20 lines; songs and action rhymes; crafts, activities, and games. Pays 25¢ a word for stories; $3 a line for poetry, on publication. Guidelines. Web site: www.cricketmag.com.

MUSE—The Cricket Magazine Group, 332 S. Michigan Ave., Suite 1100, Chicago, IL 60604. Submissions Ed. Ten times a year. Articles, 1,000 to 2,500 words, on problems connected with a discipline or area of practical knowledge, for children ages 8 to 14. Guidelines. Query with resumé, writing samples, list of possible topics, and SASE. Pays 50¢ a word, within 60 days of acceptance. E-mail: muse@caruspub.com. Web site: www.musemag.com.

MY FRIEND—Pauline Books & Media, Daughters of St. Paul, 50 St. Pauls Ave., Boston, MA 02130-3491. Sister Kathryn James Hermes, Ed. "The Catholic Magazine for Kids." Fun stories, 150 to 900 words, with Christian values for 6- to 12-years-olds. Buys first rights. Pays $35 to $100 for stories, $5 for fillers. Query for artwork. Guidelines. E-mail: myfriend@pauline.org. Web site: www.pauline.org.

NATIONAL GEOGRAPHIC WORLD—1145 17th St. N.W., Washington, DC 20036-4688. Julie Agnone, Acting Deputy Ed. Picture magazine for young readers, ages 8 and older. Natural history, adventure, archaeology, geography, science, the environment, and human interest. Proposals for picture stories only. No unsolicited manuscripts.

NATURE FRIEND—2727 TR 421, Sugarcreek, OH 44681. Marvin Wengerd, Ed. Monthly. Articles for children that "increase their awareness of God; teach them to be kind to animals, plants, and nature; and illustrate spiritual lessons." Also publishes fillers and games. Pays 5¢ per word for articles; $15 for games and fillers. SASE and $4.00 for guidelines.

NEW MOON, THE MAGAZINE FOR GIRLS AND THEIR DREAMS—P.O. Box 3620, Duluth, MN 55803-3620. Deb Mylin, Bridget Grosser, Man. Eds. "Our goal is to celebrate girls and support their efforts to hang on to their voices, strengths, and dreams as they move from being girls to becoming women." Profiles of girls (written by girls) and women, 600 to 1,000 words. Science and math experiments, 600 words. Submissions from both girls and women. Pays 6¢ to 12¢ a word, on publication. Also publishes companion newsletter, *New Moon Network: For Adults Who Care About Girls*. See Web site for guidelines: www.newmoon.org. E-mail: girl@newmoon.org.

ODYSSEY: ADVENTURES IN SCIENCE—(formerly *Odyssey: Science That's Out of This World*) Cobblestone Publishing, 30 Grove St., Suite C, Peterborough, NH 03458. Elizabeth Lindstrom, Ed. Features, 750 to 1,000 words, on science and technology, for 10 to 16-year-olds. Science-related fiction, myths, legends, and science fiction stories. Activities. Pays 20¢ to 25¢ a word, on publication. Guidelines and themes.

ON THE LINE—616 Walnut, Scottdale, PA 15683-1999. Mary Clemens Meyer, Ed. Monthly magazine for 9- to 14-year-olds. Nature, general nonfiction, and how-to articles, 350 to 500 words; fiction, 1,000 to 1,800 words; poetry, puzzles, cartoons. Pays to 5¢ a word, on acceptance.

OWL MAGAZINE—The Owl Group, Bayard Press, 179 John St., Suite 500, Toronto, Ont., Canada M5T 3G5. Elizabeth Siegel, Ed. Articles, 500 to 1,000 words, for 9- to 12-year-olds, about animals, science, people, technology, new discoveries, activities. Does not publish fiction. Pays varying rates, on acceptance. Enclose $2.00 money order and SAE for reply. Guidelines. E-mail: owl@owlkids.com. Web site: www.owlkids.com.

PLAYS, THE DRAMA MAGAZINE FOR YOUNG PEOPLE—P.O. Box 600160, Newton, MA 02460. Elizabeth Preston, Ed. Wholesome one-act comedies, dramas, skits, satires, farces, and creative dramatic material suitable for school productions at junior high, middle, and lower grade levels. Plays with modern settings preferred. Also uses dramatized classics, folktales and fairy tales, puppet plays. No religious plays or musicals. Pays good rates, on acceptance. Buys all rights. Query for classics, folk and fairy tales. Guidelines.

POCKETS—P.O. Box 340004, Nashville, TN 37203-0004. Janet Knight, Ed. Ecumenical thematic magazine for 6- to 11-year-olds. Fiction and scripture stories, 600 to 1,400 words; short poems; games and activities; role model stories; and stories about children involved in environmental, community, and peace/justice issues. Pays 14¢ a word, $2 per line for poetry, on acceptance. Guidelines and themes available upon request with an SASE. Annual fiction contest; send SASE for details. For sample copy send a 7 1/2 x 10 1/2 SASE

($1.10 postage). E-mail: pockets@upperroom.org. Website: www.upperroom. org/pockets.

POWER AND LIGHT—6401 The Paseo, Kansas City, MO 64131. Matt Price, Preteen Ed. Emily Freeburg, Ed. Asst. Nonfiction: hot topics and relevant issues, 400 to 500 words, for grades 5 and 6, with Christian emphasis. Pays 5¢ a word for multi-use rights, 1³/₄¢ a word for reprints. Pays $15 for cartoons and puzzles. E-mail: mprice@nazarene.org.

R-A-D-A-R—See *Kidz Chat.*

RANGER RICK—National Wildlife Federation, 8925 Leesburg Pike, Vienna, VA 22184. Gerald Bishop, Ed. Photographers and artists wishing to send unsolicited portfolios should first write for photo and art guidelines. No unsolicited article queries or manuscripts. Web site: www.nwf.org/rrick.

SCIENCEWORLD—Scholastic, Inc., 555 Broadway, New York, NY 10012-3999. Mark Bregman, Ed. Science articles, 750 words, and news articles, 200 words, on life science, earth science, physical science, technology, environmental science and/or health for readers in grades 7 to 10 (ages 12 to 15). "Articles should include current, exciting science news. Writing should be lively and show an understanding of teens' perspectives and interests." Pays $100 to $125 for news items; $200 to $650 for features. Query with a well-researched proposal, suggested sources, 2 to 3 clips of your work, and SASE.

SKIPPING STONES—P.O. Box 3939, Eugene, OR 97403. Arun N. Toké, Exec. Ed. "A Multicultural Children's Magazine." Articles, approximately 500 to 750 words, about relationships (support groups and community), peace and justice, living abroad, outstanding moments in your life, inspirations and role models, religions, nature, traditions, and cultural celebrations in other countries, for 8- to 16-year-olds. "Especially invited to submit are youth from diverse backgrounds. We print art, poetry, songs, games, stories, and photographs from around the world and include many different languages (with English translation)." Payment is one copy, on publication. Annual Youth Honor Awards due June 25, 2000; send SASE for guidelines. Query for upcoming themes. E-mail: skipping@efn.org. Web site: www.efn.org/~skipping.

SOCCER JR.—27 Unquowa Rd., Fairfield, CT 06430. Joe Provey, Ed. Fiction and fillers about soccer for readers ages 8 and up. Pays $450 for a feature or story; $250 for department pieces, on acceptance. Query. E-mail: soccerjrol@aol.com. Web site: www.soccerjr.com.

SPIDER—Carus Publishing Co., P.O. Box 300, Peru, IL 61354. Attn: Submissions Ed. Fiction, 300 to 1,000 words, for 6- to 9-year-olds: realistic, easy-to-read stories, fantasy, folk and fairy tales, science fiction, fables, myths. Articles, 300 to 800 words, on nature, animals, science, technology, environment, foreign culture, history (include short bibliography with articles). Serious, humorous, or nonsense poetry, to 20 lines. Puzzles, activities, and games, to 4 pages. Pays 25¢ a word, $3 per line for poetry, on publication. Web site: www.cricketmag.com.

SPORTS ILLUSTRATED FOR KIDS—1271 Ave. of the Americas, New York, NY 10020. Stephen Malley, Deputy Man. Ed. Articles, 1,000 words, (submit to Bob Der) and short features, 500 to 600 words, (submit to Nick Friedman) for 8- to 13-year-olds. "Most articles are staff-written. Department pieces are the best bet for free lancers." Read magazine and guidelines to learn about specific departments. Puzzles and games (submit to Nick Friedman). No fiction or poetry. Pays $500 for departments, $1,000 to $1,250 for articles, on acceptance. Query required.

STONE SOUP, THE MAGAZINE BY YOUNG WRITERS AND ARTISTS—Box 83, Santa Cruz, CA 95063-0083. Gerry Mandel, Ed. Stories, free-verse poems, plays, book reviews by children under 14. "Preference given to writing based on real-life experiences." Pays $25. E-mail: editor@stone soup.com. Web site: www.stonesoup.com.

STORY FRIENDS—Mennonite Publishing House, Scottdale, PA 15683. Rose Stutzman, Ed. Stories, 350 to 800 words, for 4- to 9-year-olds, on Christian faith and values in everyday experiences. Poetry. Pays to 5¢ a word, to $10 per poem, on acceptance.

STORYWORKS—555 Broadway, New York, NY 10012-3919. Lauren Tarshis, Ed. Bimonthly. Illustrated stories; plays and poetry with multicultural emphasis; and writing activities, all aimed at young readers. Query. Payment varies.

SUPERSCIENCE—Scholastic, Inc., 555 Broadway, New York, NY 10012. Attn: Ed. Science news and hands-on experiments for grades 4 through 6. Article topics are staff-generated and assigned to writers; send resumé and children's and science writing clips. Include large SASE for editorial calendar and sample issue. Pays $50 to $650, on acceptance.

SURPRISES—3000 N. 2nd St., Minneapolis, MN 55411-1608. Emily Meinke, Ed. Bimonthly. Articles, 50 to 250 words, for readers 5 to 11. Puzzles, games, artwork. Pays $25 to $100, on publication.

TOUCH—P.O. Box 7259, Grand Rapids, MI 49510. Carol Smith, Man. Ed. Upbeat fiction and features, 500 to 1,000 words, for Christian girls ages 8 to 14; personal life, nature, crafts. Puzzles. Pays 2½¢ a word, extra for photos, on publication. Query with SASE for theme update. E-mail: carol@gemsgc. org. Web site: www.gospelcom.net/gems.

TURTLE MAGAZINE FOR PRESCHOOL KIDS—1100 Waterway Blvd., Box 567, Indianapolis, IN 46206. Terry Harshman, Ed. Heavily illustrated articles with an emphasis on health and nutrition for 2- to 5-year-olds. Humorous, entertaining fiction. Also, crafts, recipes, activities, and simple science experiments. Simple poems. Action rhymes and read-aloud stories, to 300 words. Pays to 22¢ a word for stories; from $25 for poems; payment varies for activities. Pays on publication. Buys all rights. Send SASE for guidelines. Web site: www.turtlemag.org.

U.S. KIDS, A WEEKLY READER MAGAZINE—P.O. Box 567, Indianapolis, IN 46206. Nancy S. Axelrad, Ed. Articles, 400 words, for readers 6 to 9, on real children involved in health, fitness, sports, nutrition, and activities. Also interested in buying science fiction, nature, etc. Some poetry. No longer buying fiction. Web site: www.uskidsmag.org.

WILD OUTDOOR WORLD—Box 1329, Helena, MT 59624. Carolyn Cunningham, Ed. Dir. Articles, 600 to 800 words, on North American wildlife, for readers ages 8 to 12. Pays $100 to $300, on acceptance. Query. E-mail: wowgirl@uswest.net.

ZILLIONS—Consumers Union of the United States, 101 Truman Ave., Yonkers, NY 10703-9925. Charlotte Baecher, Ed. Bimonthly. Articles, up to 1,000 words, on consumer education (money, product testing, health, etc.), for kids ages 8 to 12. "We are the *Consumer Reports* for kids." Pays $500 to $2,000, on publication. Guidelines.

YOUNG ADULT MAGAZINES

ALIVE NOW!—P.O. Box 34004, Nashville, TN 37203-0004. Attn: Ed. Short essays, 250 to 400 words, with Christian emphasis for adults and young adults. Poetry, one page. B&W photos. Pays $20 to $30, on publication. Query with SASE for themes. E-mail: alivenow@upperroom.org. Web site: www. upperroom.org/alivenow/.

ALL ABOUT YOU—6420 Wilshire Blvd., Los Angeles, CA 90048-5515. Roxanne Camron, Ed. Dir. Beth Mayall, Ed. Articles, 1,000 to 1,500 words, on issues of interest to middle school girls. Payment varies, on acceptance. Queries.

BEAUTIFUL CHRISTIAN TEEN—7 Bergoo Rd., Webster Springs, WV 26288-9703. Kimberly Short Wolfe, Ed. Bimonthly. Articles on a wide variety of topics that teach and develop Christian girls. Query. Payment varies.

BOYS' LIFE—1325 W. Walnut Hill Ln., P.O. Box 152079, Irving, TX 75015-2079. Published monthly by the Boy Scouts of America. Articles and fiction, 500 to 1,500 words, for 8- to 18-year-old boys. Pays from $350 for major articles, $750 for fiction, on acceptance. Query for articles; send complete manuscript for fiction. SASE. Web site: www.bsa.scouting.org.

BRIO—Focus on Family, 8605 Explorer Dr., Colorado Springs, CO 80920. Susie Shellenberger, Ed. Articles of interest to Christian teen girls: profiles, how-to pieces, adventures that show the fun Christian teens can have together. Fiction, to 2,000 words, with realistic character development, good dialogue, and a plot that teen girls will be drawn to. Stories may contain a spiritual slant but should not be preachy. Short humorous pieces. Pays 8¢ to 12¢ a word, on acceptance. Web site: www.briomag.com.

CAMPUS LIFE—465 Gundersen Dr., Carol Stream, IL 60188. Chris Lutes, Ed. Articles reflecting Christian values and world view, for high school and college students. Humor, general fiction, and true, first-person experiences. "If we have a choice of fiction, how-to, and a strong first-person story, we'll go with the true story every time." Photo-essays, cartoons. Pays 15¢ to 20¢ a word, on acceptance. Query only. E-mail: cledit@aol.com. Web site: www. campuslife.net.

CICADA—P.O. Box 300, Peru, IL 61354. Submissions Ed. Bimonthly literary magazine. Articles on personal experience with coming-of-age theme, 2,000 to 5,000 words; realistic, contemporary, historical fiction, science fiction, fantasy, and humor, 2,000 to 15,000 words; poetry, to 25 lines; and book reviews, to 700 words. Send complete manuscript with SASE. Guidelines available. Pays to 25¢ per word for prose and $3 per line for poetry, on publication. E-mail: cicada@caruspub.com. Web site: www.cricketmag.com. E-mail: amelia@lightspeed.net.

THE CLAREMONT REVIEW—4980 Wesley Rd., Victoria, BC, Canada V84 1Y9. Eds. Biannual. Fiction with a strong voice, 500 to 3,000 words, and poetry that stirs the heart by young adults 13 to 19. Photos welcome. Submit complete manuscript with SASE (IRC if outside Canada); guidelines available. Pays copy. E-mail: aurora@home.com. Web site: www.members. home.net/review.

COLLEGE BOUND MAGAZINE—Ramholtz Publishing, Inc., 2071 Clove Rd., Suite 206, Staten Island, NY 10304. Gina LaGuardia, Ed. Features, 600 to 1,000 words, and department pieces, 50 to 300 words, that offer high school students a view of college life. Especially interested in personal accounts by current college students. Pays $25 to $100, on publication. E-mail: editorial @collegebound.net. Web site: www.collegebound.net.

COSMOGIRL!—1790 Broadway, 20th Fl., New York, NY 10019. Autumn Madrano, Ed. Teen version of *Cosmopolitan*, for girls 12 to 17. Articles, 900 words, about outstanding young women; first-person narratives of interesting or unusual happenings in the lives of young women; fillers, 150 words, of how the readers can get involved in social issues. "Must be snappy, teen-friendly style without appearing patronizing." Query. Payment varies, on publication. E-mail: amadrano@hearst.com. Web site: www.cosmogirl.com.

CRACKED—3 E. 54th St., 15 Fl., New York, NY 10022-3108. Lou Silverstone, Andy Simmons, Eds. Cartoon humor, one to 5 pages, for 10- to 15-year-old readers. Cartoons/comic book style work; no short stories or poetry. "Read magazine before submitting." Pays $100 per page, on acceptance. E-mail: dkulpa@globefl.com. Web site: www.cracked.com.

ENCOUNTER: MEETING GOD FACE-TO-FACE—(formerly *Straight*) 8121 Hamilton Ave., Cincinnati, OH 45231. Heather E. Wallace, Ed. Articles on current situations and issues for Christian teens. Humor. Well-constructed fiction, to 1,100 words, showing teens using Christian principles. Poetry by teenagers. Photos. Pays about 6¢ to 8¢ a word, on acceptance. Guidelines. No electronic submissions. E-mail: kcarr@standardpub.com. Web site: www.standardpub.com.

ENTERTAINMENTEEN—470 Park Ave. South, New York, NY 10016. Hedy End, Ed. Lifestyle monthly aimed at 14- to 17-year-old girls. The articles include interviews and profiles of popular teen celebrities: actors, actresses, singers, and musicians. Fillers, humor, and jokes also welcome. Payment varies and is made on publication.

GUIDEPOSTS FOR TEENS—P.O. Box 638, Chesterton, IN 46304. Betsy Kohn, Ed. Bimonthly. "Value-centered" articles. First-person true stories about teens in dangerous, miraculous, and inspiring situations, 700 to 2,000 words. How-to pieces, 750 to 1,000 words; quizzes and humor with a spiritual point, 250 to 750 words. Queries preferred; send SASE for guidelines. Pays $25 to $100 for fillers and $175 to $500 for stories and departments, on acceptance. E-mail: gp4t@guideposts.org. Web site: www.gp4k.com.

JUMP—21100 Erwin St., Woodland Hills, CA 91367-3712. Lori Berger, Ed.-in-Chief Published ten times a year. "Written for girls who are into sports, strong minds, and living with a healthy lifestyle." Articles include the latest news in beauty, style, sports, music, body and soul, etc. Query. Payment varies.

KEYNOTER—3636 Woodview Trace, Indianapolis, IN 46268. Amy L. Wiser, Exec. Ed. Articles, 1,300 to 1,500 words, for high school leaders: general-interest features; self-help; contemporary teenage problems. No fillers, poetry, first-person accounts, or fiction. Pays $150 to $350, on acceptance. Query preferred. E-mail: keynoter@kiwanis.org. Web site: www.keyclub.org.

LATINGIRL: THE HISPANIC TEEN MAGAZINE—*Latingirl Maga-*

zine, 33–41 Newark St., Suite 1, Hoboken, New Jersey 07030. Jeanette Del Valle, Sr. Ed. Bimonthly that "addresses the lives and aspirations of Latin female teens." Articles on fashion, beauty, health, relationships, education, and entertainment. Query with clips. Payment varies, made on publication. Web site: www.latingirlmag.com.

LISTEN MAGAZINE—55 W. Oak Ridge Dr., Hagerstown, MD 21740. Larry Becker, Ed. Articles, 1,200 to 1,500 words, providing teens with "a vigorous, positive, educational approach to the problems arising from the use of tobacco, alcohol, and other drugs." Pays $50 to $200, on acceptance.

THE LOOK—P.O. Box 272, Cranford, NJ 07016-0272. John R. Hawks, Pub. Articles, 1,500 to 3,000 words, on fashion, student life, employment, relationships, and profiles of interest to local (NJ) readers ages 16 to 26. Also, beach stories and articles about the New Jersey shore. Pays $30 to $200, on publication. E-mail: jrhawks@thelookmag.com. Web site: www.thelook mag.com.

MERLYN'S PEN: FICTION, ESSAYS, AND POEMS BY AMERICA'S TEENS—P.O. Box 1058, Dept. WR, East Greenwich, RI 02818. R. James Stahl, Ed. Writing by students in grades 6 through 12. Short stories and essays, to 5,000 words; reviews; travel pieces; and poetry, to 200 lines. Responds in 10 weeks. Pays $20 to $200, plus copies. Guidelines. Please download cover sheet at www.merlynspen.com. E-mail: merlynspen@aol.com.

THE NEW YORK TIMES UPFRONT—(formerly *Scholastic Update*) 555 Broadway, New York, NY 10012-3999. Herbert Buchsbaum, Ed. Biweekly. News articles, 500 words or 1,000 to 1,500 words, for teenagers. Pays $150 to $1,000, on acceptance. Send SASE for guidelines before querying. Web site: www.nytimes.com/upfront.

REACT—Parade Publications, 711 Third Ave., New York, NY 10017. Susan Byrne, Man. Ed. Weekly. Articles, to 800 words, on national and international news, entertainment, sports, social issues related to teenagers, and profiles of notable young people for readers 12 to 17. Payment varies, on acceptance. Query with related clips. Web site: www.react.com.

SCHOLASTIC UPDATE—See *The New York Times UpFront.*

SCIENCE WORLD—Scholastic, Inc., 555 Broadway, New York, NY 10012-3999. Attn: Eds. Articles, 750 words, on life science, earth science, physical science, environmental science, or health science for 7th to 10th graders (ages 12 to 15). Science news pieces, 200 words. Submit well-researched proposal, including suggested sources, 2 to 3 clips of your work, and SASE. Pays $100 to $125 for news items; $200 to $650 for features.

SEVENTEEN—850 Third Ave., New York, NY 10022. Tamara Glenny, Deputy Ed. Articles, to 2,500 words, on subjects of interest to teenagers. Sophisticated, well-written fiction, 1,000 to 3,500 words, for young adults. Personal essays, to 1,200 words, by writers 25 and younger for "Voice." Pays varying rates, on acceptance. Request guidelines with an SASE. E-mail: tamaraglenny@primediamags.com. Web site: www.seventeen.com.

SISTERS IN STYLE—233 Park Ave. S., 5th Fl., New York, NY 10003. Cynthia Marie Horner, Ed. Dir. Bimonthly. "For Today's Young Black Woman." Beauty and fashion articles, quizzes, and advice for African-American teens. No fiction or poetry. Payment varies, on publication. Query.

STRAIGHT—See *Encounter: Meeting God Face-To-Face.*

'TEEN—6420 Wilshire Blvd., Los Angeles, CA 90048-5515. Attn: Ed. Short stories, 2,500 to 4,000 words: mystery, teen situations, adventure, romance, humor for teens. Pays from $250 to $450, on acceptance. Buys all rights.

TEEN LIFE—1445 Boonville Ave., Springfield, MO 65802-1894. Tammy Bicket, Ed. Not currently accepting material. Articles, 500 to 1,000 words, and fiction, to 1,200 words, for 13- to 19-year-olds; strong evangelical emphasis. Interviews with Christian athletes and other well-known Christians; true stories; up-to-date factual articles. No freelance material.

TEEN VOICES—P.O. Box 120–027, Boston, MA 02112-0027. Shannon Berning, Man. Ed. Quarterly. Fiction and nonfiction, 200 to 400 words; and poetry, any length. Submissions by teenage girls only. Photo of writer and short bio preferred. Pays in copies. E-mail: womenexp@teenvoices.com. Web site: www.teenvoices.com.

TIGER BEAT—Sterling/MacFadden Partnership, 233 Park Ave. S., New York, NY 10003. Louise Barile, Ed. Articles, to 4 pages, on young people in show business and the music industry. Pays varying rates, on acceptance. Query.

WHAT MAGAZINE—108–93 Lombard Ave., Winnipeg, Manitoba, Canada R3B 3B1. Leslie Malkin, Ed. Published 5 times a year and distributed in high schools. Articles, 650 to 2,000 words, on contemporary pop-cultural issues for teenage readers. Pays $100 to $300 (Canadian), on publication. Queries preferred. E-mail: what@m2ci.mb.ca.

YM—375 Lexington Ave., 8th Fl., New York, NY 10017-5514. Mary Witherell, Man. Ed. Articles, to 2,500 words, on entertainment, lifestyle, fashion, beauty, relationships, health, for women ages 14 to 19. Payment varies, on acceptance. Query with clips.

YOU!—29963 Mulholland Hwy., Agoura Hills, CA 91301. Attn: Submissions Ed. Articles, 200 to 1,000 words, on topics related to teenagers, especially moral issues, faith, and contemporary pop culture viewed from the Catholic/Christian perspective. No payment. E-mail: youmag@earthlink.net. Web site: www.youmagazine.com.

YOUNG AND ALIVE—P.O. Box 6097, Lincoln, NE 68506. Gaylena Gibson, Ed. Quarterly. Feature articles, 800 to 1,400 words, for blind and visually impaired young adults on adventure, biography, camping, careers, health, history, hobbies, holidays, marriage, nature, practical Christianity, sports, and travel. Photos. Pays 3¢ to 5¢ a word, $5 to $10 for photos, on acceptance. Guidelines, available on request.

YOUNG SALVATIONIST—The Salvation Army, 615 Slaters Ln., P.O. Box 269, Alexandria, VA 22313. Tim Clark, Man. Ed. Articles for teens, 600 to 1,200 words, with Christian perspective; fiction, 800 to 1,200 words; short fillers. Pays 10¢ to 15¢ a word, on acceptance.

YOUTH UPDATE—St. Anthony Messenger Press, 1615 Republic St., Cincinnati, OH 45210. Attn: Ed. Articles on timely topics for Catholic teens. Avoid cuteness, glib phrases and clichés, academic or erudite approaches, preachiness. Pays 15¢ a word, on acceptance. Query with outline and SASE. No on-line queries. E-mail: stanthony@americancatholic.org. Web site: www.americancatholic.org.

THE DRAMA MARKET

Community, regional, and civic theaters and college dramatic groups offer the best opportunities today for playwrights to see their work produced, whether on the stage or in dramatic readings. Indeed, aspiring playwrights will be encouraged to hear that many well-known playwrights received their first recognition in the regional theaters. Payment is generally nominal, but regional and university theaters usually buy only the right to produce a play, and all further rights revert to the author. Since most directors like to work closely with authors on any revisions necessary, theaters will often pay the playwright's expenses while in residence during rehearsals. The thrill of seeing your play come to life on the stage is one of the pleasures of being on hand for rehearsals and performances. In addition to producing plays and giving dramatic readings, many theaters also sponsor competitions or new play festivals.

Aspiring playwrights should query college and community theaters in their region to find out which ones are interested in seeing original scripts. Dramatic associations of interest to playwrights include the Dramatists Guild (1501 Broadway, Suite 701, New York, NY 10036), and Theatre Communications Group, Inc. (355 Lexington Ave., New York, NY 10017), which publishes the annual *Dramatists Sourcebook. The Playwright's Companion,* published by Feedback Theatrebooks (305 Madison Ave., Suite 1146, New York, NY 10165), is an annual directory of theaters, play publishers, and prize contests seeking scripts. See the *Organizations for Writers* list for details on dramatists' associations.

Some of the theaters on this list require that playwrights submit all or some of the following with scripts-cast list, synopsis, resumé, recommendations, return postcard-and with scripts and queries, SASEs must always be enclosed.

While the almost unlimited television offerings on commercial, educational, and cable TV stations, in addition to the hundreds of films released yearly, may lead free-lance writers to believe that opportunities to sell movie and television scripts are infinite, unfortunately, this is not true. With few exceptions, TV and film producers and programmers will read scripts and queries submitted only through recognized agents. (For a list of agents, see page 872.) Writers who want to try their hand at writing directly for this very limited market should be prepared to learn the special techniques and acceptable format of scriptwriting, either by taking a workshop through a university or at a writers conference, or by reading one or more of the many books that have been written on this subject. Also, experience in playwriting and knowledge of dramatic structure gained through working in amateur, community, or professional theaters can be helpful.

REGIONAL & UNIVERSITY THEATERS

ACTORS THEATRE OF LOUISVILLE—316 W. Main St., Louisville, KY 40202. Michael Bigelow Dixon, Lit. Mgr. Ten-minute comedies and dramas, to 10 pages. Longer one-act and full-length plays accepted from literary agents, and from playwrights with letter of recommendation from another professional theatre. SASE. Annual contest. Guidelines.

ACTORS' PLAYHOUSE AT THE MIRACLE THEATRE—280 Miracle Mile, Coral Gables, FL 33134. Earl Maulding. One-act musicals, children's plays, adaptations, and bilingual material (Spanish/English). Maximum 8 actors to play any number of roles; suitable for touring. Enclose resumé, recommendations, cast list, synopsis, and score or lead sheet, with vocal tape. Allow 3 to 6 months for response. Pay is made following production and is negotiable.

A. D. PLAYERS—2710 W. Alabama, Houston, TX 77098. Attn: Lit. Mgr. Jeannette Clift George, Artistic Dir. Full-length or one-act comedies, dramas, musicals, children's plays, and adaptations with Christian world view. Submit scripts and cast list with SASE. Readings. Pays negotiable rates. E-mail: adplayers@itern.org. Web site: www.adplayers.org.

ALABAMA SHAKESPEARE FESTIVAL—The State Theatre, 1 Festival Dr., Montgomery, AL 36117-4605. Gwen Orel, Lit. Mgr. Full-length scripts with southern and/or African-American themes, issues, or history; and scripts with southern and/or African-American authors. One work per author; query. Web site: www.asf.net. E-mail: asfmail@mindspring.com.

ALLIANCE THEATRE COMPANY—1280 Peachtree St. N.E., Atlanta, GA 30309. Attn: Lit. Dept. Dramas, comedies, and musicals, especially those that speak to a culturally diverse community; plays with compelling stories and engaging characters, told in adventurous or stylish ways. No unsolicited manuscripts or telephone inquiries. Letter of inquiry with synopsis and no more than 10 pages of sample dialogue accepted only with SASE for reply. E-mail: Freddie.Ashley@woodruffcenter.org. Web site: www.alliancetheatre.org.

AMERICAN LITERATURE THEATRE PROJECT—Fountain Theatre, 5060 Fountain Ave., Los Angeles, CA 90029. Simon Levy, Prod. Dramaturg. One-act and full-length stage adaptations of classic and contemporary American literature. Sets and cast size are unrestricted. Send synopsis and SAS postcard. Rate of payment is standard, as set by the Dramatists Guild.

AMERICAN LIVING HISTORY THEATER—P.O. Box 752, Greybull, WY 82426. Dorene Ludwig, Artistic Dir. One-act, (one or 2 characters preferred) historically accurate (primary source materials only) dramas dealing with marketable American historical and literary characters and events. Submit treatment and letter with SASE. Responds within 6 months. Pays varying rates.

AMERICAN THEATRE OF ACTORS—314 W. 54th St., New York, NY 10019. James Jennings, Artistic Dir. Full-length dramas for a cast of 2 to 6. Submit complete play and SASE. Reports in one to 2 months.

ARENA STAGE—1101 Sixth St. S.W., Washington, DC 20024. Cathy Madison, Lit. Mgr. Manuscripts accepted from D.C.-metro area writers; send synopsis, 10 pages of dialogue, bio, and reviews if available. Currently looking for American settings and themes.

ARKANSAS REPERTORY THEATRE COMPANY—601 S. Main, P.O. Box 110, Little Rock, AR 72203-0110. Brad Mooy, Lit. Mgr. Full-length comedies, dramas, and musicals; prefer up to 8 characters. Send synopsis, cast list, resumé, and return postage; do not send complete manuscript. Reports in 3 months.

BARTER THEATER—P.O. Box 867, Abingdon, VA 24212-0867. Richard Rose, Artistic Dir. Full-length dramas, comedies, adaptations, and children's plays. Submit synopsis, dialogue sample, and SASE. Allow 6 to 8 months for report. Royalty policies consistent with industry standard. E-mail: barter@naxs.com.

BERKSHIRE THEATRE FESTIVAL—Box 797, Stockbridge, MA 01262. Kate Maguire, Producing Dir. Full-length comedies, musicals, and dramas; cast to 8. Submit through agent only. Web site: www.berkshiretheatre.org.

BOARSHEAD THEATER—425 S. Grand Ave., Lansing, MI 48933. John Peakes, Artistic Dir. Full-length comedies and dramas with simple sets and cast of up to 10. Send precis, 5 to 10 pages of dialogue, cast list with descriptions, and SAS postcard for reply; do not send complete manuscript.

CALIFORNIA UNIVERSITY THEATRE—, California, PA 15419. Dr. Richard J. Helldobler, Chairman. Unusual, avant-garde, and experimental one-act and full-length comedies and dramas, children's plays, and adaptations. Cast size varies. Submit synopsis with short, sample scene(s). Payment available.

CENTER STAGE—700 N. Calvert St., Baltimore, MD 21202. Charlotte Stoudt, Resident Dramaturg. Full-length comedies, dramas, translations, adaptations. No unsolicited manuscripts. Send synopsis, a few sample pages, resumé, cast list, and production history. Allow 8 to 10 weeks for reply.

CHILDSPLAY, INC.—Box 517, Tempe, AZ 85280. David Saar, Artistic Dir. Multigenerational plays running 45 to 120 minutes: dramas, musicals, and adaptations for family audiences. Productions may need to travel. Submissions accepted July through December. Send synopsis and 10-page dialogue sample. Reports in 2 to 6 months. Web site: www.tempe.gov/childsplay. E-mail: childsplayaz@juno.com.

CIRCLE IN THE SQUARE THEATRE SCHOOL—1633 Broadway, New York, NY 10019-6795. Dr. Rhonda R. Dodd, Assoc. Dir. Accepts scripts, tapes, and sheet music for children's theatre performed by 4 to 6 adult actors. Prefer multi-cultural or American historical themes, 35 to 45 minutes in length, may include music. E-mail: circleinthesquare@worldnet.att.net. Web site: www.circlesquare.org.

CITY THEATRE COMPANY—57 S. 13th St., Pittsburgh, PA 15203. Carlyn Ann Aquiline, Literary Man. Full-length comedies, musicals, and dramas. We seek innovative contemporary plays of substance and ideas. No unsolicited or e-mail submissions. Agent submissions or query with resume, detailed synopsis, character breakdown, 15- to 20-page dialogue sample, development/production history, and SASE. Web site: www. citytheatre-phg.org. Royalty.

CLASSIC STAGE COMPANY—136 E. 13th St., New York, NY 10003. Barry Edelstein, Artistic Dir. Produces full-length translations and adaptations of classic literature. Submit synopsis with cast list and ten pages of sample dialogue. No unsolicited scripts.

THE CONSERVATORY THEATRE ENSEMBLE—c/o Tamalpais High School, 700 Miller Ave., Mill Valley, CA 94941. Susan Brashear, Artistic Dir. Comedies, dramas, children's plays, adaptations, and scripts addressing high school issues for larger casts (8 to 20). "Plays with flexible casting and adaptable to 'ensemble' style are encouraged." "One-act plays of approximately 30 minutes are especially needed, as we produce 50 short plays each season using teenage actors." Send synopsis and resumé. E-mail: suebrash@earthlink.net.

CROSSROADS THEATRE CO.—7 Livingston Ave., New Brunswick,

NJ 08901. Ricardo Khan, Artistic Dir. Full-length and one-act dramas, comedies, musicals, and adaptations; issue-oriented experimental plays that offer honest, imaginative, and insightful examinations of the African-American experience. Also interested in African and Caribbean plays and plays exploring cross-cultural issues. No unsolicited scripts; queries only, with synopsis, cast list, resumé, and SASE. E-mail: crossroads@10p.com. Web site: www.cross roadstheatre.org.

DELAWARE THEATRE COMPANY—200 Water St., Wilmington, DE 19801-5030. Cleveland Morris, Artistic Dir. Full-length comedies, dramas, and musicals. Prefer cast of no more than 10. SASE required. Reports in 6 months. No longer accepting unsolicited manuscripts, except from local authors. Agent submissions in the form of synopses or letters of inquiries will be considered. The "Connections" competition has been suspended for the time being. Web site: www.delawaretheatre.org.

DENVER CENTER THEATRE COMPANY—1050 13th St., Denver, CO 80204. Bruce K. Sevy, Assoc. Artistic Dir./New Play Development. New play festival in June. Primus prize to female playwright. Send SASE; request guidelines and information.

DETROIT REPERTORY THEATRE—13103 Woodrow Wilson Ave., Detroit, MI 48238. Barbara Busby, Lit. Mgr. Full-length comedies and dramas. Scripts accepted October to April. Enclose SASE. Pays royalty.

STEVE DOBBINS PRODUCTIONS—650 Geary Blvd., San Francisco, CA 94102. Alan Ramos, Lit. Dir. No unsolicited manuscripts.

DORSET THEATRE FESTIVAL—Box 519, Dorset, VT 05251. Jill Charles, Artistic Dir. Accepts queries or scripts from resident writers only. Residencies at Dorset Colony House for Writers available September to May; inquire. E-mail: theatre@sover.net. Web site: www.theatredirectories.com.

EAST WEST PLAYERS—244 S. San Pedro St., # 301, Los Angeles, CA 90012. Tim Dang, Artistic Dir. Ken Narasaki, Lit. Mgr. Produces 1 to 3 new plays annually. Original plays, translations, adaptations, musicals, and youth theater, "all of which must illuminate the Asian or Asian-American experience, or resonate in a significant fashion if cast with Asian-American actors." Readings. Prefer to see query letter with synopsis and 10 pages of dialogue; complete scripts also considered. Reports in 5 to 6 weeks for query; 6 to 9 months for complete script. E-mail: info@eastwestplayers.org. Web site: www.eastwestplayers.org.

ENSEMBLE STUDIO THEATRE—549 W. 52nd St., New York, NY 10019. Attn: Lit. Mgr. Send full-length or one-act comedies and dramas with resumé and SASE, September to April. Specializing in developmental theatre.

FLORIDA STUDIO THEATRE—1241 N. Palm Ave., Sarasota, FL 33577. James Ashford, Casting & Lit. Coord. Highly theatrical, innovative plays with universal themes. Query with synopsis and SASE. Also accepting musicals and musical revues. E-mail: james@fst2000.org. Web site:www. fst2000.org.

WILL GEER THEATRICUM BOTANICUM—Box 1222, Topanga, CA 90290. Attn: Lit. Dir. All types of scripts for outdoor theater, with large playing area. Submit synopsis with SASE. Pays varying rates. E-mail: theatri cum@mindspring.com. Web site: www.theatricum.com.

THE GOODMAN THEATRE—170 N. Dearborn Street., Chicago, IL

60601. Susan V. Booth, Lit. Mgr. Queries from recognized literary agents or producing organizations required for full-length comedies or dramas. No unsolicited scripts. E-mail: staff@goodman-theatre.org. Web site: www.goodman theatre.org.

THE GUTHRIE THEATER—725 Vineland Pl., Minneapolis, MN 55403. Attn: Lit. Dept. Full-length dramas and adaptations of world literature, classic masterworks, oral traditions, and folktales. No unsolicited scripts; send query with synopsis, resumé, professional recommendation, and SASE. Reports in 3 to 4 months. E-mail: joh@guthrietheater.org.

HIPPODROME STATE THEATRE—25 S.E. Second Pl., Gainesville, FL 32601. Tamerin Dygert, Dramaturg. Full-length plays with unit sets and casts of up to 6. Agent submissions and professional recommendations only; no unsolicited material. Submissions accepted May through August. Send synopsis only, with reviews and professional recommendation.

HOLLYWOOD THESPIAN COMPANY—12838 Kling St., Studio City, CA 91604-1127. Rai Tasco, Artistic Dir. Full-length comedies and dramas for integrated cast. Include cast list and SAS postcard with submission.

HORIZON THEATRE COMPANY—P. O. Box 5376, Station E, Atlanta, GA 31107. Jeff and Lisa Adler, Artistic Dirs. Full-length comedies, dramas, and satires. Encourages submissions by women writers. Cast of no more than 10. Submit synopsis with cast list, resumé, and recommendations. Pays percentage. Readings. Reports in 6 months.

HUNTINGTON THEATRE COMPANY—264 Huntington Ave., Boston, MA 02115-4606. Nicholas Martin, Artistic Dir. Accepts agent submissions only.

ILLINOIS THEATRE CENTER—371 Artists' Walk, P.O. Box 397, Park Forest, IL 60466. Attn: Producing Dir. Full-length comedies, dramas, musicals, and adaptations, for unit/fragmentary sets, and up to 8 cast members. Send summary and SAS postcard. No unsolicited manuscripts. Pays negotiable rates. Workshops and readings offered.

INVISIBLE THEATRE—1400 N. First Ave., Tucson, AZ 85719. Deborah Dickey, Lit. Mgr. Letter of introduction from theatre professional must accompany submissions for full-length comedies, dramas, musicals, and adaptations. Submit after October 2000. Cast of up to 10; simple set. Also one-act plays. Pays royalty.

KUMU KAHUA THEATRE—46 Merchant St., Honolulu, HI 96813. Harry Wong III, Artistic Dir. Full-length plays especially relevant to life in Hawaii. Prefer simple sets for arena productions. Submit resumé and synopsis. Pays $50 per performance. Readings. Contests.

LOS ANGELES DESIGNERS' THEATRE—P.O. Box 1883, Studio City, CA 91614-0883. Richard Niederberg, Artistic Dir. Full-length comedies, dramas, musicals, fantasies, or adaptations. Religious, political, social, and controversial themes encouraged. Nudity, "adult" language, etc., O.K. "Please detail in the cover letter what the writer's proposed involvement with the production would be beyond the usual. Do not submit material that needs to be returned." Send proposals; not scripts. Payment varies. E-mail: LADESIGNERS@Juno.com.

LOVE CREEK PRODUCTIONS—162 Nesbit St., Weehawken, NJ 07087. Cynthia Granville-Callahan, Lit. Man. Stages one-act and full-length plays. One-Act Festival Series, cutting edge and eclectic one acts; Developmental Series, full-length plays and evenings of one-acts by single author; and Love Creek Mainstage, extended runs. Please send SASE for guidelines before submitting material.

THE MAGIC THEATRE—Fort Mason Ctr., Bldg. D, San Francisco, CA 94123. Laura Owens, Lit. Mgr. Comedies and dramas. "Special interest in political, non-linear, and multicultural work for mainstage productions." Query with synopsis, resumé, first 10 to 20 pages of script, and SASE; no unsolicited manuscripts. Pays varying rates.

MANHATTAN THEATRE CLUB—311 W. 43rd St., New York, NY 10036. Attn: Christian Parker, Literary Man. Full-length and one-act comedies, dramas, and musicals. No unsolicited manuscripts or queries; agent submissions only. Annual playwriting fellowship for emerging writers. Visit web site: www.mtc-nyc.org. E-mail: info@mtc-nyc.org.

METROSTAGE—1201 N. Royal St., Alexandria, VA 22314. Carolyn Griffin, Prod. Art. Dir. Full-length comedies, dramas, and children's plays; casts of no more than 8. Send synopsis, 10 page dialogue sample, resumé, reading/production history, and return post card to P.O. Box 329, Alexandria, VA 22313. Responds in 2 months.

MILL MOUNTAIN THEATRE—One Market Sq., Second Fl., Roanoke, VA 24011-1437. Literary Dept. One-act comedies and dramas, 25 to 30 minutes. Send SASE for guidelines for new play competition. Payment varies. E-mail: mmtmail@millmountain.org. Web site: www.millmountain.org.

MISSOURI REPERTORY THEATRE—4949 Cherry St., Kansas City, MO 64110. Felicia Londré, Dramaturg. Full-length comedies and dramas. Query with synopsis, cast list, resumé, and SAS postcard. Royalty. Allow 6 months for response. E-mail: theatre@umkc.edu. Web site: www.missourirep theatre.org.

MUSICAL THEATRE WORKS—440 Lafayette St., New York, NY 10003. Lonny Price, Art. Dir. Please call or write for submission guidelines.

NATIONAL BLACK THEATRE—2033 Fifth Ave., Harlem, NY 10035. Attn: Tunde Samuel. Drama, musicals, and children's plays. "Scripts should reflect African and African-American lifestyle. Historical, inspirational, and ritualistic forms appreciated." Workshops and readings.

NATIONAL PLAYWRIGHTS CONFERENCE, EUGENE O'NEILL THEATRE CENTER—234 W. 44th St., Suite 901, New York, NY 10036. James Houghton, Artistic Dir. Annual competition to select new stage plays and teleplays/screenplays for development during the summer at organization's Waterford, CT, location. Submission deadline: December 1. Send #10-size SASE in the fall for guidelines. Pays stipend of $1,000, plus travel/living expenses during conference in July 2001. Send SASE for guidelines to Mary McCabe, Man. Dir. Deadline is November 15, 2000.

NEW ENSEMBLE ACTORS THEATRE PROJECT OF SALT & PEPPER MIME CO.—320 E. 90th St., #1B, New York, NY 10128. Ms. Scottie Davis, Dir. 10 minute plays, one-acts, all genres, conducive to "nontraditional" casting, surreal sets with mimetic concepts. One- or 4-person cast. Scripts reviewed from May to December. Works also considered for readings, critiques, storyplayers, and experimental development. Logging fee/Application required.

NEW THEATRE, INC.—P.O. Box 173, Boston, MA 02117-0173. Attn: NEWorks Submissions Program. New full-length scripts for readings, workshop, and main stage productions. Include SASE.

NEW TUNERS/THE THEATRE BUILDING—1225 W. Belmont Ave., Chicago, IL 60657. John Sparks, Artistic Dir. Full-length musicals only, for cast to 15; no wing/fly space. Send query with brief synopsis, cassette tape of score, cast list, resumé, SASE, and SAS postcard. Pays on royalty basis.

NEW YORK STATE THEATRE INSTITUTE—155 River St., Troy, NY 12180. Attn: Patricia Di Benedetto Snyder, Producing Artistic Dir. Emphasis on new, full-length plays and musicals for family audiences. Query with synopsis and cast list. Payment varies.

ODYSSEY THEATRE ENSEMBLE—2055 S. Sepulveda Blvd., Los Angeles, CA 90025. Ron Sossi, Artistic Dir. Full-length comedies, dramas, musicals, and adaptations: provocative subject matter, or plays that stretch and explore the possibilities of theater. Query Sally Essex-Lopresti, Lit. Mgr., with synopsis, 8 to 10 pages of sample dialogue, and resumé. Pays variable rates. Allow 2 to 6 months for reply to script; 2 to 4 weeks for queries. Workshops and readings.

OLDCASTLE THEATRE COMPANY—Bennington Center for the Arts, P.O. Box 1555, Bennington, VT 05201. Eric Peterson, Dir. Full-length comedies, dramas, and musicals for a small cast (up to 10). Submit synopsis and cast list in the winter. Reports in 6 months. Offers workshops and readings. Pays expenses for playwright to attend rehearsals. Royalty.

PENGUIN REPERTORY COMPANY—Box 91, Stony Point, Rockland County, NY 10980. Joe Brancato, Artistic Dir. Full-length comedies and dramas with cast size to 5. Submit script, resumé, and SASE. Payment varies.

PEOPLE'S LIGHT AND THEATRE COMPANY—39 Conestoga Rd., Malvern, PA 19355. Alda Cortese, Lit. Mgr. Full-length comedies, dramas, adaptations. No unsolicited manuscripts; query with synopsis and 10 pages of script. Reports in 6 months. Payment negotiable.

PIER ONE THEATRE—Box 894, Homer, AK 99603. Lance Petersen, Lit. Dir. Full-length and one-act comedies, dramas, musicals, children's plays, and adaptations. Submit complete script; include piano score with musicals. Pays 8% of ticket sales for mainstage musicals; other payment varies. E-mail: lance@xyz.net. Web site: www.pieronetheatre.org.

PLAYHOUSE ON THE SQUARE—51 S. Cooper in Overton Sq., Memphis, TN 38104. Jackie Nichols, Artistic Dir. Full-length comedies, dramas; cast of up to 15. Contest deadline is April for fall production. Pays $500.

PLAYWRIGHTS HORIZONS—416 W. 42nd St., New York, NY 10036. Address Literary Dept. Full-length, original comedies, dramas, and musicals by American authors. No one-acts or screenplays. Synopses discouraged; send script, resumé and SASE, include tape for musicals. Off Broadway contract. Web sites: www.playwrightshorizons.org.

PLAYWRIGHTS' PLATFORM—Massachusetts College of Art, Office 164 Brayton Rd., Boston, MA 02135. Attn: Lit. Dir. Script development workshops and public readings for New England playwrights only. Full-length and one-act plays of all kinds. No sexist or racist material. Residents of New England send scripts with short synopsis, resumé, SAS postcard, and SASE. Readings conducted at Massachusetts College of Art (Boston). Web site: www.theatermirror.com.

POPLAR PIKE PLAYHOUSE—7653 Old Poplar Pike, Germantown, TN 38138. Frank Bluestein, Artistic Dir. Full-length and one-act comedies, dramas, musicals, and children's plays. Submit synopsis with SAS postcard and resumé. Pays $300. E-mail: efblue@aol.com. Web site: www.ppp.org.

PRINCETON REPERTORY COMPANY—44 Nassau St., Suite 350, Princeton, NJ 08542. Victoria Liberatori, Artistic Dir. Submit synopsis (no more than two pages), cast list, resumé, and three pages of dialogue sample. Responds within one year.

THE REPERTORY THEATRE OF ST. LOUIS—Box 191730, St. Louis, MO 63119. Attn: S. Gregg Query with brief synopsis, technical requirements, and cast size. Unsolicited manuscripts will be returned unread. E-mail: sgregg@repstl.org.

ROUND HOUSE THEATRE—12210 Bushey Dr., Silver Spring, MD 20902. Nick Olcott, Assoc. Artistic Dir. Full-length comedies, dramas, and adaptations; cast of up to 10; prefer simple set. Send one-page synopsis with 3 or 4 sample pages, cast list, and technical requirements. No unsolicited manuscripts.

SEATTLE REPERTORY THEATRE—155 Mercer St., Seattle, WA 98109. Sharon Ott, Artistic Dir. Full-length comedies, dramas, and adaptations. No unsolicited submissions.

SOCIETY HILL PLAYHOUSE—507 S. 8th St., Philadelphia, PA 19147. Walter Vail, Dramaturg. Full-length dramas, comedies, and musicals with up to 6 cast members and simple set. Submit synopsis and SASE. Reports in 6 months. Nominal payment. Web site: www.erols.com/shp.

SOUTH COAST REPERTORY—P. O. Box 2197, Costa Mesa, CA 92628. John Glore, Lit. Mgr. Full-length comedies, dramas, musicals, juveniles. Query with synopsis and resumé. Payment varies. Web site: www.scr.org.

SOUTHERN APPALACHIAN REPERTORY THEATRE—P.O. Box 1720, Mars Hill, NC 28754. James W. Thomas, Artistic Dir. Full-length comedies, dramas, musicals, and plays including (but not limited to) scripts with Appalachian theme. Submit resumé, recommendations, full script, and SASE. Send SASE for information on Southern Appalachian Playwright's Conference (held in April each year). Pays $500 royalty if play is selected for production during the summer season. Deadline for submissions is October 31 each year. E-mail: sart@mhc.edu. Web site: www.sartheatre.com

STAGES REPERTORY THEATRE—3201 Allen Pkwy., #101, Houston, TX 77019. Rob Bundy, Artistic Dir. Southwest Festival of New Plays: Children's Theatre Playwright Division, Texas Playwrights' Division, Women Playwrights' Division, and Hispanic Playwrights' Division. Submissions accepted October 1 through December 31 only. Send for guidelines on each theme. Web site: www.stagestheatre.com.

MARK TAPER FORUM—135 N. Grand Ave., Los Angeles, CA 90012. Pier Carlo Talenti, Lit. Man. Full-length comedies, dramas, musicals, 50-minute juveniles, adaptations. Query. Web site: www.taperahmanson.org.

THE TEN MINUTE MUSICALS PROJECT—Box 461194, W. Hollywood, CA 90046. Michael Koppy, Prod. One-act musicals. Include audio cassette, libretto, and lead sheets with submission. "We are looking for complete short musicals." Pays $250. Phone: 323–651–4899.

THEATER OF THE FIRST AMENDMENT—George Mason University, Institute of the Arts MSN 3E6, Fairfax, VA 22030. Rick Davis, Artistic Dir. Full-length and one-act comedies, drama, and adaptations. Send synopsis and resumé with return post card.

THEATRE AMERICANA—Box 245, Altadena, CA 91003-0245. Attn: Playreading Chair. Full-length comedies and dramas, preferably with American theme. No children's plays or musicals. Language and subject matter should be suitable for a community audience. Send bound manuscript with cast list, resumé, and SASE, by February 1. No payment. Allow 3 to 6 months for reply. Submit no more than 2 entries per season.

THEATRE/TEATRO—Bilingual Foundation of the Arts, 421 N. Ave., #19, Los Angeles, CA 90031. Agustin Coppola, Lit. Mgr. Margarita Galban, Artistic Dir. Full-length plays about the Hispanic experience; small casts. Submit manuscript with SASE. Pays negotiable rates.

THEATREWORKS—1100 Hamilton Ct., Menlo Park, CA 94025. Attn: Lit. Dept. Full-length comedies, dramas, and musicals. Submit complete script or synopsis with SAS postcard and SASE, cast list, theatre resumé, and production history. For musicals, include cassette of up to 6 songs and lyrics for all songs. Responds in 4 months for submissions made March to July; 5 months for submissions August to January. Payment is negotiable.

THEATREWORKS/USA—151 W. 26th St., 7th Fl., New York, NY 10001. Literary Manager One-hour children's musicals and plays with music for 5-person cast. Playwrights must be within commutable distance to New York City. Submit outline or treatment, sample scenes, and music in spring, summer. Pays royalty and commission.

WALNUT STREET THEATRE COMPANY—825 Walnut St., Philadelphia, PA 19107. Beverly Elliott, Lit. Mgr. Mainstage: Full-length comedies, dramas, musicals, and popular, upbeat adaptations; also, one- to 4-character plays for studio stage. Submit 10 to 20 sample pages with SAS postcard, character breakdown, and synopsis. Musical submissions must include an audio cassette or CD. Responds only with SASE. Reports in 6 months. Payment varies.

THE WESTERN STAGE—156 Homestead Ave., Salinas, CA 93901. Michael Roddy, Dramaturg. Alan Harrison, Man. Dir. Ongoing submissions; send query. Prefers adaptations of works of literary significance and/or large cast shows. Two or more shows chosen to workshop yearly.

PLAY PUBLISHERS

AMELIA—329 E St., Bakersfield, CA 93304. Frederick A. Raborg, Jr., Ed. One-act comedies and dramas; no longer than 45 minutes running time. Responds in 2 to 3 months. Payment is $35, on acceptance. E-mail: amelia@lightspeed.net.

ANCHORAGE PRESS—Box 8067, New Orleans, LA 70182. Attn: Ed. Plays and musicals that have been proven in multiple production, for children ages 6 to 18. "We publish 8 to 10 new playbooks and one to 3 new hardcover books each year." Royalty.

BAKER'S PLAYS—P.O. Box 69922, Quincy, MA 02269-9222. Ray Pape, Assoc. Ed. Full-length plays, one-act plays for young audiences, musicals, chancel dramas. Prefers produced plays; plays suitable for high school, community and regional theaters; "Plays from Young Authors" division features plays by high school playwrights. Send resumé; include press clippings if play has been produced. Responds within 2 to 6 months. E-mail: info@bakers plays.com. Web site: www.bakersplays.com.

CALLALOO—Dept. of English, Univ. of Virginia P.O. Box 400121, Charlottesville, VA 22904-4121. Charles H. Rowell, Ed. One-act dramas or excerpts of longer dramas by and about African-American, Caribbean, and African Diaspora writers. Scripts read year-round. Responds in 4 to 6 months. Payment varies, on publication, usually in offprints and complimentary copies. E-mail: callaloo@virginia.edu. Web site: www.people.virginia.edu/~callaloo.

COLLAGES & BRICOLAGES—P.O. Box 360, Shippenville, PA 16254. Marie-José Fortis, Ed. One-act avant-garde comedies and dramas, maximum 25 pages. Manuscripts read August through November; responds in one to 3 months. Payment is in copies. E-mail: cb@penn.com.

CONCORDIA PUBLISHING HOUSE—Church Resource Development, 3558 S. Jefferson Ave., St. Louis, MO 63118-3968. Drama Resources Ed. No longer accepting unsolicited materials.

CONFRONTATION—Dept. of English, C.W. Post of L.I.U., Greenvale, NY 11548. Martin Tucker, Ed. One-act comedies, dramas, and adaptations. Manuscripts read September through May. Responds in 6 to 8 weeks. Pays $25 to $100, on publication.

CONTEMPORARY DRAMA SERVICE—Meriwether Publishing Co., Box 7710, 885 Elkton Dr., Colorado Springs, CO 80903. Arthur Zapel, Ed. Easy-to-stage comedies, skits, one-acts, large-cast musicals, and full-length comedy plays for schools and churches. (Junior high through college level; no elementary level material.) Adaptations of classics and improvised material for classroom use. Character education plays and comedy monologues and duets. Chancel drama for Christmas and Easter church use. Enclose synopsis. Books on theater arts subjects, scene books, monologue books, and anthologies. Textbooks for speech and drama. Pays by fee arrangement or royalty.

DRAMATIC PUBLISHING COMPANY — 311 Washington St., Woodstock, IL 60098. Linda Habjan, Ed. Full-length and one-act plays and musicals for the professional, stock, amateur, and children's theater market. Send SASE. Royalty. Responds within 4 to 6 months. E-mail: plays@dramaticpublishing. com. Web site: www.dramaticpublishing.com.

DRAMATICS—Educational Theatre Assoc., 2343 Auburn Ave., Cincinnati, OH 45219. Don Corathers, Ed. One-act and full-length plays for high school production. Pays $100 to $400 for one-time, non-exclusive publication rights, on acceptance. E-mail: dcorathers@etassoc.org. Web site: www.etassoc. org.

ELDRIDGE PUBLISHING COMPANY—P. O. Box 1595, Venice, FL 34284. Nancy Vorhis, Ed. Dept. One-act and full-length plays and musicals suitable for performance by schools, churches, and community theatre groups. Comedies, tragedies, dramas, skits, spoofs, and religious plays (all holidays). Submit complete manuscript with cover letter, biography, and SASE. Responds in 2 months. Flat fee for religious plays, royalties for full-length plays and one-acts; paid on publication. E-mail: info@histage.com. Web site: http.//www.his tage.com.

FOURTEEN HILLS: THE SFSU REVIEW—Creative Writing Dept., San Francisco State Univ., 1600 Holloway Ave., San Francisco, CA 94132-1722. Biannual. Fiction, creative nonfiction, poetry, and plays. Submissions read August through February only. Send complete manuscript and SASE; no simultaneous or e-mail submissions. No payment. E-mail: hills@sfsu.edu. Web site: http://mercury.sfsu.edu/~hill/14hills.html.

SAMUEL FRENCH, INC.—45 W. 25th St., New York, NY 10010. Submissions editor. Full-length plays and musicals. One-act plays, 20 to 45 minutes. Children's plays, 45 to 60 minutes. Web site: www.samuelfrench.com.

THE GOODMAN THEATRE—200 S. Columbus Dr., Chicago, IL 60603. Susan V. Booth, Dir. of New Play Development. Full-length plays, translations, musicals, solo pieces. Queries from recognized literary agents or producing organizations required. No unsolicited manuscripts; send synopsis, professional recommendation, and letter of inquiry.

HEUER PUBLISHING COMPANY—P.O. Box 248, Cedar Rapids, IA 52406. C. Emmett McMullen, Ed. One-act comedies and dramas for contest work; two- and three-act comedies, mysteries, farces, and musicals, with one interior setting, for middle school and high school production. Pays royalty or flat fee. E-mail: editor@hitplays.com. Web site: www.hitplays.com.

I. E. CLARK PUBLICATIONS— P.O. Box 246, Schulenburg, TX 78956. Donna Cozzaglio, Ed. One-act and full-length plays and musicals, for children, young adults, and adults. Serious drama, comedies, classics, fairytales, melodramas, and holiday plays. "We seldom publish a play that has not been produced." Responds in 2 to 6 months. Royalty. E-mail: ieclark@cvtv.net. Web site: www.ieclark.com.

LYNX EYE—c/o Scribblefest Literary Group, 1880 Hill Dr., Los Angeles, CA 90041. Pam McCully, Kathryn Morrison, Co-Eds. One-act plays, 500 to 5,000 words, for thoughtful adults who enjoy interesting reading and writing. Also, short stories, vignettes, novel excerpts, essays, satires; poetry, to 30 lines. Pays $10, on acceptance.

NATIONAL DRAMA SERVICE—MSN 158, 127 Ninth Ave. N., Nashville, TN 37234. Attn: Ed. Scripts, 2 to 7 minutes long: drama in worship, puppets, clowns, Christian comedy, mime, movement, readers theater, creative worship services, and monologues. "We publish dramatic material that communicates the message of Christ. We want scripts that will give even the smallest church the opportunity to enhance their ministry with drama." Payment varies, on acceptance. Guidelines. E-mail: churchdrama@earthlink.net.

PIONEER DRAMA SERVICE—P. O. Box 4267, Englewood, CO 80155. Attn: Ed. Full-length and one-act plays as well as musicals, melodramas, and children's theatre. No unproduced plays or plays with largely male casts. Simple sets preferred. Query preferred. Royalty. E-mail: editors@pioneerdra ma.com. Web site: www.pioneerdrama.com.

PLAYERS PRESS, INC.—P.O. Box 1132, Studio City, CA 91614-0132. Robert W. Gordon, Ed. One-act and full-length comedies, dramas, and musicals. "No manuscript will be considered unless it has been produced." Query with manuscript-size SASE and 2 #10 SASEs for correspondence. Include resumé and/or biography. Responds in 3 to 12 months. Royalty.

PLAYS, THE DRAMA MAGAZINE FOR YOUNG PEOPLE—P.O. Box 600160, Newton, MA 02460. Elizabeth Preston, Ed. One-act plays, with simple contemporary sets, for production by young people, 7 to 17: comedies, dramas, farces, skits, holiday plays. Also adaptations of classics, biography plays, puppet plays, and creative dramatics. No musicals or plays with religious themes. Maximum lengths: lower grades and skits, 10 double-spaced pages; middle grades, 15 pages; junior and senior high, 20 pages. Guidelines. Pays good rates, on acceptance. Query for adaptations of folk tales and classics. Buys all rights.

PRISM INTERNATIONAL—Dept. of Creative Writing, Univ. of British Columbia, Buch E462, 1866 Main Mall, Vancouver, BC, Canada V6T 1Z1. Jennica Harper, Drama Ed. One-act plays and translations of contemporary work. Responds in 4 to 6 months. Pays $20 per page, on publication, $10 per page web rights. Send request with SASE for rules to register for new drama contest. E-mail: prism@interchange.ubc.ca. Web site: www.arts.ubc.ca/prism.

RAG MAG—P.O. Box 12, Goodhue, MN 55027. Beverly Voldseth, Ed. Semiannual. Full-length and one-act comedies and dramas. SASE for guidelines. Send complete play. No plays read May through August. Pays in copy.

ROCKFORD REVIEW—P.O. Box 858, Rockford, IL 61105. David Ross, Ed. Published tri-quarterly by Rockford Writers Guild. One-act comedies, dramas, and satires, to 1,300 words. "We prefer genuine or satirical human dilemmas with coping or non-coping outcomes that illuminate the human condition." Publishes one to 2 plays per issue. Pays in copies (plus invitation to attend reading-reception in the summer). Two $25 Editor's Choice Prizes awarded each issue. Samples $5. E-mail: dragonldy@prodigy.net. Web site: www.welcome.to/rwg.

SMITH AND KRAUS, INC.—P.O. Box 127, Main St., Lyme, NH 03768. Marisa Smith, Pres. Publishes monologue and scene anthologies, biographies of playwrights, translations, books on career developement (in theater) and the art of theater, and teaching texts for young actors (K-12). Does not accept full-length and one-act plays unless the play in question has been produced within the year and is therefore eligible for the "Best Scene and Monologue Series for the Year." Does not return manuscripts. Response time is 3 months. Pays on publication. E-mail: sandk@sover.net. Web site: www.smithkraus.com

BOOK PUBLISHERS

The following list includes the major book publishers for adult and juvenile fiction and nonfiction and a representative number of small publishers from across the country, as well as a number of university presses.

Before submitting a complete manuscript to an editor, it is advisable to send a brief query letter describing the proposed book, and an SASE. The letter should also include information about the author's special qualifications for dealing with a particular topic and any previous publication credits. An outline of the book (or a synopsis for fiction) and a sample chapter may also be included.

While it is common practice to submit a book manuscript to only one publisher at a time, it is becoming more and more acceptable to submit the same query or proposal to more than one editor simultaneously. When sending multiple queries, *always* make note of it in each submission.

Book manuscripts may be packaged in typing paper boxes (available from a stationery store) and sent by first-class mail, or, more common and less expensive, by "Special Fourth Class Rate—Manuscript." For rates, details of insurance, and so forth, inquire at your local post office. With any submission to a publisher, be sure to enclose sufficient postage for the manuscript's return.

Royalty rates for hardover books usually start at 10% of the retail price of the book and increase after a certain number of copies have been sold. Paperbacks generally have a somewhat lower rate, about 5% to 8%. It is customary for the publishing company to pay the author a cash advance against royalties when the book contract is signed or when the finished manuscript is received. Some publishers pay on a flat-fee basis.

While most of the publishers on this list consider either unsolicited manuscripts or queries, an increasing number now read only agented submissions. Since finding an agent is not an easy task, especially for newcomers, writers are advised to try to sell their manuscripts directly to the publisher first.

Writers seeking publication of their book-length poetry manuscripts are encouraged to enter contests that offer publication as the prize (see *Literary Prize Offers*, page 81?); many presses that once considered unsolicited poetry manuscripts by emerging or unpublished writers now limit their reading of such manuscripts to those entered in their contests for new writers.

ABINGDON PRESS—P.O. Box 801, Nashville, TN 37202. Joseph A. Crowe, Ed. General-interest books: mainline, social issues, marriage/family, self-help, exceptional people. Query with outline and one or 2 sample chapters. Guidelines.

ACADEMIC PRESS—Harcourt, Brace & Co., 525 B St., Suite 1900, San Diego, CA 92101. Attn: Ed. Dept. Scientific and technical books and journals for research-level scientists, students, and professionals; upper-level undergraduate and graduate science texts.

ACTIVITY RESOURCES—P.O. Box 4875, Hayward, CA 94540. Mary Laycock. Math educational material only. "Our main focus is on grades K through 8." Submit complete manuscript. Royalty. E-mail: info@activity resources.com. Web site: www.activityresources.com.

ADAMS-BLAKE PUBLISHING—8041 Sierra St., Fair Oaks, CA 95628. Monica Blane, Ed. Books on business, careers, and technology. Query or send complete manuscript. Multiple submissions accepted. Royalty. See www.adams-blake.com for guidelines.

ADAMS-HALL PUBLISHING—P.O. Box 491002, Los Angeles, CA 90049. Sue Ann Bacon, Marketing Dir. Business and personal finance books with wide market appeal. Query with proposed book idea, a listing of current competitive books, author qualifications, the reason that the book is unique, and SASE. Royalty.

ADAMS MEDIA COPORATION—260 Center St., Holbrook, MA 02343. Edward Walters, Ed.-in-Chief. Nonfiction trade books on business and careers, financial planning, self-improvement, family and parenting, relationships, pets, humor, inspiration, and historical biography. Query with outline, at least 2 sample chapters, and SASE. Unsolicted material without SASE will not be returned. Royalty and work for hire. Web site: www.adamsmedia.com.

ADDISON WESLEY LONGMAN—One Jacob Way, Reading, MA 01867-3999. Attn: Ed. Dept. Adult nonfiction on current topics including science, health, psychology, business, biography, child care, etc. Specializing in literary nonfiction. Royalty.

ADRENALINE BOOKS—See *Thunder's Mouth Press.*

AFRICAN AMERICAN IMAGES—1909 W. 95th St., Chicago, IL 60643. Attn: Ed. Publishes books from an Africentric frame of reference that promote self-esteem, collective values, liberation, and skill development. Solutions for African Americans. Juvenile fiction and nonfiction as well. Responds within 10 weeks. Multiple queries are accepted, and payment is made on a royalty basis. Send complete manuscript.

ALABASTER—See *Multnomah Publishers.*

ALASKA NORTHWEST BOOKS—Imprint of Graphic Arts Center Publishing Co., P.O. Box 10306, Portland, OR 97296-0306. Tricia Brown, Acq. Ed. Nonfiction, 50,000 to 100,000 words, with an emphasis on natural world and history of Alaska and the Pacific Northwest: travel books; cookbooks; field guides; children's books; outdoor recreation; natural history; native culture; lifestyle. Send query or sample chapters with outline. Guidelines.

ALGONQUIN BOOKS OF CHAPEL HILL—Box 2225, Chapel Hill, NC 27515. Shannon Ravenel, Ed. Dir. Trade books, literary fiction and nonfiction, for adults.

ALLWORTH PRESS—10 E. 23rd St., Suite 210, New York, NY 10010. Nicole Potter, Ed. Helpful books for professional artists, designers, writers, and photographers. Query with outline and sample chapters. Royalty.

ALPINE PUBLICATIONS—225 S. Madison Ave., Loveland, CO 80537. B.J. McKinney, Pub. Nonfiction books, 35,000 to 60,000 words, on dogs and horses. Submit outline and sample chapters or complete manuscript. Royalty.

ALYSON PUBLICATIONS—6922 Hollywood Blvd., Suite 100, Los Angeles, CA 90028. Attn: Ed. Gay and lesbian adult fiction and nonfiction books, from 65,000 words. *Alyson Wonderland* imprint: Children and young adult with gay and lesbian themes. Query with outline only. Royalty. See www.alyson.com for guidelines.

AMERICAN PARADISE PUBLISHING—P.O. Box 781, St. John, USVI 00831. Pamela Gaffin, Ed. "We are interested in 'hopelessly local' books, between 80 and 300 pages. We need useful, practical books that help our Virgin Island readers lead better and more enjoyable lives." Guidebooks, cookbooks, how-to books, books on sailing, yacht cruising, hiking, snorkeling, sportfishing, local history, and West Indian culture, specifically aimed at Caribbean readers/tourists. Query with outline and sample chapters. Royalty. E-mail: pam@viaccess.net. Web site: www.americanparadisepublishing.com.

ANCHOR BOOKS—The Knopf Publishing Group, 299 Park Ave., New York, NY 10171. Ed. Adult trade paperbacks and hardcovers. Original fiction, nonfiction, multicultural, sociology, psychology, philosophy, women's interest, etc. No unsolicited manuscripts.

ANCHORAGE PRESS—Box 8067, New Orleans, LA 70182. Attn: Acquisitions Ed. Dramatic publishers. Plays for children ages 4 to 18. "We publish 8 to 10 new playbooks and one to 3 new hardcover books each year." Royalty.

ANHINGA PRESS—P.O. Box 10595, Tallahassee, FL 32302-0595. Rick Campbell, Ed. Poetry books. (Publishes 3 books a year.) Query or send complete manuscripts. Flat fee. Annual poetry prize of $2,000 plus publication; send #10 SASE for details. E-mail: info@anhinga.org. Web site: www. anhinga.org.

ANVIL PRESS—P.O. Box 1575, Bentall Centre, Vancouver, BC, Canada V6C 2P7. Brian Kaufman, Ed. Contemporary literary fiction, nonfiction, and poetry. Submit query and outline with 20 to 30 sample pages, or 8 to 12 poems. No multiple queries. Pays in royalties. Canadian authors only. Web site: www. anvilpress.com.

APPALACHIAN MOUNTAIN CLUB BOOKS—5 Joy St., Boston, MA 02108. Attn: Ed. Dept. Regional (New England) and national nonfiction titles, 250 to 400 pages, for adult audience; juvenile and young adult nonfiction. Topics include guidebooks on non-motorized backcountry recreation, nature, outdoor recreation skills (how-to books), mountain history/biography, search and rescue, conservation, and environmental management. Query with outline and sample chapters. Multiple queries considered. Royalty.

ARABESQUE—See *Kensington Publishing Co.*

ARCADE PUBLISHING—141 Fifth Ave., New York, NY 10010. Richard Seaver, Pub./Ed., Jeannette Seaver, Assoc. Pub., Cal Barksdale, Webb Younce, Eds. Fiction and nonfiction. No unsolicited manuscripts. Query.

ARCHON BOOKS—See *Shoe String Press.*

ARCHWAY/MINSTREL BOOKS—Pocket Books, 1230 Ave. of the Americas, New York, NY 10020. Patricia MacDonald, V.P./ Ed. Dir. No unsolicited material.

ARONSON INC., PUBLISHERS, JASON —230 Livingston St., Northvale, NJ 07647. Arthur Kurzweil, Ed. Nonfiction on all aspects of Jewish life, including such topics as anti-semitism, the Bible, Hasidic thought, genealogy, medicine, folklore and storytelling, interfaith relations, the Holocaust, the Talmud, women's studies, and travel. Send complete manuscript or query with outline and sample chapters. Payment is in royalties.

ARTE PUBLICO PRESS —University of Houston, 4800 Calhoun, Houston, TX 77204-2090. *Pinata Books.* Publishes contemporary and historical literature by U.S. Hispanics in both English and Spanish; novels, short stories, poetry, drama, and autobiographies. Query with outline and sample chapters, or send complete manuscript. Payment is in royalties. Web site: www.arte.uh.edu.

AVALON BOOKS—160 Madison Ave., New York, NY 10016. Wilhelm H. Mickelsen, Pres. Erin Cartwright, Ed. Hardcover books, 40,000 to 50,000 words: romances, mysteries, and westerns. No explicit sex. Query with first 3 chapters and outline. SASE for guidelines. E-mail: avalonbooks@att.net. Web site: www.avalonbooks.com.

AVERY PUBLISHING GROUP—120 Old Broadway, Garden City Park, NY 11040. Attn: Man. Ed. Nonfiction, from 40,000 words, on health, childbirth, child care, healthful cooking. Query. Royalty.

AVISSON PRESS, INC.—3007 Taliaferro Rd., Greensboro, NC 27408. Martin L. Hester, Exec. Ed. Helpful nonfiction books on health, lifestyle, finance, etc., for older Americans; books on teenage issues, teen problems, and parenting; young adult biography (for readers 10 to 18). Query with outline or sample chapter, bio and SASE. Royalty.

AVON BOOKS—See *HarperCollins Children's Books.*

BAEN BOOKS—Baen Publishing Enterprises, P.O. Box 1403, Riverdale, NY 10471-1403. Jim Baen, Pres./Ed.-in-Chief. Strongly plotted science fiction; innovative fantasy. Query with synopsis and manuscript. Advance and royalty. Guidelines available for letter-sized SASE.

BAKER BOOK HOUSE—P. O. Box 6287, Grand Rapids, MI 49516-6287. Rebecca Cooper, Asst. Ed. Religious nonfiction: books for trade, clergy, seminarians, collegians. Literary fiction. Query first with sample chapters. Pays in royalties. Imprint: *Brazos Press.*Web site: www.bakerbooks.com.

BALBOA—See *Tiare Publications.*

BALLAD—See *Kensington Publishing Corp.*

BALLANTINE BOOKS—1540 Broadway, 11th Fl., New York, NY 10036. Attn: Editorial Dept. General fiction and nonfiction. Accepts material only through agents. Web site: www.randomhouse.com/bb.

BALSAM PRESS—36 E. 22nd St., 9th Fl., New York, NY 10010. Barbara Krohn, Exec. Ed. General and illustrated adult nonfiction. Query. Royalty.

BANTAM SPECTRA BOOKS—1540 Broadway, New York, NY 10036. Anne Lesley Groell, Ed. Patrick LoBrutto, Sr. Ed. Science fiction and fantasy, with emphasis on storytelling and characterization. First three chapters and synopsis with SASE; no unsolicited manuscripts. Royalty.

BANTAM, DOUBLEDAY, DELL—Div. of Random House, 1540 Broadway, New York, NY 10036. Irwyn Applebaum, Pres./Pub. Adult fiction and nonfiction. Mass-market titles, submit queries to the following imprints: *Crime Line*, crime and mystery fiction; *Domain*, frontier fiction, historical sagas, traditional westerns; *Spectra*, science fiction and fantasy; *Bantam Nonfiction*, wide variety of commercial nonfiction, including true crime, health and nutrition, sports, reference. Agented queries and manuscripts only.

BARRON'S EDUCATIONAL SERIES, INC.—250 Wireless Blvd., Hauppauge, NY 11788. Wayne Barr, Acquisitions Dir. Juvenile nonfiction (science, nature, history, hobbies, and how-to) and picture books for ages 3 to 6. Adult nonfiction (business, pet care, childcare, sports, test preparation, cookbooks, foreign language instruction). Query with SASE. Guidelines. E-mail: editors@barrons.com. Web site: www.barrons.com.

BAUHAN, PUBLISHER, WILLIAM L.—Box 443, Dublin, NH 03444. William L. Bauhan, Ed. Biographies, fine arts, gardening, architecture, and history books with an emphasis on New England. Submit query with outline and sample chapter. E-mail: wlbinc@aol.com. Web site: www.bauhanpublishing. com.

BAYLOR UNIVERSITY PRESS—P.O. Box 97363, Baylor Univ., Waco, TX 76798-7363. David Holcomb, Acq. Ed. Scholarly nonfiction, especially oral history and church-state issues. Query with outline. Royalty. E-mail: david holcomb@baylor.edu. Web site: www.baylor.edu/~bupress.

BEACON PRESS—25 Beacon St., Boston, MA 02108. Attn: Helene Atwan. General nonfiction: world affairs, women's studies, anthropology, history, philosophy, religion, gay and lesbian studies, nature writing, African-American studies, Latino studies, Asian-American studies, Native-American studies. Series: "Concord Library" (nature writing); "Barnard New Women Poets." Query. Agented manuscripts only.

BEAR & COMPANY, INC.—P.O. Drawer 2860, Santa Fe, NM 87504. Attn: Acquisitions. Nonfiction "that will help transform our culture philosophically, environmentally, and spiritually." Query with outline, sample chapters, and SASE. Royalty. E-mail: bearco@bearco.com.

BEHRMAN HOUSE—11 Edison Place, Springfield, NJ 07081. Hebrew language and Judaica textbooks for children. Adult Jewish nonfiction. Query with outline and sample chapters. Flat fee or royalty. Web site: www.behrman house.com.

BELLWETHER-CROSS PUBLISHING—18319 Highway 20 W., E. Dubuque, IL 61025. Educational materials in most disciplines from high school through college. Also, trade nonfiction in a variety of topics. For educational materials, query with proposed book idea, list of current competitive books, and bio. For trade nonfiction, query with outline and sample chapters. SASE. Royalty. E-mail: jwhite@shepherd-inc.com. Web site: www.bellwether cross.com.

BENCHMARK BOOKS—99 White Plains Rd., Tarrytown, NY 10591-9001. Kate Nunn, Ed. Dir. Books, 3,000 to 30,000 words, for young readers (grades K up) on science, sports, the arts, history, wildlife, math, and social studies. Series include: "Cultures of the World," "Cultures of the Past," "Ecosystems of North America," "Celebrate the States," "Rulers and Their Times," and "We Can Read!" among others. Query with outline. Royalty or flat fee. No single-title submissions.

BERKLEY PUBLISHING GROUP —375 Hudson St., New York, NY 10014. General-interest fiction and nonfiction; science fiction, suspense, and mystery novels; romance. Submit through agent only. Publishes both reprints and originals. Paperback books, except for some hardcover mysteries and science fiction. Query required.

BERKSHIRE HOUSE PUBLISHERS—480 Pleasant St., Suite 5, Lee, MA 02138. Philip Rich, Ed. Dir. Nonfiction, 70,000 to 95,000 words, on travel to specific regional USA destinations and recreation in the Berkshires. Query with table of contents, sample chapter, resumé, and SASE; guidelines available. Multiple queries considered. Pays in royalties. Professional travel writers only. E-mail: philipr@berkshirehouse.com or info@berkshirehouse.com. Web site: www.berkshirehouse.com.

THE BESS PRESS—3565 Harding Ave., Honolulu, HI 96816. Revé Shapard, Ed. Nonfiction books about Hawaii and the Pacific for adults, children, and young adults. Query. Royalty. E-mail: editor@besspress.com. Web site: www.besspress.com.

BETHANY HOUSE PUBLISHERS—11400 Hampshire Ave. S., Minneapolis, MN 55438. Carol Johnson, VP/Ed. Religious fiction and nonfiction. Adults: personal growth books; divorce; euthanasia; women's issues; spirituality; abortion; and cults. Send synopsis, three sample chapters, bio, and SASE to Sharon Madison. Children and teens: First chapter books, 6,000 to 7,500 words, of biblical lessons and Christian faith for ages 7 to 10; imaginative stories and believable characters, 20,000 to 40,000 words, for middle-grade readers; and for teens of ages 12 to 17, at least 40,000-word stories with strong plots and realistic characters. Send synopsis, three sample chapters, bio, and SASE. Payment is in royalties.

BEYOND WORDS PUBLISHING—20827 N.W. Cornell Rd., Suite 500, Hillsboro, OR 97124. Attn: Adult Acquisitions Ed. or Children's Acquisitions Ed. Books on personal growth, women, and spiritual issues. Adult nonfiction books, 150 to 250 pages. Children's picture books, 32, 48, 60, or 80 pages. Submit outline and sample chapters for adult titles; complete manuscript for juvenile titles. Royalty.

BICK PUBLISHING HOUSE—307 Neck Rd., Madison, CT 06443. Dale Carlson, Ed. Books, 64 to 250 pages, on wildlife rehabilitation, special needs/disabilities, psychology. Submit outline and sample chapters. Royalty.

BINFORD & MORT PUBLISHING—5245 N.E. Elam Young Pkwy., Suite C, Hillsboro, OR 97124. P.L. Gardenier, Ed. Nonfiction on subjects related to the Pacific Coast and the Northwest. Lengths vary. Query. Royalty. E-mail: polly@binfordandmort.com. Web site: www.binfordandmort.com.

BLACK BELT PRESS—Black Belt Publishing, P.O. Box 551, Montgomery, AL 36101. Attn: Submission Ed. Regional titles of national interest: history, especially African American or civil rights, biography, folklore, contemporary Southern fiction and poetry. Query with cover letter, synopsis or outline, author bio, and SASE for reply. Royalty varies. E-mail: info@black belt.com. Web site: www.black-belt.com.

BLACKBIRCH PRESS, INC.—260 Amity Rd., P.O. Box 3573, Woodbridge, CT 06525. Attn: Ed. Publishes books in a series, for 6- to 16-year-olds. Series include "The Library of Famous Women" and "Building America." E-mail queries acceptable: staff@blackbirch.com. Web site: www.blackbirch. com.

BLAIR, PUBLISHER, JOHN F.—1406 Plaza Dr., Winston-Salem, NC 27103. Carolyn Sakowski, Pres. Books, 70,000 to 100,000 words: biography, history, folklore, and guidebooks, with southeastern tie-in. Query. Royalty. No electronic submissions. E-mail: blairpub@aol.com. Web site: www.blair pub.com.

BLOOMBERG PRESS—100 Business Park Dr., P.O. Box 888, Princeton, NJ 08542-0888. Kathleen Peterson, Sr. Ed. Nonfiction, varying lengths, on topics such as investing, finance, e-commerce, and small business. Query with outline and sample chapter or send complete manuscript. SASE. Pays varying rates. Royalty. Web site: www.bloomberg.com/books.

BLUE DOLPHIN PUBLISHING, INC.—P.O. Box 8, Nevada City, CA 95959. Paul M. Clemens, Ed. Books, 200 to 300 pages, on comparative spiritual traditions, lay and transpersonal psychology, self-help, health, healing, and "whatever helps people grow in their social awareness and conscious evolution." Query with outline, sample chapters, and SASE. Royalty.

BLUE HERON PUBLISHING—1234 S.W. Stark St., Portland, OR

97205. Daniel Urban, Acq. Ed. Books on writing and teaching writing for adults and young adults. Northwestern and Western fiction for adults, universities and high schools (especially multicultural themes), political mysteries, cookbooks. SASE for guidelines or e-mail guidelines@blueheronpublishing.com. Query. Web site: www.blueheronpublishing.com.

BOA EDITIONS, LTD.—260 East Ave., Rochester, NY 14604. Steven Huff, Thomas Ward, Eds. Books of poetry, approximately 70 pages. Query. Royalty.

BOB JONES UNIVERSITY PRESS—See *Journey Books.*

BONUS BOOKS—160 E. Illinois St., Chicago, IL 60611. Devon Freeny, Assist. Ed. Nonfiction; topics vary widely. Query with sample chapters and SASE. Royalty. E-mail: bb@bonus-books.com. Web site: www.bonus-books. com.

BOUQUET—See *Kensington Publishing Corp.*

BOTTOM DOG PRESS, INC.—Firelands College, Huron, OH 44839. Larry Smith, Dir. Collections of personal essays, fiction, 50 to 160 pages, and poetry for book publication (50 poems). Subjects should be midwestern or working class in focus. "Interested writers should query first." Do not send manuscripts. Royalty.

BOYDS MILLS PRESS—815 Church St., Honesdale, PA 18431. Beth Troop, Manuscript Coord. Hardcover trade books for children. Fiction: picture books; middle-grade fiction with fresh ideas and involving story; young adult novels of literary merit. Nonfiction should be "fun, entertaining, and informative." Send outline and sample chapters for young adult novels and nonfiction, complete manuscripts for all other categories. Royalty. Web site: www.boyds millspress.com.

BRANDEN PUBLISHING COMPANY—17 Station St., Box 843, Brookline Village, MA 02447. Attn: Ed. Dept. Novels, biographies, and autobiographies. Especially books by or about women, 250 to 350 pages. Also considers queries on history, computers, business, performance arts, and translations. Query only with SASE. Royalty. Web site: www.branden.com.

BRASSEY'S, INC.—(formerly *Batsford Brassey's, Inc.*) 22841 Quicksilver Dr., Dulles, VA 20166. Don McKeon, Pub. Nonfiction books, 75,000 to 130,000 words. National and international affairs, history, foreign policy, defense, military biography, sports, and transportation. No fiction. Query with synopsis, author bio, outline, sample chapters, and SASE. Royalty. E-mail: djacobs@booksintl.com.

BRAZILLER PUBLISHERS, GEORGE—171 Madison Ave., Suite 1103, New York, NY 10016. Attn: Ed. Dept. Fiction and nonfiction. Art history, collections of essays and short stories, anthologies. Send art history manuscripts to Art Ed.; others to Fiction Ed. Send outline with sample chapters.

BRAZOS PRESS—Division of Baker Book House, P.O. Box 6287, Grand Rapids, MI 49516-6287. Rodney Clapp, Ed. Dir. Titles that concentrate on theology, cultural criticism, and Christian spirituality, in the range of 50,000 words-plus. Query. Pays in royalties.

BREAKAWAY BOOKS—Box 24, Halcottsville, NY 12438. Garth Battista, Pub. Literary sports novels or collections of essays or stories. "Our goal is to bring to light literary writing on the athletic experience." Royalty. Send queries to: Garth@breakawaybooks.com. Web site: www.breakawaybooks.com.

BRIDGE WORKS—Box 1798, Bridgehampton, NY 11932. Barbara Phillips, Pres./Ed. Dir. Mainstream adult literary fiction and nonfiction, 50,000 to 75,000 words. Royalty. Query first with SASE.

BRISTOL PUBLISHING ENTERPRISES—P.O. Box 1737, San Leandro, CA 94577. Patricia Hall, Ed. Cookbooks. Query with outline, sample chapters, resumé, and SASE. Royalty.

BROADMAN AND HOLMAN PUBLISHERS—127 Ninth Ave. N., Nashville, TN 37234-0115. Richard P. Rosenbaum, Jr., V. P. Trade, academic, religious and inspirational nonfiction. Query with SASE. Royalty. Guidelines.

BUCKNELL UNIVERSITY PRESS—Bucknell Univ., Lewisburg, PA 17837. Greg Clingham, Dir. Scholarly nonfiction. Query. Royalty.

BULFINCH PRESS—3 Center Plaza, Boston, MA 02108. Attn: Ed. Dept. Illustrated fine art and photography books. Query with outline or proposal, sample artwork, bio, and SASE. Web site: www.bulfinch.com.

BURFORD BOOKS—32 Morris Ave., Springfield, NJ 07081. Peter Burford, Pub. Books, 100 to 300 pages, related to sports, the outdoors, and military history. Query with outline. Royalty. E-mail: info@burfordbooks.com.

C&T PUBLISHING—1651 Challenge Dr., Concord, CA 94520. Barbara Kuhn, Ed.-in-Chief. Quilting books, 64 to 200 finished pages. "Our focus is how-to, although we will consider picture, inspirational, or history books on quilting." Send query, outline, or sample chapters. Multiple queries considered. Royalty.

CALENDAR ISLANDS PUBLISHERS—477 Congress St., Suite 404–406, Portland, ME 04101. Peter Stillman, Ed. Nonfiction, on teaching English from junior high level through college. Query with outline and sample chapter; multiple queries considered. Pays in royalties.

CALYX BOOKS—P.O. Box B, Corvallis, OR 97339. Margarita Donnelly, Micki Reaman, Eds. Feminist publisher. Novels, short stories, poetry, nonfiction, translations, and anthologies by women. Send SASE or e-mail calyx@proaxis.com for guidelines before submitting.

CANDLEWICK PRESS—2067 Massachusetts Ave., Cambridge, MA 02140. Karen Lotz, Pres. and Pub. Elizabeth Bicknell, Ed. Dir. Children's books. No unsolicited material. E-mail: bigbear@candlewick.com.

CAPSTONE PRESS, INC.—P.O. Box 669, Mankato, MN 56001. Helen Moore, Ed. High interest/low-reading level and early reader nonfiction for children; specifically, reluctant and new readers. Send SASE for author brochure. Query with references and resumé; do not send complete manuscript. Flat fee. Web site: www.capstone-press.com.

CAROLRHODA BOOKS—241 First Ave. N., Minneapolis, MN 55401. Rebecca Poole, Ed. Complete manuscripts for ages 4 to 12: biography, science, nature, history, photo-essays; historical fiction. Guidelines. Hardcover. Accepts submissions from March 1 to 31 and from October 1 to 31. E-mail: info@lernerbooks.com. Web site: www.lernerbooks.com.

CAROUSEL PRESS—P.O. Box 6038, Berkeley, CA 94706-0038. Carole T. Meyers, Ed. Travel guides, especially round-ups. Send letter, table of contents, and sample chapter. "We publish one or 2 new books each year and will consider out-of-print books that the author wants to update." Modest advance and royalty. E-mail: info@carousel-press.com. Web site: www.carousel press.com.

CARROLL AND GRAF PUBLISHERS, INC.—19 W. 21st St., Suite 601, New York, NY 10001. Kent E. Carroll, Exec. Ed. General fiction and nonfiction. No unagented submissions.

CASABLANCA PRESS—Imprint of Sourcebooks, Inc., 121 N. Washington St., Naperville, IL 60540. Todd Stocke, Ed. Nonfiction, specializing in self-help, relationship, and gift. Query with outline and sample chapters. Pays in royalties.

CATBIRD PRESS—16 Windsor Rd., North Haven, CT 06473. Robert Wechsler, Ed. Adult fiction and nonfiction with "a fresh, sophisticated approach." Translations, especially Czech, German, and French. Query with outline and sample chapters. Accepts multiple queries and pays on a royalty basis. Web site: www.catbirdpress.com.

CATHOLIC UNIVERSITY PRESS OF AMERICA—240 Leahy Hall, 620 Michigan Ave. N.E., Washington DC 20064. Dr. David J. McGonagle, Ed. Scholarly works and serious studies related to the humanities and social sciences, namely ecclesiastical and secular history; literature; social studies; and theology. Query the editor with outline and sample chapters. Payment is in royalties.

CELESTIAL ARTS—See *Ten Speed Press.*

CHARLESBRIDGE PUBLISHING—85 Main St., Watertown, MA 02472. Attn: Submissions Ed. Children's nonfiction picture books under *Charlesbridge* imprint, fiction picture books under *Talewinds* or *Whispering Coyote* imprint. Send complete manuscript. Exclusive submissions only: must indicate on envelope and cover letter. Pays royalty or flat fee. E-mail: trade editorial@charlesbridge.com. Web site: www.charlesbridge.com.

CHATHAM PRESS—P. O. Box A, Old Greenwich, CT 06870. Roger H. Lourie, Man. Dir. Books on the Northeast coast, gardening, New England maritime subjects, and the ocean. Large photography volumes. Query with outline, sample chapters, illustrations, and SASE. Royalty.

CHECKMARK BOOKS—Facts on File, Inc., 11 Penn Plaza, New York, NY 10001-2006. Laurie Likoff, Ed. Dir. Focuses on careers, education, health, popular history and culture, fashion, and fitness. "We are looking for materials that fit a particular market niche and are high-quality, with a strong reference component." No memoirs, autobiographies, or fiction. Query, with sample chapters or outline. Payment is advance against royalties. Web site: www. factsonfile.com

CHELSEA GREEN PUBLISHING CO.—P.O. Box 428, White River Junction, VT 05001. Stephen Morris, Acting Ed.-in-Chief. Nonfiction: natural history, environmental issues, solar energy and shelter, organic agriculture, and ecological lifestyle books with strong backlist potential. Query with outline and SASE. Royalty. Web site: www.chelseagreen.com.

CHELSEA HOUSE PUBLISHERS—1974 Sproul Rd., Broomall, PA 19008. Attn: Acquisitions Ed. Juvenile books (for ages 8 up) for publication in a series format. Series include: "Women of Achievement" and "Overcoming Adversity," among others. No unsolicited manuscripts. Query with writing sample and SASE for consideration of assignments. Flat fee.

CHICAGO REVIEW PRESS—814 N. Franklin St., Chicago, IL 60610. Cynthia Sherry, Ed. Nonfiction: activity books for children, general nonfiction, architecture, parenting, how-to, and regional gardening and other regional topics. Query with outline and sample chapters. E-mail: publish@ipgbook.com. Web site: www.ipgbook.com.

CHILD AND FAMILY PRESS—Child Welfare League of America, 440 First St. N.W., Third Fl., Washington, DC 20001-2085. Juvenile picture books, fiction, and nonfiction, 24 to 32 pages, on various child welfare topics. Also, adult nonfiction on parenting and family topics. Submit complete manuscript. Multiple queries are considered. Pays in royalties. Web: www.cwla.org.

CHILDREN'S BOOK PRESS—246 First St., Suite 101, San Francisco, CA 94105. Submissions Ed. Bilingual and multicultural picture books, 750 to 1,500 words, for children in grades K through 6. "We publish folktales and contemporary stories reflecting the traditions and culture of minorities and new immigrants in the U.S. Ultimately, we want to help encourage a more international, multicultural perspective on the part of all young people." Query. Pays advance on royalties.

CHILDREN'S PRESS—Grolier Publishing Co., Sherman Turnpike, Danbury, CT 06816. Attn: Submissions Ed. Science, social studies, and biography, to 25,000 words, for supplementary use in libraries and classrooms. Royalty or outright purchase. Currently overstocked; not accepting unsolicited manuscripts. No phone inquiries.

CHINA BOOKS—2929 24th St., San Francisco, CA 94110. Greg Jones, Sr. Ed. Books relating to China or Chinese culture. Adult nonfiction, varying lengths. Juvenile picture books, fiction, nonfiction, and young adult books. Query. Royalty. More information available at www.chinabooks.com.

CHRONICLE BOOKS—85 Second St., San Francisco, CA 94105. Attn: Ed. Dept. Fiction, art, photography, architecture, design, nature, food, giftbooks. Children's books. Send proposal or complete manuscript for fiction with SASE. Web site: www.chroniclebooks.com.

CLARION BOOKS—215 Park Ave. S., New York, NY 10003. Dinah Stevenson, Ed. Dir. No unsolicited material.

CLARKSON N. POTTER, PUBLISHERS—201 E. 50th St., New York, NY 10022. Lauren Shakely, Ed. Dir. Illustrated trade books about such topics as cooking, gardening, and decorating. Submissions accepted through agents only.

CLEIS PRESS—P.O. Box 14684, San Francisco, CA 94114. Frédérique Delacoste, Ed. Fiction and nonfiction, 200 pages, by women. No poetry. Send SASE with 2 first-class stamps for catalogue before querying. Royalty.

CLOVER PARK PRESS—P.O. Box 5067-T, Santa Monica, CA 90409-5067. Martha Grant, Acquisitions Ed. Nonfiction adult books on California (history, natural history, travel, culture, or the arts), biographies of extraordinary women, nature, exploration, scientific/medical discovery, adventure. Query with outline, sample chapter, author bio, and SASE. E-mail: cloverpark pr@loop.com. Web site: www.loop.com/~cloverparkpr.

COFFEE HOUSE PRESS—27 N. 4th St., Suite 400, Minneapolis, MN 55401. Attn: Chris Fischbach. Literary fiction, poetry. Query with SASE. Web site: www.coffeehousepress.org.

CONARI PRESS—2550 Ninth St., Suite 101, Berkeley, CA 94710. Heather McArthur, Man. Ed. Adult nonfiction: women's issues, personal growth, parenting, and spirituality. Submit outline, sample chapters, and 6½″×9½″ SASE. Royalty.

CONCORDIA PUBLISHING HOUSE—3558 S. Jefferson Ave., St. Louis, MO 63118. Attn: Book Development. Practical family books and devotionals. Must have explicit Christian content. No poetry. Query. Royalty.

CONFLUENCE PRESS—Lewis-Clark State College, 500 8th Ave., Lewiston, ID 83501-2698. James R. Hepworth, Dir. Literary fiction, essay collections, literary criticism, regional history, natural history, biography, and poetry. SASE for guidelines. Royalty.

COPPER BEECH BOOKS—See *The Millbrook Press.*

COPPER CANYON PRESS—P.O. Box 271, Port Townsend, WA 98368. Sam Hamill, Ed. Poetry books only. No unsolicited manuscripts. Annual Hayden Carruth Award for first, second and third books. Send SASE for guidelines. Royalty. Web site: www.coppercanyonpress.org.

CORNELL UNIVERSITY PRESS—Sage House, 512 E. State St., Ithaca, NY 14850. Frances Benson, Ed.-in-Chief. Scholarly nonfiction, 60,000 to 120,000 words. Query with outline. Royalty. Web site: www.cornellpress. cornell.edu.

COTLER BOOKS, JOANNA—See *HarperCollins Children's Books.*

COUNCIL OAK BOOKS—1290 Chestnut St., Suite 2, San Francisco, CA 94109. Kevin Bentley, Ed. General trade spirituality, new age, memoirs, diaries, letters of historical nature, and Native American spirituality. Do not send complete manuscript; query editor and include SASE. Multiple queries are considered. Payment is in royalties.

COUNTERPOINT—1627 I St. N.W., Suite 500, Washington, DC 20006. Ed. Adult literary nonfiction, including art, religion, history, biography, science, and current affairs; literary fiction. All submissions through agent only. Royalty.

CRAFTSMAN BOOK COMPANY—6058 Corte del Cedro, P.O. Box 6500, Carlsbad, CA 92018. Laurence D. Jacobs, Ed. How-to construction and estimating manuals and software for professional builders, 450 pages. Query. Royalty. Paperback. E-mail: jacobs@costbook.com. Web sites: www. craftsman-book.com or www.costbook.com.

CREATIVE HOMEOWNER PRESS—24 Park Way, Box 38, Upper Saddle River, NJ 07458. Timothy O. Bakke, Ed. Nonfiction, including home improvement how-to, home design, decorating, and landscape and gardening. Queries preferred. Pays flat fee.

CRICKET BOOKS—Carus Publishing, 332 S. Michigan Ave., Suite 1100, Chicago, IL 60604. Publishes chapter books, middle-grade novels, and occasional young-adult fiction along the same lines as the material published in their magazines, *Spider, Cricket,* and *Cicada.* Submit complete manuscript. Response time is 10 to 12 weeks. Payment is on a royalty basis. Web site: www.cricketbooks.net.

CRIME LINE—See *Bantam, Doubleday, Dell.*

CROCODILE BOOKS, USA—Interlink Publishing, 46 Crosby St., Northampton, MA 01060. Publishes high-quality picture books from around the world, fiction and nonfiction for ages 3 to 8. Query with sample illustrations. Multiple queries are not considered. Pays in royalties. Web site: www.interlink books.com.

CROSS CULTURAL PUBLICATIONS, INC.—P.O. Box 506, Notre Dame, IN 46556. Cyriac K. Pullapilly, Gen. Ed. Nonfiction, to 250 pages, that promotes intercultural or interfaith understanding. Send proposal with table of contents, resumé, and SASE. Multiple queries considered. Pays in royalties. E-mail: crosscult@aol.com. Web site: www.crossculturalpub.com.

THE CROSSING PRESS—P.O. Box 1048, Freedom, CA 95019. Elaine Goldman Gill, Pub. Natural and alternative health, spirituality, personal growth, self-help, empowerment, and cookbooks. Royalty. E-mail: elaine@crossing press.com. Web site: www.crossingpress.com.

CROWN BOOKS FOR YOUNG READERS—1540 Broadway, 19th Fl., New York, NY 10036. Children's nonfiction (science, sports, nature, music, and history) and picture books for ages 3 and up. Send complete manuscript and SASE for picture books to: Submissions Editorial Dept.

CUMBERLAND HOUSE PUBLISHING—431 Harding Industrial Dr., Nashville, TN 37211. Tilly Katz, Ed. Adult nonfiction, to 100,000 words, and mysteries. Query with outline and sample chapters. Royalty.

CURBSTONE PRESS—321 Jackson St., Willimantic, CT 06226. Alexander Taylor, Pub./Ed. Fiction, nonfiction, poetry books, and picture books that reflect a commitment to social change, with an emphasis on contemporary writing from Latin America and Latino communities in the U.S. Agented material only. Royalty.

DA CAPO PRESS—10 East 53rd St., 19th Fl., New York, NY 10022. Andrea Schulz, Sr. Ed. Trade nonfiction including performing arts and history. Query with outline and sample chapters. Pays on royalty basis.

DALKEY ARCHIVE PRESS—Illinois State Univ., Campus Box 4241, Normal, IL 61790-4241. John O'Brien, Sr. Ed. Avant-garde, experimental fiction, publishes only reprints "of the highest literary quality." No unsolicited manuscripts.

DANIEL AND COMPANY, JOHN—P.O. Box 21922, Santa Barbara, CA 93121. John Daniel, Pub. Books, to 200 pages, in the field of belles lettres and literary memoirs; stylish and elegant writing; essays and short fiction dealing with social issues; one poetry title per year. Send synopsis or outline with no more than 50 sample pages and SASE. Allow 6 to 8 weeks for response. Royalty. E-mail: dandd@danielpublishing.com. Web site: www.danielpub lishing.com.

DAVIES-BLACK PUBLISHING—3803 E. Bayshore Rd., Palo Alto, CA 94303. Alan R. Shrader, Acquisitions Dir. Books, 250 to 400 manuscript pages. Professional and trade titles in business and careers. Web site: www.cppdb.com.

DAVIS PUBLICATIONS, INC.—50 Portland St., Worcester, MA 01608. Books, 100 to 300 manuscript pages, for the art education market; mainly for teachers of art, grades K through 12. Must have an educational component. Grades K through 8, address Claire M. Golding; grades 9 through 12, address Helen Ronan. Query with outline and sample chapters. Royalty.

DAW BOOKS, INC.—375 Hudson St., 3rd Fl., New York, NY 10014-3658. Elizabeth R. Wollheim, Pres. & Pub. Sheila E. Gilbert, Exec. V.P. & Pub.

Peter Stampfel, Submissions Ed. Science fiction and fantasy, 85,000 words and up. No short stories, collections, or anthologies. Royalty. E-mail: daw@pen guinputnam.com. Web site: www.dawbooks.com.

DAWN PUBLICATIONS—P.O. Box 2010, Nevada City, CA 95959. Glenn J. Hovemann, Ed. Dept. Nature awareness books for children. Children's picture books with a positive, uplifting message to awaken a sense of appreciation and kinship with nature. For children's works, submit complete manuscript with SASE and specify intended age. Royalty. See web site for guidelines: www.dawnpub.com.

DAYBREAK BOOKS—Rodale, Inc., 400 S. 10th St., Emmaus, PA 18098. Neil Wertheimer, Ed. Four main categories: motivation, inspiration, self-help, and spiritual. Thematic interests include grief/loss, loneliness, and relationships. Send proposal, bio, table of contents, and two or three sample chapters to Sally A. Reith, Acq. Ed. Flat fee.

DEARBORN FINANCIAL PUBLISHING, INC.—155 N. Wacker Dr., Chicago, IL 60606-1719. Carol Luitjens, V.P. Cynthia Zigmund, Ed. Dir. Professional and consumer books and courses on financial services, real estate, banking, small business, investing, etc. Query with outline and sample chapters. Royalty and flat fee.

DEE PUBLISHER, INC., IVAN R.—1332 N. Halsted St., Chicago, IL 60622-2637. Ivan R. Dee, Pres. Nonfiction books on history, politics, biography, literature, and theater. Query with outline and sample chapters. Royalty. E-mail: elephant@ivanrdee.com. Web site: www.ivanrdee.com.

DEL REY BOOKS—1540 Broadway, 11th Fl.-J, New York, NY 10036. Shelly Shapiro, Ed. Dir. Steve Saffel and Chris Schluep, Eds. Science fiction and fantasy, 60,000 to 120,000 words; first novelists welcome. No unsolicited submissions. Royalty. E-mail: delrey@randomhouse.com. See Web site for details: www.randomhouse.com/delrey.

DELACORTE PRESS—Bantam Dell Publishing, 1540 Broadway, New York, NY 10036. Jackie Cantor, Tom Spain, Eds. General adult fiction and nonfiction. Accepts material from agents only. Web site: www.random house.com.

DELACORTE PRESS BOOKS FOR YOUNG READERS—1540 Broadway, New York, NY 10036. Attn: Ed. Dept. Unsolicited young adult manuscripts are accepted only for the Delacorte Press Prize for a first young adult novel. This must be a work of fiction written for ages 12 to 18, by a previously unpublished author. Send SASE for rules and guidelines.

DELL BOOKS—1540 Broadway, New York, NY 10036. Commercial fiction (including romance, mystery, and westerns) and nonfiction (including health, war, and spirituality). Agented submissions only.

DEVIN-ADAIR PUBLISHERS, INC.—P.O. Box A, Old Greenwich, CT 06870. J. Andrassi, Ed. Books on conservative affairs, Irish topics, photography, Americana, self-help, health, gardening, cooking, and ecology. Send outline, sample chapters, and SASE. Royalty.

DIAL BOOKS FOR YOUNG READERS—345 Hudson St., New York, NY 10014. Garen Thomas, Ed. Lively, unique picture books for children ages 2 to 4, and some middle-grade novels. Send complete manuscript for picture books; outline and two sample chapters for novels.

DIAL PRESS—1540 Broadway, New York, NY 10036. Susan Kamil, VP & Ed. Dir. Quality fiction and nonfiction. *No unsolicited material.* Web site: www.randomhouse.com.

DIMI PRESS—3820 Oak Hollow Ln. S.E., Salem, OR 97302-4774. Dick Lutz, Pres. Books on unusual things in nature, e.g., unique animals, different cultures, astonishing natural events or disasters. Also, books on travel (no travel guides). Query. Royalty. E-mail: dickbook@earthlink.net. Web site: www. members.aol.com/dickbook/dimipress.html.

DK INK—Imprint of Dorling Kindersley, 95 Madison Ave., New York, NY 10016. Neal Porter, VP & Pub. Picture books and fiction for middle-grade and older readers. Send outline and sample chapter. Payment in royalty or flat fees.

DOMAIN—See *Bantam, Doubleday, Dell.*

DOUBLEDAY AND CO.—Division of *Bantam Doubleday Dell,* 1540 Broadway, New York, NY 10036. Stephen Rubin, Pub./Pres. Proposals from literary agents only. No unsolicited material.

DUETS—See *Harlequin Books/Canada.*

DUNNE BOOKS, THOMAS—175 Fifth Ave., New York, NY 10010. Thomas L. Dunne, Ed. Adult fiction (mysteries, trade, etc.) and nonfiction (history, biographies, science, politics, humor, etc.). Query with outline, sample chapters, and SASE. Royalty.

DUQUESNE UNIVERSITY PRESS—600 Forbes Ave., Pittsburgh, PA 15282. Attn: Ed. Dept. Scholarly publications in the humanities and social sciences; creative nonfiction (book-length only) by emerging writers. Send SASE for guidelines. Web site: www.dug.edu/dupress.

DUTTON CHILDREN'S BOOKS—345 Hudson St., New York, NY 10014. Lucia Monfried, Assoc. Pub. & Ed.-in-Chief. Picture books, easy-to-read books; fiction and nonfiction for preschoolers to young adults. No unsolicited submissions.

EAKIN PRESS—P.O. Drawer 90159, Austin, TX 78709-0159. Melissa Roberts, Sr. Ed. Adult nonfiction, 60,000 to 80,000 words: Texana, regional cookbooks, Mexico and the Southwest, WWII, military. Children's books: history, culture, geography, etc., of Texas and the Southwest. Juvenile picture books, 5,000 to 10,000 words; fiction, 20,000 to 30,000 words; young adult fiction, 25,000 to 40,000 words. Query; responds in 90 days. Royalty. E-mail: eakinpub@sig.net.

EASTERN WASHINGTON UNIVERSITY PRESS—Mail Stop 1, Eastern Washington Univ., 705 W. 1st Ave., Spokane, WA 99201. Attn: Eds. Literary essays, history, social commentary, and other academic subjects. Limited fiction and well-researched historical novels (one title every 2 years or so). One or 2 books of poetry, 60 to 150 pages, each year. "We are a small regional university press, publishing titles that reflect our regional service, our international contacts, our strong creative writing program, and research and interests of our exceptional faculty." Send complete manuscript, query with outline, or Mac-compatible diskette. Royalty.

EERDMANS PUBLISHING COMPANY, INC., WM. B.—255 Jefferson Ave. S.E., Grand Rapids, MI 49503. Jon Pott, Ed.-in-Chief. Protestant, Roman Catholic, and Orthodox theological nonfiction; religious history and biography; ethics; philosophy; literary studies; spiritual growth. For children's religious books, query Judy Zylstra, Ed., Eerdmans Books for Young Readers. Royalty.

ELEMENT BOOKS—160 North Washington St., 4th Floor, Boston, MA 02114. Holly Schmidt, Acquisitions Ed. Books on world religions, ancient wisdom, astrology, meditation, women's studies, and alternative health and healing. Study recent catalogue. Query with outline and sample chapters. Royalty. No phone calls, please. E-mail: publishers@elementboston.com.

ELEMENT CHILDREN'S BOOKS—160 N. Washington St., 4th Fl., Boston, MA 02114. Barry Cunningham, Ed. Publishes picture books (ages 4 to 8) and nonfiction books for ages 8 and up. Send SASE and queries to editor. Payment is made on a royalty basis. Web site: www.elementbooks.com.

ENCANTO—See *Kensington Publishing Corp.*

ENSLOW PUBLISHERS, INC.—P.O. Box 398, 40 Industrial Rd., Berkeley Heights, NJ 07922-0398. Brian D. Enslow, Ed./Pub. No fiction; nonfiction books for young people only. Areas of emphasis are children's and young adult books for ages 10 to 18 in the fields of social studies, science, and biography. Also reference books for all ages and easy reading books for teenagers.

ENTREPRENEUR BOOKS—2445 McCabe Way, Irvine, CA 92614. Marla Markman, Man. Ed. Trade paperbacks, 80,000 words, and business start-up guides, 30,000 to 60,000 words. Include sidebars, information boxes, and graphics. Topics include raising money, sales and marketing, staffing, etc. Payment varies from $6,000 to $15,000 (depending on type of book), with half as an advance and half upon completion of the manuscript.

EPICENTER PRESS—P.O. Box 82368, Kenmore, WA 98028. Kent Sturgis, Pub. Quality nonfiction trade books, contemporary western art and photography titles, emphasizing Alaska. "We are a regional press whose interests include but are not limited to the arts, history, environment, and diverse cultures and lifestyles of the North Pacific and high latitudes."

ERIKSSON, PUBLISHER, PAUL S.—P.O. Box 125, Forest Dale, VT 05745. Attn: Ed. Dept. General nonfiction (send outline and cover letter); some fiction (send 3 chapters with an SASE and query). Royalty.

EVANS & CO., INC., M.—216 E. 49th St., New York, NY 10017. Attn: Ed. Dept. Books on health, self-help, popular psychology, and cookbooks. Limited list of commercial fiction. Query with outline, sample chapter, and SASE. Royalty. E-mail: mevans@3prynet.com.

EVENT HORIZON PRESS—P.O. Box 2006, Palm Springs, CA 92263. Joseph Cowles, Pub. Adult fiction and nonfiction. Currently overstocked; no unsolicited manuscripts.

EXCALIBUR PUBLICATIONS—P.O. Box 35369, Tucson, AZ 85740-5369. Alan M. Petrillo, Ed. Books on military history, firearms history, antique arms and accessories, military personalities, tactics and strategy, history of battles. Query with outline and 1st chapter with any two other consecutive chapters. SASE. Royalty or flat fee.

FACTS ON FILE, INC.—11 Penn Plaza, New York, NY 10001. Reference and trade books on science, health, literature, language, history, the performing arts, ethnic studies, popular culture, sports, etc. (No fiction, poetry, computer books, technical books or cookbooks.) Query with outline, sample chapter, and SASE. Royalty. Hardcover.

FAIRVIEW PRESS—2450 Riverside Ave. S., Minneapolis, MN 55454. Lane Stiles, Dir. Stephanie Billecke, Ed. Adult books, 80,000 words, on aging, grief & bereavement, health, medicine, and patient education. Query with outline and sample chapters. Royalty. E-mail: press@webx.fairview.org. Web site: www.fairview.press.org.

FARRAR, STRAUS & GIROUX—19 Union Sq. W., New York, NY 10003. Adult and juvenile literary fiction and nonfiction.

FREDERICK FELL PUBLISHERS, INC.—(formerly *Lifetime Books, Inc.*) 2131 Hollywood Blvd., Hollywood, FL 33020. Virginia Wells, Sr. Ed. Nonfiction (200 to 300 pages): general interest, how-to, self-help, cooking, hobby, business, health, and inspiration. Query with letter or outline and sample chapter, SASE. Royalty. Send 9x12 SASE with 5 first-class stamps for catalogue.

THE FEMINIST PRESS AT THE CITY UNIVERSITY OF NEW YORK—The Graduate School & University Center, 365 Fifth Ave, New York, NY 10016. Florence Howe, Pub. Reprints of significant "lost" fiction, original memoirs, autobiographies, biographies; multicultural anthologies; handbooks; bibliographies. "We are especially interested in international literature, women and peace, women and music, and women of color." Royalty. Web site: www. feministpress.org.

FIREBRAND BOOKS—141 The Commons, Ithaca, NY 14850. Nancy K. Bereano, Ed. Feminist and lesbian fiction and nonfiction. Royalty. Paperback and library edition cloth.

FIRESIDE BOOKS—1230 Ave. of the Americas, New York, NY 10020. No unsolicited manuscripts.

FIRST STORY PRESS—1800 Business Park Dr., Suite 205, Clarksville, TN 37040. Judith Pierson, Ed. Children's picture books of varying lengths. Currently overstocked.

FODOR'S TRAVEL GUIDES—201 E. 50th St., New York, NY 10022. Karen Cure, Ed. Dir. Travel guides for both foreign and US destinations. "For our Gold Guides, our flagship series, we generally hire writers who live in the area they will write about or who have a very intimate knowledge of the area they will cover; we're open to new ideas beyond our Gold Guides as well." Gold Guides follow established format. Send writing sample, and, for proposals for new books, a sample chapter, outline, and statement about your guide's intended audience. Email: kcure@randomhouse.com. Web site: www. fodors.com.

FORGE—Tom Doherty Associates, 175 Fifth Ave., 14th Fl., New York, NY 10010. Melissa Ann Singer, Sr. Ed. General fiction; limited nonfiction, from 80,000 words. Query with complete synopsis and first 3 chapters to William Smith, Ed. Asst. Advance and royalty.

FORUM—c/o Prima Publishing, 3000 Lava Ridge Ct., Roseville, CA 95661. Steven Martin, Pub. Serious nonfiction books on current affairs, business, public policy, libertarian/conservative thought, high-level management, individual empowerment, and historical biography. Submit outline and sample chapters. Royalty.

FREE SPIRIT PUBLISHING—400 First Ave. N., Suite 616, Minneapolis, MN 55401-1724. Katrina Wentzel, Ed. Asst. Nonfiction self-help for kids and teens, with an emphasis on school success, self-awareness, self-esteem, creativity, social action, life skills, and special needs. Creative classroom activities for teachers; adult books on raising, counseling, or educating children. Queries only. Request free catalog and guidelines. Advance and royalty. E-mail: help4kids@freespirit.com. Web site: www.freespirit.com.

FRONT STREET BOOKS, INC.—20 Battery Park Ave., #403, Asheville, NC 28801. Stephen Roxburgh, Pres./Pub. Fiction, poetry, and picture books for children and young adults. Query with sample chapters. Royalty. E-mail: staff@frontstreetbooks.com. Web site: www.frontstreetbooks.com.

FRONT STREET/CRICKET BOOKS—Imprint of *Front Street,* 332 S. Michigan Ave., Suite 1100, Chicago, IL 60604. Submissions Ed. Novels for readers 7 to 12. Please send complete manuscripts. Pays royalties. Web site: www.cricketbooks.net.

FULCRUM PUBLISHING—16100 Table Mountain Parkway, Suite 300, Golden, CO 80403. Attn: Submissions Dept. Adult trade nonfiction: gardening, travel, nature, history, education, and Native American culture; focus on western regional topics. No fiction. Send cover letter, sample chapters, table of contents, author credentials, and market analysis. Royalty.

GERINGER BOOKS, LAURA—See *HarperCollins Children's Books.*

GIBBS SMITH PUBLISHER—P.O. Box 667, Layton, UT 84041. Madge Baird, Ed. Dir. Adult nonfiction. Query. Royalty. Web site: www.gibbs-smith.com.

GIBBS SMITH, JUNIOR—P.O. Box 667, Layton, UT 84041. Suzanne Taylor, Ed. Juvenile books: western/cowboy; activity; how-to; nature/environment; and humor. Fiction picture books, to 1,000 words; nonfiction books, to 10,000 words, for readers 4 to 12. Royalty. No e-mail submissions, please. Web site: www.gibbs-smith.com.

GINIGER CO. INC., THE K.S.—250 W. 57th St., Suite 414, New York, NY 10107. Attn: Ed. Dept. General nonfiction. Query with SASE; no unsolicited manuscripts. Royalty.

GLOBE PEQUOT PRESS, THE—6 Business Park Rd., Box 833, Old Saybrook, CT 06475. Elizabeth Taylor, Submissions Ed. Nonfiction with national and regional focus; travel; outdoor recreation; home-based business. Query with sample chapter, contents, and one-page synopsis. SASE required. Royalty or flat fee.

GODINE PUBLISHER, DAVID R.—9 Hamilton Place, Boston, MA 02108. No unsolicited manuscripts. Royalty. E-mail: infor@godine.com. Web site: www.godine.com.

GOLD EAGLE—See *Worldwide Library.*

GOLDEN BOOKS FAMILY ENTERTAINMENT—888 Seventh Ave., New York, NY 10106-4100. Ed. Children's fiction and nonfiction: picture books, storybooks, concept books, novelty books. No unsolicited manuscripts. Royalty or flat fee.

GOLDEN WEST PUBLISHERS—4113 N. Longview, Phoenix, AZ 85014. Hal Mitchell, Ed. Cookbooks and nonfiction Western history and travel books. Currently seeking writers for state and regional cookbooks. Query. Royalty or flat fee. E-mail: goldwest@goodnet.com. Web site: www.goldenwest publishers.com.

GRAYWOLF PRESS—2402 University Ave., Suite 203, St. Paul, MN 55114. Attn: Ed. Dept. Literary fiction (short story collections and novels), poetry, and essays. No e-mail submissions. Web site: www.graywolfpress.org.

GREAT QUOTATIONS—1967 Quincy Ct., Glendale Heights, IL 60139. Diane Voreis, Ed. General adult titles, 80 to 365 pages, with strong, clever, descriptive titles and brief, upbeat text. "We publish small, quick-read gift books." Query with outline and sample chapters or send complete manuscript. Royalty.

GREEN LIGHT READERS—See *Harcourt Inc./Children's Book Div.*

GREENWILLOW BOOKS—Imprint of *HarperCollins Children's Books,* 1350 Ave. of the Americas, New York, NY 10019. Susan Hirschman, Pub. Children's books for all ages. Picture books.

GROSSET AND DUNLAP, INC.—Div. of Putnam Publishing Group, 345 Hudson St., New York, NY 10014. Jane O'Connor, Pub. Mass-market children's books. Not currently accepting unsolicited manuscripts. Royalty.

GROVE/ATLANTIC MONTHLY PRESS—841 Broadway, 4th Fl., New York, NY 10003-4793. Morgan Entrekin, Pub. Distinguished fiction and nonfiction. Query; no unsolicited manuscripts. Royalty.

GRYPHON HOUSE, INC.—P.O. Box 207, Beltsville, MD 20705. Kathy Charner, Ed.-in-Chief. Resource books, 150 to 500 pages, for parents and teachers of young children from birth to 8 years old. Query with outline and sample chapters. Royalty.

GULLIVER BOOKS—See *Harcourt Inc./Children's Book Div.*

HACHAI PUBLISHING—156 Chester Ave., Brooklyn, NY 11218. Dina Rosenfeld, Ed. Full-color children's picture books, 32 pages, for readers ages 2 to 8; Judaica, Bible tales. Query or send complete manuscript. Flat fee. E-mail: info@hachai.com. Web site: www.hachai.com.

HAMBLETON-HILL PUBLISHING—See *Ideals Children's Books.*

HANCOCK HOUSE PUBLISHERS, LTD.—1431 Harrison Ave., Blaine, WA 98230. Attn: Ed. Dept. Adult nonfiction: guidebooks, biographies, natural history, popular science, conservation, animal husbandry, and falconry. Some juvenile nonfiction. Query with outline and sample chapters or send complete manuscript. Multiple queries considered. Royalty. E-mail: sales@ hancockhouse.com. Web sites: www.hancockhouse.com or www.hancock wildlife.org.

HARCOURT BRACE BIG BOOKS—See *Harcourt Inc./Children's Book Div.*

HARCOURT BRACE PROFESSIONAL PUBLISHING—525 B St., Suite 1900, San Diego, CA 92101-4495. Attn: Sidney Bernstein, V.P. & Pub. Professional books for practitioners in accounting, auditing, tax and financial planning, law, business management. Query. Royalty and work-for-hire. E-mail: sbernstein@harcourt.com. Web site: www.harcourt.com.

HARCOURT CHILDREN'S BOOKS—See *Harcourt Inc./Children's Book Div.*

HARCOURT INC.—525 B St., Suite 1900, San Diego, CA 92101. Attn:

Ed. Dept. No unsolicited manuscripts, queries, or illustrations for adult or children's books.

HARCOURT INC./CHILDREN'S BOOK DIV.—(formerly *Harcourt Brace & Co. Children's Book Div.)* 525 B St., Suite 1900, San Diego, CA 92101-4495. Juvenile fiction and nonfiction for beginning readers through young adults under the following imprints: *Gulliver Books, Red Wagon Books, Odyssey Classics, Silver Whistle, Magic Carpet Books, Harcourt Children's Books, Harcourt Young Classics, Green Light Readers, Harcourt Paperbacks, Voyager Books/Libros Viajeros.* No unsolicited submissions or queries.

HARCOURT PAPERBACKS—See *Harcourt Inc./Children's Book Div.*

HARCOURT YOUNG CLASSICS—See *Harcourt Inc./Children's Book Div.*

HARLEQUIN BOOKS/CANADA—225 Duncan Mill Rd., Don Mills, Ont., Canada M3B 3K9. Randall Toye, Ed. Dir. *Mira Books*: Dianne Moggy, Ed. Dir. Contemporary women's fiction, to 100,000 words. Query. *Harlequin Superromance*: Paula Eykelhof, Sr. Ed. Contemporary romance, to 85,000 words, with a mainstream edge. Query. *Harlequin Temptation*: Birgit Davis-Todd, Sr. Ed. Sensuous, humorous contemporary romances, to 60,000 words. *Duets*: Birgit Davis-Todd, Sr. Ed. The lighter side of love, to 55,000 words. Query.

HARLEQUIN BOOKS/U.S.—300 E. 42nd St., 6th Fl., New York, NY 10017. Denise O'Sullivan, Assoc. Sr. Ed. Contemporary romances, 70,000 to 75,000 words. Send for tip sheets, SASE. *Harlequin American Romances*, Melissa Jeglinski, Assoc. Sr. Ed.: bold, exciting romantic adventures, "where anything is possible and dreams come true." *Harlequin Intrigue*, Denise O'Sullivan, Assoc. Sr. Ed.: set against a backdrop of mystery and suspense, worldwide locales. Query. Paperback.

HARPER SAN FRANCISCO—353 Sacramento St., Suite 500, San Francisco, CA 94111-3653. Attn: Acquisitions Ed. Books on spirituality and religion. No unsolicited manuscripts; query required.

HARPERCOLLINS CHILDREN'S BOOKS—1350 Ave. of the Americas, New York, NY 10019. Picture books, chapter books, and fiction and nonfiction for middle-grade and young adult readers. "Our imprints (*Avon, HarperFestival, HarperTempest, HarperTrophy, Joanna Cotler Books, Laura Geringer Books,* and *Greenwillow Books*) are committed to producing imaginative and responsible children's books. All publish from preschool to young adult titles." Guidelines. Royalty.

HARPERCOLLINS PUBLISHERS—10 E. 53rd St., New York, NY 10022-5299. Adult Trade Department: Address Man. Ed. Fiction, nonfiction (biography, history, etc.), reference. Submissions from agents only. College texts: Address College Dept. No unsolicited manuscripts; query only.

HARPERCOLLINS SAN FRANCISCO—See *Harper San Francisco.*

HARPERFESTIVAL—See *HarperCollins Children's Books*

HARPERPRISM—10 E. 53rd St., New York, NY 10022-5299. John Douglas, Exec. Ed. Science fiction/fantasy. No unsolicited manuscripts; query.

HARPERTEMPEST—See *HarperCollins Children's Books.*

HARPERTROPHY—See *HarperCollins Children's Books.*

HARVARD COMMON PRESS—535 Albany St., Boston, MA 02118.

Bruce Shaw, Pub. Adult nonfiction: cookbooks, travel guides, books on child-care and parenting, health, small business, etc. Send outline, analysis of competing books, and sample chapters or complete manuscript. SASE. Royalty.

HARVARD UNIVERSITY PRESS—79 Garden St., Cambridge, MA 02138-1499. Mary Ann Lane, Managing Ed. No free-lance submissions: "We hire no writers." Web site: www.hup.harvard.edu.

HATHERLEIGH PRESS—5–22 46 Ave., Suite 200, Long Island, NY 11101. Kevin Moran, Ed. Nonfiction on health, fitness, and self-help. Query with sample chapter and SASE. Multiple queries considered. Pays royalties or flat fee. E-mail: kevin@hatherleigh.com. Web site: www.hatherleigh.com.

HAWORTH PRESS, INC.—10 Alice St., Binghamton, NY 13904-1580. Bill Palmer, Ed. Scholarly press interested in research-based adult nonfiction: psychology, social work, gay and lesbian studies, women's studies, family and marriage; some recreation and entertainment. Send outline with sample chapters or complete manuscript. Royalty.

HAY HOUSE—P.O. Box 5100, Carlsbad, CA 92018-5100. Attn: Ed. Dir. Self-help books on health, self-awareness, spiritual growth, astrology, psychology, philosophy, women's and men's issues, metaphysics, and the environment. Query with outline, a few sample chapters, and SASE. Royalties. E-mail: jkramer@hayhouse.com. Web site: www.hayhouse.com.

HAZELDEN EDUCATIONAL MATERIALS—Box 176, Center City, MN 55012. Self-help books, curricula, videos, audios, and pamphlets relating to addiction, recovery, spirituality, mental health, chronic illness, family issues, and wholeness. Query with outline and sample chapters. Multiple queries considered. Royalty.

HEALTH COMMUNICATIONS, INC.—3201 S.W. 15th St., Deerfield Beach, FL 33442. Christine Belleris, Ed. Dir. Books, 250 pages, on self-help, recovery, inspiration, and personal growth for adults. Query with outline and 2 sample chapters and SASE. Royalty. E-mail: editorial@hcibooks.com. Web site: www.hci-online.com.

HEALTH PRESS—P.O. Box 1388, Santa Fe, NM 87504. K. Schwartz, Ed. Health-related adult and children's books, 100 to 300 pages. "We're seeking cutting-edge, original manuscripts that will excite, educate, and help readers." Author must have credentials, or preface/intro must be written by M.D., Ph.D., etc. Controversial topics are desired; must be well researched and documented. Submit outline, table of contents, and first chapter with SASE. Royalty.

HEARST BOOKS—See *William Morrow and Co., Inc.*

HEARTSONG PRESENTS—Barbour Publishing, Inc., P.O. Box 719, Uhrichsville, OH 44683. Rebecca Germany, Man. Ed. Contemporary and historical romances, 50,000 to 55,000 words, that present a conservative, evangelical Christian world view. Pays flat fee. E-mail: info@heartsongpresents.com. Web site: www.barbourbooks.com.

HEBREW UNION COLLEGE PRESS—3101 Clifton Ave., Cincinnati, OH 45220. Barbara Selya, Ed. Scholarly books, 200 pages, on very specific topics in Judaic studies. "Our usual print run is 500 books, and our target audience is mainly rabbis and professors." Query with outline and sample chapters. No payment. E-mail: hucpress@huc.edu.

HEINEMANN—361 Hanover St., Portsmouth, NH 03801. Attn: Ed.

Dept. Practical theatre, drama education, professional education, K-12, and literacy education. Query. Web site: www.heinemann.com or www.heinemann drama.com.

HEMINGWAY WESTERN STUDIES SERIES—Boise State University, 1910 University Dr., Boise, ID 83725. Tom Trusky, Ed. Artists' and eccentric format books (multiple editions) relating to Rocky Mountain environment, race, religion, gender and other public issues. Guidelines.

HIGGINSON BOOK COMPANY—148 Washington St., Salem, MA 01970. Attn: Ed. Dept. Nonfiction genealogy and local history only, 20 to 1,000 pages. Specializes in reprints. Query. Royalty. E-mail: higginsn@cove.com. Web site: www.higginsonbooks.com.

HIGHSMITH PRESS—P.O. Box 800, Fort Atkinson, WI 53538-0800. Donald Sager, Pub. Adult books, 80 to 200 pages, on professional library science and education. Teacher activity and curriculum resource books, 48 to 240 pages, for pre-K through 12. Query with outline and sample chapters. Royalty. Guidelines available at web site: www.hpress.highsmith.com. E-mail: hpress@ highsmith.com.

HIPPOCRENE BOOKS—171 Madison Ave., New York, NY 10016. George Blagowidow, Ed. Dir. Language instruction books and foreign language dictionaries, international cookbooks, travel guides, military history, Polish interest books. Send outline and sample chapters with SASE for reply. Multiple queries considered. Royalty. Web site: www.hippocrenebooks.com.

HOLIDAY HOUSE, INC.—425 Madison Ave., New York, NY 10017. Michelle Troy, V.P. General juvenile fiction and nonfiction. Query with SASE. Royalty. Hardcover only.

HOLT AND CO., HENRY—115 W. 18th St., New York, NY 10011. Distinguished works of biography, history, fiction, and natural history; humor; child activity books; parenting books; books for the entrepreneurial business person; and health books. "Virtually all submissions come from literary agents or from writers whom we publish."

HOME BUILDER PRESS—National Assoc. of Home Builders, 1201 15th St. N.W., Washington, DC 20005-2800. Doris M. Tennyson, Sr. Acquisitions Ed. How-to and business management books, 150 to 200 manuscript pages, for builders, remodelers, developers, other building industry professionals, and consumers. Writers should be experts in homebuilding, remodeling, land development, sales, marketing, or related aspects of the building industry. Query with outline and sample chapter. Royalty. For author's packet TW look on the web site: www.builderbooks.com. E-mail: dtennyson@nahb.com.

HOMESTEAD PUBLISHING—P.O. Box 193, Moose, WY 83012. Carl Schreier, Pub. Fiction, guidebooks, art, history, natural history, and biography. Royalty.

HORIZON BOOKS—Christian Publications, 3825 Hartzdale Dr., Camp Hill, PA 17011. George McPeek, Ed. Adult and young adult nonfiction, from 35,000 to 50,000 words, on a variety of topics from an evangelical Christian perspective. Query; multiple queries considered. Pays in royalties.

HOUGHTON MIFFLIN COMPANY—222 Berkeley St., Boston, MA 02116-3764. Attn: Ed. Dept. Fiction: literary, historical. Nonfiction: history, biography, psychology. No unsolicited submissions. Children's book division, address Children's Trade Books: picture books, fiction, and nonfiction for all ages. Query. Royalty.

HOWELL PRESS—1713–2D Allied Ln., Charlottesville, VA 22903. Ed. Nonfiction, especially history, transportation, cooking, gardening, motor sports, aviation, regional topics, Civil War, and quilting. Query with outline and sample chapters; multiple queries are considered. Imprint: *Rockbridge Publishing*. Pays either royalty or flat fee, as negotiated. E-mail: howellpress@aol.com. Web site: www.howellpress.com.

HP BOOKS—375 Hudson St., New York, NY 10014. Attn: Ed. Dept. How-tos on cooking, automotive topics. Query with SASE.

HUMANICS PUBLISHING GROUP—P.O. Box 7400, Atlanta, GA 30357. W. Arthur Bligh, Acquisitions Ed. Inspiring trade books, 100 to 300 pages: self-help, spiritual, instructional, philosophy, and health for body, mind, and soul. Also, children's educational books/teacher resource guides for grades K through 6. "We are interested in books that people go to for help, guidance, and inspiration." Query with outline and SASE required. Royalty. E-mail: dshadovitz@lrp.com. Web site: www.hrexecutive.com.

HUNGRY MIND PRESS—See *Ruminator Books.*

HUNTER HOUSE PUBLISHERS—P.O. Box 2914, Alameda, CA 94501-0914. Nonfiction for health, family, and community. Topics include health, women's health, personal growth, sexuality and relationships, violence intervention and prevention, and counseling resources. Send for guidelines. E-mail: acquisitions@hunterhouse.com. Web site: www.hunterhouse.com.

HUNTER PUBLISHING, INC.—130 Campus Dr., Edison, NJ 08818. Kim André, Acquisitions Dept. Travel guides to the U.S., South America, and the Caribbean. E-mail: hunterp@bellsouth.net. Web site: www.hunterpublishing.com.

HYSTERIA PUBLICATIONS—Div. of *Sourcebooks, Inc.,* P.O. Box 38581, Bridgeport, CT 06605. Deborah Werksman, Ed. Humorous books that are "progressive, provocative, liberating, funny, and insightful," 96 to 112 finished pages. Also acquires gift, self-help, parenting, business, and media for *Sourcebooks.* Query with sample chapters or complete manuscript. SASE for guidelines. Royalty. E-mail: laugh@hysteriabooks.com. Web site: www.hysteriabooks.com.

IDEALS CHILDREN'S BOOKS—Imprint of Hambleton-Hill Publishing, 1501 County Hospital Rd., Nashville, TN 37218. Seeks only submissions from members of the Society of Children's Book Writers and Illustrators, agented authors, and previously published writers submitting with a list of writing credits. E-mail: publish@aol.com.

IMPACT PUBLISHERS, INC.—P.O. Box 6016, Atascadero, CA 93423-6016. Attn: Acquisitions Ed. Popular and professional psychology books, from 200 pages. Personal growth, relationships, families, communities, and health for adults. Children's books for "Little Imp" series on issues of self-esteem. "Writers must have advanced degrees and professional experience in human-service fields." Query with outline and sample chapters. Royalty. E-mail: editor@impactpublishers.com. Web site: www.impactpublishers.com.

INNER TRADITIONS INTERNATIONAL, INC.—One Park St., Rochester, VT 05767. Jon Graham, Acquisitions Ed. Books representing the spiritual, cultural, and mythic traditions of the world, focusing on inner wisdom and the perennial philosophies and alternative modalities of healing. Query. Royalty. E-mail: jon@innertraditions.com or submissions@innertraditions.com. Web site: www.innertraditions.com.

INNISFREE PRESS, INC.—136 Roumfort Rd., Philadelphia, PA 19119-1632. Marcia Broucek, Ed. Adult nonfiction, from 40,000 to 60,000 words, on spiritual issues. "No fiction, poetry, or disease 'survival' stories." Accepts multiple queries and pays on a royalty basis. Query with outline and sample chapters. E-mail: innisfreep@aol.com. Web site: www.innisfree press.com.

INSTRUCTOR BOOKS—See *Scholastic Professional Books.*

INTERNATIONAL MARINE—Div. of McGraw-Hill, Box 220, Camden, ME 04843. Jonathan Eaton, Ed. Dir. Books on boating (sailing and power). Imprint: *Seven Seas Press.*

INTIMATE MOMENTS—See *Silhouette Books.*

IRONWEED PRESS—P.O. Box 754208, Parkside Station, Forest Hills, NY 11375. Attn: Ed. Multicultural fiction, especially Asian fiction, to 50,000 words. Biographies and scholarly works, same length. Accepts multiple queries and pays on a royalty basis. Query with outline, sample chapters, or complete manuscript.

ISLAND PRESS—1718 Connecticut Ave. N.W., Suite 300, Washington, DC 20009. Dan Sayre, Ed.-in-Chief. Nonfiction focusing on natural history, literary science, the environment, and natural resource management. "We want solution-oriented material to solve environmental problems. For our imprint, *Shearwater Books*, we want books that express new insights about nature and the environment." Query or send manuscript. SASE required.

JAI PRESS, INC.—100 Prospect St., P.O. Box 811, Stamford, CT 06904. Roger A. Dunn, Man. Dir. & Pub. Research and technical reference books on such subjects as business, economics, management, sociology, political science, computer science, life sciences, and chemistry. Query or send complete manuscript. Royalty. E-mail: r.a.dunn@elsevier.com. Web site: www.jai-ablex.com.

JALMAR PRESS—P.O. Box 1185, Torrance, CA 90505. Dr. Bradley L. Winch, Pub. Nonfiction books for parents, teachers, and caregivers. No picture books. "Our emphasis is on helping children and adults live from the inside out so that they become personally and socially responsible." Special interest in peaceful conflict resolution, whole brain learning, self-esteem, emotional intelligence, stress management, and character education. Multiple queries considered. Submit outline. Royalty.

JAMES BOOKS, ALICE—Univ. of Maine at Farmington, 98 Main St., Farmington, ME 04938. Peg Peoples, Program Dir. Cooperative publishes books of poetry (48 to 72 pages) by writers through two annual competitions. The New England/New York Competition publishes manuscripts by writers living in New England (deadline is September); authors become active cooperative members. The Beatrice Hawley Competition is open to poets nationwide (deadline is December); authors do not become members. Also offers Jane Kenyon Chapbook Award (deadline June). "We emphasize the publication of poetry by women, but also welcome all manuscripts of high literary quality. Authors paid $1,000 award for NE/NY Award and Beatrice Hawley Award." Request guidelines with SASE. Web site: www.umf.maine.edu/~ajb.

JIST PUBLISHING—(formerly *Jist Works*) 8902 Otis Ave., Indianapolis, IN 46216-1033. Michael Cunningham, Ed.-in-Chief. Career and "life decision" books for people at all reading and academic levels. Also business, welfare-to-work titles, and trade topics for consumers. Query with outline and sample chapters. Payment made on a royalty or flat fee basis.

THE JOHNS HOPKINS UNIVERSITY PRESS—2715 N. Charles St., Baltimore, MD 21218. No unsolicited poetry or fiction considered.

JOHNSON BOOKS, INC.—1880 S. 57th Ct., Boulder, CO 80301. Stephen Topping, Ed. Dir. Nonfiction: environmental subjects, archaeology, geology, natural history, astronomy, travel guides, outdoor guidebooks, fly fishing, regional. Proposal. Royalty.

JONA BOOKS—P.O. Box 336, Bedford, IN 47421. Joe Glasgow, Ed. Nonfiction: biographies, Native American history, old west, and military history. Fiction: action adventure, alternative history, historical fiction, mysteries, and military science fiction. Contracts negotiated; no advances. SASE for guidelines. Web site: www.kiva.net/~jonabook. E-mail: jonabooks@kiva.net.

JONATHAN DAVID PUBLISHERS, INC.—68–22 Eliot Ave., Middle Village, NY 11379. Alfred J. Kolatch, Ed.-in-Chief. General nonfiction (how-to, sports, cooking and food, self-help, etc.) and books on Judaica. Query with outline, sample chapter, resumé, and SASE. Royalty or outright purchase. Web site: www.jdbooks.com.

JOURNEY BOOKS—Division of Bob Jones University Press, 1700 Wade Hampton Blvd., Greenville, SC 29614. Gloria Repp, Ed. Books for young readers, ages 6 to 12, that reflect "the highest Christian standards of thought, feeling, and action." Fiction, 8,000 to 40,000 words. Nonfiction, 10,000 to 30,000 words. Young adult books, 40,000 to 60,000 words. Read guidelines, then submit sample chapters. Pays on royalty or flat fee basis. E-mail: jb@bjup.com. Web site: www.bjup.com.

JOVE BOOKS—375 Hudson Street, New York, NY 10014. Fiction and nonfiction. No unsolicited manuscripts.

JUDSON PRESS—American Baptist Churches, P.O. Box 851, Valley Forge, PA 19482-0851. Randy Frame, Ed. Adult, juvenile, and young adult nonfiction of varying lengths. Publishes practical Christian resources for pastors and laity on church life, devotional materials, Baptist heritage and identity materials, and African American church resources. Query with proposal, table of contents, estimated length of book, sample chapters, target audience, expected completion date, and bio. Send for guidelines. Pays in royalties. Web site: www.judsonpress.com.

JUST US BOOKS—356 Glenwood Ave., East Orange, NJ 07017. No unsolicited material. E-mail: justusbooks@aol.com. Web site: www.justus books.com.

KALMBACH BOOKS—21027 Crossroads Cir., Waukesha, WI 53187. Dick Christianson, Ed.-in-Chief. Adult nonfiction, 18,000 to 50,000 words, on scale modeling, railroading, model railroading, and toy trains. Send outline with sample chapters. Accepts multiple queries. Royalty. E-mail: rchristianson@ kalmbach.com. Web site: www.kalmbachbooks.com.

KAR-BEN COPIES—6800 Tildenwood Ln., Rockville, MD 20852. Judye Groner, Ed. Books on Jewish themes for preschool and elementary children (to age 9): picture books, fiction, and nonfiction. Complete manuscript preferred; SASE. Royalty. Web site: www.karben.com.

KEATS PUBLISHING, INC.—2020 Ave. of the Stars, Suite 300, Los Angeles, CA 90067. Peter Hoffman, Sr. Ed. Health, nutrition, alternative and complimentary medicine, preventive health care, New Age, and spirituality. Royalty.

KENSINGTON PUBLISHING CORP.—(*Kensington Books, Pinnacle, Zebra* and *Arabesque* imprints) 850 Third Ave., 16th Fl., New York, NY 10022. Paul Dinas, Ed.-in-Chief. Ann LaFarge, Exec. Ed. Popular fiction; historical and contemporary romance, thrillers, true crime, alternative health, nonfiction. Regencies (80,000 words); *Ballad* historical romances (90–100,000 words); *Bouquet* contemporary romances (70–72,000 words); *Precious Gem* contemporary romances (50–55,000 words); Precious Gem historical romances (972,000 words); *Arabesque* multicultural romances (80–100,000 words); *Encanto* Hispanic romances in English & Spanish (50,000 words). Agented material only. SASE for guidelines. Web: www.kensingtonbooks.com.

KENT STATE UNIVERSITY PRESS—Kent State Univ., Kent, OH 44242. John T. Hubbell, Dir. Joanna Hildebrand Craig, Ed.-in-Chief. Interested in scholarly works in history and literary criticism of high quality, any titles of regional interest for Ohio, scholarly biographies, archaeological research, the arts, and general nonfiction. E-mail: jhildebr@kent.edu. Web site: www.bookmasters.com/ksu-press.

KIDS CAN PRESS—29 Birch Ave., Toronto, Ontario, Canada M4V 1E2. Acq. Ed. Picture books, 24 pages; juvenile nonfiction, 24 to 144 pages; and young adult novels, to 256 pages. Query with outline and sample chapters or complete manuscript with SASE (IRC coupon or postal order). Multiple queries considered. E-mail: info@kidscan.com.

KNOPF BOOKS FOR YOUNG READERS, ALFRED A.—1540 Broadway, New York, NY 10036. Distinguished juvenile fiction and nonfiction. Query; no unsolicited manuscripts. Royalty. Guidelines.

KNOPF, INC., ALFRED A.—299 Park Avenue, New York, NY 10171. Attn: Sr. Ed. Distinguished adult fiction and general nonfiction. Query for nonfiction.

KRAUSE PUBLICATIONS, INC.—700 E. State St., Iola, WI 54990-0001. Paul Kennedy, Acq. Ed. Antiques and collectibles, sewing and crafts, automotive topics, numismatics, sports, philatelics, outdoors, guns and knives, toys, records and comics. E-mail: kennedyp@krause.com.

KREGEL PUBLICATIONS—P.O. Box 2607, Grand Rapids, MI 49501-2607. Dennis Hillman, Ed. Evangelical Christian publisher interested in pastoral ministry, Christian education, family and marriage, devotional books, and biblical studies. No poetry, general fiction, or cartoons. Query editor with summary, target audience, brief bio, an outline or table of contents, two sample chapters, and an SASE. Allow six to eight weeks for a response. Payment is on a royalty basis.

LANDOLL, INC./AMERICAN EDUCATION PUBLISHING—425 Orange St., Ashland, OH 44805. Attn: Ed. Dir. Children's books. Submit writing samples and resume for consideration as a free-lance, flat-fee writer.

LARK BOOKS—50 College St., Asheville, NC 28801. Carol Taylor, Pub. Distinctive books for creative people in crafts, how-to, leisure activities, and "coffee table" categories. Query with outline. Royalty.

LEADERSHIP PUBLISHERS, INC.—P.O. Box 8358, Des Moines, IA

50301-8358. Dr. Lois F. Roets, Ed. Reference books for teachers of talented and gifted students, grades K to 12, and teacher reference books. No fiction or poetry. Send SASE for catalogue and writer's guidelines before submitting. "We're getting too many manuscripts that have nothing to do with our area of publication." Query or outline. Royalty for books; flat fee for booklets.

LEE & LOW BOOKS—95 Madison Ave., New York, NY 10016. Philip Lee, Pub. Louise May, Sr. Ed. Focus is on fiction and nonfiction picture books for children ages 2 to 10. "Our goal is to meet the growing need for books that address children of color and to provide books on subjects and stories they can identify with. Of special interest are stories set in contemporary America. Folklore and animal stories not considered." Include SASE. Advance/royalty. E-mail: info@leeandlow.com. Web site: www.leeandlow.com.

LEVINE BOOKS, ARTHUR A.—Imprint of Scholastic, Inc., 555 Broadway, New York, NY 10012. Arthur A. Levine, Ed. Dir. Beautiful picture books and literary fiction for children of all ages. Web site: www.scholastic.com.

LIFETIME BOOKS, INC.—See *Frederick Fell Publishers, Inc.*

LIMELIGHT BOOKS—See *Tiare Publications.*

LINCOLN-HERNDON PRESS, INC.—818 S. Dirksen Pkwy., Springfield, IL 62703. James E. Myers, Pub. American humor that reveals American history. Humor collections. Query. E-mail: lhp@cityscape.net. Web site: www.lincolnherndon.com.

LINNET BOOKS, LINNET PROFESSIONAL BOOKS—See *Shoe String Press.*

LITTLE, BROWN & CO.—1271 Avenue of the Americas, New York, NY 10020. No unsolicited manuscripts.

LITTLE, BROWN & CO. CHILDREN'S BOOK DEPT.—3 Center Plaza, Boston, MA 02108. Attn: Ed. Dept. Juvenile fiction and nonfiction and picture books. No unsolicited manuscripts. Accepts agented material only. Web site: www.littlebrown.com.

LITTLE TIGER PRESS—N16 W23390 Stoneridge Dr., Waukesha, WI 53188. Acquisitions Ed. No unsolicited manuscripts.

LLEWELLYN PUBLICATIONS—P.O. Box 64383, St. Paul, MN 55164-0383. Nancy J. Mostad, Acquisitions Mgr. Books, from 75,000 words, on subjects of self-help, how-to, alternative health, astrology, metaphysics, new age, and the occult. Metaphysical/occult fiction. "We're interested in any kind of story (mystery, historical, gothic, occult, metaphysical adventure), just as long as the theme is authentic occultism, and the work is both entertaining and educational." Query with sample chapters. Multiple queries considered. Royalty.

LONGSTREET PRESS—2140 Newmarket Pkwy., Suite 122, Marietta, GA 30067. Editorial Dept. Nonfiction, varying lengths, appealing to a general audience. Query with outline and sample chapters. Accepts very little fiction, and only through an agent. SASE. Allow 5 months for response. Royalty.

LOUISIANA STATE UNIVERSITY PRESS—P.O. Box 25053, Baton Rouge, LA 70894-5053. Attn: Ed. Dir. Scholarly adult nonfiction, dealing with the U.S. South, its history and its culture. Query with outline and sample chapters. Royalty. E-mail: lsupress@lsu.edu. Web site: www.lsupress.edu.

LOVE INSPIRED—See *Silhouette Books.*

LUCENT BOOKS—P.O. Box 289011, San Diego, CA 92198-9011. Lori Shein, Man. Ed. Books, 18,000 to 25,000 words, for junior high/middle school students. "Overview" series: current issues (political, social, historical, environmental topics). Other series include "World History," "The Way People Live" (exploring daily life and culture of communities worldwide, past and present), "Modern Nations." No unsolicited material; work is by assignment only. Flat fee. Query for guidelines and catalogue. Web site: www.lucent books.com.

LYONS PRESS—123 W. 18th St., New York, NY 10011. Becky Kohlr, Ed. Books, 100 to 300 pages, on cooking, gardening, sports, woodworking, natural history, and science. Query with outline. Royalty.

MCCLANAHAN BOOK CO.—23 W. 26th St., New York, NY 10010. Kenn Goin, Ed. Dir. Mass-market books for children, preschool to third grade. "Most books published as part of a series." Majority of work is done on a work for hire basis. Flat fee. Query; no unsolicited manuscripts accepted.

MCELDERRY BOOKS, MARGARET K.—1230 6th Ave., New York, NY 10020. Emma D. Dryden, Exec. Ed. Children's and young adult books, including picture books; quality fiction; fantasy; beginning chapter books; humor; and realism. Request guidelines before querying.

MCFARLAND & COMPANY, INC., PUBLISHERS—Box 611, Jefferson, NC 28640. Robert Franklin, Pres./Ed.-in-Chief. Steve Wilson, Sr. Ed., Virginia Tobiassen, Ed. Scholarly and reference books, from 225 manuscript pages, in many fields, except mathematical sciences. Particularly interested in general reference, performing arts, sports, automotive history, women's studies, and African American studies. No fiction, new age, inspirational, children's, poetry, or exposés. Submit complete manuscripts or query with outline and sample chapters. Royalty. E-mail: info@mcfarlandpub.com. Web site: www. mcfarlandpub.com.

MCGREGOR PUBLISHING—4532 W. Kennedy Blvd., Suite 233, Tampa, FL 33609. Lonnie Herman, Pub. Nonfiction, especially biography, sports, self-help. Query with outline and sample chapters. Royalty. E-mail: mcgregpub@aol.com.

MACMURRAY & BECK, INC.—4101 E. Louisiana Ave., Suite 100, Denver, CO 80246. Frederick Ramey, Exec. Dir. Quality fiction and narrative nonfiction.

MADISON BOOKS—4720 Boston Way, Lanham, MD 20706. James E. Lyons, Pub. Full-length nonfiction: history, biography, contemporary affairs, trade reference. Query required. Royalty.

MADLIBS—See *Price Stern Sloan, Inc.*

MAGIC CARPET BOOKS—See *Harcourt Inc./Children's Book Div.*

MAGINATION PRESS—750 First St., N.E., Washington, DC 20002. Darcie Conner Johnston, Ed. Children's picture books dealing with the psychotherapeutic treatment or resolution of serious childhood problems. Picture books for children 4 to 11; nonfiction for children 8 to 18. Most books are written by mental health professionals. Submit complete manuscript. Royalty. Web site: www.maginationpress.com.

MARKOWSKI INTERNATIONAL PUBLISHERS—See *Possibility Press.*

MARLOWE AND COMPANY—See *Thunder's Mouth Press.*

MEADOWBROOK PRESS—5451 Smetana Dr., Minnetonka, MN 55343. Meagan McGinnis, Submissions Ed. Upbeat, useful books, 60,000 words, on pregnancy, childbirth, and parenting; shorter works of humor, party planning, and children's activities; fiction anthologies and humorous poetry for children; adult light verse. Send for guidelines; include SASE with all submissions. Royalty or flat fee. Web site: www.meadowbrookpress.com.

MENASHA RIDGE PRESS—700 S. 28th St., Suite 206, Birmingham, AL 35233. Bud Zehmer, Sr. Acquisitions Ed. Outdoor/action travel guidebooks (mountain biking, canoeing, backpacking, etc.), to 224 pages. Query with sample chapters and table of contents. Pays flat fee or royalty. E-mail: bzehmer@menasharidge.com. Web site: www.menasharidge.com.

MID-LIST PRESS—4324 12th Ave. S., Minneapolis, MN 55407-3218. Marianne Nora, Assoc. Pub. Collections of short fiction and poetry, novels, and creative nonfiction. Interested in publishing "high literary merit and fresh artistic vision by new and emerging writers and by writers ignored, marginalized, or excluded from publication by commercial and mainstream publishers." Query. Royalty. Send #10 SASE for guidelines. E-mail: guide@midlist.org. Web site: www.midlist.org.

MILKWEED EDITIONS—1011 Washington Ave., S., Suite 300, Minneapolis, MN 55415. Emilie Buchwald, Ed. "We publish excellent award-winning fiction, poetry, essays, and nonfiction about the natural world, the kind of writing that makes for good reading." Publishes about 17 books a year. Send SASE for guidelines before submitting manuscript. Royalty. Also publishes *Milkweeds for Young Readers*: high-quality novels for middle grades. E-mail: editorial@milkweed.org. Web site: www.milkweed.org.

THE MILLBROOK PRESS—P.O. Box 335, 2 Old New Milford Rd., Brookfield, CT 06804. Bridget Noujaim, Ed. Asst. Nonfiction for early elementary grades through grades 7 and up, appropriate for the school and public library market, encompassing curriculum-related topics and extracurricular interests. Some picture books. Imprint: *Copper Beech Books.* Query with outline, sample chapter, and SASE. Request submission guidelines first. Allow 6 to 8 weeks for response. Royalty. Web site: www.millbrookpress.com.

MINSTREL BOOKS—See *Archway/Minstrel Books.*

MIRA BOOKS—See *Harlequin Books/Canada.*

THE MIT PRESS—5 Cambridge Center, Cambridge, MA 02142. Larry Cohen, Ed.-in-Chief. Books on computer science/artificial intelligence; cognitive sciences; economics; finance; architecture; aesthetic and social theory; linguistics; technology studies; environmental studies; and neuroscience.

MONDO PUBLISHING—980 Ave. of the Americas, 2nd Fl., New York, NY 10018. Gina Shaw, Sr. Ed. Picture books, nonfiction, and early chapter books for readers ages 4 to 10. "We want to create beautiful books that children can read on their own and find so enjoyable that they'll want to come back to them time and time again." Query; no unsolicited manuscripts. Royalty.

MONTANA HISTORICAL SOCIETY—P.O. Box 201201, Helena, MT

59620. Martha Kohl, Ed. Books on Montana history. Query. Royalty. E-mail: mkohlmhs@aol.com. Web site: www.his.state.mt.us.

MOODY PRESS—820 N. LaSalle Blvd., Chicago, IL 60610-3284. Acquisitions Coordinator. Christian material including personal experiences, new Bible translations, and Bible study material, and some juvenile books; no picture books. Send complete manuscript or three sample chapters, outline, table of contents, introduction, and target audience of proposed book. Payment is in royalties.

MOREHOUSE PUBLISHING—4775 Linglestown Rd., Harrisburg, PA 17112. Mark Fretz, Ed. Dir. Theology, pastoral care, church administration, spirituality, Anglican studies, history of religion, books for children. Query with outline, contents, and sample chapter and SASE. Royalty. Web site: www.morehousepublishing.com.

MORGAN REYNOLDS, INC.—620 S. Elm St., Suite 384, Greensboro, NC 27406. John Riley, Pub. Young adult biography and history, 20,000 words. Queries preferred. Multiple queries considered. Pays in royalties. Send SASE for guidelines. Web site: www.morganreynolds.com.

MORROW AND CO., INC., WILLIAM—The Hearst Corp., 1350 Ave. of the Americas, New York, NY 10019. Attn: Eds. Adult fiction and nonfiction: no unsolicited manuscripts. Betty Kelly, V.P. & Ed.-in-Chief. *Mulberry Books* (children's paperbacks), Paulette Kaufmann, Ed. Dir.; *Hearst Books* (general nonfiction), Jacqueline Deval, VP & Pub., Elizabeth Rice, Ed. Dir.

MOUNTAIN PRESS PUBLISHING—1301 S. 3rd W., P.O. Box 2399, Missoula, MT 59806. Attn: Kathleen Ort, Ed.-in-Chief. Nonfiction, 300 pages: natural history, field guides, geology, Western history, and Americana. Query with outline and sample chapters; multiple queries discouraged. Royalty.

MULTNOMAH BOOKS—See *Multnomah Publishers*.

MULTNOMAH PUBLISHERS—204 W. Adams Ave., P.O. Box 1720, Sisters, OR 97759. Attn: Ed. Evangelical, Christian publishing house with two imprints: *Multnomah Books*, message-driven, clean, moral, uplifting fiction, and nonfiction; address Ed. Dept. *Alabaster*, contemporary women's fiction that upholds strong Christian values; address Karen Ball, Ed. Submit 2 or 3 sample chapters with outline, cover letter, and SASE. Royalty. Web site: www.Mult nomahBooks.com

MUSTANG PUBLISHING CO., INC.—Box 770426, Memphis, TN 38177. Rollin A. Riggs, Ed. Nonfiction for 18- to 40-year-olds, specializing in travel, humor, and how-to. Send queries for 100- to 300-page books, with outlines and sample chapters. No phone calls. Royalty. SASE required. Web site: www.mustangpublishing.com.

THE MYSTERIOUS PRESS—Time/Life Bldg., 1271 Ave. of the Americas, New York, NY 10020. William Malloy, Ed.-in-Chief. Mystery/suspense novels. Agented manuscripts only.

NAIAD PRESS, INC.—Box 10543, Tallahassee, FL 32302. Barbara Grier, Ed. Adult fiction, 48,000 to 50,000 words, with lesbian themes and characters: mysteries, romances, gothics, ghost stories, westerns, regencies, spy novels, etc. Query with letter and one-page précis only. Royalty. Web site: www.naiadpress.com.

NAL—(formerly *Topaz*) 375 Hudson St., New York, NY 10014. Audrey LaFehr, Ex. Ed. Query.

NATIONAL GEOGRAPHIC CHILDREN'S BOOKS—1145 17th St. N.W., Washington DC, 20036-4688. Nancy Laties Feresten, Pub. Dir. Nonfiction for ages 2 to 12, with adventure, exploration, science, nature, geography, history, and the multicultural society of special interest. Submit complete manuscript for shorter books, and an outline and sample chapters for longer books with a SASE.

NATUREGRAPH PUBLISHERS—P.O. Box 1047, Happy Camp, CA 96039. Barbara Brown, Ed. Nonfiction: Native-American culture, natural history, outdoor living, land, Indian lore, and how-to. Query. Royalty.

THE NAVAL INSTITUTE PRESS—Annapolis, MD 21402. Attn: Acquisitions Dept. Nonfiction, 60,000 to 100,000 words: military histories; biographies; ship guides. Occasional military fiction, 75,000 to 110,000 words. Query with outline and sample chapters. Royalty.

NEW CANAAN PUBLISHING COMPANY—P.O. Box 752, New Canaan, CT 06840. Kathy Mittelstadt, Ed. Juvenile fiction, to 40,000 words, for readers ages 5 to 16. "We want children's books with strong educational and moral content." Submit complete manuscript. No multiple queries. Royalty.

NEW HORIZON PRESS—P.O. Box 669, Far Hills, NJ 07931. Joan Dunphy, Ed.-in-Chief. True stories, 96,000 words, of uncommon hero's advancing a social cause or wrong, especially true crime. First-time authors welcome, small advances, normal royalties. Query.

NEW LEAF PRESS, INC.—P.O. Box 726, Green Forest, AR 72638. Jim Fletcher, Acquisitions Ed. Nonfiction, 100 to 400 pages, for Christian readers: how to live the Christian life, devotionals, gift books. Query with outline and sample chapters. Royalty.

NEW READERS PRESS—1320 Jamesville Ave., Box 131, Syracuse, NY 13210. Julie Gehring, Ed. Fiction, 5,000 to 9,000 words, for adults who read at low levels for use in basic and ESL programs, volunteer literacy programs, and job training programs. Guidelines. Query; no unsolicited manuscripts. Royalty. Web site: www.newreaderpress.com.

NEW VICTORIA PUBLISHERS—P.O. Box 27, Norwich, VT 05055. Rebecca Béguin, Ed. Lesbian feminist fiction and nonfiction, including mystery, biography, history, fantasy; some humor and education. Guidelines. Query with outline and sample chapters; SASE. Royalty.

NEW WORLD LIBRARY—14 Pamaron Way, Novato, CA 94949. Attn: Submissions Ed. Inspirational and practical nonfiction books on spirituality, personal growth, health and wellness, business and prosperity, religion, recovery, multicultural studies, and women's studies. "Dedicated to awakening individual and global potential." Query with outline, sample chapter, and SASE. Multiple queries accepted. Royalty. E-mail: escort@nwlib.com. Web site: www.nwlib.com.

NEW YORK UNIVERSITY PRESS—838 Broadway, New York, NY 10003. Scholarly nonfiction. Submit proposal with sample chapters and curriculum vitae.

NEWCASTLE PUBLISHING—13419 Saticoy St., N. Hollywood, CA 91605. Daryl Jacoby, Pub. Nonfiction manuscripts, 200 to 250 pages, for older adults on personal health, health care issues, psychology, and relationships. "We are not looking for fads or trends. We want books with a long shelf life." Multiple queries considered. Royalty.

NORTHEASTERN UNIVERSITY PRESS—360 Huntington Ave., 416 CP, Boston, MA 02115. William Frohlich, Elizabeth Swayze, and John Weingartner, Eds. Nonfiction, 50,000 to 200,000 words: trade and scholarly titles in music, criminal justice, women's studies, ethnic studies, law, society, and American history. Submit query with outline and sample chapter. Royalty. E-mail: univpress@lynx.neu.edu. Web site: www.neu.edu/nupress

NORTHERN ILLINOIS UNIVERSITY PRESS—DeKalb, IL 60115. Mary L. Lincoln, Dir. Books, 250 to 450 typescript pages, for scholars and informed general readers. Submit history, regional topics, literature and Russian studies topics to Mary Lincoln; philosophy, politics, anthropology, economics, and other social sciences to Martin Johnson. Query with outline. Royalty.

NORTHLAND PUBLISHING—See *Rising Moon.*

NORTHWORD PRESS—5900 Green Oak Dr., Minnetonka, MN 55343. Acq. Ed. Nonfiction nature and wildlife books for children and adults. Send SASE with 7 first-class stamps for catalogue and SASE for guidelines. Royalty or flat fee.

NORTON AND CO., INC., W.W.—500 Fifth Ave., New York, NY 10110. Attn: Ed. High-quality literary fiction and nonfiction. No occult, paranormal, religious, genre fiction (formula romance, science fiction, westerns), arts and crafts, young adult, or children's books. Send outline, three sample chapters and SASE to Editorial Department. Web site: www.wwnorton.com.

NTC/CONTEMPORARY PUBLISHING GROUP—4255 W. Touhy Ave., Lincolnwood, IL 60712-1975. John T. Nolan, Vice Pres. and Pub. Trade nonfiction, 100 to 400 pages, on health, fitness, sports, cooking, business, popular culture, finance, women's issues, quilting, crafts, and general reference. Query with outline, sample chapter, and SASE. Royalty.

ODYSSEY CLASSICS—See *Harcourt Inc./Children's Book Div.*

OHIO UNIVERSITY PRESS/SWALLOW PRESS—Scott Quadrangle, Athens, OH 45701. David Sanders, Dir. Scholarly nonfiction, 300 to 400 manuscript pages, especially Victorian studies, contemporary history, regional studies, African studies. *Swallow Press*: general interest and frontier Americana. Query with outline and sample chapters. Royalty. Annual Hollis Summers Poetry Award Competition. Contest guidelines available at: www.ohiou.edu/oupress/.

OLIN FREDERICK, INC.—5338 Lakeside Blvd., Dunkirk, NY 14048. Political nonfiction including works of critique, assessment, and debate of current issues, as well as biography, history, economics, health and medicine, business, political fiction, and poetry. All material should be focused on "revealing the truth about issues in the government." Query with outline, synopsis, author bio, and SASE. No sample chapters. Pays in royalties. Web site: www.olin frederick.com. E-mail: olinfred@aol.com.

THE OLIVER PRESS—Charlotte Square, 5707 W. 36th St., Minneapolis, MN 55416. Denise Sterling, Ed. Collective biographies for young adults. Submit proposals for books, 20,000 to 25,000 words, on people who have made an impact in such areas as history, politics, crime, science, and business. Contracts negotiated.

ORCHARD BOOKS—95 Madison Ave., New York, NY 10016. Rebecca Davis, Sr. Ed. Ana Cerro, Sarah Caguiat, Eds. Juvenile fiction. Picture books and middle-grade fiction, 100 to 150 pages. Limited amount of nonfiction. No unsolicited manuscripts. Query only. No electronic submissions. Web site: www.publishing.grolier.com.

ORCHISES PRESS—P.O. Box 20602, Alexandria, VA 22320-1602. Roger Lathbury, Ed. Nonfiction books, 128 to 500 pages; and intellectually sophisticated, technically expert poetry books, 48 to 128 pages. No fiction. Query with sample chapters. Royalty.

OREGON STATE UNIVERSITY PRESS—101 Waldo Hall, Corvallis, OR 97331. Attn: Ed. Dept. Scholarly books in a limited range of disciplines and books of particular importance to the Pacific Northwest, especially dealing with the history, natural history, culture, and literature of the region or with natural resource issues. Query with summary of manuscript. E-mail: osu press@orst.edu. Web site: www.osu.orst.edu/dept/press.

OSBORNE/MCGRAW HILL—2600 Tenth St., Berkeley, CA 94710. Scott Rogers, Ed.-in-Chief. Computer books for general and technical audience. Query. Royalty.

OUR SUNDAY VISITOR PUBLISHING—200 Noll Plaza, Huntington, IN 46750. Jacquelyn M. Lindsey, Mike Dubruiel, Acquisitions Eds. Catholic-oriented books of various lengths. No fiction. Query with outline and sample chapters. Royalty. E-mail: booksed@osv.com. Web site: www.osv.com.

THE OVERLOOK PRESS—386 W. Broadway, 4th Fl., New York, NY 10012. Tracy Carns, Pub. Dir. Literary fiction, some fantasy/science fiction, foreign literature in translation, general nonfiction, including art, architecture, design, film, history, biography, crafts/lifestyle, martial arts, Hudson Valley regional interest, and children's books. Query with outline, sample chapters and SASE. Royalty.

OWEN PUBLISHERS, INC., RICHARD C.—Children's Book Dept., P.O. Box 585, Katonah, NY 10536. Janice Boland, Ed. Fiction and nonfiction. Brief storybooks, approximately 45 to 200 words, suitable for 5- and 7-year-old beginning readers for the "Books for Young Learners" collection. Also articles and fiction, 100 to 700 words, that interest, inform, inspire, fascinate, and entertain, for 7- and 8-year-olds for "Books for Fluent Readers" collection. Royalties for writers. Flat fee for illustrators. Writers must send SASE for guidelines before submitting.

OXFORD UNIVERSITY PRESS—198 Madison Ave., New York, NY 10016. Attn: Ed. Dept. Authoritative books on literature, history, philosophy, etc.; college textbooks, medical, scientific, technical and reference books. Query. Royalty.

PANTHEON BOOKS—The Knopf Publishing Group, 299 Park Ave., New York, NY 10171. Attn: Ed. Dept. Quality fiction and nonfiction. Query required. Royalty.

PARA PUBLISHING—P.O. Box 8206–238, Santa Barbara, CA 93118-8206. Dan Poynter, Ed. Adult nonfiction books on parachutes and skydiving only. Author must present evidence of having made at least 1,000 jumps. Query. Royalty. E-mail: info@parapublishing.com. Web site: www.parapublishing.com.

PARACLETE PRESS—P.O. Box 1568, Orleans, MA 02653. Attn: Editorial Review Committee. Adult nonfiction and fiction, 170 to 300 pages. Christian classics, Christian fiction, personal testimonies, and devotionals. Query with summary of proposed book and its target audience, estimated length of book, table of contents, and one or two sample chapters. Multiple queries accepted. Payment is royalties.

PARAGON HOUSE—2700 University Ave. W., Suite 200, St. Paul, MN 55114-1016. Gordon Anderson, Pub. Scholarly nonfiction, including philosophy, religion, spiritual health, biography, and current affairs. Query with sample chapters, summary table of contents, and SASE. Pays in royalties. E-mail: paragon@paragonhouse.com. Web site: www.paragonhouse.com.

PARENTING PRESS—P.O. Box 75267, Seattle, WA 98125. Elizabeth Crary, Pres. Children's books that build social skills, teach problem-solving techniques, and explore feelings or teach safety; for children up to age 12. Fiction must have a learning component to the story. Send query explaining how your book is different from others on the market on a similar topic, why you're qualified to write the book, and ways in which you can promote the book.

PASSPORT BOOKS—4255 W. Touhy Ave., Lincolnwood, IL 60712. Ed. Adult nonfiction, 200 to 400 pages, picture books up to 120 pages, and juvenile nonfiction. Send outline and sample chapters for books on foreign language to Christofer Brown; for travel and culture to Adam Miller. Multiple queries considered. Royalty and flat fee.

PAULIST PRESS—997 Macarthur Blvd., Mahwah, NJ 07430. Donald F. Brophy, Man. Ed. Adult nonfiction, 120 to 250 pages, on ecumenical theology, Roman Catholic studies, liturgy, spirituality, church history, ethics, education, and philosophy. Also publishes a limited number of story books for children. Query Maria Maggi with SASE. For juvenile books, submit complete manuscript with one sample illustration. No multiple submissions. Pays flat fees or royalties.

PEACHTREE PUBLISHERS, LTD.—494 Armour Cir. N.E., Atlanta, GA 30324. Attn: Ed. Dept. Wide variety of juvenile and young adult books, fiction and nonfiction. No religious material, science fiction/fantasy, romance, mystery/detective, and historical fiction; no business, scientific, or technical books. Send outline and sample chapters. SASE required. Royalty.

PELICAN PUBLISHING CO., INC.—P.O. Box 3110, Gretna, LA 70054. Nina Kooij, Ed.-in-Chief. General nonfiction: Americana, regional, architecture, travel, cookbooks, history, collectibles, business, children's picture books. Royalty. Web site: www.pelicanpub.com.

PENGUIN PUTNAM BOOKS—375 Hudson St., New York, NY 10014. Attn: Ed. Dept. Adult fiction and nonfiction paperbacks. Royalty. Web site: www.penguinputnam.com.

THE PERMANENT PRESS—4170 Noyac Rd., Sag Harbor, NY 11963. Judith Shepard, Ed. Original and arresting novels. Query. Royalty. Web site: www.thepermanentpress.com.

PERSEUS PUBLISHING—11 Cambridge Center, Cambridge, MA 02142. David Goehring, V-P and Pub. Adult nonfiction, varying lengths, on science, business, psychology, parenting, and health. Query with outline and sample chapters. Pays on royalty basis.

PERSPECTIVES PRESS—P.O. Box 90318, Indianapolis, IN 46290-

0318. Pat Johnston, Pub. Nonfiction on infertility, adoption, closely related reproductive health and child welfare issues (foster care, etc.). "Writers must read our guidelines before submitting." Query. Royalty. See web site for guidelines: www.perspectivespress.com. E-mail: ppress@iquest.net.

PHILOMEL BOOKS—345 Hudson St., New York, NY 10014. Patricia Lee Gauch, VP & Pub. Michael Green, Sr. Ed. Juvenile picture books and young adult fiction, particularly fantasy and historical. Fresh, original work with compelling characters and "a sense of the dramatic." Query required.

PINATA BOOKS—Imprint of Arte Publico Press, University of Houston, 4800 Calhoun, Houston, TX 77204-2090. Picture books, fiction, and autobiographies for children and young adults. Query with outline and sample chapters, or send complete manuscript. Payment is in royalties. Web site: www.arte.uh.edu.

PINEAPPLE PRESS—P.O. Box 3899, Sarasota, FL 34230. June Cussen, Ed. Serious fiction and nonfiction, Florida-oriented, 60,000 to 125,000 words. Query with outline, sample chapters, and SASE. Royalty. E-mail: info@pineapplepress.com. Web site: www.pineapplepress.com.

PINNACLE BOOKS—850 Third Ave., New York, NY 10022. Paul Dinas, Ed.-in-Chief. Nonfiction books: true crime, celebrity biographies, and humor. Unsolicited material not accepted. Web site: www.kensingtonbooks.com.

PIPPIN PRESS—229 E. 85th St., Gracie Sta., Box 1347, New York, NY 10028. Barbara Francis, Pub. Small chapter books for children ages 7 to 10, with historical fiction and fantasy themes, as well as ethnic stories and humorous mysteries; imaginative nonfiction for children of all ages. Query with SASE only; no unsolicited manuscripts. Royalty.

PLANET DEXTER—One Jacob Way, Reading, MA 01867-3999. Jess Brallier, Pub. Nonfiction books for children ages 8 to 12. All products developed internally. No unsolicited submissions.

PLAYERS PRESS, INC.—P.O. Box 1132, Studio City, CA 91614. Robert Gordon, Ed. Plays and musicals for children and adults; juvenile and adult nonfiction related to theatre, film, television, and the performing arts. Lengths vary. Query. Royalty.

PLEASANT COMPANY—8400 Fairway Pl., Middleton, WI 58562-0998. Erin Falligant, Submissions Ed. Books, 40,000 to 60,000 words, for 10- to 13-year-old girls: historical mystery/suspense, contemporary fiction, and contemporary advice and activity. "We have a small 'concept-driven' list and do not use inexperienced writers." Query with outline and sample chapters or send complete manuscript. Pays on a flat fee or royalty basis.

POCKET BOOKS—1230 Ave. of the Americas, New York, NY 10020. Adult and young adult fiction and nonfiction. Mystery line: police procedurals, private eye, and amateur sleuth novels, 60,000 to 70,000 words. Royalty.

POISONED PEN PRESS—6962 E. 1st Ave., #103, Scottsdale, AZ 85251. Louis Silverstein, Ed. Adult mysteries only. Pays on a royalty basis. Query with outline, sample chapters, and SASE. E-mail: louis@poisonedpenpress.com. Web site: www.poisonedpenpress.com.

POPULAR PRESS—Bowling Green State Univ., Bowling Green, OH

43403. Ms. Pat Browne, Ed. Nonfiction, 250 to 400 pages, examining some aspect of popular culture. Query with outline. Flat fee or royalty.

POSSIBILITY PRESS—(formerly *Markowski Publishers, Success Publishers*) One Oakglade Cir., Hummelstown, PA 17036. Marjorie L. Markowski, Ed. Nonfiction, 30,000 to 50,000 words: personal development, self-help, sales and marketing, leadership training, network marketing, motivation, and success topics. "Our mission is to help the people of the world grow and become the best they can be." SASE for guidelines. Query with outline and 3 sample chapters. Royalty. E-mail: PossPress@aol.com.

PRAEGER PUBLISHERS—88 Post Rd. W., Westport, CT 06881-5007. Attn: Pub. General nonfiction; scholarly and textbooks in the social sciences. Query with outline. Royalty. Web site: www.praeger.com.

PRECIOUS GEM—See *Kensington Publishing Corp.*

PRESIDIO PRESS—505-B San Marin Dr., Suite 300, Novato, CA 94945-1340. Attn: Ed. Dept. Nonfiction: military history and military affairs, from 90,000 words. Fiction: selected military and action-adventure works from 100,000 words. Query. Royalty.

PRICE STERN SLOAN, INC.—Penguin Putnam Books for Young Readers, 345 Hudson St., New York, NY 10014. Ed. Witty or edgy middle-grade fiction and nonfiction, calendars, and novelty juvenile titles. Imprints include *Troubador Press, Wee Sing, MadLibs.* Royalty. No longer accepting unsolicited manuscripts.

PRIMA PUBLISHING—3000 Lava Ridge Ct., Roseville, CA 95661. Ben Dominitz, Pub. Alice Feinstein, Ed. Dir. Susan Silva, Jamie Miller, David Richardson, Lorna Eby, Denise Sternad, Eds. Nonfiction on variety of subjects, including business, health, cooking, self-help, entertainment, computers, inspiration, home and family, parenting and education. "We want books with originality, written by highly qualified individuals." Advance against royalty.

PROMPT PUBLICATIONS—2647 Waterfront Pkwy. E. Dr., Indianapolis, IN 46214-2041. Attn: Acquisitions Ed. Nonfiction softcover technical books on electronics, how-to, troubleshooting and repair, electrical engineering, video and sound equipment, etc., for all levels of technical experience. Query with outline, sample chapters, author bio, and SASE. Royalty. E-mail: atripp@ wwsams.com. Web site: www.hwsams.com.

PRUETT PUBLISHING COMPANY—7464 Arapahoe Rd., Suite A-9, Boulder, CO 80303. Jim Pruett, Pub. Nonfiction: outdoors and recreation, western U.S. history, travel, natural history and the environment, fly fishing. Query. Royalty.

PUTNAM'S SONS, G.P.—345 Hudson St., New York, NY 10014. Attn: Children's Ed. Dept. General trade nonfiction and fiction for ages 2 to 18. Mostly picture books and middle-grade novels. No unsolicited manuscripts. Royalty. Web site: www.penguinputnam.com.

QED PRESS—155 Cypress St., Fort Bragg, CA 95437. Cynthia Frank, Ed. Health & healing, self-help, and how to fold paper airplanes. Query with outline and sample chapters. Royalty. E-mail: publishing@cypresshouse.com. Web site: www.cypresshouse.com.

QUEST BOOKS—Theosophical Publishing House, 306 W. Geneva Rd., P. O. Box 270, Wheaton, IL 60189-0270. Dr. Christine Merritt, Ed. Nonfiction books on Eastern and Western religion and philosophy, holistic health, healing, transpersonal psychology, men's and women's spirituality, creativity, meditation, yoga, ancient wisdom. Query Vija Bremanis with outline and sample chapters. Pays in royalties or flat fees.

QUIXOTE PRESS—1854 345th Ave., Wever, IA 52658. Bruce Carlson, Pres. Adult fiction and nonfiction including humor, folklore, and regional cookbooks; some juvenile fiction. Query with sample chapters and outline. Royalty.

RAGGED MOUNTAIN PRESS—Div. of McGraw-Hill, Box 220, Camden, ME 04843. Jonathan Eaton, Ed. Dir. Tom McCarthy, Acquisitions Ed. Books on outdoor recreation.

RAINBOW BOOKS, INC.—Box 430, Highland City, FL 33846. Betsy Lampe, Ed. Adult mysteries, to 75,000 words. Self-help and how-to nonfiction, of varying lengths. Send SASE for guidelines. Pays royalties.

RAINTREE STECK-VAUGHN PUBLISHERS—466 Southern Blvd., Chatham, NJ 07928. Walter Kossmann, Frank Sloan, Eds. Nonfiction books, 5,000 to 30,000 words, for school and library market: biographies for grades 3 and up; and science, social studies, and history books for primary grades through high school. Query with outline and sample chapters; SASE required. Flat fee or royalty.

RANDOM HOUSE BOOKS FOR YOUNG READERS—1540 Broadway, New York, NY 10036. Kate Klimo, Pub. Dir. Fiction and nonfiction for beginning readers; paperback fiction line for 7- to 9-year-olds. No unsolicited manuscripts. Agented material only.

RED CRANE BOOKS—2008 Rosina St., Suite B, Santa Fe, NM 87505. Marianne O'Shaughnessy, Ed. Art and folk art, bilingual material with Spanish and English, cookbooks, gardening, herbal guides, natural history, novels, social and political issues and social history. No children's books. Send a short synopsis, 2 sample chapters, resumé, and SASE.

RED SAGE PUBLISHING, INC.—P.O. Box 4844, Seminole, FL 33775. Alexandria Kendall, Acquisitions Ed. Novella submissions for anthologies. Sensual romantic fiction, 20,000 to 30,000 words. "Love scenes should be sophisticated, erotic, and emotional. Push the envelope beyond the normal romance novel." Query with first 10 pages and synopsis. Royalty. E-mail: ale kendall@aol.com. Web site: www.redsagepub.com.

THE RED SEA PRESS—11-D Princess Rd., Suites D, E, F, Lawrenceville, NJ 08648. Kassahun Checole, Pub. Adult nonfiction, 360 double-spaced manuscript pages. "We focus on nonfiction material with a specialty on the Horn of Africa." Query. Royalty.

RED WAGON BOOKS—Imprint of Harcourt Inc./Children's Book Div., 525 B St., Suite 1900, San Diego, CA 92101-4495. Attn: Acquisitions Ed. No unsolicited manuscripts. Query with SASE.

REGNERY PUBLISHING, INC.—One Massachusetts Ave., N.W., Washington, DC 20001. Attn: Ed. Dept. Nonfiction books. Query. Royalty.

RISING MOON—Imprint of Northland Publishing, P.O. Box 1389, Flagstaff, AZ 86002-1389. Aimee Jackson, Ed. Picture books for children ages 5 to 8. Send complete manuscript. Fiction and nonfiction, ages 8 to 12; no longer accepts unsolicited manuscripts. Interested in material on contemporary subjects. Considers multiple queries and pays on a royalty basis. E-mail: editorial @northlandpub.com. Web site: www.northlandpub.com.

RISING TIDE PRESS—3831 N. Oracle Rd., Tucson, AZ 85705. Debra Tobin, Brenda Kazen, Eds. Books for, by, and about women. Fiction, 60,000 to 80,000 words: romance, mystery, and young adult and adventure, science fiction/fantasy. Nonfiction, 40,000 to 60,000 words. Royalty. Reports in 3 months. SASE for guidelines or e-mail milestonepress@gateway.net.

RIZZOLI INTERNATIONAL PUBLICATIONS, INC.—300 Park Ave. S., New York, NY 10010. Children's Book Ed. Original manuscripts that introduce children to fine art, folk art, and architecture of all cultures for a small list. Nonfiction and fiction for all ages. Query with SASE or response card. Royalty.

ROC—375 Hudson St., New York, NY 10014. Science fiction, fantasy. Send agented manuscripts to Laura Anne Gilman, Exec. Ed.; unagented manuscripts to Jennifer Heddle, Asst. Ed. E-mail: roc@penguinputnam.com. Web site: www.penguinputnam.com.

ROCKBRIDGE PUBLISHING—Imprint of Howell Press, Inc., P.O. Box 351, Berryville, VA 22611. Katherine Tennery, Ed. Book-length nonfiction on the Civil War, Virginia history, and travel guides to Virginia. Query. Royalty. E-mail: cwpub@visuallink.com. Web site: www.rockbpub.com.

RODALE—400 S. 10th St., Emmaus, PA 18098. Books on health (men's, women's, alternative, senior), gardening, cookbooks, spirituality, fitness, and pets. Query with resumé, table of contents/outline, and two sample chapters. Royalty and outright purchase. "We have a large in-house writing staff; the majority of our books are conceived and developed in-house. We're always looking for truly competent free-lancers to write chapters for books." Payment on a work-for-hire basis.

RUMINATOR BOOKS—(formerly *Hungry Mind Press*) 1648 Grand Ave., St. Paul, MN 55105. Pearl Kilbride, Ed. Fiction; memoirs; contemporary affairs; cultural criticism; travel essays; nonfiction. No genre fiction, self-help, or poetry. "Books that examine the human experience or comment on social and cultural mores." Query with outline and sample chapters. Royalty. E-mail: books@ruminator.com. Web site: www.ruminator.com.

RUNNING PRESS—125 S. 22nd St., Philadelphia, PA 19103. Attn: Asst. to Ed. Dir. Trade nonfiction: art, craft, how-to, self-help, science, lifestyles. Young adult books and interactive packages. Query with outline or table of contents and two- to three-page writing sample. Royalty for some projects; flat fee for others. Web site: www.runningpress.com.

RUTGERS UNIVERSITY PRESS—100 Joyce Kilmer Ave., Piscataway, NJ 08854-8099. Paula Kantenwein, Ed. Asst. Nonfiction, 70,000 to 100,000 words. Query with outline and sample chapters. Royalty. Send Humanities proposals to Theresa Liu; Science and Social Sciences proposals to Suzanne Kellam. Web site: www.rutgerspress.rutgers.edu.

RUTLEDGE HILL PRESS—P.O. Box 141000, Nashville, TN 37214-1000. Mike Towle, Ed. Market-specific nonfiction. Query with outline and sample chapters. Royalty. E-mail: tmengesrhp@aol.com. Web site: www.rutledge hillpress.com.

ST. ANTHONY MESSENGER PRESS—1615 Republic St., Cincinnati, OH 45210-1298. Lisa Biedenbach, Man. Ed. Inspirational nonfiction for Catholics, supporting a Christian lifestyle in our culture; prayer aids, scripture, church history, education, practical spirituality, parish ministry, liturgy resources, Franciscan resources, family-based religious education program, and children's books. Query with 500-word summary. Royalty. E-mail: stanthony@american catholic.org. Web site: www.americancatholic.org.

ST. MARTIN'S PRESS—175 Fifth Ave., New York, NY 10010. Attn: Ed. Dept. General adult fiction and nonfiction. Query. Royalty.

SAINT MARY'S PRESS—702 Terrace Heights, Winona, MN 55987-1320. Stephan Nagel, Ed.-in-Chief. Progressive Catholic publisher. Fiction, to 40,000 words, for young adults ages 11 to 17, "that gives insight into the struggle of teens to become healthy, hopeful adults and also sheds light on Catholic experience, history, or cultures." Query with outline and sample chapter. Royalty.

SANDLAPPER PUBLISHING, INC.—P.O. Drawer 730, Orangeburg, SC 29116-0730. Amanda Gallman, Book Ed. Nonfiction books on South Carolina history, culture, cuisine. Query with outline, sample chapters, and SASE. No phone calls, please. E-mail: agallman@theisp.net.

SASQUATCH BOOKS—615 2nd Ave., Suite 260, Seattle, WA 98104. Attn: Ed. Dept. Regional books on a wide range of nonfiction topics: travel, natural history, gardening, cooking, history, and public affairs. Books should have a Pacific Northwest and/or West Coast subject or theme. Query with SASE. Royalty. E-mail: books@sasquatchbooks.com. Web site: www.sasquatchbooks.com.

SCARECROW PRESS—4720 Boston Way, Lanham, MD 20706. Shirley Lambert, Assoc. Pub. Reference works and bibliographies, from 150 pages, especially in the areas of library and information science, cinema, TV, radio, music and theater, mainly for use by libraries. Query or send complete manuscript; multiple queries considered. Royalty. Web: www.scarecrowpress.com. New division: educational administration.

SCHOCKEN BOOKS—299 Park Ave., New York, NY 10171. Attn: Ed. Dept. Fiction and general nonfiction: Judaica, women's studies, education, history, religion, psychology, cultural studies. Query with book proposal/outline and 2 sample chapters. Royalty. E-mail: dzeidel@randomhouse.com. Web site: www.randomhouse.com/knopf/.

SCHOLASTIC, INC.—555 Broadway, New York, NY 10012. No unsolicited manuscripts.

SCHOLASTIC PROFESSIONAL BOOKS—555 Broadway, New York, NY 10012-3999. Attn: Adriane Rozier. Books by and for teachers of kindergarten through eighth grade. *Instructor Books*: practical, activity/resource books on teaching reading and writing, science, math, etc. *Teaching Strategies Books*: 64 to 96 pages on new ideas, practices, and approaches to teaching. Query with outline, sample chapters or activities, contents page, and resumé. Flat fee or royalty. Multiple queries considered. 8 1/2″ × 11″ SASE for guidelines.

SCHWARTZ BOOKS, ANNE—Atheneum Publishers, 1230 Ave. of the Americas, New York, NY 10020. Anne Schwartz, Ed. Dir. Picture books, juvenile fiction, and nonfiction as well as illustrated collections. Query letter only; no unsolicited manuscripts. Web site: www.simonsays.com.

SCOTT FORESMAN—1900 E. Lake Ave., Glenview, IL 60025. Paul

McFall, Pres. Elementary textbooks. Royalty or flat fee. Must have proper educational credentials in order to submit.

SEAL PRESS—3131 Western Ave., Suite 410, Seattle, WA 98121-1041. Jennie Goode, Man Ed. Feminist/women's studies books: popular culture and lesbian studies; parenting; domestic violence; health and recovery; sports and outdoors. Query. Royalty. E-mail: sealpress@sealpress.com.

SEVEN SEAS PRESS—See *International Marine*.

SEVEN STORIES PRESS—140 Watts St., New York, NY 10013. Small press. Fiction and nonfiction. Query with SASE. Royalty.

17TH STREET PRODUCTIONS (formerly *Daniel Weiss Associates*)—33 W. 17th St., New York, NY 10011. Ann Brashares, Les Morgenstein, Co-Pres. Book packager. Young adult books, 36,000 words; middle-grade books, 29,000 words; elementary books, 10,000 to 12,000 words. Royalty and flat fee.

SHAMBHALA PUBLICATIONS, INC.—Horticultural Hall, 300 Massachusetts Ave., Boston, MA 02115. Peter Turner, Exec. Ed. Eastern religion, especially Buddhism and Taoism, as well as psychology, self-help, and philosophy. Query Laura Stone with outline and sample chapters. Payment is in flat fees and royalty. E-mail: editors@shambhala.com.

SHEARWATER BOOKS—See *Island Press*.

SHOE STRING PRESS—P.O. Box 657, 2 Linsley St., North Haven, CT 06473-2517. Diantha C. Thorpe, Ed./Pub. Books for children and teenagers, including juvenile nonfiction for ages 10 and older. Resources for teachers and librarians that share high standards of scholarship and practical experience. Imprints include *Linnet Books, Archon Books,* and *Linnet Professional Publications*. Submit outline and sample chapters. Royalty. E-mail: sspbooks@aol.com. Web site: www.shoestringpress.com.

SIERRA CLUB BOOKS—85 Second St., San Francisco, CA 94105. Attn: Ed. Dept. Nonfiction: environment, natural history, the sciences, outdoors and regional guidebooks, nature photography; literary nonfiction. Query with SASE. Royalty. E-mail: sierra.letters@sierraclub.org. Web site: www.sierra club.org/books.

SILHOUETTE BOOKS—300 E. 42nd St., New York, NY 10017. Isabel Swift, V.P. Ed. Tara Gavin, Ed. Dir. *Silhouette Romance*: Mary Theresa Hussey, Sr. Ed. Contemporary romances, 53,000 to 58,000 words. *Special Edition*: Karen Taylor Richman, Sr. Ed. Sophisticated contemporary romances, 75,000 to 80,000 words. *Silhouette Desire*: Joan Marlow Golan, Ed. Sensuous contemporary romances, 53,000 to 60,000 words. *Intimate Moments*: Leslie Wainger, Exec. Sr. Ed. Sensuous, exciting contemporary romances, 80,000 words. Historical romance: 95,000 to 105,000 words, and more; query with synopsis and 3 sample chapters to Tracy Farrell, Sr. Ed. *Love Inspired* (*Steeple Hill* imprint): Inspirational Christian romances, 70,000 to 75,000 words. Query with synopsis and SASE to appropriate editor. Tipsheets available.

SILVER MOON PRESS—160 Fifth Ave., Suite 622, New York, NY 10010. Web site: www.silvermoonpress.com.

SILVER WHISTLE—See *Harcourt Inc./Children's Book Div.*

SIMON & SCHUSTER—1230 Ave. of the Americas, New York, NY

10020. Adult books. No unsolicited material; manuscripts must be submitted by an agent.

SIMON & SCHUSTER BOOKS FOR YOUNG READERS—1230 Ave. of the Americas, New York, NY 10020. Stephanie Owens Lurie, Assoc. Pub./V.P./Ed. Dir. Books for ages preschool through high school: picture books to young adult; nonfiction for all age levels. Hardcover only. Request guidelines before querying. SASE required for reply.

SMITH AND KRAUS, INC.—P.O. Box 127, Main St., Lyme, NH 03768. Marisa Smith, Pres. Material of interest to the theatre community, collections of major American playwrights, annuals; monologues, scenes, and plays that have been published in the current theatrical year; plays and material for grades K through 12. Nonfiction on stagecraft, design, costuming, and makeup. No manuscripts returned. Response time is 3 months. Pays on publication. E-mail: saudk@sover.net. Web site: www.smithkraus.com.

SOHO PRESS—853 Broadway, New York, NY 10003. Juris Jurjevics, Pub. Mysteries, thrillers, and contemporary fiction and nonfiction, from 60,000 words. Send SASE and complete manuscript. Royalty. Web site: www.soho press.com.

SOURCEBOOKS—121 N. Washington St., Naperville, IL 60540. Todd Stocke, Ed. General nonfiction, how-to and reference titles, including business; parenting; self-help; new age; gift-oriented; humor; law; and health. Imprint: *Casablanca Press.* Query with outline and sample chapters. Royalty.

SOUTH END PRESS—7 Brookline St., #1, Cambridge, MA 02139-4146. Acq. Ed. Nonfiction on leftist politics. Query with sample chapters; multiple queries are accepted. Pays royalties. E-mail: southend@igc.org. Web site: www.llbs.org/sep/sep.htm.

SOUTHERN ILLINOIS UNIVERSITY PRESS—P.O. Box 3697, Carbondale, IL 62902-3697. James Simmons, Ed. Dir. Nonfiction on the humanities, 200 to 300 pages. Query with outline and sample chapters. Royalty. E-mail: jdsin@siu.edu. Web site: www.siu.ed/~siupress

SOUTHERN METHODIST UNIVERSITY PRESS—Box 415, Dallas, TX 75275-0415. Kathryn Lang, Sr. Ed. Literary fiction. Nonfiction: scholarly studies in religion; medical ethics (death and dying); film; theater; scholarly works on Texas or Southwest. No juvenile material, science fiction, or poetry. Query. Royalty.

SPECIAL EDITION—See *Silhouette Books.*

SPECTACLE LANE PRESS—Box 1237, Mt. Pleasant, SC 29465-1237. Attn: Ed. Dept. Humor books, 500 to 5,000 words, on subjects of strong, current interest, illustrated with cartoons. Buys text or text/cartoon packages. Occasional nonfiction, non-humor books on provocative subjects of popular appeal. Advance against royalties. E-mail: jaskar44@aol.com.

SPECTRA—See *Bantam Books.*

SPHINX PRESS—Imprint of *Sourcebooks, Inc.,* 1725 Clearwater/Largo Rd., Clearwater, FL 33756. Mark Warda, Ed. Nonfiction; legal self-help. Query with outline and sample chapters. Pays in royalties.

SPINSTERS INK—32 E. First St., #330, Duluth, MN 55802. Nancy Walker, Acquisitions Ed. Adult fiction and nonfiction books, 200-plus pages, that deal with significant issues in women's lives from a feminist perspective and encourage change and growth. Main characters and/or narrators must be women. Query with synopsis. No e-mail queries. Royalty. Web site: www. spinsters-ink.com.

STACKPOLE BOOKS—5067 Ritter Rd., Mechanicsburg, PA 17055. Judith Schnell, Ed. Dir. Books on the outdoors, nature, fishing, flyfishing, climbing, paddling, sports, sporting literature, history, and military reference. Query. Royalty; advance. Unsolicited materials will not be returned. E-mail: jschnell-@stackpolebooks.com. Web site: www.stackpolebooks.com.

STA-KRIS, INC.—P.O. Box 714, Grantsburg, WI 54840. Kathy Wagoner, Pres. Nonfiction adult-level gift books that portray universal feelings, truths, and values or have a special-occasion theme. Query with bio, list of credits, complete manuscript, and SASE. E-mail: stakris@win.bright.net. Web site: www.stakris.com.

STANDARD PUBLISHING—8121 Hamilton Ave., Cincinnati, OH 45231. Attn: Acquisitions Ed. Christian education resources and children's books. Request guidelines to find out current editorial needs.

STANFORD UNIVERSITY PRESS—Stanford University, Stanford, CA 94305-2235. Norris Pope, Dir. "For the most part, we publish academic scholarship." No original fiction or poetry. Query with outline and sample chapters. Royalty. Web site: www.sup.org.

STARBURST PUBLISHERS—Box 4123, Lancaster, PA 17604. David A. Robie, Ed. Dir. Health, inspiration, Christian, and self-help books. Query with outline for nonfiction book, synopsis for fiction book, and 3 sample chapters. Royalty. SASE. E-mail: editorial@starburstpublishers.com. Web site: www.starburstpublishers.com.

STARRHILL PRESS—Black Belt Publishing, LLC, P.O. Box 551, Montgomery, AL 36101. Jim Davis, Ed. Affordable, succinct titles on American arts and letters. High-quality nonfiction, including gardening, health, history, music, and travel. National and international audience. Query with cover letter, outline, author bio, and SASE for reply. Royalty varies. E-mail: info@black-belt.com. Web site: www.black-belt.com.

STEEPLE HILL—See *Silhouette Books*.

STEERFORTH PRESS—105–106 Chelsea St., Box 70, S. Royalton, VT 05068. Michael Moore, Ed. Adult nonfiction and some literary fiction. Fifteen books a year: novels; serious works of history, biography, politics, current affairs. Query with SASE. Royalty.

STEMMER HOUSE PUBLISHERS, INC.—2627 Caves Rd., Owings Mills, MD 21117. Barbara Holdridge, Ed. Adult nonfiction and juvenile picture books. Specializes in art, design, cookbooks, horticultural, and children's titles. Query with SASE. Royalty.

STERLING PUBLISHING CO., INC.—387 Park Ave. S., New York, NY 10016. Steven E. Magnusan, V.P., Editorial. Frances Gilbert, Juvenile Ed. How-to, hobby, woodworking, alternative health and healing, fiber arts, crafts, dolls and puppets, ghosts, wine, nature, oddities, new consciousness, puzzles, juvenile humor and activities, juvenile nature and science, medieval history, Celtic topics, gardening, alternative lifestyle, business, pets, recreation, sports and games books, reference, and home decorating. Query with outline, sample chapter, and sample illustrations. Royalty. E-mail: sterlingpub.com.

STODDART PUBLISHING COMPANY—34 Lesmill Rd., North York, Ontario, Canada M3B 2T6. Literary fiction and nonfiction, including business, politics, humor, and sports. Query with an outline and sample chapters; multiple queries are accepted. Pays on royalty basis. Web site: www.genpub.com.

STONEYDALE PRESS—523 Main St., Box 188, Stevensville, MT 59870. Dale A. Burk, Ed. Adult nonfiction, primarily how-to, on outdoor recreation with emphasis on big game hunting; some regional history of Northern Rockies. "We're a very specialized market. Query with outline and sample chapters essential." Royalty. E-mail: daleburk@montana.com.

STORY LINE PRESS—Three Oaks Farm, P.O. Box 1240, Ashland, OR 97520-0055. Robert McDowell, Ed. Fiction, nonfiction, and poetry of varying lengths. Query. Royalty. E-mail: mail@storylinepress.com. Web site: www. storylinepress.com.

STRAWBERRY HILL PRESS—3848 S.E. Division St., Portland, OR 97202-1641. Carolyn Soto, Ed. Nonfiction: biography, autobiography, history, cooking, health, how-to, philosophy, performance arts, and Third World. Query with sample chapters, outline, and SASE. Royalty.

SUCCESS PUBLISHERS—See *Possibility Press.*

SWALLOW PRESS—See *Ohio University Press/Swallow Press.*

SYRACUSE UNIVERSITY PRESS—621 Skytop Rd., Ste. 110, Syracuse, NY 13244-5290. E-mail: twalsh01@syr.edu. Web site: www.sumweb. syr.edu/supress/.

TALEWINDS—See *Charlesbridge Publishing.*

TEACHING STRATEGIES BOOKS—See *Scholastic Professional Books.*

TEMPLE UNIVERSITY PRESS—1601 N. Broad St., USB 306, Philadelphia, PA 19122-6099. Janet Francendese, Ed. Adult nonfiction. Query with outline and sample chapters. Royalty.

TEN SPEED PRESS—P.O. Box 7123, Berkeley, CA 94707. Attn: Ed. Dept. Self-help and how-to on careers, recreation, etc.; natural science, history, cookbooks. Imprints include: *Tricycle Press* and *Celestial Arts.* Query with outline, sample chapters, and SASE. Paperback. Royalty.

THIRD WORLD PRESS—P.O. Box 19730, Chicago, IL 60619. Attn: Ed. Board. "Progressive Black Publishing." Adult fiction, nonfiction, and poetry, as well as juvenile fiction and young adult books. Query with outline. Royalty. Send SASE or e-mail twpress3@aol.com for guidelines.

THUNDER'S MOUTH PRESS—Avalon Publishing Group, 841 Broadway, 4th Fl., New York, NY 10003. Neil Ortenberg, Pub. Nonfiction: popular culture, music, and biography, to 300 pages. Royalty. Under *Adrenaline Books* imprint, publishes extreme adventure sports stories. Also publishes *Marlowe and Company* line; adult trade nonfiction focusing on health, religion, spriritu-ality, and self-help. Royalty. Please, no e-mail submissions.

TIA CHUCHA PRESS—P.O. Box 476969, Chicago, IL 60647. Luis Rodriguez, Ed. Poetry, 60 to 100 pages. Annual deadline: June 30. Royalty. E-mail: guildcomplex@earthlink.net. Web site: www.nupress.nwu.edu/guild.

TIARE PUBLICATIONS—P.O. Box 493, Lake Geneva, WI 53147. Gerry L. Dexter, Ed. General nonfiction, *Limelight* imprint; jazz discographies and commentaries, *Balboa* imprint. Query with outline and sample chapters. Royalties. E-mail: info@tiare.com. Web site: www.tiare.com.

TILBURY HOUSE—2 Mechanic St., #3, Gardiner, ME 04345. Attn: Acquisitions Ed. Children's books that deal with cultural diversity or the environment, appeal to children and parents as well as the educational market, and offer possibilities for developing a separate teacher's guide. Adult books: nonfiction books about Maine or the Northeast. Query with outline and sample chapters. Web site: www.tilburyhouse.com.

TOPAZ—See *NAL.*

TRICYCLE PRESS—Ten Speed Press, P.O. Box 7123, Berkeley, CA 94707. Nicole Geiger, Pub. Children's books: Picture books, submit complete manuscripts. Activity books, submit about 20 pages and complete outline. "Real life" books that help children cope with issues. SASE required. Do not send original artwork. Responds in 10 to 20 weeks. Royalty. Please read catalog or visit our web site before submitting. Guidelines available. Send SASE. Web site: www.tenspeed.com.

TRINITY PRESS INTERNATIONAL—Morehouse Group, P.O. Box 1321, Harrisburg, PA 17105. Henry L. Carrigan, Jr., Ed. Serious studies and research in Bible and theology/religion, interfaith studies, African-American religious life and thought, biblical interpretation, and methodology. Query with outline and sample chapters or send complete manuscript. Multiple queries are considered. Payment is in royalties.

TROUBADOR PRESS—See *Price Stern Sloan, Inc.*

TSR, INC.—See *Wizards of the Coast.*

TURTLE BOOKS—866 United Nations Plaza, Suite 525, New York, NY 10017. John Whitman, Pub. Children's picture books only. Submit complete manuscript with SASE. Royalty.

TURTLE PRESS—P.O. Box 290206, Wethersfield, CT 06129-0206. Cynthia Kim, Ed. Nonfiction, varying lengths, on all aspects of martial arts and Eastern philosophy. Query. Royalty. E-mail: editorial@turtlepress.com. Web site: www.turtlepress.com.

TWENTY-FIRST CENTURY BOOKS—The Millbrook Press, P.O. Box 335, 2 Old New Milford Rd., Brookfield, CT 06804. Attn: Submissions Ed. Juvenile nonfiction, 10,000 to 30,000 words, for use in school and public libraries. Science, history, health, and social studies books for grades 5 and up. No fiction, workbooks, or picture books. Also accepts single titles for middle-grade and young adult readers. "Books are published primarily in series of four or more; not all titles in a series are necessarily by the same author." Query with SASE. Royalty.

TYNDALE HOUSE—351 Executive Dr., Carol Stream, IL 60188. Ron Beers, V.P. Adult fiction and nonfiction on subjects of concern to Christians. No unsolicited manuscripts. SASE for guidelines.

UAHC PRESS—633 Third Ave., New York, NY 10017. Rabbi Hara Person, Man. Ed. Religious educational titles on or related to Judaism. Adult nonfiction; textbooks for Jewish education; juvenile picture books and nonfiction; and young adult nonfiction titles. Query with outline. Royalty. Web site: www.uahcpress.com.

THE UNIVERSITY OF AKRON PRESS—374-B Bierce Library,

Akron, OH 44325-1703. Michael J. Carley, Dir. Five nonfiction series on: Ohio History & Culture, Technology & the Environment, Law & Government, European History, and Canadian Studies. Query with outline and chapters. Poetry, 60 to 100 pages, through the Akron Poetry Prize, Elton Glaser, Poetry Ed. Send SASE for poetry guidelines. Pays in royalties. See web site for prospective author suggestions: www.uakron.edu/uapress.

UNIVERSITY OF ARIZONA PRESS—1230 N. Park Ave., Suite 102, Tucson, AZ 85719-4140. Christine R. Szuter, Dir. Cynthia Maude, Ed.-in-Chief. Patti Hartmann, Acquiring Ed. Scholarly and popular nonfiction: Arizona, American West, anthropology, archaeology, behavioral sciences, environmental science, geography, Latin America, Native Americans, natural history, space sciences, women's studies. Query with outline, sample chapters, and current curriculum vitae or resumé. Royalty.

UNIVERSITY OF CALIFORNIA PRESS—2120 Berkeley Way, Berkeley, CA 94720. Attn: Acquisitions Dept. Scholarly nonfiction. Query with cover letter, outline, sample chapters, curriculum vitae, and SASE. E-mail: ucpress.comments@ucop.edu. Web site: www.ucpress.edu.

UNIVERSITY OF GEORGIA PRESS—330 Research Dr., Athens, GA 30602-4901. Karen Orchard, Dir. Short story collections and poetry, scholarly nonfiction and literary criticism, Southern and American history, regional studies, biography and autobiography. For nonfiction, query with outline and sample chapters. Poetry collections considered in Sept. and Jan. only; short fiction in April and May only. A $15 fee is required for all poetry and fiction submissions. Royalty. SASE for competition guidelines. E-mail: mnunnell@ugapress.uga.edu. Web site: www.uga.edu/ugapress.

UNIVERSITY OF ILLINOIS PRESS—1325 S. Oak St., Champaign, IL 61820. Willis G. Regier, Dir. Scholarly and regional nonfiction. Rarely considers multiple submissions. Query. Royalty.

UNIVERSITY OF IOWA PRESS—100 Kuhl House, Iowa City, IA 52242-1000. Holly Carver, Dir. Nonfiction. Short fiction and poetry published only through annual competitions. Query with SASE. Pay varies. E-mail: holly carver@uiowa.edu. Web site: www.uiowa.edu/~uipress.

UNIVERSITY OF MINNESOTA PRESS—111 Third Ave. S., Suite 290, Minneapolis, MN 55401-2520. Nonfiction: literary and cultural theory, social and political theory; communications/media; anthropology; geography; international relations; Native American studies; regional titles, 50,000 to 225,000 words. Query with detailed prospectus or introduction, table of contents, sample chapter, and resumé. Royalty. E-mail: ump@tc.umn.edu. Web site: www.upress.umn.edu.

UNIVERSITY OF MISSOURI PRESS—2910 LeMone Blvd., Columbia, MO 65201-8227. Beverly Jarrett, Dir./Ed.in-Chief. Mr. Clair Wilcox, Acquisitions Ed. Scholarly books on American and European history; American, British, and Latin American literary criticism; political philosophy; intellectual history; regional studies; and short fiction. E-mail: upress@umsystem.edu. Web site: www.system.missouri.edu/upress.

UNIVERSITY OF NEBRASKA PRESS—233 N. 8th St., Lincoln, NE 68588-0255. Attn: Ed.-in-Chief. Specializes in the history of the American West, Native-American studies, literary and cultural nonfiction, fiction in translation, music, Jewish studies, and sports history. Send proposals with summary, a sample chapter, and resumé. Write for guidelines for annual North American Indian Prose Award. E-mail: pressmail@unl.edu. Web site: www.nebraska press.unl.edu.

UNIVERSITY OF NEVADA PRESS—MS 166, Reno, NV 89557. Margaret Dalrymple, Ed.-in-Chief. Fiction, nonfiction, and poetry. Nonfiction areas include history, biography, political science, natural history, regional (Nevada), mining, gaming, and Basque studies. Query first, with outline or table of contents, a synopsis, the estimated length and completion date of the manuscript, and resumé. Payment is on a royalty basis. E-mail: dalrympl@scs.unr.edu.

UNIVERSITY OF NEW MEXICO PRESS—University of New Mexico, Albuquerque, NM 87131. Elizabeth C. Hadas, Ed. Dir. David V. Holtby, Larry Ball, Dana Asbury, and Barbara Guth, Eds. Scholarly nonfiction on social and cultural anthropology, archaeology, Western history, art, and photography. Query. Royalty. E-mail: unmpress@unm.edu. Web site: www.unmpress.com.

UNIVERSITY OF NORTH TEXAS PRESS—P.O. Box 311336, Denton, TX 76203-1336. Frances B. Vick, Dir. Karen DeVinney, Man. Ed. Books on Western Americana, Texan culture, history (including regional), women's studies, multicultural studies, and folklore. Series include: "War and the Southwest" (perspectives, histories, and memories of war from authors living in the Southwest); "Western Life Series"; and "Texas Writers" (critical biographies of Texas writers). Send manuscript or query with sample chapters; no multiple queries. Royalty. E-mail: devinney@unt.edu. Web site: www.unt.edu/untpress.

UNIVERSITY OF PENNSYLVANIA PRESS—4200 Pine St., Philadelphia, PA 19104-4011. Eric Halpern, Dir. Scholarly nonfiction. Query. E-mail: custserv@pobox.upenn.edu. Web site: www.upenn.edu/pennpress.

UNIVERSITY OF PITTSBURGH PRESS—3347 Forbes Ave., Pittsburgh, PA 15261. Attn: Editor. Scholarly nonfiction (philosophy of science, Latin American studies, political science, urban environmental history, culture, composition, and literacy). For poetry send SASE for rules and reading periods.

UNIVERSITY OF SOUTH CAROLINA PRESS—937 Assembly St., Carolina Plaza, 8th Fl., Columbia, SC 29208. Acquisitions Ed. Books on history, literature, rhetoric, and religious studies. No original fiction. Submit outline with sample chapters. Royalty. Web site: www.sc.edu/uscpress.

UNIVERSITY OF TENNESSEE PRESS—293 Communications Bldg., Knoxville, TN 37996-0325. Attn: Joyce Harrison. Nonfiction, American topics only, and humanities disciplines only, 200 to 400 manuscript pages. No poetry, translations, children's books, plays, or textbooks. Query with outline and sample chapters. Royalty. Web site: www.sunsite.utk.edu/utpress.

UNIVERSITY OF TEXAS PRESS—Div. of University of Texas, Box 7819, Austin, TX 78713-7819. Joanna Hitchcock, Dir. Nonfiction books, 75,000 to 100,000 words. "Our press is located in the heart of Texas, but our books know no regional or even national boundaries." Query with outline. Royalty.

UNIVERSITY OF WISCONSIN PRESS—2537 Daniels St., Madison, WI 53718-6772. Attn: Acquisitions Ed. Trade nonfiction, scholarly books and regional titles on the Midwest. Offers Brittingham Prize in Poetry and Pollak Prize in Poetry; query for details. E-mail: uniscpress@uwpress.wisc.edu. Web site: www.wisc.edu/wisconsinpress/.

UNIVERSITY PRESS OF MISSISSIPPI—3825 Ridgewood Rd., Jackson, MS 39211-6492. Seetha Srinivasan, Dir. & Ed.-in-Chief. Scholarly and trade titles in American literature, history, and culture; southern studies; African-American, women's and American studies; popular culture; folklife; art and architecture; natural sciences; health; and other liberal arts. E-mail: press @inl.state.ms.us. Web site: www.upress.state.ms.us.

THE UPPER ROOM MINISTRIES—1908 Grand Ave., Nashville, TN 37202. Stephen D. Bryant, Ed. and Pub. Adult and juvenile nonfiction. Christian devotional and spiritual formation that fit into one of the following five categories: "Opening Our Hearts and Minds to God," "Walking Together with Christ," "Preparing the Spiritual Way for Emerging Generations," "Maturing as Spiritual Leaders," and "Realizing Our Oneness in Christ." No fiction or poetry. Query with outline, sample chapters, and SASE. Multiple queries considered. Payment is in royalties.

VANDAMERE PRESS—P.O. Box 5243, Arlington, VA 22205. Jerry Frank, Assoc. Acquisitions Ed. General trade, fiction and nonfiction, including history, military, parenting, and healthcare/disability studies. Also books about the nation's capital for a national audience. Prefer to see outline with sample chapter for nonfiction; for fiction send 4 or 5 sample chapters. Author resumé essential. Multiple queries considered. Royalty. SASE required.

VIKING—375 Hudson St., New York, NY 10014. Paul Slovak and Ivan Held, Assoc. Pubs. Fiction and nonfiction, including psychology, sociology, child-rearing and development, cookbooks, sports, and popular culture. Query. Royalty.

VIKING CHILDREN'S BOOKS—345 Hudson St., New York, NY 10014. Judy Carey, Assoc. Ed. Fiction and nonfiction, including biography, history, and sports, for ages 7 to 14. Humor and picture books for ages 3 to 8. Query Children's Book Dept. with outline and sample chapter. For picture books, send entire manuscript. SASE required. Advance and royalty.

VINTAGE BOOKS—299 Park Ave., New York, NY 10171. Attn: Ed. Dept. Quality fiction and serious nonfiction. Query with sample chapters for fiction; query for nonfiction. Web site: www.vintagebooks.com.

VOYAGER BOOKS/LIBROS VIAJEROS—See *Harcourt Inc./Children's Book Div.*

VOYAGEUR PRESS—123 N. Second St., Stillwater, MN 55082. Todd R. Berger, Acquisitions Ed. Books, 15,000 to 100,000 words, on wildlife, travel, Americana, collectibles, natural history, and regional topics. "Photography is very important for most of our books." Guidelines. Query with outline and sample chapters. Royalty. E-mail: tberger@voyageurpress.com. Web site: www.voyageurpress.com.

WALKER AND COMPANY—435 Hudson St., New York, NY 10014. Attn: Ed. Dept. Adult fiction: mysteries. Adult nonfiction: biography, history, science, natural history, health, psychology, popular science, and music. Juvenile nonfiction, including biography, science, history, music, and nature. Juvenile fiction: Picture books, middle grade and young adult novels. Query with synopsis and SASE. Guidelines. Royalty. Web site: www.walkerbooks.com.

WARNER BOOKS—1271 Ave. of the Americas, New York, NY 10020. No unsolicited manuscripts or proposals. Web site: www.twbookmark.com.

WASHINGTON SQUARE PRESS—1230 Ave. of the Americas, New York, NY 10020. Nancy Miller, Dir. Paperback reprints only.

WASHINGTON STATE UNIVERSITY PRESS—Cooper Publications Bldg., P.O. Box 645910, Pullman, WA 99164-5910. Glen Lindeman, Acq. Ed. Books on northwest history, prehistory, natural history, culture and politics, 200 to 350 pages. Query. Royalty.

WASHINGTON WRITERS PUBLISHING HOUSE—P.O. Box 15271, Washington, DC 20003. Attn: Ed. Dept. Poetry books, 50 to 60 pages, by writers in the greater Washington, DC and Baltimore area only. Send SASE for guidelines.

WEE SING—See *Price Stern Sloan, Inc.*

WEISER, INC., SAMUEL—Box 612, York Beach, ME 03910. Eliot Stearnes, Ed. Nonfiction, including psychology, Eastern philosophy, esoteric studies, and alternative health. Query with sample chapters or complete manuscript. Multiple queries accepted. Pays royalty. E-mail: email@weiserbooks. com. Web site: www.weiserbooks.com.

WEISS ASSOCIATES, DANIEL—See *17th Street Productions.*

WESLEYAN UNIVERSITY PRESS—110 Mt. Vernon St., Middletown, CT 06459-0433. Tom Radko, Dir. Wesleyan Poetry series: 64 to 136 pages. Query. Royalty.

WESTMINSTER JOHN KNOX PRESS—100 Witherspoon St., Louisville, KY 40202-1396. Richard Brown, Dir. Books that inform, interpret, challenge, and encourage religious faith and living. Query Karen Kaye, Asst. Ed.; do not send complete manuscript. Payment is in royalties. Send SASE for guidelines.

WHISPERING COYOTE PRESS—Imprint of *Charlesbridge Publishing,* 7130 Alexander Dr., Dallas, TX 75214. Harold Underdown, Sr. Ed., Charlesbridge. All submissions should go to Charlesbridge Publishing Inc., 85 Main St., Watertown, MA 02472. Include SASE with sufficient postage for return of manuscript. Response time is two months. Payment is in royalties.

WHITE PINE PRESS—P.O. Box 236, Buffalo, NY 14201. Elaine La-Mattina, Ed. Novels, books of short stories, and essay collections, 250 to 350 pages. Query with outline and sample chapters. Pays in copies. E-mail: wpine@whitepine.org. Web site: www.whitepine.org.

WHITECAP BOOKS—351 Lynn Ave., N. Vancouver, BC, Canada V7J 2C4. Robert McCullough, Dir. of Pub. Operations. Juvenile books, 32 to 84 pages, and adult books, varying lengths, on such topics as natural history, gardening, cookery, and regional subjects. Query with table of contents, synopsis, and one sample chapter. Royalty and flat fee. E-mail: whitecap@whitecap.ca. Web site: www.whitecap.ca.

WHITMAN & CO., ALBERT—6340 Oakton, Morton Grove, IL 60053. Kathleen Tucker, Ed. Picture books for children ages 2 to 8; novels, biographies, mysteries, and nonfiction for middle-grade readers. Send SASE for guidelines. Send complete manuscript for picture books, 3 chapters and outline for longer fiction; query for nonfiction. Royalty.

WHITSTON PUBLISHING COMPANY—P.O. Box 958, Troy, NY 12181-0988. Michael Laddin, Ed. Publishes nonfiction in: arts, literature, humanities, psychology, science, medicine, and critical theory; bibliographies, reference works, and academic titles. Pays in royalties. Send queries, outlines, sample chapters or manuscripts.

WILDERNESS PRESS—1200 5th St., Berkeley, CA 94710. Caroline Winnett, Pub. Nonfiction: outdoor sports, recreation, and travel in the western U.S. Royalty. E-mail: mail@wildernesspress.com. Web site: www.wilderness press.com.

WILEY & SONS, INC., JOHN—605 Third Ave., New York, NY 10158-0012. Attn: Ed. Dept. Nonfiction: science/technology; business/management; travel; cooking; biography; psychology; computers; language; history; current affairs; health; finance. Send proposals with outline, bio, market information, and sample chapter. Royalty.

WILEY CHILDREN'S BOOKS—605 Third Ave., New York, NY 10158-0012. Kate Bradford, Ed. Nonfiction books, 96 to 128 pages, for 8- to 12-year-old children. Query. Royalty.

WILLIAMSON PUBLISHING CO.—P.O. Box 185, Charlotte, VT 05445. Attn: Susan Williamson. Award-winning active learning books for kids, parents, and teachers (pre-kindergarten to 8). No children's picture books or fiction. Writers must send annotated table of contents, 2 sample chapters, and SASE. E-mail: jean@williamsonbooks.com. Web site: www.williamson books.com.

WILLOW CREEK PRESS—9931 Hwy. 70 W., P.O. Box 147, Minocqua, WI 54548. Andrea Donner, Man. Ed. Books, 25,000 to 50,000 words, on nature, wildlife, and outdoor sports. Query with sample chapters. Include SASE for return of materials. No fiction. Royalty. E-mail: info@willowcreekpress. com. Web site: www.willowcreekpress.com.

WILSHIRE BOOK COMPANY—12015 Sherman Rd., N. Hollywood, CA 91605-3781. Melvin Powers, Pub. Nonfiction: self-help, motivation/inspiration/spiritual, psychology, recovery, how-to, entrepreneurship, mail order, horsemanship, and Internet marketing; minimum, 60,000 words. Fiction: allegories that teach principles of psychological/spiritual growth. Send synopsis/detailed chapter outline, 3 chapters, and SASE. Royalty.

WINDSWEPT HOUSE PUBLISHERS—Rte. 3 198, Mt. Desert, ME 04660-0159. Ed. Children's picture books; young adult novels; adult fiction and nonfiction. No unsolicited manuscripts. Send SASE for copy of new guidelines. E-mail: windswt@acadia.net. Web site: www.booknotes.com/windswept/.

WIZARDS OF THE COAST—(formerly *TSR, Inc.*) P.O. Box 707, Renton, WA 98057-0707. Attn: Manuscript Ed. Epic game-related high fantasy, gritty, action-oriented fantasy, some science fiction, about 100,000 words. Query. Advance royalty. Send SASE for guidelines. Web site: www.wizards. com.

WOODBINE HOUSE—6510 Bells Mill Rd., Bethesda, MD 20817. Susan Stokes, Ed. Books for or about people with disabilities only. Current needs include parenting, reference, special ed., picture books, and novels or nonfiction chapter books for young readers. Query or submit complete manuscript with SASE. Guidelines. Royalty. E-mail: info@woodbinehouse.com. Web site: www.woodbinehouse.com.

WORD PUBLISHING—545 Marriott Dr., Suite 750, Box 141000, Nashville, TN 37214. David Moberg, Pub. and Exec. VP. Fiction and nonfiction, 65,000 to 95,000 words, dealing with the relationship and/or applications of biblical principles to everyday life. Royalty. No unsolicited manuscripts.

WORKMAN PUBLISHING CO., INC.—708 Broadway, New York,

NY 10003. Attn: Ed. Dept. General nonfiction. Normal contractual terms based on agreement.

WORLDWIDE LIBRARY—225 Duncan Mill Rd., Don Mills, Ont., Canada M3B 3K9. Randall Toye, Ed. Dir. Feroze Mohammed, Sr. Ed. Action adventure series for *Gold Eagle* imprint; mystery fiction reprints only. No unsolicited manuscripts. E-mail: ferozemohammed@harlequin.ca.

WORLDWIDE MEDIA—27324 Camino Capistrano, Suite 211, Laguna Niguel, CA 92677. Helen J. Lee, Acquisitions Dir. International literary agency and syndicate specializing in licensing foreign rights to books and magazine articles in the fields of business, management, celebrity biographies, self-help, and occult in all genres of global appeal. Previously published books and/or magazine articles only. No poetry. Query first with SASE.

WYRICK & COMPANY—1-A Pinckney St., Charleston, SC 29401. Charles L. Wyrick, Jr., Ed.-in-Chief. Publishes fiction (particularly set in the South) and nonfiction, including illustrated books on gardening, fine arts, and antiques; food and cooking; history and memoirs; photography; travel and guide books. Queries, proposals, and manuscripts are accepted. Send SASE. Allow four to six weeks for response. Pays in royalties. E-mail: bookguys@mindspring.com.

YALE UNIVERSITY PRESS—Box 209040, New Haven, CT 06520-9040. Adult nonfiction, 400 manuscript pages. Query. Royalty.

ZEBRA—See *Kensington Publishing Corp.*

ZOLAND BOOKS—384 Huron Ave., Cambridge, MA 02138. Roland Pease, Pub. & Ed. Dir. Fiction; nonfiction of literary interest, including art and photography; and poetry. Queries preferred. Pays royalties. Web site: www.zolandbooks.com. E-mail: info@zolandbooks.com.

ZONDERVAN PUBLISHING HOUSE—5300 Patterson S.E., Grand Rapids, MI 49530. Attn: Manuscript Review. Christian titles. General fiction and nonfiction; academic and professional books. Query with outline, two sample chapters, and SASE. Royalty. Guidelines. E-mail: zpub@zph.com No proposals, manuscripts, or queries accepted via e-mail. Web site: www.zondervan.com.

SYNDICATES

Syndicates buy material from writers and artists to sell to newspapers all over the country and the world. Authors are paid either a percentage of the gross proceeds or an outright fee. Of course, features by people well known in their fields have the best chance of being syndicated. In general, syndicates want columns that have been popular in a local newspaper or magazine. Since most syndicated fiction has been published previously in magazines or books, beginning fiction writers should try to sell their stories to magazines before submitting them to syndicates.

Always query syndicates before sending manuscripts, since their needs change frequently, and be sure to enclose SASEs with queries and manuscripts.

ARKIN MAGAZINE SYNDICATE—300 Bayview Dr., Suite A-8, N. Miami Beach, FL 33160. Mitzi Roberg, Ed. Dir. Articles, 750 to 2,200 words, for trade and professional magazines. Must have small-business slant, be written in layman's language, and offer solutions to business problems. Articles should apply to many businesses, not just a specific industry. No columns. Pays 3¢ to 10¢ a word, on acceptance. SASE required; query not necessary.

CONTEMPORARY FEATURES SYNDICATE—P. O. Box 1258, Jackson, TN 38302-1258. Lloyd Russell, Ed. Articles, 1,000 to 10,000 words: how-to, money savers, business, etc. Self-help pieces for small business. Pays from $25, on acceptance. Query.

HARRIS & ASSOCIATES FEATURES—15915 Caminito Aire Puro, San Diego, CA 92128. Dick Harris, Ed. Sports- and family-oriented features, to 1,200 words; fillers and short humor, 500 to 800 words. Queries preferred. Pays varying rates.

HISPANIC LINK NEWS SERVICE—1420 N St. N.W., Washington, DC 20005. Charles A. Ericksen, Ed. Trend articles, opinion and personal experience pieces, and general features with Hispanic focus, 650 to 700 words; editorial cartoons. Pays $25 for op-ed columns and cartoons, on acceptance. Send SASE for guidelines.

THE HOLLYWOOD INSIDE SYNDICATE—Box 49957, Los Angeles, CA 90049-0957. John Austin, Dir. Feature articles, 750 to 2,500 words, on TV and film personalities with B&W photo(s). Article suggestions for 3-part series. Pieces on unusual medical and scientific breakthroughs. Pays on percentage basis for features, negotiated rates for ideas, on publication. E-mail: holywood@e32.net.

KING FEATURES SYNDICATE—235 E. 45th St., New York, NY 10017. Paul Eberhart, Exec. Ed. Columns, comics. "We do not consider or buy individual articles. We are interested in ideas for nationally syndicated columns." Submit cover letter, six sample columns of 650 words each, bio sheet and any additional clips, and SASE. No simultaneous submissions. Query with SASE for guidelines. Web site: www.kingfeatures.com.

LOS ANGELES TIMES SYNDICATE—Times Mirror Sq., Los Angeles, CA 90053. Commentary, features, columns, editorial cartoons, comics, puzzles and games; news services and online products. Send SASE for submission guidelines. Web site: www.lats.com.

NATIONAL NEWS BUREAU—P.O. Box 43039, Philadelphia, PA 19129. Harry Jay Katz, Ed. Articles, 500 to 1,500 words, interviews, consumer news, how-tos, travel pieces, reviews, entertainment pieces, features, etc. Pays on publication.

NEW YORK TIMES SYNDICATION SALES—122 E. 42nd St., New York, NY 10168. Gloria Brown Anderson, Pres. and Ed.-in-Chief. Carolee Morrison, International Ed. Articles on international, seasonal, health, lifestyle, and entertainment topics, to 1,500 words (Previously published or unpublished). Query with published article or tear sheet and SASE. No calls please. Pays 50% royalty on collected sales.

NEWSPAPER ENTERPRISE ASSOCIATION—200 Madison Ave., 4th Fl., New York, NY 10016. Alleen Barber, Man. Ed. Ideas for new concepts in syndicated columns. No single stories or stringers. Payment by contractual arrangement.

SINGER MEDIA CORP.—#106, 1030 Calle Cordillera, San Clemente, CA 92673. Helen J. Lee, V.P. International syndication, some domestic. Subjects must be of global interest. Features: celebrity interviews and profiles, women's, health, fitness, self-help, business, computer, etc., all lengths; psychological quizzes; puzzles (no word puzzles), single-panel cartoons (with no bubbles), and games for children or adults. Pays 50%.

TRIBUNE MEDIA SERVICES—435 N. Michigan Ave., #1400, Chicago, IL 60611. Fred Schecker, Ed. Continuing columns, comic strips, features, electronic databases, puzzles and word games. Query with clips. Web site: www.tms.tribune.com.

UNITED FEATURE SYNDICATE—200 Madison Ave., 4th Fl., New York, NY 10016-3903. Alleen Barber, Man. Ed./NEA No one-shots or series. Payment by contractual arrangement. Send samples with SASE. Call (212) 293-8500 or write for submission guidelines.

LITERARY PRIZE OFFERS

Writers seeking the thrill of competition should review the extensive list of literary prize offers, many of them designed to promote the as-yet-unpublished author. All of the competitions listed here are for unpublished manuscripts and usually offer publication in addition to a cash prize. The prestige that comes with winning some of the more established awards can do much to further a writer's career, as editors, publishers, and agents are likely to consider the future work of the prize winner more closely.

There are hundreds of literary contests open to writers in all genres, and the following list covers a representative number of them. The summaries given below are intended merely as guides; since submission requirements are more detailed than space allows, writers should send an SASE for complete guidelines before entering any contest. Writers are also advised to check the monthly "Prize Offers" column of *The Writer* Magazine (Kalmbach Publishing Co., 21027 Crossroads Circle, P.O. Box 1612, Waukesha, WI 53187-1612) for additional contest listings and up-to-date contest requirements. Deadlines are annual unless otherwise noted.

ACADEMY OF AMERICAN POETS—Walt Whitman Award, 584 Broadway, Suite 1208, New York, NY 10012-3250. An award of $5,000 plus publication and a one-month residency at the Vermont Studio Center is offered for a book-length poetry manuscript by a poet who has not yet published a volume of poetry. Deadline: November 15. Entry fee.

ACADEMY OF MOTION PICTURE ARTS AND SCIENCES—The Nicholl Fellowships, 8949 Wilshire Blvd., Beverly Hills, CA 90211-1972. Up to five fellowships of $25,000 each are awarded for original screenplays that display exceptional craft and engaging storytelling. Deadline: May 1. Entry fee.

ACTORS THEATRE OF LOUISVILLE—Ten-Minute Play Contest, 316 W. Main St., Louisville, KY 40202-4218. A prize of $1,000 is offered for a previously unproduced ten-page script. Deadline: December 1.

AMERICAN ACADEMY OF ARTS AND LETTERS—Richard Rodgers Awards, 633 W. 155th St., New York, NY 10032. Offers subsidized productions or staged readings in New York City by a nonprofit theater for a musical, play with music, thematic review, or any comparable work. Deadline: November 1.

AMERICAN ANTIQUARIAN SOCIETY—Fellowships for Historical Research, 185 Salisbury St., Worcester, MA 01609-1634. Attn: John B. Hench. At least three fellowships are awarded to creative and performing artists, writers, film makers, and journalists for research on pre-20th century American history. Residencies are four to eight weeks; travel expenses and stipends of $1,200 per month are offered. Deadline: October 5, 1999.

THE AMERICAN-SCANDINAVIAN FOUNDATION—Translation Prize, 725 Park Ave., New York, NY 10021. A prize of $2,000 is awarded for an outstanding English translation of poetry, fiction, drama, or literary prose originally written in Danish, Finnish, Icelandic, Norwegian, or Swedish. Second prize is $500. Deadline: June 1.

ANHINGA PRESS—Anhinga Prize for Poetry, P.O. Box 10595, Tallahassee, FL 32302-0595. A $2,000 prize will be awarded for an unpublished full-length collection of poetry, 48 to 72 pages, by a poet who has published no more than one full-length collection. Deadline: March 15. Entry fee.

ARMY MAGAZINE—Essay Contest, Box 1560, Arlington, VA 22210. Prizes of $1,000, $500, and $250 plus publication are awarded for essays on a given theme. Deadline: May 31.

THE ASSOCIATED WRITING PROGRAMS—Awards Series, Tallwood House, Mail Stop 1E3, George Mason Univ., Fairfax, VA 22030. In the categories of poetry, short fiction, the novel, and nonfiction, the prize is book publication and a $2,000 honorarium. Deadline: February 29. Entry fee.

ASSOCIATION OF JEWISH LIBRARIES—Sydney Taylor Manuscript Competition, 1327 Wyntercreek Ln., Dunwoody, GA 30338. Attn: Paula Sandfelder, Coordinator. Offers $1,000 for the best fiction manuscript, 64 to 200 pages, by an unpublished book author, writing for readers 8 to 11. Stories must have a positive Jewish focus. Deadline: January 15.

BAKER'S PLAYS—High School Playwriting Contest, P.O. Box 69922, Quincy, MA 02269. Plays about the high school experience, written by high school students, are eligible for awards of $500, $250, and $100. Deadline: January 31.

BANKS CHANNEL BOOKS—Carolina Novel Award, P.O. Box 4446, Wilmington, NC 28406. Awards publication plus a $1,000 advance for an original, unpublished novel by a North or South Carolina writer. Deadline: July 31 of even-numbered years. Entry fee.

BANTAM DOUBLEDAY DELL BOOKS FOR YOUNG READERS—Marguerite de Angeli Prize, Dept. BFYR, 1540 Broadway, New York,

NY 10036. A prize of $1,500 and a $3,500 advance against royalties is awarded for a middle-grade fiction manuscript that explores the diversity of the American experience. Open to U.S. and Canadian writers who have not previously published a novel for middle-grade readers. Deadline: June 30.

BARNARD COLLEGE—New Women Poets Prize, Women Poets at Barnard, Columbia Univ., 3009 Broadway, New York, NY 10027-6598. Attn: Directors. A prize of $1,500 and publication by Beacon Press is offered for an unpublished poetry manuscript, 50 to 100 pages, by a female poet who has never published a book of poetry. Deadline: October 15.

THE BELLETRIST REVIEW—Fiction Contest, Marmarc Publications, P.O. Box 596, Plainville, CT 06062-0596. Prize of $200 plus publication is awarded for an unpublished short story, 2,500 to 5,000 words. Deadline: July 15. Entry fee.

THE BELLINGHAM REVIEW—Tobias Wolff Award in Fiction/Annie Dillard Award in Nonfiction/49th Parallel Poetry Award, MS-9053, Western Washington Univ., Bellingham, WA 98225. Tobias Wolff Award in Fiction: Offers prizes of $500 plus publication, $250, and $100 for a short story or novel excerpt. Deadline: March 1. Annie Dillard Award in Nonfiction: Offers prizes of $500 plus publication, $250, and $100 for previously unpublished essays. Deadline: March 1. 49th Parallel Poetry Award: Offers publication and prizes of $500, $250, and $100 for individual poems. Deadline: November 30. Entry fees.

BEVERLY HILLS THEATRE GUILD/JULIE HARRIS PLAYWRIGHT AWARD—2815 N. Beachwood Dr., Los Angeles, CA 90068-1923. Attn: Marcella Meharg. Offers prize of $5,000, $2,000, and $1,000 for an unpublished full-length play. Deadline: November 1.

THE BEVERLY HILLS THEATRE GUILD PLAY COMPETITION FOR CHILDREN'S THEATRE—2815 N. Beachwood Dr., Los Angeles, CA 90068-1923. A prize of $750 is awarded to the winning playscript, 40 to 50 minutes playing time, suitable for children ages 7 to 14. Runner-up receives $250. Deadline: February 28. Entry fee.

BIRMINGHAM-SOUTHERN COLLEGE—Hackney Literary Awards, Box 549003, Birmingham, AL 35254. A prize of $5,000 is awarded for an unpublished novel, any length. Deadline: September 30. Also, a $5,000 prize is shared for the winning short story, to 5,000 words, and poem of up to 50 lines. Deadline: December 31. Entry fees.

BLUE MOUNTAIN CENTER—Richard J. Margolis Award, 294 Washington St., Suite 610, Boston, MA 02108. A prize of $1,000 is awarded annually to a promising journalist or essayist whose work combines warmth, humor, wisdom, and a concern with social issues. Applications should include up to 30 pages of published or unpublished work. Deadline: June 1.

BOISE STATE UNIVERSITY—The Rocky Mountain Artists' Book Competition, Hemingway Western Studies Center, Boise, ID 83725. Tom Trusky, Ed. A prize of $500 and publication is awarded for up to 3 books; manuscripts (text and/or visual content) and proposals are considered for the short-run printing of books on public issues, especially the Inter-Mountain West. Deadline: year-round.

BOSTON REVIEW—Poetry Contest, *Boston Review*, E53–407 MIT, Cambridge, MA 02139. Annual poetry contest for original, unpublished poems, up to ten pages. Winner receives $1,000 plus publication in *Boston Review*. Send up to five poems. Deadline: June 15. Entry fee.

BOX TURTLE PRESS, INC.—Mudfish Poetry Prize, 184 Franklin St., New York, NY 10013. Awards $500 plus publication in *Mudfish*. Deadline: April 30. Entry fee.

ARCH AND BRUCE BROWN FOUNDATION—P.O. Box 45231, Phoenix, AZ 85064. Offers $1,000 grants for gay and lesbian-positive fiction. Deadline: May 31.

BUCKNELL UNIVERSITY—The Philip Roth Residence in Creative Writing, Stadler Center for Poetry, Bucknell Univ., Lewisburg, PA 17837. Attn: Cynthia Hogue, Dir. The fall residency, which includes studio, lodging, meals, and a $1,000 stipend, may be used by a writer, over 21, not currently enrolled in a university, to work on a first or second book. The residency is awarded in odd-numbered years to a fiction writer, and in even-numbered years to a poet. Deadline: March 1.

CASE WESTERN RESERVE UNIVERSITY—Marc A. Klein Playwriting Award, Dept. of Theater Arts, 10900 Euclid Ave., Cleveland, OH 44106-7077. A prize of $1,000 plus production is offered for an original, previously unproduced full-length play by a student currently enrolled at an American college or university. Deadline: May 15.

CENTER FOR BOOK ARTS—Poetry Chapbook Prize, Center for Book Arts, 626 Broadway, 5th Floor, New York, NY 10012. Offers $1,000, publication and a public reading for poetry manuscript, to 500 lines. Deadline: December 31. Entry fee.

CHELSEA AWARD COMPETITION—P.O. Box 1040, York Beach, ME 03910. Attn: Ed. Prizes of $750 plus publication are awarded for the best unpublished short fiction and poetry. Deadlines: June 15 (fiction); December 15 (poetry). Entry fees.

THE CHICAGO TRIBUNE—Nelson Algren Awards, 435 N. Michigan Ave., Chicago, IL 606ll. A first prize of $5,000 and three runner-up prizes of $1,000 are awarded for outstanding unpublished short stories, 2,500 to 10,000 words, by American writers. Deadline: February 1.

CLAREMONT GRADUATE SCHOOL—Kingsley Tufts Poetry Awards, 160 E. 10th St., Claremont, CA 91711. An award of $50,000 is given an American poet whose work is judged most worthy. An award of $5,000 is given to an emerging poet whose work displays extraordinary promise. Books of poetry published or manuscripts completed in the calendar year are considered. Deadline: September 15.

CLEVELAND STATE UNIVERSITY POETRY CENTER—Poetry Center Prize, Dept. of English, Rhodes Tower, Rm. 1815, 1983 E. 24th St., Cleveland, OH 44115-2440. Publication and $1,000 are awarded for a previously unpublished book-length volume of poetry. Deadline: March 1. Entry fee.

COALITION FOR THE ADVANCEMENT OF JEWISH EDUCATION—David Dornstein Memorial Creative Writing Contest, 261 W. 35th St., Floor 12A, New York, NY 10001. Publication and prizes of $700, $200, and $100 are awarded for the three best original, previously unpublished short stories, to 5,000 words, on a Jewish theme or topic, by writers age 18 to 35. Deadline: December 31.

COLONIAL PLAYERS, INC.—Promising Playwright Award, 98 Tower Dr., Stevensville, MD 21666. Attn: Fran Marchano. A prize of $750 plus possible production will be awarded for the best full-length play by a resident of MD, DC, VA, WV, DE, or PA. Deadline: December 31 (of even-numbered years).

COLORADO STATE UNIVERSITY—Colorado Prize for Poetry, *Colorado Review,* Dept. of English, Fort Collins, CO 80523. Offers $1,500 plus publication for a book-length collection of original poems. Deadline: January 10. Entry fee.

COMMUNITY CHILDREN'S THEATRE OF KANSAS CITY—8021 E. 129th Terrace, Grandview, MO 64030. Attn: Mrs. Blanche Sellens, Dir. A prize of $500, plus production, is awarded for the best play, up to one hour long, to be performed by adults for elementary school audiences. Deadline: January 31.

COMMUNITY WRITERS ASSOCIATION—CWA Writing Contest, P.O. Box 12, Newport, RI 02840-0001. A prize of $500 is offered for short stories, to 2,000 words, and poetry, any length. Deadline: June 1. Entry fee.

EUGENE V. DEBS FOUNDATION—Bryant Spann Memorial Prize, Dept. of History, Indiana State Univ., Terre Haute, IN 47809. Offers a prize of $1,000 for a published or unpublished article or essay on themes relating to social protest or human equality. Deadline: April 30.

DEEP SOUTH WRITERS CONFERENCE—Contest Clerk, Drawer 44691, Univ. of Southwestern Louisianna, Lafayette, LA 70504-4691. Prizes ranging from $50 to $300 are offered for unpublished manuscripts in the following categories: Fiction (including science fiction); Novel; Nonfiction; Poetry; Drama; and French literature. Deadline: July 15. Miller Award: offers $500 for a play dealing with some aspect of the life of Edward de Vere (1550-1604), the 17th Earl of Oxford. Deadline: July 15 (of odd-numbered years). Entry fee.

DELACORTE PRESS—Prize for First Young Adult Novel, Random House, Inc., 1540 Broadway, New York, NY 10036. A writer who has not previously published a young adult novel may submit a book-length manuscript with a contemporary setting suitable for readers ages 12 to 18. The prize is $1,500, plus a $6,000 advance, and hardcover and paperback publication. Deadline: December 31.

DRURY COLLEGE—Playwriting Contest, 900 N. Benton Ave., Springfield, MO 65802. Attn: Sandy Asher, Writer-in-Residence. Prizes of $300 and two $150 honorable mentions, plus possible production, are awarded for original, previously unproduced one-act plays. Deadline: December 1 (of even-numbered years).

DUBUQUE FINE ARTS PLAYERS—One-Act Playwriting Contest, 330 Clarke Dr., Dubuque, IA 52001. Attn: Jennifer G. Stabenow, Coordinator. Prizes of $600, $300 and $200 plus possible production are awarded for unproduced, original one-act plays of up to 40 minutes. Deadline: January 31. Entry fee.

DUKE UNIVERSITY—Dorothea Lange-Paul Taylor Prize, Prize Committee, Center for Documentary Studies, Box 90802, Duke Univ., Durham, NC 27708-0802. A grant of up to $10,000 is awarded to a writer and photographer working together in the formative stages of a documentary project that will ultimately result in a publishable work. Deadline: January 31. Entry fee.

ELF: ECLECTIC LITERARY FORUM—Ruth Cable Memorial Prize, P.O. Box 392, Tonawanda, NY 14150. Awards of $500 and three $50 prizes are given for poems up to 50 lines. Short Fiction Prize awards $500 plus publication and two $50 prizes for stories, to 3,500 words. Deadline: March 31. Fiction deadline: August 31. Entry fee.

EMPORIA STATE UNIVERSITY—Bluestem Award, English Dept., Emporia State Univ., Emporia, KS 66801-5087. A prize of $1,000 plus publication is awarded for a previously unpublished book of poems by a U.S. author. Deadline: March 1. Entry fee.

THE FLORIDA REVIEW—The Editors' Awards (specify Fiction, Nonfiction, or Poetry), Dept. of English, Univ. of Central Florida, Orlando, FL 32816-0001. Attn: Russell Kesler, Ed. Prizes of $500 plus publication are offered for short stories, essays, and creative nonfiction to 7,500 words, as well as groups of 3 to 5 poems, to 25 lines. Deadline: March 15. Entry fee.

FLORIDA STUDIO THEATRE—Shorts Contest, 1241 N. Palm Ave., Sarasota, FL 34236. Attn: Christian Angermann. Short scripts, songs, and other performance pieces on a given theme are eligible for a prize of $500. Deadline: February 15.

THE FORMALIST—Howard Nemerov Sonnet Award, 320 Hunter Dr., Evansville, IN 47711. A prize of $1,000 plus publication is offered for a previously unpublished, original sonnet. Deadline: June 15. Entry fee.

FOUR WAY BOOKS—Intro Prize in Poetry, P.O. Box 535, Village Sta., New York, NY 10014. Attn: K. Clarke. Awards $3,500 ($2,000 honorarium plus $1,500 author tour money) and publication for a book-length collection of poems by a U.S. poet. Deadline: March 31. Entry fee.

GEORGE MASON UNIVERSITY—Greg Grummer Award in Poetry, 4400 Univ. Dr., Fairfax, VA 22030-4444. A prize of $500 plus publication is offered for an outstanding previously unpublished poem. Deadline: December 15. Entry fee.

GEORGE WASHINGTON UNIVERSITY—Jenny McKean Moore Writer-in-Washington, Dept. of English, Washington, DC 20052. Attn: Prof. Christopher Sten. A salaried teaching position for two semesters is offered to a creative writer (of various mediums in alternate years) having "significant publications and a demonstrated commitment to teaching. The writer need not have conventional academic credentials." Deadline: November 15.

THE GEORGETOWN REVIEW FICTION AND POETRY CONTEST—P.O. Box 6309, Southern Station, Hattiesburg, MS 39406-6309. A prize of $1,000 for a short story of no more than 25 pages or 6,500 words and $500 for a single poem, any length, plus publication and subscription. Deadline: October 1. Entry fee.

GLIMMER TRAIN PRESS—Semiannual Short Story Award for New Writers, 710 S.W. Madison St., #504, Portland, OR 97205. Writers whose fiction has never appeared in a nationally distributed publication are eligible to enter their stories of 1,200 to 7,500 words. Prizes are $1,200 plus publication, $500, and $300. Deadlines: March 31; September 30. Entry fee.

GREENFIELD REVIEW LITERARY CENTER—North American

Native Authors First Book Awards, P.O. Box 308, 2 Middle Grove Rd., Greenfield Center, NY 12833. Attn: Joseph Bruchac, Dir. Native Americans of American Indian, Aleut, Inuit, or Metis ancestry who have not yet published a book are eligible to enter poetry, 64 to 100 pages, and prose, 200 to 300 pages (fiction or nonfiction) for $500 prizes plus publication. Deadline: March 15.

GROLIER POETRY PRIZE—6 Plympton St., Cambridge, MA 02138. Two $150 honorariums are awarded for poetry manuscripts of up to 10 double-spaced pages, including no more than five previously unpublished poems, by writers who have not yet published a book of poems. Deadline: May 1. Entry fee.

HEEKIN GROUP FOUNDATION—Fiction Fellowships Competition, Box 1534, Sisters, OR 97759. Awards the following fellowships to beginning career writers: two $1,500 Tara Fellowships in Short Fiction; two $3,000 James Fellowships for a Novel in Progress; one $2,000 Mary Molloy Fellowship for a Juvenile Novel in Progress (address H.G.F., P.O. Box 209, Middlebury, VT 05753); and one $2,000 Cuchulain Fellowhip for Rhetoric (Essay). Writers who have never published a novel, a children's novel, more than five short stories in national publication, or an essay are eligible to enter. Deadline: December 1. Entry fee.

HELICON NINE EDITIONS—Literary Prizes, 3607 Pennsylvania, Kansas City, MO 64111. Marianne Moore Poetry Prize: offers $1,000 for an original unpublished poetry manuscript of at least 48 pages. Willa Cather Fiction Prize: offers $1,000 for an original novella or short story collection, from 150 to 300 pages. Deadline: May 1. Entry fee.

LORIAN HEMINGWAY SHORT STORY COMPETITION—P.O. Box 993, Key West, FL 33041. Awards a $1,000 prize to an original, unpublished work short story, to 3,000 words by a writer whose fiction has never appeared in a nationally distributed publication. Deadline: June 1. Entry fee.

HIGHLIGHTS FOR CHILDREN—Fiction Contest, 803 Church St., Honesdale, PA 18431. Three $1,000 prizes plus publication are offered for stories on a given subject, up to 900 words. Deadline: February 28.

RUTH HINDMAN FOUNDATION—H.E. Francis Award, Dept. of English, Univ. of Alabama, Huntsville, AL 35899. A prize of $1,000 is awarded for a short story of up to 5,000 words. Deadline: December 31. Entry fee.

L. RON HUBBARD'S WRITERS OF THE FUTURE CONTEST—P.O. Box 1630, Los Angeles, CA 90078. Unpublished fiction writers are eligible to enter science fiction or fantasy short stories under 10,000 words, or novellas under 17,000 words. Quarterly prizes: $1,000, $750, and $500. Annual prize: $4,000. Deadlines: March 31; June 30; September 30; December 31.

INSTITUTE OF HISPANIC CULTURE—José Martí Award, 3315 Sul Ross, Houston, TX 77098. Prizes of $1,000, $600, and $400 are awarded for essays, 15 to 20 pages, on a given theme. Deadline: August 31.

INTERNATIONAL QUARTERLY—Crossing Boundaries Awards, P.O. Box 10521, Tallahassee, FL 32303-0521. Offers four prizes of $500 each plus publication for poetry, fiction, nonfiction, and "Crossing Boundaries," a category that includes "atypical work and innovative or experimental writing." Manuscripts, to 5,000 words; up to 5 poems per poetry submission. Deadline: March 1. Entry fee.

IUPUI CHILDREN'S THEATRE—Playwriting Competition, Indiana

University-Purdue University at Indianapolis, 425 University Blvd., Suite 309, Indianapolis, IN 46202. Offers four $1,000 prizes plus staged readings for plays for young people. Deadline: September 1 (of even-numbered years).

ALICE JAMES BOOKS—Beatrice Hawley Award, Univ. of Maine at Farmington, 98 Main St., Farmington, ME 04938. A prize of publication plus 100 free copies is offered for the best poetry manuscript, 60 to 70 pages. Deadline: December 1. Entry fee.

JOE JEFFERSON PLAYERS ORIGINAL PLAY COMPETITION— P.O. Box 66065, Mobile, AL 36660. A prize of $1,000 plus production is offered for an original, previously unproduced play. Deadline: March 1.

JEWISH COMMUNITY CENTER THEATRE—Dorothy Silver Playwriting Competition, 3505 Mayfield Rd., Cleveland Heights, OH 44118. Attn: Elaine Rembrandt, Dir. Offers $1,000 and a staged reading for an original, previously unproduced full-length play, on some aspect of the Jewish experience. Deadline: December 15.

CHESTER H. JONES FOUNDATION—National Poetry Competition, P. O. Box 498, Chardon, OH 44024. Prizes of $1,000, $750, $500, $250, and $100, as well as several $50 and $10 prizes are awarded for original, unpublished poems of up to 32 lines. Deadline: March 31. Entry fee.

JAMES JONES SOCIETY—First Novel Fellowship, c/o Dept. of English, Wilkes Univ., Wilkes-Barre, PA 18766. An award of $2,500 is offered for a first novel-in-progress by an American. Deadline: March 1. Entry fee.

THE JOURNAL: THE LITERARY MAGAZINE OF O.S.U.—The Ohio State Univ. Press, 1070 Carmack Rd., Columbus, OH 43210-1002. Attn: David Citino, Poetry Ed. Awards $1,000 plus publication for at least 48 pages of original, unpublished poetry. Deadline: September 30. Entry fee.

KALLIOPE: A JOURNAL OF WOMEN'S ART—Sue Saniel Elkind Poetry Contest, Florida Community College at Jacksonville, 3939 Roosevelt Blvd., Jacksonville, FL 32205. Publication and $1,000 are awarded for the best poem, under 50 lines, written by a woman. Deadline: November 1. Entry fee.

KEATS/KERLAN MEMORIAL FELLOWSHIP—The Ezra Jack Keats Memorial Fellowship Committee, 109 Walter Library, 117 Pleasant St. S.E., Univ. of Minnesota, Minneapolis, MN 55455. A $1,500 fellowship is awarded to a talented writer and/or illustrator of children's books who wishes to use the Kerlan Collection for furtherance of his or her artistic development. Deadline: May 1.

KENT STATE UNIVERSITY PRESS—Stan and Tom Wick Poetry Prize, P.O. Box 5190, Kent, OH 44242-0001. Publication and $1,000 are offered for a book of poems, 48 to 68 pages, by a writer who has not previously published a collection of poetry. Deadline: May 1. Entry fee.

LOVE CREEK PRODUCTIONS—One-Act Play Festivals, 162 Nesbit St., Weehawken, NJ 07087-6817. One-act plays and theme-based plays are awarded production or staged readings. Deadlines vary.

AMY LOWELL POETRY TRAVELLING SCHOLARSHIP— Choate, Hall & Stewart, Exchange Pl., 53 State St., Boston, MA 02109-2891. Attn: F. Davis Dassori. A scholarship of approximately $29,000 is awarded for a poet to spend the year abroad to advance the art of poetry. Deadline: October 15.

THE MADISON REVIEW—Dept. of English, 600 N. Park St., Helen C. White Hall, Univ. of Wisconsin-Madison, Madison, WI 53706. Phyllis Smart Young Prize in Poetry: awards $500 plus publication for a group of three unpublished poems. Chris O'Malley Prize in Fiction: awards $500 plus publication for an unpublished short story. Deadline: September 30. Entry fees.

MIDDLEBURY COLLEGE—Katharine Bakeless Nason Prizes, c/o Bread Loaf Writers' Conference, Middlebury College, Middlebury, VT 05753. Attn: Carol Knauss. Publication and fellowships to the Bread Loaf Writers' Conference are offered for previously unpublished first books of poetry, fiction, and nonfiction. Deadline: March 1. Entry fee.

MID-LIST PRESS—First Series Awards, 4324 12th Ave. S., Minneapolis, MN 55407-3218. Publication and an advance against royalties are awarded for first books in the following categories: a novel in any genre, from 50,000 words; poetry, from 65 pages; short fiction, from 50,000 words; creative nonfiction, from 50,000 words. Deadline: February 1 (novel and poetry); July 1 (short fiction and creative nonfiction). Entry fees.

MIDWEST RADIO THEATRE WORKSHOP—MRTW Script Competition, 115 Dikeman St., Hempstead, NY 11550. Workshop Script Contest: offers $800 in prizes, to be divided among two to four winners, and free workshop participation for contemporary radio scripts, 25 to 30 minutes long. Deadline: November 15. Entry fee.

MILL MOUNTAIN THEATRE—New Play Competition, 2nd Fl., One Market Square, Roanoke, VA 24011-1437. Attn: Jo Weinstein. Offers a $1,000 prize and staged reading, with possible full production, for an unpublished, unproduced, full-length or one-act play or musical. Cast size to ten. Deadline: January 1.

MISSISSIPPI REVIEW—Prize for Short Fiction and Poetry, The Center for Writers, Univ. of Southern Mississippi, Box 5144, Hattiesburg, MS 39406-5144. Attn: R. Fortenberry. Publication and $1,000 are offered for the best short story; $500 plus publication for the best poem. Deadline: May 31. Entry fee.

THE MISSOURI REVIEW—Editors' Prize, 1507 Hillcrest Hall, UMC, Columbia, MO 65211. Publication plus $1,500 is awarded for a short fiction manuscript (25 pages); $1,000 for an essay (25 pages); and $1,500 for poetry (10 pages). Deadline: October 15. Entry fee.

THE MOUNTAINEERS BOOKS—The Barbara Savage/"Miles from Nowhere" Memorial Award, 1001 S. W. Klickitat Way, Suite 201, Seattle, WA 98134. Offers a $3,000 cash award, plus publication and a $12,000 guaranteed advance against royalties for an outstanding unpublished, book-length manuscript of a nonfiction, personal-adventure narrative. Deadline: May 1 (of even-numbered years).

NATIONAL ENDOWMENT FOR THE ARTS—Nancy Hanks Center, 1100 Pennsylvania Ave. N.W., Room 720, Washington, DC 20506. Attn: Dir., Literature Program. Offers fellowships to writers and translators of poetry, fiction, plays, and creative nonfiction. Deadline: varies.

NATIONAL FEDERATION OF STATE POETRY SOCIETIES—Poetry Manuscript Contest, 3520 State Rt. 56, Mechanicsburg, OH 43044. Attn: Amy Zook, Chairman. A prize of $1,000 is awarded for the best manuscript of poetry, 35 to 60 pages. Deadline: October 15. Entry fee.

NATIONAL POETRY SERIES—P.O. Box G, Hopewell, NJ 08525.

Attn: Coordinator. Sponsors Annual Open Competition for unpublished book-length poetry manuscripts. Five manuscripts are selected for publication, and each winner receives a $1,000 award. Deadline: February 15. Entry fee.

NEW ENGLAND POETRY CLUB—Annual Contests, 11 Puritan Rd., Arlington, MA 02172. Attn: Virginia Thayer. Prizes range from $100 to $500 in various contests for members, nonmembers, and students. Deadline: April 15. Entry fee.

NEW ENGLAND THEATRE CONFERENCE—John Gassner Memorial Playwriting Award, c/o Dept. of Theatre, Northeastern Univ., 360 Huntington Ave., Boston, MA 02115. A $1,000 first prize and a $500 second prize are offered for unpublished, unproduced full-length plays written by New England residents or members of the NETC. Deadline: April 15. Entry fee.

NEW ISSUES PRESS/WESTERN MICHIGAN UNIVERSITY—New Issues Poetry Prize, Western Michigan Univ., Kalamazoo, MI 49008-5092. Attn: Herbert Scott, Ed. Awards $1,000 plus publication for a book-length collection of poetry by a poet who has never before published a full-length collection. Deadline: November 30. Entry fee.

THE GREEN ROSE PRIZE IN POETRY—*New Issues Poetry,* Western Michigan University, 1201 Oliver St., Kalamazoo, MI 49008. Open to poets who have had one or more full-length collections of poetry published, the winner receives a prize of $1,000 plus publication. Deadline: September 30. Entry fee.

NEW LETTERS—University of Missouri-Kansas City, 5100 Rockhill Rd., Kansas City, MO 64110-2499. Offers $750 for the best short story, to 5,000 words; $750 for the best group of three to six poems; $500 for the best essay, to 5,000 words. The work of each winner and first runner-up will be published. Deadline: May 15. Entry fee.

NEW YORK UNIVERSITY PRESS—New York University Press Prizes, 70 Washington Sq. S., 2nd Fl., New York, NY 10012-1091. Awards $1,000 plus publication to a book-length poetry manuscript and a book-length fiction manuscript. Deadline: May 1.

NIMROD/HARDMAN AWARDS—*Nimrod International Journal,* 600 S. College Ave., Tulsa, OK 74104-3189. Katherine Anne Porter Prize: offers prizes of $2,000 and $1,000 for fiction, to 7,500 words. Pablo Neruda Prize: offers prizes of $2,000 and $1,000 for one long poem or a selection of poems. Deadline: April 15. Entry fees.

NORTH CAROLINA WRITERS' NETWORK—International Literature Prizes, 3501 Hwy. 54 West, Studio C, Chapel Hill, NC 27516. Thomas Wolfe Fiction Prize: offers $500 for a previously unpublished short story or novel excerpt. Deadline: August 31. Paul Green Playwrights Prize: offers $500 for a previously unproduced, unpublished play. Deadline: September 30. Randall Jarrell Poetry Prize: offers $500 for a previously unpublished poem. Deadline: November 1. Entry fees.

NORTHEASTERN UNIVERSITY PRESS—Samuel French Morse Poetry Prize, English Dept., 406 Holmes Hall, Northeastern Univ., Boston, MA 02115. Attn: Prof. Guy Rotella, Chairman. Offers $1,000 plus publication for a full-length poetry manuscript by a U.S. poet who has published no more than one book of poems. Deadline: August 1 (for inquiries); September 15 (for entries). Entry fee.

NORTHERN KENTUCKY UNIVERSITY—Y.E.S. New Play Festival, Dept. of Theatre, FA 227, Nunn Dr., Highland Hts., KY 41099-1007. Attn: Sandra Forman, Project Dir. Awards three $400 prizes plus production for previously unproduced full-length plays and musicals. Deadline: October 31 (of even-numbered years).

NORTHERN MICHIGAN UNIVERSITY—Mildred & Albert Panowski Playwriting Competition, Forest Roberts Theatre, Northern Michigan Univ., 1401 Presque Isle Ave., Marquette, MI 49855-5364. Awards $2,000, plus production for an original, full-length, previously unproduced and unpublished play. Deadline: November 20.

O'NEILL THEATER CENTER—National Playwrights Conference, 234 W. 44th St., Suite 901, New York, NY 10036. Attn: Mary F. McCabe. Offers stipend, staged readings, and room and board at the conference, for new stage and television plays. Deadline: December 1. Entry fee.

OFF CENTER THEATER—Women Playwright's Festival, Tampa Bay Performing Arts Center, P.O. Box 518, Tampa, FL 33601. A $1,000 prize, production, and travel are offered for the best play about women, written by a woman; runner-up receives staged reading. Deadline: September 15. Entry fee.

OHIO UNIVERSITY PRESS—Hollis Summers Poetry Prize, Scott Quadrangle, Athens, OH 45701. A $500 prize plus publication is awarded for an original collection of poetry, 60 to 95 pages. Deadline: October 31. Entry fee.

OLD DOMINION UNIVERSITY—Vassar Miller Prize in Poetry, c/o English Dept., Old Dominion University, Norfolk, VA 23529. Attn: Scott Cairns, Series Ed. Awards $1,000 plus publication by the University of North Texas Press for an original, unpublished poetry manuscript, 50 to 80 pages. Deadline: November 30. Entry fee.

PASSAGES NORTH—Elinor Benedict Poetry Prize, Dept. of English, Northern Michigan Univ., 1401 Presque Isle Ave., Marquette, MI 49855. $500 prize for unpublished poem. Deadline: December 1. Entry fee.

PATHWAY PRODUCTIONS—National Playwriting Contest, 9561 E. Daines Dr., Temple City, CA 91780. (E-mail: PathWayPro@earthlink.net) Awards $200 plus a workshop production to plays for and about teenagers. Deadline April 1.

PEN WRITERS FUND—PEN American Center, 568 Broadway, New York, NY 10012. Attn: India Amos, Writers Fund Coordinator. Grants and interest-free loans of up to $500 are available to published writers or produced playwrights facing unanticipated financial emergencies. If the emergency is due to HIV- and AIDS-related illness, professional writers and editors qualify through the Fund for Writers and Editors with AIDS; all decisions are confidential. Deadline: year-round.

PEN WRITING AWARDS FOR PRISONERS—PEN American Center, 568 Broadway, New York, 10012. County, state, and federal prisoners are eligible to enter one unpublished manuscript, to 5,000 words, in each of these categories: fiction, drama, and nonfiction. Prisoners may submit up to 10 poems (any form) in the poetry category (to 20 pages total) in the poetry category. Prizes of $100, $50, and $25 are awarded in each category. Deadline: September 1.

PEREGRINE SMITH POETRY SERIES—Gibbs Smith, Publisher,

P.O. Box 667, Layton, UT 84041. Offers a $500 prize plus publication for a previously unpublished 64-page poetry manuscript. Deadline: April 30. Entry fee.

PETERLOO POETS—Open Competition, 2 Kelly Gardens, Calstock, Cornwall PL18 9SA, U.K. Prizes totalling 5,100 British pounds, including a grand prize of £4,000 plus publication, are awarded for poems of up to 40 lines. Deadline: March 1. Entry fee.

PHILADELPHIA FESTIVAL OF WORLD CINEMA—"Set in Philadelphia" Screenwriting Competition, 3701 Chestnut St., Philadelphia, PA 19104-3195. A $5,000 prize is awarded for the best screenplay, 85 to 130 pages, set primarily in the greater Philadelphia area. Deadline: January 1. Entry fee.

PIG IRON PRESS—Kenneth Patchen Competition, P.O. Box 237, Youngstown, OH 44501. Awards paperback publication, $500, and 20 copies of the winning manuscript of fiction (in even-numbered years) and poetry (in odd-numbered years). Deadline: December 31. Entry fee.

PIONEER DRAMA SERVICE—Shubert Fendrich Memorial Playwriting Contest, P.O. Box 4267, Englewood, CO 80155-4267. A prize of publication plus a $1,000 advance is offered for a previously produced, though unpublished, full-length play suitable for community theater. Deadline: March 1.

PLAYBOY—College Fiction Contest, 680 N. Lake Shore Dr., Chicago, IL 60611. Prizes of $3,000 plus publication, and $500, are offered for a short story, up to 25 pages, by a college student. Deadline: January 1.

THE PLAYWRIGHTS' CENTER—Jerome Fellowships, 2301 Franklin Ave. E., Minneapolis, MN 55406. Five emerging playwrights are offered a $7,000 stipend and 12-month residency; housing and travel are not provided. Deadline: September 16.

POCKETS—Fiction Contest, c/o Lynn W. Gilliam, Assoc. Ed., P.O. Box 189, Nashville, TN 37202-0189. A $1,000 prize goes to the author of the winning 1,000- to 1,600-word story for children in grades 1 to 6. Deadline: August 15.

POETS AND PATRONS OF CHICAGO—Poets and Patrons of Chicago, 1206 Hutchings, Glenview, IL 60025. Attn: Agnes Wathall Tatera. Prizes are $75 and $25 for original, unpublished poems of up to 40 lines. Deadline: September 1.

POETS CLUB OF CHICAGO—130 Windsor Park Dr., C-323, Carol Stream, IL 60188. Attn: LaVone Holt. Shakespearean/Petrarchan Sonnet Contest, with prizes of $50, $35, and $15. Deadline: September 1.

PRISM INTERNATIONAL—Short Fiction Contest, Creative Writing Dept., Univ. of B.C., E462-1866 Main Mall, Vancouver, B.C., V6T 1Z1. Publication, a $2,000 first prize, and five $200 prizes are awarded for stories of up to 25 pages. Deadline: December 31. Entry fee.

RIVER CITY—Writing Awards in Fiction, Dept. of English, Univ. of Memphis, Memphis, TN 38152. Awards of $2,000 plus publication, $500, and $300 are offered for previously unpublished short stories, to 7,500 words. Deadline: December 1. Entry fee.

ROME ART & COMMUNITY CENTER—Milton Dorfman Poetry Prize, 308 W. Bloomfield St., Rome, NY 13440. Offers prizes of $500, $200, and $100 for the best original, unpublished poems. Deadline: November 1. Entry fee.

ST. MARTIN'S PRESS/MALICE DOMESTIC CONTEST—Thomas Dunne Books, 175 Fifth Ave., New York, NY 10010. Offers publication plus a $10,000 advance against royalties, for a best first traditional mystery novel. Deadline: October 15.

ST. MARTIN'S PRESS/PRIVATE EYE NOVEL CONTEST—PWA Contest, 175 Fifth Ave., New York, NY 10010. Co-sponsored by Private Eye Writers of America. The writer of the best first private eye novel, from 60,000 words, receives publication plus $10,000 against royalties. Deadline: August 1.

SARABANDE BOOKS—Poetry and Short Fiction Prizes, P.O. Box 4999, Louisville, KY 40204. Prizes are $2,000, publication, and a standard royalty contract in the competition for the Kathryn A. Morton Prize in Poetry (for a collection of poems, from 48 pages) and the Mary McCarthy Prize in Short Fiction (for a collection of short stories or novellas, 150 to 300 pages). Deadline: February 15. Entry fee.

SHENANARTS—Shenandoah International Playwrights Retreat, Rt. 5, Box 167-F, Staunton, VA 24401. Full fellowships are offered to playwrights to attend the four-week retreat held each August. Each year the retreat focuses on plays having to do with a specific region of the world. Deadline: February 1.

SIENA COLLEGE—International Playwrights' Competition, Siena College, 515 Loudon Rd., Loudonville, NY 12211-1462. Offers $2,000 plus campus residency expenses for the winning full-length script; no musicals. Deadline: June 30 (of even-numbered years).

SILVERFISH REVIEW PRESS—The Gerald Cable Book Award, P.O. Box 3541, Eugene, OR 97403. Attn: Rodger Moody, Series Ed. Awards $1,000 plus publication to a book-length manuscript of poetry by an author who has not yet published a full-length collection. Deadline: November 1. Entry fee.

SNAKE NATION PRESS—Fiction and Poetry Contests, 110 #2 W. Force St., Valdosta, GA 31601. Attn: Nancy Phillips. Violet Reed Haas Prize: Offers publication plus $500 for a previously unpublished book of poetry, 50 to 75 pages. Deadline: January 15. *Snake Nation Review* Contest Issues: Prizes are publication plus $300, $200, and $100 for short stories; $100, $75, and $50 for poems. Deadlines: April 1; September 1. Entry fee.

SONORA REVIEW—Contests, Univ. of Arizona, Dept. of English, Tucson, AZ 85721. Poetry, Nonfiction Contest: offers $250 plus publication for the best poem; $100 plus publication for the best nonfiction. Deadline: July 1 for poetry and nonfiction. Short Story Contest: offers $250 plus publication for the best short story. Deadline: December 1. Entry fees.

THE SOUTHERN ANTHOLOGY—The Southern Prize, 2851 Johnston St., #123, Lafayette, LA 70503. A prize of $600 and publication are awarded for the best original, previously unpublished short story or novel excerpt, up to 7,500 words, or poem. Deadline: May 30. Entry fee.

SOUTHERN POETRY REVIEW—Guy Owen Poetry Prize, Southern Poetry Review, Advancement Studies Dept., Central Piedmont Community College, Charlotte, NC 28235. Attn: Ken McLaurin, Ed. A prize of publication plus $500 is awarded for the best original, previously unpublished poem. Deadline: April 30. Entry fee.

THE SOW'S EAR PRESS—19535 Pleasant View Dr., Abingdon, VA 24211-6827. Chapbook Competition: offers a prize of $500 plus 50 published copies for the best poetry manuscript, as well as two $100 prizes. Deadline: April 30. Poetry Competition: offers prizes of $500, $100, and $50 for a previously unpublished poem of any length. Deadline: October 31. Entry fees.

SPOON RIVER POETRY REVIEW—Editors' Prize, 4240 Dept. of English, Illinois State Univ., Normal, IL 61790-4240. Publication and a $500 prize, as well as two $100 prizes, are awarded for single poems. Deadline: May 1. Entry fee.

STATE UNIVERSITY OF NEW YORK AT STONY BROOK—Short Fiction Prize, Dept. of English, Humanities Bldg., State Univ., Stony Brook, NY 11794-5350. Attn: Carolyn McGrath. A prize of $1,000 is offered for the best short story, up to 5,000 words, written by an undergraduate currently enrolled full-time in an American or Canadian college. Deadline: February 28.

STORY LINE PRESS—Nicholas Roerich Poetry Prize, Three Oaks Farm, P.O. Box 1240, Ashland, OR 97520-0055. A prize of $1,000 plus publication is awarded for an original book of poetry by a poet who has never before published a book of poetry. Deadline: October 31. Entry fee.

SUNY FARMINGDALE—Paumanok Poetry Award, English Dept., Knapp Hall, SUNY Farmingdale, Farmingdale, NY 11735. Prizes of $1,000 and two $500 prizes are offered for entries of three to five poems. Deadline: September 15. Entry fee.

SYRACUSE UNIVERSITY PRESS—John Ben Snow Prize, 1600 Jamesville Ave., Syracuse, NY 13244-5160. Attn: Dir. Awards a $1,500 advance, plus publication, for an unpublished book-length nonfiction manuscript about New York State, especially upstate or central New York. Deadline: December 31.

TEN MINUTE MUSICALS PROJECT—Box 461194, W. Hollywood, CA 90046. Attn: Michael Koppy, Prod. Musicals of 7 to 20 minutes are eligible for a $250 advance against royalties and musical anthology productions at theaters in the U.S. and Canada. Deadline: August 31.

DAVID THOMAS CHARITABLE TRUST—Open Competitions, P.O. Box 4, Nairn IV12 4HU, Scotland, UK. The trust sponsors a number of theme-based poetry and short story contests open to beginning writers, with prizes ranging from £25 to £1,200. Deadline: varies. Entry fee.

TRITON COLLEGE—Salute to the Arts Poetry Contest, 2000 Fifth Ave., River Grove, IL 60171. Winning original, unpublished poems, to 60 lines, on designated themes, are published by Triton College. Deadline: April 1.

UNICO NATIONAL—Ella T. Grasso Literary Award Contest, 72 Burroughs Pl., Bloomfield, NJ 07003. A prize of $1,000 is awarded for the best essay or short story, 1,500 to 2,000 words, on the Italian-American experience; two $250 prizes also awarded. Deadline: April 1.

U.S. NAVAL INSTITUTE—Arleigh Burke Essay Contest, *Proceedings Magazine*, 291 Wood Rd., Annapolis, MD 21402-5034. Awards prizes of $3,000, $2,000, and $1,000 plus publication, for essays on the advancement of professional, literary, or scientific knowledge in the naval or maritime services, and the advancement of the knowledge of sea power. Deadline: December 31. Also sponsors several smaller contests; deadlines vary.

UNIVERSITIES WEST PRESS—Emily Dickinson Award in Poetry, Universities West Press, P.O. Box 22310, Flagstaff, AZ 86002-2310. A prize of $1,000 plus publication is awarded for an unpublished poem. Deadline: August 31. Entry fee.

UNIVERSITY OF AKRON PRESS—The Akron Poetry Prize, 374B Bierce Library, Akron, OH 44325-1703. Publication and $500 are offered for a previously unpublished collection of poems. Deadline: June 30. Entry fee.

UNIVERSITY OF CALIFORNIA IRVINE—Chicano/Latino Literary Contest, Dept. of Spanish and Portuguese, UCI, Irvine, CA 92697-5275. Attn: Alejandro Morales, Dir. A first prize of $1,000 plus publication, and prizes of $500 and $250 are awarded in alternating years for poetry, drama, novels, and short stories. Deadline: April 30.

UNIVERSITY OF GEORGIA PRESS—Flannery O'Connor Award for Short Fiction, Univ. of Georgia Press, 330 Research Dr., Athens, GA 30602-4901. Two prizes of $1,000 plus publication are awarded for book-length collections of short fiction. Deadline: July 31. Entry fees.

UNIVERSITY OF GEORGIA PRESS CONTEMPORARY POETRY SERIES—Athens, GA 30602-4901. Offers publication of manuscripts from poets who have published at least one volume of poetry. Deadline: January 31. Publication of book-length poetry manuscripts is offered to poets who have never had a book of poems published. Deadline: September 30. Entry fee.

UNIVERSITY OF HAWAII AT MANOA—Kumu Kahua Playwriting Contest, Dept. of Drama and Theatre, 1770 East-West Rd., Honolulu, HI 96822. Awards $500 and $400 for full-length plays on the Hawaiian experience; $200 for plays on any topic. Also conducts contest for plays written by Hawaiian residents. Deadline: January 1.

UNIVERSITY OF IOWA—Iowa Publication Awards for Short Fiction, Iowa Writers' Workshop, 102 Dey House, Iowa City, IA 52242-1000. The John Simmons Short Fiction Award and the Iowa Short Fiction Award, both for unpublished full-length collections of short stories, offer publication under a standard contract. Deadline: September 30.

UNIVERSITY OF IOWA PRESS—The Iowa Poetry Prize, 100 Kuhl House, Iowa City, IA 52242-1000. Two $1,000 prizes, plus publication, are awarded for poetry manuscripts, 50 to 150 pages, by writers who have published at least one book of poetry. Deadline: May 31.

UNIVERSITY OF MASSACHUSETTS PRESS—Juniper Prize, Amherst, MA 01003. Offers a prize of $1,000 plus publication for a book-length manuscript of poetry; awarded in odd-numbered years to writers who have never published a book of poetry, and in even-numbered years to writers who have published a book or chapbook of poetry. Deadline: September 30. Entry fee.

UNIVERSITY OF NEBRASKA-OMAHA—Awards in Poetry and Fiction, *The Nebraska Review*, Univ. of Nebraska-Omaha, Omaha, NE 68182-0324. Offers $500 each plus publication to the winning short story (to 5,000 words) and the winning poem (or group of poems). Deadline: November 30. Entry fee.

UNIVERSITY OF NEBRASKA PRESS—North American Indian Prose Award, 312 N. 14th St., Lincoln, NE 68588-0484. Previously unpublished book-length manuscripts of biography, autobiography, history, literary criticism, and essays will be judged for originality, literary merit, and familiarity with North American Indian life. A $1,000 advance and publication are offered. Deadline: July 1.

UNIVERSITY OF PITTSBURGH PRESS—3347 Forbes Ave., Pittsburgh, PA 15261. Agnes Lynch Starrett Poetry Prize: offers $3,000 plus publication in the Pitt Poetry Series for a book-length collection of poems by a poet who has not yet published a volume of poetry. Deadline: April 30. Entry fee. Drue Heinz Literature Prize: offers $10,000 plus publication and royalty contract for an unpublished collection of short stories or novellas, 150 to 300 pages, by a writer who has previously published a book-length collection of fiction or at least three short stories or novellas in nationally distributed magazines. Deadline: June 30.

UNIVERSITY OF SOUTHERN CALIFORNIA—Ann Stanford Poetry Prize, Master of Professional Writing Program, WPH 404, Univ. of Southern California, Los Angeles, CA 90089-4034. Publication plus prizes of $750, $250, and $100 are awarded; submit up to five poems. Deadline: April 15. Entry fee.

UTAH STATE UNIVERSITY PRESS—May Swenson Poetry Award, Utah State Univ. Press, Logan, UT 84322-7800. Awards $750, plus publication and royalties to a collection of poems, 50 to 100 pages. Deadline: September 30. Entry fee.

VETERANS OF FOREIGN WARS—Voice of Democracy Audio Essay Competition, VFW National Headquarters, 406 W. 34th St., Kansas City, MO 64111. Several national scholarships totalling over $120,000 are awarded to high school students for short, tape-recorded essays. Themes change annually. Deadline: November 1.

YALE UNIVERSITY PRESS—Yale Series of Younger Poets Prize, Box 209040, Yale Sta., New Haven, CT 06520-9040. Attn: Ed. Series publication is awarded for a book-length manuscript of poetry written by a poet under 40 who has not previously published a volume of poems. Deadline: February 29. Entry fee.

WRITERS COLONIES

Writers colonies offer solitude and freedom from everyday distractions so that writers can concentrate on their work. Though some colonies are quite small, with space for just three or four writers at a time, others can provide accommodations for as many as thirty or forty. The length of a residency may vary, too, from a couple of weeks to five or six months. These programs have strict admissions policies, and writers must submit a formal application or letter of intent, a resumé, writing samples, and letters of recommendation. As an alternative to the traditional writers colony, a few of the organizations listed offer writing rooms for writers who live nearby. Write for application information first, enclosing a stamped, self-addressed envelope. Residency fees are subject to change.

THE EDWARD F. ALBEE FOUNDATION, INC.
14 Harrison St.
New York, NY 10013
(212) 266-2020
David Briggs, *Foundation Secretary*
   located on Long Island, "The Barn," or the William Flanagan Memorial Creative Persons Center, is maintained by the Albee Foundation. "The standards for admission are, simply, talent and need." Twelve writers are accepted each season for one-month residencies, available from June 1 to October 1; applications, including writing samples, project description, and resumé, are accepted from January 1 to April 1. There is no fee, though residents are responsible for their own food and travel expenses.

ALTOS DE CHAVÓN
c/o Parsons School of Design
2 W. 13th St., Rm. 707
New York, NY 10011
(212) 229-5370
Stephen D. Kaplan, *Arts/Education Director*
   Altos de Chavón is a nonprofit center for the arts in the Dominican Republic committed to education, design innovation, international creative exchange, and the promotion of Dominican culture. Residencies average 12 weeks and provide the emerging or established artist an opportunity to live and work in a setting of architectural and natural beauty. All artists are welcome to apply, though writers should note there are no typewriters, the library is oriented more toward the design profession, and the apartments housing writers also accommodate university students. Two to three writers are chosen each year for the program. The fee is $350 per month for an apartment with kitchenette; linen and cleaning services are available at an extra cost. Applications include a letter of interest, writing sample, and resumé; deadline for application is July 15.

MARY ANDERSON CENTER FOR THE ARTS
101 St. Francis Dr.
Mount St. Francis, IN 47146
(812) 923-8602
e-mail: maca@iglou.com
Debra Carmody, *Executive Director*
   Founded in 1989, the artists' residency and retreat is situated on the grounds of a Franciscan friary. Space is available for seven residents at a time, including private rooms, working space, and a visual artists' studio; meals are provided. Two-week to three-month residencies are available and are granted based on project proposal and the artist's body of work; applications are accepted year-round. Fees are $30 per day, but can be reduced in some cases. There is a non-refundable $15 application fee.

ATLANTIC CENTER FOR THE ARTS
1414 Art Center Ave.
New Smyrna Beach, FL 32168
(904) 427-6975; (800) 393-6975
web site: www.atlantic-centerarts.org
Nicholas Conroy, *Program Director*

The center is located on the east coast of central Florida, with 67 acres of pristine hammockland on a tidal estuary. All buildings, connected by raised wooden walkways, are handicapped accessible and air conditioned. The center provides a unique environment for sharing ideas, learning, and collaborating on interdisciplinary projects. Master artists meet with talented artists for readings and critiques, with time out for individual work. Residencies are one to three weeks. Fees are $100 a week for tuition and $25 a day for housing; off-site, tuition-only plans are available; financial aid is limited. Application deadlines vary.

BLUE MOUNTAIN CENTER
Blue Mountain Lake, NY 12812-0109
(518) 352-7391
e-mail: bmcl@telenet.net
Harriet Barlow, *Director*
Hosts month-long residencies for artists and writers from mid-June to late October. Established fiction and nonfiction writers, poets, and playwrights whose work evinces social and ecological concern are eligible; 14 residents are accepted per session. Residents are not charged for their time at Blue Mountain, although all visitors are invited to contribute to the studio construction fund. There is no application form; apply by sending a brief biographical sketch, a plan for work at Blue Mountain, five to 10 slides or a writing sample of any length, an indication of preference for an early summer, late summer, or fall residence, and a $20 application fee, attention: *Admissions Committee*. Applications are due February 1.

BYRDCLIFFE ARTS COLONY
Artists' Residency Program
Woodstock Guild
34 Tinker St.
Woodstock, NY 12498
(914) 679-2079; fax: (914) 679-4529
e-mail: wguild@ulster.net
web site: www.woodstockguild.org
Attn: *Director*
The Villetta Inn, located on the 400-acre arts colony, offers private studios and separate bedrooms, a communal kitchen, and a peaceful environment for fiction writers, poets, playwrights, and visual artists. One-month residencies are offered from June to September. Fee is $500 per month. Submit application, resumé, writing sample, and two letters of recommendation; the deadline is April 1. Send SASE for application.

THE CAMARGO FOUNDATION
125 Park Square Ct.
400 Sibley St.
St. Paul, MN 55101-1982
Dr. William Reichard, *U.S. Secretariat*
The Camargo Foundation maintains a center of studies in France for the benefit of nine scholars and graduate students each semester who wish to pursue projects in the humanities and social sciences relative to France and Francophone culture. In addition, one artist, one composer, and one

writer are accepted each semester. The foundation offers furnished apartments and a reference library in the city of Cassis. Research should be at an advanced stage and not require resources unavailable in the Marseilles-Aix-Cassis region. Fellows must be in residence at the foundation; the award is exclusively a residential grant. Application materials include: application form, curriculum vitae, three letters of recommendation, and project description. Writers, artists, and composers are required to send work samples. Applications are due February 1.

CENTRUM
P.O. Box 1158
Port Townsend, WA 98368
(360) 385-3102; fax: (360) 385-2470
e-mail: ted@centrum.org
web site: www.centrum.org
Ted Senecal, *Program Coordinator*
Writers and other creative artists are awarded one week to 2 month residencies between September and May. Applicants selected by a peer jury receive free housing. A few stipends of $300 or less are available for selected Seattle area artists. Previous residents may return on a space-available basis for a rental fee. Applications are due August 19th. The application fee is $10.

DJERASSI RESIDENT ARTISTS PROGRAM
2325 Bear Gulch Rd.
Woodside, CA 94062
(650) 747-1250; fax: (650) 747-0105
e-mail: drap@djerassi.org
web site: www.djerassi.org
The Djerassi Resident Artists Program offers four-week residencies, at no cost, to artists in the disciplines of literature (prose, poetry, drama/playwrights/screenwriters), choreography, music composition, visual arts, and media arts/new genres. There is a $25 application fee. The Program is located in a spectacular rural setting in the Santa Cruz Mountains, one hour south of San Francisco. The postmark deadline for accepting applications is February 15, 2001 for a residency in the year 2002. Request applications by sending an SASE. Application forms are also available on web site.

DORLAND MOUNTAIN ARTS COLONY
Box 6
Temecula, CA 92593
(909) 302-3837; fax: (909) 696-2855
e-mail: dorland@ez2.net
web site: www.ez2.net/dorland/
Attn: *Admissions Committee*
Dorland is a nature preserve and "retreat for creative people" located in the Palomar Mountains of Southern California. "Without electricity, residents find a new, natural rhythm for their work." Novelists, playwrights, poets, nonfiction writers, composers, and visual artists are encouraged to apply for residencies of one to two months. The fee of $300 a month includes cottage, fuel, and firewood. Send SASE for application; deadlines are March 1 and September 1.

DORSET COLONY HOUSE
Box 510
Dorset, VT 05251
(802) 867-2223
John Nassivera, *Director*
   Writers and playwrights are offered low-cost rooms with kitchen facilities at the historic Colony House in Dorset, Vermont. Residencies are one week to one month, and are available in the fall and spring. Applications are accepted year-round, and up to eight writers stay at a time. The fee is $125 per week; financial aid is limited. For more information, send SASE.

FINE ARTS WORK CENTER IN PROVINCETOWN
24 Pearl St.
Provincetown, MA 02657
Hunter O'Hanian, *Executive Director*
   Fellowships, including living and studio space and monthly stipends, are available at the Fine Arts Work Center on Cape Cod, for fiction writers and poets to work independently. Residencies are for seven months, October through April; apply before December 1 deadline. Five poets and five fiction writers are accepted. Send SASE for details; indicate that you are a writer in the request.

GLENESSENCE WRITERS COLONY
1447 West Ward Ave.
Ridgecrest, CA 93555
(760) 446-5894
Allison Swift, *Director*
   Glenessence is a luxury villa located in the Upper Mojave Desert, offering private rooms with bath, pool, spa, courtyard, shared kitchen, fitness center, and library. Children, pets, and smoking are prohibited. Residencies are offered at $565 per month; meals are not provided. Reservations are made on a first-come basis. Seasonal: January through May.

THE TYRONE GUTHRIE CENTRE
Annaghmakerrig, Newbliss
County Monaghan
Ireland
(353) 47–54003; fax: (353) 47–54380
e-mail: thetgc@indigo.ie
web site: www.tyroneguthrie.ie
Regina Doyle, *Acting Director*
   Set on a 450-acre country estate, the center offers peace and seclusion to writers and other artists to enable them to get on with their work. All art forms are represented. One- to three-month residencies are offered throughout the year, at the rate of 2,000 pounds per month; financial assistance is available to Irish citizens only. A number of longer term self-catering houses in the old farmyard are also available at £300 per week. Writers chosen on the basis of c.v., samples of published work, and outline of intended project. Writers may apply for acceptance year-round.

THE HAMBIDGE CENTER
P.O. Box 339
Rabun Gap, GA 30568

(706) 746-5718; fax: (706) 746-9933
e-mail: Hambidge@rabun.net
web site: www.rabun.net/~Hambidge
    The Hambidge Center for Creative Arts and Sciences is located on 600 pristine acres of quiet woods in the north Georgia mountains. Eight private cottages are available for fellows. All fellowships are partially underwritten, residents are asked to contribute $125 per week. Two-week to six-week residencies, year-round, are offered to serious artists from all disciplines. Send SASE for application form. Application deadlines: November 1 for May to October; May 1 for November to April.

HEADLANDS CENTER FOR THE ARTS
944 Fort Barry
Sausalito, CA 94965
(415) 331-2787
    Programs at the Headlands Center, located on 13,000 acres of open coastal space, are available to residents of Ohio, New Jersey, North Carolina, and California. Application requirements vary by state. Applications are due in June and decisions are announced in October for residencies beginning in February. There are no residency or application fees. Send SASE for more information.

HEDGEBROOK
2197 E. Millman Rd.
Langley, WA 98260
(360) 321-4786
web site: www.hedgebrook.org
    Hedgebrook provides women writers, published or not, of all ages and from all cultural backgrounds, with a natural place to work. Established in 1988, the retreat is located on 30 acres of farmland and woods on Whidbey Island in Washington State. Each writer has her own cottage, equipped with electricity and woodstove. A bathhouse serves all six cottages. Writers gather for dinner in the farmhouse every evening and frequently read in the living room/library afterwards. Limited travel scholarships are available. Residencies range from one week to two months. March 15 is the application deadline for residencies from early-June to mid-November; October 1 for mid-January to early May. Applicants are chosen by a selection committee composed of writers. There is a $15 fee to apply; send SASE for application.

KALANI OCEANSIDE RETREAT, INSTITUTE FOR CULTURE AND WELLNESS
Artist-in-Residence Program
RR2, Box 4500
Pahoa-Beach Road, HI 96778
(808) 965-7828; (800) 800-6886; fax: (808) 965-0527
e-mail: kalani@kalani.com
web site: www.kalani.com
Richard Koob, *Program Coordinator*
    Located in a rural coastal setting of 113 botanical acres, Kalani Oceanside Retreat hosts and sponsors educational programs "with the aloha experience that is its namesake: harmony of heaven and earth." Residencies range from two weeks to two months and are available throughout the year.

Fees range from $38 to $68 per day, meals available at additional fee. Applications accepted year-round.

THE MACDOWELL COLONY
100 High St.
Peterborough, NH 03458
(603) 924-3886
web site: www.macdowellcolony.org
Pat Dodge, *Admissions Coordinator*
Studios, room, and board are available for writers to work without interruption in a woodland setting. Through 2001, writers are given a stipend of up to $1,000 depending on financial need. Selection is competitive. Apply by January 15 for stays May through August; April 15 for September through December; and September 15 for January through April. Residencies last up to eight weeks, and 80 to 90 writers are accepted each year. Send SASE for application.

THE MILLAY COLONY FOR THE ARTS
444 East Hill Rd.
P.O. Box 3
Austerlitz, NY 12017-0003
(518) 392-3103
Gail Giles, *Director of Admissions*
At Steepletop, the former home of Edna St. Vincent Millay, writers are provided studios, universally accessible living quarters, and meals at no cost. Residencies last one month. Application deadlines are February 1, May 1, and September 1. Send SASE or e-mail (application@millaycolony.org) for application.

MILLETT FARM: AN ART COLONY FOR WOMEN
295 Bowery
New York, NY 10003
Kate Millett, *Director*
Summer residencies are offered to women writers and visual artists at a picturesque tree farm in rural New York. In return for housing, all residents contribute four hours of work each weekday morning and contribute $80 a week toward meals. Preference is given to writers who can stay all summer or at least six weeks. Also, one week intensive master class with Kate Millett. For more information send an SASE.

MOLASSES POND WRITERS' RETREAT AND WORKSHOP
RR 1, Box 85C
Milbridge, ME 04658
(207) 546-2506
Martha Barron Barrett and Sue Wheeler, *Coordinators*
Led by published authors who teach writing at the University of New Hampshire, this one-week workshop is held in June and includes time set aside for writing, as well as manuscript critique and writing classes. Up to 10 writers participate, staying in a colonial farmhouse with private bed/work rooms for each participant and common areas for meals and classes. The $450 fee covers lodging, meals, and tuition. No children's literature or poetry. Submit statement of purpose and 15 to 20 pages of fiction or nonfiction between February 15 and March 1.

MONTANA ARTISTS REFUGE
Box 8
Basin, MT 59631
(406) 225-3500
e-mail: mtrefuge@pop.mcn.net
  Writers are offered living space in a relaxed and unpretentious atmosphere, where they can work with other artists or in solitude. Residencies, which include kitchen facilities and private phone, range from three months to one year, and rents range from $400 to $600 per month. Financial aid is available. Deadline for summer (May—Sept.) is November 1 each year. Applications for other dates are ongoing. Send SASE for information.

JENNY McKEAN MOORE WRITER-IN-WASHINGTON
Dept. of English
The George Washington University
Washington, DC 20052
Fax: (202) 994-7915
e-mail: Faymos@gwu.edu
Attn: Prof. Faye Moskowitz
  The fellowship allows for a writer to teach two paid semesters (salary: $48,000) at The George Washington University. Teaching duties include a fiction workshop each semester for students from the metropolitan community who may have had little formal education; and one class each semester for university students. Fiction and poetry alternate years. Applications include letter, indicating publications and other projects, extent of teaching experience, and other qualifications.The application must also include a resumé and fifteen to twenty-five sample pages of your work. The application deadline is November 15.

NEW YORK MILLS ARTS RETREAT AND REGIONAL CULTURAL CENTER
24 N. Main Ave.
P.O. Box 246
New York Mills, MN 56567
(218) 385-3339; fax: (218) 385-3366
e-mail: nymills@uslink.net
Kent Scheer, *Retreat Coordinator*
  Five to seven emerging artists, writers, filmmakers, or musicians are accepted during the nine month season. Each artist receives financial assistance through a stipend, ranging from $750 for a two-week residency to $1,500 for four weeks, provided by the Jerome Foundation. Retreatants live in a small house in the heart of this community of 1,000 people. There is a review process twice a year; the deadlines are April 1 and October 1.

THE NORTHWOOD UNIVERSITY
Alden B. Dow Creativity Center
4000 Whiting Dr.
Midland, MI 48640-2398
(517) 837-4478; fax: (517) 837-4468
e-mail: creativity@northwood.edu
web site: www.northwood.edu/abd

The Fellowship Program allows individuals time away from their on-going daily routines to pursue their project ideas without interruption. A project idea should be innovative, creative, and have potential for impact in its field. Four ten-week residencies, lasting from early-June to mid-August, are awarded yearly. There is a $10 application fee. A $750 stipend plus room and board are provided. No spouses or families. Applications are due December 31.

OX-BOW
37 S. Wabash Ave.
Chicago, IL 60603
(312) 899-7455
One-week residencies are available mid-June to mid-August for writers who wish to reside and work in a secluded, natural environment. Recipients are required to pay $380 room and board, per week. Primarily a program for the visual arts, the mission of Ox-Bow is to nurture the creative process through instruction, example, and community. Resident writers are encouraged to present a reading of their work and to participate in the community life at Ox-Bow. For application form write or call. Application deadline is May 14.

RAGDALE FOUNDATION
1260 N. Green Bay Rd.
Lake Forest, IL 60045
(847) 234-1063; fax: (847) 234-1075
e-mail: ragdalel@aol.com
web site: http://nsn.nslsilus.org/lfkhome/ragdale
Suellen Rocca, *Admissions*
Uninterrupted time and peaceful space allow writers a chance to finish works in progress, to begin new works, to solve thorny creative problems, and to experiment in new genres. The foundation is located 30 miles north of Chicago, on 55 acres of prairie. Residencies of two weeks to two months are available for writers, artists, and composers. The fee is $15 a day; some full and partial fee waivers available, based solely on financial need. Send SASE for deadline information. Application fee: $20.

SASKATCHEWAN WRITERS GUILD
Writers/Artists Colonies and Individual Retreats
P.O. Box 3986
Regina, Saskatchewan S4P 3R9
Canada
(306) 565-8785
e-mail: skcolony@attglobal.net
web site: www.skwriter.com/colonies.html
Attn: *Colony Coordinator*
The Saskatchewan Colonies are at two locations: St. Peter's Abbey, near Humboldt, provides a six-week summer colony (July–August) and a two-week winter colony in February, for up to eight writers and artists at a time; applicant stays vary. Individual retreats of up to two weeks are offered year-round at St. Peter's, for up to three residents at a time. Only Canadian residents are eligible for individual retreats. Emma Lake, near

Prince Albert, is the site of a two-week colony in August. A fee of $125 (Saskatchewan Writers Guild members) or $175 (nonmembers) per week includes room and board. Submit resumé, short project description, two references, and a 10-page writing sample. Among applicants of equal ability, priority is given to Saskatchewan residents. December 1 deadline for winter colony; May 1 deadline for summer colonies. Apply at least four weeks in advance of preferred dates for individual retreats.

THE JOHN STEINBECK ROOM
Long Island University
Southampton College Library
Southampton, NY 11968
(631) 287-8382
Robert Gerbereux, *Library Director*
    The John Steinbeck Room at Long Island University provides a basic research facility to writers who have either a current contract with a book publisher or a confirmed assignment from a magazine editor. The room is available for a period of six months with one six-month renewal permissible. Send SASE for application.

THE THURBER HOUSE RESIDENCIES
c/o Thurber House
77 Jefferson Ave.
Columbus, OH 43215
(614) 464-1032; fax: (614) 228-7445
e-mail: thhouse@thurberhouse.org
web site: www.thurberhouse.org
Michael J. Rosen, *Literary Director*
    Residencies in the restored home of James Thurber are awarded to journalists, poets, and playwrights. Residents work on their own writing projects, and in addition to other duties, teach one class at the Ohio State University. A stipend of $6,000 per quarter is provided. A letter of interest and curriculum vitae must be received by December 15, at which time applications are reviewed for the upcoming academic year.

UCROSS FOUNDATION
Residency Program
30 Big Red Lane
Clearmont, WY 82835
(307) 737-2291; fax: (307) 737-2322
e-mail: ucross@wyoming.com
web site: ucrossfoundation.org
Sharon Dynak, *Executive Director*
    Residencies, two to eight weeks, in the foothills of the Big Horn Mountains in Wyoming, allow writers, artists, and scholars to concentrate on their work without interruption. Two residency sessions are scheduled annually: February to June and August to December. There is no charge for room, board, or studio space. Application deadlines are March 1 for the fall session and October 1 for the spring session. Send SASE for more information.

VERMONT STUDIO CENTER

P.O. Box 613
Johnson, VT 05656
(802) 635-2727; fax: (802) 635-2730;
e-mail: info@vscvt.org
web site: www.vermontstudiocenter.org
Attn: *Registrar*

The Vermont Studio Center offers 4- to 12-week Independent Residencies year-round for up to 12 writers of fiction. nonfiction, and poetry. All VSC Writing Residencies receive a private studio space, room, meals, and access to the community at large (24 painters, 12 sculptors, 2 printmakers), as well as optional readings and private writing conferences with prominent Visiting Writers. A one-month Residency is $3,200. Full Fellowships, VSC Grants, and Work-Exchange Aid are available. Application deadlines are February 15th, June 15th, and Spetember 30th. Application fee is $25.

VILLA MONTALVO ARTIST RESIDENCY PROGRAM

P.O. Box 158
Saratoga, CA 95071
(408) 961-5818; fax (408) 961-5850
e-mail: kfunk@villamontalvo.org
web site: www.villamontalvo.org
Kathryn Funk, *Artist Residency Director*

Villa Montalvo, in the foothills of the Santa Cruz Mountains south of San Francisco, offers one- to three-month residencies free of charge to writers, visual artists, and composers. Several merit-based fellowships are available. The application deadlines are September 1 and March 1; send self-addressed label and 55¢ postage to receive brochure and application form. Application fee is $20.

VIRGINIA CENTER FOR THE CREATIVE ARTS

Box VCCA
Sweet Briar, VA 24595
(804) 946-7236; fax: (804) 946-7239
e-mail: vcca@vcca.com
web site: www.vcca.com
Suny Monk, *Executive Director*

A working retreat for writers, composers, and visual artists in Virginia's Blue Ridge Mountains. Residencies from two weeks to two months are available year-round. Application deadlines are the 15th of January, May, and September; about 300 residents are accepted each year. A limited amount of financial assistance is available. Send SASE for more information.

THE WRITERS ROOM

10 Astor Pl., 6th Fl.
New York, NY 10003
(212) 254-6995; fax: (212) 533-6059
e-mail: writersroom@writersroom.org
web site: www.writersroom.org
Donna Brodie, *Executive Director*

Located in the East Village, The Writers Room provides subsidized work space to all types of writers at all stages of their careers. "We offer urban writers a quiet place to escape from noisy neighbors, children, room-mates, and other distractions of city life." The Room holds 30 desks sepa-rated by partitions, a typing room with five desks, a kitchen, and a library. Open 24 hours a day, 365 days a year. There is a one-time $50 application fee; fees for the three-month period include $185 for a "floater" desk. Part-time memberships at reduced rates are also available. Call, fax or write for application (no visits without appointment).

THE WRITERS STUDIO
The Mercantile Library Association
17 E. 47th St.
New York, NY 10017
(212) 755-6710
Harold Augenbraum, *Director*
The Writers Studio is a quiet place in which writers can rent space conducive to the production of good work. A carrel, locker, small reference collection, electrical outlets, and membership in the Mercantile Library of New York are available at the cost of $200 per three-month residency. Submit application, resumé, and writing samples; applications are consid-ered year-round.

HELENE WURLITZER FOUNDATION OF NEW MEXICO
Box 1891
Taos, NM 87571
(505) 758-2413; fax: (505) 758-2559
Rent-free and utility-free studios in Taos are offered to writers and creative artists in all media. "All artists are given the opportunity to be free of the shackles of a 9-to-5 routine." Residency is usually three months. The foundation is open from April 1 through September 30 and on a lim-ited basis October through March. Residencies are assigned into the year 2002. Send an SASE for application and guidelines.

YADDO
Box 395
Saratoga Springs, NY 12866-0395
(518) 584-0746; fax: (518) 584-1312
e-mail: CHWAIT@yaddo.org
Candace Wait, *Program Coordinator*
Visual artists, writers, choreographers, film/video artists, performance artists, composers, and collaborators are invited for stays from two weeks to two months. Room, board, and studio space are provided. No stipends. Deadlines are January 15 and August 1. There is a $20 application fee; send SASE for form.

WRITERS CONFERENCES

Each year, hundreds of writers conferences are held across the country. The following list, arranged by state, represents a sampling of conferences; each listing includes the location of the conference, the month during which it is usually held, and the name and address of the person from whom specific information may be received. Writers are advised to write directly to conference directors for full details. Always enclose an SASE. Additional conferences are listed annually in the May issue of *The Writer* Magazine (Kalmbach Publishing Co., 21027 Crossroads Circle, P.O. Box 1612, Waukesha, WI 53187-1612).

ALABAMA

WRITING TODAY—Birmingham, AL. March. Martha Ross, Dir., Writing Today, Birmingham-Southern College, Box 549003, Birmingham, AL 35254.

SCBWI "WRITING & ILLUSTRATING FOR KIDS"—Birmingham, AL. October. Joan Broerman, Reg. Adv., Southern Breeze, SCBWI, P.O. Box 26282, Birmingham, AL 35260 .

ALASKA

SITKA SYMPOSIUM ON HUMAN VALUES & THE WRITTEN WORD—Sitka, AK. June. Carolyn Servid, Dir., The Island Institute, P.O. Box 2420, Sitka, AK 99835.

NATIONAL FEDERATION OF PRESS WOMEN ANNUAL CONFERENCE—Anchorage, AK. September. Carol S. Pierce, Dir., NFPW, Box 5556, Arlington, VA 22205.

ARIZONA

DESERT DREAMS—Phoenix, AZ. March, April. Alison Kinnaird, P.O. Box 1771, Chandler, AZ 85244-1771.

ARKANSAS

ARKANSAS WRITER'S CONFERENCE—Little Rock, AR. June. Barbara Mulkey, Dir., 78 Maple Ct., Little Rock, AR 72212.

OZARK CREATIVE WRITERS CONFERENCE—Eureka Springs, AR. October. Marsha Camp, Robinwood Dr., Little Rock, AR 72227.

CALIFORNIA

SAN DIEGO STATE UNIVERSITY ANNUAL WRITERS' CONFERENCE—San Diego, CA. January. Diane Dunaway, Coord., 8465 Jane St., San Diego, CA 92129.

JACK LONDON'S WRITERS' CONFERENCE—S. San Francisco, CA. March. Mariann M. Jackson, Dir., 327 B St., Redwood City, CA 94063-1017.

IWWG EARLY SPRING IN CALIFORNIA CONFERENCE—Santa Cruz, CA. March. Hannelore Hahn, Dir., IWWG, P.O. Box 810, Gracie Station, New York, NY 10028.

WRITERS' FORUM—Pasadena, CA. March. Meredith Brucker, Dir., Pasadena City College, 1570 E. Colorado Blvd., Pasadena, CA 91106-2003.

MOUNT HERMON CHRISTIAN WRITERS CONFERENCE—

Mount Hermon, CA. April. David R. Talbott, Dir., P.O. Box 413, Mount Hermon, CA 95041. Web site: www.mounthermon.org.

FOOTHILL WRITERS' CONFERENCE—Los Altos Hills, CA. June. Kim Wolterbeek, Dir., Foothill Writers' Conference, 12345 El Monte Rd., Los Altos Hills, CA 94022.

WRITERS' AND ILLUSTRATORS' CONFERENCE IN CHILDREN'S LITERATURE—Los Angeles, CA. August. Lin Oliver, Dir., SCBWI, 8271 Beverly Blvd., Los Angeles, CA 90048.

AMERICAN TRANSLATORS ASSOCIATION ANNUAL CONFERENCE—Los Angeles, CA. October. Walter Bacak, Dir., ATA, 225 Reinekers La., Suite 590, Alexandria, VA 22314.

CAT WRITERS' ASSOCIATION WRITERS' CONFERENCE—Anaheim, CA. November. Amy D. Shojai, Dir., Cat Writers' Assoc., P.O. Box 1904, Sherman, TX 75091.

WRITING AND EDITING SEMINARS—Various dates and locations, CA. Louise Purwin Zobel, 23350 Sereno, Villa 30, Cupertino, CA 95014.

COLORADO

COLORADO CHRISTIAN WRITERS' CONFERENCE—Estes Park, CO. May. Marlene Bagnull, Dir., 316 Blanchard Rd., Drexel Hill, PA 19026.

STEAMBOAT SPRINGS WRITERS' CONFERENCE—Steamboat Springs, CO. July. Harriet Freiberger, Dir., P.O. Box 774284, Steamboat Springs, CO 80477.

THE PUBLISHING INSTITUTE AT THE UNIVERSITY OF DENVER—Denver, CO. July–August. Elizabeth Geiser, Dir., Publishing Institute, 2075 S. University Blvd., #D-114, Denver, CO 80210.

CONNECTICUT

WESLEYAN WRITERS' CONFERENCE—Middletown, CT. June. Anne Greene, Dir., Wesleyan Writers' Conference, Wesleyan Univ., Middletown, CT 06459.

DISTRICT OF COLUMBIA

WASHINGTON INDEPENDENT WRITERS SPRING WRITER'S CONFERENCE—Washington, DC. May. Isolde Chapin, Dir., 220 Woodward Bldg., 733 15th St. N.W., Washington, DC 20005.

ROMANCE WRITERS OF AMERICA CONFERENCE—Washington, DC. July. Allison Kelley, RWA Exec. Dir., 3707 FM 1960 W., Suite 555, Houston, TX 77068.

FLORIDA

KEY WEST LITERARY SEMINAR—Key West, FL. January. Contact Miles Frieden: www.KeyWestLiterarySeminar.org or call 1-888-293-9291.

KEY WEST WRITERS' WORKSHOP—Key West, FL. January–March. Director, 5901 College Rd., Key West, FL 33040.

FLORIDA SUNCOAST WRITERS' CONFERENCE—St. Petersburg,

FL. February. Betty Moss, Dir., Dept. of English, Univ. of South Florida, Tampa, FL 33620.

SOUTHWEST FLORIDA WRITERS' CONFERENCE—Ft. Myers, FL. March. Jeri Magg, 723 Sand Dollar Dr., Sanibel, FL 33957.

SOUTH FLORIDA WRITERS CONFERENCE—Coral Gables, FL. March. Judith Welsh, Dir., National Writers Association, P.O. Box 570415, Miami, FL 33257-0415.

SLEUTH FEST—Ft. Lauderdale, FL. March, April. Dianne Ell, Dir., 1432 S.E. 8th St., Deerfield Beach, FL 33441.

MARJORIE KINNAN RAWLINGS WRITERS WORKSHOP— Gainesville, Cross Creek, FL. June, July. Norma Homan, Dir., MKR Writers Workshop, P.O. Box 12246, Gainesville, FL 32604.

FLORIDA REGION SCBWI CONFERENCE—Palm Springs, FL. September. Barbara Casey, Reg. Adv., 2158 Portland Ave., Wellington, FL 33414.

GEORGIA

SPRING MINGLE—Atlanta, GA. March. Joan Broerman, Reg. Adv., Southern Breeze SCBWI, P.O. Box 26282, Birmingham, AL 35260.

SANDHILLS WRITERS CONFERENCE—Augusta, GA. March. Anthony Kellman, Dir., Augusta State Univ., Dept. of Language, Literature, & Communications, Augusta, GA 30904.

SOUTHEASTERN WRITER'S ASSOC. SUMMER WORKSHOP— St. Simons Island, GA. June. Cappy Hall-Rearick, Pres., 114 Gould St., St. Simons Island, GA 31522.

ILLINOIS

MISSISSIPPI VALLEY WRITERS' CONFERENCE—Rock Island, IL. June. David R. Collins, Dir., 3403 45th St., Moline, IL 61265.

WRITE-TO-PUBLISH CONFERENCE—Wheaton, IL. June. Lin Johnson, Dir., 9731 N. Fox Glen Dr., #6F, Niles, IL 60714-4222. E-mail: linjohnson@compuserve.com.

OF DARK AND STORMY NIGHTS—Rolling Meadows, IL. June. Bill Spurgeon, Dir., P.O. Box 1944, Muncie, IN 47308-1944.

ANNUAL ROMANCE WRITERS OF AMERICA CONFERENCE— Chicago, IL. July, August. Director, 13700 Veterans Memorial, #315, Houston, TX 77014.

AUTUMN AUTHORS' AFFAIR—near Chicago, IL. Autumn. Nancy McCann, Dir., 1507 Burnham Ave., Calumet City, IN 60409.

INDIANA

BUTLER UNIVERSITY CHILDREN'S LITERATURE CONFERENCE—Indianapolis, IN. January. Valiska Gregory, Dir., Butler University, 4600 Sunset Dr., Indianapolis, IN 46208.

INDIANA UNIVERSITY WRITERS' CONFERENCE—Bloomington, IN. June. Romayne Rubinas, Dir., IU Writers' Conference, Ballantine Hall 464, Bloomington, IN 47405.

MIDWEST WRITERS WORKSHOP—Muncie, IN. July. Earl Conn, Dir., Ball State Univ., Dept. of Journalism, Muncie, IN 47306.

NATIONAL FEDERATION OF PRESS WOMEN—Indianapolis, IN. September. National Federation of Press Women, P.O. Box 5556, Arlington, VA 22205.

KANSAS

WRITERS' WORKSHOP IN SCIENCE FICTION—Lawrence, KS. July. James Gunn, Dir., Univ. of Kansas, English Dept., Lawrence, KS 66045.

KENTUCKY

GREEN RIVER NOVELS-IN-PROGRESS WORKSHOP—Louisville, KY. March. Mary E. O'Dell, Dir., Green River Writers, Inc., 11906 Locust Rd., Middletown, KY 40243-1413.

WRITERS' RETREAT WORKSHOP—Erlanger, KY. May, June. Gail Provost Stockwell, Dir., P.O. Box 139, S. Lancaster, MA 01561.

ANNUAL APPALACHIAN WRITERS WORKSHOP—Hindman, KY. July. Mike Mullins, Dir., Hindman Settlement School, Box 844, Hindman, KY 41822.

GREEN RIVER WORKSHOP WEEKEND & WRITERS RETREAT—Louisville, KY. July. Mary E. O'Dell, Dir., Green River Writers, Inc., 11906 Locust Rd., Middletown, KY 40243-1413.

MAINE

DOWNEAST MAINE WRITER'S WORKSHOPS—Stockton Springs, ME. July, August. Janet J. Barron, Dir., P.O. Box 446, Stockton Springs, ME 04981.

IN CELEBRATION OF CHILDREN'S LITERATURE—Gorham, ME. July. Joyce Martin, Dir., Univ. of Southern Maine, 305 Bailey Hall, Gorham, ME 04038.

STONECOAST WRITERS CONFERENCE—Freeport, ME. July, August. Barbara Hope, Dir., Univ. of Southern Maine, 96 Falmouth St., Portland, ME 04104.

STATE OF MAINE WRITERS' CONFERENCE—Ocean Park, ME. August. June A. Knowles, Mary E. Pitts, 18 Hill Rd., Belmont, MA 02478.

MARYLAND

SANDY COVE CHRISTIAN WRITERS' CONFERENCE—North East, MD. October. Jim Watkins, Dir., Sandy Cove Ministries, 60 Sandy Cove Rd., North East, MD 21901-5436.

MASSACHUSETTS

BOOK ARTS WORKSHOPS—Kingston, MA. May, June, July. Lilas Cingolani, Dir., Box 52, Kingston, MA 02364.

CAPE COD WRITERS CONFERENCE—Craigville Beach, MA. August. Cape Cod Writers' Center, P.O. Box 186, Barnstable, MA 02630.

TRURO CENTER FOR THE ARTS AT CASTLE HILL WRITERS WORKSHOPS—Truro, MA. Various dates. Mary Stackhouse, Dir., P.O. Box 756, Truro, MA 02666.

MICHIGAN

40TH ANNUAL WRITERS' CONFERENCE, SPONSORED AT OAKLAND UNIVERSITY—Rochester, MI. October. Gloria J. Boddy, Dir., Oakland Univ., 231 Varner Hall, Rochester, MI 48309-4401.

MINNESOTA

HOW TO WRITE A CHILDREN'S PICTURE BOOK—Coon Rapids, MN. June. Brenda Dickenson, Dir., Cont. Education Dept., 11200 Mississippi Blvd. N.W., Coon Rapids, MN 55433-3499.

SPLIT ROCK ARTS PROGRAM—Duluth, MN. July, August. Andrea Gilats, Dir., 360 Coffey Hall, 1420 Eckles Ave., St. Paul, MN 55108-6084. Web site: www.cce.umn.edu/splitrockarts/

WRITING TO SELL 16TH ANNUAL WORKSHOP—Minneapolis, MN. August. Joyce Banaszak, Dir., Minneapolis Writers Workshop, P.O. Box 24356, Minneapolis, MN 55424.

MISSISSIPPI

SPRINGMINGLE '01—Jackson, MS. February. Joan Broerman, Reg. Advisor, Southern Breeze, SCBWI, P.O. Box 26282, Birmingham, AL 35260.

NATCHEZ LITERARY CELEBRATION—Natchez, MS. June. Carolyn Vance Smith, Dir., P.O. Box 894, Natchez, MS 39121.

MISSOURI

WRITING AND LITERATURE CAMP—Springfield, MO. June. Dr. John Bushman, Dir., The Writing Conference, P.O. Box 27288, Shawnee Mission, KS 66225-7288.

NEW LETTERS WEEKEND WRITERS' CONFERENCE—Kansas City, MO. June. James McKinley, Dir., UMKC, Arts & Sciences Cont. Ed., 4825 Troost, Room 215, Kansas City, MO 64110.

AMERICAN TRANSLATORS ASSOCIATION ANNUAL CONFERENCE—St. Louis, MO. November. Walter Bacak, Dir., 1800 Diagonal Rd., #220, Alexandria, VA 22314.

NEW HAMPSHIRE

MOLASSES POND WRITER'S RETREAT/WORKSHOP—Wakefield, NH. June. Martha Barron Barrett, Dir., RR1, Box 85, Milbridge, ME 04658.

ODYSSEY FANTASY WRITING WORKSHOP—Manchester, NH. June, July. Jeanne Cavelos, Dir., Odyssey, 20 Levesque La., Mount Vernon, NH 03057.

NEW ENGLAND WRITERS CONFERENCE—Hanover, NH. July. Dr. Frank & Susan Anthony, Dirs., Box 483, Windsor, VT 05089.

ANNUAL FESTIVAL OF POETRY—Franconia, NH. August. Donald Sheehan, Dir., P.O. Box 74, Franconia, NH 03580.

NEW JERSEY

THE COLLEGE OF NEW JERSEY WRITERS' CONFERENCE— Ewing, NJ. April. Jean Hollander, Dir., The College of New Jersey, Dept. of English, P.O. Box 7718, Ewing, NJ 08628-0718.

NEW MEXICO

WRITING WOMEN'S LIVES—Santa Fe, NM. May. Robin Jones, Dir., Recursos, 826 Camino del Monte Rey, Santa Fe, NM 87505.

TAOS SCHOOL OF WRITING—Taos Ski Valley, NM. July. Norman Zollinger, Dir., P.O. Box 20496, Albuquerque, NM 87154.

SANTA FE WRITER'S CONFERENCE—Santa Fe, NM. July. Robin Jones, Dir., Recursos, 826 Camino del Monte Rey, Santa Fe, NM 87505.

WRITING YOURSELF—Santa Fe, NM. October. Stephen Lewis, Dir., Recursos, 826 Camino del Monte Rey, Santa Fe, NM 87505.

GLORIETA CHRISTIAN WRITERS' CONFERENCE—Glorieta, NM. October. Mona Gansberg Hodgson, Dir.,Glorieta Conference Center, P.O. Box 8, Glorieta, NM 87535-0008. Web site: www.monahodgson.com.

NEW YORK

BIG APPLE WRITING WORKSHOPS—New York, NY. April, October. Hannelore Hahn, Dir., IWWG, P.O. Box 810, Gracie Station, New York, NY 10028.

THE WRITERS' CENTER AT CHAUTAUQUA—Chautauqua, NY. June, August. Mary Jean Irion, Dir., 149 Kready Ave., Millersville, PA 17551.

MARYMOUNT MANHATTAN COLLEGE WRITER'S CONFERENCE—New York, NY. June. Lewis Burke Frumkes, Dir., The Writing Center, Marymount Manhattan College, 221 E. 71st St., New York, NY 10021.

MANHATTANVILLE'S SUMMER WRITERS' WORKSHOPS— Purchase, NY. June. Ruth Dowd, Dir., Manhattanville College, 2900 Purchase St., Purchase, NY 10577.

FEMINIST WOMEN'S WRITING WORKSHOPS—Geneva, NY. July. Margo Gumosky, Dir., P.O. Box 6583, Ithaca, NY 14851.

NEW YORK STATE SUMMER WRITERS' INSTITUTE—Saratoga Springs, NY. July. Robert Boyers, Dir., NYSSWI, Skidmore College, Saratoga Springs, NY 12866.

ROBERT QUACKENBUSH'S CHILDREN'S BOOK WRITING & ILLUSTRATING WORKSHOPS—New York, NY. July. Robert Quackenbush, Dir., Quackenbush Studios, 460 E. 79th St., New York, NY 10021.

"REMEMBER THE MAGIC" SUMMER CONFERENCE—Saratoga Springs, NY. August. Hannelore Hahn, Dir., IWWG, P.O. Box 810, Gracie Station, New York, NY 10028.

NORTH CAROLINA

NORTH CAROLINA WRITERS' NETWORK SPRING GALA— Chapel Hill, NC. June. Bobbie Collins-Perry, Dir., P.O. Box 954, Carrboro, NC 27510.

NORTH CAROLINA WRITERS' NETWORK'S ANNUAL FALL CONFERENCE—Fayetteville, NC. November. Bobbi Collins-Perry, Dir., P.O. Box 954. Carrboro, NC 27510.

OHIO

WESTERN RESERVE WRITERS' MINI CONFERENCE—Kirtland, OH. March. Lea Leever Oldham, Dir., 34200 Ridge Rd., #110, Willoughby, OH 44094.

HUDSON WRITERS' MINI CONFERENCE—Hudson, OH. May. Lea Leever Oldham, Dir., 34200 Ridge Rd., #110, Willoughby, OH 44094.

THE HEIGHTS WRITER'S CONFERENCE—Beachwood, OH. May. Lavern Hall, Dir.,Writer's World Press, 35 N. Chillicothe Rd., Suite D, Aurora, OH 44202.

KENYON REVIEW WRITERS WORKSHOP—Gambier, OH. June, July. David Lynn, Dir., Kenyon Review Summer Programs, Sunset Cottage, Kenyon College, Gambier, OH 43022.

VALLEY WRITERS' CONFERENCE—Youngstown, OH. August. Nancy Christie, Dir., P.O. Box 4610, Youngstown, OH 44515.

ANTIOCH WRITERS' WORKSHOP—Yellow Springs, OH. August. Tara Muller & Barbara Calarese, Dirs., P.O. Box 494, Yellow Springs, OH 45387.

SKYLINE WRITERS' CONFERENCE—N. Royalton, OH. August. Lilie Kilburn, Dir., Skyline Writers' Club, P.O. Box 33343, N. Royalton, OH 44133.

WESTERN RESERVE WRITERS & FREELANCE CONFER-ENCE—Kirtland, OH. September. Lea Leever Oldham, Dir., 34200 Ridge Rd., #110, Willoughby, OH 44094.

COLUMBUS WRITERS CONFERENCE—Columbus, OH. September. Angela Palazzolo, Dir., P.O. Box 20548, Columbus, OH 43220.

CLEVELAND HEIGHTS/UNIVERSITY HEIGHTS WRITERS MINI CONFERENCE—Cleveland Heights, OH. October. Lea Leever Oldham, Dir., 34200 Ridge Rd., #110, Willoughby, OH 44094.

OKLAHOMA

NORTHWEST OKLAHOMA WRITERS' WORKSHOP—Enid, OK. April. Bev Walton-Porter, Dir., Enid Writers Club, P.O. Box 5994, Enid, OK 73702.

SHORT COURSE ON PROFESSIONAL WRITING—Norman, OK. June. J. Madison Davis, Dir., Univ. of Oklahoma, 226 Copeland Hall, Norman, OK 73019.

OREGON

FISHTRAP GATHERING & WORKSHOPS—Wallowa Lake, OR. February, July. Rich Wandschneider, Dir., Fishtrap, P.O. Box 38, Enterprise, OR 97828.

THE FLIGHT OF THE MIND WRITING WORKSHOPS FOR WOMEN—McKenzie Bridge, OR. June–July. Ruth Gundle, Dir., Flight of the Mind, 622 S.E. 29th Ave., Portland, OR 97214.

WILLAMETTE WRITERS CONFERENCE—Portland, OR. August. Cherie Walter, Dir., Willamette Writers, 9045 S.W. Barbur Blvd., Suite 5A, Portland, OR 97219

COOS BAY WRITERS CONFERENCE—Coos Bay, OR. Summer. Mary Scheirman, Dir., 2463 Union, North Bend, OR 97459.

PENNSYLVANIA

GREATER PHILADELPHIA CHRISTIAN WRITERS CONFERENCE—Glenside, PA. August. Marlene Bagnull, Dir., 316 Blanchard Rd., Drexel Hill, PA 19026.

PENNWRITERS ANNUAL CONFERENCE—Grantville, PA. May. Elizabeth Darrach, Dir., 492 Letort Rd., Millersville, PA 17551-9660.

ST. DAVID'S CHRISTIAN WRITERS' CONFERENCE—Beaver Falls, PA. June. Audrey Stallsmith, Registrar, 87 Pines Rd. E., Hadley, PA 16130.

BUCKNELL SEMINAR FOR YOUNGER POETS—Lewisburg, PA. June. Cynthia Hogue, Dir., Bucknell Univ., Stadler Center for Poetry, Lewisburg, PA 17837.

LIGONIER VALLEY WRITERS CONFERENCE—Ligonier, PA. July. Dr. Kirk Weixel, Dir., P.O. Box B, Ligonier, PA 15658.

MID-ATLANTIC MYSTERY—Philadelphia, PA. October. Deen Kogan, Dir., 507 S. 8th St., Philadelphia, PA 19147.

RHODE ISLAND

NEW ENGLAND SCREENWRITERS CONFERENCE—Providence, RI. August. Robert Hofmann, Dir., Community Writers Assoc., P.O. Box 312, Providence, RI 02901-0312.

SOUTH CAROLINA

SOUTH CAROLINA PLAYWRIGHTS' CONFERENCE—Beaufort, SC. June. Bill Rauch, Dir., 1001 Bay St., Beaufort, SC 29902.

SOUTH CAROLINA WRITERS WORKSHOP—Myrtle Beach, FL. October. South Carolina Writers Workshop, P.O. Box 7104, Columbia, SC 29202.

TENNESSEE

AMERICAN CHRISTIAN WRITERS CONFERENCES—Various locations and dates. Reg A. Forder, Dir., P.O. Box 110390, Nashville, TN 37222. (800) 21-WRITE.

SEWANEE WRITERS CONFERENCE—Sewanee, TN. July, August. Wyatt Prunty, Dir., 310 St. Luke's Hall, 735 University Ave., Sewanee, TN 37383.

TEXAS

CRAFTING THE STORY—Austin, TX. February. Jim Bob McMillan, Dir., Austin Writers League, 1501 W. 5th St., Suite E-2, Austin, TX 78703.

WRITER'S ROUNDTABLE CONFERENCE—Dallas, TX. March, April. Deborah Morris, Dir., P.O. Box 461572, Garland, TX 75046-1572.

AGENTS! AGENTS! AGENTS! & EDITORS TOO!—Austin, TX. July. Jim Bob McMillan, Dir., Austin Writers League, 1501 W. 5th St., Suite E-2, Austin, TX 78703. Web site: www.writersleague.org.

CAT WRITERS ASSOCIATION WRITERS CONFERENCE—Houston, TX. November. Kim Thornton, Dir., 22841 Orchid Creek La., Lake Forest, CA 92630.

UTAH

SAN JUAN WRITERS' WORKSHOP—Bluff, UT. March. Scott Russel Sanders, Canyonlands Field Institute, P.O. Box 68, Moab, UT 84532.

SOUTHERN UTAH WRITERS CONFERENCE—Cedar City, UT. July. David Lee, Dir., Southern Utah Univ., School of Cont. Ed., Cedar City, UT 84720.

DESERT WRITERS WORKSHOP—Moab, UT. November. Ann Haymond Zwinger (Nonfiction), Alison Hawthorne Deming (Poetry), or Roy Porvin (Fiction), Canyonlands Field Institute, P.O. Box 68, Moab, UT 84532.

VERMONT

WILDBRANCH WORKSHOP IN OUTDOOR, NATURAL HISTORY, & ENVIRONMENTAL WRITING—Craftsbury Common, VT. June. David W. Brown, Dir., Wildbranch, Sterling College, Craftsbury Common, VT 05827.

BREAD LOAF WRITERS' CONFERENCE—Ripton, VT. August. Michael Collier, Dir., Bread Loaf Writers' Conference, Middlebury College, Middlebury, VT 05753.

VIRGINIA

HIGHLAND SUMMER CONFERENCE—Radford, VA. June. Dr. Grace Toney Edwards, Dir., c/o Jo Ann Asbury, Radford Univ., P.O. Box 7014, Radford, VA 24142.

SHENANDOAH INTERNATIONAL PLAYWRIGHT'S RETREAT—Staunton, VA. July–September. Robert Graham Small, Dir., Pennyroyal Farm, Rt. 5, Box 167-F, Staunton, VA 24401.

WASHINGTON

WRITER'S WEEKEND AT THE BEACH—Ocean Park, WA. February. Birdie Etchison, Dir., P.O. Box 877, Ocean Park, WA 98640.

SCBWI WASHINGTON REGION WRITING & ILLUSTRATING FOR CHILDREN—Seattle, WA. April. Sue Ford, Reg. Advisor, SCBWI, 14816 205th Ave. S.E., Renton, WA 98059-8926. Web site: www.scbwi-washington.org.

CLARION WEST SCIENCE FICTION & SCIENCE FICTION WRITERS WORKSHOP—Seattle, WA. June, July. Leslie Howle, Dir., 340 15th Ave. E., Suite 350, Seattle, WA 98112.

PORT TOWNSEND WRITERS' CONFERENCE—Port Townsend, WA. July. Sam Hamill, Dir., Centrum, Box 1158, Port Townsend, WA 98368.

TOUCH OF SUCCESS SEMINARS—San Juan Islands, WA (aboard yacht). August. Bill Thomas, Dir., Box 201, Quilcene, WA 98376.

WISCONSIN

GREEN LAKE WRITERS CONFERENCE—Green Lake, WI. June, July. Blythe Ann Cooper, Dir., Green Lake Conference Center, 2511 State Hwy. 23, Green Lake, WI 54941.

WISCONSIN FALL RETREAT FOR WORKING WRITERS—Racine, WI. October. Patricia Curtis Pfitsch, Dir., Rt. 1, Box 137, Gays Mills, WI 54631.

WYOMING

JACKSON HOLE WRITERS CONFERENCE—Jackson Hole, WY. July. Barbara Barnes, Dir., P.O. Box 3972, Laramie, WY 82071.

STATE ARTS COUNCILS

State arts councils sponsor grants, fellowships, and other programs for writers. To be eligible for funding, a writer *must* be a resident of the state in which he is applying. Write or call for more information; 1–800 numbers are toll free for in-state calls only; numbers preceded by TDD indicate Telecommunications Device for the Deaf; TTY indicates Teletypewriter.

ALABAMA STATE COUNCIL ON THE ARTS
201 Monroe St., Suite 110
Montgomery, AL 36130
(334) 242-4076; fax: (334) 240-3269
e-mail: staff@arts.state.al.us
web site: www.state.art.al.us
Albert B. Head, *Executive Director*

ALASKA STATE COUNCIL ON THE ARTS
411 W. 4th Ave., Suite 1E
Anchorage, AK 99501-2343
(907) 269-6610; fax: (907) 269-6601
e-mail: info@aksca.org
Shannon Planchon, *Grants Officer*

ARIZONA COMMISSION ON THE ARTS
417 W. Roosevelt
Phoenix, AZ 85003
(602) 255-5882; fax: (602) 256-0282
e-mail: jbernstein@ArizonaArts.org
web site: http://az.arts.asu.edu/artscomm
Attn: Jill Bernstein, *Public Information and Literature Dir.*

ARKANSAS ARTS COUNCIL
1500 Tower Bldg., 323 Center St.
Little Rock, AR 72201
(501) 324-9766; fax: (501) 324-9154
e-mail: info@dah.state.ar.us
web site: www.arkansasarts.com
James E. Mitchell, *Executive Director*

CALIFORNIA ARTS COUNCIL
1300 I St., Suite 930
Sacramento, CA 95814
1–800–201–6201; fax: (916) 322-6575
e-mail: cac@cwo.com
web site: www.cac.ca.gov
Adam Gottlieb, *Communications Director*

COLORADO COUNCIL ON THE ARTS
750 Pennsylvania St.
Denver, CO 80203-3699
(303) 894-2617; fax: (303) 894-2615
e-mail: coloarts@artswire.org
Fran Holden, *Executive Director*

CONNECTICUT COMMISSION ON THE ARTS
1 Financial Plaza
Hartford, CT 06103
(860) 566-4770; fax: (860) 566-6462
John Ostrout, *Executive Director*

DELAWARE DIVISION OF THE ARTS
(For Delaware residents only)
Carvel State Bldg.
820 N. French St.
Wilmington, DE 19801
(302) 577-8278; fax: (302) 577-6561
web site: www.artsdel.org
Kristin Pleasanton, *Art and Artist Services Coordinator*

FLORIDA ARTS COUNCIL
Dept. of State, Div. of Cultural Affairs
The Capitol
Tallahassee, FL 32399-0250
(850) 487-2980; fax: (850) 922-5259
TTY: (850) 488-5779
web site: www.dos.state.fl.us
Attn: Ms. Peg Richardson

GEORGIA COUNCIL FOR THE ARTS
260 14th St. N.W., Suite 401
Atlanta, GA 30318
(404) 685-2787; fax: (404) 685-2788
Ann Davis, *Grants Manager, Literature*

HAWAII STATE FOUNDATION ON CULTURE AND THE ARTS
44 Merchant St.
Honolulu, HI 96813
(808) 586-0300; fax: (808) 586-0308
e-mail: sfca@sfca.state.hi.us
web site: www.state.hi.us/sfca
Ronald Yamakawa, *Interim Executive Director*

IDAHO COMMISSION ON THE ARTS
Box 83720
Boise, ID 83720-0008
(208) 334-2119; fax (208) 334-2488
e-mail: cconley@ica.state.id.us
Attn: Cort Conley

ILLINOIS ARTS COUNCIL
100 W. Randolph, Suite 10–500
Chicago, IL 60601
(312) 814-6750; (800) 237-6994; fax: (312) 814-1471
Loretta Brockmezor, *Director of Lit. Programs*

INDIANA ARTS COMMISSION
402 W. Washington St., Rm. 072
Indianapolis, IN 46204-2741
(317) 232-1268; TDD: (317) 233-3001; fax: (317) 232-5595
web site: www.state.in.us1ac
Dorothy Ilgen, *Executive Director*

IOWA ARTS COUNCIL
600 E. Locust
Des Moines, IA 50319-0290
(515) 282-6500; fax: (515) 242-6498
Attn: Stephen Poole

KANSAS ARTS COMMISSION
700 S.W. Jackson, Suite 1004
Topeka, KS 66603-3761
(785) 296-3335; fax: (785) 296-4989; TTY: (800) 766-3777
e-mail: KAC@arts.state.KS.US
web site: http://arts.state.KS.US
David Wilson, *Executive Director*

KENTUCKY ARTS COUNCIL
300 West Broadway
Frankfort, KY 40601-1950
(502) 564-3757; (888) 833-ARTS; fax: (502) 564-2839
e-mail: kyarts@mail.state.ky.us
web site: www.kyarts.org
Attn: Gerri Combs, *Executive Director*

LOUISIANA DIVISION OF THE ARTS
Box 44247
Baton Rouge, LA 70804
(225) 342-8180; fax: (225) 342-8173
e-mail: jborders@crt.state.la.us
web site: www.crt.state.la.us
James Borders, *Executive Director*

MAINE ARTS COMMISSION
25 State House Station
Augusta, ME 04333-0025
(207) 287-2724; fax: (207) 287-2335; TDD: (207) 287-6740
web site: www.mainearts.com
Alden C. Wilson, *Director*

MARYLAND STATE ARTS COUNCIL
Literature Program
125 W. Ostend St., Suite E
Baltimore, MD 21230
(410) 767-6450; fax: (410) 333-1062
e-mail: rturner@mdbusiness.state.md.us
web site: www.msac.org
Rory Turner, *Literature Program Coordinator*

MASSACHUSETTS CULTURAL COUNCIL
120 Boylston St., 2nd Floor
Boston, MA 02116-4802
(617) 727-3668; (800) 232-0960; TTY: (617) 338-9153
fax: (617) 727-0044
e-mail: mcc@art.state.ma.us
web site: www.massculturalcouncil.org
Attn: Michael Brady

MICHIGAN COUNCIL FOR ARTS AND CULTURAL AFFAIRS
525 W. Ottawa
P.O. Box 30705
Lansing, MI 48909-8205
(517) 241-4011; fax: (517) 241-3979
web site: www.cis.state.mi.us
Betty Boone, *Executive Director*

MINNESOTA STATE ARTS BOARD
Park Square Court
400 Sibley St., Suite 200
St. Paul, MN 55101-1928
(651) 215-1600; (800) 8MN-ARTS; fax: (651) 215-1602
e-mail: Amy.Frimpong@arts.state.mn.us
web site: www.arts.state.mn.us
Amy Frimpong, *Artist Assistance Program Associate*

COMPAS: WRITERS & ARTISTS IN THE SCHOOLS
304 Landmark Center
75 W. Fifth St.
St. Paul, MN 55102
(651) 292-3254; fax: (651) 292-3258
web site: www.compas.org
Daniel Gabriel, *Director*

MISSISSIPPI ARTS COMMISSION
239 N. Lamar St., Suite 207
Jackson, MS 39201
(601) 359-6030; fax: (601) 359-6008
web site: www.arts.state.ms.us
Lynn Adams Wilkins, *Community Arts Director*

MISSOURI ARTS COUNCIL
Wainwright Office Complex
111 N. 7th St., Suite 105
St. Louis, MO 63101-2188
(314) 340-6845; fax: (314) 340-7215
e-mail: dburns@mail.state.mo.us
web site: www.missouriartscouncil.org
David Burns, *Program Specialist, Music & Literature*

MONTANA ARTS COUNCIL
P.O. Box 202201
Helena, MT 59620-2201
(406) 444-6430; fax: (406) 444-6548
e-mail: mac@state.mt.us
web site: www.art.state.mt.us
Arlynn Fishbaugh, *Executive Director*

NEBRASKA ARTS COUNCIL
3838 Davenport St.
Omaha, NE 68131-2329
(402) 595-2122; fax: (402) 595-2334
web site: www.nebraskaartscouncil.org
Jennifer Severin, *Executive Director*

NEVADA ARTS COUNCIL
602 N. Curry St.
Carson City, NV 89703
(702) 687-6680; fax: (702) 687-6688
web site: dmla.clan.lib.nv.us
Susan Boskoff, *Executive Director*

NEW HAMPSHIRE STATE COUNCIL ON THE ARTS
Phenix Hall
40 N. Main St.
Concord, NH 03301-4974
(603) 271-2789; fax: (603) 271-3584; TDD: (800) 735-2964
web site: www.state.nh.us/nharts
Audrey Sylvester, *Artist Services Coordinator*

NEW JERSEY STATE COUNCIL ON THE ARTS
Artist Services
P.O. Box 306
Trenton, NJ 08625
(609) 292-6130; fax: (609) 989-1440
e-mail: Beth@arts.sos.state.nj.us
web site: www.njartscouncil.org
Beth Vogel, *Program Officer, Arts Education & Artists Services*

NEW MEXICO ARTS
P.O. Box 1450
Santa Fe, NM 87501
(505) 827-6490; fax: (505) 827-6043
e-mail: rforrest@oca.state.nm.us
Randy Forrester, *Program Coordinator*

NEW YORK STATE COUNCIL ON THE ARTS
915 Broadway
New York, NY 10010
(212) 387-7022; fax: (212) 387-7164/7168
e-mail: KMASTERSON@NYSCA.org
Kathleen Masterson, *Director, Literature Program*

NORTH CAROLINA ARTS COUNCIL
Dept. of Cultural Resources
Raleigh, NC 27601-2807
(919) 733-2111 ext. 22; fax: (919) 733-4834
e-mail: dmcgill@ncacmail.dcr.state.nc.us
Deborah McGill, *Literature Director*

NORTH DAKOTA COUNCIL ON THE ARTS
418 E. Broadway, Suite 70
Bismarck, ND 58501-4086
e-mail: comserv@state.nd.us
web site: www.state.nd.us/arts
(701) 328-3954; fax: (701) 328-3963

OHIO ARTS COUNCIL
727 E. Main St.
Columbus, OH 43205-1796
(614) 466-2613; fax: (614) 466-4494
web site: www.oac.state.oh.us
Bob Fox, *Literature Program Coordinator*

OKLAHOMA ARTS COUNCIL
P.O. Box 52001-2001
Oklahoma City, OK 73152-2001
(405) 521-2931; fax: (405) 521-6418
e-mail: okarts@arts.state.ok.us
web site: www.state.ok.us/~arts
Betty Price, *Executive Director*

OREGON ARTS COMMISSION
775 Summer St. N.E.
Salem, OR 97310
(503) 986-0082; fax: (503) 986-0260;
e-mail: oregon.artscomm@state.or.us
web site: http://art.econ.state.or.us
Attn: *Assistant Director*

PENNSYLVANIA COUNCIL ON THE ARTS
Room 216, Finance Bldg.
Harrisburg, PA 17120
(717) 787-6883; fax (717) 783-2538
web site: http://artsnet.org/pca/
James Woland, *Literature Program*

INSTITUTO DE CULTURA PUERTORRIQUENA
P.O. Box 9024184
San Juan, PR 00902-4184
Dr. Jose Ramon de la Torre, *Executive Director*

RHODE ISLAND STATE COUNCIL ON THE ARTS
95 Cedar St., Suite 103
Providence, RI 02903
(401) 222-3880; fax: (401) 521-1351
e-mail: info@risca.state.ri.us
web site: www.risca.state.ri.us
Randall Rosenbaum, *Executive Director*

SOUTH CAROLINA ARTS COMMISSION
1800 Gervais St.
Columbia, SC 29201
(803) 734-8696; fax: (803) 734-8526
e-mail: goldstsa@arts.state.sc.us
web site: www.state.sc.us/arts
Sara June Goldstein, *Director, Literary Arts Program*

SOUTH DAKOTA ARTS COUNCIL
800 Governors Dr.
Pierre, SD 57501-2294
(605) 773-3131; fax: (605) 773-6962
e-mail: <sdac@stlib.state.sd.us>
web site: www.sdarts.org
Attn: Dennis Holub, *Executive Director*

TENNESSEE ARTS COMMISSION
401 Charlotte Ave.
Nashville, TN 37243-0780
(615) 741-1701; fax: (615) 741-8559
web site: www.arts.state.tn.us
Attn: Literary Arts Director

TEXAS COMMISSION ON THE ARTS
P.O. Box 13406
Austin, TX 78711-3406
(512) 463-5535; fax: (512) 475-2699
Attn: Gaye Greever McElwain

UTAH ARTS COUNCIL
617 E. South Temple
Salt Lake City, UT 84102-1177
(801) 236-7553; fax: (801) 236-7556
Guy Lebeda, *Literary Coordinator*

VERMONT ARTS COUNCIL
136 State St., Drawer 33
Montpelier, VT 05633-6001
(802) 828-3291; fax: (802) 828-3363
e-mail: info@arts.vca.state.vt.us
web site: www.state.vt.us/vermont-arts
Michele Bailey, Director of Artist Programs

VIRGINIA COMMISSION FOR THE ARTS
223 Governor St.
Richmond, VA 23219
(804) 225-3132; fax: (804) 225-4327
e-mail: pbaggett.arts@state.va.us
web site: www.artswire.org/~vacomm
Peggy J. Baggett, *Executive Director*

WASHINGTON STATE ARTS COMMISSION
234 E. 8th Ave.
P.O. Box 42675
Olympia, WA 98504-2675
(360)586-2421; fax: (360) 586-5351
e-mail: bitsyb@wsac.wa.gov
web site: www.wa.gov/art
Bitsy Bidwell, *Community Arts Development Manager*

WEST VIRGINIA DIVISION OF CULTURE & HISTORY
WV Commission on the Arts
Culture and History Division
The Cultural Center, Capitol Complex
1900 Kanawha Blvd. E.
Charleston, WV 25305-0300
(304) 558-0220; fax: (304) 558-2779
e-mail: debbie.haught@wvculture.org
web site: www.wvculture.org

WISCONSIN ARTS BOARD
101 E. Wilson St., 1st Floor
Madison, WI 53702
(608) 266-0190; fax: (608) 267-0380
e-mail: artsboard@arts.state.wi.us
web site: www.arts.state.wi.us
George Tzougros, *Executive Director*

WYOMING ARTS COUNCIL
2320 Capitol Ave.
Cheyenne, WY 82002
(307) 777-7742; fax: (307) 777-5499
e-mail: mshay@missc.state.wy.us
Michael Shay, *Literature Program Manager*

ORGANIZATIONS FOR WRITERS

ACADEMY OF AMERICAN POETS
584 Broadway, Suite 1208
New York, NY 10012
(212) 274-0343; fax: (212) 274-9427
web site: http://www.poets.org.
Jonathan Galassi, *President*
    The Academy was founded in 1934 to support American poets at all stages of their careers and to foster the appreciation of contemporary poetry. The largest organization in the country dedicated specifically to the art of poetry, the Academy sponsors programs nationally. In addition to the Walt Whitman Award, these include the Academy Fellowship for distinguished poetic achievement; the Tanning Prize for outstanding and proven mastery in the art of poetry; the Lenore Marshall Poetry Prize; the James Laughlin Award; the Raiziss/de Palchi Translation Award; the Harold Morton Landon Translation Award; poetry prizes at more than 160 colleges and universities; a national series of poetry readings and poets' residencies; and the American Poets Fund and the Atlas Fund, which provide financial assistance to poets and non-commercial publishers of poetry, respectively. Membership is open to all. Annual dues: $25 and up.

AMERICAN SOCIETY OF JOURNALISTS AND AUTHORS, INC.
1501 Broadway, Suite 302
New York, NY 10036
(212) 997-0947
e-mail: ASJA@compuserve.com
web site: http://www.asja.org
Alexandra Owens, *Executive Director*
    A nationwide organization of independent writers of nonfiction dedicated to promoting high standards of nonfiction writing through monthly meetings, annual writers' conferences, etc. The ASJA produces a free electronic bulletin board for free-lance writers on contract issues in the new-media age, and the organization offers extensive benefits and services in-

cluding referral services, numerous discount services, and the opportunity to explore professional issues and concerns with other writers. Members also receive a monthly newsletter with confidential market information. Membership is open to professional free-lance writers of nonfiction; qualifications are judged by the membership committee. Call or write for application details.

THE ASSOCIATED WRITING PROGRAMS
Tallwood House, Mail Stop 1E3
George Mason University
Fairfax, VA 22030
(703) 993-4301; fax: (703) 993-4302
web site: http://www.awpwriter.org
Attn: *Membership*
   The AWP seeks to serve writers and teachers in need of community, support, information, inspiration, contacts, and ideas. *The Writer's Chronicle* provides publishing opportunities, job listings, and an active exchange of ideas on writing and teaching, including an annual conference. Members receive six issues of *The Writer's Chronicle* and seven issues of *AWP Job List*. Publications include *The AWP Official Guide to Creative Writing Programs*. Annual dues: $57, *individual*; $37, *student*.

THE AUTHORS GUILD, INC.
330 W. 42nd St., 29th Fl.
New York, NY 10036-6902
(212) 563-5904; fax: (212) 564-5363
e-mail: staff@authorsguild.org
web site: www.authorsguild.org
Attn: *Membership Committee*
   As the largest organization of published writers in America, membership offers writers free reviews of publishing and agency contracts, access to group health insurance, and seminars on subjects of concern to authors. The Authors Guild also lobbies on behalf of all authors on issues such as copyright, taxation, and freedom of expression. A writer who has published a book in the last seven years with an established publisher, or has published three articles in periodicals of general circulation within the last eighteen months is eligible for active voting membership. An unpublished writer who has received a contract offer may be eligible for associate membership. All members of the Authors Guild automatically become members of its parent organization, the Authors League of America. First year annual dues: $90.

THE AUTHORS LEAGUE OF AMERICA, INC.
330 W. 42nd St.
New York, NY 10036-6902
(212) 564-8350; fax: (212) 564-5363
e-mail: Authors@pipeline.com
Attn: *Membership Committee*
   A national organization representing over 14,000 authors and dramatists on matters of joint concern, such as copyright, taxes, and freedom of expression. Membership is restricted to authors and dramatists who are members of the Authors Guild and the Dramatists Guild.

THE DRAMATISTS GUILD OF AMERICA, INC.
1501 Broadway, Suite 701
New York, NY 10036-3909
(212) 398-9366
John Weidman, *President*; Christopher Wilson, *Executive Director*

The national professional association of playwrights, composers, and lyricists, the guild was established to protect dramatists' rights and to improve working conditions. Services include use of the guild's contracts; a toll-free number for members in need of business advice; access to discount tickets; access to third-party health insurance programs and a group term life insurance plan; and numerous seminars. The Frederick Loew room is available to members for readings and rehearsals at a nominal fee. Publications currently include *The Dramatists Guild Resource Directory*, and *The Dramatists Magazine*. All playwrights, produced or not, are eligible for membership. Annual dues: $125, *active*; $75, *associate*; $35, *student*.

INTERNATIONAL ASSOCIATION OF CRIME WRITERS (NORTH AMERICAN BRANCH)
P.O. Box 8674
New York, NY 10116-8674
(212) 243-8966; fax: (815) 361-1477
e-mail: mfrisque@igc.org
Jim Weikart, *President*

This international association was founded in 1987 to promote communications among crime writers worldwide, encourage translation of crime writing into other languages, and defend authors against censorship and other forms of tyranny. The IACW sponsors a number of conferences, publishes a quarterly newsletter, *Border Patrol*, and annually awards the Hammett prize for literary excellence in crime writing to a work of fiction or nonfiction by a U.S. or Canadian author. Membership is open to published authors of crime fiction, nonfiction, and screenplays. Agents, editors, and booksellers in the mystery field are also eligible to apply. Annual dues: $50.

INTERNATIONAL ASSOCIATION OF THEATRE FOR CHILDREN AND YOUNG PEOPLE
724 Second Ave. S.
Nashville, TN 37210
(615) 254-5719; fax: (615) 254-3255
e-mail: USASSITEJ@aol.com

The development of professional theater for young audiences and international exchange are the organization's primary mandates. Provides a link between professional theaters, artists, directors, training institutions, and arts agencies; sponsors festivals and forums for interchange among theaters and theater artists. Annual dues: $65, *individual*; $35, *retiree*; $30, *student*.

THE INTERNATIONAL WOMEN'S WRITING GUILD
Box 810, Gracie Station
New York, NY 10028-0082
(212) 737-7536; fax: (212) 737-9469
e-mail: iwwg@iwwg-com

web site: http://www.iwwg.com

Hannelore Hahn, *Executive Director & Founder*

Founded in 1976, serving as a network for the personal and professional empowerment of women through writing. Services include six issues of a 32-page newsletter, a list of literary agents, independent small presses, and publishing services, access to health insurance plan at group rates, access to writing conferences and related events throughout the U.S., including the annual "Remember the Magic" summer conference at Skidmore College in Saratoga Springs, NY, regional writing clusters, and year-round supportive networking. Any woman may join regardless of portfolio. Annual dues: $35; $45 *international.*

MIDWEST RADIO THEATRE WORKSHOP
KOPN
915 E. Broadway
Columbia, MO 65201
(573) 874-5676; fax: (314) 499-1662
e-mail: mrtw@mrtw.org

Sue Zizza, *Director*

Founded in 1979, the MRTW is the only national resource for American radio dramatists, providing referrals, technical assistance, educational materials, and workshops. MRTW coordinates an annual national radio script contest, publishes an annual radio scriptbook, and distributes a script anthology with primer. Send SASE for more information.

MYSTERY WRITERS OF AMERICA, INC.
17 E. 47th St., 6th Fl.
New York, NY 10017
(212) 888-8171; fax: (212) 888-8107

Mary Beth Becker, *Executive Director*

The MWA exists for the purpose of raising the prestige of mystery and detective writing, and of defending the rights and increasing the income of all writers in the field of mystery, detection, and fact crime writing. Each year, the MWA presents the Edgar Allan Poe Awards for the best mystery writing in a variety of fields. The four classifications of membership are: *active*, open to any writer who has made a sale in the field of mystery, suspense, or crime writing; *associate*, for professionals in allied fields; *corresponding*, for writers living outside the U.S.; *affiliate*, for unpublished writers. Annual dues: $65; $32.50 *corresponding members.*

NATIONAL ASSOCIATION OF SCIENCE WRITERS, INC.
P.O. Box 294
Greenlawn, NY 11740
(516) 757-5664
e-mail: diane@nasw.ORG

Diane McGurgan, *Executive Director*

The NASW promotes the dissemination of accurate information regarding science through all media, and conducts a varied program to increase the flow of news from scientists, to improve the quality of its presentation, and to communicate its meaning to the reading public. Anyone who has been actively engaged in the dissemination of science information is eligible to apply for membership. Members must be principally involved in reporting on science through newspapers, magazines, TV, or other media that reach the public directly. Also, members report on science through limited-circulation publications and other media. Annual dues: $60.

NATIONAL CONFERENCE OF EDITORIAL WRITERS
6223 Executive Blvd.
Rockville, MD 20852
(301) 984-3015; fax: (301) 231-0026
e-mail: ncewhqs@erols.com
web site: www.ncew.org
A nonprofit professional organization established in 1947, NCEW exists to improve the quality of editorial pages and broadcast editorials, and to promote high standards among opinion writers and editors . The association offers members networking opportunities, regional meetings, page exchanges, foreign tours, educational opportunities and seminars, an annual convention, and a subscription to the quarterly journal *The Masthead.* Membership is open to opinion writers and editors for general-circulation newspapers, radio or television stations, and syndicated columnists; teachers and students of journalism; and others who determine editorial policy. Annual dues are based on circulation or broadcast audience and range from $85 to $150 (journalism educators: $75; students: $50).

THE NATIONAL LEAGUE OF AMERICAN PEN WOMEN, INC.
The Pen Arts Building
1300 17th St. N.W.
Washington, DC 20036-1973
(202) 785-1997; fax: (202) 452-6868
e-mail: NLAPW1@juno.com
web site: http://members.aol.com/penwomen/pen.htm
Judith La Fourest, *National President*
Founded in 1897, the league promotes development of the creative talents of professional women in the arts. Membership is through local branches in the categories of Art, Letters, and Music.

THE NATIONAL WRITERS ASSOCIATION
3140 S. Peoria, #295
Aurora, CO 80014
(303) 841-0246; fax: (303) 751-8593
web site: www.nationalwriters.com
Sandy Whelchel, *Executive Director*
New and established writers, poets, and playwrights throughout the U.S. and worldwide may become members of the NWA, a full-time, customer-service-oriented association founded in 1937. Members receive a quarterly newsletter, *Authorship*, and may attend the annual June conference. Annual dues: $85, *professional*; $65, *regular*; add $25 outside the U.S.

NATIONAL WRITERS UNION
113 University Place, 6th Fl.
New York, NY 10003
(212) 254-0279
e-mail: nwu@nwu.org
web site: www.nwu.org

Jonathan Tasini, *President*

Dedicated to bringing about equitable payment and fair treatment of free-lance writers through collective action. Membership is over 6,000 and includes book authors, poets, cartoonists, journalists, and technical writers in 17 chapters nationwide. The union offers its members contract and agent information, group health insurance, press credentials, grievance handling, a quarterly magazine, and sample contracts and resource materials. It sponsors workshops and seminars across the country. Membership is open to writers who have published a book, play, three articles, five poems, one short story or an equivalent amount of newsletter, publicity, technical, commercial, government, or institutional copy, or have written an equivalent amount of unpublished material and are actively seeking publication. Annual dues: $95 to $210.

NEW DRAMATISTS
424 W. 44th St.
New York, NY 10036
(212) 757-6960
web site: www.newdramatists.org
Todd London, *Artistic Director*

New Dramatists is dedicated to finding gifted playwrights and giving them the time, space, and tools to develop their craft. Services include readings and workshops; a director-in-residence program; national script distribution for members; artist work spaces; international playwright exchange programs; script copying facilities; and a free ticket program. Membership is open to residents of New York City and the surrounding tri-state area. National memberships are offered to those outside the area who can spend time in NYC in order to take advantage of programs. Apply between July 15 and September 15. No annual dues.

NORTHWEST PLAYWRIGHTS GUILD
318 S.W. Palatine Hill Rd.
Portland, OR 97219
(503) 452-4778
e-mail: bjscript@teleport.com
web site: www.nwpg.org
Bill Johnson, *Office Manager*

The guild supports and promotes playwrights living in the Northwest through play development, staged readings, and networking for play competitions and production opportunities. Members receive monthly and quarterly newsletters. Annual dues: $25.

OUTDOOR WRITERS ASSOCIATION OF AMERICA, INC.
158 Lower Georges Valley Rd.
Spring Mills, PA 16875
e-mail: eking4owaa@cs.com
web site: www.owaa.org
Eileen King, *Meeting Director*

A non-profit, international organization representing professional communicators who report and reflect upon America's diverse interests in the outdoors. Membership, by nomination only, includes a monthly publication, *Outdoors Unlimited*; annual conference; annual membership directory; contests.

PEN AMERICAN CENTER
568 Broadway
New York, NY 10012
(212) 334-1660; fax (212) 334-2181
e-mail: pen@pen.org
web site: www.pen.org
Michael Roberts, *Executive Director*

PEN American Center is one of more than 130 centers worldwide that compose International PEN. The 2,600 members of the American Center are poets, playwrights, essayists, editors, and novelists, as well as literary translators and those agents who have made a substantial contribution to the literary community. PEN American headquarters is in New York City, and branches are located in Boston, Chicago, New Orleans, Portland, Oregon, and San Francisco. Among the activities, programs, and services sponsored are literary events and awards, outreach projects to encourage reading, assistance to writers in financial need, and international and domestic human rights campaigns on behalf of many writers, editors, and journalists censored or imprisoned because of their writing. Membership is open to writers who have published two books of literary merit, as well as editors, agents, playwrights, and translators who meet specific standards; apply to membership committee.

THE PLAYWRIGHTS' CENTER
2301 Franklin Ave. E.
Minneapolis, MN 55406
(612) 332-7481; fax (612) 332-6037
e-mail: pwcenter@mtn.org
web site: www.pwcenter.org
Carlo Cuesta, *Executive Director*

The Playwrights' Center fuels the theater by providing services that support playwrights and playwriting. Members receive applications for all programs, a calendar of events, eligibility to participate in special activities, including classes, outreach programs, and PlayLabs. For membership information, contact Ronnell Wheeler, Membership Coordinator. Annual dues: $40.

POETRY SOCIETY OF AMERICA
15 Gramercy Park
New York, NY 10003
(212) 254-9628; fax: (212) 673-2352
1 (888) USA-POEM, for a free brochure
web site: www.poetrysociety.org
Rebecca Wolff, *Programs Associate*

Founded in 1910, the PSA seeks to raise the awareness of poetry, to deepen the understanding of it, and to encourage more people to read, listen to, and write poetry. To this end, the PSA presents national series of readings including "Tributes in Libraries" and "Poetry in Public Places," and mounts poetry posters on mass transit vehicles through "Poetry in Motion." The PSA also offers annual contests for poetry, seminars, poetry festivals, and publishes a journal. Annual dues: from $40 ($25 for students).

POETS AND WRITERS, INC.
72 Spring St.
New York, NY 10012
(212) 226-3586; fax: (212) 226-3963
web site: http://www.pw.org
Elliot Figman, *Executive Director*

Poets & Writers, Inc., was founded in 1970 to foster the development of poets and fiction writers and to promote communication throughout the literary community. A non-membership organization, it offers information for writers; *Poets & Writers Magazine* and other publications; as well as support for readings and workshops at a wide range of venues.

PUBLICATION RIGHTS CLEARINGHOUSE
National Writers Union
113 University Pl., 6th Fl.
New York, NY 10003
(212) 254-0279; fax: (212) 254-0673
e-mail: nwu@nwu.org
web site: www.nwu.org

Publication Rights Clearinghouse, the collective-licensing agency of the National Writers Union, was created in 1996 to help writers license and collect royalties for the reuse of their published works in electronic databases and other media. It is modeled after similar organizations that have long existed in the music industry. Writers license non-exclusive secondary rights to the PRC; the PRC licenses those rights to secondary users and distributes payment to the writers. Enrollment is open to both NWU members and non-members.

ROMANCE WRITERS OF AMERICA
3707 FM 1960 West, Suite 555
Houston, TX 77068
(713) 440-6885; fax: (713) 440-7510
Allison Kelley, *Executive Director*

An international organization with over 150 local chapters across the U.S., Canada, Europe, and Australia; membership is open to any writer, published or unpublished, interested in the field of romantic fiction. Annual dues of $65, plus $10 application fee for new members; benefits include annual conference, contest, market information, and monthly professional journal, *Romance Writers' Report.*

SCIENCE-FICTION AND FANTASY WRITERS OF AMERICA, INC.
532 La Guardia Pl., #632
New York, NY 10012-1428
Robert J. Sawyer, *Pres.*

An organization whose purpose it is to foster and further the professional interests of science fiction and fantasy writers. Presents the annual Nebula Award for excellence in the field and publishes the *Bulletin* and *SFWA Handbook* for its members (also available to non-members).

Any writer who has sold a work of science fiction or fantasy is eligible for membership. Annual dues: $50, *active* ; $35, *affiliate*; plus $10 installation fee; send for application and information.

SISTERS IN CRIME
P.O. Box 442124
Lawrence, KS 66044-8933
e-mail: sistersincrime@juno.com
web site: www.sistersincrime.org
Barbara Burnett Smith, *President*
Sisters in Crime was founded in 1986 to combat discrimination against women in the mystery field, educate publishers and the general public as to inequalities in the treatment of female authors, and raise the level of awareness of their contribution to the field. Membership is open to all and includes writers, readers, editors, agents, booksellers, and librarians. Publications include a quarterly newsletter and Books in Print membership directory. Annual dues: $35, U.S.; $40, foreign. Members interested in mysteries for young readers may join Mysteries for Minors (Katherine Hall Page, Chair, P.O. Box 442124, Lawrence, KS 66044-8933) with no additional dues.

SOCIETY OF AMERICAN TRAVEL WRITERS
4101 Lake Boone Trail, Suite 201
Raleigh, NC 27607
(919) 787-5181; fax: (919) 787-4916
Cathy Korr
The Society of American Travel Writers represents writers and other professionals who strive to provide travelers with accurate reports on destinations, facilities, and services. Active membership is limited to travel writers and free lancers who have a steady volume of published or distributed work about travel. Application fees: $250, *active*; $500, *associate*. Annual dues: $130, *active*; $250, *associate*.

SOCIETY OF CHILDREN'S BOOK WRITERS & ILLUSTRATORS
8271 Beverly Blvd.
Los Angeles, CA 90048
(323) 782-1010; fax: (323) 782-1892
e-mail:scbwi@scbwi.org
web site: www.scbwi.org
Lin Oliver, *Executive Director*
A national organization of authors, editors, publishers, illustrators, librarians, and educators, the SCBWI offers a variety of services to people who write, illustrate, or share an interest in children's literature. Full memberships are open to those who have had at least one children's book or story published. Associate memberships are open to all those with an interest in children's literature. Annual dues: $50.

SOCIETY OF ENVIRONMENTAL JOURNALISTS
P.O. Box 27280
Philadelphia, PA 19118
(215) 836-9970; fax: (215) 836-9972
e-mail: SEJ@SEJ.ORG
web site: http://www.SEJ.org
Beth Parke, *Executive Director*
Dedicated to improving the quality, accuracy, and visibility of environmental reporting, the society serves 1,200 members with a quarterly

newsletter, the *SEJournal*, national and regional conferences, World Wide Web (www.SEJ.org), and membership directory. Annual dues: $40; $30, *student*.

SOCIETY OF PROFESSIONAL JOURNALISTS
16 S. Jackson St.
Greencastle, IN 46135-0077
(765) 653-3333; fax: (765) 653-4631
web site: http://spj.org
  With 13,500 members and 300 chapters, the Society seeks to serve the interests of print, broadcast, and wire journalists. Services include legal counsel on journalism issues, jobs-for-journalists career search newsletter, professional development seminars, and awards that encourage journalism. Members receive *Quill*, a monthly magazine that explores current issues in the field. SPJ promotes ethics and freedom of information programs. Annual dues: $70, *professional*; $35, *student*.

THE SONGWRITERS GUILD FOUNDATION
1560 Broadway, Suite 1306
New York, NY 10036
(212) 768-7902; fax: (212) 768-9048
George Wurzbach, *National Projects Director*
  Open to published and unpublished songwriters, the Guild provides members with songwriter-publisher contracts, reviews contracts, collects royalties from publishers, offers group health and life insurance plans, conducts workshops and critique sessions, and provides a newsletter. Annual dues: $55, *associate*; $70 and up, *full member*.

THEATRE COMMUNICATIONS GROUP
355 Lexington Ave.
New York, NY 10017
(212) 697-5230; fax (212) 983-4847
web site: www.tcg.org
Terence Nemeth, *Vice President, Publications*
  Theatre Communications Group (TCG), the national organization for the American theatre, offers a wide array of services in line with its mission: to strengthen, nurture, and promote the not-for-profit American theatre. Through artistic and management programs, advocacy activities, and publications, TCG seeks to increase the organizational efficiency of member theatres, cultivate and celebrate the artistic talent and achievements of the field, and promote a larger public understanding of and appreciation for the theatre field. Individual members receive *American Theatre* magazine. Annual dues: $35, *individual*.

WESTERN WRITERS OF AMERICA, INC.
1012 Fair St.
Franklin, TN 37064
(615) 791-1444
e-mail: Tncrutch@aol.com
web site: www.westernwriters.org
James A. Crutchfield, *Secretary/Treasurer*
  Membership is open to qualified professional writers of fiction and nonfiction related to the history and literature of the American West. Its

chief purpose is to promote a more widespread distribution, readership, and appreciation of the West and its literature. Holds annual convention in the last week of June. Sponsors annual Spur Awards, Owen Wister Award, and Medicine Pipe Bearer's Award for published work and produced screenplays. Annual dues: $75.

WRITERS GUILD OF AMERICA, EAST, INC.
555 W. 57th St.
New York, NY 10019
(212) 767-7800; fax: (212) 582-1909
web site: http://www.wgaeast.org
Mona Mangan, *Executive Director*

WRITERS GUILD OF AMERICA, WEST, INC.
7000 W. 3rd St.
Los Angeles, CA 90048
(213) 951-4000; fax: (213) 782-4800
web site: www.wga.org
Brian Walton, *Executive Director*
    The Writers Guild of America (East and West) represents writers in motion pictures, broadcast, cable and new media industries, including news and entertainment. In order to qualify for membership, a writer must fulfill current requirements for employment or sale of material in one of these fields.
    The basic dues are $25 per quarter for both organizations. In addition, there are quarterly dues based on percentage of the member's earnings in any one of the fields over which the guild has jurisdiction. The initiation fee is $1,500 for WGAE, for writers living east of the Mississippi, and $2,500 for WGAW, for those living west of the Mississippi.

WRITERS INFORMATION NETWORK, THE PROFESSIONAL ASSOCIATION FOR CHRISTIAN WRITERS
P.O. Box 11337
Bainbridge Island, WA 98110
(206) 842-9103; fax: (206) 842-0536
e-mail: WritersInfoNetwork@juno.com
web site: http://www.bluejaypub.com/win/
Elaine Wright Colvin, *Director/Publisher*
    W.I.N. was founded in 1983 to provide a link between Christian writers and the religious publishing industry. Offered are a bimonthly magazine, *The WIN-Informer Magazine*, and market news, editorial services, advocacy and grievance procedures, referral services, and conferences. Annual dues: $33; $37, *foreign*.

LITERARY AGENTS

As the number of book publishers that will consider only agented submissions grows, more writers are turning to agents to sell their manuscripts.

The agents in the following list handle both literary and dramatic material. Included in each listing are such important details as type of material represented, submission procedure, and commission. Since agents derive their income from the sales of their clients' work, they must represent writers who are selling fairly regularly to good markets. Nonetheless, many of the agents listed here note they will consider unpublished writers. Always query an agent first, and enclose a self-addressed, stamped envelope; most agents will not respond without it. Do not send any manuscripts until the agent has asked you to do so; and be wary of agents who charge fees for reading manuscripts. All of the following agents have indicated they do *not* charge reading fees, however some charge for copyright fees, manuscript retyping, photocopies, copies of books for use in the sale of other rights, and long distance calls.

To learn more about agents and their role in publishing, the Association of Authors' Representatives, Inc., publishes a canon of ethics as well as an up-to-date list of AAR members, available for $7 (check or money order) and a 55¢ legal-size SASE. Write to: Association of Authors' Representatives, P.O. Box 237201, Ansonia Station, New York, NY 10023, or visit their web site: www.aar-online.org.

Another good source which lists agents and their policies is *Literary Market Place,* a directory found in most libraries.

BRET ADAMS LTD.—448 W. 44th St., New York, NY 10036. (212) 765-5630; fax: (212) 265-2212. E-mail: badamsltd@aol.com. Attn: Bruce Ostler, Bret Adams, Melissa Hardy. Stage plays, musicals, teleplays, screenplays. Query with synopsis, bio, resume, and SASE. Rarely considers unproduced writers. Commission: 10%.

LEE ALLAN AGENCY—7464 N. 107th St., Milwaukee, WI 53224-3706. Attn: Mr. Lee A. Matthias. Adult genre fiction, nonfiction. Screenplays. Unpublished writers considered. Query with SASE. Commission: 15% books; 10% scripts. Fees: photocopying, overnight shipping, telephone. "Go to a bookstore and locate the exact place in the store where your book would be displayed. If it realistically fits a popular market niche, is not derivative or imitative, meets the size constraints, and you can't make it any better yourself, you are ready to find an agent."

JAMES ALLEN LITERARY AGENT—538 E. Harford St., P.O. Box 909, Milford, PA 18337. Attn: James Allen. All types of adult fiction except Westerns; considers very few new authors. Query with 2- to 3-page synopsis; no multiple queries. Commission: 10% domestic; 20% foreign, film/TV. Representatives in Hollywood and all principle foreign countries.

MARCIA AMSTERDAM AGENCY—41 W. 82nd St., #9A, New York, NY 10024. Attn: Marcia Amsterdam. Adult and young adult fiction; mainstream nonfiction. Screenplays and teleplays: comedy, romance, psychological suspense. Query with resumé; multiple queries O.K.; two-week exclusive for requested submissions. Commission: 15% books; 10% scripts.

ARTISTS MANAGEMENT GROUP/RENAISSANCE, L.L.C.—9465 Wilshire Blvd., Beverly Hills, CA 90212. Tel: (310) 860-8000; fax: (310) 860-8130. Literary fiction and nonfiction. Unpublished, unproduced novelists considered. Please fax Mr. Joel Gotler. Query with bio and resumé. Commission: 15%.

THE AXELROD AGENCY—49 Main St., Chatham, NY 12037. Attn: Steven Axelrod. Adult fiction and nonfiction. No science fiction, fantasy, or westerns. Unpublished writers considered. Query; multiple queries O.K. Commission: 15% domestic; 20% foreign.

MALAGA BALDI LITERARY AGENCY—204 W. 84th St., Suite 3C, New York, NY 10024. Tel: (212) 579-5075; fax: (212) 579-5078. E-mail: mbaldi@aol.com. Attn: Malaga Baldi. Adult fiction and nonfiction. Unpublished writers considered. Query first. "If I am interested, I ask for proposal, outline, and sample pages for nonfiction, complete manuscript for fiction." Multiple queries O.K. Commission: 15%. Response time: 10 weeks minimum.

THE BALKIN AGENCY—P.O. Box 222, Amherst, MA 01004. Fax: (413) 548-9836. E-mail: balkin@crocker.com. Attn: Rick Balkin. Adult nonfiction. Unpublished writers considered. Query with outline; no multiple queries. Commission: 15% domestic; 20% foreign. "Most interested in serious nonfiction."

VIRGINIA BARBER AGENCY—See *The Writers Shop.*

BARNWOOD PRESS & AGENCY—72 Hudson Point Lane, Ossining, NY 10562. Attn: Diana Dehli Gould. Fax: (914) 923-1604. E-mail: Dianagould@aol.com. Literary fiction and nonfiction. Special interest in travel, biography, and women's subjects. No science fiction, fantasy, genre romance, or children's books. Query with SASE. Commission: 15% domestic; 20% foreign.

LORETTA BARRETT BOOKS—101 Fifth Ave., New York, NY 10003. Attn: Loretta Barrett. Adult fiction and nonfiction. Unpublished writers considered. Query with outline and SASE; include sample pages for nonfiction only. Commission: 15%. Response time: 4 weeks.

REID BOATES LITERARY AGENCY—Box 328, 69 Cooks Crossroad, Pittstown, NJ 08867-0328. Attn: Reid Boates. Adult mainstream nonfiction. New clients by referral only. Commission: 15%.

BOOK DEALS, INC.—417 N. Sangamon St., Chicago, IL 60622. Caroline Carney, President. General-interest adult fiction and nonfiction. Query with outline, first 20 pages, and bio. Commission: 15% domestic; 20% foreign.

GEORGES BORCHARDT, INC.—136 E. 57th St., New York, NY 10022. Fax: (212) 838-6518. Adult fiction and nonfiction. Unpublished writers considered by recommendation only. No unsolicited queries or submissions. Commission: 15%.

BRANDT & BRANDT LITERARY AGENTS—1501 Broadway, New York, NY 10036. Adult fiction and nonfiction. Unpublished writers considered occasionally. Unsolicited query by letter only; no multiple queries. Commission: 15%.

THE HELEN BRANN AGENCY—94 Curtis Rd., Bridgewater, CT 06752. Fax: (860) 355-2572. E-mail: helenbrannagency@ibm.net. Attn: Carol White. Adult fiction and nonfiction. Unpublished writers considered. Commission: 15%.

ANDREA BROWN LITERARY AGENCY, INC.—P.O. Box 371027, Montara, CA 94037. Attn: Laura Rennert. Juvenile fiction and nonfiction only. Unpublished writers considered. Query with outline, sample pages, bio and resumé, and SASE; no faxes. Commission: 15% domestic; 20% foreign.

KNOX BURGER IN ASSOCIATION WITH HAROLD OBER ASSO-

CIATES, INC.—425 Madison Ave., New York, NY 10017. Adult fiction and nonfiction. Highly selective. Query with SASE; no multiple queries. Commission: 15%.

SHEREE BYKOFSKY ASSOCIATES, INC.—16 W. 36th St., 13th Fl., New York, NY 10018. Web site: www.shereebee.com. Mostly adult nonfiction; some adult fiction. Unpublished writers considered. One-page query with SASE. Multiple queries O.K. if indicated as such. Commission: 15%.

MARTHA CASSELMAN—P.O. Box 342, Calistoga, CA 94515-0342. Martha Casselman, Agent. Nonfiction, especially interested in cookbooks. Unpublished writers considered. Query with outline, bio/resumé, and SASE for return. Multiple queries O.K. if noted as such. Commission: 15%.

CASTIGLIA LITERARY AGENCY—1155 Camino del Mar, Suite 510, Del Mar, CA 92014. Tel: (858) 755-8761; fax: (858) 755-7065. Attn: Julie Castiglia, Winifred Golden. Fiction: commercial, ethnic and literary. Nonfiction: psychology, health, women's issues, science, biography, spirituality, Eastern religions, finance, business, and technology. Query with sample page and SASE. No multiple queries. Commission: 15%. "Please do not query by phone. Attend workshops and writers' conferences before approaching an agent."

HY COHEN LITERARY AGENCY, LTD.—P.O. Box 43770, Upper Montclair, NJ 07043. Fax: (973) 783-9867. E-mail: cogency@home.com. Attn: Hy Cohen. Adult fiction, nonfiction, and juvenile. Unpublished writers considered. Unsolicited queries and manuscripts O.K., "with SASE, please!" Multiple submissions recommended. Commission: 10% domestic; 20% foreign.

RUTH COHEN, INC.—P.O. Box 7626, Menlo Park, CA 94025. Attn: Ruth Cohen. Adult mysteries and women's fiction; quality juvenile fiction and nonfiction. Unpublished writers seriously considered. Query with first 10 pages, synopsis, bio and resumé, and SASE. Commission: 15%.

DON CONGDON ASSOCIATES, INC.—156 Fifth Ave., Suite 625, New York, NY 10010. Adult fiction and nonfiction. Query with outline; no multiple queries. Commission: 10% domestic.

THE DOE COOVER AGENCY—P.O. Box 668, Winchester, MA 01890. Attn: Doe Coover, Colleen Mohyde. Adult literary and commercial fiction and general nonfiction including social sciences, journalism, science, business, biography, memoir, and cookbooks. Unpublished writers considered. Query with outline, bio/resumé, and SASE; no unsolicited manuscripts. Commission: 15%.

RICHARD CURTIS ASSOCIATES, INC.—171 E. 74th St., 2nd Fl., New York, NY 10021. Attn: Pam Valvera. Adult fiction and nonfiction. Unpublished writers considered. Query with outline, bio/resumé, two chapters, and SASE; no multiple queries. Commission: 15% domestic; 20% foreign.

CURTIS BROWN LTD.—10 Astor Pl., New York, NY 10003. General trade fiction and nonfiction; also juvenile. Unpublished writers considered. Query with SASE; no multiple queries. Commission: unspecified.

SANDRA DIJKSTRA LITERARY AGENCY—1155 Camino del Mar, Suite 515C, Del Mar, CA 92014. Attn: Sandra Zane. Adult and children's fiction and nonfiction. Query with outline and bio/resumé. For fiction, submit first 50 pages and synopsis; for nonfiction, submit proposal. Commission: 15% domestic, 20% foreign. SASE.

THE JONATHAN DOLGER AGENCY — 49 E. 96th St., 9B, New York, NY 10128. Attn: Tom Wilson. Adult trade fiction and nonfiction. Considers unpublished writers. Query with outline and SASE. Commission: 15%. "No category mysteries, romance, or science fiction."

DWYER & O'GRADY, INC. — P.O. Box 239, Lempster, NH 03605. Attn: Elizabeth O'Grady. Specialize in children's books for ages 6 to 12. Require strong story line, dialogue, and character development. Not seeking new clients at this time. Commission: 15% domestic, 20% foreign, film, and merchandise.

JANE DYSTEL LITERARY MANAGEMENT, INC. — One Union Square W., Suite 904, New York, NY 10003. Web site: www.dystel.com. Attn: Jane Dystel, Miriam Goderich, Todd Keithley, Jo Fagan, Stacey Glick. Adult fiction and nonfiction; some picture books and children's books. Unpublished writers considered. Query with bio/resumé, sample pages, and outline; no multiple queries. Commission: 15%.

EDUCATIONAL DESIGN SERVICES — P.O. Box 253, Wantaugh, NY 11793. E-mail: edselzer@aol.com. Attn: Bertram L. Linder. Educational texts only. Unpublished writers considered. Query with outline, sample pages or complete manuscript, bio/resumé, and SASE. No multiple queries. Commission: 15% domestic, 25% foreign.

ETHAN ELLENBERG LITERARY AGENCY — 548 Broadway, Suite 5E, New York, NY 10012. E-mail: ellenbergagent@aol.com. Ethan Ellenberg, Agent. Commercial and literary fiction and nonfiction, including health, new age, pop-science, biography, and cookbooks. Specialize in first novels, thrillers, children's books, romance, science fiction and fantasy. No poetry or short stories. Query with cover letter, first 3 chapters, synopsis, and SASE. Responds in 4 to 6 weeks. Commission: 15% domestic; 20% foreign.

ANN ELMO AGENCY — 60 E. 42nd St., New York, NY 10165. Adult fiction, nonfiction, and plays. Juvenile for middle grades and up. No picture books. Unpublished writers considered. Please query first with outline, sample pages, and bio/resumé. No multiple queries. Commission: 15% domestic, 10% foreign.

FELICIA ETH — 555 Bryant St., Suite 350, Palo Alto, CA 94301. Attn: Felicia Eth. Mostly adult nonfiction; some fiction. Unpublished writers considered. Query with outline, sample pages, and bio/resumé. Multiple queries O.K. if noted. Commission: 15% domestic; 20% foreign. "I am a small, very selective agent. My preference is for provocative, original subjects presented in a strong creative voice."

FARBER LITERARY AGENCY — 14 E. 75th St., New York, NY 10021. Attn: Ann Farber. Adult fiction, nonfiction, and stage plays; juvenile books. Considers unpublished writers. Query with outline, sample pages, and SASE. Commission: 15% "with services of attorney."

JOYCE FLAHERTY — 816 Lynda Ct., St. Louis, MO 63122. Tel: (212) 861-7075; fax: (212) 861-7076. Attn: Joyce Flaherty. Adult fiction and nonfiction. Query with outline or proposal, first chapter, and bio. SASE. Commission: 15% domestic; 30% foreign.

FLANNERY LITERARY — 1140 Wickfield Ct., Naperville, IL 60563-3303. Attn: Jennifer Flannery. Juvenile fiction and nonfiction, from board books through young adult novels. Unpublished writers considered. Query with SASE (no phone or fax queries); multiple queries O.K. Commission: 15%.

FOGELMAN LITERARY AGENCY—7515 Greenville Ave., Suite 712, Dallas, TX 75231. Tel: (214) 361-9956. Web site: www.fogelman.com. Attn: Linda M. Kruger. Romance. Nonfiction. Query with SASE. Commission: 15% domestic; 10% foreign.

ROBERT A. FREEDMAN DRAMATIC AGENCY, INC.—1501 Broadway, Suite 2310, New York, NY 10036. Attn: Robert A. Freedman or Selma Luttinger. Screenplays, teleplays, and stage plays. Send query, outline, and bio/resumé; multiple queries O.K. Commission: 10%.

SAMUEL FRENCH, INC.—45 W. 25th St., New York, NY 10010. Stage plays. Unpublished writers considered. Query with complete manuscript; unsolicited and multiple queries O.K.

GELFMAN SCHNEIDER—250 W. 57th St., Suite 2515, New York, NY 10107. Attn: Jane Gelfman. Adult fiction and nonfiction. Unpublished writers only considered if recommended by other writers or teachers. Query with outline, sample pages, and bio; no multiple queries. Commission: 15% domestic; 20% foreign.

GOODMAN ASSOCIATES—500 West End Ave., New York, NY 10024. Attn: Elise Simon Goodman. Adult fiction and nonfiction. Unpublished writers considered. Query with outline, sample pages, and bio/resumé. Multiple queries O.K. Commission: 15% domestic; 20% foreign.

GRAYBILL & ENGLISH, L.L.C.—1920 N. St. N.W., Suite 620, Washington, DC 20036. Attn: Nina Graybill. Adult commercial and literary fiction and nonfiction. For nonfiction, query with SASE and proposal or outline; for fiction, query with SASE and synopsis and up to 3 sample chapters. Multiple queries O.K. Commission: 15% domestic, 20% foreign.

SANFORD J. GREENBURGER—55 Fifth Ave., 15th Fl., New York, NY 10003. Attn: Faith Hornby Hamlin. Nonfiction, including sports books, health, business, psychology, parenting, science, biography, gay; juvenile books. Unpublished writers with strong credentials considered. Query with outline, sample pages, bio, and SASE; multiple queries O.K. Commission: 15% domestic; 20% foreign.

THE CHARLOTTE GUSAY LITERARY AGENCY—10532 Blythe, Los Angeles, CA 90064. Tel: (310) 559-0831; fax: (310) 559-2639. E-mail (for queries only): gusay1@aol.com. Web site: mediastudio.com/gusay. Adult mainstream and literary fiction, nonfiction, and some young adult novels for film. Screenplays/Books to Film. "Query with one-page outline and SASE. Then if we request to see your project, for fiction send a one-page synopsis and the first three chapters. For nonfiction, send the proposal, which includes overview, contents, bio, audience/marketing, and first three chapters. Multiple queries are discouraged, but if you do so, please advise." Commission: 10% dramatic, 15% literary.

JOY HARRIS LITERARY AGENCY, INC.—156 Fifth Ave., Suite 617, New York, NY 10010. E-mail: joyharris@jhlitagent.com. Adult fiction and nonfiction. Unpublished writers considered. Query with outline, sample pages, and bio/resumé. No multiple queries. Commission: 15%.

HEACOCK LITERARY AGENCY, INC.—P.O. Box 927, Main Branch, Malibu, CA 90265-0927. Tel: (310) 589-1775; fax: (310) 589-2825. E-mail:

gracebooks@aol.com. Attn: Rosalie Grace Heacock, Pres. Adult nonfiction. Published and unpublished writers welcome to query with outline, bio/resumé, and SASE. Queries unaccompanied by SASE will not be answered. No multiple queries. Commission: 15%.

FREDERICK HILL ASSOCIATES—1842 Union St., San Francisco, CA 94123. Attn: Irene Moore. Branch office: 505 N. Robertson Blvd., Los Angeles, CA 90048. Adult fiction and nonfiction. Unpublished writers considered. Query with outline and bio/resumé; multiple queries O.K. Commission: 15% domestic, 20% foreign.

JOHN L. HOCHMANN BOOKS—320 E. 58th St., New York, NY 10022. Attn: John L. Hochmann. Mainly nonfiction: biography, social history, health and food, college textbooks. Represent published authors, but unpublished writers considered, "provided they demonstrate thorough knowledge of their subjects." Query with outline, sample pages, bio/resumé, and SASE. No multiple queries. Commission: 15% for domestic/Canadian; plus 15% foreign language and U.K. "Do not submit jacket copy. Submit detailed outlines and proposals that include evaluations of competing books."

BARBARA HOGENSON AGENCY—165 West End Ave., Suite 19-C, New York, NY 10023. Attn: Barbara Hogenson. Adult fiction, nonfiction. Screenplays and stage plays. Query with bio and synopsis, SASE; multiple queries O.K. Commission: 10% scripts; 15% books.

IMG LITERARY AGENCY—825 7th Ave., New York, NY 10019. Attn: Mark Reiter, Carolyn Krupp, and David McCormick. Adult fiction and nonfiction. Unpublished writers considered. Query with outline, sample pages, and bio/resumé. No multiple queries. Commission: 15% domestic.

SHARON JARVIS & CO.—Toad Hall, Inc., RR2, Box 2090, Laceyville, PA 18623. Fax: (570) 869-2942. E-mail: toadhallco@aol.com. Web site: www.laceyville.com/toad-hall. Adult fiction and nonfiction. Unpublished writers considered. Query with bio or resumé, and outline or synopsis. No unsolicited manuscripts. Commission: 15%. "Pay attention to what's selling and what's commercial."

JCA LITERARY AGENCY, INC.—27 W. 20th St., Suite 1103, New York, NY 10011. E-mail: jeff@jcalit.com. Adult fiction and nonfiction. Unpublished writers considered. Query with sample pages; multiple queries O.K. Commission: 15% domestic, 20% foreign.

NATASHA KERN LITERARY AGENCY, INC.—P.O. Box 2908, Portland, OR 97208-2908. Attn: Natasha Kern. Adult nonfiction including investigative journalism, popular psychology and sociology, self-help, natural science, New Age/inspiration, health and alternative health, parenting, business, animals, controversial, gay, and women's issues, celebrity biographies, gardening, etc.; and fiction, including mainstream women's, medical and historical thrillers, mysteries, psychological suspense, magical realism, novels of the West, romance, and mainstream historical and contemporary novels. See web site www.natashakern.com for detailed submission instructions. For fiction, query with SASE; for nonfiction, send book proposal with SASE. Commission: 15% domestic; 20% foreign.

KIDDE, HOYT & PICARD—335 E. 51st St., New York, NY 10022. Tel: (212) 755-9461; fax: (212) 223-2501. Attn: Katharine Kidde, Laura Langlie. Mainstream, literary, and romantic fiction; general nonfiction. Writers should have been published to be considered. Query; include past writing experience, credits. Multiple queries O.K. Commission: 15%.

KIRCHOFF/WOHLBERG, INC.—866 United Nations Plaza, Suite 525, New York, NY 10017. Attn: Liza Voges. Juvenile fiction and nonfiction only. Unpublished writers considered. Query; multiple submissions O.K. Commission: 15%.

HARVEY KLINGER, INC.—301 W. 53rd St., New York, NY 10019. Attn: Harvey Klinger, Laurie E. Liss, David Dunton. Commercial and literary fiction and nonfiction. Unpublished writers considered. Query with outline and bio/resumé. No multiple queries. Commission: 15% domestic, 25% foreign.

BARBARA S. KOUTS—P.O. Box 560, Bellport, NY 11713. Attn: Barbara S. Kouts. Adult fiction, nonfiction, and juvenile for all ages. Unpublished writers considered. Query with bio/resumé. Multiple queries O.K. Commission: 15%.

PETER LAMPACK AGENCY, INC.—551 Fifth Ave., Suite 1613, New York, NY 10176. Attn: Loren Soeiro, Agent. E-mail: renbopla@aol.com. Adult fiction and nonfiction including mainstream, mystery, suspense, thrillers, and literature. No poetry, romance, science fiction, fantasy, horror, or Westerns. No theatrical plays, screenplays, or teleplays. Unpublished writers considered. Query with synopsis/outline, up to 10 sample pages, SASE, and bio/resumé. Commission: 15% domestic; 20% foreign.

MICHAEL LARSEN/ELIZABETH POMADA—1029 Jones St., San Francisco, CA 94109. E-mail: larsenpoma@aol.com. Attn: M. Larsen, nonfiction; E. Pomada, fiction. Fiction: literary, commercial, and genre. Nonfiction: general, including biography, business, nature, health, history, arts, travel. Unpublished writers welcome. Query for fiction with first 10 pages, synopsis, SASE, and phone number; send #10 SASE for brochure. For nonfiction, query with SASE. Commission: 15%. For more information see web site: www. larsen-pomada.com.

THE MAUREEN LASHER AGENCY—P.O. Box 888, Pacific Palisades, CA 90272. E-mail: mlasherlaca@aol.com. Attn: Ann Cashman. Adult fiction and nonfiction. Unpublished writers considered. Query with outline, sample pages, and bio/resumé. No multiple queries. Commission: 15%.

ELLEN LEVINE LITERARY AGENCY, INC.—15 E. 26th St., Suite 1801, New York, NY 10010. Attn: Elizabeth Kaplan, Diana Finch, Louise Quayle. Adult fiction and nonfiction. Query with SASE. Commission: 15%.

LICHTMAN, TRISTER, SINGER & ROSS—See *Gail Ross Literary Agency.*

NANCY LOVE LITERARY AGENCY—250 E. 65th St., New York, NY 10021. Tel: (212) 980-3499. Attn: Daniel Genis. Adult fiction: mysteries and thrillers; and nonfiction: health, parenting, inspirational, current affairs, biography, memoirs, psychology. Unpublished writers considered. For nonfiction, query with proposal; for fiction, query with first chapter. Commission: 15%.

MCINTOSH & OTIS, INC.—353 Lexington Ave., New York, NY 10016. Adult fiction, nonfiction, and screenplays; juvenile fiction and nonfiction. Unpublished writers considered. Query with sample pages; include SASE. Allow 4 to 6 weeks for response. Commission: 15%.

DONALD MAASS LITERARY AGENCY—157 W. 57th St., Suite 703,

New York, NY 10019. Attn: Donald Maass, Pres. Jennifer Jackson, Associate. Michelle Brummer, Asst. Adult fiction: science fiction, fantasy, mystery, suspense, horror, frontier, romance, mainstream, literary. Unpublished writers considered. Query with first 5 sample pages, synopsis, and SASE. Commission: 15% domestic; 20% foreign.

GINA MACCOBY LITERARY AGENCY—P.O. Box 60, Chappaqua, NY 10514. Adult fiction and nonfiction; juvenile for all ages. No computer books, horror, science fiction, diet books, or cookbooks. Unpublished writers considered. Query with SASE; multiple queries O.K. Commission: 15%. No unsolicited manuscripts.

CAROL MANN LITERARY AGENCY—55 Fifth Ave., New York, NY 10003. Attn: Carol Mann. 30% fiction; 70% nonfiction, including health, fitness, inspiration, alternative medicine, and self-help. Query with outline, sample pages, bio and resumé, and SASE. Commission: 15%.

MANUS ASSOCIATES, INC.—417 E. 57th St., Suite 5D, New York, NY 10022. Fax: (650) 470-5159. E-mail: manuslit@lit.com. Web site: www. manuslit.com. Attn: Janet Wilkens Manus. West Coast office: 375 Forest Ave., Palo Alto, CA 94301. Adult fiction and nonfiction. No science fiction/fantasy, category romance, westerns, children's, or original screenplays. Unpublished writers considered. Query with synopsis, three sample chapters, and bio/ resumé. Multiple queries O.K. "on occasion." Commission: 15%.

THE MARTON AGENCY, INC.—One Union Square W., Rm. 612, New York, NY 10003-3303. Fax: (212) 691-9061. E-mail: martonagcy@aol. com. Attn: Tonda Marton. Plays only. Not considering new work at this time. Commission: 10%.

JED MATTES, INC.—2095 Broadway, #302, New York, NY 10023-2895. Adult fiction and nonfiction. Unpublished writers considered. Query. Commission: 15% domestic; 20% foreign.

HELMUT MEYER LITERARY AGENCY—330 E. 79th St., New York, NY 10021. Attn: Helmut Meyer, Literary Agent. Adult nonfiction. Telephone query or query by mail with outline, sample pages, and bio/resumé. No multiple queries. Commission: 15%.

HENRY MORRISON, INC.—Box 235, Bedford Hills, NY 10507. Tel: (914) 666-3500; fax: (914) 241-7846. Adult fiction and nonfiction; book-length only. Unpublished writers considered. Query with outline; multiple queries O.K. Commission: 15% domestic; 25% foreign. Fees: photocopying, shipping. "We are concentrating on a relatively small list of clients, and work toward building them in the U.S. and international marketplaces. We tend to avoid autobiographical novels and extremely literary novels, but always seek good nonfiction on major political and historical subjects."

MULTIMEDIA PRODUCT DEVELOPMENT, INC.—410 S. Michigan Ave., Suite 724, Chicago, IL 60605. Tel: (312) 922-3063; fax (312) 922-1905. E-mail: mpdev@aol.com. Jane Jordan Browne, Pres. Adult fiction and nonfiction, as well as juvenile fiction and nonfiction. "We are interested in commercial, overnight sellers in the areas of mainstream fiction and nonfiction." No short stories, poems, screenplays, articles, or software. Query with bio and SASE. "We do not accept e-mail or fax queries." Commission: 15% domestic; 20% foreign.

JEAN V. NAGGAR LITERARY AGENCY—216 E. 75th St., New

York, NY 10021. Attn: Jean Naggar, Frances Kuffel, or Alice Tasman. Adult mainstream fiction and nonfiction. Very few unpublished writers considered. Query with outline, SASE, bio, and resumé. Commission: 15% domestic, 20% foreign.

RUTH NATHAN AGENCY—53 E. 34th St., Suite 809, New York, NY 10016. Decorative arts, show business, biography. Selected historical fiction, pre-1500. No unsolicited queries. Commission: 15%. "To writers seeking an agent: Please note what my specialties are. Do not send science fiction, fantasy, children's books, or business books. Unsolicited manuscripts are not accepted."

NEW ENGLAND PUBLISHING ASSOCIATES—P.O. Box 5, Chester, CT 06412. Tel: (860) 345-7323; fax: (860) 345-3660. E-mail: nepa@nepa.com. Adult nonfiction, especially women's studies, history, biography, literature, business, science, crime, law, and reference. Unpublished writers considered. Query with outline, sample pages, and bio/resumé. See web site for submission guidelines: http://www.nepa.com. Commission: 15% domestic; 20% foreign.

THE RICHARD PARKS AGENCY—138 E. 16th St., 5B, New York, NY 10003. Tel: (212) 254-9067. Attn: Richard Parks. Adult nonfiction; fiction by referral only. Unpublished writers considered. Query with bio and resumé. Commission: 15% domestic; 20% foreign. "No phone calls, e-mails, or faxed queries, please."

JAMES PETER ASSOCIATES, INC.—P.O. Box 670, Tenafly, NJ 07670. Attn: Bert Holtje. Adult nonfiction. Unpublished writers considered. Query with outline, sample pages, and bio/resumé. No multiple queries. Commission: 15% domestic, 20% foreign.

ALISON PICARD, LITERARY AGENT—P.O. Box 2000, Cotuit, MA 02635. Attn: Alison Picard. Adult fiction, nonfiction, and juvenile. Unpublished writers considered. Query; multiple queries O.K. Commission: 15%.

PINDER LANE & GARON-BROOKE ASSOCIATES, LTD.—159 W. 53rd St., #14-E, New York, NY 10019. Tel: (212) 489-0880. E-mail: pinderl@interport.net. Attn: Jean Free. Adult fiction and nonfiction including thrillers, romance, contemporary, biography, lifestyle, and health. Unpublished writers considered. Query with outline, bio/resumé, and SASE; no multiple queries. Commission: 15% domestic, 30% foreign.

SUSAN ANN PROTTER—110 W. 40th St., Suite 1408, New York, NY 10018. Fax: (212) 840-1132. E-mail: sapla@aol.com. Adult fiction and nonfiction only, specializing in mysteries, crime, thrillers and science fiction; health, psychology, parenting, self-help, biographies, history, popular science, medicine, and alternative medicine. Query by mail only, with description, bio/resumé, synopsis, and SASE. Commission: 15%.

RAINES & RAINES—71 Park Ave., Suite 4A, New York, NY 10016. Attn: Keith Korman, Joan Raines, Theron Raines. Adult fiction, nonfiction, and juvenile for all ages. Query; no multiple queries. Commission: 15% domestic; 20% foreign. "Keep query to one page."

HELEN REES LITERARY AGENCY—123 N. Washington St., Boston, MA 02114. Literary and commercial fiction and nonfiction. No short stories, science fiction, children's, religious, sports, occult, or poetry. Unpublished writers considered. Query with outline and bio/resumé. No multiple queries. Commission: 15%.

JODY REIN BOOKS, INC.—7741 S. Ash Ct., Littleton, CO 80122.

Web site: jodyreinbooks.com. Attn: Jody Rein. Literary and commercial adult nonfiction. Query with SASE. Commission: 15%.

GAIL ROSS LITERARY AGENCY—(formerly *Lichtman, Trister, Singer & Ross*) 1666 Connecticut Ave. N.W., Suite 500, Washington, DC 20009. Web site: www.gailross.com. Attn: Jenne Land. Adult nonfiction. Unpublished writers considered. Query with outline, sample pages, resumé, and SASE. Multiple queries O.K. Commission: 15%.

JANE ROTROSEN AGENCY, LLC.—318 E. 51st St., New York, NY 10022. Attn: Ruth Kagle. Adult fiction and nonfiction. Unpublished writers considered. Query with outline and bio; no unsolicited manuscripts. Commission: 15% U.S. and Canada; 20% foreign and film/TV.

THE PETER RUBIE LITERARY AGENCY—240 W. 35th St., Suite 500, New York, NY 10001. Web site: www.prlit.com. Attn: Peter Rubie. Adult fiction and nonfiction. Jennifer DeChiara, children's books. Unpublished writers considered. Query with outline, sample pages, bio, and resumé; multiple queries O.K. Commission: 15% U.S.; 20% foreign.

PESHA RUBINSTEIN LITERARY AGENCY—1392 Rugby Rd., Teaneck, NJ 07666. Attn: Pesha Rubinstein. Commercial fiction: mysteries, women's fiction, and thrillers; nonfiction; humor; and juvenile. Unpublished writers considered. Query with first 10 pages, synopsis, and SASE. Commission: 15% domestic, 20% foreign.

RUSSELL & VOLKENING, INC.—50 W. 29th St., #7E, New York, NY 10001. Adult and juvenile fiction and nonfiction; specializing in literary fiction and narrative nonfiction. Queries for juvenile books should be addressed to Jennie Dunham. No screenplays, horror, romance, science fiction, or poetry. Unpublished writers considered. Query with letter and SASE.

SANDUM & ASSOCIATES—144 E. 84th St., New York, NY 10028. Attn: Howard E. Sandum. Primarily nonfiction. Query with sample pages and bio/resumé. Multiple queries O.K. Commission: 15% domestic; 10% when foreign or TV/film subagents are used. "We do not consider manuscripts in genres such as science fiction, romance, or horror unless surpassing literary qualities are present."

BOBBE SIEGEL, RIGHTS AND LITERARY AGENT—41 W. 83rd St., New York, NY 10024. Attn: Bobbe Siegel. Adult fiction and nonfiction. No children's books, poetry, short stories, romances, cookbooks, or humor. Unpublished writers considered. Query; multiple queries O.K. SASE required. Commission: 15%.

JACQUELINE SIMENAUER LITERARY AGENCY—P.O. Box 1039, Barnegat, NJ 08005. Tel: (609) 607-1780. E-mail: JacSimLit@aol.com. Jacqueline Simenauer, Doris Walfield, nonfiction. Fran Pardi, fiction. Nonfiction: Medical, how-to/self help, pop psychology, women's issues, health, alternative health, spirituality, parenting, New Age, fitness, diet, nutrition, travel, current issues, true crime, business, men's issues, celebrities, reference, cookbooks, social issues. Fiction: literary and mainstream commercial. Query with SASE. Multiple queries O.K. Commission: 15% domestic; 20% foreign.

PHILIP G. SPITZER LITERARY AGENCY—50 Talmage Farm Ln., East Hampton, NY 11937. Tel: (631) 329-3650; fax: (631) 329-3651. E-mail: spitzer516@aol.com. Attn: Philip Spitzer. Adult fiction and nonfiction. Query. Commission: 15% domestic; 20% foreign.

GUNTHER STUHLMANN, AUTHOR'S REPRESENTATIVE—P.O. Box 276, Becket, MA 01223. Attn: Barbara Ward. Literary fiction and nonfiction, especially biography, letters, and history. No mysteries, romance, science fiction, or adventure. Unpublished writers sometimes considered. Query with SASE; no multiple queries. Commission: 10% North America; 15% Britain and Commonwealth; 20% foreign.

THE TANTLEFF OFFICE—375 Greenwich St., Suite 700, New York, NY 10013. Attn: Charmaine Ferenczi, stage plays. John Santoianni, stage plays, film and television. Jack Tantleff, stage plays, film and television. Jill Bock, film and television. Stage plays, screenplays, teleplays. Unpublished writers considered. Query with synopsis, up to 10 sample pages, bio/resumé; multiple queries O.K. Commission: 10% scripts.

WALES LITERARY AGENCY, INC.—108 Hayes St., Seattle, WA 98109. E-mail: waleslit@aol.com. Attn: Elizabeth Wales, Adrienne Reed. Mainstream and literary fiction and nonfiction, including women's, nature writing, multicultural stories, and animal stories. Unpublished writers considered. Query with outline, sample pages, and SASE. Multiple queries O.K. Commission: 15%.

JOHN A. WARE LITERARY AGENCY—392 Central Park W., New York, NY 10025. Tel: (212) 866-4733; fax: (212) 866-4734. Attn: John Ware. Adult fiction and nonfiction. "Literate, accessible, noncategory fiction, plus thrillers and mysteries." Nonfiction: biography, history, current affairs, investigative journalism, social criticism, Americana and folklore, science. Unpublished writers considered. Query letter only, with SASE; multiple queries O.K. Commission: 15% domestic, 20% foreign.

WATKINS/LOOMIS AGENCY—133 E. 35th St., Suite One, New York, NY 10016. Attn: Katherine Fausset. Adult literary fiction and nonfiction. Unpublished writers considered. Query with SASE by mail only; no multiple queries. Commission: 15%.

SANDRA WATT & ASSOCIATES—1750 N. Sierra Bonita, Los Angeles, CA 90046. Attn: Sandra Watt. Adult fiction (mystery, thrillers, women's novels, detective) and nonfiction (spiritual, New Age, animals, humor, anthropology, art, true crime, and gardening. Unpublished writers considered. Query with outline; multiple submissions O.K. Commission: 15%. "We're probably a bit old-fashioned in loving a great story."

WIESER & WIESER, INC.—25 E. 21st St., 6th Fl., New York, NY 10010. Attn: Olga Wieser, Jake Elwell. Adult fiction and nonfiction. Unpublished writers considered. Query with outline, sample pages, bio/resumé, and SASE. Commission: 15%.

WRITERS HOUSE—21 W. 26th St., New York, NY 10010. Attn: Front desk. Adult fiction and nonfiction for all ages, including young adult. Unpublished writers considered. "Query with one-page letter on what your project is about, why it's unique, and why you're the ideal author to write it." No multiple queries. Commission: 15% domestic; 20% foreign.

THE WRITERS SHOP—(formerly *Virginia Barber Agency*) 101 5th Ave., New York, NY 10003. Tel: (212) 255-6515; fax: (212) 691-9418. Adult fiction and nonfiction. No unsolicited manuscripts. Query with outline, sample pages, bio/resumé, and SASE. No multiple queries. Commission: 15%; 20% domestic.

Glossary

Advance—The amount a publisher pays a writer before a book is published; it is deducted from the royalties earned from sales of the finished book.

Agented material—Submissions from literary or dramatic agents to a publisher. Some publishing companies accept agented material only.

All rights—Some magazines purchase all rights to the material they publish, which means that they can use it as they wish, as many times as they wish. They cannot purchase all rights unless the writer gives them written permission to do so.

Assignment—A contract, written or oral, between an editor and writer, confirming that the writer will complete a specific project by a certain date, and for a certain fee.

B&W—Abbreviation for black-and-white photographs.

Book outline—Chapter-by-chapter summary of a book, frequently in paragraph form, allowing an editor to evaluate the book's content, tone, and pacing, and determine whether he or she wants to see the entire manuscript for possible publication.

Book packager—Company that puts together all the elements of a book, from initial concept to writing, publishing, and marketing it. Also called **book producer** or **book developer**.

Byline—Author's name as it appears on a published piece.

Clips—Copies of a writer's published work, often used by editors to evaluate the writer's talent.

884

Column inch—One inch of a typeset column; often serves as a basis for payment.

Contributor's copies—Copies of a publication sent to a writer whose work is included in it.

Copy editing—Line-by-line editing to correct errors in spelling, grammar, and punctuation, and inconsistencies in style. Differs from **content editing**, which evaluates flow, logic, and overall message.

Copy —Manuscript pages before they are set into type.

Copyright —Legal protection of creative works from unauthorized use. Under the law, copyright is secured automatically when the work is set down for the first time in written or recorded form.

Cover letter—A brief letter that accompanies a manuscript or book proposal. A cover letter is *not* a query letter (see definition, page 887).

Deadline —The date on which a written work is due at the editor's office, agreed to by author and editor.

Draft —A complete version of an article, story, or book. **First drafts** are often called **rough drafts**.

Fair use—A provision of the copyright law allowing brief passages of copyrighted material to be quoted without infringing on the owner's rights.

Feature—An article that is generally longer than a news story and whose main focus is an issue, trend, or person.

Filler—Brief item used to fill out a newspaper or magazine column; could be a news item, joke, anecdote, or puzzle.

First serial rights—The right of a magazine or newspaper to publish a work for the first time in any periodical. After that, all rights revert to the writer.

Ghostwriter—Author of books, articles, and speeches that are credited to someone else.

Glossy—Black-and-white photo with a shiny, rather than a matte, finish.

Hard copy—The printed copy of material written on a computer.

Honorarium—A modest, token fee paid by a publication to an author in gratitude for a submission.

International reply coupon (IRC)—Included with any correspondence or submission to a foreign publication; allows the editor to reply by mail without incurring cost.

Kill fee—Fee paid for an article that was assigned but subsequently not published; usually a percentage of the amount that would have been paid if the work had been published.

Lead time—Time between the planning of a magazine or book and its publication date.

Libel—A false accusation or published statement that causes a person embarrassment, loss of income, or damage to reputation.

Little magazines—Publications with limited circulation whose content often deals with literature or politics.

Mass market—Books appealing to a very large segment of the reading public and often sold in such outlets as drugstores, supermarkets, etc.

Masthead—A listing of the names and titles of a publication's staff members.

Ms—Abbreviation for manuscript; mss is the plural abbreviation.

Multiple submissions—Also called **simultaneous submissions**. Complete manuscripts sent simultaneously to different publications. Once universally discouraged by editors, the practice is gaining more acceptance, though some still frown on it. **Multiple queries** are generally accepted, however, since reading them requires less of an investment in time on the editor's part.

On speculation—Editor agrees to consider a work for publication "on speculation," without any guarantee that he or she will ultimately buy the work.

One-time rights—Editor buys manuscript from writer and agrees to publish it one time, after which the rights revert to the author for subsequent sales.

Op-ed—A newspaper piece, usually printed opposite the editorial page, that expresses a personal viewpoint on a timely news item.

Over-the-transom—Describes the submission of unsolicited material by a free-lance writer; the term harks back to the time when mail was delivered through the open window above an office door.

Payment on acceptance—Payment to writer when manuscript is submitted.

Payment on publication—Payment to writer when manuscript is published.

Pen name—A name other than his or her legal name that an author uses on written work.

Public domain—Published material that is available for use without permission, either because it was never copyrighted or because its copyright term is expired. Works published at least 75 years ago are considered in the public domain.

Q-and-A format—One type of presentation for an interview article, in which questions are printed, followed by the interviewee's answers.

Query letter—A letter—usually no longer than one page—in which a writer proposes an article idea to an editor.

Rejection slip—A printed note in which a publication indicates that it is not interested in a submission.

Reporting time—The weeks or months it takes for an editor to evaluate a submission.

Reprint rights—The legal right of a magazine or newspaper to print an article, story, or poem after it has already appeared elsewhere.

Royalty—A percentage of the amount received from retail sales of a book, paid to the author by the publisher. For hardcovers, the royalty is generally 10% on the first 5,000 copies sold; 12½% on the next 5,000 sold; 15% thereafter. Paperback royalties range from 4% to 8%, depending on whether it's a trade or mass-market book.

SASE—Self-addressed, stamped envelope, required with all submissions that the author wishes returned—either for return of material or (if you don't need material returned) for editor's reply.

Slush pile—The stack of unsolicited manuscripts in an editor's office.

Tear sheets—The pages of a magazine or newspaper on which an author's work is published.

Unsolicited submission—A manuscript that an editor did not specifically ask to see.

Vanity publisher—Also called **subsidy publisher**. A publishing company that charges an author all costs of printing his or her book. No reputable book publisher operates on this subsidy basis.

Work for hire—When a work is written on a "for hire" basis, all rights in it become the property of the publisher. Though the work-for-hire clause applies mostly to work done by regular employees of a company, some editors offer work-for-hire agreements to free lancers. Think carefully before signing such agreements, however, since by doing so you will essentially be signing away your rights and will not be able to try to resell your work on your own.

Writers guidelines—A formal statement of a publication's editorial needs, payment schedule, deadlines, and other essential information.

INDEX TO MARKETS

Insights into IFR

**KPMG's practical guide to
International Financial Reporting Stand**

7th Edition 2010/11

The KPMG International Standards Group

SWEET & MAXWELL

 THOMSON REUTERS

...sed on specific facts and circumstances. In many instances, further interpreta-... in order for an entity to apply IFRSs to its own facts, circumstances and individual ...s. Further, some of the information contained in this publication is based on the KPMG ...ernational Standards Group's interpretations of IFRSs, which may change as practice and implementation guidance continue to develop. Users are cautioned to read this publication in conjunction with the actual text of the standards and implementation guidance issued, and to consult their professional advisers before concluding on accounting treatments for their own transactions.

The KPMG International Standards Group is part of KPMG IFRG Limited.

ISBN 978-0-414-04456-2

Printed and bound in Italy by L.E.G.O. S.p.A.